UNIVERSITY CASEBOOK SERIES®

THE POLICE FUNCTION

EIGHTH EDITION

GEORGE E. DIX

George R. Killam, Jr. Chair of Criminal Law,
University of Texas

FOUNDATION
PRESS

University Casebook Series is a trademark registered in the U.S. Patent and Trademark Office.

© 1986, 2000 FOUNDATION PRESS
© 2012 By THOMSON REUTERS/FOUNDATION PRESS
© 2017 LEG, Inc. d/b/a West Academic
  444 Cedar Street, Suite 700
  St. Paul, MN 55101
  1-877-888-1330

Printed in the United States of America

ISBN: 978-1-68328-124-5

PREFACE

This eighth edition of The Police Function follows the general organization of the earlier editions. Border-related law enforcement activity, however, is no longer covered due to the complexity of that subject and the need to expand coverage of other areas in which Supreme Court case law has increased.

Footnotes and textual citations to authority have been deleted from principal cases and note quotations from cases without specific indication of those omissions. The omission of unreprinted opinions in principal cases is noted only when the existence of such opinions is useful in understanding the procedural or precedential significance of the opinions reprinted.

GEORGE E. DIX

December 24, 2016

SUMMARY OF CONTENTS

TABLE OF CONTENTS

TABLE OF CASES

The principal cases are in bold type.

UNIVERSITY CASEBOOK SERIES®

THE POLICE FUNCTION

EIGHTH EDITION

PRELUDE: THE CRIMINAL JUSTICE PROCESS

Analysis

National Advisory Commission on Criminal Justice Standards
  and Goals, Courts 11–15 (1973)
Editors' Introduction: Federal and State Constitutional Provisions Affecting Law
  Enforcement Conduct

National Advisory Commission on Criminal Justice Standards and Goals, Courts 11–15 (1973)

* * *

ARREST

The first formal contact of an accused with the criminal justice system is likely to be an arrest by a police officer. In most cases, the arrest will be made upon the police officer's own evaluation that there is sufficient basis for believing that a crime had been committed by the accused. However, the arrest may be made pursuant to a warrant; in this case, the police officer or some other person will have submitted the evidence against the accused to a judicial officer, who determines whether the evidence is sufficient to justify an arrest. In some situations, the accused may have no formal contact with the law until he has been indicted by a grand jury. Following such an indictment, a court order may be issued authorizing police officers to take the accused into custody. But these are exceptional situations. Ordinarily, the arrest is made without any court order and the court's contact with the accused comes only after the arrest.

* * *

INITIAL JUDICIAL APPEARANCE

In all jurisdictions, a police officer or other person making an arrest must bring the arrested person before a judge within a short period of time. It is at this initial appearance that most accused have their first contact with the courts. This initial appearance is usually before a lower court—a justice of the peace or a magistrate. * * * Often by the time of the initial appearance, the prosecution will have prepared a formal document called a complaint, which charges the defendant with a specific crime.

At the initial appearance, several things may occur. First, the defendant will be informed of the charges against him, usually by means of the complaint. Second, he will be informed of his rights, including his constitutional privilege against self-incrimination. Third, if the case is one in which the accused will be provided with an attorney at State expense, the mechanical process of assigning the attorney at least may begin at this stage. Fourth, unless the defendant is convicted of an offense at this point, arrangements may be made concerning the release of the defendant before further proceedings. This may take the traditional form of setting bail, that is, establishment of an amount of security the defendant himself or a professional bondsman whom he may hire must deposit with the court (or assume the obligation to pay) to assure that the defendant does appear for later proceedings. Pre-trial release, in some jurisdictions, also may take the form of being released on one's own recognizance, that is, release simply upon the defendant's promise to appear at a later time. * * *

In addition to these matters collateral to the issue of guilt, it is at the initial appearance that judicial inquiry into the merits of the case begins. If the charge is one the lower court has authority to try, the defendant may be asked how he pleads. If he pleads guilty, he may be convicted at this point. If he pleads not guilty, a trial date may be set and trial held later in this court.

However, if the charge is more serious, the court must give the defendant the opportunity for a judicial evaluation to determine whether there is enough evidence to justify putting him to trial in the higher court. In this type of case, the judge at the initial appearance ordinarily will ask the defendant whether he wants a preliminary hearing. If the defendant does, the matter generally is continued, or postponed to give both the prosecution and the defense time to prepare their cases.

The matter will be taken up again later in the lower court at the preliminary hearing. At this proceeding, the prosecutor introduces evidence to try to prove the defendant's guilt. He need not convince the court of the defendant's guilt beyond a reasonable doubt, but need only establish that there is enough evidence from which an average person (juror) could conclude that the defendant was guilty of the crime charged. If this evidence is produced, the court may find that the prosecution has established probable cause to believe the defendant guilty.

At this preliminary hearing the defendant may cross-examine witnesses produced by the prosecution and present evidence himself. If the court finds at the end of the preliminary hearing that probable cause does not exist, it dismisses the complaint. This does not ordinarily prevent the prosecution from bringing another charge, however. If the court finds that probable cause does exist, it orders that the defendant be bound over to the next step in the prosecution. As a practical matter, the preliminary hearing also serves the function of giving the defendant and his attorney a look at the case the prosecution will produce at trial. It gives a defense attorney the opportunity to cross-examine witnesses he later will have to confront. This informal previewing function may be more valuable to defendants than the theoretical function of the preliminary hearing.

FILING OF FORMAL CRIMINAL CHARGE

Generally, it is following the decision of the lower court to bind over a defendant that the formal criminal charge is made in the court that would try the case if it goes to formal trial. If no grand jury action is to be taken, this is a simple step consisting of the prosecutor's filing a document called an information. But in many jurisdictions the involvement of the grand jury makes the process more complex. There, the decision at the preliminary hearing simply is to bind the defendant over for consideration by the grand jury. In these areas, the prosecutor then must go before the grand jury and again present his evidence. Only if the grand jury determines that there is probable cause does it act. Its action—consisting of issuing a document called an indictment—constitutes the formal charging of the defendant. If it does not find probable cause, it takes no action and the prosecution is dismissed.

In some jurisdictions, it is not necessary to have both a grand jury inquiry and a preliminary hearing. In most Federal jurisdictions, for example, if a defendant has been indicted by a grand jury he no longer has a right to a preliminary hearing, on the theory that he is entitled to only one determination as to whether probable cause exists.

Although the defendant is entitled to participate in the preliminary hearing, he has no right to take part in a grand jury inquiry. Traditionally, he has not been able to ascertain what went on in front of the grand jury, although increasingly the law has given him the right, after the fact, to know.

Following the formal charge—whether it has been by indictment or information—any of a variety of matters that require resolution may arise. The defendant's competency to stand trial may be in issue. This requires the court to resolve the question of whether the defendant is too ill mentally or otherwise impaired to participate meaningfully in his trial. If he is sufficiently impaired, trial must be postponed until he regains his competency.

The defendant also may challenge the validity of the indictment or information or the means by which they were issued. For example, he may assert that those acts with which he is charged do not constitute a crime under the laws of the jurisdiction. Or, if he was indicted by a grand jury, he may assert that the grand jury was selected in a manner not consistent with State or Federal law and, therefore, that the indictment is invalid.

A defendant also may—and in some jurisdictions must—raise, before trial, challenges to the admissibility of certain evidence, especially evidence seized by police officers in a search or statements obtained from him by interrogation. In view of the rapid growth of legal doctrine governing the admissibility of statements of defendants and evidence obtained by police search and seizure, resolution of the issues raised by defendants' challenges to the admissibility of such evidence may be more complex and time-consuming than anything involved in determining guilt or innocence.

* * *

ARRAIGNMENT

In view of the potential complexity of pretrial matters, much of the significant activity in a criminal prosecution already may have occurred at the time the defendant makes his first formal appearance before the court that is to try him. This first appearance—the arraignment—is the point at which he is asked to plead to the charge. He need not plead, in which case a plea of not guilty automatically is entered for him. If he pleads guilty, the law requires that certain precautions be taken to assure that this plea is made validly. Generally, the trial judge accepting the plea first must inquire of the defendant whether he understands the charge against him and the penalties that may be imposed. The judge also must assure himself that there is some reasonable basis in the facts of the case for the plea. This may involve requiring the prosecution to present some of its evidence to assure the court that there is evidence tending to establish guilt.

TRIAL

Unless the defendant enters a guilty plea, the full adversary process is put into motion. The prosecution now must establish to a jury or a judge the guilt of the defendant beyond a reasonable doubt. If the defendant elects to have the case tried by a jury, much effort is expended on the selection of a jury. Prospective jurors are questioned to ascertain whether they might be biased and what their views on numerous matters might be. Both sides have the right to have a potential juror rejected on the ground that he may be biased. In addition, both have the right to reject a limited number of potential jurors without having to state any reason. When the jury has been selected and convened, both sides may make opening statements explaining what they intend to prove or disprove.

The prosecution presents its evidence first, and the defendant has the option of making no case and relying upon the prosecution's inability to establish guilt beyond a reasonable doubt. He also has the option of presenting evidence tending to disprove the prosecution's case or tending to prove additional facts constituting a defense under applicable law. Throughout, however, the burden remains upon the prosecution. Procedurally, this is effectuated by defense motions to dismiss, which often are made after the prosecution's case has been presented and after all of the evidence is in. These motions in effect assert that the prosecution's case is so weak that no reasonable jury could conclude beyond a reasonable doubt that the defendant was guilty. If the judge grants the motion, he is in effect determining that no jury could reasonably return a verdict of guilty. This not only results in a dismissal of the prosecution but also prevents the prosecution from bringing another charge for the same crime.

After the evidence is in and defense motions are disposed of, the jury is instructed on the applicable law. Often both defense and prosecution lawyers submit instructions which they ask the court to read to the jury, and the court chooses from those and others it composes itself. It is in the formulation of these instructions that many issues regarding the definition of the applicable law arise and must be resolved. After—or sometimes before—the instructions are read, both sides present formal arguments to the jury. The jury then retires for its deliberations.

Generally, the jury may return only one of two verdicts: guilty or not guilty. A verdict of not guilty may be misleading; it may mean not that the jury believed that the defendant was not guilty but rather that the jury determined that the prosecution had not established guilt by the criterion—beyond a reasonable doubt—the law imposes. If the insanity defense has been raised, the jury may be told it should specify if insanity is the reason for acquittal; otherwise, there is no need for explanation. If a guilty verdict is returned, the court formally enters a judgment of conviction unless there is a legally sufficient reason for not doing so.

The defendant may attack his conviction, usually by making a motion to set aside the verdict and order a new trial. In his attack, he may argue that evidence was improperly admitted during the trial, that the evidence was so weak that no reasonable jury could have found that it established guilt beyond a reasonable doubt, or that there is newly discovered evidence which, had it been available at the time of trial, would have changed the result. If the court grants a motion raising one of these arguments, the effect generally is not to acquit the defendant but merely to require the holding of a new trial.

SENTENCING

Sentencing then follows. (If the court has accepted a plea of guilty, this step follows acceptance of the plea.) In an increasing number of jurisdictions, an investigation called the presentence report is conducted by professional probation officers. This involves investigation of the offense, the offender and his background, and any other matters of potential value to the sentencing judge. Following submission of the report to the court, the defendant is given the opportunity to comment upon the appropriateness of sentencing. In some jurisdictions, this has developed into a more extensive court hearing on sentencing issues, with the defendant given the opportunity to present evidence as well as argument for leniency. Sentencing itself generally is the responsibility of the judge, although in some jurisdictions juries retain that authority.

APPEAL

Following the conclusion of the proceeding in the trial court, the matter shifts to the appellate courts. In some jurisdictions, a defendant who is convicted of a minor offense in a lower court has the right to a new trial (trial de novo) in a higher court. But in most situations—and in all cases involving serious offenses—the right to appeal is limited to the right to have an appellate court examine the record of the trial proceedings for error. If error is found, the appellate court either may take definitive action—such as ordering that the prosecution be dismissed—or it may set aside the conviction and remand the case for a new trial. The latter gives the prosecution the opportunity to obtain a valid conviction. Generally, a time limit is placed upon the period during which an appeal may be taken.

COLLATERAL ATTACK

Even if no appeal is taken or the conviction is upheld, the courts' participation in the criminal justice process is not necessarily ended. To some extent, a convicted defendant who has either exhausted his appeal rights or declined to exercise them within the appropriate time limits can seek further relief by means of collateral attack upon the conviction. This method involves a procedure collateral to the standard process of conviction and appeal.

Traditionally this relief was sought by applying for a writ of habeas corpus on the ground that the conviction under which the applicant was held was invalid. Many jurisdictions have found this vehicle too cumbersome for modern problems and have developed special procedures for collateral attacks. * * *

Editors' Introduction: Federal and State Constitutional Provisions Affecting Law Enforcement Conduct

Law enforcement conduct, and the admissibility of evidence developed by such conduct, is affected by law emanating from numerous sources other than the United States Constitution. Nevertheless, because of the United States Supreme Court's "constitutionalization" of criminal procedure, several provisions of the federal document—applicable to the states by virtue of the Fourteenth Amendment—have taken on immense significance for law enforcement activity. Much of the case law in these materials is devoted to exploring the content of these provisions. The text of these is as follows:

Amendment IV

The right of the people to be secure in their persons, houses, papers, and effects, against unreasonable searches and seizures, shall not be violated, and no Warrants shall issue, but upon probable cause, supported by Oath or affirmation, and particularly describing the place to be searched, and the persons or things to be seized.

Amendment V

No person * * * shall be compelled in any criminal case to be a witness against himself, nor be deprived of life, liberty, or property, without due process of law * * * .

Amendment VI

In all criminal prosecutions, the accused shall enjoy the right * * * to have the Assistance of Counsel for his defense.

Amendment XIV, Section 1

No State shall * * * deprive any person of life, liberty, or property, without due process of law; nor deny to any person within its jurisdiction the equal protection of the laws.

———

State constitutions usually have provisions analogous and sometimes identical to those provisions. Article 1 of the Utah constitution, for example, contains the following provisions:

Section 12. Right of accused persons

In criminal prosecutions the accused shall have the right to appear and defend in person and by counsel * * * . The accused shall not be compelled to give evidence against himself.

Section 14. Unreasonable searches forbidden—Issuance of warrant

The right of the people to be secure in their persons, houses, papers and effects against unreasonable searches and seizures shall not be violated; and no warrant shall issue but upon probable cause supported by oath or affirmation, particularly describing the place to be searched and the person or thing to be seized.

Other state provisions differ more significantly from their federal counterparts. Article 1, Section 4 of the Washington Constitution, for example, provides:

No person shall be disturbed in his private affairs, or his home invaded, without authority of law.

Obviously, a state cannot—by constitutional provision or otherwise—deprive litigants in its courts of rights which they have by virtue of the United States Constitution. But it is equally obvious that states can—by constitutional provision or otherwise—give their citizens more protection than those citizens are afforded by the federal Constitution.

Even if a state constitutional provision is phrased similarly or identically to an analogous federal constitutional provision, the state courts need not construe the state provision as having the same content as the United States Supreme Court has given to the federal provision.

State judicial willingness to "independently" construe state constitutional provisions was at least initially sometimes labeled "new federalism." See, e.g., Wilkes, The New Federalism in Criminal Procedure: State Court Evasion of the Burger Court, 62 Ky.L.J. 421 (1974).

The Iowa Supreme Court noted in 2010 that its older decisions 'embrace' what has been called a 'lockstep' approach to interpretation of state constitutional provisions * * * [u]nder [which] a state court adopts prevailing federal authority in its interpretation of parallel state constitutional provisions, even though theoretically recognizing their independent nature." It continued:

> [W]e now hold that, while United States Supreme Court cases are entitled to respectful consideration, we will engage in independent analysis of the content of our state search and seizure provisions. A Fourth Amendment opinion of the United States Supreme Court * * * is no more binding upon our interpretation of [the search and seizure provision] of the Iowa Constitution than is a case decided by another state supreme court under a search and seizure provision of that state's constitution. The degree to which we follow United States Supreme Court precedent, or any other precedent, depends solely upon its ability to persuade us with the reasoning of the decision.

State v. Ochoa, 792 N.W.2d 260, 267 (Iowa 2010).

The New York Court of Appeals elaborated on its "noninterpretive" approach to deciding whether a state constitutional provision would be construed more broadly than a federal provision containing no material difference in terminology:

> A noninterpretive review "proceeds from a judicial perception of sound policy, justice and fundamental fairness" and seeks to discover, for example,
>
> > "any preexisting State statutory or common law defining the scope of the individual right in question; the history and traditions of the State in its protection of that individual right; any identification of the right in the State Constitution as being one of peculiar State or local concern; and any distinctive attitudes of the State citizenry toward the definition, scope or protection of the individual right."
>
> A finding of these factors suggests that a broader reading of the state constitutional provision could be appropriate.

In re Nassau County Grand Jury Subpoena Duces Tecum Dated June 24, 2003, 4 N.Y.3d 665, 674, 830 N.E.2d 1118, 1123–24, 797 N.Y.S.2d 790, 795–96 (2005). See also, State v. Ketelson, 150 N.M. 137, ¶ 10, 257 P.3d 957, 961 (2011) (state supreme court construing state constitutional provision may diverge from federal precedent "for three reasons: 'a flawed federal analysis, structural differences between state and federal government, or distinctive state characteristics' ").

State tribunals may, of course, construe state provisions as conferring no more rights upon citizens, suspects or defendants than the Supreme Court construes the federal provisions as providing, and in fact many state courts do so. Often state courts doing this characterize Supreme Court interpretations of the federal provisions as "strongly persuasive." State v. Johnson, 354 S.W.3d 627, 632 (Mo.2011).

State courts' independence applies only to matters of *state* law. In Arkansas v. Sullivan, 532 U.S. 769, 121 S.Ct. 1876 (2001) (per curiam), the Arkansas Supreme Court reasoned that even if the officer's conduct in the case did not violate the Fourth Amendment as interpreted in United States Supreme Court case law, "there is nothing that prevents this court from interpreting the U.S. Constitution more broadly than the United States Supreme Court, which has the effect of providing more rights." Summarily reversing, the Supreme Court explained:

> The Arkansas Supreme Court's alternative holding, that it may interpret the United States Constitution to provide greater protection than this Court's own federal constitutional precedents provide, is foreclosed by *Oregon v. Hass*, 420 U.S. 714, 95 S.Ct. 1215, 43 L.Ed.2d 570 (1975). There, we observed that the Oregon Supreme Court's statement that it could " 'interpret the Fourth Amendment more restrictively than interpreted by the United States Supreme Court' " was "not the law and surely must be inadvertent error." We reiterated in *Hass* that while "a State is free as a matter of its own law to impose greater restrictions on police activity than those this Court holds to be necessary upon federal constitutional standards," it "may not impose such greater restrictions as a matter of federal constitutional law when this Court specifically refrains from imposing them."

532 U.S. at 770, 121 S.Ct. at 1878.

On remand, the Arkansas court explicitly rested its result on *state* constitutional grounds. State v. Sullivan, 348 Ark. 647, 74 S.W.3d 215 (2002).

These materials emphasize the federal constitutional provisions and their construction. But full treatment of these issues in state litigation cannot ignore "new federalism" and state law arguments independent of federal constitutional ones.

CHAPTER 1

THE EXCLUSIONARY SANCTION

Analysis

A. Adoption of the Federal Constitutional Exclusionary Sanction
B. Scope of Exclusionary Sanctions: Standing, Fruit of the Poisonous Tree, Independent Source and Attenuation of the Taint
C. Exceptions to Exclusionary Requirements

EDITORS' INTRODUCTION: EXCLUSIONARY RULES

The most dramatic development in American criminal procedure has been its "constitutionalization." To a significant extent, the requirements imposed by local statutes, case law and court rules have been eclipsed by the development of federal constitutional requirements. Constitutionalization of certain evidence matters by federal constitutional exclusionary requirements has been particularly important.

The major federal constitutional requirements affecting law enforcement conduct and the admissibility in a criminal trial of evidence obtained by law enforcement efforts are set out in the Editors' Introduction to these materials. These are, of course, binding on the states because of the Fourteenth Amendment. This chapter considers the enforcement of these provisions and other legal requirements by rules excluding evidence obtained in violation of their terms. The substance of these provisions is considered throughout much of the remainder these materials; the basic contours of the Fourth and Fifth Amendments are addressed in Chapter 2.

Requirements that evidence offered by the prosecution at a criminal trial be rejected because of impropriety in the process of gathering it are often referred to as "exclusionary rules." In one sense, any legal rule resulting in evidence being held inadmissible is "exclusionary." But in common legal usage, the phrase "exclusionary rule" has come to mean a legal requirement mandating exclusion of evidence because of the illegal manner in which it was obtained. Exclusion is usually imposed without regard to whether the illegality affects the reliability of the evidence. The traditional requirement that out-of-court confessions given by defendants be "voluntary" (discussed in Chapter 6) is an exclusionary rule under this definition. But in its original form, the prohibition against the use of involuntary confessions appears to have been based more upon a perception that coercion rendered confessions unreliable than upon the desirability of responding to illegality in the interrogation process by holding the fruits of that illegality inadmissible.

Discussions are often conducted in terms of what is assumed to be "the exclusionary rule," as if only one doctrine or legal requirement is involved. This is simply not the case. "[T]he exclusionary rule" usually describes the federal constitutional requirement—announced in Mapp v. Ohio, reprinted in this chapter—that evidence obtained in violation of the Fourth Amendment be excluded from state criminal trials. But *Mapp* is not the only legal requirement mandating exclusion of evidence because of impropriety in the manner in which it was obtained. Other federal constitutional provisions also require exclusion of evidence obtained in violation of their requirements. Moreover, the exclusionary requirements attaching to the various federal constitutional provisions are not necessarily the same. As is developed later in these materials, for example, the extent to which evidence derived from a violation must be excluded may differ significantly depending upon whether the underlying violation is of the Fourth Amendment's requirements or, instead, of judicially-developed rules based upon the Fifth Amendment.

Evidence obtained by conduct violating state legal requirements but not a federal constitutional provision may be inadmissible as a matter of state law. If state law imposes such a requirement, the details of that requirement—as, for example, the number and scope of exceptions sometime permitting the use of illegally seized evidence—may not be the same as the details of the Fourth Amendment federal constitutional exclusionary rule.

Conceptually, then, it is best to regard exclusionary requirements as consisting of a number of potentially quite different exclusionary demands imposed by various legal requirements. There could be as many exclusionary rules as there are legal requirements that might be violated in the obtaining of evidence.

The Fourth Amendment exclusionary rule announced in Mapp v. Ohio has generated the most controversy. Consequently, these materials emphasize that holding and its development. Showings that evidence was obtained in violation of other legal requirements present distinguishable although related exclusionary rule issues.

Exclusionary rule concerns are presented throughout these materials. Chapters 2 through 6 address a variety of issues concerning law enforcement authority to make searches and seizures. Action taken beyond this authority may invoke exclusionary sanctions. While exclusionary rule considerations are less pervasive in the material addressed in Chapters 7 through 9, they are nevertheless present and important. Chapter 1 is limited to the exclusionary sanction and its procedural aspects: When, if ever, is it appropriate? If it applies, when does it require the exclusion of challenged evidence? What exceptions to the general rule of exclusion do and should exist?

A. ADOPTION OF THE FEDERAL CONSTITUTIONAL EXCLUSIONARY SANCTION

EDITORS' INTRODUCTION

Exclusion of evidence resulting from improper law enforcement conduct was not a notion original with the United States Supreme Court. The Vermont court, for example, embraced an exclusionary rule as a matter of state law in State v. Slamon, 73 Vt. 212, 50 A. 1097 (1901). Nevertheless, the Supreme Court's adoption of this sanction for violation of federal constitutional rights is largely responsible for the pervasive impact exclusionary rules have on modern criminal procedure.

The Court's position in the case law culminating in the case reprinted in this part, Mapp v. Ohio, reflects both a break from evidence law tradition and the Court's prior position. In Adams v. New York, 192 U.S. 585, 24 S.Ct. 372 (1904), the Court rejected a state defendant's complaint regarding the use in his trial of evidence seized in violation of the Fourth Amendment. Where such evidence shows the accused's guilt, the Court explained, "the weight of authority as well as reason limits the inquiry to the competency of the proffered testimony, and the courts do not stop to inquire as to the means by which the evidence was obtained." This traditional position—that the manner in which otherwise competent evidence was obtained does not affect its admissibility—was supported by two major considerations: the need to have all available relevant evidence bearing on the important issues posed in criminal litigation, and the inconvenience, disruption, and other costs involved in making the complex and collateral inquiries determining whether challenged evidence was in fact improperly obtained.

A major issue posed by *Mapp* is the role history should play in construction of those federal constitutional provisions applicable to law enforcement conduct. Some members of the Supreme Court believe many aspects of the Fourth Amendment's contents should be determined or informed by the "intent" or contemplation of the framers as reflected in then-current law. Thus in Wyoming v. Houghton, 526 U.S. 295, 299, 119 S.Ct. 1297, 1300 (1999), Justice Scalia—writing for the Court—explained that "[i]n determining whether a particular governmental action violates [the Fourth Amendment], we inquire first whether the action was regarded as an unlawful search or seizure under the common law when the amendment was framed." Only if that inquiry provides no answer, he continued, is the Court to balance competing policy considerations in assessing the action's reasonableness. Should the Court have taken a similar approach in *Mapp*, and inquired whether under the common law in effect when the Fourth Amendment was framed a defendant such as *Mapp* was entitled to have excluded evidence improperly obtained?

The major argument against the approach applied by Justice Scalia in *Houghton* is its failure to take into account the vast difference between the common law context and modern criminal justice. In another decision relying heavily upon the common law position, the Supreme Court cautioned against excessive reliance upon this source:

> The significance accorded to [common law] authority * * * must be kept in perspective, for our decisions in this area have not "simply frozen into constitutional law those enforcement practices that existed at the time of the Fourth Amendment's passage." The common-law rules governing searches and arrests evolved in a society far simpler than ours is today. Crime has changed, as have the means of law enforcement, and it would therefore be naive to assume that those actions a constable could take in an English or American village three centuries ago should necessarily govern what we, as a society, now regard as proper. Instead, the Amendment's prohibition against "unreasonable searches and seizures" must be interpreted "in light of contemporary norms and conditions."

Steagald v. United States, 451 U.S. 204, 218 n. 10, 101 S.Ct. 1642, 1651 n. 10 (1981).

Mapp v. Ohio

Supreme Court of the United States, 1961.
367 U.S. 643, 81 S.Ct. 1684.

■ MR. JUSTICE CLARK delivered the opinion of the Court.

Appellant stands convicted of knowingly having had in her possession and under her control certain lewd and lascivious books, pictures, and photographs * * * though "based primarily upon the introduction in evidence of lewd and lascivious books and pictures unlawfully seized during an unlawful search of defendant's home * * * ." * * *

On May 23, 1957, three Cleveland police officers arrived at appellant's residence in that city pursuant to information that "a person [was] hiding out in the home, who was wanted for questioning in connection with a recent bombing, and that there was a large amount of policy paraphernalia being hidden in the home." * * * [B]ut appellant, after telephoning her attorney, refused to admit them without a search warrant. * * *

The officers again sought entrance some three hours later when four or more additional officers arrived on the scene. When Miss Mapp did not come to the door immediately, at least one of the several doors to the house was forcibly opened and the policemen gained admittance. Meanwhile Miss Mapp's attorney arrived, but the officers, having secured their own entry, and continuing in their defiance of the law, would permit him neither to see Miss Mapp nor to enter the house. It appears that Miss Mapp was halfway down the stairs from the upper floor to the front door when the officers, in this highhanded manner, broke into the hall. She demanded to see the search warrant. A paper, claimed to be a warrant, was held up by one of the officers. She grabbed the "warrant" and placed it in her bosom. A struggle ensued in which the officers recovered the piece of paper and as a result of which they handcuffed appellant because she had been "belligerent" in resisting their official rescue of the "warrant" from her person. * * * The obscene materials for possession of which she was ultimately convicted were discovered in the course of [a] widespread search.

At the trial no search warrant was produced by the prosecution, nor was the failure to produce one explained or accounted for. * * * The Ohio Supreme Court believed a "reasonable argument" could be made that the conviction should be reversed "because the 'methods' employed to obtain the [evidence] were such as to 'offend "a sense of justice," ' but the court found determinative the fact that the evidence had not been taken 'from defendant's person by the use of brutal or offensive physical force against defendant.' "

* * *

The State says that even if the search were made without authority, or otherwise unreasonably, it is not prevented from using the unconstitutionally seized evidence at trial, citing *Wolf v. People of the State of Colorado*, 1949, 338 U.S. 25, at page 33, 69 S.Ct. 1359 * * * , in which this Court did indeed hold "that in a prosecution in a State court for a State crime the Fourteenth Amendment does not forbid the admission of evidence obtained by an unreasonable search and seizure." On this appeal * * * it is urged once again that we review that holding.

I.

Seventy-five years ago, in *Boyd v. United States*, 1886, 116 U.S. 616, 630, 6 S.Ct. 524, 532, 29 L.Ed. 746, considering the Fourth and Fifth Amendments as running "almost into each other" on the facts before it, this Court held that the doctrines of those Amendments

"apply to all invasions on the part of the government and its employes of the sanctity of a man's home and the privacies of life. It is not the breaking of his doors, and the rummaging of his drawers, that constitutes the essence of the offence; but it is the invasion of his indefeasible right of personal security, personal liberty and private property * * * . Breaking into a house and opening boxes and drawers are circumstances of aggravation; but any forcible and compulsory extortion of a man's own testimony or of his private papers to be used as evidence to convict him of crime or to forfeit his goods, is within the condemnation * * * [of those Amendments]."

* * *

Less than 30 years after *Boyd*, this Court, in *Weeks v. United States*, 1914, [232 U.S. 383, 393, 34 S.Ct. 341, 344, 58 L.Ed. 652,] * * *

[s]pecifically dealing with the use of * * * evidence unconstitutionally seized, * * * concluded:

> "If letters and private documents can thus be seized and held and used in evidence against a citizen accused of an offense, the protection of the Fourth Amendment declaring his right to be secure against such searches and seizures is of no value, and, so far as those thus placed are concerned, might as well be stricken from the Constitution. The efforts of the courts and their officials to bring the guilty to punishment, praiseworthy as they are, are not to be aided by the sacrifice of those great principles established by years of endeavor and suffering which have resulted in their embodiment in the fundamental law of the land."

* * * Thus, in the year 1914, in the *Weeks* case, this Court "for the first time" held that "in a federal prosecution the Fourth Amendment barred the use of evidence secured through an illegal search and seizure."

* * * There are in the cases of this Court some passing references to the *Weeks* rule as being one of evidence. But the plain and unequivocal language of *Weeks* * * * to the effect that the *Weeks* rule is of constitutional origin, remains entirely undisturbed. * * *

II.

In 1949, 35 years after *Weeks* was announced, this Court, in *Wolf v. People of the State of Colorado*, supra, again for the first time, discussed the effect of the Fourth Amendment upon the States through the operation of the Due Process Clause of the Fourteenth Amendment. It said:

> "[W]e have no hesitation in saying that were a State affirmatively to sanction such police incursion into privacy it would run counter to the guaranty of the Fourteenth Amendment." * * *

Nevertheless, after declaring that the "security of one's privacy against arbitrary intrusion by the police" is "implicit in 'the concept of ordered liberty' and as such enforceable against the States through the Due Process Clause," * * * and announcing that it "stoutly adhere[d]" to the *Weeks* decision, the Court decided that the *Weeks* exclusionary rule would not then be imposed upon the States as "an essential ingredient of the right." * * * The Court's reasons for not considering essential to the right to privacy, as a curb imposed upon the States by the Due Process Clause, that which decades before had been posited as part and parcel of the Fourth Amendment's limitation upon federal encroachment of individual privacy, were bottomed on factual considerations.

While they are not basically relevant to a decision that the exclusionary rule is an essential ingredient of the Fourth Amendment as the right it embodies is vouchsafed against the States by the Due Process

Clause, we will consider the current validity of the factual grounds upon which *Wolf* was based.

The Court in *Wolf* * * * stated that "[t]he contrariety of views of the States" on the adoption of the exclusionary rule of *Weeks* was "particularly impressive" * * *; and, in this connection that it could not "brush aside the experience of States which deem the incidence of such conduct by the police too slight to call for a deterrent remedy * * * by overriding the [States'] relevant rules of evidence." * * * While in 1949, prior to the *Wolf* case, almost two-thirds of the States were opposed to the use of the exclusionary rule, now, despite the *Wolf* case, more than half of those since passing upon it, by their own legislative or judicial decision, have wholly or partly adopted or adhered to the *Weeks* rule. * * * Significantly, among those now following the rule is California, which, according to its highest court, was "compelled to reach that conclusion because other remedies have completely failed to secure compliance with the constitutional provisions * * *." *People v. Cahan*, 1955, 44 Cal.2d 434, 445, 282 P.2d 905, 911. In connection with this California case, we note that the second basis elaborated in *Wolf* in support of its failure to enforce the exclusionary doctrine against the States was that "other means of protection" have been afforded "the right to privacy." The experience of California that such other remedies have been worthless and futile is buttressed by the experience of other States. The obvious futility of relegating the Fourth Amendment to the protection of other remedies has, moreover, been recognized by this Court since *Wolf.*

* * *

It, therefore, plainly appears that the factual considerations supporting the failure of the *Wolf* Court to include the *Weeks* exclusionary rule when it recognized the enforceability of the right to privacy against the States in 1949, while not basically relevant to the constitutional consideration, could not, in any analysis, now be deemed controlling.

III.

Some five years after *Wolf*, in answer to a plea made here Term after Term that we overturn its doctrine on applicability of the *Weeks* exclusionary rule, this Court indicated that such should not be done until the States had "adequate opportunity to adopt or reject the [*Weeks*] rule." *Irvine v. People of State of California*, [1954, 347 U.S. 128, 134, 74 S.Ct. 381, 384, 98 L.Ed. 561] * * *. Today we once again examine *Wolf*'s constitutional documentation of the right to privacy free from unreasonable state intrusion, and, after its dozen years on our books, are led by it to close the only courtroom door remaining open to evidence secured by official lawlessness in flagrant abuse of that basic right, reserved to all persons as a specific guarantee against that very same unlawful conduct. We hold that all evidence obtained by searches and seizures in violation of the Constitution is, by that same authority, inadmissible in a state court.

IV.

Since the Fourth Amendment's right of privacy has been declared enforceable against the States through the Due Process Clause of the Fourteenth, it is enforceable against them by the same sanction of exclusion as is used against the Federal Government. Were it otherwise, then just as without the *Weeks* rule the assurance against unreasonable federal searches and seizures would be "a form of words", valueless and undeserving of mention in a perpetual charter of inestimable human liberties, so too, without that rule the freedom from state invasions of privacy would be so ephemeral and so neatly severed from its conceptual nexus with the freedom from all brutish means of coercing evidence as not to merit this Court's high regard as a freedom "implicit in 'the concept of ordered liberty.' " * * * In short, the admission of the new constitutional right by *Wolf* could not consistently tolerate denial of its most important constitutional privilege, namely, the exclusion of the evidence which an accused had been forced to give by reason of the unlawful seizure. To hold otherwise is to grant the right but in reality to withhold its privilege and enjoyment. Only last year the Court itself recognized that the purpose of the exclusionary rule "is to deter—to compel respect for the constitutional guaranty in the only effectively available way—by removing the incentive to disregard it." *Elkins v. United States*[, 1960, 364 U.S. 206, 217, 80 S.Ct. 1437, 1444, 4 L.Ed.2d (1669)].

* * *

V.

Moreover, our holding that the exclusionary rule is an essential part of both the Fourth and Fourteenth Amendments is not only the logical dictate of prior cases, but it also makes very good sense. There is no war between the Constitution and common sense. Presently, a federal prosecutor may make no use of evidence illegally seized, but a State's attorney across the street may, although he supposedly is operating under the enforceable prohibitions of the same Amendment. Thus the State, by admitting evidence unlawfully seized, served to encourage disobedience to the Federal Constitution which it is bound to uphold. * * *

Federal-state cooperation in the solution of crime under constitutional standards will be promoted, if only by recognition of their now mutual obligation to respect the same fundamental criteria in their approaches. "However much in a particular case insistence upon such rules may appear as a technicality that inures to the benefit of a guilty person, the history of the criminal law proves that tolerance of shortcut methods in law enforcement impairs its enduring effectiveness." *Miller v. United States*, 1958, 357 U.S. 301, 313, 78 S.Ct. 1190, 1197, 2 L.Ed.2d 1332. Denying shortcuts to only one of two cooperating law enforcement agencies tends naturally to breed legitimate suspicion of "working arrangements" whose results are equally tainted. * * *

There are those who say, as did Justice (then Judge) Cardozo, that under our constitutional exclusionary doctrine "[t]he criminal is to go free because the constable has blundered." *People v. Defore*, [1926, 242 N.Y. 13, 21, 150 N.E. 585, 587]. In some cases this will undoubtedly be the result. But, as was said in *Elkins*, "there is another consideration—the imperative of judicial integrity." * * * The criminal goes free, if he must, but it is the law that sets him free. Nothing can destroy a government more quickly than its failure to observe its own laws, or worse, its disregard of the charter of its own existence. As Mr. Justice Brandeis, dissenting, said in *Olmstead v. United States*, 1928, 277 U.S. 438, 485, 48 S.Ct. 564, 575, 72 L.Ed. 944: "Our government is the potent, the omnipresent teacher. For good or for ill, it teaches the whole people by its example. * * * If the government becomes a lawbreaker, it breeds contempt for law; it invites every man to become a law unto himself; it invites anarchy." Nor can it lightly be assumed that, as a practical matter, adoption of the exclusionary rule fetters law enforcement. Only last year this Court expressly considered that contention and found that "pragmatic evidence of a sort" to the contrary was not wanting. *Elkins v. United States*, supra. The Court noted that

> "The federal courts themselves have operated under the exclusionary rule of *Weeks* for almost half a century; yet it has not been suggested either that the Federal Bureau of Investigation has thereby been rendered ineffective, or that the administration of criminal justice in the federal courts has thereby been disrupted. Moreover, the experience of the states is impressive * * * . The movement towards the rule of exclusion has been halting but seemingly inexorable." * * *

The ignoble shortcut to conviction left open to the State tends to destroy the entire system of constitutional restraints on which the liberties of the people rest. Having once recognized that the right to privacy embodied in the Fourth Amendment is enforceable against the States, and that the right to be secure against rude invasions of privacy by state officers is, therefore, constitutional in origin, we can no longer permit that right to remain an empty promise. Because it is enforceable in the same manner and to like effect as other basic rights secured by the Due Process Clause, we can no longer permit it to be revocable at the whim of any police officer who, in the name of law enforcement itself, chooses to suspend its enjoyment. Our decision, founded on reason and truth, gives to the individual no more than that which the Constitution guarantees him, to the police officer no less than that to which honest law enforcement is entitled, and, to the courts, that judicial integrity so necessary in the true administration of justice.

The judgment of the Supreme Court of Ohio is reversed and the cause remanded for further proceedings not inconsistent with this opinion.

Reversed and remanded.

■ [The concurring opinions of JUSTICES BLACK and DOUGLAS and the dissenting opinion of JUSTICE HARLAN, joined by JUSTICES FRANKFURTER and WHITTAKER, are omitted.]

NOTES

1. **Exclusionary Sanctions for Fifth and Sixth Amendment Violations.** Following *Mapp,* the Supreme Court virtually without discussion assumed the federal constitution requires exclusion of evidence obtained in violation of the defendant's Fifth Amendment privilege against compelled self-incrimination, Miranda v. Arizona, 384 U.S. 436, 86 S.Ct. 1602 (1966), the Sixth Amendment right to counsel, Brewer v. Williams, 430 U.S. 387, 97 S.Ct. 1232 (1977), and the Sixth Amendment right to counsel during certain pretrial identification procedures, Gilbert v. California, 388 U.S. 263, 87 S.Ct. 1951 (1967).

2. **Judicial Integrity.** In post-*Mapp* case law, the Supreme Court refined its view as to the policy considerations supporting the Fourth Amendment exclusionary rule developed in that case. *Mapp,* for example, relied in part upon what it called "judicial integrity." This has clearly become considerably less significant. Fifteen years after *Mapp* the Court commented:

> Judicial integrity clearly does not mean that the courts must never admit evidence obtained in violation of the Fourth Amendment. * * *
>
> The primary meaning of "judicial integrity" in the context of evidentiary rules is that the courts must not commit or encourage violations of the Constitution. In the Fourth Amendment area, however, * * * the violation is complete by the time the evidence is presented to the court. The focus therefore must be on the question whether the admission of the evidence encourages violations of Fourth Amendment rights. * * * [T]his inquiry is essentially the same as the inquiry into whether exclusion would serve a deterrent purpose.

United States v. Janis, 428 U.S. 433, 458 n. 35, 96 S.Ct. 3021, 3034 n. 35 (1976).

3. **Remedial Function.** Is the *Mapp* exclusionary requirement supportable on the ground it provides an appropriate remedy for the wrong done to the person unreasonably searched or seized? The Court has stated:

> Post-*Mapp* decisions have established that the [exclusionary] rule is not a personal constitutional right. It is not calculated to redress the injury to the privacy of the victim of the search or seizure, for any "[r]eparation comes too late." *Linkletter v. Walker*, 381 U.S. 618, 637, 85 S.Ct. 1731, 14 L.Ed.2d 601 (1965). * * *

Stone v. Powell, 428 U.S. 465, 484–86, 96 S.Ct. 3037, 3047 (1976).

4. **Systemic Prevention.** Most discussions of the exclusionary sanction assume it works by consciously deterring particular officers from engaging in conduct they know will violate suspects' Fourth Amendment

rights. But the sanction may prevent violations in other ways. In Stone v. Powell, 428 U.S. 465, 96 S.Ct. 3037 (1976), the Court commented:

> [W]e have assumed that the immediate effect of exclusion will be to discourage law enforcement officials from violating the Fourth Amendment by removing the incentive to disregard it. More importantly, over the long term, this demonstration that our society attaches serious consequences to violation of constitutional rights is thought to encourage those who formulate law enforcement policies, and the officers who implement them, to incorporate Fourth Amendment ideals into their value system.

428 U.S. at 492, 96 S.Ct. at 3051. Even if exclusion of evidence does not cause law enforcement officials and officers to incorporate Fourth Amendment ideals into their internal value system, it may cause them to encourage compliance with the provision's requirements by the development of specific and practical guidelines and training programs. Some commentators refer to these processes by which exclusion might affect law enforcement behavior as "systemic deterrence." See Christopher Slobogin, Why Liberals Should Chuck the Exclusionary Rule, 1999 Ill.L.Rev. 363, 393 (1999).

5. **Injunctive Judicial Relief.** An alternative to exclusion of evidence as a device for changing law enforcement officers' behavior is the granting of judicial injunctive relief, particularly injunctive relief in federal litigation against local law enforcement agencies. Private parties seeking such injunctive remedies are sometimes impeded by the requirement that they show they are at risk of future harm by virtue of the police practices they want enjoined. City of Los Angeles v. Lyons, 461 U.S. 95, 111, 103 S.Ct. 1660, 1670 (1983). Nevertheless, they sometimes succeed. Floyd v. City of New York, 959 F.Supp.2d 540 (S.D.N.Y.2013), and Floyd v. City of New York, 959 F.Supp.2d 668 (S.D.N.Y.2013), discussed in Chapter 4, resulted in significant changes in New York City's "stop, question, and frisk" practices.

The Violent Crime Control and Law Enforcement Act of 1994 added to the United States Code, among other things, 42 U.S.C. § 14141. Under this provision, it is unlawful "to engage in a pattern or practice of conduct by law enforcement officers * * * that deprives persons of rights, privileges, or immunities secured or protected by the Constitution or laws of the United States." The United States Attorney General, on reasonable cause to believe that a violation of the provision has occurred, is authorized "in a civil action [to] obtain appropriate equitable and declaratory relief to eliminate the pattern or practice." See Stephen Rushin, Federal Enforcement of Police Reform, 82 Fordham L. Rev. 3189 (2014). In practice, the Department of Justice has negotiated settlements with local police departments it is prepared to proceed against, and this has resulted in judicially-approved settlements that can be enforced by the courts. See Stephen Rushin, Structural Reform Litigation in American Police Departments, 99 Minn. L.Rev. 1343, 1377 (2015) (Department has agreed to 24 settlements and 12 of these have resulted in appointment of external monitors for the police agencies involved). One commentator suggested that in the long run, enactment of this federal statute might be more significant than Mapp v.

Ohio. William J. Stuntz, The Pathological Politics of Criminal Law, 100 Mich. L. Rev. 505, 538 n. 134 (2001).

6. **Other Uses of Unconstitutionally Obtained Evidence.** In determining whether a federal constitutional exclusionary rule should be expanded beyond a prohibition against using unconstitutionally obtained evidence at trial to prove the defendant's guilt, the Court has utilized a balancing analysis. That analysis asks how much the functions of the rule would be increased by the additional exclusion of evidence that would result from the potential expansion. Addressing this generally involves primarily a consideration of the incremental deterrence that would be accomplished. The Court then weighs against this incremental deterrence the costs of so expanding the rule, and inquires whether the incremental deterrence is worth the cost. See United States v. Calandra, 414 U.S. 338, 349–52, 94 S.Ct. 613, 620–22 (1974).

In Pennsylvania Board of Probation and Parole v. Scott, 524 U.S. 357, 118 S.Ct. 2014 (1998), for example, the Court addressed whether evidence obtained in violation of the Fourth Amendment could be used at a parole violation hearing to prove a convicted and paroled defendant violated the conditions of parole. By a 5-to-4 vote, it held such evidence could be so used. Justice Thomas' opinion for the Court first stressed the cost of exclusion:

> Because the exclusionary rule precludes consideration of reliable, probative evidence, it imposes significant costs: it undeniably detracts from the truthfinding process and allows many who would otherwise be incarcerated to escape the consequences of their actions. * * * [O]ur cases have repeatedly emphasized that the rule's "costly toll" upon truth-seeking and law enforcement objectives presents a high obstacle for those urging application of the rule.

524 U.S. at 364–65, 118 S.Ct. at 2020. These costs are particularly high in the parole context, the Court continued, because states give up the right to continue incarceration of convicted persons on the condition they abide by the terms and conditions of parole release. Therefore, states have an "overwhelming interest" in enforcing these terms and limits, and this interest would be frustrated by application of the exclusionary rule. Further, application of the exclusionary rule would compel the states to transform parole revocation proceedings from "a 'productive and discretionary' effort to promote the best interests of both parolees and society into trial-like proceedings less attuned to the interests of the parolee."

The deterrent effect of applying the exclusionary rule to parole revocation would not, the *Scott* majority added, outweigh these costs. Officers will often be unaware that suspects are parolees, and thus "the remote possibility that the subject is a parolee and that the evidence may be admitted at a parole revocation proceeding surely has little, if any, effect on the officer's incentives."

The state court held the Fourth Amendment exclusionary rule should apply to parole revocation proceedings but only upon proof officers who engaged in the challenged search or seizure were aware of the suspect's status as a parolee. Rejecting this view, *Scott* first indicated this "piecemeal approach" would add to exclusionary rule procedure an undesirable need to inquire into officers' knowledge of parolees' status. Even in these cases, it added, deterrence would be minimal. Police officers aware of a suspect's parolee status will be deterred by the inadmissibility of illegally-seized evidence at criminal trials. Parole officers' relationship with parolees "is more supervisory than adversarial." This means "the harsh deterrent of exclusion [from parole revocation proceedings] is unwarranted," because adequate deterrence can be achieved by "other deterrents as departmental training and discipline and the threat of damages actions."

For these reasons, the *Scott* majority declined "to extend the operation of the exclusionary rule beyond the criminal trial context" as urged by Scott.

Four members of the Court disagreed:

> [T]he majority does not see that in the investigation of criminal conduct by someone known to be on parole, Fourth Amendment standards will have very little deterrent sanction unless evidence offered for parole revocation is subject to suppression for unconstitutional conduct. * * * [P]arole revocation will frequently be pursued instead of prosecution as the course of choice * * * . * * * [W]ithout a suppression remedy in revocation proceedings, there will often be no influence capable of deterring Fourth Amendment violations when parole revocation is a possible response to new crime. Suppression in the revocation proceeding cannot be looked upon, then, as furnishing merely incremental or marginal deterrence over and above the effect of exclusion in criminal prosecution. Instead, it will commonly provide the only deterrence to unconstitutional conduct when the incarceration of parolees is sought, and the reasons that support the suppression remedy in prosecution therefore support it in parole revocation.

524 U.S. at 378–79, 118 S.Ct. at 2027 (Souter, J., dissenting).

In *Calandra*, using a similar analysis, the Court held the Fourth Amendment exclusionary rule does not apply before a grand jury. Thus a suspect questioned by a grand jury has no right to avoid questions based on information obtained in violation of his Fourth Amendment rights. Any increase in deterrence resulting from extending the exclusionary rule to grand juries would be "speculative and undoubtedly minimal," the Court reasoned, and applying the exclusionary demand in this area might delay and impede grand jury investigations. 414 U.S. at 351–52, 94 S.Ct. at 621–22.

The same approach used in *Calandra* and *Scott* was applied in Stone v. Powell, 428 U.S. 465, 96 S.Ct. 3037 (1976), to determine whether state criminal defendants who had unsuccessfully sought suppression of evidence in their state trials on Fourth Amendment grounds could seek reconsideration of the matters in federal habeas corpus proceedings. Unless such state defendants were denied in the state trial an opportunity for full and fair litigation of their Fourth Amendment claims, the Court held, the *Mapp* exclusionary requirement did not entitle them to seek federal habeas corpus relief. If permitting state defendants to seek such relief in federal court would increase the deterrent effect of the exclusionary requirement—a matter on which the Court expressed doubt—this increased deterrence would be outweighed by the costs of so expanding the rule.

Much the same approach has been taken in the Court's consideration of proposed exceptions to the general requirements of exclusion. Exceptions in general, and the "good faith" exception in particular, are addressed in Subchapter C of this chapter.

7. **Actual Effect of Exclusion of Evidence.** Do exclusionary requirements affect law enforcement conduct? If so, how do they do so? What costs are paid for these requirements? These are matters that in theory should be subject to empirical study. Engaging in such study, however, is difficult because there are few opportunities to compare police actions subject to exclusionary sanctions and similar actions not so limited.

Many efforts to conduct such research on the effectiveness of the federal constitutional rules were reviewed in T. Perrin, H. Caldwell, C. Chase, and R. Fagan, It It's Broken, Fix It: Moving Beyond the Exclusionary Rule, 83 Iowa L. Rev. 669, 678–710 (1998). Some involved analysis of statistics regarding arrests, convictions, and suppression motions, others were conducted by direct observation of police officers, and a number undertook to survey police officers and others regarding their knowledge and attitudes. Perrin and his colleagues concluded the research is subject to methodological criticism but in general fails to support the promise that *Mapp* would "dramatically and beneficially impact[ ] police practices." They elaborated:

> The most that can be said is that *Mapp* has probably made officers more aware of the Fourth Amendment, and has increased the number of warrants they obtain, although it is less certain that it has actually affected their performance of their other duties. One costly effect of the exclusionary rule that emerges from the studies in that it has encouraged police officers to falsify their reports and their testimony.
>
> The studies show that *Mapp* has significantly increased the number of suppression motions filed * * * . The filing of these motions has driven up the cost of processing cases, and it beyond dispute that a number of apparently guilty defendants go free as a result of the rule.

83 Iowa L.Rev. at 710–11.

In 1984, the Supreme Court noted the developing research and commented on some interpretations of the leading study of the costs of *Mapp*:

> Researchers have only recently begun to study extensively the effects of the exclusionary rule on the disposition of felony arrests. One study suggests that the rule results in the nonprosecution or nonconviction of between 0.6% and 2.35% of individuals arrested for felonies. Davies, A Hard Look at What We Know (and Still Need to Learn) About the "Costs" of the Exclusionary Rule: The NIJ Study and Other Studies of "Lost" Arrests, 1983 A.B.F.Res.J. 611, 621. The estimates are higher for particular crimes the prosecution

of which depends heavily on physical evidence. Thus, the cumulative loss due to nonprosecution or nonconviction of individuals arrested on felony drug charges is probably in the range of 2.8% to 7.1%. Davies' analysis of California data suggests that screening by police and prosecutors results in the release because of illegal searches or seizures of as many as 1.4% of all felony arrestees, that 0.9% of felony arrestees are released, because of illegal searches or seizures, at the preliminary hearing or after trial, and that roughly 0.5% of all felony arrestees benefit from reversals on appeal because of illegal searches. * * *

Many * * * researchers have concluded that the impact of the exclusionary rule is insubstantial, but the small percentages with which they deal mask a large absolute number of felons who are released because the cases against them were based in part on illegal searches or seizures. * * *

United States v. Leon, 468 U.S. 897, 908 n. 6, 104 S.Ct. 3405, 3412 n. 6 (1984).

Christopher Slobogin, Why Liberals Should Chuck the Exclusionary Rule, 1999 Ill.L.Rev. 363, 369, 394 (1999), agreeing generally with Perrin, Caldwell, Chase, and Fagan, observed "we do not know how much the [exclusionary] rule deters, * * * [and, given the limitations of empirical inquiry, w]e probably never will." With regard to "systemic" deterrence or prevention, he concluded that "the systemic deterrent effect of the exclusionary rule is just not powerful enough to overcome a police culture that is unsympathetic to rules that restrict investigative powers."

8. **Nonconstitutional Illegality.** When evidence is obtained in violation of a nonconstitutional legal requirement—such as a federal or state statute—whether exclusion is possible or required presents a more difficult question. Clearly, there is no federal or state constitutional right to have evidence excluded because of a statutory violation. A few states have statutory provisions or court rules requiring exclusion in many such situations. E.g., Vernon's Ann.Tex.Code Crim.Pro. art. 38.23 (evidence obtained in violation of "any provisions of the Constitution or laws of the State of Texas" must be excluded); Alaska Evid.R. 412 (evidence "illegally obtained" is not to be used in a criminal prosecution). Sometimes specific statutory requirements explicitly direct exclusion.

Courts differ in their willingness to find unexpressed legislative "intentions" that violations of statutes are to result in exclusion of evidence. The Supreme Court has held without explanation that violation of a federal statute requiring prior announcement before entering premises to execute a warrant required exclusion. Miller v. United States, 357 U.S. 301, 78 S.Ct. 1190 (1958). In addition, the Supreme Court has held it has a "supervisory power" giving it authority to sometimes require exclusion of evidence obtained in violation of nonconstitutional legal requirements. McNabb v. United States, 318 U.S. 332, 63 S.Ct. 608 (1943). State courts may have a similar power. See People v. Dyla, 142 A.D.2d 423, 536 N.Y.S.2d 799 (1988). The Supreme Court has in recent cases been unwilling to exercise its supervisory power to create or develop "new" exclusionary requirements. See United States v. Payner, 447 U.S. 727, 100 S.Ct. 2439 (1980); United States v. Caceres, 440 U.S. 741, 99 S.Ct. 1465 (1979).

Some versions of nonconstitutional exclusionary requirements require more than a showing that the evidence was obtained as a result of a violation of the legal requirement involved. Federal Rule of Criminal Procedure 41 governs search warrants. Some federal courts hold that evidence must be excluded because of a violation of the rule's requirements only if either the defendant shows "prejudice"—the search might not have occurred or would not have been so abrasive if the rule had been followed—or intentional and deliberate disregard of the rule. United States v. Krueger, 809 F.3d 1109, 1113–14 (10th Cir. 2015). Others direct exclusion if the defendant shows a reckless disregard of the rule's requirements. United States v. Beckmann, 786 F.3d 672, 680 (8th Cir. 2015).

B. SCOPE OF EXCLUSIONARY SANCTIONS: STANDING, FRUIT OF THE POISONOUS TREE, INDEPENDENT SOURCE AND ATTENUATION OF THE TAINT

EDITORS' INTRODUCTORY NOTE: EXCLUSIONARY SANCTION ISSUES, REQUIREMENTS AND EXCEPTIONS

Determinations that law enforcement officers engaged in activity during the preparation of the prosecution's case and that this activity violated the Fourth Amendment or some other legal requirement that triggers an exclusionary sanction does not complete the inquiry into the admissibility of evidence obtained by the officers. In fact, the Supreme Court's post-*Mapp* case law has greatly increased the complexity of two subissues needing consideration: (1) what evidence is rendered inadmissible by demonstrated law enforcement misconduct; and (2) what persons are able to invoke the exclusionary remedy?

In considering the issues presented by these cases, it may be useful to first identify those matters a defendant seeking exclusion of evidence must establish to make a basic case for exclusion. These might usefully be distinguished from "exceptions" to the requirement of exclusion triggered by the making of such a basic case.

The distinction may be useful in litigation because it may determine which party has the burden of persuasion. Although the Supreme Court has never comprehensively addressed the allocation of the burden[s] of persuasion in litigation under the federal constitutional exclusionary sanction, there is widespread agreement that a defendant seeking to have evidence suppressed must prove (1) illegality sufficient to trigger the exclusionary sanction; (2) the defendant's right to invoke that sanction ("standing"); and (3) that the challenged evidence was obtained as a factual result of the illegality or, as courts often put the matter, that the evidence was "fruit of the poisonous tree." There is also widespread agreement that if the prosecution responds by relying on an "exception" to the general requirement of exclusion, the prosecution bears the burden of persuasion regarding the exception.

Whatever the allocation of the burden of persuasion, that burden is not high. In general, the Court announced in United States v. Matlock, 415 U.S. 164, 178 n. 14, 94 S.Ct. 988, 996 n. 14 (1974), the controlling standard of proof at suppression hearings should impose no greater burden than proof by a preponderance of the evidence.

The principal case in this part is an early one, but the opinion demonstrates the interrelationship among the issues presented by many instances of exclusionary sanction litigation. The propriety of the arrests of the defendants was in dispute. Four members of the Supreme Court, in a dissenting opinion by Justice Clark, took the position that neither arrest was constitutionally impermissible. For present purposes, assume the arrests were constitutionally unreasonable and consider what effect those arrests should have upon the admissibility of the various evidence offered by the prosecution against each of the defendants.

Wong Sun v. United States

Supreme Court of the United States, 1963.
371 U.S. 471, 83 S.Ct. 407.

■ MR. JUSTICE BRENNAN delivered the opinion of the Court.

The petitioners were tried without a jury in the District Court for the Northern District of California under a two-count indictment for violation of the Federal Narcotics Laws * * * . They were acquitted under the first count which charged a conspiracy, but convicted under the second count which charged the substantive offense of fraudulent and knowing transportation and concealment of illegally imported heroin. The Court of Appeals for the Ninth Circuit, one judge dissenting, affirmed the convictions. We granted certiorari. * * * .

About 2 a.m. on the morning of June 4, 1959, federal narcotics agents in San Francisco, after having had one Hom Way under surveillance for six weeks, arrested him and found heroin in his possession. Hom Way, who had not before been an informant, stated after his arrest that he had bought an ounce of heroin the night before from one known to him only as "Blackie Toy," proprietor of a laundry on Leavenworth Street.

About 6 a. m. that morning six or seven federal agents went to a laundry at 1733 Leavenworth Street. The sign above the door of this establishment said "Oye's Laundry." It was operated by the petitioner James Wah Toy. There is, however, nothing in the record which identifies James Wah Toy and "Blackie Toy" as the same person. The other federal officers remained nearby out of sight while Agent Alton Wong, who was of Chinese ancestry, rang the bell. When petitioner Toy appeared and opened the door, Agent Wong told him that he was calling for laundry and dry cleaning. Toy replied that he didn't open until 8 o'clock and told the agent to come back at that time. Toy started to close the door. Agent

Wong thereupon took his badge from his pocket and said, "I am a federal narcotics agent." Toy immediately "slammed the door and started running" down the hallway through the laundry to his living quarters at the back where his wife and child were sleeping in a bedroom. Agent Wong and the other federal officers broke open the door and followed Toy down the hallway to the living quarters and into the bedroom. Toy reached into a nightstand drawer. Agent Wong thereupon drew his pistol, pulled Toy's hand out of the drawer, placed him under arrest and handcuffed him. There was nothing in the drawer and a search of the premises uncovered no narcotics.

One of the agents said to Toy " * * * [Hom Way] says he got narcotics from you." Toy responded, "No, I haven't been selling any narcotics at all. However, I do know somebody who has." When asked who that was, Toy said, "I only know him as Johnny. I don't know his last name." However, Toy described a house on Eleventh Avenue where he said Johnny lived; he also described a bedroom in the house where he said "Johnny kept about a piece"[2] of heroin, and where he and Johnny had smoked some of the drug the night before. The agents left immediately for Eleventh Avenue and located the house. They entered and found one Johnny Yee in the bedroom. After a discussion with the agents, Yee took from a bureau drawer several tubes containing in all just less than one ounce of heroin, and surrendered them. Within the hour Yee and Toy were taken to the Office of the Bureau of Narcotics. Yee there stated that the heroin had been brought to him some four days earlier by petitioner Toy and another Chinese known to him only as "Sea Dog."

Toy was questioned as to the identity of "Sea Dog" and said that "Sea Dog" was Wong Sun. Some agents, including Agent Alton Wong, took Toy to Wong Sun's neighborhood where Toy pointed out a multifamily dwelling where he said Wong Sun lived. Agent Wong rang a downstairs door bell and a buzzer sounded, opening the door. The officer identified himself as a narcotics agent to a woman on the landing and asked "for Mr. Wong." The woman was the wife of petitioner Wong Sun. She said that Wong Sun was "in the back room sleeping." Alton Wong and some six other officers climbed the stairs and entered the apartment. One of the officers went into the back room and brought petitioner Wong Sun from the bedroom in handcuffs. A thorough search of the apartment followed, but no narcotics were discovered.

Petitioner Toy and Johnny Yee were arraigned before a United States Commissioner on June 4 on a complaint * * * . Later that day, each was released on his own recognizance. Petitioner Wong Sun was arraigned on a similar complaint filed the next day and was also released on his own recognizance. Within a few days, both petitioners and Yee were interrogated at the office of the Narcotics Bureau by Agent William Wong, also of Chinese ancestry. The agent advised each of the three of

---

[2] A "piece" is approximately one ounce.

his right to withhold information which might be used against him, and stated to each that he was entitled to the advice of counsel, though it does not appear that any attorney was present during the questioning of any of the three. The officer also explained to each that no promises or offers of immunity or leniency were being or could be made.

The agent interrogated each of the three separately. After each had been interrogated the agent prepared a statement in English from rough notes. The agent read petitioner Toy's statement to him in English and interpreted certain portions of it for him in Chinese. Toy also read the statement in English aloud to the agent, said there were corrections to be made, and made the corrections in his own hand. Toy would not sign the statement, however; in the agent's words "he wanted to know first if the other persons involved in the case had signed theirs." Wong Sun had considerable difficulty understanding the statement in English and the agent restated its substance in Chinese. Wong Sun refused to sign the statement although he admitted the accuracy of its contents.

Hom Way did not testify at petitioners' trial. The Government offered Johnny Yee as its principal witness but excused him after he invoked the privilege against self-incrimination and flatly repudiated the statement he had given to Agent William Wong. That statement was not offered in evidence nor was any testimony elicited from him identifying either petitioner as the source of the heroin in his possession, or otherwise tending to support the charges against the petitioners.

The statute expressly provides that proof of the accused's possession of the drug will support a conviction under the statute unless the accused satisfactorily explains the possession. The Government's evidence tending to prove the petitioners' possession (the petitioners offered no exculpatory testimony) consisted of four items which the trial court admitted over timely objections that they were inadmissible as "fruits" of unlawful arrests or of attendant searches: (1) the statements made orally by petitioner Toy in his bedroom at the time of his arrest; (2) the heroin surrendered to the agents by Johnny Yee; (3) petitioner Toy's pretrial unsigned statement; and (4) petitioner Wong Sun's similar statement. The dispute below and here has centered around the correctness of the rulings of the trial judge allowing these items in evidence.

The Court of Appeals held that the arrests of both petitioners were illegal because not based on " 'probable cause' within the meaning of the Fourth Amendment" * * * [but] nevertheless [also] held that the four items of proof were not the "fruits" of the illegal arrests and that they were therefore properly admitted in evidence.

The Court of Appeals rejected [an] additional [contention] of the petitioners. [This] was that there was insufficient evidence to corroborate the petitioners' unsigned admissions of possession of narcotics. The court held that the narcotics in evidence surrendered by Johnny Yee, together with Toy's statements in his bedroom at the time of arrest corroborated petitioners' admissions. * * *

We believe that significant differences between the cases of the two petitioners require separate discussion of each. We shall first consider the case of petitioner Toy.

I.

The Court of Appeals found there was [not] probable cause for Toy's arrest. Giving due weight to that finding, we think it is amply justified by the facts clearly shown on this record. * * *

II.

It is conceded that Toy's declarations in his bedroom are to be excluded if they are held to be "fruits" of the agents' unlawful action.

In order to make effective the fundamental constitutional guarantees of sanctity of the home and inviolability of the person, this Court held nearly half a century ago that evidence seized during an unlawful search could not constitute proof against the victim of the search. The exclusionary prohibition extends as well to the indirect as the direct products of such invasions. *Silverthorne Lumber Co. v. United States*, 251 U.S. 385, 40 S.Ct. 182, 64 L.Ed. 319. Mr. Justice Holmes, speaking for the Court in that case, in holding that the Government might not make use of information obtained during an unlawful search to subpoena from the victims the very documents illegally viewed, expressed succinctly the policy of the broad exclusionary rule:

> "The essence of a provision forbidding the acquisition of evidence in a certain way is that not merely evidence so acquired shall not be held before the Court but that it shall not be used at all. Of course this does not mean that the facts thus obtained become sacred and inaccessible. If knowledge of them is gained from an independent source they may be proved like any others, but the knowledge gained by the Government's own wrong cannot be used by it in the way proposed."

The exclusionary rule has traditionally barred from trial physical, tangible materials obtained either during or as a direct result of an unlawful invasion. It follows * * * that the Fourth Amendment may protect against the overhearing of verbal statements as well as against the more traditional seizure of "papers and effects." Similarly, testimony as to matters observed during an unlawful invasion has been excluded in order to enforce the basic constitutional policies. Thus, verbal evidence which derives so immediately from an unlawful entry and an unauthorized arrest as the officers' action in the present case is no less the "fruit" of official illegality than the more common tangible fruits of the unwarranted intrusion. Nor do the policies underlying the exclusionary rule invite any logical distinction between physical and verbal evidence. * * * [T]he danger in relaxing the exclusionary rules in the case of verbal evidence would seem too great to warrant introducing such a distinction.

The Government argues that Toy's statements to the officers in his bedroom, although closely consequent upon the invasion which we hold unlawful, were nevertheless admissible because they resulted from "an intervening independent act of a free will." This contention, however, takes insufficient account of the circumstances. Six or seven officers had broken the door and followed on Toy's heels into the bedroom where his wife and child were sleeping. He had been almost immediately handcuffed and arrested. Under such circumstances it is unreasonable to infer that Toy's response was sufficiently an act of free will to purge the primary taint of the unlawful invasion.

* * *

III.

We now consider whether the exclusion of Toy's declarations requires also the exclusion of the narcotics taken from Yee, to which those declarations led the police. The prosecutor candidly told the trial court that "we wouldn't have found those drugs except that Mr. Toy helped us to." Hence this is not the case envisioned by this Court where the exclusionary rule has no application because the Government learned of the evidence "from an independent source," nor is this a case in which the connection between the lawless conduct of the police and the discovery of the challenged evidence has "become so attenuated as to dissipate the taint." We need not hold that all evidence is "fruit of the poisonous tree" simply because it would not have come to light but for the illegal actions of the police. Rather, the more apt question in such a case is "whether, granting establishment of the primary illegality, the evidence to which instant objection is made has been come at by exploitation of that illegality or instead by means sufficiently distinguishable to be purged of the primary taint." Maguire, Evidence of Guilt, 221 (1959). We think it clear that the narcotics were "come at by the exploitation of that illegality" and hence that they may not be used against Toy.

IV.

It remains only to consider Toy's unsigned statement. We need not decide whether, in light of the fact that Toy was free on his own recognizance when he made the statement, that statement was a fruit of the illegal arrest. Since we have concluded that his declarations in the bedroom and the narcotics surrendered by Yee should not have been admitted in evidence against him, the only proofs remaining to sustain his conviction are his and Wong Sun's unsigned statements. Without scrutinizing the contents of Toy's ambiguous recitals, we conclude that no reference to Toy in Wong Sun's statement constitutes admissible evidence corroborating any admission by Toy. We arrive at this conclusion upon two clear lines of decisions which converge to require it. One line of our decisions establishes that criminal confessions and admissions of guilt require extrinsic corroboration; the other line of precedents holds that an out-of-court declaration made after arrest may not be used at trial against one of the declarant's partners in crime.

It is a settled principle of the administration of criminal justice in the federal courts that a conviction must rest upon firmer ground than the uncorroborated admission or confession of the accused. We observed in *Smith v. United States*, 348 U.S. 147, 153, 75 S.Ct. 194, 197, 99 L.Ed. 192, that the requirement of corroboration is rooted in "a long history of judicial experience with confessions and in the realization that sound law enforcement requires police investigations which extend beyond the words of the accused." * * * Wong Sun's unsigned confession does not furnish competent corroborative evidence. The second governing principle, likewise well settled in our decisions, is that an out-of-court declaration made after arrest may not be used at trial against one of the declarant's partners in crime. While such a statement is "admissible against the others where it is in furtherance of the criminal undertaking * * * all such responsibility is at an end when the conspiracy ends." *Fiswick v. United States*, 329 U.S. 211, 217, 67 S.Ct. 224, 227, 91 L.Ed. 196. * * *

V.

We turn now to the case of the other petitioner, Wong Sun. We have no occasion to disagree with the finding of the Court of Appeals that his arrest, also, was without probable cause or reasonable grounds. At all events no evidentiary consequences turn upon that question. For Wong Sun's unsigned confession was not the fruit of that arrest, and was therefore properly admitted at trial. On the evidence that Wong Sun had been released on his own recognizance after a lawful arraignment, and had returned voluntarily several days later to make the statement, we hold that the connection between the arrest and the statement had "become so attenuated as to dissipate the taint." * * *

We must then consider the admissibility of the narcotics surrendered by Yee. Our holding, supra, that this ounce of heroin was inadmissible against Toy does not compel a like result with respect to Wong Sun. The exclusion of the narcotics as to Toy was required solely by their tainted relationship to information unlawfully obtained from Toy, and not by any official impropriety connected with their surrender by Yee. The seizure of this heroin invaded no right of privacy of person or premises which would entitle Wong Sun to object to its use at his trial.

However, for the reasons that Wong Sun's statement was incompetent to corroborate Toy's admissions contained in Toy's own statement, any references to Wong Sun in Toy's statement were incompetent to corroborate Wong Sun's admissions. Thus, the only competent source of corroboration for Wong Sun's statement was the heroin itself. We cannot be certain, however, on this state of the record, that the trial judge may not also have considered the contents of Toy's statement as a source of corroboration. Petitioners raised as one ground of objection to the introduction of the statements the claim that each statement, "even if it were a purported admission or confession or declaration against interest of a defendant * * * would not be binding upon the other defendant." The trial judge, in allowing the statements in, apparently overruled all of petitioners' objections, including this one. Thus we presume that he considered all portions of both statements as bearing upon the guilt of both petitioners.

We intimate no view one way or the other as to whether the trial judge might have found in the narcotics alone sufficient evidence to corroborate Wong Sun's admissions that he delivered heroin to Yee and smoked heroin at Yee's house around the date in question. But because he might, as the factfinder, have found insufficient corroboration from the narcotics alone, we cannot be sure that the scales were not tipped in favor of conviction by reliance upon the inadmissible Toy statement. * * * We therefore hold that petitioner Wong Sun is also entitled to a new trial.

The judgment of the Court of Appeals is reversed and the case is remanded to the District Court for further proceedings consistent with this opinion.

It is so ordered.

Judgment of Court of Appeals reversed and case remanded to the District Court.

■ [The concurring opinion of JUSTICE DOUGLAS and the dissenting opinion of JUSTICE CLARK, joined by JUSTICES HARLAN, STEWART and WHITE, are omitted.]

NOTES

1.   The requirement that a confession be corroborated is discussed in Chapter 6.

2.   **"Standing" or the "Personal Nature" of Federal Constitutional Rights.** The doctrine which precluded Wong Sun from successfully objecting to the introduction of the heroin on the same grounds as were successful for Toy has traditionally been described as a requirement of "standing." Application of the requirement to specific search situations is explored further in Subchapter C of Chapter 2.

In Rakas v. Illinois, 439 U.S. 128, 99 S.Ct. 421 (1978) (reprinted in part in Chapter 2), however, the Supreme Court appeared to "dispens[e] with the rubric of standing." Cases containing standing discussions, it explained, simply applied the principle that Fourth Amendment rights are personal in nature. Whether particular defendants can challenge particular law enforcement conduct should be discussed in those terms:

> Analyzed in these terms, the question is whether the challenged search or seizure violated the Fourth Amendment rights of a criminal defendant who seeks to exclude the evidence obtained during it. That inquiry in turn requires a determination of whether the disputed search and seizure has infringed an interest of the defendant which the Fourth Amendment was designed to protect. * * * [T]his aspect of the analysis belongs more

properly under the heading of substantive Fourth Amendment doctrine rather than under the heading of standing * * * .

439 U.S. at 140, 99 S.Ct. at 429. The majority emphasized the abandonment of standing rubric would not change either the basic inquiry or the outcome of cases. But the shift, it explained, should focus concern on "the extent of a particular defendant's rights under the Fourth Amendment, rather than on any theoretically separate, but invariably intertwined concept of standing." Further, this approach should result in particular decisions resting on "sounder logical footing."

Earlier, the Court had defended the requirement of standing on its merits:

> Fourth Amendment rights are personal rights which, like some other constitutional rights, may not be vicariously asserted. * * * There is no necessity to exclude evidence against one defendant in order to protect the rights of another. No rights of the victim of an illegal search are at stake when the evidence is offered against some other party. The victim can and very probably will object for himself when and if it becomes important for him to do so. * * * [None of our cases] hold that anything which deters illegal searches is thereby commanded by the Fourth Amendment. The deterrent values of preventing the incrimination of those whose rights the police have violated have been considered sufficient to justify the suppression of probative evidence even though the case against the defendant is weakened or destroyed. We adhere to that judgment. But we are not convinced that the additional benefits of extending the exclusionary rule to other defendants would justify further encroachment upon the public interest in prosecuting those accused of crime and having them acquitted or convicted on the basis of all the evidence which exposes the truth.

Alderman v. United States, 394 U.S. 165, 174–75, 89 S.Ct. 961, 966–97 (1969).

In *Rakas*, the Court rejected a proposal that it permit any criminal defendant at whom a search was "directed" to challenge the admissibility of evidence obtained as a result of that search. It explained it was unwilling to increase the amount of reliable evidence that would be rendered unavailable by the exclusionary rule. It also quoted with approval Justice Harlan's argument in *Alderman* that such a "target" rule would involve excessive administrative costs in the form of lengthy hearings to determine whether or not particular defendants were the "targets" of particular police action.

3. **Fruit of the Poisonous Tree.** In holding Toy's bedroom statements inadmissible, *Wong Sun* applied what is often called the "fruit of the poisonous tree" rule. Once a defendant establishes a violation of his Fourth Amendment rights, the defendant is entitled to suppression of all "fruit of [that] poisonous tree." Nardone v. United States, 308 U.S. 338, 341, 60 S.Ct. 266, 268 (1939). This position is sometimes stated as the "derivative evidence" rule—all evidence derived from a violation of the defendant's rights must be suppressed. The "core rationale" for this rule, the Court has

explained, is "that this admittedly drastic and socially costly course is needed to deter police from violations" of the protections involved. Nix v. Williams, 467 U.S. 431, 442–43, 104 S.Ct. 2501, 2508 (1984).

The "fruits" rule is not applied in some situations, as where police illegality consists of a violation of *Miranda* requirements. Admissibility of evidence obtained as a result of a *Miranda* violation is developed in Chapter 6.

A defendant seeking to invoke the "fruits" doctrine must establish that the challenged evidence was obtained by police as a factual result of a violation of his rights. Murray v. United States, 487 U.S. 533, 108 S.Ct. 2529 (1988). Obviously, evidence obtained by law enforcement officers *before* they violated a defendant's rights is not the "fruit" of the violation and hence is not subject to challenge. See Waller v. Georgia, 467 U.S. 39, 104 S.Ct. 2210 (1984).

Murray illustrates the difficulty sometimes involved in showing the required factual causation. Federal officers conducting a drug investigation observed several suspicious vehicles enter and leave a warehouse in South Boston. About 2:30 p.m. and without a search warrant, the officers went to the warehouse, forced open the door, and entered. While inside, they observed burlap-wrapped bales. They then, without seizing or disturbing those bales, left the warehouse. Later, the officers applied for a search warrant for the warehouse. The application relied upon other information possessed by the officers at the time of their first entry and did not mention they had already entered the structure. The warrant issued about 10:45 p.m. Pursuant to that warrant, the officers entered the warehouse and seized 270 bales of marijuana—including the bales observed during the earlier entry—as well as other incriminating items. Murray and Carter were charged with conspiracy to possess and distribute the marijuana. Before trial, they moved to suppress the evidence obtained from the warehouse on the ground it was the "fruit" of the officers' first and unreasonable warrantless entry of the warehouse. The Court of Appeals held that this motion should have been granted. By a 4–3 vote, with two justices not participating, the Supreme Court vacated and remanded. Knowledge that the marijuana was in the warehouse, Justice Scalia wrote for the majority, was obtained in the first and presumably-unreasonable search of the warehouse. But such knowledge as well as the marijuana itself were acquired in the second and reasonable search pursuant to the warrant. If the search pursuant to the warrant was "genuinely independent" of the first search, the evidence would be admissible. This "independent source" rule, he explained, is based on the need to limit exclusion of evidence to those situations in which rejecting it is necessary to deter improper police activity. Deterrence is adequately accomplished by placing the police in the position they would have occupied had the illegal search not occurred. It does not require placing them in a *worse* position. Excluding evidence having an independent source would be to unjustifiably place the police in such a worse position; they would be deprived of evidence that they in fact obtained independently of their improper conduct.

But this doctrine requires that the manner in which the evidence was obtained be "genuinely independent" of the illegal search. "This would not have been the case," Justice Scalia explained, "if the agents' decision to seek the warrant was prompted by what they had seen during the initial entry, or if information obtained during that entry was presented to the Magistrate and affected his decision to issue the warrant." The lower courts determined the officers had not revealed to the magistrate issuing the search warrant any information from the illegal entry. But no finding was made as to whether or not the officers would have sought a warrant for the warehouse if they had not earlier entered it. The matter was therefore remanded to the District Court for a determination as to whether the search pursuant to the warrant was an independent source of the challenged evidence in the sense that the opinion defined independent source.

4.   **Independent Source.** Justice Holmes's discussion in *Silverthorne Lumber Co.*, quoted in *Wong Sun*, referred to evidence gained from "an independent source." If evidence is obtained by police after they violated a defendant's rights, but not as a consequence of that violation, the evidence is often said to have such an independent source and, as a result, is admissible despite officers' intrusion upon the defendant's rights.

If the prosecution argues challenged evidence is admissible under the independent source doctrine, which side has the burden of persuasion? This may depend upon how the doctrine is conceptualized. If it is an exception to the general rule that all evidence proved fruit of a poisonous tree must be suppressed, the prosecution would most likely have the burden of establishing its applicability. Independent source may, on the other hand, be simply a label for a conclusion that a defendant has failed to establish that the challenged evidence was obtained as a factual result of the official misconduct. A defendant probably has the burden of establishing that challenged evidence was obtained as a factual result of unreasonable law enforcement conduct. Thus independent source would seem to be only a theory on which the prosecution can argue that the defendant has failed to meet his burden of persuasion regarding the necessary causal link.

In general, the Supreme Court has not made clear either the nature of independent source or the placement of the burden of persuasion. It has, however, addressed the situation in which a defendant establishes a lineup was conducted in violation of his Sixth Amendment right to counsel, and a witness identified him at that lineup. The prosecution can escape suppression of the witness's in-court identification testimony only if it establishes—by clear and convincing evidence—the in-court testimony of that witness's in-court identification testimony would be based on a source independent of the tainted lineup. United States v. Wade, 388 U.S. 218, 240, 87 S.Ct. 1926 1939 (1967) (reprinted in Chapter 9). This holding may rest upon a perception that independent source, as applied in lineup situations, involves such an unusually difficult and speculative inquiry that error can be avoided only by placing the burden of persuasion on the prosecution. Cf., Nix v. Williams. 467 U.S. 431, 444 n. 5, 104 S.Ct. 2501, 2509 n. 5 (1984). In other situations, the burden of proof may remain on the defendant to show the challenged evidence was discovered as a factual result of the illegality, although only by a preponderance of the evidence.

5. **Defendant's Presence as "Fruit."** The Supreme Court recognized one qualification to the general rule that "fruit of the poisonous tree" must be excluded: the defendant's physical presence for trial and punishment is never the excludable "fruit" of improper law enforcement conduct. Illegal police activity, the Court made clear, affects only the admissibility of evidence; it does not affect the jurisdiction of the trial court or otherwise serve as a basis for dismissing the prosecution. Ker v. Illinois, 119 U.S. 436, 7 S.Ct. 225 (1886). In United States v. Blue, 384 U.S. 251, 86 S.Ct. 1416 (1966), the Court explained its adherence to this approach despite *Mapp* and the "constitutionalization" of the exclusionary rule:

> So drastic a step [as barring the prosecution altogether] might advance marginally some of the ends served by the exclusionary rules, but it would also increase to an intolerable degree interference with the public interest in having the guilty brought to book.

384 U.S. at 225, 86 S.Ct. at 1419.

6. **Attenuation of the Taint.** As the principal case makes clear, the "fruit of the poisonous tree" doctrine is subject to the qualification that "fruit" of a violation of the defendant's rights becomes admissible if the prosecution establishes that the "taint" of the constitutional violation was "attenuated" when the challenged evidence was obtained. "Evidence is admissible [under the attenuation of taint doctrine] when the connection between unconstitutional police conduct and the evidence is remote or has been interrupted by some intervening circumstance, so that 'the interest protected by the constitutional guarantee that has been violated would not be served by suppression of the evidence obtained.'" Utah v. Strieff, ___ U.S.___, ___, 136 S.Ct. 2056, 2061 (2016).

Applying the attenuation doctrine, *Strieff* added, involves evaluation of the causal link between the government's unlawful act and the discovery of evidence:

> The three factors articulated in *Brown v. Illinois,* 422 U.S. 590, 95 S.Ct. 2254, 45 L.Ed.2d 416 (1975), guide our analysis. First, we look to the "temporal proximity" between the unconstitutional conduct and the discovery of evidence to determine how closely the discovery of evidence followed the unconstitutional search. Second, we consider "the presence of intervening circumstances." Third, and "particularly" significant, we examine "the purpose and flagrancy of the official misconduct."

___ U.S. at ___, 136 S.Ct. at 2061–62.

In *Strieff,* an officer—Fackrell—detained Strieff after seeing Strieff leave a suspected drug house. He, however, lacked sufficient information to establish reasonable suspicion as required by Fourth Amendment law. During the detention, the officer learned there was an outstanding warrant for Strieff's arrest and he arrested Strieff on that warrant. A search incident to the arrest revealed drugs and related paraphernalia. Was the taint of the unreasonable detention attenuated by the time the contraband was discovered? By a 5-to-3 vote, the Court held it was. The majority explained:

The first factor, temporal proximity between the initially unlawful stop and the search, favors suppressing the evidence. Our precedents have declined to find that this factor favors attenuation unless "substantial time" elapses between an unlawful act and when the evidence is obtained. Here, however, Officer Fackrell discovered drug contraband on Strieff's person only minutes after the illegal stop. * * * [S]uch a short time interval counsels in favor of suppression * * *

In contrast, the second factor, the presence of intervening circumstances, strongly favors the State. * * * [T]he existence of a valid warrant favors finding that the connection between unlawful conduct and the discovery of evidence is "sufficiently attenuated to dissipate the taint." That principle applies here.

In this case, the warrant was valid, it predated Officer Fackrell's investigation, and it was entirely unconnected with the stop. And once Officer Fackrell discovered the warrant, he had an obligation to arrest Strieff. * * * Officer Fackrell's arrest of Strieff thus was a ministerial act that was independently compelled by the pre-existing warrant. And once Officer Fackrell was authorized to arrest Strieff, it was undisputedly lawful to search Strieff as an incident of his arrest to protect Officer Fackrell's safety.

Finally, the third factor, "the purpose and flagrancy of the official misconduct," also strongly favors the State. The exclusionary rule exists to deter police misconduct. The third factor of the attenuation doctrine reflects that rationale by favoring exclusion only when the police misconduct is most in need of deterrence—that is, when it is purposeful or flagrant.

Officer Fackrell was at most negligent. In stopping Strieff, Officer Fackrell made two good-faith mistakes. First, he had not observed what time Strieff entered the suspected drug house, so he did not know how long Strieff had been there. Officer Fackrell thus lacked a sufficient basis to conclude that Strieff was a short-term visitor who may have been consummating a drug transaction. Second, because he lacked confirmation that Strieff was a short-term visitor, Officer Fackrell should have asked Strieff whether he would speak with him, instead of demanding that Strieff do so. Officer Fackrell's stated purpose was to "find out what was going on [in] the house." Nothing prevented him from approaching Strieff simply to ask. But these errors in judgment hardly rise to a purposeful or flagrant violation of Strieff's Fourth Amendment rights.

While Officer Fackrell's decision to initiate the stop was mistaken, his conduct thereafter was lawful. The officer's decision to run the warrant check was a "negligibly burdensome precautio[n]" for officer safety. And Officer Fackrell's actual search of Strieff was a lawful search incident to arrest.

Moreover, there is no indication that this unlawful stop was part of any systemic or recurrent police misconduct. To the contrary, all the evidence suggests that the stop was an isolated instance of negligence that occurred in connection with a bona fide investigation of a suspected drug house. Officer Fackrell saw Strieff leave a suspected drug house. And his suspicion about the house was based on an anonymous tip and his personal observations.

Applying these factors, we hold that the evidence discovered on Strieff's person was admissible because the unlawful stop was sufficiently attenuated by the pre-existing arrest warrant. Although the illegal stop was close in time to Strieff's arrest, that consideration is outweighed by two factors supporting the State. The outstanding arrest warrant for Strieff's arrest is a critical intervening circumstance that is wholly independent of the illegal stop. The discovery of that warrant broke the causal chain between the unconstitutional stop and the discovery of evidence by compelling Officer Fackrell to arrest Strieff. And, it is especially significant that there is no evidence that Officer Fackrell's illegal stop reflected flagrantly unlawful police misconduct.

___ U.S. at ___, 136 S.Ct. at 2062–63.

7. **Testimony of Witness as Excludable Fruit.** When, if ever, should the fruits of the poisonous tree doctrine include testimony of a witness whose identity was discovered in violation of a defendant's constitutional rights? In United States v. Ceccolini, 435 U.S. 268, 98 S.Ct. 1054 (1978), Biro, a local police officer, entered Ceccolini's place of business to talk with Lois Hennessey, a friend and an employee of the shop. During the course of the conversation he noticed an envelope with money sticking out of it lying on the drawer of the cash register behind the counter. Biro picked up the envelope and, upon examining its contents, discovered it contained not only money but policy (gambling) slips. He placed the envelope back on the register and, without telling his friend what he had seen, asked her to whom the envelope belonged. She replied the envelope belonged to Ceccolini and that he had instructed her to give it to someone. The officer related what he had observed and been told to local police detectives who, in turn, gave the information to an FBI agent. Ceccolini had already been the subject of an FBI gambling investigation. An agent interviewed Ms. Hennessey at her home and she agreed to provide information about the envelope to the agent. Ceccolini was subpoenaed before a grand jury, where he denied any knowledge of a policy operation run from his shop. Ms. Hennessey testified about the envelope and the grand jury indicted Ceccolini for committing perjury in his grand jury testimony. The District Court and the Court of Appeals concluded that Biro's examination of the envelope was an unreasonable search and that the trial testimony of the store employee was a fruit of that illegality.

The Supreme Court disagreed. Writing for the Court, Justice Rehnquist concluded that although there was a causal connection between the initial illegality and the employee's testimony, the taint had been dissipated:

> [W]e hold that the Court of Appeals erred in holding that the degree of attenuation was not sufficient to dissipate the connection between the illegality and the testimony. The evidence indicates overwhelmingly that the testimony given by the witness was an act of her own free will in no way coerced or even induced by official authority as a result of Biro's discovery of the policy slips. Nor were the slips themselves used in questioning Hennessey. Substantial periods of time elapsed between the time of the illegal search and the initial contact with the witness, on the one hand, and between the latter and the testimony at trial on the other. While the particular knowledge to which Hennessey testified at trial can be logically traced back to Biro's discovery of the policy slips both the identity of Hennessey and her relationship with the respondent was well known to those investigating the case. There is in addition, not the slightest evidence to suggest that Biro entered the shop or picked up the envelope with the intent of finding tangible evidence bearing on an illicit gambling operation, much less any suggestion that he entered the shop and searched with the intent of finding a willing and knowledgeable witness to testify against respondent. Application of the exclusionary rule in this situation could not have the slightest deterrent effect on the behavior of an officer such as Biro. The cost of permanently silencing Hennessey is too great for an even-handed system of law enforcement to bear in order to secure such a speculative and very likely negligible deterrent effect.
>
> Obviously no mathematical weight can be assigned to any of the factors which we have discussed, but just as obviously they all point to the conclusion that the exclusionary rule should be invoked with much greater reluctance where the claim is based on a causal relationship between a constitutional violation and the discovery of a live witness than when a similar claim is advanced to support suppression of an inanimate object.

435 U.S. at 279–80, 98 S.Ct. at 1062. Justices Marshall and Brennan dissented.

8.   **Limits on Fruits Doctrine.** The Supreme Court refused in 1984 to apply the general rule that all evidence obtained as a factual result of conduct violating Fourth Amendment standards must be suppressed. In New York v. Harris, 495 U.S. 14, 110 S.Ct. 1640 (1990), officers had probable cause to believe Harris committed a homicide but obtained no warrant. They nevertheless entered his home and placed him under arrest. This warrantless entry violated the Fourth Amendment; the warrant requirement in this context is considered in Chapter 4. Harris was warned of his rights and admitted the killing. He was taken to the stationhouse, warned again, and signed a written incriminating statement. Later, ignoring Harris's expressed desire to remain silent, police videotaped an interview

with him. The trial court suppressed the oral statement made at his home and the videotaped statement, but admitted the written statement despite the earlier violation of his Fourth Amendment rights.

The Supreme Court held admission of the statement this was proper, applying what the dissenters characterized as a "newly-fashioned *per se* rule." No need existed to inquire whether the taint of the improper entry became attenuated, Justice White reasoned for the majority, because that analysis is necessary only if the challenged evidence is the product or fruit of the Fourth Amendment violation. The illegality of the officers' entry and Harris's arrest in his home, he continued, did not render unlawful Harris's continued custody once he was removed from the house:

> Harris's statement taken at the police station was not the product of being in unlawful custody. Neither was it the fruit of having been arrested in the home rather than someplace else. * * * [T]he police had a justification to question Harris prior to his arrest; therefore, his subsequent statement was not an exploitation of the illegal entry into Harris' home.

495 U.S. at 19, 110 S.Ct. at 1644. Therefore:

> [W]here the police have probable cause to arrest a suspect, the exclusionary rule does not bar the State's use of a statement made by the defendant outside of his home, even though the statement is taken after an arrest made in the home in violation of [the Fourth Amendment].

495 U.S. at 21, 110 S.Ct. at 1644–45.

Its decision, the Court explained further, implemented the principle that penalties, including exclusion of evidence, must bear some relation to the purposes of the legal requirement violated. The underlying rule requiring a warrant for arrests in the home was designed to protect the physical integrity of the home. "[I]t was not intended to grant criminal suspects, like Harris, protection for statements made outside their premises where the police have probable cause to arrest the suspects for committing a crime." Once incriminating evidence gathered from arresting the suspect in his home, the purpose of the rule is vindicated. Moreover, the threat of suppression of such evidence retains the principal incentive for officers to comply with the warrant requirement. Suppression of statements obtained after the suspect is removed would provide only "minimal" incremental deterrence.

C. EXCEPTIONS TO EXCLUSIONARY REQUIREMENTS

EDITORS' INTRODUCTION: EXCLUSIONARY SANCTION EXCEPTIONS

The federal constitutional requirement that evidence obtained as a result of a violation of a defendant's Fourth, Fifth, or Sixth Amendment rights be excluded from evidence is subject to exceptions. Initially, however, it is necessary to consider what are exceptions as contrasted with failures to meet the requirements for triggering the exclusionary sanction.

Attenuation of Taint and Independent Source

Several of these matters have already been addressed. The last subchapter of this chapter considered the attenuation of taint doctrine rendering certain evidence admissible.

As the last part similarly developed, the independent source doctrine also renders challenged evidence admissible at the behest of the prosecution. There is some question, however, whether independent source is properly conceptualized as an exception to the general requirement of exclusion. It may be a description of certain situations in which defendants failed to carry the burden of proving challenged evidence was obtained as factual results of the law enforcement conduct.

Impeachment of Testifying Defendant

Generally, the exceptions permit the use of evidence to prove defendants' guilt. One, however, allows use of evidence only for the limited purpose of impeaching the credibility of testifying defendants.

Evidence obtained in violation of a defendant's Fourth Amendment rights can be used, if the defendant takes the witness stand at trial, to impeach the defendant's credibility. Harris v. New York, 401 U.S. 222, 91 S.Ct. 643 (1971). It may even be used to contradict answers given by a testifying defendant on cross-examination, as long as the testimony is in response to questions "plainly within the scope of the defendant's direct examination." United States v. Havens, 446 U.S. 620, 627, 100 S.Ct. 1912, 1916 (1980). The exception applies to other federal constitutional exclusionary requirements. See Michigan v. Harvey, 494 U.S. 344, 350–53, 110 S.Ct. 1176, 1180–81 (1990) (evidence obtained in violation of the defendant's Sixth Amendment right to counsel could be used to impeach).

In support of the impeachment exception, the Court has stressed the great need for such evidence, as it limits defendants' ability to give possibly perjurious testimony. It has characterized the possibility that the exception will encourage impermissible law enforcement conduct as purely "speculative." Thus:

> Assuming that the exclusionary rule has a deterrent effect on proscribed police conduct, sufficient deterrence flows when the evidence in question is made unavailable to the prosecution in its case in chief.

Harris v. New York, 401 U.S. at 225, 91 S.Ct. at 645, reaffirmed in *Havens*, 446 U.S. at 627, 100 S.Ct. at 1916–17. The *Harris* dissenters argued an impeachment exception "will seriously undermine the achievement of [the exclusionary rule's deterrent] objective," and is inconsistent with the exclusionary rule's objective of preserving the courts from the taint of aiding and abetting the law-breaking police officer. *Harris*, 401 U.S. at 232, 91 S.Ct. at 649 (Brennan, J., dissenting).

In *Harris*, the Court made clear the exception would apply only if "the trustworthiness of the evidence satisfies legal standards." A confession obtained in a manner rendering it involuntary therefore cannot be used to impeach the defendant if he testifies at trial. Mincey v. Arizona, 437 U.S. 385, 402, 98 S.Ct. 2408, 2418 (1978).

The Supreme Court—by a close 5-to-4 vote—refused to expand the *Harris* impeachment exception into a broader rule permitting the use of unconstitutionally obtained evidence to rebut *any* evidence offered by the defense. James v. Illinois, 493 U.S. 307, 110 S.Ct. 648 (1990). The balancing approach used in *Harris*, the *James* majority reasoned, did not support this narrowing of the exclusionary sanction. Permitting such rebuttal use of unconstitutionally obtained evidence, the Court acknowledged, might deter some perjurious testimony. It would also, however, discourage defendants from producing even legitimate defenses. Nondefendant witnesses cannot be "controlled" by defense counsel as effectively as defendant witnesses, so calling such witnesses might often result in accidentally rendering improperly obtained evidence admissible. Defendants would with some frequency, then, refrain from presenting defense witnesses. Moreover, once law enforcement officers learned of the expanded exception they would have significant incentive to proceed in violation of suspects' rights because the more extensive use that could be made of the fruits of their action would make such activity worthwhile. Thus expansion of the exception would significantly weaken the exclusionary sanction's deterrent effect.

Inevitable Discovery Exception

Two exceptions to exclusionary sanctions attaching to violations of federal constitutional rights were recognized in the Supreme Court's 1983 term. The first was developed in Nix v. Williams, 467 U.S. 431, 104 S.Ct. 2501 (1984).

Williams was convicted of the murder of a young girl. Following his first trial, the Supreme Court determined he was interrogated in violation of his Sixth and Fourteenth Amendments right to counsel and consequently the statements he made during this interrogation were improperly admitted into evidence at his trial. Brewer v. Williams, 430 U.S. 387, 97 S.Ct. 1232 (1977). In addition, however, Williams revealed to the interrogating officers the location of the victim's body. Using this information, officers found the body. At Williams's second trial, the prosecution did not offer into evidence his incriminating statements nor did it show Williams directed police to the body. It did, however, offer evidence of the condition of the body as found, articles and photographs of clothing found on the body, and the results of medical and chemical tests performed on the body. In support of its offer of this evidence, the prosecution showed that, at the time of Williams' interrogation, a search for the body was underway and that 200 volunteers were involved. This search was called off when Williams began to cooperate with law enforcement officers. But, the state's witness testified, had the search not been called off it would have resulted in discovery of the body after three to five additional hours of searching. The trial judge admitted the evidence on the ground that the prosecution showed that, if Williams had not been improperly interrogated, the victim's body would nevertheless have been found and therefore evidence resulting from the body's discovery was admissible. Williams was again convicted and later sought invalidation of that conviction in federal habeas corpus litigation.

The Supreme Court found no violation of Williams's federal constitutional rights in the use of the evidence. All nine members of the Court agreed the exclusionary sanction attaching to the violation of Williams's Sixth and Fourteenth Amendments right to counsel is subject to an "ultimate or inevitable discovery" exception:

> [W]hen * * * the evidence in question would inevitably have been discovered without reference to the police error or misconduct, there is no nexus [between the error and the evidence] sufficient to provide a taint and the evidence is admissible.

467 U.S. at 448, 104 S.Ct. at 2511.

The rationale for this exception, Chief Justice Burger explained for the Court, is the same as that for the "independent source" rule discussed in Subchapter B of this chapter. The need to deter unlawful police conduct is sufficiently met if police engaging in misconduct are put in the same position they would have been in had the misconduct not occurred. This need does not, however, justify putting law enforcement in a worse position than it would have been in had no misconduct taken place. Society's need for reliable evidence of offenders' guilt, on the other hand, strongly argues against any aspect of the exclusionary rules putting a law enforcement agency in a worse position than it would have been in had misconduct not taken place. Both the inevitable discovery exception and the independent source doctrine serve the purpose of assuring that misbehaving law enforcement agencies are not put in any worse position than they would have been in had they avoided the misbehavior. While the case involved the exclusionary penalty for a violation of the Sixth Amendment right to counsel, the Court's discussion strongly suggests identical exceptions will be recognized with regard to other exclusionary rules, including that adopted in *Mapp* for violations of the Fourth Amendment.

All members of the Court agreed the inevitable discovery exception should not be qualified by requiring the prosecution, as a condition of invoking it, to show the officers acted without "bad faith." Such a condition, the Court reasoned, would in no way further the purpose of the inevitable discovery exception. The members of the Court split, however, on the appropriate burden of proof. Justice Brennan, joined by Justice Marshall, reasoned:

The inevitable discovery exception necessarily implicates a hypothetical finding that differs in kind from the factual finding that precedes application of the independent source rule. To ensure that this hypothetical finding is narrowly confined to circumstances that are functionally equivalent to an independent source, and to protect fully the fundamental rights served by the exclusionary rule, I would require clear and convincing evidence before concluding that the government had met its burden of proof on this issue.

467 U.S. at 459, 104 S.Ct. at 2517 (Brennan, J., dissenting). The Court, however, rejected Justice Brennan's characterization of the analysis and conclusion as to the appropriate burden of proof:

[I]nevitable discovery involves no speculative elements but focuses on demonstrated historical facts capable of ready verification or impeachment and does not require a departure from the usual burden of proof [by a preponderance of the evidence] at suppression hearings.

467 U.S. at 444 n. 5, 104 S.Ct. at 2509 n. 5.

"Good Faith" Exception

Later in the same term as *Williams* the Court decided United States v. Leon, 468 U.S. 897, 104 S.Ct. 3405 (1984). *Leon* recognized what is often—but perhaps improperly—called the "good faith" exception. This exception is developed in the principal cases in this subchapter.

Leon itself involved a search conducted pursuant to a search warrant issued on information falling short of the constitutionally required probable cause. The majority turned to what it described as the seldom-discussed rationale for suppressing evidence obtained pursuant to a search warrant. For several reasons, it concluded that exclusion's behavioral effect on judges and magistrates could not support the sanction:

First, the exclusionary rule is designed to deter police misconduct rather than to punish the errors of judges and magistrates. Second, there exists no evidence suggesting that judges and magistrates are inclined to ignore or subvert the Fourth Amendment or that lawlessness among these actors requires application of the extreme sanction of exclusion.

Third, and most important, we discern no basis, and are offered none, for believing that exclusion of evidence seized pursuant to a warrant will have a significant deterrent effect on the issuing judge or magistrate. Many of the factors that indicate that the exclusionary rule cannot provide an effective "special" or "general" deterrent for individual offending law enforcement officers apply as well to judges or magistrates. And, to the extent that the rule is thought to operate as a "systemic" deterrent on a wider audience, it clearly can have no such effect on individuals empowered to issue search warrants. Judges and magistrates are not adjuncts to the law enforcement team; as neutral judicial officers, they have no stake in the outcome of particular criminal prosecutions. The threat of exclusion thus cannot be expected significantly to deter them. Imposition of the exclusionary sanction is not necessary meaningfully to inform judicial officers of their errors, and we cannot conclude that admitting evidence obtained pursuant to a warrant while at the same time declaring that the warrant was somehow defective will in any way reduce judicial officers' professional incentives to comply with the Fourth Amendment, encourage them to repeat their mistakes, or lead to the granting of all colorable warrant requests.

468 U.S. at 916–917, 104 S.Ct. at 3417–18. Nor could considerations relating to the integrity of the courts support exclusion. Use of illegally obtained evidence offends the integrity of the courts only if that use encourages violations of the Fourth Amendment. Thus, "[a]bsent unusual circumstances," the integrity of the courts is not implicated by use of evidence obtained in reasonable reliance on a warrant. 468 U.S. at 921 n. 22, 104 S.Ct. at 3419 n. 22.

The Court continued:

> We have frequently questioned whether the exclusionary rule can have any deterrent effect when the offending officers acted in the objectively reasonable belief that their conduct did not violate the Fourth Amendment. * * *

> This is particularly true, we believe, when an officer acting with objective good faith has obtained a search warrant from a judge or magistrate and acted within its scope. In most such cases, there is no police illegality and thus nothing to deter. It is the magistrate's responsibility to determine whether the officer's allegations establish probable cause and, if so, to issue a warrant comporting in form with the requirements of the Fourth Amendment. In the ordinary case, an officer cannot be expected to question the magistrate's probable-cause determination or his judgment that the form of the warrant is technically sufficient. "[O]nce the warrant issues, there is literally nothing more the policeman can do in seeking to comply with the law." Penalizing the officer for the magistrate's error, rather than his own, cannot logically contribute to the deterrence of Fourth Amendment violations.

468 U.S. at 918–21, 104 S.Ct. at 3418–19.

The Court noted the exception was qualified:

> Suppression * * * remains an appropriate remedy if the magistrate or judge in issuing a warrant was misled by information in an affidavit that the affiant knew was false or

would have known was false except for his reckless disregard of the truth. The exception we recognize today will also not apply in cases where the issuing magistrate wholly abandoned his judicial role; in such circumstances, no reasonably well trained officer should rely on the warrant. Nor would an officer manifest objective good faith in relying on a warrant based on an affidavit "so lacking in indicia of probable cause as to render official belief in its existence entirely unreasonable." Finally, depending on the circumstances of the particular case, a warrant may be so facially deficient—i.e., in failing to particularize the place to be searched or the things to be seized—that the executing officers cannot reasonably presume it to be valid.

468 U.S. at 923, 104 S.Ct. at 3421.

Despite the use of "good faith" terminology, the Court added: "We emphasize that the standard of reasonableness we adopt is an objective one." It explained:

[W]e * * * eschew inquiries into the subjective beliefs of law enforcement officers who seize evidence pursuant to a subsequently invalidated warrant. * * * [W]e believe that "sending state and federal courts on an expedition into the minds of police officers would produce a grave and fruitless misallocation of judicial resources." *Massachusetts v. Painten*, 389 U.S. 560, 565, 88 S.Ct. 660, 663, 19 L.Ed.2d 770 (1968) (WHITE, J., dissenting). Accordingly, our good-faith inquiry is confined to the objectively ascertainable question whether a reasonably well trained officer would have known that the search was illegal despite the magistrate's authorization. In making this determination, all of the circumstances—including whether the warrant application had previously been rejected by a different magistrate—may be considered.

468 U.S. at 923 n. 23, 104 S.Ct. at 3420 n. 23. In addition: "The objective standard we adopt, moreover, requires officers to have a reasonable knowledge of what the law prohibits." 468 U.S. at 919 n. 20, 104 S.Ct. at 3419 n. 20.

What would make a search warrant so clearly defective that a reasonable officer could not rely on it? The matter was addressed in Groh v. Ramirez, 540 U.S. 551, 124 S.Ct. 1284 (2004). Although *Groh* involved whether an officer who executed a warrant had qualified immunity from civil liability for the search, the Court made clear that both qualified immunity and the "good faith" exception to the exclusionary rule demand the same objective reasonableness of officers.

In *Groh*, a federal officer prepared an application for a search warrant for the Ramirez residence. In that application, he described in detail various weapons, explosive devices, and receipts pertaining to the purchase or manufacture of such weapons and devices for which the officer sought authority to search. The officer also used a form to prepare a warrant. In that portion of the form calling for a description of the person or property to be seized, the officer mistakenly inserted a description of the premises to be searched. The warrant form did not purport to incorporate the application. Then the officer presented the application, an affidavit, and the warrant form to a Magistrate Judge who signed the filled-in warrant form.

As a result, the warrant contained no description of any things for which the search was to be conducted. Could a reasonable officer nevertheless believe the warrant and search valid? A majority of the Court held not. That majority explained:

> Given that the particularity requirement is set forth in the text of the Constitution, no reasonable officer could believe that a warrant that plainly did not comply with that requirement was valid. Moreover, because [Groh] himself prepared the invalid warrant, he may not argue that he reasonably relied on the Magistrate's assurance that the warrant contained an adequate description of the things to be seized and was therefore valid. In fact, the guidelines of [Groh's] own department placed him on notice that he might be liable for executing a manifestly invalid warrant. * * * And even a cursory reading of the warrant in this case—perhaps just a simple glance—would have revealed a glaring deficiency that any reasonable police officer would have known was constitutionally fatal.

540 U.S. at 563–64, 124 S.Ct. at 1293–94.

A showing that the officers submitted a search warrant application to a magistrate only after obtaining approval of the application from a superior officer and a deputy district attorney "support[ed]" the argument that an officer could reasonably have believed the facts supported a finding of probable cause. Messerschmidt v. Millender, ___ U.S. ___, ___, 132 S.Ct. 1235, 1249 (2012).

The good faith exception was extended to warrantless searches made pursuant to an invalid statute in Illinois v. Krull, 480 U.S. 340, 107 S.Ct. 1160 (1987). A Chicago police officer made a warrantless inspection of a junkyard, believing that the Illinois statute authorizing such inspections was valid. But the statute authorizing inspections of this sort was later held invalid. Nevertheless, the Supreme Court held, the evidence was admissible because of the officer's reliance on the statute. *Krull*, therefore, extended *Leon* to at least certain searches conducted without warrants. *Leon*'s analysis, Justice Blackmun explained for the *Krull* majority, indicated a *Leon*-like exception covering the facts before it should be recognized:

> The application of the exclusionary rule to suppress evidence obtained by an officer acting in objectively reasonable reliance on a statute would have as little deterrent effect on the officer's

actions as would the exclusion of evidence when an officer acts in objectively reasonable reliance on a warrant. Unless a statute is clearly unconstitutional, an officer cannot be expected to question the judgment of the legislature that passed the law. * * *

Any difference between our holding in *Leon* and our holding in the instant case * * * must rest on a difference between the effect of the exclusion of evidence on judicial officers and the effect of the exclusion on legislators. * * * We noted in *Leon* as an initial matter that the exclusionary rule was aimed at deterring police misconduct. Thus, legislators, like judicial officers, are not the focus of the rule. * * *

There is no evidence suggesting that Congress or state legislatures have enacted a significant number of statutes permitting warrantless administrative searches violative of the Fourth Amendment. * * * Thus, we are given no basis for believing that legislators are inclined to subvert their oaths and the Fourth Amendment and that "lawlessness among these actors requires application of the extreme sanction of exclusion." * * * There is nothing to indicate that applying the exclusionary rule to evidence seized pursuant to [an invalid] statute prior to the declaration of its invalidity will act as a significant, additional deterrent. Moreover, to the extent that application of the exclusionary rule could provide some incremental deterrent, that possible benefit must be weighed against the "substantial social costs exacted by the exclusionary rule." When we indulge in such weighing, we are convinced that applying the exclusionary rule in this context is unjustified.

480 U.S. at 351–53, 107 S.Ct. at 1168–69. But, the Court continued, the *Krull* exception is subject to certain constraints:

A statute cannot support objectively reasonable reliance if, in passing the statute, the legislature wholly abandoned its responsibility to enact constitutional laws. Nor can a law enforcement officer be said to have acted in good-faith reliance upon a statute if its provisions are such that a reasonable officer should have known that the statute was unconstitutional. As we emphasized in *Leon,* the standard of reasonableness we adopt is an objective one; the standard does not turn on the subjective good faith of individual officers.

480 U.S. at 355, 107 S.Ct. at 1170.

Turning to the case before it, the majority concluded any such defects as existed in the Illinois statute were not so obvious that an objectively reasonable police officer would have realized the statute was unconstitutional. The officer "relied, in objective good faith, on a statute that appeared legitimately to allow a warrantless administrative search of [Krull's] business," and the evidentiary products of his actions were therefore admissible against Krull. The majority assumed the officer acted within the scope of the statute, but indicated this could be explored on remand:

> At this juncture, we decline the State's invitation to recognize an exception for an officer who erroneously but in good faith believes he is acting within the scope of a statute. * * * [S]uch a ruling * * * does not follow inexorably from today's decision. As our opinion makes clear, the question whether the exclusionary rule is applicable in a particular context depends significantly upon the actors who are making the relevant decision that the rule is designed to influence. The answer to this question might well be different when police officers act outside the scope of a statute, albeit in good faith. In that context, the relevant actors are not legislators or magistrates, but police officers who concededly are "engaged in the often competitive enterprise of ferreting out crime."

480 U.S. at 360 n. 17, 107 S.Ct. at 1172 n. 17. Justice O'Connor, joined by Justices Brennan, Marshall and Stevens, dissented.

Herring v. United States

Supreme Court of the United States, 2009.
555 U.S. 135, 129 S.Ct. 695.

■ CHIEF JUSTICE ROBERTS delivered the opinion of the Court.

The Fourth Amendment forbids "unreasonable searches and seizures," and this usually requires the police to have probable cause or a warrant before making an arrest. What if an officer reasonably believes there is an outstanding arrest warrant, but that belief turns out to be wrong because of a negligent bookkeeping error by another police employee? * * *

I

On July 7, 2004, Investigator Mark Anderson learned that Bennie Dean Herring had driven to the Coffee County Sheriff's Department to retrieve something from his impounded truck. Herring was no stranger to law enforcement, and Anderson asked the county's warrant clerk, Sandy Pope, to check for any outstanding warrants for Herring's arrest. When she found none, Anderson asked Pope to check with Sharon Morgan, her counterpart in neighboring Dale County. After checking Dale County's computer database, Morgan replied that there was an active arrest warrant for Herring's failure to appear on a felony charge. Pope relayed the information to Anderson and asked Morgan to fax over a copy of the warrant as confirmation. Anderson and a deputy followed Herring as he left the impound lot, pulled him over, and arrested him. A search incident to the arrest revealed methamphetamine in Herring's pocket, and a pistol (which as a felon he could not possess) in his vehicle.

There had, however, been a mistake about the warrant. The Dale County sheriff's computer records are supposed to correspond to actual arrest warrants, which the office also maintains. But when Morgan went to the files to retrieve the actual warrant to fax to Pope, Morgan was unable to find it. She called a court clerk and learned that the warrant had been recalled five months earlier. Normally when a warrant is recalled the court clerk's office or a judge's chambers calls Morgan, who enters the information in the sheriff's computer database and disposes of the physical copy. For whatever reason, the information about the recall of the warrant for Herring did not appear in the database. Morgan immediately called Pope to alert her to the mixup, and Pope contacted Anderson over a secure radio. This all unfolded in 10 to 15 minutes, but Herring had already been arrested and found with the gun and drugs, just a few hundred yards from the sheriff's office.

Herring was indicted in the District Court for the Middle District of Alabama for illegally possessing the gun and drugs * * * . He moved to suppress the evidence on the ground that his initial arrest had been illegal because the warrant had been rescinded. The Magistrate Judge recommended denying the motion because the arresting officers had acted in a good-faith belief that the warrant was still outstanding. * * * The District Court adopted the Magistrate Judge's recommendation, and the Court of Appeals for the Eleventh Circuit affirmed.

* * *

Other courts have required exclusion of evidence obtained through similar police errors, so we granted Herring's petition for certiorari to resolve the conflict. * * *

These principles are reflected in the holding of [*United States v. Leon*, 468 U.S. 897, 104 S.Ct. 3405, 82 L.Ed.2d 677 (1984)]: When police act under a warrant that is invalid for lack of probable cause, the exclusionary rule does not apply if the police acted "in objectively reasonable reliance" on the subsequently invalidated search warrant. We (perhaps confusingly) called this objectively reasonable reliance "good faith." * * *

II

[W]e accept the parties' assumption that there was a Fourth Amendment violation. The issue is whether the exclusionary rule should be applied.

A

The Fourth Amendment protects "[t]he right of the people to be secure in their persons, houses, papers, and effects, against unreasonable searches and seizures," but "contains no provision expressly precluding the use of evidence obtained in violation of its commands." Nonetheless, our decisions establish an exclusionary rule that, when applicable, forbids the use of improperly obtained evidence at trial. We have stated that this judicially created rule is "designed to safeguard Fourth

Amendment rights generally through its deterrent effect." *United States v. Calandra,* 414 U.S. 338, 348, 94 S.Ct. 613, 38 L.Ed.2d 561 (1974).

In analyzing the applicability of the rule, *Leon* admonished that we must consider the actions of all the police officers involved. The Coffee County officers did nothing improper. Indeed, the error was noticed so quickly because Coffee County requested a faxed confirmation of the warrant.

The Eleventh Circuit concluded, however, that somebody in Dale County should have updated the computer database to reflect the recall of the arrest warrant. The court also concluded that this error was negligent, but did not find it to be reckless or deliberate. That fact is crucial to our holding that this error is not enough by itself to require "the extreme sanction of exclusion."

B

1.   The fact that a Fourth Amendment violation occurred—*i.e.,* that a search or arrest was unreasonable—does not necessarily mean that the exclusionary rule applies. Indeed, exclusion "has always been our last resort, not our first impulse," *Hudson v. Michigan,* 547 U.S. 586, 591, 126 S.Ct. 2159, 165 L.Ed.2d 56 (2006), and our precedents establish important principles that constrain application of the exclusionary rule.

First, the exclusionary rule is not an individual right and applies only where it " 'result[s] in appreciable deterrence.' " We have repeatedly rejected the argument that exclusion is a necessary consequence of a Fourth Amendment violation. Instead we have focused on the efficacy of the rule in deterring Fourth Amendment violations in the future.[2]

In addition, the benefits of deterrence must outweigh the costs. * * * The principal cost of applying the rule is, of course, letting guilty and possibly dangerous defendants go free-something that "offends basic concepts of the criminal justice system."

Shortly thereafter we extended these holdings to warrantless administrative searches performed in good-faith reliance on a statute later declared unconstitutional. Finally, in [*Arizona v. Evans,* 514 U.S. 1, 10, 115 S.Ct. 1185, 131 L.Ed.2d 34 (1995)], we applied this good-faith rule to police who reasonably relied on mistaken information in a court's database that an arrest warrant was outstanding. We held that a mistake made by a judicial employee could not give rise to exclusion for three reasons: The exclusionary rule was crafted to curb police rather than judicial misconduct; court employees were unlikely to try to subvert the Fourth Amendment; and "most important, there [was] no basis for believing that application of the exclusionary rule in [those] circumstances" would have any significant effect in deterring the errors. *Evans* left unresolved "whether the evidence should be suppressed if

---

[2]   Justice GINSBURG's dissent champions what she describes as " 'a more majestic conception' of . . . the exclusionary rule," which would exclude evidence even where deterrence does not justify doing so. Majestic or not, our cases reject this conception * * * .

police personnel were responsible for the error,"[3] an issue not argued by the State in that case, but one that we now confront.

* * *

2.   The extent to which the exclusionary rule is justified by these deterrence principles varies with the culpability of the law enforcement conduct. As we said in *Leon,* "an assessment of the flagrancy of the police misconduct constitutes an important step in the calculus" of applying the exclusionary rule. Similarly, * * * we [later] elaborated that "evidence should be suppressed 'only if it can be said that the law enforcement officer had knowledge, or may properly be charged with knowledge, that the search was unconstitutional under the Fourth Amendment.' "

Anticipating the good-faith exception to the exclusionary rule, Judge Friendly wrote that "[t]he beneficent aim of the exclusionary rule to deter police misconduct can be sufficiently accomplished by a practice . . . outlawing evidence obtained by flagrant or deliberate violation of rights." The Bill of Rights as a Code of Criminal Procedure, 53 Calif. L.Rev. 929, 953 (1965) (footnotes omitted).

Indeed, the abuses that gave rise to the exclusionary rule featured intentional conduct that was patently unconstitutional. * * * [F]lagrant conduct was at issue in *Mapp v. Ohio,* 367 U.S. 643, 81 S.Ct. 1684, 6 L.Ed.2d 1081 (1961) * * * . Officers forced open a door to Ms. Mapp's house, kept her lawyer from entering, brandished what the court concluded was a false warrant, then forced her into handcuffs and canvassed the house for obscenity. An error that arises from nonrecurring and attenuated negligence is thus far removed from the core concerns that led us to adopt the rule in the first place. And in fact since *Leon,* we have never applied the rule to exclude evidence obtained in violation of the Fourth Amendment, where the police conduct was no more intentional or culpable than this.

3.   To trigger the exclusionary rule, police conduct must be sufficiently deliberate that exclusion can meaningfully deter it, and sufficiently culpable that such deterrence is worth the price paid by the justice system. As laid out in our cases, the exclusionary rule serves to deter deliberate, reckless, or grossly negligent conduct, or in some circumstances recurring or systemic negligence. The error in this case does not rise to that level.[4]

---

[3]   We thus reject [the] suggestion that *Evans* was entirely "premised on a distinction between judicial errors and police errors." Were that the only rationale for our decision, there would have been no reason for us expressly and carefully to leave police error unresolved. * * *

[4]   We do not quarrel with Justice GINSBURG's claim that "liability for negligence . . . creates an incentive to act with greater care," and we do not suggest that the exclusion of this evidence could have *no* deterrent effect. But our cases require any deterrence to "be weighed against the 'substantial social costs exacted by the exclusionary rule,' " and here exclusion is not worth the cost.

* * *

4. We do not suggest that all recordkeeping errors by the police are immune from the exclusionary rule. In this case, however, the conduct at issue was not so objectively culpable as to require exclusion. In *Leon* we held that "the marginal or nonexistent benefits produced by suppressing evidence obtained in objectively reasonable reliance on a subsequently invalidated search warrant cannot justify the substantial costs of exclusion." The same is true when evidence is obtained in objectively reasonable reliance on a subsequently recalled warrant.

If the police have been shown to be reckless in maintaining a warrant system, or to have knowingly made false entries to lay the groundwork for future false arrests, exclusion would certainly be justified under our cases should such misconduct cause a Fourth Amendment violation. We said as much in *Leon,* explaining that an officer could not "obtain a warrant on the basis of a 'bare bones' affidavit and then rely on colleagues who are ignorant of the circumstances under which the warrant was obtained to conduct the search." Petitioner's fears that our decision will cause police departments to deliberately keep their officers ignorant, are thus unfounded.

The dissent also adverts to the possible unreliability of a number of databases not relevant to this case. In a case where systemic errors were demonstrated, it might be reckless for officers to rely on an unreliable warrant system. But there is no evidence that errors in Dale County's system are routine or widespread. Officer Anderson testified that he had never had reason to question information about a Dale County warrant, and both Sandy Pope and Sharon Morgan testified that they could remember no similar miscommunication ever happening on their watch. * * * Because no such showings were made here, the Eleventh Circuit was correct to affirm the denial of the motion to suppress.

* * *

Petitioner's claim that police negligence automatically triggers suppression cannot be squared with the principles underlying the exclusionary rule, as they have been explained in our cases. In light of our repeated holdings that the deterrent effect of suppression must be substantial and outweigh any harm to the justice system, we conclude that when police mistakes are the result of negligence such as that described here, rather than systemic error or reckless disregard of constitutional requirements, any marginal deterrence does not "pay its way." In such a case, the criminal should not "go free because the constable has blundered."

The judgment of the Court of Appeals for the Eleventh Circuit is affirmed.

It is so ordered.

■ JUSTICE GINSBURG, with whom JUSTICE STEVENS, JUSTICE SOUTER, and JUSTICE BREYER join, dissenting.

* * *

I would * * * hold the [exclusionary] rule dispositive of this case: "[I]f courts are to have any power to discourage [police] error of [the kind here at issue], it must be through the application of the exclusionary rule." *Arizona v. Evans,* 514 U.S. 1, 22–23, 115 S.Ct. 1185, 131 L.Ed.2d 34 (1995) (STEVENS, J., dissenting). The unlawful search in this case was contested in court because the police found methamphetamine in Herring's pocket and a pistol in his truck. But the "most serious impact" of the Court's holding will be on innocent persons "wrongfully arrested based on erroneous information [carelessly maintained] in a computer data base."

* * *

II

A

The Court states that the exclusionary rule is not a defendant's right; rather, it is simply a remedy applicable only when suppression would result in appreciable deterrence that outweighs the cost to the justice system.

* * *

B

Others have described "a more majestic conception" of the Fourth Amendment and its adjunct, the exclusionary rule. *Evans,* 514 U.S., at 18, 115 S.Ct. 1185 (STEVENS, J., dissenting). Protective of the fundamental "right of the people to be secure in their persons, houses, papers, and effects," the Amendment "is a constraint on the power of the sovereign, not merely on some of its agents." I share that vision of the Amendment.

The exclusionary rule is "a remedy necessary to ensure that" the Fourth Amendment's prohibitions "are observed in fact." The rule's service as an essential auxiliary to the Amendment earlier inclined the Court to hold the two inseparable.

Beyond doubt, a main objective of the rule "is to deter—to compel respect for the constitutional guaranty in the only effectively available way—by removing the incentive to disregard it." But the rule also serves other important purposes: It "enabl[es] the judiciary to avoid the taint of partnership in official lawlessness," and it "assur[es] the people—all potential victims of unlawful government conduct—that the government would not profit from its lawless behavior, thus minimizing the risk of seriously undermining popular trust in government." *United States v. Calandra,* 414 U.S. 338, 357, 94 S.Ct. 613, 38 L.Ed.2d 561 (1974) (Brennan, J., dissenting).

The exclusionary rule, it bears emphasis, is often the only remedy effective to redress a Fourth Amendment violation. Civil liability will not lie for "the vast majority of [F]ourth [A]mendment violations—the frequent infringements motivated by commendable zeal, not condemnable malice." Criminal prosecutions or administrative sanctions against the offending officers and injunctive relief against widespread violations are an even farther cry.

III

The Court maintains that Herring's case is one in which the exclusionary rule could have scant deterrent effect and therefore would not "pay its way." I disagree.

A

The exclusionary rule, the Court suggests, is capable of only marginal deterrence when the misconduct at issue is merely careless, not intentional or reckless. The suggestion runs counter to a foundational premise of tort law—that liability for negligence, *i.e.,* lack of due care, creates an incentive to act with greater care. * * *

B

Is the potential deterrence here worth the costs it imposes? In light of the paramount importance of accurate recordkeeping in law enforcement, I would answer yes * * * .

Electronic databases form the nervous system of contemporary criminal justice operations. In recent years, their breadth and influence have dramatically expanded. Police today can access databases that include not only the updated National Crime Information Center (NCIC), but also terrorist watchlists, the Federal Government's employee eligibility system, and various commercial databases. Moreover, States are actively expanding information sharing between jurisdictions. As a result, law enforcement has an increasing supply of information within its easy electronic reach.

The risk of error stemming from these databases is not slim. Herring's *amici* warn that law enforcement databases are insufficiently monitored and often out of date. Government reports describe, for example, flaws in NCIC databases, terrorist watchlist databases, and databases associated with the Federal Government's employment eligibility verification system.

Inaccuracies in expansive, interconnected collections of electronic information raise grave concerns for individual liberty. * * *

C

The Court assures that "exclusion would certainly be justified" if "the police have been shown to be reckless in maintaining a warrant system, or to have knowingly made false entries to lay the groundwork for future false arrests." This concession provides little comfort.

First, by restricting suppression to bookkeeping errors that are deliberate or reckless, the majority leaves Herring, and others like him, with no remedy for violations of their constitutional rights. There can be no serious assertion that relief is available under 42 U.S.C. § 1983. The arresting officer would be sheltered by qualified immunity, and the police department itself is not liable for the negligent acts of its employees. Moreover, identifying the department employee who committed the error may be impossible.

Second, I doubt that police forces already possess sufficient incentives to maintain up-to-date records. The Government argues that police have no desire to send officers out on arrests unnecessarily, because arrests consume resources and place officers in danger. The facts of this case do not fit that description of police motivation. Here the officer wanted to arrest Herring and consulted the Department's records to legitimate his predisposition.

Third, even when deliberate or reckless conduct is afoot, the Court's assurance will often be an empty promise: How is an impecunious defendant to make the required showing? If the answer is that a defendant is entitled to discovery (and if necessary, an audit of police databases), then the Court has imposed a considerable administrative burden on courts and law enforcement.

IV

Negligent recordkeeping errors by law enforcement threaten individual liberty, are susceptible to deterrence by the exclusionary rule, and cannot be remedied effectively through other means. Such errors present no occasion to further erode the exclusionary rule. The rule "is needed to make the Fourth Amendment something real; a guarantee that does not carry with it the exclusion of evidence obtained by its violation is a chimera." In keeping with the rule's "core concerns," suppression should have attended the unconstitutional search in this case.

* * *

For the reasons stated, I would reverse the judgment of the Eleventh Circuit.

■ JUSTICE BREYER, with whom JUSTICE SOUTER joins, dissenting.

* * *

Distinguishing between police recordkeeping errors and judicial ones not only is consistent with our precedent, but also is far easier for courts to administer than THE CHIEF JUSTICE's case-by-case, multifactored inquiry into the degree of police culpability. I therefore would apply the exclusionary rule when police personnel are responsible for a recordkeeping error that results in a Fourth Amendment violation.

The need for a clear line, and the recognition of such a line in our precedent, are further reasons in support of the outcome that Justice GINSBURG's dissent would reach.

Davis v. United States

Supreme Court of the United States, 2011.
564 U.S. 229, 131 S.Ct. 2419.

■ JUSTICE ALITO delivered the opinion of the Court.

The * * * question here is whether to apply [the Fourth Amendment exclusionary] sanction when the police conduct a search in compliance with binding precedent that is later overruled. * * *

I

The question presented arises in this case as a result of a shift in our Fourth Amendment jurisprudence on searches of automobiles incident to arrests of recent occupants.

A

[T]his Court's decision in * * * *New York v. Belton,* 453 U.S. 454, 458–459, 101 S.Ct. 2860, 69 L.Ed.2d 768 (1981)[,] * * * was widely understood to have set down a simple, bright-line rule. Numerous courts read the decision to authorize automobile searches incident to arrests of recent occupants, regardless of whether the arrestee in any particular case was within reaching distance of the vehicle at the time of the search. * * *

[In] * * * *Arizona v. Gant,* 556 U.S. 332, 129 S.Ct. 1710, 173 L.Ed.2d 485 (2009)[,] the Court adopted a new, two-part rule under which an automobile search incident to a recent occupant's arrest is constitutional (1) if the arrestee is within reaching distance of the vehicle during the search, or (2) if the police have reason to believe that the vehicle contains "evidence relevant to the crime of arrest."

B

The search at issue in this case took place a full two years before this Court announced its new rule in *Gant.* On an April evening in 2007, police officers in Greenville, Alabama, conducted a routine traffic stop that eventually resulted in the arrests of driver Stella Owens (for driving while intoxicated) and passenger Willie Davis (for giving a false name to police). The police handcuffed both Owens and Davis, and they placed the arrestees in the back of separate patrol cars. The police then searched the passenger compartment of Owens's vehicle and found a revolver inside Davis's jacket pocket.

Davis was indicted in the Middle District of Alabama on one count of possession of a firearm by a convicted felon. [He moved to suppress the revolver.] The District Court denied the motion, and Davis was convicted on the firearms charge.

While Davis's appeal was pending, this Court decided *Gant.* The Eleventh Circuit, in the opinion below, applied *Gant*'s new rule and held that the vehicle search incident to Davis's arrest "violated [his] Fourth Amendment rights." As for whether this constitutional violation warranted suppression, the Eleventh Circuit viewed that as a separate issue [and] declined to apply the exclusionary rule and affirmed Davis's conviction. We granted certiorari.

II

The * * * Fourth Amendment protects the "right of the people to be secure in their persons, houses, papers, and effects, against unreasonable searches and seizures." The Amendment says nothing about suppressing evidence obtained in violation of this command. That rule—the exclusionary rule—is a "prudential" doctrine, created by this Court to "compel respect for the constitutional guaranty." Exclusion is "not a personal constitutional right," nor is it designed to "redress the injury" occasioned by an unconstitutional search. The rule's sole purpose, we have repeatedly held, is to deter future Fourth Amendment violations. Our cases have thus limited the rule's operation to situations in which this purpose is "thought most efficaciously served." Where suppression fails to yield "appreciable deterrence," exclusion is "clearly . . . unwarranted."

Real deterrent value is a "necessary condition for exclusion," but it is not "a sufficient" one. The analysis must also account for the "substantial social costs" generated by the rule. Exclusion exacts a heavy toll on both the judicial system and society at large. It almost always requires courts to ignore reliable, trustworthy evidence bearing on guilt or innocence. And its bottom-line effect, in many cases, is to suppress the truth and set the criminal loose in the community without punishment. Our cases hold that society must swallow this bitter pill when necessary, but only as a "last resort." For exclusion to be appropriate, the deterrence benefits of suppression must outweigh its heavy costs.

Admittedly, there was a time when our exclusionary-rule cases were not nearly so discriminating in their approach to the doctrine. "Expansive dicta" in several decisions suggested that the rule was a self-executing mandate implicit in the Fourth Amendment itself. * * * In time, however, we came to acknowledge the exclusionary rule for what it undoubtedly is—a "judicially created remedy" of this Court's own making. We abandoned the old, "reflexive" application of the doctrine, and imposed a more rigorous weighing of its costs and deterrence benefits. In a line of cases beginning with *United States v. Leon*, 468 U.S. 897, 104 S.Ct. 3405, 82 L.Ed.2d 677 [(1984)], we also recalibrated our cost-benefit analysis in exclusion cases to focus the inquiry on the "flagrancy of the police misconduct" at issue.

The basic insight of the *Leon* line of cases is that the deterrence benefits of exclusion "var[y] with the culpability of the law enforcement conduct" at issue. When the police exhibit "deliberate," "reckless," or "grossly negligent" disregard for Fourth Amendment rights, the deterrent value of exclusion is strong and tends to outweigh the resulting costs. But when the police act with an objectively "reasonable good-faith belief" that their conduct is lawful, or when their conduct involves only simple, "isolated" negligence, the " 'deterrence rationale loses much of its force,' " and exclusion cannot "pay its way."

The Court has over time applied this "good-faith" exception across a range of cases. * * *

III

The question in this case is whether to apply the exclusionary rule when the police conduct a search in objectively reasonable reliance on binding judicial precedent. * * * The search incident to Davis's arrest in this case followed the Eleventh Circuit's * * * precedent to the letter. Although the search turned out to be unconstitutional under *Gant,* all agree that the officers' conduct was in strict compliance with then-binding Circuit law and was not culpable in any way.

Under our exclusionary-rule precedents, this acknowledged absence of police culpability dooms Davis's claim. Police practices trigger the harsh sanction of exclusion only when they are deliberate enough to yield "meaningfu[l]" deterrence, and culpable enough to be "worth the price paid by the justice system." The conduct of the officers here was neither of these things. The officers who conducted the search did not violate Davis's Fourth Amendment rights deliberately, recklessly, or with gross negligence. Nor does this case involve any "recurring or systemic negligence" on the part of law enforcement. The police acted in strict compliance with binding precedent, and their behavior was not wrongful. Unless the exclusionary rule is to become a strict-liability regime, it can have no application in this case.

Indeed, in 27 years of practice under *Leon*'s good-faith exception, we have "never applied" the exclusionary rule to suppress evidence obtained as a result of nonculpable, innocent police conduct. If the police in this case had reasonably relied on a warrant in conducting their search, or on an erroneous warrant record in a government database, the exclusionary rule would not apply. And if Congress or the Alabama Legislature had enacted a statute codifying the precise holding of the Eleventh Circuit's [case law], we would swiftly conclude that " '[p]enalizing the officer for the legislature's error . . . cannot logically contribute to the deterrence of Fourth Amendment violations.' " The same should be true of Davis's attempt here to " '[p]enaliz[e] the officer for the [appellate judges'] error.' "

About all that exclusion would deter in this case is conscientious police work. Responsible law-enforcement officers will take care to learn "what is required of them" under Fourth Amendment precedent and will conform their conduct to these rules. But by the same token, when binding appellate precedent specifically *authorizes* a particular police practice, well-trained officers will and should use that tool to fulfill their crime-detection and public-safety responsibilities. An officer who conducts a search in reliance on binding appellate precedent does no more than " 'ac[t] as a reasonable officer would and should act' " under the circumstances. The deterrent effect of exclusion in such a case can only be to discourage the officer from " 'do[ing] his duty.' "

That is not the kind of deterrence the exclusionary rule seeks to foster. We have stated before, and we reaffirm today, that the harsh sanction of exclusion "should not be applied to deter objectively reasonable law enforcement activity." Evidence obtained during a search conducted in reasonable reliance on binding precedent is not subject to the exclusionary rule.

IV

Justice BREYER's dissent and Davis argue that, although the police conduct in this case was in no way culpable, other considerations should prevent the good-faith exception from applying. We are not persuaded.

A

1

The principal argument of both the dissent and Davis is that the exclusionary rule's availability to enforce new Fourth Amendment precedent is a retroactivity issue, see *Griffith v. Kentucky,* 479 U.S. 314, 107 S.Ct. 708, 93 L.Ed.2d 649 (1987), not a good-faith issue. * * *

[In *Griffith*,] the Court * * * held that newly announced rules of constitutional criminal procedure must apply "retroactively to all cases, state or federal, pending on direct review or not yet final, with no exception."

2

The dissent and Davis argue that applying the good-faith exception in this case is "incompatible" with our retroactivity precedent under *Griffith.* We think this argument conflates what are two distinct doctrines.

Our retroactivity jurisprudence is concerned with whether, as a categorical matter, a new rule is available on direct review as a *potential* ground for relief. Retroactive application under *Griffith* lifts what would otherwise be a categorical bar to obtaining redress for the government's violation of a newly announced constitutional rule. Retroactive application does not, however, determine what "appropriate remedy" (if any) the defendant should obtain. Remedy is a separate, analytically distinct issue. As a result, the retroactive application of a new rule of substantive Fourth Amendment law *raises* the question whether a suppression remedy applies; it does not answer that question.

When this Court announced its decision in *Gant,* Davis's conviction had not yet become final on direct review. *Gant* therefore applies retroactively to this case. Davis may invoke its newly announced rule of substantive Fourth Amendment law as a basis for seeking relief. The question, then, becomes one of remedy, and on that issue Davis seeks application of the exclusionary rule. But exclusion of evidence does not automatically follow from the fact that a Fourth Amendment violation occurred. The remedy is subject to exceptions and applies only where its "purpose is effectively advanced."

The * * * good-faith exception, however, is * * * an established limit on the *remedy* of exclusion than is inevitable discovery. Its application here neither contravenes *Griffith* nor denies retroactive effect to *Gant*.

* * *

B

Davis also contends that applying the good-faith exception to searches conducted in reliance on binding precedent will stunt the development of Fourth Amendment law. With no possibility of suppression, criminal defendants will have no incentive, Davis maintains, to request that courts overrule precedent.

1

This argument is difficult to reconcile with our modern understanding of the role of the exclusionary rule. We have never held that facilitating the overruling of precedent is a relevant consideration in an exclusionary-rule case. Rather, we have said time and again that the *sole* purpose of the exclusionary rule is to deter misconduct by law enforcement.

We have also repeatedly rejected efforts to expand the focus of the exclusionary rule beyond deterrence of culpable police conduct. * * * [T]he exclusionary rule should [not] be modified to serve a purpose other than deterrence of culpable law-enforcement conduct.

2

And in any event, applying the good-faith exception in this context will not prevent judicial reconsideration of prior Fourth Amendment precedents. In most instances, as in this case, the precedent sought to be challenged will be a decision of a Federal Court of Appeals or State Supreme Court. But a good-faith exception for objectively reasonable reliance on binding precedent will not prevent review and correction of such decisions. This Court reviews criminal convictions from 12 Federal Courts of Appeals, 50 state courts of last resort, and the District of Columbia Court of Appeals. If one or even many of these courts uphold a particular type of search or seizure, defendants in jurisdictions in which the question remains open will still have an undiminished incentive to litigate the issue. This Court can then grant certiorari, and the development of Fourth Amendment law will in no way be stunted.

Davis argues that Fourth Amendment precedents of *this* Court will be effectively insulated from challenge under a good-faith exception for reliance on appellate precedent. But this argument is overblown. For one thing, it is important to keep in mind that this argument applies to an exceedingly small set of cases. * * *

At most, Davis's argument might suggest that—to prevent Fourth Amendment law from becoming ossified—the petitioner in a case that results in the overruling of one of this Court's Fourth Amendment precedents should be given the benefit of the victory by permitting the suppression of evidence in that one case. Such a result would undoubtedly be a windfall to this one random litigant. But the exclusionary rule is "not a personal constitutional right." It is a "judicially created" sanction, specifically designed as a "windfall" remedy to deter future Fourth Amendment violations. The good-faith exception is a judicially created exception to this judicially created rule. Therefore, in a future case, we could, if necessary, recognize a limited exception to the good-faith exception for a defendant who obtains a judgment over-ruling one of our Fourth Amendment precedents.

But this is not such a case. Davis did not secure a decision overturning a Supreme Court precedent; the police in his case reasonably relied on binding Circuit precedent. That sort of blameless police conduct, we hold, comes within the good-faith exception and is not properly subject to the exclusionary rule.

* * *

It is one thing for the criminal "to go free because the constable has blundered." It is quite another to set the criminal free because the constable has scrupulously adhered to governing law. Excluding evidence in such cases deters no police misconduct and imposes substantial social costs. We therefore hold that when the police conduct a search in objectively reasonable reliance on binding appellate precedent, the exclusionary rule does not apply. The judgment of the Court of Appeals for the Eleventh Circuit is

Affirmed.

■ JUSTICE SOTOMAYOR, concurring in the judgment.

Under our precedents, the primary purpose of the exclusionary rule is "to deter future Fourth Amendment violations." Accordingly, we have held, application of the exclusionary rule is unwarranted when it " 'does not result in appreciable deterrence.' " In the circumstances of this case, where "binding appellate precedent specifically *authorize*[d] a particular police practice," in accord with the holdings of nearly every other court in the country—application of the exclusionary rule cannot reasonably be expected to yield appreciable deterrence. I am thus compelled to conclude that the exclusionary rule does not apply in this case and to agree with the Court's disposition.

This case does not present the markedly different question whether the exclusionary rule applies when the law governing the constitutionality of a particular search is unsettled. * * * Whether exclusion would deter Fourth Amendment violations where appellate precedent does not specifically authorize a certain practice and, if so, whether the benefits of exclusion would outweigh its costs are questions unanswered by our previous decisions.

The dissent suggests that today's decision essentially answers those questions, noting that an officer who conducts a search in the face of unsettled precedent "is no more culpable than an officer who follows erroneous 'binding precedent.'" The Court does not address this issue. In my view, whether an officer's conduct can be characterized as "culpable" is not itself dispositive. We have never refused to apply the exclusionary rule where its application would appreciably deter Fourth Amendment violations on the mere ground that the officer's conduct could be characterized as nonculpable. Rather, an officer's culpability is relevant because it may inform the overarching inquiry whether exclusion would result in appreciable deterrence. Whatever we have said about culpability, the ultimate questions have always been, one, whether exclusion would result in appreciable deterrence and, two, whether the benefits of exclusion outweigh its costs.

As stated, whether exclusion would result in appreciable deterrence in the circumstances of this case is a different question from whether exclusion would appreciably deter Fourth Amendment violations when the governing law is unsettled. The Court's answer to the former question in this case thus does not resolve the latter one.

■ JUSTICE BREYER, with whom JUSTICE GINSBURG joins, dissenting.

In 2009, in *Arizona v. Gant,* 556 U.S. 332, 129 S.Ct. 1710, 173 L.Ed.2d 485, this Court held that a police search of an automobile without a warrant violates the Fourth Amendment if the police have previously removed the automobile's occupants and placed them securely in a squad car. * * *

I agree with the Court about *whether Gant'*s new rule applies. It does apply. * * *

The Court goes on, however, to decide *how Gant'* s new rule will apply. And here it adds a fatal twist. While conceding that, like the search in *Gant,* this search violated the Fourth Amendment, it holds that, unlike Gant, this defendant is not entitled to a remedy. That is because the Court finds a new "good faith" exception which prevents application of the normal remedy for a Fourth Amendment violation, namely, suppression of the illegally seized evidence. * * *

At this point I can no longer agree with the Court. * * *

[One] problem concerns fairness. Today's holding * * * "violates basic norms of constitutional adjudication." It treats the defendant in a case announcing a new rule one way while treating similarly situated defendants whose cases are pending on appeal in a different way. * * *

Of course, the Court may, as it suggests, avoid this unfairness by refusing to apply the exclusionary rule even to the defendant in the very case in which it announces a "new rule." But that approach would make matters worse. What would then happen in the lower courts? How would courts of appeals, for example, come to reconsider their prior decisions when other circuits' cases lead them to believe those decisions may be wrong? Why would a defendant seek to overturn any such decision? After all, if the (incorrect) circuit precedent is clear, then even if the defendant wins (on the constitutional question), he loses (on relief). To what extent then could this Court rely upon lower courts to work out Fourth Amendment differences among themselves—through circuit reconsideration of a precedent that other circuits have criticized?

Perhaps more important, the Court's rationale for creating its new "good faith" exception threatens to undermine well-settled Fourth Amendment law. The Court correctly says that pre-*Gant* Eleventh Circuit precedent had held that a *Gant*-type search was constitutional; hence the police conduct in this case, consistent with that precedent, was "innocent." But the Court then finds this fact sufficient to create a new "good faith" exception to the exclusionary rule. It reasons that the "sole purpose" of the exclusionary rule "is to deter future Fourth Amendment violations." Those benefits are sufficient to justify exclusion where "police exhibit deliberate, reckless, or grossly negligent disregard for Fourth Amendment rights." But those benefits do not justify exclusion where, as here, the police act with "simple, isolated negligence" or an "objectively reasonable good-faith belief that their conduct is lawful."

If the Court means what it says, what will happen to the exclusionary rule, a rule that the Court adopted nearly a century ago for federal courts, and made applicable to state courts a half century ago through the Fourteenth Amendment? The Court has thought of that rule not as punishment for the individual officer or as reparation for the individual defendant but more generally as an effective way to secure enforcement of the Fourth Amendment's commands. This Court has deviated from the "suppression" norm in the name of "good faith" only a handful of times and in limited, atypical circumstances * * * .

The fact that such exceptions are few and far between is understandable. Defendants frequently move to suppress evidence on Fourth Amendment grounds. In many, perhaps most, of these instances the police, uncertain of how the Fourth Amendment applied to the particular factual circumstances they faced, will have acted in objective good faith. Yet, in a significant percentage of these instances, courts will find that the police were wrong. And, unless the police conduct falls into one of the exceptions previously noted, courts have required the suppression of the evidence seized.

But an officer who conducts a search that he believes complies with the Constitution but which, it ultimately turns out, falls just outside the Fourth Amendment's bounds is no more culpable than an officer who follows erroneous "binding precedent." Nor is an officer more culpable where circuit precedent is simply suggestive rather than "binding," where it only describes how to treat roughly analogous instances, or where it just does not exist. Thus, if the Court means what it now says, if it would place determinative weight upon the culpability of an individual officer's conduct, and if it would apply the exclusionary rule only where a Fourth Amendment violation was "deliberate, reckless, or grossly negligent," then the "good faith" exception will swallow the exclusionary rule. Indeed, our broad dicta in *Herring*—dicta the Court repeats and expands upon today—may already be leading lower courts in this direction.

Any such change (which may already be underway) would affect not "an exceedingly small set of cases," but a very large number of cases, potentially many thousands each year. And since the exclusionary rule is often the only sanction available for a Fourth Amendment violation, the Fourth Amendment would no longer protect ordinary Americans from "unreasonable searches and seizures." It would become a watered-down Fourth Amendment, offering its protection against only those searches and seizures that are *egregiously* unreasonable.

* * *

For these reasons, with respect, I dissent.

CHAPTER 2

CONSTITUTIONAL DOCTRINES RELATING TO LAW ENFORCEMENT CONDUCT

Analysis

A. Scope of the Basic Doctrines
B. Officers' "Intent" and Pretext Motivation
C. The Fourth Amendment's Prohibition Against Unreasonable Searches and Seizures

---

Exclusionary sanctions of the sort considered in Chapter 1 come into operation only if there has been a violation of underlying legal requirements. In constitutional terms, challenges to law enforcement conduct usually rest on provisions guaranteeing protection from compelled self-incrimination, rights to privacy and freedom from unreasonable searches and seizures, rights to the assistance of counsel, and general rights to due process of law. Major federal provisions and illustrative state provisions are set out in the Introduction at the beginning of these materials.

This chapter develops the basic content of the major federal constitutional provisions. Subchapter A provides an opportunity to compare several of these provisions as they apply to the extraction of a sample of a suspect's blood. Subchapter B considers the significance of law enforcement officers' subjective states of mind in legal analysis of the officers' conduct. Subchapter C then focuses on the Fourth Amendment. The Fifth Amendment privilege against compelled self-incrimination applies primarily to law enforcement efforts to obtain confessions and other self-incriminating admissions; this is the subject of Chapter 6, and the Fifth Amendment privilege is considered at length in that chapter.

A. SCOPE OF THE BASIC DOCTRINES

Before considering in detail the impact of the major doctrines, it is important to consider the framework for analyzing situations under these doctrines. The principal case in this section addresses the relevance of these doctrines to a single police activity—the extraction from a suspect of a sample of blood. It is important to distinguish two matters. First, what are the "threshold" issues determining whether the doctrine applies? Second, *if* the doctrine applies, what requirements does it impose upon law enforcement conduct?

Schmerber v. California

Supreme Court of the United States, 1966.
384 U.S. 757, 86 S.Ct. 1826.

■ MR. JUSTICE BRENNAN delivered the opinion of the Court.

Petitioner was convicted in Los Angeles Municipal Court of the criminal offense of driving an automobile while under the influence of intoxicating liquor. He had been arrested at a hospital while receiving treatment for injuries suffered in an accident involving the automobile that he had apparently been driving. At the direction of a police officer, a blood sample was then withdrawn from petitioner's body by a physician at the hospital. The chemical analysis of this sample revealed a percent by weight of alcohol in his blood at the time of the offense which indicated intoxication, and the report of this analysis was admitted in evidence at the trial. Petitioner objected to receipt of this evidence of the analysis on the ground that the blood had been withdrawn despite his refusal, on the advice of his counsel, to consent to the test. He contended that in that circumstance the withdrawal of the blood and the admission of the analysis in evidence denied him due process of law under the Fourteenth Amendment, as well as specific guarantees of the Bill of Rights secured against the States by that Amendment: his privilege against self-incrimination under the Fifth Amendment; * * * and his right not to be subjected to unreasonable searches and seizures in violation of the Fourth Amendment. The Appellate Department of the California Superior Court rejected these contentions and affirmed the conviction. In view of constitutional decisions since we last considered these issues in *Breithaupt v. Abram*, 352 U.S. 432, 77 S.Ct. 408, 1 L.Ed.2d 448 [(1957)] we granted certiorari. We affirm.

I.

The Due Process Clause Claim

[In *Rochin v. California*, 342 U.S. 165, 72 S.Ct. 205, 96 L.Ed. 183 (1952), officers lacking probable cause had entered Rochin's house through an open door. Forcing open the door to Rochin's second floor room, they found Rochin partly dressed and sitting on a bed, upon which his wife was lying. When they asked about two capsules which were on a night stand next to the bed, Rochin grabbed the capsules and swallowed them despite the efforts of the three officers to prevent this. Rochin was then taken to a hospital, where a doctor forced an emetic solution through a tube into his stomach, causing him to vomit. In the vomited matter were found the two capsules which were used in evidence in his later prosecution for possession of the morphine in the capsules. The Supreme Court held that the resulting conviction violated due process:

> This is conduct that shocks the conscience. Illegally breaking into the privacy of [Rochin], the struggle to open his mouth and remove what was there, the forcible extraction of his stomach contents—this course of proceeding by agents of government to

obtain evidence is bound to offend even hardened sensibilities. They are methods too close to the rack and screw to permit of constitutional differentiation.

342 U.S. at 172, 72 S.Ct. at 209–10, 96 L.Ed. at 190. Petitioner argues that *Rochin* controls here.]

Breithaupt was also a case in which police officers caused blood to be withdrawn from the driver of an automobile involved in an accident, and in which there was ample justification for the officer's conclusion that the driver was under the influence of alcohol. There, as here, the extraction was made by a physician in a simple, medically acceptable manner in a hospital environment. There, however, the driver was unconscious at the time the blood was withdrawn and hence had no opportunity to object to the procedure. We affirmed the conviction there resulting from the use of the test in evidence, holding that under such circumstances the withdrawal did not offend "that 'sense of justice' of which we spoke in *Rochin*." *Breithaupt* thus requires the rejection of petitioner's due process argument, and nothing in the circumstances of this case or in supervening events persuades us that this aspect of *Breithaupt* should be overruled.

II.

The Privilege Against Self-incrimination Claim

Breithaupt summarily rejected an argument that the withdrawal of blood and the admission of the analysis report involved in that state case violated the Fifth Amendment privilege of any person not to "be compelled in any criminal case to be a witness against himself," citing *Twining v. State of New Jersey*, 211 U.S. 78, 29 S.Ct. 14, 53 L.Ed. 97. But that case, holding that the protections of the Fourteenth Amendment do not embrace this Fifth Amendment privilege, has been succeeded by *Malloy v. Hogan*, 378 U.S. 1, 8, 84 S.Ct. 1489, 1493, 12 L.Ed.2d 653 [(1964)]. We there held that "[t]he Fourteenth Amendment secures against state invasion the same privilege that the Fifth Amendment guarantees against federal infringement—the right of a person to remain silent unless he chooses to speak in the unfettered exercise of his own will, and to suffer no penalty * * * for such silence." We therefore must now decide whether the withdrawal of the blood and admission in evidence of the analysis involved in this case violated petitioner's privilege. We hold that the privilege protects an accused only from being compelled to testify against himself, or otherwise provide the State with evidence of a testimonial or communicative nature,[5] and that the

---

[5] A dissent suggests that the report of the blood test was "testimonial" or "communicative," because the test was performed in order to obtain the testimony of others, communicating to the jury facts about petitioner's condition. Of course, all evidence received in court is "testimonial" or "communicative" if these words are thus used. But the Fifth Amendment relates only to acts on the part of the person to whom the privilege applies, and we use these words subject to the same limitations. A nod or headshake is as much a "testimonial" or "communicative" act in this sense as are spoken words. But the terms as we use them do not

withdrawal of blood and use of the analysis in question in this case did not involve compulsion to these ends.

It could not be denied that in requiring petitioner to submit to the withdrawal and chemical analysis of his blood the State compelled him to submit to an attempt to discover evidence that might be used to prosecute him for a criminal offense. He submitted only after the police officer rejected his objection and directed the physician to proceed. The officer's direction to the physician to administer the test over petitioner's objection constituted compulsion for the purposes of the privilege. The critical question, then, is whether petitioner was thus compelled "to be a witness against himself."

If the scope of the privilege coincided with the complex of values it helps to protect, we might be obliged to conclude that the privilege was violated. In *Miranda v. Arizona*, 384 U.S. 436, at 460, 86 S.Ct. 1602, at 1620, 16 L.Ed.2d 694, at 715 [(1966)], the Court said of the interests protected by the privilege: "All these policies point to one overriding thought: the constitutional foundation underlying the privilege is the respect a government—state or federal—must accord to the dignity and integrity of its citizens. To maintain a 'fair state-individual balance,' to require the government 'to shoulder the entire load,' * * * to respect the inviolability of the human personality, our accusatory system of criminal justice demands that the government seeking to punish an individual produce the evidence against him by its own independent labors, rather than by the cruel, simple expedient of compelling it from his own mouth." The withdrawal of blood necessarily involves puncturing the skin for extraction, and the percent by weight of alcohol in that blood, as established by chemical analysis, is evidence of criminal guilt. Compelled submission fails on one view to respect the "inviolability of the human personality." Moreover, since it enables the State to rely on evidence forced from the accused, the compulsion violates at least one meaning of the requirement that the State procure the evidence against an accused "by its own independent labors."

As the passage in *Miranda* implicitly recognizes, however, the privilege has never been given the full scope which the values it helps to protect suggest. History and a long line of authorities in lower courts have consistently limited its protection to situations in which the State seeks to submerge those values by obtaining the evidence against an accused through "the cruel, simple expedient of compelling it from his own mouth. * * * In sum, the privilege is fulfilled only when the person is guaranteed the right 'to remain silent unless he chooses to speak in the unfettered exercise of his own will.'" The leading case in this Court is *Holt v. United States*, 218 U.S. 245, 31 S.Ct. 2, 54 L.Ed. 1021 [(1910)]. There the question was whether evidence was admissible that the accused, prior to trial and over his protest, put on a blouse that fitted

---

apply to evidence of acts noncommunicative in nature as to the person asserting the privilege, even though, as here, such acts are compelled to obtain the testimony of others.

him. It was contended that compelling the accused to submit to the demand that he model the blouse violated the privilege. Mr. Justice Holmes, speaking for the Court, rejected the argument as "based upon an extravagant extension of the 5th Amendment," and went on to say: "[T]he prohibition of compelling a man in a criminal court to be witness against himself is a prohibition of the use of physical or moral compulsion to extort communications from him, not an exclusion of his body as evidence when it may be material. The objection in principle would forbid a jury to look at a prisoner and compare his features with a photograph in proof."

It is clear that the protection of the privilege reaches an accused's communications, whatever form they might take * * * . On the other hand, both federal and state courts have usually held that it offers no protection against compulsion to submit to fingerprinting, photographing, or measurements, to write or speak for identification, to appear in court, to stand, to assume a stance, to walk, or to make a particular gesture. The distinction which has emerged, often expressed in different ways, is that the privilege is a bar against compelling "communications" or "testimony," but that compulsion which makes a suspect or accused the source of "real or physical evidence" does not violate it.

Although we agree that this distinction is a helpful framework for analysis, we are not to be understood to agree with past applications in all instances. There will be many cases in which such a distinction is not readily drawn. Some tests seemingly directed to obtain "physical evidence," for example, lie detector tests measuring changes in body function during interrogation, may actually be directed to eliciting responses which are essentially testimonial. To compel a person to submit to testing in which an effort will be made to determine his guilt or innocence on the basis of physiological responses, whether willed or not, is to evoke the spirit and history of the Fifth Amendment. Such situations call to mind the principle that the protection of the privilege "is as broad as the mischief against which it seeks to guard." *Counselman v. Hitchcock*, 142 U.S. 547, 562, 12 S.Ct. 195, 198 [(1892)].

In the present case, however, no such problem of application is presented. Not even a shadow of testimonial compulsion upon or enforced communication by the accused was involved either in the extraction or in the chemical analysis. Petitioner's testimonial capacities were in no way implicated; indeed, his participation, except as a donor, was irrelevant to the results of the test, which depend on chemical analysis and on that alone.[9] Since the blood test evidence, although an incriminating product

---

[9] This conclusion would not necessarily govern had the State tried to show that the accused had incriminated himself when told that he would have to be tested. Such incriminating evidence may be an unavoidable by-product of the compulsion to take the test, especially for an individual who fears the extraction or opposes it on religious grounds. If it wishes to compel persons to submit to such attempts to discover evidence, the State may have to forego the advantage of any *testimonial* products of administering the test—products which would fall

of compulsion, was neither petitioner's testimony nor evidence relating to some communicative act or writing by the petitioner, it was not inadmissible on privilege grounds.

* * *

IV.

The Search and Seizure Claim

* * *

The values protected by the Fourth Amendment * * * substantially overlap those the Fifth Amendment helps to protect. History and precedent have required that we today reject the claim that the Self-Incrimination Clause of the Fifth Amendment requires the human body in all circumstances to be held inviolate against state expeditions seeking evidence of crime. But if compulsory administration of a blood test does not implicate the Fifth Amendment, it plainly involves the broadly conceived reach of a search and seizure under the Fourth Amendment. That Amendment expressly provides that "[t]he right of the people to be secure in their *persons*, houses, papers, and effects, against unreasonable searches and seizures, shall not be violated * * *." (Emphasis added.) It could not reasonably be argued, and indeed respondent does not argue, that the administration of the blood test in this case was free of the constraints of the Fourth Amendment. Such testing procedures plainly constitute searches of "persons," and depend antecedently upon seizures of "persons," within the meaning of that Amendment.

Because we are dealing with intrusions into the human body rather than with state interferences with property relationships or private papers—"houses, papers, and effects"—we write on a clean slate. Limitations on the kinds of property which may be seized under warrant, as distinct from the procedures for search and the permissible scope of search, are not instructive in this context. We begin with the assumption that once the privilege against self-incrimination has been found not to bar compelled intrusions into the body for blood to be analyzed for alcohol content, the Fourth Amendment's proper function is to constrain, not against all intrusions as such, but against intrusions which are not justified in the circumstances, or which are made in an improper manner. In other words, the questions we must decide in this case are whether the police were justified in requiring petitioner to submit to the blood test, and whether the means and procedures employed in taking his blood respected relevant Fourth Amendment standards of reasonableness.

In this case, as will often be true when charges of driving under the influence of alcohol are pressed, these questions arise in the context of an arrest made by an officer without a warrant. Here, there was plainly

---

within the privilege. Indeed, there may be circumstances in which the pain, danger, or severity of an operation would almost inevitably cause a person to prefer confession to undergoing the "search," and nothing we say today should be taken as establishing the permissibility of compulsion in that case. But no such situation is presented in this case. * * *

probable cause for the officer to arrest petitioner and charge him with driving an automobile while under the influence of intoxicating liquor. The police officer who arrived at the scene shortly after the accident smelled liquor on petitioner's breath, and testified that petitioner's eyes were "bloodshot, watery, sort of a glassy appearance." The officer saw petitioner again at the hospital, within two hours of the accident. There he noticed similar symptoms of drunkenness. He thereupon informed petitioner "that he was under arrest and that he was entitled to the services of an attorney, and that he could remain silent, and that anything that he told me would be used against him in evidence."

While early cases suggest that there is an unrestricted "right on the part of the government always recognized under English and American law, to search the person of the accused when legally arrested, to discover and seize the fruits or evidences of crime," the mere fact of a lawful arrest does not end our inquiry. The suggestion of these cases apparently rests on two factors—first, there may be more immediate danger of concealed weapons or of destruction of evidence under the direct control of the accused; second, once a search of the arrested person for weapons is permitted, it would be both impractical and unnecessary to enforcement of the Fourth Amendment's purpose to attempt to confine the search to those objects alone. Whatever the validity of these considerations in general, they have little applicability with respect to searches involving intrusions beyond the body's surface. The interests in human dignity and privacy which the Fourth Amendment protects forbid any such intrusions on the mere chance that desired evidence might be obtained. In the absence of a clear indication that in fact such evidence will be found, these fundamental human interests require law officers to suffer the risk that such evidence may disappear unless there is an immediate search.

Although the facts which established probable cause to arrest in this case also suggested the required relevance and likely success of a test of petitioner's blood for alcohol, the question remains whether the arresting officer was permitted to draw these inferences himself, or was required instead to procure a warrant before proceeding with the test. Search warrants are ordinarily required for searches of dwellings, and absent an emergency, no less could be required where intrusions into the human body are concerned. The requirement that a warrant be obtained is a requirement that inferences to support the search "be drawn by a neutral and detached magistrate instead of being judged by the officer engaged in the often competitive enterprise of ferreting out crime." The importance of informed, detached and deliberate determinations of the issue whether or not to invade another's body in search of evidence of guilt is indisputable and great.

The officer in the present case, however, might reasonably have believed that he was confronted with an emergency, in which the delay necessary to obtain a warrant, under the circumstances, threatened "the destruction of evidence." We are told that the percentage of alcohol in the blood begins to diminish shortly after drinking stops, as the body functions to eliminate it from the system. Particularly in a case such as this, where time had to be taken to bring the accused to a hospital and to investigate the scene of the accident, there was no time to seek out a magistrate and secure a warrant. Given these special facts, we conclude that the attempt to secure evidence of blood-alcohol content in this case was an appropriate incident to petitioner's arrest.

Similarly, we are satisfied that the test chosen to measure petitioner's blood-alcohol level was a reasonable one. Extraction of blood samples for testing is a highly effective means of determining the degree to which a person is under the influence of alcohol. Such tests are a commonplace in these days of periodic physical examinations and experience with them teaches that the quantity of blood extracted is minimal, and that for most people the procedure involves virtually no risk, trauma, or pain. Petitioner is not one of the few who on grounds of fear, concern for health, or religious scruple might prefer some other means of testing, such as the "breathalyzer" test petitioner refused. * * * We need not decide whether such wishes would have to be respected.

Finally, the record shows that the test was performed in a reasonable manner. Petitioner's blood was taken by a physician in a hospital environment according to accepted medical practices. We are thus not presented with the serious questions which would arise if a search involving use of a medical technique, even of the most rudimentary sort, were made by other than medical personnel or in other than a medical environment—for example, if it were administered by police in the privacy of the stationhouse. To tolerate searches under these conditions might be to invite an unjustified element of personal risk of infection and pain.

We thus conclude that the present record shows no violation of petitioner's right under the Fourth and Fourteenth Amendments to be free of unreasonable searches and seizures. It bears repeating, however, that we reach this judgment only on the facts of the present record. The integrity of an individual's person is a cherished value of our society. That we today hold that the Constitution does not forbid the States minor intrusions into an individual's body under stringently limited conditions in no way indicates that it permits more substantial intrusions, or intrusions under other conditions.

Affirmed.

NOTES

1.   When *Schmerber* permits the taking of a blood sample without a warrant is addressed further in Subchapter A(1) of Chapter 5.

2.   **Providing Voice Samples as Nontestimonial Activity.** In United States v. Wade, 388 U.S. 218, 87 S.Ct. 1926 (1967), the Court held

that police did not violate the Fifth Amendment by requiring Wade to say at a lineup the words uttered by a robber—"put the money in the bag." Wade was required, the Court reasoned, only to use his voice in demonstrating its physical characteristics. See also, United States v. Dionisio, 410 U.S. 1, 93 S.Ct. 764 (1973) (Fifth Amendment not implicated by subpoena directing suspect to appear at prosecutor's office and read into a recording device from a transcript); United States v. Mara, 410 U.S. 19, 93 S.Ct. 774 (1973) (Fifth Amendment not implicated by compulsion to prepare and provide exemplar of handwriting or printing).

3. **Testimonial Aspects of Field Sobriety Tests.** The Court discussed the Fifth Amendment requirement that a compelled act be "testimonial" and the rationale for this demand in Pennsylvania v. Muniz, 496 U.S. 582, 110 S.Ct. 2638 (1990), involving the processing—and videotaping—of a suspect arrested for driving while intoxicated. Requiring the arrestee to speak to demonstrate the slurred nature of his speech, all justices agreed, did not involve compelled testimonial activity. "Requiring a suspect to reveal the physical manner in which he articulates words, like requiring him to reveal the physical properties of the sound produced by his voice ... does not, without more, compel him to provide a 'testimonial' response for purposes of the privilege." Having him perform sobriety tests (the "horizontal gaze nystagus" test, the "walk and turn" test and the "one leg stand" test), eight of the justices also held, did not implicate the Fifth Amendment. But asking him the date of his sixth birthday (apparently to determine if he could calculate that from his date of birth), a 5 to 4 majority concluded, did demand testimonial activity. It rejected the argument, accepted by the four dissenters, that this question simply sought a demonstration of the physiological functioning of the suspect's brain, and thus was no different from requiring him to demonstrate his ability to articulate words. Justice Brennan explained for the majority:

> We recently explained in *Doe v. United States*, 487 U.S. 201, 108 S.Ct. 2341, 101 L.Ed.2d 184 (1988), that "in order to be testimonial, an accused's communication must itself, explicitly or implicitly, relate a factual assertion or disclose information." We reached this conclusion after addressing our reasoning in *Schmerber*, supra, and its progeny:

>> The Court accordingly held that the privilege was not implicated in [the line of cases beginning with *Schmerber*] because the suspect was not required "to disclose any knowledge he might have," or "to speak his guilt." It is the "extortion of information from the accused," the attempt to force him "to disclose the contents of his own mind," that implicates the Self-Incrimination Clause. * * * "unless some attempt is made to secure a communication—written, oral or otherwise—upon which reliance is to be placed as involving (the accused's) consciousness of the facts and the operations of his mind in expressing it, the demand made upon him is not a testimonial one." 8 Wigmore § 2265, p. 386.

487 U.S., at 210–211, 108 S.Ct. at 2348.

After canvassing the purposes of the privilege recognized in prior cases, we concluded that "[t]hese policies are served when the privilege is asserted to spare the accused from having to reveal, directly or indirectly, his knowledge of facts relating him to the offense or from having to share his thoughts and beliefs with the Government."

This definition of testimonial evidence reflects an awareness of the historical abuses against which the privilege against self-incrimination was aimed. "Historically, the privilege was intended to prevent the use of legal compulsion to extract from the accused a sworn communication of facts which would incriminate him. Such was the process of the ecclesiastical courts and the Star Chamber—the inquisitorial method of putting the accused upon his oath and compelling him to answer questions designed to uncover uncharged offenses, without evidence from another source. The major thrust of the policies undergirding the privilege is to prevent such compulsion." At its core, the privilege reflects our fierce "unwillingness to subject those suspected of crime to the cruel trilemma of self-accusation, perjury or contempt," that defined the operation of the Star Chamber, wherein suspects were forced to choose between revealing incriminating private thoughts and forsaking their oath by committing perjury. See *United States v. Nobles*, 422 U.S. 225, 233, 95 S.Ct. 2160, 2167, 45 L.Ed.2d 141 (1975) ("The Fifth Amendment privilege against compulsory self-incrimination . . . protects 'a private inner sanctum of individual feeling and thought and proscribes state intrusion to extract self-condemnation' ").

We need not explore the outer boundaries of what is "testimonial" today, for our decision flows from the concept's core meaning. Because the privilege was designed primarily to prevent "a recurrence of the Inquisition and the Star Chamber, even if not in their stark brutality," it is evident that a suspect is "compelled . . . to be a witness against himself" at least whenever he must face the modern-day analog of the historic trilemma—either during a criminal trial where a sworn witness faces the identical three choices, or during custodial interrogation where . . . the choices are analogous and hence raise similar concerns. Whatever else it may include, therefore, the definition of "testimonial" evidence . . . must encompass all responses to questions that, if asked of a sworn suspect during a criminal trial, could place the suspect in the "cruel trilemma." This conclusion is consistent with our recognition in *Doe* that "[t]he vast majority of verbal statements thus will be testimonial" because "[t]here are very few instances in which a verbal statement, either oral or written, will not convey information or assert facts." Whenever a suspect is asked for a response requiring him to communicate an express or implied assertion of fact or belief, the suspect confronts the "trilemma" of truth, falsity, or silence and hence the response (whether based on truth or falsity) contains a testimonial component.

496 U.S. at 594–97, 110 S.Ct. at 2646–48.

Turning to the facts of the case, it continued:

> When [the officer] asked Muniz if he knew the date of his sixth birthday and Muniz, for whatever reason, could not remember or calculate that date, he was confronted with the trilemma. By hypothesis the inherently coercive environment created by the custodial interrogation precluded the option of remaining silent. Muniz was left with the choice of incriminating himself by admitting that he did not then know the date of his sixth birthday, or answering untruthfully by reporting a date that he did not then believe to be accurate (an incorrect guess would be incriminating as well as untruthful). The content of his truthful answer supported an inference that his mental faculties were impaired, because his assertion (he did not know the date of his sixth birthday) was different from the assertion (he knew the date was (correct date)) that the trier of fact might reasonably have expected a lucid person to provide. Hence, the incriminating inference of impaired mental faculties stemmed, not just from the fact that Muniz slurred his response, but also from a testimonial aspect of that response.

496 U.S. at 599, 110 S.Ct. at 2649. The Court did not reach whether asking Muniz to count out loud while performing the physical sobriety tests involved "testimonial" activity. During one test, he counted accurately and thus his responses were not incriminating. During another, he failed to count and did not argue that his silence had any "independent incriminating significance."

4. **Compulsion Must Be "Impermissible."** The Fifth Amendment is violated only if compulsion to engage in testimonial and self-incriminating activity is impermissible. Many states provide under "implied consent" statutes that, under certain circumstances, a person suspected of driving while intoxicated may be "requested" by an officer to provide a blood or breath sample but may not be forced to provide the sample if he refuses. Such a refusal is itself often admissible against the suspect if he does not provide the requested sample. In South Dakota v. Neville, 459 U.S. 553, 103 S.Ct. 916 (1983), the Court held that whether or not such a refusal is "testimonial," the Fifth Amendment does not bar use of such evidence because no "impermissible compulsion" is imposed upon the suspect. *Schmerber,* the Court observed, clearly permits a State under certain circumstances to force a person to submit to a blood test:

> Given * * * that the offer of taking a blood-alcohol test is clearly legitimate, the action becomes no *less* legitimate when the State offers a second option of refusing the test, with the attendant penalties of making that choice.

459 U.S. at 563, 103 S.Ct. at 923 (emphasis in original).

5. The application of the privilege against compelled self-incrimination to subpoenas requiring the production of documents is

considered in Chapter 8. Fifth Amendment self-incrimination principles are examined more fully in the setting of police interrogation in Chapter 6.

6.   **Requirement That Compelled Activity Be "Incriminating."** The Fifth Amendment bars law enforcement officers compelling a person to engage in testimonial activity only when that activity is "incriminating." In Minnesota v. Murphy, 465 U.S. 420, 104 S.Ct. 1136 (1984), the Supreme Court, in dicta, indicated revocation of probation is not "incrimination" within the meaning of the privilege. Thus, probationers can apparently be compelled, without violation of the privilege, to answer questions that might result in revocation of probation but that pose "no realistic threat of incrimination in a separate criminal proceeding."

7.   **Due Process Prohibition Against Conduct Shocking the Conscience.** *Schmerber* discussed the due process claim based on *Rochin* as an independent potential basis for excluding the evidence obtained from a blood withdrawal. Is the due process prohibition against law enforcement conduct that "shocks the conscience" still a viable independent basis for challenging the admissibility of evidence? County of Sacramento v. Lewis, 523 U.S. 833, 118 S.Ct. 1708 (1998), indicated yes and suggested the requirements for such an attack. In *Lewis*, the Court addressed the civil liability of officers' employing governmental entity for damages based on the Lewis's death, caused by a vehicle collision resulting from a high speed police chase. The plaintiff argued the officers' actions violated suspect Lewis's right to substantive due process. Discussing *Rochin*, the Court commented that the case "today would be treated under the Fourth Amendment, albeit with the same result." This is apparently because the officers' actions in *Rochin* would now constitute unreasonable searches and seizures and the resultant evidence would be inadmissible under *Mapp*.

The law enforcement action in *Lewis*, however, was held at most an *attempted* seizure, and thus not within the Fourth Amendment's prohibition against unreasonable seizures. Nevertheless, *Lewis* indicated a high speed chase could constitute an actionable violation of substantive due process under *Rochin* if the officers acted with "intent to harm [the] suspects physically or to worsen their legal plight * * * ." In *Rochin*, it added, "it was not the ultimate purpose of the [officers] to harm the plaintiff, but they apparently acted with full appreciation of what the Court described as the brutality of their acts." This appreciation of the brutality of the conduct apparently sufficed to trigger substantive due process in *Rochin*.

EDITORS' NOTE: DIMENSIONS OF FOURTH AMENDMENT "REASONABLENESS" AND "STANDARDIZED PROCEDURES"

Schmerber's analysis of the Fourth Amendment issue illustrates several aspects of that body of law that will be developed and explored in the material that follows.

First, *Schmerber* assumed a general Fourth Amendment rule— subject of course to exceptions—that a search of a dwelling or one involving an intrusion into the human body requires a search warrant. Is such a rule appropriate? The literal terms of the Fourth Amendment impose no such requirement, and in fact have little to offer concerning when a search warrant is necessary. Would the spirit and purpose of the Fourth Amendment be better served if the Court did not focus upon a need to fit a warrantless search into one of the exceptions to a general rule that a warrant is necessary? The Court might instead scrutinize each search for reasonableness under a more flexible standard.

Second, *Schmerber* recognized a general Fourth Amendment requirement that a search or seizure be based upon sufficient facts indicating that the action would be successful. With regard to a search, this evidence must indicate that seizable items will be found if the search is made. In the case of a search made pursuant to a search warrant, the Fourth Amendment explicitly requires these facts amount to "probable cause." This is considered in Chapter 3.

As a general rule, that same requirement—probable cause—also applies when a search is made under an exception to the requirement of a warrant. *Schmerber* addressed the reasonableness of the search at issue in the case—the insertion of a needle into the suspect's arm to seek blood believed to contain alcohol indicating he had been intoxicated. Whether it required probable cause is not entirely clear from the language used.

As is explored in more detail later in these materials, the Court has recognized that some searches and some seizures can be supported by less than probable cause. Chapter 4, for example, explores investigatory field stops which require only "reasonable suspicion" that the person is involved in criminal activity.

In some situations, as will also be addressed later, the Fourth Amendment permits so-called "suspicionless" police action. In these situations, the law enforcement action is reasonable even in the absence of any information suggesting the person or item is seizable or that the search will disclose contraband or evidence of criminal guilt. Certain checkpoint stops of motorists, for example, are reasonable simply because the driver is passing the point where the checkpoint is located. These are considered in Chapter 4.

Third, *Schmerber* inquired into the reasonableness of the means chosen to make the search—an extraction of a blood sample—and the reasonableness of manner in which that extraction was made in the case. Sometimes, apparently, the Fourth Amendment requires more than that a warrant be utilized (or an exception shown applicable) and that adequate supporting facts be known.

Another aspect of Fourth Amendment reasonableness not discussed in *Schmerber* but applied in some situations is a demand that the law enforcement actions be taken pursuant to "standardized procedures."

In Colorado v. Bertine, 479 U.S. 367, 107 S.Ct. 738 (1987), the Court reaffirmed that the Fourth Amendment permits certain inventory inspections of the contents of seized automobiles. It stressed that in the case before it "the police * * * were following standardized procedures." 479 U.S. at 372, 107 S.Ct. at 741. *Bertine*'s emphasis upon "standardized procedures" was developed into a Fourth Amendment requirement in Florida v. Wells, 495 U.S. 1, 110 S.Ct. 1632 (1990).

Officers in *Wells* examined the contents of a suitcase found in an impounded car. The state court held the search improper because no evidence was produced that the police agency had any policy concerning opening of closed containers found during inventory searches. The Supreme Court affirmed, reasoning that "absent [a policy with respect to the opening of closed containers encountered during an inventory search], the instant search was not sufficiently regulated to satisfy the Fourth Amendment * * * ." Chief Justice Rehnquist, writing for the majority, explained:

> Our view that standardized criteria or established routine must regulate the opening of containers found during inventory searches is based on the principle that an inventory search must not be a ruse for a general rummaging in order to discover incriminating evidence. The policy or practice governing inventory searches should be designed to produce an inventory. The individual police officer must not be allowed so much latitude that inventory inspections are turned into "a purposeful and general means of discovering evidence of crime," *Bertine,* supra, 479 U.S., at 376, 107 S.Ct., at 744 (Blackmun, J., concurring).

495 U.S. at 4, 110 S.Ct. at 1635.

The *Wells* majority disapproved, however, the state court's comment that under *Bertine* the policy must mandate that either all or no containers be opened:

> A police officer may be allowed sufficient latitude whether a particular container should or should not be opened in light of the nature of the search and characteristics of the container itself. Thus, while policies of opening all containers or of opening no containers are unquestionably permissible, it would be equally permissible, for example, to allow the opening of closed containers whose contents officers determine they are unable to ascertain from examining the containers' exteriors. The allowance of the exercise of judgment based on concerns relevant to the purposes of an inventory search does not violate the Fourth Amendment.

495 U.S. at 4, 110 S.Ct. at 1635.

When the Fourth Amendment mandates such standardized procedures, and what criteria such procedures must meet when they are required, is not always clear. Chapter 4, for example, explores "suspicionless" stops of motorists passing through checkpoints. Whether such checkpoints have been established or operated pursuant to "guidelines"—perhaps a kind of standardized procedure—may affect their constitutional validity.

B. OFFICERS' "INTENT" AND PRETEXT MOTIVATION

EDITORS' INTRODUCTION: THE CONSTITUTIONAL SIGNIFICANCE OF OFFICERS' MOTIVATION

An important question under federal constitutional limits on law enforcement conduct is the extent to which an officer's subjective intent, motivation or awareness is controlling or even relevant.

In *Schmerber*, for example, the Fourth Amendment reasonableness of defendant Schmerber's arrest required probable cause—a certain amount of information indicating he had violated the prohibition against driving while intoxicated. But was it also necessary that the arresting officers have actually believed he committed this offense? Must the officers have been actually motivated by a desire to pursue Schmerber's prosecution for this offense?

Traditionally, the issue has often been put negatively: Is otherwise permissible law enforcement conduct rendered unconstitutional because the evidence shows a "pretext" motivation?

Precisely what constitutes pretext motivation as the term is used here requires some elaboration. In the principal case that follows, there is some indication that the officers believed defendant Whren and his companions were involved in illegal drug activity and wanted an opportunity to observe them and their truck at close range and perhaps to question them. As developed in Chapter 4, an investigatory stop is permissible only upon "reasonable suspicion" that the stopped person is involved in criminal activity. The officers may have lacked this reasonable suspicion. They did, however, almost certainly have probable cause to believe the driver of the vehicle violated several traffic laws for which a stop could be made.

When the case is litigated and the prosecution defends the stop as one "for" violations of the traffic law, must the prosecution show that the officers were in some sense motivated by a desire to enforce the traffic laws? Or, can Whren and his companions establish that the stop was unreasonable because the officers were motivated instead by a desire to investigate their suspicions of drug activity which were not supported enough to permit an investigatory stop "for" that purpose?

The issue arises most frequently in the Fourth Amendment context. But it can be presented in other situations. Miranda v. Arizona, 384 U.S. 436, 86 S.Ct. 1602 (1966), for example, does not apply in some situations in which considerations of public safety would be served by immediate questioning of a suspect in custody. That exception to *Miranda* might apply only upon proof that the questioning officer was actually motivated by what the officer perceived was the need to address an immediate and serious risk to public safety.

Whren v. United States

Supreme Court of the United States, 1996.
517 U.S. 806, 116 S.Ct. 1769.

■ JUSTICE SCALIA delivered the opinion of the Court.

In this case we decide whether the temporary detention of a motorist who the police have probable cause to believe has committed a civil traffic violation is inconsistent with the Fourth Amendment's prohibition against unreasonable seizures unless a reasonable officer would have been motivated to stop the car by a desire to enforce the traffic laws.

I

On the evening of June 10, 1993, plainclothes vice-squad officers of the District of Columbia Metropolitan Police Department were patrolling a "high drug area" of the city in an unmarked car. Their suspicions were aroused when they passed a dark Pathfinder truck with temporary license plates and youthful occupants waiting at a stop sign, the driver looking down into the lap of the passenger at his right. The truck remained stopped at the intersection for what seemed an unusually long time—more than 20 seconds. When the police car executed a U-turn in order to head back toward the truck, the Pathfinder turned suddenly to its right, without signaling, and sped off at an "unreasonable" speed. The policemen followed, and in a short while overtook the Pathfinder when it stopped behind other traffic at a red light. They pulled up alongside, and Officer Ephraim Soto stepped out and approached the driver's door, identifying himself as a police officer and directing the driver, petitioner Brown, to put the vehicle in park. When Soto drew up to the driver's window, he immediately observed two large plastic bags of what appeared to be crack cocaine in petitioner Whren's hands. Petitioners were arrested, and quantities of several types of illegal drugs were retrieved from the vehicle.

Petitioners were charged in a four-count indictment with violating various federal drug laws * * * . At a pretrial suppression hearing, they challenged the legality of the stop and the resulting seizure of the drugs. * * * The District Court denied the suppression motion * * * .

Petitioners were convicted of the counts at issue here. The Court of Appeals affirmed the convictions. * * * We granted certiorari.

II

The Fourth Amendment guarantees "[t]he right of the people to be secure in their persons, houses, papers, and effects, against unreasonable searches and seizures." Temporary detention of individuals during the stop of an automobile by the police, even if only for a brief period and for a limited purpose, constitutes a "seizure" of "persons" within the meaning of this provision. An automobile stop is thus subject to the constitutional imperative that it not be "unreasonable" under the circumstances. As a general matter, the decision to stop an automobile is reasonable where the police have probable cause to believe that a traffic violation has occurred.

Petitioners accept that Officer Soto had probable cause to believe that various provisions of the District of Columbia traffic code had been violated. See 18 D.C. Mun. Regs. §§ 2213.4 (1995) ("An operator shall . . . give full time and attention to the operation of the vehicle"); 2204.3 ("No person shall turn any vehicle . . . without giving an appropriate signal"); 2200.3 ("No person shall drive a vehicle . . . at a speed greater than is reasonable and prudent under the conditions"). They argue, however, that "in the unique context of civil traffic regulations" probable cause is not enough. Since, they contend, the use of automobiles is so heavily and minutely regulated that total compliance with traffic and safety rules is nearly impossible, a police officer will almost invariably be able to catch any given motorist in a technical violation. This creates the temptation to use traffic stops as a means of investigating other law violations, as to which no probable cause or even articulable suspicion exists. Petitioners, who are both black, further contend that police officers might decide which motorists to stop based on decidedly impermissible factors, such as the race of the car's occupants. To avoid this danger, they say, the Fourth Amendment test for traffic stops should be, not the normal one (applied by the Court of Appeals) of whether probable cause existed to justify the stop; but rather, whether a police officer, acting reasonably, would have made the stop for the reason given.

A

Petitioners contend that the standard they propose is consistent with our past cases' disapproval of police attempts to use valid bases of action against citizens as pretexts for pursuing other investigatory agendas. We are reminded that in *Florida v. Wells*, 495 U.S. 1, 4, 110 S.Ct. 1632, 1635, 109 L.Ed.2d 1 (1990), we stated that "an inventory search must not be used as a ruse for a general rummaging in order to discover incriminating evidence"; that in *Colorado v. Bertine*, 479 U.S. 367, 372, 107 S.Ct. 738, 741, 93 L.Ed.2d 739 (1987), in approving an inventory search, we apparently thought it significant that there had been "no showing that the police, who were following standard procedures, acted in bad faith or for the sole purpose of investigation"; and that in *New York v. Burger*, 482 U.S. 691, 716–717, n. 27, 107 S.Ct. 2636, 2651, n. 27, 96 L.Ed.2d 601 (1987), we observed, in upholding the constitutionality of a warrantless administrative inspection, that the search did not appear to be "a 'pretext' for obtaining evidence of . . . violation of . . . penal laws." But only an undiscerning reader would regard these cases as endorsing the principle that ulterior motives can invalidate police conduct that is justifiable on the basis of probable cause to believe that a violation of law has occurred. In each case we were addressing the validity of a search conducted in the absence of probable cause. Our quoted statements simply explain that the exemption from the need for probable cause (and warrant), which is accorded to searches made for the purpose of inventory or administrative regulation, is not accorded to searches that are not made for those purposes.

* * *

* * * Petitioners' difficulty is not simply a lack of affirmative support for their position. Not only have we never held, outside the context of inventory search or administrative inspection (discussed above), that an officer's motive invalidates objectively justifiable behavior under the Fourth Amendment; but we have repeatedly held and asserted the contrary. In *United States v. Villamonte-Marquez*, 462 U.S. 579, 584, n. 3, 103 S.Ct. 2573, 2577, n. 3, 77 L.Ed.2d 22 (1983), we held that an otherwise valid warrantless boarding of a vessel by customs officials was not rendered invalid "because the customs officers were accompanied by a Louisiana state policeman, and were following an informant's tip that a vessel in the ship channel was thought to be carrying marihuana." We flatly dismissed the idea that an ulterior motive might serve to strip the agents of their legal justification. In *United States v. Robinson*, 414 U.S. 218, 94 S.Ct. 467, 38 L.Ed.2d 427 (1973), we held that a traffic-violation arrest (of the sort here) would not be rendered invalid by the fact that it was "a mere pretext for a narcotics search;" and that a lawful postarrest search of the person would not be rendered invalid by the fact that it was not motivated by the officer-safety concern that justifies such searches. And in *Scott v. United States*, 436 U.S. 128, 138, 98 S.Ct. 1717, 1723, 56 L.Ed.2d 168 (1978), in rejecting the contention that wiretap evidence was subject to exclusion because the agents conducting the tap had failed to make any effort to comply with the statutory requirement that unauthorized acquisitions be minimized, we said that "[s]ubjective intent alone ... does not make otherwise lawful conduct illegal or unconstitutional." We described *Robinson* as having established that "the fact that the officer does not have the state of mind which is hypothecated by the reasons which provide the legal justification for the officer's action does not invalidate the action taken as long as the circumstances, viewed objectively, justify that action."

We think these cases foreclose any argument that the constitutional reasonableness of traffic stops depends on the actual motivations of the individual officers involved. We of course agree with petitioners that the Constitution prohibits selective enforcement of the law based on considerations such as race. But the constitutional basis for objecting to intentionally discriminatory application of laws is the Equal Protection Clause, not the Fourth Amendment. Subjective intentions play no role in ordinary, probable-cause Fourth Amendment analysis.

B

Recognizing that we have been unwilling to entertain Fourth Amendment challenges based on the actual motivations of individual officers, petitioners disavow any intention to make the individual officer's subjective good faith the touchstone of "reasonableness." They insist that the standard they have put forward—whether the officer's conduct deviated materially from usual police practices, so that a reasonable officer in the same circumstances would not have made the stop for the reasons given—is an "objective" one.

But although framed in empirical terms, this approach is plainly and indisputably driven by subjective considerations. Its whole purpose is to prevent the police from doing under the guise of enforcing the traffic code what they would like to do for different reasons. Petitioners' proposed standard may not use the word "pretext," but it is designed to combat nothing other than the perceived "danger" of the pretextual stop, albeit only indirectly and over the run of cases. Instead of asking whether the individual officer had the proper state of mind, the petitioners would have us ask, in effect, whether (based on general police practices) it is plausible to believe that the officer had the proper state of mind.

Why one would frame a test designed to combat pretext in such fashion that the court cannot take into account actual and admitted pretext is a curiosity that can only be explained by the fact that our cases have foreclosed the more sensible option. If those cases were based only upon the evidentiary difficulty of establishing subjective intent, petitioners' attempt to root out subjective vices through objective means might make sense. But they were not based only upon that, or indeed even principally upon that. Their principal basis—which applies equally to attempts to reach subjective intent through ostensibly objective means—is simply that the Fourth Amendment's concern with "reasonableness" allows certain actions to be taken in certain circumstances, whatever the subjective intent. But even if our concern had been only an evidentiary one, petitioners' proposal would by no means assuage it. Indeed, it seems to us somewhat easier to figure out the intent of an individual officer than to plumb the collective consciousness of law enforcement in order to determine whether a "reasonable officer" would have been moved to act upon the traffic violation. While police manuals and standard procedures may sometimes provide objective assistance, ordinarily one would be reduced to speculating about the hypothetical reaction of a hypothetical constable— an exercise that might be called virtual subjectivity.

Moreover, police enforcement practices, even if they could be practicably assessed by a judge, vary from place to place and from time to time. We cannot accept that the search and seizure protections of the Fourth Amendment are so variable, and can be made to turn upon such trivialities. * * *

III

In what would appear to be an elaboration on the "reasonable officer" test, petitioners argue that the balancing inherent in any Fourth Amendment inquiry requires us to weigh the governmental and individual interests implicated in a traffic stop such as we have here. That balancing, petitioners claim, does not support investigation of minor traffic infractions by plainclothes police in unmarked vehicles; such investigation only minimally advances the government's interest in traffic safety, and may indeed retard it by producing motorist confusion and alarm—a view said to be supported by the Metropolitan Police Department's own regulations generally prohibiting this practice. And as for the Fourth Amendment interests of the individuals concerned, petitioners point out that our cases acknowledge that even ordinary traffic stops entail "a possibly unsettling show of authority"; that they at best "interfere with freedom of movement, are inconvenient, and consume time" and at worst "may create substantial anxiety." That anxiety is likely to be even more pronounced when the stop is conducted by plainclothes officers in unmarked cars.

It is of course true that in principle every Fourth Amendment case, since it turns upon a "reasonableness" determination, involves a balancing of all relevant factors. With rare exceptions not applicable here, however, the result of that balancing is not in doubt where the search or seizure is based upon probable cause. * * *

Where probable cause has existed, the only cases in which we have found it necessary actually to perform the "balancing" analysis involved searches or seizures conducted in an extraordinary manner, unusually harmful to an individual's privacy or even physical interests—such as, for example, seizure by means of deadly force, unannounced entry into a home, entry into a home without a warrant, or physical penetration of the body. The making of a traffic stop out-of-uniform does not remotely qualify as such an extreme practice, and so is governed by the usual rule that probable cause to believe the law has been broken "outbalances" private interest in avoiding police contact.

Petitioners urge as an extraordinary factor in this case that the "multitude of applicable traffic and equipment regulations" is so large and so difficult to obey perfectly that virtually everyone is guilty of violation, permitting the police to single out almost whomever they wish for a stop. But we are aware of no principle that would allow us to decide at what point a code of law becomes so expansive and so commonly violated that infraction itself can no longer be the ordinary measure of the lawfulness of enforcement. And even if we could identify such exorbitant codes, we do not know by what standard (or what right) we would decide, as petitioners would have us do, which particular provisions are sufficiently important to merit enforcement.

For the run-of-the-mine case, which this surely is, we think there is no realistic alternative to the traditional common-law rule that probable cause justifies a search and seizure.

* * *

Here the District Court found that the officers had probable cause to believe that petitioners had violated the traffic code. That rendered the stop reasonable under the Fourth Amendment, the evidence thereby discovered admissible, and the upholding of the convictions by the Court of Appeals for the District of Columbia Circuit correct.

Judgment affirmed.

NOTES

1. **Pretext Arrests.** *Whren* was reaffirmed and applied to an arrest in Arkansas v. Sullivan, 532 U.S. 769, 121 S.Ct. 1876 (2001) (per curiam).

2. **Law Enforcement Actions Based on Less than Probable Cause.** Does or should *Whren* apply to law enforcement action not requiring probable cause, as for example where reasonable suspicion is sufficient? In United States v. Knights, 534 U.S. 112, 122 S.Ct. 587 (2001), the Court applied *Whren* to the search of a probationer's residence which is reasonable if supported by reasonable suspicion. It explained only that the case presented no basis for examining "official purpose" because—citing *Whren*— "our holding rests on ordinary Fourth Amendment analysis that considers all of the circumstances of a search * * *." *Whren* applies, it suggested, except in "some special needs and administrative search cases" such as suspicionless stops of motorist at highway checkpoints. 534 U.S. at 122, 122 S.Ct. at 593. Justice Souter alone indicated he would "reserve the question whether *Whren*'s holding * * * should apply to searches based only upon reasonable suspicion." 534 U.S. at 123, 122 S.Ct. at 593 (Souter, J., concurring).

EDITORS' NOTE: PRETEXT MOTIVATION UNDER STATE LAW

Despite *Whren*, state constitutional provisions may provide a basis for challenging law enforcement conduct as a pretext.

The Washington Supreme Court reaffirmed in State v. Ladson, 138 Wash.2d 343, 979 P.2d 833, 842 n. 10 (1999), that pretextual stops are unreasonable under the Washington constitution. Rejecting the Supreme Court's reasoning in *Whren*, the state tribunal explained the state constitution "requires we look beyond the formal justification for the stop to the actual one." It continued:

> We note if we were to depart from our holdings and allow pretextual traffic stops, Washington citizens would lose their privacy every time they enter their automobiles. The traffic code is sufficiently extensive in its regulation that "[w]hether it be for failing to signal while changing lanes, driving with a headlight out, or not giving 'full time and attention' to the operation of the vehicle, virtually the entire driving population is in violation of some regulation as soon as they get in their cars, or shortly thereafter." Peter Shakow, Let He Who Never Has Turned

Without Signaling Cast the First Stone: An Analysis of Whren
v. United States, 24 Am. J.Crim. L. 627, 633 (1997) (footnote
omitted). Thus, nearly every citizen would be subject to a *Terry*
stop simply because he or she is in his or her car. But we have
repeatedly affirmed that Washingtonians retain their privacy
while in the automobile and we will do so today.

138 Wash.2d at 358 n. 10, 979 P.2d at 842 n. 10. In determining whether
a particular stop is pretextual, the *Ladson* court added, a court "should
consider the totality of the circumstances, including both the subjective
intent of the officer as well as the objective reasonableness of the officer's
behavior." Courts applying the *Ladson* analysis are likely to often give
controlling significance to an officer's subjective motive. Thus in State v.
DeSantiago, 97 Wash.App. 446, 983 P.2d 1173 (1999), the stop at issue
was for a left turn made improperly because DeSantiago did not turn into
the left hand lane of the street into which the turn was made. The trial
court found the officer followed DeSantiago because he had observed
DeSantiago leave a "narcotics hot spot" and "was looking for a basis to
stop the vehicle." This established subjective pretext motivation, and for
this reason the stop was unreasonable.

A pretext doctrine was adopted as a matter of state constitutional
law in State v. Sullivan, 348 Ark. 647, 74 S.W.3d 215 (2002). But the next
year the court made clear the doctrine applied only to arrests and not to
traffic stops. It based the distinction "on the heightened intrusiveness
associated with an arrest," and the absence of state case law applying the
pretext approach to otherwise valid traffic stops. State v. Harmon, 353
Ark. 568, 113 S.W.3d 75 (2003). An intermediate New Mexico court held
that pretext stops violate the state constitution. State v. Ochoa, 146 N.M.
32, 206 P.3d 143, 155–56 (2008), cert. granted 145 N.M. 572, 203 P.3d
103 (2008), cert. quashed 147 N.M. 464, 225 P.3d 794 (2009).

By a 4–3 vote, the New York Court of Appeals refused to adopt as a
matter of state constitutional law the position rejected in *Whren*. See
People v. Robinson, 97 N.Y.2d 341, 767 N.E.2d 638, 741 N.Y.S.2d 147
(2001). All seven judges agreed that a purely subjective approach was not
appropriate.

C. THE FOURTH AMENDMENT'S PROHIBITION AGAINST UNREASONABLE SEARCHES AND SEIZURES

Perhaps in part because of the limited applicability of the Fifth
Amendment, the Fourth Amendment's prohibition against unreasonable
searches and seizures has become the major federal constitutional
vehicle for regulating police conduct in gathering evidence. Several
threshold issues presented by efforts to invoke this prohibition are
considered in this portion of the materials. The first three subsections
consider when law enforcement conduct constitutes a "search" or a
"seizure" so as to invoke the Fourth Amendment. The fourth subsection

then addresses the effect of the requirement of standing and a narrow conception of what constitutes a search. But first the Introduction discusses the limitation of the Fourth Amendment to official conduct.

EDITORS' INTRODUCTION: PRIVATE PARTY SEARCHES AND SEIZURES

The Fourth Amendment's application is limited by the Supreme Court's position that it constrains only governmental action and does not apply to the conduct of a person acting purely in a private capacity. The leading case on private party searches is Burdeau v. McDowell, 256 U.S. 465, 41 S.Ct. 574 (1921). The petitioner moved for return of private papers wrongfully taken from his office by private persons and turned over to the government. The Court disposed of his Fourth Amendment claim with the following comments:

> The Fourth Amendment gives protection against unlawful searches and seizures, and * * * its protection applies to governmental action. Its origin and history clearly show that it was intended as a restraint upon the activities of sovereign authority, and was not intended to be a limitation upon other than governmental agencies * * * .

> In the present case the record clearly shows that no official of the federal government had anything to do with the wrongful seizure of the petitioner's property, or any knowledge thereof until several months after the property had been taken from him and was in the possession of the Cities Service Company. It is manifest that there was no invasion of the security afforded by the Fourth Amendment against unreasonable searches and seizure, as whatever wrong was done was the act of individuals in taking the property of another. A portion of the property so taken and held was turned over to the prosecuting officers of the federal government. We assume that petitioner has an unquestionable right of redress against those who illegally and wrongfully took his private property under the circumstances here disclosed, but with such remedies we are not now concerned.

256 U.S. at 475, 41 S.Ct. at 576.

The Court continued to apply this approach, although leaving open the possibility that involvement of governmental officers in stimulating or conducting a search by a private person might render that search within the scope of the Fourth Amendment. See United States v. Jacobsen, 466 U.S. 109, 113, 104 S.Ct. 1652, 1656 (1984); Walter v. United States, 447 U.S. 649, 100 S.Ct. 2395 (1980). In Coolidge v. New Hampshire, 403 U.S. 443, 91 S.Ct. 2022 (1971), for example, the murder suspect's wife was interviewed at the couple's home while he was in custody. In response to officers' inquiries concerning guns owned by her husband and the clothing he wore the day of the crime, she—apparently on her own initiative—obtained guns and clothing and offered them to the officers. Rejecting Coolidge's argument that this was a search despite Burdeau v. McDowell, the Court explained:

> The question presented here is whether the conduct of the police officers at the Coolidge house was such as to make her actions their actions for purposes of the Fourth and Fourteenth Amendment and their attendant exclusionary rules. The test * * * is whether Mrs. Coolidge, in light of all the circumstances of the case, must be regarded as having acted as an "instrument" or agent of the state when she produced her husband's belongings. * * * Mrs. Coolidge described her own motive as that of clearing her husband, and that she believed that she had nothing to hide. * * * The two officers who questioned her behaved, as her own testimony shows, with perfect courtesy. There is not the slightest implication of an attempt of their part to coerce or dominate her, or, for that matter, to direct her actions by the more subtle techniques of suggestion that are available to officials in circumstances like these.

403 U.S. at 487–89, 91 S.Ct. at 2048–50.

1. POLICE ACTIVITY CONSTITUTING A "SEARCH"

EDITORS' INTRODUCTION: THE *KATZ* CRITERION FOR IDENTIFYING SEARCHES AND THE REASONABLENESS OF SEARCHES

Whether law enforcement conduct constitutes a search for purposes of the Fourth Amendment is often determined by application of a standard derived from Katz v. United States, 389 U.S. 347, 88 S.Ct. 507 (1967). Whether conduct constituting a search is reasonable is generally determined by whether it is based on probable cause and is either supported by a warrant or within an exception to the general requirement of a warrant.

Katz and the Reasonable Expectation of Privacy Test

Prior to *Katz,* Fourth Amendment case law defining searches focused to some extent upon whether police had intruded in some physical sense into a protected area. In Silverman v. United States, 365 U.S. 505, 81 S.Ct. 679 (1961), for example, the Court held that officers engaged in a search when they used a "spike mike" to overhear conversations in an adjacent row house. The discussion suggested that this result was based on the showing officers inserted the microphone into a wall of the suspects house until it touched a heating duct. Thus the police conducted "an unauthorized physical penetration into the premises."

In *Katz,* federal officers attached an electronic listening and recording device to the outside of a public telephone booth that they anticipated Katz would use. Katz did use the booth, and the officers were able to overhear his end of the conversation. Finding the officers engaged in a "search," the Court stressed this conclusion did not turn upon whether the phone booth was a protected area physically penetrated by the officers' actions. Instead it explained:

> What a person knowingly exposes to the public, even in his own home or office, is not a subject of Fourth Amendment protection. * * * But what he seeks to preserve as private, even in an area accessible to the public, may be constitutionally protected.

389 U.S. at 351, 88 S.Ct. at 511. Later cases, however, often cite and use language from a concurring opinion by Justice Harlan:

> My understanding of the rule [determining the protection provided by the Fourth Amendment] is that there is a twofold requirement, first that a person have exhibited an actual (subjective) expectation of privacy and, second, that the expectation be one that society is prepared to recognize as "reasonable."

389 U.S. at 361, 88 S.Ct. at 516 (Harlan, J., concurring). Thus a search was conducted in *Katz* because when Katz used the telephone booth, he subjectively believed his conversation would be private between him and the other party, that belief was one that society recognized as objectively reasonable, and the officers' actions in intercepting the conversation violated that reasonable expectation.

"Plain View" Observations

The definition of law enforcement activity constituting a search is closely related to one use of the term, "plain view." As the Supreme Court noted in Horton v. California, 496 U.S. 128, 133 n. 4, 110 S.Ct. 2301, 2306 n. 4 (1990) (reprinted later in this chapter), the term sometimes describes a situation in which an officer has merely observed an item "left in plain view." In these situations, characterization of the facts as presenting plain view—what might be best termed a "plain view observation"— means the observation was not a search. This is because the location of the item in plain view means the owner had no reasonable expectation of privacy in information obtainable by looking at the item. As *Horton* makes clear, this use of the term plain view must be distinguished from its use in describing or justifying a *seizure* of an item. This use generally reflects a conclusion that an officer's action, although constituting a seizure, was nevertheless reasonable under the Fourth Amendment requirements applicable to seizures of items.

In the principal case reprinted in the following subsection of this chapter, for example, the question is whether the officers engaged in unreasonable searches by going on the land. Suppose Fourth Amendment law established the officers engaged in no searches by entering upon the land of the defendants. In that case, the officers' observations of the marijuana were plain view observations; neither getting to the place where the observations were made nor making the observation involved an intrusion upon a reasonable expectation of privacy harbored by the defendants. Had the officers also seized the marijuana, the case would present a much different question—the reasonableness of what was clearly a seizure. This seizure would probably have been defended by the prosecution as a reasonable—although warrantless—plain view seizure.

Law Enforcement Conduct Revealing Only Criminal Information

Law enforcement conduct may escape characterization as a search if it can reveal only information which, because of its criminal nature, permits no reasonable expectation of privacy.

In United States v. Jacobsen, 466 U.S. 109, 104 S.Ct. 1652 (1984), federal officers took small amounts of a suspicious substance found in plastic bags and subjected them to field tests to determine whether the substance was cocaine. This action was held not to involve a search, on the assumption that the tests could reveal nothing other than whether or not the substance was cocaine. Congress criminalized even private possession of cocaine; "thus governmental conduct that can reveal whether a substance is cocaine and no other arguably 'private' fact, compromises no legitimate privacy interest."

Dog Sniffing as a Search

In United States v. Place, 462 U.S. 696, 103 S.Ct. 2637 (1983), the Court held that exposure of luggage, located in a public place, to "sniffing" by a drug detecting dog did not amount to a "search." The Court explained:

> A "canine sniff" by a well-trained dog * * * does not require opening the luggage. It does not expose noncontraband items that otherwise would remain hidden from public view, as does, for example, an officer's rummaging through the contents of the luggage. Thus, the manner in which information is obtained through this investigative technique is much less intrusive than a typical search. Moreover, the sniff discloses only the presence or absence of narcotics, a contraband item. Thus, despite the fact that the sniff tells the authorities something about the contents of the luggage, the information obtained is limited. This limited disclosure also ensures that the owner of the property is not subjected to the embarrassment and inconvenience entailed in less discriminate and more intrusive investigative methods.

462 U.S. at 707, 103 S.Ct. at 2644.

Whether *Place* rested in part on an assumption that drug-sniffing dogs are infallible or at least highly reliable was at issue in Illinois v. Caballes, 543 U.S. 405, 407, 125 S.Ct. 834, 837 (2005), discussed further in Chapter 4. Justice Souter in his *Caballes* dissent argued this was the case and—convinced new evidence shows such dogs are wrong quite often—therefore *Place* should be overruled. The *Caballes* majority, however, rejected this and implicitly reaffirmed *Place*. It noted that the record in *Caballes* contained no evidence or finding concerning the error rate of these dogs and that the trial judge in the case found the sniff and alert of the specific dog involved sufficiently reliable to support the search. It also added that even if an alert is erroneous, the sniff and alert does not reveal any "legitimate private information." 543 U.S. at 409, 125 S.Ct. at 838.

How a court should determine whether a specific alert by a particular drug dog is sufficient to constitute the probable cause needed to support a search is developed in an Editors' Note in Subchapter D(2) of Chapter 4.

Bringing a drug-sniffing dog along on an approach to a residence door is considered in Subsection C(1)(c) that follows.

Examination of Trash as a Search

Whether law enforcement examination of a suspect's trash constitutes a search was considered in California v. Greenwood, 486 U.S. 35, 108 S.Ct. 1625 (1988). Suspicious Greenwood might be involved in drug trafficking, a police officer asked the trash collector to pick up the plastic garbage bags from Greenwood's curb and turn them over to the officer rather than mixing them with other trash. Before going past Greenwood's curb, the garbage collector removed all previously-collected trash from his truck. He then collected the bags from Greenwood's curb and gave them to the officer, who found items indicating that Greenwood used narcotics. Police used this information was used to procure a search warrant for Greenwood's residence. Drugs were found during execution of that warrant. Greenwood and Dyanne Van Houten were arrested at the premises. After their release on bail, officers again inspected their trash and a search pursuant to another warrant disclosed additional drugs. The state courts held the officers' examinations of the trash constituted unreasonable searches under the Fourth Amendment. Reversing, a majority of the Supreme Court found no Fourth Amendment search in the officers' conduct:

> [Respondents] assert * * * that they had, and exhibited, an expectation of privacy with respect to the trash that was searched by the police: The trash, which was placed on the street for collection at a fixed time, was contained in opaque plastic bags, which the garbage collector was expected to pick up, mingle with the trash of others, and deposit at the garbage dump. The trash was only temporarily on the street, and there was little likelihood that it would be inspected by anyone.

> It may well be that respondents did not expect that the contents of their garbage bags would become known to the police or any other members of the public. An expectation of privacy does not give rise to Fourth Amendment protection, however, unless society is prepared to accept that expectation as objectively reasonable.

Here, we conclude that respondents exposed their garbage to the public sufficiently to defeat their claim to Fourth Amendment protection. It is common knowledge that plastic garbage bags left on or at the side of a public street are readily accessible to animals, children, scavengers, snoops, and other members of the public. Moreover, respondents placed their refuse at the curb for the express purpose of conveying it to a third party, the trash collector, who might himself have sorted through respondents' trash or permitted others, such as the police, to do so. Accordingly, having deposited their garbage "in an area particularly suited for public inspection, and, in a manner of speaking, public consumption, for the express purpose of having strangers take it," *United States v. Reicherter*, 647 F.2d 397, 399 (3d Cir.1981), respondents could have had no reasonable expectation of privacy in the inculpatory items that they discarded.

486 U.S. at 39–41, 108 S.Ct. at 1628–29.

Manipulation of Luggage as a Search

A law enforcement officer's manipulation of a bus passenger's luggage was held a search in Bond v. United States, 529 U.S. 334, 120 S.Ct. 1462 (2000). The Court set out the facts:

* * * Steven Dewayne Bond was a passenger on a Greyhound bus that left California bound for Little Rock, Arkansas. The bus stopped, as it was required to do, at the permanent Border Patrol checkpoint in Sierra Blanca, Texas. Border Patrol Agent Cesar Cantu boarded the bus to check the immigration status of its passengers. After reaching the back of the bus, having satisfied himself that the passengers were lawfully in the United States, Agent Cantu began walking toward the front. Along the way, he squeezed the soft luggage which passengers had placed in the overhead storage space above the seats.

[Bond] was seated four or five rows from the back of the bus. As Agent Cantu inspected the luggage in the compartment above [Bond's] seat, he squeezed a green canvas bag and noticed that it contained a "brick-like" object. [Bond] admitted that the bag was his and agreed to allow Agent Cantu to open it. Upon opening the bag, Agent Cantu discovered a "brick" of methamphetamine. The brick had been wrapped in duct tape until it was oval-shaped and then rolled in a pair of pants.

The Government conceded that Bond had a privacy interest in the bag. It argued, however, that by placing the bag in the overhead compartment he lost any reasonable expectation that the bag would not be physically manipulated. Bond, in response, argued that Cantu's manipulation exceeded the "casual contact" a reasonable person expects as a result of placing a bag in such a location.

Siding with Bond, the Supreme Court first stressed that the visual observation decisions, considered in the first subsection that follows, were not controlling because the case before it involved tactile observation. "Physically invasive inspection," it explained, "is simply more intrusive than purely visual inspection." Further, passengers have a particularly important privacy interest in carry-on luggage used to transport personal items desired to be close at hand, although not as important an interest as individuals have in being free of tactile exploration of their bodies and clothing.

The Court then turned to whether, under *Katz*, the Fourth Amendment protected Bond's expectation that his carry-on bag would not be manipulated as Cantu manipulated it:

> When a bus passenger places a bag in an overhead bin, he expects that other passengers or bus employees may move it for one reason or another. Thus, a bus passenger clearly expects that his bag may be handled. He does not expect that other passengers or bus employees will, as a matter of course, feel the bag in an exploratory manner. But this is exactly what the agent did here. We therefore hold that the agent's physical manipulation of petitioner's bag violated the Fourth Amendment.

529 U.S. at 338–39, 120 S.Ct. at 1464.

Searches Permissible on Less than Probable Cause

Generally, law enforcement activity constituting a search is reasonable under the Fourth Amendment only if: (a) it is conducted pursuant to a search warrant; and (b) it is supported by probable cause to believe it will result in obtaining information that a crime has been committed or the identity of a person who has committed a crime. A number of exceptions to the requirement of a warrant have also been developed; these exceptions are addressed in Chapter 5. As Chapter 5 also demonstrates, the Supreme Court has sometimes been willing to hold law enforcement activity constituting a seizure reasonable on less than such probable cause. The Court has been reluctant, however, to characterize searches—at least of items rather than persons—as permissible on such a relaxed standard.

This reluctance was reflected in Arizona v. Hicks, 480 U.S. 321, 107 S.Ct. 1149 (1987). An officer, properly present in an apartment to look for someone who had shot through the floor into the apartment below, moved some suspicious stereo equipment slightly to permit him to see serial numbers on the items. This movement of the equipment was a search, because it enabled the officer to obtain information—the serial numbers—otherwise unavailable to him. Justice O'Connor, joined in dissent by the Chief Justice and Justice Powell, characterized the action as not a "full-blown search" but rather a "cursory inspection of an item in view." Since the action intruded upon privacy interests less than a full-blown search, it should be reasonable on less than is required for such a full-blown search. Specifically, Justice O'Connor argued that it should require not probable cause but only "reasonable suspicion." Reasonable suspicion is used in several contexts as the standard for determining the Fourth Amendment reasonableness of relatively-nonintrusive law enforcement activity; its content—as applied to certain nonarrest detentions of suspects—is addressed in Part C(1) of Chapter 4. Reasonable suspicion requires some objective basis for a belief that "seizable" items or information will be found by a search, but it clearly does not demand as firm a basis for this belief as is required for probable cause. Justice O'Connor explained specifically:

> [T]he balance of the governmental and privacy interests strongly supports a reasonable suspicion standard for the cursory examination of items in plain view. The additional intrusion caused by an inspection of an item in plain view for its serial number is minuscule. * * *
>
> Weighed against this * * * are rather major gains in law enforcement. The use of identification numbers in tracing stolen property is a powerful law enforcement tool. Serial numbers are far more helpful and accurate in detecting stolen property than simple police recollection of the evidence. Given the prevalence of mass produced goods in our national economy, a serial number is often the only sure method of detecting stolen property.

480 U.S. at 338–39, 107 S.Ct. at 1159–60 (O'Connor, J., dissenting). Justice Scalia's opinion for the Court, however, rejected this approach:

> [A] truly cursory inspection—one that involves merely looking at what is already exposed to view, without disturbing it—is not a "search" for Fourth Amendment purposes, and therefore does not even require reasonable suspicion. We are unwilling to send police and judges into a new thicket of Fourth Amendment law, to seek a creature of uncertain description that is neither a plain-view inspection nor yet a "full-blown search."

480 U.S. at 328–29, 107 S.Ct. at 1154.

* * *

The three following units consider several particularly important aspects of the question of when a search is involved: physical entry of private property and law enforcement activity facilitated by electronic or canine assistance. In each of the principal cases, the police failed to obtain a warrant; if their activities were searches, those search would be unreasonable and the evidence unavailable to the prosecution. But on a more general level, characterizing such activity as a search does not mean the Fourth Amendment prohibits police from engaging in the conduct. Rather, the conduct becomes subject to the requirements of Fourth Amendment reasonableness. The Fourth Amendment should be construed as applicable to law enforcement conduct sufficiently intruding upon privacy concerns to justify its *regulation*—not its *prohibition*—by application of the Fourth Amendment's requirement of reasonableness. Does the Court properly follow this approach in the principal cases?

a. ENTRY ONTO "OPEN FIELDS"

When officers physically go on real property, do they engage in a search? To what extent does the answer to this question depend upon the efforts the person in possession or control of the property has taken to preserve from others what is or occurs on the property?

Oliver v. United States

Supreme Court of the United States, 1984.
466 U.S. 170, 104 S.Ct. 1735.

■ JUSTICE POWELL delivered the opinion of the Court.

The "open fields" doctrine, first enunciated by this Court in *Hester v. United States*, 265 U.S. 57, 44 S.Ct. 445, 68 L.Ed. 898 (1924), permits police officers to enter and search a field without a warrant. We granted certiorari * * * to clarify confusion that has arisen as to the continued vitality of the doctrine.

I

* * * Acting on reports that marijuana was being raised on the farm of petitioner Oliver, two narcotics agents of the Kentucky State Police went to the farm to investigate.[1] Arriving at the farm, they drove past petitioner's house to a locked gate with a "No Trespassing" sign. A footpath led around one side of the gate. The agents walked around the gate and along the road for several hundred yards, passing a barn and a parked camper. At that point, someone standing in front of the camper shouted, "No hunting is allowed, come back here." The officers shouted back that they were Kentucky State Police officers, but found no one when they returned to the camper. The officers resumed their investigation of the farm and found a field of marijuana over a mile from petitioner's home.

Petitioner was arrested and indicted for "manufactur[ing]" a "controlled substance." After a pretrial hearing, the District Court suppressed evidence of the discovery of the marijuana fields. Applying *Katz v. United States*, 389 U.S. 347, 357, 88 S.Ct. 507, 514, 19 L.Ed.2d 576 (1967), the court found that petitioner had a reasonable expectation that the fields would remain private because petitioner "had done all that

---

[1]   It is conceded that the police did not have a warrant authorizing the search, that there was no probable cause for the search and that no exception to the warrant requirement is applicable.

could be expected of him to assert his privacy in the area of farm that was searched." He had posted no trespassing signs at regular intervals and had locked the gate at the entrance to the center of the farm. Further, the court noted that the fields themselves are highly secluded: they are bounded on all sides by woods, fences and embankments and cannot be seen from any point of public access. The court concluded that this was not an "open" field that invited casual intrusion.

The Court of Appeals for the Sixth Circuit, sitting *en banc,* reversed the district court. The court concluded that *Katz,* upon which the District Court relied, had not impaired the vitality of the open fields doctrine of *Hester.* * * * We granted certiorari.

* * *

II

The rule announced in *Hester v. United States* was founded upon the explicit language of the Fourth Amendment. That Amendment indicates with some precision the places and things encompassed by its protections. As Justice Holmes explained for the Court in his characteristically laconic style: "[T]he special protection accorded by the Fourth Amendment to the people in their 'persons, houses, papers, and effects,' is not extended to the open fields. The distinction between the latter and the house is as old as the common law."

Nor are the open fields "effects" within the meaning of the Fourth Amendment. In this respect, it is suggestive that James Madison's proposed draft of what became the Fourth Amendment preserves "[t]he rights of the people to be secured in their persons, their houses, their papers, and their other property, from all unreasonable searches and seizures. . . ." Although Congress' revisions of Madison's proposal broadened the scope of the Amendment in some respects, the term "effects" is less inclusive than "property" and cannot be said to encompass open fields.[7] We conclude, as did the Court in deciding *Hester v. United States*, that the government's intrusion upon the open fields is not one of those "unreasonable searches" proscribed by the text of the Fourth Amendment.

III

This interpretation of the Fourth Amendment's language is consistent with the understanding of the right to privacy expressed in our Fourth Amendment jurisprudence. Since *Katz v. United States*, 389 U.S. 347, 88 S.Ct. 507, 19 L.Ed.2d 576 (1967), the touchstone of Amendment analysis has been the question whether a person has a "constitutionally protected reasonable expectation of privacy." 389 U.S., at 360, 88 S.Ct., at 516 (Harlan, J., concurring). The Amendment does

---

[7]   The Framers would have understood the term "effects" to be limited to personal, rather than real, property. See generally, *Doe v. Dring*, 2 M. & S. 448, 454 (1814) (discussing prior cases); 2 Blackstone, Commentaries 16, 384–385.

not protect the merely subjective expectation of privacy, but only "those expectations that society is prepared to recognize as 'reasonable.' "

A

No single factor determines whether an individual legitimately may claim under the Fourth Amendment that a place should be free of government intrusion not authorized by warrant. In assessing the degree to which a search infringes upon individual privacy, the Court has given weight to such factors as the intention of the Framers of the Fourth Amendment, the uses to which the individual has put a location, and our societal understanding that certain areas deserve the most scrupulous protection from government invasion. These factors are equally relevant to determining whether the government's intrusion upon open fields without a warrant or probable cause violates reasonable expectations of privacy and is therefore a search proscribed by the Amendment.

In this light, the rule of *Hester v. United States*, supra, that we reaffirm today, may be understood as providing that an individual may not legitimately demand privacy for activities conducted out of doors in fields, except in the area immediately surrounding the home. This rule is true to the conception of the right to privacy embodied in the Fourth Amendment. The Amendment reflects the recognition of the Founders that certain enclaves should be free from arbitrary government interference. For example, the Court since the enactment of the Fourth Amendment has stressed "the overriding respect for the sanctity of the home that has been embedded in our traditions since the origins of the Republic."

In contrast, open fields do not provide the setting for those intimate activities that the Amendment is intended to shelter from government interference or surveillance. There is no societal interest in protecting the privacy of those activities, such as the cultivation of crops, that occur in open fields. Moreover, as a practical matter these lands usually are accessible to the public and the police in ways that a home, an office or commercial structure would not be. It is not generally true that fences or no trespassing signs effectively bar the public from viewing open fields in rural areas. And * * * petitioner Oliver * * * concede[s] that the public and police lawfully may survey lands from the air.[9] For these reasons, the asserted expectation of privacy in open fields is not an expectation that "society recognizes as reasonable."[10]

---

[9] In practical terms, petitioner Oliver's * * * analysis merely would require law enforcement officers, in most situations, to use aerial surveillance to gather the information necessary to obtain a warrant or to justify warrantless entry onto the property. It is not easy to see how such a requirement would advance legitimate privacy interests.

[10] The dissent conceives of open fields as bustling with private activity as diverse as lovers' trysts and worship services. But in most instances police will disturb no one when they enter upon open fields. These fields, by their very character as open and unoccupied, are unlikely to provide the setting for activities whose privacy is sought to be protected by the Fourth Amendment. One need think only of the vast expanse of some western ranches or of the undeveloped woods of the Northwest to see the unreality of the dissent's conception. Further, the Fourth Amendment provides ample protection to activities in the open fields that might

The historical underpinnings of the "open fields" doctrine also demonstrate that the doctrine is consistent with respect for "reasonable expectations of privacy." As Justice Holmes, writing for the Court, observed in *Hester,* the common law distinguished "open fields" from the "curtilage," the land immediately surrounding and associated with the home. The distinction implies that only the curtilage, not the neighboring open fields, warrants the Fourth Amendment protections that attach to the home. At common law, the curtilage is the area to which extends the intimate activity associated with the "sanctity of a man's home and the privacies of life," and therefore has been considered part of home itself for Fourth Amendment purposes. Thus, courts have extended Fourth Amendment protection to the curtilage; and they have defined the curtilage, as did the common law, by reference to the factors that determine whether an individual reasonably may expect that an area immediately adjacent to the home will remain private. Conversely, the common law implies, as we reaffirm today, that no expectation of privacy legitimately attaches to open fields.[11]

We conclude, from the text of the Fourth Amendment and from the historical and contemporary understanding of its purposes, that an individual has no legitimate expectation that open fields will remain free from warrantless intrusion by government officers.

B

Petitioner Oliver * * * contend[s], to the contrary, that the circumstances of a search sometimes may indicate that reasonable expectations of privacy were violated; and that courts therefore should analyze these circumstances on a case-by-case basis. The language of the Fourth Amendment itself answers their contention.

Nor would a case-by-case approach provide a workable accommodation between the needs of law enforcement and the interests protected by the Fourth Amendment. Under this approach, police officers would have to guess before every search whether landowners had erected fences sufficiently high, posted a sufficient number of warning signs, or located contraband in an area sufficiently secluded to establish a right of privacy. The lawfulness of a search would turn on "[a] highly sophisticated set of rules, qualified by all sorts of ifs, ands, and buts and requiring the drawing of subtle nuances and hairline distinctions. . . ."

---

implicate an individual's privacy. An individual who enters a place defined to be "public" for Fourth Amendment analysis does not lose all claims to privacy or personal security. For example, the Fourth Amendment's protections against unreasonable arrest or unreasonable seizure of effects upon the person remain fully applicable.

[11] [P]etitioner Oliver * * * has [not] contended that the property searched was within the curtilage. Nor is it necessary in this case to consider the scope of the curtilage exception to the open fields doctrine or the degree of Fourth Amendment protection afforded the curtilage, as opposed to the home itself. It is clear, however, that the term "open fields" may include any unoccupied or undeveloped area outside of the curtilage. An open field need be neither "open" nor a "field" as those terms are used in common speech. For example, * * * , a thickly wooded area nonetheless may be an open field as that term is used in construing the Fourth Amendment.

New York v. Belton, 453 U.S. 454, 458, 101 S.Ct. 2860, 2863, 69 L.Ed.2d 768 (1981) (quoting LaFave, "Case-By-Case Adjudication" versus "Standardized Procedures": The Robinson Dilemma, 1974 S.Ct.Rev. 127, 142). This Court repeatedly has acknowledged the difficulties created for courts, police and citizens by an *ad hoc,* case-by-case definition of Fourth Amendment standards to be applied in differing factual circumstances. The *ad hoc* approach not only makes it difficult for the policeman to discern the scope of his authority; it also creates a danger that constitutional rights will be arbitrarily and inequitably enforced.[12]

IV

In any event, while the factors that petitioner Oliver * * * urge[s] the courts to consider may be relevant to Fourth Amendment analysis in some contexts, these factors cannot be decisive on the question whether the search of an open field is subject to the Amendment. Initially, we reject the suggestion that steps taken to protect privacy establish that expectations of privacy in an open field are legitimate. It is true, of course, that petitioner Oliver * * * , in order to conceal [his] criminal activities, planted the marijuana upon secluded land and erected fences and no trespassing signs around the property. And it may be that because of such precautions, few members of the public stumbled upon the marijuana crops seized by the police. Neither of these suppositions demonstrates, however, that the expectation of privacy was *legitimate* in the sense required by the Fourth Amendment. The test of legitimacy is not whether the individual chooses to conceal assertedly "private" activity. Rather, the correct inquiry is whether the government's intrusion infringes upon the personal and societal values protected by the Fourth Amendment. As we have explained, we find no basis for concluding that a police inspection of open fields accomplishes such an infringement.

Nor is the government's intrusion upon an open field a "search" in the constitutional sense because that intrusion is a trespass at common law. The existence of a property right is but one element in determining whether expectations of privacy are legitimate. * * *

The common law may guide consideration of what areas are protected by the Fourth Amendment by defining areas whose invasion by others is wrongful. The law of trespass, however, forbids intrusions upon land that the Fourth Amendment would not proscribe. For trespass law extends to instances where the exercise of the right to exclude vindicates

---

[12] The clarity of the open fields doctrine that we reaffirm today is not sacrificed, as the dissent suggests, by our recognition that the curtilage remains within the protections of the Fourth Amendment. Most of the many millions of acres that are "open fields" are not close to any structure and so not arguably within the curtilage. And, for most homes, the boundaries of the curtilage will be clearly marked; and the conception defining the curtilage—as the area around the home to which the activity of home life extends—is a familiar one easily understood from our daily experience. The occasional difficulties that courts might have in applying this, like other, legal concepts, do not argue for the unprecedented expansion of the Fourth Amendment advocated by the dissent.

no legitimate privacy interest.[15] Thus, in the case of open fields, the general rights of property protected by the common law of trespass have little or no relevance to the applicability of the Fourth Amendment.

V

We conclude that the open fields doctrine, as enunciated in *Hester,* is consistent with the plain language of the Fourth Amendment and its historical purposes. Moreover, Justice Holmes' interpretation of the Amendment in *Hester* accords with the "reasonable expectation of privacy" analysis developed in subsequent decisions of this Court. We therefore affirm * * * .

It is so ordered.

■ JUSTICE WHITE, concurring in part and in the judgment.

I concur in the judgment and join Parts I and II of the Court's opinion. These parts dispose of the issue before us; there is no need to go further and deal with the expectation of privacy matter. However reasonable a landowner's expectations of privacy may be, those expectations cannot convert a field into a "house" or an "effect."

■ JUSTICE MARSHALL, with whom JUSTICE BRENNAN and JUSTICE STEVENS join, dissenting.

* * *

[One] ground for the Court's decision is its contention that any interest a landowner might have in the privacy of his woods and fields is not one that "society is prepared to recognize as 'reasonable.' " The mode of analysis that underlies this assertion is certainly more consistent with our prior decisions than that discussed above. But the Court's conclusion cannot withstand scrutiny.

As the Court acknowledges, we have traditionally looked to a variety of factors in determining whether an expectation of privacy asserted in a physical space is "reasonable." Though those factors do not lend themselves to precise taxonomy, they may be roughly grouped into three categories. First, we consider whether the expectation at issue is rooted in entitlements defined by positive law. Second, we consider the nature of the uses to which spaces of the sort in question can be put. Third, we consider whether the person claiming a privacy interest manifested that interest to the public in a way that most people would understand and

---

[15] The law of trespass recognizes the interest in possession and control of one's property and for that reason permits exclusion of unwanted intruders. But it does not follow that the right to exclude conferred by trespass law embodies a privacy interest also protected by the Fourth Amendment. To the contrary, the common law of trespass furthers a range of interests that have nothing to do with privacy and that would not be served by applying the strictures of trespass law to public officers. Criminal laws against trespass are prophylactic: they protect against intruders who poach, steal livestock and crops or vandalize property. And the civil action of trespass serves the important function of authorizing an owner to defeat claims of prescription by asserting his own title. In any event, unlicensed use of property by others is presumptively unjustified, as anyone who wishes to use the property is free to bargain for the right to do so with the property owner. For these reasons, the law of trespass confers protections from intrusion by others far broader than those required by Fourth Amendment interests.

respect. When the expectations of privacy asserted by petitioner Oliver * * * [is] examined through these lenses, it becomes clear that those expectations are entitled to constitutional protection.

A

We have frequently acknowledged that privacy interests are not coterminous with property rights. However, because "property rights reflect society's explicit recognition of a person's authority to act as he wishes in certain areas, [they] should be considered in determining whether an individual's expectations of privacy are reasonable." * * *

It is undisputed that Oliver * * * owned the land into which the police intruded. That fact alone provides considerable support for their assertion of legitimate privacy interests in their woods and fields. But even more telling is the nature of the sanctions that Oliver * * * could invoke, under local law, for violation of [his] property rights. * * * [A] knowing entry upon fenced or otherwise enclosed land, or upon unenclosed land conspicuously posted with signs excluding the public, constitutes criminal trespass. * * * Thus, positive law not only recognizes the legitimacy of Oliver's * * * insistence that strangers keep off their land, but subjects those who refuse to respect their wishes to the most severe of penalties—criminal liability. Under these circumstances, it is hard to credit the Court's assertion that Oliver's * * * expectations of privacy were not of a sort that society is prepared to recognize as reasonable.

B

The uses to which a place is put are highly relevant to the assessment of a privacy interest asserted therein. If, in light of our shared sensibilities, those activities are of a kind in which people should be able to engage without fear of intrusion by private persons or government officials, we extend the protection of the Fourth Amendment to the space in question, even in the absence of any entitlement derived from positive law.

Privately-owned woods and fields that are not exposed to public view regularly are employed in a variety of ways that society acknowledges deserve privacy. Many landowners like to take solitary walks on their property, confident that they will not be confronted in their rambles by strangers or policemen. Others conduct agricultural businesses on their property. Some landowners use their secluded spaces to meet lovers, others to gather together with fellow worshippers, still others to engage in sustained creative endeavor. Private land is sometimes used as a refuge for wildlife, where flora and fauna are protected from human intervention of any kind. Our respect for the freedom of landowners to use their posted "open fields" in ways such as these partially explains the seriousness with which the positive law regards deliberate invasions of such spaces, and substantially reinforces the landowners' contention that their expectations of privacy are "reasonable."

C

Whether a person "took normal precautions to maintain his privacy" in a given space affects whether his interest is one protected by the Fourth Amendment. The reason why such precautions are relevant is that we do not insist that a person who has a right to exclude others exercise that right. A claim to privacy is therefore strengthened by the fact that the claimant somehow manifested to other people his desire that they keep their distance.

Certain spaces are so presumptively private that signals of this sort are unnecessary; a homeowner need not post a "do not enter" sign on his door in order to deny entrance to uninvited guests. Privacy interests in other spaces are more ambiguous, and the taking of precautions is consequently more important; placing a lock on one's footlocker strengthens one's claim that an examination of its contents is impermissible. Still other spaces are, by positive law and social convention, presumed accessible to members of the public *unless* the owner manifests his intention to exclude them.

Undeveloped land falls into the last-mentioned category. If a person has not marked the boundaries of his fields or woods in a way that informs passersby that they are not welcome, he cannot object if members of the public enter onto the property. There is no reason why he should have any greater rights as against government officials. Accordingly, we have held that an official may, without a warrant, enter private land from which the public is not excluded and make observations from that vantage point. Fairly read, the case on which the majority so heavily relies, *Hester v. United States*, 265 U.S. 57, 44 S.Ct. 445, 68 L.Ed. 898 (1924), affirms little more than the foregoing unremarkable proposition. From aught that appears in the opinion in that case, the defendants, fleeing from revenue agents who had observed them committing a crime, abandoned incriminating evidence on private land from which the public had not been excluded. Under such circumstances, it is not surprising that the Court was unpersuaded by the defendants' argument that the entry onto their fields by the agents violated the Fourth Amendment.

A very different case is presented when the owner of undeveloped land has taken precautions to exclude the public. As indicated above, a deliberate entry by a private citizen onto private property marked with "no trespassing" signs will expose him to criminal liability. I see no reason why a government official should not be obliged to respect such unequivocal and universally understood manifestations of a landowner's desire for privacy.

In sum, examination of the three principal criteria we have traditionally used for assessing the reasonableness of a person's expectation that a given space would remain private indicates that interests of the sort asserted by Oliver * * * are entitled to constitutional protection. An owner's right to insist that others stay off his posted land is firmly grounded in positive law. Many of the uses to which such land may be put deserve privacy. And, by marking the boundaries of the land with warnings that the public should not intrude, the owner has dispelled any ambiguity as to his desires.

The police in these cases proffered no justification for their invasions of Oliver's * * * privacy interests; * * * the entry [was not] legitimated by a warrant or by one of the established exceptions to the warrant requirement. I conclude, therefore, that the searches of [the] land violated the Fourth Amendment, and the evidence obtained in the course of [the search] should have been suppressed.

III

A clear, easily administrable rule emerges from the analysis set forth above: Private land marked in a fashion sufficient to render entry thereon a criminal trespass under the law of the state in which the land lies is protected by the Fourth Amendment's proscription of unreasonable searches and seizures. One of the advantages of the foregoing rule is that it draws upon a doctrine already familiar to both citizens and government officials. In each jurisdiction, a substantial body of statutory and case law defines the precautions a landowner must take in order to avail himself of the sanctions of the criminal law. The police know that body of law, because they are entrusted with responsibility for enforcing it against the public; it therefore would not be difficult for the police to abide by it themselves.

By contrast, the doctrine announced by the Court today is incapable of determinate application. Police officers, making warrantless entries upon private land, will be obliged in the future to make on-the-spot judgments as to how far the curtilage extends, and to stay outside that zone. In addition, we may expect to see a spate of litigation over the question of how much improvement is necessary to remove private land from the category of "unoccupied or undeveloped area" to which the "open fields exception" is now deemed applicable.

The Court's holding not only ill serves the need to make constitutional doctrine "workable for application by rank and file, trained police officers," it withdraws the shield of the Fourth Amendment from privacy interests that clearly deserve protection. * * *

I dissent.

EDITORS' NOTE: THE PROTECTED CURTILAGE

The role played by the concept of the "curtilage" in defining the scope of Fourth Amendment coverage was confirmed and the definition of curtilage fleshed out in United States v. Dunn, 480 U.S. 294, 107 S.Ct. 1134 (1987).

Federal officers, suspecting Dunn of manufacturing controlled substances, went to his Texas ranch on the evening of November 5, 1980. The ranch's 198 acres were completely encircled by a "perimeter fence" and contained a number of internal fenced areas. About a half-mile from a public road, one internal fenced enclosure included the ranch house and a greenhouse. Approximately fifty yards from this fence were two barns. The larger of the two was enclosed by a wooden fence; locked waist-high gates prevented entry into the barn and a netting material was stretched from the ceiling of the barn to the top of the fence gates. The officers crossed over the perimeter fence, climbed a barbed wire fence and the fence surrounding the large barn front and approached the barn. They walked under the overhang and up to the locked gates. By shining a flashlight through the netting, they observed a drug laboratory. At no point did the officers physically enter the barn. Using the information obtained by looking into the barn, they obtained a search warrant and by executing the warrant they seized evidence of Dunn's manufacture of controlled substances. This evidence was held inadmissible by the intermediate federal court on the ground it was the product of a warrantless—and therefore unreasonable—search.

The Supreme Court reversed, concluding that under *Oliver* the officers did not engage in a search. Whether the officers' approach to the barn constituted a search, Justice White explained for the Court, depended upon whether the barn was within the protected curtilage. Turning to the meaning of that term, he continued:

> [W]e believe that curtilage questions should be resolved with particular reference to four factors: the proximity of the area claimed to be curtilage to the home, whether the area is included within an enclosure surrounding the home, the nature of the uses to which the area is put, and the steps taken by the resident to protect the area from observation by people passing by. We do not suggest that combining these factors produces a finely tuned formula that, when mechanically applied, yields a "correct" answer to all extent-of-curtilage questions. Rather, these factors are useful analytical tools only to the degree that, in any given case, they bear upon the centrally relevant consideration—whether the area in question is so intimately tied to the home itself that it should be placed under the home's "umbrella" of Fourth Amendment protection.

480 U.S. at 301, 107 S.Ct. at 1139–40.

Applying this approach to the facts of *Dunn* led the Court "with little difficulty" to conclude the barn and the area immediately surrounding it lay outside the protected curtilage. First, the 50 yards separating the barn from the house—a "substantial distance"—rendered it "in isolation." Second, the fence surrounding the ranch house demarked "a specific area of land immediately adjacent to the house that is readily identifiable as part and parcel of the house," and the barn was not within it. Third, the officers had substantial information from surveillance and smells emanating from the barn indicating it was used for the manufacture of drugs. This information indicated "the use to which the barn was being put could not fairly be characterized as so associated with the activities and privacies of domestic life that the officers should have deemed the barn as part of [the] home." Finally, Dunn had done little to protect the barn area from observation by those "standing in the open fields." The fences were designed to corral livestock and did not bar observations.

The majority also rejected Dunn's argument that, regardless of whether the barn was within the curtilage of the ranch house, the officers' actions intruded upon a protected privacy interest related to the barn and his use of it. Assuming the barn protected from entry by the Fourth Amendment, the Court stressed it was situated on an "open field." The officers' progression up to the barn involved only entry onto "open fields" and did not constitute a "search," regardless of whether the objects they observed from this vantage point lay within an area that might be protected by the Fourth Amendment.

b.   ASSISTED OBSERVATIONS

EDITORS' INTRODUCTION

Officers who merely observe or listen from a public vantage point and thereby obtain information do not ordinarily search. A person has no reasonable expectation of privacy in what the person knowingly exposes to the public.

Situations are more problematic when officers enhance their capabilities. This can involve placing themselves in a particularly advantageous vantage point—as when they use an aircraft to observe activity in a residential yard. Or it can involve enhancing their ability to obtain information from a particular vantage point—as when they use powerful lenses to observe or photograph matters.

Katz v. United States, 389 U.S. 347, 88 S.Ct. 507 (1967), itself established that mechanical interception of spoken words is sometimes a "search," and thus gave rise to the law dealing with wiretapping and electronic surveillance. Generally, electronic surveillance has become a specialized area affected not only by constitutional case law but also by elaborate statutory provisions. Further treatment of this area is beyond the scope of these materials. Several other kinds of what might be called assisted observations, however, can be addressed here.

If, because of darkness, an officer cannot see what is in a parked car but shines a flashlight into the car and observes incriminating items, does the flashlight make the officer's action a search? A plurality of the Court, with no disagreement from the other justices, indicated that "the use of artificial means to illuminate a darkened area," like the use of "a marine glass or a field glass," does not constitute a search. Texas v. Brown, 460 U.S. 730, 740, 103 S.Ct. 1535, 1542 (1983) (opinion of Rehnquist, J., announcing the judgment of the Court).

Use of more sophisticated means of watching and listening, however, has given the Court more difficulty.

In California v. Ciraolo, 476 U.S. 207, 106 S.Ct. 1809 (1986), officers observed the back yard of a house while flying in a fixed-wing aircraft at 1,000 feet. Although the yard was within the curtilage of the house and a fence shielded the yard from observation from the street, this was held not a search subject to the Fourth Amendment. The police, like the public, were free to inspect the backyard from the vantage point of an aircraft flying in the navigable airspace as this plane was: "In an age where private and commercial flight in the public airways is routine, it is unreasonable for respondent to expect that his marijuana plants were constitutionally protected from being observed with the naked eye from an altitude of 1,000 feet. The Fourth Amendment simply does not require the police traveling in the public airways at this altitude to obtain a warrant in order to observe what is visible to the naked eye."

In Dow Chemical Company v. United States, 476 U.S. 227, 106 S.Ct. 1819 (1986), investigators for the Environmental Protection Agency (EPA) used an airplane equipped with a precision aerial mapping camera to photograph Dow's Midland, Michigan plant from altitudes of 12,000, 3,000 and 1,200 feet. The plant was a 2,000 acre facility surrounded by a fence. Precautions were not taken to conceal all of the manufacturing equipment in the plant from aerial view. Nevertheless, its desire to protect trade secret information caused Dow to remain concerned about aerial photography. Low-flying planes were identified when possible and efforts made to obtain possession of any photographs taken. A majority of the Court concluded the EPA's actions did not constitute a search for Fourth Amendment purposes:

> Admittedly, Dow's enclosed plant complex * * * does not fall precisely within the "open fields" doctrine. The area at issue here can perhaps be seen as falling somewhere between "open fields" and curtilage, but lacking some of the critical characteristics of both. Dow's inner manufacturing areas are elaborately secured to ensure they are not open or exposed to the public from the ground. Any actual physical entry by EPA into any enclosed area would raise significantly different questions * * * . The narrow issue raised by [Dow] * * * concerns aerial observation of a 2,000 acre outdoor manufacturing facility without physical entry.
>
> * * *
>
> It may well be, as the Government concedes, that surveillance of private property by using highly sophisticated surveillance equipment not generally available to the public, such as satellite technology, might be constitutionally proscribed absent a warrant. But the photographs here are not so revealing of intimate details as to raise constitutional concerns. Although they undoubtedly give EPA more detailed

information than naked-eye views, they remain limited to an outline of the facility's buildings and equipment. The mere fact that human vision is enhanced somewhat, at least to the degree here, does not give rise to constitutional problems.

476 U.S. at 236–38, 106 S.Ct. at 1826.

Three years later in Florida v. Riley, 488 U.S. 445, 109 S.Ct. 693 (1989), a split Court declined to hold inadmissible evidence derived from observations made by officers in a helicopter flying 400 feet above a partially covered greenhouse. A majority of the justices seemed to agree that whether this was a search depended on whether members of the public travel by helicopter at 400 feet of altitude with sufficient regularity that Riley's expectation of privacy from this kind of aerial observation was unreasonable. See 488 U.S. at 454–55, 109 S.Ct. at 699 (O'Connor, J., concurring in the judgment). Four justices concluded that the prosecution had the burden of proof on this and failed to meet it. Justice O'Connor, in contrast, concluded the burden was on Riley and he failed to meet it. She therefore joined the result of the plurality, which reasoned that the case was controlled by *Ciraolo*.

Kyllo v. United States

Supreme Court of the United States, 2001.
533 U.S. 27, 121 S.Ct. 2038.

■ JUSTICE SCALIA delivered the opinion of the Court.

This case presents the question whether the use of a thermal-imaging device aimed at a private home from a public street to detect relative amounts of heat within the home constitutes a "search" within the meaning of the Fourth Amendment.

I

In 1991 Agent William Elliott of the United States Department of the Interior came to suspect that marijuana was being grown in the home belonging to petitioner Danny Kyllo, part of a triplex on Rhododendron Drive in Florence, Oregon. Indoor marijuana growth typically requires high-intensity lamps. In order to determine whether an amount of heat was emanating from petitioner's home consistent with the use of such lamps, at 3:20 a.m. on January 16, 1992, Agent Elliott and Dan Haas used an Agema Thermovision 210 thermal imager to scan the triplex. Thermal imagers detect infrared radiation, which virtually all objects emit but which is not visible to the naked eye. The imager converts radiation into images based on relative warmth—black is cool, white is hot, shades of gray connote relative differences; in that respect, it operates somewhat like a video camera showing heat images. The scan of Kyllo's home took only a few minutes and was performed from the passenger seat of Agent Elliott's vehicle across the street from the front of the house and also from the street in back of the house. The scan showed that the roof over the garage and a side wall of petitioner's home were relatively hot compared to the rest of the home and substantially warmer than neighboring homes in the triplex. Agent Elliott concluded that petitioner was using halide lights to grow marijuana in his house, which indeed he was. Based on tips from informants, utility bills, and the thermal imaging, a Federal Magistrate Judge issued a warrant authorizing a search of petitioner's home, and the agents found an indoor growing operation involving more than 100 plants. Petitioner was indicted on one count of manufacturing marijuana * * * . He unsuccessfully moved to suppress the evidence seized from his home and then entered a conditional guilty plea.

The Court of Appeals for the Ninth Circuit * * * affirmed * * * . We granted certiorari.

II

[T]he * * * question whether or not a Fourth Amendment "search" has occurred is not * * * simple under our precedent. The permissibility of ordinary visual surveillance of a home used to be clear because, well into the 20th century, our Fourth Amendment jurisprudence was tied to common-law trespass. Visual surveillance was unquestionably lawful because " 'the eye cannot by the laws of England be guilty of a trespass.' " We have since decoupled violation of a person's Fourth Amendment rights from trespassory violation of his property, but the lawfulness of warrantless visual surveillance of a home has still been preserved. * * *

The present case involves officers on a public street engaged in more than naked-eye surveillance of a home. We have previously reserved judgment as to how much technological enhancement of ordinary perception from such a vantage point, if any, is too much. * * *

III

It would be foolish to contend that the degree of privacy secured to citizens by the Fourth Amendment has been entirely unaffected by the advance of technology. * * * The question we confront today is what limits there are upon this power of technology to shrink the realm of guaranteed privacy.

The [*Katz v. United States*, 389 U.S. 347, 88 S.Ct. 507, 19 L.Ed.2d 576 (1967)] test—whether the individual has an expectation of privacy that society is prepared to recognize as reasonable—has often been criticized as circular, and hence subjective and unpredictable. While it may be difficult to refine *Katz* when the search of areas such as telephone booths, automobiles, or even the curtilage and uncovered portions of residences is at issue, in the case of the search of the interior of homes— the prototypical and hence most commonly litigated area of protected privacy—there is a ready criterion, with roots deep in the common law, of the minimal expectation of privacy that *exists,* and that is acknowledged to be *reasonable.* To withdraw protection of this minimum expectation would be to permit police technology to erode the privacy guaranteed by the Fourth Amendment. We think that obtaining by sense-enhancing technology any information regarding the interior of the home that could not otherwise have been obtained without physical "intrusion into a constitutionally protected area," constitutes a search-at least where (as here) the technology in question is not in general public use. This assures preservation of that degree of privacy against government that existed when the Fourth Amendment was adopted. On the basis of this criterion, the information obtained by the thermal imager in this case was the product of a search.

The Government maintains, however, that the thermal imaging must be upheld because it detected "only heat radiating from the external surface of the house." The dissent makes this its leading point, contending that there is a fundamental difference between what it calls "off-the-wall" observations and "through-the-wall surveillance." But just as a thermal imager captures only heat emanating from a house, so also a powerful directional microphone picks up only sound emanating from a house—and a satellite capable of scanning from many miles away would pick up only visible light emanating from a house. We rejected such a mechanical interpretation of the Fourth Amendment in *Katz,* where the eavesdropping device picked up only sound waves that reached the exterior of the phone booth. Reversing that approach would leave the homeowner at the mercy of advancing technology—including imaging technology that could discern all human activity in the home. While the technology used in the present case was relatively crude, the rule we adopt must take account of more sophisticated systems that are already in use or in development.[3]

The Government also contends that the thermal imaging was constitutional because it did not "detect private activities occurring in private areas." * * * The Fourth Amendment's protection of the home has never been tied to measurement of the quality or quantity of information obtained. * * *

Limiting the prohibition of thermal imaging to "intimate details" would not only be wrong in principle; it would be impractical in application, failing to provide "a workable accommodation between the needs of law enforcement and the interests protected by the Fourth Amendment." To begin with, there is no necessary connection between the sophistication of the surveillance equipment and the "intimacy" of the details that it observes—which means that one cannot say (and the police cannot be assured) that use of the relatively crude equipment at issue here will always be lawful. The Agema Thermovision 210 might disclose,

---

[3]   The ability to "see" through walls and other opaque barriers is a clear, and scientifically feasible, goal of law enforcement research and development. The National Law Enforcement and Corrections Technology Center, a program within the United States Department of Justice, features on its Internet Website projects that include a "Radar-Based Through-the-Wall Surveillance System," "Handheld Ultrasound Through the Wall Surveillance," and a "Radar Flashlight" that "will enable law enforcement officers to detect individuals through interior building walls." www.nlectc.org/techproj/ (visited May 3, 2001). Some devices may emit low levels of radiation that travel "through-the-wall," but others, such as more sophisticated thermal-imaging devices, are entirely passive, or "off-the-wall" as the dissent puts it.

for example, at what hour each night the lady of the house takes her daily sauna and bath—a detail that many would consider "intimate"; and a much more sophisticated system might detect nothing more intimate than the fact that someone left a closet light on. We could not, in other words, develop a rule approving only that through-the-wall surveillance which identifies objects no smaller than 36 by 36 inches, but would have to develop a jurisprudence specifying which home activities are "intimate" and which are not. And even when (if ever) that jurisprudence were fully developed, no police officer would be able to know *in advance* whether his through-the-wall surveillance picks up "intimate" details- and thus would be unable to know in advance whether it is constitutional.

* * *

We have said that the Fourth Amendment draws "a firm line at the entrance to the house." That line, we think, must be not only firm but also bright-which requires clear specification of those methods of surveillance that require a warrant. While it is certainly possible to conclude from the videotape of the thermal imaging that occurred in this case that no "significant" compromise of the homeowner's privacy has occurred, we must take the long view, from the original meaning of the Fourth Amendment forward.

* * *

Where, as here, the Government uses a device that is not in general public use, to explore details of the home that would previously have been unknowable without physical intrusion, the surveillance is a "search" and is presumptively unreasonable without a warrant.

* * *

The judgment of the Court of Appeals is reversed; the case is remanded for further proceedings consistent with this opinion.

It is so ordered.

■ JUSTICE STEVENS, with whom THE CHIEF JUSTICE, JUSTICE O'CONNOR, and JUSTICE KENNEDY join, dissenting.

* * *

There is no need for the Court to craft a new rule to decide this case, as it is controlled by established principles from our Fourth Amendment jurisprudence. One of those core principles, of course, is * * * that searches and seizures of property in plain view are presumptively reasonable. * * * That is the principle implicated here.

While the Court "take[s] the long view" and decides this case based largely on the potential of yet-to-be-developed technology that might allow "through-the-wall surveillance," this case involves nothing more than off-the-wall surveillance by law enforcement officers to gather information exposed to the general public from the outside of petitioner's home. All that the infrared camera did in this case was passively measure heat emitted from the exterior surfaces of petitioner's home; all that those measurements showed were relative differences in emission levels, vaguely indicating that some areas of the roof and outside walls were warmer than others. * * * [N]o details regarding the interior of petitioner's home were revealed. * * *

Indeed, the ordinary use of the senses might enable a neighbor or passerby to notice the heat emanating from a building, particularly if it is vented, as was the case here. Additionally, any member of the public might notice that one part of a house is warmer than another part or a nearby building if, for example, rainwater evaporates or snow melts at different rates across its surfaces. * * *

Notwithstanding the implications of today's decision, there is a strong public interest in avoiding constitutional litigation over the monitoring of emissions from homes, and over the inferences drawn from such monitoring. Just as "the police cannot reasonably be expected to avert their eyes from evidence of criminal activity that could have been observed by any member of the public," so too public officials should not have to avert their senses or their equipment from detecting emissions in the public domain such as excessive heat, traces of smoke, suspicious odors, odorless gases, airborne particulates, or radioactive emissions, any of which could identify hazards to the community. In my judgment, monitoring such emissions with "sense-enhancing technology" and drawing useful conclusions from such monitoring, is an entirely reasonable public service.

On the other hand, the countervailing privacy interest is at best trivial. After all, homes generally are insulated to keep heat in, rather than to prevent the detection of heat going out, and it does not seem to me that society will suffer from a rule requiring the rare homeowner who both intends to engage in uncommon activities that produce extraordinary amounts of heat, and wishes to conceal that production from outsiders, to make sure that the surrounding area is well insulated. * * *

[T]he Court has fashioned a rule that is intended to provide essential guidance for the day when "more sophisticated systems" gain the "ability to 'see' through walls and other opaque barriers." The newly minted rule encompasses "obtaining [1] by sense-enhancing technology [2] any information regarding the interior of the home [3] that could not otherwise have been obtained without physical intrusion into a constitutionally protected area . . . [4] at least where (as here) the technology in question is not in general public use." In my judgment, the Court's new rule is at once too broad and too narrow, and is not justified by the Court's explanation for its adoption. * * * I would not erect a constitutional impediment to the use of sense-enhancing technology unless it provides its user with the functional equivalent of actual presence in the area being searched.

Despite the Court's attempt to draw a line that is "not only firm but also bright," the contours of its new rule are uncertain because its protection apparently dissipates as soon as the relevant technology is "in general public use." Yet how much use is general public use is not even hinted at by the Court's opinion * * * . In any event, * * * this criterion is somewhat perverse because it seems likely that the threat to privacy will grow, rather than recede, as the use of intrusive equipment becomes more readily available.

It is clear, however, that the category of "sense-enhancing technology" covered by the new rule is far too broad. It would, for example, embrace potential mechanical substitutes for dogs trained to react when they sniff narcotics. But in *United States v. Place,* 462 U.S. 696, 707, 103 S.Ct. 2637, 77 L.Ed.2d 110 (1983), we held that a dog sniff that "discloses only the presence or absence of narcotics" does "not constitute a 'search' within the meaning of the Fourth Amendment," and it must follow that sense-enhancing equipment that identifies nothing but illegal activity is not a search either. * * *

The application of the Court's new rule to "any information regarding the interior of the home," is also unnecessarily broad. If it takes sensitive equipment to detect an odor that identifies criminal conduct and nothing else, the fact that the odor emanates from the interior of a home should not provide it with constitutional protection. * * *

The two reasons advanced by the Court as justifications for the adoption of its new rule are both unpersuasive. First, the Court suggests that its rule is compelled by our holding in *Katz,* because in that case, as in this, the surveillance consisted of nothing more than the monitoring of waves emanating from a private area into the public domain. Yet there are critical differences between the cases. In *Katz,* the electronic listening device attached to the outside of the phone booth allowed the officers to pick up the content of the conversation inside the booth, making them the functional equivalent of intruders because they gathered information that was otherwise available only to someone inside the private area; it would be as if, in this case, the thermal imager presented a view of the heat-generating activity inside petitioner's home. By contrast, the thermal imager here disclosed only the relative amounts of heat radiating from the house; it would be as if, in *Katz,* the listening device disclosed only the relative volume of sound leaving the booth, which presumably was discernible in the public domain. * * *

Second, the Court argues that the permissibility of "through-the-wall surveillance" cannot depend on a distinction between observing "intimate details" such as "the lady of the house [taking] her daily sauna and bath," and noticing only "the nonintimate rug on the vestibule floor" or "objects no smaller than 36 by 36 inches." This entire argument assumes, of course, that the thermal imager in this case could or did perform "through-the-wall surveillance" that could identify any detail "that would previously have been unknowable without physical intrusion." In fact, the device could not, and did not, enable its user to identify either the lady of the house, the rug on the vestibule floor, or anything else inside the house, whether smaller or larger than 36 by 36 inches. * * *

Although the Court is properly and commendably concerned about the threats to privacy that may flow from advances in the technology available to the law enforcement profession, it has unfortunately failed to heed the tried and true counsel of judicial restraint. Instead of concentrating on the rather mundane issue that is actually presented by the case before it, the Court has endeavored to craft an all-encompassing rule for the future. It would be far wiser to give legislators an unimpeded opportunity to grapple with these emerging issues rather than to shackle them with prematurely devised constitutional constraints.

I respectfully dissent.

United States v. Jones

Supreme Court of the United States, 2012.
___ U.S. ___, 132 S.Ct. 945.

■ JUSTICE SCALIA delivered the opinion of the Court.

We decide whether the attachment of a Global-Positioning-System (GPS) tracking device to an individual's vehicle, and subsequent use of that device to monitor the vehicle's movements on public streets, constitutes a search or seizure within the meaning of the Fourth Amendment.

I

In 2004 respondent Antoine Jones, owner and operator of a nightclub in the District of Columbia, came under suspicion of trafficking in narcotics and was made the target of an investigation by a joint FBI and Metropolitan Police Department task force. Officers employed various investigative techniques, including visual surveillance of the nightclub, installation of a camera focused on the front door of the club, and a pen register and wiretap covering Jones's cellular phone.

Based in part on information gathered from these sources, * * * [Government] agents installed a GPS tracking device on the undercarriage of [Jones'] Jeep [Grand Cherokee] while it was parked in a public parking lot. Over the next 28 days, the Government used the device to track the vehicle's movements, and once had to replace the device's battery when the vehicle was parked in a * * * public lot * * *. By means of signals from multiple satellites, the device established the vehicle's location within 50 to 100 feet, and communicated that location by cellular phone to a Government computer. It relayed more than 2,000 pages of data over the 4-week period.

The Government * * * obtained a multiple-count indictment charging Jones and several alleged co-conspirators with * * * conspiracy to distribute and possess with intent to distribute five kilograms or more of cocaine and 50 grams or more of cocaine base * * * . Before trial, Jones filed a motion to suppress evidence obtained through the GPS device. The District Court granted the motion only in part, suppressing the data obtained while the vehicle was parked in the garage adjoining Jones's residence. It held the remaining data admissible, because " '[a] person traveling in an automobile on public thoroughfares has no reasonable expectation of privacy in his movements from one place to another.' " * * * The Government introduced at trial the * * * GPS-derived locational data * * * , which connected Jones to the alleged conspirators' stash house that contained $850,000 in cash, 97 kilograms of cocaine, and 1 kilogram of cocaine base. The jury returned a guilty verdict, and the District Court sentenced Jones to life imprisonment.

The United States Court of Appeals for the District of Columbia Circuit reversed the conviction because of admission of the evidence obtained by warrantless use of the GPS device which, it said, violated the Fourth Amendment. * * * We granted certiorari.

II

A

The Fourth Amendment provides in relevant part that "[t]he right of the people to be secure in their persons, houses, papers, and effects, against unreasonable searches and seizures, shall not be violated." It is beyond dispute that a vehicle is an "effect" as that term is used in the Amendment. We hold that the Government's installation of a GPS device on a target's vehicle, and its use of that device to monitor the vehicle's movements, constitutes a "search."

It is important to be clear about what occurred in this case: The Government physically occupied private property for the purpose of obtaining information. We have no doubt that such a physical intrusion would have been considered a "search" within the meaning of the Fourth Amendment when it was adopted. * * * In [*Entick v. Carrington,* 95 Eng. Rep. 807 (C.P. 1765)], Lord Camden expressed in plain terms the significance of property rights in search-and-seizure analysis:

> "[O]ur law holds the property of every man so sacred, that no man can set his foot upon his neighbour's close without his leave; if he does he is a trespasser, though he does no damage at all; if he will tread upon his neighbour's ground, he must justify it by law."

The text of the Fourth Amendment reflects its close connection to property, since otherwise it would have referred simply to "the right of the people to be secure against unreasonable searches and seizures"; the phrase "in their persons, houses, papers, and effects" would have been superfluous.

Consistent with this understanding, our Fourth Amendment jurisprudence was tied to common-law trespass, at least until the latter half of the 20th century. * * *

Our later cases, of course, have deviated from that exclusively property-based approach. In *Katz v. United States,* 389 U.S. 347, 351, 88 S.Ct. 507, 19 L.Ed.2d 576 (1967), we said that "the Fourth Amendment protects people, not places," and found a violation in attachment of an eavesdropping device to a public telephone booth. Our later cases have applied the analysis of Justice Harlan's concurrence in that case, which said that a violation occurs when government officers violate a person's "reasonable expectation of privacy."

The Government contends that the Harlan standard shows that no search occurred here, since Jones had no "reasonable expectation of privacy" in the area of the Jeep accessed by Government agents (its underbody) and in the locations of the Jeep on the public roads, which were visible to all. But we need not address the Government's contentions, because Jones's Fourth Amendment rights do not rise or fall with the *Katz* formulation. At bottom, we must "assur[e] preservation of that degree of privacy against government that existed when the Fourth Amendment was adopted." As explained, for most of our history the Fourth Amendment was understood to embody a particular concern for government trespass upon the areas ("persons, houses, papers, and effects") it enumerates. *Katz* did not repudiate that understanding * * * [or] narrow the Fourth Amendment's scope.[5]

The Government contends that several of our post-*Katz* cases foreclose the conclusion that what occurred here constituted a search. It relies principally on two cases in which we rejected Fourth Amendment challenges to "beepers," electronic tracking devices that represent another form of electronic monitoring. The first case, [*United States v. Knotts,* 460 U.S. 276, 281, 103 S.Ct. 1081, 75 L.Ed.2d 55 (1983)], upheld against Fourth Amendment challenge the use of a "beeper" that had been placed in a container of chloroform, allowing law enforcement to monitor the location of the container. We said that there had been no infringement of Knotts' reasonable expectation of privacy since the information obtained—the location of the automobile carrying the container on public roads, and the location of the off-loaded container in open fields near Knotts' cabin—had been voluntarily conveyed to the public. But as we have discussed, the *Katz* reasonable-expectation-of-privacy test has been *added to,* not *substituted for,* the common-law trespassory test. The holding in *Knotts* addressed only the former, since the latter was not at issue. The beeper had been placed in the container before it came into Knotts' possession, with the consent of the then-owner. Knotts did not challenge that installation, and we specifically declined to consider its effect on the Fourth Amendment analysis. *Knotts* would be relevant, perhaps, if the Government were making the

---

[5]   * * * [It is irrelevant] that, if analyzed separately, neither the installation of the device nor its use would constitute a Fourth Amendment search. Of course not. A trespass on "houses" or "effects," or a *Katz* invasion of privacy, is not alone a search unless it is done to obtain information; and the obtaining of information is not alone a search unless it is achieved by such a trespass or invasion of privacy.

argument that what would otherwise be an unconstitutional search is not such where it produces only public information. The Government does not make that argument, and we know of no case that would support it.

The second "beeper" case, *United States v. Karo,* 468 U.S. 705, 104 S.Ct. 3296, 82 L.Ed.2d 530 (1984), does not suggest a different conclusion. There we addressed the question left open by *Knotts,* whether the installation of a beeper in a container amounted to a search or seizure. As in *Knotts,* at the time the beeper was installed the container belonged to a third party, and it did not come into possession of the defendant until later. Thus, the specific question we considered was whether the installation "*with the consent of the original owner* constitute[d] a search or seizure . . . when the container is delivered to a buyer having no knowledge of the presence of the beeper." (emphasis added). We held not. The Government, we said, came into physical contact with the container only before it belonged to the defendant Karo; and the transfer of the container with the unmonitored beeper inside did not convey any information and thus did not invade Karo's privacy. That conclusion is perfectly consistent with the one we reach here. Karo accepted the container as it came to him, beeper and all, and was therefore not entitled to object to the beeper's presence, even though it was used to monitor the container's location. Jones, who possessed the Jeep at the time the Government trespassorily inserted the information-gathering device, is on much different footing.[7]

* * *

Finally, the Government's position gains little support from our conclusion in *Oliver v. United States,* 466 U.S. 170, 104 S.Ct. 1735, 80 L.Ed.2d 214 (1984), that officers' information-gathering intrusion on an "open field" did not constitute a Fourth Amendment search even though it was a trespass at common law. Quite simply, an open field, unlike the curtilage of a home, is not one of those protected areas enumerated in the Fourth Amendment. The Government's physical intrusion on such an area—unlike its intrusion on the "effect" at issue here—is of no Fourth Amendment significance.[8]

B

* * * [E]ven assuming that the concurrence is correct to say that "[t]raditional surveillance" of Jones for a 4-week period "would have required a large team of agents, multiple vehicles, and perhaps aerial

---

[7]   The Government also points to *Cardwell v. Lewis,* 417 U.S. 583, 94 S.Ct. 2464, 41 L.Ed.2d 325 (1974), in which the Court rejected the claim that the inspection of an impounded vehicle's tire tread and the collection of paint scrapings from its exterior violated the Fourth Amendment. Whether the plurality said so because no search occurred or because the search was reasonable is unclear.

[8]   Thus, our theory is *not* that the Fourth Amendment is concerned with "*any* technical trespass that led to the gathering of evidence." The Fourth Amendment protects against trespassory searches only with regard to those items ("persons, houses, papers, and effects") that it enumerates. The trespass that occurred in *Oliver* may properly be understood as a "search," but not one "in the constitutional sense."

assistance," our cases suggest that such visual observation is constitutionally permissible. It may be that achieving the same result through electronic means, without an accompanying trespass, is an unconstitutional invasion of privacy, but the present case does not require us to answer that question.

And answering it affirmatively leads us needlessly into additional thorny problems. The concurrence posits that "relatively short-term monitoring of a person's movements on public streets" is okay, but that "the use of longer term GPS monitoring in investigations *of most offenses*" is no good. That introduces yet another novelty into our jurisprudence. There is no precedent for the proposition that whether a search has occurred depends on the nature of the crime being investigated. And even accepting that novelty, it remains unexplained why a 4-week investigation is "surely" too long and why a drug-trafficking conspiracy involving substantial amounts of cash and narcotics is not an "extraordinary offens[e]" which may permit longer observation. What of a 2-day monitoring of a suspected purveyor of stolen electronics? Or of a 6-month monitoring of a suspected terrorist? We may have to grapple with these "vexing problems" in some future case where a classic trespassory search is not involved and resort must be had to *Katz* analysis; but there is no reason for rushing forward to resolve them here.

III

The Government argues in the alternative that even if the attachment and use of the device was a search, it was reasonable—and thus lawful—under the Fourth Amendment because "officers had reasonable suspicion, and indeed probable cause, to believe that [Jones] was a leader in a large-scale cocaine distribution conspiracy." We have no occasion to consider this argument. The Government did not raise it below, and the D.C. Circuit therefore did not address it. We consider the argument forfeited.

The judgment of the Court of Appeals for the D.C. Circuit is affirmed.

It is so ordered.

■ JUSTICE SOTOMAYOR, concurring.

I join the Court's opinion because I agree that a search within the meaning of the Fourth Amendment occurs, at a minimum, "[w]here, as here, the Government obtains information by physically intruding on a constitutionally protected area." * * * The Government usurped Jones' property for the purpose of conducting surveillance on him, thereby invading privacy interests long afforded, and undoubtedly entitled to, Fourth Amendment protection.

Of course, the Fourth Amendment is not concerned only with trespassory intrusions on property. * * * As the majority's opinion makes clear, however, *Katz*'s reasonable-expectation-of-privacy test augmented, but did not displace or diminish, the common-law trespassory test that preceded it. * * * JUSTICE ALITO's approach, which discounts altogether the constitutional relevance of the Government's physical intrusion on Jones' Jeep, erodes that longstanding protection for privacy expectations inherent in items of property that people possess or control. By contrast, the trespassory test applied in the majority's opinion reflects an irreducible constitutional minimum: When the Government physically invades personal property to gather information, a search occurs. The reaffirmation of that principle suffices to decide this case.

Nonetheless, as JUSTICE ALITO notes, physical intrusion is now unnecessary to many forms of surveillance. With increasing regularity, the Government will be capable of duplicating the monitoring undertaken in this case by enlisting factory- or owner-installed vehicle tracking devices or GPS-enabled smartphones. In cases of electronic or other novel modes of surveillance that do not depend upon a physical invasion on property, the majority opinion's trespassory test may provide little guidance. But "[s]ituations involving merely the transmission of electronic signals without trespass would *remain* subject to *Katz* analysis." As JUSTICE ALITO incisively observes, the same technological advances that have made possible nontrespassory surveillance techniques will also affect the *Katz* test by shaping the evolution of societal privacy expectations. Under that rubric, I agree with JUSTICE ALITO that, at the very least, "longer term GPS monitoring in investigations of most offenses impinges on expectations of privacy."

In cases involving even short-term monitoring, some unique attributes of GPS surveillance relevant to the *Katz* analysis will require particular attention. GPS monitoring generates a precise, comprehensive record of a person's public movements that reflects a wealth of detail about her familial, political, professional, religious, and sexual associations. The Government can store such records and efficiently mine them for information years into the future. And because GPS monitoring is cheap in comparison to conventional surveillance techniques and, by design, proceeds surreptitiously, it evades the ordinary checks that constrain abusive law enforcement practices: "limited police resources and community hostility."

Awareness that the Government may be watching chills associational and expressive freedoms. And the Government's unrestrained power to assemble data that reveal private aspects of identity is susceptible to abuse. The net result is that GPS monitoring— by making available at a relatively low cost such a substantial quantum of intimate information about any person whom the Government, in its unfettered discretion, chooses to track—may "alter the relationship between citizen and government in a way that is inimical to democratic society."

I would take these attributes of GPS monitoring into account when considering the existence of a reasonable societal expectation of privacy in the sum of one's public movements. I would ask whether people reasonably expect that their movements will be recorded and aggregated in a manner that enables the Government to ascertain, more or less at will, their political and religious beliefs, sexual habits, and so on. I do not regard as dispositive the fact that the Government might obtain the fruits of GPS monitoring through lawful conventional surveillance techniques. * * *

More fundamentally, it may be necessary to reconsider the premise that an individual has no reasonable expectation of privacy in information voluntarily disclosed to third parties. This approach is ill suited to the digital age, in which people reveal a great deal of information about themselves to third parties in the course of carrying out mundane tasks. People disclose the phone numbers that they dial or text to their cellular providers; the URLs that they visit and the e-mail addresses with which they correspond to their Internet service providers; and the books, groceries, and medications they purchase to online retailers. Perhaps, as JUSTICE ALITO notes, some people may find the "tradeoff" of privacy for convenience "worthwhile," or come to accept this "diminution of privacy" as "inevitable," and perhaps not. I for one doubt that people would accept without complaint the warrantless disclosure to the Government of a list of every Web site they had visited in the last week, or month, or year. But whatever the societal expectations, they can attain constitutionally protected status only if our Fourth Amendment jurisprudence ceases to treat secrecy as a prerequisite for privacy. I would not assume that all information voluntarily disclosed to some member of the public for a limited purpose is, for that reason alone, disentitled to Fourth Amendment protection.

Resolution of these difficult questions in this case is unnecessary, however, because the Government's physical intrusion on Jones' Jeep supplies a narrower basis for decision. I therefore join the majority's opinion.

■ JUSTICE ALITO, with whom JUSTICE GINSBURG, JUSTICE BREYER, and JUSTICE KAGAN join, concurring in the judgment.

This case requires us to apply the Fourth Amendment's prohibition of unreasonable searches and seizures to a 21st-century surveillance technique, the use of a Global Positioning System (GPS) device to monitor a vehicle's movements for an extended period of time. Ironically, the Court has chosen to decide this case based on 18th-century tort law. By attaching a small GPS device[1] to the underside of the vehicle that respondent drove, the law enforcement officers in this case engaged in conduct that might have provided grounds in 1791 for a suit for trespass to chattels. And for this reason, the Court concludes, the installation and use of the GPS device constituted a search.

---

[1]   Although the record does not reveal the size or weight of the device used in this case, there is now a device in use that weighs two ounces and is the size of a credit card.

This holding, in my judgment, is unwise. It strains the language of the Fourth Amendment; it has little if any support in current Fourth Amendment case law; and it is highly artificial.

I would analyze the question presented in this case by asking whether respondent's reasonable expectations of privacy were violated by the long-term monitoring of the movements of the vehicle he drove.

I

A

The Fourth Amendment prohibits "unreasonable searches and seizures," and the Court makes very little effort to explain how the attachment or use of the GPS device fits within these terms. The Court does not contend that there was a seizure. * * *

The Court does claim that the installation and use of the GPS constituted a search, but this conclusion is dependent on the questionable proposition that these two procedures cannot be separated for purposes of Fourth Amendment analysis. If these two procedures are analyzed separately, it is not at all clear from the Court's opinion why either should be regarded as a search. It is clear that the attachment of the GPS device was not itself a search; if the device had not functioned or if the officers had not used it, no information would have been obtained. And the Court does not contend that the use of the device constituted a search either. On the contrary, the Court accepts the holding in *United States v. Knotts,* 460 U.S. 276, 103 S.Ct. 1081, 75 L.Ed.2d 55 (1983), that the use of a surreptitiously planted electronic device to monitor a vehicle's movements on public roads did not amount to a search.

The Court argues—and I agree—that "we must 'assur[e] preservation of that degree of privacy against government that existed when the Fourth Amendment was adopted.'" But it is almost impossible to think of late 18th-century situations that are analogous to what took place in this case. (Is it possible to imagine a case in which a constable secreted himself somewhere in a coach and remained there for a period of time in order to monitor the movements of the coach's owner?) The Court's theory seems to be that the concept of a search, as originally understood, comprehended any technical trespass that led to the gathering of evidence, but we know that this is incorrect. At common law, any unauthorized intrusion on private property was actionable, but a trespass on open fields, as opposed to the "curtilage" of a home, does not fall within the scope of the Fourth Amendment because private property outside the curtilage is not part of a "hous[e]" within the meaning of the Fourth Amendment. See *Oliver v. United States,* 466 U.S. 170, 104 S.Ct. 1735, 80 L.Ed.2d 214 (1984); *Hester v. United States,* 265 U.S. 57, 44 S.Ct. 445, 68 L.Ed. 898 (1924).

B

The Court's reasoning in this case is very similar to that in the Court's early decisions involving wiretapping and electronic eavesdropping, namely, that a technical trespass followed by the gathering of evidence constitutes a search. * * *

Katz v. United States, 389 U.S. 347, 88 S.Ct. 507, 19 L.Ed.2d 576 (1967), finally did away with the old approach, holding that a trespass was not required for a Fourth Amendment violation. * * *

Under [the *Katz*] approach, as the Court later put it when addressing the relevance of a technical trespass, "an actual trespass is neither necessary *nor sufficient* to establish a constitutional violation." *United States v. Karo,* 468 U.S. 705, 713, 104 S.Ct. 3296, 82 L.Ed.2d 530 (1984) (emphasis added). * * *

II

The majority * * * is hard pressed to find support in post-*Katz* cases for its trespass-based theory.

III

Disharmony with a substantial body of existing case law is only one of the problems with the Court's approach in this case.

I will briefly note [several] others. First, the Court's reasoning largely disregards what is really important (the *use* of a GPS for the purpose of long-term tracking) and instead attaches great significance to something that most would view as relatively minor (attaching to the bottom of a car a small, light object that does not interfere in any way with the car's operation). Attaching such an object is generally regarded as so trivial that it does not provide a basis for recovery under modern tort law. But under the Court's reasoning, this conduct may violate the Fourth Amendment. By contrast, if long-term monitoring can be accomplished without committing a technical trespass—suppose, for example, that the Federal Government required or persuaded auto manufacturers to include a GPS tracking device in every car—the Court's theory would provide no protection.

Second, the Court's approach leads to incongruous results. If the police attach a GPS device to a car and use the device to follow the car for even a brief time, under the Court's theory, the Fourth Amendment applies. But if the police follow the same car for a much longer period using unmarked cars and aerial assistance, this tracking is not subject to any Fourth Amendment constraints.

In the present case, the Fourth Amendment applies, the Court concludes, because the officers installed the GPS device after respondent's wife, to whom the car was registered, turned it over to respondent for his exclusive use. But if the GPS had been attached prior to that time, the Court's theory would lead to a different result. * * *

[Finally], the Court's reliance on the law of trespass will present particularly vexing problems in cases involving surveillance that is carried out by making electronic, as opposed to physical, contact with the item to be tracked. For example, suppose that the officers in the present case had followed respondent by surreptitiously activating a stolen vehicle detection system that came with the car when it was purchased. Would the sending of a radio signal to activate this system constitute a trespass to chattels? Trespass to chattels has traditionally required a physical touching of the property. In recent years, courts have wrestled with the application of this old tort in cases involving unwanted electronic contact with computer systems, and some have held that even the transmission of electrons that occurs when a communication is sent from one computer to another is enough. But may such decisions be followed in applying the Court's trespass theory? Assuming that what matters under the Court's theory is the law of trespass as it existed at the time of the adoption of the Fourth Amendment, do these recent decisions represent a change in the law or simply the application of the old tort to new situations?

IV

A

The *Katz* expectation-of-privacy test avoids the problems and complications noted above, but it is not without its own difficulties. It involves a degree of circularity, and judges are apt to confuse their own expectations of privacy with those of the hypothetical reasonable person to which the *Katz* test looks. In addition, the *Katz* test rests on the assumption that this hypothetical reasonable person has a well-developed and stable set of privacy expectations. But technology can change those expectations. Dramatic technological change may lead to periods in which popular expectations are in flux and may ultimately produce significant changes in popular attitudes. New technology may provide increased convenience or security at the expense of privacy, and many people may find the tradeoff worthwhile. And even if the public does not welcome the diminution of privacy that new technology entails, they may eventually reconcile themselves to this development as inevitable.

On the other hand, concern about new intrusions on privacy may spur the enactment of legislation to protect against these intrusions. This is what ultimately happened with respect to wiretapping. After *Katz,* Congress did not leave it to the courts to develop a body of Fourth Amendment case law governing that complex subject. Instead, Congress promptly enacted a comprehensive statute, see 18 U.S.C. §§ 2510–2522 (2006 ed. and Supp. IV), and since that time, the regulation of wiretapping has been governed primarily by statute and not by case law. * * *

B

Recent years have seen the emergence of many new devices that permit the monitoring of a person's movements. In some locales, closed-circuit television video monitoring is becoming ubiquitous. On toll roads, automatic toll collection systems create a precise record of the movements of motorists who choose to make use of that convenience. Many motorists purchase cars that are equipped with devices that permit a central station to ascertain the car's location at any time so that roadside assistance may be provided if needed and the car may be found if it is stolen.

Perhaps most significant, cell phones and other wireless devices now permit wireless carriers to track and record the location of users—and as of June 2011, it has been reported, there were more than 322 million wireless devices in use in the United States. For older phones, the accuracy of the location information depends on the density of the tower network, but new "smart phones," which are equipped with a GPS device, permit more precise tracking. For example, when a user activates the GPS on such a phone, a provider is able to monitor the phone's location and speed of movement and can then report back real-time traffic conditions after combining ("crowdsourcing") the speed of all such phones on any particular road. Similarly, phone-location-tracking services are offered as "social" tools, allowing consumers to find (or to avoid) others who enroll in these services. The availability and use of these and other new devices will continue to shape the average person's expectations about the privacy of his or her daily movements.

V

In the pre-computer age, the greatest protections of privacy were neither constitutional nor statutory, but practical. Traditional surveillance for any extended period of time was difficult and costly and therefore rarely undertaken. The surveillance at issue in this case— constant monitoring of the location of a vehicle for four weeks—would have required a large team of agents, multiple vehicles, and perhaps aerial assistance. Only an investigation of unusual importance could have justified such an expenditure of law enforcement resources. Devices like the one used in the present case, however, make long-term monitoring relatively easy and cheap. In circumstances involving dramatic technological change, the best solution to privacy concerns may be legislative. A legislative body is well situated to gauge changing public attitudes, to draw detailed lines, and to balance privacy and public safety in a comprehensive way.

To date, however, Congress and most States have not enacted statutes regulating the use of GPS tracking technology for law enforcement purposes. The best that we can do in this case is to apply existing Fourth Amendment doctrine and to ask whether the use of GPS tracking in a particular case involved a degree of intrusion that a reasonable person would not have anticipated.

Under this approach, relatively short-term monitoring of a person's movements on public streets accords with expectations of privacy that our society has recognized as reasonable. But the use of longer term GPS monitoring in investigations of most offenses impinges on expectations of privacy. For such offenses, society's expectation has been that law enforcement agents and others would not—and indeed, in the main, simply could not—secretly monitor and catalogue every single movement of an individual's car for a very long period. In this case, for four weeks, law enforcement agents tracked every movement that respondent made in the vehicle he was driving. We need not identify with precision the point at which the tracking of this vehicle became a search, for the line was surely crossed before the 4-week mark. Other cases may present more difficult questions. But where uncertainty exists with respect to whether a certain period of GPS surveillance is long enough to constitute a Fourth Amendment search, the police may always seek a warrant.[11] We also need not consider whether prolonged GPS monitoring in the context of investigations involving extraordinary offenses would similarly intrude on a constitutionally protected sphere of privacy. In such cases, long-term tracking might have been mounted using previously available techniques.

* * *

For these reasons, I conclude that the lengthy monitoring that occurred in this case constituted a search under the Fourth Amendment. I therefore agree with the majority that the decision of the Court of Appeals must be affirmed.

NOTE

When *Jones* was returned to the district court, the Government proceeded to retry Jones. He moved to suppress the results of other evidence the Government had secured, specifically four months of cellular phone data tending to show somewhat the same movements as were suggested by the GPS evidence held inadmissible by the Supreme Court. The cell site data had been obtained pursuant to court orders issued under the Stored Communication Act, 18 U.S.C. § 2703. These orders do not require a showing of probable cause but only that the sought information would be relevant and material to an ongoing criminal investigation. Jones contended that obtaining this information was a search and required a warrant issued on probable cause. The district judge held that if any Fourth Amendment violation occurred, the good faith exception to the exclusionary sanction rendered the evidence admissible. United States v. Jones, 908 F. Supp. 2d 203, 205 (D.D.C. 2012). In January of 2013, with Jones representing himself, a trial was held and a mistrial resulted. On May 1, 2013—again acting pro se—Jones pled guilty to conspiracy and was sentenced to fifteen years imprisonment. The next year he unsuccessfully sought to collaterally attack his conviction on the ground that he received ineffective assistance of counsel in the pretrial proceedings before he undertook to represent himself. Jones

---

[11] * * * In the courts below the Government did not argue, and has not argued here, that the Fourth Amendment does not impose [the] restrictions [that a warrant be obtained and complied with] and that the violation of these restrictions does not demand the suppression of evidence obtained using the tracking device. Because it was not raised, that question is not before us.

v. State, 2014 WL 3538084 (D.D.C. 2014) (unpublished memorandum opinion).

c. APPROACHING THE HOME WITH OR WITHOUT A DRUG-SNIFFING DOG

As a general rule, law enforcement officers may—without either a warrant or grounds for a warrant—approach a residence in a manner that under convention a private citizen may do. The officers often do this to seek an opportunity to talk with the occupants for one or more of a variety of reasons. They may seek to determine whether there are innocent explanations for suspicious circumstances or reports. They may hope to obtain incriminating admissions from the occupants, or perhaps to persuade the occupants to consent to a search of the premises. Alternatively, their purpose may be to have an opportunity to make observations that support suspicion of criminal activity.

The principal case that follows raises the question of when if ever officers' actions in approaching a residence triggers Fourth Amendment search warrant and probable cause demands despite the general rule exempting such "knock and talk" approaches from Fourth Amendment scrutiny.

Florida v. Jardines

Supreme Court of the United States, 2013.
___ U.S. ___, 133 S.Ct. 1409.

■ JUSTICE SCALIA delivered the opinion of the Court.

We consider whether using a drug-sniffing dog on a homeowner's porch to investigate the contents of the home is a "search" within the meaning of the Fourth Amendment.

I

In 2006, Detective William Pedraja of the Miami-Dade Police Department received an unverified tip that marijuana was being grown in the home of respondent Joelis Jardines. One month later, the Department and the Drug Enforcement Administration sent a joint surveillance team to Jardines' home. Detective Pedraja was part of that team. He watched the home for fifteen minutes and saw no vehicles in the driveway or activity around the home, and could not see inside because the blinds were drawn. Detective Pedraja then approached Jardines' home accompanied by Detective Douglas Bartelt, a trained canine handler who had just arrived at the scene with his drug-sniffing dog. The dog was trained to detect the scent of marijuana, cocaine, heroin, and several other drugs, indicating the presence of any of these substances through particular behavioral changes recognizable by his handler.

Detective Bartelt had the dog on a six-foot leash, owing in part to the dog's "wild" nature, and tendency to dart around erratically while searching. As the dog approached Jardines' front porch, he apparently sensed one of the odors he had been trained to detect, and began energetically exploring the area for the strongest point source of that odor. As Detective Bartelt explained, the dog "began tracking that airborne odor by . . . tracking back and forth," engaging in what is called "bracketing," "back and forth, back and forth." Detective Bartelt gave the dog "the full six feet of the leash plus whatever safe distance [he could] give him" to do this—he testified that he needed to give the dog "as much distance as I can." And Detective Pedraja stood back while this was occurring, so that he would not "get knocked over" when the dog was "spinning around trying to find" the source.

After sniffing the base of the front door, the dog sat, which is the trained behavior upon discovering the odor's strongest point. Detective Bartelt then pulled the dog away from the door and returned to his vehicle. He left the scene after informing Detective Pedraja that there had been a positive alert for narcotics.

On the basis of what he had learned at the home, Detective Pedraja applied for and received a warrant to search the residence. When the warrant was executed later that day, Jardines attempted to flee and was arrested; the search revealed marijuana plants, and he was charged with trafficking in cannabis.

At trial, Jardines moved to suppress the marijuana plants on the ground that the canine investigation was an unreasonable search. The trial court granted the motion, and the Florida Third District Court of Appeal reversed. On a petition for discretionary review, the Florida Supreme Court quashed the decision of the Third District Court of Appeal and approved the trial court's decision to suppress, holding (as relevant here) that the use of the trained narcotics dog to investigate Jardines' home was a Fourth Amendment search unsupported by probable cause, rendering invalid the warrant based upon information gathered in that search.

We granted certiorari, limited to the question of whether the officers' behavior was a search within the meaning of the Fourth Amendment.

II

The Fourth Amendment * * * establishes a simple baseline, one that for much of our history formed the exclusive basis for its protections: When "the Government obtains information by physically intruding" on persons, houses, papers, or effects, "a 'search' within the original meaning of the Fourth Amendment" has "undoubtedly occurred." *United States v. Jones,* 565 U.S. ___, ___, n. 3, 132 S.Ct. 945, 950–951, 181 L.Ed.2d 911 (2012). By reason of our decision in *Katz v. United States,* 389 U.S. 347, 88 S.Ct. 507, 19 L.Ed.2d 576 (1967), property rights "are not the sole measure of Fourth Amendment violations,"—but though

Katz may add to the baseline, it does not subtract anything from the Amendment's protections "when the Government *does* engage in [a] physical intrusion of a constitutionally protected area."

That principle renders this case a straightforward one. The officers were gathering information in an area belonging to Jardines and immediately surrounding his house—in the curtilage of the house, which we have held enjoys protection as part of the home itself. And they gathered that information by physically entering and occupying the area to engage in conduct not explicitly or implicitly permitted by the homeowner.

A

* * *

[W]hen it comes to the Fourth Amendment, the home is first among equals. At the Amendment's "very core" stands "the right of a man to retreat into his own home and there be free from unreasonable governmental intrusion." *Silverman v. United States,* 365 U.S. 505, 511, 81 S.Ct. 679, 5 L.Ed.2d 734 (1961). This right would be of little practical value if the State's agents could stand in a home's porch or side garden and trawl for evidence with impunity; the right to retreat would be significantly diminished if the police could enter a man's property to observe his repose from just outside the front window.

We therefore regard the area "immediately surrounding and associated with the home"—what our cases call the curtilage—as "part of the home itself for Fourth Amendment purposes." * * *

While the boundaries of the curtilage are generally "clearly marked," the "conception defining the curtilage" is at any rate familiar enough that it is "easily understood from our daily experience." Here there is no doubt that the officers entered it: The front porch is the classic exemplar of an area adjacent to the home and "to which the activity of home life extends."

B

Since the officers' investigation took place in a constitutionally protected area, we turn to the question of whether it was accomplished through an unlicensed physical intrusion. While law enforcement officers need not "shield their eyes" when passing by the home "on public thoroughfares," an officer's leave to gather information is sharply circumscribed when he steps off those thoroughfares and enters the Fourth Amendment's protected areas. In permitting, for example, visual observation of the home from "public navigable airspace," we were careful to note that it was done "in a physically nonintrusive manner." *Entick v. Carrington,* 2 Wils. K.B. 275, 95 Eng. Rep. 807 (K.B.1765), a case "undoubtedly familiar" to "every American statesman" at the time of the Founding, states the general rule clearly: "[O]ur law holds the property of every man so sacred, that no man can set his foot upon his neighbour's close without his leave." As it is undisputed that the detectives had all four of their feet and all four of their companion's firmly planted on the constitutionally protected extension of Jardines' home, the only question is whether he had given his leave (even implicitly) for them to do so. He had not.

"A license may be implied from the habits of the country," notwithstanding the "strict rule of the English common law as to entry upon a close." *McKee v. Gratz,* 260 U.S. 127, 136, 43 S.Ct. 16, 67 L.Ed. 167 (1922) (Holmes, J.). We have accordingly recognized that "the knocker on the front door is treated as an invitation or license to attempt an entry, justifying ingress to the home by solicitors, hawkers and peddlers of all kinds." *Breard v. Alexandria,* 341 U.S. 622, 626, 71 S.Ct. 920, 95 L.Ed. 1233 (1951). This implicit license typically permits the visitor to approach the home by the front path, knock promptly, wait briefly to be received, and then (absent invitation to linger longer) leave. Complying with the terms of that traditional invitation does not require fine-grained legal knowledge; it is generally managed without incident by the Nation's Girl Scouts and trick-or-treaters.[2] Thus, a police officer not armed with a warrant may approach a home and knock, precisely because that is "no more than any private citizen might do." *Kentucky v. King,* 563 U.S. ___, ___, 131 S.Ct. 1849, 1862, 179 L.Ed.2d 865 (2011).

But introducing a trained police dog to explore the area around the home in hopes of discovering incriminating evidence is something else. There is no customary invitation to do *that.* An invitation to engage in canine forensic investigation assuredly does not inhere in the very act of hanging a knocker.[3] To find a visitor knocking on the door is routine (even if sometimes unwelcome); to spot that same visitor exploring the front path with a metal detector, or marching his bloodhound into the garden before saying hello and asking permission, would inspire most of us to— well, call the police. The scope of a license—express or implied—is limited not only to a particular area but also to a specific purpose. Consent at a traffic stop to an officer's checking out an anonymous tip that there is a body in the trunk does not permit the officer to rummage through the

---

[2] With this much, the dissent seems to agree—it would inquire into " 'the appearance of things,' 'what is "typica[l]" for a visitor, what might cause "alarm" to a "resident of the premises," what is "expected" of "ordinary visitors," and what would be expected from a " 'reasonably respectful citizen.' " These are good questions. But their answers are incompatible with the dissent's outcome, which is presumably why the dissent does not even try to argue that it would be customary, usual, reasonable, respectful, ordinary, typical, nonalarming, etc., for a stranger to explore the curtilage of the home with trained drug dogs.

[3] The dissent insists that our argument must rest upon "the particular instrument that Detective Bartelt used to detect the odor of marijuana"—the dog. It is not the dog that is the problem, but the behavior that here involved use of the dog. We think a typical person would find it " 'a cause for great alarm' " (the kind of reaction the dissent quite rightly relies upon to justify its no-night-visits rule) to find a stranger snooping about his front porch *with or without* a dog. The dissent would let the police do whatever they want by way of gathering evidence so long as they stay on the base-path, to use a baseball analogy—so long as they "stick to the path that is typically used to approach a front door, such as a paved walkway." From that vantage point they can presumably peer into the house through binoculars with impunity. That is not the law, as even the State concedes.

trunk for narcotics. Here, the background social norms that invite a visitor to the front door do not invite him there to conduct a search.[4]

The State points to our decisions holding that the subjective intent of the officer is irrelevant. But those cases merely hold that a stop or search *that is objectively reasonable* is not vitiated by the fact that the officer's real reason for making the stop or search has nothing to do with the validating reason. Thus, the defendant will not be heard to complain that although he was speeding the officer's real reason for the stop was racial harassment. Here, however, the question before the court is precisely *whether* the officer's conduct was an objectively reasonable search. As we have described, that depends upon whether the officers had an implied license to enter the porch, which in turn depends upon the purpose for which they entered. Here, their behavior objectively reveals a purpose to conduct a search, which is not what anyone would think he had license to do.

III

The State argues that investigation by a forensic narcotics dog by definition cannot implicate any legitimate privacy interest. The State cites for authority our decisions in *United States v. Place,* 462 U.S. 696, 103 S.Ct. 2637, 77 L.Ed.2d 110 (1983), *United States v. Jacobsen,* 466 U.S. 109, 104 S.Ct. 1652, 80 L.Ed.2d 85 (1984), and *Illinois v. Caballes,* 543 U.S. 405, 125 S.Ct. 834, 160 L.Ed.2d 842 (2005), which held, respectively, that canine inspection of luggage in an airport, chemical testing of a substance that had fallen from a parcel in transit, and canine inspection of an automobile during a lawful traffic stop, do not violate the "reasonable expectation of privacy" described in *Katz.*

Just last Term, we considered an argument much like this. *Jones* held that tracking an automobile's whereabouts using a physically-mounted GPS receiver is a Fourth Amendment search. The Government argued that the *Katz* standard "show[ed] that no search occurred," as the defendant had "no 'reasonable expectation of privacy'" in his whereabouts on the public roads—a proposition with at least as much support in our case law as the one the State marshals here. But because the GPS receiver had been physically mounted on the defendant's automobile (thus intruding on his "effects"), we held that tracking the vehicle's movements was a search: a person's "Fourth Amendment rights do not rise or fall with the *Katz* formulation." The *Katz* reasonable-expectations test "has been *added to,* not *substituted for,*" the traditional property-based understanding of the Fourth Amendment, and so is

---

[4]   The dissent argues, citing *King,* that "gathering evidence—even damning evidence—is a lawful activity that falls within the scope of the license to approach." That is a false generalization. What *King* establishes is that it is not a Fourth Amendment search to approach the home in order to speak with the occupant, *because all are invited to do that.* The mere "purpose of discovering information," in the course of engaging in that permitted conduct does not cause it to violate the Fourth Amendment. But no one is impliedly invited to enter the protected premises of the home in order to do nothing but conduct a search.

unnecessary to consider when the government gains evidence by physically intruding on constitutionally protected areas.

Thus, we need not decide whether the officers' investigation of Jardines' home violated his expectation of privacy under *Katz*. One virtue of the Fourth Amendment's property-rights baseline is that it keeps easy cases easy. That the officers learned what they learned only by physically intruding on Jardines' property to gather evidence is enough to establish that a search occurred.

For a related reason we find irrelevant the State's argument (echoed by the dissent) that forensic dogs have been commonly used by police for centuries. This argument is apparently directed to our holding in *Kyllo v. United States,* 533 U.S. 27, 121 S.Ct. 2038, 150 L.Ed.2d 94 (2001), that surveillance of the home is a search where "the Government uses a device that is not in general public use" to "explore details of the home that would previously have been unknowable *without physical intrusion.*" (emphasis added). But the implication of that statement (*inclusio unius est exclusio alterius*) is that when the government uses a physical intrusion to explore details of the home (including its curtilage), the antiquity of the tools that they bring along is irrelevant.

3

The government's use of trained police dogs to investigate the home and its immediate surroundings is a "search" within the meaning of the Fourth Amendment. The judgment of the Supreme Court of Florida is therefore affirmed.

It is so ordered.

■ JUSTICE KAGAN, with whom JUSTICE GINSBURG and JUSTICE SOTOMAYOR join, concurring.

For me, a simple analogy clinches this case—and does so on privacy as well as property grounds. A stranger comes to the front door of your home carrying super-high-powered binoculars. He doesn't knock or say hello. Instead, he stands on the porch and uses the binoculars to peer through your windows, into your home's furthest corners. It doesn't take long (the binoculars are really very fine): In just a couple of minutes, his uncommon behavior allows him to learn details of your life you disclose to no one. Has your "visitor" trespassed on your property, exceeding the license you have granted to members of the public to, say, drop off the mail or distribute campaign flyers? Yes, he has. And has he also invaded your "reasonable expectation of privacy," by nosing into intimacies you sensibly thought protected from disclosure? *Katz v. United States,* 389 U.S. 347, 360, 88 S.Ct. 507, 19 L.Ed.2d 576 (1967) (Harlan, J., concurring). Yes, of course, he has done that too.

That case is this case in every way that matters. Here, police officers came to Joelis Jardines' door with a super-sensitive instrument, which they deployed to detect things inside that they could not perceive unassisted. The equipment they used was animal, not mineral. * * *

Detective Bartelt's dog was not your neighbor's pet, come to your porch on a leisurely stroll. * * * [D]rug-detection dogs are highly trained tools of law enforcement, geared to respond in distinctive ways to specific scents so as to convey clear and reliable information to their human partners. They are to the poodle down the street as high-powered binoculars are to a piece of plain glass. Like the binoculars, a drug-detection dog is a specialized device for discovering objects not in plain view (or plain smell). And as in the hypothetical above, that device was aimed here at a home—the most private and inviolate (or so we expect) of all the places and things the Fourth Amendment protects. Was this activity a trespass? Yes, as the Court holds today. Was it also an invasion of privacy? Yes, that as well.

The Court today treats this case under a property rubric; I write separately to note that I could just as happily have decided it by looking to Jardines' privacy interests. A decision along those lines would have looked . . . well, much like this one. It would have talked about " 'the right of a man to retreat into his own home and there be free from unreasonable governmental intrusion.' " It would have insisted on maintaining the "practical value" of that right by preventing police officers from standing in an adjacent space and "trawl[ing] for evidence with impunity." It would have explained that " 'privacy expectations are most heightened' " in the home and the surrounding area. And it would have determined that police officers invade those shared expectations when they use trained canine assistants to reveal within the confines of a home what they could not otherwise have found there.

It is not surprising that in a case involving a search of a home, property concepts and privacy concepts should so align. The law of property "naturally enough influence[s]" our "shared social expectations" of what places should be free from governmental incursions. And so the sentiment "my home is my own," while originating in property law, now also denotes a common understanding—extending even beyond that law's formal protections—about an especially private sphere. Jardines' home was his property; it was also his most intimate and familiar space. The analysis proceeding from each of those facts, as today's decision reveals, runs mostly along the same path.

* * *

With these further thoughts, suggesting that a focus on Jardines' privacy interests would make an "easy cas[e] easy" twice over, I join the Court's opinion in full.

■ JUSTICE ALITO, with whom THE CHIEF JUSTICE, JUSTICE KENNEDY, and JUSTICE BREYER join, dissenting.

The Court's decision in this important Fourth Amendment case is based on a putative rule of trespass law that is nowhere to be found in the annals of Anglo-American jurisprudence.

The law of trespass generally gives members of the public a license to use a walkway to approach the front door of a house and to remain there for a brief time. This license is not limited to persons who intend to speak to an occupant or who actually do so. (Mail carriers and persons delivering packages and flyers are examples of individuals who may lawfully approach a front door without intending to converse.) Nor is the license restricted to categories of visitors whom an occupant of the dwelling is likely to welcome; as the Court acknowledges, this license applies even to "solicitors, hawkers and peddlers of all kinds." (internal quotation marks omitted). And the license even extends to police officers who wish to gather evidence against an occupant (by asking potentially incriminating questions).

According to the Court, however, the police officer in this case, Detective Bartelt, committed a trespass because he was accompanied during his otherwise lawful visit to the front door of respondent's house by his dog, Franky. Where is the authority evidencing such a rule? Dogs have been domesticated for about 12,000 years; they were ubiquitous in both this country and Britain at the time of the adoption of the Fourth Amendment; their acute sense of smell has been used in law enforcement for centuries. Yet the Court has been unable to find a single case—from the United States or any other common-law nation—that supports the rule on which its decision is based. Thus, trespass law provides no support for the Court's holding today.

The Court's decision is also inconsistent with the reasonable-expectations-of-privacy test that the Court adopted in *Katz v. United States,* 389 U.S. 347, 88 S.Ct. 507, 19 L.Ed.2d 576 (1967). A reasonable person understands that odors emanating from a house may be detected from locations that are open to the public, and a reasonable person will not count on the strength of those odors remaining within the range that, while detectible by a dog, cannot be smelled by a human.

For these reasons, I would hold that no search within the meaning of the Fourth Amendment took place in this case, and I would reverse the decision below.

I

The opinion of the Court may leave a reader with the mistaken impression that Detective Bartelt and Franky remained on respondent's property for a prolonged period of time and conducted a far-flung exploration of the front yard. But that is not what happened.

Detective Bartelt and Franky approached the front door via the driveway and a paved path—the route that any visitor would customarily use—and Franky was on the kind of leash that any dog owner might employ. As Franky approached the door, he started to track an airborne odor. He held his head high and began "bracketing" the area (pacing back and forth) in order to determine the strongest source of the smell. Detective Bartelt knew "the minute [he] observed" this behavior that

Franky had detected drugs. Upon locating the odor's strongest source, Franky sat at the base of the front door, and at this point, Detective Bartelt and Franky immediately returned to their patrol car.

A critical fact that the Court omits is that, as respondent's counsel explained at oral argument, this entire process—walking down the driveway and front path to the front door, waiting for Franky to find the strongest source of the odor, and walking back to the car—took approximately a minute or two. Thus, the amount of time that Franky and the detective remained at the front porch was even less. The Court also fails to mention that, while Detective Bartelt apparently did not personally smell the odor of marijuana coming from the house, another officer who subsequently stood on the front porch, Detective Pedraja, did notice that smell and was able to identify it.

II

The Court concludes that the conduct in this case was a search because Detective Bartelt exceeded the boundaries of the license to approach the house that is recognized by the law of trespass, but the Court's interpretation of the scope of that license is unfounded.

A

It is said that members of the public may lawfully proceed along a walkway leading to the front door of a house because custom grants them a license to do so. *Breard v. Alexandria,* 341 U.S. 622, 626, 71 S.Ct. 920, 95 L.Ed. 1233 (1951). This rule encompasses categories of visitors whom most homeowners almost certainly wish to allow to approach their front doors—friends, relatives, mail carriers, persons making deliveries. But it also reaches categories of visitors who are less universally welcome— "solicitors," "hawkers," "peddlers," and the like. The law might attempt to draw fine lines between categories of welcome and unwelcome visitors, distinguishing, for example, between tolerable and intolerable door-to-door peddlers (Girl Scouts selling cookies versus adults selling aluminum siding) or between police officers on agreeable and disagreeable missions (gathering information about a bothersome neighbor versus asking potentially incriminating questions). But the law of trespass has not attempted such a difficult taxonomy. See *Desnick v. American Broadcasting Cos.,* 44 F.3d 1345, 1351 (C.A.7 1995) ("[C]onsent to an entry is often given legal effect even though the entrant has intentions that if known to the owner of the property would cause him for perfectly understandable and generally ethical or at least lawful reasons to revoke his consent").

Of course, this license has certain spatial and temporal limits. A visitor must stick to the path that is typically used to approach a front door, such as a paved walkway. A visitor cannot traipse through the garden, meander into the backyard, or take other circuitous detours that veer from the pathway that a visitor would customarily use.

Nor, as a general matter, may a visitor come to the front door in the middle of the night without an express invitation.

Similarly, a visitor may not linger at the front door for an extended period. The license is limited to the amount of time it would customarily take to approach the door, pause long enough to see if someone is home, and (if not expressly invited to stay longer), leave.

As I understand the law of trespass and the scope of the implied license, a visitor who adheres to these limitations is not necessarily required to ring the doorbell, knock on the door, or attempt to speak with an occupant. For example, mail carriers, persons making deliveries, and individuals distributing flyers may leave the items they are carrying and depart without making any attempt to converse. A pedestrian or motorist looking for a particular address may walk up to a front door in order to check a house number that is hard to see from the sidewalk or road. A neighbor who knows that the residents are away may approach the door to retrieve an accumulation of newspapers that might signal to a potential burglar that the house is unoccupied.

As the majority acknowledges, this implied license to approach the front door extends to the police. As we recognized in *Kentucky v. King,* 563 U.S. ___, 131 S.Ct. 1849, 179 L.Ed.2d 865 (2011), police officers do not engage in a search when they approach the front door of a residence and seek to engage in what is termed a "knock and talk," *i.e.,* knocking on the door and seeking to speak to an occupant for the purpose of gathering evidence. Even when the objective of a "knock and talk" is to obtain evidence that will lead to the homeowner's arrest and prosecution, the license to approach still applies. In other words, gathering evidence—even damning evidence—is a lawful activity that falls within the scope of the license to approach. And when officers walk up to the front door of a house, they are permitted to see, hear, and smell whatever can be detected from a lawful vantage point.

B

Detective Bartelt did not exceed the scope of the license to approach respondent's front door. He adhered to the customary path; he did not approach in the middle of the night; and he remained at the front door for only a very short period (less than a minute or two).

The Court concludes that Detective Bartelt went too far because he had the "*objectiv*[e] . . . *purpose* to conduct a search." (emphasis added). What this means, I take it, is that anyone aware of what Detective Bartelt did would infer that his subjective purpose was to gather evidence. But if this is the Court's point, then a standard "knock and talk" and most other police visits would likewise constitute searches. With the exception of visits to serve warrants or civil process, police almost always approach homes with a purpose of discovering information. That is certainly the objective of a "knock and talk." The Court offers no meaningful way of distinguishing the "objective purpose" of a "knock and talk" from the "objective purpose" of Detective Bartelt's conduct here.

The Court contends that a "knock and talk" is different because it involves talking, and "all are invited" to do that. But a police officer who approaches the front door of a house in accordance with the limitations already discussed may gather evidence by means other than talking. The officer may observe items in plain view and smell odors coming from the house. So the Court's "objective purpose" argument cannot stand.

What the Court must fall back on, then, is the particular instrument that Detective Bartelt used to detect the odor of marijuana, namely, his dog. But in the entire body of common-law decisions, the Court has not found a single case holding that a visitor to the front door of a home commits a trespass if the visitor is accompanied by a dog on a leash. On the contrary, the common law allowed even unleashed dogs to wander on private property without committing a trespass.

The Court responds that "[i]t is not the dog that is the problem, but the behavior that here involved use of the dog." But where is the support in the law of trespass for *this* proposition? Dogs' keen sense of smell has been used in law enforcement for centuries. * * * If bringing a tracking dog to the front door of a home constituted a trespass, one would expect at least one case to have arisen during the past 800 years. But the Court has found none.

For these reasons, the real law of trespass provides no support for the Court's holding today. While the Court claims that its reasoning has "ancient and durable roots," its trespass rule is really a newly struck counterfeit.

III

The concurring opinion attempts to provide an alternative ground for today's decision, namely, that Detective Bartelt's conduct violated respondent's reasonable expectations of privacy. But * * * I see no basis for concluding that the occupants of a dwelling have a reasonable expectation of privacy in odors that emanate from the dwelling and reach spots where members of the public may lawfully stand.

It is clear that the occupant of a house has no reasonable expectation of privacy with respect to odors that can be smelled by human beings who are standing in such places. And I would not draw a line between odors that can be smelled by humans and those that are detectible only by dogs.

Consider the situation from the point of view of the occupant of a building in which marijuana is grown or methamphetamine is manufactured. Would such an occupant reason as follows? "I know that odors may emanate from my building and that atmospheric conditions, such as the force and direction of the wind, may affect the strength of those odors when they reach a spot where members of the public may lawfully stand. I also know that some people have a much more acute sense of smell than others, and I have no idea who might be standing in one of the spots in question when the odors from my house reach that location. In addition, I know that odors coming from my building, when they reach these locations, may be strong enough to be detected by a dog. But I am confident that they will be so faint that they cannot be smelled by any human being." Such a finely tuned expectation would be entirely unrealistic, and I see no evidence that society is prepared to recognize it as reasonable.

* * *

IV

The conduct of the police officer in this case did not constitute a trespass and did not violate respondent's reasonable expectations of privacy. I would hold that this conduct was not a search, and I therefore respectfully dissent.

NOTE

If officers may approach a residence, must they do so via the front door? The issue was raised by Carroll v. Carman, ___ U.S. ___, 135 S. Ct. 348 (2014) (per curiam), in which two Pennsylvania police officers—Jeremy Carroll and Brian Roberts—were searching for one Zita believed to have stolen a car and two loaded handguns. A report indicated that Zita might have fled to the home of Andrew and Karen Carman. The officers arrived at the Carmans around 2:30 p.m. Further:

> The Carmans' house sat on a corner lot—the front of the house faced a main street while the left (as viewed from the front) faced a side street. The officers initially drove to the front of the house, but after discovering that parking was not available there, turned right onto the side street. As they did so, they saw several cars parked side-by-side in a gravel parking area on the left side of the Carmans' property. The officers parked in the "first available spot," at "the far rear of the property."
>
> The officers exited their patrol cars. As they looked toward the house, the officers saw a small structure (either a carport or a shed) with its door open and a light on. Thinking someone might be inside, Officer Carroll walked over, "poked [his] head" in, and said "Pennsylvania State Police." No one was there, however, so the officers continued walking toward the house. As they approached, they saw a sliding glass door that opened onto a ground-level deck. Carroll thought the sliding glass door "looked like a customary entryway," so he and Officer Roberts decided to knock on it.
>
> As the officers stepped onto the deck, a man came out of the house and "belligerent[ly] and aggressively approached" them. The officers identified themselves, explained they were looking for Michael Zita, and asked the man for his name. The man refused to answer. Instead, he turned away from the officers and appeared to reach for his waist. Carroll grabbed the man's right arm to make

sure he was not reaching for a weapon. The man twisted away from Carroll, lost his balance, and fell into the yard.

At that point, a woman came out of the house and asked what was happening. The officers again explained that they were looking for Zita. The woman then identified herself as Karen Carman, identified the man as her husband, Andrew Carman, and told the officers that Zita was not there. In response, the officers asked for permission to search the house for Zita. Karen Carman consented, and everyone went inside.

The officers searched the house, but did not find Zita. They then left. The Carmans were not charged with any crimes.

The Carmans sued Officer Carroll in Federal District Court under 42 U.S.C. § 1983, claiming that Carroll entered their property in violation of the Fourth Amendment when he went into their backyard and onto their deck without a warrant. A jury found for the Carmans. This was upheld on appeal by the Third Circuit, which reasoned that under clearly established Fourth Amendment law officers engaged in a "knock and talk" investigation must "begin their encounter at the front door, where they have an implied invitation to go."

The Supreme Court reversed, holding that the lower tribunals had erred in failing to accord Carroll qualified immunity:

> We do not decide today whether * * * a police officer may conduct a "knock and talk" at any entrance that is open to visitors rather than only the front door. "But whether or not the constitutional rule applied by the court below was correct, it was not 'beyond debate.'" The Third Circuit therefore erred when it held that Carroll was not entitled to qualified immunity.

___ U.S. at ___, 135 S.Ct. at 352.

2. DEFINITION AND REASONABLENESS OF ACTIVITY CONSTITUTING A "SEIZURE" OF PROPERTY

EDITORS' INTRODUCTION: SEIZURES OF ITEMS UNDER FOURTH AMENDMENT LAW

The Fourth Amendment protects against unreasonable "seizures" as well as "searches." The principal case that follows considered seizures of property. A person as well as an item may, of course, be seized. Seizures of persons raise quite different issues, and this topic is addressed in Chapter 4.

Definition of "Seizures." Whether police activity concerning a place or item constitutes a "seizure" turns not upon whether that activity intrudes upon privacy interests but rather whether it constitutes a meaningful interference with the suspect's possessory interests. United States v. Jacobsen, 466 U.S. 109, 113, 104 S.Ct. 1652, 1656 (1984). In United States v. Karo, 468 U.S. 705, 104 S.Ct. 3296 (1984), the defense urged that a seizure occurred when Karo took possession of a can of ether which, unbeknownst to him, contained a beeping device placed there by federal officers. Rejecting this, the Court explained:

> Although the can may have contained an unknown and unwanted foreign object, it cannot be said that anyone's possessory interest was interfered with in any meaningful way. At most, there was a technical trespass on the space occupied by the beeper.

468 U.S. at 712, 104 S.Ct. at 3302.

Items Subject to Seizure. Officers are clearly entitled—if other requirements are met—to seize items which they have sufficient reason to believe are seizable. Seizable items include stolen property and other "fruits" of criminal conduct, instrumentalities used in the commission of crime, or contraband, i.e., items—such as drugs—the possession of which is prohibited by law. But seizure of items of "mere evidence"—items which are of concern or value to public officers only because they constitute evidence of the commission of a crime or of someone's guilt of a crime—was at one time barred by the Fourth Amendment. Gouled v. United States, 255 U.S. 298, 311, 41 S.Ct. 261, 265 (1921). In Warden v. Hayden, 387 U.S. 294, 87 S.Ct. 1642 (1967), the Supreme Court abandoned this rule, holding that the Fourth Amendment did not absolutely bar seizure of mere evidence. No significant objective of the Amendment is served by the distinction, the Court noted, and citizens can be adequately protected from improper searches whether the object of those searches is to find and seize mere evidence or items subject to seizure under traditional doctrines.

The traditional list of items subject to seizure—contraband, instrumentalities and fruits of crime, and evidence—may be incomplete. Law enforcement officers may sometimes have authority to assume possession of items not coming within these categories. For example, an officer who arrests a suspect in or near the suspect's automobile may, under some circumstances, have authority to seize the automobile to protect the suspect's interest or to protect the officer from later claims that by his actions he subjected the automobile to increased risk of vandalism or other harm.

Need for Probable Cause. Does a seizure require probable cause to believe the item seized one to which the officers are entitled to possession, i.e., probable cause to believe that the item is contraband, an instrument or fruit of a crime or evidence? The plurality discussion in Coolidge v. New Hampshire, 403 U.S. 443, 91 S.Ct. 2022 (1971), considered at length in the principal case, suggested a "plain view" seizure requires it be "immediately apparent" to the officer that the item is subject to seizure. In Arizona v. Hicks, 480 U.S. 321, 107 S.Ct. 1149 (1987), the Court addressed specifically whether probable cause was necessary for the plain view seizure of an item which officers came upon during a warrantless but reasonable search of an apartment:

We now hold that probable cause is required. To say otherwise would cut the "plain view" doctrine loose from its theoretical and practical moorings. The theory of that doctrine consists of extending to nonpublic places such as the home * * * the police's longstanding authority to make warrantless seizures in public places of such objects as weapons and contraband. And the practical justification for that extension is the desirability of sparing police, whose viewing of the object in the course of a lawful search is as legitimate as it would have been in a public place, the inconvenience and the risk—to themselves or to preservation of the evidence—of going to obtain a warrant. Dispensing with the need for a warrant is worlds apart from permitting a lesser standard of *cause* for the seizure than a warrant would require, i.e., the standard of probable cause. No reason is apparent why an object should routinely be seizable on lesser grounds, during an unrelated search and seizure, than would have been needed to obtain a warrant for the same object if it had been known to be on the premises.

480 U.S. at 326–27, 107 S.Ct. at 1153.

Searches of Seized Items. If an item containing other items or perhaps information—a "container"—is "seized" under the Fourth Amendment and that seizure is "reasonable," a "search" of that seized item may not necessarily be reasonable.

In United States v. Chadwick, 433 U.S. 1, 97 S.Ct. 2476 (1977), officers observed two Amtrak rail passengers arrive in Boston, and suspected the large footlocker they brought contained contraband. A trained dog released near the footlocker signaled it contained a controlled substance. Chadwick met the two passengers and the footlocker was placed in the trunk of Chadwick's car, parked outside the rail station. While the trunk of the car was still open, officers arrested all three and seized the footlocker. The footlocker was taken to the federal building in Boston. An hour and a half after the arrests, the footlocker was opened and searched. It was locked with a padlock and a regular trunk lock; the evidence did not establish how the officers opened it. Marijuana was found inside. Assuming the officers constitutionally seized the footlocker, the Court nevertheless held their search of it unreasonable because they obtained no warrant:

> Once law enforcement authorities have reduced luggage or other personal property not immediately associated with the person of [an] arrestee to their exclusive control, and there is no longer any danger that the arrestee might gain access to the property to seize a weapon or destroy evidence, a search of that property is no longer an incident of the arrest.
>
> Here the search was conducted more than an hour after federal agents had gained exclusive control of the footlocker and long after [the arrestees] were securely in custody; the search

therefore cannot be viewed as incidental to the arrest or as justified by any other exigency. Even though on this record the issuance of a warrant by a judicial officer was reasonably predictable, a line must be drawn. In our view, where no exigency is shown to support the need for an immediate search, the Warrant Clause places the line at the point where the property to be searched comes under the exclusive dominion of police authority.

433 U.S. at 15, 97 S.Ct. at 2485–86.

Chadwick has given rise to significant difficulties, especially with regard to "containers" found in automobiles. These issues are considered in Chapters 4 and 5.

* * *

Fourth Amendment discussion, culminating in the principal case, has focused upon when, if ever, the Fourth Amendment requires judicial authorization for a seizure, in the form of a warrant or a specific provision in a warrant authorizing seizure of the property.

Horton v. California

Supreme Court of the United States, 1990.
496 U.S. 128, 110 S.Ct. 2301.

■ JUSTICE STEVENS delivered the opinion of the Court.

In this case we revisit an issue that was considered, but not conclusively resolved, in *Coolidge v. New Hampshire*, 403 U.S. 443, 91 S.Ct. 2022, 29 L.Ed.2d 564 (1971): Whether the warrantless seizure of evidence of crime in plain view is prohibited by the Fourth Amendment if the discovery of the evidence was not inadvertent. * * *

I

Petitioner was convicted of the armed robbery of Erwin Wallaker, the treasurer of the San Jose Coin Club. When Wallaker returned to his home after the Club's annual show, he entered his garage and was accosted by two masked men, one armed with a machine gun and the other with an electrical shocking device, sometimes referred to as a "stun gun." The two men shocked Wallaker, bound and handcuffed him, and robbed him of jewelry and cash. During the encounter sufficient conversation took place to enable Wallaker subsequently to identify petitioner's distinctive voice. His identification was partially corroborated by a witness who saw the robbers leaving the scene, and by evidence that petitioner had attended the coin show.

Sergeant LaRault, an experienced police officer, investigated the crime and determined that there was probable cause to search petitioner's home for the proceeds of the robbery and for the weapons used by the robbers. His affidavit for a search warrant referred to police reports that described the weapons as well as the proceeds, but the warrant issued by the Magistrate only authorized a search for the proceeds, including three specifically described rings.

Pursuant to the warrant, LaRault searched petitioner's residence, but he did not find the stolen property. During the course of the search, however, he discovered the weapons in plain view and seized them. Specifically, he seized an Uzi machine gun, a .38 caliber revolver, two stun guns, a handcuff key, a San Jose Coin Club advertising brochure, and a few items of clothing identified by the victim.[1] LaRault testified that while he was searching for the rings, he also was interested in finding other evidence connecting petitioner to the robbery. Thus, the seized evidence was not discovered "inadvertently."

The trial court refused to suppress the evidence found in petitioner's home and, after a jury trial, petitioner was found guilty and sentenced to prison. The California Court of Appeal affirmed. * * * The California Supreme Court denied petitioner's request for review.

* * *

II

* * *

The right to security in person and property protected by the Fourth Amendment may be invaded in quite different ways by searches and seizures. A search compromises the individual interest in privacy; a seizure deprives the individual of dominion over his or her person or property. The "plain view" doctrine is often considered an exception to the general rule that warrantless searches are presumptively unreasonable, but this characterization overlooks the important difference between searches and seizures.[5] If an article is already in plain view, neither its observation nor its seizure would involve any invasion of privacy. A seizure of the article, however, would obviously invade the owner's possessory interest. If "plain view" justifies an exception from an otherwise applicable warrant requirement, therefore, it must be an exception that is addressed to the concerns that are implicated by seizures rather than by searches.

The criteria that generally guide "plain view" seizures were set forth in *Coolidge v. New Hampshire*, 403 U.S. 443, 91 S.Ct. 2022, 29 L.Ed.2d 564 (1971). The Court held that the seizure of two automobiles parked in plain view on the defendant's driveway in the course of arresting the defendant violated the Fourth Amendment. Accordingly, particles of gun powder that had been subsequently found in vacuum sweepings from one of the cars could not be introduced in evidence against the defendant. The

---

[1] Although the officer viewed other handguns and rifles, he did not seize them because there was no probable cause to believe they were associated with criminal activity.

[5] "It is important to distinguish 'plain view,' as used in *Coolidge* to justify seizure of an object, from an officer's mere observation of an item left in plain view. Whereas the latter generally involves no Fourth Amendment search, the former generally does implicate the Amendment's limitations upon seizures of personal property." Texas v. Brown, 460 U.S. 730, 738 n. 4, 103 S.Ct. 1535, 1541 n. 4, 75 L.Ed.2d 502 (1983) (opinion of REHNQUIST, J.).

State endeavored to justify the seizure of the automobiles, and their subsequent search at the police station, on four different grounds, including the "plain view" doctrine. The scope of that doctrine as it had developed in earlier cases was fairly summarized in these three paragraphs from Justice Stewart's opinion:

> It is well established that under certain circumstances the police may seize evidence in plain view without a warrant. But it is important to keep in mind that, in the vast majority of cases, ANY evidence seized by the police will be in plain view, at least at the moment of seizure. The problem with the "plain view" doctrine has been to identify the circumstances in which plain view has legal significance rather than being simply the normal concomitant of any search, legal or illegal.

> An example of the applicability of the "plain view" doctrine is the situation in which the police have a warrant to search a given area for specified objects, and in the course of the search come across some other article of incriminating character. Where the initial intrusion that brings the police within plain view of such an article is supported, not by a warrant, but by one of the recognized exceptions to the warrant requirement, the seizure is also legitimate. Thus the police may inadvertently come across evidence while in "hot pursuit" of a fleeing suspect. And an object that comes into view during a search incident to arrest that is appropriately limited in scope under existing law may be seized without a warrant. Finally, the "plain view" doctrine has been applied where a police officer is not searching for evidence against the accused, but nonetheless inadvertently comes across an incriminating object.

> What the "plain view" cases have in common is that the police officer in each of them had a prior justification for an intrusion in the course of which he came inadvertently across a piece of evidence incriminating the accused. The doctrine serves to supplement the prior justification—whether it be a warrant for another object, hot pursuit, search incident to lawful arrest, or some other legitimate reason for being present unconnected with a search directed against the accused—and permits the warrantless seizure. Of course, the extension of the original justification is legitimate only where it is immediately apparent to the police that they have evidence before them; the "plain view" doctrine may not be used to extend a general exploratory search from one object to another until something incriminating at last emerges.

Justice Stewart then described the two limitations on the doctrine that he found implicit in its rationale: First, "that plain view ALONE is never enough to justify the warrantless seizure of evidence,"; and second, "that the discovery of evidence in plain view must be inadvertent."

Justice Stewart's analysis of the "plain view" doctrine did not command a majority and * * * the discussion is "not a binding precedent." * * *

III

Justice Stewart concluded that the inadvertence requirement was necessary to avoid a violation of the express constitutional requirement that a valid warrant must particularly describe the things to be seized. He explained:

> The rationale of the exception to the warrant requirement, as just stated, is that a plain-view seizure will not turn an initially valid (and therefore limited) search into a "general" one, while the inconvenience of procuring a warrant to cover an inadvertent discovery is great. But where the discovery is anticipated, where the police know in advance the location of the evidence and intend to seize it, the situation is altogether different. The requirement of a warrant to seize imposes no inconvenience whatever, or at least none which is constitutionally cognizable in a legal system that regards warrantless searches as "per se unreasonable" in the absence of "exigent circumstances."
>
> If the initial intrusion is bottomed upon a warrant that fails to mention a particular object, though the police know its location and intend to seize it, then there is a violation of the express constitutional requirement of "Warrants . . . particularly describing . . . [the] things to be seized."

We find two flaws in this reasoning. First, evenhanded law enforcement is best achieved by the application of objective standards of conduct, rather than standards that depend upon the subjective state of mind of the officer. The fact that an officer is interested in an item of evidence and fully expects to find it in the course of a search should not invalidate its seizure if the search is confined in area and duration by the terms of a warrant or a valid exception to the warrant requirement. If the officer has knowledge approaching certainty that the item will be found, we see no reason why he or she would deliberately omit a particular description of the item to be seized from the application for a search warrant. Specification of the additional item could only permit the officer to expand the scope of the search. On the other hand, if he or she has a valid warrant to search for one item and merely a suspicion concerning the second, whether or not it amounts to probable cause, we fail to see why that suspicion should immunize the second item from seizure if it is found during a lawful search for the first. * * *

Second, the suggestion that the inadvertence requirement is necessary to prevent the police from conducting general searches, or from converting specific warrants into general warrants, is not persuasive because that interest is already served by the requirements that no warrant issue unless it "particularly describ[es] the place to be searched and the persons or things to be seized," and that a warrantless search be circumscribed by the exigencies which justify its initiation. Scrupulous adherence to these requirements serves the interests in limiting the area and duration of the search that the inadvertence requirement inadequately protects. Once those commands have been satisfied and the officer has a lawful right of access, however, no additional Fourth Amendment interest is furthered by requiring that the discovery of evidence be inadvertent. If the scope of the search exceeds that permitted by the terms of a validly issued warrant or the character of the relevant exception from the warrant requirement, the subsequent seizure is unconstitutional without more. * * *

In this case, the scope of the search was not enlarged in the slightest by the omission of any reference to the weapons in the warrant. Indeed, if the three rings and other items named in the warrant had been found at the outset—or if petitioner had them in his possession and had responded to the warrant by producing them immediately—no search for weapons could have taken place. * * * Justice White's dissenting opinion in *Coolidge* is instructive:

> Police with a warrant for a rifle may search only places where rifles might be and must terminate the search once the rifle is found; the inadvertence rule will in no way reduce the number of places into which they may lawfully look.

As we have already suggested, by hypothesis the seizure of an object in plain view does not involve an intrusion on privacy.[11] If the interest in privacy has been invaded, the violation must have occurred before the object came into plain view and there is no need for an inadvertence limitation on seizures to condemn it. The prohibition against general searches and general warrants serves primarily as a protection against unjustified intrusions on privacy. But reliance on privacy concerns that support that prohibition is misplaced when the inquiry concerns the scope of an exception that merely authorizes an officer with a lawful right of access to an item to seize it without a warrant.

In this case the items seized from petitioner's home were discovered during a lawful search authorized by a valid warrant. When they were discovered, it was immediately apparent to the officer that they constituted incriminating evidence. He had probable cause, not only to obtain a warrant to search for the stolen property, but also to believe that the weapons and handguns had been used in the crime he was investigating. The search was authorized by the warrant, the seizure was authorized by the "plain view" doctrine. The judgment is affirmed.

---

[11] Even if the item is a container, its seizure does not compromise the interest in preserving the privacy of its contents because it may only be opened pursuant to either a search warrant, see * * * *United States v. Chadwick*, 433 U.S. 1, 97 S.Ct. 2476, 53 L.Ed.2d 538 (1977) * * * , or one of the well-delineated exceptions to the warrant requirement.

It is so ordered.

■ JUSTICE BRENNAN, with whom JUSTICE MARSHALL joins, dissenting.

* * *

The Fourth Amendment * * * protects two distinct interests. The prohibition against unreasonable searches and the requirement that a warrant "particularly describ[e] the place to be searched" protect an interest in privacy. The prohibition against unreasonable seizures and the requirement that a warrant "particularly describ[e] . . . the . . . things to be seized" protect a possessory interest in property. The Fourth Amendment, by its terms, declares the privacy and possessory interests to be equally important. * * *

The Amendment protects these equally important interests in precisely the same manner: by requiring a neutral and detached magistrate to evaluate, before the search or seizure, the government's showing of probable cause and its particular description of the place to be searched and the items to be seized. Accordingly, just as a warrantless search is per se unreasonable absent exigent circumstances, so too a seizure of personal property is "per se unreasonable within the meaning of the Fourth Amendment unless it is accomplished pursuant to a judicial warrant issued upon probable cause and particularly describing the items to be seized." * * *

The plain view doctrine is an exception to the general rule that a seizure of personal property must be authorized by a warrant. As Justice Stewart explained in *Coolidge,* we accept a warrantless seizure when an officer is lawfully in a location and inadvertently sees evidence of a crime because of "the inconvenience of procuring a warrant" to seize this newly discovered piece of evidence. But "where the discovery is anticipated, where the police know in advance the location of the evidence and intend to seize it," the argument that procuring a warrant would be "inconvenient" loses much, if not all, of its force. Barring an exigency, there is no reason why the police officers could not have obtained a warrant to seize this evidence before entering the premises. The rationale behind the inadvertent discovery requirement is simply that we will not excuse officers from the general requirement of a warrant to seize if the officers know the location of evidence, have probable cause to seize it, intend to seize it, and yet do not bother to obtain a warrant particularly describing that evidence. To do so would violate "the express constitutional requirement of 'Warrants . . . particularly describing . . . [the] things to be seized,' and would 'fly in the face of the basic rule that no amount of probable cause can justify a warrantless seizure.' "

* * *

The * * * majority explains that it can see no reason why an officer who "has knowledge approaching certainty" that an item will be found in a particular location "would deliberately omit a particular description of the item to be seized from the application for a search warrant." * * *

[T]here are[, however,] a number of instances in which a law enforcement officer might deliberately choose to omit certain items from a warrant application even though he has probable cause to seize them, knows they are on the premises, and intends to seize them when they are discovered in plain view. For example, the warrant application process can often be time-consuming, especially when the police attempt to seize a large number of items. An officer interested in conducting a search as soon as possible might decide to save time by listing only one or two hard-to-find items, such as the stolen rings in this case, confident that he will find in plain view all of the other evidence he is looking for before he discovers the listed items. Because rings could be located almost anywhere inside or outside a house, it is unlikely that a warrant to search for and seize the rings would restrict the scope of the search. An officer might rationally find the risk of immediately discovering the items listed in the warrant—thereby forcing him to conclude the search immediately—outweighed by the time saved in the application process.

* * *

* * * I respectfully dissent.

3.   APPLYING THE "STANDING" REQUIREMENT

As *Wong Sun* and the material in Subchapter B of Chapter 1 make clear, the Supreme Court has traditionally limited defendants to claims that evidence was obtained in violation of their own federal constitutional rights. Application of this "standing" requirement has presented the greatest difficulty in search and seizure cases. Once a court determines officers' activity constitutes a "search," a "seizure," or both, it is often faced with a further and sometimes difficult determination as to whose Fourth Amendment interests were infringed upon by the searches or seizures that occurred. These determinations are the subject of the principal case in this subsection.

Rakas v. Illinois

Supreme Court of the United States, 1978.
439 U.S. 128, 99 S.Ct. 421.

■ MR. JUSTICE REHNQUIST delivered the opinion of the Court.

Petitioners were convicted of armed robbery in the Circuit Court of Kankakee County, Ill., and their convictions were affirmed on appeal. At their trial, the prosecution offered into evidence a sawed-off rifle and rifle shells that had been seized by police during a search of an automobile in which petitioners had been passengers. Neither petitioner is the owner of the automobile and neither has ever asserted that he owned the rifle or shells seized. The Illinois Appellate Court held that petitioners lacked standing to object to the allegedly unlawful search and seizure and denied their motion to suppress the evidence. We granted certiorari * * * .

I.

Because we are not here concerned with the issue of probable cause, a brief description of the events leading to the search of the automobile will suffice. A police officer on a routine patrol received a radio call notifying him of a robbery of a clothing store in Bourbonnais, Ill., and describing the getaway car. Shortly thereafter, the officer spotted an automobile which he thought might be the getaway car. After following the car for some time and after the arrival of assistance, he and several other officers stopped the vehicle. The occupants of the automobile, petitioners and two female companions, were ordered out of the car and after the occupants had left the car, two officers searched the interior of the vehicle. They discovered a box of rifle shells in the glove compartment, which had been locked, and a sawed-off rifle under the front passenger seat. After discovering the rifle and the shells, the officer took petitioners to the station and placed them under arrest.

Before trial petitioners moved to suppress the rifle and shells seized from the car on the ground that the search violated the Fourth and Fourteenth Amendments. They conceded that they did not own the automobile and were simply passengers; the owner of the car had been the driver of the vehicle at the time of the search. Nor did they assert that they owned the rifle or the shells seized. The prosecutor challenged petitioners' standing to object to the lawfulness of the search of the car because neither the car, the shells nor the rifle belonged to them. The trial court agreed that petitioners lacked standing and denied the motion to suppress the evidence. In view of this holding, the court did not determine whether there was probable cause for the search and seizure. On appeal after petitioners' conviction, the Appellate Court of Illinois, Third Judicial District, affirmed the trial court's denial of petitioners' motion to suppress because it held that "without a proprietary or other similar interest in an automobile, a mere passenger therein lacks standing to challenge the legality of the search of the vehicle." * * * The Illinois Supreme Court denied petitioners leave to appeal.

II.

* * *

[The Court first rejected petitioners' argument that the traditional standing requirement should be relaxed or broadened. After adhering to its traditional position, the Court further commented, that "the type of standing requirement * * * reaffirmed today is more properly subsumed under substantive Fourth Amendment doctrine." This aspect of the decision is discussed in Subchapter B of Chapter 1. Editors.]

Analyzed in [proper] terms, the question is whether the challenged search or seizure violated the Fourth Amendment rights of a criminal defendant who seeks to exclude the evidence obtained during it. That inquiry in turn requires a determination of whether the disputed search and seizure has infringed an interest of the defendant which the Fourth

Amendment was designed to protect. We are under no illusion that by dispensing with the rubric of standing * * * we have rendered any simpler the determination of whether the proponent of a motion to suppress is entitled to contest the legality of a search and seizure. But by frankly recognizing that this aspect of the analysis belongs more properly under the heading of substantive Fourth Amendment doctrine than under the heading of standing, we think the decision of this issue will rest on sounder logical footing.

C.

Here petitioners, who were passengers occupying a car which they neither owned nor leased, seek to analogize their position to that of the defendant in *Jones v. United States*, 362 U.S. 257, 80 S.Ct. 725, 4 L.Ed.2d 697 (1960). In *Jones*, petitioner was present at the time of the search of an apartment which was owned by a friend. The friend had given Jones permission to use the apartment and a key to it, with which Jones had admitted himself on the day of the search. He had a suit and shirt at the apartment and had slept there "maybe a night," but his home was elsewhere. At the time of the search, Jones was the only occupant of the apartment because the lessee was away for a period of several days. Under these circumstances, this Court stated that while one wrongfully on the premises could not move to suppress evidence obtained as a result of searching them, "anyone legitimately on premises where a search occurs may challenge its legality." Petitioners argue that their occupancy of the automobile in question was comparable to that of Jones in the apartment and that they therefore have standing to contest the legality of the search—or as we have rephrased the inquiry, that they, like Jones, had their Fourth Amendment rights violated by the search.

We do not question the conclusion in *Jones* that the defendant in that case suffered a violation of his personal Fourth Amendment rights if the search in question was unlawful. Nonetheless, we believe that the phrase "legitimately on premises" coined in *Jones* creates too broad a gauge for measurement of Fourth Amendment rights. For example, applied literally, this statement would permit a casual visitor who has never seen, or been permitted to visit the basement of another's house to object to a search of the basement if the visitor happened to be in the kitchen of the house at the time of the search. Likewise, a casual visitor who walks into a house one minute before a search of the house commences and leaves one minute after the search ends would be able to contest the legality of the search. The first visitor would have absolutely no interest or legitimate expectation of privacy in the basement, the second would have none in the house, and it advances no purpose served by the Fourth Amendment to permit either of them to object to the lawfulness of the search.

We think that *Jones* on its facts merely stands for the unremarkable proposition that a person can have a legally sufficient interest in a place other than his own home so that the Fourth Amendment protects him from unreasonable governmental intrusion into that place. In defining the scope of that interest, we adhere to the view expressed in *Jones* and echoed in later cases that arcane distinctions developed in property and tort law between guests, licensees, invitees, and the like, ought not to control. But the *Jones* statement that a person need only be "legitimately on premises" in order to challenge the validity of the search of a dwelling place cannot be taken in its full sweep beyond the facts of that case.

* * *

Our BROTHER WHITE in dissent expresses the view that by rejecting the phrase "legitimately on [the] premises" as the appropriate measure of Fourth Amendment rights, we are abandoning a thoroughly workable, "bright line" test in favor of a less certain analysis of whether the facts of a particular case give rise to a legitimate expectation of privacy. If "legitimately on premises" were the successful litmus test of Fourth Amendment rights that he assumes it is, his approach would have at least the merit of easy application, whatever it lacked in fidelity to the history and purposes of the Fourth Amendment. But a reading of lower court cases that have applied the phrase "legitimately on premises," and of the dissent itself, reveals that this expression is not a shorthand summary for a bright line rule which somehow encapsulates the "core" of the Fourth Amendment's protections.

The dissent itself shows that the facile consistency it is striving for is illusory. The dissenters concede that "there comes a point when use of an area is shared with so many that one simply cannot reasonably expect seclusion." But surely the "point" referred to is not one demarcating a line which is black on one side and white on another; it is inevitably a point which separates one shade of gray from another. We are likewise told by the dissent that a person "legitimately on *private* premises * * * , though his privacy is *not absolute*, is entitled to expect that he is sharing it only with those persons and that governmental officials will intrude only with *consent* or by complying with the Fourth Amendment." (emphasis added). This single sentence describing the contours of the supposedly easily applied rule virtually abounds with unanswered questions: What are "private" premises? Indeed, what are the "premises?" It may be easy to describe the "premises" when one is confronted with a one-room apartment, but what of the case of a 10-room house, or of a house with an attached garage that is searched? Also, if one's privacy is not absolute, how is it bounded? If he risks governmental intrusion "with consent," who may give that consent?

Again, we are told by the dissent that the Fourth Amendment assures that "*some* expectations of privacy are justified and will be protected from official intrusion." (emphasis added). But we are not told which of many possible expectations of privacy are embraced within this sentence. And our dissenting Brethren concede that "perhaps the Constitution provides some degree less protection for the personal freedom from unreasonable governmental intrusion when one does not have a possessory interest in the invaded private place." But how much "less" protection is available when one does not have such a possessory interest?

* * *

D.

Judged by the foregoing analysis, petitioners' claims must fail. They asserted neither a property nor a possessory interest in the automobile, nor an interest in the property seized. And as we have previously indicated, the fact that they were "legitimately on [the] premises" in the sense that they were in the car with the permission of its owner is not determinative of whether they had a legitimate expectation of privacy in the particular areas of the automobile searched. It is unnecessary for us to decide here whether the same expectations of privacy are warranted in a car as would be justified in a dwelling place in analogous circumstances. We have on numerous occasions pointed out that cars are not to be treated identically with houses or apartments for Fourth Amendment purposes. But here petitioners' claim is one which would fail even in an analogous situation in a dwelling place since they made no showing that they had any legitimate expectation of privacy in the glove compartment or area under the seat of the car in which they were merely passengers. Like the trunk of an automobile, these are areas in which a passenger *qua* passenger simply would not normally have a legitimate expectation of privacy.

Jones v. United States, 362 U.S. 257, 80 S.Ct. 725, 4 L.Ed.2d 697 (1960), involved significantly different factual circumstances. Jones not only had permission to use the apartment of his friend, but had a key to the apartment with which he admitted himself on the day of the search and kept possessions in the apartment. Except with respect to his friend, Jones had complete dominion and control over the apartment and could exclude others from it. * * *

IV.

The Illinois courts were therefore correct in concluding that it was unnecessary to decide whether the search of the car might have violated the rights secured to someone else by the Fourth and Fourteenth Amendments to the United States Constitution. Since it did not violate any rights of these petitioners, their judgment of conviction is

Affirmed.

■ MR. JUSTICE WHITE, with whom MR. JUSTICE BRENNAN, MR. JUSTICE MARSHALL, and MR. JUSTICE STEVENS, join, dissenting.

* * * My Brethren in the majority assertedly do not deny that automobiles warrant at least some protection from official interference with privacy. Thus, the next step is to decide who is entitled, vis à vis the State, to enjoy that privacy. The answer to that question must be found by determining "whether petitioner had an interest in connection with the searched premises that gave rise to 'a reasonable expectation [on his part] of freedom from governmental intrusion' upon those premises."

[This does not only] supply the relevant inquiry, it also directs us to the proper answer. * * * *Jones* * * * held that one of those protected interests is created by legitimate presence on the searched premises, even absent any possessory interest. This makes unquestionable sense. We have concluded on numerous occasions that the entitlement to an expectation of privacy does not hinge on ownership * * * .

* * *

[O]ne consistent theme in our decisions under the Fourth Amendment has been, until now, that "the Amendment does not shield only those who have title to the searched premises." *Mancusi v. DeForte*, 392 U.S. 364, 367, 88 S.Ct. 2120, 2123, 20 L.Ed.2d 1154 (1968). Though there comes a point when use of an area is shared with so many that one simply cannot reasonably expect seclusion, short of that limit a person legitimately on private premises knows the others allowed there and, though his privacy is not absolute, is entitled to expect that he is sharing it only with those persons and that governmental officials will intrude only with consent or by complying with the Fourth Amendment.

It is true that the Court asserts that it is not limiting the Fourth Amendment bar against unreasonable searches to the protection of property rights, but in reality it is doing exactly that.[14] Petitioners were in a private place with the permission of the owner, but the Court states that that is not sufficient to establish entitlement to a legitimate expectation of privacy. But if that is not sufficient, what would be? * * * .[15] * * *

* * *

* * * If the owner of the car had not only invited petitioners to join her but had said to them, "I give you a temporary possessory interest in my vehicle so that you will share the right to privacy that the Supreme Court says that I own," then apparently the majority would reverse. But people seldom say such things, though they may mean their invitation to encompass them if only they had thought of the problem. If the nonowner

---

[14] The Court's reliance on property law concepts is additionally shown by its suggestion that visitors could "contest the lawfulness of the seizure of evidence or the search if their own property were seized during the search." What difference should that property interest make to constitutional protection against unreasonable searches, which is concerned with privacy? Contrary to the Court's suggestion, a legitimate passenger in a car expects to enjoy the privacy of the vehicle whether or not he happens to carry some item along for the ride. We have never before limited our concern for a person's privacy to those situations in which he is in possession of personal property. Even a person living in a barren room without possessions is entitled to expect that the police will not intrude without cause.

[15] Jones had permission to use the apartment, had slept in it one night, had a key, had left a suit and a shirt there, and was the only occupant at the time of the search. Petitioners here had permission to be in the car and were occupying it at the time of the search. Thus the only distinguishing fact is that Jones could exclude others from the apartment by using his friend's key. But petitioners and their friend the owner had excluded others by entering the automobile and shutting the doors. Petitioners did not need a key because the owner was present. * * *

were the spouse or child of the owner, would the Court recognize a sufficient interest? If so, would distant relatives somehow have more of an expectation of privacy than close friends? What if the nonowner were driving with the owner's permission? Would nonowning drivers have more of an expectation of privacy than mere passengers? What about a passenger in a taxicab? * * *

* * * The *Jones* rule is relatively easily applied by police and courts; the rule announced today will not provide law enforcement officials with a bright line between the protected and the unprotected. Only rarely will police know whether one private party has or has not been granted a sufficient possessory or other interest by another private party. Surely in this case the officers had no such knowledge. The Court's rule will ensnare defendants and police in needless litigation over factors that should not be determinative of Fourth Amendment rights.

More importantly, the ruling today undercuts the force of the exclusionary rule in the one area in which its use is most certainly justified—the deterrence of bad-faith violations of the Fourth Amendment. This decision invites police to engage in patently unreasonable searches every time an automobile contains more than one occupant. Should something be found, only the owner of the vehicle, or of the item, will have standing to seek suppression, and the evidence will presumably be usable against the other occupants. The danger of such bad faith is especially high in cases such as this one where the officers are only after the passengers and can usually infer accurately that the driver is the owner. The suppression remedy for those owners in whose vehicles something is found and who are charged with crime is small consolation for all those owners *and* occupants whose privacy will be needlessly invaded by officers following mistaken hunches not rising to the level of probable cause but operated on in the knowledge that someone in a crowded car will probably be unprotected if contraband or incriminating evidence happens to be found. After this decision, police will have little to lose by unreasonably searching vehicles occupied by more than one person.

* * *

NOTES

1.   **Privacy in Premises.** Whether a search of premises violates the privacy rights of persons on the premises is, as the Court noted in *Rakas*, potentially a different question than that resolved in *Rakas*. The premises issue was addressed in two post-*Rakas* decisions.

In Minnesota v. Olson, 495 U.S. 91, 110 S.Ct. 1684 (1990), Olson was arrested in a duplex unit used as a residence by Luanne and Julie Bergstrom. Olson, with permission of the Bergstroms, spent the previous night in the duplex (sleeping on t he floor) and had a change of clothes with him. At issue was whether Olson could contest the reasonableness of police entry of the duplex. The Supreme Court held that he could: "Olson's status as an overnight guest is alone enough to show that he had an expectation of privacy in the home that society is prepared to recognize as reasonable." Jones v. United States, distinguished in *Rakas,* was controlling, Justice White explained, despite the State's argument that Olson, unlike Jones, was never left alone in the unit and was never given a key to it.

> That the guest has a host who has ultimate control of the house is not inconsistent with the guest having a legitimate expectation of privacy. * * * [H]osts will more likely than not respect the privacy interests of their guests, who are entitled to a legitimate expectation of privacy despite the fact that they have no legal interest in the premises and do not have the legal authority to determine who may or may not enter the household.

495 U.S. at 99, 110 S.Ct. at 1689. Chief Justice Rehnquist and Justice Blackmun dissented without opinion.

Olson was developed in Minnesota v. Carter, 525 U.S. 83, 119 S.Ct. 469 (1998). The question was whether Carter and Johns had a privacy interest in an apartment located in Eagan, Minnesota, and leased by Kimberly Thompson. Carter and Johns lived in Chicago and came to the apartment for the sole purpose of packaging cocaine for resale. They had never been in the apartment before and were in it for about 2 and 1/2 hours. In return for the brief use of the apartment, Carter and Johns gave Thompson one-eighth of an ounce of the cocaine. At issue in the case was whether Carter and Johns could challenge the admissibility of certain evidence on the ground it was the result of an observation of the packaging process in the apartment that Carter and Johns contended was an unreasonable search. The Court held Carter and Johns had no protected privacy interest in the premises and thus could not challenge any search that might have been involved in the observation:

> The text of the Amendment suggests that its protections extend only to people in "their" houses. But we have held that in some circumstances a person may have a legitimate expectation of privacy in the house of someone else. In *Minnesota v. Olson*, 495 U.S. 91, 110 S.Ct. 1684, 109 L.Ed.2d 85 (1990), for example, we decided that an overnight guest in a house had the sort of expectation of privacy that the Fourth Amendment protects. * * *

> Respondents here were obviously not overnight guests, but were essentially present for a business transaction and were only in the home a matter of hours. There is no suggestion that they had a previous relationship with Thompson, or that there was any other purpose to their visit. Nor was there anything similar to the overnight guest relationship in *Olson* to suggest a degree of acceptance into the household. While the apartment was a dwelling place for Thompson, it was for these respondents simply a place to do business.

> Property used for commercial purposes is treated differently for Fourth Amendment purposes than residential property. "An expectation of privacy in commercial premises, however, is

different from, and indeed less than, a similar expectation in an individual's home." *New York v. Burger*, 482 U.S. 691, 700, 107 S.Ct. 2636, 96 L.Ed.2d 601 (1987). And while it was a "home" in which respondents were present, it was not their home. * * *

If we regard the overnight guest in Minnesota v. Olson as typifying those who may claim the protection of the Fourth Amendment in the home of another, and one merely "legitimately on the premises" as typifying those who may not do so, the present case is obviously somewhere in between. But the purely commercial nature of the transaction engaged in here, the relatively short period of time on the premises, and the lack of any previous connection between respondents and the householder, all lead us to conclude that respondents' situation is closer to that of one simply permitted on the premises. We therefore hold that any search which may have occurred did not violate their Fourth Amendment rights.

525 U.S. at 88–91, 119 S.Ct. at 470–74. Four members of the Court disagreed. They reasoned that "when a homeowner or lessor personally invites a guest into her home to share in a common endeavor, whether it be for conversation, to engage in leisure activities, or for business purposes licit or illicit, that guest should share his host's shelter against unreasonable searches and seizures." 525 U.S. at 106, 119 S.Ct. at 481–82 (Ginsburg, J., dissenting), 525 U.S. at 103, 119 S.Ct. at 480 (Breyer, J., concurring in the judgment) (agreeing with Justice Ginsburg that the respondents can claim Fourth Amendment protection but concluding further that the challenged observation did not violate that protection).

2. **Permission to Use a Place for Storage.** Suppose Rakas had testified he owned the rifle and shells and the owner of the automobile permitted him to use the car a repository for his property. Would he have established a protected privacy interest in at least that portion of the car the owner permitted him to use for storage of his property?

The issue was presented in Rawlings v. Kentucky, 448 U.S. 98, 100 S.Ct. 2556 (1980). Rawlings, the petitioner before the Supreme Court, Vannessa Cox and several others were detained by Bowling Green officers while other officers applied for a search warrant. One officer approached Cox and directed her to empty the contents of her purse onto a nearby coffee table. She complied. The contents of her purse included a jar containing 1,800 tablets of LSD and other controlled substances. She turned to Rawlings— standing next to her—and told him "to take what was his." Rawlings claimed ownership of the controlled substances. At his trial for possession of and trafficking in those substances, could he challenge the officer's search of Cox's purse? The Court described the testimony explaining the situation as follows:

Petitioner testified that he had flown into Bowling Green about a week before his arrest to look for a job and perhaps to attend the local university. He brought with him at that time the drugs later found in Cox's purse. Initially, petitioner stayed in the house where the arrest took place as the guest of Michael Swank, who shared the house with Marquess and Saddler. While at a party at that house, he met Cox and spent at least two nights of the next week on a couch at Cox's house.

On the morning of petitioner's arrest, Cox had dropped him off at Swank's house where he waited for her to return from class. At that time, he was carrying the drugs in a green bank bag. When Cox returned to the house to meet him, petitioner dumped the contents of the bank bag into Cox's purse. Although there is dispute over the discussion that took place, petitioner testified that he "asked her if she would carry this for me, and she said, 'yes'. . . ." Petitioner then left the room to use the bathroom and, by the time he returned, discovered that the police had arrived * * * .

During Rawlings' testimony, the following exchange took place:

Q: Did you feel that Vanessa Cox's purse would be free from the intrusion of the officers as you sat there [waiting for the warrant?] When you put the pills in her purse, did you feel that they would be free from governmental intrusion?

A: No, sir.

The state court, emphasizing Rawlings' admission he did not believe Cox's purse would be free from governmental intrusion, held Rawlings failed to show that the search of the purse violated his reasonable expectation of privacy.

The Supreme Court affirmed. It explained:

We believe that the record in this case supports [the state court's] conclusion. Petitioner, of course, bears the burden of proving * * * that he had a legitimate expectation of privacy in [the] purse. At the time petitioner dumped thousands of dollars worth of illegal drugs into Cox's purse, he had known her for only a few days. According to Cox's uncontested testimony, petitioner had never sought or received access to her purse prior to that sudden bailment. Nor did petitioner have any right to exclude other persons from access to Cox's purse. In fact, Cox testified that Bob Stallons, a longtime acquaintance and frequent companion of Cox's, had free access to her purse and on the very morning of the arrest had rummaged through its contents in search of a hairbrush. Moreover, even assuming that petitioner's version of the bailment is correct and that Cox did consent to the transfer of possession, the precipitous nature of the transaction hardly supports a reasonable inference that petitioner took normal precautions to maintain his privacy. * * * [T]he record also contains a frank admission by petitioner that he had no subjective expectation that Cox's purse would remain free from governmental intrusion * * * .

Petitioner contends nevertheless that, because he claimed ownership of the drugs in Cox's purse, he should be entitled to challenge the search regardless of his expectation of privacy. We disagree. While petitioner's ownership of the drugs is undoubtedly one fact to be considered in this case, *Rakas* emphatically rejected the notion that "arcane" concepts of property law ought to control the ability to claim the protections of the Fourth Amendment. * * *

In sum, we find no reason to overturn the lower court's conclusion that petitioner had no legitimate expectation of privacy in Cox's purse at the time of the search.

448 U.S. at 104–06, 100 S.Ct. at 2561–62.

3.   **Standing to Challenge a "Stop."** Could Rakas have challenged the *stop* made by the officers? Almost certainly he could have under Brendlin v. California, 551 U.S. 249, 127 S.Ct. 2400 (2007). *Brendlin* pointed out that—as is developed in Chapter 4—whether a passenger in an automobile that is pulled over by a police officer is seized for Fourth Amendment purposes depends on whether a reasonable person in the passenger's position would feel free to decline the officer's requests or otherwise terminate the encounter with the officer. Under this standard, Brendlin—a front seat passenger in a car driven by another—was seized when an officer signaled the driver to pull over:

A traffic stop necessarily curtails the travel a passenger has chosen just as much as it halts the driver, diverting both from the stream of traffic to the side of the road, and the police activity that normally amounts to intrusion on "privacy and personal security" does not normally (and did not here) distinguish between passenger and driver. An officer who orders one particular car to pull over acts with an implicit claim of right based on fault of some sort, and a sensible person would not expect a police officer to allow people to come and go freely from the physical focal point of an investigation into faulty behavior or wrongdoing.

551 U.S. at 257, 127 S.Ct. at 2407.

CHAPTER 3

ISSUANCE AND EXECUTION OF ARREST AND SEARCH WARRANTS

Analysis

Searches must, as a general Fourth Amendment rule, be conducted pursuant to search warrants issued and executed in compliance with the amendment's requirements. Seizure of persons, as is developed in Chapter 4, sometimes require the authority of an arrest warrant. This chapter addresses issues raised when law enforcement officials act pursuant to these warrants.

A. WARRANTS GENERALLY

EDITORS' NOTE: WARRANTS, THEIR USE AND BASIC FOURTH AMENDMENT REQUIREMENTS

A warrant is a court order authorizing or commanding a law enforcement officer to arrest an identified person or search a specified place for and to seize specific items, or for both arrest and search. It also typically commands the officer executing the warrant to bring the person or items seized to the issuing magistrate. For obvious reasons, a judge, or sometimes a clerk, issues a warrant *ex parte*, that is, without notice to the person whose arrest is sought or whose property will be searched. The warrant is issued upon presentation of information believed justifying the arrest or search. When an arrest warrant is sought, that information is presented in a document usually called a complaint. When a search warrant is desired, the document of application is ordinarily called simply an affidavit. The warrant may be executed by any law enforcement officer in the jurisdiction of the issuing judge; the executing officers are not necessarily the same persons supplying the information upon which issuance was based.

Warrants play an important role in the theory of Fourth Amendment law. The Fourth Amendment itself concludes with the admonition that "no Warrants shall issue, but upon probable cause supported by Oath or affirmation, and particularly describing the place to be searched, and the persons or things to be seized." The Supreme Court has made clear that Fourth Amendment law should encourage law enforcement officers to use arrest and search warrants. Use of warrants is preferred because the warrant process interposes a decision by an impartial official—called a magistrate when performing warrant issuance functions—between the desires of the police to apprehend violators and citizens' privacy and liberty. Whether grounds exist for an arrest or search—whether probable cause exists—is determined by a person with no vested interest in finding that such grounds do exist. This is preferable to litigating the matters in response to a defendant's motion to suppress evidence because the warrant process can prevent unreasonable searches and arrests rather than respond to an after-the-fact demonstration that an unreasonable search or arrest occurred.

The warrant process regulates but does not bar those police actions to which it applies. This point was made by Justice Jackson in language that has been repeated numerous times in Supreme Court opinions:

> The point of the Fourth Amendment, which often is not grasped by zealous officers, is not that it denies law enforcement the support of the usual inferences which reasonable men draw from evidence. Its protection consists in requiring that those inferences be drawn by a neutral and detached magistrate instead of being judged by the officer engaged in the often competitive enterprise of ferreting out crime.

Johnson v. United States, 333 U.S. 10, 13–14, 68 S.Ct. 367, 369 (1948).

Warrants involve the judiciary in the investigative process before certain action is taken by law enforcement. This should often prevent violation of the Fourth Amendment right to be free from unreasonable searches and seizures, which is obviously preferable to efforts after-the-fact to remedy violations that have taken place. Furthermore, use of the warrant process to prevent improper law enforcement actions avoids the difficult task of litigating after-the-fact whether a violation occurred and of then selecting an appropriate remedy if a violation is found. Finally, when an arrest or search warrant has been issued, it gives specific instructions to law enforcement officers as to what they may and may not do in execution of the warrant. It also subjects further investigative effort to supervision of the judiciary by requiring a report of action taken under the warrant in the form of a return (and inventory of items seized) on a search warrant or, with respect to an arrest warrant, the presentation of the arrestee before the court.

In fact, arrest warrants are far less significant than search warrants. This is in part because Fourth Amendment law requires an arrest warrant be used only in very limited situations; the limited Fourth Amendment need for an arrest warrant is addressed in Chapter 4. Fourth Amendment theory generally requires that an arrest warrant be issued and drafted under the same rules applicable to search warrants. Because an arrest warrant is seldom needed, however, courts only rarely reach the validity of arrest warrants.

Use of Search Warrants in Actual Practice

The extent to which the warrant process actually functions in the manner intended by Fourth Amendment theory has been the subject of much speculation. An extensive empirical study of search warrant practices was, however, conducted by the National Center for State Courts. The results are reported in Van Duizend, Sutton and Cater, The Search Warrant Process: Preconceptions, Perceptions, and Practices (National Center for State Courts, undated). Probably the most important part of the study consisted of examining 844 search warrant cases and resulting prosecutions in seven different cities. In addition, interviews with police, judges, prosecutors and defense lawyers were conducted in these seven cities and direct observations of the warrant issuing process were undertaken in one location.

The study confirmed that officers seek search warrants in relatively few investigations and that they conduct the vast majority of searches without warrants. In regard to search warrants issued, an average (or "mean") of 38% involved drug offenses and 29% concerned property crimes. But an average of 21% were used in investigations of violent offenses. An average of 40% of the warrants were issued in part upon the basis of information received from a confidential informant—that is, an unidentified informant.

Many of the judges issuing warrants perceived themselves as performing a role independent of law enforcement, but a few saw their role as "assisting the police." Often, officers were able, by "judge shopping," to avoid submitting a request for a warrant to a judge known as particularly demanding. Because of difficulty in locating rejected applications, the study could not address how often warrant applications were rejected. But the authors suggested the rate of "outright rejection" was probably "extremely low." On the other hand, warrant applications were often reviewed and screened by a superior police official or a prosecutor. While this review apparently led to few "screening outs," the process sometimes resulted in the officer being requested to add further information to the application. Similarly, judicial officers who did not reject applications with some frequency required additional information from applying officers. The judge's review was seldom lengthy. Of the warrant proceedings directly observed, 65% lasted 2.5 minutes or less. Only 11% lasted longer than five minutes.

In all of the cities studied, searches conducted pursuant to those warrants actually served resulted in the discovery of something which the officers thought worth seizing in at least 90% of the cases. In an average of over one third of the cases, officers seized items not specifically identified in the warrant.

Motions to suppress evidence were filed in a significant number of the prosecutions arising out of the searches. But they were seldom granted. Of 347 warrant-related prosecutions studied, motions to suppress evidence were granted in only 17. In at least 12 of these 17, convictions were nevertheless obtained.

Interviewed police officers often complained of the delay involved in applying for and getting a search warrant and of the resulting loss of "good cases." But the study found little relationship between the delay and the actual loss of cases.

In regard to "bottom lines," the study concluded the search warrant requirement has several beneficial effects. First, it requires officers to "at least contemplate" the requirement of probable cause before a search, and this reflection induces a higher standard of care than they would otherwise use. Second, it produces "a multi-layered review that reduces the likelihood that a search will occur in the absence of probable cause." Finally, it provides a clear and tangible record permitting a more objective later evaluation of the search. On the other hand, the study concluded "it was clear in many cases that the review process was largely perfunctory," and that there was "infrequent but significant" evidence of efforts undermining "and sometimes entirely defeat[ing]" the integrity of the review process. But "the most striking and significant—and perhaps the most troubling—discovery," the report concluded, was the infrequency with which the search warrant process was invoked. It is perceived as "burdensome, time-consuming, intimidating, frustrating, and confusing." Many easier methods of obtaining incriminating evidence or of developing a case against a suspect exist. "It is not surprising * * * ," the report concluded, "that many officers tend to regard the warrant option as a last resort." Id., at 148–49.

Does the study suggest reason to rethink the central role of warrants in the theory of Fourth Amendment law? Or, to the extent that there are deficiencies in warrant practice, should efforts be focused upon making practice more closely correspond with theory?

The Foundation Requirement—A Neutral and Detached Magistrate

As a basic foundation requirement for an effective search or arrest warrant, the Supreme Court has mandated the issuing person be an individual sufficiently likely to perform the tasks the Fourth Amendment requires—a critical and independent evaluation of the sufficiently of the information offered to justify the warrant

Generally, courts assume the person issuing a warrant must be a "judicial officer" or a "magistrate." In Shadwick v. Tampa, 407 U.S. 345, 92 S.Ct. 2119 (1972), however, the Court noted that the constitutional validity of a warrant "does not turn on the labeling of the issuing party." It explained:

> [A]n issuing magistrate must meet two tests. He must be neutral and detached, and he must be capable of determining

whether probable cause exists for the requested arrest or search.

407 U.S. at 350, 92 S.Ct. at 2123. In *Shadwick* itself, the Court held misdemeanor arrest warrants for violations of a city ordinance could be issued by clerks of a municipal court, rather than by the judge of the court. No showing had been made, it emphasized, that these clerks were affiliated with prosecutors or police or that they were partial in any sense. Nor had any demonstration been made that the clerks were incapable of determining probable cause. It was not considering, the Court stressed, whether "someone completely outside the sphere of the judicial branch" could issue warrants. Nor did *Shadwick* address whether court clerks could issue arrest warrants for more serious offenses or search warrants.

Where those issuing warrants were subject to some institutional risk of bias in favor of those applying for warrants, the Court held the resulting warrants unreasonable. An attorney general actively involved in an investigation, then, could not issue a search warrant for that investigation. Coolidge v. New Hampshire, 403 U.S. 443, 450, 91 S.Ct. 2022, 2029 (1971). A justice of the peace paid $5.00 for each search warrant issued but nothing for a search warrant application denied was held to have a direct, personal, and substantial pecuniary interest favoring the issuance of warrants. Consequently, a search under a warrant issued by such a judicial officer was unreasonable. Connally v. Georgia, 429 U.S. 245, 97 S.Ct. 546 (1977).

Further, the conduct of a judicial officer in the specific case may show the officer lacked the Fourth Amendment capacity to issue an effective warrant. Thus in In Lo-Ji Sales, Inc. v. New York, 442 U.S. 319, 99 S.Ct. 2319 (1979), upon a showing two obscene films had been purchased by a police officer at a bookstore, a Town Justice issued a search warrant for other copies of the films. In addition, the warrant authorized the officers to seize the "following" items "that the Court independently [on examination] has determined to be" obscene. No items were listed. But the Justice accompanied the officers to the bookstore and there examined numerous items. Those he found obscene he included in the warrant. The Court held that this violated the Fourth Amendment:

> The Town Justice did not manifest that neutrality and detachment demanded of a judicial officer when presented with a warrant application for a search and seizure. We need not question the subjective belief of the Town Justice in the propriety of his actions, but the objective facts of record manifest an erosion of whatever neutral and detached posture existed at the outset. He allowed himself to become a member, if not the leader, of the search party which was essentially a police operation.

442 U.S. at 326–27, 99 S.Ct. at 2324. It continued:

> We do not suggest, of course, that a "neutral and detached magistrate" loses his character as such merely because he leaves his regular office in order to make himself readily available to law enforcement officers who may wish to seek the issuance of warrants by him. * * * But * * * [in] this case * * * the Town Justice undertook not merely to issue a warrant, but to participate with the police and prosecutors in its execution.

442 U.S. at 328 n. 6, 99 S.Ct. 2325 n. 6.

Need for a "Local" Magistrate

Traditionally, a judicial officer is sometimes authorized to issue warrants permitting law enforcement action only in the judge's jurisdiction. For example, prior to 2001 Rule 41(a) of the Federal Rules of Criminal Procedure authorized a federal magistrate judge to issue a warrant "for a search of property or for a person within the [magistrate judge's federal] district." A warrant could issue for law enforcement action beyond the judge's district "if the property or person is within the district when the warrant is sought but might move outside the district before the warrant is executed." Rule 41 now, as a general rule, provides that "a magistrate judge with authority in the district * * * has authority to issue a warrant to search for and seize a person or property located within the district * * * ." Fed.R.Crim.P. 41(b)(1).

The Uniting and Strengthening America by Providing Appropriate Tools Required to Intercept and Obstruct Terrorism (USA PATRIOT) Act of 2001, Public Law 107–56, added what is now Rule 41(b)(3)'s provision that:

> a magistrate judge—in an investigation of domestic terrorism or international terrorism—with authority in any district in which activities related to the terrorism may have occurred has authority to issue a warrant for a person or property within or outside that district * * * .

* * *

This chapter addresses separately several major aspects of Fourth Amendment "warrant law." First, it considers the requirement that the warrant be issued on a showing of probable cause and several related issues. Second, it addresses limitations on the manner of gaining entry to execute the warrant and some related limits on execution of warrants. Finally, it turns to the terms of the warrant and their role in the warrant's execution.

Sample Search Warrant

Examination of a sample warrant may make clearer the issues raised by search and arrest warrants. The next three pages contain the basic documents related to the search at issue in Hudson v. Michigan 547

U.S. 586, 126 S.Ct. 2159 (2006), reprinted in Subchapter C of this chapter. First is the affidavit—the document requesting the search warrant and setting out the facts on which the applicant based that request. The second is the search warrant itself. Third is the return made by the officers who executed the warrant to the magistrate who issued it, containing an inventory of items seized.

AFFIDAVIT

State of Michigan   **Search Warrant And Affidavit**
      SS

    On Aug 26, 1998 this affiant, met with SOI #1633 to formulate plans to make a controlled purchase from the location of 4469 W. Jeffries. The affiant searched the SOI for money, narcotics, and weapons, none were found. The affiant issued the SOI an amount of Secret Service Funds with instructions to attempt a purchase from this location. The SOI was observed to go directly to the location of **4469 W. Jeffries** walk to the front door of the location, stay a short amount of time and then return directly to the affiant. The SOI turned over to the affiant an amount of **Cocaine** and stated she/he had purchased it from the above described seller, inside the previously mentioned location. The SOI was again searched for money, narcotics, and weapons, with negative results and released by this affiant.

    On Aug 26, 1998 the affiant conveyed this same **Cocaine** to Police Headquarters where PO. Javier Johnson conducted an analysis and found it to test positive for the presence of Cocaine. The affiant then sealed the Cocaine in LSF # 440231 and placed it the Narcotic Division safe.

    Wherefore the affiant has probable cause to believe the above listed items and the above described seller will be found at this location on **W. Jeffries** and seeks to remove same. Affiant also believes from past experiences, during the execution of numerous raids in the City of Detroit that illegal firearms will be found on the premises to protect the seller(s) and to safeguard the narcotic enterprise.

_____
             Affiant

Subscribed, sworn to, and approved, before me and issued under my hand this 27th day of Aug, 1998.

_____   _____
Assistant Prosecuting Attorney   Judge or Magistrate of 36th District
P#_____   **Wayne County State of Michigan**
Page 2 of 2

SEARCH WARRANT

- **STATE OF MICHIGAN**   **1027 SEARCH WARRANT AND AFFIDAVIT**
- **COUNTY OF WAYNE SS**

TO THE SHERIFF OR ANY PEACE OFFICER OF SAID COUNTY: P.O. C. Muhammad

Affiant having subscribed and sworn to affidavit for search warrant, am satisfied that probable cause exists.

Therefore, in the name of the people of the State of Michigan, I command that you search the following place: The entire premises and curtilage of 4469 W. Jeffries. 4469 W. Jeffries is described as single family, 2 story Brn abestos dwelling located on the W. side of the Jeffries between Breckenridge and a dead end of street. 4469 W. Jeffries is located in the City of Detroit, County of Wayne, and the State of Michigan. The search is to include the seller: B/M early 40's 5'8 165lbs. Light - Medium Complexion

Also to seize, secure, tabulate, and make a return according to the law, the following property and all things: All suspected controlled substance; all monies , records used in connection with the manufacture, delivery or sale of controlled substance, all firearms used in connection with the above described activities, all evidence of ownership, occupancy, possession or control of premises.

The following facts are sworn to by the affiant in support of the issuance of this warrant:

The affiant is a sworn member of the Detroit Police Narcotics Division assigned to the investigation of violations of the Controlled Substance Act. Affiant is working in conjunction with credible and reliable SOI #1633 who has been utilized over 10 separate occasions. resulting in the arrest of over 5 individuals for narcotic related offenses, and convictions of over 3 persons in court.

_____
                       Affiant

Subscribed, sworn to, and approved, before me and issued under my hand this of 27th day of August, 1998

_____   _____

Assistant Prosecuting Attorney   **Judge/Magistrate of 36th**
P#_____   **Court, Wayne County State of**
                                         Michigan

page 1 of 2

RETURN

STATE OF MICHIGAN
COUNTY OF WAYNE

RETURN TO SEARCH WARRANT

I hereby certify and return that by virtue of the within Search Warrant to me directed, I have searched for the goods and chattels therein named, at the place therein described. *

(* Strike either (1) or (2), whichever is inapplicable.)

(1) and that I have such goods and chattels before the Court, described as follows:

1- PLASTIC Baggie Cont 5 2/L oz crack cocaine
1- PLASTIC Baggie Cont 23 2/L Rocks oz crack Cocaine
1- PLASTIC Baggie Cont 2 smaller Plastic Baggies Each Cont 24 2/L Rocks oz crack Cocaine
$ 225.00 Narcotic Proceeds
$ 20.00 Narcotic Proceeds
1- S+W 38 Special 6 Shot 3½" Barrel Serial # 65744 loaded w/ 3 live Rds

1- unknown Name 12 gA Shotgun Serial # altered

Por letter address To Becker Hudson Jr From 36th Dist Ct
Narcotic Paraphernalia Empty Ziplocks + 1-ceramic crack Pipe

1- 3½" glass Stem crack Pipe

~~(2) and that I have been unable to find such goods and chattels.~~

_____
Municipal Police Officer
Sheriff   Deputy Sheriff

DATED AT: 1535
this 27 day of August 1998
ADDRESS: 4469 Jeffries

B. THE SHOWING OF PROBABLE CAUSE

The essence of the warrant process is the judicial scrutiny of the information submitted as justification for the warrant's issuance. Effective scrutiny requires, of course, that the information presented be sufficient and adequately detailed. The information required to support a warrant's issuance is considered in the first subchapter. A defendant's later ability to challenge the accuracy of this information is addressed in the next subchapter.

1. THE INITIAL SHOWING BEFORE THE MAGISTRATE

EDITORS' INTRODUCTION: THE "PROBABLE CAUSE" SHOWING

The specific terms of the Fourth Amendment prohibit the issuance of a warrant except "upon probable cause supported by Oath or affirmation." A warrant application often is accompanied by a written and sworn affidavit setting out the facts which the applying officers believe constitute the required probable cause. In many cases, then, the issuing magistrate's function consists largely of reviewing the affidavit to determine if the alleged information rises to this level.

There is probably no federal constitutional requirement that all or even any of the information submitted to the magistrate be written. Statutes and court rules sometimes authorize a warrant's issuance in whole or in part upon oral information. Rule 41(d) of the Federal Rules of Criminal Procedure requires, as a general rule, a search warrant issue on the basis of a sworn affidavit. But Rule 41(d)(2)(B) further provides: "The judge may wholly or partially dispense with a written affidavit and base a warrant on sworn testimony if doing so is reasonable under the circumstances." Under Rule 41(d)(2)(A), if an affidavit is submitted, "the judge may require the affiant to appear personally and may examine under oath the affiant and any witness the affiant produces."

Generally, however, magistrates to whom affidavits are submitted do not demand further facts and act on the basis of the written affidavits. Therefore, the magistrate's task is usually one of reviewing the affidavit "on its face"—probably assuming the correctness of the facts alleged—to determine if those facts establish probable cause. Insofar as this is the process, no critical consideration of whether the facts alleged are correct occurs until and if the defendant later challenges the accuracy of the "face" of the affidavit. Defendants' ability to make such challenges is considered later in this chapter.

Some jurisdictions provide for warrants to issue by an electronic process. Federal Rule 41(d)(3), for example, provides that "[i]n accordance with Rule 4.1, a magistrate judge may issue a warrant based on information communicated by telephone or other reliable electronic means." Under Rule 4.1, where application for a warrant is made by telephone, the applicant prepares a "duplicate original" warrant and transmits its contents "verbatim" to the magistrate. The magistrate can then sign the original warrant (which is before the magistrate) and authorize the applicant to sign the magistrate's name to the duplicate original.

Rule 4.1(b)(2) requires that information under oath electronically transmitted to the magistrate be recorded verbatim. The recording must be transcribed and the transcription certified as accurate and filed. Finally:

> Absent a finding of bad faith, evidence obtained from a warrant issued under this rule is not subject to suppression on the ground that issuing the warrant in this manner was unreasonable under the circumstances.

Fed.R.Crim.P. 4.1(c).

The Supreme Court decisions addressing the sufficiency of warrant affidavits involve situations in which the information submitted for a warrant consists in part of information from persons other than the affiant. The leading—or at least the seminal—case is Aguilar v. Texas, 378 U.S. 108, 84 S.Ct. 1509 (1964). Two police officers submitted to a Justice of the Peace an application for a search warrant for Aguilar's home. In support, they provided an affidavit which stated:

> Affiants have received reliable information from a credible person and do believe that heroin, marijuana, barbiturates and other narcotics and narcotics paraphernalia are being kept at the above described premises for the purpose of sale and use contrary to the provisions of the law.

The justice issued the warrant; the officers executed it and found drugs. These drugs were admitted into evidence at Aguilar's trial. Finding constitutional error, the Supreme Court reasoned the guiding principles must be that the magistrate must decide independently whether probable cause exists and not accept without question the officers' "mere conclusion." These principles require an affidavit permitting the magistrate to perform these tasks. Further:

> Although an affidavit may be based on hearsay information and need not reflect the direct personal observations of the affiant, the magistrate must be informed of some of the underlying circumstances from which the informant concluded that the narcotics were where he claimed they were, and some of the underlying circumstances from which the officer concluded that the informant, whose identity need not be disclosed, was "credible" or his information "reliable." Otherwise, "the inferences from the facts which lead to the complaint" will be drawn not "by a neutral and detached magistrate," as the Constitution requires, but instead, by a police officer * * * , or, as in this case, by an unidentified informant.

378 U.S. at 114–15, 84 S.Ct. at 1514.

This approach was developed further in Spinelli v. United States, 393 U.S. 410, 89 S.Ct. 584 (1969). Evidence of gambling activities was obtained in a search pursuant to a warrant of an apartment located in St. Louis. The affidavit on which the warrant was issued recited in part:

> The Federal Bureau of Investigation has been informed by a confidential reliable informant that William Spinelli is operating a handbook and accepting wagers and disseminating wagering information by means of the telephones which have

been assigned the numbers WYdown 4–0029 and WYdown 4–0136.

In addition, the affidavit recited that telephone company records disclosed the phones to which those numbers were assigned were located in a specific apartment under the name of Grace B. Hagen. Further, the affidavit stated federal agents conducting surveillance had observed Spinelli enter the apartment once, and on several other occasions they observed him in the parking lot of the apartment building or in its vicinity. Holding the warrant invalid, a majority of the Court noted that the tip met neither prong of *Aguilar.* It then suggested a tip was not sufficient under *Aguilar* might nevertheless establish probable cause for either of two reasons. First, the tip might describe the suspect's criminal activity in sufficient detail that a magistrate could infer from this detail that the informant had gained the information in a reliable way. Second, other reliable information might sufficiently corroborate parts of the information in the tip to justify a magistrate in concluding that the tip's ultimate and incriminating assertions could be relied upon. Neither method "cured" the *Spinelli* affidavit, however. The detailed information in the tip concerning the telephones was a "meager report" that "could easily have been obtained from an offhand remark heard at a neighborhood bar." The corroborating evidence gathered by the federal agents "at most * * * indicated that Spinelli could have used the telephones specified by the informant for some purpose."

As the principal case in this subsection makes clear, the *Aguilar-Spinelli* approach has not survived further consideration.

Illinois v. Gates

Supreme Court of the United States, 1983.
462 U.S. 213, 103 S.Ct. 2317.

■ JUSTICE REHNQUIST delivered the opinion of the Court.

Respondents Lance and Susan Gates were indicted for violation of state drug laws after police officers, executing a search warrant, discovered marijuana and other contraband in their automobile and home. Prior to trial the Gates moved to suppress evidence seized during this search. The Illinois Supreme Court affirmed the decisions of lower state courts granting the motion. It held that the affidavit submitted in support of the State's application for a warrant to search the Gates' property was inadequate under this Court's decisions in *Aguilar v. Texas,* 378 U.S. 108, 84 S.Ct. 1509, 12 L.Ed.2d 723 (1964) and *Spinelli v. United States,* 393 U.S. 410, 89 S.Ct. 584, 21 L.Ed.2d 637 (1969).

* * *

II

* * * A chronological statement of events usefully introduces the issues at stake. Bloomingdale, Ill., is a suburb of Chicago located in

DuPage County. On May 3, 1978, the Bloomingdale Police Department received by mail an anonymous handwritten letter which read as follows:

"This letter is to inform you that you have a couple in your town who strictly make their living on selling drugs. They are Sue and Lance Gates, they live on Greenway, off Bloomingdale Rd. in the condominiums. Most of their buys are done in Florida. Sue his wife drives their car to Florida, where she leaves it to be loaded up with drugs, then Lance flys down and drives it back. Sue flys back after she drops the car off in Florida. May 3 she is driving down there again and Lance will be flying down in a few days to drive it back. At the time Lance drives the car back he has the trunk loaded with over $100,000.00 in drugs. Presently they have over $100,000.00 worth of drugs in their basement.

They brag about the fact they never have to work, and make their entire living on pushers.

I guarantee if you watch them carefully you will make a big catch. They are friends with some big drugs dealers, who visit their house often.

Lance & Susan Gates

Greenway

in Condominiums"

The letter was referred by the Chief of Police of the Bloomingdale Police Department to Detective Mader, who decided to pursue the tip. Mader learned, from the office of the Illinois Secretary of State, that an Illinois driver's license had been issued to one Lance Gates, residing at a stated address in Bloomingdale. He contacted a confidential informant, whose examination of certain financial records revealed a more recent address for the Gates, and he also learned from a police officer assigned to O'Hare Airport that "L. Gates" had made a reservation on Eastern Airlines flight 245 to West Palm Beach, Fla., scheduled to depart from Chicago on May 5 at 4:15 p.m.

Mader then made arrangements with an agent of the Drug Enforcement Administration for surveillance of the May 5 Eastern Airlines flight. The agent later reported to Mader that Gates had boarded the flight, and that federal agents in Florida had observed him arrive in West Palm Beach and take a taxi to the nearby Holiday Inn. They also reported that Gates went to a room registered to one Susan Gates and that, at 7:00 a.m. the next morning, Gates and an unidentified woman left the motel in a Mercury bearing Illinois license plates and drove northbound on an interstate frequently used by travelers to the Chicago area. In addition, the DEA agent informed Mader that the license plate number on the Mercury was registered to a Hornet station wagon owned by Gates. The agent also advised Mader that the driving time between West Palm Beach and Bloomingdale was approximately 22 to 24 hours.

Mader signed an affidavit setting forth the foregoing facts, and submitted it to a judge of the Circuit Court of DuPage County, together with a copy of the anonymous letter. The judge of that court thereupon issued a search warrant for the Gates' residence and for their automobile. The judge, in deciding to issue the warrant, could have determined that the *modus operandi* of the Gates had been substantially corroborated. As the anonymous letter predicted, Lance Gates had flown from Chicago to West Palm Beach late in the afternoon of May 5th, had checked into a hotel room registered in the name of his wife, and, at 7:00 a.m. the following morning, had headed north, accompanied by an unidentified woman, out of West Palm Beach on an interstate highway used by travelers from South Florida to Chicago in an automobile bearing a license plate issued to him.

At 5:15 a.m. on May 7th, only 36 hours after he had flown out of Chicago, Lance Gates, and his wife, returned to their home in Bloomingdale, driving the car in which they had left West Palm Beach some 22 hours earlier. The Bloomingdale police were awaiting them, searched the trunk of the Mercury, and uncovered approximately 350 pounds of marijuana. A search of the Gates' home revealed marijuana, weapons, and other contraband. The Illinois Circuit Court ordered suppression of all these items, on the ground that the affidavit submitted to the Circuit Judge failed to support the necessary determination of probable cause to believe that the Gates' automobile and home contained the contraband in question. This decision was affirmed in turn by the Illinois Appellate Court and by a divided vote of the Supreme Court of Illinois.

The Illinois Supreme Court concluded—and we are inclined to agree—that, standing alone, the anonymous letter sent to the Bloomingdale Police Department would not provide the basis for a magistrate's determination that there was probable cause to believe contraband would be found in the Gates' car and home. The letter provides virtually nothing from which one might conclude that its author is either honest or his information reliable; likewise, the letter gives absolutely no indication of the basis for the writer's predictions regarding the Gates' criminal activities. Something more was required, then, before a magistrate could conclude that there was probable cause to believe that contraband would be found in the Gates' home and car.

The Illinois Supreme Court also properly recognized that Detective Mader's affidavit might be capable of supplementing the anonymous letter with information sufficient to permit a determination of probable cause. In holding that the affidavit in fact did not contain sufficient additional information to sustain a determination of probable cause, the Illinois court applied a "two-pronged test," derived from our decision in *Spinelli v. United States*, 393 U.S. 410, 89 S.Ct. 584, 21 L.Ed.2d 637 (1969). The Illinois Supreme Court, like some others, apparently understood *Spinelli* as requiring that the anonymous letter satisfy each of two independent requirements before it could be relied on. According to this view, the letter, as supplemented by Mader's affidavit, first had to adequately reveal the "basis of knowledge" of the letter writer—the particular means by which he came by the information given in his report. Second, it had to provide facts sufficiently establishing either the "veracity" of the affiant's informant, or, alternatively, the "reliability" of the informant's report in this particular case.

The Illinois court * * * found that the test had not been satisfied. First, the "veracity" prong was not satisfied because, "there was simply no basis [for] * * * conclud[ing] that the anonymous person [who wrote the letter to the Bloomingdale Police Department] was credible." The court indicated that corroboration by police of details contained in the letter might never satisfy the "veracity" prong, and in any event, could not do so if, as in the present case, only "innocent" details are corroborated. In addition, the letter gave no indication of the basis of its writer's knowledge of the Gates' activities. The Illinois court understood *Spinelli* as permitting the detail contained in a tip to be used to infer that the informant had a reliable basis for his statements, but it thought that the anonymous letter failed to provide sufficient detail to permit such an inference. Thus, it concluded that no showing of probable cause had been made.

We agree with the Illinois Supreme Court that an informant's "veracity," "reliability" and "basis of knowledge" are all highly relevant in determining the value of his report. We do not agree, however, that these elements should be understood as entirely separate and independent requirements to be rigidly exacted in every case, which the opinion of the Supreme Court of Illinois would imply. Rather, as detailed below, they should be understood simply as closely intertwined issues that may usefully illuminate the common-sense, practical question whether there is "probable cause" to believe that contraband or evidence is located in a particular place.

III

This totality of the circumstances approach is far more consistent with our prior treatment of probable cause than is any rigid demand that specific "tests" be satisfied by every informant's tip. Perhaps the central teaching of our decisions bearing on the probable cause standard is that it is a "practical, nontechnical conception." * * * [P]robable cause is a fluid concept—turning on the assessment of probabilities in particular factual contexts—not readily, or even usefully, reduced to a neat set of legal rules. Informants' tips doubtless come in many shapes and sizes from many different types of persons. * * * Rigid legal rules are ill-suited to an area of such diversity. * * *

Moreover, the "two-pronged test" directs analysis into two largely independent channels—the informant's "veracity" or "reliability" and his "basis of knowledge." There are persuasive arguments against according these two elements such independent status. Instead, they are better understood as relevant considerations in the totality of circumstances analysis that traditionally has guided probable cause determinations: a deficiency in one may be compensated for, in determining the overall reliability of a tip, by a strong showing as to the other, or by some other indicia of reliability. * * * Unlike a totality of circumstances analysis, which permits a balanced assessment of the relative weights of all the various indicia of reliability (and unreliability) attending an informant's tip, the "two-pronged test" has encouraged an excessively technical dissection of informants' tips, with undue attention being focused on isolated issues that cannot sensibly be divorced from the other facts presented to the magistrate.

* * *

We * * * have recognized that affidavits "are normally drafted by nonlawyers in the midst and haste of a criminal investigation. Technical requirements of elaborate specificity once exacted under common law pleading have no proper place in this area." Likewise, search and arrest warrants long have been issued by persons who are neither lawyers nor judges, and who certainly do not remain abreast of each judicial refinement of the nature of "probable cause." The rigorous inquiry into the *Spinelli* prongs and the complex superstructure of evidentiary and analytical rules that some have seen implicit in our *Spinelli* decision, cannot be reconciled with the fact that many warrants are—quite properly—issued on the basis of nontechnical, commonsense judgments of laymen applying a standard less demanding than those used in more formal legal proceedings. Likewise, given the informal, often hurried context in which it must be applied, the "built-in subtleties," of the "two-pronged test" are particularly unlikely to assist magistrates in determining probable cause.

Similarly, we have repeatedly said that after-the-fact scrutiny by courts of the sufficiency of an affidavit should not take the form of *de novo* review. A magistrate's "determination of probable cause should be paid great deference by reviewing courts."

If the affidavits submitted by police officers are subjected to the type of scrutiny some courts have deemed appropriate, police might well resort to warrantless searches, with the hope of relying on consent or some other exception to the warrant clause that might develop at the time of the search. * * * Reflecting this preference for the warrant process, the traditional standard for review of an issuing magistrate's probable cause determination has been that so long as the magistrate had a "substantial basis for . . . conclud[ing]" that a search would uncover evidence of wrongdoing, the Fourth Amendment requires no more. *Jones v. United States*, 362 U.S. 257, 271, 80 S.Ct. 725, 736, 4 L.Ed.2d 697 (1960). We think reaffirmation of this standard better serves the purpose of encouraging recourse to the warrant procedure and is more consistent with our traditional deference to the probable cause determinations of magistrates than is the "two-pronged test."

Finally, the direction taken by decisions following *Spinelli* poorly serves "the most basic function of any government": "to provide for the security of the individual and of his property." The strictures that inevitably accompany the "two-pronged test" cannot avoid seriously impeding the task of law enforcement. If, as the Illinois Supreme Court apparently thought, that test must be rigorously applied in every case, anonymous tips seldom would be of greatly diminished value in police work. Ordinary citizens, like ordinary witnesses, generally do not provide extensive recitations of the basis of their everyday observations. Likewise, as the Illinois Supreme Court observed in this case, the veracity of persons supplying anonymous tips is by hypothesis largely unknown, and unknowable. As a result, anonymous tips seldom could survive a rigorous application of either of the *Spinelli* prongs. Yet, such tips, particularly when supplemented by independent police investigation, frequently contribute to the solution of otherwise "perfect crimes." While a conscientious assessment of the basis for crediting such tips is required by the Fourth Amendment, a standard that leaves virtually no place for anonymous citizen informants is not.

For all these reasons, we conclude that it is wiser to abandon the "two-pronged test" established by our decisions in *Aguilar* and *Spinelli*.[11] In its place we reaffirm the totality of the circumstances analysis that traditionally has informed probable cause determinations. The task of the issuing magistrate is simply to make a practical, common-sense decision whether, given all the circumstances set forth in the affidavit before him, including the "veracity" and "basis of knowledge" of persons supplying hearsay information, there is a fair probability that contraband or evidence of a crime will be found in a particular place. And the duty of a reviewing court is simply to ensure that the magistrate had a "substantial basis for * * * conclud[ing]" that probable cause existed. We are convinced that this flexible, easily applied standard will better achieve the accommodation of public and private interests that the Fourth Amendment requires than does the approach that has developed from *Aguilar* and *Spinelli*.

Our earlier cases illustrate the limits beyond which a magistrate may not venture in issuing a warrant. A sworn statement of an affiant that "he has cause to suspect and does believe that" liquor illegally brought into the United States is located on certain premises will not do. *Nathanson v. United States*, 290 U.S. 41, 54 S.Ct. 11, 78 L.Ed. 159 (1933). An affidavit must provide the magistrate with a substantial basis for determining the existence of probable cause, and the wholly conclusory

---

11   * * *

Whether the allegations submitted to the magistrate in *Spinelli* would, under the view we now take, have supported a finding of probable cause, we think it would not be profitable to decide. There are so many variables in the probable cause equation that one determination will seldom be a useful "precedent" for another. Suffice it to say that while we in no way abandon *Spinelli's* concern for the trustworthiness of informers and for the principle that it is the magistrate who must ultimately make a finding of probable cause, we reject the rigid categorization suggested by some of its language.

statement at issue in *Nathanson* failed to meet this requirement. An officer's statement that "affiants have received reliable information from a credible person and believe" that heroin is stored in a home, is likewise inadequate. *Aguilar v. Texas*, 378 U.S. 108, 84 S.Ct. 1509, 12 L.Ed.2d 723 (1964). As in *Nathanson,* this is a mere conclusory statement that gives the magistrate virtually no basis at all for making a judgment regarding probable cause. Sufficient information must be presented to the magistrate to allow that official to determine probable cause; his action cannot be a mere ratification of the bare conclusions of others. In order to ensure that such an abdication of the magistrate's duty does not occur, courts must continue to conscientiously review the sufficiency of affidavits on which warrants are issued. But when we move beyond the "bare bones" affidavits present in cases such as *Nathanson* and *Aguilar,* this area simply does not lend itself to a prescribed set of rules, like that which had developed from *Spinelli.* Instead, the flexible, commonsense standard * * * better serves the purposes of the Fourth Amendment's probable cause requirement.

* * *

IV

Our decisions applying the totality of circumstances analysis outlined above have consistently recognized the value of corroboration of details of an informant's tip by independent police work. * * *

Our decision in *Draper v. United States*, 358 U.S. 307, 79 S.Ct. 329, 3 L.Ed.2d 327 (1959), however, is the classic case on the value of corroborative efforts of police officials. There, an informant named Hereford reported that Draper would arrive in Denver on a train from Chicago on one of two days, and that he would be carrying a quantity of heroin. The informant also supplied a fairly detailed physical description of Draper, and predicted that he would be wearing a light colored raincoat, brown slacks and black shoes, and would be walking "real fast." Hereford gave no indication of the basis for his information.

On one of the stated dates police officers observed a man matching this description exit a train arriving from Chicago; his attire and luggage matched Hereford's report and he was walking rapidly. We explained in *Draper* that, by this point in his investigation, the arresting officer "had personally verified every facet of the information given him by Hereford except whether petitioner had accomplished his mission and had the three ounces of heroin on his person or in his bag. And surely, with every other bit of Hereford's information being thus personally verified, [the officer] had 'reasonable grounds' to believe that the remaining unverified bit of Hereford's information—that Draper would have the heroin with him—was likewise true."

The showing of probable cause in the present case was fully as compelling as that in *Draper.* Even standing alone, the facts obtained through the independent investigation of Mader and the DEA at least suggested that the Gates were involved in drug trafficking. In addition to being a popular vacation site, Florida is well-known as a source of narcotics and other illegal drugs. Lance Gates' flight to Palm Beach, his brief, overnight stay in a motel, and apparent immediate return north to Chicago in the family car, conveniently awaiting him in West Palm Beach, is as suggestive of a prearranged drug run, as it is of an ordinary vacation trip.

In addition, the magistrate could rely on the anonymous letter, which had been corroborated in major part by Mader's efforts—just as had occurred in *Draper*. The Supreme Court of Illinois reasoned that *Draper* involved an informant who had given reliable information on previous occasions, while the honesty and reliability of the anonymous informant in this case were unknown to the Bloomingdale police. While this distinction might be an apt one at the time the police department received the anonymous letter, it became far less significant after Mader's independent investigative work occurred. The corroboration of the letter's predictions that the Gates' car would be in Florida, that Lance Gates would fly to Florida in the next day or so, and that he would drive the car north toward Bloomingdale all indicated, albeit not with certainty, that the informant's other assertions also were true. "Because an informant is right about some things, he is more probably right about other facts,"—including the claim regarding the Gates' illegal activity. This may well not be the type of "reliability" or "veracity" necessary to satisfy some views of the "veracity prong" of *Spinelli,* but we think it suffices for the practical, commonsense judgment called for in making a probable cause determination. It is enough, for purposes of assessing probable cause, that "corroboration through other sources of information reduced the chances of a reckless or prevaricating tale," thus providing "a substantial basis for crediting the hearsay."

Finally, the anonymous letter contained a range of details relating not just to easily obtained facts and conditions existing at the time of the tip, but to future actions of third parties ordinarily not easily predicted. The letter writer's accurate information as to the travel plans of each of the Gates was of a character likely obtained only from the Gates themselves, or from someone familiar with their not entirely ordinary travel plans. If the informant had access to accurate information of this type a magistrate could properly conclude that it was not unlikely that he also had access to reliable information of the Gates' alleged illegal activities.[14] Of course, the Gates' travel plans might have been learned

---

[14] The dissent seizes on one inaccuracy in the anonymous informant's letter—its statement that Sue Gates would fly from Florida to Illinois, when in fact she drove—and argues that the probative value of the entire tip was undermined by this allegedly "material mistake." We have never required that informants used by the police be infallible, and can see no reason to impose such a requirement in this case. Probable cause, particularly when police have obtained a warrant, simply does not require the perfection the dissent finds necessary.

Likewise, there is no force to the dissent's argument that the Gates' action in leaving their home unguarded undercut the informant's claim that drugs were hidden there. Indeed, the line-by-line scrutiny that the dissent applies to the anonymous letter is akin to that we find

from a talkative neighbor or travel agent; under the "two-pronged test" developed from *Spinelli,* the character of the details in the anonymous letter might well not permit a sufficiently clear inference regarding the letter writer's "basis of knowledge." But, as discussed previously, probable cause does not demand the certainty we associate with formal trials. It is enough that there was a fair probability that the writer of the anonymous letter had obtained his entire story either from the Gates or someone they trusted. And corroboration of major portions of the letter's predictions provides just this probability. It is apparent, therefore, that the judge issuing the warrant had a "substantial basis for ... conclud[ing]" that probable cause to search the Gates' home and car existed. The judgment of the Supreme Court of Illinois therefore must be

Reversed.

■ JUSTICE BRENNAN, with whom JUSTICE MARSHALL joins, dissenting.

Although I join Justice Stevens' dissenting opinion and agree with him that the warrant is invalid even under the Court's newly announced "totality of the circumstances" test, I write separately to dissent from the Court's unjustified and ill-advised rejection of the two-prong test for evaluating the validity of a warrant based on hearsay announced in *Aguilar v. Texas*, 378 U.S. 108, 84 S.Ct. 1509, 12 L.Ed.2d 723 (1964), and refined in *Spinelli v. United States*, 393 U.S. 410, 89 S.Ct. 584, 21 L.Ed.2d 637 (1969).

* * *

Although the rules drawn from the [*Aguilar-Spinelli* line of cases] are cast in procedural terms, they advance an important underlying substantive value: Findings of probable cause, and attendant intrusions, should not be authorized unless there is some assurance that the information on which they are based has been obtained in a reliable way by an honest or credible person. As applied to police officers, the rules focus on the way in which the information was acquired. As applied to informants, the rules focus both on the honesty or credibility of the informant and on the reliability of the way in which the information was acquired. Insofar as it is more complicated, an evaluation of affidavits based on hearsay involves a more difficult inquiry. This suggests a need

inappropriate in reviewing magistrate's decisions. The dissent apparently attributes to the magistrate who issued the warrant in this case the rather implausible notion that persons dealing in drugs always stay at home, apparently out of fear that to leave might risk intrusion by criminals. If accurate, one could not help sympathizing with the self-imposed isolation of people so situated. In reality, however, it is scarcely likely that the magistrate ever thought that the anonymous tip "kept one spouse" at home, much less that he relied on the theory advanced by the dissent. The letter simply says that Sue would fly from Florida to Illinois, without indicating whether the Gates made the bitter choice of leaving the drugs in their house, or those in their car, unguarded. The magistrate's determination that there might be drugs or evidence of criminal activity in the Gates' home was well-supported by the less speculative theory, noted in text, that if the informant could predict with considerable accuracy the somewhat unusual travel plans of the Gates, he probably also had a reliable basis for his statements that the Gates kept a large quantity of drugs in their home and frequently were visited by other drug traffickers there.

to structure the inquiry in an effort to insure greater accuracy. The standards announced in *Aguilar,* as refined by *Spinelli,* fulfill that need. The standards inform the police of what information they have to provide and magistrates of what information they should demand. The standards also inform magistrates of the subsidiary findings they must make in order to arrive at an ultimate finding of probable cause. *Spinelli,* properly understood, directs the magistrate's attention to the possibility that the presence of self-verifying detail might satisfy *Aguilar*'s basis of knowledge prong and that corroboration of the details of a tip might satisfy *Aguilar*'s veracity prong. By requiring police to provide certain crucial information to magistrates and by structuring magistrates' probable cause inquiries, *Aguilar* and *Spinelli* assure the magistrate's role as an independent arbiter of probable cause, insure greater accuracy in probable cause determinations, and advance the substantive value identified above.

* * *

■ JUSTICE STEVENS, with whom JUSTICE BRENNAN joins, dissenting.

The fact that Lance and Sue Gates made a 22 hour nonstop drive from West Palm Beach, Florida, to Bloomingdale, Illinois, only a few hours after Lance had flown to Florida provided persuasive evidence that they were engaged in illicit activity. That fact, however, was not known to the magistrate when he issued the warrant to search their home.

What the magistrate did know at that time was that the anonymous informant had not been completely accurate in his or her predictions. The informant had indicated that "Sue drives their car to Florida *where she leaves it to be loaded up with drugs. . . . Sue flies back after she drops the car off in Florida.*" (emphasis added). Yet Detective Mader's affidavit reported that she "left the West Palm Beach area driving the Mercury northbound."

The discrepancy between the informant's predictions and the facts known to Detective Mader is significant for three reasons. First, it cast doubt on the informant's hypothesis that the Gates already had "over $100,000 worth of drugs in their basement." The informant had predicted an itinerary that always kept one spouse in Bloomingdale, suggesting that the Gates did not want to leave their home unguarded because something valuable was hidden within. That inference obviously could not be drawn when it was known that the pair was actually together over a thousand miles from home.

Second, the discrepancy made the Gates' conduct seem substantially less unusual than the informant had predicted it would be. It would have been odd if, as predicted, Sue had driven down to Florida on Wednesday, left the car, and flown right back to Illinois. But the mere facts that Sue was in West Palm Beach with the car, that she was joined by her husband at the Holiday Inn on Friday, and that the couple drove north together the next morning are neither unusual nor probative of criminal activity.

Third, the fact that the anonymous letter contained a material mistake undermines the reasonableness of relying on it as a basis for making a forcible entry into a private home.

Of course, the activities in this case did not stop when the magistrate issued the warrant. The Gates drove all night to Bloomingdale, the officers searched the car and found 400 pounds of marijuana, and then they searched the house. However, none of these subsequent events may be considered in evaluating the warrant, and the search of the house was legal only if the warrant was valid. I cannot accept the Court's casual conclusion that, *before the Gates arrived in Bloomingdale,* there was probable cause to justify a valid entry and search of a private home. No one knows who the informant in this case was, or what motivated him or her to write the note. Given that the note's predictions were faulty in one significant respect, and were corroborated by nothing except ordinary innocent activity, I must surmise that the Court's evaluation of the warrant's validity has been colored by subsequent events.

* * *

EDITORS' NOTE: "ANTICIPATORY" WARRANTS AND PROBABLE CAUSE

So-called "anticipatory" search warrants were addressed in United States v. Grubbs, 547 U.S. 90, 126 S.Ct. 1494 (2006). Defining the warrants at issue, the Court explained:

> An anticipatory warrant is "a warrant based upon an affidavit showing probable cause that at some future time (but not presently) certain evidence of crime will be located at a specified place." 2 W. LaFave, Search and Seizure § 3.7(c), p. 398 (4th ed. 2004). Most anticipatory warrants subject their execution to some condition precedent other than the mere passage of time— a so-called "triggering condition."

547 U.S. at 94, 126 S.Ct. at 1498.

In *Grubbs*, defendant Grubbs ordered a videotape containing child pornography from a Web site actually operated by federal agents. Federal officers arranged for a "controlled delivery" of the videotape to his residence and then—but before the delivery—applied for a warrant for those premises. The affidavit submitted in support of the application provided:

> Execution of this search warrant will not occur unless and until the parcel has been received by a person(s) and has been physically taken into the residence * * *. At that time, and not before, this search warrant will be executed * * *.

A warrant issued simply authorizing a search of the residence. It made no reference to the delivery of the videotape as a prerequisite to the search.

The Court of Appeals held that the results of the search should have been suppressed because the warrant itself failed to specify the condition precedent to the search authorization. A unanimous Supreme Court reversed, holding the warrant and search reasonable.

First, the Court rejected the proposition that anticipatory warrants are categorically unconstitutional because they issue on less than the constitutionally-required probable cause:

> Because the probable-cause requirement looks to whether evidence will be found *when the search is conducted,* all warrants are, in a sense, "anticipatory." In the typical case where the police seek permission to search a house for an item they believe is already located there, the magistrate's determination that there is probable cause for the search amounts to a prediction that the item will still be there when the warrant is executed. * * * Thus, when an anticipatory warrant is issued, "the fact that the contraband is not presently located at the place described in the warrant is immaterial, so long as there is probable cause to believe that it will be there when the search warrant is executed."

> Anticipatory warrants are, therefore, no different in principle from ordinary warrants. They require the magistrate to determine (1) that it is *now probable* that (2) contraband, evidence of a crime, or a fugitive *will be* on the described premises (3) when the warrant is executed. It should be noted, however, that where the anticipatory warrant places a condition (other than the mere passage of time) upon its execution, the first of these determinations goes not merely to what will probably be found *if* the condition is met. (If that were the extent of the probability determination, an anticipatory warrant could be issued for every house in the country, authorizing search and seizure *if* contraband should be delivered—though for any single location there is no likelihood that contraband will be delivered.) Rather, the probability determination for a conditioned anticipatory warrant looks also to the likelihood that the condition will occur, and thus that a proper object of seizure will be on the described premises. In other words, for a conditioned anticipatory warrant to comply with the Fourth Amendment's requirement of probable cause, two prerequisites of probability must be satisfied. It must be true not only that *if* the triggering condition occurs "there is a fair probability that contraband or evidence of a crime will be found in a particular place," but also that there is probable cause to believe the triggering condition *will occur.* The supporting affidavit must provide the magistrate with sufficient information to evaluate both aspects of the probable-cause determination.

547 U.S. at 95–97, 126 S.Ct. at 1499–1500 (emphasis in original).

Second, the Court rejected the reasoning of the court below that the Fourth Amendment's particularity requirement demands that the triggering condition of an anticipatory warrant be set out in the warrant itself. The Fourth Amendment, it held, "specifies only two matters that must be 'particularly describ[ed]' in the warrant: 'the place to be searched' and 'the persons or things to be seized.'" Thus the triggering condition need not be in the warrant itself and of course need not be described particularly. 547 U.S. at 97–98, 126 S.Ct. at 1500–01.

2. NEED TO TEST EACH PROVISION OF A WARRANT AND "SEVERABILITY" OF PROVISIONS

EDITORS' NOTE: ANALYSIS OF MULTI-PROVISION WARRANTS

Warrants, particularly search warrants, often contain multiple grants of authority to the executing officers. The search warrant from Hudson v. Michigan reproduced at the beginning of this chapter, for example, authorized executing officers to search for and seizure not only "[a]ll suspected controlled substance[s]" but also certain records, evidence of ownership and control of the premises, and "all firearms used in connection with the * * * described activities."

Analysis of such multi-provision warrants has not been addressed by the Supreme Court. Lower courts are in agreement, however, that each provision must be considered separately. Each must be tested for support in the showing on which the warrant issued and—under the case law discussed later in this chapter—for specificity. The *Hudson* warrant, for example, might have been issued on a showing that would permit the magistrate to find probable cause to believe that controlled substances were in the premises but not that any firearms would be found there. The authorization to search for and seize firearms, then, might be invalid, although the authorization to search for and seize controlled substances might be fully effective.

Many courts faced with these situations apply what is called the "severance doctrine." This "allows a court, under certain circumstances, to strike out any constitutionally deficient items in the particularity portion of a warrant and to determine the propriety of the search on the basis of the valid remainder." State v. Browne, 291 Conn. 720, 745–51, 970 A.2d 81, 97–100 (2009). Application of this doctrine will be addressed further in Subchapter D of this chapter, considering the effect of the terms of a search warrant on officers' power to search and seize.

3. CHALLENGING FACTUAL STATEMENTS IN THE AFFIDAVIT

Prior to the principal case in this unit, many courts took the position that whether there was probable cause for issuance of an arrest or search warrant could be determined only from the face of the affidavit or complaint. The facts alleged were to be accepted as true and the sole question for debate was whether they established probable cause. To some extent, this position—barring defendants from attacking the "face" of a warrant affidavit—was based on the perception that the appropriate inquiry was whether the magistrate had probable cause to issue the warrant. If the magistrate had probable cause, no significance was attached to the fact the officer who applied for the warrant may not have had probable cause justifying a request for a warrant.

The principal case in this subsection requires defendants, to some extent, be permitted to challenge the accuracy of the facts in a warrant affidavit. Consider separately (although not necessarily in this order) what facts a defendant must establish to prevail on a challenge of this sort and what a defendant must do in order to have a factual hearing where he can establish those facts.

Franks v. Delaware

Supreme Court of the United States, 1978.
438 U.S. 154, 98 S.Ct. 2674.

■ MR. JUSTICE BLACKMUN delivered the opinion of the Court.

This case presents an important and longstanding issue of Fourth Amendment law. Does a defendant in a criminal proceeding ever have the right, under the Fourth and Fourteenth Amendments, subsequent to the *ex parte* issuance of a search warrant, to challenge the truthfulness of factual statements made in an affidavit supporting the warrant?

In the present case the Supreme Court of Delaware held, as a matter of first impression for it, that a defendant under *no* circumstances may so challenge the veracity of a sworn statement used by police to procure a search warrant. We reverse, and we hold that, where the defendant makes a substantial preliminary showing that a false statement knowingly and intentionally, or with reckless disregard for the truth, was included by the affiant in the warrant affidavit, and if the allegedly false statement is necessary to the finding of probable cause, the Fourth Amendment requires that a hearing be held at the defendant's request. In the event that at that hearing the allegation of perjury or reckless disregard is established by the defendant by a preponderance of the evidence, and, with the affidavit's false material set to one side, the affidavit's remaining content is insufficient to establish probable cause, the search warrant must be voided and the fruits of the search excluded to the same extent as if probable cause was lacking on the face of the affidavit.

I.

The controversy over the veracity of the search warrant affidavit in this case arose in connection with petitioner Jerome Franks' state conviction for rape, kidnapping, and burglary. On Friday, March 5, 1976, Mrs. Cynthia Bailey told police in Dover, Delaware, that she had been confronted in her home earlier that morning by a man with a knife, and that he had sexually assaulted her. She described her assailant's age, race, height, build, and facial hair, and gave a detailed description of his clothing as consisting of a white thermal undershirt, black pants with a silver or gold buckle, a brown leather three-quarter length coat, and a dark knit cap that he wore pulled down around his eyes.

That same day, petitioner Franks coincidentally was taken into custody for an assault involving a 15-year-old girl, Brenda B. _____, six days earlier. After his formal arrest, and while awaiting a bail hearing in Family Court, petitioner allegedly stated to Robert McClements, the youth officer accompanying him, that he was surprised the bail hearing was "about Brenda B. _____. I know her. I thought you said Bailey. I don't know her." * * *

On the following Monday, March 8, officer McClements happened to mention the courthouse incident to a detective, Ronald R. Brooks, who was working on the Bailey case. On March 9, detective Brooks and detective Larry D. Gray submitted a sworn affidavit to a justice of the peace in Dover, in support of a warrant to search petitioner's apartment.[1] In paragraph 8 of the affidavit's "probable cause page" mention was made of petitioner's statement to McClements. In paragraph 10, it was noted that the description of the assailant given to the police by Mrs. Bailey included the above mentioned clothing. Finally, the affidavit also described the attempt made by police to confirm that petitioner's typical outfit matched that of the assailant. Paragraph 15 recited: "On Tuesday, 3/9/76, your affiant contacted Mr. James Williams and Mr. Wesley Lucas of the Delaware Youth Center where Jerome Franks is employed and did have personal conversation with both these people." Paragraphs 16 and 17 respectively stated: "Mr. James Williams revealed to your affiant that the normal dress of Jerome Franks does consist of a white knit thermal undershirt and a brown leather jacket," and "Mr. Wesley Lucas revealed to your affiant that in addition to the thermal undershirt and jacket, Jerome Franks often wears a large green knit hat."

The warrant was issued on the basis of this affidavit. Pursuant to the warrant, police searched petitioner's apartment and found a white thermal undershirt, a knit hat, dark pants, and a leather jacket, and, on petitioner's kitchen table, a single-blade knife. All these ultimately were introduced in evidence at trial.

Prior to the trial, however, petitioner's counsel filed a written motion to suppress the clothing and the knife found in the search; this motion alleged that the warrant on its face did not show probable cause and that the search and seizure were in violation of the Fourth and Fourteenth Amendments. At the hearing on the motion to suppress, defense counsel orally amended the challenge to include an attack on the veracity of the warrant affidavit; he also specifically requested the right to call as

---

[1]   The affidavit is reproduced as Appendix A of this opinion.

witnesses detective Brooks, Wesley Lucas of the Youth Center, and James D. Morrison, formerly of the Youth Center.[2] Counsel asserted that Lucas and Morrison would testify that neither had been personally interviewed by the warrant affiants, and that, although they might have talked to another police officer, any information given by them to that officer was "somewhat different" from what was recited in the affidavit. Defense counsel charged that the misstatements were included in the affidavit not inadvertently, but in "bad faith." * * *

In rebuttal, the State's attorney argued in detail (a) that [Delaware law] contemplated that any challenge to a search warrant was to be limited to questions of sufficiency based on the face of the affidavit; [and] (b) that, purportedly, a majority of the States whose practice was not dictated by statute observed such a rule * * * . * * * The State objected to petitioner's "going behind [the warrant affidavit] in any way," and argued that the court must decide petitioner's motion "on the four corners" of the affidavit.

The trial court sustained the State's objection to petitioner's proposed evidence. The motion to suppress was denied, and the clothing and knife were admitted as evidence at the ensuing trial. Petitioner was convicted [and] sentenced to two consecutive terms of 25 years each and an additional consecutive life sentence.

On appeal, the Supreme Court of Delaware affirmed. It agreed with what it deemed to be the "majority rule" that no attack upon the veracity of a warrant affidavit could be made:

> "We agree with the majority rule for two reasons. First, it is the function of the issuing magistrate to determine the reliability of information and credibility of affiants in deciding whether the requirement of probable cause has been met. There has been no need demonstrated for interfering with this function. Second, neither the probable cause nor suppression hearings are adjudications of guilt or innocence; the matters asserted by defendant are more properly considered in a trial on the merits."

Because of this resolution, the Delaware Supreme Court noted that there was no need to consider petitioner's "other contentions, relating to the evidence that would have been introduced for impeachment purposes."

Franks' petition for certiorari presented only the issue whether the trial court had erred in refusing to consider his allegation of misrepresentation in the warrant affidavit. Because of the importance of

---

[2] The references in paragraphs 15 and 16 of the warrant affidavit's probable cause page to "James Williams" appear to have been intended as references to James D. Morrison, who was petitioner's supervisor at the Youth Center. This misapprehension on the part of the State continued until shortly before trial. Eleven days prior to trial, the prosecution requested the clerk of the Kent County Superior Court to summon "James Williams, Delaware Youth Center," for petitioner's trial. In his return on the summons, Record Document No. 15, the Kent County sheriff stated that he "[s]erved the within summons upon * * * James Williams (Morrison)." The summons actually delivered was made out in the name of James Morrison.

the question, and because of the conflict among both state and federal courts, we granted certiorari.

II.

* * *

Respondent * * * suggests that any error here was harmless. Assuming, *arguendo*, respondent says, that petitioner's Fourth Amendment claim was valid, and that the warrant should have been tested for veracity and the evidence excluded, it is still clear beyond a reasonable doubt that the evidence complained of did not contribute to petitioner's conviction. This contention falls of its own weight. The sole issue at trial was that of consent. Petitioner admitted that he had engaged in sexual relations with Mrs. Bailey on the day in question. She testified that she had not consented to this, and that petitioner, upon first encountering her in the house, had threatened her with a knife to force her to submit. Petitioner claimed that she had given full consent and that no knife had been present. To corroborate its contention that consent was lacking, the State introduced in evidence a stainless steel wooden-handled kitchen knife found by the detectives on the kitchen table in petitioner's apartment four days after the alleged rape. Defense counsel objected to its admission, arguing that Mrs. Bailey had not given any detailed description of the knife alleged to be involved in the incident and had claimed to have seen the knife only in "pitch blackness." The State obtained its admission, however, as a knife that matched the description contained in the search warrant, and Mrs. Bailey testified that the knife allegedly used was, like the knife in evidence, single-edged and not a pocket knife, and that the knife in evidence was the same length and thickness as the knife used in the crime. The State carefully elicited from detective Brooks the fact that this was the only knife found in petitioner's apartment. Although respondent argues that the knife was presented to the jury as "merely exemplary of the generic class of weapon testimonially described by the victim," the State at trial clearly meant to suggest that this was the knife that had been used against Mrs. Bailey. Had the warrant been quashed, and the knife excluded from the trial as evidence, we cannot say with any assurance that the jury would have reached the same decision on the issue of consent, particularly since there was other countervailing evidence on that issue.

* * *

III.

Whether the Fourth and Fourteenth Amendments, and the derivative exclusionary rule made applicable to the States under *Mapp v. Ohio*, 367 U.S. 643, 81 S.Ct. 1684, 6 L.Ed.2d 1081 (1961), ever mandate that a defendant be permitted to attack the veracity of a warrant affidavit after the warrant has been issued and executed, is a question that encounters conflicting values. The bulwark of Fourth Amendment protection, of course, is the Warrant Clause, requiring that, absent certain exceptions, police obtain a warrant from a neutral and disinterested magistrate before embarking upon a search. In deciding today, that, in certain circumstances, a challenge to a warrant's veracity must be permitted, we derive our ground from language of the Warrant Clause itself, which surely takes the affiant's good faith as its premise: "[N]o warrants shall issue, but upon probable cause, supported by Oath or affirmation * * * ." Judge Frankel, in *United States v. Halsey*, 257 F.Supp. 1002, 1005 (S.D.N.Y.1966), aff'd, Docket No. 31369 (CA2, June 12, 1967) (unreported), put the matter simply: "[W]hen the Fourth Amendment demands a factual showing sufficient to comprise 'probable cause,' the obvious assumption is that there will be a *truthful* showing" (emphasis in original). This does not mean "truthful" in the sense that every fact recited in the warrant affidavit is necessarily correct, for probable cause may be founded upon hearsay and upon information received from informants, as well as upon information within the affiant's own knowledge that sometimes must be garnered hastily. But surely it is to be "truthful" in the sense that the information put forth is believed or appropriately accepted by the affiant as true. It is established law that a warrant affidavit must set forth particular facts and circumstances underlying the existence of probable cause, so as to allow the magistrate to make an independent evaluation of the matter. If an informant's tip is the source of information, the affidavit must recite "some of the underlying circumstances from which the informant concluded" that relevant evidence might be discovered, and "some of the underlying circumstances from which the officer concluded that the informant, whose identity need not be disclosed, * * * was 'credible' or his information 'reliable.' " Because it is the magistrate who must determine independently whether there is probable cause, it would be an unthinkable imposition upon his authority if a warrant affidavit, revealed after the fact to contain a deliberately or recklessly false statement, were to stand beyond impeachment.

In saying this, however, one must give cognizance to competing values that lead us to impose limitations. They perhaps can best be addressed by noting the arguments of respondent and others against allowing veracity challenges. The arguments are several:

First, respondent argues that the exclusionary rule is not a personal constitutional right, but only a judicially created remedy extended where its benefit as a deterrent promises to outweigh the societal cost of its use. * * * Respondent argues that applying the exclusionary rule to another situation—the deterrence of deliberate or reckless untruthfulness in a warrant affidavit—is not justified * * * [because] interfering with a criminal conviction in order to deter official misconduct is a burden too great to impose on society.

Second, respondent argues that a citizen's privacy interests are adequately protected by a requirement that applicants for a warrant submit a sworn affidavit and by the magistrate's independent determination of sufficiency based on the face of the affidavit. Applying the exclusionary rule to attacks upon veracity would weed out a minimal number of perjurious government statements, says respondent, but would overlap unnecessarily with existing penalties against perjury, including criminal prosecutions, departmental discipline for misconduct, contempt of court, and civil actions.

Third, it is argued that the magistrate already is equipped to conduct a fairly vigorous inquiry into the accuracy of the factual affidavit supporting a warrant application. He may question the affiant, or summon other persons to give testimony at the warrant proceeding. The incremental gain from a post-search adversary proceeding, it is said, would not be great.

Fourth, it is argued that it would unwisely diminish the solemnity and moment of the magistrate's proceeding to make his inquiry into probable cause reviewable in regard to veracity. The less final, and less deference paid to, the magistrate's determination of veracity, the less initiative will he use in that task. Denigration of the magistrate's function would be imprudent insofar as his scrutiny is the last bulwark preventing any particular invasion of privacy before it happens.

Fifth, it is argued that permitting a post-search evidentiary hearing on issues of veracity would confuse the pressing issue of guilt or innocence with the collateral question as to whether there had been official misconduct in the drafting of the affidavit. The weight of criminal dockets, and the need to prevent diversion of attention from the main issue of guilt or innocence, militate against such an added burden on the trial courts. And if such hearings were conducted routinely, it is said, they would be misused by defendants as a convenient source of discovery. Defendants might even use the hearings in an attempt to force revelation of the identity of informants.

Sixth and finally, it is argued that a post-search veracity challenge is inappropriate because the accuracy of an affidavit in large part is beyond the control of the affiant. An affidavit may properly be based on hearsay, on fleeting observations, and on tips received from unnamed informants whose identity often will be properly protected from revelation under *McCray v. Illinois*, 386 U.S. 300, 87 S.Ct. 1056, 18 L.Ed.2d 62 (1967).

None of these considerations is trivial. Indeed, because of them, the rule announced today has a limited scope, both in regard to when exclusion of the seized evidence is mandated, and when a hearing on allegations of misstatements must be accorded. But neither do the considerations cited by respondent and others have a fully controlling weight; we conclude that they are insufficient to justify an *absolute* ban on post-search impeachment of veracity. On this side of the balance, also, there are pressing considerations:

First, a flat ban on impeachment of veracity could denude the probable cause requirement of all real meaning. The requirement that a warrant not issue "but upon probable cause, supported by Oath or affirmation," would be reduced to a nullity if a police officer was able to use deliberately falsified allegations to demonstrate probable cause, and, having misled the magistrate, then was able to remain confident that the ploy was worthwhile. It is this specter of intentional falsification that, we think, has evoked such widespread opposition to the flat nonimpeachment rule * * *. On occasion, of course, an instance of deliberate falsity will be exposed and confirmed without a special inquiry either at trial, or at a hearing on the sufficiency of the affidavit. A flat nonimpeachment rule would bar reexamination of the warrant even in these cases.

Second, the hearing before the magistrate not always will suffice to discourage lawless or reckless misconduct. The pre-search proceeding is necessarily *ex parte*, since the subject of the search cannot be tipped off to the application for a warrant lest he destroy or remove evidence. The usual reliance of our legal system on adversary proceedings itself should be an indication that an *ex parte* inquiry is likely to be less vigorous. The magistrate has no acquaintance with the information that may contradict the good faith and reasonable basis of the affiant's allegations. The pre-search proceeding will frequently be marked by haste, because of the understandable desire to act before the evidence disappears; this urgency will not always permit the magistrate to make an extended independent examination of the affiant or other witnesses.

Third, the alternative sanctions of a perjury prosecution, administrative discipline, contempt, or a civil suit are not likely to fill the gap. Mapp v. Ohio, supra, implicitly rejected the adequacy of these alternatives. * * *

Fourth, allowing an evidentiary hearing, after a suitable preliminary proffer of material falsity, would not diminish the importance and solemnity of the warrant-issuing process. It is the *ex parte* nature of the initial hearing, rather than the magistrate's capacity, that is the reason for the review. A magistrate's determination is presently subject to review before trial as to *sufficiency* without any undue interference with the dignity of the magistrate's function. Our reluctance today to extend the rule of exclusion beyond instances of deliberate misstatements, and those of reckless disregard, leaves a broad field where the magistrate is the sole protection of a citizen's Fourth Amendment rights, namely, in instances where police have been merely negligent in checking or recording the facts relevant to a probable cause determination.

Fifth, the claim that a post-search hearing will confuse the issue of the defendant's guilt with the issue of the State's possible misbehavior is footless. The hearing will not be in the presence of the jury. An issue extraneous to guilt already is examined in any probable cause determination or review of probable cause. Nor, if a sensible threshold showing is required and sensible substantive requirements for suppression are maintained, need there be any new large-scale commitment of judicial resources; many claims will wash out at an early stage, and the more substantial ones in any event would require judicial resources for vindication if the suggested alternative sanctions were truly to be effective. The requirement of a substantial preliminary showing should suffice to prevent the misuse of a veracity hearing for purposes of discovery or obstruction. And because we are faced today with only the question of the integrity of the affiant's representations as to his own activities, we need not decide, and we in no way predetermine, the difficult question whether a reviewing court must ever require the revelation of the identity of an informant once a substantial preliminary showing of falsity has been made. *McCray v. Illinois*, the Court's earlier disquisition in this area, concluded only that the Due Process Clause of the Fourteenth Amendment did not require the State to expose an informant's identity routinely, upon a defendant's mere demand, when there was ample evidence in the probable cause hearing to show that the informant was reliable and his information credible.

Sixth and finally, as to the argument that the exclusionary rule should not be extended to a "new" area, we cannot regard any such extension really to be at issue here. Despite the deep skepticism of Members of this Court as to the wisdom of extending the exclusionary rule to collateral areas, such as civil or grand jury proceedings, the Court has not questioned, in the absence of a more efficacious sanction, the continued application of the rule to suppress evidence from the State's case where a Fourth Amendment violation has been substantial and deliberate. We see no principled basis for distinguishing between the question of the sufficiency of an affidavit, which also is subject to a post-search reexamination, and the question of its integrity.

IV.

In sum, and to repeat with some embellishment what we stated at the beginning of this opinion: There is, of course, a presumption of validity with respect to the affidavit supporting the search warrant. To mandate an evidentiary hearing, the challenger's attack must be more than conclusory and must be supported by more than a mere desire to cross-examine. There must be allegations of deliberate falsehood or of reckless disregard for the truth, and those allegations must be accompanied by an offer of proof. They should point out specifically the portion of the warrant affidavit that is claimed to be false; and they should be accompanied by a statement of supporting reasons. Affidavits or sworn or otherwise reliable statements of witnesses should be furnished, or their absence satisfactorily explained. Allegations of negligence or innocent mistake are insufficient. The deliberate falsity or reckless disregard whose impeachment is permitted today is only that of the affiant, not of any nongovernmental informant. Finally, if these requirements are met, and if, when material that is the subject of the alleged falsity or reckless disregard is set to one side, there remains sufficient content in the warrant affidavit to support a finding of probable cause, no hearing is required. On the other hand, if the remaining content is insufficient, the defendant is entitled, under the Fourth Amendment, to his hearing. Whether he will prevail at that hearing is, of course, another issue.

Because of Delaware's absolute rule, its courts did not have occasion to consider the proffer put forward by petitioner Franks. Since the framing of suitable rules to govern proffers is a matter properly left to the States, we decline ourselves to pass on petitioner's proffer. The judgment of the Supreme Court of Delaware is reversed, and the case is remanded for further proceedings not inconsistent with this opinion.

It is so ordered.

APPENDIX A TO OPINION OF THE COURT

J.P.Court #7

IN THE MATTER OF: Jerome Franks, B/M, DOB: 10/9/54 and 222 S. Governors Ave., Apt. #3, Dover, Delaware. A two room apartment located on the South side, second floor, of a white block building on the west side of S. Governors Avenue, between Loockerman Street and North Street, in the City of Dover. The ground floor of this building houses Wayman's Barber Shop.

STATE OF DELAWARE

ss:

COUNTY OF KENT

Be it remembered that on this 9th day of March A.D. 1976 before me John Green, personally appeared Det. Ronald R. Brooks and Det. Larry Gray of the Dover Police Department who being by me duly sworn depose and say:

That they have reason to believe and do believe that in the 222 S. Governors Avenue, Apartment #3, Dover, Delaware. A two room apartment located on the South side second floor of a white block building on the west side of S. Governors Avenue between Loockerman Street and North Street in the City of Dover. The ground floor of this building houses Wayman's Barber Shop the occupant of which is Jerome Franks. There has been and/or there is now located and/or concealed certain property in said house, place, conveyance and/or on the person or persons of the occupants thereof, consisting of property, papers, articles, or things which are the instruments of criminal offense, and/or obtained in the commission of a crime, and/or designated to be used in the commission of a crime, and not reasonably calculated to be used for any other purpose and/or the possession of which is unlawful, papers, articles, or things which are of an evidentiary nature pertaining to the commission of a crime or crimes specified therein and in particular, a white knit thermal undershirt; a brown ¾ length leather jacket with a tie-belt; a pair of black mens pants; a dark colored knit hat; a long thin bladed knife or other instruments or items relating to the crime.

Articles, or things were, are, or will be possessed and/or used in violation of Title 11, Sub-Chapter D, Section 763, Delaware Code in that [See attached probable cause page].

Wherefore, affiants pray that a search warrant may be issued authorizing a search of the aforesaid 222 S. Governors Avenue, Apartment #3, Dover, Delaware. A two room apartment located on the south side second floor of a white block building on the west side of S. Governors Avenue between Loockerman St. and North Street, in the City of Dover in the manner provided by law.

/s/ Det. Ronald R. Brooks

Affiant

/s/ Det. Larry D. Gray

Affiant

Sworn to (or affirmed) and subscribed before me this 9th day of March A.D. 1976.

/s/ John [illegible] Green

Judge Ct 7

The facts tending to establish probable cause for the issuance of this search warrant are:

1. On Saturday, 2/28/76, Brenda L. B. _____, W/F/15, reported to the Dover Police Department that she had been kidnapped and raped.

2. An investigation of this complaint was conducted by Det. Boyce Failing of the Dover Police Department.

3. Investigation of the aforementioned complaint revealed that Brenda B. _____, while under the influence of drugs, was taken to 222 S. Governors Avenue, Apartment 3, Dover, Delaware.

4. Investigation of the aforementioned complaint revealed that 222 S. Governors Avenue, Apartment #3, Dover, Delaware, is the residence of Jerome Franks, B/M DOB: 10/9/54.

5. Investigation of the aforementioned complaint revealed that on Saturday, 2/29/76, Jerome Franks did have sexual contact with Brenda B. _____ without her consent.

6. On Thursday, 3/4/76 at the Dover Police Department, Brenda B. _____, revealed to Det. Boyce Failing that Jerome Franks was the person who committed the Sexual Assault against her.

7. On Friday, 3/5/76, Jerome Franks was placed under arrest by Cpl. Robert McClements of the Dover Police Department, and charged with Sexual Misconduct.

8. On 3/5/76 at Family Court in Dover, Delaware, Jerome Franks did, after being arrested on the charge of Sexual Misconduct, make a statement of Cpl. Robert McClements, that he thought the charge was concerning Cynthia Bailey not Brenda B. _____.

9. On Friday, 3/5/76, Cynthia C. Bailey, W/F/21 of 132 North Street, Dover, Delaware, did report to Dover Police Department that she had been raped at her residence during the night.

10. Investigation conducted by your affiant on Friday, 3/5/76, revealed the perpetrator of the crime to be an unknown black male, approximately 5'7", 150 lbs., dark complexion, wearing white thermal undershirt, black pants with a belt having a silver or gold buckle, a brown leather ¾ length coat with a tie belt in the front, and a dark knit cap pulled around the eyes.

11. Your affiant can state, that during the commission of this crime, Cynthia Bailey was forced at knife point and with the threat of death to engage in sexual intercourse with the perpetrator of the crime.

12. Your affiant can state that entry was gained to the residence of Cynthia Bailey through a window located on the east side of the residence.

13. Your affiant can state that the residence of Jerome Franks is within a very short distance and direct sight of the residence of Cynthia Bailey.

14. Your affiant can state that the description given by Cynthia Bailey of the unknown black male does coincide with the description of Jerome Franks.

15. On Tuesday, 3/9/76, your affiant contacted Mr. James Williams and Mr. Wesley Lucas of the Delaware Youth Center where Jerome Franks is employed and did have personal conversation with both these people.

16. On Tuesday, 3/9/76, Mr. James Williams revealed to your affiant that the normal dress of Jerome Franks does consist of a white knit thermal undershirt and a brown leather jacket.

17. On Tuesday, 3/9/76, Mr. Wesley Lucas revealed to your affiant that in addition to the thermal undershirt and jacket, Jerome Franks often wears a dark green knit hat.

18. Your affiant can state that a check of official records reveals that in 1971 Jerome Franks was arrested for the crime of rape and subsequently convicted with Assault with intent to Rape.

NOTES

1. On remand in *Franks*, the Delaware Supreme Court held that even if paragraphs 15 through 17 were set aside in their entirety, the remaining allegations were sufficient to establish probable cause. Consequently, Franks' proffer of evidence to contradict the facts alleged in the affidavit was insufficient and the trial judge did not err in failing to hold an evidentiary hearing. The conviction was, therefore, again upheld by that court. Franks v. State, 398 A.2d 783 (Del.1979).

2. **Availability of Informant's Identity.** A defendant's ability to determine whether there is any viable basis for attacking a warrant under *Franks* may depend upon his ability to determine the identity of the informant whose information was relied upon in the showing of probable cause. But does the Fourth Amendment ever give a defendant a right to that information in order to determine whether a *Franks* challenge is possible?

Defendants' right under the Fourth Amendment to the identity of an informant whose information was used to support law enforcement action challenged on Fourth Amendment grounds was addressed in McCray v. Illinois, 386 U.S. 300, 87 S.Ct. 1056 (1967), noted several times in the principal case. McCray complained of the trial court's refusal to require officers to disclose the name of the informant on whose tip they made a warrantless arrest of McCray. Roviaro v. United States, 353 U.S. 53, 77 S.Ct. 623 (1957), *McCray* suggested, held that federal procedural law and perhaps due process require the disclosure of an informant's identity when the facts show the informant may have information bearing on the accused's guilt or innocence. This obligation to disclose an informant's identity did not apply, the Court continued, to situations such as McCray's, where defendants sought similar information only to challenge the evidence's admissibility on Fourth Amendment exclusionary rule grounds. Thus the trial court's refusal to require disclosure to McCray did not violate his Fourth Amendment rights.

The Court left unclear whether *McCray* simply held that on the facts of the case the defendant failed to make a persuasive enough case for his need for the informant's identity or, rather, that no defendant could ever establish a right to disclosure of an informant's identity for purposes of litigating a Fourth Amendment right to exclusion of evidence. *McCray*'s discussion leaves open the possibility that some defendants may, under some quite limited circumstances, have a Fourth Amendment right to disclosure of this information. Perhaps such a right exists only if the trial judge hears all other evidence and determines a reliable resolution of the Fourth Amendment issue is difficult or impossible without further information that might become available if the defendant is permitted to know and perhaps interview the informant.

In at least some warrant situations, it is arguable the *Franks* right to challenge the accuracy of a search warrant affidavit is of no significance unless the defendant has the right to find out the identity of the informant and to inquire of that informant whether the affidavit accurately states what he told officers. Despite *McCray*, then, *Franks* suggests defendants sometimes may have a Fourth Amendment right to an informant's identity to determine whether, on the facts of the case, *Franks* permits a challenge to the affidavit's accuracy and the warrant's validity.

Whatever the constitutional demands, local statutes and court rules sometimes give defendants some right to informants' identities to investigate the validity of possible challenges to evidence's admissibility. The Model Code of Pre-Arraignment Procedure would require disclosure of the identity of an informant where the information relied upon to establish probable cause includes a report of information from that informant unless the judge finds "that the issue of [probable] cause can be fairly determined without such disclosure." Model Code of Pre-Arraignment Procedure § 290.4 (Official Draft, 1975). Disclosure would not be required, however, if (a) the evidence at issue was seized under a search warrant; or (b) the prosecution produced "substantial corroboration of the informant's existence and reliability" consisting of testimony of someone other than the person to whom the informant gave his information. For purposes of deciding whether a "fair" determination can be made without disclosure, the judge is authorized to require the prosecution, *in camera,* to disclose the informant's identity or to produce the informant for questioning by the judge. Is this approach inconsistent with *Roviaro* and *McCray*? Perhaps *McCray* can be read as a case in which the trial judge implicitly found on the facts before him that a "fair" determination of whether the officers had probable cause could be made without requiring disclosure.

C. ENTERING THE PREMISES AND SIMILAR ASPECTS OF THE EXECUTION OF WARRANTS

EDITORS' INTRODUCTION: ANNOUNCEMENT DEMANDS AND RELATED REQUIREMENTS FOR EXECUTION OF WARRANTS

Officers' executions of warrants—especially search warrants—are often affected by numerous statutory and perhaps court rule requirements. Those requirements govern matters such as the time of day or night the warrant may be executed, the need to serve the warrant upon, or present it to, those on the premises when the officers arrive, and the making of a "return" to the issuing magistrate indicating the warrant has been executed and, perhaps, in the case of a search warrant specifying the items seized during the search.

These requirements raise two related issues of particular importance: First, to what if any extent do the Fourth Amendment or similar state constitutional provisions embody some version of these requirements? Second, what if any is the effect of violating these requirements upon the admissibility of evidence obtained during execution of the warrants?

Basic Entry and Announcement Requirements

The most controversial of these execution requirements has been that demanding that before entering premises to execute a warrant, or at least before certain kinds of entry, officers announce their identity and purpose and perhaps comply with other requirements related to entry. Often the issue is posed negatively: when are so-called "no-knock" entries—those involving no such announcement—permitted?

Statutes in many jurisdictions address the matter. For example, a federal statute, 18 U.S.C.A. § 3109, provides:

> The officer may break open any outer or inner door or window of a house, or any part of a house, or anything therein, to execute a search warrant, if, after notice of his authority and purpose, he is refused admittance or when necessary to liberate himself or a person aiding him in the execution of a warrant.

In Miller v. United States, 357 U.S. 301, 78 S.Ct. 1190 (1958), and Sabbath v. United States, 391 U.S. 585, 88 S.Ct. 1755 (1968), the Supreme Court held the "validity" of an entry made to effect an arrest without a warrant must comply with criteria identical to those set out in the statute, apparently as a matter of nonconstitutional law applicable to arrests made by federal officers. Evidence obtained in a search related to an entry violating these provisions cannot be used in a federal criminal trial.

Whether the Fourth Amendment ever requires announcement prior to entry remained uncertain until the Supreme Court addressed the issue in Wilson v. Arkansas, 514 U.S. 927, 115 S.Ct. 1914 (1995). Holding that the Arkansas court below erred in concluding the Fourth Amendment imposed no "knock and announce" requirement for execution of a search warrant, Justice Thomas's *Wilson* opinion for the Court reviewed the common law authority requiring announcement and continued:

> Our own cases have acknowledged that the common-law principle of announcement is "embedded in Anglo-American law," but we have never squarely held that this principle is an element of the reasonableness inquiry under the Fourth Amendment. We now so hold. Given the longstanding common-law endorsement of the practice of announcement, we have little doubt that the Framers of the Fourth Amendment thought that the method of an officer's entry into a dwelling was among the factors to be considered in assessing the reasonableness of a search or seizure. Contrary to the decision below, we hold that in some circumstances an officer's unannounced entry into a home might be unreasonable under the Fourth Amendment.
>
> This is not to say, of course, that every entry must be preceded by an announcement. The Fourth Amendment's flexible requirement of reasonableness should not be read to mandate a rigid rule of announcement that ignores countervailing law enforcement interests. * * * [T]he common-law principle of announcement was never stated as an inflexible rule requiring announcement under all circumstances.

* * *

[B]ecause the common-law rule was justified in part by the belief that announcement generally would avoid "the destruction or breaking of any house . . . by which great damage and inconvenience might ensue," courts acknowledged that the presumption in favor of announcement would yield under circumstances presenting a threat of physical violence. Similarly, courts held that an officer may dispense with announcement in cases where a prisoner escapes from him and retreats to his dwelling. Proof of "demand and refusal" was deemed unnecessary in such cases because it would be a "senseless ceremony" to require an officer in pursuit of a recently escaped arrestee to make an announcement prior to breaking the door to retake him. Finally, courts have indicated that unannounced entry may be justified where police officers have reason to believe that evidence would likely be destroyed if advance notice were given.

We need not attempt a comprehensive catalog of the relevant countervailing factors here. For now, we leave to the lower courts the task of determining the circumstances under which an unannounced entry is reasonable under the Fourth Amendment.

514 U.S. at 934–36, 115 S.Ct. at 1918–19.

The Court further explained the basis for the *Wilson* holding in Richards v. Wisconsin, 520 U.S. 385, 117 S.Ct. 1416 (1997):

The State asserts that the intrusion on individual interests effectuated by a no-knock entry is minimal because the execution of the warrant itself constitutes the primary intrusion on individual privacy and that the individual privacy interest cannot outweigh the generalized governmental interest in effective and safe law enforcement. While it is true that a no-knock entry is less intrusive than, for example, a warrantless search, the individual interests implicated by an unannounced, forcible entry should not be unduly minimized. As we observed in [*Wilson*], the common law recognized that individuals should have an opportunity to themselves comply with the law and to avoid the destruction of property occasioned by a forcible entry. These interests are not inconsequential. Additionally, when police enter a residence without announcing their presence, the residents are not given any opportunity to prepare themselves for such an entry. The State pointed out at oral argument that, in Wisconsin, most search warrants are executed during the late night and early morning hours. The brief interlude between announcement and entry with a warrant may be the opportunity that an individual has to pull on clothes or get out of bed.

520 U.S. at 393 n. 5, 117 S.Ct. at 1421 n. 5.

Wilson made clear the Fourth Amendment sometimes requires announcement. It did not, however, address the effect of officers' failure to announce on the admissibility of evidence obtained in the post-entry search.

In *Miller* and *Sabbath*, the Court assumed entry of premises to make an arrest, if made in violation of the federal statute, rendered the arrest "unlawful," and evidence that would otherwise be admissible as seized in a search incident to the defendant's arrest must be suppressed.

Entries Requiring Announcement

What entries require the announcement specified in *Wilson*? In Sabbath v. United States 391 U.S. 585, 88 S.Ct. 1755 (1968), the entry at issue was made by officers who knocked on the door of the premises and, upon receiving no answer after a few seconds passed, opened the unlocked door and entered. Sabbath argued that the entry violated 18 U.S.C. § 3109. The Government argued in response that "the use of 'force' is an indispensable element of the statute," and since no force was used on the facts, the entry was not subject to the statute. Rejecting the Government's contention, the Court explained:

> Considering the purposes of § 3109, it would indeed be a "grudging application" to hold, as the Government urges, that the use of "force" is an indispensable element of the statute. To be sure, the statute uses the phrase "break open" and that connotes some use of force. But linguistic analysis seldom is adequate when a statute is designed to incorporate fundamental values and the ongoing development of the common law. * * * [Lower courts have] held that § 3109 applies to entries effected by the use of a passkey, which requires no more force than does the turning of a doorknob. An unannounced intrusion into a dwelling—what § 3109 basically proscribes—is no less an unannounced intrusion whether officers break down a door, force open a chain lock on a partially open door, open a locked door by use of a passkey, or, as here, open a closed but unlocked door. The protection afforded by, and the values inherent in, § 3109 must be "governed by something more than the fortuitous circumstance of an unlocked door." *Keiningham v. United States*, 109 U.S.App.D.C. 272, 276, 287 F.2d 126, 130 (1960).

391 U.S. at 589–90, 88 S.Ct. at 1758. "We do not deal here with entries obtained by ruse," the Court added, "which have been viewed as involving no 'breaking.' "

"No Knock" Entries

Wilson's indication that some unannounced entries would be reasonable was developed in Richards v. Wisconsin, 520 U.S. 385, 117 S.Ct. 1416 (1997). *Richards* explained:

> In order to justify a "no-knock" entry, the police must have
> a reasonable suspicion that knocking and announcing their
> presence, under the particular circumstances, would be
> dangerous or futile, or that it would inhibit the effective
> investigation of the crime by, for example, allowing the
> destruction of evidence. This standard—as opposed to a
> probable cause requirement—strikes the appropriate balance
> between the legitimate law enforcement concerns at issue in the
> execution of search warrants and the individual privacy
> interests affected by no-nock entries. This showing is not high,
> but the police should be required to make it whenever the
> reasonableness of a no-knock entry is challenged.

520 U.S. at 394–95, 117 S.Ct. at 1421–22. The Court held that the
Wisconsin court had erred in reading into the Fourth Amendment a
blanket *per se* rule permitting no knock entries in all felony drug cases.
It nevertheless found that on the facts of *Richards* the unannounced
entry was permissible.

Magistrate's Authorization for No-Knock Entry

What is the constitutionally necessary role of the magistrate issuing
a warrant in determining the propriety of no-knock entry? In *Richards*,
the police officers applying for the search warrant requested a warrant
authorizing no-knock entry and submitted to the magistrate a "proposed"
warrant containing such authorization. The magistrate, however,
explicitly deleted this authorization from the warrant before issuing it.
In arguing that the no-knock entry was unreasonable, Richards
emphasized the magistrate's judgment that such entry was not justified.
The Court, however, found this of little or no significance:

> [The magistrate's denial of permission to make a no-knock
> entry] does not alter the reasonableness of the officers' decision,
> which must be evaluated as of the time they entered the hotel
> room. At the time the officers obtained the warrant, they did not
> have evidence sufficient, in the judgment of the magistrate, to
> justify a no-knock warrant. Of course, the magistrate could not
> have anticipated in every particular the circumstances that
> would confront the officers when they arrived at Richards' hotel
> room. These actual circumstances * * * justified the officers'
> ultimate decision to enter without first announcing their
> presence and authority.

520 U.S. at 395–96, 117 S.Ct. at 1422. Commenting more generally, the
Court added:

> A number of States give magistrate judges the authority to
> issue "no-knock" warrants if the officers demonstrate ahead of
> time a reasonable suspicion that entry without prior
> announcement will be appropriate in a particular context.

The practice of allowing magistrates to issue no-knock warrants seems entirely reasonable when sufficient cause to do so can be demonstrated ahead of time. But, as the facts of this case demonstrate, a magistrate's decision not to authorize a no-knock entry should not be interpreted to remove the officers' authority to exercise independent judgment concerning the wisdom of a no-knock entry at the time the warrant is being executed.

520 U.S. at 396 n. 7, 117 S.Ct. at 1422 n. 7.

"Sneak and Peek" Warrants

The Uniting and Strengthening America by Providing Appropriate Tools Required to Intercept and Obstruct Terrorism (USA PATRIOT) Act of 2001, Public Law 107–56, had some impact on the execution of ordinary search warrants. 18 U.S.C. § 3103a previously provided that "[i]n addition to [other] grounds for issuing a warrant * * *, a warrant may be issued to search for and seize any property that constitutes evidence of a criminal offense in violation of the laws of the United States." The 2001 legislation and further amendments in 2006 added the following to section 3103a:

(b) Delay.—With respect to the issuance of any warrant or court order under this section, or any other rule of law, to search for and seize any property or material that constitutes evidence of a criminal offense in violation of the laws of the United States, any notice required, or that may be required, to be given may be delayed if—

(1) the court finds reasonable cause to believe that providing immediate notification of the execution of the warrant may have an adverse result (as defined in section 2705, except if the adverse results constitute only of unduly delaying a trial);

(2) the warrant prohibits the seizure of any tangible property, any wire or electronic communication * * *, or * * * any stored wire or electronic information, except where the court finds reasonable necessity for the seizure; and

(3) the warrant provides for the giving of such notice within a reasonable period not to exceed 30 days after the date of its execution, or on a later date certain if the facts of the case justify a longer period of delay.

(c) Extensions of delay.—Any period of delay authorized by this section may be extended by the court for good cause shown, subject to the condition that extensions should only be granted upon an updated showing of the need for further delay and that each additional delay should be limited to periods of 90 days or less, unless the facts of the case justify a longer period of delay.

Under 18 U.S.C. § 2705:

(2) An adverse result * * * is—

(A) endangering the life or physical safety of an individual;

(B) flight from prosecution;

(C) destruction of or tampering with evidence;

(D) intimidation of potential witnesses; or

(E) otherwise seriously jeopardizing an investigation or unduly delaying a trial.

The amended statute authorizes so-called "sneak and peek" search warrants, which permit officers to enter, search, and leave without providing notice to the occupants of the premises. See United States v. Espinoza, 2005 WL 3542519 (E.D.Wash.2005) (warrant authorizing delayed notice must "strictly comply with the requirements of [section 3103a]").

The 2006 amendments added a requirement that federal judges issuing or denying warrants authorizing delayed notice make reports to the Administrative Office of the United States Courts. After 2007, that office is to make annual reports to Congress concerning the use of delayed notice warrants.

Grounds for Immediate Forcible Entry Developed After Announcement Made

The announcement requirement generally required both an announcement and delay in entering the premises until the occupants permit the entry or the officers have reason to believe the occupants are denying the officers entry. What this means in practice was developed in United States v. Banks, 540 U.S. 31, 124 S.Ct. 521 (2003), involving the execution of a search warrant for Banks's two-bedroom apartment based on information that he was selling cocaine. Officers arrived about 2:00 p.m., called out "police search warrant," and rapped hard enough on the front door to be heard by officers at the rear door. After waiting 15 to 20 seconds and receiving no response, the officers broke open the front door with a battering ram and entered. Banks emerged dripping from a shower and later testified he heard nothing until the crash that opened the door. Officers found cocaine and evidence of drug dealing.

Acknowledging that the officers at the time of arrival did not have grounds for a "no knock" entry, the unanimous Court held that the 15 to 20 second delay excused the officers from any need to wait further before forcibly entering the premises. Whether the delay was sufficient to enable an occupant to get to the door to respond to the officers' demand, the Court explained, was not controlling. Rather, the question was whether the lack of response gave the officers reason to believe the situation presented a sufficient risk of loss of the items sought:

> [T]he issue comes down to whether it was reasonable to suspect imminent loss of evidence after the 15 to 20 seconds the officers waited prior to forcing their way. * * * [T]his call is a close one, [but] we think that after 15 or 20 seconds without a response, police could fairly suspect that cocaine would be gone if they were reticent any longer. Courts of Appeals have, indeed, routinely held similar wait times to be reasonable in drug cases with similar facts including easily disposable evidence (and some courts have found even shorter ones to be reasonable enough).

540 U.S. at 38, 124 S.Ct. at 526. Essentially, the circumstances developing after the announcement excused the officers from complying with the requirement of further delay before forcible entry.

Service of the Warrant

Statutory provisions often require some sort of service of the warrant. For example, Fed.R.Crim.P. 41(d) provides that an officer taking property under a search warrant "shall give to the person from whom or from whose premises the property was taken a copy of the warrant * * * or shall leave the copy * * * at the place from which the property was taken."

In Groh v. Ramirez, 540 U.S. 551, 124 S.Ct. 1284 (2004), the Supreme Court observed:

> It is true * * * that neither the Fourth Amendment nor Rule 41 of the Federal Rules of Criminal Procedure requires the executing officer to serve the warrant on the owner before commencing the search. Rule 41(f)(3) provides that "[t]he officer executing the warrant must: (A) give a copy of the warrant and a receipt for the property taken to the person from whom, or from whose premises, the property was taken; or (B) leave a copy of the warrant and receipt at the place where the officer took the property." Quite obviously, in some circumstances—a surreptitious search by means of a wiretap, for example, or the search of empty or abandoned premises—it will be impracticable or imprudent for the officers to show the warrant in advance. Whether it would be unreasonable to refuse a request to furnish the warrant at the outset of the search when, as in this case, an occupant of the premises is present and poses no threat to the officers' safe and effective performance of their mission, is a question that this case does not present.

540 U.S. at 562 n. 5, 124 S.Ct. at 1290 n. 5.

Would Fourth Amendment policies be furthered by a requirement of service of the warrant? In United States v. Pulliam, 748 F.3d 967, 972–73 (10th Cir. 2014), the defendant argued that service of a complete copy of the search warrant (and any other documents incorporated into the warrant) is necessary to allow persons on the premises to ensure officers executing warrants adhere to the limits on their authority to search and seize. Rejecting this, the court observed that in United States v. Grubbs, 547 U.S. 90, 98, 126 S.Ct. 1494, 1501 (2006), the Supreme Court had commented that the Fourth Amendment does not protect property owners by giving them license to engage officers in debate over the substance of a search warrant. Rather, it provides a post-search opportunity to challenge the admissibility of evidence or to seek compensation for damages.

Destruction of Property in Entering

The relationship between no-knock entry under *Wilson* and *Richards* and destruction of property was addressed in United States v. Ramirez, 523 U.S. 65, 118 S.Ct. 992 (1998). Officers with a search warrant made an unannounced entry into Ramirez's home to locate and arrest Shelby, a violent escaped prison inmate. The officers believed there were weapons in the garage. As they entered, the officers broke a window in the garage and pointed a gun through it to dissuade any occupants from rushing to those weapons. The lower courts held that an unannounced entry involving destruction of property requires a higher degree of exigency than other such entries and that this heightened standard had not been met. The Supreme Court rejected this approach:

> Neither [*Wilson* nor *Richards*] explicitly addressed the question whether the lawfulness of a no-knock entry depends on whether property is damaged in the course of the entry. It is obvious from their holdings, however, that it does not. Under *Richards*, a no-knock entry is justified if police have a "reasonable suspicion" that knocking and announcing would be dangerous, futile, or destructive to the purposes of the investigation. Whether such a "reasonable suspicion" exists depends in no way on whether police must destroy property in order to enter.

> This is not to say that the Fourth Amendment speaks not at all to the manner of executing a search warrant. The general touchstone of reasonableness which governs Fourth Amendment analysis governs the method of execution of the warrant. Excessive or unnecessary destruction of property in the course of a search may violate the Fourth Amendment, even though the entry itself is lawful and the fruits of the search not subject to suppression.

523 U.S. at 70–71, 118 S.Ct. at 996. Given what the officers knew about Shelby, it continued, they had reasonable suspicion that announcement might be dangerous as required by *Richards* for no-knock entry. The Court then concluded:

> As for the manner in which the entry was accomplished, the police here broke a single window in respondent's garage. They

did so because they wished to discourage Shelby, or any other occupant of the house, from rushing to the weapons that the informant had told them respondent might have kept there. Their conduct was clearly reasonable and we conclude that there was no Fourth Amendment violation.

523 U.S. at 71–72, 118 S.Ct. at 997. Since it found no Fourth Amendment violation, the Court added, it was not required to decide whether unreasonable damage to property in the course of an entry to execute a search warrant would require suppression of evidence found in a search conducted after that entry.

Delay in Execution of a Warrant

Statutory provisions and court rules often direct that search warrants be executed within specified times of their issuance, and permit the magistrate issuing a warrant to further limit the time for execution. Federal Rule of Criminal Procedure 41(e), for example, mandates that a search warrant "must command the officer to * * * execute the warrant within a specified time no longer than 14 days."

What is the effect of execution of a warrant beyond such time limits? In Sgro v. United States, 287 U.S. 206, 53 S.Ct. 138 (1932), the Supreme Court considered the admissibility of evidence obtained pursuant to a federal search warrant. The warrant was subject to a since-repealed statute directing such warrants be executed within ten days and specifically adding, "[A]fter the expiration of this time the warrant, unless executed, is void." Officers did not execute the warrant within ten days of its initial issuance, but took it back to the issuing magistrate who changed the date on it and "thus reissued [it]." It was executed soon thereafter. An issuing magistrate has no authority to simply and summarily redate a warrant, the Court held, and that was what was done in the case. Thus the redating of the warrant was ineffective. The Court then assumed without discussion execution of the warrant after the expiration of the ten day period required suppression of the evidence obtained.

Does *Sgro* mean the Fourth Amendment somehow incorporates legislatively-mandated timing requirements? Perhaps the language of the statute convinced the Court that Congress intended any evidence obtained by executing a warrant beyond the ten day period be inadmissible—not as a matter of federal constitutional law but as a matter of legislative mandate. In any case, execution of a search warrant beyond the time frame imposed by Rule 41 has been said to require exclusion of the resulting evidence only if "(1) there was prejudice in the sense that the search might not have occurred or would not have been so abrasive if the Rule had been followed, or (2) there is evidence of intentional and deliberate disregard of a provision in the Rule." United States v. Burgess, 576 F.3d 1078, 1097 (10th Cir.2009).

Search warrants may become subject to challenge due to passage of time within generally permissible time periods for execution, such as the 14 day window provided for in the federal rule. In United States v. Williams, 10 F.3d 590 (8th Cir.1993), for example, a warrant for an apartment issued on October 22, 1992, for an apartment. It was based on information from an informant that on that same day the informant saw a kilogram of cocaine, in its original packaging from Colombia, and $25,000.00 in currency inside the apartment. After the warrant was issued, the officer learned from the informant the kilo of cocaine was distributed; the officer therefore did not execute the warrant immediately. On October 29, however, the officer had the informant telephone Williams. The informant learned Williams received another shipment of cocaine. Consequently, the officer executed the warrant at 1:15 a.m. on October 30. Williams contended that the delay in executing the warrant, although within what was then the ten day requirement of Rule 41, nevertheless was unreasonable and rendered the search constitutionally unreasonable. By the time of the search, he reasoned, the information on which the warrant was issued was "stale" and failed to establish probable cause to believe that at the time the warrant was executed cocaine was on the premises. "Whether the period of delay between issuance and execution of a warrant is reasonable," the court explained in rejecting this contention, "necessarily depends upon the facts and circumstances of each case." Specifically, a court must consider the nature of the criminal activity involved and the kind of property sought to determine whether the passage of the time so increased the likelihood that the property sought was no longer on the premises. At some point, this likelihood is high enough to destroy the probable cause originally existing. On the facts of Williams, the court concluded, the eight day delay did not have this effect:

> [T]he continuing and ongoing nature of cocaine trafficking supports the continued existence of probable cause. It is reasonable for law enforcement officers to conclude that large-scale drug operations continued at the same location for a period of time.

10 F.3d at 595. "[T]he better practice," the court nevertheless acknowledged, would have been for the officer to have obtained a new warrant based on the information obtained on the 29th.

Nighttime Execution

What if any limits are there upon the time of day or night officers may execute a search warrant, and what are the effects of violating these requirements? Statutes and court rules often require nighttime execution of a warrant be authorized by the issuing magistrate. These provisions sometimes explicitly require any such authorization be supported by information made available to the issuing magistrate. Federal Rule of Criminal Procedure 41(e)(2)(a)(ii), for example, provides that a search warrant "must command the officer to * * * execute the warrant during the daytime, unless the judge for good cause expressly authorizes execution at another time * * * ."

In Gooding v. United States, 416 U.S. 430, 94 S.Ct. 1780 (1974), the United States Supreme Court construed 21 U.S.C.A. § 879(a), governing execution of certain search warrants for drugs. The statute provides:

> A search warrant relating to offenses involving controlled substances may be served at any time of the day or night if the judge or United States magistrate issuing the warrant is satisfied that there is probable cause to believe that grounds exist for the warrant and for its service at this time.

Relying on the legislative history of this statute, the Court held that the statute requires for nighttime execution of a warrant only a showing that the contraband is likely to be on the premises at that time. It does *not* require any showing that nighttime execution is necessary, justified in any sense, or even preferable to daytime execution. Although the majority did not explicitly address whether the Fourth Amendment requires a specific justification for nighttime execution of a search warrant, the Court's failure to mention any such possibility suggests it was not receptive to the argument—made in dissent—that any special showing is constitutionally required.

When a nighttime search in violation of Rule 41(e)(2)(a)(ii) requires exclusion is not clear. See United States v. Kelley, 652 F.3d 915, 918 n. 3 (8th Cir.2011) ("when Rule 41(e)(2)(A)(ii) applies and has been violated, [we consider] 'whether the night search prejudiced the defendants or whether there was reckless disregard of the proper procedure for a night search by the officials involved' "). A state court held the defendant was not prejudiced by improper execution of a warrant at 10:18 p.m. when the occupants were awake and clothed and permitted daytime execution shortly after 6:00 a.m. would have been more abrasive. State v. Deen, 2015 WY 5, ¶¶ 12–18, 340 P3d 1036, 1040–41 (Wyo. 2015).

The Minnesota Supreme Court in State v. Jackson, 742 N.W.2d 163 (Minn.2007), took a much different approach. Under a Minnesota statute, a search warrant may be executed at night only if it is issued on an affidavit setting out facts showing a nighttime search "is necessary to prevent the loss, destruction, or removal of the objects of the search or to protect the searchers or the public." The court held this statute reflected a Fourth Amendment requirement. Evidence obtained by a search under a warrant lacking the required showing had to be exclusion both because of the violation of the statute and under Fourth Amendment law. The court explained in part:

> Given the historical aversion to nighttime searches, the historical recognition of the unique status of persons in their home at night, the Supreme Court's recognition of the especially intrusive nature of nighttime searches of a home and the holdings of several federal courts that nighttime searches

implicate the reasonableness requirement of the Fourth Amendment, we conclude that the search of a home at night is a factor to be considered in determining whether a search is reasonable under the Fourth Amendment. We further conclude that in order to be constitutionally reasonable, nighttime searches require additional justification beyond the probable cause required for a daytime search.

742 N.W.2d at 176–77. Accord, Yanez-Marquez v. Lynch, 789 F3d 434, 467 (4th Cir.2015) ("we hold that the nighttime execution of a daytime warrant violates the Fourth Amendment, absent consent or exigent circumstances").

Hudson v. Michigan

Supreme Court of the United States, 2006.
547 U.S. 586, 126 S.Ct. 2159.

■ JUSTICE SCALIA delivered the opinion of the Court, except as to Part IV.

We decide whether violation of the "knock-and-announce" rule requires the suppression of all evidence found in the search.

I

Police obtained a warrant authorizing a search for drugs and firearms at the home of petitioner Booker Hudson. They discovered both. Large quantities of drugs were found, including cocaine rocks in Hudson's pocket. A loaded gun was lodged between the cushion and armrest of the chair in which he was sitting. Hudson was charged under Michigan law with unlawful drug and firearm possession.

This case is before us only because of the method of entry into the house. When the police arrived to execute the warrant, they announced their presence, but waited only a short time—perhaps "three to five seconds"—before turning the knob of the unlocked front door and entering Hudson's home. Hudson moved to suppress all the inculpatory evidence, arguing that the premature entry violated his Fourth Amendment rights.

The Michigan [courts refused to suppress the evidence, reasoning] that suppression is inappropriate when entry is made pursuant to warrant but without proper " 'knock and announce.' " * * * We granted certiorari.

II

[*Wilson v. Arkansas*, 514 U.S. 927, 931–932, 115 S.Ct. 1914, 131 L.Ed.2d 976 (1995)] * * * specifically declined to decide whether the exclusionary rule is appropriate for violation of the knock-and-announce requirement. That question is squarely before us now.

III

A

* * *

Suppression of evidence * * * has always been our last resort, not our first impulse. The exclusionary rule generates "substantial social costs," which sometimes include setting the guilty free and the dangerous at large. We have therefore been "cautio[us] against expanding" it, and "have repeatedly emphasized that the rule's 'costly toll' upon truth-seeking and law enforcement objectives presents a high obstacle for those urging [its] application." We have rejected "[i]ndiscriminate application" of the rule, and have held it to be applicable only "where its remedial objectives are thought most efficaciously served,"—that is, "where its deterrence benefits outweigh its 'substantial social costs.'"

* * *

[E]xclusion may not be premised on the mere fact that a constitutional violation was a "but-for" cause of obtaining evidence. Our cases show that but-for causality is only a necessary, not a sufficient, condition for suppression. In this case, of course, the constitutional violation of an illegal manner of entry was not a but-for cause of obtaining the evidence. Whether that preliminary misstep had occurred or not, the police would have executed the warrant they had obtained, and would have discovered the gun and drugs inside the house. But even if the illegal entry here could be characterized as a but-for cause of discovering what was inside, we have "never held that evidence is 'fruit of the poisonous tree' simply because 'it would not have come to light but for the illegal actions of the police.'" Rather, but-for cause, or "causation in the logical sense alone," can be too attenuated to justify exclusion. * * *

Attenuation can occur, of course, when the causal connection is remote. Attenuation also occurs when, even given a direct causal connection, the interest protected by the constitutional guarantee that has been violated would not be served by suppression of the evidence obtained. * * *

[C]ases excluding the fruits of unlawful warrantless searches say nothing about the appropriateness of exclusion to vindicate the interests protected by the knock-and-announce requirement. Until a valid warrant has issued, citizens are entitled to shield "their persons, houses, papers, and effects," U.S. Const., Amdt. 4, from the government's scrutiny. Exclusion of the evidence obtained by a warrantless search vindicates that entitlement. The interests protected by the knock-and-announce requirement are quite different—and do not include the shielding of potential evidence from the government's eyes.

One of those interests is the protection of human life and limb, because an unannounced entry may provoke violence in supposed self-defense by the surprised resident. Another interest is the protection of property. * * * The knock-and-announce rule gives individuals "the opportunity to comply with the law and to avoid the destruction of property occasioned by a forcible entry." And thirdly, the knock-and-announce rule protects those elements of privacy and dignity that can be destroyed by a sudden entrance. It gives residents the "opportunity to prepare themselves for" the entry of the police. "The brief interlude between announcement and entry with a warrant may be the opportunity that an individual has to pull on clothes or get out of bed." In other words, it assures the opportunity to collect oneself before answering the door.

What the knock-and-announce rule has never protected, however, is one's interest in preventing the government from seeing or taking evidence described in a warrant. Since the interests that were violated in this case have nothing to do with the seizure of the evidence, the exclusionary rule is inapplicable.

B

Quite apart from the requirement of unattenuated causation, the exclusionary rule has never been applied except "where its deterrence benefits outweigh its 'substantial social costs.' " The costs here are considerable. In addition to the grave adverse consequence that exclusion of relevant incriminating evidence always entails (viz., the risk of releasing dangerous criminals into society), imposing that massive remedy for a knock-and-announce violation would generate a constant flood of alleged failures to observe the rule, and claims that any asserted * * * justification for a no-knock entry, had inadequate support. The cost of entering this lottery would be small, but the jackpot enormous: suppression of all evidence, amounting in many cases to a get-out-of-jail-free card. Courts would experience as never before the reality that "[t]he exclusionary rule frequently requires extensive litigation to determine whether particular evidence must be excluded." * * *

Another consequence of the incongruent remedy Hudson proposes would be police officers' refraining from timely entry after knocking and announcing. As we have observed, the amount of time they must wait is necessarily uncertain. If the consequences of running afoul of the rule were so massive, officers would be inclined to wait longer than the law requires—producing preventable violence against officers in some cases, and the destruction of evidence in many others. * * *

Next to these "substantial social costs" we must consider the deterrence benefits, existence of which is a necessary condition for exclusion. To begin with, the value of deterrence depends upon the strength of the incentive to commit the forbidden act. Viewed from this perspective, deterrence of knock-and-announce violations is not worth a lot. Violation of the warrant requirement sometimes produces incriminating evidence that could not otherwise be obtained. But ignoring knock-and-announce can realistically be expected to achieve absolutely nothing except the prevention of destruction of evidence and the avoidance of life-threatening resistance by occupants of the premises-dangers which, if there is even "reasonable suspicion" of their existence, suspend the knock-and-announce requirement anyway. Massive deterrence is hardly required.

It seems to us not even true, as Hudson contends, that without suppression there will be no deterrence of knock-and-announce violations at all. * * *

We cannot assume that exclusion in this context is necessary deterrence simply because we found that it was necessary deterrence in different contexts and long ago. That would be forcing the public today to pay for the sins and inadequacies of a legal regime that existed almost half a century ago. Dollree Mapp could not turn to 42 U.S.C. § 1983 for meaningful relief; *Monroe v. Pape*, 365 U.S. 167, 81 S.Ct. 473, 5 L.Ed.2d 492 (1961), which began the slow but steady expansion of that remedy, was decided the same Term as [*Mapp v. Ohio*, 367 U.S. 643, 81 S.Ct. 1684, 6 L.Ed.2d 1081 (1961)]. It would be another 17 years before the § 1983 remedy was extended to reach the deep pocket of municipalities. Citizens whose Fourth Amendment rights were violated by federal officers could not bring suit until 10 years after *Mapp,* with this Court's decision in *Bivens v. Six Unknown Fed. Narcotics Agents*, 403 U.S. 388, 91 S.Ct. 1999, 29 L.Ed.2d 619 (1971).

* * *

Another development over the past half-century that deters civil-rights violations is the increasing professionalism of police forces, including a new emphasis on internal police discipline. * * * [W]e now have increasing evidence that police forces across the United States take the constitutional rights of citizens seriously. There have been "wide-ranging reforms in the education, training, and supervision of police officers." S. Walker, Taming the System: The Control of Discretion in Criminal Justice 1950–1990, p. 51 (1993). Numerous sources are now available to teach officers and their supervisors what is required of them under this Court's cases, how to respect constitutional guarantees in various situations, and how to craft an effective regime for internal discipline. Failure to teach and enforce constitutional requirements exposes municipalities to financial liability. Moreover, modern police forces are staffed with professionals; it is not credible to assert that internal discipline, which can limit successful careers, will not have a deterrent effect. There is also evidence that the increasing use of various forms of citizen review can enhance police accountability.

In sum, the social costs of applying the exclusionary rule to knock-and-announce violations are considerable; the incentive to such violations is minimal to begin with, and the extant deterrences against them are substantial—incomparably greater than the factors deterring warrantless entries when *Mapp* was decided. Resort to the massive remedy of suppressing evidence of guilt is unjustified.

* * *

For the foregoing reasons we affirm the judgment of the Michigan Court of Appeals.

It is so ordered.

■ JUSTICE KENNEDY, concurring in part and concurring in the judgment.

* * *

Today's decision does not address any demonstrated pattern of knock-and-announce violations. If a widespread pattern of violations were shown, and particularly if those violations were committed against persons who lacked the means or voice to mount an effective protest, there would be reason for grave concern. * * *

In this case the relevant evidence was discovered not because of a failure to knock-and-announce, but because of a subsequent search pursuant to a lawful warrant. The Court in my view is correct to hold that suppression was not required. * * * [T]he Court's holding is fully supported by Parts I through III of its opinion. I accordingly join those Parts and concur in the judgment.

■ JUSTICE BREYER, with whom JUSTICE STEVENS, JUSTICE SOUTER, and JUSTICE GINSBURG join, dissenting.

* * *

[T]he driving legal purpose underlying the exclusionary rule, namely, the deterrence of unlawful government behavior, argues strongly for suppression. * * * Indeed, this Court in *Mapp* held that the exclusionary rule applies to the States in large part due to its belief that alternative state mechanisms for enforcing the Fourth Amendment's guarantees had proved "worthless and futile."

Why is application of the exclusionary rule any the less necessary here? Without such a rule, as in *Mapp*, police know that they can ignore the Constitution's requirements without risking suppression of evidence discovered after an unreasonable entry. As in *Mapp*, some government officers will find it easier, or believe it less risky, to proceed with what they consider a necessary search immediately and without the requisite constitutional (say, warrant or knock-and-announce) compliance.

Of course, the State or the Federal Government may provide alternative remedies for knock-and-announce violations. But that circumstance was true of *Mapp* as well. What reason is there to believe that those remedies (such as private damages actions under 42 U.S.C. § 1983), which the Court found inadequate in *Mapp,* can adequately deter unconstitutional police behavior here?

The cases reporting knock-and-announce violations are legion. Indeed, these cases of reported violations seem sufficiently frequent and serious as to indicate "a widespread pattern." Yet the majority, like Michigan and the United States, has failed to cite a single reported case in which a plaintiff has collected more than nominal damages solely as a result of a knock-and-announce violation. * * *

* * * The majority's "substantial social costs" argument is an argument against the Fourth Amendment's exclusionary principle itself. And it is an argument that this Court, until now, has consistently rejected.

III

* * *

A

The majority * * * argues that "the constitutional violation of an illegal manner of entry was not a but-for cause of obtaining the evidence." But taking causation as it is commonly understood in the law, I do not see how that can be so. See W. Keeton, D. Dobbs, R. Keeton, & D. Owen, Prosser and Keeton on Law of Torts 266 (5th ed.1984). Although the police might have entered Hudson's home lawfully, they did not in fact do so. Their unlawful behavior inseparably characterizes their actual entry; that entry was a necessary condition of their presence in Hudson's home; and their presence in Hudson's home was a necessary condition of their finding and seizing the evidence. At the same time, their discovery of evidence in Hudson's home was a readily foreseeable consequence of their entry and their unlawful presence within the home.

Moreover, separating the "manner of entry" from the related search slices the violation too finely. * * * [W]e have described a failure to comply with the knock-and-announce rule, not as an independently unlawful event, but as a factor that renders the search "constitutionally defective."

The Court nonetheless accepts Michigan's argument that the requisite but-for-causation is not satisfied in this case because, whether or not the constitutional violation occurred (what the Court refers to as a "preliminary misstep"), "the police would have executed the warrant they had obtained, and would have discovered the gun and drugs inside the house." As support for this proposition, Michigan rests on this Court's inevitable discovery cases.

This claim, however, misunderstands the inevitable discovery doctrine. Justice Holmes in [*Silverthorne Lumber Co. v. United States*, 251 U.S. 385, 40 S.Ct. 182, 64 L.Ed. 319 (1920)], in discussing an "independent source" exception, set forth the principles underlying the inevitable discovery rule. That rule does not refer to discovery that would have taken place if the police behavior in question had (contrary to fact) been lawful. The doctrine does not treat as critical what hypothetically could have happened had the police acted lawfully in the first place. Rather, "independent" or "inevitable" discovery refers to discovery that did occur or that would have occurred (1) despite (not simply in the absence of) the unlawful behavior and (2) independently of that unlawful behavior. The government cannot, for example, avoid suppression of evidence seized without a warrant (or pursuant to a defective warrant) simply by showing that it could have obtained a valid warrant had it sought one. Instead, it must show that the same evidence "inevitably would have been discovered by lawful means." "What a man could do is not at all the same as what he would do." Austin, Ifs And Cans, 42 Proceedings of the British Academy 109, 111–112 (1956).

* * *

Of course, had the police entered the house lawfully, they would have found the gun and drugs. But that fact is beside the point. The question is not what police might have done had they not behaved unlawfully. The question is what they did do. Was there set in motion an independent chain of events that would have inevitably led to the discovery and seizure of the evidence despite, and independent of, that behavior? The answer here is "no."

* * *

C

The majority * * * says that evidence should not be suppressed once the causal connection between unlawful behavior and discovery of the evidence becomes too "attenuated." But the majority then makes clear that it is not using the word "attenuated" to mean what this Court's precedents have typically used that word to mean, namely, that the discovery of the evidence has come about long after the unlawful behavior took place or in an independent way, i.e., through " 'means sufficiently distinguishable to be purged of the primary taint.' " *Wong Sun v. United States*, 371 U.S. 471, 487–488, 83 S.Ct. 407, 9 L.Ed.2d 441 (1963).

Rather, the majority gives the word "attenuation" a new meaning * * * . "Attenuation," it says, "also occurs when, even given a direct causal connection, the interest protected by the constitutional guarantee that has been violated would not be served by suppression of the evidence obtained." The interests the knock-and-announce rule seeks to protect, the Court adds, are "human life" (at stake when a householder is "surprised"), "property" (such as the front door), and "those elements of privacy and dignity that can be destroyed by a sudden entrance," namely, "the opportunity to collect oneself before answering the door." Since none of those interests led to the discovery of the evidence seized here, there is no reason to suppress it.

* * *

[But] whether the interests underlying the knock-and-announce rule are implicated in any given case is, in a sense, beside the point. * * * [F]ailure to comply with the knock-and-announce rule renders the related search unlawful. And where a search is unlawful, the law insists upon suppression of the evidence consequently discovered, even if that evidence or its possession has little or nothing to do with the reasons underlying the unconstitutionality of a search. * * *

IV

There is perhaps one additional argument implicit in the majority's approach. The majority says * * * that the "cost" to a defendant of "entering this lottery," i.e., of claiming a "knock-and-announce" violation, "would be small, but the jackpot enormous"—namely, a potential "get-out-of-jail-free card." It adds that the "social costs" of applying the exclusionary rule here are not worth the deterrence benefits. * * * [O]ne is left with a simple unvarnished conclusion, namely, that in this kind of case, a knock-and-announce case, "[r]esort to the massive remedy of suppressing evidence of guilt is unjustified." Why is that judicial judgment, taken on its own, inappropriate? Could it not be argued that the knock-and-announce rule, a subsidiary Fourth Amendment rule, is simply not important enough to warrant a suppression remedy? Could the majority not simply claim that the suppression game is not worth the candle?

The answer, I believe, is "no." That "no" reflects history, a history that shows the knock-and-announce rule is important. That "no" reflects precedent, precedent that shows there is no pre-existing legal category of exceptions to the exclusionary rule into which the knock-and-announce cases might fit. That "no" reflects empirical fact, experience that provides confirmation of what common sense suggests: without suppression there is little to deter knock-and-announce violations.

* * *

[W]ith respect, I dissent.

D. PARTICULARITY DEMANDED OF WARRANTS AND RELATED LIMITS ON EXECUTION OF WARRANTS

The Fourth Amendment reasonableness of a search or arrest pursuant to a warrant may be affected by the manner in which that search or arrest is carried out as well as by the procedure followed in issuing the warrant. Some, although not all, Fourth Amendment requirements affecting the execution of warrants flow from limits imposed by the terms of the warrants themselves; this is particularly true with regard to search warrants. It is therefore useful to consider together the Fourth Amendment requirements governing what the warrant itself must specify and the often-related requirements applicable to the manner in which officers execute warrants.

In connection with the material in this subchapter, reconsider Horton v. California, 496 U.S. 128, 110 S.Ct. 2301 (1990), reprinted in Subchapter C of Chapter 2, concerning the right of officers executing a search warrant to seize undescribed items found in "plain view" during the course of the search.

EDITORS' INTRODUCTION: PARTICULARITY AND ITS EFFECT ON EXECUTION OF THE WARRANT

The terms of the Fourth Amendment provide in part that "no Warrants shall issue, but * * * particularly describing the place to be searched, and the persons or things to be seized." Compared to the probable cause requirement for warrant issuance, the mandate of particularity in the warrant has received relatively little attention from the Supreme Court. It is clear, however, the particularity requirement is related to the execution of the warrant and is designed to limit the officers' activity under the warrant. Without a warrant describing with precision the place to be searched and the things to be seized, the Court has observed, "officers are free to determine for themselves the extent of their search and the precise objects to be seized." Trupiano v. United States, 334 U.S. 699, 710, 68 S.Ct. 1229, 1235 (1948).

Construing Warrants by Reference to the Affidavit. The actual document constituting the search or arrest warrant is often a different one than the document constituting the affidavit on which the warrant issues. There may also be a document constituting an application for the warrant. Warrants often incorporate other documents by explicit reference to them. The search warrant descriptions discussed later in this Introduction are sometimes contained only in the affidavit or application. The warrant itself may authorize officers to search the premises described in the affidavit.

In Groh v. Ramirez, 540 U.S. 551, 124 S.Ct. 1284 (2004), the Government argued that a search warrant lacking any description of the items to be searched for and seized was saved by a description in the application for the warrant. The Court responded:

> The fact that the *application* adequately described the "things to be seized" does not save the *warrant* from its facial invalidity. The Fourth Amendment by its terms requires particularity in the warrant, not in the supporting documents. And for good reason: "The presence of a search warrant serves a high function," and that high function is not necessarily vindicated when some other document, somewhere, says something about the objects of the search, but the contents of that document are neither known to the person whose home is being searched nor available for her inspection. We do not say that the Fourth Amendment prohibits a warrant from cross-referencing other documents. Indeed, most Courts of Appeals have held that a court may construe a warrant with reference to a supporting application or affidavit if the warrant uses appropriate words of incorporation, and if the supporting document accompanies the warrant. But in this case the warrant did not incorporate other documents by reference, nor did either the affidavit or the application (which had been placed

under seal) accompany the warrant. Hence, we need not further explore the matter of incorporation.

540 U.S. at 557–558, 124 S.Ct. at 1289–90.

The Place to Be Searched. Until the case reprinted in this subchapter, the Supreme Court seldom addressed the requirement that the place to be searched be described with precision. In United States v. Karo, 468 U.S. 705, 104 S.Ct. 3296 (1984), however, the Court indirectly considered the scope of this Fourth Amendment demand. The discussion makes clear that the Court regards the precision requirements as having sufficient flexibility to accommodate use of warrants for law enforcement activity other than traditional searches of premises easily described.

In *Karo*, the Government concealed an electronic beeping device in a can of chemicals which was then transferred to Karo; law enforcement officers used the device to trace Karo's movements in his car. Karo contended that the Government's concealment of the device in the car was a search. In response, the Government urged that if this was a search, no valid warrant could be obtained for it because the Government would not be able to describe the "place to be searched" with adequate precision. In fact, it suggested, the very purpose of the use of the beeper was to determine the place to be searched, i.e., the place to which the can of chemicals would be taken. The Court rejected the Government's argument:

> [I]t will still be possible to describe the object into which the beeper is to be placed, the circumstances that led agents to wish to install the beeper, and the length of time for which beeper surveillance is requested. In our view, this information will suffice to permit issuance of a warrant authorizing beeper installation and surveillance.

468 U.S. at 718, 104 S.Ct. at 3305.

Things to Be Seized. As to the purpose of the mandate that "things to be seized" be described with precision in a search warrant, the Supreme Court has offered:

> The requirement * * * makes general searches under [warrants] impossible and prevents the seizure of one thing under a warrant describing another. As to what is to be taken, nothing is left to the discretion of the officer executing the warrant.

Marron v. United States, 275 U.S. 192, 196, 48 S.Ct. 74, 76 (1927).

Groh v. Ramirez, 540 U.S. 551, 124 S.Ct. 1284 (2004), held that a search warrant containing no description of the items to be seized at all was completely ineffective. The Court explained:

> [U]nless the particular items described in the affidavit are also set forth in the warrant itself (or at least incorporated by reference, and the affidavit present at the search), there can be

no written assurance that the Magistrate actually found probable cause to search for, and to seize, every item mentioned in the affidavit. In this case, for example, it is at least theoretically possible that the Magistrate was satisfied that the search for weapons and explosives was justified by the showing in the affidavit, but not convinced that any evidentiary basis existed for rummaging through respondents' files and papers for receipts pertaining to the purchase or manufacture of such items. Or, conceivably, the Magistrate might have believed that some of the weapons mentioned in the affidavit could have been lawfully possessed and therefore should not be seized. The mere fact that the Magistrate issued a warrant does not necessarily establish that he agreed that the scope of the search should be as broad as the affiant's request. * * *

We have long held, moreover, that the purpose of the particularity requirement is not limited to the prevention of general searches. A particular warrant also "assures the individual whose property is searched or seized of the lawful authority of the executing officer, his need to search, and the limits of his power to search." *United States v. Chadwick,* 433 U.S. 1, 9, 97 S.Ct. 2476, 53 L.Ed.2d 538 (1977) * * * .

540 U.S. at 560, 124 S.Ct. at 1291–92.

Groh was a civil action by Ramirez for damages. The defendant contended that he orally described the objects of the search to persons present when the officers arrived and to the absent Ramirez by telephone. Thus, he argued, the goals of the particularity requirement were met and the search was reasonable. The Court did not reach whether such oral notice might make the search reasonable. Since the specific issue in the case was whether summary judgment should have been granted and the plaintiffs contended that the defendant orally stated only that he was seeking "an explosive device in a box," the Court had to assume the plaintiffs' version was correct. 540 U.S. at 562–63, 124 S.Ct. at 1293.

The Court's comment in *Marron* that officers executing warrants have no discretion as to what is to be seized is, to some extent, incorrect. Under the "plain view seizure rule" (considered in Subchapter C(2) of Chapter 2), officers may sometimes seize items not described in the search warrant if they have probable cause to believe the items are subject to seizure and they come upon the items while searching within the terms of the warrant.

Marron and *Groh* both suggest that the description of things to be seized may limit the officers' authority to *search* within the described premises.

This is illustrated by Stanley v. Georgia, 394 U.S. 557, 89 S.Ct. 1243 (1969). Officers searched Stanley's residence under a warrant authorizing them to search the premises for, and to seize, numerous categories of items related to bookmaking. While searching desk drawers in a bedroom, they discovered three reels of eight millimeter film. Using Stanley's projector and screen, they viewed the films. This screening convinced the officers—apparently with good cause—the films were obscene and, therefore, they seized them. At Stanley's trial for possession of the films, the films were admitted into evidence over his objection. A majority of the Supreme Court reversed Stanley's conviction on other grounds and did not reach the propriety of the officers' actions. Justice Stewart, however, concurred on the ground the officers, by examining the film as they did, had gone beyond their authority to search under the warrant. Consequently, he reasoned, the films had been improperly seized:

> To condone what happened here is to invite a governmental official to use a seemingly precise and legal warrant only as a ticket to get into a man's home, and, once inside, to launch forth upon unconfined searches and indiscriminate seizures as if armed with all the unbridled and illegal power of a general warrant.

394 U.S. at 572, 89 S.Ct. at 1251–52. Under this approach, when did the officers' conduct become improper? Did the warrant authorize them to look into closed desk drawers? Almost certainly so, since the bookmaking items might well have been located there. But did it authorize them to examine the film in such a manner as was necessary to determine its contents? to screen the film as they did? Perhaps this turns upon whether the officers could reasonably have anticipated that this action— examining the film—would enable them to locate and seize those items which the warrant specified.

If the specificity of description of the things to be searched for and seized in a search warrant limits the officers' right to search the premises, this may help explain the requirement of specificity applicable to those descriptions. Only a specific warrant can limit the officers to a search of no greater scope or intensity than is necessary to locate the items which the officers have reason to believe are in the premises.

Specificity of the Description of Things to be Seized. In several cases, the Supreme Court has addressed the constitutionally-required specificity in regard to "things." In Stanford v. Texas, 379 U.S. 476, 85 S.Ct. 506 (1965), a search warrant was issued listing various materials believed related to the operation of the Communist Party in Texas. The Court invalidated the resulting conviction on the ground the warrant offended the requirement of particularity:

> We need not decide in the present case whether the description of the things to be seized would have been too generalized to pass constitutional muster, had the things been weapons, narcotics or "cases of whiskey." * * * The point is that it was not any contraband of that kind which was ordered to be seized, but

literary material—"books, records, pamphlets, cards, receipts, lists, memoranda, pictures, recordings and other written instruments concerning the Communist Party of Texas and the operation of the Communist Party in Texas." The indiscriminate sweep of that language is constitutionally intolerable. To hold otherwise would be false to the terms of the Fourth Amendment, false to its meaning, and false to its history.

379 U.S. at 486, 85 S.Ct. at 512.

In Andresen v. Maryland, 427 U.S. 463, 96 S.Ct. 2737 (1976), on the other hand, the warrant listed numerous documents believed related to the fraudulent transfer of a specifically described piece of realty. It concluded with authorization to seize "other fruits, instrumentalities and evidence of crime at this [time] unknown." The Court construed this as limited to other evidence relating to the crime committed by transfer of the identified lot. As so construed, it concluded, the warrant did not authorize the officers to conduct a search for evidence of other crimes and, therefore, was sufficiently precise. Andresen did not argue it was constitutionally necessary for the warrant to describe the evidence of the crime more specifically. But he did contend the list of the specified documents constituted a prohibited "general warrant." The Court responded:

> We disagree. Under investigation was a complex real estate scheme whose existence could be proved only by piecing together many bits of evidence. * * * The complexity of an illegal scheme may not be used as a shield to avoid detection when the State has demonstrated probable cause to believe that a crime has been committed and probable cause to believe that evidence of this crime is in the suspect's possession. * * *

427 U.S. at 482 n. 10, 96 S.Ct. at 2749 n. 10. Apparently, this means that the complexity of a crime under investigation sometimes causes difficulty in predicting in advance of a search what documents would constitute evidence of its commission. *Andresen* seems to hold that this justifies some relaxation of the specificity requirement. The things sought in *Stanford* (or the things that might have been seized under the warrant in that case) were more likely protected by the First Amendment than the items sought in *Andresen*. This may help explain the demand for greater specificity on the facts of *Stanford*.

Partially Invalid Warrants and Severability. This chapter earlier—in Subchapter B(2)—addressed the rule that invalid provisions of a search warrant will often be "severable" from valid provisions and not affect the admissibility of evidence obtained by law enforcement activity supported by those valid provisions. This rule is frequently applied when some provisions are invalid because they are imprecise.

Nevertheless, sometimes severability does not save a challenged search warrant. This was the case in Cassady v. Goering, 567 F.3d 628

(10th Cir.2009), in which a search warrant issued on facts establishing probable cause to believe marijuana was being grown on Cassady's farm. The court described the warrant:

> The warrant * * * authorized the search of the entire farm, including Mr. Cassady's house, and the seizure of "[a]ny & all narcotics," "[a]ny and all illegal contraband" and various specific items mostly related to a narcotics operation. In addition, * * * the warrant expressly permitted the search and seizure of "all other evidence of criminal activity" as well as personal property that was stolen, embezzled, or otherwise illegal; or was designed, intended, or had been used to commit a criminal offense; or would be material evidence in a criminal prosecution in Colorado or any other state; or the seizure of which was expressly required, authorized, or permitted by any Colorado statute.

The Tenth Circuit explained its "extensive, multi-step analysis for determining when the severability doctrine may be applied:"

> After dividing the warrant into sections, we evaluate the constitutionality of each part. If at least one part passes constitutional muster (*i.e.*, is sufficiently particularized and supported by probable cause), we determine whether the valid sections are distinguishable from the invalid sections. As we [have] explained * * * , "[t]he mere fact that one or more parts of a search warrant are valid, however, does not mean that the severance doctrine is *automatically* applicable. Instead, ... some part of the warrant must be *both* constitutionally valid *and* distinguishable from the invalid portions in order for severability to apply." Severance is permissible where "each of the categories of items to be seized describes distinct subject matter in language not linked to language of other categories, and each valid category retains its significance when isolated from rest of the warrant." Notably, this does not end the inquiry, however: "[t]otal suppression may still be required even where a part of the warrant is valid (and distinguishable) if the invalid portions so predominate the warrant that the warrant in essence authorizes a general, exploratory rummaging in a person's belongings."

567 F.3d at 635, quoting from United States v. Sells, 463 F.3d 1148 (10th Cir.2006). Applying this analysis, the court assumed the language authorizing search for and seizure of narcotics and related illegal contraband was adequately precise and supported by the showing of probable cause. Nevertheless, it held the severability rule inapplicable. The search warrant was consequently wholly ineffective.

Relying heavily upon *Cassady*, a federal district judge held invalid a warrant containing several valid provisions but also authorizing a search for and seizure of "any and all other documents, instrumentalists [*sic*], video recordings, audio recordings, or substances which constitute evidence of the commission of or constitute fruits of or which property has been used as the mean [*sic*] of committing violations of the Illinois Compiled Statutes." "[S]everance isn't usually available," the judge observed, "where a warrant contains a general, 'all evidence of crime' search clause." United States v. Conklin, 2016 WL 35550, at *5–6 (S.D. Ill. 2016), appeal dismissed.

Persons to Be Seized. The terms of the Fourth Amendment also require that at least certain warrants describe "persons * * * to be seized" with particularity. Presumably, this requirement applies to arrest warrants. When is a person described with sufficient particularity? Is a name sufficient? A name and a date of birth? A physical description without a name? In Visor v. State, 660 S.W.2d 816 (Tex.Crim.App.1983), the arrest warrant described the person to be arrested as an "unknown black female." Holding this aspect of the warrant ineffective, the court observed that to uphold it "would be to approve a general warrant prohibited by the federal constitution."

* * *

The principal case in this section addresses the criterion for determining whether a warrant is sufficiently precise for Fourth Amendment purposes. In addition, however, it considers the demands upon officers who in the process of executing a warrant discover the warrant is not as precise—at least "as applied"—as they previously thought.

Maryland v. Garrison

Supreme Court of the United States, 1987.
480 U.S. 79, 107 S.Ct. 1013.

■ JUSTICE STEVENS delivered the opinion of the Court.

Baltimore police officers obtained and executed a warrant to search the person of Lawrence McWebb and "the premises known as 2036 Park Avenue third floor apartment." When the police applied for the warrant and when they conducted the search pursuant to the warrant, they reasonably believed that there was only one apartment on the premises described in the warrant. In fact, the third floor was divided into two apartments, one occupied by McWebb and one by respondent. Before the officers executing the warrant became aware that they were in a separate apartment occupied by respondent, they had discovered the contraband that provided the basis for respondent's conviction for violating Maryland's Controlled Substances Act. The question presented is whether the seizure of that contraband was prohibited by the Fourth Amendment.

The trial court denied respondent's motion to suppress the evidence seized from his apartment, and the Maryland Special Court of Appeals affirmed. The Court of Appeals of Maryland reversed and remanded with instructions to remand the case for a new trial.

There is no question that the warrant was valid and was supported by probable cause. The trial court found, and the two appellate courts did not dispute, that after making a reasonable investigation, including a verification of information obtained from a reliable informant, an exterior examination of the three-story building at 2036 Park Avenue, and an inquiry of the utility company, the officer who obtained the warrant reasonably concluded that there was only one apartment on the third floor and that it was occupied by McWebb. When six Baltimore police officers executed the warrant, they fortuitously encountered McWebb in front of the building and used his key to gain admittance to the first floor hallway and to the locked door at the top of the stairs to the third floor. As they entered the vestibule on the third floor, they encountered respondent, who was standing in the hallway area. The police could see into the interior of both McWebb's apartment to the left and respondent's to the right, for the doors to both were open. Only after respondent's apartment had been entered and heroin, cash, and drug paraphernalia had been found did any of the officers realize that the third floor contained two apartments. As soon as they became aware of that fact, the search was discontinued. All of the officers reasonably believed that they were searching McWebb's apartment. No further search of respondent's apartment was made.

The matter on which there is a difference of opinion concerns the proper interpretation of the warrant. A literal reading of its plain language, as well as the language used in the application for the warrant, indicates that it was intended to authorize a search of the entire third floor.[3] [T]he Court of Appeals[, however,] concluded that the warrant [authorized a search of McWebb's apartment only and thus] did not authorize the search of respondent's apartment and the police had no justification for making a warrantless entry into his premises.

* * *

In our view, the case presents two separate constitutional issues, one concerning the validity of the warrant and the other concerning the reasonableness of the manner in which it was executed. We shall discuss the questions separately.

---

[3]   The warrant states:

"Affidavit having been made before me by Detective Albert Marcus, Baltimore Police Department, Narcotic Unit, that he has reason to believe that on the person of Lawrence Meril McWebb . . . (and) that on the premises known as 2036 Park Avenue third floor apartment, described as a three story brick dwelling with the numerals 2–0–3–6 affixed to the front of same in the City of Baltimore, there is now being concealed certain property. . . .

You are therefor commanded, with the necessary and proper assistants, to search forthwith the person/premises herein above described for the property specified, executing this warrant and making the search. . . ."

I

The Warrant Clause of the Fourth Amendment categorically prohibits the issuance of any warrant except one "particularly describing the place to be searched and the persons or things to be seized." The manifest purpose of this particularity requirement was to prevent general searches. By limiting the authorization to search to the specific areas and things for which there is probable cause to search, the requirement ensures that the search will be carefully tailored to its justifications, and will not take on the character of the wide-ranging exploratory searches the Framers intended to prohibit. Thus, the scope of a lawful search is "defined by the object of the search and the places in which there is probable cause to believe that it may be found. Just as probable cause to believe that a stolen lawnmower may be found in a garage will not support a warrant to search an upstairs bedroom, probable cause to believe that undocumented aliens are being transported in a van will not justify a warrantless search of a suitcase."

In this case there is no claim that the "persons or things to be seized" were inadequately described or that there was no probable cause to believe that those things might be found in "the place to be searched" as it was described in the warrant. With the benefit of hindsight, however, we now know that the description of that place was broader than appropriate because it was based on the mistaken belief that there was only one apartment on the third floor of the building at 2036 Park Avenue. The question is whether that factual mistake invalidated a warrant that undoubtedly would have been valid if it had reflected a completely accurate understanding of the building's floor plan. Plainly, if the officers had known, or even if they should have known, that there were two separate dwelling units on the third floor of 2036 Park Avenue, they would have been obligated to exclude respondent's apartment from the scope of the requested warrant. But we must judge the constitutionality of their conduct in light of the information available to them at the time they acted. Those items of evidence that emerge after the warrant is issued have no bearing on whether or not a warrant was validly issued. Just as the discovery of contraband cannot validate a warrant invalid when issued, so is it equally clear that the discovery of facts demonstrating that a valid warrant was unnecessarily broad does not retroactively invalidate the warrant. The validity of the warrant must be assessed on the basis of the information that the officers disclosed, or had a duty to discover and to disclose, to the issuing magistrate.[10] On the basis of that information, we agree with the

---

[10] Arguments can certainly be made that the police in this case should have been able to ascertain that there was more than one apartment on the third floor of this building. It contained seven separate dwelling units and it was surely possible that two of them might be on the third floor. But the record also establishes that Officer Marcus made specific inquiries to determine the identity of the occupants of the third floor premises. The officer went to 2036 Park Avenue and found that it matched the description given by the informant: a three-story brick dwelling with the numerals 2–0–3–6 affixed to the front of the premises. The officer "made a check with the Baltimore Gas and Electric Company and discovered that the premises of 2036

conclusion of all three Maryland courts that the warrant, insofar as it authorized a search that turned out to be ambiguous in scope, was valid when it issued.

II

The question whether the execution of the warrant violated respondent's constitutional right to be secure in his home is somewhat less clear. We have no difficulty concluding that the officers' entry into the third-floor common area was legal; they carried a warrant for those premises, and they were accompanied by McWebb, who provided the key that they used to open the door giving access to the thirdfloor common area. If the officers had known, or should have known, that the third floor contained two apartments before they entered the living quarters on the third floor, and thus had been aware of the error in the warrant, they would have been obligated to limit their search to McWebb's apartment. Moreover, as the officers recognized, they were required to discontinue the search of respondent's apartment as soon as they discovered that there were two separate units on the third floor and therefore were put on notice of the risk that they might be in a unit erroneously included within the terms of the warrant. The officers' conduct and the limits of the search were based on the information available as the search proceeded. While the purposes justifying a police search strictly limit the permissible extent of the search, the Court has also recognized the need to allow some latitude for honest mistakes that are made by officers in the dangerous and difficult process of making arrests and executing search warrants.

In *Hill v. California*, 401 U.S. 797, 91 S.Ct. 1106, 28 L.Ed.2d 484 (1971), we considered the validity of the arrest of a man named Miller based on the mistaken belief that he was Hill. The police had probable cause to arrest Hill and they in good faith believed that Miller was Hill when they found him in Hill's apartment. As we explained:

> "The upshot was that the officers in good faith believed Miller was Hill and arrested him. They were quite wrong as it turned out, and subjective good-faith belief would not in itself justify either the arrest or the subsequent search. But sufficient probability, not certainty, is the touchstone of reasonableness under the Fourth Amendment and on the record before us the officers' mistake was understandable and the arrest a reasonable response to the situation facing them at the time."

Park Ave. third floor was in the name of Lawrence McWebb." Officer Marcus testified at the suppression hearing that he inquired of the Baltimore Gas and Electric Company in whose name the third floor apartment was listed: "I asked if there is a front or rear or middle room. They told me, one third floor was only listed to Lawrence McWebb." The officer also discovered from a check with the Baltimore police department that the police records of Lawrence McWebb matched the address and physical description given by the informant. The Maryland courts that are presumptively familiar with local conditions were unanimous in concluding that the officer reasonably believed McWebb was the only tenant on that floor. Because the evidence supports their conclusion, we accept that conclusion for the purpose of our decision.

While *Hill* involved an arrest without a warrant, its underlying rationale that an officer's reasonable misidentification of a person does not invalidate a valid arrest is equally applicable to an officer's reasonable failure to appreciate that a valid warrant describes too broadly the premises to be searched. Under the reasoning in *Hill,* the validity of the search of respondent's apartment pursuant to a warrant authorizing the search of the entire third floor depends on whether the officers' failure to realize the overbreadth of the warrant was objectively understandable and reasonable. Here it unquestionably was. The objective facts available to the officers at the time suggested no distinction between McWebb's apartment and the third-floor premises.[12]

For that reason, the officers properly responded to the command contained in a valid warrant even if the warrant is interpreted as authorizing a search limited to McWebb's apartment rather than the entire third floor. Prior to the officers' discovery of the factual mistake, they perceived McWebb's apartment and the third-floor premises as one and the same; therefore their execution of the warrant reasonably included the entire third floor.[13] Under either interpretation of the warrant, the officers' conduct was consistent with a reasonable effort to ascertain and identify the place intended to be searched within the meaning of the Fourth Amendment.

The judgment of the Court of Appeals is reversed, and the case is remanded for further proceedings not inconsistent with this opinion.

It is so ordered.

■ JUSTICE BLACKMUN, with whom JUSTICE BRENNAN and JUSTICE MARSHALL join, dissenting.

* * *

I

* * *

* * * The words of the warrant were plain and distinctive: the warrant directed the officers to seize marijuana and drug paraphernalia on the person of McWebb and in McWebb's apartment, i.e., "on the premises known as 2036 Park Avenue third floor apartment." * * * Accordingly, * * * the warrant was limited in its description to the third floor apartment of McWebb, then the search of an additional

---

[12] Nothing McWebb did or said after he was detained outside 2036 Park Avenue would have suggested to the police that there were two apartments on the third floor. McWebb provided the key that opened the doors on the first floor and on the third floor. The police could reasonably have believed that McWebb was admitting them to an undivided apartment on the third floor. When the officers entered the foyer on the third floor, neither McWebb nor Garrison informed them that they lived in separate apartments.

[13] We expressly distinguish the facts of this case from a situation in which the police know there are two apartments on a certain floor of a building, and have probable cause to believe that drugs are being sold out of that floor, but do not know in which of the two apartments the illegal transactions are taking place. A search pursuant to a warrant authorizing a search of the entire floor under those circumstances would present quite different issues from the ones before us in this case.

apartment—respondent's—was warrantless and is presumed unreasonable "in the absence of some one of a number of well defined 'exigent circumstances.' " Because the State has not advanced any such exception to the warrant requirement, the evidence obtained as a result of this search should have been excluded.[3]

II

[T]he Court * * * analyzes the police conduct here in terms of "mistake." * * * [But even if] there is no Fourth Amendment violation where the officers' mistake is reasonable, it is questionable whether that standard was met in this case. The "place" at issue here is a small multiple-occupancy building. Such forms of habitation are now common in this country, particularly in neighborhoods with changing populations and of declining affluence. Accordingly, any analysis of the "reasonableness" of the officers' behavior here must be done with this context in mind.

The efforts of Detective Marcus, the officer who procured the search warrant, do not meet a standard of reasonableness, particularly considering that the detective knew the search concerned a unit in a multiple-occupancy building. Upon learning from his informant that McWebb was selling marijuana in his third floor apartment, Marcus inspected the outside of the building. He did not approach it, however, to gather information about the configuration of the apartments. Had he done so, he would have discovered, as did another officer on the day of executing the warrant, that there were seven separate mailboxes and bells on the porch outside the main entrance to the house. Although there is some dispute over whether names were affixed near these boxes and bells, their existence alone puts a reasonable observer on notice that the three-story structure (with, possibly, a basement) had seven individual units. The detective, therefore, should have been aware that further investigation was necessary to eliminate the possibility of more than one unit's being located on the third floor. Moreover, when Detective Marcus' informant told him that he had purchased drugs in McWebb's apartment, it appears that the detective never thought to ask the informant whether McWebb's apartment was the only one on the third floor. These efforts, which would have placed a slight burden upon the detective, are necessary in order to render reasonable the officer's behavior in seeking the warrant.

---

[3] If the officers were confused about the residence of respondent when they encountered him in the third floor vestibule * * *, they might have been justified in detaining him temporarily as an occupant of McWebb's apartment. The officers asserted that, upon entering the vestibule, they observed marijuana lying upon a dresser in respondent's bedroom, the door to respondent's apartment being open. Although it is not entirely clear that the drug could have been seized immediately under the "plain view" exception to the warrant requirement, for this would depend upon whether the officers' "access to the object has some prior Fourth Amendment justification," the officers probably would have had probable cause to obtain a search warrant and conceivably could have impounded respondent's apartment while seeking the warrant. Nothing, however, justified the full-scale search of respondent's apartment in which the officers engaged.

Moreover, even if one believed that Marcus' efforts in providing information for issuance of the warrant were reasonable, I doubt whether the officers' execution of the warrant could meet such a standard. * * *

In my view, * * * the "objective facts" should have made the officers aware that there were two different apartments on the third floor well before they discovered the incriminating evidence in respondent's apartment. Before McWebb happened to drive up while the search party was preparing to execute the warrant, one of the officers, Detective Shea, somewhat disguised as a construction worker, was already on the porch of the row house and was seeking to gain access to the locked first-floor door that permitted entrance into the building. From this vantage point he had time to observe the seven mailboxes and bells; indeed, he rang all seven bells, apparently in an effort to summon some resident to open the front door to the search party. A reasonable officer in Detective Shea's position, already aware that this was a multiunit building and now armed with further knowledge of the number of units in the structure, would have conducted at that time more investigation to specify the exact location of McWebb's apartment before proceeding further. For example, he might have questioned another resident of the building.

It is surprising, moreover, that the Court places so much emphasis on the failure of McWebb to volunteer information about the exact location of his apartment. * * * [I]t would * * * have been reasonable for the officers, aware of the problem, from Detective Shea's discovery, in the specificity of their warrant, to ask McWebb whether his apartment was the only one on the third floor. As it is, the officers made several requests of and questioned McWebb, * * * and yet failed to ask him the question, obvious in the circumstances, concerning the exact location of his apartment.

Moreover, a reasonable officer would have realized the mistake in the warrant during the moments following the officers' entrance to the third floor. The officers gained access to the vestibule separating McWebb's and respondent's apartments through a locked door for which McWebb supplied the key. There, in the open doorway to his apartment, they encountered respondent, clad in pajamas and wearing a halfbody cast as a result of a recent spinal operation. Although the facts concerning what next occurred are somewhat in dispute, it appears that respondent, together with McWebb and the passenger from McWebb's car, were shepherded into McWebb's apartment across the vestibule from his own. Once again, the officers were curiously silent. The informant had not led the officers to believe that anyone other than McWebb lived in the third-floor apartment; the search party had McWebb, the person targeted by the search warrant, in custody when it gained access to the vestibule; yet when they met respondent on the third floor, they simply asked him who he was but never where he lived. Had they done so, it is likely that they would have discovered the mistake in the warrant before they began their search.

Finally and most importantly, even if the officers had learned nothing from respondent, they should have realized the error in the warrant from their initial security sweep. Once on the third floor, the officers first fanned out through the rooms to conduct a preliminary check for other occupants who might pose a danger to them. * * * [T]he two apartments were almost a mirror image of each other—each had a bathroom, a kitchen, a living room, and a bedroom. Given the somewhat symmetrical layout of the apartments, it is difficult to imagine that, in the initial security sweep, a reasonable officer would not have discerned that two apartments were on the third floor, realized his mistake, and then confined the ensuing search to McWebb's residence.

Accordingly, even if a reasonable error on the part of police officers prevents a Fourth Amendment violation, the mistakes here, both with respect to obtaining and executing the warrant, are not reasonable and could easily have been avoided.

I respectfully dissent.

NOTES

1.   **Search of Persons on Premises.** The extent to which a search warrant does and can authorize officers to search persons on the premises to be searched pursuant to a warrant was addressed in Ybarra v. Illinois, 444 U.S. 85, 100 S.Ct. 338 (1979). In support of the warrant application, officers recounted an informant's tip that he had observed tinfoil packets on the person of "Greg," bartender at the Aurora Tap Tavern, and behind the bar. He also previously observed such packets in the same places. The informant knew from experience that such tinfoil packets are a common method of packaging heroin. In addition, Greg told the informant that he would have heroin for sale on March 1. A warrant was obtained authorizing the search of "the Aurora Tap Tavern" and "the person of 'Greg,' the bartender," for controlled substances. An Illinois statute purported to authorize officers executing a search warrant to detain and search "any person in the place at the time" either to protect themselves from attack or to prevent disposal or concealment of items described in the warrant. Ill.Rev.Stat., ch. 38, section 108–9. When, on March 1, the warrant was executed, Ybarra was one of about a dozen persons in the bar. He was first "frisked" and then more thoroughly searched. Drugs were found. Addressing the officers' right under the warrant to search Ybarra, the Court first indicated the warrant did not authorize such a search given the specific authorization to search the person of "Greg:"

> Had the issuing judge intended that the warrant would or could authorize a search of every person found within the tavern, he would hardly have specifically authorized the search of "Greg" alone. "Greg" was an employee of the tavern, and the complaint upon which the search warrant was issued gave every indication that he would be present at the tavern on March 1.

444 U.S. at 90 n. 2, 100 S.Ct. at 342 n. 2. It then suggested the warrant *could not* constitutionally be read as authorizing such a search. The officers' probable cause, the Court stressed, did not extend to Ybarra and others like him. Moreover:

> The Fourth Amendment directs that "no Warrants shall issue, but upon probable cause . . . and particularly describing the place to be searched, and the persons or things to be seized." Thus, "open-ended" or "general" warrants are constitutionally prohibited. It follows that a warrant to search a place cannot normally be construed to authorize a search of each individual in that place. The warrant for the Aurora Tap Tavern provided no basis for departing from this general rule. Consequently, we need not consider situations where the warrant itself authorizes the search of unnamed persons in a place and is supported by probable cause to believe that persons who will be in the place at the time of the search will be in possession of illegal drugs.

444 U.S. at 92 n. 4, 100 S.Ct. at 342 n. 4.

Finally, the prosecution asked that the Court recognize a "new" exception to the warrant requirement:

> to permit evidence searches of persons who, at the commencement of the search, are on "compact" premises subject to a search warrant, at least where the police have a "reasonable belief" that such persons "are connected with" drug trafficking and "may be concealing or carrying away the contraband."

Rejecting this request, the Court explained the "long-prevailing" standard of probable cause embodies the appropriate compromise between citizens' interests and law enforcement; the Court was unprepared to deviate from that standard in this situation.

The State also defended the first frisk of Ybarra as a permissible weapons search under Terry v. Ohio, 392 U.S. 1, 88 S.Ct. 1868 (1968). This aspect of the case is discussed in Chapter 4.

2. **Detention of Persons "Associated with" Premises.** In some situations, a warrant may authorize the detention of persons associated with the searched premises. Should the limitations on searching persons present when a search warrant is executed apply to the occupants of a private residence being searched?

In Michigan v. Summers, 452 U.S. 692, 101 S.Ct. 2587 (1981), law officers were approaching Summers' home to execute a search warrant for contraband when they observed him leave the residence. They detained him while the home was searched. When the search revealed narcotics, they arrested Summers, whom they knew owned the premises, and searched his person, finding still more narcotics. He was prosecuted for possession of the drugs found on his person. The state argued the authority to search premises granted by the warrant implicitly included the authority to search persons on those premises, just as that authority included authorization to search furniture and containers in which the particular things described might be concealed. But the Court, in an opinion authored by Justice Stevens, did not rule on that contention because it found the search warrant implicitly authorized the temporary detention of Summers while the search was conducted and that the discovery of the contraband in respondent's home gave the police authority to arrest him for its possession. The search of his person was justified as a search incident to his lawful arrest. Justices Stewart, Brennan and Marshall dissented.

3. **Detention of Occupants Beyond Immediate Vicinity of Premises to Be Searched.** Whether officers' right to detain occupants of the premises to be searched applies to person no longer in the immediate vicinity of the premises was at issue in Bailey v. United States, ___ U.S. ___, 133 S.Ct. 1031 (2013). Officers preparing to execute a search warrant for a residence observed Bailey and another man leave the premises and drive away in a car. The officers followed the two men and stopped them about a mile from the residence. Both men were frisked, questioned, handcuffed, and returned to the residence. In a later prosecution, Bailey challenged as inadmissible fruits of his detention a key found in his pocket during the frisk and statements he made during his detention.

Three member of the Court regarded the challenged evidence admissible under Michigan v. Summers, discussed in Note 2. The rationale of Summers, they reasoned, permits detention of persons observed leaving premises to be searched under a warrant if the detention is made as soon as is reasonably practical. Some delay in making the stop of Bailey was reasonable to avoid endangering the safe and successful execution of the warrant, these justices concluded, and the officers made the stop as soon as circumstances permitted. ___ U.S. at ___, 133 S.Ct. at 1045 (Breyer, J., dissenting).

The *Bailey* majority, however, held that *Summers* and its rationale permit only detention of occupants encountered in the immediate vicinity of the premises to be searched. Occupants encountered beyond that area, the majority reasoned in part, pose less danger to officers than those encountered at the premises and little danger of interfering with the officers' search. Detentions beyond the immediate vicinity of the premises will more often than those at the premises be made within the view of others and thus often will be more intrusive.

With regard to the meaning of "immediate vicinity," the Court explained:

> [Bailey] was detained at a point beyond any reasonable understanding of the immediate vicinity of the premises in question; and so this case presents neither the necessity nor the occasion to further define the meaning of immediate vicinity. In closer cases courts can consider a number of factors to determine whether an occupant was detained within the immediate vicinity of the premises to be searched, including the lawful limits of the premises, whether the occupant was within the line of sight of his dwelling, the ease of reentry from the occupant's location, and other relevant factors.

___ U.S. at ___, 133 S.Ct. at 1042.

4. **Other Aspects of Treatment of Persons on Searched Premises.** The Supreme Court expanded on officers' power to deal with those found on premises searched under a warrant in several post-*Summers* cases.

Muehler v. Mena, 544 U.S. 93, 125 S.Ct. 1465 (2005), arose out of an investigation of a gang-related shooting. Officers obtained a search warrant for the residence of one gang member for deadly weapons and evidence of gang membership. The suspect was believed armed and dangerous. Executing the warrant at 7:00 a.m., officers found four persons in the premises including Iris Mena. Mena was asleep in her bed when the officers entered. She was handcuffed at gunpoint and taken to a converted garage where she and the others were kept in the handcuffs and guarded by one or two officers while the search was made. This took from 2 to 3 hours. During that time, an Immigration and Naturalization Service officer questioned her and requested her immigration documentation. Mena later, invoking 42 U.S.S. § 1983, sued the officers who conducted the search on the ground that they had used excessive force in detaining her and detained her longer than was reasonable. She obtained a jury verdict and judgment and this was affirmed on appeal to the court of appeals. The Supreme Court held that the court of appeals erred in upholding the judgment on the grounds that it specified.

The Court first held that the detention and initial handcuffing were reasonable under Fourth Amendment law:

> Mena's detention was, under *Summers,* plainly permissible. An officer's authority to detain incident to a search is categorical; it does not depend on the "quantum of proof justifying detention or the extent of the intrusion to be imposed by the seizure." Thus, Mena's detention for the duration of the search was reasonable under *Summers* because a warrant existed to search 1363 Patricia Avenue and she was an occupant of that address at the time of the search.

> Inherent in *Summers'* authorization to detain an occupant of the place to be searched is the authority to use reasonable force to effectuate the detention. Indeed, *Summers* itself stressed that the risk of harm to officers and occupants is minimized "if the officers routinely exercise unquestioned command of the situation."

> The officers' use of force in the form of handcuffs to effectuate Mena's detention in the garage, as well as the detention of the three other occupants, was reasonable because the governmental interests outweigh the marginal intrusion. The imposition of correctly applied handcuffs on Mena, who was already being lawfully detained during a search of the house, was undoubtedly a separate intrusion in addition to detention in the converted garage. The detention was thus more intrusive than that which we upheld in *Summers.*

> But this was no ordinary search. The governmental interests in not only detaining, but using handcuffs, are at their maximum

when, as here, a warrant authorizes a search for weapons and a wanted gang member resides on the premises. In such inherently dangerous situations, the use of handcuffs minimizes the risk of harm to both officers and occupants. Though this safety risk inherent in executing a search warrant for weapons was sufficient to justify the use of handcuffs, the need to detain multiple occupants made the use of handcuffs all the more reasonable.

544 U.S. at 98–100, 125 S.Ct. at 1470–71. Nor could the court of appeals have held that the jury verdict was supportable on the ground that the duration of the use of the handcuffs made the detention unreasonable:

> The duration of a detention can, of course, affect the balance of interests * * * . However, the 2 to 3 hour detention in handcuffs in this case does not outweigh the government's continuing safety interests. * * * [T]his case involved the detention of four detainees by two officers during a search of a gang house for dangerous weapons. We conclude that the detention of Mena in handcuffs during the search was reasonable.

544 U.S. at 100, 125 S.Ct. at 1471.

The court of appeals also erred in concluding that the questioning of Mena about her immigration status violated the Fourth Amendment:

> This holding, it appears, was premised on the assumption that the officers were required to have independent reasonable suspicion in order to question Mena concerning her immigration status because the questioning constituted a discrete Fourth Amendment event. But the premise is faulty. We have "held repeatedly that mere police questioning does not constitute a seizure." *Florida v. Bostick,* 501 U.S. 429, 434, 111 S.Ct. 2382, 115 L.Ed.2d 389 (1991) "[E]ven when officers have no basis for suspecting a particular individual, they may generally ask questions of that individual; ask to examine the individual's identification; and request consent to search his or her luggage." *Bostick, supra,* at 434–435, 111 S.Ct. 2382 (citations omitted). As the Court of Appeals did not hold that the detention was prolonged by the questioning, there was no additional seizure within the meaning of the Fourth Amendment. Hence, the officers did not need reasonable suspicion to ask Mena for her name, date and place of birth, or immigration status.

544 U.S. at 100–01, 125 S.Ct. at 1471.

Mena argued further that she was detained beyond the time the officers completed the tasks incident to the search. The court of appeals had not addressed this contention, and the Supreme Court also declined to reach it.

Actions during execution of a search warrant were again at issue in Los Angeles County, California v. Rettele, 550 U.S. 609, 127 S.Ct. 1989 (2007). Sheriff's deputies investigating a fraud and identity-theft ring had four African-American suspects, one of whom had registered a handgun. The deputies also had information that the suspects resided in a specific home and obtained a warrant authorizing a search of that residence. Unknown to the deputies, the residence had been sold. At 7:15 a.m., the deputies knocked on the door. When one Chase Hall answered, the deputies ordered him to lie face down on the ground. The deputies entered a bedroom and found Judy Sadler and Max Rettle in bed. Despite protests by Sadler and Rettle that they were not clothed, the deputies required them to get out of the bed. Several minutes later, Sadler and Rettle were permitted to dress. Hall, Sadler and Rettle were Caucasian.

The Supreme Court held that the deputies acted constitutionally:

> In executing a search warrant officers may take reasonable action to secure the premises and to ensure their own safety and the efficacy of the search. The test of reasonableness under the Fourth Amendment is an objective one. Unreasonable actions include the use of excessive force or restraints that cause unnecessary pain or are imposed for a prolonged and unnecessary period of time.

> The orders by the police to the occupants, in the context of this lawful search, were permissible, and perhaps necessary, to protect the safety of the deputies. Blankets and bedding can conceal a weapon, and one of the suspects was known to own a firearm, factors which underscore this point. The Constitution does not require an officer to ignore the possibility that an armed suspect may sleep with a weapon within reach.

> The deputies needed a moment to secure the room and ensure that other persons were not close by or did not present a danger. Deputies were not required to turn their backs to allow Rettle and Sadler to retrieve clothing or to cover themselves with the sheets. Rather, "[t]he risk of harm to both the police and the occupants is minimized if the officers routinely exercise unquestioned command of the situation."

> This is not to say, of course, that the deputies were free to force Rettle and Sadler to remain motionless and standing for any longer than necessary. * * * [But] there is no allegation that the deputies prevented Sadler and Rettele from dressing longer than necessary to protect their safety. Sadler was unclothed for no more than two minutes, and Rettele for only slightly more time than that.

550 U.S. at 613, 127 S.Ct. at 1993.

5. **Return of the Warrant and Inventories of Seized Items.** The manner in which officers deal with seized property during and after a search pursuant to a search warrant may raise significant issues.

Statutes or court rules often require search warrants be in some sense returned to the issuing magistrate and persons on the searched premises be provided with an inventory of items seized. Fed.R.Crim.P. 41(f)(1)(D), for example, provides: "The officer executing the warrant must promptly return it—together with a copy of the inventory—to the magistrate judge designated on the warrant. The officer may do so by reliable electronic means." As this suggests, an officer is required to compile an inventory of items taken. This must be done "in the presence of another officer and the person from whom, or from whose premises, the property was taken." Rule 41(f)(1)(B). Further:

> The officer executing the warrant must give a copy of the warrant and a receipt for the property taken to the person from whom, or from whose premises, the property was taken or leave a copy of the warrant and receipt at the place where the officer took the property.

Rule 41(f)(1)(c).

Are there circumstances in which failure to observe these requirements means the Fourth Amendment is violated? If so, does this demand the exclusion of evidence obtained in the search?

In Cady v. Dombrowski, 413 U.S. 433, 93 S.Ct. 2523 (1973), the officers failed to list all items seized on the inventory filed with the court issuing the search warrant. The Court rejected the argument that this failure required the exclusion of the unlisted items:

> As these items were constitutionally seized, we do not deem it constitutionally significant that they were not listed in the return of the warrant. The ramification of that "defect," if such it was, is purely a question of state law.

413 U.S. at 449, 93 S.Ct. at 2532.

Lower courts have tended to follow the same approach, characterizing return provisions as "technical requirements" and holding that their violation does not trigger exclusion of evidence. E.g., State v. Roy, 167 NH 276, 283–84, 111 A3d 1061, 1068–69 (2015) (showing that officers made return on a warrant only after the seven-day period required by statute did not require exclusion of evidence seized in search under the warrant).

CHAPTER 4

DETENTIONS OF PERSONS AND RELATED SEARCHES

Analysis

EDITORS' INTRODUCTION: DETENTIONS, SEIZURES AND THEIR CHARACTERIZATION

This chapter addresses law enforcement detentions of persons suspected of crime—"seizures" of the person in the language of the Fourth Amendment—and related searches. A lawful detention may, in theory at least, create civil or possibly even criminal liability on the part of the officer. In many circumstances, however, the legality of an arrest or other detention is of practical significance only if it is accompanied by or leads to a search yielding incriminating evidence. Should such evidence be offered against the suspect at trial and challenged, its admissibility is often affected by the validity of the detention.

At one time, all detentions were regarded as indistinguishable from one another and characterized as arrests. This is no longer the case. Case law, much of it involving the Fourth Amendment requirement that "seizures" of the person be "reasonable," distinguishes a variety of detentions. Given the different requirements that have developed for different detentions and the variation in the searches that can be made in relation to different types of detentions, how a detention is characterized is often important. See generally, LaFave, "Seizures" Typology: Classifying Detentions of the Person to Resolve Warrant, Grounds, and Search Issues, 17 U.Mich.J.L.Reform 417 (1984).

This chapter begins with the problem of determining whether any detention at all has occurred. It then considers detentions or seizures constituting "arrests," the benchmark of Fourth Amendment analysis in this area. After this, it addresses field detentions for investigation—so-called *Terry* stops—and the right to make weapon searches where no arrest has occurred. Next, the chapter considers certain non-arrest detentions of persons in automobiles, specifically traffic stops, detentions arguably different from both arrests and field detentions for investigation. Finally, attention turns to roadblock stops.

A. DETERMINING WHETHER A PERSON IS DETAINED OR SEIZED

EDITORS' INTRODUCTION: DEFINING "SEIZURES" OF THE PERSON

Whether confrontations between police officers and suspects involve "seizures" as that term is used in the Fourth Amendment has long presented a difficult problem. Until the principal case, the Supreme Court's case law appeared to indicate that whether a seizure occurred depended upon how a reasonable person would react to the officer's actions.

In 1984, the Court indicated that "police questioning, by itself" is unlikely to result in a seizure. Only if an officer, "by means of physical force or show of authority," restrains a person's liberty has the person been seized. An officer seizes a person by approaching him and posing questions, therefore, only if "the circumstances of the encounter are so intimidating as to demonstrate that a reasonable person would have believed he was not free to leave if he [did not respond]." Immigration and Naturalization Service v. Delgado, 466 U.S. 210, 216, 104 S.Ct. 1758, 1762 (1984).

The standard was applied in Michigan v. Chesternut, 486 U.S. 567, 108 S.Ct. 1975 (1988). Four Detroit officers were engaged in routine patrol in a marked police cruiser. As the cruiser came to an intersection, one officer saw a car pull over to the curb and an occupant alight. This person approached Chesternut, standing alone on the corner. Chesternut saw the cruiser as it approached; he immediately turned and ran. The cruiser caught up with him and drove alongside him for a short distance. During this time, the officers observed Chesternut pull several packets from his pocket and discard them. Chesternut then stopped and one officer examined the discarded packets. Concluding that the packets contained codeine, the officers placed Chesternut under arrest. A search revealed other drugs, including heroin. After Chesternut was charged with drug offenses, a magistrate held he had been unlawfully seized before he discarded the codeine. This holding was affirmed on appeal in reliance upon state court holdings that any police pursuit was a seizure. Since the officers did not have reasonable suspicion when their pursuit of Chesternut began, the state courts reasoned, their seizure of him was unreasonable.

A unanimous Supreme Court reversed. Justice Blackmun, writing for the Court, rejected both the position that any pursuit is a seizure and the view that no seizure can occur until and if the officer actually apprehends the person. Instead, he indicated, the Court would continue to apply its traditional "contextual approach." Under this approach, "the police can be said to have seized an individual 'only if, in view of all of the circumstances surrounding the incident, a reasonable person would have believed that he was not free to leave.'" Applying this standard, the Court found no seizure occurred before Chesternut discarded the packets:

> [T]he police conduct involved here would not have communicated to the reasonable person an attempt to capture or otherwise intrude upon [the person's] freedom of movement. The record does not reflect that the police activated a siren or flashers; or that they commanded [Chesternut] to halt, or displayed any weapons; or that they operated the car in an aggressive manner to block [Chesternut's] course or otherwise control the direction or speed of his movement. While the very presence of a police car driving parallel to a running pedestrian could be somewhat intimidating, this kind of police presence does not, standing alone, constitute a seizure.

486 U.S. at 575, 108 S.Ct. at 1980. Consequently, the prosecution was not required to establish the reasonableness of the officers' actions prior to Chesternut's discarding of the packets.

California v. Hodari D.

Supreme Court of the United States, 1991.
499 U.S. 621, 111 S.Ct. 1547.

■ JUSTICE SCALIA delivered the opinion of the Court.

Late one evening in April 1988, Officers Brian McColgin and Jerry Pertoso were on patrol in a high-crime area of Oakland, California. They were dressed in street clothes but wearing jackets with "Police" embossed on both front and back. Their unmarked car proceeded west on Foothill Boulevard, and turned south onto 63rd Avenue. As they rounded the corner, they saw four or five youths huddled around a small red car parked at the curb. When the youths saw the officers' car approaching they apparently panicked, and took flight. The respondent here, Hodari D., and one companion ran west through an alley; the others fled south. The red car also headed south, at a high rate of speed.

The officers were suspicious and gave chase. McColgin remained in the car and continued south on 63rd Avenue; Pertoso left the car, ran back north along 63rd, then west on Foothill Boulevard, and turned south on 62nd Avenue. Hodari, meanwhile, emerged from the alley onto 62nd and ran north. Looking behind as he ran, he did not turn and see Pertoso until the officer was almost upon him, whereupon he tossed away what appeared to be a small rock. A moment later, Pertoso tackled Hodari, handcuffed him, and radioed for assistance. Hodari was found to be carrying $130 in cash and a pager; and the rock he had discarded was found to be crack cocaine.

In the juvenile proceeding brought against him, Hodari moved to suppress the evidence relating to the cocaine. The court denied the motion without opinion. The California Court of Appeal reversed, holding that Hodari had been "seized" when he saw Officer Pertoso running towards him, that this seizure was unreasonable under the Fourth Amendment, and that the evidence of cocaine had to be suppressed as the fruit of that illegal seizure..The California Supreme Court denied the State's application for review. We granted certiorari.

As this case comes to us, the only issue presented is whether, at the time he dropped the drugs, Hodari had been "seized" within the meaning of the Fourth Amendment. If so, respondent argues, the drugs were the fruit of that seizure and the evidence concerning them was properly excluded. If not, the drugs were abandoned by Hodari and lawfully recovered by the police, and the evidence should have been admitted. * * *

We have long understood that the Fourth Amendment's protection against "unreasonable . . . seizures" includes seizure of the person. From the time of the founding to the present, the word "seizure" has meant a "taking possession," 2 N. Webster, An American Dictionary of the English Language 67 (1828). For most purposes at common law, the word connoted not merely grasping, or applying physical force to, the animate or inanimate object in question, but actually bringing it within physical control. * * * To constitute an arrest, however—the quintessential "seizure of the person" under our Fourth Amendment jurisprudence—the mere grasping or application of physical force with lawful authority, whether or not it succeeded in subduing the arrestee, was sufficient. See, e.g., *Whithead v. Keyes*, 85 Mass. 495, 501 (1862) ("[A]n officer effects an arrest of a person whom he has authority to arrest, by laying his hand on him for the purpose of arresting him, though he may not succeed in stopping and holding him"). * * *

To say that an arrest is effected by the slightest application of physical force, despite the arrestee's escape, is not to say that for Fourth Amendment purposes there is a continuing arrest during the period of fugitivity. If, for example, Pertoso had laid his hands upon Hodari to arrest him, but Hodari had broken away and had then cast away the cocaine, it would hardly be realistic to say that that disclosure had been made during the course of an arrest. The present case, however, is even one step further removed. It does not involve the application of any physical force; Hodari was untouched by Officer Pertoso at the time he discarded the cocaine. His defense relies instead upon the proposition that a seizure occurs "when the officer, by means of physical force *or show of authority*, has in some way restrained the liberty of a citizen." *Terry v. Ohio*, 392 U.S. 1, 19, n. 16, 88 S.Ct. 1868, 1879, n. 16, 20 L.Ed.2d 889 (1968) (emphasis added). Hodari contends (and we accept as true for purposes of this decision) that Pertoso's pursuit qualified as a "show of authority" calling upon Hodari to halt. The narrow question before us is whether, with respect to a show of authority as with respect to application of physical force, a seizure occurs even though the subject does not yield. We hold that it does not.

The language of the Fourth Amendment, of course, cannot sustain respondent's contention. The word "seizure" readily bears the meaning of a laying on of hands or application of physical force to restrain movement, even when it is ultimately unsuccessful. ("She seized the purse-snatcher, but he broke out of her grasp.") It does not remotely apply, however, to the prospect of a policeman yelling "Stop, in the name of the law!" at a fleeing form that continues to flee. That is no seizure. Nor can the result respondent wishes to achieve be produced—indirectly, as it were—by suggesting that Pertoso's uncomplied—with show of authority was a common-law arrest, and then appealing to the principle that all common-law arrests are seizures. An arrest requires either physical force (as described above) or, where that is absent, submission to the assertion of authority.

* * *

We do not think it desirable, even as a policy matter, to stretch the Fourth Amendment beyond its words and beyond the meaning of arrest, as respondent urges. Street pursuits always place the public at some risk, and compliance with police orders to stop should therefore be encouraged. Only a few of those orders, we must presume, will be without adequate basis, and since the addressee has no ready means of identifying the deficient ones it almost invariably is the responsible course to comply. Unlawful orders will not be deterred, moreover, by sanctioning through the exclusionary rule those of them that are not obeyed. Since policemen do not command "Stop!" expecting to be ignored, or give chase hoping to be outrun, it fully suffices to apply the deterrent to their genuine, successful seizures.

Respondent contends that his position is sustained by the so-called *Mendenhall* test, formulated by Justice Stewart's opinion in *United States v. Mendenhall*, 446 U.S. 544, 554, 100 S.Ct. 1870, 1877, 64 L.Ed.2d 497 (1980), and adopted by the Court in later cases: "[A] person has been 'seized' within the meaning of the Fourth Amendment only if, in view of all the circumstances surrounding the incident, a reasonable person would have believed that he was not free to leave." In seeking to rely upon that test here, respondent fails to read it carefully. It says that a person has been seized "only if," not that he has been seized "whenever"; it states a necessary, but not a sufficient, condition for seizure—or, more precisely, for seizure effected through a "show of authority." *Mendenhall* establishes that the test for existence of a "show of authority" is an objective one: not whether the citizen perceived that he was being ordered to restrict his movement, but whether the officer's words and actions would have conveyed that to a reasonable person. Application of this objective test was the basis for our decision in the other case principally relied upon by respondent, [*Michigan v. Chesternut*, 486 U.S. 567, 108 S.Ct. 1975, 100 L.Ed.2d 565 (1988)], where we concluded that the police cruiser's slow following of the defendant did not convey the message that he was not free to disregard the police and go about his business. We did not address in *Chesternut*, however, the question whether, if the *Mendenhall* test was met—if the message that the defendant was not free to leave had been conveyed—a Fourth Amendment seizure would have occurred.

* * *

[A]ssuming that Pertoso's pursuit in the present case constituted a "show of authority" enjoining Hodari to halt, since Hodari did not comply with that injunction he was not seized until he was tackled. The cocaine abandoned while he was running was in this case not the fruit of a seizure, and his motion to exclude evidence of it was properly denied. We reverse the decision of the California Court of Appeal, and remand for further proceedings not inconsistent with this opinion.

It is so ordered.

■ JUSTICE STEVENS, with whom JUSTICE MARSHALL joins, dissenting.

* * *

The first question * * * is whether the common law should define the scope of the outer boundaries of the constitutional protection against unreasonable seizures. Even if, contrary to settled precedent, traditional common-law analysis were controlling, it would still be necessary to decide whether the unlawful attempt to make an arrest should be considered a seizure within the meaning of the Fourth Amendment, and whether the exclusionary rule should apply to unlawful attempts.

* * *

Whatever else one may think of today's decision, it unquestionably represents a departure from earlier Fourth Amendment case law. * * *

Because the facts of this case are somewhat unusual, it is appropriate to note that the same issue would arise if the show of force took the form of a command to "freeze," a warning shot, or the sound of sirens accompanied by a patrol car's flashing lights. In any of these situations, there may be a significant time interval between the initiation of the officer's show of force and the complete submission by the citizen. At least on the facts of this case, the Court concludes that the timing of the seizure is governed by the citizen's reaction, rather than by the officer's conduct. One consequence of this conclusion is that the point at which the interaction between citizen and police officer becomes a seizure occurs, not when a reasonable citizen believes he or she is no longer free to go, but, rather, only after the officer exercises control over the citizen.

In my view, our interests in effective law enforcement and in personal liberty would be better served by adhering to a standard that "allows the police to determine in advance whether the conduct contemplated will implicate the Fourth Amendment." The range of possible responses to a police show of force, and the multitude of problems that may arise in determining whether, and at which moment, there has been "submission," can only create uncertainty and generate litigation.

* * *

It seems equally clear to me that the constitutionality of a police officer's show of force should be measured by the conditions that exist at the time of the officer's action. A search must be justified on the basis of the facts available at the time it is initiated; the subsequent discovery of evidence does not retroactively validate an unconstitutional search. The same approach should apply to seizures; the character of the citizen's response should not govern the constitutionality of the officer's conduct.

If an officer effects an arrest by touching a citizen, apparently the Court would accept the fact that a seizure occurred, even if the arrestee should thereafter break loose and flee. In such a case, the constitutionality of the seizure would be evaluated as of the time the officer acted. That category of seizures would then be analyzed in the same way as searches, namely, was the police action justified when it took place? It is anomalous, at best, to fashion a different rule for the subcategory of "show of force" arrests.

In cases within this new subcategory, there will be a period of time during which the citizen's liberty has been restrained, but he or she has not yet completely submitted to the show of force. A motorist pulled over by a highway patrol car cannot come to an immediate stop, even if the motorist intends to obey the patrol car's signal. If an officer decides to make the kind of random stop forbidden by *Delaware v. Prouse*, 440 U.S. 648, 99 S.Ct. 1391, 59 L.Ed.2d 660 (1979), and, after flashing his lights, but before the vehicle comes to a complete stop, sees that the license plate has expired, can he justify his action on the ground that the seizure became lawful after it was initiated but before it was completed? In an airport setting, may a drug enforcement agent now approach a group of passengers with his gun drawn, announce a "baggage search," and rely on the passengers' reactions to justify his investigative stops? The holding of today's majority fails to recognize the coercive and intimidating nature of such behavior and creates a rule that may allow such behavior to go unchecked.

The deterrent purposes of the exclusionary rule focus on the conduct of law enforcement officers and on discouraging improper behavior on their part, and not on the reaction of the citizen to the show of force. In the present case, if Officer Pertoso had succeeded in tackling respondent before he dropped the rock of cocaine, the rock unquestionably would have been excluded as the fruit of the officer's unlawful seizure. Instead, under the Court's logic-chopping analysis, the exclusionary rule has no application because an attempt to make an unconstitutional seizure is beyond the coverage of the Fourth Amendment, no matter how outrageous or unreasonable the officer's conduct may be.

It is too early to know the consequences of the Court's holding. If carried to its logical conclusion, it will encourage unlawful displays of force that will frighten countless innocent citizens into surrendering whatever privacy rights they may still have. * * *

I respectfully dissent.

NOTE

Law enforcement conduct that under *Hodari D.* does not constitute a seizure may become a seizure by means other than submission or capture in the ordinary sense of the latter term. In Scott v. Harris, 550 U.S. 372, 381, 127 S.Ct. 1769, 1776 (2007), for example, the parties agreed (and the Court apparently accepted) that an officer's decision to terminate a car chase by ramming the officer's vehicle into the suspect's vehicle constituted a seizure.

EDITORS' NOTE: SEIZURE OF A STATIONARY SUSPECT

Hodari D. involved a claim that a seizure occurred while the suspect was moving. Whether a person approached while stationary has been seized presents a somewhat different question. Florida v. Bostick, 501 U.S. 429, 111 S.Ct. 2382 (1991) and United States v. Drayton, 536 U.S. 194, 122 S.Ct. 2105 (2002), raised the issue in the context of "bus sweeps." In *Bostick*, the Court remanded the case for the state courts to address under the correct legal standard whether a person seated on a bus was seized when approached by officers. That standard, it continued, requires in the context presented the state courts not focus upon whether the person felt "free to leave":

> When police attempt to question a person who is walking down the street or through an airport lobby, it makes sense to inquire whether a reasonable person would feel free to continue walking. But when the person is seated on a bus and has no desire to leave, the degree to which a reasonable person would feel that he or she could leave is not an accurate measure of the coercive effect of the encounter. * * * In such a situation, the appropriate inquiry is whether a reasonable person would feel free to decline the officers' requests or otherwise terminate the encounter. This formulation follows logically from prior cases and breaks no new ground. We have said before that the crucial test is whether, taking into account all of the circumstances surrounding the encounter, the police conduct would "have communicated to a reasonable person that he was not at liberty to ignore the police presence and go about his business." Where the encounter takes place is one factor, but it is not the only one. And * * * an individual may decline an officer's request without fearing prosecution. We have consistently held that a refusal to cooperate, without more, does not furnish the minimal level of objective justification needed for a detention or seizure.

501 U.S. at 435–37, 111 S.Ct. at 2387.

In *Drayton*, the Court applied this approach. It first set out the facts:

> On February 4, 1999, respondents Christopher Drayton and Clifton Brown, Jr., were traveling on a Greyhound bus en

route from Ft. Lauderdale, Florida, to Detroit, Michigan. The bus made a scheduled stop in Tallahassee, Florida. The passengers were required to disembark so the bus could be refueled and cleaned. As the passengers reboarded, the driver checked their tickets and then left to complete paperwork inside the terminal. As he left, the driver allowed three members of the Tallahassee Police Department to board the bus as part of a routine drug and weapons interdiction effort. The officers were dressed in plain clothes and carried concealed weapons and visible badges.

Once onboard Officer Hoover knelt on the driver's seat and faced the rear of the bus. He could observe the passengers and ensure the safety of the two other officers without blocking the aisle or otherwise obstructing the bus exit. Officers Lang and Blackburn went to the rear of the bus. Blackburn remained stationed there, facing forward. Lang worked his way toward the front of the bus, speaking with individual passengers as he went. He asked the passengers about their travel plans and sought to match passengers with luggage in the overhead racks. To avoid blocking the aisle, Lang stood next to or just behind each passenger with whom he spoke.

According to Lang's testimony, passengers who declined to cooperate with him or who chose to exit the bus at any time would have been allowed to do so without argument. * * * Lang sometimes informed passengers of their right to refuse to cooperate. On the day in question, however, he did not.

Respondents were seated next to each other on the bus. Drayton was in the aisle seat, Brown in the seat next to the window. Lang approached respondents from the rear and leaned over Drayton's shoulder. He held up his badge long enough for respondents to identify him as a police officer. With his face 12-to-18 inches away from Drayton's, Lang spoke in a voice just loud enough for respondents to hear:

> "I'm Investigator Lang with the Tallahassee Police Department. We're conducting bus interdiction [sic], attempting to deter drugs and illegal weapons being transported on the bus. Do you have any bags on the bus?"

Both respondents pointed to a single green bag in the overhead luggage rack. Lang asked, "Do you mind if I check it?," and Brown responded, "Go ahead." Lang handed the bag to Officer Blackburn to check. The bag contained no contraband.

Officer Lang noticed that both respondents were wearing heavy jackets and baggy pants despite the warm weather. In Lang's experience drug traffickers often use baggy clothing to conceal weapons or narcotics. The officer thus asked Brown if he had any weapons or drugs in his possession. And he asked Brown: "Do you mind if I check your person?" Brown answered, "Sure," and cooperated by leaning up in his seat, pulling a cell phone out of his pocket, and opening up his jacket. Lang reached across Drayton and patted down Brown's jacket and pockets, including his waist area, sides, and upper thighs. In both thigh areas, Lang detected hard objects similar to drug packages detected on other occasions. Lang arrested and handcuffed Brown. Officer Hoover escorted Brown from the bus.

Lang then asked Drayton, "Mind if I check you?" Drayton responded by lifting his hands about eight inches from his legs. Lang conducted a pat-down of Drayton's thighs and detected hard objects similar to those found on Brown. He arrested Drayton and escorted him from the bus. A further search revealed that respondents had duct-taped plastic bundles of powder cocaine between several pairs of their boxer shorts. Brown possessed three bundles containing 483 grams of cocaine. Drayton possessed two bundles containing 295 grams of cocaine.

In their prosecution for federal drug offenses, Drayton and Brown moved to suppress the cocaine. The trial court denied the motion but on appeal the Court of Appeals held the motion should have been granted. The Supreme Court reversed:

> [T]he police did not seize respondents when they boarded the bus and began questioning passengers. The officers gave the passengers no reason to believe that they were required to answer the officers' questions. When Officer Lang approached respondents, he did not brandish a weapon or make any intimidating movements. He left the aisle free so that respondents could exit. He spoke to passengers one by one and in a polite, quiet voice. Nothing he said would suggest to a reasonable person that he or she was barred from leaving the bus or otherwise terminating the encounter.
>
> There were ample grounds for the District Court to conclude that "everything that took place between Officer Lang and [respondents] suggests that it was cooperative" and that there "was nothing coercive [or] confrontational" about the encounter. There was no application of force, no intimidating movement, no overwhelming show of force, no brandishing of weapons, no blocking of exits, no threat, no command, not even an authoritative tone of voice. It is beyond question that had this encounter occurred on the street, it would be constitutional. The fact that an encounter takes place on a bus does not on its own transform standard police questioning of citizens into an illegal seizure. Indeed, because many fellow passengers are present to witness officers' conduct, a reasonable person may feel even

more secure in his or her decision not to cooperate with police on a bus than in other circumstances.

Respondents make much of the fact that Officer Lang displayed his badge. [But wearing or displaying of a badge does not] * * * constitute a seizure. * * *

Officer Hoover's position at the front of the bus also does not tip the scale in respondents' favor. Hoover did nothing to intimidate passengers, and he said nothing to suggest that people could not exit and indeed he left the aisle clear. * * *

536 U.S. at 205–06, 122 S.Ct. at 2111–12. Even after Brown was arrested, Drayton's status did not change:

The arrest of one person does not mean that everyone around him has been seized by police. If anything, Brown's arrest should have put Drayton on notice of the consequences of continuing the encounter by answering the officers' questions. Even after arresting Brown, Lang addressed Drayton in a polite manner and provided him with no indication that he was required to answer Lang's questions.

536 U.S. at 206, 122 S.Ct. at 2113. Having concluded that neither Brown nor Drayton were seized, the majority determined their consents were voluntary and hence effective.

Three members of the Court concluded that Drayton and Brown had been seized:

It is very hard to imagine that either Brown or Drayton would have believed that he stood to lose nothing if he refused to cooperate with the police, or that he had any free choice to ignore the police altogether. No reasonable passenger could have believed that, only an uncomprehending one.

536 U.S. at 212, 122 S.Ct. at 2116 (Souter, J., dissenting). The dissenters would not have reached the question of the voluntariness of the consent.

The analysis of *Bostick* and *Drayton* applies, the Court made clear in Brendlin v. California, 551 U.S. 249, 127 S.Ct. 2400 (2007), "[w]hen the actions of the police do not show an unambiguous intent to restrain or when an individual's submission to a show of governmental authority takes the form of passive acquiescence * * * ." In *Brendlin*, a front seat passenger in an automobile was held to have been seized when the driver pulled over in response to a police officer's signal. The officer's show of force would be considered by a reasonable passenger as directed to all occupants of the vehicle, the Court explained, and once the vehicle came to a stop Brendlin submitted by staying inside.

A person in a vehicle that was required to stop to accommodate an officer's stop of another vehicle would not be seized, the Court commented in *Brendlin*, because that person "would not perceive a show of authority as directed at him or his car." It also added:

California claims that, under today's rule, "all taxi cab and bus passengers would be 'seized' under the Fourth Amendment when the cab or bus driver is pulled over by the police for running a red light." But the relationship between driver and passenger is not the same in a common carrier as it is in a private vehicle, and the expectations of police officers and passengers differ accordingly. In those cases, as here, the crucial question would be whether a reasonable person in the passenger's position would feel free to take steps to terminate the encounter.

551 U.S. at 262 n. 6, 127 S.Ct. at 2410 n. 6.

B. ARRESTS AND ASSOCIATED SEARCHES

The right to search arising by virtue of effectuation of certain "arrests" is quite broad. It is at least broader than the right to search arising when other detentions are made. Among the reasons why it is important to identify those detentions constituting arrests, therefore, is that characterizing detentions will often determine officers' right to search because of those detentions.

EDITORS' INTRODUCTION: ARRESTS AND THEIR VALIDITY

Arrests pose a number of problems under both federal constitutional law and—in many jurisdictions—as a matter of local law.

Definition of Arrest. The increased complexity of the law relating to detentions makes the definition of arrest more difficult. In part, this is because the definition may be called into play to distinguish arrests from other detentions. One court—with these considerations in mind—offered:

The classic definition of arrest consists of " ' . . . the apprehending or restraining of one's person, in order to be forthcoming to answer an alleged or suspected crime.' " E. Fisher, *Laws of Arrest* 7 (1967) (quoting 4 W. Blackstone, *Commentaries* 288, 289). The necessary first step in determining whether there has been an arrest is to ask whether the individual was free to leave the presence of the police.

A second element of arrest is the likelihood that the present confinement will be accompanied by future interference with the individual's freedom of movement. This element reflects the common law notion that an arrest is more than a present confinement. To be an arrest, confinement should simply be the initial action in criminal prosecution.

State v. Rupe, 101 Wash.2d 664, 683–84, 683 P.2d 571, 584 (1984). This definition suggest an arrest requires a certain intention on the part of the officer. See, e.g., State v. Ellingson, 13 Neb.App. 931, 938–939, 703 N.W.2d 273, 281 (Neb.App.2005) ("An arrest is taking custody of another person for the purpose of holding or detaining him or her to answer a criminal charge.").

"Custodial" and Other Arrests. The Supreme Court's case law sometimes refers to "custodial" arrests. The Court has never developed precisely what is meant by this term. Perhaps, however, the Court intends to distinguish those arrests that will result in the release of the suspect in the field from those that will result in the suspect's being removed to some other location—a stationhouse or courtroom—for further "processing." The distinction between custodial arrests and other detentions is considered later in this chapter in the material on so-called "traffic stops."

"Formal" Arrests. The Supreme Court's cases also refer to "formal" arrests. Berkemer v. McCarty, 468 U.S. 420, 441, 104 S.Ct. 3138, 3151 (1984); Rawlings v. Kentucky, 448 U.S. 98, 111, 100 S.Ct. 2556, 2564 (1980). Again, however, the Court has not defined this term. It seems likely, however, the Court regards a "formal" arrest as a detention accompanied by the officer's expressed announcement to the detained person that the officer is making an arrest.

Some jurisdictions require such an announcement. In a number of jurisdictions, for example, an officer is directed to inform the person of the officer's authority and the reason or cause for the arrest. Exceptions are commonly provided for situations in which the suspect's flight or resistance make such action by the officer impractical. E.g., Mich.Code Crim.Pro. § 764.19; N.Y.—McKinney's Crim.Pro.L. § 00140.15(2). Nevertheless, lower courts have held that compliance with provisions such as these is not necessary to the making of a valid arrest under state law. E.g., Williams v. State, 278 Ark. 9, 12, 642 S.W.2d 887, 889 (1982). The Supreme Court has never indicated that the Fourth Amendment requires such an announcement. Nor has an announcement of this sort been required by the lower courts as a matter of federal constitutional law. As one federal court stated, "the determination of whether an arrest has occurred for Fourth Amendment purposes does not depend upon whether the officers announced that they were placing the suspects under arrest." United States v. Rose, 731 F.2d 1337, 1342 (8th Cir.1984).

Arrests for Minor Offenses. Four members of the Supreme Court argued in Atwater v. City of Lago Vista, 532 U.S. 318, 121 S.Ct. 1536 (2001), that if a crime is punishable only by a fine, the governmental interest in taking a suspect into custody for that offense is outweighed by the suspect's interest in liberty. Consequently, Justice O'Connor concluded:

> Giving police officers constitutional carte blanche to effect an arrest whenever there is probable cause to believe a fine-only misdemeanor has been committed is irreconcilable with the Fourth Amendment's command that seizures be reasonable. Instead, I would require that when there is probable cause to believe that a fine-only offense has been committed, the police

officer should issue a citation unless the officer is "able to point to specific and articulable facts which, taken together with rational inferences from those facts, reasonably warrant [the additional] intrusion" of a full custodial arrest.

532 U.S. at 365–66, 121 S.Ct. at 1563–64 (O'Connor, J., dissenting).

The *Atwater* majority, however, rejected any such Fourth Amendment limitation on arrests. Neither the common law nor more recent American law generally accepted such a limitation on the arrest power. Any rule limiting the power to arrest would require officers to make difficult judgments as to whether only fine-only offenses were committed or whether particular situations came within exceptions to the general rule barring arrests, such as an exception for cases in which the offender presents a continuing danger to the community. Further, the majority commented on the lack of evidence of any "epidemic" of full arrests for minor offenses justifying a new Fourth Amendment limitation on law enforcement. "If an officer has probable cause to believe that an individual has committed even a very minor criminal offense in his presence," the majority concluded, "he may, without violating the Fourth Amendment, arrest the offender." 532 U.S. at 354, 121 S.Ct. at 1557.

Warrant Requirements—Arrests. Arrests may be made pursuant to arrest warrants, issued by magistrates on the basis of information found by those magistrates to constitute probable cause to believe the persons guilty of offenses. Rule 4 of the Federal Rules of Criminal Procedure, for example, authorizes issuance of an arrest warrant.

Such warrants are, however, seldom required as a matter of Fourth Amendment law. In United States v. Watson, 423 U.S. 411, 96 S.Ct. 820 (1976), the Supreme Court considered whether the Fourth Amendment requires—in the absence of exigent circumstances—that an arrest warrant be procured for an arrest in a public place. The Court noted long and widespread acceptance of the common law rule that a warrantless arrest for a felony was permissible, even if the felony was not committed in the presence of the officer, if the officer had probable cause to believe the suspect guilty. Congressional enactments authorizing such arrests reflected the understanding of that body that the Fourth Amendment did not require more. Thus, the Court concluded:

> Law enforcement officers may find it wise to seek arrest warrants where practicable to do so, and their judgments about probable cause may be more readily accepted where backed by a warrant issued by a magistrate. But we decline to transform this judicial preference into a constitutional rule when the judgment of the Nation and Congress has for so long been to authorize warrantless public arrests on probable cause rather than to encumber criminal prosecutions with endless litigation with respect to the existence of exigent circumstances, whether it was practicable to get a warrant, whether the suspect was about to flee, and the like.

423 U.S. at 423–24, 96 S.Ct. at 827–28.

In regard to misdemeanors, the law is less clear. At common law, a warrantless arrest was permitted for a misdemeanor only if the offense was a breach of the peace and committed in the presence of the officer. See Commonwealth v. Reeves, 223 Pa.Super. 51, 52–53, 297 A.2d 142, 143 (1972). Many American jurisdictions, however, permit warrantless misdemeanor arrests in more circumstances. Warrantless arrests are, for example, often permitted for any misdemeanor committed in the presence of the officer. Sometimes state statutory authority or case law is broader.

Post-Arrest Requirement of Judicial Determination of Probable Cause. Although the Fourth Amendment does not require a warrant for an arrest, it imposes a post-arrest requirement of a magistrate's determination of probable cause:

> Maximum protection of individual rights could be assured by requiring a magistrate's review of the factual justification prior to any arrest, but such a requirement would constitute an intolerable handicap for legitimate law enforcement. Thus, while the Court has expressed a preference for the use of arrest warrants when feasible, it has never invalidated an arrest supported by probable cause solely because the officers failed to secure a warrant.

> Under this practical compromise, a policeman's on-the-scene assessment of probable cause provides legal justification for arresting a person suspected of crime, and for a brief period of detention to take the administrative steps incident to arrest. Once the suspect is in custody, however, the reasons that justify dispensing with the magistrate's neutral judgment evaporate. There no longer is any danger that the suspect will escape or commit further crimes while the police submit their evidence to a magistrate. And, while the State's reasons for taking summary action subside, the suspect's need for a neutral determination of probable cause increases significantly. The consequences of prolonged detention may be more serious than the interference occasioned by arrest. Pretrial confinement may imperil the suspect's job, interrupt his source of income, and impair his family relationships. Even pretrial release may be accompanied by burdensome conditions that effect a significant restraint of liberty. When the stakes are this high, the detached judgment of a neutral magistrate is essential if the Fourth Amendment is to furnish meaningful protection from unfounded interference with liberty. Accordingly, we hold that the Fourth Amendment requires a judicial determination of probable cause as a prerequisite to extended restraint of liberty following arrest.

Gerstein v. Pugh, 420 U.S. 103, 113–114, 95 S.Ct. 854, 862–63 (1975). County of Riverside v. McLaughlin, 500 U.S. 44, 111 S.Ct. 1661 (1991), made clear that promptness generally requires such probable cause determinations be made within 48 hours of arrests.

Warrant Requirements—Search for Person to Be Arrested. When an arrest requires entry into premises to find the suspect and arrest him, it is clear the Fourth Amendment's warrant requirement comes into play. In Payton v. New York, 445 U.S. 573, 100 S.Ct. 1371 (1980), officers entered the suspects' residences seeking them for purposes of arrest. Such activity, the Court reasoned, breaches the entrance of an individual's home just as does a search for evidence. "Absent exigent circumstance," it concluded, "that threshold may not reasonably be crossed without a warrant." It then continued:

> [W]e note the State's suggestion that only a search warrant based on probable cause to believe the suspect is at home at a given time can adequately protect the privacy interests at stake, and since such a warrant requirement is manifestly impractical, there need be no warrant of any kind. We find this ingenious argument unpersuasive. It is true that an arrest warrant requirement may afford less protection than a search warrant requirement, but it will suffice to interpose the magistrate's determination of probable cause between the zealous officer and the citizen. If there is sufficient evidence of a citizen's participation in a felony to persuade a judicial officer that his arrest is justified, it is constitutionally reasonable to require him to open his doors to the officers of the law. Thus, for Fourth Amendment purposes, an arrest warrant founded on probable cause implicitly carries with it the limited authority to enter a dwelling in which the suspect lives when there is reason to believe the suspect is within.

445 U.S. at 602–03, 100 S.Ct. at 1388.

But when the premises entered are not those of the suspect, a different situation is presented. In Steagald v. United States, 451 U.S. 204, 101 S.Ct. 1642 (1981), federal drug Enforcement Administration agents had a warrant for the arrest of Lyons. Two days after receiving a tip from an informant that Lyons could be found at a particular residence, they searched that residence. They did not find Lyons but discovered a substantial quantity of cocaine. This was admitted at Steagald's trial for possession of that substance. Finding constitutional error, the Supreme Court held the absence of a valid search warrant rendered the search of the premises for Lyons unreasonable:

> [W]hile the [arrest] warrant * * * may have protected Lyons from an unreasonable seizure, it did absolutely nothing to protect [Steagald's] privacy interest in being free from an unreasonable invasion and search of his home. Instead, [Steagald's] only protection from an illegal entry and search was

the agent's personal determination of probable cause. In the absence of exigent circumstances, we have consistently held that such judicially untested determinations are not reliable enough to justify an entry into a person's home to arrest him without a warrant, or a search of a home for objects in the absence of a search warrant. We see no reason to depart from this settled course when the search of a home is for a person rather than an object.

451 U.S. at 213–14, 101 S.Ct. at 1648.

In *Steagald,* Steagald and one Gaultney were apprehended standing outside the house; Gaultney's wife was inside when it was searched. Before the Supreme Court, the Government urged that Steagald had failed to demonstrate he had an expectation of privacy in the house. The Court, however, concluded the Government had effectively conceded in the lower courts that Steagald had a privacy interest in the premises and that it could therefore not challenge the matter before the Court.

The warrant requirement here, just as the general search warrant requirement, is subject to an emergency exception. The matter was addressed in Welsh v. Wisconsin, 466 U.S. 740, 104 S.Ct. 2091 (1984). Information from a witness led police officers to believe Welsh had, while intoxicated, driven his automobile off the highway into a field, abandoned it, and gone to his nearby residence. Police went to his residence, entered, and—upon finding Welsh lying naked in bed—placed him under arrest for driving a motor vehicle under the influence of an intoxicant. They took him to the station where he refused to submit to a breathalyzer test. Subsequently, authorities began proceedings to revoke his driver's license, based upon his refusal to submit to the breathalyzer test. Under Wisconsin law, if his arrest had been unlawful his refusal to submit to the breathalyzer test would have been reasonable and that refusal could not serve as the basis for revocation. The state courts ultimately rejected Welsh's argument that his arrest violated the Fourth Amendment, despite the officers' failure to obtain a warrant. The officers' actions were reasonable, they reasoned, in view of their "hot pursuit," the risk of harm to the public and Welsh himself, and the need for an immediate arrest and breath test before the alcohol in Welsh's blood disappeared from his system.

The Supreme Court reversed. Justice Brennan, writing for the Court, acknowledged that some "emergency conditions" would sometimes justify warrantless home arrests. But, he continued:

> [A]n important factor to be considered when determining whether any exigency exists is the gravity of the underlying offense for which the arrest is being made. * * * [A]pplication of the exigent-circumstances exception in the context of a home entry should rarely be sanctioned where there is probable cause to believe that only a minor offense, such as the kind at issue in this case, has been committed.

466 U.S. at 753, 104 S.Ct. at 2099. Under Wisconsin law, first offense driving while intoxicated was a noncriminal civil forfeiture offense for which the maximum penalty was a $200 fine. Turning to the facts of the case, the Court continued:

> [T]he claim of hot pursuit is unconvincing because there was no immediate or continuous pursuit of the petitioner from the scene of a crime. Moreover, because the petitioner had already arrived home and had abandoned his car at the scene of the accident, there was little remaining threat to the public safety. Hence, the only potential emergency claimed by the State was the need to ascertain the petitioner's blood-alcohol level.
>
> Even assuming, however, that the underlying facts would support a finding of this exigent circumstance, mere similarity to other cases involving the imminent destruction of evidence is not sufficient. [Wisconsin's classification of driving while intoxicated as a civil offense for which no imprisonment is possible] * * * is the best indication of the state's interest in precipitating an arrest, and is one that can easily be identified both by the courts and by officers faced with a decision to arrest. Given this expression of the state's interest, a warrantless home arrest cannot be upheld simply because evidence of the petitioner's blood-alcohol level might have dissipated while the police obtained a warrant.

466 U.S. at 753–54, 104 S.Ct. at 2099–2100.

In view of this conclusion, the Court found "no occasion to consider whether the Fourth Amendment might impose an absolute ban on warrantless home arrests for certain minor offenses."

The Supreme Court had earlier applied a "hot pursuit" sort of exception to the warrant requirement in this context. In United States v. Santana, 427 U.S. 38, 96 S.Ct. 2406 (1976), officers in an automobile pulled up in front of Santana's residence. She was standing in the door. When the officers shouted, "Police," displayed their badges and advanced, she "retreated" into the vestibule of her house. The officers—without a warrant—followed her into the vestibule and arrested her. No constitutional defect was found in the officers' actions. While she was in her doorway, the Court reasoned, Santana was in a "public place" and, under *Watson,* no warrant was required. Where the police follow in "true 'hot pursuit,'" a suspect may not, by retreating into a house, "defeat an arrest which has been set in motion in a public place * * * ."

The Court in Stanton v. Sims, ___ U.S. ___, 134 S.Ct. 3 (2013) (per curiam), left undecided whether an officer with probable cause to believe a suspect committed a misdemeanor and in hot pursuit of that suspect may enter residential premises without a warrant to arrest the suspect.

Entry to Arrest—Announcement Requirement. Where officers rely upon a search warrant as authority to enter premises and search those premises for a suspect they have grounds to arrest, the propriety of the officers' actions in gaining entry is undoubtedly governed by the rules relating to entry to execute a search warrant, discussed in Chapter 3. In other situations, however, must officers make some sort of preliminary announcements—as, for example, to their purpose—and perhaps also a request for admission before entering?

In Miller v. United States, 357 U.S. 301, 78 S.Ct. 1190 (1958), the Government conceded that the validity of an entry to make an arrest without a warrant was to be tested by criteria identical to those which 18 U.S.C.A. § 3109 (set out in the Editors' Introduction to Subchapter C of Chapter 3) imposes upon entry to execute a search warrant. Since the officers in *Miller* failed to give notice of their authority and purpose before breaking to enter to locate and arrest Miller, the entry, Miller's arrest, and the search incident to the arrest were held invalid and the evidence obtained in the search was inadmissible. The Court reached a similar result in Sabbath v. United States, 391 U.S. 585, 88 S.Ct. 1755 (1968). *Miller* and *Sabbath* may, of course, reflect only the Court's application of federal statutory law. However, the Supreme Court's Fourth Amendment case law concerning entry to execute a search warrant, covered in Chapter 3, suggests that entry to make an arrest is subject to similar requirements. Thus, *Miller* and *Sabbath* may reflect a constitutionally-required construction of the federal statute. Consider whether in light of the material in Chapter 3, violation of this announcement requirement demands exclusion of evidence obtained after the entry.

Probable Cause Requirement—In General. Although the warrant requirement has relatively little application to the reasonableness of an arrest, the Fourth Amendment's requirement of probable cause has substantial significance:

> Whether [an] arrest was constitutionally valid depends * * * upon whether, at the moment the arrest was made, the officers had probable cause to make it—whether at that moment the facts and circumstances within their knowledge and of which they had reasonably trustworthy information were sufficient to warrant a prudent man in believing that the [suspect] had committed or was committing an offense.

Beck v. Ohio, 379 U.S. 89, 91, 85 S.Ct. 223, 225 (1964).

Probable Cause—Intended or Announced Basis for Arrest. Whren v. United States, 517 U.S. 806, 116 S.Ct. 1769 (1996) (reprinted in Chapter 2), holding "pretext" challenges unavailable to traffic stops, was reaffirmed and applied to an arrest in Arkansas v. Sullivan, 532 U.S. 769, 121 S.Ct. 1876 (2001) (per curiam).

What if any constitutional consequences flow from officers' announcement when an arrest is made of some specific legal basis for that action? This was addressed in Devenpeck v. Alford, 543 U.S. 146, 125 S.Ct. 588 (2004).

After being told that Jerome Alford had activated "wig-wag" headlights (which flash the left and right lights alternately) on his vehicle, Washington State Police officers stopped him to investigate their concerns that he was impersonating a police officer. When they observed that he had an operating tape recorder on the seat, they told him he was being arrested for a violation of Washington's Privacy Act, which prohibits recording certain conversations without the permission of the participants. After the charge was dismissed, Alford sued the officers asserting a federal cause of action under 42 U.S.C. § 1983, and a state cause of action for unlawful arrest and imprisonment. Both claims rested upon the allegation that the defendant officers arrested him without probable cause in violation of the Fourth and Fourteenth Amendments. A jury returned a verdict for the defendants.

On appeal, this was reversed. The court of appeals rejected the officers' contention that the arrest could be justified as one on probable cause to believe Alford committed the offenses of impersonating a law-enforcement officer and obstructing a law-enforcement officer. It applied a rule that when an arrest is announced by an officer as resting on a particular offense, it can be later upheld as one for a different offense only if that different offense is a crime involving the same conduct as that relied upon by the officer and is "closely related" to that offense. Since the defendants had stated that the arrest was for violation of the Privacy Act, they could not later defend it as an arrest for impersonating an officer or obstructing an officer because these were not closely related to the possible Privacy Act violation.

A unanimous Supreme Court (with the Chief Justice not participating) reversed, holding the defendants were not, as a matter of Fourth Amendment law, limited to defending the arrest as one for an offense closely related to that the officers announced at the time of the arrest. The Court explained:

> Our cases make clear that an arresting officer's state of mind (except for the facts that he knows) is irrelevant to the existence of probable cause. That is to say, his subjective reason for making the arrest need not be the criminal offense as to which the known facts provide probable cause. * * *
>
> The rule that the offense establishing probable cause must be "closely related" to, and based on the same conduct as, the offense identified by the arresting officer at the time of arrest is inconsistent with this precedent. Such a rule makes the lawfulness of an arrest turn upon the motivation of the arresting officer—eliminating, as validating probable cause, facts that played no part in the officer's expressed subjective reason for making the arrest, and offenses that are not "closely related" to that subjective reason.

543 U.S. at 153–54, 125 S.Ct. at 593–94. It continued:

> [T]he "closely related offense" rule is condemned by its perverse consequences. While it is assuredly good police practice to inform a person of the reason for his arrest at the time he is taken into custody, we have never held that to be constitutionally required. Hence, the predictable consequence of a rule limiting the probable cause inquiry to offenses closely related to (and supported by the same facts as) those identified by the arresting officer is not, as respondent contends, that officers will cease making sham arrests on the hope that such arrests will later be validated, but rather that officers will cease providing reasons for arrest. And even if this option were to be foreclosed by adoption of a statutory or constitutional requirement, officers would simply give every reason for which probable cause could conceivably exist.

543 U.S. at 155, 125 S.Ct. at 595 (incorporating footnote into text).

Probable Cause—Cooperative Action and "Collective" Information. Given the complexity of many criminal offenses and the mobility of many suspects, investigations often involve more than one officer and, in fact, officers of several jurisdictions. Action by law enforcement officers may be taken upon request of other officers, perhaps ones of another jurisdiction. When one officer or agency makes an arrest upon the request of another officer or police agency, what information is to be considered in determining if probable cause exists?

In United States v. Hensley, 469 U.S. 221, 105 S.Ct. 675 (1985), the Court explained:

> [W]hen evidence is uncovered during a search incident to an arrest in reliance merely on a flyer or bulletin, its admissibility turns on whether the officers who *issued* the flyer possessed probable cause to make the arrest. It does not turn on whether those relying on the flyer were themselves aware of the specific facts which led their colleagues to seek their assistance. In an era when criminal suspects are increasingly mobile and increasingly likely to flee across jurisdictional boundaries, this rule is a matter of common sense: it minimizes the volume of information concerning suspects that must be transmitted to other jurisdictions and enables police in one jurisdiction to act promptly in reliance on information from another jurisdiction.

469 U.S. at 231, 105 S.Ct. at 681.

Excessive Force. Traditionally, the amount of force permissible to make an arrest has been a matter of nonconstitutional law. In Tennessee v. Garner, 471 U.S. 1, 105 S.Ct. 1694 (1985), however, the Supreme Court held excessive deadly force in making an otherwise proper arrest renders that arrest "unreasonable" under the Fourth Amendment. Such reasonableness, the Court explained, depends not simply upon whether there are grounds for arrest—that is, probable cause—"but also on how [the arrest] is carried out." In Graham v. Connor, 490 U.S. 386, 109 S.Ct. 1865 (1989), it held that nondeadly but excessive force could have the same effect.

Traditional law permitted officers to use deadly force whenever they reasonably believed that necessary to make the arrest of a person reasonably believed to have committed a felony. *Garner* defined acceptable deadly force for purposes of the Fourth Amendment rule more narrowly. Use of deadly force, the Court concluded, is unreasonable if used against a nondangerous suspect. Putting the holding affirmatively, it explained:

> Where the officer has probable cause to believe that the suspect poses a threat of serious physical harm, either to the officer or to others, it is not constitutionally unreasonable to prevent escape by using deadly force. Thus, if the suspect threatens the officer with a weapon or there is probable cause to believe that he has committed a crime involving the infliction or threatened infliction of serious physical harm, deadly force may be used if necessary to prevent escape, and if, where feasible, some warning has been given.

471 U.S. at 11–12, 105 S.Ct. at 1701. On the facts of *Garner,* the Court held the officer's reasonable belief the suspect had committed nighttime burglary was *not* sufficient to justify the use of the fatal gunfire there at issue to stop the suspect.

The significance of the deadly/nondeadly force distinction was deemphasized in Scott v. Harris, 550 U.S. 372, 382–83, 127 S.Ct. 1769, 1777–78 (2007), in which the Court stressed that the ultimate question is whether the officer's actions—however labeled—"were reasonable." *Scott* held reasonable the actions of an officer (Scott) in ramming Harris's fleeing automobile in an effort to terminate a ten mile high speed chase. "[I]n judging whether Scott's actions were reasonable," the Court explained, "we must consider the risk of bodily harm that Scott's actions posed to [Harris] in light of the threat to the public that Scott was trying to eliminate." Harris, it continued, "posed an actual and imminent threat to the lives of any pedestrians who might have been present, to other civilian motorists, and to the officers involved in the chase." Further, "Scott's actions posed a high likelihood of serious injury or death to respondent—though not the near *certainty* of death posed by, say, shooting a fleeing felon in the back of the head, or pulling alongside a fleeing motorist's car and shooting the motorist."

Garner, Graham and *Scott* were civil cases in which damages were sought under 42 U.S.C.A. § 1983 on the theory that the officers' use of force had made the arrests unreasonable. When, if ever, will force that is excessive under these cases render evidence inadmissible? Suppose, for example, in *Garner* the officer's gunfire had not killed Garner but had disabled him and thus enabled the officer to arrest him. Suppose further in a search incident to this arrest, items taken from the burglarized premises were found on Garner's person. Would these items be inadmissible because of the excessive force?

One federal court of appeals held—relying in part on Hudson v. Michigan, 547 U.S. 586, 126 S.Ct. 2159 (2006), reprinted in Subchapter C of Chapter 3—that in light of the availability of civil damages the use of excessive force in making an arrest does not give rise to a Fourth Amendment right to suppression of evidence obtained because of that arrest. United States v. Watson, 558 F.3d 702, 704–05 (7th Cir.2009). *Watson* was reaffirmed in United States v. Collins, 714 F.3d 540, 543–45 (7th Cir.2013) (per curiam). Several other courts have reached the same result. State v. Sandberg, 611 P.2d 44 (Alaska 1980); State v. Herr, 828 N.W.2d 896, 346 Wis.2d 603 (App. 2013), appeal dismissed.

1. SEARCHES INCIDENT TO ARRESTS

EDITORS' INTRODUCTION: SEARCHES INCIDENT TO ARRESTS AND THOSE PART OF STATIONHOUSE PROCESSING

The occurrence of a valid arrest itself brings into play a right to make certain searches. This power to search because of an arrest is the subject of the present unit.

The Supreme Court described the background of this search power:

> The search-incident-to-arrest doctrine has an ancient pedigree. Well before the Nation's founding, it was recognized that officers carrying out a lawful arrest had the authority to make a warrantless search of the arrestee's person. * * *

> One Fourth Amendment historian has observed that, prior to American independence, "[a]nyone arrested could expect that not only his surface clothing but his body, luggage, and saddlebags would be searched and, perhaps, his shoes, socks, and mouth as well." W. Cuddihy, The Fourth Amendment: Origins and Original Meaning: 602–1791, p. 420 (2009).

> No historical evidence suggests that the Fourth Amendment altered the permissible bounds of arrestee searches. On the contrary, legal scholars agree that "the legitimacy of body searches as an adjunct to the arrest process had been thoroughly established in colonial times, so much so that their constitutionality in 1789 can not be doubted." *Id.,* at 752.

> Few reported cases addressed the legality of such searches before the 19th century, apparently because the point was not much contested. In the 19th century, the subject came up for discussion more often, but court decisions and treatises alike confirmed the searches' broad acceptance.

When this Court first addressed the question, we too confirmed (albeit in dicta) "the right on the part of the Government, always recognized under English and American law, to search the person of the accused when legally arrested to discover and seize the fruits or evidence of crime." *Weeks v. United States,* 232 U.S. 383, 392, 34 S.Ct. 341, 58 L.Ed. 652 (1914). The exception quickly became a fixture in our Fourth Amendment case law.

Birchfield v. North Dakota, ___ U.S. ___, ___, 136 S.Ct. 2160, 2174–75 (2016).

Although the rule permitting a search incident to arrest is often referred to as an exception to the requirement of a warrant, the Court has noted that "the label 'exception' is something of a misnomer in this context, as warrantless searches incident to arrest occur with far greater frequency than searches conducted pursuant to a warrant." Riley v. California, ___ U.S. ___, ___, 134 S.Ct. 2473, 2482 (2014).

This power to search a suspect incident to an arrest must be distinguished from what may be done as part of later processing of an arrested suspect. The Supreme Court addressed authorities' right to search at the stationhouse in Illinois v. Lafayette, 462 U.S. 640, 103 S.Ct. 2605 (1983). LaFayette was arrested and handcuffed at a theater for disturbing the peace. He carried a "purse-type shoulder bag" with him to the police station. Upon arrival at the station, officers took him to the "booking room" and examined the bag's contents; they found amphetamines. These were admitted into evidence at LaFayette's prosecution for possession of a controlled substance. The Supreme Court found no constitutional error, reasoning "it is not 'unreasonable' for police, as part of the routine procedure incident to incarcerating an arrested person, to search any container or article in his possession, in accordance with established inventory procedures." Characterizing an inventory search as "not an independent legal consent but rather an incidental administrative step following arrest and preceding incarceration," the majority explained its holding:

> At the stationhouse, it is entirely proper for police to remove and list or inventory property found on the person or in the possession of an arrested person who is to be jailed. A range of governmental interests support such an inventory process. It is not unheard of for persons employed in police activities to steal property taken from arrested persons; similarly, arrested persons have been known to make false claims regarding what was taken from their possession at the stationhouse. A standardized procedure for making a list or inventory as soon as reasonable after reaching the stationhouse not only deters false claims but also inhibits theft or careless handling of articles taken from the arrested person. Arrested persons have also been known to injure themselves—or others—with belts, knives,

drugs or other items on their persons while being detained. Dangerous instrumentalities—such as razor blades, bombs, or weapons—can be concealed in innocent-looking articles taken from the arrestee's possession. The bare recital of these mundane realities justifies reasonable measures by police to limit these risks—either while the items are in police possession or at the time they are returned to the arrestee upon his release. Examining all the items removed from the arrestee's person or possession and listing or inventorying them is an entirely reasonable administrative procedure. It is immaterial whether the police actually fear any particular package or container; the need to protect against such risks arises independent of a particular officer's subjective concerns. Finally, inspection of an arrestee's personal property may assist the police in ascertaining or verifying his identity.

462 U.S. at 646, 103 S.Ct. at 2609–10. These interests, the Court added, may sometimes be greater than those supporting a search immediately after arrest:

> Consequently, the scope of a stationhouse search will often vary from that made at the time of arrest. Police conduct that would be impractical or unreasonable—or embarrassingly intrusive— on the street can more readily—and privately—be performed at the station. For example, the interest supporting a search incident to arrest would hardly justify disrobing an arrestee on the street, but the practical necessities of routine jail administration may even justify taking a prisoner's clothing from him before confining him, although that step would be rare.

462 U.S. at 645, 103 S.Ct. at 2609. It was not, the majority noted, addressing the circumstances in which a strip search of an arrestee "may or may not be appropriate."

The Illinois court had held the search of LaFayette's shoulder bag unreasonable because the State's interests could be served by less intrusive methods, such as placing the bag in a secured locker or sealing it in a plastic bag. Granting this might have been so, a majority of the Supreme Court rejected the position that the Fourth Amendment required the Illinois police to use such less intrusive methods:

> The reasonableness of any particular governmental activity does not necessarily or invariably turn on the existence of alternative "less intrusive" means. * * * We are hardly in a position to second-guess police departments as to what practical administrative method will best deter theft by and false claims against its employees and preserve the security of the stationhouse. * * *

> Even if less intrusive means existed of protecting some particular types of property, it would be unreasonable to expect police officers in the everyday course of business to make fine and subtle distinctions in deciding which containers or items may be searched and which must be sealed as a unit.

462 U.S. at 647–48, 103 S.Ct. at 2610. But the Court apparently intended to limit inventory inspections to situations in which the suspect was to be more than "booked." It noted uncertainty in the record as to whether LaFayette was to be incarcerated after being booked for disturbing the peace. "That," it offered, "is an appropriate inquiry on remand."

Perhaps the most troublesome aspect of the right to search incident to arrests is defining the scope of the permissible search. This is the subject of the principal case that follows.

Chimel v. California

Supreme Court of the United States, 1969.
395 U.S. 752, 89 S.Ct. 2034.

■ MR. JUSTICE STEWART delivered the opinion of the Court.

This case raises basic questions concerning the permissible scope under the Fourth Amendment of a search incident to a lawful arrest.

The relevant facts are essentially undisputed. Late in the afternoon of September 13, 1965, three police officers arrived at the Santa Ana, California, home of the petitioner with a warrant authorizing his arrest for the burglary of a coin shop. The officers knocked on the door, identified themselves to the petitioner's wife, and asked if they might come inside. She ushered them into the house, where they waited 10 or 15 minutes until the petitioner returned home from work. When the petitioner entered the house, one of the officers handed him the arrest warrant and asked for permission to "look around." The petitioner objected, but was advised that "on the basis of the lawful arrest," the officers would nonetheless conduct a search. No search warrant had been issued.

Accompanied by the petitioner's wife, the officers then looked through the entire three-bedroom house, including the attic, the garage, and a small workshop. In some rooms the search was relatively cursory. In the master bedroom and sewing room, however, the officers directed the petitioner's wife to open drawers and "to physically move contents of the drawers from side to side so that [they] might view any items that would have come from [the] burglary." After completing the search, they seized numerous items—primarily coins, but also several medals, tokens, and a few other objects. The entire search took between 45 minutes and an hour.

At the petitioner's subsequent state trial on two charges of burglary, the items taken from his house were admitted into evidence against him, over his objection that they had been unconstitutionally seized. He was convicted, and the judgments of conviction were affirmed by both the California Court of Appeal, and the California Supreme Court. Both courts accepted the petitioner's contention that the arrest warrant was invalid because the supporting affidavit was set out in conclusory terms, but held that since the arresting officers had procured the warrant "in good faith," and since in any event they had had sufficient information to constitute probable cause for the petitioner's arrest, that arrest had been lawful. From this conclusion the appellate courts went on to hold that the search of the petitioner's home had been justified, despite the absence of a search warrant, on the ground that it had been incident to a valid arrest. * * *

Without deciding the question, we proceed on the hypothesis that the California courts were correct in holding that the arrest of the petitioner was valid under the Constitution. This brings us directly to the question whether the warrantless search of the petitioner's entire house can be constitutionally justified as incident to that arrest. The decisions of this Court bearing upon that question have been far from consistent * * * .

Approval of a warrantless search incident to a lawful arrest seems first to have been articulated by the Court in 1914 as dictum in *Weeks v. United States*, 232 U.S. 383, 34 S.Ct. 341, 58 L.Ed. 652. * * *

That statement made no reference to any right to search the *place* where an arrest occurs, but was limited to a right to search the "person." * * *

In 1950 * * * came *United States v. Rabinowitz*, 339 U.S. 56, 70 S.Ct. 430, 94 L.Ed. 653, the decision upon which California primarily relies in the case now before us. In *Rabinowitz*, federal authorities had been informed that the defendant was dealing in stamps bearing forged overprints. On the basis of that information they secured a warrant for his arrest, which they executed at his one-room business office. At the time of the arrest, the officers "searched the desk, safe, and file cabinets in the office for about an hour and a half," and seized 573 stamps with forged overprints. The stamps were admitted into evidence at the defendant's trial, and this Court affirmed his conviction, rejecting the contention that the warrantless search had been unlawful. The Court held that the search in its entirety fell within the principle giving law enforcement authorities "[t]he right 'to search the place where the arrest is made in order to find and seize things connected with the crime * * * .'" * * *

Rabinowitz has come to stand for the proposition, *inter alia*, that a warrantless search "incident to a lawful arrest" may generally extend to the area that is considered to be in the "possession" or under the "control" of the person arrested. And it was on the basis of that proposition that the California courts upheld the search of the petitioner's entire house in this case. That doctrine, however, at least in the broad sense in which it was applied by the California courts in this case, can withstand neither historical nor rational analysis.

Even limited to its own facts, the *Rabinowitz* decision was * * * hardly founded on an unimpeachable line of authority. * * * Nor is the rationale by which the State seeks here to sustain the search of the petitioner's house supported by a reasoned view of the background and purpose of the Fourth Amendment.

* * *

Only last Term in *Terry v. Ohio*, 392 U.S. 1, 88 S.Ct. 1868, 20 L.Ed.2d 889, we emphasized that "the police must, whenever practicable, obtain advance judicial approval of searches and seizures through the warrant procedure," and that "[t]he scope of [a] search must be 'strictly tied to and justified by' the circumstances which rendered its initiation permissible." * * *

A similar analysis underlies the "search incident to arrest" principle, and marks its proper extent. When an arrest is made, it is reasonable for the arresting officer to search the person arrested in order to remove any weapons that the latter might seek to use in order to resist arrest or effect his escape. Otherwise, the officer's safety might well be endangered, and the arrest itself frustrated. In addition, it is entirely reasonable for the arresting officer to search for and seize any evidence on the arrestee's person in order to prevent its concealment or destruction. And the area into which an arrestee might reach in order to grab a weapon or evidentiary items must, of course, be governed by a like rule. A gun on a table or in a drawer in front of one who is arrested can be as dangerous to the arresting officer as one concealed in the clothing of the person arrested. There is ample justification, therefore, for a search of the arrestee's person and the area "within his immediate control" construing that phrase to mean the area from within which he might gain possession of a weapon or destructible evidence.

There is no comparable justification, however, for routinely searching any room other than that in which an arrest occurs—or, for that matter, for searching through all the desk drawers or other closed or concealed areas in that room itself. Such searches, in the absence of well-recognized exceptions, may be made only under the authority of a search warrant. The "adherence to judicial processes" mandated by the Fourth Amendment requires no less.

* * *

It is argued in the present case that it is "reasonable" to search a man's house when he is arrested in it. Under such an unconfined analysis, Fourth Amendment protection in this area would approach the evaporation point. It is not easy to explain why, for instance, it is less subjectively "reasonable" to search a man's house when he is arrested on his front lawn—or just down the street—than it is when he happens to be in the house at the time of arrest.

No consideration relevant to the Fourth Amendment suggests any point of rational limitation, once the search is allowed to go beyond the area from which the person arrested might obtain weapons or evidentiary items. The only reasoned distinction is one between a search of the person arrested and the area within his reach on the one hand and more extensive searches on the other.

The petitioner correctly points out that one result of decisions such as *Rabinowitz* * * * is to give law enforcement officials the opportunity to engage in searches not justified by probable cause, by the simple expedient of arranging to arrest suspects at home rather than elsewhere. We do not suggest that the petitioner is necessarily correct in his assertion that such a strategy was utilized here but the fact remains that had he been arrested earlier in the day, at his place of employment rather than at home, no search of his house could have been made without a search warrant.

* * *

Rabinowitz * * * [has] been the subject of critical commentary for many years, and [has] been relied upon less and less in our own decisions. It is time, for the reasons we have stated, to hold that * * * [it is] no longer to be followed.

Application of sound Fourth Amendment principles to the facts of this case produces a clear result. The search here went far beyond the petitioner's person and the area from within which he might have obtained either a weapon or something that could have been used as evidence against him. There was no constitutional justification, in the absence of a search warrant, for extending the search beyond that area. The scope of the search was, therefore, "unreasonable" under the Fourth and Fourteenth Amendments and the petitioner's conviction cannot stand.

Reversed.

■ MR. JUSTICE WHITE, with whom MR. JUSTICE BLACK joins, dissenting.

* * *

* * * An arrest itself may often create an emergency situation making it impracticable to obtain a warrant before embarking on a related search. * * * [A]ssuming that there is probable cause to search premises at the spot where a suspect is arrested, it seems to me unreasonable to require the police to leave the scene in order to obtain a search warrant when they are already legally there to make a valid arrest, and when there must almost always be a strong possibility that confederates of the arrested man will in the meanwhile remove the items for which the police have probable cause to search. This must so often be the case that it seems to me as unreasonable to require a warrant for a search of the premises as to require a warrant for search of the person and his very immediate surroundings.

* * *

NOTES

1. **Establishing the Arrest.** Is it important when—or even whether—an "arrest" occurs? In Rawlings v. Kentucky, 448 U.S. 98, 100 S.Ct. 2556 (1980), Rawlings was present when officers searched his companion's purse; they found 1,800 tablets of LSD and a variety of other controlled substances. When the companion told Rawlings to "take what was his," he claimed ownership of all the substances. One of the officers searched Rawlings and found $4,500 in a shirt pocket and a knife in a sheath at his side. Rawlings was then placed under "formal arrest." Challenging the admissibility of the money and the knife, Rawlings argued the search could not be justified as incident to his arrest since the arrest did not occur until after the search. A majority of the Court experienced "no difficulty" in rejecting this claim:

> Once [Rawlings] admitted ownership of the sizable quantity of drugs found in [the] purse, the police clearly had probable cause to place [him] under arrest. Where the formal arrest followed quickly on the heels of the challenged search of [Rawlings'] person, we do not believe it particularly important that the search preceded the arrest rather than vice versa.

448 U.S. at 111, 100 S.Ct. at 2564.

2. **Need for Case-Specific Justification.** Do officers need reason to believe a particular search incident to an arrest would be fruitful? In United States v. Robinson, 414 U.S. 218, 94 S.Ct. 467 (1973), District of Columbia police officer Jenks stopped Robinson's automobile to arrest him on probable cause to believe Robinson was driving after revocation of his motor vehicle operator's license. Jenks then searched Robinson:

> Jenks felt an object in the left breast pocket of the heavy coat [Robinson] was wearing, but testified that he "couldn't tell what it was" and also that he "couldn't actually tell the size of it." Jenks then reached into the pocket and pulled out the object, which turned out to be a "crumpled up cigarette package." Jenks testified that at this point he still did not know what was in the package:
>
> > "As I felt the package I could feel objects in the package but I couldn't tell what they were * * *. I knew they weren't cigarettes."
>
> The officer then opened the cigarette pack and found 14 gelatin capsules of white powder which he thought to be, and which later analysis proved to be, heroin. Jenks then continued his search of [Robinson] to completion, feeling around his waist and trouser legs, and examining the remaining pockets. The heroin * * * was admitted into evidence at the trial which resulted in his conviction in the District Court.

The Supreme Court, reversing the Court of Appeals, held the search permissible:

[O]ur * * * fundamental disagreement with the Court of Appeals arises from its suggestion that there must be litigated in each case the issue of whether or not there was present one of the reasons supporting the authority for a search of the person incident to a lawful arrest. We do not think the long line of authorities of this Court * * * , nor what we can glean from the history of practice in this country and in England, requires such a case by case adjudication. A police officer's determination as to how and where to search the person of a suspect whom he has arrested is necessarily a quick *ad hoc* judgment which the Fourth Amendment does not require to be broken down in each instance into an analysis of each step in the search. The authority to search the person incident to a lawful custodial arrest, while based upon the need to disarm and to discover evidence, does not depend on what a court may later decide was the probability in a particular arrest situation that weapons or evidence would in fact be found upon the person of the suspect. A custodial arrest of a suspect based on probable cause is a reasonable intrusion under the Fourth Amendment; that intrusion being lawful, a search incident to the arrest requires no additional justification. It is the fact of the lawful arrest which establishes the authority to search, and we hold that in the case of a lawful custodial arrest a full search of the person is not only an exception to the warrant requirement of the Fourth Amendment, but is also a "reasonable" search under that Amendment.

414 U.S. at 235, 94 S.Ct. at 477. Justices Marshall, Douglas and Brennan dissented.

3. **Time at Which Scope of Right to Search is Determined.** In 2009, several members of the Court addressed what they saw as an ambiguity in *Chimel*:

> *Chimel* did not say whether "the area from within which [an arrestee] might gain possession of a weapon or destructible evidence" is to be measured at the time of the arrest or at the time of the search, but unless the *Chimel* rule was meant to be a specialty rule, applicable to only a few unusual cases, the Court must have intended for this area to be measured at the time of arrest.

> This is so because the Court can hardly have failed to appreciate the following two facts. First, in the great majority of cases, an officer making an arrest is able to handcuff the arrestee and remove him to a secure place before conducting a search incident to the arrest. Second, because it is safer for an arresting officer to secure an arrestee before searching, it is likely that this is what arresting officers do in the great majority of cases. (And it appears, not surprisingly, that this is in fact the prevailing practice.) Thus, if the area within an arrestee's reach were assessed, not at the time of arrest, but at the time of the search, the *Chimel* rule would rarely come into play.

Moreover, if the applicability of the *Chimel* rule turned on whether an arresting officer chooses to secure an arrestee prior to conducting a search, rather than searching first and securing the arrestee later, the rule would "create a perverse incentive for an arresting officer to prolong the period during which the arrestee is kept in an area where he could pose a danger to the officer." If this is the law, * * * "the law would truly be, as Mr. Bumble said, 'a ass.' "

I do not think that this is what the *Chimel* Court intended. Handcuffs were in use in 1969. The ability of arresting officers to secure arrestees before conducting a search—and their incentive to do so—are facts that can hardly have escaped the Court's attention. I therefore believe that the *Chimel* Court intended that its new rule apply in cases in which the arrestee is handcuffed before the search is conducted.

Arizona v. Gant, 556 U.S. 332, 361–63, 129 S.Ct. 1710, 1730 (2009) (Alito, J. dissenting).

4. **Moving and Accompanying the Suspect.** May an officer who has arrested a suspect in a public place accompany the suspect into his dwelling or into particular parts of the dwelling as an incident of the arrest? In Washington v. Chrisman, 455 U.S. 1, 102 S.Ct. 812 (1982), a campus police officer observed a student, Overdahl, exit a dormitory carrying a half-gallon bottle of gin. Overdahl appeared to be underage. The officer stopped him and asked for identification. He responded that his identification was in his dormitory room and asked whether the officer could wait until he retrieved it. The officer replied he would have to accompany Overdahl to his room, to which Overdahl responded, "O.K." Overdahl's roommate, Chrisman, was in the room when the officer and Overdahl arrived. The officer remained at the doorway while Overdahl entered the room to look for identification. While at the doorway, the officer observed what he believed to be marijuana seeds and a pipe on a desk about 8 to 10 feet away. He entered the room and confirmed his suspicions. After placing the roommates under arrest and obtaining their consent to a search of the room, the officer found additional drugs. Chrisman was prosecuted for possession of controlled substances. His conviction was overturned by the Washington Supreme Court on the ground that, although the officer could have accompanied Overdahl into the room after arresting him, he was not permitted under the Fourth Amendment to enter the room to seize evidence of crime without a warrant or exigent circumstances.

The Supreme Court reversed. The majority reasoned the Fourth Amendment permits the officer "to remain literally at [the arrestee's] elbow at all times":

[I]t is not "unreasonable" under the Fourth Amendment for a police officer, as a matter of routine, to monitor the movements of an arrested person, as his judgment dictates, following the arrest. The officer's need to ensure his own safety—as well as the integrity of the arrest—is compelling. Such surveillance is not an impermissible invasion of the privacy or personal liberty of an individual who has been arrested.

455 U.S. at 7, 102 S.Ct. at 817. The majority also concluded that since the officer could have accompanied Overdahl into the dormitory room, his remaining in the doorway did not make his entry into the room after seeing contraband in plain view a Fourth Amendment violation.

5. **Search for Dangerous Persons.** What action may officers take at the scene of an arrest to protect themselves from persons other than the individual arrested? In Maryland v. Buie, 494 U.S. 325, 334, 110 S.Ct. 1093, 1098 (1990), the Court commented that officers making an arrest in a private residence could, "as an incident to the arrest * * * , as a precautionary matter and without probable cause or reasonable suspicion, look in closets and other spaces immediately adjoining the place of arrest from which an attack could be immediately launched."

A more intensive and extensive "protective sweep" of the premises— described by the Court as "a quick and limited search of a premises, incident to an arrest and conducted to protect the safety of officers or others"— requires "articulable facts which, taken together with the rational inferences from those facts, would warrant a reasonably prudent officer in believing that the area to be swept harbors an individual posing a danger to those on the arrest scene." The Court continued:

> We should emphasize that such a protective sweep, aimed at protecting the arresting officers, if justified by the circumstances, is nevertheless not a full search of the premises, but may extend only to a cursory inspection of those spaces where a person may be found. The sweep lasts no longer than is necessary to dispel the reasonable suspicion of danger and in any event no longer than it takes to complete the arrest and depart the premises.

494 U.S. at 335, 110 S.Ct. at 1099.

6. **Taking DNA Samples.** Whether law enforcement officers may take DNA samples from arrested suspects was at issue in Maryland v. King, ___ U.S. ___, 133 S.Ct. 1958 (2013). The Maryland DNA Collection Act, Md. Pub. Saf. Code Ann. § 2–504, authorizes the taking of DNA samples from persons arrested for certain serious offenses. A sample may not be processed until the arrested person is presented before a judicial officer, who determines whether there is probable cause to believe the arrestee guilty of an offense triggering the sampling procedure. Destruction of the sample is required if probable cause is found lacking, the prosecution does not result in a conviction, or a conviction is finally held invalid without the possibility of a new trial. Analysis of the sample may only be conducted for information related to the identification of the person.

King was arrested in 2009 for felony assault and, pursuant to the Maryland statute, a DNA sample was obtained from him by a "buccal swab." This consists of wiping a small piece of filter paper or a cotton swab similar to a Q-tip against the inside cheek of the arrestee's mouth to collect skin cells. King's DNA profile was found to match that of the unidentified perpetrator of a 2003 rape. King sought suppression of this evidence of his guilt of the rape on the ground that the taking of the DNA sample from him, although authorized by statute, violated the Fourth Amendment. By a 5-to-4 vote, the Supreme Court found no constitutional violation.

The majority first held the collection of a DNA sample, since it involves an intrusion into the body, is a search. However, it involves no intrusion below the skin, is quick and painless, and does not threaten the arrestee's health or safety. Thus the intrusion is "negligible," the majority concluded, and this "is of central relevance to determining reasonableness * * * ." No search warrant is required, because no individualized suspicion is necessary and thus there would be nothing for a magistrate to evaluate. Fourth Amendment reasonableness therefore depends upon a balancing of the privacy-related concerns ("the degree to which [the search] intrudes upon an individual's privacy") and the law enforcement-related concerns ("the promotion of legitimate governmental interests"). ___ U.S. at ___, 133 S.Ct. at 1970.

"The legitimate government interest served by the Maryland DNA Collection Act," the majority reasoned, "is one that is well established: the need for law enforcement officers in a safe and accurate way to process and identify the persons and possessions they must take into custody." Accurate identification of an arrested person is necessary for a variety of reasons, including the need to assess the risk posed to those processing the person and application of the criteria for pretrial release. "DNA identification is an advanced technique superior to fingerprinting in many ways," * * * but involving no significant "additional intrusion upon the arrestee's privacy beyond that associated with fingerprinting * * * ." Collecting a DNA sample, like taking fingerprints, is therefore reasonable.

Processing of the sample, under the circumstances presented by *King*, does "not amount to a significant invasion of privacy that would render the DNA identification impermissible under the Fourth Amendment." The type of analysis conducted for identification most likely does not provide access to private information beyond identity. Further, samples are not analyzed for such information and such analysis is barred by the statute. "If in the future police analyze samples to determine, for instance, an arrestee's predisposition for a particular disease or other hereditary factors not relevant to identity," the Court observed, "that case would present additional privacy concerns not present here." ___ U.S. at ___, 133 S.Ct. at 1979.

Justice Scalia, joined by Justices Ginsburg, Sotomayor, and Kagen, dissented. Taking a DNA sample from one arrested is a suspicionless search. Such suspicionless searches are reasonable only if they serve some limited and important purpose other than general law enforcement. Insofar as the majority suggests the need to accurately identify arrestees is such a purpose, the dissenters maintained, the majority's analysis is artificial. DNA samples are sought and used not to identify arrestees but rather to determine whether arrestees have in the past committed other offenses for which they might be prosecuted. Since "the primary purpose of these DNA searches is * * * discovering evidence of criminal wrongdoing," the dissenters concluded, conducting them without individualized suspicion of some sort renders them unreasonable. ___ U.S. at ___, 133 S.Ct. at 1981–82 (Scalia, J., dissenting).

7. **Blood and Breath Tests.** Whether a breath or blood test to measure blood alcohol content (BAC) can be conducted without a search warrant incident to the arrest of a person for driving while impaired was addressed in Birchfield v. North Dakota, ___ U.S. ___, 136 S.Ct. 2160 (2016), involving three consolidated cases with three separate petitioners.

A breath test requires the person tested to blow continuously for 4 to 15 seconds into a straw-like mouthpiece connected by a tube to the test machine. "The effort [required]," the Court observed, "is no more demanding than blowing up a party balloon." Sometimes the process is repeated to obtain multiple samples to ensure the device's accuracy. Because a controlled environment increases the reliability of the testing, most breath tests designed to produce results admissible in court are not conducted at the location of the stop but rather in a police station or perhaps a police patrol vehicle or a special mobile testing facility.

The specific question in *Birchfield* was whether the Fourth Amendment permits criminal prosecution and conviction for failing to submit to or cooperate in the administration of such tests. If the Fourth Amendment requires a warrant, *Birchfield* assumed, the constitutional provision also bars making a suspect's refusal to submit to a warrantless test a crime.

Because officers making an arrest must make quick decisions as to what searches to make incident to the arrest, the reasonableness of such searches cannot depend upon complex case-by-case analyses. "[T]he legality of a search incident to arrest," *Birchfield* emphasized, "must be judged on the basis of categorical rules."

Historical information from the founding era fails to provide definitive guidance on whether breath and blood tests would have been regarded by the founders as permissible incident to a valid arrest. Consequently, the *Birchfield* majority analyzed the question before it by balancing the extent to which the searches at issue intrude upon suspects' privacy against the degree to which the searches are needed to promote legitimate governmental interests. It addressed separately breath and blood tests.

The physical intrusion of breath tests—much like using a straw to drink—is minimal. The air captured by the test is air that sooner or later would be exhaled by the natural process of breathing. This air is not a part of the person's body and "[h]umans have never been known to assert a possessory interest in or any emotional attachment to any of the air in their lungs." (emphasis removed) Breath tests are capable of revealing only one bit of information—the amount of alcohol in the subject's breath. Moreover, the tests are usually conducted out of public view and in a manner "not inherently embarrassing;" therefore they do not greatly enhance the embarrassment caused by the arrest itself.

Blood tests, in contrast, involve piercing the suspect's skin and extracting a portion of the body. Although such tests may involve "little pain or risk" and are often part of voluntary medical evaluation or treatment, for many the tests are not procedures the persons "relish." The Court added:

> In addition, a blood test, unlike a breath test, places in the hands of law enforcement authorities a sample that can be

preserved and from which it is possible to extract information beyond a simple BAC reading. Even if the law enforcement agency is precluded from testing the blood for any purpose other than to measure BAC, the potential remains and may result in anxiety for the person tested.

___ U.S. at ___, 136 S.Ct. at 2178.

Turning to the legitimate governmental interests promoted by the tests, the Court stressed the social costs of impaired driving and the value of legal requirements designed to provide suspects with an incentive to cooperate in investigations as to whether the suspects have in fact driven while impaired. Breath and blood tests provide such an incentive, the Court concluded, and thus "serve a very important function."

Also relevant, the Court made clear, is whether the warrant process if applied to BAC tests would effectively protect the privacy interests implicated. It continued:

Search warrants protect privacy in two main ways. First, they ensure that a search is not carried out unless a neutral magistrate makes an independent determination that there is probable cause to believe that evidence will be found. Second, if the magistrate finds probable cause, the warrant limits the intrusion on privacy by specifying the scope of the search—that is, the area that can be searched and the items that can be sought.

How well would these functions be performed by the warrant applications that [are] propose[d]? In order to persuade a magistrate that there is probable cause for a search warrant, the officer would typically recite the same facts that led the officer to find that there was probable cause for arrest, namely, that there is probable cause to believe that a BAC test will reveal that the motorist's blood alcohol level is over the limit. * * * [T]he facts that establish probable cause are largely the same from one drunk-driving stop to the next and consist largely of the officer's own characterization of his or her observations—for example, that there was a strong odor of alcohol, that the motorist wobbled when attempting to stand, that the motorist paused when reciting the alphabet or counting backwards, and so on. A magistrate would be in a poor position to challenge such characterizations.

As for the second function served by search warrants—delineating the scope of a search—the warrants in question here would not serve that function at all. In every case the scope of the warrant would simply be a BAC test of the arrestee. For these reasons, requiring the police to obtain a warrant in every case would impose a substantial burden but no commensurate benefit.

___ U.S. at ___, 136 S.Ct. at 2180–81.

As a bottom line, the *Birchfield* majority concluded:

> [T]he Fourth Amendment permits warrantless breath tests incident to arrests for drunk driving. The impact of breath tests on privacy is slight, and the need for BAC testing is great.
>
> We reach a different conclusion with respect to blood tests. Blood tests are significantly more intrusive, and their reasonableness must be judged in light of the availability of the less invasive alternative of a breath test. Respondents have offered no satisfactory justification for demanding the more intrusive alternative without a warrant.
>
> Because breath tests are significantly less intrusive than blood tests and in most cases amply serve law enforcement interests, we conclude that a breath test, but not a blood test, may be administered as a search incident to a lawful arrest for drunk driving. As in all cases involving reasonable searches incident to arrest, a warrant is not needed in this situation.

___ U.S. at ___, 136 S.Ct. at 2184.

Petitioner Birchfield had been convicted for refusing to submit to a warrantless blood draw. There was no indication that a breath test would have failed to satisfy the State's interest in acquiring evidence of his possible impairment and nothing to suggest exigent circumstances. His conviction was therefore reversed. Petitioner Bernard was convicted for refusing a warrantless breath test. No warrant was required for the test and therefore his conviction was upheld. Petitioner Beylund, in contrast, submitted to a warrantless blood test after police told him that the law required his submission. This raised separate issues and is discussed in Chapter 5, Subchapter C ("Consent Searches").

Justice Sotomayor, joined by Justice Ginsburg, concurred in part and dissented in part on the ground that she would hold the Fourth Amendment permitted neither breath nor blood tests incident to an arrest. Justice Thomas, concurred in the judgment and dissented in part on the basis that both blood and alcohol tests should be permitted under the exigent circumstances exception to the Fourth Amendment requirement of a search warrant.

2. INCIDENTAL SEARCHES OF VEHICLES

EDITORS' INTRODUCTION: SEARCHES OF VEHICLES INCIDENT TO ARRESTS

Searches of vehicles have given rise to particularly difficult problems. The Supreme Court's approach to these problems has been colored by—among other matters—the Court's perception that persons have a less significant privacy interest in their vehicles than in their residences. This is developed further in Subchapter D of Chapter 5, considering the "vehicle exception" to the requirement of a warrant; this exception permits warrantless searches of certain vehicles *if* the officers have probable cause to believe that the vehicles contain items the officers are entitled to seize.

As the principal case that follows makes clear, however, officers may often search vehicles incident to the arrest of person in and perhaps around those vehicles, regardless of whether those searches would be reasonable under the vehicle exception. In this principal case, the Court considered whether to adhere to the approach it took in New York v. Belton, 453 U.S. 454, 101 S.Ct. 2860 (1981).

Five year before deciding the principal case, in Thornton v. United States, 541 U.S. 615, 124 S.Ct. 2127 (2004), the Court refused to limit the right to search a vehicle under *Belton* to situations in which officers first made contact with the arrested person while that person was still an actual occupant of the vehicle. In *Thornton*, an officer—Nichols—approached Thornton after Thornton had parked and gotten out of his car. When a consent search turned up drugs, the officer arrested and handcuffed Thornton and in a search of his car found a gun. A majority held *Belton* applied and permitted a search of the vehicle incident to the arrest although the officers did not make contact with Thornton until after he had gotten out of the car.

Justice Scalia, joined by Justice Ginsburg, indicated in *Thornton* that he favored modifying *Belton* law:

> If *Belton* searches are justifiable, it is not because the arrestee might grab a weapon or evidentiary item from his car, but simply because the car might contain evidence relevant to the crime for which he was arrested. * * *

> There is nothing irrational about broader police authority to search for evidence when and where the perpetrator of a crime is lawfully arrested. The fact of prior lawful arrest distinguishes the arrestee from society at large, and distinguishes a search for evidence of *his* crime from general rummaging. Moreover, it is not illogical to assume that evidence of a crime is most likely to be found where the suspect was apprehended.

> * * *

> [I]f we are going to continue to allow *Belton* searches * * * , we should at least be honest about why we are doing so. *Belton* cannot reasonably be explained as a mere application of [*Chimel v. California*, 395 U.S. 752, 89 S.Ct. 2034, 23 L.Ed.2d 685 (1981)]. Rather, it is a return to the broader sort of search incident to arrest that we allowed before *Chimel*—limited, of course, to searches of motor vehicles, a category of "effects" which give rise to a reduced expectation of privacy and heightened law enforcement needs.

> Recasting *Belton* in these terms would have at least one important practical consequence. In *United States v. Robinson,*

414 U.S. 218, 235, 94 S.Ct. 467, 38 L.Ed.2d 427 (1973), we held that authority to search an arrestee's person does not depend on the actual presence of one of *Chimel's* two rationales in the particular case; rather, the fact of arrest alone justifies the search. That holding stands in contrast to *Rabinowitz,* where we did not treat the fact of arrest alone as sufficient, but upheld the search only after noting that it was "not general or exploratory for whatever might be turned up" but reflected a reasonable belief that evidence would be found. The two different rules make sense: When officer safety or imminent evidence concealment or destruction is at issue, officers should not have to make fine judgments in the heat of the moment. But in the context of a general evidence-gathering search, the state interests that might justify any overbreadth are far less compelling. A motorist may be arrested for a wide variety of offenses; in many cases, there is no reasonable basis to believe relevant evidence might be found in the car. I would therefore limit *Belton* searches to cases where it is reasonable to believe evidence relevant to the crime of arrest might be found in the vehicle.

In this case, as in *Belton,* petitioner was lawfully arrested for a drug offense. It was reasonable for Officer Nichols to believe that further contraband or similar evidence relevant to the crime for which he had been arrested might be found in the vehicle from which he had just alighted and which was still within his vicinity at the time of arrest. I would affirm the decision below on that ground.

541 U.S. at 629–32, 124 S.Ct. at 2135–38 (Scalia, J., concurring in the judgment).

Arizona v. Gant
Supreme Court of the United States, 2009.
556 U.S. 332, 129 S.Ct. 1710.

■ JUSTICE STEVENS delivered the opinion of the Court.

After Rodney Gant was arrested for driving with a suspended license, handcuffed, and locked in the back of a patrol car, police officers searched his car and discovered cocaine in the pocket of a jacket on the backseat. Because Gant could not have accessed his car to retrieve weapons or evidence at the time of the search, the Arizona Supreme Court held that the search-incident-to-arrest exception to the Fourth Amendment's warrant requirement, as defined in *Chimel v. California,* 395 U.S. 752, 89 S.Ct. 2034, 23 L.Ed.2d 685 (1969), and applied to vehicle searches in *New York v. Belton,* 453 U.S. 454, 101 S.Ct. 2860, 69 L.Ed.2d 768 (1981), did not justify the search in this case. * * *

I

On August 25, 1999, acting on an anonymous tip that the residence at 2524 North Walnut Avenue was being used to sell drugs, Tucson police officers Griffith and Reed knocked on the front door and asked to speak to the owner. Gant answered the door and, after identifying himself, stated that he expected the owner to return later. The officers left the residence and conducted a records check, which revealed that Gant's driver's license had been suspended and there was an outstanding warrant for his arrest for driving with a suspended license.

When the officers returned to the house that evening, they found a man near the back of the house and a woman in a car parked in front of it. After a third officer arrived, they arrested the man for providing a false name and the woman for possessing drug paraphernalia. Both arrestees were handcuffed and secured in separate patrol cars when Gant arrived. The officers recognized his car as it entered the driveway, and Officer Griffith confirmed that Gant was the driver by shining a flashlight into the car as it drove by him. Gant parked at the end of the driveway, got out of his car, and shut the door. Griffith, who was about 30 feet away, called to Gant, and they approached each other, meeting 10-to-12 feet from Gant's car. Griffith immediately arrested Gant and handcuffed him.

Because the other arrestees were secured in the only patrol cars at the scene, Griffith called for backup. When two more officers arrived, they locked Gant in the backseat of their vehicle. After Gant had been handcuffed and placed in the back of a patrol car, two officers searched his car: One of them found a gun, and the other discovered a bag of cocaine in the pocket of a jacket on the backseat.

Gant was charged with two offenses—possession of a narcotic drug for sale and possession of drug paraphernalia (*i.e.,* the plastic bag in which the cocaine was found). He moved to suppress the evidence seized from his car on the ground that the warrantless search violated the Fourth Amendment. * * *

The trial court * * * denied the motion to suppress. Relying on the fact that the police saw Gant commit the crime of driving without a license and apprehended him only shortly after he exited his car, the court held that the search was permissible as a search incident to arrest. A jury found Gant guilty on both drug counts, and he was sentenced to a 3-year term of imprisonment.

After protracted state-court proceedings, the Arizona Supreme Court concluded that the search of Gant's car was unreasonable within the meaning of the Fourth Amendment. * * *

The chorus that has called for us to revisit *Belton* includes courts, scholars, and Members of this Court who have questioned that decision's clarity and its fidelity to Fourth Amendment principles. We therefore granted the State's petition for certiorari.

II

* * *

In *Belton,* we considered *Chimel's* application to the automobile context. A lone police officer in that case stopped a speeding car in which Belton was one of four occupants. While asking for the driver's license and registration, the officer smelled burnt marijuana and observed an envelope on the car floor marked "Supergold"—a name he associated with marijuana. Thus having probable cause to believe the occupants had committed a drug offense, the officer ordered them out of the vehicle, placed them under arrest, and patted them down. Without handcuffing the arrestees, the officer " 'split them up into four separate areas of the Thruway . . . so they would not be in physical touching area of each other' " and searched the vehicle, including the pocket of a jacket on the backseat, in which he found cocaine.

* * *

[W]e held that when an officer lawfully arrests "the occupant of an automobile, he may, as a contemporaneous incident of that arrest, search the passenger compartment of the automobile" and any containers therein. That holding was based in large part on our assumption "that articles inside the relatively narrow compass of the passenger compartment of an automobile are in fact generally, even if not inevitably, within 'the area into which an arrestee might reach.' "

III

[O]ur [*Belton*] opinion has been widely understood to allow a vehicle search incident to the arrest of a recent occupant even if there is no possibility the arrestee could gain access to the vehicle at the time of the search. * * *

Under this broad reading of *Belton,* a vehicle search would be authorized incident to every arrest of a recent occupant notwithstanding that in most cases the vehicle's passenger compartment will not be within the arrestee's reach at the time of the search. To read *Belton* as authorizing a vehicle search incident to every recent occupant's arrest would thus untether the rule from the justifications underlying the *Chimel* exception—a result clearly incompatible with our statement in *Belton* that it "in no way alters the fundamental principles established in the *Chime* case regarding the basic scope of searches incident to lawful custodial arrests." Accordingly, we reject this reading of *Belton* and hold that the *Chimel* rationale authorizes police to search a vehicle incident to a recent occupant's arrest only when the arrestee is unsecured and within reaching distance of the passenger compartment at the time of the search.[4]

---

[4] Because officers have many means of ensuring the safe arrest of vehicle occupants, it will be the rare case in which an officer is unable to fully effectuate an arrest so that a real possibility of access to the arrestee's vehicle remains. But in such a case a search incident to arrest is reasonable under the Fourth Amendment.

Although it does not follow from *Chimel,* we also conclude that circumstances unique to the vehicle context justify a search incident to a lawful arrest when it is "reasonable to believe evidence relevant to the crime of arrest might be found in the vehicle." [*Thornton v. United States,* 541 U.S. 615, 632, 124 S.Ct. 2127, 158 L.Ed.2d 905 (2004)] (Scalia, J., concurring in judgment). In many cases, as when a recent occupant is arrested for a traffic violation, there will be no reasonable basis to believe the vehicle contains relevant evidence. But in others, including *Belton* and *Thornton,* the offense of arrest will supply a basis for searching the passenger compartment of an arrestee's vehicle and any containers therein.

Neither the possibility of access nor the likelihood of discovering offense-related evidence authorized the search in this case. Unlike in *Belton,* which involved a single officer confronted with four unsecured arrestees, the five officers in this case outnumbered the three arrestees, all of whom had been handcuffed and secured in separate patrol cars before the officers searched Gant's car. Under those circumstances, Gant clearly was not within reaching distance of his car at the time of the search. An evidentiary basis for the search was also lacking in this case. Whereas Belton and Thornton were arrested for drug offenses, Gant was arrested for driving with a suspended license—an offense for which police could not expect to find evidence in the passenger compartment of Gant's car. Because police could not reasonably have believed either that Gant could have accessed his car at the time of the search or that evidence of the offense for which he was arrested might have been found therein, the search in this case was unreasonable.

IV

The State * * * argues that *Belton* searches are reasonable regardless of the possibility of access in a given case because that expansive rule correctly balances law enforcement interests, including the interest in a bright-line rule, with an arrestee's limited privacy interest in his vehicle.

For several reasons, we reject the State's argument. First, the State seriously undervalues the privacy interests at stake. Although we have recognized that a motorist's privacy interest in his vehicle is less substantial than in his home, the former interest is nevertheless important and deserving of constitutional protection. * * *

At the same time as it undervalues these privacy concerns, the State exaggerates the clarity that its reading of *Belton* provides. Courts that have read *Belton* expansively are at odds regarding how close in time to the arrest and how proximate to the arrestee's vehicle an officer's first contact with the arrestee must be to bring the encounter within *Belton*'s purview and whether a search is reasonable when it commences or continues after the arrestee has been removed from the scene. The rule has thus generated a great deal of uncertainty, particularly for a rule touted as providing a "bright line."

Contrary to the State's suggestion, a broad reading of *Belton* is also unnecessary to protect law enforcement safety and evidentiary interests. Under our view, *Belton* and *Thornton* permit an officer to conduct a vehicle search when an arrestee is within reaching distance of the vehicle or it is reasonable to believe the vehicle contains evidence of the offense of arrest. Other established exceptions to the warrant requirement authorize a vehicle search under additional circumstances when safety or evidentiary concerns demand. * * *

These exceptions together ensure that officers may search a vehicle when genuine safety or evidentiary concerns encountered during the arrest of a vehicle's recent occupant justify a search. Construing *Belton* broadly to allow vehicle searches incident to any arrest would serve no purpose except to provide a police entitlement, and it is anathema to the Fourth Amendment to permit a warrantless search on that basis. For these reasons, we are unpersuaded by the State's arguments that a broad reading of *Belton* would meaningfully further law enforcement interests and justify a substantial intrusion on individuals' privacy.

V

* * *

We do not agree * * * that consideration of police reliance interests requires a different result. Although it appears that the State's reading of *Belton* has been widely taught in police academies and that law enforcement officers have relied on the rule in conducting vehicle searches during the past 28 years, many of these searches were not justified by the reasons underlying the *Chimel* exception. Countless individuals guilty of nothing more serious than a traffic violation have had their constitutional right to the security of their private effects violated as a result. The fact that the law enforcement community may view the State's version of the *Belton* rule as an entitlement does not establish the sort of reliance interest that could outweigh the countervailing interest that all individuals share in having their constitutional rights fully protected. * * *

VI

Police may search a vehicle incident to a recent occupant's arrest only if the arrestee is within reaching distance of the passenger compartment at the time of the search or it is reasonable to believe the vehicle contains evidence of the offense of arrest. When these justifications are absent, a search of an arrestee's vehicle will be unreasonable unless police obtain a warrant or show that another exception to the warrant requirement applies. The Arizona Supreme Court correctly held that this case involved an unreasonable search. Accordingly, the judgment of the State Supreme Court is affirmed.

It is so ordered.

■ JUSTICE SCALIA, concurring.

* * * In my view we should simply abandon the *Belton-Thornton* charade of officer safety and overrule those cases. I would hold that a vehicle search incident to arrest is *ipso facto* "reasonable" only when the object of the search is evidence of the crime for which the arrest was made, or of another crime that the officer has probable cause to believe occurred. Because respondent was arrested for driving without a license (a crime for which no evidence could be expected to be found in the vehicle), I would hold in the present case that the search was unlawful.

* * *

No other Justice, however, shares my view that application of *Chimel* in this context should be entirely abandoned. It seems to me unacceptable for the Court to come forth with a 4-to-1-to-4 opinion that leaves the governing rule uncertain. I am therefore confronted with the choice of either leaving the current understanding of *Belton* and *Thornton* in effect, or acceding to what seems to me the artificial narrowing of those cases adopted by Justice STEVENS. The latter, as I have said, does not provide the degree of certainty I think desirable in this field; but the former opens the field to what I think are plainly unconstitutional searches—which is the greater evil. I therefore join the opinion of the Court.

■ JUSTICE BREYER, dissenting.

I agree with JUSTICE ALITO that *New York v. Belton,* 453 U.S. 454, 101 S.Ct. 2860, 69 L.Ed.2d 768 (1981), is best read as setting forth a bright-line rule that permits a warrantless search of the passenger compartment of an automobile incident to the lawful arrest of an occupant—regardless of the danger the arrested individual in fact poses. I also agree with JUSTICE STEVENS, however, that the rule can produce results divorced from its underlying Fourth Amendment rationale. For that reason I would look for a better rule—were the question before us one of first impression.

The matter, however, is not one of first impression, and that fact makes a substantial difference. The *Belton* rule has been followed not only by this Court * * * , but also by numerous other courts. Principles of *stare decisis* must apply, and those who wish this Court to change a well-established legal precedent—where, as here, there has been considerable reliance on the legal rule in question—bear a heavy burden. I have not found that burden met. Nor do I believe that the other considerations ordinarily relevant when determining whether to overrule a case are satisfied. I consequently join JUSTICE ALITO's dissenting opinion with the exception of Part II-E.

■ JUSTICE ALITO, with whom THE CHIEF JUSTICE and JUSTICE KENNEDY join, and with whom JUSTICE BREYER joins except as to Part II-E, dissenting.

* * *

I

Although the Court refuses to acknowledge that it is overruling *Belton* * * *, there can be no doubt that it does so.

* * *

The precise holding in *Belton* could not be clearer. The Court stated unequivocally: "[W]e hold that when a policeman has made a lawful custodial arrest of the occupant of an automobile, he may, as a contemporaneous incident of that arrest, search the passenger compartment of that automobile." (footnote omitted).

* * *

II

* * *

C

* * * The *Belton* rule has not proved to be unworkable. On the contrary, the rule was adopted for the express purpose of providing a test that would be relatively easy for police officers and judges to apply. The Court correctly notes that even the *Belton* rule is not perfectly clear in all situations. Specifically, it is sometimes debatable whether a search is or is not contemporaneous with an arrest, but that problem is small in comparison with the problems that the Court's new two-part rule will produce.

The first part of the Court's new rule—which permits the search of a vehicle's passenger compartment if it is within an arrestee's reach at the time of the search—reintroduces the same sort of case-by-case, fact-specific decisionmaking that the *Belton* rule was adopted to avoid. As the situation in *Belton* illustrated, there are cases in which it is unclear whether an arrestee could retrieve a weapon or evidence in the passenger compartment of a car.

Even more serious problems will also result from the second part of the Court's new rule, which requires officers making roadside arrests to determine whether there is reason to believe that the vehicle contains evidence of the crime of arrest. What this rule permits in a variety of situations is entirely unclear.

* * *

E

* * * The Court is harshly critical of *Belton*'s reasoning, but the problem that the Court perceives cannot be remedied simply by overruling *Belton*. *Belton* represented only a modest—and quite defensible—extension of *Chimel,* as I understand that decision.

* * *

Unfortunately, *Chimel* did not say whether "the area from within which [an arrestee] might gain possession of a weapon or destructible evidence" [that is subject to search incident to arrest] is to be measured at the time of the arrest or at the time of the search, but unless the *Chimel* rule was meant to be a specialty rule, applicable to only a few unusual cases, the Court must have intended for this area to be measured at the time of arrest.

* * *

The *Belton* Court, in my view, proceeded on the basis of this interpretation of *Chimel*. * * * [T]hat is why the *Belton* Court was able to say that its decision "in no way alter[ed] the fundamental principles established in the *Chimel* case regarding the basic scope of searches incident to lawful custodial arrests." Viewing *Chimel* as having focused on the time of arrest, *Belton*'s only new step was to eliminate the need to decide on a case-by-case basis whether a particular person seated in a car actually could have reached the part of the passenger compartment where a weapon or evidence was hidden. For this reason, if we are going to reexamine *Belton,* we should also reexamine the reasoning in *Chimel* on which *Belton* rests.

F

The Court, however, does not reexamine *Chimel* and thus leaves the law relating to searches incident to arrest in a confused and unstable state. The first part of the Court's new two-part rule—which permits an arresting officer to search the area within an arrestee's reach at the time of the search—applies, at least for now, only to vehicle occupants and recent occupants, but there is no logical reason why the same rule should not apply to all arrestees.

The second part of the Court's new rule, which the Court takes uncritically from JUSTICE SCALIA's separate opinion in *Thornton,* raises doctrinal and practical problems that the Court makes no effort to address. Why, for example, is the standard for this type of evidence-gathering search "reason to believe" rather than probable cause? And why is this type of search restricted to evidence of the offense of arrest? * * *

Nor is it easy to see why an evidence-gathering search incident to arrest should be restricted to the passenger compartment. The *Belton* rule was limited in this way because the passenger compartment was considered to be the area that vehicle occupants can generally reach, but since the second part of the new rule is not based on officer safety or the preservation of evidence, the ground for this limitation is obscure.

III

* * * I would simply apply *Belton* and reverse the judgment below.

3. INCIDENTAL SEARCHES OF CELL PHONES

Riley v. California

Supreme Court of the United States, 2014.
___ U.S. ___, 134 S.Ct. 2473.

■ CHIEF JUSTICE ROBERTS delivered the opinion of the Court.

Th[is case raises the] question: whether the police may, without a warrant, search digital information on a cell phone seized from an individual who has been arrested.

I

* * *

[P]etitioner David Riley was stopped by a police officer for driving with expired registration tags. In the course of the stop, the officer also learned that Riley's license had been suspended. The officer impounded Riley's car, pursuant to department policy, and another officer conducted an inventory search of the car. Riley was arrested for possession of concealed and loaded firearms when that search turned up two handguns under the car's hood.

An officer searched Riley incident to the arrest and found items associated with the "Bloods" street gang. He also seized a cell phone from Riley's pants pocket. According to Riley's uncontradicted assertion, the phone was a "smart phone," a cell phone with a broad range of other functions based on advanced computing capability, large storage capacity, and Internet connectivity. The officer accessed information on the phone and noticed that some words (presumably in text messages or a contacts list) were preceded by the letters "CK"—a label that, he believed, stood for "Crip Killers," a slang term for members of the Bloods gang.

At the police station about two hours after the arrest, a detective specializing in gangs further examined the contents of the phone. The detective testified that he "went through" Riley's phone "looking for evidence, because ... gang members will often video themselves with guns or take pictures of themselves with the guns." Although there was "a lot of stuff" on the phone, particular files that "caught [the detective's] eye" included videos of young men sparring while someone yelled encouragement using the moniker "Blood." The police also found photographs of Riley standing in front of a car they suspected had been involved in a shooting a few weeks earlier.

Riley was ultimately charged, in connection with that earlier shooting, with firing at an occupied vehicle, assault with a semiautomatic firearm, and attempted murder. The State alleged that Riley had committed those crimes for the benefit of a criminal street gang, an aggravating factor that carries an enhanced sentence. Prior to trial, Riley moved to suppress all evidence that the police had obtained from his cell phone. He contended that the searches of his phone violated the Fourth Amendment, because they had been performed without a warrant and were not otherwise justified by exigent circumstances. The trial court rejected that argument. At Riley's trial, police officers testified about the photographs and videos found on the phone, and some of the photographs were admitted into evidence. Riley was convicted on all three counts and received an enhanced sentence of 15 years to life in prison.

The California Court of Appeal affirmed[, reasoning] that the Fourth Amendment permits a warrantless search of cell phone data incident to an arrest, so long as the cell phone was immediately associated with the arrestee's person.

The California Supreme Court denied Riley's petition for review, and we granted certiorari.

* * *

II

* * *

Th[is case] concern[s] the reasonableness of a warrantless search incident to a lawful arrest. * * *

Although the existence of the exception [to the warrant requirement] for such searches has been recognized for a century, its scope has been debated for nearly as long. That debate has focused on the extent to which officers may search property found on or near the arrestee. Three related precedents[, *Chimel v. California*, 395 U.S. 752, 89 S.Ct. 2034, 23 L.Ed.2d 685 (1969), *United States v. Robinson*, 414 U. S. 218, 94 S.Ct. 467, 38 L.Ed.2d 427 (1973), and *Arizona v. Gant*, 556 U. S. 332, 129 S.Ct. 1710, 173 L.Ed.2d 485 (2009),] set forth the rules governing such searches * * * .

III

Th[is] case[ ] require[s] us to decide how the search incident to arrest doctrine applies to modern cell phones, which are now such a pervasive and insistent part of daily life that the proverbial visitor from Mars might conclude they were an important feature of human anatomy. A smart phone of the sort taken from Riley was unheard of ten years ago; a significant majority of American adults now own such phones. Even less sophisticated phones * * * , which have already faded in popularity * * * , have been around for less than 15 years. [Such] phones are based on technology nearly inconceivable just a few decades ago, when *Chimel* and *Robinson* were decided.

Absent more precise guidance from the founding era, we generally determine whether to exempt a given type of search from the warrant requirement "by assessing, on the one hand, the degree to which it intrudes upon an individual's privacy and, on the other, the degree to which it is needed for the promotion of legitimate governmental interests." Such a balancing of interests supported the search incident to arrest exception in *Robinson*, and a mechanical application of *Robinson* might well support the warrantless searches at issue here.

But while *Robinson*'s categorical rule strikes the appropriate balance in the context of physical objects, neither of its rationales has much force with respect to digital content on cell phones. On the government interest side, *Robinson* concluded that the two risks identified in *Chimel*—harm to officers and destruction of evidence—are present in all custodial arrests. There are no comparable risks when the search is of digital data. In addition, *Robinson* regarded any privacy interests retained by an individual after arrest as significantly diminished by the fact of the arrest itself. Cell phones, however, place vast quantities of personal information literally in the hands of individuals. A search of the information on a cell phone bears little resemblance to the type of brief physical search considered in *Robinson*.

We therefore decline to extend *Robinson* to searches of data on cell phones, and hold instead that officers must generally secure a warrant before conducting such a search.

A

We * * * consider each * * * concern [discussed in *Chimel*] in turn. In doing so, we do not overlook *Robinson*'s admonition that searches of a person incident to arrest, "while based upon the need to disarm and to discover evidence," are reasonable regardless of "the probability in a particular arrest situation that weapons or evidence would in fact be found." Rather than requiring the "case-by-case adjudication" that *Robinson* rejected, we ask instead whether application of the search incident to arrest doctrine to this particular category of effects would "untether the rule from the justifications underlying the *Chimel* exception."

1

Digital data stored on a cell phone cannot itself be used as a weapon to harm an arresting officer or to effectuate the arrestee's escape. Law enforcement officers remain free to examine the physical aspects of a phone to ensure that it will not be used as a weapon—say, to determine whether there is a razor blade hidden between the phone and its case. Once an officer has secured a phone and eliminated any potential physical threats, however, data on the phone can endanger no one.

Perhaps the same might have been said of the cigarette pack seized from Robinson's pocket. Once an officer gained control of the pack, it was unlikely that Robinson could have accessed the pack's contents. But unknown physical objects may always pose risks, no matter how slight, during the tense atmosphere of a custodial arrest. The officer in *Robinson* testified that he could not identify the objects in the cigarette pack but knew they were not cigarettes. Given that, a further search was a reasonable protective measure. No such unknowns exist with respect to digital data. * * *

The United States and California both suggest that a search of cell phone data might help ensure officer safety in more indirect ways, for example by alerting officers that confederates of the arrestee are headed to the scene. There is undoubtedly a strong government interest in warning officers about such possibilities, but neither the United States nor California offers evidence to suggest that their concerns are based on actual experience. The proposed consideration would also represent a broadening of *Chimel's* concern that an *arrestee himself* might grab a weapon and use it against an officer "to resist arrest or effect his escape." And any such threats from outside the arrest scene do not "lurk[ ] in all custodial arrests." Accordingly, the interest in protecting officer safety does not justify dispensing with the warrant requirement across the board. To the extent dangers to arresting officers may be implicated in a particular way in a particular case, they are better addressed through consideration of case-specific exceptions to the warrant requirement, such as the one for exigent circumstances.

2

The United States and California focus primarily on the second *Chimel* rationale: preventing the destruction of evidence.

Riley * * * concede[s] that officers could have seized and secured [his] cell phone[ ] to prevent destruction of evidence while seeking a warrant. That is a sensible concession. And once law enforcement officers have secured a cell phone, there is no longer any risk that the arrestee himself will be able to delete incriminating data from the phone.

The United States and California argue that information on a cell phone may nevertheless be vulnerable to two types of evidence destruction unique to digital data—remote wiping and data encryption. Remote wiping occurs when a phone, connected to a wireless network, receives a signal that erases stored data. This can happen when a third party sends a remote signal or when a phone is preprogrammed to delete data upon entering or leaving certain geographic areas (so-called "geofencing"). Encryption is a security feature that some modern cell phones use in addition to password protection. When such phones lock, data becomes protected by sophisticated encryption that renders a phone all but "unbreakable" unless police know the password.

As an initial matter, these broader concerns about the loss of evidence are distinct from *Chimel's* focus on a defendant who responds to arrest by trying to conceal or destroy evidence within his reach. With respect to remote wiping, the Government's primary concern turns on the actions of third parties who are not present at the scene of arrest. And data encryption is even further afield. There, the Government focuses on the ordinary operation of a phone's security features, apart from *any* active attempt by a defendant or his associates to conceal or destroy evidence upon arrest.

We have also been given little reason to believe that either problem is prevalent. The briefing reveals only a couple of anecdotal examples of remote wiping triggered by an arrest. Similarly, the opportunities for officers to search a password-protected phone before data becomes encrypted are quite limited. Law enforcement officers are very unlikely to come upon such a phone in an unlocked state because most phones lock at the touch of a button or, as a default, after some very short period of inactivity. * * *

Moreover, in situations in which an arrest might trigger a remote-wipe attempt or an officer discovers an unlocked phone, it is not clear that the ability to conduct a warrantless search would make much of a difference. The need to effect the arrest, secure the scene, and tend to other pressing matters means that law enforcement officers may well not be able to turn their attention to a cell phone right away. Cell phone data would be vulnerable to remote wiping from the time an individual anticipates arrest to the time any eventual search of the phone is completed, which might be at the station house hours later. Likewise, an officer who seizes a phone in an unlocked state might not be able to begin his search in the short time remaining before the phone locks and data becomes encrypted.

In any event, as to remote wiping, law enforcement is not without specific means to address the threat. Remote wiping can be fully prevented by disconnecting a phone from the network. There are at least two simple ways to do this: First, law enforcement officers can turn the phone off or remove its battery. Second, if they are concerned about encryption or other potential problems, they can leave a phone powered on and place it in an enclosure that isolates the phone from radio waves. Such devices are commonly called "Faraday bags," after the English scientist Michael Faraday. They are essentially sandwich bags made of aluminum foil: cheap, lightweight, and easy to use. They may not be a complete answer to the problem, but at least for now they provide a reasonable response. In fact, a number of law enforcement agencies around the country already encourage the use of Faraday bags.

To the extent that law enforcement still has specific concerns about the potential loss of evidence in a particular case, there remain more targeted ways to address those concerns. If "the police are truly confronted with a 'now or never' situation,"—for example, circumstances suggesting that a defendant's phone will be the target of an imminent remote-wipe attempt—they may be able to rely on exigent circumstances to search the phone immediately. Or, if officers happen to seize a phone in an unlocked state, they may be able to disable a phone's automatic-lock feature in order to prevent the phone from locking and encrypting data. * * *

B

The search incident to arrest exception rests not only on the heightened government interests at stake in a volatile arrest situation, but also on an arrestee's reduced privacy interests upon being taken into police custody. * * *

The fact that an arrestee has diminished privacy interests does not mean that the Fourth Amendment falls out of the picture entirely. * * * One such example, of course, is *Chimel*. *Chimel* refused to "characteriz[e] the invasion of privacy that results from a top-to-bottom search of a man's house as 'minor.'" Because a search of the arrestee's entire house was a substantial invasion beyond the arrest itself, the Court concluded that a warrant was required.

Robinson is the only decision from this Court applying *Chimel* to a search of the contents of an item found on an arrestee's person. * * * Lower courts applying *Robinson* and *Chimel*, however, have approved searches of a variety of personal items carried by an arrestee[, such as a billfold and address book, wallet, and purse].

The United States asserts that a search of all data stored on a cell phone is "materially indistinguishable" from searches of these sorts of physical items. That is like saying a ride on horseback is materially indistinguishable from a flight to the moon. Both are ways of getting from point A to point B, but little else justifies lumping them together. Modern cell phones, as a category, implicate privacy concerns far beyond those implicated by the search of a cigarette pack, a wallet, or a purse. A conclusion that inspecting the contents of an arrestee's pockets works no substantial additional intrusion on privacy beyond the arrest itself may make sense as applied to physical items, but any extension of that reasoning to digital data has to rest on its own bottom.

1

Cell phones differ in both a quantitative and a qualitative sense from other objects that might be kept on an arrestee's person. The term "cell phone" is itself misleading shorthand; many of these devices are in fact minicomputers that also happen to have the capacity to be used as a telephone. They could just as easily be called cameras, video players, rolodexes, calendars, tape recorders, libraries, diaries, albums, televisions, maps, or newspapers.

One of the most notable distinguishing features of modern cell phones is their immense storage capacity. Before cell phones, a search of a person was limited by physical realities and tended as a general matter to constitute only a narrow intrusion on privacy. Most people cannot lug around every piece of mail they have received for the past several months, every picture they have taken, or every book or article they have read—nor would they have any reason to attempt to do so. * * *

But the possible intrusion on privacy is not physically limited in the same way when it comes to cell phones. The current top-selling smart phone has a standard capacity of 16 gigabytes (and is available with up to 64 gigabytes). Sixteen gigabytes translates to millions of pages of text, thousands of pictures, or hundreds of videos. Cell phones couple that capacity with the ability to store many different types of information: Even the most basic phones that sell for less than $20 might hold photographs, picture messages, text messages, Internet browsing history, a calendar, a thousand-entry phone book, and so on. We expect that the gulf between physical practicability and digital capacity will only continue to widen in the future.

The storage capacity of cell phones has several interrelated consequences for privacy. First, a cell phone collects in one place many distinct types of information—an address, a note, a prescription, a bank statement, a video—that reveal much more in combination than any isolated record. Second, a cell phone's capacity allows even just one type of information to convey far more than previously possible. The sum of an individual's private life can be reconstructed through a thousand photographs labeled with dates, locations, and descriptions; the same cannot be said of a photograph or two of loved ones tucked into a wallet. Third, the data on a phone can date back to the purchase of the phone, or even earlier. A person might carry in his pocket a slip of paper reminding him to call Mr. Jones; he would not carry a record of all his communications with Mr. Jones for the past several months, as would routinely be kept on a phone.

Finally, there is an element of pervasiveness that characterizes cell phones but not physical records. Prior to the digital age, people did not typically carry a cache of sensitive personal information with them as they went about their day. Now it is the person who is not carrying a cell phone, with all that it contains, who is the exception. According to one poll, nearly three-quarters of smart phone users report being within five feet of their phones most of the time, with 12% admitting that they even use their phones in the shower. A decade ago police officers searching an arrestee might have occasionally stumbled across a highly personal item such as a diary. But those discoveries were likely to be few and far between. Today, by contrast, it is no exaggeration to say that many of the more than 90% of American adults who own a cell phone keep on their person a digital record of nearly every aspect of their lives—from the mundane to the intimate. Allowing the police to scrutinize such records on a routine basis is quite different from allowing them to search a personal item or two in the occasional case.

Although the data stored on a cell phone is distinguished from physical records by quantity alone, certain types of data are also qualitatively different. An Internet search and browsing history, for example, can be found on an Internet-enabled phone and could reveal an individual's private interests or concerns—perhaps a search for certain symptoms of disease, coupled with frequent visits to WebMD. Data on a cell phone can also reveal where a person has been. Historic location information is a standard feature on many smart phones and can reconstruct someone's specific movements down to the minute, not only around town but also within a particular building.

Mobile application software on a cell phone, or "apps," offer a range of tools for managing detailed information about all aspects of a person's life. There are apps for Democratic Party news and Republican Party news; apps for alcohol, drug, and gambling addictions; apps for sharing prayer requests; apps for tracking pregnancy symptoms; apps for planning your budget; apps for every conceivable hobby or pastime; apps for improving your romantic life. There are popular apps for buying or selling just about anything, and the records of such transactions may be accessible on the phone indefinitely. There are over a million apps available in each of the two major app stores; the phrase "there's an app for that" is now part of the popular lexicon. The average smart phone user has installed 33 apps, which together can form a revealing montage of the user's life.

[A] cell phone search would typically expose to the government far *more* than the most exhaustive search of a house: A phone not only contains in digital form many sensitive records previously found in the home; it also contains a broad array of private information never found in a home in any form—unless the phone is.

2

To further complicate the scope of the privacy interests at stake, the data a user views on many modern cell phones may not in fact be stored on the device itself. Treating a cell phone as a container whose contents may be searched incident to an arrest is a bit strained as an initial matter. But the analogy crumbles entirely when a cell phone is used to access data located elsewhere, at the tap of a screen. That is what cell phones, with increasing frequency, are designed to do by taking advantage of "cloud computing." Cloud computing is the capacity of Internet-connected devices to display data stored on remote servers rather than on the device itself. Cell phone users often may not know whether particular information is stored on the device or in the cloud, and it generally makes little difference. Moreover, the same type of data may be stored locally on the device for one user and in the cloud for another.

The United States concedes that the search incident to arrest exception may not be stretched to cover a search of files accessed remotely—that is, a search of files stored in the cloud. Such a search would be like finding a key in a suspect's pocket and arguing that it allowed law enforcement to unlock and search a house. But officers searching a phone's data would not typically know whether the information they are viewing was stored locally at the time of the arrest or has been pulled from the cloud.

Although the Government recognizes the problem, its proposed solutions are unclear. It suggests that officers could disconnect a phone from the network before searching the device—the very solution whose feasibility it contested with respect to the threat of remote wiping. Alternatively, the Government proposes that law enforcement agencies "develop protocols to address" concerns raised by cloud computing. Probably a good idea, but the Founders did not fight a revolution to gain the right to government agency protocols. The possibility that a search might extend well beyond papers and effects in the physical proximity of an arrestee is yet another reason that the privacy interests here dwarf those in *Robinson*.

C

Apart from their arguments for a direct extension of *Robinson*, the United States and California offer various fallback options for permitting warrantless cell phone searches under certain circumstances. Each of the proposals is flawed and contravenes our general preference to provide clear guidance to law enforcement through categorical rules. * * *

The United States first proposes that the *Gant* standard be imported from the vehicle context, allowing a warrantless search of an arrestee's cell phone whenever it is reasonable to believe that the phone contains evidence of the crime of arrest. But *Gant* relied on "circumstances unique to the vehicle context" to endorse a search solely for the purpose of gathering evidence. * * * [T]hose unique circumstances are "a reduced expectation of privacy" and "heightened law enforcement needs" when it comes to motor vehicles. For reasons that we have explained, cell phone searches bear neither of those characteristics.

At any rate, a *Gant* standard would prove no practical limit at all when it comes to cell phone searches. In the vehicle context, *Gant* generally protects against searches for evidence of past crimes. In the cell phone context, however, it is reasonable to expect that incriminating information will be found on a phone regardless of when the crime occurred. Similarly, in the vehicle context *Gant* restricts broad searches resulting from minor crimes such as traffic violations. That would not necessarily be true for cell phones. It would be a particularly inexperienced or unimaginative law enforcement officer who could not come up with several reasons to suppose evidence of just about any crime could be found on a cell phone. Even an individual pulled over for something as basic as speeding might well have locational data dispositive of guilt on his phone. An individual pulled over for reckless driving might have evidence on the phone that shows whether he was texting while driving. The sources of potential pertinent information are virtually unlimited, so applying the *Gant* standard to cell phones would in effect give "police officers unbridled discretion to rummage at will among a person's private effects."

The United States also proposes a rule that would restrict the scope of a cell phone search to those areas of the phone where an officer reasonably believes that information relevant to the crime, the arrestee's identity, or officer safety will be discovered. This approach would again impose few meaningful constraints on officers. The proposed categories would sweep in a great deal of information, and officers would not always be able to discern in advance what information would be found where.

We also reject the United States' final suggestion that officers should always be able to search a phone's call log * * * . The Government relies on *Smith* v. *Maryland*, 442 U. S. 735, 99 S.Ct. 2577, 61 L.Ed.2d 220 (1979), which held that no warrant was required to use a pen register at telephone company premises to identify numbers dialed by a particular caller. The Court in that case, however, concluded that the use of a pen register was not a "search" at all under the Fourth Amendment. There is no dispute here that * * * officers engage[ ] in a search [when they examine a phone's call log]. Moreover, call logs typically contain more than just phone numbers; they include any identifying information that an individual might add * * * .

Finally, at oral argument California suggested a different limiting principle, under which officers could search cell phone data if they could have obtained the same information from a pre-digital counterpart. But the fact that a search in the pre-digital era could have turned up a photograph or two in a wallet does not justify a search of thousands of photos in a digital gallery. The fact that someone could have tucked a paper bank statement in a pocket does not justify a search of every bank statement from the last five years. And to make matters worse, such an analogue test would allow law enforcement to search a range of items contained on a phone, even though people would be unlikely to carry such a variety of information in physical form. In Riley's case, for example, it is implausible that he would have strolled around with video tapes, photo albums, and an address book all crammed into his pockets. But because each of those items has a pre-digital analogue, police under California's proposal would be able to search a phone for all of those items—a significant diminution of privacy.

In addition, an analogue test would launch courts on a difficult line-drawing expedition to determine which digital files are comparable to physical records. Is an e-mail equivalent to a letter? Is a voicemail equivalent to a phone message slip? It is not clear how officers could make these kinds of decisions before conducting a search, or how courts would apply the proposed rule after the fact. An analogue test would "keep defendants and judges guessing for years to come."

IV

We cannot deny that our decision today will have an impact on the ability of law enforcement to combat crime. Cell phones have become important tools in facilitating coordination and communication among members of criminal enterprises, and can provide valuable incriminating information about dangerous criminals. Privacy comes at a cost.

Our holding, of course, is not that the information on a cell phone is immune from search; it is instead that a warrant is generally required before such a search, even when a cell phone is seized incident to arrest. * * * Recent technological advances similar to those discussed here have, in addition, made the process of obtaining a warrant itself more efficient.

Moreover, even though the search incident to arrest exception does not apply to cell phones, other case-specific exceptions may still justify a warrantless search of a particular phone. "One well-recognized exception applies when ' "the exigencies of the situation" make the needs of law enforcement so compelling that [a] warrantless search is objectively reasonable under the Fourth Amendment.' " Such exigencies could include the need to prevent the imminent destruction of evidence in individual cases, to pursue a fleeing suspect, and to assist persons who are seriously injured or are threatened with imminent injury. * * *

* * *

* * * Our answer to the question of what police must do before searching a cell phone seized incident to an arrest is * * * simple—get a warrant.

We reverse the judgment of the California Court of Appeal * * * and remand the case for further proceedings not inconsistent with this opinion. * * *

It is so ordered.

JUSTICE ALITO, concurring in part and concurring in the judgment.

* * *

* * * While I agree with the holding of the Court, I would reconsider the question presented here if either Congress or state legislatures, after assessing the legitimate needs of law enforcement and the privacy interests of cell phone owners, enact legislation that draws reasonable distinctions based on categories of information or perhaps other variables.

* * *

C. FIELD DETENTIONS FOR INVESTIGATION AND RELATED SEARCHES

EDITORS' INTRODUCTION: *TERRY* "STOPS" AND "FRISKS"

Prior to a trilogy of Supreme Court decisions in 1968, the Supreme Court's case law could have been read as holding that any seizure of a person challenged under the Fourth Amendment must be supported by at least the probable cause necessary to render reasonable an arrest. In 1968, however, the Court decided Terry v. Ohio, 392 U.S. 1, 88 S.Ct. 1868 (1968), and two companion cases, Sibron v. New York and Peters v. New York, 392 U.S. 40, 88 S.Ct. 1889 (1968). Those decisions, particularly *Terry*, established that the Fourth Amendment has sufficient flexibility to permit certain law enforcement conduct—often called "stop and frisk" or "stop, question, and frisk"—on less than probable cause.

Terry and its companion cases made clear Fourth Amendment analysis requires a distinction to be drawn between investigatory "stops"—seizures of suspects for purposes of questioning or other investigation—and "frisks"—searches to locate weapons to prevent suspects from harming investigating officers. The three subparts of this subchapter address, first, so-called *Terry* stops, second, weapon searches permissible in nonarrest situations, and third the special situation in which law enforcement action is based upon concern that the suspect is in possession of a weapon. The impact of the *Terry* trilogy on Fourth Amendment law in general and the role of stop and frisk in law enforcement general policy, however, deserve preliminary discussion.

The Terry Trilogy: Fourth Amendment Flexibility

Terry noted the exclusionary sanction attaching to Fourth Amendment requirements may be less effective in preventing improper nonarrest field practices than deterring other unacceptable law enforcement conduct:

> [W]e approach the issues in this case mindful of the limitations of the judicial function in controlling the myriad daily situations in which policemen and citizens confront each other on the street. * * * Ever since its inception, the rule excluding evidence seized in violation of the Fourth Amendment has been recognized as a principal mode of discouraging lawless police conduct. * * * The exclusionary rule has its limitations, however, as a tool of judicial control. * * * [I]n some contexts the rule is ineffective as a deterrent. * * * Encounters are initiated by the police for a wide variety of purposes, some of which are wholly unrelated to a desire to prosecute for crime. Doubtless some police "field interrogation" conduct violates the Fourth Amendment. But a stern refusal by this Court to condone such activity does not necessarily render it responsive to the exclusionary rule. Regardless of how effective the rule may be where obtaining convictions is an important objective of the police, it is powerless to deter invasions of constitutionally guaranteed rights where the police either have no interest in prosecuting or are willing to forgo successful prosecution in the interest of serving some other goal.
>
> Proper adjudication of cases in which the exclusionary rule is invoked demands a constant awareness of these limitations. * * *

392 U.S. at 12–14, 88 S.Ct. at 1875–76.

The Fourth Amendment reasonableness of law enforcement conduct, *Terry* continued, must be determined by balancing the extent to which particular kinds of police conduct further governmental interests, such as those in crime detection and prevention, against the nature and extent of the conduct's intrusion on Fourth Amendment interests. The first consideration, it noted, suggests "in dealing with the rapidly unfolding and often dangerous situations on city streets the police are in need of an escalating set of flexible responses, graduated in relation to the amount of information they possess." The safety of officers engaged in legitimate investigations, of course, is an especially important objective of this area's law.

Among the factors bearing on the second consideration, *Terry* suggested, is the risk that power to make nonarrest detentions will be abused and its use or abuse experienced as particularly oppressive by minorities. Nonarrest field practices may be particularly subject to abuse, the Court noted. Further, it cited reason to fear that officers' implementation of the right to make field stops and frisks may be influenced by the race of the suspects:

> The President's Commission on Law Enforcement and Administration of Justice found that "[I]n many communities, field interrogations are a major source of friction between the police and minority groups." President's Commission on Law Enforcement and Administration of Justice, Task Force Report: The Police 183 (1967). It was reported that the friction caused by "[m]isuse of field interrogations" increases "as more police departments adopt 'aggressive patrol' in which officers are encouraged routinely to stop and question persons on the street who are unknown to them, who are suspicious, or whose purpose for being abroad is not readily evident." While the frequency with which "frisking" forms a part of field interrogation practice varies tremendously with the locale, the objective of the interrogation, and the particular officer, it cannot help but be a severely exacerbating factor in police-community tensions. This is particularly true in situations where the "stop and frisk" of youths or minority group members is "motivated by the officers' perceived need to maintain the power image of the beat officer, an aim sometimes accomplished by humiliating anyone who attempts to undermine police control of the streets."

392 U.S. at 15 n. 11, 88 S.Ct. at 1877 n. 11.

Much of the Court's discussion in *Terry* and its companion cases was very broad and obviously applied to fields stops for investigation as well as weapons searches. Nevertheless, the three 1968 cases actually decided only the constitutionality of police action, on less than probable cause, constituting weapons searches and seizures of suspects to the extent necessary to perform those protective searches.

Conducting the balancing analysis identified as necessary, the Court rejected Terry's argument that no search or seizure was reasonable unless supported by probable cause as developed in the law of arrest:

> [Terry's] argument * * * assumes that the law of arrest has already worked out the balance between the particular interests involved here—the neutralization of danger to the policeman in the investigative circumstance and the sanctity of the

individual. But this is not so. An arrest is a wholly different kind of intrusion upon individual freedom from a limited search for weapons, and the interests each is designed to serve are likewise quite different. An arrest is the initial stage of a criminal prosecution. It is intended to vindicate society's interest in having its laws obeyed, and it is inevitably accompanied by future interference with the individual's freedom of movement, whether or not trial or conviction ultimately follows. The protective search for weapons, on the other hand, constitutes a brief, though far from inconsiderable, intrusion upon the sanctity of the person. It does not follow that because an officer may lawfully arrest a person only when he is apprised of facts sufficient to warrant a belief that the person has committed or is committing a crime, the officer is equally unjustified, absent that kind of evidence, in making any intrusions short of an arrest. Moreover, a perfectly reasonable apprehension of danger may arise long before the officer is possessed of adequate information to justify taking a person into custody for the purpose of prosecuting him for a crime. [Terry's] reliance on cases which have worked out standards of reasonableness with regard to "seizures" constituting arrests and searches incident thereto is thus misplaced. It assumes that the interests sought to be vindicated and the invasions of personal security may be equated in the two cases, and thereby ignores a vital aspect of the analysis of the reasonableness of particular types of conduct under the Fourth Amendment.

Our evaluation of the proper balance that has to be struck in this type of case leads us to conclude that there must be a narrowly drawn authority to permit a reasonable search for weapons for the protection of the police officer, where he has reason to believe that he is dealing with an armed and dangerous individual, regardless of whether he has probable cause to arrest the individual for a crime.

392 U.S. at 26–27, 88 S.Ct. at 1882. The precise contours of the right to search for weapons on less than probable cause is developed in more detail in the material that follows.

In *Terry* and its companion cases, the Court appeared satisfied to set out its general approach to resolving issues in this area and to decide only the narrow question of the propriety of a weapon search and any detention necessary to accomplish that search. "We * * * decide nothing today," it stressed, "concerning the constitutional propriety of an investigative 'seizure' upon less than probable cause for purposes of 'detention' and/or interrogation." *Terry*, 392 U.S. at 19 n. 16, 88 S.Ct. at 1879 n. 16. Nevertheless, the Court's general approach strongly suggested that it would be receptive to the argument that such detentions are—at least under certain circumstances—constitutionally reasonable. In fact, the Court subsequently assumed that *Terry* established the permissibility of such stops. Consequently, nonarrest stops for investigation are widely referred to as *Terry* stops.

Statutory provisions in some jurisdictions authorize the sort of law enforcement activity discussed by the Supreme Court in the *Terry* trilogy. Probably the leading example is the New York statute, which provides:

140.50 Temporary questioning of persons in public places; search for weapons

1.   * * * [A] police officer may stop a person in a public place located within the geographical area of such officer's employment when he reasonably suspects that such person is committing, has committed or is about to commit either (a) a felony or (b) a misdemeanor defined in the penal law, and may demand of him his name, address and an explanation of his conduct.

* * *

3.   When upon stopping a person under circumstances prescribed in subdivision[ ] one * * * a police officer * * * reasonably suspects that he is in danger of physical injury, he may search such person for a deadly weapon or any instrument, article or substance readily capable of causing serious physical injury and of a sort not ordinarily carried in public places by law-abiding persons. If he finds such a weapon or instrument, or any other property possession of which he reasonably believes may constitute the commission of a crime, he may take it and keep it until the completion of the questioning, at which time he shall either return it, if lawfully possessed, or arrest such person.

Stop and Frisk in the Context of General Law Enforcement Philosophy

When New York's Attorney General in 1999 undertook a comprehensive examination of stop and frisk practices in New York City, he began by putting the formal law in conceptual context. See The New York City Police Department's "Stop & Frisk" Practices: A Report to the People of the State of New York from the Office of the Attorney General (1999) ("New York Report"). Stop and frisk, he suggested, can only be fully understood if it is considered not simply as a specific law enforcement technique to prevent, investigate, detect, and solve crime but also as part of an overall crime-fighting philosophy.

Addressing stop and frisk as part of New York City's overall law enforcement approach to crime, the report noted that New York police, like many other modern departments, embrace modern policing philosophies of "community policing" and "order maintenance"/"broken windows" theory.

"Community policing" holds that effective crime-fighting is based on a "partnership" between police and the residents of the immediate community they serve. The goal of the partnership is to ensure that police "meet the demands" of law-abiding people within their jurisdiction.

Implementing community policing, the department discovered that rank-and-file community residents were more concerned about petty crime and disorder problem than the major crimes that had preoccupied police.

The * * * impact was to increase police presence in the everyday life of the community. The cop on foot patrol—walking the neighborhood, interacting with its residents, learning the complex social dynamics of the area, and responding to low-level disorder complaints—is emblematic of the "community policing" model.

In addition, New York police adopted

a second approach known as "order maintenance" theory (or simply, "broken windows"). Order maintenance theory rests on two fundamental premises * * * .

The first premise holds that low-level disorder in the streets—graffiti, aggressive panhandling, public drunkenness and the like—makes people fearful and weakens neighborhood social controls. In this atmosphere, law-abiding civilians become more fearful and withdrawn from the daily life of the community, effectively ceding the street to the forces of greater disorder and more serious crime. As Kelling and Wilson [Broken Windows: The Police and Neighborhood Safety, Atlantic Monthly, March 1982] put it: "[I]f [one broken window] is left unrepaired, all the rest of the windows will soon be broken."

Only by actively combating low-level disorder, can police and the neighborhood residents signal to the criminal element their resolve that "law breaking of any kind will not be tolerated"—and thus begin to restore standards of behavior which make serious crime untenable.

Second, as a tactical matter, order maintenance theory "advocate[s] close collaboration between police and citizens . . . in the development of neighborhood standards" of conduct. Such standards are "to be enforced for the most part though non-arrest approaches—education, persuasion, counseling, and ordering"—so that arrest would only be resorted to when other approaches failed. In this sense, order maintenance theory and "community policing" connect and overlap to a substantial degree.

The results * * * seemed to confirm the order maintenance hypothesis. * * * [Police] discovered that persons arrested for turnstyle-jumping frequently were found to be "carrying weapons or [to] have outstanding warrants." As the progenitor of "broken windows" theory would later describe the key lesson of the * * * experience: "Restoring order reduces crime . . . at least in part because restoring order puts police in contact with persons who carry weapons and who commit serious crime." [G.L. Kelling & C.M. Coles, Fixing Broken Windows: Restoring Order and Reducing Crime in Our communities (1996).]

* * *

[T]he role of "stop & frisk" in furthering the Department's goals of order maintenance, deterrence, crime prevention, and a direct attack on gun violence is clear. Given the Department's focus on apprehending violent criminals and preventing more serious crimes by aggressively enforcing laws aimed at low-level criminality, "stop & frisk" serves as an important wedge into the criminal element.

Order maintenance theory encourages officers to intervene in instances of low-level disorder, whether observed or suspected, with approaches which fall short of arrest. A "stop" intervention provides an occasion for the police to have contact with persons presumably involved in low-level criminality— without having to effect a formal arrest, and under a lower-constitutional standard (*i.e.*, "reasonable suspicion"). Indeed, because low-level "quality of life" and misdemeanor offenses are more likely to be committed in the open, as a theoretical matter, the "reasonable suspicion" standard may be more readily satisfied as to those sorts of crimes. To the extent that "stop" encounters create points of contact between police and low-level offenders, such contacts can lead to the apprehension of persons already wanted for more serious crimes, or who might be prepared to commit them in the near future.

* * *

Finally, as implemented by the NYPD, "stop & frisk" serves the Department's No. 1 strategic goal—"getting guns off the streets of New York." Notwithstanding its origin as a technique designed to assure officer safety, "stop & frisk" plainly has been used as a method to detect and seize illegal handguns. [During a study period], fully 34% of all documented "stop & frisk" encounters by NYPD officers citywide were for suspected weapons possession.

* * *

Thus, a model which values both proactive police interventions short of arrest and an aggressive approach to low-level disorder is well served by aggressive use of "stop & frisk." More to the point, "stop & frisk" has served as an important tactical resource in promoting the Department's specific strategic crime-fighting goals.

New York Report at 47–59.

New York Stop and Frisk Practice

The New York Attorney General made an effort to determine how New York City police actually used the authority to make *Terry* stops. The results were also presented in the New York Report.

Under New York departmental policies, an officer was required to file a "UF-250" report on each incident in which a person is stopped and (a) force is used to make the stop; (b) the person stopped is frisked or searched; (c) the person stopped is arrested; or (d) the person stopped refuses to identify himself. If an incident involves a stop but none of the factors mandating a report applies, the officer may file a report. The reports are to include the race of the person stopped and the facts which led the officer to make the stop. The study analyzed 174,919 reports of stops during 1998–1999; 72.5% of the reports reflected incidents in which a report was required, and the remaining 27.5% reflected incidents in which the officer chose to file a report.

The investigators looked at which the facts set out by the officers were sufficient to constitute reasonable suspicion. The results were as follows:

facts sufficient to constitute reasonable suspicion	61.1%
facts not sufficient to constitute reasonable suspicion	15.4%
report insufficient to permit determination	23.5%
	100%

New York Report at xiii–xiv. A form was put into the insufficient to determine category if the situation suggested that additional information "readily hypothesized" might justify the stop. Thus if a form said, "moving furniture/carrying 'out of place objects,'" the investigators assumed other information available but not reported might justify the stop and they treated it as insufficient to permit determination.

Overall, one out of nine stops resulted in an arrest. The study found this "unsurprising, given the purpose of a 'stop' and the lower level of suspicion required to justify a 'stop' as opposed to an arrest." New York Report at viii.

The study provided some support for concern that field stops are made in part on racial grounds. Overall, the results were as follows

	City Population	Stops
Blacks	25.6%	50.6%
Hispanics	23.7%	33.0%
Whites	43.4%	12.9%

The disparity was most pronounced in those precincts in which a majority of the population was white.

Precincts in which minorities constituted the majority of the population tended to have more "stop & frisk" activity than precincts in which whites constituted the majority. Some, but not all, of this was accounted for by the higher crime rate in those precincts with a nonwhite majority.

Blacks were less likely to be stopped on suspicion of property crimes than whites or hispanics. But—controlling for other factors—blacks were 2.1 times more often than whites stopped on suspicion of committing a violent crime and 2.4 times more often on suspicion of carrying a weapon. Hispanics were stopped 1.7 times as often as whites on suspicion of committing a violent crime and 2.0 times as often on suspicion of carrying a weapon. New York Report at x–xi.

Floyd Litigation Challenging New York Stop and Frisk

New York City's stop and frisk practices were examined further in federal litigation, particularly by federal district judge Shira A. Scheindlin in Floyd v. City of New York, filed in 2008. See generally Jeffrey Bellin, The Inverse Relationship Between the Constitutionality and Effectiveness of New York City's "Stop and Frisk," 94 B.U. L. Rev. 1495 (2014).

The *Floyd* plaintiffs—blacks and Hispanics who were stopped—contended their constitutional rights were violated in two ways: "(1) they were stopped without a legal basis in violation of the Fourth Amendment, and (2) they were targeted for stops because of their race in violation of the Fourteenth Amendment."

In 2012, the plaintiffs' motion for class certification was granted. Floyd v. City of New York, 283 F.R.D. 153, 178 (S.D.N.Y.2012). Extensive pretrial discovery was conducted. Plaintiffs relied heavily upon analyses by Professor Jeffrey Fagan, Professor of Law at Columbia Law School and Professor of Epidemiology at the Mailman School of Public Health at Columbia University. See Floyd v. City of New York, 861 F.Supp.2d 274 (S.D.N.Y.2012) (granting in part and denying in part defendants' motion to exclude Professor Fagan's opinions on the grounds "he lacks the qualifications to make the assessments that he makes, that his methodologies are fatally flawed, and that many of his opinions constitute inadmissible conclusions of law").

Trial began on March 18, 2013 and ended on May 20 of that year. Both sides introduced expert testimony and vigorously cross-examined each others' experts. On August 12, 2013 Judge Scheidlin issued two opinions, one finding liability, Floyd v. City of New York, 959 F.Supp.2d 540 (S.D.N.Y.2013), and another addressing the relief granted, Floyd v. City of New York, 959 F.Supp.2d 668 (S.D.N.Y.2013).

In the liability opinion, Judge Scheidlin set out "the most relevant uncontested statistics culled from the UF-250 database":

- Between January 2004 and June 2012 the NYPD conducted over 4.4 million *Terry* stops.

- The number of stops per year rose sharply from 314,000 in 2004 to a high of 686,000 in 2011.

- 52% of all stops were followed by a protective frisk for weapons. A weapon was found after 1.5% of these frisks. In other words, in 98.5% of the 2.3 million frisks, no weapon was found.

- 8% of all stops led to a search into the stopped person's clothing, ostensibly based on the officer feeling an object during the frisk that he suspected to be a weapon, or immediately perceived to be contraband other than a weapon. In 9% of these searches, the felt object was in fact a weapon. 91% of the time, it was not. In 14% of these searches, the felt object was in fact contraband. 86% of the time it was not.

- 6% of all stops resulted in an arrest, and 6% resulted in a summons. The remaining 88% of the 4.4 million stops resulted in no further law enforcement action.

- In 52% of the 4.4 million stops, the person stopped was black.

- In 31% of the stops, the person stopped was Hispanic.

- In 10% of the stops, the person stopped was white.

- In 2010, New York City's resident population was roughly 23% black, 29% Hispanic, and 33% white.

- In 23% of the stops of blacks, and 24% of the stops of Hispanics, the officer recorded using force. The number for whites was 17%.

- Weapons were seized in 1.0% of the stops of blacks, 1.1% of the stops of Hispanics, and 1.4% of the stops of whites.

- Contraband other than weapons was seized in 1.8% of the stops of blacks, 1.7% of the stops of Hispanics, and 2.3% of the stops of whites.

Dr. Fagan's testimony analyzed the data on the basis of a benchmark using both population and reported crime.

The defendants and their experts—among them Dr. Dennis Smith, an Associate Professor of Public Administration at the Robert F. Wagner Graduate School of Public Service at New York University—contended that the composition of those stopped should not be compared to that of the resident population. Rather, they urged use of "a benchmark consisting of the rates at which various races appear in suspect descriptions from crime victims—in other words, 'suspect race description data.' " "The City's experts," Judge Scheidlin noted, "assumed that if officers' stop decisions were racially unbiased, then the racial distribution of stopped pedestrians would be the same as the racial distribution of the criminal suspects in the area." Those experts contended that the demonstrated disproportionate stopping of black people can be explained by the disproportionately black composition of the pool of criminals. A significant portion of the stops that resulted in no further enforcement action, Dr. Smith indicated, were stops of people who were about to commit a crime but were prevented by the stop from doing so.

Judge Scheidlin sided with the plaintiffs:

I conclude that Dr. Fagan's benchmark is the better choice. The reason is simple and reveals a serious flaw in the logic applied by the City's experts: there is no basis for assuming that the racial distribution of stopped pedestrians will resemble the racial distribution of the local criminal population *if the people stopped are not criminals*. The City defends the fact that blacks and Hispanics represent 87% of the persons stopped in 2011 and 2012 by noting that "approximately 83% of all known crime suspects and approximately 90% of all violent crime suspects were Black and Hispanic." This might be a valid comparison if the people stopped were criminals, or if they were stopped based on fitting a specific suspect description. But there was insufficient evidence to support either conclusion. To the contrary, nearly 90% of the people stopped are released without the officer finding any basis for a summons or arrest, and only 13% of stops are based on fitting a specific suspect description. There is no reason to believe that the nearly 90% of people who are stopped and then subject to no further enforcement action are criminals. As a result, there is no reason to believe that their racial distribution should resemble that of the local criminal population, as opposed to that of the local population in general. If the police are stopping people in a race-neutral way, then the racial composition of innocent people stopped should more or less mirror the racial composition of the areas where they are stopped, all other things being equal.

"Dr. Smith's theory that a significant number of * * * stops [of Blacks and Hispanics] resulted in the prevention of the suspected crime," she added, "is pure speculation and not reliable."

Fourth Amendment violations were proved, Judge Scheidlin concluded; at least 6 % of the stops—and likely more—were made without reasonable suspicion. Fourteenth Amendment violations were also established:

> Based on the expert testimony I find the following: (1) The NYPD carries out more stops where there are more black and Hispanic residents, even when other relevant variables are held constant. The racial composition of a precinct or census tract predicts the stop rate *above and beyond* the crime rate. (2) Blacks and Hispanics are more likely than whites to be stopped within precincts and census tracts, even after controlling for other relevant variables. This is so even in areas with low crime rates, racially heterogenous populations, or predominately white populations. (3) For the period 2004 through 2009, when any law enforcement action was taken following a stop, blacks were 30% more likely to be arrested (as opposed to receiving a summons) than whites, for the same suspected crime. (4) For the period 2004 through 2009, after controlling for suspected crime and precinct characteristics, blacks who were stopped were about 14% more likely—and Hispanics 9% more likely—than whites to be subjected to the use of force. (5) For the period 2004 through 2009, all else being equal, the odds of a stop resulting in any further enforcement action were 8% *lower* if the person stopped was black than if the person stopped was white. In addition, the greater the black population in a precinct, the less likely that a stop would result in a sanction. Together, these results show that blacks are likely targeted for stops based on a lesser degree of objectively founded suspicion than whites.

She added:

> [T]he evidence at trial revealed that the NYPD has an unwritten policy of targeting "the right people" for stops. In practice, the policy encourages the targeting of young black and Hispanic men based on their prevalence in local crime complaints. This is a form of racial profiling. While a person's race may be important if it fits the description of a particular crime suspect, it is impermissible to subject all members of a racially defined group to heightened police enforcement because some members of that group are criminals. The Equal Protection Clause does not permit race-based suspicion.

Judge Scheidlin held the city liable for the individual officers' actions on two theories: (a) city and police senior official were deliberately indifferent to unconstitutional stops and frisks; and (b) unconstitutional stops and frisk practices were so widespread they had the force of law.

Regarding remedies, Judge Scheidlin appointed an independent monitor to oversee the reforms she ordered. Among those reforms were revision of policies and training material, improved documentation of stop activities and the development of an improved system for monitoring, supervising and disciplining officers. In addition, she ordered pilot programs in some precincts for use of body-worn cameras to record stop activities.

The City of New York appealed from Judge Scheidlin's decisions. The Second Circuit stayed the district judge's actions pending disposition of the appeals. It also held Judge Scheidlin's actions in connection with the case compromised the appearance of impartiality and ordered that a different district judge be assigned to the case. Ligon v. City of New York, 736 F.3d 118 (2nd Cir.2013). After a new mayor of New York City was elected in late 2013, the city reversed its opposition to the district court's orders and agreed to withdraw the appeal and implement the reforms. B. Weiser and J. Goldstein, Mayor Says City Will Settle Suits on Frisk Tactics, New York Times, Jan. 31, 2014.

Several police unions sought to intervene and to continue the appellate challenge to the district court's orders. The Second Circuit, however, refused to rule on the motions to intervene and remanded the case to the district court for the parties to explore settlement. Ligon v. City of New York, 743 F.3d 362 (2nd Cir.2014).

Figures from the New York police themselves indicate that stops have declined dramatically. In 2011, 685,724 stops were reported. In 2013 and 2014, the department made 191,558 and 46,235 stops respectively. Stop-and-Frisk Data, http://www.nyclu.org/content/stop-and-frisk-data. There are indications that this was not accompanied by an increase in the city's crime. Philip Bump, The Fix, New York has essentially eliminated stop-and-frisk—and crime is still down, http://www.washingtonpost.com/blogs/the-fix/wp/2014/12/03/new-york-has-essentially-eliminated-stop-and-frisk-and-crime-is-still-down/.

New York police, however, acknowledged a 19.5% increase in homicides during the first five months of 2015. Moreover, the percent of homicides caused by gun violence rose from about 57% to 72% in that part of 2015. Gianluca Cuestas, Rocco Parascandola, Tina Moore, and Kerry Burke, Frisks down, slays up & cop big warns . . . GUNS ARE WINNING, New York Daily News, June 2, 2015. This prompted a June 1, 2015 New York Post editorial titled, "How many New Yorkers must die before the mayor brings back stop-and-frisk?"

1. FIELD DETENTIONS

Analysis is furthered by considering separately field detentions of subjects—so-called *Terry* stops—from weapons searches that may accompany many of these detentions.

a. ANALYSIS OF FIELD ENCOUNTERS

How should courts analyze situations in which a law enforcement officers and citizens come into contact—when they have what might be called an "encounter?"[1] At a minimum, the courts must ask whether the Fourth Amendment was triggered by the situation and if so, when. If the Fourth Amendment was triggered, they must ask what Fourth Amendment standards applied at critical times in the events. This second question requires the courts to decide how to characterize seizures of the person for Fourth Amendment purposes.

Florida v. Royer

Supreme Court of the United States, 1983.
460 U.S. 491, 103 S.Ct. 1319.

■ JUSTICE WHITE announced the judgment of the Court and delivered an opinion in which JUSTICES MARSHALL, POWELL and STEVENS joined.

* * *

I

On January 3, 1978, Royer was observed at Miami International Airport by two plain-clothes detectives of the Dade County, Florida, Public Safety Department assigned to the County's Organized Crime Bureau, Narcotics Investigation Section. Detectives Johnson and Magdalena believed that Royer's appearance, mannerisms, luggage, and actions fit the so-called "drug courier profile." Royer, apparently unaware of the attention he had attracted, purchased a one-way ticket to New York City and checked his two suitcases, placing on each suitcase an identification tag bearing the name "Holt" and the destination, "LaGuardia". As Royer made his way to the concourse which led to the airline boarding area, the two detectives approached him, identified themselves as policemen working out of the sheriff's office, and asked if Royer had a "moment" to speak with them; Royer said "Yes."

Upon request, but without oral consent, Royer produced for the detectives his airline ticket and his driver's license. The airline ticket, like the baggage identification tags, bore the name "Holt," while the driver's license carried respondent's correct name, "Royer." When the detectives asked about the discrepancy, Royer explained that a friend had made the reservation in the name of "Holt." Royer became noticeably

---

[1] [Some discussions use the term "encounter" to describe situations in which no seizure of the citizen occurs. In this discussion, the term is used in a broader sense to describe field contacts between officers and citizens, whether or not the Fourth Amendment is implicated.]

more nervous during this conversation, whereupon the detectives informed Royer that they were in fact narcotics investigators and that they had reason to suspect him of transporting narcotics.

The detectives did not return his airline ticket and identification but asked Royer to accompany them to a room, approximately forty feet away, adjacent to the concourse. Royer said nothing in response but went with the officers as he had been asked to do. The room was later described by Detective Johnson as a "large storage closet," located in the stewardesses' lounge and containing a small desk and two chairs. Without Royer's consent or agreement, Detective Johnson, using Royer's baggage check stubs, retrieved the "Holt" luggage from the airline and brought it to the room where respondent and Detective Magdalena were waiting. Royer was asked if he would consent to a search of the suitcases. Without orally responding to this request, Royer produced a key and unlocked one of the suitcases, which the detective then opened without seeking further assent from Royer. Drugs were found in that suitcase. According to Detective Johnson, Royer stated that he did not know the combination to the lock on the second suitcase. When asked if he objected to the detective opening the second suitcase, Royer said "no, go ahead," and did not object when the detective explained that the suitcase might have to be broken open. The suitcase was pried open by the officers and more marihuana was found. Royer was then told that he was under arrest. Approximately fifteen minutes had elapsed from the time the detectives initially approached respondent until his arrest upon the discovery of the contraband.

Prior to his trial for felony possession of marihuana, Royer made a motion to suppress the evidence obtained in the search of the suitcases. The trial court found that Royer's consent to the search was "freely and voluntarily given," and that, regardless of the consent, the warrantless search was reasonable because "the officer doesn't have the time to run out and get a search warrant because the plane is going to take off." Following the denial of the motion to suppress, Royer * * * was convicted.

The District Court of Appeal, sitting en banc, reversed Royer's conviction. * * * We granted the State's petition for certiorari * * * .

II

* * * The Florida Court of Appeal * * * concluded * * * that Royer had been seized when he gave his consent to search his luggage [and] also that the bounds of an investigative stop had been exceeded. In its view the "confinement" in this case went beyond the limited restraint of a *Terry* investigative stop, and Royer's consent was thus tainted by the illegality, a conclusion that required reversal in the absence of probable cause to arrest. The question before us is whether the record warrants that conclusion. We think that it does.

III

The State proffers three reasons for holding that when Royer consented to the search of his luggage, he was not being illegally detained. First, it is submitted that the entire encounter was consensual and hence Royer was not being held against his will at all. We find this submission untenable. Asking for and examining Royer's ticket and his driver's license were no doubt permissible in themselves, but when the officers identified themselves as narcotics agents, told Royer that he was suspected of transporting narcotics, and asked him to accompany them to the police room, while retaining his ticket and driver's license and without indicating in any way that he was free to depart, Royer was effectively seized for the purposes of the Fourth Amendment. These circumstances surely amount to a show of official authority such that "a reasonable person would have believed he was not free to leave." *United States v. Mendenhall*, 446 U.S. 544, 554, 100 S.Ct. 1870, 1877, 64 L.Ed.2d 497 (Opinion of Stewart, J.).

Second, the State submits that if Royer was seized, there existed reasonable, articulable suspicion to justify a temporary detention and that the limits of a *Terry*-type stop were never exceeded. We agree with the State that when the officers discovered that Royer was travelling under an assumed name, this fact, and the facts already known to the officers—paying cash for a one-way ticket, the mode of checking the two bags, and Royer's appearance and conduct in general—were adequate grounds for suspecting Royer of carrying drugs and for temporarily detaining him and his luggage while they attempted to verify or dispel their suspicions in a manner that did not exceed the limits of an investigative detention. We also agree that had Royer voluntarily consented to the search of his luggage while he was justifiably being detained on reasonable suspicion, the products of the search would be admissible against him. We have concluded, however, that at the time Royer produced the key to his suitcase, the detention to which he was then subjected was a more serious intrusion on his personal liberty than is allowable on mere suspicion of criminal activity.

By the time Royer was informed that the officers wished to examine his luggage, he had identified himself when approached by the officers and had attempted to explain the discrepancy between the name shown on his identification and the name under which he had purchased his ticket and identified his luggage. The officers were not satisfied, for they informed him they were narcotics agents and had reason to believe that he was carrying illegal drugs. They requested him to accompany them to the police room. Royer went with them. He found himself in a small room—a large closet—equipped with a desk and two chairs. He was alone with two police officers who again told him that they thought he was carrying narcotics. He also found that the officers, without his consent, had retrieved his checked luggage from the airlines. What had begun as a consensual inquiry in a public place had escalated into an investigatory procedure in a police interrogation room, where the police, unsatisfied with previous explanations, sought to confirm their suspicions. The officers had Royer's ticket, they had his identification, and they had seized his luggage. Royer was never informed that he was free to board his plane if he so chose, and he reasonably believed that he was being detained. At least as of that moment, any consensual aspects of the encounter had evaporated, and we cannot fault the Florida Court of Appeal for concluding that *Terry v. Ohio*[, 392 U.S. 1, 88 S.Ct. 1868, 20 L.Ed.2d 889 (1968),] and the cases following it did not justify the restraint to which Royer was then subjected. As a practical matter, Royer was under arrest. Consistent with this conclusion, the State conceded in the Florida courts that Royer would not have been free to leave the interrogation room had he asked to do so. Furthermore, the state's brief in this Court interprets the testimony of the officers at the suppression hearing as indicating that had Royer refused to consent to a search of his luggage, the officers would have held the luggage and sought a warrant to authorize the search.

We also think that the officers' conduct was more intrusive than necessary to effectuate an investigative detention otherwise authorized by the *Terry* line of cases. First, by returning his ticket and driver's license, and informing him that he was free to go if he so desired, the officers may have obviated any claim that the encounter was anything but a consensual matter from start to finish. Second, there are undoubtedly reasons of safety and security that would justify moving a suspect from one location to another during an investigatory detention, such as from an airport concourse to a more private area. There is no indication in this case that such reasons prompted the officers to transfer the site of the encounter from the concourse to the interrogation room. It appears, rather, that the primary interest of the officers was not in having an extended conversation with Royer but in the contents of his luggage, a matter which the officers did not pursue orally with Royer until after the encounter was relocated to the police room. The record does not reflect any facts which would support a finding that the legitimate law enforcement purposes which justified the detention in the first instance were furthered by removing Royer to the police room prior to the officer's attempt to gain his consent to a search of his luggage. As we have noted, had Royer consented to a search on the spot, the search could have been conducted with Royer present in the area where the bags were retrieved by Officer Johnson and any evidence recovered would have been admissible against him. If the search proved negative, Royer would have been free to go much earlier and with less likelihood of missing his flight, which in itself can be a very serious matter in a variety of circumstances.

Third, the State has not touched on the question whether it would have been feasible to investigate the contents of Royer's bags in a more expeditious way. The courts are not strangers to the use of trained dogs to detect the presence of controlled substances in luggage. There is no indication here that this means was not feasible and available. If it had been used, Royer and his luggage could have been momentarily detained while this investigative procedure was carried out. Indeed, it may be that no detention at all would have been necessary. A negative result would have freed Royer in short order; a positive result would have resulted in his justifiable arrest on probable cause.

We do not suggest that there is a litmus-paper test for distinguishing a consensual encounter from a seizure or for determining when a seizure exceeds the bounds of an investigative stop. Even in the discrete category of airport encounters, there will be endless variations in the facts and circumstances, so much variation that it is unlikely that the courts can reduce to a sentence or a paragraph a rule that will provide unarguable answers to the question whether there has been an unreasonable search or seizure in violation of the Fourth Amendment. Nevertheless, we must render judgment, and we think that the Florida Court of Appeal cannot be faulted in concluding that the limits of a *Terry*-stop had been exceeded.

IV

The State's third and final argument is that Royer was not being illegally held when he gave his consent because there was probable cause to arrest him at that time. Officer Johnson testified at the suppression hearing and the Florida Court of Appeal held that there was no probable cause to arrest until Royer's bags were opened, but the fact that the officers did not believe there was probable cause and proceeded on a consensual or *Terry*-stop rationale would not foreclose the State from justifying Royer's custody by proving probable cause and hence removing any barrier to relying on Royer's consent to search. We agree with the Florida Court of Appeal, however, that probable cause to arrest Royer did not exist at the time he consented to the search of his luggage. The facts are that a nervous young man with two American Tourister bags paid cash for an airline ticket to a "target city." These facts led to inquiry, which in turn revealed that the ticket had been bought under an assumed name. The proffered explanation did not satisfy the officers. We cannot agree with the State, if this is its position, that every nervous young man paying cash for a ticket to New York City under an assumed name and carrying two heavy American Tourister bags may be arrested and held to answer for a serious felony charge.

V

Because we affirm the Florida Court of Appeal's conclusion that Royer was being illegally detained when he consented to the search of his luggage, we agree that the consent was tainted by the illegality and was ineffective to justify the search. The judgment of the Florida Court of Appeal is accordingly

Affirmed.

■ JUSTICE BRENNAN, concurring in the result.

* * *

To the extent that the plurality endorses the legality of the officers' initial stop of Royer, it was wholly unnecessary to reach that question. For even assuming the legality of the initial stop, the plurality correctly holds, and I agree, that the officers' subsequent actions clearly exceeded the permissible bounds of a *Terry* "investigative" stop. * * *

In any event, I dissent from the plurality's view that the initial stop of Royer was legal. For plainly Royer was "seized" * * * . [The] facts clearly are not sufficient to provide the reasonable suspicion of criminal activity necessary to justify the * * * seizure * * * .

■ JUSTICE BLACKMUN, dissenting

* * *

At the suppression hearing in this case, Royer agreed that he was not formally arrested until after his suitcases were opened. In my view, it cannot fairly be said that, prior to the formal arrest, the functional equivalent of an arrest had taken place. The encounter had far more in common with automobile stops justifiable on reasonable suspicion than with the * * * functional equivalent of a formal arrest * * * .

■ JUSTICE REHNQUIST, with whom THE CHIEF JUSTICE and JUSTICE O'CONNOR join, dissenting.

* * *

I think the articulable suspicion which concededly focused upon Royer [after the officers' initial conversation with him] justified the length and nature of his detention.

The reasonableness of the officers' activity in this case did not depend upon Royer's consent to the investigation. Nevertheless, the presence of consent further justifies the action taken. * * * [I]f Royer was legally approached in the first instance and consented to accompany the detectives to the room, it does not follow that his consent went up in smoke and he was "arrested" upon entering the room. * * * [L]ogical analysis would focus on whether the environment in the room rendered the subsequent consent to a search of the luggage involuntary.

[T]here is nothing in the record which would indicate that Royer's resistance was overborne by anything * * * .

NOTES

1.   **Movement of the Suspect.** How much may an officer who has made a proper nonarrest investigatory detention move the suspect? In Dunaway v. New York, 442 U.S. 200, 99 S.Ct. 2248 (1979), officers with information—but less than probable cause—connecting Dunaway with a robbery-murder had Dunaway "picked up" at a neighbor's home. They drove him to police headquarters, placed him in an interrogation room, warned him of his rights, and questioned him. Finding that the officers' actions were "in

important respects indistinguishable from an arrest," the Court held the lack of probable cause rendered the detention invalid. The *Dunaway* holding that movement to the stationhouse is prohibited was confirmed in Hayes v. Florida, 470 U.S. 811, 105 S.Ct. 1643 (1985).

2. **Stationhouse Detentions on Reasonable Suspicion.** In Davis v. Mississippi, 394 U.S. 721, 89 S.Ct. 1394 (1969), the Court indicated in dictum that stationhouse detentions for fingerprinting might be permissible upon less than probable cause:

> It is arguable * * * that, because of the unique nature of the fingerprinting process, * * * detentions [for fingerprinting] might, under narrowly defined circumstances, be found to comply with the Fourth Amendment even though there is no probable cause in the traditional sense. Detention for fingerprinting may constitute a much less serious intrusion upon personal security than other types of police searches and detentions. Fingerprinting involves none of the probing into an individual's private life and thoughts that mark an interrogation or search. Nor can fingerprint detention be employed repeatedly to harass any individual, since the police need only one set of each person's prints. Furthermore, fingerprinting is an inherently more reliable and effective crime-stopping tool than eyewitness identification or confessions and is not subject to such abuses as the improper lineup and the "third degree." Finally, because there is no danger of destruction of fingerprints, the limited detention need not come unexpectedly or at an inconvenient time. For this same reason, the general requirement that the authorization of a judicial officer be obtained in advance of detention would seem not to admit of any exception in the fingerprinting context.

394 U.S. at 727–28, 89 S.Ct. at 1397–98. The court reaffirmed this suggestion in Hayes v. Florida, 470 U.S. 811, 817, 105 S.Ct. 1643, 1647 (1985), noting a number of jurisdictions, in reliance on the *Davis* suggestion, had enacted provisions for judicial authorizations for fingerprinting detentions.

3. **Length of the Detention.** How long may a non-arrest investigatory detention last? In United States v. Place, 462 U.S. 696, 103 S.Ct. 2637 (1983), dealing with detention of luggage as discussed later in these Notes, the Court declined "to adopt any outside time limitation for a permissible *Terry* stop:"

> We understand the desirability of providing law enforcement authorities with a clear rule to guide their conduct. Nevertheless, we question the wisdom of a rigid time limitation. Such a limit would undermine the equally important need to allow authorities to graduate their responses to the demands of any particular situation.

462 U.S. at 710 n. 10, 103 S.Ct. at 2646 n. 10. But it then continued:

> The [90-minute] length of the detention of [Place's] luggage alone precludes the conclusion that the seizure was reasonable in the absence of probable cause. Although we have recognized the

reasonableness of seizures longer than * * * momentary ones * * *, the brevity of the invasion of the individual's Fourth Amendment interests is an important factor in determining whether the seizure is so minimally intrusive as to be justifiable on reasonable suspicion. Moreover, in assessing the effect of the length of the detention, we take into account whether the police diligently pursue their investigation. We note that here the New York agents knew the time of Place's scheduled arrival at LaGuardia [Airport], had ample time to arrange for their additional investigation at that location, and thereby could have minimized the intrusion on [Place's] Fourth Amendment interests. * * * [W]e have never approved a seizure of the person for the prolonged 90-minute period involved here and cannot do so on the facts presented by this case.

462 U.S. at 709–10, 103 S.Ct. at 2645–46.

The permissible length of investigatory detentions was again addressed in United States v. Sharpe, 470 U.S. 675, 105 S.Ct. 1568 (1985). Drug Enforcement Administration agent Cooke was patrolling a coastal road in North Carolina and observed a pickup truck (driven by Savage) and a Pontiac (driven by Sharpe) traveling "in tandem." After observing the pickup truck was heavily loaded, Cooke called for assistance. Highway patrol officer Thrasher, driving a marked patrol car, responded. Within approximately a minute of Thrasher's joining the "procession," the truck and the Pontiac turned off the highway onto a campground road and—despite the 35 mph speed limit—progressed at 55 to 60 mph until the road looped back onto the highway. The officers decided to stop the vehicles and Thrasher pulled aside the Pontiac (which was in the lead), turned on his flashing light, and motioned for the driver to pull over. As the Pontiac pulled over, the pickup truck "cut" between the Pontiac and the patrol car and continued down the highway. Thrasher pursued the truck and Cooke pulled over behind the Pontiac. Cooke obtained identification from Sharpe, the driver of the Pontiac. When he was unable to make radio contact with Thrasher, he called local police, directed them to "maintain the situation," and joined Thrasher.

Thrasher had stopped and secured identification from the driver of the truck, Savage. Savage explained that the truck belonged to a friend (and produced a bill of sale) and that he was taking the truck to have its shock absorbers repaired. Thrasher told Savage that the two would await the arrival of a DEA agent. Savage became nervous and asked for his identification; Thrasher told him that he was not free to leave. Cooke arrived at the scene about 15 minutes after the truck had been stopped. When Cooke stated that he believed the truck contained marihuana and twice asked for permission to search it, Savage twice refused. Cooke stepped on the rear of the truck, noting that it did not sink. He then put his nose against the rear window, reported that he could smell marihuana, and searched the vehicle. Bales of marihuana were found and Savage was placed under arrest. Cooke then returned to the Pontiac and arrested Sharpe; this was about 30 to 40 minutes from the time the Pontiac was stopped. At the trial of Sharpe and Savage for possession of the marihuana, the marihuana was admitted into evidence. On appeal, the Court of Appeals reversed, reasoning that the detentions of Sharpe and Savage were too long to be supported on less than probable cause and that these detentions tainted the discovery and seizure of the marihuana.

The Supreme Court reversed. Writing for the Court, Chief Justice Burger reaffirmed that the Fourth Amendment imposes no "hard-and-fast" time limit upon the duration of a *Terry* stop:

> In assessing whether a detention is too long in duration to be justified as an investigative stop, we consider it appropriate to examine whether the police diligently pursued a means of investigation that was likely to confirm or dispel their suspicions quickly, during which time it was necessary to detain the defendant. A court making this assessment should take care to consider whether the police are acting in a swiftly developing situation, and in such cases the court should not indulge in unrealistic second-guessing. * * * The question is not simply whether some other alternative was available, but whether the police acted unreasonably in failing to recognize or pursue it.

470 U.S. at 686–87, 105 S.Ct. at 1575–76.

On the facts before it, the Court concluded, Cooke pursued the investigation with regard to Savage in a diligent and reasonable manner. Most of the delay was attributable to Savage's actions in maneuvering around the Pontiac and Thrasher's patrol car, which required separate stops of the two vehicles. The Court assumed this was a conscious effort by Savage to elude the officers, but commented that Savage's actions would also justify the delay even if they were "innocent." To affirm the decision of the lower court with regard to Savage's 20 minute detention, the majority concluded, would be to "effectively establish a *per se* rule that a 20-minute detention is too long to be justified under the *Terry* doctrine." This, the Court indicated, it was unwilling to do. In regard to Sharpe's detention, the Court found no reason to consider the validity of its 30 to 40 minute duration. The challenged evidence was obtained by searching the truck and was not "fruit" of any improper detention of Sharpe as may have taken place.

4. **Investigatory "Detentions" of Items.** Some seizures of items as well as persons may be made upon less than probable cause. In United States v. Place, 462 U.S. 696, 103 S.Ct. 2637 (1983), Drug Enforcement Administration officers approached Place at New York's LaGuardia airport after he aroused suspicion while departing from Miami and upon arrival in New York. Discrepancies were noted concerning the addresses placed on his two pieces of luggage. At both Miami and New York, he volunteered to officers who approached him that he had recognized them as police officers. At New York, he falsely claimed that his baggage had been searched in Miami. He refused to consent to a search of the luggage at the New York airport. One of the agents then informed him that the officers would take the luggage to a federal judge and apply for a search warrant. He added that Place was free to accompany the officers (and the luggage). Place declined the invitation, but obtained a number at which the officers indicated they could be reached. The officers took the bags to another airport where, one

hour and thirty minutes later, a trained narcotics detention dog reacted positively to the smaller bag but "ambiguously" to the larger one. As it was late on Friday, the agents retained the bags until Monday, when they obtained a search warrant. The smaller bag was found to contain cocaine. Applying the principles of *Terry,* the Supreme Court concluded certain seizures of personal luggage on the basis of "reasonable, articulable suspicion, premised on objective facts," would be reasonable under the Fourth Amendment. Balancing the relevant interests, the Court noted a substantial governmental interest in a brief seizure of luggage believed to contain drugs. On the other hand, some brief seizures of luggage intrude only minimally upon the owner's Fourth Amendment protected interests:

> [W]e conclude that when an officer's observations lead him reasonably to believe that a traveler is carrying luggage that contains narcotics, the principles of *Terry* and its progeny would permit the officer to detain the luggage briefly to investigate the circumstances that aroused his suspicion, provided that the investigative detention is properly limited in scope.

462 U.S. at 706, 103 S.Ct. at 2644. But—as discussed earlier in these Notes— the Court further concluded the length of the detention exceeded what was permissible on less than probable cause.

b.   REQUIREMENT OF REASONABLE SUSPICION

EDITORS' INTRODUCTION: REASONABLE SUSPICION

The Supreme Court's case law after *Terry* and its companion decisions clearly regards law enforcement as constitutionally permitted to seize and briefly detain persons for purposes of investigation on less than the probable cause required for an arrest. What factual basis is required for such action? Post-*Terry* decisions sometimes used somewhat different terminology to describe the required basis, but the Court appears to have settled on "reasonable suspicion" as the standard.

What is this required reasonable suspicion? In Alabama v. White, 496 U.S. 325, 110 S.Ct. 2412 (1990), the Court explained in general terms:

> Reasonable suspicion is a less demanding standard than probable cause not only in the sense that reasonable suspicion can be established with information that is different in quantity or content than that required to establish probable cause, but also in the sense that reasonable suspicion can arise from information that is less reliable than that required to show probable cause. * * * Reasonable suspicion, like probable cause, is dependent upon both the content of information possessed by police and its degree of reliability. Both factors—quantity and quality—are considered in the "totality of the circumstances— the whole picture," that must be taken into account when evaluating whether there is reasonable suspicion. * * *

496 U.S. at 330, 110 S.Ct. at 2416. The case reprinted in this section presents an interesting application of this standard. Several specific aspects of reasonable suspicion as the standard for nonarrest investigatory field detentions, however, merit preliminary consideration.

Reasonable Suspicion as Applied

What specific facts support valid nonarrest field detentions is obviously a difficult question. The Supreme Court has addressed the problem in a number of contexts.

Several cases involved informant tips. In Adams v. Williams, 407 U.S. 143, 92 S.Ct. 1921 (1972), an informant approached a police cruiser and informed the officer a person seated in a nearby vehicle was carrying narcotics and had a gun at his waist. The officer knew the informant and had received information from him in the past. On the other hand, this information involved claims of homosexual activity in a local railroad station and the followup investigation resulted in neither confirmation nor arrests. The officer located the person described by the informant and detained him. Upholding the detention, the Supreme Court rejected the proposition that the necessary reasonable cause must be based upon the officer's personal observation. While the tip may not have amounted to probable cause justifying an arrest, it did support the action taken:

> This is a stronger case than obtains in the case of an anonymous telephone tip. The informant here came forward personally to give information that was immediately verifiable at the scene. Indeed, * * * the informant might have been subject to immediate arrest for making a false complaint had [the] investigation proved the tip incorrect.

407 U.S. at 146–47, 92 S.Ct. at 1923.

An anonymous tip was at issue in Alabama v. White, 496 U.S. 325, 110 S.Ct. 2412 (1990). The facts were as follows:

> On April 22, 1987, at approximately 3 p.m., Corporal B.H. Davis of the Montgomery Police Department received a telephone call from an anonymous person, stating that Vanessa White would be leaving 235-C Lynwood Terrace Apartments at a particular time in a brown Plymouth station wagon with the right taillight lens broken, that she would be going to Dobey's Motel, and that she would be in possession of about an ounce of cocaine inside a brown attache case. Corporal Davis and his partner, Corporal P.A. Reynolds, proceeded to the Lynwood Terrace Apartments. The officers saw a brown Plymouth station wagon with a broken right taillight in the parking lot in front of the 235 building. The officers observed [White] leave the 235 building, carrying nothing in her hands, and enter the station wagon. They followed the vehicle as it drove the most direct route to Dobey's Motel. When the vehicle reached the Mobile Highway, on which Dobey's Motel is located, Corporal Reynolds

requested a patrol unit to stop the vehicle. The vehicle was stopped at approximately 4:18 p.m., just short of Dobey's Motel.

Relying heavily upon Illinois v. Gates, reprinted in Chapter 3, the Court held *Gates'* totality of the circumstances approach should be taken, with appropriate accommodation for the less demanding standard applicable in field stop situations. It declined to conclude that an anonymous caller's tip alone could never provide reasonable suspicion. Further, the range of detailed assertions in the tip before it suggested that it was reliable. Nevertheless, the Court—after acknowledging the case was a close one— finally concluded the tip lacked sufficient indicia of reliability to itself constitute reasonable suspicion. But the tip and the officers' corroboration of some information in it adequately supported suspicion White was engaged in criminal activity:

> What was important was the caller's ability to predict [White's] *future behavior,* because it demonstrated inside information—a special familiarity with [White's] affairs. The general public would have no way of knowing that [White] would shortly leave the building, get in the described car, and drive the most direct route to Dobey's Motel. Because only a small number of people are generally privy to an individual's itinerary, it is reasonable for police to believe that a person with access to such information is likely to also have access to reliable information about that individual's illegal activities. When significant aspects of the caller's predictions were verified, there was reason to believe not only that the caller was honest but also that he was well informed, at least well enough to justify the stop.

496 U.S. at 332, 110 S.Ct. at 2417 (emphasis in original).

In Navarette v. California, ___ U.S. ___, 134 S.Ct. 1683 (2014), the Humbolt County, California, 911 team of the California Highway Patrol (CHP) received a call and relayed to a CHP team in neighboring Humboldt County the following message: " 'Showing southbound Highway 1 at mile marker 88, Silver Ford 150 pickup. Plate of 8-David-94925. Ran the reporting party off the roadway and was last seen approximately five [minutes] ago.' " At 3:47 p.m., the information was broadcast to CHP officers. At 4:00 p.m., a CHP officer driving north saw the truck near milemarker 69, followed it for five minutes and then pulled it over. He and another officer approached the truck and after smelling marijuana found 30 pounds of the substance in the bed of the truck. By a 5-to-4 vote, the Court held the stopping officer had reasonable suspicion to believe the driver of the truck stopped had run another vehicle off the road and thus the stop was reasonable. Acknowledging that—as in *White*—the case was a close one, the majority found sufficient indicia of reliability. The apparently anonymous caller claimed eyewitness knowledge of the dangerous driving. She made the report soon after being run off the road and "[t]hat sort of contemporaneous report has long been treated as especially reliable." Further, the caller used the 922 emergency system, which "has some features that allow for identifying and tracing callers, and thus provide some safeguards against making false reports with immunity." In addition, the report concerned not simply completed criminal conduct but ongoing impaired driving that had already resulted in a dangerous incident.

The four *Navarette* dissenters stressed—among other considerations—that the stopping officer's own observations detracted from the credibility of the report. During the five minutes he followed the truck, the officer observed only driving that was irreproachable. Further, "the State offers no evidence to suggest that the [occupants during this time] even did anything *suspicious,* such as suddenly slowing down, pulling off to the side of the road, or turning somewhere to see whether they were being followed." ___ U.S. at ___, 134 S.Ct. at 1696 (Scalia J., dissenting).

A leading decision finding reasonable suspicion lacking is Brown v. Texas, 443 U.S. 47, 99 S.Ct. 2637 (1979). The Court described the facts as follows:

> At 12:45 on the afternoon of December 9, 1977, officers Venegas and Soleto of the El Paso Police Department were cruising in a patrol car. They observed [Brown] and another man walking in opposite directions away from one another in an alley. Although the two men were a few feet apart when they were first seen, officer Venegas later testified that both officers believed the two had been together or were about to meet until the patrol car appeared.

The area had a high incidence of drug traffic. Brown was stopped because, as one officer testified, the situation "looked suspicious" and the officers had never seen Brown in the area before. The Supreme Court held the stop unreasonable:

> Officer Venegas testified at [Brown's] trial that the situation in the alley "looked suspicious," but he was unable to point to any facts supporting that conclusion. There is no indication in the record that it was unusual for people to be in the alley. The fact that [Brown] was in a neighborhood frequented by drug users, standing alone, is not a basis for concluding that [Brown] himself was engaged in criminal conduct. * * * When pressed, Officer Venegas acknowledged that the only reason he stopped [Brown] was to ascertain his identity. The record suggests an understandable desire to assert a police presence; however that purpose does not negate Fourth Amendment guarantees.

443 U.S. at 52, 99 S.Ct. at 2641.

The Supreme Court elaborated on reasonable suspicion analysis in United States v. Arvizu, 534 U.S. 266, 122 S.Ct. 744 (2002). A border patrol agent—Stoddard—stopped Arvizu's minivan on a remote and unpaved road near Douglas, Arizona. After obtaining Arvizu's consent, Stoddard searched the vehicle and found marijuana. The District Court concluded that given all of the circumstances the agent had reasonable suspicion for the stop. Reversing, the Ninth Circuit took a restrictive approach to the issue:

> "What factors law enforcement officers may consider in deciding to stop and question citizens minding their own business should, if possible, be carefully circumscribed and clearly articulated. When courts invoke multi-factor tests, balancing of interests or fact-specific weighing of circumstances, this introduces a troubling degree of uncertainty and unpredictability into the process; no one can be sure whether a particular combination of factors will justify a stop until a court has ruled on it." [*United States v. Montero-Camargo*, 208 F.3d 1122, 1142 (9th Cir.2000) (en banc)] (Kozinski, J. concurring). Thus we attempt here to describe and clearly delimit the extent to which certain factors may be considered by law enforcement officers in making stops such as the stop involved here.

Dividing the factors considered by the District Court into two groups, the Court of Appeals first held that seven were entitled to little or no weight at all. These included Stoddard's testimony that the minivan slowed down when approaching him parked off the road; Stoddard's testimony that the driver failed to acknowledge the parked agent; Stoddard's observation that the children sitting in the back appeared to have their knees at a high level suggesting their feet were on something; and Stoddard's testimony that the children in the van waived at him in an odd manner. Three were properly considered: Stoddard's knowledge that the road was used by persons smuggling illegally entered aliens; observation of the minivan near the time of the border agents' shift chance, a time often chosen by smugglers; and the agent's experience that minivans of the sort driven by Arvizu were often used by smugglers. But these three together were insufficient to constitute reasonable suspicion.

A unanimous Supreme Court reversed, disapproving of the intermediate court's approach to the case:

> When discussing how reviewing courts should make reasonable-suspicion determinations, we have said repeatedly that they must look at the "totality of the circumstances" of each case to see whether the detaining officer has a "particularized and objective basis" for suspecting legal wrongdoing. This process allows officers to draw on their own experience and specialized training to make inferences from and deductions about the cumulative information available to them that "might well elude an untrained person."

> Our cases have recognized that the concept of reasonable suspicion is somewhat abstract. But we have deliberately avoided reducing it to " 'a neat set of legal rules.' " * * *

We think that the approach taken by the Court of Appeals here departs sharply from the teachings of these cases. The court's evaluation and rejection of seven of the listed factors in isolation from each other does not take into account the "totality of the circumstances," as our cases have understood that phrase.

The Court of Appeals' view that it was necessary to "clearly delimit" an officer's consideration of certain factors to reduce "troubling . . . uncertainty," also runs counter to our cases and underestimates the usefulness of the reasonable-suspicion standard in guiding officers in the field. * * *

Having considered the totality of the circumstances and given due weight to the factual inferences drawn by the law enforcement officer and District Court Judge, we hold that Stoddard had reasonable suspicion to believe that [Arvizu] was engaged in illegal activity. It was reasonable for Stoddard to infer from his observations, his registration check, and his experience as a border patrol agent that [Arvizu] had set out from Douglas along a little-traveled route used by smugglers to avoid [a nearby] checkpoint. Stoddard's knowledge further supported a commonsense inference that [Arvizu] intended to pass through the area at a time when officers would be leaving their backroads patrols to change shifts. The likelihood that [Arvizu] and his family were on a picnic outing was diminished by the fact that the minivan had turned away from the known recreational areas accessible to the east on Rucker Canyon Road. Corroborating this inference was the fact that recreational areas farther to the north would have been easier to reach by taking [an alternative route passing through the checkpoint], as opposed to the 40-to-50-mile trip on unpaved and primitive roads. The children's elevated knees suggested the existence of concealed cargo in the passenger compartment. Finally, * * * Stoddard's assessment of [Arvizu]'s reactions upon seeing him and the children's mechanical-like waving, which continued for a full four to five minutes, were entitled to some weight.

[Arvizu] argues that we must rule in his favor because the facts suggested a family in a minivan on a holiday outing. A determination that reasonable suspicion exists, however, need not rule out the possibility of innocent conduct. Undoubtedly, each of these factors alone is susceptible to innocent explanation, and some factors are more probative than others. Taken together, we believe they sufficed to form a particularized and objective basis for Stoddard's stopping the vehicle, making the stop reasonable within the meaning of the Fourth Amendment.

534 U.S. at 273–78, 122 S.Ct. at 750–52.

Officers' Mistake About the Law

An officer may have reasonable suspicion (or even probable cause) despite a mistake about the facts. But what if an officer is mistaken about the law? The issue was presented in Hein v. North Carolina, ___ U.S. ___, 135 S. Ct. 530 (2014). An officer observed a vehicle with two brake lights, only one of which went on when the driver braked. He stopped the car, believing that North Carolina law required two working brake lights, or at least that a vehicle with two brake lights have both of them functioning. As a result of the stop, the officer found cocaine in the stopped vehicle. Later in appellate litigation, the state's statutory law was held to require only one working brake light. Hein, a passenger in the vehicle, was charged with a drug offense and moved to suppress the cocaine. The state courts ultimately held the officer reasonably—but mistakenly—believed the applicable law defined as a crime the operation of a vehicle without two working brake lights and thus—based on his observation—the officer had reasonable suspicion that the driver was committing a traffic offense.

In the Supreme Court, Justice Sotomayor disagreed: "I would hold that determining whether a search or seizure is reasonable requires evaluating an officer's understanding of the facts against the actual state of the law." The rule that officers need not be correct on the facts "has been justified in large part based on the recognition that officers are generally in a superior position, relative to courts, to evaluate those facts and their significance as they unfold. In other words, the leeway we afford officers' factual assessments is rooted not only in our recognition that police officers operating in the field have to make quick decisions but also in our understanding that police officers have the expertise to 'dra[w] inferences and mak[e] deductions . . . that might well elude an untrained person.'" The same, she continued, cannot be said of matters of law:

> After all, the meaning of the law is not probabilistic in the same way that factual determinations are. Rather, "the notion that the law is definite and knowable" sits at the foundation of our legal system. And it is courts, not officers, that are in the best position to interpret the laws.

___ U.S. at ___, 135 S.Ct. at 543 (Sotomayor, J., dissenting). She added that an officer's mistake of law will often be relevant to whether a situation is covered by "the exception to the exclusionary rule for good-faith police errors." ___ U.S. at ___, 135 S.Ct. at 544.

An eight-justice majority rejected Justice Sotomayor's analysis. It explained:

> The question here is whether reasonable suspicion can rest on a mistaken understanding of the scope of a legal prohibition. We hold that it can.
>
> As * * * we have repeatedly affirmed, "the ultimate touchstone of the Fourth Amendment is 'reasonableness.'" To

be reasonable is not to be perfect, and so the Fourth Amendment allows for some mistakes on the part of government officials, giving them "fair leeway for enforcing the law in the community's protection." We have recognized that searches and seizures based on mistakes of fact can be reasonable. * * * The limit is that "the mistakes must be those of reasonable men."

But reasonable men make mistakes of law, too, and such mistakes are no less compatible with the concept of reasonable suspicion. Reasonable suspicion arises from the combination of an officer's understanding of the facts and his understanding of the relevant law. The officer may be reasonably mistaken on either ground. Whether the facts turn out to be not what was thought, or the law turns out to be not what was thought, the result is the same: the facts are outside the scope of the law. There is no reason, under the text of the Fourth Amendment or our precedents, why this same result should be acceptable when reached by way of a reasonable mistake of fact, but not when reached by way of a similarly reasonable mistake of law.

___ U.S. at ___, 135 S.Ct. at 536.

Justice Kagen, joined by Justice Ginsburg, wrote separately to stress several points, including her perception of the standard for determining whether an officer reasonably believed the law covered the facts:

A court tasked with deciding whether an officer's mistake of law can support a seizure * * * faces a straightforward question of statutory construction. If the statute is genuinely ambiguous, such that overturning the officer's judgment requires hard interpretive work, then the officer has made a reasonable mistake. But if not, not. As the Solicitor General made the point at oral argument, the statute must pose a "really difficult" or "very hard question of statutory interpretation." And indeed, both North Carolina and the Solicitor General agreed that such cases will be "exceedingly rare."

___ U.S. at ___, 135 S.Ct. at 541 (Kagen, J., concurring).

Illinois v. Wardlow

Supreme Court of the United States, 2000.
528 U.S. 119, 120 S.Ct. 673.

■ CHIEF JUSTICE REHNQUIST delivered the opinion of the Court.

Respondent Wardlow fled upon seeing police officers patrolling an area known for heavy narcotics trafficking. Two of the officers caught up with him, stopped him and conducted a protective pat-down search for weapons. Discovering a .38-caliber handgun, the officers arrested Wardlow. * * *

On September 9, 1995, Officers Nolan and Harvey were working as uniformed officers in the special operations section of the Chicago Police Department. The officers were driving the last car of a four car caravan converging on an area known for heavy narcotics trafficking in order to investigate drug transactions. The officers were traveling together because they expected to find a crowd of people in the area, including lookouts and customers.

As the caravan passed 4035 West Van Buren, Officer Nolan observed respondent Wardlow standing next to the building holding an opaque bag. Respondent looked in the direction of the officers and fled. Nolan and Harvey turned their car southbound, watched him as he ran through the gangway and an alley, and eventually cornered him on the street. Nolan then exited his car and stopped respondent. He immediately conducted a protective pat-down search for weapons because in his experience it was common for there to be weapons in the near vicinity of narcotics transactions. During the frisk, Officer Nolan squeezed the bag respondent was carrying and felt a heavy, hard object similar to the shape of a gun. The officer then opened the bag and discovered a .38-caliber handgun with five live rounds of ammunition. The officers arrested Wardlow.

The Illinois trial court denied respondent's motion to suppress, finding the gun was recovered during a lawful stop and frisk. Following a stipulated bench trial, Wardlow was convicted of unlawful use of a weapon by a felon. The Illinois [courts] reversed Wardlow's conviction, concluding that the gun should have been suppressed because Officer Nolan did not have reasonable suspicion sufficient to justify an investigative stop pursuant to *Terry v. Ohio*, 392 U.S. 1, 88 S.Ct. 1868, 20 L.Ed.2d 889 (1968).

* * *

This case, involving a brief encounter between a citizen and a police officer on a public street, is governed by the analysis we first applied in *Terry*. In *Terry*, we held that an officer may, consistent with the Fourth Amendment, conduct a brief, investigatory stop when the officer has a reasonable, articulable suspicion that criminal activity is afoot. While "reasonable suspicion" is a less demanding standard than probable cause and requires a showing considerably less than preponderance of the evidence, the Fourth Amendment requires at least a minimal level of objective justification for making the stop. The officer must be able to articulate more than an "inchoate and unparticularized suspicion or 'hunch' " of criminal activity.[2]

Nolan and Harvey were among eight officers in a four car caravan that was converging on an area known for heavy narcotics trafficking,

---

[2]   We granted certiorari solely on the question of whether the initial stop was supported by reasonable suspicion. Therefore, we express no opinion as to the lawfulness of the frisk independently of the stop.

and the officers anticipated encountering a large number of people in the area, including drug customers and individuals serving as lookouts. It was in this context that Officer Nolan decided to investigate Wardlow after observing him flee. An individual's presence in an area of expected criminal activity, standing alone, is not enough to support a reasonable, particularized suspicion that the person is committing a crime. But officers are not required to ignore the relevant characteristics of a location in determining whether the circumstances are sufficiently suspicious to warrant further investigation. Accordingly, we have previously noted the fact that the stop occurred in a "high crime area" among the relevant contextual considerations in a *Terry* analysis. *Adams v. Williams*, 407 U.S. 143, 144 and 147–148, 92 S.Ct. 1921, 32 L.Ed.2d 612 (1972).

In this case, moreover, it was not merely respondent's presence in an area of heavy narcotics trafficking that aroused the officers' suspicion but his unprovoked flight upon noticing the police. Our cases have also recognized that nervous, evasive behavior is a pertinent factor in determining reasonable suspicion. Headlong flight—wherever it occurs— is the consummate act of evasion: it is not necessarily indicative of wrongdoing, but it is certainly suggestive of such. In reviewing the propriety of an officer's conduct, courts do not have available empirical studies dealing with inferences drawn from suspicious behavior, and we cannot reasonably demand scientific certainty from judges or law enforcement officers where none exists. Thus, the determination of reasonable suspicion must be based on commonsense judgments and inferences about human behavior. We conclude Officer Nolan was justified in suspecting that Wardlow was involved in criminal activity, and, therefore, in investigating further.

Such a holding is entirely consistent with our decision in *Florida v. Royer*, 460 U.S. 491, 103 S.Ct. 1319, 75 L.Ed.2d 229 (1983), where we held that when an officer, without reasonable suspicion or probable cause, approaches an individual, the individual has a right to ignore the police and go about his business. And any "refusal to cooperate, without more, does not furnish the minimal level of objective justification needed for a detention or seizure." But unprovoked flight is simply not a mere refusal to cooperate. Flight, by its very nature, is not "going about one's business"; in fact, it is just the opposite. Allowing officers confronted with such flight to stop the fugitive and investigate further is quite consistent with the individual's right to go about his business or to stay put and remain silent in the face of police questioning.

Respondent and *amici* also argue that there are innocent reasons for flight from police and that, therefore, flight is not necessarily indicative of ongoing criminal activity. This fact is undoubtedly true, but does not establish a violation of the Fourth Amendment. Even in *Terry*, the conduct justifying the stop was ambiguous and susceptible of an innocent explanation. The officer observed two individuals pacing back and forth in front of a store, peering into the window and periodically conferring. All of this conduct was by itself lawful, but it also suggested that the individuals were casing the store for a planned robbery. *Terry* recognized that the officers could detain the individuals to resolve the ambiguity.

In allowing such detentions, *Terry* accepts the risk that officers may stop innocent people. Indeed, the Fourth Amendment accepts that risk in connection with more drastic police action; persons arrested and detained on probable cause to believe they have committed a crime may turn out to be innocent. The *Terry* stop is a far more minimal intrusion, simply allowing the officer to briefly investigate further. If the officer does not learn facts rising to the level of probable cause, the individual must be allowed to go on his way. But in this case the officers found respondent in possession of a handgun, and arrested him for violation of an Illinois firearms statute. No question of the propriety of the arrest itself is before us.

The judgment of the Supreme Court of Illinois is reversed, and the cause is remanded for further proceedings not inconsistent with this opinion.

It is so ordered.

■ JUSTICE STEVENS, with whom JUSTICE SOUTER, JUSTICE GINSBURG, and JUSTICE BREYER join, concurring in part and dissenting in part.

The State of Illinois asks this Court to announce a "bright-line rule" authorizing the temporary detention of anyone who flees at the mere sight of a police officer. Respondent counters by asking us to adopt the opposite *per se* rule—that the fact that a person flees upon seeing the police can never, by itself, be sufficient to justify a temporary investigative stop * * * .

The Court today wisely endorses neither *per se* rule. Instead, it rejects the proposition that "flight is . . . necessarily indicative of ongoing criminal activity," adhering to the view that "[t]he concept of reasonable suspicion . . . is not readily, or even usefully, reduced to a neat set of legal rules," but must be determined by looking to "the totality of the circumstances—the whole picture." Abiding by this framework, the Court concludes that "Officer Nolan was justified in suspecting that Wardlow was involved in criminal activity."

Although I agree with the Court's rejection of the *per se* rules proffered by the parties, unlike the Court, I am persuaded that in this case the brief testimony of the officer who seized respondent does not justify the conclusion that he had reasonable suspicion to make the stop. * * *

Guided by [its] totality-of-the-circumstances test, the Court concludes that Officer Nolan had reasonable suspicion to stop respondent. In this respect, my view differs from the Court's. The entire justification for the stop is articulated in the brief testimony of Officer

Nolan. Some facts are perfectly clear; others are not. This factual insufficiency leads me to conclude that the Court's judgment is mistaken.

Respondent Wardlow was arrested a few minutes after noon on September 9, 1995. Nolan was part of an eight-officer, four-car caravan patrol team. The officers were headed for "one of the areas in the 11th District [of Chicago] that's high [in] narcotics traffic." The reason why four cars were in the caravan was that "[n]ormally in these different areas there's an enormous amount of people, sometimes lookouts, customers." Officer Nolan testified that he was in uniform on that day, but he did not recall whether he was driving a marked or an unmarked car.

Officer Nolan and his partner were in the last of the four patrol cars that "were all caravaning eastbound down Van Buren." Nolan first observed respondent "in front of 4035 West Van Buren." Wardlow "looked in our direction and began fleeing." Nolan then "began driving southbound down the street observing [respondent] running through the gangway and the alley southbound," and observed that Wardlow was carrying a white, opaque bag under his arm. After the car turned south and intercepted respondent as he "ran right towards us," Officer Nolan stopped him and conducted a "protective search," which revealed that the bag under respondent's arm contained a loaded handgun.

This terse testimony is most noticeable for what it fails to reveal. Though asked whether he was in a marked or unmarked car, Officer Nolan could not recall the answer. He was not asked whether any of the other three cars in the caravan were marked, or whether any of the other seven officers were in uniform. Though he explained that the size of the caravan was because "[n]ormally in these different areas there's an enormous amount of people, sometimes lookouts, customers," Officer Nolan did not testify as to whether anyone besides Wardlow was nearby 4035 West Van Buren. Nor is it clear that that address was the intended destination of the caravan. As the Appellate Court of Illinois interpreted the record, "it appears that the officers were simply driving by, on their way to some unidentified location, when they noticed defendant standing at 4035 West Van Buren."[16] Officer Nolan's testimony also does not reveal how fast the officers were driving. It does not indicate whether he saw respondent notice the other patrol cars. And it does not say whether the caravan, or any part of it, had already passed Wardlow by before he began to run.

* * *

No other factors sufficiently support a finding of reasonable suspicion. Though respondent was carrying a white, opaque bag under his arm, there is nothing at all suspicious about that. Certainly the time

---

[16] Of course, it would be a different case if the officers had credible information respecting that specific street address which reasonably led them to believe that criminal activity was afoot in that narrowly defined area.

of day—shortly after noon—does not support Illinois' argument. Nor were the officers "responding to any call or report of suspicious activity in the area." Officer Nolan did testify that he expected to find "an enormous amount of people," including drug customers or lookouts, and the Court points out that "[i]t was in this context that Officer Nolan decided to investigate Wardlow after observing him flee." This observation, in my view, lends insufficient weight to the reasonable suspicion analysis; indeed, in light of the absence of testimony that anyone else was nearby when respondent began to run, this observation points in the opposite direction.

The State, along with the majority of the Court, relies as well on the assumption that this flight occurred in a high crime area. Even if that assumption is accurate, it is insufficient because even in a high crime neighborhood unprovoked flight does not invariably lead to reasonable suspicion. On the contrary, because many factors providing innocent motivations for unprovoked flight are concentrated in high crime areas, the character of the neighborhood arguably makes an inference of guilt less appropriate, rather than more so. Like unprovoked flight itself, presence in a high crime neighborhood is a fact too generic and susceptible to innocent explanation to satisfy the reasonable suspicion inquiry.

It is the State's burden to articulate facts sufficient to support reasonable suspicion. In my judgment, Illinois has failed to discharge that burden. I am not persuaded that the mere fact that someone standing on a sidewalk looked in the direction of a passing car before starting to run is sufficient to justify a forcible stop and frisk.

I therefore respectfully dissent from the Court's judgment to reverse the court below.

EDITORS' NOTE: STOPS FOR MINOR, POSSESSORY, PAST AND FUTURE OFFENSES

Are stops on reasonable suspicion reasonable if that reasonable suspicion concerns certain minor or possessory offenses, completed offenses, or those not actually begun? In United States v. Hensley, 469 U.S. 221, 105 S.Ct. 675 (1985), discussed later in this Note, the Court was careful to limit its approval of investigatory stops to those involving past *serious* offenses—those constituting felonies. "We need not and do not decide today," it commented, "whether *Terry* stops to investigate all past crimes, however serious, are permitted."

Possessory Offenses

The nature of some offenses may suggest too high a risk that *Terry* stops to investigate them might be abused. In Adams v. Williams, 407 U.S. 143, 92 S.Ct. 1921 (1972), the officer's suspicion concerned the suspect's possible commission of crimes consisting of possessing items— possession of drugs and possession of a prohibited weapon. One of the judges in the Court of Appeals urged stops not be permitted for such possessory crimes. "There is too much danger," he reasoned, "that, instead of the stop being the object and the protective frisk an incident thereto, the reverse will be true." Williams v. Adams, 436 F.2d 30, 38 (2d Cir.1970) (Friendly, J., dissenting), reversed 441 F.2d 394 (2d Cir.1971) (en banc) (per curiam). Justice Brennan adopted this position in the Supreme Court. 407 U.S. at 151–53, 92 S.Ct. at 1926–27 (Brennan, J., dissenting). The opinion of the Court, written by then-Justice Rehnquist, did not address the matter.

Reasonable Suspicion Concerning Past and Future Offenses

The Court has somewhat offhanded suggested *Terry* and later decisions settled the constitutionality of investigatory stops for past and future offenses as well as those being committed at the time of the stop. "Under the Fourth Amendment [ ] we have held," the Court commented in Berkemer v. McCarty, 468 U.S. 420, 439, 104 S.Ct. 3138, 3150 (1984), "a policeman who lacks probable cause but whose 'observations lead him reasonably to suspect' that a particular person has committed, is committing, or is about to commit a crime, may detain that person briefly in order to 'investigate the circumstances that provoke suspicion.'"

Until United States v. Hensley, 469 U.S. 221, 105 S.Ct. 675 (1985), however, the cases decided by the Court—many of which were discussed earlier in this chapter—all involved situations in which the suspected criminal activity was yet to be completed when the officers intervened. In *Hensley*, the Court acknowledged it had never actually held a nonarrest *Terry* stop constitutionally permissible on probable cause to believe the suspect had committed an offense in the past. Hensley had been stopped on reasonable suspicion that he had been involved in a robbery committed twelve days earlier. The Court treated the question whether stops for investigation are permissible for completed past offenses as a significant one, and addressed the matter at length. Application of the balancing analysis used to determine the reasonableness of nonarrest stops, it acknowledged, must be somewhat different in past crime situations:

> The factors in the balance may be somewhat different when a stop to investigate past criminal activity is involved rather than a stop to investigate ongoing criminal conduct. * * * [O]ne general interest present in the context of ongoing or imminent criminal activity is "that of effective crime prevention and detention." A stop to investigate an already completed crime does not necessarily promote the interest of crime prevention as directly as a stop to investigate suspected ongoing criminal activity. Similarly, the exigent circumstances which require a police officer to step in before a crime is committed or completed are not necessarily as pressing long afterwards. Public safety may be less threatened by a suspect in a past crime who now appears to be going about his lawful business than it is by a

suspect who is currently in the process of violating the law. Finally, officers making a stop to investigate past crimes may have a wider range of opportunity to choose the time and circumstances of the stop.

469 U.S. at 228–29, 105 S.Ct. at 680. Nevertheless, the Court concluded in some situations the law enforcement interests at stake outweigh the interests of individuals in being free of relatively nonintrusive *Terry* stops. Disclaiming a decision on whether its holding would apply to less serious crimes, the Court concluded that "if police have a reasonable suspicion, grounded in specific and articulable facts, that a person they encounter was involved in or is wanted in connection with a completed felony, then a *Terry* stop may be made to investigate that suspicion."

Neither *Hensley* nor any other of the Court's decisions has actually passed on the reasonableness of an investigatory stop based on reasonable suspicion the person would commit a crime *in the future*. *Hensley* characterized *Terry* itself as a case in which "police stopped or seized a person because they suspected he was about to commit a crime." But *Terry* in fact passed only on the seizure of Terry to the extent necessary to conduct the weapons search. Arguably the Court was careful to avoid, at this early stage in the development of nonarrest detention law, any definitive decision on stops to investigate concern that a person will commit a future crime. In *Terry*'s companion cases, the parties sought to have the Court pass on the constitutionality of New York's "stop-and-frisk" law, set out earlier in the Editors' Introduction to Subchapter C of this chapter, which authorized an officer to stop a person "whom [the officer] reasonably suspects is committing, has committed or *is about to commit*" one of the specific offenses. In neither case, however, did the Court address the facial validity of the statute generally or, in particular, the authorization to stop those reasonably suspected of being "about to commit" an offense.

If officers are permitted by the Fourth Amendment to make investigatory stops regarding future offenses, whether *Terry*'s facts justified such a stop arguably presented a quite difficult question. The Supreme Court acknowledged the reasonableness of detentions on less than probable cause only in the 1968 trilogy of decisions. It may have believed that the courts should have more opportunity to address investigatory stop situations before the Supreme Court resolved particularly difficult subquestions concerning the scope of the stop authority. The facts of *Terry* were as follows:

> Officer McFadden testified that while he was patrolling in plain clothes in downtown Cleveland at approximately 2:30 in the afternoon of October 31, 1963, his attention was attracted by two men, Chilton and Terry, standing on the corner of Huron Road and Euclid Avenue. He had never seen the two men before, and he was unable to say precisely what first drew his eye to them. However, he testified that he had been a policeman for 39

years and a detective for 35 and that he had been assigned to patrol this vicinity of downtown Cleveland for shoplifters and pickpockets for 30 years. He explained that he had developed routine habits of observation over the years and that he would "stand and watch people or walk and watch people at many intervals of the day." He added: "Now, in this case when I looked over they didn't look right to me at the time."

His interest aroused, Officer McFadden took up a post of observation in the entrance to a store 300 to 400 feet away from the two men. "I get more purpose to watch them when I seen their movements,' " he testified. He saw one of the men leave the other one and walk southwest on Huron Road, past some stores. The man paused for a moment and looked in a store window, then walked on a short distance, turned around and walked back toward the corner, pausing once again to look in the same store window. He rejoined his companion at the corner, and the two conferred briefly. Then the second man went through the same series of motions, strolling down Huron Road, looking in the same window, walking on a short distance, turning back, peering in the store window again, and returning to confer with the first man at the corner. The two men repeated this ritual alternately between five and six times apiece—in all, roughly a dozen trips. At one point, while the two were standing together on the corner, a third man approached them and engaged them briefly in conversation. This man then left the two others and walked west on Euclid Avenue. Chilton and Terry resumed their measured pacing, peering and conferring. After this had gone on for 10 to 12 minutes, the two men walked off together, heading west on Euclid Avenue, following the path taken earlier by the third man. By this time Officer McFadden had become thoroughly suspicious. He testified that after observing their elaborately casual and oft-repeated reconnaissance of the store window on Huron Road, he suspected the two men of "casing a job, a stick-up," and that he considered it his duty as a police officer to investigate further. He added that he feared "they may have a gun." Thus, Officer McFadden followed Chilton and Terry and saw them stop in front of Zucker's store to talk to the same man who had conferred with them earlier on the street corner. Deciding that the situation was ripe for direct action, Officer McFadden approached the three men, identified himself as a police officer and asked for their names. At this point his knowledge was confined to what he had observed. He was not acquainted with any of the three men by name or by sight, and he had received no information concerning them from any other source. When the men "mumbled something" in response to his inquiries, Officer McFadden grabbed petitioner Terry, spun him around so that they were facing the other two, with Terry between McFadden and the others, and patted down the outside of his clothing. In the left breast pocket of Terry's overcoat Officer McFadden felt a pistol. He reached inside the overcoat pocket, but was unable to remove the gun. At this point, keeping Terry between himself and the others, the officer ordered all three men to enter Zucker's store. As they went in, he removed Terry's overcoat completely, removed a .38-caliber revolver from the pocket and ordered all three men to face the wall with their hands raised. Officer McFadden proceeded to pat down the outer clothing of Chilton and the third man, Katz. He discovered another revolver in the outer pocket of Chilton's overcoat, but no weapons were found on Katz. The officer testified that he only patted the men down to see whether they had weapons, and that he did not put his hands beneath the outer garments of either Terry or Chilton until he felt their guns. So far as appears from the record, he never placed his hands beneath Katz' outer garments. Officer McFadden seized Chilton's gun, asked the proprietor of the store to call a police wagon, and took all three men to the station, where Chilton and Terry were formally charged with carrying concealed weapons.

If McFadden seized Terry when he confronted him and his companions in front of Zucker's store and requested their names, was that stop constitutionally permissible? Finding McFadden could constitutionally search the trio for weapons, the Court explained:

> [O]n the facts and circumstances Officer McFadden detailed before the trial judge a reasonably prudent man would have been warranted in believing petitioner was armed and thus presented a threat to the officer's safety while he was investigating his suspicious behavior. The actions of Terry and Chilton were consistent with McFadden's hypothesis that these men were contemplating a daylight robbery—which, it is reasonable to assume, would be likely to involve the use of weapons—and nothing in their conduct from the time he first noticed them until the time he confronted them and identified himself as a police officer gave him sufficient reason to negate that hypothesis. Although the trio had departed the original scene, there was nothing to indicate abandonment of an intent to commit a robbery at some point. Thus, when Officer McFadden approached the three men gathered before the display window at Zucker's store he had observed enough to make it quite reasonable to fear that they were armed * * * .

392 U.S. at 28, 88 S.Ct. at 1883. The Court did not, however, reach whether McFadden could seize Terry to question him about any plans he might have had to commit robbery.

Perhaps the difficulty of predicting whether suspects will commit future crimes means that stops on reasonable suspicion this will occur are unacceptable. Or, perhaps such stops are acceptable only if an officer has reasonable suspicion the suspect is—in the words of the New York statute—*about to* commit an offense. Arguably predictions concerning whether suspects will quite soon engage in criminal activity are more accurate than other predictions, and therefore only stops for relatively imminent future offenses are reasonable. If investigatory stops are permissible only upon reasonable suspicion that the suspect is about to commit an offense, could McFadden have reasonably suspected that Terry and his companions were *about to* commit the robbery McFadden reasonably suspected the three had in mind?

c.   SEEKING IDENTIFICATION DURING FIELD STOPS

What if any limits are placed on officers' ability to question a person stopped on reasonable suspicion is addressed in Chapter 6 on Interrogation and Confessions. Arguably, officers' authority to seek identifying information from such a suspect is a different matter.

Hiibel v. Sixth Judicial District Court of Nevada, Humboldt County, et al.

Supreme Court of the United States, 2004.
542 U.S. 177, 124 S.Ct. 2451.

■ JUSTICE KENNEDY delivered the opinion of the Court.

The petitioner was arrested and convicted for refusing to identify himself during a stop allowed by *Terry v. Ohio,* 392 U.S. 1, 88 S.Ct. 1868, 20 L.Ed.2d 889 (1968). He challenges his conviction under the Fourth and Fifth Amendments to the United States Constitution, applicable to the States through the Fourteenth Amendment.

I

The sheriff's department in Humboldt County, Nevada, received an afternoon telephone call reporting an assault. The caller reported seeing a man assault a woman in a red and silver GMC truck on Grass Valley Road. Deputy Sheriff Lee Dove was dispatched to investigate. When the officer arrived at the scene, he found the truck parked on the side of the road. A man was standing by the truck, and a young woman was sitting inside it. The officer observed skid marks in the gravel behind the vehicle, leading him to believe it had come to a sudden stop.

The officer approached the man and explained that he was investigating a report of a fight. The man appeared to be intoxicated. The officer asked him if he had "any identification on [him]," which we understand as a request to produce a driver's license or some other form of written identification. The man refused and asked why the officer wanted to see identification. The officer responded that he was conducting an investigation and needed to see some identification. The unidentified man became agitated and insisted he had done nothing wrong. The officer explained that he wanted to find out who the man was and what he was doing there. After continued refusals to comply with the officer's request for identification, the man began to taunt the officer by placing his hands behind his back and telling the officer to arrest him and take him to jail. This routine kept up for several minutes: the officer asked for identification 11 times and was refused each time. After warning the man that he would be arrested if he continued to refuse to comply, the officer placed him under arrest.

We now know that the man arrested on Grass Valley Road is Larry Dudley Hiibel. Hiibel was charged with "willfully resist[ing], delay[ing], or obstruct[ing] a public officer in discharging or attempting to discharge any legal duty of his office" in violation of Nev.Rev.Stat. (NRS) § 199.280 (2003). The government reasoned that Hiibel had obstructed the officer in carrying out his duties under § 171.123, a Nevada statute that defines the legal rights and duties of a police officer in the context of an investigative stop. Section 171.123 provides in relevant part:

> "1. Any peace officer may detain any person whom the officer encounters under circumstances which reasonably indicate that the person has committed, is committing or is about to commit a crime.
>
> . . .
>
> "3. The officer may detain the person pursuant to this section only to ascertain his identity and the suspicious circumstances surrounding his presence abroad. Any person so detained shall identify himself, but may not be compelled to answer any other inquiry of any peace officer."

Hiibel was tried in the Justice Court of Union Township. The court agreed that Hiibel's refusal to identify himself as required by § 171.123 "obstructed and delayed Dove as a public officer in attempting to discharge his duty" in violation of § 199.280. Hiibel was convicted and fined $250. The Sixth Judicial District Court affirmed, rejecting Hiibel's argument that the application of § 171.123 to his case violated the Fourth and Fifth Amendments. On review the Supreme Court of Nevada [also affirmed]. We granted certiorari.

II

NRS § 171.123(3) is an enactment sometimes referred to as a "stop and identify" statute.

Stop and identify statutes often combine elements of traditional vagrancy laws with provisions intended to regulate police behavior in the course of investigatory stops. The statutes vary from State to State, but all permit an officer to ask or require a suspect to disclose his identity. * * * In some States, a suspect's refusal to identify himself is a misdemeanor offense or civil violation; in others, it is a factor to be considered in whether the suspect has violated loitering laws. In other States, a suspect may decline to identify himself without penalty.

* * *

The Court has recognized * * * constitutional limitations on the scope and operation of stop and identify statutes. In *Brown v. Texas,* 443 U.S. 47, 52, 99 S.Ct. 2637, 61 L.Ed.2d 357 (1979), the Court invalidated a conviction for violating a Texas stop and identify statute on Fourth Amendment grounds. The Court ruled that the initial stop was not based on specific, objective facts establishing reasonable suspicion to believe the suspect was involved in criminal activity. Absent that factual basis for detaining the defendant, the Court held, the risk of "arbitrary and abusive police practices" was too great and the stop was impermissible. Four Terms later, the Court invalidated a modified stop and identify statute on vagueness grounds. See *Kolender v. Lawson,* 461 U.S. 352, 103 S.Ct. 1855, 75 L.Ed.2d 903 (1983). The California law in *Kolender* required a suspect to give an officer " 'credible and reliable' " identification when asked to identify himself. The Court held that the statute was void because it provided no standard for determining what a suspect must do to comply with it, resulting in " 'virtually unrestrained power to arrest and charge persons with a violation.' "

The present case begins where our prior cases left off. Here there is no question that the initial stop was based on reasonable suspicion, satisfying the Fourth Amendment requirements noted in *Brown.* Further, the petitioner has not alleged that the statute is unconstitutionally vague, as in *Kolender.* Here the Nevada statute is narrower and more precise. The statute in *Kolender* had been interpreted to require a suspect to give the officer "credible and reliable" identification. In contrast, the Nevada Supreme Court has interpreted NRS § 171.123(3) to require only that a suspect disclose his name. As we understand it, the statute does not require a suspect to give the officer a driver's license or any other document. Provided that the suspect either states his name or communicates it to the officer by other means—a choice, we assume, that the suspect may make—the statute is satisfied and no violation occurs.

III

Hiibel argues that his conviction cannot stand because the officer's conduct violated his Fourth Amendment rights. We disagree.

* * *

Obtaining a suspect's name in the course of a *Terry* stop serves important government interests. Knowledge of identity may inform an officer that a suspect is wanted for another offense, or has a record of violence or mental disorder. On the other hand, knowing identity may help clear a suspect and allow the police to concentrate their efforts elsewhere. Identity may prove particularly important in cases such as this, where the police are investigating what appears to be a domestic assault. Officers called to investigate domestic disputes need to know whom they are dealing with in order to assess the situation, the threat to their own safety, and possible danger to the potential victim.

Although it is well established that an officer may ask a suspect to identify himself in the course of a *Terry* stop, it has been an open question whether the suspect can be arrested and prosecuted for refusal to answer. * * *

[T]he Fourth Amendment does not impose obligations on the citizen but instead provides rights against the government. As a result, the Fourth Amendment itself cannot require a suspect to answer questions. This case concerns a different issue, however. Here, the source of the legal obligation arises from Nevada state law, not the Fourth Amendment. Further, the statutory obligation does not go beyond answering an officer's request to disclose a name. * * *

The principles of *Terry* permit a State to require a suspect to disclose his name in the course of a *Terry* stop. The reasonableness of a seizure under the Fourth Amendment is determined "by balancing its intrusion on the individual's Fourth Amendment interests against its promotion of legitimate government interests." *Delaware v. Prouse,* 440 U.S. 648, 654, 99 S.Ct. 1391, 59 L.Ed.2d 660 (1979). The Nevada statute satisfies that standard. The request for identity has an immediate relation to the purpose, rationale, and practical demands of a *Terry* stop. The threat of criminal sanction helps ensure that the request for identity does not become a legal nullity. On the other hand, the Nevada statute does not alter the nature of the stop itself: it does not change its duration. A state law requiring a suspect to disclose his name in the course of a valid *Terry* stop is consistent with Fourth Amendment prohibitions against unreasonable searches and seizures.

Petitioner argues that the Nevada statute circumvents the probable cause requirement, in effect allowing an officer to arrest a person for being suspicious. According to petitioner, this creates a risk of arbitrary police conduct that the Fourth Amendment does not permit. * * * Petitioner's concerns are met by the requirement that a *Terry* stop must be justified at its inception and "reasonably related in scope to the circumstances which justified" the initial stop. Under these principles, an officer may not arrest a suspect for failure to identify himself if the request for identification is not reasonably related to the circumstances justifying the stop. * * * It is clear in this case that the request for identification was "reasonably related in scope to the circumstances which justified" the stop. The officer's request was a commonsense inquiry, not an effort to obtain an arrest for failure to identify after a *Terry* stop yielded insufficient evidence. The stop, the request, and the State's requirement of a response did not contravene the guarantees of the Fourth Amendment.

IV

Petitioner further contends that his conviction violates the Fifth Amendment's prohibition on compelled self-incrimination. The Fifth Amendment states that "[n]o person . . . shall be compelled in any criminal case to be a witness against himself." To qualify for the Fifth Amendment privilege, a communication must be testimonial, incriminating, and compelled. See *United States v. Hubbell,* 530 U.S. 27, 34–38, 120 S.Ct. 2037, 147 L.Ed.2d 24 (2000).

Respondents urge us to hold that the statements NRS § 171.123(3) requires are nontestimonial, and so outside the Clause's scope. We decline to resolve the case on that basis. "[T]o be testimonial, an accused's communication must itself, explicitly or implicitly, relate a factual assertion or disclose information." *Doe v. United States,* 487 U.S. 201, 210, 108 S.Ct. 2341, 101 L.Ed.2d 184 (1988). Stating one's name may qualify as an assertion of fact relating to identity. Production of identity documents might meet the definition as well. As we noted in *Hubbell,* acts of production may yield testimony establishing "the existence, authenticity, and custody of items [the police seek]." Even if these required actions are testimonial, however, petitioner's challenge must fail because in this case disclosure of his name presented no reasonable danger of incrimination.

The Fifth Amendment * * * "protects against any disclosures that the witness reasonably believes could be used in a criminal prosecution or could lead to other evidence that might be so used." * * *

In this case petitioner's refusal to disclose his name was not based on any articulated real and appreciable fear that his name would be used to incriminate him, or that it "would furnish a link in the chain of evidence needed to prosecute" him. *Hoffman v. United States,* 341 U.S. 479, 486, 71 S.Ct. 814, 95 L.Ed. 1118 (1951). As best we can tell, petitioner refused to identify himself only because he thought his name was none of the officer's business. Even today, petitioner does not explain how the disclosure of his name could have been used against him in a criminal case. While we recognize petitioner's strong belief that he should not have to disclose his identity, the Fifth Amendment does not override the Nevada Legislature's judgment to the contrary absent a reasonable belief that the disclosure would tend to incriminate him.

The narrow scope of the disclosure requirement is also important. One's identity is, by definition, unique; yet it is, in another sense, a universal characteristic. Answering a request to disclose a name is likely to be so insignificant in the scheme of things as to be incriminating only in unusual circumstances. In every criminal case, it is known and must be known who has been arrested and who is being tried. Even witnesses who plan to invoke the Fifth Amendment privilege answer when their names are called to take the stand. Still, a case may arise where there is a substantial allegation that furnishing identity at the time of a stop would have given the police a link in the chain of evidence needed to convict the individual of a separate offense. In that case, the court can then consider whether the privilege applies, and, if the Fifth Amendment has been violated, what remedy must follow. We need not resolve those questions here.

The judgment of the Nevada Supreme Court is

Affirmed.

■ JUSTICE STEVENS, dissenting.

* * * [T]he broad constitutional right to remain silent, which derives from the Fifth Amendment's guarantee that "[n]o person . . . shall be compelled in any criminal case to be a witness against himself," U.S. Const., Amdt. 5, is not as circumscribed as the Court suggests, and does not admit even of the narrow exception defined by the Nevada statute.

* * * The protections of the Fifth Amendment are directed squarely toward those who are the focus of the government's investigative and prosecutorial powers. In a criminal trial, the indicted defendant has an unqualified right to refuse to testify and may not be punished for invoking that right. The unindicted target of a grand jury investigation enjoys the same constitutional protection even if he has been served with a subpoena. So does an arrested suspect during custodial interrogation in a police station.

There is no reason why the subject of police interrogation based on mere suspicion, rather than probable cause, should have any lesser protection. * * *

The * * * compelled statement at issue in this case is clearly testimonial. * * *

[T]he Court * * * concludes that the State can compel the disclosure of one's identity because it is not "incriminating." But our cases have afforded Fifth Amendment protection to statements that are "incriminating" in a much broader sense than the Court suggests. * * * By "incriminating" we have meant disclosures that "could be used in a criminal prosecution or could lead to other evidence that might be so used,"—communications, in other words, that "would furnish a link in the chain of evidence needed to prosecute the claimant for a federal crime," *Hoffman v. United States,* 341 U.S. 479, 486, 71 S.Ct. 814, 95 L.Ed. 1118 (1951). Thus, "[c]ompelled testimony that communicates information that may 'lead to incriminating evidence' is privileged even if the information itself is not inculpatory."

[I]t is clear that the disclosure of petitioner's identity is protected. The Court reasons that we should not assume that the disclosure of petitioner's name would be used to incriminate him or that it would furnish a link in a chain of evidence needed to prosecute him. But why else would an officer ask for it? * * *

A person's identity obviously bears informational and incriminating worth, "even if the [name] itself is not inculpatory." A name can provide the key to a broad array of information about the person, particularly in the hands of a police officer with access to a range of law enforcement databases. And that information, in turn, can be tremendously useful in a criminal prosecution. It is therefore quite wrong to suggest that a person's identity provides a link in the chain to incriminating evidence "only in unusual circumstances."

The officer in this case told petitioner, in the Court's words, that "he was conducting an investigation and needed to see some identification." As the target of that investigation, petitioner, in my view, acted well within his rights when he opted to stand mute. Accordingly, I respectfully dissent.

■ JUSTICE BREYER, with whom JUSTICE SOUTER and JUSTICE GINSBURG join, dissenting.

[P]olice may conduct a *Terry* stop only within circumscribed limits. And one of those limits invalidates laws that compel responses to police questioning.

* * * [In 1984] the Court wrote that an "officer may ask the [*Terry*] detainee a moderate number of questions to determine his identity and to try to obtain information confirming or dispelling the officer's suspicions. *But the detainee is not obliged to respond.*" *Berkemer v. McCarty,* 468 U.S. 420, 439, 104 S.Ct. 3138, 82 L.Ed.2d 317 (1984) (emphasis added).

[T]he Court's statement in *Berkemer,* while technically dicta, is the kind of strong dicta that the legal community typically takes as a statement of the law. And that law has remained undisturbed for more than 20 years.

There is no good reason now to reject this generation-old statement of the law. There are sound reasons rooted in Fifth Amendment considerations for adhering to this Fourth Amendment legal condition circumscribing police authority to stop an individual against his will. Administrative considerations also militate against change. Can a State, in addition to requiring a stopped individual to answer "What's your name?" also require an answer to "What's your license number?" or "Where do you live?" Can a police officer, who must know how to make a *Terry* stop, keep track of the constitutional answers? After all, answers to any of these questions may, or may not, incriminate, depending upon the circumstances.

Indeed, as the majority points out, a name itself—even if it is not "Killer Bill" or "Rough 'em up Harry"—will sometimes provide the police with "a link in the chain of evidence needed to convict the individual of a separate offense." The majority reserves judgment about whether compulsion is permissible in such instances. How then is a police officer in the midst of a *Terry* stop to distinguish between the majority's ordinary case and this special case where the majority reserves judgment?

The majority presents no evidence that the rule enunciated by * * * the *Berkemer* Court, which for nearly a generation has set forth a settled *Terry* stop condition, has significantly interfered with law enforcement. Nor has the majority presented any other convincing justification for change. I would not begin to erode a clear rule with special exceptions.

I consequently dissent.

2.   WEAPON SEARCHES OR "FRISKS"

EDITORS' INTRODUCTION: SEARCHING FOR WEAPONS ON LESS THAN PROBABLE CAUSE

In *Terry*, the Supreme Court held Officer McFadden's search of Terry for weapons was, at its inception, reasonable despite McFadden's lack of probable cause to believe Terry in possession of a weapon. Subsequent decisions have confirmed that *Terry* established the reasonableness of such a search on less than probable cause:

> *Terry* * * * held that "[w]hen an officer is justified in believing that the individual whose suspicious behavior he is investigating at close range is armed and presently dangerous to the officer or others," the officer may conduct a patdown search "to determine whether the person is in fact carrying a weapon" * * * [A] protective search [is] permitted without a warrant and on the basis of reasonable suspicion less than probable cause * * * .

Minnesota v. Dickerson, 508 U.S. 366, 373, 113 S.Ct. 2130, 2136 (1993).

Terry made clear the Fourth Amendment limits not only when such a search may be conducted but the manner in which it may be made. After concluding that McFadden's search of Terry was reasonable at its inception, the Court in *Terry* turned to whether McFadden's search was reasonable in Fourth Amendment terms "as conducted." It explained:

> The manner in which the seizure and search were conducted is, of course, as vital a part of the inquiry as whether they were warranted at all. * * *
>
> We need not develop at length in this case * * * the limitations which the Fourth Amendment places upon a protective seizure and search for weapons. * * * Suffice it to note that such a search, unlike a search without a warrant incident to a lawful arrest, is not justified by any need to prevent the disappearance or destruction of evidence of crime. The sole justification of the search in the present situation is the protection of the police officer and others nearby, and it must therefore be confined in scope to an intrusion reasonably designed to discover guns, knives, clubs, or other hidden instruments for the assault of the police officer.

The scope of the search in this case presents no serious problem in light of these standards. Officer McFadden patted down the outer clothing of petitioner and his two companions. He did not place his hands in their pockets or under the outer surface of their garments until he had felt weapons, and then he merely reached for and removed the guns. * * * Officer McFadden confined his search strictly to what was minimally necessary to learn whether the men were armed and to disarm them once he discovered the weapons. He did not conduct a general exploratory search for whatever evidence of criminal activity he might find.

392 U.S. at 28–30, 88 S.Ct. at 1883–84.

In Sibron v. New York, 392 U.S. 40, 88 S.Ct. 1889 (1968), a companion case to *Terry*, the Court further developed limits on weapons searches. The Court stated *Sibron*'s facts as follows:

Sibron * * * was convicted of the unlawful possession of heroin. He moved before trial to suppress the heroin seized from his person by the arresting officer, Brooklyn Patrolman Anthony Martin. * * * At the hearing on the motion to suppress, Officer Martin testified that while he was patrolling his beat in uniform on March 9, 1965, he observed Sibron "continually from the hours of 4:00 P.M. to 12:00, midnight * * * in the vicinity of 742 Broadway." He stated that during this period of time he saw Sibron in conversation with six or eight persons whom he (Patrolman Martin) knew from past experience to be narcotics addicts. The officer testified that he did not overhear any of these conversations, and that he did not see anything pass between Sibron and any of the others. Late in the evening Sibron entered a restaurant. Patrolman Martin saw Sibron speak with three more known addicts inside the restaurant. Once again, nothing was overheard and nothing was seen to pass between Sibron and the addicts. Sibron sat down and ordered pie and coffee, and, as he was eating Patrolman Martin approached him and told him to come outside. Once outside, the officer said to Sibron, "You know what I am after." According to the officer, Sibron "mumbled something and reached into his pocket." Simultaneously, Patrolman Martin thrust his hand into the same pocket, discovering several glassine envelopes, which, it turned out, contained heroin.

* * * Patrolman Martin * * * [never] seriously suggest[ed] that he was in fear of bodily harm and that he searched Sibron in self-protection to find weapons.

The Court concluded Officer Martin lacked probable cause to arrest until after the heroin was seized. It then turned to the reasonableness of the officer's conduct under *Terry*. As to whether the officer was entitled under *Terry* to frisk Sibron, the Court observed:

> The suspect's mere act of talking with a number of known addicts over an eight-hour period no more gives rise to reasonable fear of life or limb on the part of the police officer than it justifies an arrest for committing a crime. Nor did Patrolman Martin urge that when Sibron put his hand in his pocket, he feared that he was going for a weapon and acted in self-defense. His opening statement to Sibron—"You know what I am after"—made it abundantly clear that he sought narcotics, and his testimony at the hearing left no doubt that he thought there were narcotics in Sibron's pocket.

392 U.S. at 64, 88 S.Ct. at 1903. Finally, the Court concluded, even if the officer had been authorized to frisk Sibron, the officer's actions went beyond a self-protective search and constituted a search for evidence:

> [W]ith no attempt at an initial limited exploration for arms, Patrolman Martin thrust his hand into Sibron's pocket and took from him envelopes of heroin. His testimony shows that he was looking for narcotics, and he found them. The search was not reasonably limited in scope to the accomplishment of the only goal which might conceivably have justified its inception—the protection of the officer by disarming a potentially dangerous man.

392 U.S. at 65, 88 S.Ct. at 1904.

Minnesota v. Dickerson

Supreme Court of the United States, 1993.
508 U.S. 366, 113 S.Ct. 2130.

■ JUSTICE WHITE delivered the opinion of the Court.

In this case, we consider whether the Fourth Amendment permits the seizure of contraband detected through a police officer's sense of touch during a protective pat-down search.

I

On the evening of November 9, 1989, two Minneapolis police officers were patrolling an area on the city's north side in a marked squad car. At about 8:15 p.m., one of the officers observed respondent leaving a 12-unit apartment building on Morgan Avenue North. The officer, having previously responded to complaints of drug sales in the building's hallways and having executed several search warrants on the premises, considered the building to be a notorious "crack house." According to testimony credited by the trial court, respondent began walking toward the police but, upon spotting the squad car and making eye contact with one of the officers, abruptly halted and began walking in the opposite direction. His suspicion aroused, this officer watched as respondent turned and entered an alley on the other side of the apartment building. Based upon respondent's seemingly evasive actions and the fact that he had just left a building known for cocaine traffic, the officers decided to stop respondent and investigate further.

The officers pulled their squad car into the alley and ordered respondent to stop and submit to a patdown search. The search revealed no weapons, but the officer conducting the search did take an interest in a small lump in respondent's nylon jacket. The officer later testified: "[A]s I pat-searched the front of his body, I felt a lump, a small lump, in the front pocket. I examined it with my fingers and it slid and it felt to be a lump of crack cocaine in cellophane." The officer then reached into respondent's pocket and retrieved a small plastic bag containing one fifth of one gram of crack cocaine. Respondent was arrested and charged in Hennepin County District Court with possession of a controlled substance.

Before trial, respondent moved to suppress the cocaine. The trial court first concluded that the officers were justified under *Terry v. Ohio,* 392 U.S. 1, 88 S.Ct. 1868, 20 L.Ed.2d 889 (1968), in stopping respondent to investigate whether he might be engaged in criminal activity. The court further found that the officers were justified in frisking respondent to ensure that he was not carrying a weapon. Finally, analogizing to the "plain-view" doctrine, under which officers may make a warrantless seizure of contraband found in plain view during a lawful search for other items, the trial court ruled that the officers' seizure of the cocaine did not violate the Fourth Amendment:

> "To this Court there is no distinction as to which sensory perception the officer uses to conclude that the material is contraband. An experienced officer may rely upon his sense of smell in DWI stops or in recognizing the smell of burning marijuana in an automobile. The sound of a shotgun being racked would clearly support certain reactions by an officer. The sense of touch, grounded in experience and training, is as reliable as perceptions drawn from other senses. 'Plain feel,' therefore, is no different than plain view and will equally support the seizure here."

His suppression motion having failed, respondent proceeded to trial and was found guilty.

On appeal, the Minnesota Supreme Court affirmed [the intermediate court's reversal of the conviction]. * * * [T]he State Supreme Court held that both the stop[2] and the frisk[3] of respondent were valid under *Terry,* but found the seizure of the cocaine to be unconstitutional.

---

[2] [The Minnesota court explained that Dickerson's "evasive conduct after eye contact with police, combined with his departure from a building with a history of drug activity, justified police in reasonably suspecting criminal activity [and] therefore * * * the stop was valid." *State v. Dickerson*, 481 N.W.2d 840, 843 (Minn.1992).]

[3] [The Minnesota court explained that "the defendant's suspicious behavior, the history of drug activity in the immediate vicinity and [the officer's] personal experience in seizing guns from the building the defendant left justified a pat search." 481 N.W.2d at 843.]

The court expressly refused "to extend the plain view doctrine to the sense of touch" on the grounds that "the sense of touch is inherently less immediate and less reliable than the sense of sight" and that "the sense of touch is far more intrusive into the personal privacy that is at the core of the [F]ourth [A]mendment." The court thus appeared to adopt a categorical rule barring the seizure of any contraband detected by an officer through the sense of touch during a patdown search for weapons. The court further noted that "[e]ven if we recognized a 'plain feel' exception, the search in this case would not qualify" because "[t]he pat search of the defendant went far beyond what is permissible under *Terry*." As the State Supreme Court read the record, the officer conducting the search ascertained that the lump in respondent's jacket was contraband only after probing and investigating what he certainly knew was not a weapon.

We granted certiorari to resolve a conflict among the state and federal courts over whether contraband detected through the sense of touch during a patdown search may be admitted into evidence. We now affirm.

II

A

* * *

Terry * * * held that "[w]hen an officer is justified in believing that the individual whose suspicious behavior he is investigating at close range is armed and presently dangerous to the officer or to others," the officer may conduct a patdown search "to determine whether the person is in fact carrying a weapon." * * * [A] protective search * * * must be strictly "limited to that which is necessary for the discovery of weapons which might be used to harm the officer or others nearby." If the protective search goes beyond what is necessary to determine if the suspect is armed, it is no longer valid under *Terry* and its fruits will be suppressed. *Sibron v. New York*, 392 U.S. 40, 65–66, 88 S.Ct. 1889, 1904, 20 L.Ed.2d 917 (1968).

These principles were settled 25 years ago when, on the same day, the Court announced its decisions in *Terry* and *Sibron*. The question presented today is whether police officers may seize nonthreatening contraband detected during a protective patdown search of the sort permitted by *Terry*. We think the answer is clearly that they may, so long as the officer's search stays within the bounds marked by *Terry*.

B

* * *

* * * Under [the "plain-view"] doctrine, if police are lawfully in a position from which they view an object, if its incriminating character is immediately apparent, and if the officers have a lawful right of access to the object, they may seize it without a warrant. If, however, the police

lack probable cause to believe that an object in plain view is contraband without conducting some further search of the object—i.e., if "its incriminating character [is not] 'immediately apparent,' "—the plain-view doctrine cannot justify its seizure.

We think that this doctrine has an obvious application by analogy to cases in which an officer discovers contraband through the sense of touch during an otherwise lawful search. The rationale of the plain view doctrine is that if contraband is left in open view and is observed by a police officer from a lawful vantage point, there has been no invasion of a legitimate expectation of privacy and thus no "search" within the meaning of the Fourth Amendment—or at least no search independent of the initial intrusion that gave the officers their vantage point. The warrantless seizure of contraband that presents itself in this manner is deemed justified by the realization that resort to a neutral magistrate under such circumstances would often be impracticable and would do little to promote the objectives of the Fourth Amendment. The same can be said of tactile discoveries of contraband. If a police officer lawfully pats down a suspect's outer clothing and feels an object whose contour or mass makes its identity immediately apparent, there has been no invasion of the suspect's privacy beyond that already authorized by the officer's search for weapons; if the object is contraband, its warrantless seizure would be justified by the same practical considerations that inhere in the plain view context.

* * *

III

It remains to apply these principles to the facts of this case. Respondent has not challenged the finding made by the trial court and affirmed by both the Court of Appeals and the State Supreme Court that the police were justified under *Terry* in stopping him and frisking him for weapons. Thus, the dispositive question before this Court is whether the officer who conducted the search was acting within the lawful bounds marked by *Terry* at the time he gained probable cause to believe that the lump in respondent's jacket was contraband. The State District Court did not make precise findings on this point, instead finding simply that the officer, after feeling "a small, hard object wrapped in plastic" in respondent's pocket, "formed the opinion that the object . . . was crack . . . cocaine." The District Court also noted that the officer made "no claim that he suspected this object to be a weapon," a finding affirmed on appeal. The Minnesota Supreme Court, after "a close examination of the record," held that the officer's own testimony "belies any notion that he 'immediately' " recognized the lump as crack cocaine. Rather, the court concluded, the officer determined that the lump was contraband only after "squeezing, sliding and otherwise manipulating the contents of the defendant's pocket"—a pocket which the officer already knew contained no weapon.

Under the State Supreme Court's interpretation of the record before it, it is clear that the court was correct in holding that the police officer in this case overstepped the bounds of the "strictly circumscribed" search for weapons allowed under *Terry*. Where, as here, "an officer who is executing a valid search for one item seizes a different item," this Court rightly "has been sensitive to the danger * * * that officers will enlarge a specific authorization, furnished by a warrant or an exigency, into the equivalent of a general warrant to rummage and seize at will." *Texas v. Brown*, 460 U.S. [730,] 748, 103 S.Ct. [1535,] 1546–47[, 75 L.Ed.2d 502 (1983)] (Stevens, J., concurring in judgment). Here, the officer's continued exploration of respondent's pocket after having concluded that it contained no weapon was unrelated to "[t]he sole justification of the search [under *Terry*:] . . . the protection of the police officer and others nearby." It therefore amounted to the sort of evidentiary search that *Terry* expressly refused to authorize, and that we have condemned in subsequent cases.

* * * Although the officer was lawfully in a position to feel the lump in respondent's pocket, because *Terry* entitled him to place his hands upon respondent's jacket, the court below determined that the incriminating character of the object was not immediately apparent to him. Rather, the officer determined that the item was contraband only after conducting a further search, one not authorized by *Terry* or by any other exception to the warrant requirement. Because this further search of respondent's pocket was constitutionally invalid, the seizure of the cocaine that followed is likewise unconstitutional.

IV

For these reasons, the judgment of the Minnesota Supreme Court is

Affirmed.

■ CHIEF JUSTICE REHNQUIST, with whom JUSTICE BLACKMUN and JUSTICE THOMAS join, concurring in part and dissenting in part.

I join Parts I and II of the Court's opinion. Unlike the Court, however, I would vacate the judgment of the Supreme Court of Minnesota and remand the case to that court for further proceedings.

The Court, correctly in my view, states that "the dispositive question before this Court is whether the officer who conducted the search was acting within the lawful bounds marked by *Terry* at the time he gained probable cause to believe that the lump in respondent's jacket was contraband." The Court then goes on to point out that the state trial court did not make precise findings on this point, but accepts the appellate findings made by the Supreme Court of Minnesota. I believe that these findings, like those of the trial court, are imprecise and not directed expressly to the question of the officer's probable cause to believe that the lump was contraband. Because the Supreme Court of Minnesota employed a Fourth Amendment analysis which differs significantly from that now adopted by this Court, I would vacate its judgment and remand the case for further proceedings there in the light of this Court's opinion.

NOTES

1. **Grounds for Weapons Search.** What constitutes grounds for a *Terry* weapons search has been addressed by the Supreme Court in several additional cases. In Adams v. Williams, 407 U.S. 143, 92 S.Ct. 1921 (1972), the officer—Sgt. Connolly—was told the suspect was carrying drugs and had a gun at his waist. It was 2:15 a.m. when the officer approached the suspect seated in a car; the area was known to the officer as a high crime rate area. He tapped on the car window and asked the suspect to open the door. The suspect instead rolled down the window. At that point, the officer reached into the car and "removed" a loaded revolver from the suspect's waistband. The Court upheld the action, explaining:

> Sgt. Connolly had ample reason to fear for his safety. When Williams rolled down his window, rather than complying with the policeman's request to step out of the car so that his movements could more easily be seen, the revolver allegedly at Williams' waist became an even greater threat. Under these circumstances the policeman's action in reaching to the spot where the gun was thought to be hidden constituted a limited intrusion designed to insure his safety, and we conclude that it was reasonable.

407 U.S. at 147–48, 92 S.Ct. at 1924.

In Pennsylvania v. Mimms, 434 U.S. 106, 98 S.Ct. 330 (1977) (per curiam), an officer stopped a car driven by Mimms to issue him a traffic citation for having an expired license plate. When Mimms stepped out of the car, the officer observed a large bulge under Mimms' sports jacket. Under *Terry*, the Court held, the bulge permitted the officer to conclude Mimms posed a serious and present danger to the officer's safety. Thus, the officer properly conducted a pat down of Mimms. The pat down revealed Mimms was in fact armed.

The matter was again considered in Ybarra v. Illinois, 444 U.S. 85, 100 S.Ct. 338 (1979). Officers obtained a valid search warrant authorizing the search of the Aurora Tap Tavern and Greg, the bartender. When the officers entered the tavern in late afternoon, between 9 and 13 customers—including Ybarra—were present. All were "frisked" and the officer felt "a cigarette pack with objects in it" in Ybarra's pocket; he did not at that time remove it. Several minutes later, Ybarra was searched again, this time more thoroughly. Drugs were found in the cigarette package. The State argued the first patdown frisk was permissible under *Terry* and since this revealed probable cause to believe Ybarra was in possession of drugs, the second and thorough search was permissible as an exigent circumstances search made on probable cause. Without addressing whether the frisk gave rise to probable cause, a majority of the Court held the frisk invalid:

> The initial frisk of Ybarra was simply not supported by a reasonable belief that he was armed and presently dangerous, a belief which this Court has invariably held must form the predicate

to a patdown of a person for weapons. When the police entered the Aurora Tap Tavern * * * , the lighting was sufficient for them to observe the customers. Upon seeing Ybarra, they neither recognized him as a person with a criminal history nor had any particular reason to believe that he might be inclined to assault them. Moreover, as Police Agent Johnson later testified, Ybarra, whose hands were empty, gave no indication of possessing a weapon, made no gestures or other actions indicative of an intent to commit an assault, and acted generally in a manner that was not threatening. At the suppression hearing, the most Agent Johnson could point to was that Ybarra was wearing a 3/4-length lumber jacket, clothing which the State admits could be expected on almost any tavern patron in Illinois in early March. In short, the State is unable to articulate any specific fact that would have justified a police officer at the scene in even suspecting that Ybarra was armed and dangerous.

* * * The "narrow scope" of the *Terry* exception does not permit a frisk for weapons on less than reasonable belief or suspicion directed at the person to be frisked, even though that person happens to be on premises where an authorized narcotics search is taking place.

444 U.S. at 92–94, 100 S.Ct. at 343.

2. **Need to Begin with Patdown.** Is a weapons search under *Terry* always required to begin with a patdown? In Adams v. Williams, discussed in note 1 above, the officer apparently conducted no patdown but rather reached into the automobile and "removed" a gun from the suspect's waistband. The Court upheld the constitutionality of this action but did not discuss the officer's failure to conduct a preliminary patdown. How might this be justified?

3. STOP AND FRISK ON SUSPICION OF CARRYING A FIREARM

EDITORS' INTRODUCTION: STOP AND FRISK FOR FIREARMS

Where police concern is that a person on the street is carrying a handgun, the situation is arguably different from other field situations.

In these situations, is any legitimate investigatory purpose served by a stop? An officer may, of course, wish to search the person to determine whether the person in fact has a handgun. Arguably, however, the right to make a weapons frisk in field situations is not a legitimate objective in itself but only a way of assuring officers' safety as they conduct investigations supported on other grounds. If a stop is made only because it triggers the opportunity to frisk for weapons, perhaps the right to stop is being misused.

Whatever the Fourth Amendment theory, it seems clear that the authority permitted officers under Terry v. Ohio, 392 U.S. 1, 88 S.Ct.

1868 (1968) and subsequent case law is in fact used to conduct searches as ends in themselves. The report on New York "stop & frisk" practices, quoted earlier in this chapter, asserted that in practice stop and frisk often served not as a basis for protecting officers while they conduct investigations concerning other suspected crimes but rather as a means of determining by search whether in fact suspects are illegally carrying handguns.

Perhaps generally-applicable criteria for limiting law enforcement field practices should be relaxed where officers fear a person in a public place has a handgun. When the case reprinted in this subsection was in the Florida Supreme Court, two members of that tribunal urged that the officers' actions should be evaluated under a version of the Fourth Amendment reasonable suspicion requirement requiring less rigorous corroboration of an anonymous tip than is otherwise demanded:

> I would * * * recognize a "firearm exception" to the general rule that the corroboration of only the innocent details of an anonymous tip does not provide police officers with a reasonable suspicion of criminal activity. In my view, this holding is necessary because the great risk of harm to the public and police in such a situation substantially outweighs the limited privacy intrusion to the suspect. Such a holding is true to the dictates of *Terry.* *"The officer need not be absolutely certain that the individual is armed; the issue is whether a reasonably prudent [person] in the circumstances would be warranted in the belief that his safety or that of others was in danger."* *Terry,* 392 U.S. at 27, 88 S.Ct. 1868 (emphasis added). Clearly, it is reasonable in today's society for law enforcement officers confronted with the circumstances presented in this case to conduct a stop and frisk.

> I strongly emphasize that this holding should apply only to investigatory stop and frisks supported by reliable anonymous tips regarding individuals possessing illegally concealed firearms. * * *

J.L. v. State, 727 So.2d 204, 214–15 (Fla.1998) (Overton, J., dissenting).

Florida v. J. L.
Supreme Court of the United States, 2000.
529 U.S. 266, 120 S.Ct. 1375.

■ JUSTICE GINSBURG delivered the opinion of the Court.

The question presented in this case is whether an anonymous tip that a person is carrying a gun is, without more, sufficient to justify a police officer's stop and frisk of that person. We hold that it is not.

I

On October 13, 1995, an anonymous caller reported to the Miami-Dade Police that a young black male standing at a particular bus stop and wearing a plaid shirt was carrying a gun. So far as the record reveals, there is no audio recording of the tip, and nothing is known about the informant. Sometime after the police received the tip—the record does not say how long—two officers were instructed to respond. They arrived at the bus stop about six minutes later and saw three black males "just hanging out [there]." One of the three, respondent J. L., was wearing a plaid shirt. Apart from the tip, the officers had no reason to suspect any of the three of illegal conduct. The officers did not see a firearm, and J. L. made no threatening or otherwise unusual movements. One of the officers approached J. L., told him to put his hands up on the bus stop, frisked him, and seized a gun from J. L.'s pocket. The second officer frisked the other two individuals, against whom no allegations had been made, and found nothing.

J.L., who was at the time of the frisk "10 days shy of his 16th birth[day]," was charged under state law with carrying a concealed firearm without a license and possessing a firearm while under the age of 18. He moved to suppress the gun as the fruit of an unlawful search, and the trial court granted his motion. The intermediate appellate court reversed, but the Supreme Court of Florida quashed that decision and held the search invalid under the Fourth Amendment.

* * *

We granted certiorari * * * .

II

* * * [T]he officers' suspicion that J. L. was carrying a weapon arose not from any observations of their own but solely from a call made from an unknown location by an unknown caller. Unlike a tip from a known informant whose reputation can be assessed and who can be held responsible if her allegations turn out to be fabricated, "an anonymous tip alone seldom demonstrates the informant's basis of knowledge or veracity." As we have recognized, however, there are situations in which an anonymous tip, suitably corroborated, exhibits "sufficient indicia of reliability to provide reasonable suspicion to make the investigatory stop." The question we here confront is whether the tip pointing to J. L. had those indicia of reliability.

* * *

The tip in the instant case lacked the moderate indicia of reliability [required]. The anonymous call concerning J. L. provided no predictive information and therefore left the police without means to test the informant's knowledge or credibility. That the allegation about the gun turned out to be correct does not suggest that the officers, prior to the frisks, had a reasonable basis for suspecting J. L. of engaging in unlawful conduct: The reasonableness of official suspicion must be measured by what the officers knew before they conducted their search. All the police had to go on in this case was the bare report of an unknown, unaccountable informant who neither explained how he knew about the gun nor supplied any basis for believing he had inside information about J. L. * * *

Florida contends that the tip was reliable because its description of the suspect's visible attributes proved accurate: There really was a young black male wearing a plaid shirt at the bus stop. The United States as *amicus curiae* makes a similar argument, proposing that a stop and frisk should be permitted "when (1) an anonymous tip provides a description of a particular person at a particular location illegally carrying a concealed firearm, (2) police promptly verify the pertinent details of the tip except the existence of the firearm, and (3) there are no factors that cast doubt on the reliability of the tip. . . ." Brief for United States 16. These contentions misapprehend the reliability needed for a tip to justify a *Terry* stop.

An accurate description of a subject's readily observable location and appearance is of course reliable in this limited sense: It will help the police correctly identify the person whom the tipster means to accuse. Such a tip, however, does not show that the tipster has knowledge of concealed criminal activity. The reasonable suspicion here at issue requires that a tip be reliable in its assertion of illegality, not just in its tendency to identify a determinate person.

A second major argument advanced by Florida and the United States as *amicus* is, in essence, that the standard *Terry* analysis should be modified to license a "firearm exception." Under such an exception, a tip alleging an illegal gun would justify a stop and frisk even if the accusation would fail standard pre-search reliability testing. We decline to adopt this position.

Firearms are dangerous, and extraordinary dangers sometimes justify unusual precautions. Our decisions recognize the serious threat that armed criminals pose to public safety; *Terry*'s rule, which permits protective police searches on the basis of reasonable suspicion rather than demanding that officers meet the higher standard of probable cause, responds to this very concern. But an automatic firearm exception to our established reliability analysis would rove too far. Such an exception would enable any person seeking to harass another to set in motion an intrusive, embarrassing police search of the targeted person simply by placing an anonymous call falsely reporting the target's unlawful carriage of a gun. Nor could one securely confine such an exception to allegations involving firearms. Several Courts of Appeals have held it *per se* foreseeable for people carrying significant amounts of illegal drugs to be carrying guns as well. If police officers may properly conduct *Terry* frisks on the basis of bare-boned tips about guns, it would be reasonable to maintain under the above-cited decisions that the police should similarly have discretion to frisk based on bare-boned tips about narcotics. [T]he Fourth Amendment is not so easily satisfied.

The facts of this case do not require us to speculate about the circumstances under which the danger alleged in an anonymous tip might be so great as to justify a search even without a showing of reliability. We do not say, for example, that a report of a person carrying a bomb need bear the indicia of reliability we demand for a report of a person carrying a firearm before the police can constitutionally conduct a frisk. Nor do we hold that public safety officials in quarters where the reasonable expectation of Fourth Amendment privacy is diminished, such as airports, and schools, cannot conduct protective searches on the basis of information insufficient to justify searches elsewhere.

Finally, the requirement that an anonymous tip bear standard indicia of reliability in order to justify a stop in no way diminishes a police officer's prerogative, in accord with *Terry*, to conduct a protective search of a person who has already been legitimately stopped. We speak in today's decision only of cases in which the officer's authority to make the initial stop is at issue. In that context, we hold that an anonymous tip lacking indicia of reliability * * * does not justify a stop and frisk whenever and however it alleges the illegal possession of a firearm.

The judgment of the Florida Supreme Court is affirmed.

It is so ordered.

D. TRAFFIC STOPS

There is probably wide-spread consensus that a traffic stop—or at least a "routine" traffic stop—is different from an arrest or even an investigatory stop. Whether that is adequately reflected in the formal law, however, is open to question. That formal law is addressed in this subchapter.

1. TRAFFIC STOPS AS A DISTINGUISHABLE TYPE OF DETENTION

EDITORS' INTRODUCTION: TRAFFIC STOPS AS A DISTINGUISHABLE KIND OF DETENTION

The Supreme Court and lower tribunals have long assumed that traffic stops are a type of detention different from arrests or investigatory field stops. Nevertheless, the case law arguably fails to make clear how, in at least some situations, a traffic stop should be distinguished from an arrest and a field stop.

The Supreme Court first referred to traffic stops in United States v. Robinson, 414 U.S. 218, 94 S.Ct. 467 (1973). In a discussion of searches incident to custodial arrest, it noted the court below "discussed its understanding of the law where the police officer makes what the court characterized as 'a routine traffic stop,' i.e., where the officer would simply issue a notice of violation and allow the offender to proceed." Since *Robinson* involved "a full-custody arrest of the violator," the Court did not reach the question discussed by the lower tribunal.

Citations as Alternatives to Custodial Arrest

The major alternative to "a full-custody arrest" as a law enforcement officer's response to observing a traffic offense, of course, is the issuance of what is varyingly called a citation, a "ticket," or in the language of the lower court in *Robinson*, a "notice of violation." A citation directs the cited person to appear, generally in a specified court, at some future time to respond to the official contention that the person has committed an offense or violation. Failure to appear is generally a criminal offense. In many jurisdictions—including, as the first principal case in this part indicates, Iowa—local nonconstitutional law gives officers considerable discretion whether, in the case of a traffic offense, to issue a citation or rather make a full custody arrest.

Some jurisdictions, however, limit officers' authority to make a full custody arrest for some minor offenses. A Minnesota rule, for example, provides:

> Law enforcement officers acting without a warrant, who have decided to proceed with prosecution, shall issue citations to persons subject to lawful arrest for misdemeanors, unless it reasonably appears to the officer that arrest or detention is necessary to prevent bodily harm to the accused or another or further criminal conduct, or that there is a substantial likelihood that the accused will fail to respond to a citation. The citation may be issued in lieu of an arrest, or if an arrest has been made, in lieu of continued detention.

Minn.R.Crim.Pro. 6.01, subd.1(1)(a).

Atwater v. City of Lago Vista, 532 U.S. 318, 121 S.Ct. 1536 (2001), discussed in the Editors' Introduction to Subchapter B of this chapter, appears to hold that at least many and perhaps all custodial arrests made on probable cause to believe the persons committed traffic offenses are constitutionally reasonable. Whren v. United States, 517 U.S. 806, 116 S.Ct. 1769 (1996) (reprinted in Chapter 2), held constitutional "pretext" challenges unavailable to traffic stops, at least if those are made on probable cause.

In Arkansas v. Sullivan, 532 U.S. 769, 121 S.Ct. 1876 (2001) (per curiam), Justice Ginsburg, joined by Justices Stevens, O'Connor, and Breyer, commented:

> In *Atwater*, which recognized no constitutional limitation on arrest for a fine-only misdemeanor offense, this Court relied in part on a perceived "dearth of horribles demanding redress." Although I joined a dissenting opinion questioning the relevance of the Court's conclusion on that score, I hope the Court's

perception proves correct. But if it does not, if experience demonstrates "anything like an epidemic of unnecessary minor-offense arrests," I hope the Court will reconsider its recent precedent.

532 U.S. at 773, 121 S.Ct. at 1879 (Ginsburg, J., concurring). Justice Ginsburg seemed to regard a traffic offense arrest made for purposes of pursuing suspicions of drug trafficking as a "horrible" demanding redress. Was she correct?

Multiple Functions of Traffic Law Enforcement

The complexity of the law in this area is undoubtedly affected by the nature of traffic law's role in policing. Certainly, to some extent, law enforcement agencies properly regard traffic laws themselves as deserving of enforcement:

> [T]raffic problems are a quality-of-life issue nearly everywhere. If the essence of community policing is to be sensitive to citizen concerns, we cannot afford to ignore traffic enforcement. Citizens need to feel safe on the streets and highways—not only from careless and drunk drivers, but also from the violent quarrels that sometimes occur when hot-tempered, aggressive individuals act out because another driver "cut them off."

Earl M. Sweeney, Traffic Enforcement: New Uses for an Old Tool, 68 Police Chief 45 (1996).

Aggressive traffic law enforcement may—perhaps because of the increase in resulting visibility of police officers—further other law enforcement objectives. Sweeney, for example, added:

> Many cities that are plagued by gang activities, illegal guns, open-air drug markets and drive-by shootings have discovered that saturating an area with traffic patrol shuts down these illegal operations.

In addition, traffic enforcement may be used as a means of investigating suspicions that particular persons are involved in more serious criminal behavior. Sweeney continued:

> [A]n alert police officer who "looks beyond the traffic ticket" and uses the motor vehicle stop to "sniff out" possible criminal behavior may be our most effective tool for interdicting criminals. Serious lawbreakers almost always have aggressive personalities that also show up in their driving behavior. They drive after drinking, speed, cross over solid center lines, run red lights and stop signs, and neglect to register their vehicles or renew their driver's licenses. And they pass through our communities every day on their way to or from holdups and burglaries, or en route in the transport of drugs or illegal loads of hazardous wastes. Many of them are apprehended in routine

traffic stops—and still more could be—if we re-emphasized traffic patrol.

If traffic enforcement is a valuable tool for use against serious crime, how is it best used? In 1997, Indianapolis police implemented "directed patrol" programs in two high crime areas. In the first ("east"), officers tended to stop vehicles for any observed violation in order to create a sense of significantly increased police presence. In the second ("north") area, officers again used traffic stops but focused upon those motorists specifically suspected of involvement in nontraffic criminal activity. Officers made more stops in the first area, and every 100 stops resulted in 24.5 citations, 14.5 arrests, 1.1 felony arrests, and 0.34 seizures of illegal guns. In the second area, every 100 stops resulted in 49.2 citations, 30.6 arrests, 2.9 felony arrests and 0.085 seizures of illegal guns. Total gun crimes actually increased somewhat in the first area but dropped 29 percent in the second. Office of Justice Program, U.S. Department of Justice, Promising Strategies to Reduce Gun Violence 53–54, 95–96 (1999). This, of course, suggests that simply vigorous traffic enforcement is less effective than using stops to follow through on suspicions developed by other methods. But the more extensive use of warnings rather than citations in the first area may have muted the "zero tolerance" message the police sought to convey by the increased police activity.

A major issue, of course, is whether the legal rules relating to traffic stops should be affected by the likelihood that traffic stops are sometimes used for purposes other than simply enforcing traffic laws themselves.

Definition and Requirements of Traffic Stops

Judicial discussions—including those in the Supreme Court's case law—often assume traffic stops are self-defining. This, however, is not necessarily the case. Moreover, there is some question as to the basis required for a traffic stop. Further—as the first principal case reprinted here makes clear—there remains some question as to what officers may do during a traffic stop.

Implicit in a traffic stop is some particularized information suggesting the driver has committed a violation of a traffic law. As is discussed in the Editors' Introduction to the next subchapter of this chapter (Subchapter E), the Supreme Court has held the Fourth Amendment prohibits random or "suspicionless" stops of motorists to determine whether they lack valid driver's licenses or registration documents for the vehicles. Delaware v. Prouse, 440 U.S. 648, 99 S.Ct. 1391 (1979), so holding, made clear some focused showing of at least a basis for suspecting a driver of committing an offense is necessary for a traffic stop.

In *Whren*, the Supreme Court observed that an "[a]utomobile stop"— by which the Court apparently meant a routine traffic stop—"is reasonable where the police have probable cause to believe that a traffic violation has occurred." But is a traffic stop reasonable *only* if such probable cause exists? Or would a traffic stop to issue a citation be constitutionally permissible on reasonable suspicion the driver has committed a traffic violation? The issue seldom arises, of course, because traffic stops are nearly always supported by officers' testimony that they observed the drivers commit acts constituting violations of the traffic laws. Since such testimony constitutes probable cause, the cases present no occasion to consider whether less than probable cause might support a traffic stop. In *Whren*, for example, the parties apparently agreed that the officers had probable cause to believe the suspects committed multiple traffic violations.

The Supreme Court again in 2009 described a traffic stop as a situation in which "[t]here is probable cause to believe that the driver has committed a minor vehicular offense." Arizona v. Johnson, 555 U.S. 323, 331, 129 S.Ct. 781, 787 (2009), quoting from Maryland v. Wilson, 519 U.S. 408, 413, 117 S.Ct. 882, 882 (1997). The Second Circuit, however, agreed with what it described as the position of majority of the federal circuits: probable cause is not required. "[N]o Fourth Amendment violation aris[es] from a traffic stop supported by a reasonable suspicion that a traffic violation has occurred." United States v. Stewart, 551 F.3d 187, 191 (2d Cir.2009).

The Supreme Court of Pennsylvania held that Fourth Amendment law (and Pennsylvania state constitutional law) *sometimes* permit a "traffic stop" on reasonable suspicion. This is permitted when the traffic offense is one for which "a post-stop investigation is normally feasible." This is the case if the offense is driving while impaired, and in this situation the stop is essentially a *Terry* stop for that investigation. It added:

> However, a vehicle stop based solely on offenses not "investigatable" cannot be justified by a mere reasonable suspicion, because the purposes of a *Terry* stop do not exist— maintaining the *status quo* while investigating is inapplicable where there is nothing further to investigate. An officer must have probable cause to make a constitutional vehicle stop for such offenses.

Commonwealth v. Chase, 599 Pa. 80, 94, 960 A.2d 108, 116 (2008).

Knowles v. Iowa

Supreme Court of the United States, 1998.
525 U.S. 113, 119 S.Ct. 484.

■ CHIEF JUSTICE REHNQUIST delivered the opinion of the Court.

An Iowa police officer stopped petitioner Knowles for speeding, but issued him a citation rather than arresting him. The question presented is whether such a procedure authorizes the officer, consistently with the

Fourth Amendment, to conduct a full search of the car. We answer this question "no."

Knowles was stopped in Newton, Iowa, after having been clocked driving 43 miles per hour on a road where the speed limit was 25 miles per hour. The police officer issued a citation to Knowles, although under Iowa law he might have arrested him. The officer then conducted a full search of the car, and under the driver's seat he found a bag of marijuana and a "pot pipe." Knowles was then arrested and charged with violation of state laws dealing with controlled substances.

Before trial, Knowles moved to suppress the evidence so obtained. He argued that the search could not be sustained under the "search incident to arrest" exception recognized in *United States v. Robinson*, 414 U.S. 218, 94 S.Ct. 467, 38 L.Ed.2d 427 (1973), because he had not been placed under arrest. At the hearing on the motion to suppress, the police officer conceded that he had neither Knowles' consent nor probable cause to conduct the search. He relied on Iowa law dealing with such searches.

Iowa Code Ann. § 321.485(1)(a) (West 1997) provides that Iowa peace officers having cause to believe that a person has violated any traffic or motor vehicle equipment law may arrest the person and immediately take the person before a magistrate. Iowa law also authorizes the far more usual practice of issuing a citation in lieu of arrest or in lieu of continued custody after an initial arrest.[1] See Iowa Code Ann. § 805.1(1) (West Supp.1997). Section 805.1(4) provides that the issuance of a citation in lieu of an arrest "does not affect the officer's authority to conduct an otherwise lawful search." The Iowa Supreme Court has interpreted this provision as providing authority to officers to conduct a full-blown search of an automobile and driver in those cases where police elect not to make a custodial arrest and instead issue a citation—that is, a search incident to citation.

Based on this authority, the trial court denied the motion to suppress and found Knowles guilty. The Supreme Court of Iowa, sitting en banc, affirmed by a divided vote. * * * [T]he Iowa Supreme Court upheld the constitutionality of the search under a bright-line "search incident to citation" exception to the Fourth Amendment's warrant requirement, reasoning that so long as the arresting officer had probable cause to make a custodial arrest, there need not in fact have been a custodial arrest. We granted certiorari * * * . * * * Knowles did not argue below, and does not argue here, that the statute could never be lawfully applied. The question we therefore address is whether the search at issue, authorized as it was by state law, nonetheless violates the Fourth Amendment.

---

[1] Iowa law permits the issuance of a citation in lieu of arrest for most offenses for which an accused person would be "eligible for bail." See Iowa Code Ann. § 805.1(1) (West Supp.1997). In addition to traffic and motor vehicle equipment violations, this would permit the issuance of a citation in lieu of arrest for such serious felonies as second-degree burglary, and first-degree theft, both bailable offenses under Iowa law. The practice in Iowa of permitting citation in lieu of arrest is consistent with law reform efforts.

In *Robinson*, supra, we noted the two historical rationales for the "search incident to arrest" exception: (1) the need to disarm the suspect in order to take him into custody, and (2) the need to preserve evidence for later use at trial. But neither of these underlying rationales for the search incident to arrest exception is sufficient to justify the search in the present case.

We have recognized that the first rationale—officer safety—is " 'both legitimate and weighty.' " The threat to officer safety from issuing a traffic citation, however, is a good deal less than in the case of a custodial arrest. In *Robinson*, we stated that a custodial arrest involves "danger to an officer" because of "the extended exposure which follows the taking of a suspect into custody and transporting him to the police station." We recognized that "[t]he danger to the police officer flows from the fact of the arrest, and its attendant proximity, stress, and uncertainty, and not from the grounds for arrest." A routine traffic stop, on the other hand, is a relatively brief encounter and "is more analogous to a so-called '*Terry* stop' . . . than to a formal arrest." *Berkemer v. McCarty*, 468 U.S. 420, 437, 104 S.Ct. 3138, 82 L.Ed.2d 317 (1984). See also *Cupp v. Murphy*, 412 U.S. 291, 296, 93 S.Ct. 2000, 36 L.Ed.2d 900 (1973) ("Where there is no formal arrest . . . a person might well be less hostile to the police and less likely to take conspicuous, immediate steps to destroy incriminating evidence").

This is not to say that the concern for officer safety is absent in the case of a routine traffic stop. It plainly is not. But while the concern for officer safety in this context may justify the "minimal" additional intrusion of ordering a driver and passengers out of the car, it does not by itself justify the often considerably greater intrusion attending a full field-type search. Even without the search authority Iowa urges, officers have other, independent bases to search for weapons and protect themselves from danger. For example, they may order out of a vehicle both the driver, and any passengers; perform a "patdown" of a driver and any passengers upon reasonable suspicion that they may be armed and dangerous; conduct a "*Terry* patdown" of the passenger compartment of a vehicle upon reasonable suspicion that an occupant is dangerous and may gain immediate control of a weapon; and even conduct a full search of the passenger compartment, including any containers therein, pursuant to a custodial arrest.

Nor has Iowa shown the second justification for the authority to search incident to arrest—the need to discover and preserve evidence. Once Knowles was stopped for speeding and issued a citation, all the evidence necessary to prosecute that offense had been obtained. No further evidence of excessive speed was going to be found either on the person of the offender or in the passenger compartment of the car.

Iowa nevertheless argues that a "search incident to citation" is justified because a suspect who is subject to a routine traffic stop may attempt to hide or destroy evidence related to his identity (e. g., a driver's license or vehicle registration), or destroy evidence of another, as yet undetected crime. As for the destruction of evidence relating to identity, if a police officer is not satisfied with the identification furnished by the driver, this may be a basis for arresting him rather than merely issuing a citation. As for destroying evidence of other crimes, the possibility that an officer would stumble onto evidence wholly unrelated to the speeding offense seems remote.

In *Robinson*, we held that the authority to conduct a full field search as incident to an arrest was a "bright-line rule," which was based on the concern for officer safety and destruction or loss of evidence, but which did not depend in every case upon the existence of either concern. Here we are asked to extend that "bright-line rule" to a situation where the concern for officer safety is not present to the same extent and the concern for destruction or loss of evidence is not present at all. We decline to do so. The judgment of the Supreme Court of Iowa is reversed, and the cause remanded for further proceedings not inconsistent with this opinion.

It is so ordered.

NOTES

1. **Distinguishing Traffic Stops from Arrests.** Often, as in Iowa, an officer has authority to either issue a motor a citation for a traffic offense or make a full custody arrest. If in such situations the officer searches before actually issuing a citation, how should the courts determine whether the situation is an arrest permitting an incidental search or rather a nonarrest traffic stop that under *Knowles* does not permit such a search? The issue was raised during oral argument in *Knowles*. One member of the Court inquired of counsel for Knowles, Paul Rosenberg:

QUESTION:	* * * Suppose the officer had just said, I'm placing you under arrest, and he said those words before he searched the driver and the passenger and the inside of the car. * * *
MR. ROSENBERG:	If he had done that, then it would have been a valid search incident to a lawful arrest.
QUESTION:	So, the whole thing turns on whether the officer says you're under * * * arrest or here's a ticket.
MR. ROSENBERG:	Yes * * * .

During the argument by counsel for Iowa, Bridget A. Chambers, the following exchange took place:

MS. CHAMBERS:	* * * [U]nder Iowa law officers can arrest, search, and then subsequently release on citation. * * *
QUESTION:	Excuse me. They can arrest, search, and then say never mind the arrest?
MS. CHAMBERS:	Yes.
QUESTION:	Wow.

(Laughter.)

The questioning of Ms. Chambers continued:

QUESTION:	[T]he usual rule is there can be a search incident to an arrest. You want to turn it around and have an arrest incident to a search. And it seems to me that that's an abuse of authority. * * * If the officer arrests not intending really to arrest, that's an abuse of authority. You're not really proposing that this could happen, are you?
MS. CHAMBERS:	We're certainly not advocating that that should happen, and we're certainly not * * * encouraging that. * * * [W]e think it could conceivably happen, and * * * [it is likely that this] wouldn't violate the Fourth Amendment * * * .

2. **"Frisks" of Automobiles.** Under certain circumstances officers' right to conduct a protective weapons search extends beyond the person of a motorist and includes some parts of the automobile. Such searches are sometimes permissible during traffic stops.

In Michigan v. Long, 463 U.S. 1032, 103 S.Ct. 3469 (1983), two Michigan sheriff's deputies, Howell and Lewis, were on routine patrol in a rural area. Shortly after midnight, they observed a car driven erratically and at excessive speed. When it swerved into a ditch, they stopped to investigate. Long, the only occupant of the vehicle, met the officers at the rear of the car which protruded from the ditch onto the road. Howell asked Long to produce his operator's license; Long did not respond until the request was repeated. When asked to produce the registration for the vehicle, Long again failed to respond. When this request was repeated, Long turned and walked towards the front open door on the driver's side of the vehicle. The officers followed Long and observed a large hunting knife on the floorboard of the vehicle. They then stopped Long and conducted a patdown; they found no weapons.

Shining a flashlight into the car, one deputy noticed "something" protruding from under the armrest on the front seat. He entered the car, knelt, and lifted the armrest, revealing an open leather pouch on the seat. The officer then "determined" that the pouch contained marihuana. At issue before the Supreme Court was the propriety of the officers' action leading to the discovery of the marihuana as a *Terry*-type weapons search conducted on less than probable cause.

Neither *Terry*'s language nor its rationale, Justice O'Connor concluded for the Court, required the right to search for weapons during a nonarrest detention be restricted to the person of the detained suspect. To the contrary, suspects confronted while in automobiles present special dangers to officers' safety because of their access to weapons that might be in the vehicles. Consequently, during a nonarrest detention of a suspect:

> the search of the passenger compartment of an automobile, limited to those areas in which a weapon might be placed or hidden, is permissible if the police officer possessed a reasonable belief based on "specific and articulable facts which, taken together with the rational inferences from those facts, reasonably warrant" the officers in believing that the suspect is dangerous and the suspect may gain immediate control of weapons. * * * If, while conducting a legitimate *Terry* search of the interior of the automobile, the officer should * * * discover contraband other than weapons, he clearly cannot be required to ignore the contraband, and the Fourth Amendment does not require its suppression in such circumstances.

463 U.S. at 1049–50, 103 S.Ct. at 3480–81. Turning to the facts before it, the Court held the deputies entertained the requisite reasonable fear for their safety. The rural nature of the area and late time of the stop were relevant. Further, the officers had reason to believe Long intoxicated and their pre-search observations disclosed a knife in the car. Although Long was, in some sense, under the "control" of the officers, he might still have been able to obtain and use weapons in the car. If released after the detention, he would in any event have had access to any such weapons. Even if methods other than the search were available to the officers to assure their safety, in contexts such as this in which quick decisions are crucial, the Court has "not required that officers adopt alternative means to ensure their safety in order to avoid the intrusion involved in a *Terry* encounter." Once begun, the search was properly limited. It was restricted to "those areas to which Long would generally have immediate control, and that could contain a weapon." Examining the contents of the pouch was permissible, since the trial court determined the pouch "could have contained a weapon."

3. **Removal of Driver and Passengers from Stopped Vehicle.** Some protective action by officers during a traffic stop does not require even the justification demanded by the Court for the search in *Long*. This is the case, for example, with removal of persons from a stopped vehicle.

In Pennsylvania v. Mimms, 434 U.S. 106, 98 S.Ct. 330 (1977) (per curiam), an officer stopped Mimms for driving an automobile with an expired license plate, intending to issue a traffic citation. The officer asked Mimms to step out of the car and produce his owner's card and operator's license. When Mimms complied, the officer noticed a large bulge under Mimms' sports jacket. A frisk resulted in discovery of a revolver. The state court held ordering Mimms out of his car was unreasonable because the officer lacked any reason to believe criminal activity was afoot or Mimms posed a danger; the State conceded the officer had no reason to fear Mimms particularly. Reversing, the Supreme Court held the officer's action permissible. Conversing with a driver while standing exposed to traffic, it emphasized, creates a risk of injury to the officer. On the other hand, given the fact that the motorist had already been stopped, the additional intrusion involved in requiring the motorist to get out of the car "can only be described as *de minimis*." Once the officer observed the bulge in Mimms' jacket, the Court continued, *Terry* justified the officer's further action:

> The bulge in the jacket permitted the officer to conclude that Mimms was armed and thus posed a serious and present danger to the safety of the officer. In these circumstances, any man of "reasonable caution" would likely have conducted the "pat-down."

434 U.S. at 112, 98 S.Ct. at 334.

In Maryland v. Wilson, 519 U.S. 408, 117 S.Ct. 882 (1997), *Mimms* was extended and the Court held that an officer making a traffic stop may order passengers to get out of a vehicle during the stop. Under *Mimms*, the Court reasoned, the reasonableness of such action depends on a balance between the public interests implicated and individuals' interest in personal security free of arbitrary interference by officers. Passenger removal furthers the same "legitimate and weighty" need for officer safety as was involved in *Mimms*. In fact, the Court added, "the fact that there is more than one occupant of the vehicle increases the possible sources of harm to the officer." That the persons involved are passengers rather than drivers does not significantly reduce the risk:

> It would seem that the possibility of a violent encounter stems not from the ordinary reaction of a motorist stopped for a speeding violation, but from the fact that evidence of a more serious crime might be encountered during the stop. And the motivation of a passenger to employ violence to prevent apprehension of such a crime is every bit as great as that of the driver.

519 U.S. at 413, 117 S.Ct. at 886.

Considering the public interest side of the balance, the Court acknowledged the case for suspicionless removal of passengers is "in one sense" weaker than that for removal of drivers. Although there is probable cause to believe the driver has committed an offense, there is no similar basis for stopping or detaining the passengers. Therefore, the passengers' personal liberty interests weigh more heavily against removal than did those of drivers. Nevertheless, the Court found this weightier liberty interest of minimal significance:

> [A]s a practical matter, the passengers are already stopped by virtue of the stop of the vehicle. The only change in their

circumstances which will result from ordering them out of the car is that they will be outside of, rather than inside of, the stopped car.

519 U.S. at 413–14, 117 S.Ct. at 886. Consequently, "the additional intrusion on the passenger is minimal." The risk of harm to those involved "is minimized if the officers routinely exercise unquestioned command of the situation." The Fourth Amendment therefore permits officers making traffic stops to order passengers to get out of the cars pending completion of the stops.

Maryland urged the Court to hold an officer may forcibly detain a passenger for the duration of a stop. Wilson had not been detained after he was directed to get out of the car, the Court responded, and therefore the Court did not reach, and expressly reserved comment on, officers' power to detain passengers.

In Arizona v. Johnson, 555 U.S. 323, 129 S.Ct. 781 (2009), however, the Court assumed that at least as a general rule, all passengers in a vehicle stopped as part of a routine traffic stop are seized and such seizures are reasonable. It stated:

> A lawful roadside stop begins when a vehicle is pulled over for investigation of a traffic violation. The temporary seizure of driver and passengers ordinarily continues, and remains reasonable, for the duration of the stop. Normally, the stop ends when the police have no further need to control the scene, and inform the driver and passengers they are free to leave.

555 U.S. at 332, 129 S.Ct. at 788.

4.   **Weapon Frisks of Occupants.** Officers making a traffic stop may make patdown weapons frisks of any passengers as well as drivers, if the officers have reasonable suspicion that the person patted down may be armed and dangerous. Arizona v. Johnson, 555 U.S. 323, 332–33, 129 S.Ct. 781, 787–88 (2009).

5.   **Questioning Occupants.** In Arizona v. Johnson, 555 U.S. 323, 129 S.Ct. 781 (2009), the Court commented:

> An officer's inquiries into matters unrelated to the justification for the traffic stop, this Court has made plain, do not convert the encounter into something other than a lawful seizure, so long as those inquiries do not measurably extend the duration of the stop.

555 U.S. at 333, 129 S.Ct. at 788.

2.   DURATION AND EXTENSION OF A TRAFFIC STOP

Are there Fourth Amendment limits on the duration of a traffic stop? In Ohio v. Robinette, 519 U.S. 33, 117 S.Ct. 417 (1996), Deputy Newsome stopped Robinette for speeding, asked for and received his driver's license, and ran a computer check which indicated that Robinette had no prior violations. Next:

> Newsome then asked Robinette to step out of his car, turned on his mounted video camera, issued a verbal warning to Robinette, and returned his license.

At this point, Newsome asked, "One question before you get gone: [A]re you carrying any illegal contraband in your car? Any weapons of any kind, drugs, anything like that?" Robinette answered "no" to these questions, after which Deputy Newsome asked if he could search the car. Robinette consented. In the car, Deputy Newsome discovered a small amount of marijuana and, in a film container, a pill which was later determined to be methylenedioxymethamphetamine (MDMA).

The Supreme Court granted review primarily to address the state court's holding that Robinette's consent was ineffective; this aspect of the case is discussed in Chapter 5. Robinette contended, however, the Court should not reach the consent issue because the state court had held the evidence inadmissible on an alternative basis. Before Newsome returned to Robinette's vehicle, he had determined not to give Robinette a ticket but rather to pursue his suspicion that Robinette might be in possession of drugs. "When the motivation behind a police officer's continued detention of a person stopped for a traffic violation is not related to the purpose of the original, constitutional stop, and when that continued detention is not based on articulable facts giving rise to a suspicion of some separate illegal activity justifying an extension of the detention," the state court explained, "the continued detention constitutes an illegal seizure." Thus the consent and search were all the tainted "fruit" of a detention that had become unreasonable.

The Supreme Court, however, disagreed:

> We think that under our recent decision in *Whren v. United States*, 517 U.S. 806, 116 S.Ct. 1769, 135 L.Ed.2d 89 (1996) [reprinted in Chapter 2] * * *, the subjective intentions of the officer did not make the continued detention of respondent illegal under the Fourth Amendment. As we made clear in *Whren*, " 'the fact that [an] officer does not have the state of mind which is hypothecated by the reasons which provide the legal justification for the officer's action does not invalidate the action taken as long as the circumstances, viewed objectively, justify that action.' * * * Subjective intentions play no role in ordinary, probable-cause Fourth Amendment analysis." * * *

519 U.S. at 38, 117 S.Ct. at 420–21. It is not clear the Supreme Court intended by this discussion to reject the possibility that Deputy Newsome may have impermissibly extended the traffic stop. *Robinette* appears to reject only the state court's holding that the stop became unreasonable because the officer's subjective motivation had shifted from traffic matters to drug concerns.

On remand in *Robinette*, the Ohio Supreme Court reanalyzed the situation. In recognition of *Whren*, it first held that a continued detention resulting from a traffic stop becomes unreasonable "[w]hen [the] police officer's objective justification to continue detention * * * is not related to the purpose of the original stop," unless it is justified on some other ground. The Fourth Amendment permissibility of brief stops at sobriety checkpoints, the court continued, establishes the weight properly given to the strong policy in favor of quelling the drug trade. This policy also permits an officer who has made a proper traffic stop, pursuant to a drug interdiction policy, to briefly detain the motorist in order to ask him whether he is carrying any illegal drugs or weapons.

If during that continued detention reasonable suspicion develops, the Ohio court added, the officer may detain the motorist for a more in-depth investigation that may include soliciting consent to search. But where, as in *Robinette*, the questioning does not give rise to reasonable suspicion, the officer cannot reasonably continue to detain the motorist "to ask for and execute an intrusive search." State v. Robinette, 80 Ohio St.3d 234, 241, 685 N.E.2d 762, 768 (1997). Thus Robinette's detention became unreasonable, apparently after he responded negatively to Newsome's inquiries about drugs and weapons.

Issues concerning the possible limits on the duration of traffic stops are often presented by contentions related to the use of drug-sniffing dogs during the stops. This is the case in the principal decision that follows, decided ten years after Illinois v. Caballes, 543 U.S. 405, 125 S.Ct. 834 (2005).

In *Caballes*, defendant Caballes was stopped for speeding. As one officer prepared a citation, another walked a drug-sniffing dog around the stopped vehicle. The dog alerted and on this basis the vehicle was searched and marijuana was found. The state court held the use of the dog required reasonable suspicion and this was lacking, so the trial court erred in failing to suppress the marijuana. A split Supreme Court reversed. Relying on United States v. Place, 462 U.S. 696, 103 S.Ct. 2637 (1983), discussed in the Editors' Introduction to Subchapter 2(C)(1), the majority reasoned that use of the dog in *Caballes* as in *Place* did not intrude upon constitutionally-protected privacy and thus need not be shown by the prosecution to be reasonable in any sense.

Justice Souter in dissent reasoned that *Place* relied heavily upon an assumption that drug-sniffing dogs are extremely reliable, an assumption that he believed had become untenable. As a result, s sniff by such a dog should be viewed as putting into play a procedure that results in an intrusion into the privacy of the vehicle's interior. Realistically, in other words, a sniff is part of a process clearly constituting a search and should require at least some basis for believing those with a privacy interest in the vehicle to be in possession of contraband. 543 U.S. at 413, 125 S.Ct. at 840 (Souter, J., dissenting) ("in practice the government's use of a trained narcotics dog functions as a limited search to reveal undisclosed facts about private enclosures, to be used to justify a further and complete search of the enclosed area").

Justice Ginsburg also dissented in *Caballes* but on somewhat different grounds. She explained:

A drug-detection dog is an intimidating animal. Injecting such an animal into a routine traffic stop changes the character of the encounter between the police and the motorist. The stop becomes broader, more adversarial, and (in at least some cases) longer. Caballes—who, as far as [the officers] knew, was guilty solely of driving six miles per hour over the speed limit—was exposed to the embarrassment and intimidation of being investigated, on a public thoroughfare, for drugs. Even if the drug sniff is not characterized as a Fourth Amendment "search,", the sniff surely broadened the scope of the traffic-violation-related seizure.

543 U.S. at 421–22, 125 S.Ct. at 845 (Ginsburg, J., dissenting).

Rodriguez v. United States
Supreme Court of the United States, 2015.
___ U.S. ___, 135 S. Ct. 1609.

■ JUSTICE GINSBURG delivered the opinion of the Court.

In *Illinois v. Caballes,* 543 U.S. 405, 125 S.Ct. 834, 160 L.Ed.2d 842 (2005), this Court held that a dog sniff conducted during a lawful traffic stop does not violate the Fourth Amendment's proscription of unreasonable seizures. This case presents the question whether the Fourth Amendment tolerates a dog sniff conducted after completion of a traffic stop. We hold that a police stop exceeding the time needed to handle the matter for which the stop was made violates the Constitution's shield against unreasonable seizures. * * *

I

Just after midnight on March 27, 2012, police officer Morgan Struble observed a Mercury Mountaineer veer slowly onto the shoulder of Nebraska State Highway 275 for one or two seconds and then jerk back onto the road. Nebraska law prohibits driving on highway shoulders, and on that basis, Struble pulled the Mountaineer over at 12:06 a.m. Struble is a K-9 officer with the Valley Police Department in Nebraska, and his dog Floyd was in his patrol car that night. Two men were in the Mountaineer: the driver, Dennys Rodriguez, and a front-seat passenger, Scott Pollman.

Struble approached the Mountaineer on the passenger's side. After Rodriguez identified himself, Struble asked him why he had driven onto the shoulder. Rodriguez replied that he had swerved to avoid a pothole. Struble then gathered Rodriguez's license, registration, and proof of insurance, and asked Rodriguez to accompany him to the patrol car. Rodriguez asked if he was required to do so, and Struble answered that he was not. Rodriguez decided to wait in his own vehicle.

After running a records check on Rodriguez, Struble returned to the Mountaineer. Struble asked passenger Pollman for his driver's license and began to question him about where the two men were coming from and where they were going. Pollman replied that they had traveled to Omaha, Nebraska, to look at a Ford Mustang that was for sale and that they were returning to Norfolk, Nebraska. Struble returned again to his patrol car, where he completed a records check on Pollman, and called for a second officer. Struble then began writing a warning ticket for Rodriguez for driving on the shoulder of the road.

Struble returned to Rodriguez's vehicle a third time to issue the written warning. By 12:27 or 12:28 a.m., Struble had finished explaining the warning to Rodriguez, and had given back to Rodriguez and Pollman the documents obtained from them. As Struble later testified, at that point, Rodriguez and Pollman "had all their documents back and a copy of the written warning. I got all the reason[s] for the stop out of the way[,] . . . took care of all the business."

Nevertheless, Struble did not consider Rodriguez "free to leave." Although justification for the traffic stop was "out of the way," Struble asked for permission to walk his dog around Rodriguez's vehicle. Rodriguez said no. Struble then instructed Rodriguez to turn off the ignition, exit the vehicle, and stand in front of the patrol car to wait for the second officer. Rodriguez complied. At 12:33 a.m., a deputy sheriff arrived. Struble retrieved his dog and led him twice around the Mountaineer. The dog alerted to the presence of drugs halfway through Struble's second pass. All told, seven or eight minutes had elapsed from the time Struble issued the written warning until the dog indicated the presence of drugs. A search of the vehicle revealed a large bag of methamphetamine.

Rodriguez was indicted in the United States District Court for the District of Nebraska on one count of possession with intent to distribute 50 grams or more of methamphetamine * * * . He moved to suppress the evidence seized from his car on the ground, among others, that Struble had prolonged the traffic stop without reasonable suspicion in order to conduct the dog sniff.

After receiving evidence, a Magistrate Judge recommended that the motion be denied. The Magistrate Judge found no probable cause to search the vehicle independent of the dog alert. He further found that no reasonable suspicion supported the detention once Struble issued the written warning. He concluded, however, that under Eighth Circuit precedent, extension of the stop by "seven to eight minutes" for the dog sniff was only a *de minimis* intrusion on Rodriguez's Fourth Amendment rights and was therefore permissible.

The District Court adopted the Magistrate Judge's factual findings and legal conclusions and denied Rodriguez's motion to suppress. * * * Rodriguez entered a conditional guilty plea and was sentenced to five years in prison.

The Eighth Circuit affirmed. The "seven- or eight-minute delay" in this case, the opinion noted, resembled delays that the court had previously ranked as permissible. The Court of Appeals thus ruled that the delay here constituted an acceptable "*de minimis* intrusion on Rodriguez's personal liberty." Given that ruling, the court declined to reach the question whether Struble had reasonable suspicion to continue Rodriguez's detention after issuing the written warning.

We granted certiorari to resolve a division among lower courts on the question whether police routinely may extend an otherwise-completed traffic stop, absent reasonable suspicion, in order to conduct a dog sniff.

II

A seizure for a traffic violation justifies a police investigation of that violation. "[A] relatively brief encounter," a routine traffic stop is "more analogous to a so-called '*Terry* stop' . . . than to a formal arrest." Like a *Terry* stop, the tolerable duration of police inquiries in the traffic-stop context is determined by the seizure's "mission"—to address the traffic violation that warranted the stop. Because addressing the infraction is the purpose of the stop, it may "last no longer than is necessary to effectuate th[at] purpose." Authority for the seizure thus ends when tasks tied to the traffic infraction are—or reasonably should have been—completed.

Our decisions in *Caballes* and [*Arizona v. Johnson*, 555 U.S. 323, 129 S.Ct. 781, 172 L.Ed.2d 694 (2009),] heed these constraints. In both cases, we concluded that the Fourth Amendment tolerated certain unrelated investigations that did not lengthen the roadside detention. *Johnson*, 555 U.S., at 327–328, 129 S.Ct. 781 (questioning); *Caballes*, 543 U.S., at 406, 408, 125 S.Ct. 834 (dog sniff). In *Caballes*, however, we cautioned that a traffic stop "can become unlawful if it is prolonged beyond the time reasonably required to complete th[e] mission" of issuing a warning ticket. And we repeated that admonition in *Johnson*: The seizure remains lawful only "so long as [unrelated] inquiries do not measurably extend the duration of the stop." An officer, in other words, may conduct certain unrelated checks during an otherwise lawful traffic stop. But contrary to JUSTICE ALITO's suggestion [in dissent in this case], he may not do so in a way that prolongs the stop, absent the reasonable suspicion ordinarily demanded to justify detaining an individual.

Beyond determining whether to issue a traffic ticket, an officer's mission includes "ordinary inquiries incident to [the traffic] stop." Typically such inquiries involve checking the driver's license, determining whether there are outstanding warrants against the driver, and inspecting the automobile's registration and proof of insurance. These checks serve the same objective as enforcement of the traffic code: ensuring that vehicles on the road are operated safely and responsibly.

A dog sniff, by contrast, is a measure aimed at "detect[ing] evidence of ordinary criminal wrongdoing." Candidly, the Government acknowledged at oral argument that a dog sniff, unlike the routine measures just mentioned, is not an ordinary incident of a traffic stop. Lacking the same close connection to roadway safety as the ordinary inquiries, a dog sniff is not fairly characterized as part of the officer's traffic mission.

In advancing its *de minimis* rule, the Eighth Circuit relied heavily on our decision in *Pennsylvania v. Mimms,* 434 U.S. 106, 98 S.Ct. 330, 54 L.Ed.2d 331 (1977) (*per curiam*). In *Mimms,* we reasoned that the government's "legitimate and weighty" interest in officer safety outweighs the "*de minimis*" additional intrusion of requiring a driver, already lawfully stopped, to exit the vehicle. The Eighth Circuit, echoed in Justice THOMAS's dissent, believed that the imposition here similarly could be offset by the Government's "strong interest in interdicting the flow of illegal drugs along the nation's highways."

Unlike a general interest in criminal enforcement, however, the government's officer safety interest stems from the mission of the stop itself. Traffic stops are "especially fraught with danger to police officers," so an officer may need to take certain negligibly burdensome precautions in order to complete his mission safely. On-scene investigation into other crimes, however, detours from that mission. So too do safety precautions taken in order to facilitate such detours. Thus, even assuming that the imposition here was no more intrusive than the exit order in *Mimms,* the dog sniff could not be justified on the same basis. Highway and officer safety are interests different in kind from the Government's endeavor to detect crime in general or drug trafficking in particular.

The Government argues that an officer may "incremental[ly]" prolong a stop to conduct a dog sniff so long as the officer is reasonably diligent in pursuing the traffic-related purpose of the stop, and the overall duration of the stop remains reasonable in relation to the duration of other traffic stops involving similar circumstances. The Government's argument, in effect, is that by completing all traffic-related tasks expeditiously, an officer can earn bonus time to pursue an unrelated criminal investigation. The reasonableness of a seizure, however, depends on what the police in fact do. In this regard, the Government acknowledges that "an officer always has to be reasonably diligent." How could diligence be gauged other than by noting what the officer actually did and how he did it? If an officer can complete traffic-based inquiries expeditiously, then that is the amount of "time reasonably required to complete [the stop's] mission." As we said in *Caballes* and reiterate today, a traffic stop "prolonged beyond" that point is "unlawful." The critical question, then, is not whether the dog sniff occurs before or after the officer issues a ticket, as JUSTICE ALITO supposes, but whether conducting the sniff "prolongs"—*i.e.,* adds time to—"the stop."

III

The Magistrate Judge found that detention for the dog sniff in this case was not independently supported by individualized suspicion, and the District Court adopted the Magistrate Judge's findings. The Court of Appeals, however, did not review that determination. The question whether reasonable suspicion of criminal activity justified detaining Rodriguez beyond completion of the traffic infraction investigation, therefore, remains open for Eighth Circuit consideration on remand.

* * *

For the reasons stated, the judgment of the United States Court of Appeals for the Eighth Circuit is vacated, and the case is remanded for further proceedings consistent with this opinion.

It is so ordered.

■ JUSTICE KENNEDY, dissenting.

My join in JUSTICE THOMAS' dissenting opinion does not extend to Part III. Although the issue discussed in that Part was argued here, the Court of Appeals has not addressed that aspect of the case in any detail. In my view the better course would be to allow that court to do so in the first instance.

■ JUSTICE THOMAS, with whom JUSTICE ALITO joins, and with whom JUSTICE KENNEDY joins as to all but Part III, dissenting.

Ten years ago, we explained that "conducting a dog sniff [does] not change the character of a traffic stop that is lawful at its inception and otherwise executed in a reasonable manner." *Illinois v. Caballes,* 543 U.S. 405, 408, 125 S.Ct. 834, 160 L.Ed.2d 842 (2005). The only question here is whether an officer executed a stop in a reasonable manner when he waited to conduct a dog sniff until after he had given the driver a written warning and a backup unit had arrived, bringing the overall duration of the stop to 29 minutes. Because the stop was reasonably executed, no Fourth Amendment violation occurred. The Court's holding to the contrary cannot be reconciled with our decision in *Caballes* or a number of common police practices. It was also unnecessary, as the officer possessed reasonable suspicion to continue to hold the driver to conduct the dog sniff. I respectfully dissent.

I

* * *

Although a traffic stop "constitutes a 'seizure' of 'persons' within the meaning of [the Fourth Amendment]," such a seizure is constitutionally "reasonable where the police have probable cause to believe that a traffic violation has occurred." But "a seizure that is lawful at its inception can violate the Fourth Amendment if its manner of execution unreasonably infringes interests protected by the Constitution."

Because Rodriguez does not dispute that Officer Struble had probable cause to stop him, the only question is whether the stop was otherwise executed in a reasonable manner. I easily conclude that it was. Approximately 29 minutes passed from the time Officer Struble stopped Rodriguez until his narcotics-detection dog alerted to the presence of drugs. That amount of time is hardly out of the ordinary for a traffic stop by a single officer of a vehicle containing multiple occupants even when no dog sniff is involved. During that time, Officer Struble conducted the ordinary activities of a traffic stop—he approached the vehicle, questioned Rodriguez about the observed violation, asked Pollman about their travel plans, ran serial warrant checks on Rodriguez and Pollman, and issued a written warning to Rodriguez. And when he decided to conduct a dog sniff, he took the precaution of calling for backup out of concern for his safety.

As *Caballes* makes clear, the fact that Officer Struble waited until after he gave Rodriguez the warning to conduct the dog sniff does not alter this analysis. ecause "the use of a well-trained narcotics-detection dog . . . generally does not implicate legitimate privacy interests," "conducting a dog sniff would not change the character of a traffic stop that is lawful at its inception and otherwise executed in a reasonable manner." The stop here was "lawful at its inception and otherwise executed in a reasonable manner." As in *Caballes,* "conducting a dog sniff [did] not change the character of [the] traffic stop," and thus no Fourth Amendment violation occurred.

II

Rather than adhere to the reasonableness requirement that we have repeatedly characterized as the "touchstone of the Fourth Amendment," the majority constructed a test of its own that is inconsistent with our precedents.

A

The majority's rule requires a traffic stop to "en[d] when tasks tied to the traffic infraction are—or reasonably should have been—completed." "If an officer can complete traffic-based inquiries expeditiously, then that is the amount of time reasonably required to complete the stop's mission" and he may hold the individual no longer. The majority's rule thus imposes a one-way ratchet for constitutional protection linked to the characteristics of the individual officer conducting the stop: If a driver is stopped by a particularly efficient officer, then he will be entitled to be released from the traffic stop after a shorter period of time than a driver stopped by a less efficient officer. Similarly, if a driver is stopped by an officer with access to technology that can shorten a records check, then he will be entitled to be released from the stop after a shorter period of time than an individual stopped by an officer without access to such technology.

I "cannot accept that the search and seizure protections of the Fourth Amendment are so variable and can be made to turn upon such trivialities." * * *

B

As if that were not enough, the majority also limits the duration of the stop to the time it takes the officer to complete a narrow category of "traffic-based inquiries." According to the majority, these inquiries include those that "serve the same objective as enforcement of the traffic code: ensuring that vehicles on the road are operated safely and responsibly." Inquiries directed to "detecting evidence of ordinary criminal wrongdoing" are not traffic-related inquiries and thus cannot count toward the overall duration of the stop.

The combination of that definition of traffic-related inquiries with the majority's officer-specific durational limit produces a result demonstrably at odds with our decision in *Caballes. Caballes* expressly anticipated that a traffic stop could be *reasonably* prolonged for officers to engage in a dog sniff. We explained that no Fourth Amendment violation had occurred in *Caballes,* where the "duration of the stop . . . was entirely justified by the traffic offense and the ordinary inquiries incident to such a stop," but suggested a different result might attend a case "involving a dog sniff that occurred during an *unreasonably* prolonged traffic stop." (emphasis added). The dividing line was whether the overall duration of the stop exceeded "the time reasonably required to complete th[e] mission," not, as the majority suggests, whether the duration of the stop "in fact" exceeded the time necessary to complete the traffic-related inquiries.

The majority's approach draws an artificial line between dog sniffs and other common police practices. The lower courts have routinely confirmed that warrant checks are a constitutionally permissible part of a traffic stop, and the majority confirms that it finds no fault in these measures. Yet its reasoning suggests the opposite. Such warrant checks look more like they are directed to "detecting evidence of ordinary criminal wrongdoing" than to "ensuring that vehicles on the road are operated safely and responsibly." Perhaps one could argue that the existence of an outstanding warrant might make a driver less likely to operate his vehicle safely and responsibly on the road, but the same could be said about a driver in possession of contraband. A driver confronted by the police in either case might try to flee or become violent toward the officer. But under the majority's analysis, a dog sniff, which is directed at uncovering that problem, is not treated as a traffic-based inquiry. Warrant checks, arguably, should fare no better. The majority suggests that a warrant check is an ordinary inquiry incident to a traffic stop because it can be used " 'to determine whether the apparent traffic violator is wanted for one or more previous traffic offenses.' " But * * * such checks are a "manifest[ation of] the 'war on drugs' motivation so often underlying [routine traffic] stops," and thus are very much like the dog sniff in this case.

Investigative questioning rests on the same basis as the dog sniff. "Asking questions is an essential part of police investigations." And the lower courts have routinely upheld such questioning during routine traffic stops. The majority's reasoning appears to allow officers to engage in *some* questioning aimed at detecting evidence of ordinary criminal wrongdoing. But it is hard to see how such inquiries fall within the "seizure's 'mission' [of] address[ing] the traffic violation that warranted the stop," or "attend[ing] to related safety concerns." Its reasoning appears to come down to the principle that dogs are different.

C

On a more fundamental level, the majority's inquiry elides the distinction between traffic stops based on probable cause and those based on reasonable suspicion. Probable cause is *the* "traditional justification" for the seizure of a person. This Court created an exception to that rule in *Terry v. Ohio,* 392 U.S. 1, 88 S.Ct. 1868, 20 L.Ed.2d 889 (1968), permitting "police officers who suspect criminal activity to make limited intrusions on an individual's personal security based on less than probable cause." Reasonable suspicion is the justification for such seizures.

Traffic stops can be initiated based on probable cause or reasonable suspicion. Although the Court has commented that a routine traffic stop is "more analogous to a so-called '*Terry* stop' than to a formal arrest," it has rejected the notion "that a traffic stop supported by probable cause may not exceed the bounds set by the Fourth Amendment on the scope of a *Terry* stop." *Berkemer v. McCarty,* 468 U.S. 420, 439, and n. 29, 104 S.Ct. 3138, 82 L.Ed.2d 317 (1984) (citation omitted).

Although all traffic stops must be executed reasonably, our precedents make clear that traffic stops justified by reasonable suspicion are subject to additional limitations that those justified by probable cause are not. A traffic stop based on reasonable suspicion, like all *Terry* stops, must be "justified at its inception" and "reasonably related in scope to the circumstances which justified the interference in the first place." It also "cannot continue for an excessive period of time or resemble a traditional arrest." By contrast, a stop based on probable cause affords an officer considerably more leeway. In such seizures, an officer may engage in a warrantless arrest of the driver, a warrantless search incident to arrest of the driver, and a warrantless search incident to arrest of the vehicle if it is reasonable to believe evidence relevant to the crime of arrest might be found there.

The majority casually tosses this distinction aside. It asserts that the traffic stop in this case, which was undisputedly initiated on the basis of probable cause, can last no longer than is in fact necessary to effectuate the mission of the stop. And, it assumes that the mission of the stop was merely to write a traffic ticket, rather than to consider making a custodial arrest. In support of that durational requirement, it relies primarily on cases involving *Terry* stops.

* * *

By strictly limiting the tasks that define the durational scope of the traffic stop, the majority accomplishes today what the *Caballes* dissent could not: strictly limiting the scope of an officer's activities during a traffic stop justified by probable cause. In doing so, it renders the difference between probable cause and reasonable suspicion virtually meaningless in this context. That shift is supported neither by the Fourth Amendment nor by our precedents interpreting it. And, it results in a constitutional framework that lacks predictability. Had Officer Struble arrested, handcuffed, and taken Rodriguez to the police station for his traffic violation, he would have complied with the Fourth Amendment. But because he made Rodriguez wait for seven or eight extra minutes until a dog arrived, he evidently committed a constitutional violation. Such a view of the Fourth Amendment makes little sense.

III

Today's revision of our Fourth Amendment jurisprudence was also entirely unnecessary. Rodriguez suffered no Fourth Amendment violation here for an entirely independent reason: Officer Struble had reasonable suspicion to continue to hold him for investigative purposes. * * *

Officer Struble testified that he first became suspicious that Rodriguez was engaged in criminal activity for a number of reasons. When he approached the vehicle, he smelled an "overwhelming odor of air freshener coming from the vehicle," which is, in his experience, "a common attempt to conceal an odor that [people] don't want . . . to be smelled by the police." He also observed, upon approaching the front window on the passenger side of the vehicle, that Rodriguez's passenger, Scott Pollman, appeared nervous. Pollman pulled his hat down low, puffed nervously on a cigarette, and refused to make eye contact with him. The officer thought he was "more nervous than your typical passenger" who "do[esn't] have anything to worry about because [t]hey didn't commit a [traffic] violation."

Officer Struble's interactions with the vehicle's occupants only increased his suspicions. When he asked Rodriguez why he had driven onto the shoulder, Rodriguez claimed that he swerved to avoid a pothole. But that story could not be squared with Officer Struble's observation of the vehicle slowly driving off the road before being jerked back onto it. And when Officer Struble asked Pollman where they were coming from and where they were going, Pollman told him they were traveling from Omaha, Nebraska, back to Norfolk, Nebraska, after looking at a vehicle they were considering purchasing. Pollman told the officer that he had neither seen pictures of the vehicle nor confirmed title before the trip. As

Officer Struble explained, it "seemed suspicious" to him "to drive . . . approximately two hours . . . late at night to see a vehicle sight unseen to possibly buy it," and to go from Norfolk to Omaha to look at it because "[u]sually people leave Omaha to go get vehicles, not the other way around" due to higher Omaha taxes.

These facts, taken together, easily meet our standard for reasonable suspicion. * * * Taking into account all the relevant facts, Officer Struble possessed reasonable suspicion of criminal activity to conduct the dog sniff.

* * *

I would conclude that the police did not violate the Fourth Amendment here. Officer Struble possessed probable cause to stop Rodriguez for driving on the shoulder, and he executed the subsequent stop in a reasonable manner. * * * I respectfully dissent.

■ JUSTICE ALITO, dissenting.

This is an unnecessary, impractical, and arbitrary decision. It addresses a purely hypothetical question: whether the traffic stop in this case *would be* unreasonable if the police officer, prior to leading a drug-sniffing dog around the exterior of petitioner's car, did not already have reasonable suspicion that the car contained drugs. In fact, however, the police officer *did have* reasonable suspicion, and, as a result, the officer was justified in detaining the occupants for the short period of time (seven or eight minutes) that is at issue.

* * *

Not only does the Court reach out to decide a question not really presented by the facts in this case, but the Court's answer to that question is arbitrary. The Court refuses to address the real Fourth Amendment question: whether the stop was unreasonably prolonged. Instead, the Court latches onto the fact that Officer Struble delivered the warning prior to the dog sniff and proclaims that the authority to detain based on a traffic stop ends when a citation or warning is handed over to the driver. The Court thus holds that the Fourth Amendment was violated, not because of the length of the stop, but simply because of the sequence in which Officer Struble chose to perform his tasks.

This holding is not only arbitrary; it is perverse since Officer Struble chose that sequence for the purpose of protecting his own safety and possibly the safety of others. Without prolonging the stop, Officer Struble could have conducted the dog sniff while one of the tasks that the Court regards as properly part of the traffic stop was still in progress, but that sequence would have entailed unnecessary risk. At approximately 12:19 a.m., after collecting Pollman's driver's license, Officer Struble did two things. He called in the information needed to do a records check on Pollman (a step that the Court recognizes was properly part of the traffic stop), and he requested that another officer report to the scene. Officer Struble had decided to perform a dog sniff but did not want to do that without another officer present. When occupants of a vehicle who know that their vehicle contains a large amount of illegal drugs see that a drug-sniffing dog has alerted for the presence of drugs, they will almost certainly realize that the police will then proceed to search the vehicle, discover the drugs, and make arrests. Thus, it is reasonable for an officer to believe that an alert will increase the risk that the occupants of the vehicle will attempt to flee or perhaps even attack the officer.

In this case, Officer Struble was concerned that he was outnumbered at the scene, and he therefore called for backup and waited for the arrival of another officer before conducting the sniff. As a result, the sniff was not completed until seven or eight minutes after he delivered the warning. But Officer Struble could have proceeded with the dog sniff while he was waiting for the results of the records check on Pollman and before the arrival of the second officer. The drug-sniffing dog was present in Officer Struble's car. If he had chosen that riskier sequence of events, the dog sniff would have been completed before the point in time when, according to the Court's analysis, the authority to detain for the traffic stop ended. Thus, an action that would have been lawful had the officer made the *unreasonable* decision to risk his life became unlawful when the officer made the *reasonable* decision to wait a few minutes for backup. Officer Struble's error—apparently—was following prudent procedures motivated by legitimate safety concerns. The Court's holding therefore makes no practical sense. And nothing in the Fourth Amendment, which speaks of *reasonableness,* compels this arbitrary line.

The rule that the Court adopts will do little good going forward. It is unlikely to have any appreciable effect on the length of future traffic stops. Most officers will learn the prescribed sequence of events even if they cannot fathom the reason for that requirement. (I would love to be the proverbial fly on the wall when police instructors teach this rule to officers who make traffic stops.)

For these reasons and those set out in Justice THOMAS's opinion, I respectfully dissent.

NOTE

In Ohio v. Robinette, 519 U.S. 33, 117 S.Ct. 417 (1996), discussed in the note preceeding *Rodriguez*, the State of Ohio argued that after the traffic stop of Robinette ended, he voluntarily remained at the scene to discuss the stopping officer's concern that he was transporting controlled substances. At issue was the effectiveness of consent to search the vehicle given during this discussion.

The Ohio Supreme Court held the prosecution was barred from establishing the consent was "an independent act of free will" by the officer's failure to follow what the court found to be the applicable Fourth Amendment law:

This case demonstrates the need for this court to draw a bright line between the conclusion of a valid seizure and the beginning of a consensual exchange. * * *

The transition between detention and a consensual exchange can be so seamless that the untrained eye may not notice that it has occurred. The undetectability of that transition may be used by police officers to coerce citizens into answering questions that they need not answer, or to allow a search of a vehicle that they are not legally obligated to allow.

The present case offers an example of the blurring between a legal detention and an attempt at consensual interaction. Even assuming that Newsome's detention of Robinette was legal through the time when Newsome handed back Robinette's driver's license, Newsome then said, "One question *before you get gone*: are you carrying any illegal contraband in your car?" (Emphasis added.) Newsome tells Robinette that before he leaves Newsome wants to know whether Robinette is carrying any contraband. Newsome does not ask if he may ask a question, he simply asks it, implying that Robinette must respond before he may leave. The interrogation then continues. Robinette is never told that he is free to go or that he may answer the question at his option.

Most people believe that they are validly in a police officer's custody as long as the officer continues to interrogate them. The police officer retains the upper hand and the accouterments of authority. That the officer lacks legal license to continue to detain them is unknown to most citizens, and a reasonable person would not feel free to walk away as the officer continues to address him.

We are aware that consensual encounters between police and citizens are an important, and constitutional, investigative tool. However, citizens who have not been detained immediately prior to being encountered and questioned by police are more apt to realize that they need not respond to a police officer's questions. A "consensual encounter" immediately following a detention is likely to be imbued with the authoritative aura of the detention. Without a clear break from the detention, the succeeding encounter is not consensual at all.

Therefore, we are convinced that the right, guaranteed by the federal and Ohio Constitutions, to be secure in one's person and property requires that citizens stopped for traffic offenses be clearly informed by the detaining officer when they are free to go after a valid detention, before an officer attempts to engage in a consensual interrogation. Any attempt at consensual interrogation must be preceded by the phrase "At this time you legally are free to go" or by words of similar import.

73 Ohio St.3d at 654–55, 653 N.E.2d at 698–99.

The United States Supreme Court disagreed:

We have long held that the "touchstone of the Fourth Amendment is reasonableness." Reasonableness, in turn, is measured in objective terms by examining the totality of the circumstances.

In applying this test we have consistently eschewed bright-line rules, instead emphasizing the fact-specific nature of the reasonableness inquiry. * * *

The Fourth Amendment test for a valid consent to search is that the consent be voluntary, and "[v]oluntariness is a question of fact to be determined from all the circumstances." The Supreme Court of Ohio having held otherwise, its judgment is reversed, and the case is remanded for further proceedings not inconsistent with this opinion.

519 U.S. at 39–40, 117 S.Ct. at 421.

On remand, the Ohio court addressed the voluntariness of Robinette's consent under, among other cases, Schneckloth v. Bustamonte, 412 U.S.218, 93 S.Ct.2041 (1973) (reprinted in Chapter 4). It concluded the consent was not voluntary:

Newsome's words did not give Robinette any indication that he was free to go, but rather implied just the opposite—that Robinette was not free to go until he answered Newsome's additional questions. The timing of Newsome's immediate transition from giving Robinette the warning for speeding into questioning regarding contraband and the request to search is troubling. * * *

When these factors are combined with a police officer's superior position of authority, any reasonable person would have felt compelled to submit to the officer's questioning. While Newsome's questioning was not expressly coercive, the circumstances surrounding the request to search made the questioning impliedly coercive. * * * [A]n officer has discretion to issue a ticket rather than a warning to a motorist if the motorist becomes uncooperative. From the totality of the circumstances, it appears that Robinette merely submitted to "a claim of lawful authority" rather than consenting as a voluntary act of free will.

State v. Robinette, 80 Ohio St.3d 234, 244–45, 685 N.E.2d 762, 770–71 (1997).

EDITORS' NOTE: DETERMINING WHETHER A DOG ALERT CONSTITUTES PROBABLE CAUSE

How should a court determine whether an alert to a vehicle by a narcotic-detention dog constitutes the probable cause necessary to permit a search of that vehicle? This was addressed in Florida v. Harris, ___ U.S. ___, 133 S.Ct. 1050 (2013).

The Florida Supreme Court had held that in such cases the State must demonstrate the dog's reliability in a particular way:

> "[T]he State must present * * *. the dog's training and certification records, an explanation of the meaning of the particular training and certification, field performance records (including any unverified alerts), and evidence concerning the experience and training of the officer handling the dog, as well as any other objective evidence known to the officer about the dog's reliability."

Harris v. State, 71 So.3d 756, 775 (Fla.2011). Elaborating, it stressed the need for "evidence of the dog's performance history in the field," including "how often the dog has alerted in the field without illegal contraband having been found." 71 S.3d at 769.

A unanimous Supreme Court reversed. It explained:

> A police officer has probable cause to conduct a search when "the facts available to [him] would 'warrant a [person] of reasonable caution in the belief'" that contraband or evidence of a crime is present. The test for probable cause is not reducible to "precise definition or quantification." "Finely tuned standards such as proof beyond a reasonable doubt or by a preponderance of the evidence . . . have no place in the [probable-cause] decision." All we have required is the kind of "fair probability" on which "reasonable and prudent [people,] not legal technicians, act."
>
> In evaluating whether the State has met this practical and common-sensical standard, we have consistently looked to the totality of the circumstances. We have rejected rigid rules, bright-line tests, and mechanistic inquiries in favor of a more flexible, all-things-considered approach.

___U.S. at ___, 133 S.Ct. at 1055. The Florida court, by creating "a strict evidentiary checklist, whose every item the State must tick off," "flouted this established approach to determining probable cause." Treating "records of a dog's field performance as the gold standard in evidence" was particularly inappropriate:

> [E]vidence of a dog's satisfactory performance in a certification or training program can itself provide sufficient reason to trust his alert. If a bona fide organization has certified a dog after testing his reliability in a controlled setting, a court can presume (subject to any conflicting evidence offered) that the dog's alert provides probable cause to search. The same is true, even in the absence of formal certification, if the dog has recently and successfully completed a training program that evaluated his proficiency in locating drugs. * * *

A defendant, however, must have an opportunity to challenge such evidence of a dog's reliability, whether by cross-examining the testifying officer or by introducing his own fact or expert witnesses. The defendant, for example, may contest the adequacy of a certification or training program, perhaps asserting that its standards are too lax or its methods faulty. So too, the defendant may examine how the dog (or handler) performed in the assessments made in those settings. Indeed, evidence of the dog's (or handler's) history in the field * * * . And even assuming a dog is generally reliable, circumstances surrounding a particular alert may undermine the case for probable cause—if, say, the officer cued the dog (consciously or not), or if the team was working under unfamiliar conditions.

___ U.S. at ___, 133 S.Ct. at 1057–58.

Applying the correct approach, the Court held the record supported the trial judge's determination that the alert by the dog at issue—Aldo— as handled by Officer Wheetley gave rise to probable cause to search Harris's vehicle:

> The State * * * introduced substantial evidence of Aldo's training and his proficiency in finding drugs. The State showed that two years before alerting to Harris's truck, Aldo had successfully completed a 120-hour program in narcotics detection, and separately obtained a certification from an independent company. And although the certification expired after a year, the Sheriff's Office required continuing training for Aldo and Wheetley. The two satisfied the requirements of another, 40-hour training program one year prior to the search at issue. And Wheetley worked with Aldo for four hours each week on exercises designed to keep their skills sharp. Wheetley testified, and written records confirmed, that in those settings Aldo always performed at the highest level.

___ U.S. at ___, 133 S.Ct. at 1058.

3. RACE-RELATED ISSUES IN THE USE OF TRAFFIC STOPS

Commonwealth v. Lora

Supreme Judicial Court of Massachusetts, 2008.
451 Mass. 425, 886 N.E.2d 688.

■ Present: MARSHALL, C.J., GREANEY, IRELAND, SPINA, COWIN, CORDY, & BOTSFORD, JJ.

■ CORDY, J.

In this case, * * * we granted the defendant's application for direct appellate review [and we address issues relating to racial profiling and traffic stops]. * * *

1. Background.

a. Traffic stop.

On the evening of December 20, 2001, State Trooper Brendhan Shugrue was patrolling Interstate Route 290 in Auburn (Route 290). At approximately 9:10 p.m., he approached a motor vehicle traveling ahead of him in the left lane. * * *

Shugrue followed the vehicle for three-quarters mile to an area within several hundred yards of the border between Auburn and Worcester. He observed that the two occupants of the vehicle were dark skinned (the defendant, Andres Lora, is Hispanic). He activated the cruiser's blue lights and stopped the vehicle for traveling in the left lane while the center and right lanes were unoccupied.[6] Shugrue approached the vehicle from the passenger's side and asked the driver for his license and registration. * * *

Shugrue * * * directed his flashlight inside the vehicle, where he observed a small glassine bag on the driver's side floor containing white powder.

Shugrue immediately asked Lora to step out of the vehicle and frisked him. He then retrieved the glassine bag, which appeared to contain cocaine, and radioed the State police barracks to request assistance. Trooper William Pinkes arrived at the scene ten to fifteen minutes later. The troopers then proceeded to search the vehicle. Shugrue discovered substantially more cocaine in the trunk. Pinkes then placed Lora and the driver under arrest.

A grand jury subsequently returned an indictment charging Lora with trafficking in cocaine * * * .

b. Motion to suppress.

On March 27, 2003, Lora filed a motion to suppress the cocaine as the fruit of an unconstitutional search. He contended that Shugrue initiated the traffic stop because the occupants of the vehicle were dark skinned, and not solely because the operator of the vehicle committed a traffic violation by driving in the left lane. In other words, he claimed that Shugrue impermissibly engaged in the practice of racial profiling [in violation of the Fourteenth Amendment to the United States Constitution and arts. 1 and 10 of the Massachusetts Declaration of Rights].

Lora sought to prove that the stop of the vehicle in which he was traveling was the product of racial profiling by establishing that Shugrue had a history of disproportionately stopping and citing nonwhite motorists for motor vehicle violations. To that end, defense counsel filed

---

[6] General Laws c. 89, § 4B, states in relevant part: "Upon all ways the driver of a vehicle shall drive in the lane nearest the right side of the way when such lane is available for travel, except when overtaking another vehicle or when preparing for a left turn. . . ." Andres Lora concedes that the vehicle in which he was traveling was in violation of this statutory provision.

an affidavit stating that he had reviewed 256 citations issued by Trooper Shugrue between August 22, 2001, and February 18, 2002.[11] The affidavit pointed out that during this time period, Shugrue cited the operators of fifty-one vehicles driving on the stretch of Route 290 that passes through Auburn. Sixteen of the operators cited (or 31.37 per cent) were identified as Hispanic, and six (or 11.76 per cent) as African-American.[13]

Defense counsel then compared the percentage of citations issued to each racial group with the racial composition of the town of Auburn, as tabulated by the 2000 United States census (census). White residents accounted for 97.5 per cent of the population of Auburn; Hispanic residents, one per cent; and African-American residents, .6 per cent. Implicitly assuming that the demographics of the town of Auburn mirror the demographics of those driving on Route 290 through Auburn, defense counsel argued that Shugrue cited minority drivers at a rate wildly disproportionate to their representation in the local Auburn population. This type of comparison is known as census benchmarking. Using this analytical framework, defense counsel contended that a Hispanic driver would be 31.37 times more likely to be cited than an average motorist; and an African-American driver would be 19.60 times more likely to be cited than an average motorist. By contrast, white drivers were only .5631 times as likely to be pulled over as an average motorist (or, in other words, about one-half as likely).

In his affidavit, defense counsel cast these numbers as percentage increases, labeled "differentials" rather than multiples. The discrepancy between the proportion of Hispanics living in Auburn and the proportion of the Hispanics stopped by Shugrue was not, therefore, described as 31.37 times greater than expected, but rather was described as resulting in a 3,137 per cent "differential." * * *

Defense counsel's affidavit also included information regarding traffic citations issued by Shugrue along the stretch of Route 290 passing through the city of Worcester. In that same period, i.e., between August 22, 2001, and February 18, 2002, Shugrue cited eighty-nine motorists. Seventy-four, or 83.15 per cent, of the motorists cited were white; seven, or 7.87 per cent, were Hispanic; and six, or 6.74 per cent, were African-American. According to the census, white residents account for 77.1 per cent of the population of Worcester; Hispanic residents, 15.1 per cent; and African-American residents, 8.0 per cent. Defense counsel again used census benchmarking to compare the racial composition of the citations to the racial composition of the inhabitants of Worcester. Using the same implicit assumption that the demographics of Worcester accurately reflected the demographics of motorists driving on Route 290 in

---

[11] The records reviewed were Shugrue's citations, which demonstrate only which motorists were cited, and do not account for motorists who may have been stopped but not cited.

[13] The records denote only the race of the operator of the vehicle, not the race of any other occupants.

Worcester, defense counsel calculated that white motorists were 1.08 times more likely to be cited than an average motorist (that is, slightly more likely). Hispanic motorists were .52 times as likely to be cited as an average motorist (that is, about one-half as likely), while African-American drivers were .84 times as likely to be cited (that is, slightly less likely).

At the hearing on the motion to suppress, Lora introduced Shugrue's citation history * * * . Troopers Shugrue and Pinkes testified on behalf of the Commonwealth, contending that the traffic stop was motivated solely by the operator's failure to keep to the right * * * . After taking the matter under advisement, the judge allowed Lora's motion to suppress. In his decision, the judge found that * * * the record left "no reasonable conclusion but that Shugrue stopped the motor vehicle in which the Defendant was a passenger because of the race of the operator and the race of the Defendant." Therefore, the trooper "violated the Defendant's rights pursuant to the Fourteenth Amendment . . . and Articles 1 and 10 . . . when he stopped and searched his vehicle."

* * *

c.   Motion for rehearing and the joint motion to vacate.

Following the judge's decision, the Commonwealth filed a motion for reconsideration. * * * The motion for reconsideration was allowed, and the judge ordered the scheduling of another evidentiary hearing.

Before the evidentiary hearing took place, the Commonwealth shared with defense counsel the evidence that it anticipated presenting at the hearing * * * . After defense counsel had the opportunity to review [the evidence] and discuss its contents with Lora, he joined the Commonwealth in filing a motion to vacate the suppression order * * * .

The judge held a hearing on the joint motion to vacate the suppression order, during which he suggested that both parties were "looking to duck the issue" * * * . Consequently, the judge declined to rule on the joint motion and directed both parties to present expert testimony at the rehearing.

At the rehearing, the defense called Scott Evans, a research scientist in the department of biostatistics at Harvard School of Public Health. In preparing for his testimony, Evans reviewed only the data regarding the citations issued by Shugrue in Auburn, and compared that information to the population demographics of that town. On the basis of that data, he concluded that the chance that race was not a factor in the disparate stop rates in Auburn was "very, very minute." On cross-examination by the Commonwealth, Evans admitted that the assumption underlying his conclusion was that the demographics of the town of Auburn reflected the demographics of motorists on Interstate Route 290, and admitted that he had not considered the stops that occurred in Worcester.

The Commonwealth called [Donna M. Bishop of Northeastern University's College of Criminal Justice, holder of a doctorate in criminal justice], who testified that the census benchmarking technique used by Lora is "outmoded and no longer accepted within the scientific community because . . . it is highly likely to yield misleading and erroneous conclusions." She testified that census benchmarking assumes that the "demographic profile of the community [is] nearly identical to the demographic profile of drivers on the road where the officer was patrolling," an assumption that is "not accurate."[22] Bishop further testified that Shugrue's citations themselves demonstrate the flaw in census benchmarking: "I examined each of the citations that were given by Trooper Shugrue of [sic] motorists in Auburn . . . ninety per cent of those motorists were not from Auburn, which is conclusive evidence that a residential or a census benchmark coming from Auburn is totally inappropriate [as a point of comparison]." She went on to explain that an appropriate benchmark must include "a profile of the people who should be legitimately at more risk of being stopped and then compare that to the profile of who is actually stopped," and ideally "roadside observers [would be used to] develop a demographic profile of people who violate traffic laws in a particular location where police are patrolling and stops are being made. In that instance, the benchmark would represent fairly well the group of people who should be at risk for being stopped if no bias exists."

* * *

On December 2, 2005, the judge issued his decision affirming the earlier suppression order * * *. The single justice allowed the Commonwealth's interlocutory appeal.

2. Discussion.

* * * [I]n *Whren v. United States*, 517 U.S. 806, 813, 116 S.Ct. 1769, 135 L.Ed.2d 89 (1996), * * * the Court specifically noted, "We of course agree with petitioners that the Constitution prohibits selective enforcement of the law based on considerations such as race. * * *" * * *

a. Selective enforcement.

[T]he issue of racial profiling is * * * at base a claim that Shugrue selectively enforced the laws in contravention of the Fourteenth Amendment and arts. 1 and 10 * * *.

It is well established that "[t]he equal protection principles of the Fourteenth Amendment . . . and arts. 1 and 10 . . . prohibit discriminatory application of impartial laws." "It is equally well established, however, that prosecutors and other law enforcement officers enjoy considerable discretion in exercising some selectivity for purposes consistent with the public interest." The " 'conscious exercise of

---

[22] Bishop elaborated on the reasons for this inaccuracy, testifying that "[t]he stops in this particular case took place near a turnpike exit. Drivers on the turnpike include many nonresidents. There are commuters from other communities who are going to and from work, there are tourists and people on vacation who are passing through. . . . There is reason to believe that the resident population is not an accurate reflection of the people who are on the roadway."

some selectivity' in criminal law enforcement" is permitted "as long as the selectivity is not based on 'an unjustifiable standard such as race, religion or other arbitrary classification.' " * * *

An arrest or prosecution based on probable cause is ordinarily cloaked with a presumption of regularity. "Because we presume that criminal prosecutions are undertaken in good faith, without intent to discriminate, the defendant bears the initial burden of demonstrating selective enforcement." In order to meet this burden, the defendant must first "present evidence which raises at least a reasonable inference of impermissible discrimination," including evidence that "a broader class of persons than those prosecuted has violated the law, . . . that failure to prosecute was either consistent or deliberate, . . . and that the decision not to prosecute was based on an impermissible classification such as race, religion, or sex." Once a defendant has raised a reasonable inference of selective prosecution by presenting credible evidence that persons similarly situated to himself have been deliberately or consistently not prosecuted because of their race, "the Commonwealth must rebut that inference or suffer dismissal of the underlying complaint."

b.   Suppression as remedy.

The Commonwealth * * * "contend[s] that claims of selective enforcement must be raised in a motion to dismiss. * * *

We conclude that the application of the exclusionary rule to evidence obtained in violation of the constitutional right to the equal protection of the laws is entirely consistent with the policy underlying the exclusionary rule, is properly gauged to deter intentional unconstitutional behavior, and furthers the protections guaranteed by the Massachusetts Declaration of Rights. Consequently, if a defendant can establish that a traffic stop is the product of selective enforcement predicated on race, evidence seized in the course of the stop should be suppressed unless the connection between the unconstitutional stop by the police and the discovery of the challenged evidence has "become so attenuated as to dissipate the taint."

c.   Statistical evidence.

"Statistics may be used to make out a case of targeting minorities for prosecution of traffic offenses. . . ." *State v. Soto*, 324 N.J.Super. 66, 83, 734 A.2d 350 (1996) (unrebutted statistical evidence of disproportionate traffic stops of African-American motorists established de facto policy of targeting them for investigation and arrest). "Of course, parties may not prove discrimination merely by providing the court with statistical analyses. The statistics proffered must address the crucial question of whether one class is being treated differently from another class that is otherwise similarly situated." * * * If the evidence is introduced through expert testimony, the "expert analysis must be both relevant and reliable."

In *State v. Soto*, a New Jersey case examining racial profiling in traffic stops, the judge was presented with rigorously prepared surveys regarding both the racial makeup of motorists traveling along a stretch of the New Jersey Turnpike encompassing three exits (traffic survey) and the racial makeup of motorists observed violating speeding and other moving violation laws along that same stretch of highway (violation survey). The data from these surveys demonstrated that the racial makeup of the motorists traveling the road was 13.5 per cent black, and that the observed violators were approximately fifteen per cent black. This data were used as the benchmark for comparison with the number of "race identified" traffic stops made by the State police along the same stretch of highway. The stop data showed that 46.2 per cent of the stops were of black motorists. This disparity was calculated to be more than sixteen standard deviations over the expected norm. Further expert testimony presented by the defendants established that the surveys were well designed and performed, and statistically reliable for the analysis, and that a similarly situated black motorist was 4.85 times as likely as a white motorist to be stopped on the roadway.

Ultimately, the judge concluded that the statistical data were sufficient to support the finding of a "de facto policy" on the part of certain State troopers of targeting black motorists, which was not adequately rebutted by the State. * * *

                              * * *

We are of the view that statistical evidence may be used to meet a defendant's initial burden of producing sufficient evidence to raise a reasonable inference of impermissible discrimination. At a minimum, that evidence must establish that the racial composition of motorists stopped for motor vehicle violations varied significantly from the racial composition of the population of motorists making use of the relevant roadways, and who therefore could have encountered the officer or officers whose actions have been called into question.

d.   Lora's evidence.

[W]e turn to Lora's evidence. * * *

[T]he use of census benchmarking to compare the demographics of a small community with citation ratios on a major interstate highway, which happens to pass through it, is unreliable and not accepted in the scientific community. Such benchmarking data do not provide an adequate basis for assessing the racial composition of the drivers encountered by Shugrue on Route 290 and is inadequate to establish that similarly situated drivers of different races were treated differently. Indeed, Lora's own evidence disproves his premise of comparability: of the fifty-two motorists that Shugrue ticketed on Route 290 in Auburn, ninety per cent were not residents of Auburn. Lora therefore failed to present sufficient credible evidence of discriminatory effect. The judge's determination to the contrary was clearly erroneous, and the motion to suppress should not have been granted.

* * *

3.   Conclusion.

* * * While racial profiling evidence is relevant to assessing the constitutionality of a traffic stop, and evidence seized during a traffic stop that violates the equal protection guarantees of the Massachusetts Declaration of Rights may be suppressed, the initial burden rests on the defendant to produce evidence that similarly situated persons were treated differently because of their race. The practical weight of this burden is admittedly daunting in some cases, but not impossible. * * *

Of necessity, the important responsibility of eliminating racial considerations in the day-to-day enforcement of our laws lies principally with the executive branch of government, and no evidence was presented in this case to suggest that this is a responsibility that is being ignored. * * * The judge's order suppressing the evidence in this case is reversed.

So ordered.

NOTE

What has been described as "the most thorough and comprehensive study that has ever been done on traffic stops in the United States," Kathryne M. Young & Joan Petersilia, Keeping Track: Surveillance, Control and the Expansion of the Carceral State, 129 Harv.L.Rev. 1318 (2016) (book review), was reported in Charles R. Epp, Steven Maynard-Moody, and Donald Haider-Markel, Pulled Over, How Police Stops Define Race and Citizenship (2014).

Epp and his coauthors distinguished between what they described as "traffic-safety stops" and "investigatory stops." They categorized stops according to what the subjects reported the officers as stating was the basis for the stops. A stop was regarded as a traffic-safety stop if the officer stated it was for speeding at 7 or more mph over the limit, suspicion of driving while impaired, running a red light, reckless driving or if it was a random checkpoint stop for driving under the influence. A stop was regarded as an investigatory stop if it the officer stated it was based on a less serious offense, such as failure to signal a turn or lane change, or if no basis was offered by the officer. Epp, et al., at 59. Investigatory stops, they contended, are not made to enforce traffic laws but to investigate whether the drivers have committed criminal offenses. Id. at 8.

Their study convinced the authors that the race of the drivers—whether the drivers were African-American—influenced the making of investigatory stops but not traffic-safety stops. For investigatory stops but not traffic-safety stops, race also influenced whether the subject was threatened with arrest, searched and handcuffed.

In traffic-safety stops, officers try to carry out the stop and issuance of a citation or warning quickly and with as little interpersonal conflict as possible. In investigatory stops, on the other hand, the need for investigation sometimes requires prolonging the stop despite the risk of generating interpersonal conflict.

African-Americans recognized investigatory stops, the study concluded, and even if the officers were polite the stopped persons evaluated the stops negatively. The kind of stop rather than the manner in which a stop is carried out offended many African-Americans. Id. at 133. Experiencing a traffic-safety stop had no effect on trust in police for either whites or African-Americans. But experiencing an investigatory stop did decrease this trust, more so with regard to African-Americans than with whites. Id at 143. Accumulation of multiple investigatory stops had no effect on whites' trust in police but did erode the trust of African-Americans. Id. at 143–44.

Epp and his coauthors concluded that investigatory police stops "are the police activity that most directly contributes to the enduring racial divide in American society." Id. at 150. For whites, stops are annoyances but that also "reaffirm the driver's place as a full citizen in a rule-regulated society." For African-Americans, in contrast, stops "are the signal form of surveillance and legalized racial subordination." Id. at 150.

As a bottom line, the study represented that "the benefits of investigatory stops are modest and greatly exaggerated, yet their costs are substantial and largely unrecognized. It is time to end this failed practice." Id. at 153.

E. SOBRIETY CHECKPOINTS AND RELATED DETENTIONS

EDITORS' INTRODUCTION: SUSPICIONLESS STOPS

Arrests, *Terry* stops for investigation, and traffic stops all involve action based on suspicion focused upon the suspects. The criteria for determining the reasonableness of these seizures impose different standards for judging the adequacy of suspicion, or at least the basis for such suspicion. Those criteria all, however, address the adequacy of the facts to support a belief that the suspect is involved in criminal activity.

Some law enforcement action, in contrast, is permissible without regard to officers' suspicion the suspect is involved in criminal activity or any basis for such suspicion. This action may usefully be regarded as "suspicionless" law enforcement action.

Suspicionless action by officers is considered earlier in these materials. Thus searches incident to custodial arrests, addressed earlier in this chapter, are suspicionless in the sense they are permissible regardless of whether the officers have any subjective concern that the suspects have evidence or weapons or whether the officers have any objective information that could support such concern.

This part considers the constitutionality of suspicionless stops of persons in certain situations. Eleven years before the first principal case, the Supreme Court refused to permit suspicionless stops of motorists in a different context. In Delaware v. Prouse, 440 U.S. 648, 99 S.Ct. 1391 (1979), the Court considered Delaware's contention that its police officers were permitted by the Fourth Amendment to stop any motorist to determine whether the driver was in possession of a valid driver's license and registration for the vehicle being driven. No suspicion that the driver lacked either was required, the state argued, nor did an officer need facts that would support any such suspicion. Holding that these suspicionless stops were unreasonable, the Court explained:

> We agree that the States have a vital interest in ensuring that only those qualified to do so are permitted to operate motor vehicles, that these vehicles are fit for safe operation, and hence that licensing, registration, and vehicle inspection requirements are being observed. * * *

> The question remains, however, whether in the service of these important ends the discretionary spot check is a sufficiently productive mechanism to justify the intrusion upon Fourth Amendment interests which such stops entail. On the record before us, that question must be answered in the negative. Given the alternative mechanisms available, both those in use and those that might be adopted, we are unconvinced that the incremental contribution to highway safety of the random spot check justifies the practice under the Fourth Amendment.

> The foremost method of enforcing traffic and vehicle safety regulations * * * is acting upon observed violations. Vehicle stops for traffic violations occur countless times each day; and on these occasions, licenses and registration papers are subject to inspection and drivers without them will be ascertained. Furthermore, drivers without licenses are presumably the less safe drivers whose propensities may well exhibit themselves. * * * The contribution to highway safety made by discretionary stops selected from among drivers generally will therefore be marginal at best. Furthermore, and again absent something more than mere assertion to the contrary, we find it difficult to believe that the unlicensed driver would not be deterred by the possibility of being involved in a traffic violation or having some other experience calling for proof of his entitlement to drive but that he would be deterred by the possibility that he would be one of those chosen for a spot check. In terms of actually discovering unlicensed drivers or deterring them from driving, the spot check does not appear sufficiently productive to qualify as a reasonable law-enforcement practice under the Fourth Amendment.

> Much the same can be said about the safety aspects of automobiles as distinguished from drivers. * * *

The marginal contribution to roadway safety possibly resulting from a system of spot checks cannot justify subjecting every occupant of every vehicle on the roads to a seizure—limited in magnitude compared to other intrusions but nonetheless constitutionally cognizable—at the unbridled discretion of law-enforcement officials. * * * This kind of standardless and unconstrained discretion is the evil the Court has discerned when in previous cases it has insisted that the discretion of the official in the field be circumscribed, at least to some extent. * * *

Accordingly, we hold that except in those situations in which there is at least articulable and reasonable suspicion that a motorist is unlicensed or that an automobile is not registered, or that either the vehicle or an occupant is otherwise subject to seizure for violation of law, stopping an automobile and detaining the driver in order to check his driver's license and the registration of the automobile are unreasonable under the Fourth Amendment. This holding does not preclude the State of Delaware or other States from developing methods for spot checks that involve less intrusion or that do not involve the unconstrained exercise of discretion. Questioning of all oncoming traffic at roadblock-type stops is one possible alternative. We hold only that persons in automobiles on public roadways may not for that reason alone have their travel and privacy interfered with at the unbridled discretion of police officers.

440 U.S. at 658–63, 99 S.Ct. at 1398–1401. Justice Rehnquist dissented, noting the majority's statement concerning roadblocks "elevates the adage 'misery loves company' to a novel role in Fourth Amendment jurisprudence."

Prouse obviously invited the litigation of stops at "roadblock-type stops," and the issue was presented to the Court in the principal case that follows.

Michigan v. Sitz

Supreme Court of the United States, 1990.
496 U.S. 444, 110 S.Ct. 2481.

■ CHIEF JUSTICE REHNQUIST delivered the opinion of the Court.

This case poses the question whether a State's use of highway sobriety checkpoints violates the Fourth and Fourteenth Amendments to the United States Constitution. * * *

Petitioners, the Michigan Department of State Police and its Director, established a sobriety checkpoint pilot program in early 1986. The Director appointed a Sobriety Checkpoint Advisory Committee comprising representatives of the State Police force, local police forces, state prosecutors, and the University of Michigan Transportation Research Institute. Pursuant to its charge, the Advisory Committee created guidelines setting forth procedures governing checkpoint operations, site selection, and publicity.

Under the guidelines, checkpoints would be set up at selected sites along state roads. All vehicles passing through a checkpoint would be stopped and their drivers briefly examined for signs of intoxication. In cases where a checkpoint officer detected signs of intoxication, the motorist would be directed to a location out of the traffic flow where an officer would check the motorist's driver's license and car registration and, if warranted, conduct further sobriety tests. Should the field tests and the officer's observations suggest that the driver was intoxicated, an arrest would be made. All other drivers would be permitted to resume their journey immediately.

The first—and to date the only—sobriety checkpoint operated under the program was conducted in Saginaw County with the assistance of the Saginaw County Sheriff's Department. During the hour-and-fifteen-minute duration of the checkpoint's operation, 126 vehicles passed through the checkpoint. The average delay for each vehicle was approximately 25 seconds. Two drivers were detained for field sobriety testing, and one of the two was arrested for driving under the influence of alcohol. A third driver who drove through without stopping was pulled over by an officer in an observation vehicle and arrested for driving under the influence.

On the day before the operation of the Saginaw County checkpoint, respondents filed a complaint in the Circuit Court of Wayne County seeking declaratory and injunctive relief from potential subjection to the checkpoints. * * * During pretrial proceedings, petitioners agreed to delay further implementation of the checkpoint program pending the outcome of this litigation.

After the trial, at which the court heard extensive testimony concerning, inter alia, the "effectiveness" of highway sobriety checkpoint programs, the court ruled that the Michigan program violated the Fourth Amendment and Art. 1, § 11, of the Michigan Constitution. On appeal, the Michigan Court of Appeals affirmed the holding that the program violated the Fourth Amendment and, for that reason, did not consider whether the program violated the Michigan Constitution. After the Michigan Supreme Court denied petitioners' application for leave to appeal, we granted certiorari.

To decide this case the [lower courts] performed a balancing test derived from our opinion in *Brown v. Texas*, 443 U.S. 47, 99 S.Ct. 2637, 61 L.Ed.2d 357 (1979) [which involved] "balancing the state's interest in preventing accidents caused by drunk drivers, the effectiveness of sobriety checkpoints in achieving that goal, and the level of intrusion on an individual's privacy caused by the checkpoints." * * *

As characterized by the Court of Appeals, the trial court's findings with respect to the balancing factors were that the State has "a grave and legitimate" interest in curbing drunken driving; that sobriety checkpoint programs are generally "ineffective" and, therefore, do not significantly further that interest; and that the checkpoints' "subjective intrusion" on individual liberties is substantial. According to the court, the record disclosed no basis for disturbing the trial court's findings, which were made within the context of an analytical framework prescribed by this Court for determining the constitutionality of seizures less intrusive than traditional arrests. * * *

[*United States v.*] *Martinez-Fuerte*, [428 U.S. 543, 96 S.Ct. 3074, 49 L.Ed.2d 1116 (1976)], which utilized a balancing analysis in approving highway checkpoints for detecting illegal aliens, and Brown v. Texas, supra, are the relevant authorities here.

Petitioners concede, correctly in our view, that a Fourth Amendment "seizure" occurs when a vehicle is stopped at a checkpoint. The question thus becomes whether such seizures are "reasonable" under the Fourth Amendment.

It is important to recognize what our inquiry is NOT about. No allegations are before us of unreasonable treatment of any person after an actual detention at a particular checkpoint. As pursued in the lower courts, the instant action challenges only the use of sobriety checkpoints generally. We address only the initial stop of each motorist passing through a checkpoint and the associated preliminary questioning and observation by checkpoint officers. Detention of particular motorists for more extensive field sobriety testing may require satisfaction of an individualized suspicion standard.

No one can seriously dispute the magnitude of the drunken driving problem or the States' interest in eradicating it. * * *

Conversely, the weight bearing on the other scale—the measure of the intrusion on motorists stopped briefly at sobriety checkpoints—is slight. We reached a similar conclusion as to the intrusion on motorists subjected to a brief stop at a highway checkpoint for detecting illegal aliens. See *Martinez-Fuerte,* supra, at 558, 96 S.Ct. at 3083. We see virtually no difference between the levels of intrusion on law-abiding motorists from the brief stops necessary to the effectuation of these two types of checkpoints, which to the average motorist would seem identical save for the nature of the questions the checkpoint officers might ask. The trial court and the Court of Appeals[ ] thus[ ] accurately gauged the "objective" intrusion, measured by the duration of the seizure and the intensity of the investigation, as minimal.

With respect to what it perceived to be the "subjective" intrusion on motorists, however, the Court of Appeals found such intrusion substantial. The court first affirmed the trial court's finding that the guidelines governing checkpoint operation minimize the discretion of the officers on the scene. But the court also agreed with the trial court's conclusion that the checkpoints have the potential to generate fear and surprise in motorists. This was so because the record failed to demonstrate that approaching motorists would be aware of their option to make U-turns or turnoffs to avoid the checkpoints. On that basis, the court deemed the subjective intrusion from the checkpoints unreasonable.

We believe the Michigan courts misread our cases concerning the degree of "subjective intrusion" and the potential for generating fear and surprise. The "fear and surprise" to be considered are not the natural fear of one who has been drinking over the prospect of being stopped at a sobriety checkpoint but, rather, the fear and surprise engendered in law abiding motorists by the nature of the stop. * * * Here, checkpoints are selected pursuant to the guidelines, and uniformed police officers stop every approaching vehicle. The intrusion resulting from the brief stop at the sobriety checkpoint is for constitutional purposes indistinguishable from the checkpoint stops we upheld in *Martinez-Fuerte.*

The Court of Appeals went on to consider as part of the balancing analysis the "effectiveness" of the proposed checkpoint program. Based on extensive testimony in the trial record, the court concluded that the checkpoint program failed the "effectiveness" part of the test, and that this failure materially discounted petitioners' strong interest in implementing the program. We think the Court of Appeals was wrong on this point as well.

The actual language from Brown v. Texas, upon which the Michigan courts based their evaluation of "effectiveness," describes the balancing factor as "the degree to which the seizure advances the public interest." This passage from *Brown* was not meant to transfer from politically accountable officials to the courts the decision as to which among reasonable alternative law enforcement techniques should be employed to deal with a serious public danger. Experts in police science might disagree over which of several methods of apprehending drunken drivers is preferable as an ideal. But for purposes of Fourth Amendment analysis, the choice among such reasonable alternatives remains with the governmental officials who have a unique understanding of, and a responsibility for, limited public resources, including a finite number of police officers. * * *

Unlike [*Delaware v. Prouse*, 440 U.S. 648, 99 S.Ct. 1391, 59 L.Ed.2d 660 (1979)], this case involves neither a complete absence of empirical data nor a challenge to random highway stops. During the operation of the Saginaw County checkpoint, the detention of each of the 126 vehicles that entered the checkpoint resulted in the arrest of two drunken drivers. Stated as a percentage, approximately 1.5 percent of the drivers passing through the checkpoint were arrested for alcohol impairment. In addition, an expert witness testified at the trial that experience in other States demonstrated that, on the whole, sobriety checkpoints resulted in drunken driving arrests of around 1 percent of all motorists stopped. By way of comparison, the record from one of the consolidated cases in *Martinez-Fuerte,* showed that in the associated checkpoint, illegal aliens were found in only 0.12 percent of the vehicles passing through the checkpoint. The ratio of illegal aliens detected to vehicles stopped (considering that on occasion two or more illegal aliens were found in a single vehicle) was approximately 0.5 percent. We concluded that this "record . . . provides a rather complete picture of the effectiveness of the San Clemente checkpoint", and we sustained its constitutionality. We see no justification for a different conclusion here.

In sum, the balance of the State's interest in preventing drunken driving, the extent to which this system can reasonably be said to advance that interest, and the degree of intrusion upon individual motorists who are briefly stopped, weighs in favor of the state program. We therefore hold that it is consistent with the Fourth Amendment. The judgment of the Michigan Court of Appeals is accordingly reversed, and the cause is remanded for further proceedings not inconsistent with this opinion.

Reversed.

■ JUSTICE STEVENS, with whom JUSTICE BRENNAN and JUSTICE MARSHALL join * * * , dissenting.

[T]he record in this case makes clear that a decision holding these suspicionless seizures unconstitutional would not impede the law enforcement community's remarkable progress in reducing the death toll on our highways. * * * [I]t seems inconceivable that a higher arrest rate could not have been achieved by more conventional means. * * *

[T]he Court today * * * overvalues the law enforcement interest in using sobriety checkpoints, undervalues the citizen's interest in freedom from random, unannounced investigatory seizures, and mistakenly assumes that there is "virtually no difference" between a routine stop at a permanent, fixed checkpoint and a surprise stop at a sobriety checkpoint. I believe this case is controlled by our * * * precedent[ ] condemning suspicionless random stops of motorists for investigatory purposes. *Delaware v. Prouse,* 440 U.S. 648, 99 S.Ct. 1391, 59 L.Ed.2d 660 (1979).

* * *

There is a critical difference between a seizure that is preceded by fair notice and one that is effected by surprise. That is one reason why a border search, or indeed any search at a permanent and fixed checkpoint, is much less intrusive than a random stop. A motorist with advance notice of the location of a permanent checkpoint has an opportunity to avoid the search entirely, or at least to prepare for, and limit, the intrusion on her privacy.

No such opportunity is available in the case of a random stop or a temporary checkpoint, which both depend for their effectiveness on the element of surprise. A driver who discovers an unexpected checkpoint on a familiar local road will be startled and distressed. She may infer, correctly, that the checkpoint is not simply "business as usual," and may likewise infer, again correctly, that the police have made a discretionary decision to focus their law enforcement efforts upon her and others who pass the chosen point.

This element of surprise is the most obvious distinction between the sobriety checkpoints permitted by today's majority and the interior border checkpoints approved by this Court in *Martinez-Fuerte*. The distinction casts immediate doubt upon the majority's argument, for *Martinez-Fuerte* is the only case in which we have upheld suspicionless seizures of motorists. But the difference between notice and surprise is only one of the important reasons for distinguishing between permanent and mobile checkpoints. With respect to the former, there is no room for discretion in either the timing or the location of the stop—it is a permanent part of the landscape. In the latter case, however, although the checkpoint is most frequently employed during the hours of darkness on weekends (because that is when drivers with alcohol in their blood are most apt to be found on the road), the police have extremely broad discretion in determining the exact timing and placement of the roadblock.

There is also a significant difference between the kind of discretion that the officer exercises after the stop is made. A check for a driver's license, or for identification papers at an immigration checkpoint, is far more easily standardized than is a search for evidence of intoxication. * * *

For all these reasons, I do not believe that this case is analogous to *Martinez-Fuerte*. In my opinion, the sobriety checkpoints are instead similar to—and in some respects more intrusive than—the random investigative stops that the Court held unconstitutional in * * * *Prouse*. * * *

I respectfully dissent.

NOTE

On remand, the Michigan courts held the roadblock at issue violated the Michigan Constitution's prohibition against unreasonable searches and seizures. Sitz v. Department of State Police, 443 Mich. 744, 506 N.W.2d 209 (1993), affirming 193 Mich.App. 690, 485 N.W.2d 135 (1992).

City of Indianapolis v. Edmond

Supreme Court of the United States, 2000.
531 U.S. 32, 121 S.Ct. 447.

■ JUSTICE O'CONNOR delivered the opinion of the Court.

In *Michigan Dept. of State Police v. Sitz,* 496 U.S. 444, 110 S.Ct. 2481, 110 L.Ed.2d 412 (1990), and *United States v. Martinez-Fuerte,* 428 U.S. 543, 96 S.Ct. 3074, 49 L.Ed.2d 1116 (1976), we held that brief, suspicionless seizures at highway checkpoints for the purposes of combating drunk driving and intercepting illegal immigrants were constitutional. We now consider the constitutionality of a highway checkpoint program whose primary purpose is the discovery and interdiction of illegal narcotics.

I

In August 1998, the city of Indianapolis began to operate vehicle checkpoints on Indianapolis roads in an effort to interdict unlawful drugs. The city conducted six such roadblocks between August and November that year, stopping 1,161 vehicles and arresting 104 motorists. Fifty-five arrests were for drug-related crimes, while 49 were for offenses unrelated to drugs. The overall "hit rate" of the program was thus approximately nine percent.

The parties stipulated to the facts concerning the operation of the checkpoints by the Indianapolis Police Department (IPD) for purposes of the preliminary injunction proceedings instituted below. At each checkpoint location, the police stop a predetermined number of vehicles. Approximately 30 officers are stationed at the checkpoint. Pursuant to written directives issued by the chief of police, at least one officer approaches the vehicle, advises the driver that he or she is being stopped briefly at a drug checkpoint, and asks the driver to produce a license and registration. The officer also looks for signs of impairment and conducts an open-view examination of the vehicle from the outside. A narcotics-detection dog walks around the outside of each stopped vehicle.

The directives instruct the officers that they may conduct a search only by consent or based on the appropriate quantum of particularized suspicion. The officers must conduct each stop in the same manner until particularized suspicion develops, and the officers have no discretion to stop any vehicle out of sequence. The city agreed in the stipulation to operate the checkpoints in such a way as to ensure that the total duration of each stop, absent reasonable suspicion or probable cause, would be five minutes or less.

[C]heckpoint locations are selected weeks in advance based on such considerations as area crime statistics and traffic flow. The checkpoints are generally operated during daylight hours and are identified with lighted signs reading, "NARCOTICS CHECKPOINT ___ MILE AHEAD, NARCOTICS K-9 IN USE, BE PREPARED TO STOP." Once a group of cars has been stopped, other traffic proceeds without interruption until all the stopped cars have been processed or diverted for further processing. * * * [T]he average stop for a vehicle not subject to further processing lasts two to three minutes or less.

Respondents James Edmond and Joell Palmer were each stopped at a narcotics checkpoint in late September 1998. Respondents then filed a lawsuit on behalf of themselves and the class of all motorists who had been stopped or were subject to being stopped in the future at the Indianapolis drug checkpoints. Respondents claimed that the roadblocks violated the Fourth Amendment of the United States Constitution and the search and seizure provision of the Indiana Constitution. Respondents requested declaratory and injunctive relief for the class, as well as damages and attorney's fees for themselves.

Respondents then moved for a preliminary injunction. * * * The United States District Court for the Southern District of Indiana * * * denied the motion for a preliminary injunction, holding that the checkpoint program did not violate the Fourth Amendment. A divided panel of the United States Court of Appeals for the Seventh Circuit reversed, holding that the checkpoints contravened the Fourth Amendment. The panel denied rehearing. We granted certiorari * * * .

* * *

III

It is well established that a vehicle stop at a highway checkpoint effectuates a seizure within the meaning of the Fourth Amendment. The fact that officers walk a narcotics-detection dog around the exterior of each car at the Indianapolis checkpoints does not transform the seizure into a search. * * * [A]n exterior sniff of an automobile does not require entry into the car and is not designed to disclose any information other than the presence or absence of narcotics. * * * [A] sniff by a dog that simply walks around a car is "much less intrusive than a typical search." Rather, what principally distinguishes these checkpoints from those we have previously approved is their primary purpose.

As petitioners concede, the Indianapolis checkpoint program unquestionably has the primary purpose of interdicting illegal narcotics. * * *

We have never approved a checkpoint program whose primary purpose was to detect evidence of ordinary criminal wrongdoing. Rather, our checkpoint cases have recognized only limited exceptions to the general rule that a seizure must be accompanied by some measure of individualized suspicion. We suggested in [*Delaware v. Prouse,* 440 U.S. 648, 663, 99 S.Ct. 1391, 59 L.Ed.2d 660 (1979),] that we would not credit the "general interest in crime control" as justification for a regime of suspicionless stops. Consistent with this suggestion, each of the checkpoint programs that we have approved was designed primarily to serve purposes closely related to the problems of policing the border or the necessity of ensuring roadway safety. Because the primary purpose of the Indianapolis narcotics checkpoint program is to uncover evidence of ordinary criminal wrongdoing, the program contravenes the Fourth Amendment.

Petitioners propose several ways in which the narcotics-detection purpose of the instant checkpoint program may instead resemble the primary purposes of the checkpoints in *Sitz* and *Martinez-Fuerte*. Petitioners state that the checkpoints in those cases had the same ultimate purpose of arresting those suspected of committing crimes. Securing the border and apprehending drunk drivers are, of course, law enforcement activities, and law enforcement officers employ arrests and criminal prosecutions in pursuit of these goals. If we were to rest the case at this high level of generality, there would be little check on the ability of the authorities to construct roadblocks for almost any conceivable law enforcement purpose. Without drawing the line at roadblocks designed primarily to serve the general interest in crime control, the Fourth Amendment would do little to prevent such intrusions from becoming a routine part of American life.

Petitioners also emphasize the severe and intractable nature of the drug problem as justification for the checkpoint program. There is no doubt that traffic in illegal narcotics creates social harms of the first magnitude. The law enforcement problems that the drug trade creates likewise remain daunting and complex, particularly in light of the myriad forms of spin-off crime that it spawns. The same can be said of various other illegal activities, if only to a lesser degree. But the gravity of the threat alone cannot be dispositive of questions concerning what means law enforcement officers may employ to pursue a given purpose. Rather, in determining whether individualized suspicion is required, we must consider the nature of the interests threatened and their connection to the particular law enforcement practices at issue. We are particularly reluctant to recognize exceptions to the general rule of individualized suspicion where governmental authorities primarily pursue their general crime control ends.

Nor can the narcotics-interdiction purpose of the checkpoints be rationalized in terms of a highway safety concern similar to that present in *Sitz*. The detection and punishment of almost any criminal offense serves broadly the safety of the community, and our streets would no doubt be safer but for the scourge of illegal drugs. Only with respect to a smaller class of offenses, however, is society confronted with the type of immediate, vehicle-bound threat to life and limb that the sobriety checkpoint in *Sitz* was designed to eliminate.

Petitioners also liken the anticontraband agenda of the Indianapolis checkpoints to the antismuggling purpose of the checkpoints in *Martinez-Fuerte*. Petitioners cite this Court's conclusion in *Martinez-Fuerte* that the flow of traffic was too heavy to permit "particularized study of a given car that would enable it to be identified as a possible carrier of illegal aliens," and claim that this logic has even more force here. The problem with this argument is that the same logic prevails any time a vehicle is employed to conceal contraband or other evidence of a crime. This type of connection to the roadway is very different from the close connection to roadway safety that was present in *Sitz* * * * . Further, the Indianapolis checkpoints are far removed from the border context that was crucial in *Martinez-Fuerte.* While the difficulty of examining each passing car was ·an important factor in validating the law enforcement technique employed in *Martinez-Fuerte,* this factor alone cannot justify a regime of suspicionless searches or seizures. Rather, we must look more closely at the nature of the public interests that such a regime is designed principally to serve.

The primary purpose of the Indianapolis narcotics checkpoints is in the end to advance "the general interest in crime control." We decline to suspend the usual requirement of individualized suspicion where the police seek to employ a checkpoint primarily for the ordinary enterprise of investigating crimes. We cannot sanction stops justified only by the generalized and ever-present possibility that interrogation and inspection may reveal that any given motorist has committed some crime.

Of course, there are circumstances that may justify a law enforcement checkpoint where the primary purpose would otherwise, but for some emergency, relate to ordinary crime control. For example, as the Court of Appeals noted, the Fourth Amendment would almost certainly permit an appropriately tailored roadblock set up to thwart an imminent terrorist attack or to catch a dangerous criminal who is likely to flee by way of a particular route. The exigencies created by these scenarios are far removed from the circumstances under which authorities might simply stop cars as a matter of course to see if there just happens to be a felon leaving the jurisdiction. While we do not limit the purposes that may justify a checkpoint program to any rigid set of categories, we decline to approve a program whose primary purpose is ultimately indistinguishable from the general interest in crime control.

Petitioners argue that our prior cases preclude an inquiry into the purposes of the checkpoint program. For example, they cite *Whren v. United States,* 517 U.S. 806, 116 S.Ct. 1769, 135 L.Ed.2d 89 (1996) * * * to support the proposition that "where the government articulates and pursues a legitimate interest for a suspicionless stop, courts should not look behind that interest to determine whether the government's 'primary purpose' is valid." [*Whren,* however, does] not control the instant situation.

In *Whren,* we held that an individual officer's subjective intentions are irrelevant to the Fourth Amendment validity of a traffic stop that is justified objectively by probable cause to believe that a traffic violation has occurred. We observed that our prior cases "foreclose any argument that the constitutional reasonableness of traffic stops depends on the actual motivations of the individual officers involved." In so holding, we expressly distinguished cases where we had addressed the validity of searches conducted in the absence of probable cause.

Whren therefore reinforces the principle that, while "[s]ubjective intentions play no role in ordinary, probable-cause Fourth Amendment analysis," programmatic purposes may be relevant to the validity of Fourth Amendment intrusions undertaken pursuant to a general scheme without individualized suspicion. Accordingly, *Whren* does not preclude an inquiry into programmatic purpose in such contexts. It likewise does not preclude an inquiry into programmatic purpose here.

* * *

Petitioners argue that the Indianapolis checkpoint program is justified by its lawful secondary purposes of keeping impaired motorists off the road and verifying licenses and registrations. If this were the case, however, law enforcement authorities would be able to establish checkpoints for virtually any purpose so long as they also included a license or sobriety check. For this reason, we examine the available evidence to determine the primary purpose of the checkpoint program. While we recognize the challenges inherent in a purpose inquiry, courts routinely engage in this enterprise in many areas of constitutional jurisprudence as a means of sifting abusive governmental conduct from that which is lawful. As a result, a program driven by an impermissible purpose may be proscribed while a program impelled by licit purposes is permitted, even though the challenged conduct may be outwardly similar. While reasonableness under the Fourth Amendment is predominantly an objective inquiry, our special needs and administrative search cases demonstrate that purpose is often relevant when suspicionless intrusions pursuant to a general scheme are at issue.[2]

It goes without saying that our holding today does nothing to alter the constitutional status of the sobriety and border checkpoints that we approved in *Sitz* and *Martinez-Fuerte,* or of the type of traffic checkpoint that we suggested would be lawful in *Prouse.* The constitutionality of such checkpoint programs still depends on a balancing of the competing interests at stake and the effectiveness of the program. When law enforcement authorities pursue primarily general crime control purposes at checkpoints such as here, however, stops can only be justified by some quantum of individualized suspicion.

Our holding also does not affect the validity of border searches or searches at places like airports and government buildings, where the need for such measures to ensure public safety can be particularly acute. Nor does our opinion speak to other intrusions aimed primarily at

---

[2] Because petitioners concede that the primary purpose of the Indianapolis checkpoints is narcotics detection, we need not decide whether the State may establish a checkpoint program with the primary purpose of checking licenses or driver sobriety and a secondary purpose of interdicting narcotics. Specifically, we express no view on the question whether police may expand the scope of a license or sobriety checkpoint seizure in order to detect the presence of drugs in a stopped car.

purposes beyond the general interest in crime control. Our holding also does not impair the ability of police officers to act appropriately upon information that they properly learn during a checkpoint stop justified by a lawful primary purpose, even where such action may result in the arrest of a motorist for an offense unrelated to that purpose. Finally, we caution that the purpose inquiry in this context is to be conducted only at the programmatic level and is not an invitation to probe the minds of individual officers acting at the scene.

Because the primary purpose of the Indianapolis checkpoint program is ultimately indistinguishable from the general interest in crime control, the checkpoints violate the Fourth Amendment. The judgment of the Court of Appeals is accordingly affirmed.

It is so ordered.

■ CHIEF JUSTICE REHNQUIST, with whom JUSTICE THOMAS joins, and with whom JUSTICE SCALIA joins as to Part I, dissenting.

The State's use of a drug-sniffing dog, according to the Court's holding, annuls what is otherwise plainly constitutional under our Fourth Amendment jurisprudence: brief, standardized, discretionless, roadblock seizures of automobiles, seizures which effectively serve a weighty state interest with only minimal intrusion on the privacy of their occupants. Because these seizures serve the State's accepted and significant interests of preventing drunken driving and checking for driver's licenses and vehicle registrations, and because there is nothing in the record to indicate that the addition of the dog sniff lengthens these otherwise legitimate seizures, I dissent.

I

* * * Petitioners acknowledge that the "primary purpose" of these roadblocks is to interdict illegal drugs, but this fact should not be controlling. Even accepting the Court's conclusion that the checkpoints at issue in *United States v. Martinez-Fuerte* and *Sitz* were not primarily related to criminal law enforcement, the question whether a law enforcement purpose could support a roadblock seizure is not presented in this case. The District Court found that another "purpose of the checkpoints is to check driver's licenses and vehicle registrations," and the written directives state that the police officers are to "[l]ook for signs of impairment." The use of roadblocks to look for signs of impairment was validated by *Sitz,* and the use of roadblocks to check for driver's licenses and vehicle registrations was expressly recognized in *Delaware v. Prouse,* 440 U.S. 648, 663, 99 S.Ct. 1391, 59 L.Ed.2d 660 (1979). That the roadblocks serve these legitimate state interests cannot be seriously disputed, as the 49 people arrested for offenses unrelated to drugs can attest. And it would be speculative to conclude—given the District Court's findings, the written directives, and the actual arrests—that petitioners would not have operated these roadblocks but for the State's interest in interdicting drugs.

Because of the valid reasons for conducting these roadblock seizures, it is constitutionally irrelevant that petitioners also hoped to interdict drugs. In *Whren v. United States,* 517 U.S. 806, 116 S.Ct. 1769, 135 L.Ed.2d 89 (1996), we held that an officer's subjective intent would not invalidate an otherwise objectively justifiable stop of an automobile. The reasonableness of an officer's discretionary decision to stop an automobile, at issue in *Whren,* turns on whether there is probable cause to believe that a traffic violation has occurred. The reasonableness of highway checkpoints, at issue here, turns on whether they effectively serve a significant state interest with minimal intrusion on motorists. The stop in *Whren* was objectively reasonable because the police officers had witnessed traffic violations; so too the roadblocks here are objectively reasonable because they serve the substantial interests of preventing drunken driving and checking for driver's licenses and vehicle registrations with minimal intrusion on motorists.

Once the constitutional requirements for a particular seizure are satisfied, the subjective expectations of those responsible for it, be it police officers or members of a city council, are irrelevant. It is the objective effect of the State's actions on the privacy of the individual that animates the Fourth Amendment. Because the objective intrusion of a valid seizure does not turn upon anyone's subjective thoughts, neither should our constitutional analysis.

* * *

These stops effectively serve the State's legitimate interests; they are executed in a regularized and neutral manner; and they only minimally intrude upon the privacy of the motorists. They should therefore be constitutional.

II

The Court, unwilling to adopt the straightforward analysis that these precedents dictate, adds a new non-law-enforcement primary purpose test lifted from a distinct area of Fourth Amendment jurisprudence relating to the *searches* of homes and businesses. * * * [W]hatever sense a non-law-enforcement primary purpose test may make in the search setting, it is ill suited to brief roadblock seizures, where we have consistently looked at "the scope of the stop" in assessing a program's constitutionality.

We have already rejected [in *Sitz*] an invitation to apply the non-law-enforcement primary purpose test that the Court now finds so indispensable. * * * [S]eizures of automobiles "deal neither with searches nor with the sanctity of private dwellings, ordinarily afforded the most stringent Fourth Amendment protection." *Martinez-Fuerte, supra,* at 561, 96 S.Ct. 3074.

* * *

* * * The brief seizure of an automobile can hardly be compared to the intrusive search of the body or the home. * * *

[T]he Court's newfound non-law-enforcement primary purpose test is both unnecessary to secure Fourth Amendment rights and bound to produce wide-ranging litigation over the "purpose" of any given seizure. Police designing highway roadblocks can never be sure of their validity, since a jury might later determine that a forbidden purpose exists. Roadblock stops identical to the one that we upheld in *Sitz* 10 years ago, or to the one that we upheld 24 years ago in *Martinez-Fuerte,* may now be challenged on the grounds that they have some concealed forbidden purpose.

* * *

■ JUSTICE THOMAS, dissenting.

* * * I am not convinced that *Sitz* and *Martinez-Fuerte* were correctly decided. Indeed, I rather doubt that the Framers of the Fourth Amendment would have considered "reasonable" a program of indiscriminate stops of individuals not suspected of wrongdoing.

Respondents did not, however, advocate the overruling of *Sitz* and *Martinez-Fuerte,* and I am reluctant to consider such a step without the benefit of briefing and argument. For the reasons given by THE CHIEF JUSTICE, I believe that those cases compel upholding the program at issue here. I, therefore, join his opinion.

NOTES

1. **Programmatic Purpose.** The Court after *Edmond* further explained the nature of the inquiry permitted and in fact necessitated by *Edmond*:

> [W]e have held in the context of programmatic searches conducted without individualized suspicion—such as checkpoints to combat drunk driving or drug trafficking—that "an inquiry into *programmatic* purpose" is sometimes appropriate. But this inquiry is directed at ensuring that the purpose behind the *program* is not "ultimately indistinguishable from the general interest in crime control." It has nothing to do with discerning what is in the mind of the individual officer conducting the search.

Brigham City, Utah v. Stuart, 547 U.S. 398, 405, 126 S.Ct. 1943, 1948 (2006).

2. **Informational Checkpoint Stops.** The *Edmond*-type approach—a rule of automatic unconstitutionality—does not apply to checkpoint stops of an "information-seeking kind," the Supreme Court held in Illinois v. Lidster, 540 U.S. 419, 124 S.Ct. 885 (2004).

In *Lidster*, officers were investigating a hit-and-run incident in which a 70-year-old bicyclist was killed. The officers set up a checkpoint about a week after the incident at the same place and time of night the incident had occurred. Traffic going one way on the highway was stopped, an officer asked the occupants of each car whether they had seen anything happened there the night of the incident, and each driver was given an flyer describing the incident and asking help identifying the vehicle and driver involved. Lidster approached the checkpoint and swerved, nearly striking one of the officers. Officers conducted a sobriety test and Lidster was charged with driving under the influence of alcohol.

The Court rejected Lidster's contention that the evidence of his intoxication was obtained through an unconstitutional checkpoint stop. All of the justices agreed that the standard to be applied was not that applied in *Edmond*:

> The checkpoint stop here differs significantly from that in *Edmond*. The stop's primary law enforcement purpose was *not* to determine whether a vehicle's occupants were committing a crime, but to ask vehicle occupants, as members of the public, for their help in providing information about a crime in all likelihood committed by others. The police expected the information elicited to help them apprehend, not the vehicle's occupants, but other individuals.

* * *

> [U]nlike *Edmond,* the context here (seeking information from the public) is one in which, by definition, the concept of individualized suspicion has little role to play. Like certain other forms of police activity, say, crowd control or public safety, an information-seeking stop is not the kind of event that involves suspicion, or lack of suspicion, of the relevant individual.

> For another thing, information-seeking highway stops are less likely to provoke anxiety or to prove intrusive. The stops are likely brief. The police are not likely to ask questions designed to elicit self-incriminating information. And citizens will often react positively when police simply ask for their help as "responsible citizen[s]" to "give whatever information they may have to aid in law enforcement."

* * *

> [W]e do not believe that an *Edmond*-type rule is needed to prevent an unreasonable proliferation of police checkpoints. Practical considerations—namely, limited police resources and community hostility to related traffic tie-ups—seem likely to inhibit any such proliferation. And, of course, the Fourth Amendment's normal insistence that the stop be reasonable in context will still provide an important legal limitation on police use of this kind of information-seeking checkpoint.

> These considerations, taken together, convince us that an *Edmond*-type presumptive rule of unconstitutionality does not apply here. That does not mean the stop is automatically, or even presumptively, constitutional. It simply means that we must judge its reasonableness, hence, its constitutionality, on the basis of the individual circumstances. And * * * in judging reasonableness, we look to "the gravity of the public concerns served by the seizure, the degree to which the seizure advances the public interest, and the severity of the interference with individual liberty."

540 U.S. at 423–28, 124 S.Ct. at 889–90. Three members of the Court thought the case should be remanded for the State court to apply this analysis to the facts.

The majority, however, applied the analysis itself:

> The relevant public concern was grave. Police were investigating a crime that had resulted in a human death. No one denies the police's need to obtain more information at that time. And the stop's objective was to help find the perpetrator of a specific and known crime, not of unknown crimes of a general sort.
>
> The stop advanced this grave public concern to a significant degree. The police appropriately tailored their checkpoint stops to fit important criminal investigatory needs. The stops took place about one week after the hit-and-run accident, on the same highway near the location of the accident, and at about the same time of night. And police used the stops to obtain information from drivers, some of whom might well have been in the vicinity of the crime at the time it occurred.
>
> Most importantly, the stops interfered only minimally with liberty of the sort the Fourth Amendment seeks to protect. Viewed objectively, each stop required only a brief wait in line—a very few minutes at most. Contact with the police lasted only a few seconds. Police contact consisted simply of a request for information and the distribution of a flyer. Viewed subjectively, the contact provided little reason for anxiety or alarm. The police stopped all vehicles systematically. And there is no allegation here that the police acted in a discriminatory or otherwise unlawful manner while questioning motorists during stops.
>
> For these reasons we conclude that the checkpoint stop was constitutional.

540 U.S. at 427–28, 124 S.Ct. at 891.

CHAPTER 5

"WARRANTLESS" SEARCHES

Analysis

A. Exigent Circumstances
B. Administrative Inspections and Searches of Licensed Premises
C. Consent Searches
D. Searches and Seizures of Vehicles
E. Extraordinarily Intrusive Searches

EDITORS' INTRODUCTION: EXCEPTIONS TO BENCHMARK FOURTH AMENDMENT REQUIREMENTS

If law enforcement conduct constitutes a "search," the material in Chapters 2 and 3 made clear—as a general rule—certain benchmark Fourth Amendment requirements apply. Information amounting to "probable cause" to believe that the intrusion is justified must be present. In addition, officers must use the search warrant process and obtain a judicial determination that probable cause exists before the intrusion.

But the Fourth Amendment's reasonableness requirement has significant flexibility. In some situations, either or both of the benchmark demands may be modified or abandoned. Relaxation of these requirements was explored to some extent in Chapter 4, which considered officers' right to conduct certain searches as incidents to arrests or because of nonarrest police-citizen contacts. Other situations in which the Fourth Amendment's demands may deviate from the benchmark requirements are the subject of the present chapter.

Most of these situations involve law enforcement activity investigating whether a criminal offense has been committed and, if so, the offender's identity. But this is not always the case. Subchapter B of this chapter considers the so-called "administrative" searches. These may be conducted by inspectors not law enforcement officers. Inspectors' primary objective may be to end violation of legal but noncriminal requirements by means other than criminal prosecution of those found in noncompliance with the law's demands. Whether a noncriminal objective justifies relaxation of Fourth Amendment requirements, of course, is among the issues raised by such inspections.

Each situation discussed in this chapter presents two categories of issues. The first concerns the requirement of a search warrant. In many situations, the issue is whether this requirement should be abandoned entirely and so-called "warrantless" searches regarded as reasonable. In other situations, however, the question is whether the warrant requirement should be retained but relaxed to accommodate special needs presented by the situation. In still others, the issue is whether Fourth Amendment reasonableness should be retained and modified so as to impose *more* stringent requirements than are involved in the traditional warrant process considered in Chapter 3.

These situations are often discussed as if the only question is whether—and when—warrantless searches are reasonable. Many, however, also present issues in a second category, concerning possible changes in the traditional requirement of probable cause. If a decision is made to dispense with the warrant requirement, of course, Fourth Amendment reasonableness might still require that an officer have information amounting to probable cause before beginning the search. But in some situations persuasive arguments can be made for demanding only information meeting a less stringent standard or for dispensing entirely with any requirement that the officer have information indicating that a search is justified. Even if a warrant or court order is necessary, the standard for deciding whether that order or warrant can issue might demand less than traditional probable cause. In some situations involving unusually intrusive law enforcement conduct, the Fourth Amendment might permit a warrant to issue or a warrantless search conducted only under a *more* stringent standard than the traditional probable cause requirement.

The significance of these issues often results from the application of the plain view seizure rule, considered in Subchapter C(2) of Chapter 2. If law enforcement officers or other public officials are engaged in a proper, i.e., "reasonable," search and in the course of that search come upon items in plain view, they may often seize those items. Whether the search placing the items in the officers' plain view was proper will, in many cases, determine whether the seizure was permissible. If the officers came upon the items in the course of an unreasonable search, the discovery and seizure of the items is likely to be tainted "fruit" of the improper search.

The case law presented in this chapter consists entirely of United States Supreme Court decisions construing the Fourth Amendment requirement of reasonableness. State constitutional, statutory or case law may here as well as elsewhere impose more stringent requirements upon official activity than is mandated by the federal constitutional provision.

Several subsequent chapters address other areas of official conduct raising issues similar to those considered in this chapter. Use of grand jury subpoenas is discussed in Chapter 8. Among the issues raised in Chapter 7 is the extent to which undercover law enforcement activity so intrudes upon privacy as to justify subjecting such activity to Fourth Amendment reasonableness requirements. If the Fourth Amendment were applied to this activity, the courts would have to address the extent and nature of the regulation which Fourth Amendment reasonableness imposes.

A. EXIGENT CIRCUMSTANCES

EDITORS' INTRODUCTION: EXIGENT CIRCUMSTANCES AND THE "EMERGENCY AID" DOCTRINE

The Supreme Court has upheld certain searches without warrants upon demonstrations that the officers reasonably believed delays necessary to apply for search warrants would result in destruction of the evidence or contraband sought—"exigent circumstances." Schmerber v. California, 384 U.S. 757, 86 S.Ct. 1826 (1966) (reprinted in Chapter 2), for example, held reasonable a warrantless taking of a blood sample because delaying the process might have resulted in the suspect's body eliminating alcohol from his system. The meaning of *Schmerber* is explored further in the first unit of this subchapter.

In a sense, the exigent circumstance doctrine is a benchmark for analysis of other situations that may dispense with the need for a warrant and perhaps probable cause. In regard to the warrant requirement, many other exceptions—such as that for certain vehicles—involve situations in which a claim might be made that an emergency exists. Fitting a case within one of the other exceptions, however, dispenses with the need for the prosecution to show that *on the facts of the particular case* delay to apply for a warrant would create sufficient risk of loss of the evidence or contraband. In considering the wisdom of various other more specific exceptions and their scope, the availability of the general emergency exception might usefully be kept in mind. If a case falls without any other exception, the prosecution always has the opportunity to demonstrate that, on the facts of the particular situation, the emergency exception applies.

The exigent circumstances situation must be distinguished from the closely-related "emergency aid doctrine," the Supreme Court made clear in Brigham City, Utah v. Stuart, 547 U.S. 398, 126 S.Ct. 1943 (2006). The facts of *Stuart* were as follows:

> At about 3 a.m. [on July 23, 2000], four [Brigham City, Utah] police officers responded to a call regarding a loud party at a residence. Upon arriving at the house, they heard shouting from inside, and proceeded down the driveway to investigate. There, they observed two juveniles drinking beer in the backyard. They entered the backyard, and saw—through a screen door and windows—an altercation taking place in the kitchen of the home. According to the testimony of one of the officers, four adults were attempting, with some difficulty, to restrain a juvenile. The juvenile eventually "broke free, swung a fist and struck one of the adults in the face." The officer testified that he

observed the victim of the blow spitting blood into a nearby sink. The other adults continued to try to restrain the juvenile, pressing him up against a refrigerator with such force that the refrigerator began moving across the floor. At this point, an officer opened the screen door and announced the officers' presence. Amid the tumult, nobody noticed. The officer entered the kitchen and again cried out, and as the occupants slowly became aware that the police were on the scene, the altercation ceased.

The officers subsequently arrested respondents[, the three adult occupants,] and charged them with contributing to the delinquency of a minor, disorderly conduct, and intoxication.

The state courts held inadmissible all the evidence obtained after the officer entered the residence. They refused to uphold the entry under the exigent circumstances exception. In addition, they rejected the State's alternative reliance on an "emergency aid doctrine." The Supreme Court granted review, apparently limited to the Utah Supreme Court's holding that no emergency aid doctrine was applicable.

The Court began by making clear that an emergency aid exception to the requirement of a warrant is a part of Fourth Amendment law:

> One exigency obviating the requirement of a warrant is the need to assist persons who are seriously injured or threatened with such injury. * * * Accordingly, law enforcement officers may enter a home without a warrant to render emergency assistance to an injured occupant or to protect an occupant from imminent injury.

547 U.S. at 403, 126 S.Ct. at 1947. It then rejected both of the state tribunal's rationales for holding the exception inapplicable. First, the state court erred in holding the exception inapplicable because the officers were not subjectively motivated by a desire to protect the subjects rather than to arrest and prosecute:

> The officer's subjective motivation is irrelevant. * * * It therefore does not matter here—even if their subjective motives could be so neatly unraveled—whether the officers entered the kitchen to arrest respondents and gather evidence against them or to assist the injured and prevent further violence.

547 U.S. at 404–05, 126 S.Ct. at 1948.

Second, the state court erred in holding that the assaultive conduct observed by the officers was not serious enough to justify the entry into the residence:

> We think the officers' entry here was plainly reasonable under the circumstances. The officers were responding, at 3 o'clock in the morning, to complaints about a loud party. As they approached the house, they could hear from within "an

altercation occurring, some kind of a fight." "It was loud and it was tumultuous." The officers heard "thumping and crashing" and people yelling "stop, stop" and "get off me." * * * [F]rom the back of the house * * * they could see that a fracas was taking place inside the kitchen. A juvenile, fists clenched, was being held back by several adults. As the officers watch, he breaks free and strikes one of the adults in the face, sending the adult to the sink spitting blood.

In these circumstances, the officers had an objectively reasonable basis for believing both that the injured adult might need help and that the violence in the kitchen was just beginning. Nothing in the Fourth Amendment required them to wait until another blow rendered someone "unconscious" or "semi-conscious" or worse before entering. The role of a peace officer includes preventing violence and restoring order, not simply rendering first aid to casualties; an officer is not like a boxing (or hockey) referee, poised to stop a bout only if it becomes too one-sided.

547 U.S. at 406, 126 S.Ct. at 1949.

1. BLOOD TESTS

Schmerber v. California, 384 U.S. 757, 86 S.Ct. 1826 (1966)—reprinted in Chapter 2—addressed the need for a search warrant to support the taking of a blood sample from a person suspected of driving while impaired. In the principal case that follows, the Court explored when under *Schmerber* the exigent circumstances doctrine permits officers to proceed without a warrant.

Missouri v. McNeely

Supreme Court of the United States, 2013.
___U.S. ___, 133 S.Ct. 1552.

■ JUSTICE SOTOMAYOR announced the judgment of the Court and delivered the opinion of the Court with respect to Parts I, II-A, II-B, and IV, and an opinion with respect to Parts II-C and III, in which JUSTICE SCALIA, JUSTICE GINSBURG, and JUSTICE KAGAN join.

In *Schmerber v. California,* 384 U.S. 757, 86 S.Ct. 1826, 16 L.Ed.2d 908 (1966), this Court upheld a warrantless blood test of an individual arrested for driving under the influence of alcohol because the officer "might reasonably have believed that he was confronted with an emergency, in which the delay necessary to obtain a warrant, under the circumstances, threatened the destruction of evidence." The question presented here is whether the natural metabolization of alcohol in the bloodstream presents a *per se* exigency that justifies an exception to the Fourth Amendment's warrant requirement for nonconsensual blood testing in all drunk-driving cases. * * *

I

While on highway patrol at approximately 2:08 a.m., a Missouri police officer stopped Tyler McNeely's truck after observing it exceed the posted speed limit and repeatedly cross the centerline. The officer noticed several signs that McNeely was intoxicated, including McNeely's bloodshot eyes, his slurred speech, and the smell of alcohol on his breath. McNeely acknowledged to the officer that he had consumed "a couple of beers" at a bar, and he appeared unsteady on his feet when he exited the truck. After McNeely performed poorly on a battery of field-sobriety tests and declined to use a portable breath-test device to measure his blood alcohol concentration (BAC), the officer placed him under arrest.

The officer began to transport McNeely to the station house. But when McNeely indicated that he would again refuse to provide a breath sample, the officer changed course and took McNeely to a nearby hospital for blood testing. The officer did not attempt to secure a warrant. Upon arrival at the hospital, the officer asked McNeely whether he would consent to a blood test. Reading from a standard implied consent form, the officer explained to McNeely that under state law refusal to submit voluntarily to the test would lead to the immediate revocation of his driver's license for one year and could be used against him in a future prosecution. McNeely nonetheless refused. The officer then directed a hospital lab technician to take a blood sample, and the sample was secured at approximately 2:35 a.m. Subsequent laboratory testing measured McNeely's BAC at 0.154 percent, which was well above the legal limit of 0.08 percent.

McNeely was charged with driving while intoxicated (DWI). * * * He moved to suppress the results of the blood test, arguing in relevant part that, under the circumstances, taking his blood for chemical testing without first obtaining a search warrant violated his rights under the Fourth Amendment. The trial court agreed. * * * On appeal, the Missouri Court of Appeals stated an intention to reverse but transferred the case directly to the Missouri Supreme Court.

The Missouri Supreme Court affirmed. Recognizing that this Court's decision in *Schmerber* * * * "provide[d] the backdrop" to its analysis, the Missouri Supreme Court * * * concluded that *Schmerber* "requires more than the mere dissipation of blood-alcohol evidence to support a warrantless blood draw in an alcohol-related case." * * * Finding that this was "unquestionably a routine DWI case" in which no factors other than the natural dissipation of blood-alcohol suggested that there was an emergency, the court held that the nonconsensual warrantless blood draw violated McNeely's Fourth Amendment right to be free from unreasonable searches of his person.

We granted certiorari to resolve a split of authority on the question whether the natural dissipation of alcohol in the bloodstream establishes a *per se* exigency that suffices on its own to justify an exception to the warrant requirement for nonconsensual blood testing in drunk-driving investigations. * * *

II

A

The Fourth Amendment provides in relevant part that "[t]he right of the people to be secure in their persons, houses, papers, and effects, against unreasonable searches and seizures, shall not be violated, and no Warrants shall issue, but upon probable cause." Our cases have held that a warrantless search of the person is reasonable only if it falls within a recognized exception. That principle applies to the type of search at issue in this case, which involved a compelled physical intrusion beneath McNeely's skin and into his veins to obtain a sample of his blood for use as evidence in a criminal investigation. Such an invasion of bodily integrity implicates an individual's "most personal and deep-rooted expectations of privacy." *Winston v. Lee,* 470 U.S. 753, 760, 105 S.Ct. 1611, 84 L.Ed.2d 662 (1985).

We first considered the Fourth Amendment restrictions on such searches in *Schmerber,* where, as in this case, a blood sample was drawn from a defendant suspected of driving while under the influence of alcohol. Noting that "[s]earch warrants are ordinarily required for searches of dwellings," we reasoned that "absent an emergency, no less could be required where intrusions into the human body are concerned," even when the search was conducted following a lawful arrest. We explained that the importance of requiring authorization by a " 'neutral and detached magistrate' " before allowing a law enforcement officer to "invade another's body in search of evidence of guilt is indisputable and great."

As noted, the warrant requirement is subject to exceptions. "One well-recognized exception," and the one at issue in this case, "applies when the exigencies of the situation make the needs of law enforcement so compelling that a warrantless search is objectively reasonable under the Fourth Amendment." *Kentucky v. King,* 563 U.S. 452, 460, 131 S.Ct. 1849, 1856, 179 L.Ed.2d 865 (2011) (internal quotation marks and brackets omitted). A variety of circumstances may give rise to an exigency sufficient to justify a warrantless search, including law enforcement's need to provide emergency assistance to an occupant of a home, engage in "hot pursuit" of a fleeing suspect, or enter a burning building to put out a fire and investigate its cause. As is relevant here, we have also recognized that in some circumstances law enforcement officers may conduct a search without a warrant to prevent the imminent destruction of evidence. While these contexts do not necessarily involve equivalent dangers, in each a warrantless search is potentially reasonable because "there is compelling need for official action and no time to secure a warrant."

To determine whether a law enforcement officer faced an emergency that justified acting without a warrant, this Court looks to the totality of circumstances. We apply this "finely tuned approach" to Fourth Amendment reasonableness in this context because the police action at issue lacks "the traditional justification that . . . a warrant . . . provides." Absent that established justification, "the fact-specific nature of the reasonableness inquiry," demands that we evaluate each case of alleged exigency based "on its own facts and circumstances."[3]

Our decision in *Schmerber* applied this totality of the circumstances approach. In that case, the petitioner had suffered injuries in an automobile accident and was taken to the hospital. While he was there receiving treatment, a police officer arrested the petitioner for driving while under the influence of alcohol and ordered a blood test over his objection. After explaining that the warrant requirement applied generally to searches that intrude into the human body, we concluded that the warrantless blood test "in the present case" was nonetheless permissible because the officer "might reasonably have believed that he was confronted with an emergency, in which the delay necessary to obtain a warrant, under the circumstances, threatened 'the destruction of evidence.' "

* * *

[O]ur analysis in *Schmerber* fits comfortably within our case law applying the exigent circumstances exception. In finding the warrantless blood test reasonable in *Schmerber,* we considered all of the facts and circumstances of the particular case and carefully based our holding on those specific facts.

B

The State * * * seeks a *per se* rule for blood testing in drunk-driving cases. The State contends that whenever an officer has probable cause to believe an individual has been driving under the influence of alcohol, exigent circumstances will necessarily exist because BAC evidence is inherently evanescent. As a result, the State claims that so long as the officer has probable cause and the blood test is conducted in a reasonable manner, it is categorically reasonable for law enforcement to obtain the blood sample without a warrant.

It is true that as a result of the human body's natural metabolic processes, the alcohol level in a person's blood begins to dissipate once the alcohol is fully absorbed and continues to decline until the alcohol is

---

[3]   We have recognized a limited class of traditional exceptions to the warrant requirement that apply categorically and thus do not require an assessment of whether the policy justifications underlying the exception, which may include exigency-based considerations, are implicated in a particular case. See, *e.g., California v. Acevedo,* 500 U.S. 565, 569–570, 111 S.Ct. 1982, 114 L.Ed.2d 619 (1991) (automobile exception); *United States v. Robinson,* 414 U.S. 218, 224–235, 94 S.Ct. 467, 38 L.Ed.2d 427 (1973) (searches of a person incident to a lawful arrest). By contrast, the general exigency exception, which asks whether an emergency existed that justified a warrantless search, naturally calls for a case-specific inquiry.

eliminated. Testimony before the trial court in this case indicated that the percentage of alcohol in an individual's blood typically decreases by approximately 0.015 percent to 0.02 percent per hour once the alcohol has been fully absorbed. More precise calculations of the rate at which alcohol dissipates depend on various individual characteristics (such as weight, gender, and alcohol tolerance) and the circumstances in which the alcohol was consumed. Regardless of the exact elimination rate, it is sufficient for our purposes to note that because an individual's alcohol level gradually declines soon after he stops drinking, a significant delay in testing will negatively affect the probative value of the results. This fact was essential to our holding in *Schmerber,* as we recognized that, under the circumstances, further delay in order to secure a warrant after the time spent investigating the scene of the accident and transporting the injured suspect to the hospital to receive treatment would have threatened the destruction of evidence.

But it does not follow that we should depart from careful case-by-case assessment of exigency and adopt the categorical rule proposed by the State and its *amici.* In those drunk-driving investigations where police officers can reasonably obtain a warrant before a blood sample can be drawn without significantly undermining the efficacy of the search, the Fourth Amendment mandates that they do so. We do not doubt that some circumstances will make obtaining a warrant impractical such that the dissipation of alcohol from the bloodstream will support an exigency justifying a properly conducted warrantless blood test. That, however, is a reason to decide each case on its facts, as we did in *Schmerber,* not to accept the "considerable overgeneralization" that a *per se* rule would reflect.

The context of blood testing is different in critical respects from other destruction-of-evidence cases in which the police are truly confronted with a " 'now or never' " situation. In contrast to, for example, circumstances in which the suspect has control over easily disposable evidence, BAC evidence from a drunk-driving suspect naturally dissipates over time in a gradual and relatively predictable manner. Moreover, because a police officer must typically transport a drunk-driving suspect to a medical facility and obtain the assistance of someone with appropriate medical training before conducting a blood test, some delay between the time of the arrest or accident and the time of the test is inevitable regardless of whether police officers are required to obtain a warrant. This reality undermines the force of the State's contention, endorsed by the dissent, that we should recognize a categorical exception to the warrant requirement because BAC evidence "is actively being destroyed with every minute that passes." Consider, for example, a situation in which the warrant process will not significantly increase the delay before the blood test is conducted because an officer can take steps to secure a warrant while the suspect is being transported to a medical facility by another officer. In such a circumstance, there would be no plausible justification for an exception to the warrant requirement.

The State's proposed *per se* rule also fails to account for advances in the 47 years since *Schmerber* was decided that allow for the more expeditious processing of warrant applications, particularly in contexts like drunk-driving investigations where the evidence offered to establish probable cause is simple. The Federal Rules of Criminal Procedure were amended in 1977 to permit federal magistrate judges to issue a warrant based on sworn testimony communicated by telephone. As amended, the law now allows a federal magistrate judge to consider "information communicated by telephone or other reliable electronic means." Fed. Rule Crim. Proc. 4.1. States have also innovated. Well over a majority of States allow police officers or prosecutors to apply for search warrants remotely through various means, including telephonic or radio communication, electronic communication such as e-mail, and video conferencing. And in addition to technology-based developments, jurisdictions have found other ways to streamline the warrant process, such as by using standard-form warrant applications for drunk-driving investigations.

We by no means claim that telecommunications innovations have, will, or should eliminate all delay from the warrant-application process. Warrants inevitably take some time for police officers or prosecutors to complete and for magistrate judges to review. Telephonic and electronic warrants may still require officers to follow time-consuming formalities designed to create an adequate record, such as preparing a duplicate warrant before calling the magistrate judge. And improvements in communications technology do not guarantee that a magistrate judge will be available when an officer needs a warrant after making a late-night arrest. But technological developments that enable police officers to secure warrants more quickly, and do so without undermining the neutral magistrate judge's essential role as a check on police discretion, are relevant to an assessment of exigency. That is particularly so in this context, where BAC evidence is lost gradually and relatively predictably.

Of course, there are important countervailing concerns. While experts can work backwards from the BAC at the time the sample was taken to determine the BAC at the time of the alleged offense, longer intervals may raise questions about the accuracy of the calculation. For that reason, exigent circumstances justifying a warrantless blood sample may arise in the regular course of law enforcement due to delays from the warrant application process. But adopting the State's *per se* approach would improperly ignore the current and future technological developments in warrant procedures, and might well diminish the incentive for jurisdictions "to pursue progressive approaches to warrant acquisition that preserve the protections afforded by the warrant while meeting the legitimate interests of law enforcement."

In short, while the natural dissipation of alcohol in the blood may support a finding of exigency in a specific case, as it did in *Schmerber,* it does not do so categorically. Whether a warrantless blood test of a drunk-driving suspect is reasonable must be determined case by case based on the totality of the circumstances.

C

In an opinion concurring in part and dissenting in part, THE CHIEF JUSTICE agrees that the State's proposed *per se* rule is overbroad because "[f]or exigent circumstances to justify a warrantless search . . . there must . . . be 'no time to secure a warrant.' " But THE CHIEF JUSTICE then goes on to suggest his own categorical rule under which a warrantless blood draw is permissible if the officer could not secure a warrant (or reasonably believed he could not secure a warrant) in the time it takes to transport the suspect to a hospital or similar facility and obtain medical assistance. Although we agree that delay inherent to the blood-testing process is relevant to evaluating exigency, we decline to substitute THE CHIEF JUSTICE's modified *per se* rule for our traditional totality of the circumstances analysis.

For one thing, making exigency completely dependent on the window of time between an arrest and a blood test produces odd consequences. Under THE CHIEF JUSTICE's rule, if a police officer serendipitously stops a suspect near an emergency room, the officer may conduct a nonconsensual warrantless blood draw even if all agree that a warrant could be obtained with very little delay under the circumstances (perhaps with far less delay than an average ride to the hospital in the jurisdiction). The rule would also distort law enforcement incentives. As with the State's *per se* rule, THE CHIEF JUSTICE's rule might discourage efforts to expedite the warrant process because it categorically authorizes warrantless blood draws so long as it takes more time to secure a warrant than to obtain medical assistance. On the flip side, making the requirement of independent judicial oversight turn exclusively on the amount of time that elapses between an arrest and BAC testing could induce police departments and individual officers to minimize testing delay to the detriment of other values. THE CHIEF JUSTICE correctly observes that "[t]his case involves medical personnel drawing blood at a medical facility, not police officers doing so by the side of the road." But THE CHIEF JUSTICE does not say that roadside blood draws are necessarily unreasonable, and if we accepted THE CHIEF JUSTICE's approach, they would become a more attractive option for the police.

III

The remaining arguments advanced in support of a *per se* exigency rule are unpersuasive.

The State and several of its *amici,* including the United States, express concern that a case-by-case approach to exigency will not provide adequate guidance to law enforcement officers deciding whether to conduct a blood test of a drunk-driving suspect without a warrant. THE CHIEF JUSTICE and the dissent also raise this concern. While the desire for a bright-line rule is understandable, the Fourth Amendment will not tolerate adoption of an overly broad categorical approach that would dilute the warrant requirement in a context where significant privacy interests are at stake. Moreover, a case-by-case approach is hardly unique within our Fourth Amendment jurisprudence. Numerous police actions are judged based on fact-intensive, totality of the circumstances analyses rather than according to categorical rules, including in situations that are more likely to require police officers to make difficult split-second judgments. As in those contexts, we see no valid substitute for careful case-by-case evaluation of reasonableness here.

Next, the State and the United States contend that the privacy interest implicated by blood draws of drunk-driving suspects is relatively minimal. That is so, they claim, both because motorists have a diminished expectation of privacy and because our cases have repeatedly indicated that blood testing is commonplace in society and typically involves "virtually no risk, trauma, or pain." *Schmerber,* 384 U.S., at 771, 86 S.Ct. 1826.

But the fact that people are "accorded less privacy in . . . automobiles because of th[e] compelling governmental need for regulation," does not diminish a motorist's privacy interest in preventing an agent of the government from piercing his skin. As to the nature of a blood test conducted in a medical setting by trained personnel, it is concededly less intrusive than other bodily invasions we have found unreasonable. See *Winston,* 470 U.S., at 759–766, 105 S.Ct. 1611 (surgery to remove a bullet); *Rochin v. California,* 342 U.S. 165, 172–174, 72 S.Ct. 205, 96 L.Ed. 183 (1952) (induced vomiting to extract narcotics capsules ingested by a suspect violated the Due Process Clause). For that reason, we have held that medically drawn blood tests are reasonable in appropriate circumstances. See [*Skinner v. Railway Labor Executives' Assn.,* 489 U.S. 602, 618–633, 109 S.Ct. 1402, 103 L.Ed.2d 639 (1989)] (upholding warrantless blood testing of railroad employees involved in certain train accidents under the "special needs" doctrine). We have never retreated, however, from our recognition that any compelled intrusion into the human body implicates significant, constitutionally protected privacy interests.

Finally, the State and its *amici* point to the compelling governmental interest in combating drunk driving and contend that prompt BAC testing, including through blood testing, is vital to pursuit of that interest. They argue that is particularly so because, in addition to laws that make it illegal to operate a motor vehicle under the influence of alcohol, all 50 States and the District of Columbia have enacted laws that make it *per se* unlawful to operate a motor vehicle with a BAC of over 0.08 percent. To enforce these provisions, they reasonably assert, accurate BAC evidence is critical.

"No one can seriously dispute the magnitude of the drunken driving problem or the States' interest in eradicating it." *Michigan Dept. of State*

Police v. Sitz, 496 U.S. 444, 451, 110 S.Ct. 2481, 110 L.Ed.2d 412 (1990). Certainly we do not. While some progress has been made, drunk driving continues to exact a terrible toll on our society.

But the general importance of the government's interest in this area does not justify departing from the warrant requirement without showing exigent circumstances that make securing a warrant impractical in a particular case. To the extent that the State and its *amici* contend that applying the traditional Fourth Amendment totality-of-the-circumstances analysis to determine whether an exigency justified a warrantless search will undermine the governmental interest in preventing and prosecuting drunk-driving offenses, we are not convinced.

As an initial matter, States have a broad range of legal tools to enforce their drunk-driving laws and to secure BAC evidence without undertaking warrantless nonconsensual blood draws. For example, all 50 States have adopted implied consent laws that require motorists, as a condition of operating a motor vehicle within the State, to consent to BAC testing if they are arrested or otherwise detained on suspicion of a drunk-driving offense. Such laws impose significant consequences when a motorist withdraws consent; typically the motorist's driver's license is immediately suspended or revoked, and most States allow the motorist's refusal to take a BAC test to be used as evidence against him in a subsequent criminal prosecution.

It is also notable that a majority of States either place significant restrictions on when police officers may obtain a blood sample despite a suspect's refusal (often limiting testing to cases involving an accident resulting in death or serious bodily injury) or prohibit nonconsensual blood tests altogether. * * * We are aware of no evidence indicating that restrictions on nonconsensual blood testing have compromised drunk-driving enforcement efforts in the States that have them. And in fact, field studies in States that permit nonconsensual blood testing pursuant to a warrant have suggested that, although warrants do impose administrative burdens, their use can reduce breath-test-refusal rates and improve law enforcement's ability to recover BAC evidence.

To be sure, "States [may] choos[e] to protect privacy beyond the level that the Fourth Amendment requires." But wide-spread state restrictions on nonconsensual blood testing provide further support for our recognition that compelled blood draws implicate a significant privacy interest. They also strongly suggest that our ruling today will not "severely hamper effective law enforcement."

IV

The State argued before this Court that the fact that alcohol is naturally metabolized by the human body creates an exigent circumstance in every case. The State did not argue that there were exigent circumstances in this particular case because a warrant could not have been obtained within a reasonable amount of time. * * *

Although the Missouri Supreme Court referred to this case as "unquestionably a routine DWI case," the fact that a particular drunk-driving stop is "routine" in the sense that it does not involve " 'special facts,' " such as the need for the police to attend to a car accident, does not mean a warrant is required. Other factors present in an ordinary traffic stop, such as the procedures in place for obtaining a warrant or the availability of a magistrate judge, may affect whether the police can obtain a warrant in an expeditious way and therefore may establish an exigency that permits a warrantless search. The relevant factors in determining whether a warrantless search is reasonable, including the practical problems of obtaining a warrant within a timeframe that still preserves the opportunity to obtain reliable evidence, will no doubt vary depending upon the circumstances in the case.

Because this case was argued on the broad proposition that drunk-driving cases present a *per se* exigency, the arguments and the record do not provide the Court with an adequate analytic framework for a detailed discussion of all the relevant factors that can be taken into account in determining the reasonableness of acting without a warrant. It suffices to say that the metabolization of alcohol in the bloodstream and the ensuing loss of evidence are among the factors that must be considered in deciding whether a warrant is required. No doubt, given the large number of arrests for this offense in different jurisdictions nationwide, cases will arise when anticipated delays in obtaining a warrant will justify a blood test without judicial authorization, for in every case the law must be concerned that evidence is being destroyed. But that inquiry ought not to be pursued here where the question is not properly before this Court. Having rejected the sole argument presented to us challenging the Missouri Supreme Court's decision, we affirm its judgment.

3

We hold that in drunk-driving investigations, the natural dissipation of alcohol in the bloodstream does not constitute an exigency in every case sufficient to justify conducting a blood test without a warrant.

The judgment of the Missouri Supreme Court is affirmed.

It is so ordered.

■ JUSTICE KENNEDY, concurring in part.

I join Parts I, II-A, II-B, and IV of the opinion for the Court.

For the reasons stated below this case does not call for the Court to consider in detail the issue discussed in Part II-C and the separate opinion by THE CHIEF JUSTICE.

As to Part III, much that is noted * * * will be of relevance when this issue is explored in later cases. * * *

■ CHIEF JUSTICE ROBERTS, with whom JUSTICE BREYER and JUSTICE ALITO join, concurring in part and dissenting in part.

A police officer reading this Court's opinion would have no idea—no idea—what the Fourth Amendment requires of him, once he decides to obtain a blood sample from a drunk driving suspect who has refused a breathalyzer test. I have no quarrel with the Court's "totality of the circumstances" approach as a general matter; that is what our cases require. But the circumstances in drunk driving cases are often typical, and the Court should be able to offer guidance on how police should handle cases like the one before us.

In my view, the proper rule is straightforward. Our cases establish that there is an exigent circumstances exception to the warrant requirement. That exception applies when there is a compelling need to prevent the imminent destruction of important evidence, and there is no time to obtain a warrant. The natural dissipation of alcohol in the bloodstream constitutes not only the imminent but ongoing destruction of critical evidence. That would qualify as an exigent circumstance, except that there may be time to secure a warrant before blood can be drawn. If there is, an officer must seek a warrant. If an officer could reasonably conclude that there is not, the exigent circumstances exception applies by its terms, and the blood may be drawn without a warrant.[2]

* * *

The Court * * * contend[s] that the question presented somehow inhibits such a focused analysis in this case. It does not. The question presented is whether a warrantless blood draw is permissible under the Fourth Amendment "based upon the natural dissipation of alcohol in the bloodstream." The majority answers "It depends," and so do I. The difference is that the majority offers no additional guidance, merely instructing courts and police officers to consider the totality of the circumstances. I believe more meaningful guidance can be provided about how to handle the typical cases, and nothing about the question presented prohibits affording that guidance.

A plurality of the Court also expresses concern that my approach will discourage state and local efforts to expedite the warrant application process. That is not plausible: Police and prosecutors need warrants in a wide variety of situations, and often need them quickly. They certainly

---

[2]   This case involves medical personnel drawing blood at a medical facility, not police officers doing so by the side of the road. See *Schmerber v. California,* 384 U.S. 757, 771–772, 86 S.Ct. 1826, 16 L.Ed.2d 908 (1966) ("Petitioner's blood was taken by a physician in a hospital environment according to accepted medical practices. We are thus not presented with the serious questions which would arise if a search involving use of a medical technique, even of the most rudimentary sort, were made by other than medical personnel or in other than a medical environment—for example, if it were administered by police in the privacy of the stationhouse") * * * . A plurality of the Court suggests that my approach could make roadside blood draws a more attractive option for police, but such a procedure would pose practical difficulties and, as the Court noted in *Schmerber,* would raise additional and serious Fourth Amendment concerns.

would not prefer a slower process, just because that might obviate the need to ask for a warrant in the occasional drunk driving case in which a blood draw is necessary. The plurality's suggestion also overlooks the interest of law enforcement in the protection a warrant provides.

The Court is correct when it says that every case must be considered on its particular facts. But the pertinent facts in drunk driving cases are often the same, and the police should know how to act in recurring factual situations. Simply put, when a drunk driving suspect fails field sobriety tests and refuses a breathalyzer, whether a warrant is required for a blood draw should come down to whether there is time to secure one.

* * *

Because the Missouri courts did not apply the rule I describe above, and because this Court should not do so in the first instance, I would vacate and remand for further proceedings in the Missouri courts.

■ JUSTICE THOMAS, dissenting.

This case requires the Court to decide whether the Fourth Amendment prohibits an officer from obtaining a blood sample without a warrant when there is probable cause to believe that a suspect has been driving under the influence of alcohol. Because the body's natural metabolization of alcohol inevitably destroys evidence of the crime, it constitutes an exigent circumstance. As a result, I would hold that a warrantless blood draw does not violate the Fourth Amendment.

* * *

Once police arrest a suspect for drunk driving, each passing minute eliminates probative evidence of the crime. The human liver eliminates alcohol from the bloodstream at a rate of approximately 0.015 percent to 0.020 percent per hour, with some heavy drinkers as high as 0.022 percent per hour, depending on, among other things, a person's sex, weight, body type, and drinking history. * * *

The rapid destruction of evidence acknowledged by the parties, the majority, and *Schmerber*'s exigency determination occurs in *every* situation where police have probable cause to arrest a drunk driver. In turn, that destruction of evidence implicates the exigent-circumstances doctrine. * * * [T]he natural metabolization of blood alcohol concentration (BAC) creates an exigency once police have probable cause to believe the driver is drunk. It naturally follows that police may conduct a search in these circumstances.

* * *

The majority believes that, absent special facts and circumstances, some destruction of evidence is acceptable. This belief must rest on the assumption that whatever evidence remains once a warrant is obtained will be sufficient to prosecute the suspect. But that assumption is clearly wrong. Suspects' initial levels of intoxication and the time necessary to obtain warranted blood draws will vary widely from case to case. Even a slight delay may significantly affect probative value in borderline cases of suspects who are moderately intoxicated or suspects whose BAC is near a statutory threshold that triggers a more serious offense. Similarly, the time to obtain a warrant can be expected to vary, and there is no reason to believe it will do so in a predictable fashion.

Further, the Court nowhere explains how an officer in the field is to apply the facts-and-circumstances test it adopts. First, officers do not have the facts needed to assess how much time can pass before too little evidence remains. They will never know how intoxicated a suspect is at the time of arrest. Otherwise, there would be no need for testing. Second, they will not know how long it will take to roust a magistrate from his bed, reach the hospital, or obtain a blood sample once there. * * * The Court should not adopt a rule that requires police to guess whether they will be able to obtain a warrant before "too much" evidence is destroyed, for the police lack reliable information concerning the relevant variables.

* * *

The availability of telephonic warrant applications is not an answer to this conundrum. For one thing, Missouri still requires written warrant applications and affidavits, rendering the Court's * * * survey irrelevant to the actual disposition of this case. But even if telephonic applications were available in Missouri, the same difficulties would arise. As the majority correctly recognizes, "[w]arrants inevitably take some time for police officers or prosecutors to complete and for magistrate judges to review." During that time, evidence is destroyed, and police who have probable cause to believe a crime has been committed should not have to guess how long it will take to secure a warrant.

* * *

For the foregoing reasons, I respectfully dissent.

2. SEARCHES OF RESIDENTIAL PREMISES

Fourth Amendment standards are applied with particular rigor when the law enforcement activity at issue involves the home. "[W]hen it comes to the Fourth Amendment, the home is first among equals. At the Amendment's 'very core' stands 'the right of a man to retreat into his own home and there be free from unreasonable governmental intrusion.' *Silverman v. United States,* 365 U.S. 505, 511, 81 S.Ct. 679, 5 L.Ed.2d 734 (1961)." Florida v. Jardines, ___ U.S. ___, ___, 133 S.Ct. 1409, 1414–15 (2013). More specifically, "unwarranted 'searches and seizures inside a home' bear heightened scrutiny." Kentucky v. King, 563 U.S. 452, 474, 131 S.Ct. 1849, 1864 (2011).

This may mean that supporting a search of a residence on the basis of exigent circumstances requires more than is required in other situations. It may also mean that in some situations, exigencies permit "seizure"—or "securing"—of premises but not a search of those premises without a warrant.

Vale v. Louisiana

Supreme Court of the United States, 1970.
399 U.S. 30, 90 S.Ct. 1969.

■ MR. JUSTICE STEWART delivered the opinion of the Court.

The appellant, Donald Vale, was convicted in a Louisiana court on a charge of possessing heroin and was sentenced as a multiple offender to 15 years' imprisonment at hard labor. The Louisiana Supreme Court affirmed the conviction, rejecting the claim that evidence introduced at the trial was the product of an unlawful search and seizure. * * *

The evidence adduced at the pretrial hearing on a motion to suppress showed that on April 24, 1967, officers possessing two warrants for Vale's arrest and having information that he was residing at a specified address proceeded there in an unmarked car and set up a surveillance of the house. The evidence of what then took place was summarized by the Louisiana Supreme Court as follows:

> "After approximately 15 minutes the officers observed a green 1958 Chevrolet drive up and sound the horn and after backing into a parking place, again blew the horn. At this juncture Donald Vale, who was well known to Officer Brady having arrested him twice in the previous month, was seen coming out of the house and walk up to the passenger side of the Chevrolet where he had a close brief conversation with the driver; and after looking up and down the street returned inside of the house. Within a few minutes he reappeared on the porch, and again cautiously looked up and down the street before proceeding to the passenger side of the Chevrolet, leaning through the window. From this the officers were convinced a narcotics sale had taken place. They returned to their car and immediately drove toward Donald Vale, and as they reached within approximately three car lengths from the accused, (Donald Vale) he looked up and, obviously recognizing the officers, turned around, walking quickly toward the house. At the same time the driver of the Chevrolet started to make his get away when the car was blocked by the police vehicle. The three officers promptly alighted from the car, whereupon Officers Soule and Laumann called to Donald Vale to stop as he reached the front steps of the house, telling him he was under arrest. Officer Brady at the same time, seeing the driver of the Chevrolet, Arizzio Saucier, whom the officers knew to be a narcotic addict, place something hurriedly in his mouth, immediately placed him under arrest and joined his co-officers. Because of the transaction they had just observed they, informed Donald Vale they were going to search the house, and thereupon advised him of his constitutional rights. After they all entered the front room, Officer Laumann made a cursory inspection of the house to ascertain if anyone else was present

and within about three minutes Mrs. Vale and James Vale, mother and brother of Donald Vale, returned home carrying groceries and were informed of the arrest and impending search."

The search of a rear bedroom revealed a quantity of narcotics.

* * *

The Louisiana Supreme Court thought the search * * * supportable because it involved narcotics, which are easily removed, hidden, or destroyed. It would be unreasonable, the Louisiana court concluded, "to require the officers under the facts of the case to first secure a search warrant before searching the premises, as time is of the essence inasmuch as the officers never know whether there is anyone on the premises to be searched who could very easily destroy the evidence." Such a rationale could not apply to the present case, since by their own account the arresting officers satisfied themselves that no one else was in the house when they first entered the premises. But entirely apart from that point, our past decisions make clear that only in "a few specifically established and well-delineated" situations, may a warrantless search of a dwelling withstand constitutional scrutiny, even though the authorities have probable cause to conduct it. The burden rests on the State to show the existence of such an exceptional situation. And the record before us discloses none.

There is no suggestion that anyone consented to the search. The officers were not responding to an emergency. They were not in hot pursuit of a fleeing felon. *Warden v. Hayden*, 387 U.S. 294, 298–299, 87 S.Ct. 1642, 1645–1646, 18 L.Ed.2d 782. The goods ultimately seized were not in the process of destruction. *Schmerber v. California*, 384 U.S. 757, 770–771, 86 S.Ct. 1826, 1835–1836, 16 L.Ed.2d 908. Nor were they about to be removed from the jurisdiction.

The officers were able to procure two warrants for Vale's arrest. They also had information that he was residing at the address where they found him. There is thus no reason, so far as anything before us appears, to suppose that it was impracticable for them to obtain a search warrant as well. * * * We decline to hold that an arrest on the street can provide its own "exigent circumstance" so as to justify a warrantless search of the arrestee's house.

* * *

Reversed and remanded.

■ MR. JUSTICE BLACKMUN took no part in the consideration or decision of this case.

■ MR. JUSTICE BLACK, with whom THE CHIEF JUSTICE joins, dissenting.

* * *

[T]he police did not know * * * who else might be in the house. Vale's arrest took place near the house, and anyone observing from inside would surely have been alerted to destroy the stocks of contraband which the police believed Vale had left there. The police had already seen Saucier, the narcotics addict, apparently swallow what Vale had given him. Believing that some evidence had already been destroyed and that other evidence might well be, the police were faced with the choice of risking the immediate destruction of evidence or entering the house and conducting a search. I cannot say that their decision to search was unreasonable. * * *

[T]he Court asserts, however, that because the police obtained two warrants for Vale's arrest there is "no reason * * * to suppose that it was impracticable for them to obtain a search warrant as well." The difficulty is that the two arrest warrants on which the Court seems to rely so heavily were not issued because of any present misconduct of Vale's; they were issued because the bond had been increased for an earlier narcotics charge then pending against Vale. When the police came to arrest Vale, they knew only that his bond had been increased. There is nothing in the record to indicate that, absent the increased bond, there would have been probable cause for an arrest, much less a search. Probable cause for the search arose for the first time when the police observed the activity of Vale and Saucier in and around the house.

* * *

NOTES

1. In Minnesota v. Olson, 495 U.S. 91, 110 S.Ct. 1684 (1990), officers investigating a robbery-murder occurring about 6 a.m. on July 18, 1987 developed probable cause to believe Olson the driver of the getaway car. On July 19, they determined Olson was staying in a duplex unit occupied by Louanne and Julie Bergstrom. The occupant of the other duplex unit promised to call when Olson returned; officers were directed to stay away from the duplex in the interim. At 2:45 p.m., the neighbor called and told police Olson had returned. Officers surrounded the unit and telephoned Julie Bergstrom to tell her Olson should come out. The telephoning detective heard a male voice say, "[T]ell them I left." Julie said "Rob" had left. At 3 p.m., police entered and found Olson hiding in a closet. The Minnesota Supreme Court found this warrantless entry of the duplex was not justified by exigent circumstances. In the absence of hot pursuit, it reasoned, officers must have probable cause to believe the situation involved a risk of imminent destruction of evidence, the suspect's escape, or danger to police or persons inside or outside the dwelling. In assessing these risks, it also concluded, the crime's gravity and the likelihood the suspect is armed could be considered. Applying this standard, the state court held that the entry was unjustified. A majority of the Supreme Court held the state tribunal "applied essentially the correct standard in determining whether exigent circumstances existed." Moreover, it declined to disagree with the state court's "fact-specific application" of the standard:

> The [state] court pointed out that although a grave crime was involved, [Olson] "was known not to be the murderer but thought

to be the driver of the getaway car," and that the police had already recovered the murder weapon. "The police knew that Louanne and Julie were with the suspect in the upstairs duplex with no suggestion of danger to them. Three or four Minneapolis police squads surrounded the house. The time was 3 p.m., Sunday. . . . It was evident the suspect was going nowhere. If he came out of the house he would have been promptly apprehended." We do not disturb the state court's judgment that these facts do not add up to exigent circumstances.

495 U.S. at 100–01, 110 S.Ct. at 1690. Justice Kennedy joined with the "understanding" that the Court's discussion was not an endorsement of the state court's application of the standard. Chief Justice Rehnquist and Justice Blackmun dissented without opinion.

2. **Police-Created Exigent Circumstances.** In Kentucky v. King, 563 U.S. 452, 131 S.Ct. 1849 (2011), the Court addressed whether exigent circumstances permit a warrantless search where police themselves have some responsibility for the exigency.

Several Lexington, Kentucky uniformed police officers, including Officer Steven Cobb, were in pursuit of a suspect from whom a controlled buy of cocaine had been made. The officers believed he had entered one of two apartments and they smelled marijuana smoke emanating from one of the apartments. Then they approached the door of that apartment:

> [T]he officers banged on the left apartment door "as loud as [they] could" and announced, " 'This is the police' " or " 'Police, police, police.' " Cobb said that "[a]s soon as [the officers] started banging on the door," they "could hear people inside moving," and "[i]t sounded as [though] things were being moved inside the apartment." These noises, Cobb testified, led the officers to believe that drug-related evidence was about to be destroyed.
>
> At that point, the officers announced that they "were going to make entry inside the apartment." Cobb then kicked in the door, the officers entered the apartment, and they found three people in the front room: respondent Hollis King, respondent's girlfriend, and a guest who was smoking marijuana. The officers performed a protective sweep of the apartment during which they saw marijuana and powder cocaine in plain view. In a subsequent search, they also discovered crack cocaine, cash, and drug paraphernalia.

Later, the suspected drug dealer who was the initial target of the investigation was found in the other apartment.

Justice Ginsburg argued that the trial court erred in admitting the evidence obtained as a result of the entry. The officers had an opportunity to apply for a warrant, she reasoned. Any exigent circumstances were created by the choice of the officers to knock on the apartment door rather than seek a warrant. "The urgency [required to support an exigent circumstances search] must exist," she concluded, "when the police come on the scene, not subsequent to their arrival, prompted by their own conduct." 563 U.S. at 473, 131 S.Ct. at 1864 (Ginsburg, J., dissenting).

An eight-justice majority, in an opinion by Justice Alito, reasoned otherwise. If exigent circumstances exist and "the police did not create the exigency by engaging or threatening to engage in conduct that violates the Fourth Amendment, warrantless entry to prevent the destruction of evidence is reasonable and thus allowed."

The majority rejected a number of offered limitations on that rule, including ones that would deny officers the right to enter if it was reasonably foreseeable that the investigative tactics employed by the police would create exigent circumstances, if they acted in "bad faith," or if the officers engage in conduct that would cause a reasonable person to believe that entry is imminent and inevitable. With regard to the last proposed limitation, the Court explained:

> If [this] test were adopted, it would be extremely difficult for police officers to know how loudly they may announce their presence or how forcefully they may knock on a door without running afoul of the police-created exigency rule. And in most cases, it would be nearly impossible for a court to determine whether that threshold had been passed.

563 U.S. at 468–69, 131 S.Ct. at 1861.

Applying the adopted approach, the majority assumed—without deciding—that exigent circumstances existed. Nothing in the conduct of the officers prevented the prosecution from relying on those exigent circumstances. Contrary to King's argument, the evidence did not show the officers made a "demand" to be let into the apartment, " much less a demand that amounts to a threat to violate the Fourth Amendment." 563 U.S. at 471, 131 S.Ct. at 1863.

3. **"Hot Pursuit" Situations.** The Court in *Vale* distinguished Warden v. Hayden, 387 U.S. 294, 87 S.Ct. 1642 (1967).

In *Hayden*, two cab drivers followed the armed robber of the cab company to a residence. A description of the robber and the drivers' information was relayed to police, who arrived at the residence within minutes. They knocked on the door and told the woman who answered they had reason to believe a robber had entered the house. The officers asked to search and the woman did not object. Hayden was found in an upstairs bedroom feigning sleep, and was arrested when no other male was found in the house. One officer was attracted to a bathroom adjoining that in which Hayden was found; in the flush tank of a toilet he found a shotgun and pistol. Another officer searching the cellar for the gun or money looked in a washing machine and found a jacket and trousers resembling what the fleeing robber wore. Under the mattress of Hayden's bed the officers found ammunition for the pistol and a cap. Additional ammunition was found in the drawer of the bedroom dresser.

Upholding the admission of these items into evidence, the Supreme Court held that the entry of the premises and the search for the robber and his weapons without a warrant was reasonable, because delay might have endangered the officers or others. "[O]nly a thorough search of the house for persons or weapons could have insured that Hayden was the only man present and that the police had control of all weapons which could be used against them or to effect an escape."

4.   **Crime Scenes.** In Mincey v. Arizona, 437 U.S. 385, 98 S.Ct. 2408 (1978), the Supreme Court rejected the proposition that emergency considerations justify a broad exception to the warrant requirement for scenes of even serious offenses such as homicides. Police officers entered Mincey's apartment to arrest him for possession of drugs. A police officer was shot and killed and Mincey was wounded. Officers secured the apartment and arrested Mincey and the other occupants. There then ensued four days of searching the apartment for evidence related to the homicide; two or three hundred items were seized and inventoried. No warrant was obtained. Mincey was convicted of murder and other offenses after a trial in which some of the seized items were introduced. The Arizona Supreme Court affirmed in part, holding the search permissible without a warrant because the place searched was a "murder scene." The Supreme Court reversed. That the premises were a crime scene did not itself dispense with the warrant requirement. Considered under the emergency doctrine, the search exceeded what emergency justification the case presented:

> All the persons in Mincey's apartment had been located before the investigating homicide officers arrived there and began their search. And a four day search that included opening dresser drawers and ripping up carpets can hardly be rationalized in terms of the legitimate concerns that justify an emergency search.

437 U.S. at 393, 98 S.Ct. at 2414.

Illinois v. McArthur

Supreme Court of the United States, 2001.
531 U.S. 326, 121 S.Ct. 946.

■ JUSTICE BREYER delivered the opinion of the Court.

Police officers, with probable cause to believe that a man had hidden marijuana in his home, prevented that man from entering the home for about two hours while they obtained a search warrant. We must decide whether those officers violated the Fourth Amendment. * * *

I

A

On April 2, 1997, Tera McArthur asked two police officers to accompany her to the trailer where she lived with her husband, Charles, so that they could keep the peace while she removed her belongings. The two officers, Assistant Chief John Love and Officer Richard Skidis, arrived with Tera at the trailer at about 3:15 p.m. Tera went inside, where Charles was present. The officers remained outside.

When Tera emerged after collecting her possessions, she spoke to Chief Love, who was then on the porch. She suggested he check the trailer because "Chuck had dope in there." She added (in Love's words) that she had seen Chuck "slid[e] some dope underneath the couch."

Love knocked on the trailer door, told Charles what Tera had said, and asked for permission to search the trailer, which Charles denied. Love then sent Officer Skidis with Tera to get a search warrant.

Love told Charles, who by this time was also on the porch, that he could not reenter the trailer unless a police officer accompanied him. Charles subsequently reentered the trailer two or three times (to get cigarettes and to make phone calls), and each time Love stood just inside the door to observe what Charles did.

Officer Skidis obtained the warrant by about 5 p.m. He returned to the trailer and, along with other officers, searched it. The officers found under the sofa a marijuana pipe, a box for marijuana (called a "one-hitter" box), and a small amount of marijuana. They then arrested Charles.

B

Illinois subsequently charged Charles McArthur with unlawfully possessing drug paraphernalia and marijuana (less than 2.5 grams), both misdemeanors. McArthur moved to suppress the pipe, box, and marijuana on the ground that they were the "fruit" of an unlawful police seizure, namely, the refusal to let him reenter the trailer unaccompanied, which would have permitted him, he said, to "have destroyed the marijuana."

The trial court granted McArthur's suppression motion. The Appellate Court of Illinois affirmed, and the Illinois Supreme Court denied the State's petition for leave to appeal. We granted certiorari to determine whether the Fourth Amendment prohibits the kind of temporary seizure at issue here.

II

A

The Fourth Amendment says that the "right of the people to be secure in their persons, houses, papers, and effects, against unreasonable searches and seizures, shall not be violated." U.S. Const., Amdt. 4. Its "central requirement" is one of reasonableness. In order to enforce that requirement, this Court has interpreted the Amendment as establishing rules and presumptions designed to control conduct of law enforcement officers that may significantly intrude upon privacy interests. Sometimes those rules require warrants. We have said, for example, that in "the ordinary case," seizures of personal property are "unreasonable within the meaning of the Fourth Amendment," without more, "unless . . . accomplished pursuant to a judicial warrant," issued by a neutral magistrate after finding probable cause. *United States v. Place,* 462 U.S. 696, 701, 103 S.Ct. 2637, 77 L.Ed.2d 110 (1983).

We nonetheless have made it clear that there are exceptions to the warrant requirement. When faced with special law enforcement needs, diminished expectations of privacy, minimal intrusions, or the like, the Court has found that certain general, or individual, circumstances may render a warrantless search or seizure reasonable.

In the circumstances of the case before us, we cannot say that the warrantless seizure was *per se* unreasonable. It involves a plausible claim of specially pressing or urgent law enforcement need, *i.e.,* "exigent circumstances." Moreover, the restraint at issue was tailored to that need, being limited in time and scope, and avoiding significant intrusion into the home itself. Consequently, rather than employing a *per se* rule of unreasonableness, we balance the privacy-related and law enforcement-related concerns to determine if the intrusion was reasonable.

We conclude that the restriction at issue was reasonable, and hence lawful, in light of the following circumstances, which we consider in combination. First, the police had probable cause to believe that McArthur's trailer home contained evidence of a crime and contraband, namely, unlawful drugs. The police had had an opportunity to speak with Tera McArthur and make at least a very rough assessment of her reliability. They knew she had had a firsthand opportunity to observe her husband's behavior, in particular with respect to the drugs at issue. And they thought, with good reason, that her report to them reflected that opportunity.

Second, the police had good reason to fear that, unless restrained, McArthur would destroy the drugs before they could return with a warrant. They reasonably might have thought that McArthur realized that his wife knew about his marijuana stash; observed that she was angry or frightened enough to ask the police to accompany her; saw that after leaving the trailer she had spoken with the police; and noticed that she had walked off with one policeman while leaving the other outside to observe the trailer. They reasonably could have concluded that McArthur, consequently suspecting an imminent search, would, if given the chance, get rid of the drugs fast.

Third, the police made reasonable efforts to reconcile their law enforcement needs with the demands of personal privacy. They neither searched the trailer nor arrested McArthur before obtaining a warrant. Rather, they imposed a significantly less restrictive restraint, preventing McArthur only from entering the trailer unaccompanied. They left his home and his belongings intact—until a neutral Magistrate, finding probable cause, issued a warrant.

Fourth, the police imposed the restraint for a limited period of time, namely, two hours. As far as the record reveals, this time period was no longer than reasonably necessary for the police, acting with diligence, to obtain the warrant. Given the nature of the intrusion and the law enforcement interest at stake, this brief seizure of the premises was permissible.

B

* * *

We have found no case in which this Court has held unlawful a temporary seizure that was supported by probable cause and was designed to prevent the loss of evidence while the police diligently obtained a warrant in a reasonable period of time. But cf. *Welsh v. Wisconsin,* 466 U.S. 740, 754, 104 S.Ct. 2091, 80 L.Ed.2d 732 (1984) (holding warrantless entry into and arrest in home unreasonable despite possibility that evidence of noncriminal offense would be lost while warrant was being obtained).

C

* * * Finally, McArthur points to a case (and we believe it is the only case) that he believes offers direct support, namely, *Welsh v. Wisconsin, supra.* In *Welsh,* this Court held that police could not enter a home without a warrant in order to prevent the loss of evidence (namely, the defendant's blood alcohol level) of the "nonjailable traffic offense" of driving while intoxicated. McArthur notes that his two convictions are for misdemeanors, which, he says, are as minor, and he adds that the restraint, keeping him out of his home, was nearly as serious.

We nonetheless find significant distinctions. The evidence at issue here was of crimes that were "jailable," not "nonjailable." See Ill. Comp. Stat., ch. 720, § 550/4(a) (1998); ch. 730, § 5/5–8–3(3) (possession of less than 2.5 grams of marijuana punishable by up to 30 days in jail); ch. 720, § 600/3.5; ch. 730, § 5/5–8–3(1) (possession of drug paraphernalia punishable by up to one year in jail). In *Welsh,* we noted that, "[g]iven that the classification of state crimes differs widely among the States, the penalty that may attach to any particular offense seems to provide the clearest and most consistent indication of the State's interest in arresting individuals suspected of committing that offense." The same reasoning applies here, where class C misdemeanors include such widely diverse offenses as drag racing, drinking alcohol in a railroad car or on a railroad platform, bribery by a candidate for public office, and assault.

And the restriction at issue here is less serious. Temporarily keeping a person from entering his home, a consequence whenever police stop a person on the street, is considerably less intrusive than police entry into the home itself in order to make a warrantless arrest or conduct a search.

We have explained above why we believe that the need to preserve evidence of a "jailable" offense was sufficiently urgent or pressing to justify the restriction upon entry that the police imposed. We need not decide whether the circumstances before us would have justified a greater restriction for this type of offense or the same restriction were only a "nonjailable" offense at issue.

III

In sum, the police officers in this case had probable cause to believe that a home contained contraband, which was evidence of a crime. They reasonably believed that the home's resident, if left free of any restraint, would destroy that evidence. And they imposed a restraint that was both limited and tailored reasonably to secure law enforcement needs while protecting privacy interests. In our view, the restraint met the Fourth Amendment's demands.

The judgment of the Illinois Appellate Court is reversed, and the case is remanded for further proceedings not inconsistent with this opinion.

It is so ordered.

■ JUSTICE SOUTER, concurring.

I join the Court's opinion subject to this afterword on two points: the constitutionality of a greater intrusion than the one here and the permissibility of choosing impoundment over immediate search. Respondent McArthur's location made the difference between the exigency that justified temporarily barring him from his own dwelling and circumstances that would have supported a greater interference with his privacy and property. As long as he was inside his trailer, the police had probable cause to believe that he had illegal drugs stashed as his wife had reported and that with any sense he would flush them down the drain before the police could get a warrant to enter and search. This probability of destruction in anticipation of a warrant exemplifies the kind of present risk that undergirds the accepted exigent circumstances exception to the general warrant requirement. That risk would have justified the police in entering McArthur's trailer promptly to make a lawful, warrantless search. When McArthur stepped outside and left the trailer uninhabited, the risk abated and so did the reasonableness of entry by the police for as long as he was outside. This is so because the only justification claimed for warrantless action here is the immediate risk, and the limit of reasonable response by the police is set by the scope of the risk.

Since, however, McArthur wished to go back in, why was it reasonable to keep him out when the police could perfectly well have let him do as he chose, and then enjoyed the ensuing opportunity to follow him and make a warrantless search justified by the renewed danger of destruction? The answer is not that the law officiously insists on safeguarding a suspect's privacy from search, in preference to respecting the suspect's liberty to enter his own dwelling. Instead, the legitimacy of the decision to impound the dwelling follows from the law's strong preference for warrants, which underlies the rule that a search with a warrant has a stronger claim to justification on later, judicial review than a search without one. The law can hardly raise incentives to obtain a warrant without giving the police a fair chance to take their probable cause to a magistrate and get one.

■ JUSTICE STEVENS, dissenting.

The Illinois General Assembly has decided that the possession of less than 2.5 grams of marijuana is a class C misdemeanor. In so classifying the offense, the legislature made a concerted policy judgment that the possession of small amounts of marijuana for personal use does not constitute a particularly significant public policy concern. * * *

* * * I would affirm. As the majority explains, the essential inquiry in this case involves a balancing of the "privacy-related and law enforcement-related concerns to determine if the intrusion was reasonable." Under the specific facts of this case, I believe the majority gets the balance wrong. Each of the Illinois jurists who participated in the decision of this case placed a higher value on the sanctity of the ordinary citizen's home than on the prosecution of this petty offense. They correctly viewed that interest—whether the home be a humble cottage, a secondhand trailer, or a stately mansion—as one meriting the most serious constitutional protection. Following their analysis and the reasoning in our decision in *Welsh v. Wisconsin,* 466 U.S. 740, 104 S.Ct. 2091, 80 L.Ed.2d 732 (1984) (holding that some offenses may be so minor as to make it unreasonable for police to undertake searches that would be constitutionally permissible if graver offenses were suspected), I would affirm.

B. ADMINISTRATIVE INSPECTIONS AND SEARCHES OF LICENSED PREMISES

EDITORS' INTRODUCTION: "ADMINISTRATIVE" HOUSING CODE INSPECTIONS

The Fourth Amendment by its terms is not limited to traditional criminal investigation. Rather, it is potentially applicable to any governmental activity meeting the threshold requirements of a "search" or a "seizure." Supreme Court case law, however, has tended to dilute the requirements of the Amendment when governmental activity has a purpose other than the location of evidence to use in a criminal prosecution.

Such dilution was clearly evidenced in Frank v. Maryland, 359 U.S. 360, 79 S.Ct. 804 (1959). The Health Code of the City of Baltimore required all dwellings be kept clean and free from rodent infestation. Health inspectors having "cause to suspect" a violation were authorized to demand entry to premises for purposes of inspection. Frank was convicted and fined $20 for refusing to permit an inspector to enter his premises to look for rats. Finding no federal constitutional defect in this conviction, a majority of the Supreme Court explained:

The attempted inspection of appellant's home is merely to determine whether conditions exist which the Baltimore Health Code proscribes. If they do appellant is notified to remedy the infringing condition. No evidence for criminal prosecution is sought to be seized. * * * The power of inspection granted by the Baltimore City Code is strictly limited * * * . Valid grounds for suspicion of the existence of a nuisance must exist. * * * The inspection must be made in the day time. * * * Moreover, the inspector has no power to force entry * * * . A fine is imposed for resistance, but officials are not authorized to break past the unwilling occupant.

Thus, not only does the inspection touch at most upon the periphery of the important interests safeguarded by the Fourteenth Amendment's protection against official intrusion, but it is hedged about with safeguards designed to make the least possible demand on the individual occupant, and to cause only the slightest restriction on his claims of privacy.

359 U.S. at 366–67, 79 S.Ct. at 808–09. Against this, the Court continued, must be weighed the interests served by inspections:

Time and experience have forcefully taught that the power to inspect dwelling places, either as a matter of systematic area-by-area search or * * * to treat a specific problem, is of indispensable importance to the maintenance of community health; a power that would be greatly hobbled by the blanket requirement of the safeguards necessary for a search of evidence for criminal acts.

359 U.S. at 372, 79 S.Ct. at 811. In light of this, a five justice majority of the Court held the inspector's entry would not have been an unreasonable search. Thus Frank was properly convicted of refusing to permit it.

Frank suggested warrants are unnecessary for administrative inspections. In 1967, however, the Court held that despite *Frank* the Fourth Amendment requires warrants for nonemergency Housing Code inspections of residences. Camara v. Municipal Court, 387 U.S. 523, 87 S.Ct. 1727 (1967). But it also held warrants authorizing such inspections need not be based upon probable cause to believe that each building to be inspected contains Code violations. Several considerations justified modification of the probable cause standard for this context. Code violations are a serious problem and so limiting inspectors would render effective enforcement impossible. Moreover, since "the inspections are neither personal in nature nor aimed at the discovery of evidence of crime, they involve a relatively limited invasion of the urban citizen's privacy." Consequently, the warrant process is appropriately modified in this context so as to permit warrants to issue for "area inspections"— inspections of all premises in a particular area based on conditions in the area as a whole rather than on knowledge of conditions in particular buildings. Thus:

"probable cause" to issue a warrant to inspect must exist if reasonable legislative or administrative standards for conducting an area inspection are satisfied with respect to a particular dwelling. Such standards, which will vary with the municipal program being enforced, may be based upon the passage of time, the nature of the building (e.g., a multifamily apartment house), or the condition of the entire area, but they will not necessarily depend upon specific knowledge of the condition of the particular dwelling.

387 U.S. at 538, 87 S.Ct. at 1736. In a companion case, the Court held the same general Fourth Amendment rules apply to administrative inspections of commercial premises and added that the nature of such premises might make them subject to inspection in more situations than permit inspections of private residence. See v. City of Seattle, 387 U.S. 541, 87 S.Ct. 1737 (1967).

The principal case in this section deals with inspections of heavily regulated businesses, which are permitted under even more relaxed Fourth Amendment standards than were applied in *Camara* and *See*.

New York v. Burger

Supreme Court of the United States, 1987.
482 U.S. 691, 107 S.Ct. 2636.

■ JUSTICE BLACKMUN delivered the opinion of the Court.

This case presents the question whether the warrantless search of an automobile junkyard, conducted pursuant to a statute authorizing such a search, falls within the exception to the warrant requirement for administrative inspections of pervasively regulated industries. The case also presents the question whether an otherwise proper administrative inspection is unconstitutional because the ultimate purpose of the regulatory statute pursuant to which the search is done—the deterrence of criminal behavior—is the same as that of penal laws, with the result that the inspection may disclose violations not only of the regulatory statute but also of the penal statutes.

I

Respondent Joseph Burger is the owner of a junkyard in Brooklyn, N.Y. His business consists, in part, of the dismantling of automobiles and the selling of their parts. His junkyard is an open lot with no buildings. A high metal fence surrounds it, wherein are located, among other things, vehicles and parts of vehicles. At approximately noon on November 17, 1982, Officer Joseph Vega and four other plainclothes officers, all members of the Auto Crimes Division of the New York City Police Department, entered respondent's junkyard to conduct an inspection pursuant to N.Y.Veh. & Traf.Law § 415–a5 (McKinney 1986). On any given day, the Division conducts from 5 to 10 inspections of vehicle dismantlers, automobile junkyards, and related businesses.

Upon entering the junkyard, the officers asked to see Burger's license[3] and his "police book"—the record of the automobiles and vehicle parts in his possession. Burger replied that he had neither a license nor a police book. The officers then announced their intention to conduct a § 415–a inspection. Burger did not object. In accordance with their practice, the officers copied down the Vehicle Inspection Numbers (VINs) of several vehicles and parts of vehicles that were in the junkyard. After checking these numbers against a police computer, the officers determined that respondent was in possession of stolen vehicles and parts. Accordingly, Burger was arrested and charged with five counts of possession of stolen property and one count of unregistered operation as a vehicle dismantler * * * .

In the Kings County Supreme Court, Burger moved to suppress the evidence obtained as a result of the inspection, primarily on the ground that § 415–a5 was unconstitutional. After a hearing, the court denied the motion. * * *

The New York Court of Appeals, however, reversed. In its view, § 415–a5 violated the Fourth Amendment's prohibition of unreasonable searches and seizures. According to the Court of Appeals, "[t]he fundamental defect [of § 415–a5] * * * is that [it] authorize[s] searches undertaken solely to uncover evidence of criminality and not to enforce a comprehensive regulatory scheme. The asserted 'administrative schem[e]' here [is], in reality, designed simply to give the police an expedient means of enforcing penal sanctions for possession of stolen property." * * * [W]e granted certiorari.

II

A

The Court long has recognized that the Fourth Amendment's prohibition on unreasonable searches and seizures is applicable to commercial premises, as well as to private homes. An owner or operator of a business thus has an expectation of privacy in commercial property, which society is prepared to consider to be reasonable. This expectation exists not only with respect to traditional police searches conducted for the gathering of criminal evidence but also with respect to administrative inspections designed to enforce regulatory statutes. See *Marshall v. Barlow's, Inc.*, 436 U.S. 307, 312–313, 98 S.Ct. 1816, 1820–1821, 56 L.Ed.2d 305 (1978). An expectation of privacy in commercial premises, however, is different from, and indeed less than, a similar expectation in an individual's home. See *Donovan v. Dewey*, 452 U.S. 594, 598–599, 101

---

[3] An individual operating a vehicle-dismantling business in New York is required to have a license:

"Definition and registration of vehicle dismantlers. A vehicle dismantler is any person who is engaged in the business of acquiring motor vehicles or trailers for the purpose of dismantling the same for parts or reselling such vehicles as scrap. No person shall engage in the business of or operate as a vehicle dismantler unless there shall have been issued to him a registration in accordance with the provisions of this section. A violation of this subdivision shall be a class E felony." N.Y.Veh. & Traf.Laws 415–a1 (McKinney 1986).

S.Ct. 2534, 2537–2538, 69 L.Ed.2d 262 (1981). This expectation is particularly attenuated in commercial property employed in "closely regulated" industries. The Court observed in *Marshall v. Barlow's, Inc.*: "Certain industries have such a history of government oversight that no reasonable expectation of privacy could exist for a proprietor over the stock of such an enterprise."

The Court first examined the "unique" problem of inspections of "closely regulated" businesses in two enterprises that had "a long tradition of close government supervision." In *Colonnade Corp. v. United States*, 397 U.S. 72, 90 S.Ct. 774, 25 L.Ed.2d 60 (1970), it considered a warrantless search of a catering business pursuant to several federal revenue statutes authorizing the inspection of the premises of liquor dealers. Although the Court disapproved the search because the statute provided that a sanction be imposed when entry was refused, and because it did not authorize entry without a warrant as an alternative in this situation, it recognized that "the liquor industry [was] long subject to close supervision and inspection."

We returned to this issue in *United States v. Biswell*, 406 U.S. 311, 92 S.Ct. 1593, 32 L.Ed.2d 87 (1972), which involved a warrantless inspection of the premises of a pawn shop operator, who was federally licensed to sell sporting weapons pursuant to the Gun Control Act of 1968, 82 Stat. 1213, 18 U.S.C. § 921 et seq. While noting that "[f]ederal regulation of the interstate traffic in firearms is not as deeply rooted in history as is governmental control of the liquor industry," we nonetheless concluded that the warrantless inspections authorized by the Gun Control Act would "pose only limited threats to the dealer's justifiable expectations of privacy." We observed: "When a dealer chooses to engage in this pervasively regulated business and to accept a federal license, he does so with the knowledge that his business records, firearms, and ammunition will be subject to effective inspection."

The "*Colonnade-Biswell*" doctrine, stating the reduced expectation of privacy by an owner of commercial premises in a "closely regulated" industry, has received renewed emphasis in more recent decisions. In *Marshall v. Barlow's, Inc.,* we noted its continued vitality but declined to find that warrantless inspections, made pursuant to the Occupational Safety and Health Act of 1970, 84 Stat. 1598, 29 U.S.C. §§ 657(a), of all businesses engaged in interstate commerce fell within the narrow focus of this doctrine. However, we found warrantless inspections made pursuant to the Federal Mine Safety and Health Act of 1977, 91 Stat. 1290, 30 U.S.C. § 801 et seq., proper because they were of a "closely regulated" industry. *Donovan v. Dewey,* supra.

Indeed, in *Donovan v. Dewey,* we declined to limit our consideration to the length of time during which the business in question—stone quarries—had been subject to federal regulation. We pointed out that the doctrine is essentially defined by "the pervasiveness and regularity of the federal regulation" and the effect of such regulation upon an owner's expectation of privacy. We observed, however, that "the duration of a particular regulatory scheme" would remain an "important factor" in deciding whether a warrantless inspection pursuant to the scheme is permissible.

B

Because the owner or operator of commercial premises in a "closely regulated" industry has a reduced expectation of privacy, the warrant and probable cause requirements, which fulfill the traditional Fourth Amendment standard of reasonableness for a government search, have lessened application in this context. Rather, we conclude that, as in other situations of "special need," where the privacy interests of the owner are weakened and the government interests in regulating particular businesses are concomitantly heightened, a warrantless inspection of commercial premises may well be reasonable within the meaning of the Fourth Amendment.

This warrantless inspection, however, even in the context of a pervasively regulated business, will be deemed to be reasonable only so long as three criteria are met. First, there must be a "substantial" government interest that informs the regulatory scheme pursuant to which the inspection is made.

Second, the warrantless inspections must be "necessary to further [the] regulatory scheme." For example, in *Dewey* we recognized that forcing mine inspectors to obtain a warrant before every inspection might alert mine owners or operators to the impending inspection, thereby frustrating the purposes of the Mine Safety and Health Act—to detect and thus to deter safety and health violations.

Finally, "the statute's inspection program, in terms of the certainty and regularity of its application, [must] provid[e] a constitutionally adequate substitute for a warrant." In other words, the regulatory statute must perform the two basic functions of a warrant: it must advise the owner of the commercial premises that the search is being made pursuant to the law and has a properly defined scope, and it must limit the discretion of the inspecting officers. To perform this first function, the statute must be "sufficiently comprehensive and defined that the owner of commercial property cannot help but be aware that his property will be subject to periodic inspections undertaken for specific purposes." In addition, in defining how a statute limits the discretion of the inspectors, we have observed that it must be "carefully limited in time, place, and scope."

III

A

Searches made pursuant to § 415–a, in our view, clearly fall within this established exception to the warrant requirement for administrative inspections in "closely regulated" businesses. First, the nature of the regulatory statute reveals that the operation of a junkyard, part of which is devoted to vehicle dismantling, is a "closely regulated" business in the State of New York. The provisions regulating the activity of vehicle dismantling are extensive. An operator cannot engage in this industry without first obtaining a license, which means that he must meet the registration requirements and must pay a fee. Under § 415–a5(a), the operator must maintain a police book recording the acquisition and disposition of motor vehicles and vehicle parts, and make such records and inventory available for inspection by the police or any agent of the Department of Motor Vehicles. The operator also must display his registration number prominently at his place of business, on business documentation, and on vehicles and parts that pass through his business. Moreover, the person engaged in this activity is subject to criminal penalties, as well as to loss of license or civil fines, for failure to comply with these provisions. That other States besides New York have imposed similarly extensive regulations on automobile junkyards further supports the "closely regulated" status of this industry.

In determining whether vehicle dismantlers constitute a "closely regulated" industry, the "duration of [this] particular regulatory scheme," has some relevancy. Section 415–a could be said to be of fairly recent vintage, and the inspection provision of § 415–a5 was added only in 1979. But because the automobile is a relatively new phenomenon in our society and because its widespread use is even newer, automobile junkyards and vehicle dismantlers have not been in existence very long and thus do not have an ancient history of government oversight. * * *

The automobile junkyard business * * * is simply a new branch of an industry that has existed, and has been closely regulated, for many years. The automobile junkyard is closely akin to the secondhand shop or the general junkyard. Both share the purpose of recycling salvageable articles and components of items no longer usable in their original form. As such, vehicle dismantlers represent a modern, specialized version of a traditional activity.

In New York, general junkyards and secondhand shops long have been subject to regulation. * * * The history of government regulation of junk-related activities argues strongly in favor of the "closely regulated" status of the automobile junkyard.

Accordingly, in light of the regulatory framework governing his business and the history of regulation of related industries, an operator of a junkyard engaging in vehicle dismantling has a reduced expectation of privacy in this "closely regulated" business.

B

The New York regulatory scheme satisfies the three criteria necessary to make reasonable warrantless inspections pursuant to § 415–a5. First, the State has a substantial interest in regulating the vehicle-dismantling and automobile-junkyard industry because motor vehicle theft has increased in the State and because the problem of theft is associated with this industry. In this day, automobile theft has become a significant social problem, placing enormous economic and personal burdens upon the citizens of different States. * * * Because contemporary automobiles are made from standardized parts, the nationwide extent of vehicle theft and concern about it are understandable.

Second, regulation of the vehicle-dismantling industry reasonably serves the State's substantial interest in eradicating automobile theft. It is well established that the theft problem can be addressed effectively by controlling the receiver of, or market in, stolen property. Automobile junkyards and vehicle dismantlers provide the major market for stolen vehicles and vehicle parts. Thus, the State rationally may believe that it will reduce car theft by regulations that prevent automobile junkyards from becoming markets for stolen vehicles and that help trace the origin and destination of vehicle parts.

Moreover, the warrantless administrative inspections pursuant to § 415–a5 "are necessary to further [the] regulatory scheme." In this respect, we see no difference between these inspections and those approved by the Court in *United States v. Biswell* and *Donovan v. Dewey*. We explained in *Biswell:*

> "[I]f inspection is to be effective and serve as a credible deterrent, unannounced, even frequent, inspections are essential. In this context, the prerequisite of a warrant could easily frustrate inspection; and if the necessary flexibility as to time, scope, and frequency is to be preserved, the protections afforded by a warrant would be negligible."

Similarly, in the present case, a warrant requirement would interfere with the statute's purpose of deterring automobile theft accomplished by identifying vehicles and parts as stolen and shutting down the market in such items. Because stolen cars and parts often pass quickly through an automobile junkyard, "frequent" and "unannounced" inspections are necessary in order to detect them. In sum, surprise is crucial if the regulatory scheme aimed at remedying this major social problem is to function at all.

Third, § 415–a5 provides a "constitutionally adequate substitute for a warrant." The statute informs the operator of a vehicle dismantling business that inspections will be made on a regular basis. Thus, the vehicle dismantler knows that the inspections to which he is subject do not constitute discretionary acts by a government official but are conducted pursuant to statute. Section 415–a5 also sets forth the scope of the inspection and, accordingly, places the operator on notice as to how to comply with the statute. In addition, it notifies the operator as to who is authorized to conduct an inspection.

Finally, the "time, place, and scope" of the inspection is limited, to place appropriate restraints upon the discretion of the inspecting officers. The officers are allowed to conduct an inspection only "during [the] regular and usual business hours."[21] The inspections can be made only of vehicle-dismantling and related industries. And the permissible scope of these searches is narrowly defined: the inspectors may examine the records, as well as "any vehicles or parts of vehicles which are subject to the record keeping requirements of this section and which are on the premises."

IV

A search conducted pursuant to § 415–a5, therefore, clearly falls within the well-established exception to the warrant requirement for administrative inspections of "closely regulated" businesses. The Court of Appeals, nevertheless, struck down the statute as violative of the Fourth Amendment because, in its view, the statute had no truly administrative purpose but was "designed simply to give the police an expedient means of enforcing penal sanctions for possession of stolen property." The court rested its conclusion that the administrative goal of the statute was pretextual and that § 415–a5 really "authorize[d] searches undertaken solely to uncover evidence of criminality" particularly on the fact that, even if an operator failed to produce his police book, the inspecting officers could continue their inspection for stolen vehicles and parts. The court also suggested that the identity of the inspectors—police officers—was significant in revealing the true nature of the statutory scheme.

In arriving at this conclusion, the Court of Appeals failed to recognize that a State can address a major social problem both by way of an administrative scheme and through penal sanctions. Administrative statutes and penal laws may have the same ultimate purpose of remedying the social problem, but they have different subsidiary purposes and prescribe different methods of addressing the problem. An administrative statute establishes how a particular business in a "closely regulated" industry should be operated, setting forth rules to guide an operator's conduct of the business and allowing government officials to ensure that those rules are followed. Such a regulatory approach contrasts with that of the penal laws, a major emphasis of which is the punishment of individuals for specific acts of behavior.

* * *

Accordingly, to state that § 415–a5 is "really" designed to gather evidence to enable convictions under the penal laws is to ignore the plain administrative purposes of § 415–a, in general, and § 415–a5, in particular. If the administrative goals of § 415–a5 are recognized, the difficulty the Court of Appeals perceives in allowing inspecting officers to examine vehicles and vehicle parts even in the absence of records

---

[21] Respondent contends that § 415–a5 is unconstitutional because it fails to limit the number of searches that may be conducted of a particular business during any given period. While such limitations, or the absence thereof, are a factor in an analysis of the adequacy of a particular statute, they are not determinative of the result so long as the statute, as a whole, places adequate limits upon the discretion of the inspecting officers. * * *

evaporates. The regulatory purposes of § 415–a5 certainly are served by having the inspecting officers compare the records of a particular vehicle dismantler with vehicles and vehicle parts in the junkyard. The purposes of maintaining junkyards in the hands of legitimate-business persons and of tracing vehicles that pass through these businesses, however, also are served by having the officers examine the operator's inventory even when the operator, for whatever reason, fails to produce the police book. Forbidding inspecting officers from examining the inventory in this situation would permit an illegitimate vehicle dismantler to thwart the purposes of the administrative scheme and would have the absurd result of subjecting his counterpart who maintained records to a more extensive search.

Nor do we think that this administrative scheme is unconstitutional simply because, in the course of enforcing it, an inspecting officer may discover evidence of crimes, besides violations of the scheme itself. The discovery of evidence of crimes in the course of an otherwise proper administrative inspection does not render that search illegal or the administrative scheme suspect.

Finally, we fail to see any constitutional significance in the fact that police officers, rather than "administrative" agents, are permitted to conduct the § 415–a5 inspection. The significance respondent alleges lies in the role of police officers as enforcers of the penal laws and in the officers' power to arrest for offenses other than violations of the administrative scheme. It is, however, important to note that state police officers, like those in New York, have numerous duties in addition to those associated with traditional police work. As a practical matter, many States do not have the resources to assign the enforcement of a particular administrative scheme to a specialized agency. So long as a regulatory scheme is properly administrative, it is not rendered illegal by the fact that the inspecting officer has the power to arrest individuals for violations other than those created by the scheme itself. In sum, we decline to impose upon the States the burden of requiring the enforcement of their regulatory statutes to be carried out by specialized agents.

V

Accordingly, the judgment of the New York Court of Appeals is reversed and the case is remanded to that court for further proceedings not inconsistent with this opinion.

It is so ordered.

■ JUSTICE BRENNAN, with whom JUSTICE MARSHALL joins, and with whom JUSTICE O'CONNOR joins as to all but Part III, dissenting.

Warrantless inspections of pervasively regulated businesses are valid if necessary to further an urgent state interest, and if authorized by a statute that carefully limits their time, place, and scope. I have no objection to this general rule. Today, however, * * * the Court renders virtually meaningless the general rule that a warrant is required for administrative searches of commercial property.

I

In *See v. City of Seattle*, 387 U.S. 541, 543, 87 S.Ct. 1737, 1739, 18 L.Ed.2d 943 (1967), we held that an administrative search of commercial property generally must be supported by a warrant. We make an exception to this rule, and dispense with the warrant requirement, in cases involving "closely regulated" industries, where we believe that the commercial operator's privacy interest is adequately protected by detailed regulatory schemes authorizing warrantless inspections. See *Donovan v. Dewey*, 452 U.S. 594, 599, 101 S.Ct. 2534, 2538, 69 L.Ed.2d 262 (1981). * * *

* * * In *Dewey* * * * we clarified that * * * it is "the pervasiveness and regularity of * * * regulation that ultimately determines whether a warrant is necessary to render an inspection program reasonable under the Fourth Amendment."

The provisions governing vehicle dismantling in New York simply are not extensive. A vehicle dismantler must register and pay a fee, display the registration in various circumstances, maintain a police book, and allow inspections. Of course, the inspections themselves cannot be cited as proof of pervasive regulation justifying elimination of the warrant requirement; that would be obvious bootstrapping. Nor can registration and recordkeeping requirements be characterized as close regulation. New York City, like many States and municipalities, imposes similar, and often more stringent licensing, recordkeeping, and other regulatory requirements on a myriad of trades and businesses. Few substantive qualifications are required of an aspiring vehicle dismantler; no regulation governs the condition of the premises, the method of operation, the hours of operation, the equipment utilized, etc. * * *

In sum, if New York City's administrative scheme renders the vehicle-dismantling business closely regulated, few businesses will escape such a finding. Under these circumstances, the warrant requirement is the exception not the rule * * * .

II

Even if vehicle dismantling were a closely regulated industry, I would nonetheless conclude that this search violated the Fourth Amendment. The warrant requirement protects the owner of a business from the "unbridled discretion [of] executive and administrative officers," by ensuring that "reasonable legislative or administrative standards for conducting an . . . inspection are satisfied with respect to a particular [business]." In order to serve as the equivalent of a warrant, an administrative statute must create "a predictable and guided (governmental) presence," *Dewey,* 452 U.S., at 604, 101 S.Ct., at 2541. Section 415–a5 does not approach the level of "certainty and regularity of * * * application" necessary to provide "a constitutionally adequate substitute for a warrant."[8]

The statute does not inform the operator of a vehicle-dismantling business that inspections will be made on a regular basis; in fact, there is no assurance that any inspections at all will occur. There is neither an upper nor a lower limit on the number of searches that may be conducted at any given operator's establishment in any given time period. Neither the statute, nor any regulations, nor any regulatory body, provide limits or guidance on the selection of vehicle dismantlers for inspection. In fact, the State could not explain why Burger's operation was selected for inspection. * * *

The Court also maintains that this statute effectively limits the scope of the search. We have previously found significant that "the standards with which a [business] operator is required to comply are all specifically set forth," reasoning that a clear and complete definition of potential administrative violations constitutes an implied limitation on the scope of any inspection. Plainly, a statute authorizing a search which can uncover no administrative violations is not sufficiently limited in scope to avoid the warrant requirement. This statute fails to tailor the scope of administrative inspection to the particular concerns posed by the regulated business. I conclude that "the frequency and purpose of the inspections [are left] to the unchecked discretion of Government officers." The conduct of the police in this case underscores this point. The police removed identification numbers from a walker and a wheelchair, neither of which fell within the statutory scope of a permissible administrative search.

The Court also finds significant that an operator is on notice as to who is authorized to search the premises; I do not find the statutory limitation—to "any police officer" or "agent of the commissioner"—significant. The sole limitation I see on a police search of the premises of a vehicle dismantler is that it must occur during business hours; otherwise it is open season. The unguided discretion afforded police in this scheme precludes its substitution for a warrant.

III

The fundamental defect in § 415–a5 is that it authorizes searches intended solely to uncover evidence of criminal acts. The New York Court of Appeals correctly found that § 415–a5 authorized a search of Burger's business "solely to discover whether defendant was storing stolen property on his premises." In the law of administrative searches, one principle emerges with unusual clarity and unanimous acceptance: the

---

[8] I also dispute the contention that warrantless searches are necessary to further the regulatory scheme, because of the need for unexpected and/or frequent searches. If surprise is essential (as it usually is in a criminal case), a warrant may be obtained *ex parte*. If the State seeks to conduct frequent inspections, then the statute (or some regulatory authority) should somewhere inform the industry of that fact.

government may not use an administrative inspection scheme to search for criminal violations. * * *

Here the State has used an administrative scheme as a pretext to search without probable cause for evidence of criminal violations. It thus circumvented the requirements of the Fourth Amendment by altering the label placed on the search. * * *

Moreover, it is factually impossible that the search was intended to discover wrongdoing subject to administrative sanction. Burger stated that he was not registered to dismantle vehicles as required by § 415–a1, and that he did not have a police book, as required by § 415–a5(a). At that point he had violated every requirement of the administrative scheme. There is no administrative provision forbidding possession of stolen automobiles or automobile parts. The inspection became a search for evidence of criminal acts when all possible administrative violations had been uncovered.

The Court * * * implicitly holds that if an administrative scheme has certain goals and if the search serves those goals, it may be upheld even if no concrete administrative consequences could follow from a particular search. This is a dangerous suggestion, for the goals of administrative schemes often overlap with the goals of the criminal law. * * * If the Fourth Amendment is to retain meaning in the commercial context, it must be applied to searches for evidence of criminal acts even if those searches would also serve an administrative purpose, unless that administrative purpose takes the concrete form of seeking an administrative violation.

IV

The implications of the Court's opinion, if realized, will virtually eliminate Fourth Amendment protection of commercial entities in the context of administrative searches. No State may require, as a condition of doing business, a blanket submission to warrantless searches for any purpose. I respectfully dissent.

NOTES

1. **Inspection of Hotel Guest Information.** A Los Angeles city ordinance required hotel operators to keep paper or electronic records concerning guests, including the guest's name and address, the date and time of arrival and scheduled departure date, the rate charged and amount collected for the room; and the method of payment. The records had to be "kept on the hotel premises in the guest reception or guest check-in area or in an office adjacent" to this area for a period of 90 days. Further, these records "shall be made available to any officer of the Los Angeles Police Department for inspection," subject to the qualification that "[w]henever possible, the inspection shall be conducted at a time and in a manner that minimizes any interference with the operation of the business." A hotel operator's failure to make the guest records available for police inspection was a misdemeanor. In City of Los Angeles, Cal. v. Patel, ___ U.S. ___, 135

S.Ct. 2443 (2015), the Supreme Court held the statutory provisions facially invalid as violating the Fourth Amendment. It assumed the searches served a "special need" other than conducting criminal investigations—ensuring compliance with the recordkeeping requirement, which in turn deterred criminals from operating on the hotels' premises—and thus were a kind of administrative search. But, Justice Sotomayor explained for the majority, the scheme did not come within the Fourth Amendment rule permitting warrantless searches of property used in certain closely regulated industries.

Hotels are not regulated in a manner or degree materially different than other commercial businesses, *Patel* reasoned, and thus the industry was not sufficiently regulated to come within the rule. But even if it was a sufficiently regulated industry, the ordinance's provisions for warrantless searches are not necessary to implement the regulatory scheme. In addition, the program does not include a constitutionally adequate substitute for a warrant, because "it fails sufficiently to constrain police officers' discretion as to which hotels to search and under what circumstances." As a result, "the provision of the Los Angeles Municipal Code that requires hotel operators to make their registries available to the police on demand is facially unconstitutional because it penalizes them for declining to turn over their records without affording them any opportunity for precompliance review [before a neutral decisionmaker]."

2. **Providing the Opportunity for Precompliance Review.** In *Patel*, discussed in the last note, the Supreme Court majority addressed how the opportunity for precompliance review by a neutral decisionmaker might be made available with minimal disruption of the statutory scheme designed to deter criminals from using hotel premises for illegal activities. Justice Sotomayor's opinion explained:

> [T]his opportunity can be provided without imposing onerous burdens on those charged with an administrative scheme's enforcement. For instance, [the hotel operators] accept that the searches authorized by [the ordinance] would be constitutional if they were performed pursuant to an administrative subpoena. These subpoenas, which are typically a simple form, can be issued by the individual seeking the record—here, officers in the field— without probable cause that a regulation is being infringed. Issuing a subpoena will usually be the full extent of an officer's burden because "the great majority of businessmen can be expected in normal course to consent to inspection without warrant." * * *
>
> In those instances, however, where a subpoenaed hotel operator believes that an attempted search is motivated by illicit purposes, [the hotel operators] suggest it would be sufficient if he or she could move to quash the subpoena before any search takes place. A neutral decisionmaker, including an administrative law judge, would then review the subpoenaed party's objections before deciding whether the subpoena is enforceable. Given the limited grounds on which a motion to quash can be granted, such challenges will likely be rare. And, in the even rarer event that an officer reasonably suspects that a hotel operator may tamper with

the registry while the motion to quash is pending, he or she can guard the registry until the required hearing can occur, which ought not take long.

___ U.S. at ____, 135 S.Ct. at 2453.

3. **Inspections and Searches Related to Arson Investigations.** The Supreme Court has explored the relationship among emergency searches, "administrative" warrants, and traditional searches for criminal evidence in the context of arson investigations. In Michigan v. Tyler, 436 U.S. 499, 98 S.Ct. 1942 (1978), firemen arrived at a furniture store ablaze at midnight and extinguished the fire by 4 a.m. Two plastic containers holding flammable liquid were discovered during the course of extinguishing the fire. Investigators were not able to conduct a thorough investigation of the scene when the fire was extinguished because of the darkness and the smoke. The fire chief returned at 9 a.m. the next morning and discovered some suspicious burn marks in the carpeting. Samples of the carpet were seized. Three weeks later a state fire inspector entered the premises several times and seized more items. No warrant was obtained. Tyler was subsequently tried for arson of the store. The items seized in both inspections and evidence derived from them was admitted over defense objection and Tyler was convicted.

The Supreme Court held this constitutional error. Firefighters do not need a warrant to enter a burning building and extinguish the fire, Justice Stewart's opinion for the Court explained. Moreover:

> Prompt determination of the fire's origin may be necessary to prevent its recurrence, as through the detection of continuing dangers such as faulty wiring or a defective furnace. Immediate investigation may also be necessary to preserve evidence from intentional or accidental destruction. * * * For these reasons, officials need no warrant to remain in a building for a reasonable time to investigate the cause of a blaze after it has been extinguished.

436 U.S. at 510, 98 S.Ct. at 1950. But other entries require a warrant. Despite the fire, privacy interests may still be implicated. Burned premises are sometimes still used for living or business purposes after the fire. Private effects are often left at the scene of a fire. The court declined, however, to require a traditional search warrant for all post-fire entries. In some situations, an administrative warrant will suffice. Rejecting the argument administrative warrants serve no purpose, Justice Stewart explained for the Court:

> To secure a warrant to investigate the cause of a fire, an official must show more than the bare fact that a fire has occurred. The magistrate's duty is to assure that the proposed search will be reasonable, a determination that requires inquiry into the need for the intrusion on the one hand, and the threat of disruption of the occupant on the other. * * * Even though a fire victim's privacy must normally yield to the vital social objective of ascertaining the cause of the fire, the magistrate can perform the important function of preventing harassment by keeping that invasion to a minimum.

In addition, * * * [another] major function of the warrant is to provide the property owner with sufficient information to reassure him of the entry's legality.

436 U.S. at 507–08, 98 S.Ct. at 1949. But, Justice Stewart continued:

[I]f the investigating officials find probable cause to believe that arson has occurred and require further access to gather evidence for a possible prosecution, they may obtain a warrant only upon a traditional showing of probable cause applicable to searches for evidence of crime.

436 U.S. at 512, 98 S.Ct. at 1951. On the facts of the case, the Court concluded the entry on the morning after the fire was "no more than an actual continuation" of the firefighters' entry the previous night to extinguish the fire and to conduct an immediate investigation into its origin; therefore, no warrant was needed. But the later entries required a warrant. Since none had been secured, evidence obtained from those entries should not have been used against Tyler.

The Fourth Amendment need for a warrant to conduct post-fire inspections was before the Court again in Michigan v. Clifford, 464 U.S. 287, 104 S.Ct. 641 (1984). In *Clifford,* a majority of the Court's members appeared to reject *Tyler's* analysis. Justice Rehnquist, joined by the Chief Justice and Justices Blackmun and O'Connor, took the position that no warrant whatsoever is necessary for a post-fire investigation conducted within a reasonable time of a fire. Since the right to enter is contingent upon the happening of an event—a fire—over which authorities have no control, application of the warrant requirement is not necessary to regulate authorities' power to initiate searches. Property owners could be adequately assured of the legality of an inspection by providing inspectors with identification or by efforts to notify the owners before the inspection. 464 U.S. at 309, 104 S.Ct. at 655 (Rehnquist, J., dissenting). Justice Stevens construed the Fourth Amendment as requiring a traditional search warrant for an unannounced entry. But an entry without any warrant would be reasonable, he concluded, if the inspector had either given the owner sufficient advance notice to enable him or an agent to be present at the inspection or had made a reasonable effort to provide such notice. 464 U.S. at 303, 104 S.Ct. at 652 (Stevens, J., concurring in the judgment).

EDITORS' NOTE: DRUG TESTING AND "SPECIAL NEEDS"

Drug test cases have similarly involved consideration of the appropriate effect to give to non-prosecution objectives of official activity infringing interests protected by the Fourth Amendment.

In Ferguson v. City of Charleston, 532 U.S. 67, 121 S.Ct. 1281 (2001), the Supreme Court noted:

[In] four previous cases * * * we have considered whether comparable drug tests "fit within the closely guarded category of constitutionally permissible suspicionless searches." *Chandler v. Miller,* 520 U.S. 305, 309, 117 S.Ct. 1295, 137

L.Ed.2d 513 (1997). In three of those cases, we sustained drug tests for railway employees involved in train accidents, *Skinner v. Railway Labor Executives' Assn.*, 489 U.S. 602, 109 S.Ct. 1402, 103 L.Ed.2d 639 (1989), for United States Customs Service employees seeking promotion to certain sensitive positions, *National Treasury Employees v. Von Raab*, 489 U.S. 656, 109 S.Ct. 1384, 103 L.Ed.2d 685 (1989), and for high school students participating in interscholastic sports, *Vernonia School Dist. 47J v. Acton*, 515 U.S. 646, 115 S.Ct. 2386, 132 L.Ed.2d 564 (1995). In the fourth case, we struck down such testing for candidates for designated state offices as unreasonable. *Chandler v. Miller*, 520 U.S. 305, 117 S.Ct. 1295, 137 L.Ed.2d 513 (1997).

In each of those cases, we employed a balancing test that weighed the intrusion on the individual's interest in privacy against the "special needs" that supported the program. * * *

532 U.S. at 77–78, 121 S.Ct. at 1288. Explaining the terminology, the Court continued:

The term "special needs" first appeared in Justice Blackmun's opinion concurring in the judgment in *New Jersey v. T.L.O.*, 469 U.S. 325, 351, 105 S.Ct. 733, 83 L.Ed.2d 720 (1985). In his concurrence, Justice Blackmun agreed with the Court that there are limited exceptions to the probable-cause requirement, in which reasonableness is determined by "a careful balancing of governmental and private interests," but concluded that such a test should only be applied "in those exceptional circumstances in which special needs, beyond the normal need for law enforcement, make the warrant and probable-cause requirement impracticable. . . ." This Court subsequently adopted the "special needs" terminology * * *, concluding that, in limited circumstances, a search unsupported by either warrant or probable cause can be constitutional when "special needs" other than the normal need for law enforcement provide sufficient justification.

532 U.S. at 74 n. 7, 121 S.Ct. at 1286 n. 7.

In *Ferguson*, the Court applied this special needs balancing test to a Charleston, North Carolina program in which pregnant women seeking medical care were—if they were suspected of cocaine use—given urine tests for cocaine. If they tested positive, the threat of criminal prosecution was used to compel them to accept treatment. Some who failed to cooperate were in fact prosecuted. Those who conducted the tests were staff members of a state hospital, and "the urine tests * * * were indisputably searches within the meaning of the Fourth Amendment."

Assuming that effective consent to the tests was not shown, the court held that the warrantless and suspicionless searches could not be upheld on the basis of the special needs analysis:

> [T]he invasion of privacy in this case is far more substantial than in those cases. In the previous four cases, there was no misunderstanding about the purpose of the test or the potential use of the test results, and there were protections against the dissemination of the results to third parties. The use of an adverse test result to disqualify one from eligibility for a particular benefit, such as a promotion or an opportunity to participate in an extracurricular activity, involves a less serious intrusion on privacy than the unauthorized dissemination of such results to third parties. The reasonable expectation of privacy enjoyed by the typical patient undergoing diagnostic tests in a hospital is that the results of those tests will not be shared with nonmedical personnel without her consent. * * *
>
> The critical difference between those four drug-testing cases and this one, however, lies in the nature of the "special need" asserted as justification for the warrantless searches. In each of those earlier cases, the "special need" that was advanced as a justification for the absence of a warrant or individualized suspicion was one divorced from the State's general interest in law enforcement. * * * In this case, however, the central and indispensable feature of the policy from its inception was the use of law enforcement to coerce the patients into substance abuse treatment. This fact distinguishes this case from circumstances in which physicians or psychologists, in the course of ordinary medical procedures aimed at helping the patient herself, come across information that under rules of law or ethics is subject to reporting requirements, which no one has challenged here.

532 U.S. at 78–79, 121 S.Ct. at 1288–90. The Court rejected the argument that the programmatic purpose of the testing was the protection of the health of mothers and children and therefore sufficiently special to make the program reasonable. A purpose or interest indistinguishable from the general interest in crime control is not special. "[W]e examine all the available evidence," it explained, "to determine relevant primary purpose." Further:

> [T]hroughout the development and application of the policy, the Charleston prosecutors and police were extensively involved in the day-to-day administration of the policy. * * *
>
> While the ultimate goal of the program may well have been to get the women in question into substance abuse treatment and off of drugs, the immediate objective of the searches was to generate evidence for law enforcement purposes in order to reach that goal. The threat of law enforcement may ultimately

have been intended as a means to an end, but the direct and primary purpose of [the] policy was to ensure the use of those means. In our opinion, this distinction is critical. Because law enforcement involvement always serves some broader social purpose or objective, under respondents' view, virtually any nonconsensual suspicionless search could be immunized under the special needs doctrine by defining the search solely in terms of its ultimate, rather than immediate, purpose. Such an approach is inconsistent with the Fourth Amendment. Given the primary purpose of the Charleston program, which was to use the threat of arrest and prosecution in order to force women into treatment, and given the extensive involvement of law enforcement officials at every stage of the policy, this case simply does not fit within the closely guarded category of "special needs."

532 U.S. at 82–84, 121 S.Ct. at 1290–92.

Remanding the case for further proceedings consistent with its opinion, the Court clearly contemplated that the Court of Appeals would address whether the program assured "informed consent" that would render the tests reasonable.

Drug testing programs without law enforcement objectives are subject to even more relaxed Fourth Amendment standards. Mandatory drug testing of all middle and high school students participating in extracurricular activities was upheld in Board of Education v. Earls, 536 U.S. 822, 122 S.Ct. 2559 (2002). The Court stressed that the program "is not in any way related to the conduct of criminal investigations," and that the results of tests are not turned over to any law enforcement agency. These characteristics of the testing program, in the Court's view, assisted in reducing the invasion of the students' privacy to insignificance.

C. CONSENT SEARCHES

A search is reasonable if it is conducted within the scope of effective consent provided by a person with authority to give it. Effective consent means the absence of a warrant will not render evidence inadmissible, even if under general Fourth Amendment requirements a warrant is usually required for similar searches of the sort at issue. In addition, the officers need not have had information rising to the level of probable cause or, for that matter, any basis whatsoever for believing a search would be productive.

Consent searches present three major categories of issues. First are those related to the legal effectiveness of words appearing on their face to constitute consent to search; these are addressed in the first unit that follows. Second are those related to the authority of the consenting person to consent to the search at issue; these are addressed in the second unit. Third are questions regarding the scope of authority resulting from particular consents; these are considered in the last unit.

Need for "Consent". These questions arise, however, only if there is "consent." One court indicated that the prosecution defending a search as based on consent must first make an initial showing of "an objective manifestation of consent * * * given by word or gesture." State v. Bailey, 989 A.2d 716, 722 (Me.2010). Perhaps, in light of the cases presented in this subchapter, the showing required might be better put as one of some words or gesture that a reasonable officer would or could regard as manifesting consent.

Some courts maintain this initial showing cannot consist only of evidence that the person did not object to the officers' action. E.g., State v. Schultz, 170 Wash.2d 746, 757, 248 P.3d 484, 489 (2011) ("Individuals do not waive [the] constitutional right [to be free from unreasonable searches] by failing to object when the police storm into their homes."). One, however, commented that "[c]onsent to a search can be implied from silence or failure to object if it follows a police officer's explicit or implicit request for consent." United States v. Martinez, 410 Fed.Appx. 759, 763 (5th Cir.2011).

During a field encounter in United States v. Chrispin, 181 Fed.Appx. 935 (11th Cir.2006), an officer asked suspect Chrispin if the officer could frisk him. "[A]lthough Chrispin did not express his verbal assent to be searched, his body language—turning away from Officer Lorente and placing his hands on the police cruiser as if preparing to be searched—gave implied consent." 181 Fed.Appx. at 939.

"Implied" Consent. Blood tests to determine whether persons believed to have been driving while impaired are in fact impaired generally require a search warrant, the Supreme Court confirmed in Birchfield v. North Dakota, ___ U.S. ___, 136 S.Ct. 2160 (2016). *Birchfield* briefly considered the contention that warrantless tests of this sort might be held reasonable pursuant to the wide-spread "implied consent" laws providing that cooperating with law enforcement tests is a condition of the privilege of driving on public roadways and that this privilege is to be withdrawn if a suspect refused such cooperation. At issue in *Birchfield* was whether refusal of cooperation could constitutionally be made a criminal offense. Holding that blood tests could not be upheld on this basis, the *Birchfield* majority explained:

> Our prior opinions have referred approvingly to the general concept of implied-consent laws that impose civil penalties and evidentiary consequences on motorists who refuse to comply. Petitioners do not question the constitutionality of those laws, and nothing we say here should be read to cast doubt on them.
>
> It is another matter, however, for a State not only to insist upon an intrusive blood test, but also to impose criminal penalties on the refusal to submit to such a test. There must be

a limit to the consequences to which motorists may be deemed to have consented by virtue of a decision to drive on public roads.

> [T]he United States suggests that motorists could be deemed to have consented to only those conditions that are "reasonable" in that they have a "nexus" to the privilege of driving and entail penalties that are proportional to severity of the violation. But in the Fourth Amendment setting, * * * reasonableness is always the touchstone of Fourth Amendment analysis. And applying this standard, we conclude that motorists cannot be deemed to have consented to submit to a blood test on pain of committing a criminal offense.

___U.S. at ___,136 S.Ct. at 2185–86.

1. THE EFFECTIVENESS OF CONSENT

The Supreme Court has long recognized that not all words or actions of consent are effective. In Amos v. United States, 255 U.S. 313, 41 S.Ct. 266 (1921), for example, officers testified that they went to Amos's residence and told the only person there, Amos' wife, they had come to search the premises. She opened the nearby store and the officers entered and searched. The Court posed and resolved the issue as one of possible waiver:

> The contention that the constitutional rights of defendant were waived when his wife admitted to his home the governmental officers * * * cannot be entertained. * * * [I]t is perfectly clear that, under the implied coercion here presented, no such waiver was intended or effected.

255 U.S. at 317, 41 S.Ct. at 268.

Under what circumstances will words, action, or inaction constituting consent have full legal effect? In analyzing this problem, is it necessary or permissible to still conceptualize consent as a "waiver" of the right to be free from searches in the absence of compliance with certain requirements, such as a search warrant based on probable cause? To the extent consent operates as a waiver, perhaps it must meet standards developed in other contexts for determining the effectiveness of a waiver of federal constitutional rights. These issues are addressed in the following case.

Schneckloth v. Bustamonte

Supreme Court of the United States, 1973.
412 U.S. 218, 93 S.Ct. 2041.

■ MR. JUSTICE STEWART delivered the opinion of the Court.

* * *

I.

The respondent was brought to trial in a California court upon a charge of possessing a check with intent to defraud. He moved to suppress the introduction of certain material as evidence against him on the ground that the material had been acquired through an unconstitutional search and seizure. In response to the motion, the trial judge conducted an evidentiary hearing where it was established that the material in question had been acquired by the State under the following circumstances:

While on routine patrol in Sunnyvale, California, at approximately 2:40 in the morning, Police Officer James Rand stopped an automobile when he observed that one headlight and its license plate light were burned out. Six men were in the vehicle. Joe Alcala and the respondent, Robert Bustamonte, were in the front seat with Joe Gonzales, the driver. Three older men were seated in the rear. When, in response to the policeman's question, Gonzales could not produce a driver's license, Officer Rand asked if any of the other five had any evidence of identification. Only Alcala produced a license, and he explained that the car was his brother's. After the six occupants had stepped out of the car at the officer's request and after two additional policemen had arrived, Officer Rand asked Alcala if he could search the car. Alcala replied, "Sure, go ahead." Prior to the search no one was threatened with arrest and, according to Officer Rand's uncontradicted testimony, it "was all very congenial at this time." Gonzales testified that Alcala actually helped in the search of the car, by opening the trunk and glove compartment. In Gonzales' words: " * * * the police officer asked Joe [Alcala], he goes, 'Does the trunk open?' And Joe said, 'Yes.' He went to the car and got the keys and opened up the trunk." Wadded up under the left rear seat, the police officers found three checks that had previously been stolen from a car wash.

[Bustamonte, by means never explained, had come into possession of a checkwriting machine previously stolen from a car wash. He, Alcala, and Gonzales had cashed at least one check from the machine. On the day prior to the stop in Sunnydale, the three had gone to San Jose to find other people willing to use false identification to cash checks written on the machine. The three passengers in the rear seat of the car at the time of the stop had joined the trio for this purpose. By the time Alcala gave his consent to the search, there were four police cars and an undetermined number of officers at the scene. The facts do not suggest that the officers connected the car and its occupants with the theft of the checkwriting machine or the passing of the checks before the search. Two of the older men seated in the rear seat had given inconsistent stories concerning the situation. One officer stated that permission to search the car was sought because things "just didn't fit in right." The search was quite intensive; the officers removed the rear seat from the car. After discovery of the checks, Gonzales "cooperated" with the officers and provided information that linked Bustamonte and the others to the checkwriting machine and the scheme to cash the forged checks. Editors.]

The trial judge denied the motion to suppress, and the checks in question were admitted in evidence at Bustamonte's trial. On the basis of this and other evidence he was convicted, and the California Court of Appeals for the First Appellate District affirmed the conviction. In agreeing that the search and seizure were constitutionally valid, the appellate court applied the standard earlier formulated by the Supreme Court of California in an opinion by then Justice Traynor: "Whether in a particular case an apparent consent was in fact voluntarily given or was in submission to an express or implied assertion of authority, is a question of fact to be determined in the light of all the circumstances." The appellate court found that "[i]n the instant case the prosecution met the necessary burden of showing consent * * * since there were clearly circumstances from which the trial court could ascertain that consent had been freely given without coercion or submission to authority. Not only officer Rand, but Gonzales, the driver of the automobile, testified that Alcala's assent to the search of his brother's automobile was freely, even casually given. At the time of the request to search the automobile the atmosphere, according to Rand, was 'congenial' and there had been no discussion of any crime. As noted, Gonzales said Alcala even attempted to aid in the search." The California Supreme Court denied review.

Thereafter, the respondent sought a writ of habeas corpus in a federal district court. It was denied. On appeal, the Court of Appeals for the Ninth Circuit * * * set aside the District Court's order. The appellate court reasoned that a consent was a waiver of a person's Fourth and Fourteenth Amendment rights, and that the State was under an obligation to demonstrate not only that the consent had been uncoerced, but that it had been given with an understanding that it could be freely and effectively withheld. Consent could not be found, the court held, solely from the absence of coercion and a verbal expression of assent. Since the District Court had not determined that Alcala had *known* that his consent could be withheld and that he could have refused to have his vehicle searched, the Court of Appeals vacated the order denying the writ and remanded the case for further proceedings. We granted the State's petition for certiorari to determine whether the Fourth and Fourteenth Amendments require the showing thought necessary by the Court of Appeals.

II.

It is important to make it clear at the outset what is not involved in this case. The respondent concedes that a search conducted pursuant to a valid consent is constitutionally permissible. * * * And similarly the State concedes that "[w]hen a prosecutor seeks to rely upon consent to justify the lawfulness of a search he has the burden of proving that the consent was, in fact, freely and voluntarily given." *Bumper v. North Carolina*, 391 U.S. 543, 548, 88 S.Ct. 1788, 1792, 20 L.Ed.2d 797.

The precise question in this case, then, is what must the state prove to demonstrate that a consent was "voluntarily" given. * * *

A.

The most extensive judicial exposition of the meaning of "voluntariness" has been developed in those cases in which the Court has had to determine the "voluntariness" of a defendant's confession for purposes of the Fourteenth Amendment. * * * It is to that body of case law to which we turn for initial guidance on the meaning of "voluntariness" in the present context.

Those cases yield no talismanic definition of "voluntariness," mechanically applicable to the host of situations where the question has arisen. "The notion of 'voluntariness,'" Mr. Justice Frankfurter once wrote, "is itself an amphibian." *Culombe v. Connecticut*, 367 U.S. 568, 604–605, 81 S.Ct. 1860, 1880–1881, 6 L.Ed.2d 1037. It cannot be taken literally to mean a "knowing" choice. "Except where a person is unconscious or drugged or otherwise lacks capacity for conscious choice, all incriminating statements—even those made under brutal treatment—are 'voluntary' in the sense of representing a choice of alternatives. On the other hand, if 'voluntariness' incorporates notions of 'but-for' cause, the question should be whether the statement would have been made even absent inquiry or other official action. Under such a test, virtually no statement would be voluntary because very few people give incriminating statements in the absence of official action of some kind." It is thus evident that neither linguistics nor epistemology will provide a ready definition of the meaning of "voluntariness."

Rather, "voluntariness" has reflected an accommodation of the complex of values implicated in police questioning of a suspect. At one end of the spectrum is the acknowledged need for police questioning as a tool for the effective enforcement of criminal laws. Without such investigation, those who were innocent might be falsely accused, those who were guilty might wholly escape prosecution, and many crimes would go unsolved. In short, the security of all would be diminished. At the other end of the spectrum, is the set of values reflecting society's deeply felt belief that the criminal law cannot be used as an instrument of unfairness, and that the possibility of unfair and even brutal police tactics poses a real and serious threat to civilized notions of justice. "[I]n cases involving involuntary confessions, this Court enforces the strongly felt attitude of our society that important human values are sacrificed where an agency of the government, in the course of securing a conviction, wrings a confession out of an accused against his will."

This Court's decisions reflect a frank recognition that the Constitution requires the sacrifice of neither security nor liberty. The Due Process Clause does not mandate that the police forego all questioning, nor that they be given carte blanche to extract what they can from a suspect. "The ultimate test remains that which has been the only clearly established test in Anglo-American courts for two hundred years: the test of voluntariness. Is the confession the product of an essentially free and unconstrained choice by its maker? If it is, if he has willed to confess, it may be used against him. If it is not, if his will has been overborne and his capacity for self-determination critically impaired, the use of his confession offends due process." *Culombe v. Connecticut*, supra, 367 U.S., at 602, 81 S.Ct., at 1879.

In determining whether a defendant's will was overborne in a particular case, the Court has assessed the totality of all the surrounding circumstances—both the characteristics of the accused and the details of the interrogation. Some of the factors taken into account have included the youth of the accused, his lack of education, or his low intelligence, the lack of any advice to the accused of his constitutional rights, the length of detention, the repeated and prolonged nature of the questioning, and the use of physical punishment such as the deprivation of food or sleep. In all of these cases, the Court determined the factual circumstances surrounding the confession, assessed the psychological impact on the accused, and evaluated the legal significance of how the accused reacted.

The significant fact about all of these decisions is that none of them turned on the presence or absence of a single controlling criterion; each reflected a careful scrutiny of all the surrounding circumstances. In none of them did the Court rule that the Due Process Clause required the prosecution to prove as part of its initial burden that the defendant knew he had a right to refuse to answer the questions that were put. While the state of the accused's mind, and the failure of the police to advise the accused of his rights, were certainly factors to be evaluated in assessing the "voluntariness" of an accused's responses, they were not in and of themselves determinative.

B.

Similar considerations lead us to agree with the courts of California that the question whether a consent to a search was in fact "voluntary" or was the product of duress or coercion, express or implied, is a question of fact to be determined from the totality of all the circumstances. While knowledge of the right to refuse consent is one factor to be taken into account, the government need not establish such knowledge as the *sine qua non* of an effective consent. As with police questioning, two competing concerns must be accommodated in determining the meaning of a "voluntary" consent—the legitimate need for such searches and the equally important requirement of assuring the absence of coercion.

In situations where the police have some evidence of illicit activity, but lack probable cause to arrest or search, a search authorized by a valid consent may be the only means of obtaining important and reliable evidence. In the present case for example, while the police had reason to stop the car for traffic violations, the State does not contend that there was probable cause to search the vehicle or that the search was incident to a valid arrest of any of the occupants. Yet, the search yielded tangible evidence that served as a basis for a prosecution, and provided some assurance that others, wholly innocent of the crime, were not mistakenly brought to trial. And in those cases where there is probable cause to arrest or search, but where the police lack a warrant, a consent search may still be valuable. If the search is conducted and proves fruitless, that in itself may convince the police that an arrest with its possible stigma and embarrassment is unnecessary, or that a far more extensive search pursuant to a warrant is not justified. In short, a search pursuant to consent may result in considerably less inconvenience for the subject of the search, and, properly conducted, is a constitutionally permissible and wholly legitimate aspect of effective police activity.

But the Fourth and Fourteenth Amendments require that a consent not be coerced, by explicit or implicit means, by implied threat or covert force. For, no matter how subtly the coercion were applied, the resulting "consent" would be no more than a pretext for the unjustified police intrusion against which the Fourth Amendment is directed. * * *

The problem of reconciling the recognized legitimacy of consent searches with the requirement that they be free from any aspect of official coercion cannot be resolved by any infallible touchstone. To approve such searches without the most careful scrutiny would sanction the possibility of official coercion; to place artificial restrictions upon such searches would jeopardize their basic validity. Just as was true with confessions, the requirement of a "voluntary" consent reflects a fair accommodation of the constitutional requirements involved. In examining all the surrounding circumstances to determine if in fact the consent to search was coerced, account must be taken of subtly coercive police questions, as well as the possibly vulnerable subjective state of the person who consents. Those searches that are the product of police coercion can thus be filtered out without undermining the continuing validity of consent searches. In sum, there is no reason for us to depart in the area of consent searches, from the traditional definition of "voluntariness."

The approach of the Court of Appeals for the Ninth Circuit * * *, that the State must affirmatively prove that the subject of the search knew that he had a right to refuse consent, would, in practice, create serious doubt whether consent searches could continue to be conducted. There might be rare cases where it could be proved from the record that a person in fact affirmatively knew of his right to refuse—such as a case where he announced to the police that if he didn't sign the consent form, "you [police] are going to get a search warrant;" or a case where by prior experience and training a person had clearly and convincingly demonstrated such knowledge. But more commonly where there was no evidence of any coercion, explicit or implicit, the prosecution would nevertheless be unable to demonstrate that the subject of the search in fact had known of his right to refuse consent.

The very object of the inquiry—the nature of a person's subjective understanding—underlines the difficulty of the prosecution's burden under the rule applied by the Court of Appeals in this case. Any defendant who was the subject of a search authorized solely by his consent could effectively frustrate the introduction into evidence of the fruits of that search by simply failing to testify that he in fact knew he could refuse to consent. And the near impossibility of meeting this prosecutorial burden suggests why this Court has never accepted any such litmus-paper test of voluntariness. * * *

One alternative that would go far towards proving that the subject of a search did know he had a right to refuse consent would be to advise him of that right before eliciting his consent. That, however, is a suggestion that has been almost universally repudiated by both federal and state courts, and, we think, rightly so. For it would be thoroughly impractical to impose on the normal consent search the detailed requirements of an effective warning. Consent searches are part of the standard investigatory techniques of law enforcement agencies. They normally occur on the highway, or in a person's home or office, and under informal and unstructured conditions. The circumstances that prompt the initial request to search may develop quickly or be a logical extension of investigative police questioning. The police may seek to investigate further suspicious circumstances or to follow up leads developed in questioning persons at the scene of a crime. These situations are a far cry from the structured atmosphere of a trial where, assisted by counsel if he chooses, a defendant is informed of his trial rights. And, while surely a closer question, these situations are still immeasurably, far removed from "custodial interrogation" where * * * we found that the Constitution required certain now familiar warnings as a prerequisite to police interrogation. * * *

Consequently, we cannot accept the position of the Court of Appeals in this case that proof of knowledge of the right to refuse consent is a necessary prerequisite to demonstrating a "voluntary" consent. Rather it is only by analyzing all the circumstances of an individual consent that it can be ascertained whether in fact it was voluntary or coerced. It is this careful sifting of the unique facts and circumstances of each case that is evidenced in our prior decisions involving consent searches.

* * *

[I]f under all the circumstances it has appeared that the consent was not given voluntarily—that it was coerced by threats or force, or granted only in submission to a claim of lawful authority—then we have found the consent invalid and the search unreasonable. In *Bumper*, a 66-year-old Negro widow, who lived in a house located in a rural area at the end of an isolated mile-long dirt road, allowed four white law enforcement officials to search her home after they asserted they had a warrant to search the house. We held the alleged consent to be invalid, noting that "[w]hen a law enforcement officer claims authority to search a home under a warrant, he announces in effect that the occupant has no right to resist the search. The situation is instinct with coercion—albeit colorably lawful coercion. Where there is coercion there cannot be consent."

Implicit in all of these cases is the recognition that knowledge of a right to refuse is not a prerequisite of a voluntary consent. If the prosecution were required to demonstrate such knowledge, * * * [the] opinions would surely have focused upon the subjective mental state of the person who consented. Yet they did not.

In short, neither this Court's prior cases, nor the traditional definition of "voluntariness" requires proof of knowledge of a right to refuse as the *sine qua non* of an effective consent to a search.

C.

It is said, however, that a "consent" is a "waiver" of a person's rights under the Fourth and Fourteenth Amendments. The argument is that by allowing the police to conduct a search, a person "waives" whatever right he had to prevent the police from searching. It is argued that under the doctrine of *Johnson v. Zerbst*, 304 U.S. 458, 464, 58 S.Ct. 1019, 1023, 82 L.Ed. 1461, to establish such a "waiver" the state must demonstrate "an intentional relinquishment or abandonment of a known right or privilege."

But these standards were enunciated in *Johnson* in the context of the safeguards of a fair criminal trial. Our cases do not reflect an uncritical demand for a knowing and intelligent waiver in every situation where a person has failed to invoke a constitutional protection. As Mr. Justice Black once observed for the Court: " 'Waiver' is a vague term used for a great variety of purposes, good and bad, in the law." *Green v. United States*, 355 U.S. 184, 191, 78 S.Ct. 221, 226, 2 L.Ed.2d 199. * * *

The requirement of a "knowing" and "intelligent" waiver was articulated in a case involving the validity of a defendant's decision to forego a right constitutionally guaranteed to protect a fair trial and the reliability of the truth-determining process. *Johnson v. Zerbst*, supra, dealt with the denial of counsel in a federal criminal trial. There the Court held that under the Sixth Amendment a criminal defendant is entitled to the assistance of counsel, and that if he lacks sufficient funds to retain counsel, it is the Government's obligation to furnish him with a lawyer. * * * To preserve the fairness of the trial process the Court established an appropriately heavy burden on the government before waiver could be found—"an intentional relinquishment or abandonment of a known right or privilege."

Almost without exception the requirement of a knowing and intelligent waiver has been applied only to those rights which the Constitution guarantees to a criminal defendant in order to preserve a fair trial. Hence, and hardly surprisingly in view of the facts of *Johnson* itself, the standard of a knowing and intelligent waiver has most often been applied to test the validity of a waiver of counsel, either at trial, or upon a guilty plea. And the Court has also applied the *Johnson* criteria to assess the effectiveness of a waiver of other trial rights such as the right to confrontation, to a jury trial and to a speedy trial, and the right to be free from twice being placed in jeopardy. Guilty pleas have been carefully scrutinized to determine whether the accused knew and understood all the rights to which he would be entitled at trial, and that he had intentionally chosen to forego them. And the Court has evaluated the knowing and intelligent nature of the waiver of trial rights in trial-type situations, such as the waiver of the privilege against compulsory self-incrimination before an administrative agency or a congressional committee or the waiver of counsel in a juvenile proceeding.

The guarantees afforded a criminal defendant at trial also protect him at certain stages before the actual trial, and any alleged waiver must meet the strict standard of an intentional relinquishment of a "known" right. But the "trial" guarantees that have been applied to the "pretrial" stage of the criminal process are similarly designed to protect the fairness of the trial itself.

* * *

There is a vast difference between those rights that protect a fair criminal trial and the rights guaranteed under the Fourth Amendment. Nothing, either in the purposes behind requiring a "knowing" and "intelligent" waiver of trial rights, or in the practical application of such a requirement suggests that it ought to be extended to the constitutional guarantee against unreasonable searches and seizures.

A strict standard of waiver has been applied to those rights guaranteed to a criminal defendant to insure that he will be accorded the greatest possible opportunity to utilize every facet of the constitutional model of a fair criminal trial. Any trial conducted in derogation of that model leaves open the possibility that the trial reached an unfair result precisely because all the protections specified in the Constitution were not provided. A prime example is the right to counsel. For without that right, a wholly innocent accused faces the real and substantial danger that simply because of his lack of legal expertise he may be convicted. * * * The Constitution requires that every effort be made to see to it that a defendant in a criminal case has not unknowingly relinquished the basic protections that the Framers thought indispensable to a fair trial.

The protections of the Fourth Amendment are of a wholly different order, and have nothing whatever to do with promoting the fair ascertainment of truth at a criminal trial. Rather, * * * the Fourth Amendment protects the "security of one's privacy against arbitrary intrusion by the police. * * *" * * * The Fourth Amendment "is not an adjunct to the ascertainment of truth." The guarantees of the Fourth Amendment stand "as a protection of quite different constitutional values—values reflecting the concern of our society for the right of each individual to be let alone. To recognize this is no more than to accord those values undiluted respect."

Nor can it even be said that a search, as opposed to an eventual trial, is somehow "unfair" if a person consents to a search. While the Fourth and Fourteenth Amendments limit the circumstances under which the police can conduct a search, there is nothing constitutionally suspect in a person voluntarily allowing a search. The actual conduct of the search may be precisely the same as if the police had obtained a warrant. And, unlike those constitutional guarantees that protect a defendant at trial, it cannot be said every reasonable presumption ought to be indulged against voluntary relinquishment. We have only recently stated: "[I]t is no part of the policy underlying the Fourth and Fourteenth Amendments to discourage citizens from aiding to the utmost of their ability in the apprehension of criminals." *Coolidge v. New Hampshire*, 403 U.S. 443, 448, 91 S.Ct. 2022, 2049, 29 L.Ed.2d 564. Rather the community has a real interest in encouraging consent, for the resulting search may yield necessary evidence for the solution and prosecution of crime, evidence that may insure that a wholly innocent person is not wrongly charged with a criminal offense.

Those cases that have dealt with the application of the *Johnson v. Zerbst* rule make clear that it would be next to impossible to apply to a consent search the standard of "an intentional relinquishment or abandonment of a known right or privilege." To be true to *Johnson* and its progeny, there must be examination into the knowing and understanding nature of the waiver, an examination that was designed for a trial judge in the structured atmosphere of a courtroom. * * * It would be unrealistic to expect that in the informal, unstructured context of a consent search a policeman, upon pain of tainting the evidence obtained, could make the detailed type of examination demanded by *Johnson*. And, if for this reason a diluted form of "waiver" were found acceptable, that would itself be ample recognition of the fact that there is no universal standard that must be applied in every situation where a person forgoes a constitutional right.

Similarly, a "waiver" approach to consent searches would be thoroughly inconsistent with our decisions that have approved "third party consents." * * * [I]t is inconceivable that the Constitution could countenance the waiver of a defendant's right to counsel by a third party, or that a waiver could be found because a trial judge reasonably though mistakenly believed a defendant had waived his right to plead not guilty.

In short, there is nothing in the purposes or application of the waiver requirements of *Johnson v. Zerbst* that justifies, much less compels, the easy equation of a knowing waiver with a consent search. * * *

* * *

E.

Our decision today is a narrow one. We hold only that when the subject of a search is not in custody and the State attempts to justify a search on the basis of his consent, the Fourth and Fourteenth Amendments require that it demonstrate that the consent was in fact voluntarily given, and not the result of duress or coercion, express or implied. Voluntariness is a question of fact to be determined from all the circumstances, and while the subject's knowledge of a right to refuse is a factor to be taken into account, the prosecution is not required to demonstrate such knowledge as a prerequisite to establishing a voluntary consent. Because the California courts followed these principles in affirming the respondent's conviction, and because the Court of Appeals for the Ninth Circuit in remanding for an evidentiary hearing required more, its judgment must be reversed.

It is so ordered.

■ MR. JUSTICE MARSHALL, dissenting.

Several years ago, Mr. Justice Stewart reminded us that "[t]he Constitution guarantees * * * a society of free choice. Such a society presupposes the capacity of its members to choose." *Ginsberg v. New York*, 390 U.S. 629, 649, 88 S.Ct. 1274, 1285, 20 L.Ed.2d 195 (1968) (concurring opinion). I would have thought that the capacity to choose necessarily depends upon knowledge that there is a choice to be made. But today the Court reaches the curious result that one can choose to relinquish a constitutional right—the right to be free of unreasonable searches—without knowing that he has the alternative of refusing to accede to a police request to search. I cannot agree, and therefore dissent.

NOTES

1.   **Consent from Person in Custody.** Despite the limitations the Court placed upon its holding in the principal case, the same analysis was soon applied to consent given by an arrested person. United States v. Watson, 423 U.S. 411, 96 S.Ct. 820 (1976).

2.   **Suspect's Knowledge Search Would Be Incriminating.** Does the fact the suspect was likely aware that a search would be fruitful suggest that the suspect's consent to the search was not voluntary? In United States v. Mendenhall, 446 U.S. 544, 100 S.Ct. 1870 (1980), Mendenhall was approached by two Drug Enforcement Administration agents at the Detroit Metropolitan Airport and agreed to accompany them to a nearby office. She consented to being searched. When told that the search would require her to

remove her clothing, Mendenhall stated she had a plane to catch. The officer, however, assured her that if she were carrying no drugs "there would be no problem." After beginning to disrobe, Mendenhall took two small packages from her undergarments and handed them to the officer. One contained heroin. Upholding a lower court finding that Mendenhall's consent was voluntary, Justice Stewart's plurality opinion rejected the assertion that Mendenhall's consent was involuntary because she would not have voluntarily consented to a search she knew was likely to disclose incriminating narcotics. "[T]he question," he responded, "is not whether [she] acted in her ultimate self-interest, but whether she acted voluntarily." Nevertheless, he also noted the possibility that Mendenhall may have thought she was acting in self-interest by voluntarily cooperating with the officers in a manner she perceived would result in later more lenient treatment.

3. **Provision of Misinformation About the Law.** One of the defendants in Birchfield v. North Dakota, ___ U.S. ___, 136 S.Ct. 2160 (2016), one Beylund, had submitted to a blood test to determine blood alcohol level after an officer told him the law required him to submit. In fact, as a general rule either a search warrant or exigent circumstances were required. The state court had held Beylund's consent was voluntary on the erroneous assumption that the officer could permissibly compel a blood test. The Supreme Court noted that under *Schneckloth* the "voluntariness of consent to a search must be 'determined from the totality of all the circumstances,'" and remanded with the comment, "we leave it to the state court on remand to reevaluate Beylund's consent given the partial inaccuracy of the officer's advisory."

4. **Consent Given During Bus Drug Interdiction Efforts.** In United States v. Drayton, 536 U.S. 194, 122 S.Ct. 2105 (2002), the Supreme Court addressed the voluntariness of consent given without warnings of a right to refuse and during drug interdiction efforts aboard a bus. *Drayton* is discussed in Chapter 4.

2. AUTHORITY TO CONSENT: "THIRD PARTY" CONSENTS

EDITORS' INTRODUCTION: CONSENTS GIVEN BY THIRD PARTIES

In a substantial number of cases, law enforcement officers rely on consent provided by persons other than those against whom the discovered evidence is eventually offered at trial. The sufficiency of such consents was addressed in United States v. Matlock, 415 U.S. 164, 94 S.Ct. 988 (1974):

> This Court left open in *Amos v. United States*, 255 U.S. 313, 317, 41 S.Ct. 266, 267, 65 L.Ed. 654 (1921), the question whether a wife's permission to search the residence in which she lived with her husband could "waive his constitutional rights," but more recent authority here clearly indicates that the consent of one who possesses common authority over premises or effects is valid as against the absent, nonconsenting person with whom

that authority is shared. * * * [W]hen the prosecution seeks to justify a warrantless search by proof of voluntary consent, it is not limited to proof that consent was given by the defendant, but may show that permission to search was obtained from a third party who possessed common authority over or other sufficient relationship to the premises or effect sought to be inspected.

415 U.S. at 170–71, 94 S.Ct. at 993. The Court elaborated further:

> Common authority is * * * not to be implied from the mere property interest a third party has in the premises. The authority which justifies the third-party consent does not rest upon the law of property, with its attendant historical and legal refinements, see *Chapman v. United States*, 365 U.S. 610, 81 S.Ct. 776, 5 L.Ed.2d 828 (1961) (landlord could not validly consent to the search of a house he had rented to another), *Stoner v. California*, 376 U.S. 483, 84 S.Ct. 889, 11 L.Ed.2d 856 (1964) (night hotel clerk could not validly consent to search of customer's room) but rests rather on mutual use of the property by persons generally having joint access or control for most purposes, so that it is reasonable to recognize that any of the cohabitants has the right to permit the inspection in his own right and that the others have assumed the risk that one of their number might permit the common area to be searched.

415 U.S. at 171 n. 7, 94 S.Ct. at 993 n. 7.

In *Matlock,* the officers searched a room in a house leased by Mr. and Mrs. Marshall and occupied by Mrs. Marshall, several of her children including Gayle Graff, Graff's three-year old son, and Matlock. Matlock was arrested in the yard. Several officers, without consulting Matlock, went to the door, met Graff, and—after telling her they were looking for money and a gun—asked Graff if they could search the house. She consented. While going through an upstairs bedroom occupied by Matlock and Graff, officers found $4,995 in cash concealed in a diaper bag in the only closet in the room. At issue was the admissibility at the hearing on the motion to suppress of Graff's out-of-court statements concerning her joint occupancy of the bedroom and similar statements by both Graff and Matlock representing themselves as husband and wife. After finding the statements were admissible, the Court concluded the Government's evidence was sufficient to prove Graff's consent was "legally sufficient." But since the Court preferred that the trial court first pass on the sufficiency of the evidence in light of the *Matlock* opinion, it remanded the case for such reconsideration.

Suppose, however, the person giving consent lacks authority to give effective authorization for the search? This problem is considered in the following case.

Illinois v. Rodriguez

Supreme Court of the United States, 1990.
497 U.S. 177, 110 S.Ct. 2793.

■ JUSTICE SCALIA delivered the opinion of the Court.

* * * The present case presents an issue we expressly reserved in [*United States v. Matlock*, 415 U.S. 164, 94 S.Ct. 988, 39 L.Ed.2d 242 (1974)]: whether a warrantless entry is valid when based upon the consent of a third party whom the police, at the time of the entry, reasonably believe to possess common authority over the premises, but who in fact does not do so.

I

Respondent Edward Rodriguez was arrested in his apartment by law enforcement officers and charged with possession of illegal drugs. The police gained entry to the apartment with the consent and assistance of Gail Fischer, who had lived there with respondent for several months. The relevant facts leading to the arrest are as follows.

On July 26, 1985, police were summoned to the residence of Dorothy Jackson on South Wolcott in Chicago. They were met by Ms. Jackson's daughter, Gail Fischer, who showed signs of a severe beating. She told the officers that she had been assaulted by respondent Edward Rodriguez earlier that day in an apartment on South California. Fischer stated that Rodriguez was then asleep in the apartment, and she consented to travel there with the police in order to unlock the door with her key so that the officers could enter and arrest him. During this conversation, Fischer several times referred to the apartment on South California as "our" apartment, and said that she had clothes and furniture there. It is unclear whether she indicated that she currently lived at the apartment, or only that she used to live there.

The police officers drove to the apartment on South California, accompanied by Fischer. They did not obtain an arrest warrant for Rodriguez, nor did they seek a search warrant for the apartment. At the apartment, Fischer unlocked the door with her key and gave the officers permission to enter. They moved through the door into the living room, where they observed in plain view drug paraphernalia and containers filled with white powder that they believed (correctly, as later analysis showed) to be cocaine. They proceeded to the bedroom, where they found Rodriguez asleep and discovered additional containers of white powder in two open attache cases. The officers arrested Rodriguez and seized the drugs and related paraphernalia.

Rodriguez was charged with possession of a controlled substance with intent to deliver. He moved to suppress all evidence seized at the time of his arrest, claiming that Fischer had vacated the apartment several weeks earlier and had no authority to consent to the entry. The Cook County Circuit Court granted the motion, holding that at the time she consented to the entry Fischer did not have common authority over the apartment. * * *

The Appellate Court of Illinois affirmed the Circuit Court in all respects. The Illinois Supreme Court denied the State's Petition for Leave to Appeal, and we granted certiorari.

II

The Fourth Amendment generally prohibits the warrantless entry of a person's home, whether to make an arrest or to search for specific objects. The prohibition does not apply, however, to situations in which voluntary consent has been obtained, either from the individual whose property is searched, see *Schneckloth v. Bustamonte*, 412 U.S. 218, 93 S.Ct. 2041, 36 L.Ed.2d 854 (1973), or from a third party who possesses common authority over the premises. The State of Illinois contends that that exception applies in the present case.

As we stated in *Matlock*, "[c]ommon authority" rests "on mutual use of the property by persons generally having joint access or control for most purposes. . . ." The burden of establishing that common authority rests upon the State. On the basis of this record, it is clear that burden was not sustained. The evidence showed that although Fischer, with her two small children, had lived with Rodriguez beginning in December 1984, she had moved out on July 1, 1985, almost a month before the search at issue here, and had gone to live with her mother. She took her and her children's clothing with her, though leaving behind some furniture and household effects. During the period after July 1 she sometimes spent the night at Rodriguez's apartment, but never invited her friends there, and never went there herself when he was not home. Her name was not on the lease nor did she contribute to the rent. She had a key to the apartment, which she said at trial she had taken without Rodriguez's knowledge (though she testified at the preliminary hearing that Rodriguez had given her the key). On these facts the State has not established that, with respect to the South California apartment, Fischer had "joint access or control for most purposes." To the contrary, the Appellate Court's determination of no common authority over the apartment was obviously correct.

III

A

The State contends that, even if Fischer did not in fact have authority to give consent, it suffices to validate the entry that the law enforcement officers reasonably believed she did. * * *

B

[R]espondent asserts that permitting a reasonable belief of common authority to validate an entry would cause a defendant's Fourth Amendment rights to be "vicariously waived." We disagree. We have been unyielding in our insistence that a defendant's waiver of his trial rights cannot be given effect unless it is "knowing" and "intelligent." We would assuredly not permit, therefore, evidence seized in violation of the Fourth Amendment to be introduced on the basis of a trial court's mere "reasonable belief"—derived from statements by unauthorized persons— that the defendant has waived his objection. But one must make a distinction between, on the one hand, trial rights that derive from the violation of constitutional guarantees and, on the other hand, the nature of those constitutional guarantees themselves. As we said in *Schneckloth*:

> "There is a vast difference between those rights that protect a fair criminal trial and the rights guaranteed under the Fourth Amendment. Nothing, either in the purposes behind requiring a 'knowing' and 'intelligent' waiver of trial rights, or in the practical application of such a requirement suggests that it ought to be extended to the constitutional guarantee against unreasonable searches and seizures."

What Rodriguez is assured by the trial right of the exclusionary rule, where it applies, is that no evidence seized in violation of the Fourth Amendment will be introduced at his trial unless he consents. What he is assured by the Fourth Amendment itself, however, is not that no government search of his house will occur unless he consents; but that no such search will occur that is "unreasonable." U.S. Const., Amdt. 4. There are various elements, of course, that can make a search of a person's house "reasonable"—one of which is the consent of the person or his cotenant. The essence of respondent's argument is that we should impose upon this element a requirement that we have not imposed upon other elements that regularly compel government officers to exercise judgment regarding the facts: namely, the requirement that their judgment be not only responsible but correct.

The fundamental objective that alone validates all unconsented government searches is, of course, the seizure of persons who have committed or are about to commit crimes, or of evidence related to crimes. But "reasonableness," with respect to this necessary element, does not demand that the government be factually correct in its assessment that that is what a search will produce. * * * If a magistrate, based upon seemingly reliable but factually inaccurate information, issues a warrant for the search of a house in which the sought-after felon is not present, has never been present, and was never likely to have been present, the owner of that house suffers one of the inconveniences we all expose ourselves to as the cost of living in a safe society; he does not suffer a violation of the Fourth Amendment.

* * *

It would be superfluous to multiply * * * examples. It is apparent that in order to satisfy the "reasonableness" requirement of the Fourth Amendment, what is generally demanded of the many factual determinations that must regularly be made by agents of the government—whether the magistrate issuing a warrant, the police officer executing a warrant, or the police officer conducting a search or seizure under one of the exceptions to the warrant requirement—is not that they always be correct, but that they always be reasonable. * * *

We see no reason to depart from this general rule with respect to facts bearing upon the authority to consent to a search. Whether the basis for such authority exists is the sort of recurring factual question to which law enforcement officials must be expected to apply their judgment; and all the Fourth Amendment requires is that they answer it reasonably. The Constitution is no more violated when officers enter without a warrant because they reasonably (though erroneously) believe that the person who has consented to their entry is a resident of the premises, than it is violated when they enter without a warrant because they reasonably (though erroneously) believe they are in pursuit of a violent felon who is about to escape.

* * *

[W]hat we hold today does not suggest that law enforcement officers may always accept a person's invitation to enter premises. Even when the invitation is accompanied by an explicit assertion that the person lives there, the surrounding circumstances could conceivably be such that a reasonable person would doubt its truth and not act upon it without further inquiry. As with other factual determinations bearing upon search and seizure, determination of consent to enter must "be judged against an objective standard: would the facts available to the officer at the moment * * * 'warrant a man of reasonable caution in the belief' " that the consenting party had authority over the premises? If not, then warrantless entry without further inquiry is unlawful unless authority actually exists. But if so, the search is valid.

* * *

In the present case, the Appellate Court found it unnecessary to determine whether the officers reasonably believed that Fischer had the authority to consent, because it ruled as a matter of law that a reasonable belief could not validate the entry. Since we find that ruling to be in error, we remand for consideration of that question. The judgment of the Illinois Appellate Court is reversed and remanded for further proceedings not inconsistent with this opinion.

So ordered.

■ JUSTICE MARSHALL, with whom JUSTICE BRENNAN and JUSTICE STEVENS join, dissenting.

* * *

The * * * majority's * * * position rests on a misconception of the basis for third-party consent searches. That [consent] searches do not give rise to claims of constitutional violations rests not on the premise that they are "reasonable" under the Fourth Amendment, but on the premise that a person may voluntarily limit his expectation of privacy by

Officers subsequently obtained a warrant to search the house. During the search pursuant to the warrant, a number of drug-related items were seized. An indictment was returned charging Mr. Randolph with possession of cocaine. He moved to suppress evidence of the drugs, arguing that the search of his residence over his express objection violated his Fourth Amendment rights. The trial court denied the motion, but the Georgia appellate courts reversed.

The Supreme Court affirmed by a 5-to-3 vote, holding that the consent was not effective. Justice Souter's opinion for the Court explained:

> *Matlock* * * * not only holds that a solitary co-inhabitant may sometimes consent to a search of shared premises, but stands for the proposition that the reasonableness of such a search is in significant part a function of commonly held understanding about the authority that co-inhabitants may exercise in ways that affect each other's interests.

* * *

> [I]t is fair to say that a caller standing at the door of shared premises would have no confidence that one occupant's invitation was a sufficiently good reason to enter when a fellow tenant stood there saying, "stay out." Without some very good reason, no sensible person would go inside under those conditions. Fear for the safety of the occupant issuing the invitation, or of someone else inside, would be thought to justify entry, but the justification then would be the personal risk, the threats to life or limb, not the disputed invitation.

> The visitor's reticence without some such good reason would show not timidity but a realization that when people living together disagree over the use of their common quarters, a resolution must come through voluntary accommodation, not by appeals to authority. Unless the people living together fall within some recognized hierarchy, like a household of parent and child or barracks housing military personnel of different grades, there is no societal understanding of superior and inferior, a fact reflected in a standard formulation of domestic property law, that "[e]ach cotenant . . . has the right to use and enjoy the entire property as if he or she were the sole owner, limited only by the same right in the other cotenants." 7 R. Powell, Powell on Real Property § 50.03[1], p. 50–14 (M. Wolf gen. ed.2005). The want of any recognized superior authority among disagreeing tenants is also reflected in the law's response when the disagreements cannot be resolved. The law does not ask who has the better side of the conflict; it simply provides a right to any co-tenant, even the most unreasonable, to obtain a decree partitioning the property (when the relationship is one of co-ownership) and terminating the relationship. And while a

decree of partition is not the answer to disagreement among rental tenants, this situation resembles co-ownership in lacking the benefit of any understanding that one or the other rental co-tenant has a superior claim to control the use of the quarters they occupy together. In sum, there is no common understanding that one co-tenant generally has a right or authority to prevail over the express wishes of another, whether the issue is the color of the curtains or invitations to outsiders.

* * *

Since the co-tenant wishing to open the door to a third party has no recognized authority in law or social practice to prevail over a present and objecting co-tenant, his disputed invitation, without more, gives a police officer no better claim to reasonableness in entering than the officer would have in the absence of any consent at all.

547 U.S. at 111–14, 126 S.Ct. at 1521–23. It continued:

[W]e have to admit that we are drawing a fine line; if a potential defendant with self-interest in objecting is in fact at the door and objects, the co-tenant's permission does not suffice for a reasonable search, whereas the potential objector, nearby but not invited to take part in the threshold colloquy, loses out.

This is the line we draw, and we think the formalism is justified. So long as there is no evidence that the police have removed the potentially objecting tenant from the entrance for the sake of avoiding a possible objection, there is practical value in the simple clarity of complementary rules, one recognizing the co-tenant's permission when there is no fellow occupant on hand, the other according dispositive weight to the fellow occupant's contrary indication when he expresses it. * * * [W]e think it would needlessly limit the capacity of the police to respond to ostensibly legitimate opportunities in the field if we were to hold that reasonableness required the police to take affirmative steps to find a potentially objecting co-tenant before acting on the permission they had already received. There is no ready reason to believe that efforts to invite a refusal would make a difference in many cases, whereas every co-tenant consent case would turn into a test about the adequacy of the police's efforts to consult with a potential objector.

547 U.S. at 121–22, 126 S.Ct. at 1527–28.

In some situations, the Court stressed, searches may be permissible without consent:

The co-tenant acting on his own initiative may be able to deliver evidence to the police, and can tell the police what he knows, for use before a magistrate in getting a warrant.

Sometimes, of course, the very exchange of information like this in front of the objecting inhabitant may render consent irrelevant by creating an exigency that justifies immediate action on the police's part; if the objecting tenant cannot be incapacitated from destroying easily disposable evidence during the time required to get a warrant.

547 U.S. at 116, 126 S.Ct. at 1524 (incorporating footnote into text).

Responding to a dissent, the majority added:

[T]his case has no bearing on the capacity of the police to protect domestic victims. The dissent's argument rests on the failure to distinguish two different issues: when the police may enter without committing a trespass, and when the police may enter to search for evidence. No question has been raised, or reasonably could be, about the authority of the police to enter a dwelling to protect a resident from domestic violence; so long as they have good reason to believe such a threat exists, it would be silly to suggest that the police would commit a tort by entering, say, to give a complaining tenant the opportunity to collect belongings and get out safely, or to determine whether violence (or threat of violence) has just occurred or is about to (or soon will) occur, however much a spouse or other co-tenant objected. (And since the police would then be lawfully in the premises, there is no question that they could seize any evidence in plain view or take further action supported by any consequent probable cause.) Thus, the question whether the police might lawfully enter over objection in order to provide any protection that might be reasonable is easily answered yes. The undoubted right of the police to enter in order to protect a victim, however, has nothing to do with the question in this case, whether a search with the consent of one co-tenant is good against another, standing at the door and expressly refusing consent.

547 U.S. at 118–19, 126 S.Ct. at 1525–26.

Randolph was applied in Fernandez v. California, ___ U.S. ___, 134 S.Ct. 1126 (2014). Officers suspecting Walter Fernandez of involvement in a robbery approached an apartment occupied by Fernandez and Roxanne Rojas. Fernandez told the officers they could not enter the apartment; Rojas did not express any view on this. On the basis of probable cause to believe Fernandez had assaulted Rojas, the officers removed him from the apartment and arrested him. One hour later, the officers returned and Rojas consented to their entry and search of the apartment. The California courts held incriminating evidence found by the officers admissible against Fernandez over his contention that the officers had neither a search warrant nor effective consent. A split Supreme Court agreed.

Justice Ginsburg, joined in dissent by Justices Sotomayor and Kagen, contended "that Fernandez' objection to the search did not become null upon his arrest and removal from the scene." Thus a warrant was required. Justice Thomas's opinion for the Court, however, reasoned that *Randolph*'s rationale—based on "widely shared social expectations" or "customary social usage"—indicated that a co-tenant's objection to a search, made while the co-tenant was present, should not remain effective after the co-tenant has been removed:

> [T]he calculus of [a caller standing at the door of shared premises] would likely be quite different if the objecting tenant was not standing at the door. When the objecting occupant is standing at the threshold saying "stay out," a friend or visitor invited to enter by another occupant can expect at best an uncomfortable scene and at worst violence if he or she tries to brush past the objector. But when the objector is not on the scene (and especially when it is known that the objector will not return during the course of the visit), the friend or visitor is much more likely to accept the invitation to enter.

___ U.S. at ___, 134 S.Ct. at 1135. Thus, *Randolph* did not apply and the consent given by Rojas was effective under the general rule that "consent by one resident of jointly occupied premises is generally sufficient to justify a warrantless search."

There was agreement that Fernandez's removal and arrest was based on legitimate grounds. The case therefore did not implicate *Randolph*'s comment on the potential significance of evidence that officers removed a tenant "for the sake of avoiding a possible objection."

3. SCOPE OF CONSENT

If effective consent was given by a person with authority to provide it, defining the scope of that consent may present further problems. How extensive and intrusive a search is supported by particular words of consent? How should a court approach the task of construing words constituting consent to a search of some sort? The Supreme Court addressed these issues in the following case.

Florida v. Jimeno
Supreme Court of the United States, 1991.
500 U.S. 248, 111 S.Ct. 1801.

■ CHIEF JUSTICE REHNQUIST delivered the opinion of the Court.

* * *

This case began when a Dade County police officer, Frank Trujillo, overheard respondent, Enio Jimeno, arranging what appeared to be a drug transaction over a public telephone. Believing that respondent might be involved in illegal drug trafficking, Officer Trujillo followed his car. The officer observed respondent make a right turn at a red light without stopping. He then pulled respondent over to the side of the road in order to issue him a traffic citation. Officer Trujillo told respondent that he had been stopped for committing a traffic infraction. The officer went on to say that he had reason to believe that respondent was carrying narcotics in his car, and asked permission to search the car. He explained that respondent did not have to consent to a search of the car. Respondent stated that he had nothing to hide, and gave Trujillo permission to search the automobile. After two passengers stepped out of respondent's car, Officer Trujillo went to the passenger side, opened the door, and saw a folded, brown paper bag on the floorboard. The officer picked up the bag, opened it, and found a kilogram of cocaine inside.

Respondent was charged with possession with intent to distribute cocaine in violation of Florida law. Before trial, he moved to suppress the cocaine found in the bag on the ground that his consent to search the car did not extend to the closed paper bag inside of the car. The trial court granted the motion. It found that although respondent "could have assumed that the officer would have searched the bag" at the time he gave his consent, his mere consent to search the car did not carry with it specific consent to open the bag and examine its contents.

The Florida District Court of Appeal affirmed the trial court's decision to suppress the evidence of the cocaine. In doing so, the court established a *per se* rule that "consent to a general search for narcotics does not extend to 'sealed containers within the general area agreed to by the defendant.'" The Florida Supreme Court affirmed, relying upon its decision in *State v. Wells*, 539 So.2d 464 (1989) aff'd on other grounds, 495 U.S. 1, 110 S.Ct. 1632 (1990). We granted certiorari to determine whether consent to search a vehicle may extend to closed containers found inside the vehicle * * * .

The * * * standard for measuring the scope of a suspect's consent under the Fourth Amendment is that of "objective" reasonableness— what would the typical reasonable person have understood by the exchange between the officer and the suspect? The question before us, then, is whether it is reasonable for an officer to consider a suspect's general consent to a search of his car to include consent to examine a paper bag lying on the floor of the car. We think that it is.

The scope of a search is generally defined by its expressed object. In this case, the terms of the search's authorization were simple. Respondent granted Officer Trujillo permission to search his car, and did not place any explicit limitation on the scope of the search. Trujillo had informed respondent that he believed respondent was carrying narcotics, and that he would be looking for narcotics in the car. We think that it was objectively reasonable for the police to conclude that the general consent to search respondent's car included consent to search containers within that car which might bear drugs. A reasonable person may be expected to know that narcotics are generally carried in some form of a container. "Contraband goods rarely are strewn across the trunk or floor of a car." The authorization to search in this case, therefore, extended beyond the surfaces of the car's interior to the paper bag lying on the car's floor.

The facts of this case are therefore different from those in *State v. Wells*, supra, on which the Supreme Court of Florida relied in affirming the suppression order in this case. There the Supreme Court of Florida held that consent to search the trunk of a car did not include authorization to pry open a locked briefcase found inside the trunk. It is very likely unreasonable to think that a suspect, by consenting to the search of his trunk, has agreed to the breaking open of a locked briefcase within the trunk, but it is otherwise with respect to a closed paper bag.

Respondent argues, and the Florida trial court agreed with him, that if the police wish to search closed containers within a car they must separately request permission to search each container. But we see no basis for adding this sort of superstructure to the Fourth Amendment's basic test of objective reasonableness. A suspect may of course delimit as he chooses the scope of the search to which he consents. But if his consent would reasonably be understood to extend to a particular container, the Fourth Amendment provides no grounds for requiring a more explicit authorization. * * *

The judgment of the Supreme Court of Florida is accordingly reversed, and the case remanded for further proceedings not inconsistent with this opinion.

It is so ordered.

■ JUSTICE MARSHALL, with whom JUSTICE STEVENS joins, dissenting.

[A]nalysis of this question must start by identifying the differing expectations of privacy that attach to cars and closed containers. It is well established that an individual has but a limited expectation of privacy in the interior of his car. * * * In contrast, it is equally well established that an individual has a heightened expectation of privacy in the contents of a closed container. Luggage, handbags, paper bags, and other containers are common repositories for one's papers and effects, and the protection of these items from state intrusion lies at the heart of the Fourth Amendment. * * *

The distinct privacy expectations that a person has in a car as opposed to a closed container do not merge when the individual uses his car to transport the container. * * *

Because an individual's expectation of privacy in a container is distinct from, and far greater than, his expectation of privacy in the interior of his car, it follows that an individual's consent to a search of the interior of his car cannot necessarily be understood as extending to containers in the car. At the very least, general consent to search the car is ambiguous with respect to containers found inside the car. In my view, the independent and divisible nature of the privacy interests in cars and containers mandates that a police officer who wishes to search a suspicious container found during a consensual automobile search obtain additional consent to search the container. If the driver intended to authorize search of the container, he will say so; if not, then he will say no.[1] The only objection that the police could have to such a rule is that it would prevent them from exploiting the ignorance of a citizen who simply did not anticipate that his consent to search the car would be understood to authorize the police to rummage through his packages.

* * *

I dissent.

D. SEARCHES AND SEIZURES OF VEHICLES

Searches and seizures of vehicles have probably given rise to more Fourth Amendment difficulties than any other category of law enforcement conduct. In all of its vehicle search or seizure case law, the Supreme Court has assumed citizens' privacy interest in vehicles and their contents is less than their privacy in homes and some other places:

> One has a lesser expectation of privacy in a motor vehicle because its function is transportation and it seldom serves as one's residence or as the repository of personal effects. A car has little capacity for escaping public scrutiny. It travels public thoroughfares where both its occupants and its contents are in plain view.

Cardwell v. Lewis, 417 U.S. 583, 590, 94 S.Ct. 2464, 2469 (1974) (opinion of Blackmun, J., announcing the judgment of the Court).

Searches of vehicles may be permissible under several doctrines. The right to search a car "incident to" the arrest of a person in or near the car was considered in Chapter 4, as was the right to make a weapons search of some cars during nonarrest confrontations between officers and citizens. This subchapter addresses two additional aspects of vehicle searches. The first unit that follows presents the traditional "vehicle exception" to the requirement of a search warrant; the second unit explores officers' power to seize and inventory vehicles.

1. THE "VEHICLE" EXCEPTION TO THE SEARCH WARRANT REQUIREMENTS

EDITORS' INTRODUCTION: "AUTOMOBILE" OR "VEHICLE" EXCEPTION

A right on the part of law enforcement officers to conduct warrantless searches of automobiles independent of any right the officers may have to arrest occupants was recognized in two early Supreme Court

---

[1]   Alternatively, the police could obtain such consent in advance by asking the individual for permission to search both the car and any closed containers found inside.

cases. In Carroll v. United States, 267 U.S. 132, 45 S.Ct. 280 (1925), officers observed a car coming from the direction of Detroit, which they knew to be a location where much illicit liquor entered the United States. Several months earlier the officers, acting undercover, met with two men who agreed to sell them illicit liquor; the men came to the meeting in the same automobile. The officers stopped the car and searched it; they found 68 bottles of illicit liquor concealed under the seat upholstery. Finding the search reasonable, the Supreme Court noted there is

> a necessary difference between a search of a store, dwelling house or other structure in respect of which a proper official warrant readily may be obtained, and a search of a ship, motor boat, wagon or automobile for contraband goods, where it is not practicable to secure a warrant because the vehicle can be quickly moved out of the locality or jurisdiction in which the warrant must be sought.

267 U.S. at 153, 45 S.Ct. at 285. The right of those using public highways to free passage without interruption or search, it continued, is adequately protected by the prohibition against search of vehicles "unless there is known to a competent official authorized to search, probable cause for believing that their vehicles are carrying contraband or illegal merchandise." Transporting the liquor was in violation of the National Prohibition Act. Those transporting it were guilty of a criminal offense; the first two offenses were misdemeanors but a third conviction constituted a felony.

Carroll urged that federal law permitted a warrantless arrest for a misdemeanor only if the offense was committed in the officers' presence and consequently that the officers lacked authority to arrest him without a warrant. It followed, he argued, the officers should not be permitted to make a warrantless search related to a crime for which no warrantless arrest was permissible. The Court responded:

> The argument of defendants is based on the theory that the seizure in this case can only be * * * justified [on the ground that it was incident to a lawful arrest]. If their theory were sound, their conclusion would be. The validity of the seizure would turn wholly on the validity of the arrest without a seizure. But the theory is unsound. The right to search and the validity of the seizure are not dependent on the right to arrest. They are dependent on the reasonable cause the seizing officers has for belief that the contents of the automobile offend against the law. The seizure in such a proceeding comes before the arrest * * * . The character of the offense for which, after the contraband liquor is found and seized, the driver can be prosecuted does not affect the validity of the seizure.

267 U.S. at 158–59, 45 S.Ct. at 287. The *Carroll* approach was reaffirmed in the second leading case, Brinegar v. United States, 338 U.S. 160, 69 S.Ct. 1302 (1949), involving similar facts.

Chief Justice Burger's opinion for the Court in California v. Carney, 471 U.S. 386, 105 S.Ct. 2066 (1985), traced the evolution of the rationale for the vehicle exception as follows:

> [A]lthough ready mobility alone was perhaps the original justification for the vehicle exception, our later cases have made clear that ready mobility is not the only basis for the exception. The reasons for the vehicle exception, we have said, are twofold. "Besides the element of mobility, less rigorous warrant requirements govern because the expectation of privacy with respect to one's automobile is significantly less than that relating to one's home or office." [*South Dakota v. Opperman*, 428 U.S. 364, 367, 96 S.Ct. 3092, 49 L.Ed.2d 1000 (1976)].

* * *

> These reduced expectations of privacy derive not from the fact that the area to be searched is in plain view, but from the pervasive regulation of vehicles capable of traveling on the public roadway. As we explained in *South Dakota v. Opperman* * * *:

>> "Automobiles, unlike homes, are subjected to pervasive and continuing governmental regulations and controls, including periodic inspection and licensing requirements. As an everyday occurrence, police stop and examine vehicles when license plates or inspection stickers have expired, or if other violations, such as exhaust fumes or excessive noise, are noted, or if headlights or other safety equipment are not in proper working order."

> The public is fully aware that it is accorded less privacy in its automobiles because of this compelling governmental need for regulation. Historically, "individuals always [have] been on notice that movable vessels may be stopped and searched on facts giving rise to probable cause that the vehicle contains contraband, without the protection afforded by a magistrate's prior evaluation of those facts." [*United States v.*] *Ross*, [456 U.S. 798, 806 n. 8, 102 S.Ct. 2157, 2163 n. 8, 72 L.Ed.2d 572, 582 n. 8 (1982)].

471 U.S. at 391–92, 105 S.Ct. at 2069–70.

Chambers v. Maroney

Supreme Court of the United States, 1970.
399 U.S. 42, 90 S.Ct. 1975.

■ MR. JUSTICE WHITE delivered the opinion of the Court.

The principal question in this case concerns the admissibility of evidence seized from an automobile, in which petitioner was riding at the time of his arrest, after the automobile was taken to a police station and was there thoroughly searched without a warrant.

* * *

I

During the night of May 20, 1963, a Gulf service station in North Braddock, Pennsylvania, was robbed by two men, each of whom carried and displayed a gun. The robbers took the currency from the cash register; the service station attendant, one Stephen Kovacich, was directed to place the coins in his righthand glove, which was then taken by the robbers. Two teenagers, who had earlier noticed a blue compact station wagon circling the block in the vicinity of the Gulf station, then saw the station wagon speed away from a parking lot close to the Gulf station. About the same time, they learned that the Gulf station had been robbed. They reported to police, who arrived immediately, that four men were in the station wagon and one was wearing a green sweater. Kovacich told the police that one of the men who robbed him was wearing a green sweater and the other was wearing a trench coat. A description of the car and the two robbers was broadcast over the police radio. Within an hour, a light blue compact station wagon answering the description and carrying four men was stopped by the police about two miles from the Gulf station. Petitioner was one of the men in the station wagon. He was wearing a green sweater and there was a trench coat in the car. The occupants were arrested and the car was driven to the police station. In the course of a thorough search of the car at the station, the police found concealed in a compartment under the dashboard two .38 caliber revolvers (one loaded with dumdum bullets), a righthand glove containing small change, and certain cards bearing the name of Raymond Havicon, the attendant at a Boron service station in McKeesport, Pennsylvania, who had been robbed at gunpoint on May 13, 1963. * * *

Petitioner was indicted for both robberies. * * * The materials taken from the station wagon were introduced into evidence, Kovacich identifying his glove and Havicon the cards taken in the May 13 robbery. Petitioner was sentenced to a term of four to eight years' imprisonment for the May 13 robbery and to a term of two to seven years' imprisonment for the May 20 robbery, the sentences to run consecutively. Petitioner did not take a direct appeal from these convictions. In 1965, petitioner sought a writ of habeas corpus in the state court, which denied the writ after a brief evidentiary hearing; the denial of the writ was affirmed on appeal in the Pennsylvania appellate courts. Habeas corpus proceedings were then commenced in the United States District Court for the Western District of Pennsylvania. An order to show cause was issued. Based on the State's response and the state court record, the petition for habeas corpus was denied without a hearing. The Court of Appeals for the Third Circuit affirmed and we granted certiorari.

II

We pass quickly the claim that the search of the automobile was the fruit of an unlawful arrest. Both the courts below thought the arresting officers had probable cause to make the arrest. We agree. Having talked to the teenage observers and to the victim Kovacich, the police had ample cause to stop a light blue compact station wagon carrying four men and to arrest the occupants, one of whom was wearing a green sweater and one of whom had a trench coat with him in the car.

Even so, the search that produced the incriminating evidence was made at the police station some time after the arrest and cannot be justified as a search incident to an arrest: "Once an accused is under arrest and in custody, then a search made at another place, without a warrant, is simply not incident to the arrest." *Preston v. United States*, 376 U.S. 364, 367, 84 S.Ct. 881, 883, 11 L.Ed.2d 777 (1964).

There are, however alternative grounds arguably justifying the search of the car in this case. * * * Here * * * the police had probable cause to believe that the robbers, carrying guns and the fruits of the crime, had fled the scene in a light blue compact station wagon which would be carrying four men, one wearing a green sweater and another wearing a trench coat. As the state courts correctly held, there was probable cause to arrest the occupants of the station wagon that the officers stopped; just as obviously was there probable cause to search the car for guns and stolen money.

In terms of the circumstances justifying a warrantless search, the Court has long distinguished between an automobile and a home or office. In *Carroll v. United States*, 267 U.S. 132, 45 S.Ct. 280, 69 L.Ed. 543 (1925), the issue was the admissibility in evidence of contraband liquor seized in a warrantless search of a car on the highway. After surveying the law from the time of the adoption of the Fourth Amendment onward, the Court held that automobiles and other conveyances may be searched without a warrant in circumstances that would not justify the search without a warrant of a house or an office, provided that there is probable cause to believe that the car contains articles that the officers are entitled to seize. * * * Finding that there was probable cause for the search and seizure at issue before it, the Court affirmed the convictions.

* * *

Neither *Carroll,* supra, nor other cases in this Court require or suggest that in every conceivable circumstance the search of an auto even with probable cause may be made without the extra protection for privacy that a warrant affords. But the circumstances that furnish probable cause to search a particular auto for particular articles are most often unforeseeable; moreover, the opportunity to search is fleeting since a car is readily movable. Where this is true, as in *Carroll* and the case before us now, if an effective search is to be made at any time, either the search must be made immediately without a warrant or the car itself must be seized and held without a warrant for whatever period is necessary to obtain a warrant for the search.

In enforcing the Fourth Amendment's prohibition against unreasonable searches and seizures, the Court has insisted upon probable cause as a minimum requirement for a reasonable search permitted by the Constitution. As a general rule, it has also required the judgment of a magistrate on the probable-cause issue and the issuance of a warrant before a search is made. Only in exigent circumstances will the judgment of the police as to probable cause serve as a sufficient authorization for a search. *Carroll*, supra, holds a search warrant unnecessary where there is probable cause to search an automobile stopped on the highway; the car is movable, the occupants are alerted, and the car's contents may never be found again if a warrant must be obtained. Hence an immediate search is constitutionally permissible. * * * 9

* * *

Arguably, because of the preference for a magistrate's judgment, only the immobilization of the car should be permitted until a search warrant is obtained; arguably, only the "lesser" intrusion is permissible until the magistrate authorizes the "greater." But which is the "greater" and which the "lesser" intrusion is itself a debatable question and the answer may depend on a variety of circumstances. For constitutional purposes, we see no difference between on the one hand seizing and holding a car before presenting the probable cause issue to a magistrate and on the other hand carrying out an immediate search without a warrant. Given probable cause to search, either course is reasonable under the Fourth Amendment.

On the facts before us, the blue station wagon could have been searched on the spot when it was stopped since there was probable cause to search and it was a fleeting target for a search. The probable cause factor still obtained at the station house and so did the mobility of the car unless the Fourth Amendment permits a warrantless seizure of the car and the denial of its use to anyone until a warrant is secured. In that event there is little to choose in terms of practical consequences between an immediate search without a warrant and the car's immobilization until a warrant is obtained.[10] The same consequences may not follow where there is unforeseeable cause to search a house. But as *Carroll*,

---

[9] Following the car until a warrant can be obtained seems an impractical alternative since, among other things, the car may be taken out of the jurisdiction. Tracing the car and searching it hours or days later would of course permit instruments or fruits of crime to be removed from the car before the search.

[10] It was not unreasonable in this case to take the car to the station house. All occupants in the car were arrested in a dark parking lot in the middle of the night. A careful search at that point was impractical and perhaps not safe for the officers, and it would serve the owner's convenience and the safety of his car to have the vehicle and the keys together at the station house.

supra, held, for the purposes of the Fourth Amendment there is a constitutional difference between houses and cars.

* * *

Affirmed.

■ MR. JUSTICE HARLAN, concurring in part and dissenting in part.

* * *

Where officers have probable cause to search a vehicle on a public way, a * * * limited exception to the warrant requirement is reasonable * * *. I agree with the Court that they should be permitted to take the steps necessary to preserve evidence and to make a search possible. The Court holds that those steps include making a warrantless search of the entire vehicle on the highway * * * and indeed appears to go further and to condone the removal of the car to the police station for a warrantless search there at the convenience of the police. I cannot agree that this result is consistent with our insistence in other areas that departures from the warrant requirement strictly conform to the exigency presented.

[I]n the circumstances in which this problem is likely to occur the lesser intrusion will almost always be the simple seizure of the car for the period—perhaps a day—necessary to enable the officers to obtain a search warrant. * * * To be sure, one can conceive of instances in which the occupant, having nothing to hide and lacking concern for the privacy of the automobile, would be more deeply offended by a temporary immobilization of his vehicle than by a prompt search of it. However, such a person always remains free to consent to an immediate search, thus avoiding any delay. Where consent is not forthcoming, the occupants of the car have an interest in privacy that is protected by the Fourth Amendment even where the circumstances justify a temporary seizure. * * * The Court's endorsement of a warrantless invasion of that privacy where another course would suffice is simply inconsistent with our repeated stress on the Fourth Amendment's mandate of "adherence to judicial processes."[9]

* * *

NOTES

1. **Vehicles Subject to Search.** What vehicles are within the exception? In California v. Carney, 471 U.S. 386, 105 S.Ct. 2066 (1985), DEA agents received uncorroborated information that Carney's Dodge Mini Motor Home was being used by someone else for purposes of exchanging marihuana for sex. An agent observed Carney approach a youth in downtown San Diego;

---

[9] Circumstances might arise in which it would be impracticable to immobilize the car for the time required to obtain a warrant—for example, where a single police officer must take arrested suspects to the station, and has no way of protecting the suspects' car during his absence. In such situations it might be wholly reasonable to perform an on-the-spot search based on probable cause. However, where nothing in the situation makes impracticable the obtaining of a warrant, I cannot join the Court in shunting aside that vital Fourth Amendment safeguard.

the two went to Carney's motor home, parked in a nearby lot. The shades of the motor home were drawn and the youth remained in it for about one and one-quarter hours. After the youth left, the agents stopped him and elicited from him that he had received marihuana in return for allowing Carney sexual contacts. At the agent's request, the youth knocked on the motor home door. Carney came out. An agent immediately entered and observed marihuana and related items. The Supreme Court, in an opinion by Chief Justice Burger, held the motor home was within the vehicle exception:

> While it is true that [Carney's] vehicle possessed some, if not many of the attributes of a home, it is equally clear that the vehicle falls clearly within the scope of the exception * * *. Like the automobile in *Carroll*, [Carney's] motor home was readily mobile. Absent the prompt search and seizure, it could readily have been moved beyond the reach of the police. Furthermore, the vehicle was licensed to "operate on public streets; [was] serviced in public places; . . . and [was] subject to extensive regulation and inspection." And the vehicle was so situated that an objective observer would conclude that it was being used not as a residence, but as a vehicle. * * *
>
> Our application of the vehicle exception has never turned on the other uses to which a vehicle might be put. * * *

471 U.S. at 393–94, 105 S.Ct. at 2070. The Court added:

> We need not pass on the application of the vehicle exception to a motor home that is situated in a way or place that objectively indicates that it is being used as a residence. Among the factors that might be relevant in determining whether a warrant would be required in such a circumstance is its location, whether the vehicle is readily mobile or instead, for instance, elevated on blocks, whether the vehicle is licensed, whether it is connected to utilities, and whether it has convenient access to a public road.

471 U.S. at 394 n. 3, 105 S.Ct. at 2071 n. 3. The information available to the agents, the Court also concluded, gave them "abundant probable cause" to enter and search the vehicle for evidence of a crime. As a result, the search was "reasonable" for Fourth Amendment purposes.

2. **Vehicles Parked in Public Places.** Does *Carney* also signal another expansion of the exception? Officers did not stop Carney's motor home but instead came upon it parked in an off-the-street lot. The Court's opinion equated "a vehicle * * * being used on the highways"—like those in *Carroll* and *Chambers*—with one—like Carney's motor home—"readily capable of such use and * * * found stationary in a place not regularly used for residential purposes." Justice Stevens commented:

> Until today, * * * the Court has never decided whether the practical justifications that apply to a vehicle stopped in transit on a public way apply with the same force to a vehicle parked in a lot near a court house where it could easily be detained while a warrant is issued.

471 U.S. at 403, 105 S.Ct. at 2075 (Stevens, J., dissenting).

EDITORS' NOTE: SEARCHES OF PERSONS AND CONTAINERS FOUND IN VEHICLES

In United States v. Chadwick, 433 U.S. 1, 97 S.Ct. 2476 (1977), discussed in Subchapter C(2) of Chapter 2, the Supreme Court held that in some circumstances officers may seize a "container" but not search it until they obtain a search warrant. The Supreme Court has had particular difficulty applying *Chadwick* to containers found in vehicles. Some issues of this sort have been presented already—Subchapter B(2) of Chapter 4 considered an officer's right to search a container found in a vehicle that is being searched incident to a valid custodial arrest.

Several decisions addressed whether *Chadwick* applies to containers in vehicles searched under the vehicle exception to the warrant requirement.

Arkansas v. Sanders, 442 U.S. 753, 99 S.Ct. 2586 (1979), reflected the Court's initial approach. In *Sanders*, an informant of demonstrated reliability told a Little Rock officer that Sanders—who was known to both the informant and the officer—would arrive at a specific gate at the Municipal Airport that afternoon and would be carrying a green suitcase containing marihuana. During surveillance, the officers observed Sanders's arrive at the designated gate and followed him while he met another man and obtained a green suitcase from the airline baggage. Sanders and the other man hailed a taxi, placed the green suitcase in the trunk, and left the airport in the taxi. Several blocks from the airport, officers stopped the taxi, retrieved the green suitcase from the trunk, and searched the suitcase. They found marihuana. The Supreme Court concluded the officers had probable cause to believe the suitcase contained marihuana and that they acted properly in seizing the suitcase. But, it continued, search of the suitcase without a warrant offended the Fourth Amendment.

In United States v. Ross, 456 U.S. 798, 102 S.Ct. 2157 (1982), in contrast, an informant told the police that he had seen Ross complete a drug transaction using drugs stored in the trunk of his car. Officers stopped Ross's car, searched it, and found and searched a brown paper bag in the trunk. *Ross* held the warrantless search of the paper bag reasonable, because requiring the officers to seek a warrant for each container found in a vehicle being searched would render the power to search of little practical value. The *Chadwick-Sanders* rule—barring search of the seized container—applied only when officers had probable cause to search not an entire vehicle but only a container in a vehicle. No general right to search the vehicle would be frustrated because in these situations there was no such right to search an entire vehicle. At most, the officers had the right to search the vehicle for the container and then to seize it.

The Court reconsidered the matter in California v. Acevedo, 500 U.S. 565, 111 S.Ct. 1982 (1991), involving a situation much like that in

Sanders. The *Chadwick-Sanders* rule, the *Acevedo* majority concluded, only minimally protects privacy, in part because search warrants will often be issued if officers are required to seek warrants and the searches will then occur on that basis. Further, the rule "confused courts and police officers and impeded effective law enforcement." Consequently, the Court overruled *Sanders*. Under *Acevedo*, the search of the suitcase in *Sanders* would have been constitutionally permissible although the officers had only a right to search the vehicle insofar as was necessary to find and seize the suitcase.

Is ownership of a container relevant to whether it may be searched during a vehicle search? In Wyoming v. Houghton, 526 U.S. 295, 119 S.Ct. 1297 (1999), a Wyoming police officer made a traffic stop of an automobile driven by David Young. Houghton and another woman were passengers; both were sitting in the front seat. During the stop, the officer observed a hypodermic syringe in Young's pocket. When asked, Young acknowledged he used the syringe to take drugs. The officer then, after removing the three occupants, began to search the car. He came upon a purse in the rear seat and, as he began to search it, Houghton claimed it as hers. Nevertheless, the officer continued to search the purse and discovered methamphetamine and drug paraphernalia. The Wyoming court held the drugs and paraphernalia could not be used in Houghton's prosecution. An officer's right to search a vehicle on probable cause to believe it contains contraband, the state court reasoned, does not extend to a container the officer knows or should know belongs to a passenger not suspected of criminal activity—unless there was an opportunity for someone to conceal the contraband sought in that container.

The Supreme Court reversed. Justice Scalia's opinion for the Court reasoned that the Court's automobile cases, and *Ross* in particular, reflect a conclusion that the Framers would have regarded as reasonable a warrantless search of all containers in a vehicle regardless of ownership if those containers might conceal contraband the officer has probable cause to believe is in the vehicle. Reasonableness of a search, it continued, historically does not depend upon whether the owner of property is suspected of a crime but rather whether there is probable cause to believe seizable items are in or on the property. Further:

> [T]he balancing of the relative interests weighs decidedly in favor of allowing searches of a passenger's belongings. Passengers, no less than drivers, possess a reduced expectation of privacy with regard to the property that they transport in cars * * * .

> [T]he governmental interests at stake are substantial. Effective law enforcement would be appreciably impaired without the ability to search a passenger's personal belongings when there is reason to believe contraband or evidence of criminal wrongdoing is hidden in the car. As in all car-search

cases, the "ready mobility" of an automobile creates a risk that the evidence or contraband will be permanently lost while a warrant is obtained. In addition, a car passenger * * * will often be engaged in a common enterprise with the driver, and have the same interest in concealing the fruits or the evidence of their wrongdoing. A criminal might be able to hide contraband in a passenger's belongings as readily as in other containers in the car perhaps even surreptitiously, without the passenger's knowledge or permission. * * *

526 U.S. at 303–06, 119 S.Ct. at 1302–03.

United States v. Di Re, 332 U.S. 581, 68 S.Ct. 222 (1948), *Houghten* added, "held that probable cause to search a car did not justify a body search of a passenger." *Houghton* apparently did not disturb this holding.

Justice Breyer joined the *Houghton* majority opinion but wrote separately to comment on one aspect of the facts:

> [It is important, in my view,] that the container here at issue, a woman's purse, was found at a considerable distance from its owner, who did not claim ownership until the officer discovered her identification while looking through it. Purses are special containers. They are repositories of especially personal items that people generally like to keep with them at all times. So I am tempted to say that a search of a purse involves an intrusion so similar to a search of one's person that the same rule should govern both. However, given this Court's prior cases, I cannot argue that the fact that the container was a purse automatically makes a legal difference, for the Court has warned against trying to make that kind of distinction. But I can say that it would matter if a woman's purse, like a man's billfold, were attached to her person. It might then amount to a kind of "outer clothing," which under the Court's cases would properly receive increased protection. In this case, the purse was separate from the person, and no one has claimed that, under those circumstances, the type of container makes a difference. For that reason, I join the Court's opinion.

526 U.S. at 308, 119 S.Ct. at 1304 (Breyer, J., concurring).

2. SEIZURE AND INVENTORY OF VEHICLES

EDITORS' INTRODUCTION: IMPOUNDMENT OF VEHICLES AND INVENTORYING OF IMPOUNDED VEHICLES

Two often-related issues frequently arise regarding official exercises of control over vehicles. One is officials' authority to seize or "impound" vehicles. The other is officers' authority to examine the contents of a properly seized vehicle, most often as part of "inventorying" those contents. Unfortunately, the Supreme Court's case law has focused more upon the power to inventory than on the power to seize.

Inventory Inspections of Seized Automobiles. Just as officers may inventory personal possessions of a person to be incarcerated after arrest (see Subsection B(1) of Chapter 4), the Supreme Court held that the Fourth Amendment permits some inventory inspections of seized automobiles. The leading case is South Dakota v. Opperman, 428 U.S. 364, 96 S.Ct. 3092 (1976). At 3 A.M., a Vermillion, South Dakota police officer noted Opperman's car parked in a downtown area in violation of an ordinance prohibiting parking in such areas between 2 a.m. and 6 a.m. He issued a citation and placed it on the windshield. After another officer issued a second citation at 10 a.m., the vehicle was "inspected" and towed to the city impound lot. At the lot, an officer noted a watch on the dashboard and other items of personal property on the back seat and floorboard. The locked car doors were opened and "using a standard inventory form, pursuant to police procedures, the officer inventoried the contents of the car * * * ." The glove compartment was not locked; upon opening it, the officer discovered marihuana in a plastic bag. All items found in the car were removed to the police department for safekeeping. Opperman was prosecuted for possession of marihuana. His objection to the admissibility of the marihuana was overruled and he was convicted. Finding the police activity reasonable, a majority of the Supreme Court explained:

> When vehicles are impounded, local police departments generally follow a routine practice of securing and inventorying the automobiles' contents. These procedures developed in response to three distinct needs: the protection of the owner's property while it remains in police custody; the protection of the police against claims or disputes over lost or stolen property; and the protection of the police from potential danger. The practice has been viewed as essential to respond to incidents of theft or vandalism. In addition, police frequently attempt to determine whether a vehicle has been stolen and thereafter abandoned. * * *

> The decisions of this Court point unmistakably to the conclusion * * * that inventories pursuant to standard police procedures are reasonable.

> The Vermillion police were indisputably engaged in a caretaking search of a lawfully impounded automobile. The inventory was conducted only after the car had been impounded for multiple parking violations. The owner, having left his car illegally parked for an extended period, and thus subject to impoundment, was not present to make other arrangements for the safekeeping of his belongings. The inventory itself was prompted by the presence in plain view of a number of valuables inside the car. * * * [T]here is no suggestion whatever that this

standard procedure * * * was a pretext concealing an investigatory motive.

428 U.S. at 369, 372, 375–76, 96 S.Ct. at 3097–99, 3100. Nor, the majority continued, was the inventory unlawful in scope because it extended to items not in plain view from outside the car:

> [O]nce the policeman was lawfully inside the car to secure the personal property in plain view, it was not unreasonable to open the unlocked glove compartment, to which vandals would have had ready and unobstructed access once inside the car.

428 U.S. at 376 n. 10, 96 S.Ct. at 3100 n. 10.

Opperman's holding that certain vehicular inventory examinations are permissible was developed in the principal case in this subsection. An otherwise proper inventory examination is fatally tainted, however, if the vehicle's impoundment was an unreasonable seizure of it. Courts have considerable difficulty determining when impoundments of vehicles are reasonable.

Seizures or Impoundments of Automobiles. Despite the frequency with which police assume control over automobiles, the extent of officers' authority to impound vehicles is not well developed in case law. Police authority to impound in several situations is, however, quite settled. In *Opperman* itself, the Court commented, "The authority of police to seize and remove from the streets vehicles impeding traffic or threatening public safety and convenience is beyond challenge." Statutes in many jurisdictions authorize judicial proceedings for the forfeiture of some vehicles used illegally, such as in the commission of particular criminal offenses. When officers have probable cause to believe a vehicle subject to forfeiture under such provisions, they may seize the vehicle and hold it pending the completion of judicial forfeiture proceedings. Cf. Cooper v. California, 386 U.S. 58, 87 S.Ct. 788 (1967).

It has also been suggested that grounds for impoundment exist when—or at least when officers have reason to believe—the automobile has been abandoned or stolen, the automobile constitutes evidence of the commission of a crime or of someone's guilt of a crime, or the driver (as by reason of injury, intoxication or mental incapacitation) is unable to attend to the car. See State v. Singleton, 9 Wash.App. 327, 332–33, 511 P.2d 1396, 1399–1400 (1973).

Courts disagree regarding the propriety of vehicle impoundments made because the driver was arrested. Unfortunately, judicial discussions sometimes do not clearly distinguish between the validity of the initial impoundment and that of the inventory inspection of a vehicle properly in official custody.

Colorado v. Bertine

Supreme Court of the United States, 1987.
479 U.S. 367, 107 S.Ct. 738.

■ CHIEF JUSTICE REHNQUIST delivered the opinion of the Court.

On February 10, 1984, a police officer in Boulder, Colorado, arrested respondent Steven Lee Bertine for driving while under the influence of alcohol. After Bertine was taken into custody and before the arrival of a tow truck to take Bertine's van to an impoundment lot,[1] a backup officer inventoried the contents of the van. The officer opened a closed backpack in which he found controlled substances, cocaine paraphernalia, and a large amount of cash. Bertine was subsequently charged with driving while under the influence of alcohol, unlawful possession of cocaine with intent to dispense, sell, and distribute, and unlawful possession of methaqualone. We are asked to decide whether the Fourth Amendment prohibits the State from proving these charges with the evidence discovered during the inventory of Bertine's van. We hold that it does not.

The backup officer inventoried the van in accordance with local police procedures, which require a detailed inspection and inventory of impounded vehicles. He found the backpack directly behind the front seat of the van. Inside the pack, the officer observed a nylon bag containing metal canisters. Opening the canisters, the officer discovered that they contained cocaine, methaqualone tablets, cocaine paraphernalia, and $700 in cash. In an outside zippered pouch of the backpack, he also found $210 in cash in a sealed envelope. After completing the inventory of the van, the officer had the van towed to an impound lot and brought the backpack, money, and contraband to the police station.

After Bertine was charged with the offenses described above, he moved to suppress the evidence found during the inventory search on the ground, inter alia, that the search of the closed backpack and containers exceeded the permissible scope of such a search under the Fourth Amendment. The Colorado trial court ruled that probable cause supported Bertine's arrest and that the police officers had made the decisions to impound the vehicle and to conduct a thorough inventory search in good faith. Although noting that the inventory of the vehicle was performed in a "somewhat slipshod" manner, the District Court concluded that "the search of the backpack was done for the purpose of protecting the owner's property, protection of the police from subsequent claims of loss or stolen property, and the protection of the police from dangerous instrumentalities." The court observed that the standard

---

[1] Section 7–7–2(a)(4) of the Boulder Revised Code authorizes police officers to impound vehicles when drivers are taken into custody. Section 772(a)(4) provides:

"A peace officer is authorized to remove or cause to be removed a vehicle from any street, parking lot, or driveway when:

(4) The driver of a vehicle is taken into custody by the police department." Boulder Rev.Code § 772(a)(4) (1981).

procedures for impounding vehicles mandated a "detailed inventory involving the opening of containers and the listing of [their] contents." Based on these findings, the court determined that the inventory search did not violate Bertine's rights under the Fourth Amendment of the United States Constitution. * * *

On the State's interlocutory appeal, the Supreme Court of Colorado [disagreed]. * * * The court recognized that in *South Dakota v. Opperman*, 428 U.S. 364, 96 S.Ct. 3092, 49 L.Ed.2d 1000 (1976), we had held inventory searches of automobiles to be consistent with the Fourth Amendment, and that in *Illinois v. Lafayette*, 462 U.S. 640, 103 S.Ct. 2605, 77 L.Ed.2d 65 (1983), we had held that the inventory search of personal effects of an arrestee at a police station was also permissible under that Amendment. The Supreme Court of Colorado felt, however, that our decisions in *Arkansas v. Sanders*, 442 U.S. 753, 99 S.Ct. 2586, 61 L.Ed.2d 235 (1979), and *United States v. Chadwick*, 433 U.S. 1, 97 S.Ct. 2476, 53 L.Ed.2d 538 (1977), holding searches of closed trunks and suitcases to violate the Fourth Amendment, meant that *Opperman* and *Lafayette* did not govern this case.

We granted certiorari to consider the important and recurring question of federal law decided by the Colorado Supreme Court. As that court recognized, inventory searches are now a well-defined exception to the warrant requirement of the Fourth Amendment. The policies behind the warrant requirement are not implicated in an inventory search, nor is the related concept of probable cause:

> "The standard of probable cause is peculiarly related to criminal investigations, not routine, noncriminal procedures. . . . The probable-cause approach is unhelpful when analysis centers upon the reasonableness of routine administrative caretaking functions, particularly when no claim is made that the protective procedures are a subterfuge for criminal investigations."

For these reasons, the Colorado Supreme Court's reliance on *Arkansas v. Sanders*, supra, and *United States v. Chadwick*, supra, was incorrect. Both of these cases concerned searches solely for the purpose of investigating criminal conduct, with the validity of the searches therefore dependent on the application of the probable-cause and warrant requirements of the Fourth Amendment.

By contrast, an inventory search may be "reasonable" under the Fourth Amendment even though it is not conducted pursuant to a warrant based upon probable cause. In *Opperman*, this Court assessed the reasonableness of an inventory search of the glove compartment in an abandoned automobile impounded by the police. We found that inventory procedures serve to protect an owner's property while it is in the custody of the police, to insure against claims of lost, stolen, or vandalized property, and to guard the police from danger. In light of these strong governmental interests and the diminished expectation of privacy in an automobile, we upheld the search. In reaching this decision, we observed that our cases accorded deference to police caretaking procedures designed to secure and protect vehicles and their contents within police custody.

In our more recent decision, *Lafayette*, a police officer conducted an inventory search of the contents of a shoulder bag in the possession of an individual being taken into custody. In deciding whether this search was reasonable, we recognized that the search served legitimate governmental interests similar to those identified in *Opperman*. We determined that those interests outweighed the individual's Fourth Amendment interests and upheld the search.

In the present case, as in *Opperman* and *Lafayette*, there was no showing that the police, who were following standardized procedures, acted in bad faith or for the sole purpose of investigation. In addition, the governmental interests justifying the inventory searches in *Opperman* and *Lafayette* are nearly the same as those which obtain here. In each case, the police were potentially responsible for the property taken into their custody. By securing the property, the police protected the property from unauthorized interference. Knowledge of the precise nature of the property helped guard against claims of theft, vandalism, or negligence. Such knowledge also helped to avert any danger to police or others that may have been posed by the property.

* * *

The Supreme Court of Colorado * * * expressed the view that the search in this case was unreasonable because Bertine's van was towed to a secure, lighted facility and because Bertine himself could have been offered the opportunity to make other arrangements for the safekeeping of his property. But the security of the storage facility does not completely eliminate the need for inventorying; the police may still wish to protect themselves or the owners of the lot against false claims of theft or dangerous instrumentalities. And while giving Bertine an opportunity to make alternative arrangements would undoubtedly have been possible, we said in *Lafayette*:

> "[T]he real question is not what 'could have been achieved,' but whether the Fourth Amendment requires such steps . . .
>
> "The reasonableness of any particular governmental activity does not necessarily or invariably turn on the existence of alternative 'less intrusive' means."

We conclude that here, as in *Lafayette*, reasonable police regulations relating to inventory procedures administered in good faith satisfy the Fourth Amendment, even though courts might as a matter of hindsight be able to devise equally reasonable rules requiring a different procedure.[6]

The Supreme Court of Colorado also thought it necessary to require that police, before inventorying a container, weigh the strength of the individual's privacy interest in the container against the possibility that the container might serve as a repository for dangerous or valuable items. We think that such a requirement is contrary to our decisions in *Opperman* and *Lafayette* * * *:

> "Even if less intrusive means existed of protecting some particular types of property, it would be unreasonable to expect police officers in the everyday course of business to make fine and subtle distinctions in deciding which containers or items may be searched and which must be sealed as a unit." *Lafayette*, supra, 462 U.S., at 648, 103 S.Ct., at 2610.

* * *

We reaffirm these principles here: " '[a] single familiar standard is essential to guide police officers, who have only limited time and expertise to reflect on and balance the social and individual interests involved in the specific circumstances they confront.' " *Lafayette*, supra, 462 U.S., at 648, 103 S.Ct., at 2610.

Bertine finally argues that the inventory search of his van was unconstitutional because departmental regulations gave the police officers discretion to choose between impounding his van and parking and locking it in a public parking place. The Supreme Court of Colorado did not rely on this argument in reaching its conclusion, and we reject it. Nothing in *Opperman* or *Lafayette* prohibits the exercise of police discretion so long as that discretion is exercised according to standard criteria and on the basis of something other than suspicion of evidence of criminal activity. Here, the discretion afforded the Boulder police was exercised in light of standardized criteria, related to the feasibility and appropriateness of parking and locking a vehicle rather than impounding it.[7] There was no showing that the police chose to impound Bertine's van in order to investigate suspected criminal activity.

---

[6] We emphasize that, in this case, the trial court found that the Police Department's procedures mandated the opening of closed containers and the listing of their contents. Our decisions have always adhered to the requirement that inventories be conducted according to standardized criteria.

[T]he dissent suggests that the inventory here was not authorized by the standard procedures of the Boulder Police Department. Yet that court specifically stated that the procedure followed here was "officially authorized." In addition, the court did not disturb the trial court's finding that the police procedures for impounding vehicles required a detailed inventory of Bertine's van.

[7] In arguing that the Boulder Police Department procedures set forth no standardized criteria guiding an officer's decision to impound a vehicle, the dissent selectively quotes from the police directive concerning the care and security of vehicles taken into police custody. The dissent fails to mention that the directive establishes several conditions that must be met before an officer may pursue the park-and-lock alternative. For example, police may not park and lock the vehicle where there is reasonable risk of damage or vandalism to the vehicle or where the approval of the arrestee cannot be obtained. Not only do such conditions circumscribe the

While both *Opperman* and *Lafayette* are distinguishable from the present case on their facts, we think that the principles enunciated in those cases govern the present one. The judgment of the Supreme Court of Colorado is therefore

Reversed.

■ JUSTICE MARSHALL, with whom JUSTICE BRENNAN joins, dissenting.

[The] search [in this case]—it cannot legitimately be labeled an inventory—was unreasonable and violated the Fourth Amendment. * * * [I]t was not conducted according to standardized procedures. * * *

As the Court acknowledges, inventory searches are reasonable only if conducted according to standardized procedures. * * *

The Court today attempts to evade these clear prohibitions on unfettered police discretion by declaring that "the discretion afforded the Boulder police was exercised in light of standardized criteria, related to the feasibility and appropriateness of parking and locking a vehicle rather than impounding it." This vital assertion is flatly contradicted by the record in this case. The officer who conducted the inventory, Officer Reichenbach, testified at the suppression hearing that the decision not to "park and lock" respondent's vehicle was his "own individual discretionary decision." Indeed, application of these supposedly standardized "criteria" upon which the Court so heavily relies would have yielded a different result in this case. Since there was ample public parking adjacent to the intersection where respondent was stopped, consideration of "feasibility" would certainly have militated in favor of the "park and lock" option, not against it. I do not comprehend how consideration of "appropriateness" serves to channel a field officer's discretion; nonetheless, the "park and lock" option would seem particularly appropriate in this case, where respondent was stopped for a traffic offense and was not likely to be in custody for a significant length of time.

Indeed, the record indicates that *no* standardized criteria limit a Boulder police officer's discretion. According to a departmental directive, after placing a driver under arrest, an officer has three options for disposing of the vehicle. First, he can allow a third party to take custody. Second, the officer or the driver (depending on the nature of the arrest) may take the car to the nearest public parking facility, lock it, and take the keys. Finally, the officer can do what was done in this case: impound the vehicle, and search and inventory its contents, including closed containers.

Under the first option, the police have no occasion to search the automobile. Under the "park and lock" option, "[c]losed containers that give no indication of containing either valuables or a weapon *may not be opened and the contents searched* (i.e., inventoried)." Only if the police

───────────────

discretion of individual officers, but they also protect the vehicle and its contents and minimize claims of property loss.

choose the third option are they entitled to search closed containers in the vehicle. Where the vehicle is not itself evidence of a crime,[5] as in this case, the police apparently have totally unbridled discretion as to which procedure to use. Consistent with this conclusion, Officer Reichenbach testified that such decisions were left to the discretion of the officer on the scene.

Once a Boulder police officer has made this initial completely discretionary decision to impound a vehicle, he is given little guidance as to which areas to search and what sort of items to inventory. The arresting officer, Officer Toporek, testified at the suppression hearing as to what items would be inventoried: "That would I think be very individualistic as far as what an officer may or may not go into. I think whatever arouses his suspicious [sic] as far as what may be contained in any type of article in the car." In application, these so-called procedures left the breadth of the "inventory" to the whim of the individual officer. Clearly, "[t]he practical effect of this system is to leave the [owner] subject to the discretion of the official in the field."

Inventory searches are not subject to the warrant requirement because they are conducted by the government as part of a "community caretaking" function, "totally divorced from the detection, investigation, or acquisition of evidence relating to the violation of a criminal statute." Standardized procedures are necessary to ensure that this narrow exception is not improperly used to justify, after the fact, a warrantless investigative foray. Accordingly, to invalidate a search that is conducted without established procedures, it is not necessary to establish that the police actually acted in bad faith, or that the inventory was in fact a "pretext." By allowing the police unfettered discretion, Boulder's discretionary scheme * * * is unreasonable because of the " 'grave danger' of abuse of discretion."

* * *

NOTE

Bertine's emphasis upon the need for "standardized procedures" was developed in Florida v. Wells, 495 U.S. 1, 110 S.Ct. 1632 (1990). *Wells* is discussed in Subchapter A of Chapter 2, following Schmerber v. California.

E. EXTRAORDINARILY INTRUSIVE SEARCHES

In all of the situations covered in the preceding parts of this chapter, attention has focused on whether or to what extent the benchmark requirements of probable cause and a traditional search warrant should

---

[5] Respondent's van was not evidence of a crime within the meaning of the departmental directive; Officer Reichenbach testified that it was not his practice to impound all cars following an arrest for driving while under the influence of alcohol. The Memorandum also requires the "approval of the arrestee" before the police can "park and lock" his car. In this case, however, respondent was never advised of this option and had no opportunity to consent. At the suppression hearing, he indicated that he would have consented to such a procedure.

be abandoned or diluted. But in other situations, it is at least arguable that those requirements should not only be retained but also tightened so as to impose greater limitations on police ability to search or seize than are imposed in standard situations. One of those situations—surgical removal of evidence from the suspect's body—is covered in this subchapter.

Winston v. Lee

Supreme Court of the United States, 1985.
470 U.S. 753, 105 S.Ct. 1611.

■ JUSTICE BRENNAN delivered the opinion of the Court.

* * *

I

A

At approximately 1 a.m. on July 18, 1982, Ralph E. Watkinson was closing his shop for the night. As he was locking the door, he observed someone armed with a gun coming toward him from across the street. Watkinson was also armed and when he drew his gun, the other person told him to freeze. Watkinson then fired at the other person, who returned his fire. Watkinson was hit in the legs, while the other individual, who appeared to be wounded in his left side, ran from the scene. The police arrived on the scene shortly thereafter, and Watkinson was taken by ambulance to the emergency room of the Medical College of Virginia (MCV) Hospital.

Approximately 20 minutes later, police officers responding to another call found respondent eight blocks from where the earlier shooting occurred. Respondent was suffering from a gunshot wound to his left chest area and told the police that he had been shot when two individuals attempted to rob him. An ambulance took respondent to the MCV Hospital. Watkinson was still in the MCV emergency room and, when respondent entered that room, said "[t]hat's the man that shot me." After an investigation, the police decided that respondent's story of having been himself the victim of a robbery was untrue and charged respondent with attempted robbery, malicious wounding, and two counts of using a firearm in the commission of a felony.

B

The Commonwealth shortly thereafter moved in state court for an order directing respondent to undergo surgery to remove an object thought to be a bullet lodged under his left collarbone. The court conducted several evidentiary hearings on the motion. At the first hearing, the Commonwealth's expert testified that the surgical procedure would take 45 minutes and would involve a three to four percent chance of temporary nerve damage, a one percent chance of permanent nerve damage, and a one-tenth of one percent chance of death. At the second hearing, the expert testified that on reexamination of respondent, he discovered that the bullet was not "back inside close to the nerves and arteries," as he originally had thought. Instead, he now believed the bullet to be located "just beneath the skin." He testified that the surgery would require an incision of only one and one-half centimeters (slightly more than one-half inch), could be performed under local anesthesia, and would result in "no danger on the basis that there's no general anesthesia employed."

The state trial judge granted the motion to compel surgery. Respondent petitioned the Virginia Supreme Court for a writ of prohibition and/or a writ of habeas corpus, both of which were denied. Respondent then brought an action in the United States District Court for the Eastern District of Virginia to enjoin the pending operation on Fourth Amendment grounds. The court refused to issue a preliminary injunction, holding that respondent's cause had little likelihood of success on the merits.

On October 18, 1982, just before the surgery was scheduled, the surgeon ordered that X rays be taken of respondent's chest. The X rays revealed that the bullet was in fact lodged two and one-half to three centimeters (approximately one inch) deep in muscular tissue in respondent's chest, substantially deeper than had been thought when the state court granted the motion to compel surgery. The surgeon now believed that a general anesthetic would be desirable for medical reasons.

Respondent moved the state trial court for a rehearing based on the new evidence. After holding an evidentiary hearing, the state trial court denied the rehearing and the Virginia Supreme Court affirmed. Respondent then returned to federal court, where he moved to alter or amend the judgment previously entered against him. After an evidentiary hearing, the District Court enjoined the threatened surgery. A divided panel of the Court of Appeals for the Fourth Circuit affirmed. We granted certiorari to consider whether a State may consistently with the Fourth Amendment compel a suspect to undergo surgery of this kind in a search for evidence of a crime.

II

The Fourth Amendment protects "expectations of privacy,"—the individual's legitimate expectations that in certain places and at certain times he has "the right to be let alone—the most comprehensive of rights and the right most valued by civilized men." Putting to one side the procedural protections of the warrant requirement, the Fourth Amendment generally protects the "security" of "persons, houses, papers, and effects" against official intrusions up to the point where the community's need for evidence surmounts a specified standard, ordinarily "probable cause." Beyond this point, it is ordinarily justifiable for the community to demand that the individual give up some part of his interest in privacy and security to advance the community's vital interests in law enforcement; such a search is generally "reasonable" in the Amendment's terms.

A compelled surgical intrusion into an individual's body for evidence, however, implicates expectations of privacy and security of such magnitude that the intrusion may be "unreasonable" even if likely to produce evidence of a crime. In *Schmerber v. California*, 384 U.S. 757, 86 S.Ct. 1826, 16 L.Ed.2d 908 (1966), we addressed a claim that the State had breached the Fourth Amendment's protection of the "right of the people to be secure in their *persons* . . . against unreasonable searches and seizures" (emphasis added) when it compelled an individual suspected of drunken driving to undergo a blood test. Schmerber had been arrested at a hospital while receiving treatment for injuries suffered when the automobile he was driving struck a tree. Despite Schmerber's objection, a police officer at the hospital had directed a physician to take a blood sample from him. Schmerber subsequently objected to the introduction at trial of evidence obtained as a result of the blood test.

The authorities in *Schmerber* clearly had probable cause to believe that he had been driving while intoxicated, and to believe that a blood test would provide evidence that was exceptionally probative in confirming this belief. Because the case fell within the exigent circumstances exception to the warrant requirement, no warrant was necessary. The search was not more intrusive than reasonably necessary to accomplish its goals. Nonetheless, Schmerber argued that the Fourth Amendment prohibited the authorities from intruding into his body to extract the blood that was needed as evidence.

Schmerber noted that "[t]he overriding function of the Fourth Amendment is to protect personal privacy and dignity against unwarranted intrusion by the State." * * * [W]e observed that these values were "basic to a free society." We also noted that "[b]ecause we are dealing with intrusions into the human body rather than with state interferences with property relationships or private papers—'houses, papers, and effects'—we write on a clean slate." The intrusion perhaps implicated Schmerber's most personal and deep-rooted expectations of privacy, and the Court recognized that Fourth Amendment analysis thus required a discerning inquiry into the facts and circumstances to determine whether the intrusion was justifiable. The Fourth Amendment neither forbids nor permits all such intrusions; rather, the Amendment's "proper function is to constrain, not against all intrusions as such, but against intrusions which are not justified in the circumstances, or which are made in an improper manner."

The reasonableness of surgical intrusions beneath the skin depends on a case-by-case approach, in which the individual's interests in privacy and security are weighed against society's interests in conducting the procedure. In a given case, the question whether the community's need for evidence outweighs the substantial privacy interests at stake is a delicate one admitting of few categorical answers. We believe that

Schmerber, however, provides the appropriate framework of analysis for such cases.

Schmerber recognized that the ordinary requirements of the Fourth Amendment would be the threshold requirements for conducting this kind of surgical search and seizure. We noted the importance of probable cause. And we pointed out: "Search warrants are ordinarily required for searches of dwellings, and, absent an emergency, no less could be required where intrusions into the human body are concerned. . . . The importance of informed, detached and deliberate determinations of the issue whether or not to invade another's body in search of evidence of guilt is indisputable and great."

Beyond these standards, *Schmerber*'s inquiry considered a number of other factors in determining the "reasonableness" of the blood test. A crucial factor in analyzing the magnitude of the intrusion in *Schmerber* is the extent to which the procedure may threaten the safety or health of the individual. "[F]or most people [a blood test] involves virtually no risk, trauma, or pain." Moreover, all reasonable medical precautions were taken and no unusual or untested procedures were employed in *Schmerber,* the procedure was performed "by a physician in a hospital environment according to accepted medical practices." Notwithstanding the existence of probable cause, a search for evidence of a crime may be unjustifiable if it endangers the life or health of the suspect.

Another factor is the extent of intrusion upon the individual's dignitary interests in personal privacy and bodily integrity. Intruding into an individual's living room, eavesdropping upon an individual's telephone conversations, or forcing an individual to accompany police officers to the police station typically do not injure the physical person of the individual. Such intrusions do, however, damage the individual's sense of personal privacy and security and are thus subject to the Fourth Amendment's dictates. In noting that a blood test was "a commonplace in these days of periodic physical examinations," *Schmerber* recognized society's judgment that blood tests do not constitute an unduly extensive imposition on an individual's personal privacy and bodily integrity.

Weighed against these individual interests is the community's interest in fairly and accurately determining guilt or innocence. This interest is of course of great importance. We noted in *Schmerber* that a blood test is "a highly effective means of determining the degree to which a person is under the influence of alcohol." Moreover, there was "a clear indication that in fact [desired] evidence [would] be found" if the blood test were undertaken. Especially given the difficulty of proving drunkenness by other means, these considerations showed that results of the blood test were of vital importance if the State were to enforce its drunken driving laws. In *Schmerber,* we concluded that this state interest was sufficient to justify the intrusion, and the compelled blood test was thus "reasonable" for Fourth Amendment purposes.

III

Applying the *Schmerber* balancing test in this case, we believe that the Court of Appeals reached the correct result. The Commonwealth plainly had probable cause to conduct the search. In addition, all parties apparently agree that respondent has had a full measure of procedural protections and has been able fully to litigate the difficult medical and legal questions necessarily involved in analyzing the reasonableness of a surgical incision of this magnitude.[6] Our inquiry therefore must focus on the extent of the intrusion on respondent's privacy interests and on the State's need for the evidence.

The threats to the health or safety of respondent posed by the surgery are the subject of sharp dispute between the parties. Before the new revelations of October 18, the District Court found that the procedure could be carried out "with virtually no risk to [respondent]." On rehearing, however, with new evidence before it, the District Court held that "the risks previously involved have increased in magnitude even as new risks are being added."

The Court of Appeals examined the medical evidence in the record and found that respondent would suffer some risks associated with the surgical procedure. One surgeon had testified that the difficulty of discovering the exact location of the bullet "could require extensive probing and retracting of the muscle tissue," carrying with it "the concomitant risks of injury to the muscle as well as injury to the nerves, blood vessels and other tissue in the chest and pleural cavity." The court further noted that "the greater intrusion and the larger incisions increase the risks of infection." Moreover, there was conflict in the testimony concerning the nature and the scope of the operation. One surgeon stated that it would take 15–20 minutes, while another predicted the procedure could take up to two and one-half hours. The court properly took the resulting uncertainty about the medical risks into account.

Both lower courts in this case believed that the proposed surgery, which for purely medical reasons required the use of a general anesthetic, would be an "extensive" intrusion on respondent's personal privacy and bodily integrity. When conducted with the consent of the patient, surgery requiring general anesthesia is not necessarily demeaning or intrusive. In such a case, the surgeon is carrying out the patient's own will concerning the patient's body and the patient's right to privacy is therefore preserved. In this case, however, the Court of Appeals noted that the Commonwealth proposes to take control of respondent's body, to "drug this citizen—not yet convicted of a criminal offense—with narcotics and barbiturates into a state of unconsciousness," and then to search beneath his skin for evidence of a crime. This kind of surgery involves a

---

[6] Because the State has afforded respondent the benefit of a full adversary presentation and appellate review, we do not reach the question whether the State may compel a suspect to undergo a surgical search of this magnitude for evidence absent such special procedural protections.

virtually total divestment of respondent's ordinary control over surgical probing beneath his skin.

The other part of the balance concerns the Commonwealth's need to intrude into respondent's body to retrieve the bullet. The Commonwealth claims to need the bullet to demonstrate that it was fired from Watkinson's gun, which in turn would show that respondent was the robber who confronted Watkinson. However, although we recognize the difficulty of making determinations in advance as to the strength of the case against respondent, petitioners' assertions of a compelling need for the bullet are hardly persuasive. The very circumstances relied on in this case to demonstrate probable cause to believe that evidence will be found tend to vitiate the Commonwealth's need to compel respondent to undergo surgery. The Commonwealth has available substantial additional evidence that respondent was the individual who accosted Watkinson on the night of the robbery. No party in this case suggests that Watkinson's entirely spontaneous identification of respondent at the hospital would be inadmissible. In addition, petitioners can no doubt prove that [respondent] was found a few blocks from Watkinson's store shortly after the incident took place. And petitioners can certainly show that the location of the bullet (under respondent's left collarbone) seems to correlate with Watkinson's report that the robber "jerked" to the left. The fact that the Commonwealth has available such substantial evidence of the origin of the bullet restricts the need for the Commonwealth to compel respondent to undergo the contemplated surgery.[10]

In weighing the various factors in this case, we therefore reach the same conclusion as the courts below. The operation sought will intrude substantially on respondent's protected interests. The medical risks of the operation, although apparently not extremely severe, are a subject of considerable dispute: the very uncertainty militates against finding the operation to be "reasonable." In addition, the intrusion on respondent's privacy interests entailed by the operation can only be characterized as severe. On the other hand, although the bullet may turn out to be useful to the Commonwealth in prosecuting respondent, the Commonwealth has failed to demonstrate a compelling need for it. We believe that in these circumstances the Commonwealth has failed to demonstrate that it would be "reasonable" under the terms of the Fourth Amendment to search for evidence of this crime by means of the contemplated surgery.

---

[10] There are also some questions concerning the probative value of the bullet, even if it could be retrieved. The evidentiary value of the bullet depends on a comparison between markings, if any, on the bullet in respondent's shoulder and markings, if any, found on a test bullet that the police could fire from Watkinson's gun. However, the record supports some doubt whether this kind of comparison is possible. This is because the bullet's markings may have been corroded in the time that the bullet has been in respondent's shoulder, thus making it useless for comparison purposes. In addition, respondent argues that any given gun may be incapable of firing bullets that have a consistent set of markings. The record is devoid of any evidence that the police have attempted to test-fire Watkinson's gun, and there thus remains the additional possibility that a comparison of bullets is impossible because Watkinson's gun does not consistently fire bullets with the same markings. However, because the courts below made no findings on this point, we hesitate to give it significant weight in our analysis.

IV

The Fourth Amendment is a vital safeguard of the right of the citizen to be free from unreasonable governmental intrusions into any area in which he has a reasonable expectation of privacy. Where the Court has found a lesser expectation of privacy, or where the search involves a minimal intrusion on privacy interests, the Court has held that the Fourth Amendment's protections are correspondingly less stringent. Conversely, however, the Fourth Amendment's command that searches be "reasonable" requires that when the State seeks to intrude upon an area in which our society recognizes a significantly heightened privacy interest, a more substantial justification is required to make the search "reasonable." Applying these principles, we hold that the proposed search in this case would be "unreasonable" under the Fourth Amendment.

Affirmed.

■ JUSTICE BLACKMUN and JUSTICE REHNQUIST concur in the judgment.

■ CHIEF JUSTICE BURGER, concurring.

I join because I read the Court's opinion as not preventing detention of an individual if there are reasonable grounds to believe that natural bodily functions will disclose the presence of contraband materials secreted internally.

CHAPTER 6

INTERROGATION AND CONFESSIONS

Analysis

———————

This chapter deals with the variety of legal doctrines bearing upon the propriety of law enforcement elicitation of "confessions" and the admissibility of defendants' out-of-court admissions. Introductory Subchapter A considers several general matters. Then the next three subchapters address the major applicable federal constitutional doctrines. Subchapter B deals with the requirement of voluntariness. Subchapter C considers the Fifth Amendment demands under Miranda v. Arizona, 384 U.S. 436, 86 S.Ct. 1602 (1966). Finally, Subchapter D deals with the more general right to counsel embodied in the Sixth Amendment as it applies in this context.

A. INTRODUCTION

EDITORS' INTRODUCTION: "CONFESSION LAW"

Terminology: Confessions, Admissions, and Exculpatory Statements

When prosecutors offer defendants' out of court self-incriminating statements into evidence against them, courts sometimes distinguished between a "confession"—a statement admitting or acknowledging all facts necessary for conviction of the crime charged—and an "admission"—an acknowledgement of one or more facts that tend to establish guilt but not of all elements of the crime. Moreover, both are sometimes distinguished from an "exculpatory" statement, a statement which, at the time it was made, was intended to exculpate rather than incriminate the speaker, but which later is offered to prove the speaker's guilt. Prosecutors often use exculpatory statements by of proving that a suspect gave a false explanation of incriminating circumstances; this is offered to prove that the suspect was conscious of his or her guilt and, therefore, that the suspect is in fact guilty.

It is doubtful that these distinctions have much significance today. In any case, this chapter will use the term "confession" as including what some distinguish as admissions or exculpatory statements.

Other Legal Doctrines Generally

Other legal requirements than those considered in this chapter may have an impact on interrogation and confessions. Police questioning may, for example, implicate the general due process prohibition against the use of evidence obtained in a manner that "shocks the conscience." This prohibition was discussed in Schmerber v. California, 384 U.S. 757, 86 S.Ct. 1826 (1966), reprinted in Chapter 2.

A confession may, of course, be subject to challenge as the "fruit" of an arrest or detention made in violation of the Fourth Amendment. Nonconstitutional requirements that arrested defendants be promptly presented before a magistrate and the perhaps-related Fourth Amendment requirement of a post-arrest judicial determination of probable cause are also of concern.

Requirement of Corroboration or "Independent" Proof of the Corpus Delicti.

The doctrines discussed in this chapter relating to the admissibility of confessions must be distinguished from the very different requirement of "corroboration" imposed by many jurisdictions.

The requirement of corroboration is often put as a demand that the prosecution, in order to prove guilt beyond a reasonable doubt, produce evidence other than an out-of-court confession by the defendant. This other evidence is often required to show the corpus delicti, that is, that the crime charged was committed by someone. The evidence independent of the confession need not tend to show that the defendant committed the crime. Nor need it be sufficient in itself to prove commission of the crime beyond a reasonable doubt. The confession can be the only evidence tending to show that the defendant committed the offense; the corroborating evidence can be considered together with the confession in determining whether the prosecution has proven guilt beyond a reasonable doubt. In some states, the requirement has been incorporated into statute. Section 60.50 of New York's Criminal Procedure Law, for example, provides that a conviction is not permitted "solely upon evidence of a confession made by [the defendant] without additional proof that the offense charged has been committed."

The requirement is sometimes stated as one addressing the admissibility of a confession—a confession is not admissible unless the prosecution has first introduced other evidence showing that the charged offense was committed. But trial judges have great discretion over the order of proof. A trial judge is therefore unlikely to commit reversible error even under this formulation of the requirement by admitting a confession, if the prosecution later in the case produces other evidence showing the charged offense was committed. See generally, McCormick on Evidence § 146 (6th ed. 2006).

In some jurisdictions, the requirement is somewhat more flexible than one of independent proof of the corpus delicti. In federal litigation, for example, the Supreme Court has held that in order for a conviction to be upheld the Government must have introduced "substantial independent evidence which would tend to establish the trustworthiness of the [defendant's] statement." Opper v. United States, 348 U.S. 84, 93, 75 S.Ct. 158, 164 (1954). This is the requirement applied by the Court in Wong Sun v. United States, 371 U.S. 471, 83 S.Ct. 407 (1963), reprinted in Chapter 1. However the requirement is formulated, it is in effect a requirement that a confession be corroborated by some other evidence at trial in order to justify the conviction of the defendant.

Like the voluntariness rule, the requirement of corroboration is based upon concern regarding the accuracy of out-of-court self-incriminating statements. In *Opper* the Court explained:

> [O]ur concept of justice that finds no man guilty until proven has led our state and federal courts generally to refuse conviction on testimony concerning confessions of the accused not made by him at the trial of his case. * * * [T]he doubt persists that the zeal of the agencies of prosecution to protect the peace, the self interest of the accomplice, the maliciousness of an enemy or the aberration or weakness of the accused under the strain of suspicion may tinge or warp the facts of the confession. Admissions, retold at trial, are much like hearsay, that is, statements not made at the pending trial. They had neither the compulsion of the oath nor the test of cross examination.

348 U.S. at 89–90, 75 S.Ct. at 162–63. Despite its concern with the accuracy of confessions and trials, however, the requirement of corroboration has not been incorporated into any federal constitutional doctrine. It remains exclusively a matter of state or local definition of evidence sufficiency.

Statutory Provisions Related to Confessions

There have been relatively few legislative efforts addressing confession issues. The federal statute discussed in Subchapters B(1) and C(1) of this chapter is one of the few such efforts. The American Law Institute's Model Code of Pre-Arraignment Procedure (Official Draft, 1975) offers a more comprehensive model. Article 150 deals with Exclusion of Statements and some portions of Article 140, Conditions of Investigation During Custody of an Arrested Person, are also relevant to confession issues.

Objectives of Confession Law

A basic issue that remains largely unresolved is what ought to be the objectives of constitutional and nonconstitutional law relating to confessions. Obviously a major objective must be the avoidance of conviction of innocent defendants based on judges' and juries' reliance upon inaccurate confessions.

Should confession law also aim more broadly to pursue objectives other than the accuracy of confessions and convictions? Dix, Mistake, Ignorance, Expectation of Benefit, and the Modern Law of Confessions, 1975 Wash.U.L.Q. 275, 330–31, argued:

> A major objective of the law of confessions * * * should be * * * assuring that a person who confesses does so with as complete an understanding of his tactical position as possible. This, of course, would require awareness not only of his abstract legal rights, but also of his practical ability to implement those rights in light of his factual situation and of the tactical wisdom of asserting them.

EDITORS' NOTE: CONFESSION LAW, RELIABILITY OF CONFESSIONS AND THE ROLE OF JUDGES AND JURIES

The legal rules triggered by the manner in which confessions were obtained, unlike exclusionary rules based on illegality in obtaining evidence generally, have generated some confusion regarding the appropriate and constitutionally-permissible roles of judge and jury.

If at the trial of a criminal case the prosecution introduces evidence that the defendant made an out-of-court confession, the defense has always, of course, been permitted to argue that the judge or jury should give that evidence little or no weight. The defense may argue that the defendant did not in fact give the out-of-court statement suggested by the prosecution's evidence or that any such statement given by the defendant was not complete or accurate.

Common Law Voluntariness Requirement

When the courts developed the common law requirement that an out-of-court confession by the defendant be "voluntary" (considered in Subchapter B that follows), this was recognized as a requirement of admissibility. Under what came to be called the "orthodox" approach, whether an offered confession was voluntary was decided by the judge in ruling on admissibility of the prosecution's offered evidence. If the judge rules a confession was voluntary and thus admissible, the defendant can argue that the prosecution's evidence was not credible and can support this with additional evidence. See Bernard D. Meltzer, Involuntary Confessions: The Allocation of Responsibility Between Judge and Jury, 21 Univ. Chi. L.Rev. 317, 320 (1954).

Some jurisdictions—most notably New York—permitted or required a judge who found voluntariness in question to submit the issue to the jury, with instruction for the jury to disregard the purported confession if it found that the confession had been made but was not voluntary. Others provided that if the judge found the confession voluntary, that voluntariness issue could also be submitted to the jury for, in effect, reconsideration. Under both of these approaches, a jury to whom voluntariness was submitted was expected to first determine voluntariness and—if the confession was found to have been made and voluntary—to determine credibility, that is, how much if any weight to give the evidence that the defendant had confessed. Meltzer, 21 Univ. Chi. L. Rev. at 319–22.

There is some question whether judges and juries actually understood and applied meaningful distinctions between the standard for admissibility—voluntariness—and credibility issues. Sometimes, of course, evidence regarding the manner in which a confession was obtained was relevant to both voluntariness and credibility. Evidence that the defendant was beaten to obtain a confession, for example, indicated both that the resulting confession was not voluntary and that it may not have been reliable or credible.

Federal Constitutional Requirement of Voluntariness

In its first confession case, Hopt v. Utah, 110 U.S. 574, 4 S.Ct. 202 (1884), the United States Supreme Court made clear that an out-of court confession by a defendant is admissible in a federal criminal trial only if it is voluntary. *Hopt* was apparently decided as a matter of non-constitutional evidence law.

Thirteen years later, in Bram v. United States, 168 U.S. 532, 18 S.Ct. 183 (1897), the Court commented that "[i]n criminal trials, in the courts of the United States wherever a question arises whether a confession is incompetent because not voluntary, the issue is controlled by that portion of the fifth amendment to the constitution of the United States, commanding that no person 'shall be compelled in any criminal case, to be a witness against himself.'" The Fifth Amendment privilege, the Court continued, was a crystallization of the common law voluntariness rule existing at the time of the adoption of the Constitution.

The Fifth Amendment privilege against compelled self-incrimination was not held binding upon the states until Malloy v. Hogan, 378 U.S. 1, 84 S.Ct. 1489 (1964). But, beginning with Brown v. Mississippi, 297 U.S. 278, 56 S.Ct. 461 (1936), the Supreme Court imposed federal constitutional limitations upon the use of confessions in state criminal trials through application of the Fourteenth Amendment's general requirement of due process. Earlier cases suggested some difference between the due process requirement and the *Bram* Fifth Amendment rules. In 1966, however, the Court commented that "[t]he decisions of this Court have guaranteed the same procedural protection for the defendant whether his confession was used in a federal or state court." Miranda v. Arizona, 384 U.S. 436, 464 n. 33, 86 S.Ct. 1602, 1623 n. 33 (1966).

The rationale for the federal constitutional requirement of voluntariness evolved during this period. *Hopt* appeared to accept the common law approach that the prohibition against involuntary confessions was based primarily and perhaps entirely on what was perceived to be the unreliability of these statements. But by 1959 the Supreme Court was willing to state:

> The abhorrence of society to the use of involuntary confessions does not turn alone on their inherent untrustworthiness. It also turns on the deep-rooted feeling that the police must obey the law while enforcing the law; that in the end life and liberty can be as much endangered from illegal methods used to convict those thought to be criminals as from the actual criminals themselves.

Spano v. New York, 360 U.S. 315, 320–321, 79 S.Ct. 1202, 1205–06 (1959).

Voluntariness and Accuracy Distinguished

A federal constitutional need to distinguish carefully between voluntariness and reliability was established in Rogers v. Richmond, 365 U.S. 534, 81 S.Ct. 735 (1961). Police misrepresented to defendant Rogers that they were about to bring his wife into the stationhouse for questioning. The trial judge held the resulting confession admissible because the police pretense "had no tendency to produce a confession that was not in accord with the truth." The United States Supreme Court reversed the conviction:

> From a fair reading of * * * [the record] we cannot but conclude that the question whether Rogers' confessions were admissible was answered by reference to a legal standard which took into account the circumstance of probable truth or falsity. And this is not a permissible standard under the Due Process Clause of the Fourteenth Amendment. The attention of the trial court should have been focused * * * on the question whether the behavior of the State's law enforcement officials was such as to overbear [Roger's] will to resist and to bring about confessions not freely self-determined—a question to be answered with complete disregard of whether or not [Rogers] in fact spoke the truth.

365 U.S. at 543–44, 81 S.Ct. at 741.

Voluntariness to Be Determined, at Least Initially, by the Court

Three years after *Rogers*, in Jackson v. Denno, 378 U.S. 368, 84 S.Ct. 1774 (1964), the Court held that as developed in this line of cases, the federal constitutional requirement of voluntariness bars a procedure under which the issue of voluntariness is relegated to the jury. Essentially, *Jackson* held, a defendant is entitled to have the trial judge make a definitive decision on whether a challenged confession is voluntary. Under the New York procedure, the jury entrusted to decide voluntariness may also hear evidence suggesting the confession may be accurate and reliable even though involuntary. A jury may be unable to understand, or unwilling to respect, the rule that even a reliable involuntary confession may not be considered in determining whether the prosecution has proved the defendant's guilt. Further, a jury may be unable or unwilling to disregard the apparent reliability and accuracy of a confession in determining its voluntariness. 378 U.S. at 381–88, 84 S.Ct. at 1783–87.

Under *Jackson*, federal due process requires a fair determination by the judge that a challenged confession is voluntary. If a confession is determined voluntary, *Jackson* does not, however, bar a procedure under which this is resubmitted to the trial jury.

Burden of Proof

The federal Constitution requires only that voluntariness be proved by a preponderance of the evidence, the Court held in Lego v. Twomey, 404 U.S. 477, 92 S.Ct. 619 (1972). No basis existed, the majority reasoned, to believe that rulings made under the preponderance of the evidence standard have been unreliable or otherwise wanting in quality. Consequently, the prosecution's ability to put confessions before juries need not be further impeded by a need to prove voluntariness beyond a reasonable doubt. When a confession is challenged on *Miranda* grounds, the prosecution must show compliance with that body of law but again only by a preponderance of the evidence. Colorado v. Connelly, 479 U.S. 157, 107 S.Ct. 515 (1986).

States, of course, remain free to impose a higher standard as a matter of state law. Some do, most frequently by requiring that voluntariness be established by more than a preponderance of the evidence.

Admission of Confession as Harmless Error

Early Supreme Court discussions suggested that if on appeal an appellate court determined that the trial judge had erroneously admitted an involuntary confession, reversal of the conviction for a new trial was always necessary. Admission of such a confession, in other words, could not be "harmless error." In Arizona v. Fulminante, 499 U.S. 279, 111 S.Ct. 1246 (1991), a bare majority of the Supreme Court held that even admission of an involuntary confession could be harmless error if the appellate court is convinced beyond a reasonable doubt that the confession did not contribute to the defendant's conviction. Trial errors generally are subject to the harmless error rule, the Court concluded, and insufficient reason exists to treat involuntary confessions any differently. Admission of such a confession is not a "structural defect[ ] in the constitution of the trial mechanism, which def[ies] analysis by 'harmless error' standards." Nor is the admission of such a confession a type of error that should always require reversal because it "transcends the criminal process." On the facts of *Fulminante*, however, the State failed to meet its burden of establishing beyond a reasonable doubt that the confession did not contribute to Fulminante's conviction. Therefore, his conviction was reversed.

Error in admitting a confession inadmissible because it was obtained in violation of *Miranda*, of course, can also be harmless. Brecht v. Abrahamson, 507 U.S. 619, 113 S.Ct. 1710 (1993).

Defendants' Right to Challenge Credibility of Confession Evidence

When a confession is held admissible, a defendant is entitled to the opportunity to persuade the judge or jury passing on guilt or innocence that the confession should not be believed because of the manner in which it was elicited. Under Crane v. Kentucky, 476 U.S. 683, 106 S.Ct. 2142 (1986), this is a matter of federal constitutional right.

In *Crane*, the defense moved before trial to suppress Crane's confession to the murder for which he was to be tried. A pretrial hearing was held on the motion, at which Crane testified he had been detained for questioning in a windowless room for some time, as many as six officers had been present during the questioning, he had unsuccessfully made repeated requests to contact his family and he had been badgered into making a false confession. Several police officers' testimonies contradicted this version of the facts and the trial court held the confession admissible. At trial, the prosecution introduced the confession into evidence. The defense contended in response that contradictions in the confession and the circumstances under which it was given meant the jury should not believe it. In support of this, the defense unsuccessfully attempted to introduce before the jury evidence concerning the interrogation during which the defendant made the confession.

The state supreme court affirmed Crane's resulting conviction, reasoning that evidence relating only to the "voluntariness" of a confession is not admissible before the jury. While evidence relating to the "credibility" of the confession is admissible, the court reasoned, all of Crane's offered evidence went only to voluntariness. A unanimous Supreme Court, speaking through Justice O'Connor, reversed:

> Whether rooted directly in the due process clause of the Fourteenth Amendment or in the Compulsory Process or Confrontation clauses of the Sixth Amendment, the Constitution guarantees criminal defendants "a meaningful opportunity to present a complete defense." We break no new ground in observing that an essential component of procedural fairness is an opportunity to be heard. That opportunity would be an empty one if the State were permitted to exclude competent, reliable evidence bearing on the credibility of a confession when such evidence is central to the defendant's claim of innocence. * * *
>
> Under these principles, the Kentucky courts erred in foreclosing [Crane's] efforts to introduce testimony about the environment in which the police secured his confession. * * *

[E]vidence about the manner in which a confession was obtained is often highly relevant to its reliability and credibility.

476 U.S. at 690–91, 106 S.Ct. at 2146–47.

Crane assured a defendant of an opportunity to introduce certain evidence bearing on the reliability of a confession put into evidence by the prosecution. Whether in a jury trial a defendant is entitled to any particular instructions to the jury has not been considered by the Supreme Court.

Recent Increased Scrutiny of Confession Reliability

Reliability of confessions has come under increased scrutiny as a result of recent exonerations of convicted defendants on the basis of DNA evidence establishing the innocence of those defendants. One authority has reported that false confessions were a contributing factor to about twenty-five percent of the convictions that DNA evidence has shown were of innocent defendants. Saul M. Kassin, False Confessions, 73 Alb. L. Rev. 1227, 1228 (2010).

A traditional indicator of the reliability of confessions has been the provision by the confessing suspect of details of the crime that only the perpetrator is likely to know. Brandon L. Garrett, The Substance of False Confessions, 62 Stan. L. Rev. 1051 (2010), however, cast doubt upon this approach. Garrett examined 38 rape and murder cases in which defendants had confessed, been convicted, and then were exonerated based on DNA testing. In 36 of the 38 cases, the confessions included specific details about the crime, often involving details that only the guilty person was likely to know. In most, law enforcement officers denied providing this information to the suspects. The fact that the confessions contained these details, however, suggests that officers must have—perhaps unintentionally—conveyed this information to the suspects during the process of questioning them.

Garrett also noted that in 28 of the 38 cases, the defendants "supplied facts during the interrogation that were inconsistent with the known facts in the case." This, however, did not result in the confessions being discredited. He concluded:

> [O]ur existing criminal procedure not only ignores glaring evidence of unreliability, but it also reinforces dangers of contamination by crediting assertions of "inside knowledge" without assessing whether those facts were truly volunteered and ignoring the risk that those facts could have been disclosed.

62 Stan. L.Rev. at 1110.

In 2010, the American Psychology-Law Society, Division 41 of the American Psychological Association—motivated in part by the confessions in the DNA exoneration cases—authorized and approved a Scientific Review Paper on false confessions. Saul M. Kassin, Steven A. Drizin, Thomas Grisso, Gisli H. Gudjonsson, Richard A. Leo, Allison D.

Redlich, Police-Induced Confessions: Risk Factors and Recommendations, 34 Law & Hum. Behav. 3 (2010). Among the objectives of this project were to "review the state of the science on interviewing and interrogation by bringing together a multidisciplinary group of scholars" and "to identify the dispositional characteristics * * * that influence the voluntariness and reliability of confessions."

The Review Paper concluded that "a small but significant minority of innocent people confess under interrogation." No precise incident rate can be ascertained, however.

Some "innocent but malleable suspects, told that there is incontrovertible evidence of their involvement, come not only to capitulate in their behavior but also to believe that they may have committed the crime in question, sometimes confabulating false memories in the process." Other cases involve "compliant false confessions," which "are those in which suspects are induced through interrogation to confess to a crime they did not commit. In these cases, the suspect acquiesces to the demand for a confession to escape a stressful situation, avoid punishment, or gain a promised or implied reward."

Interrogation, the Paper observed, is designed "not to discern the truth, determine if the suspect committed the crime, or evaluate his or her denials. Rather, police are trained to interrogate only those suspects whose culpability they 'establish' on the basis of their initial investigation." Id., at 6.

The Paper singled out, "because of the consistency in which they appear in cases involving proven false confessions," three situational risk factors associated with false confessions: "interrogation time, the presentation of false evidence, and minimization." With regard to the first, it asserted that "false confessions tend to occur after long periods of time—which indicates a dogged persistence in the face of denial." "[P]rolonged isolation from significant others," as well as sleep deprivation, "constitutes a form of deprivation that can heighten a suspect's distress and incentive to remove himself or herself from the situation." "[P]esentations of false evidence can lead people to confess to crimes they did not commit. With regard to the third factor, the Paper stated:

Minimization: Promises Implied But Not Spoken

In addition to thrusting the suspect into a state of despair by the processes of confrontation, interrogators are trained to minimize the crime through "theme development," a process of providing moral justification or face-saving excuses, making confession seem like an expedient means of escape. Interrogators are thus trained to suggest to suspects that their actions were spontaneous, accidental, provoked, peer-pressured, drug-induced, or otherwise justifiable by external factors. * * *

Minimization tactics that imply leniency may well lead innocent people who feel trapped to confess. * * *

Id., at 18.

As to "dispositional risk factors for false confession," the Paper noted "the two most commonly cited concerns are a suspect's age (i.e., juvenile status) and mental impairment (i.e., mental illness, mental retardation). These common citations are because of the staggering overrepresentation of these groups in the population of proven false confessions."

Judges and jurors, the Paper continued, do not consistently discount the credibility of confessions induced by interrogation techniques associated with producing false confessions.

There are at least three reasons why people cannot easily identify as false the confessions of innocent suspects. First, generalized common sense leads people to trust confessions the way they trust other behaviors that counter self-interest. * * * [M]ost people reasonably believe that they would never confess to a crime they did not commit and have only rudimentary understanding of the predispositional and situational factors that would lead someone to do so.

A second reason is that people are typically not adept at deception detection. * * * [N]either lay people nor professionals distinguish truths from lies at high levels of accuracy. This problem extends to judgments of true and false confessions. * * *

* * * [A] third reason [is that p]olice-induced false confessions often contain content cues presumed to be associated with truthfulness. In many documented false confessions, the statements ultimately presented in court contained not only an admission of guilt but vivid details about the crime, the scene, and the victim that became known to the innocent suspect through leading questions, photographs, visits to the crime scene, and other secondhand sources invisible to the naïve observer. To further complicate matters, many false confessors state not just what they allegedly did, and how they did it, but why—as they self-report on revenge, jealousy, provocation, financial desperation, peer pressure, and other prototypical motives for crime. Some of these statements even contain apologies and expressions of remorse. To the naïve spectator, such statements appear to be voluntary, textured with detail, and the product of personal experience. Uninformed, however, this spectator mistakes illusion for reality, not realizing that the taped confession is scripted by the police theory of the case, rehearsed during hours of unrecorded questioning, directed by the questioner, and ultimately enacted on paper, tape, or camera by the suspect.

Id., at 24–25.

NOTES

1. **Improper Interrogation as a Constitutional Violation.** Does—or should—improper police interrogation constitute a violation of the federal Constitution if it does not produce a confession or if any confession produced is not offered in a criminal prosecution? If it does, such questioning might create civil liability. In Chavez v. Martinez, 538 U.S. 760, 123 S.Ct. 1994 (2003), a majority of the justices concluded that under current law, no constitutional violation arises. Four justices reasoned that the Fifth Amendment prohibits only compelling a person to be a witness in a "criminal case," If coercive police questioning results in a suspect making incriminatory statements to the interrogating officers, "it is not until their use in a criminal case that a violation of the Self-Incrimination Clause occurs * * *." 538 U.S. at 767, 123 S.Ct. at 2001 (Thomas, J., announcing the judgment of the Court). Two justices reasoned that the Court *could* read the Fifth Amendment as applicable to aggressive but unproductive questioning but *should* not. No need for such expansive civil liability to protect the core privilege against self-incrimination, they reasoned, has been established. 538 U.S. at 778–79, 123 S.Ct. at 2007 (Souter, J., concurring in the judgment).

2. **Violation of "Prompt Presentation" Requirements.** Rule 5(a) of the Federal Rules of Criminal Procedure demands presentation of an arrested person before a judicial officer without "unnecessary delay." Most if not all states have similar requirements of "prompt presentation" of arrested suspects. In part, prompt presentation minimizes the opportunity for coercive or otherwise improper interrogation techniques. At the arrestee's appearance before the magistrate, the arrestee may be given information concerning the charges pending and may be informed by the judge regarding legal rights. Moreover, provision may be made for pretrial release. What is the effect upon the admissibility of a confession of a delay in presenting the accused before a magistrate in accordance with these requirements?

In McNabb v. United States, 318 U.S. 332, 63 S.Ct. 608 (1943), the Supreme Court held that under its supervisory power it would require exclusion of a confession made by a defendant after federal officers who had the defendant in custody failed to comply with a statutory predecessor to Rule 5(a) demanding prompt presentation. The Court later applied the same exclusionary rule to Rule 5(a). Upshaw v. United States, 335 U.S. 410, 69 S.Ct. 170 (1948).

In Mallory v. United States, 354 U.S. 449, 77 S.Ct. 1356 (1957), the Court considered the meaning of "unnecessary delay" under Rule 5(a), and made clear this was to be defined so as to minimize the opportunity for custodial interrogation:

> Circumstances may justify a brief delay between arrest and arraignment, as for instance, where the story volunteered by the accused is susceptible of quick verification through third parties. But the delay must not be of a nature to give opportunity for the extraction of a confession.

354 U.S. at 455, 77 S.Ct. at 1360. The delay in the case before it, the Court held, was "unnecessary" because a magistrate was readily available and the defendant was not presented only because the officers desired the opportunity for interrogation.

The Supreme Court has never held the *McNabb-Mallory* rule in any way binding on the states. Instead, a showing that a confession was obtained during an improper delay in presenting the defendant before a magistrate is generally regarded—under federal constitutional confession law—as merely one factor to consider in determining the confession's due process voluntariness. Some state courts have, apparently as matter of state law, embellished this approach. Maryland case law, for example, provides that delay that is unnecessary and deliberate but not for the sole purpose of obtaining a confession is to be weighed against a finding that the confession was voluntary. Unnecessary and deliberate delay for the sole purpose of obtaining a confession is to be weighed "very heavily" in favor of involuntariness. Perez v. State, 168 Md.App. 248, 274–276, 896 A.2d 380, 394–396 (Md.App.2006).

States remain free, of course, to adopt—as a matter of state law— exclusionary rules requiring the suppression of confessions made during a period of delay violative of the state prompt presentation requirement. Some have. State v. Barros, 24 A.3d 1158, 1181 (R.I.2011) (confession made during unnecessary delay in presentment must be suppressed if defendant shows " '*both:* (1) that the delay in presentment was unnecessary *and* (2) that such delay was "causative" with respect to' the making of the inculpatory statement").

As a matter of federal law, Congress has modified the *McNabb-Mallory* rule. Under 18 U.S.C.A. § 3501(c), a confession offered against a federal criminal defendant is not to be excluded solely because of delay in presenting a defendant before a magistrate if the confession is voluntary and made within six hours following the defendant's taking into custody. Further, a confession obtained after a six-hour period is not to be excluded on delay grounds alone if the delay is found reasonable, considering the distance traveled to a judicial officer and the means of transportation available to the officers.

The Supreme Court in Corley v. United States, 556 U.S. 303, 129 S.Ct. 1558 (2009), addressed the effect of the statute on a confession obtained during improper delay lasting longer than the six hour "safe harbor" period. The federal statute, *Corley* held by a 5-to-4 vote, did not completely nullify the *McNabb-Mallory* rule.

> We hold that § 3501 modified *McNabb-Mallory* without supplanting it. Under the rule as revised by § 3501(c), a district court with a suppression claim must find whether the defendant confessed within six hours of arrest (unless a longer delay was "reasonable considering the means of transportation and the distance to be traveled to the nearest available [magistrate]"). If the confession came within that period, it is admissible, subject to the other Rules of Evidence, so long as it was "made voluntarily and

. . . the weight to be given [it] is left to the jury." If the confession occurred before presentment and beyond six hours, however, the court must decide whether delaying that long was unreasonable or unnecessary under the *McNabb-Mallory* cases, and if it was, the confession is to be suppressed.

556 U.S. at 322, 129 S.Ct. at 1571. The *Corley* majority was clearly influenced by its perception of the significance of the prompt presentation requirement:

It * * * counts heavily against the position of the United States that it would leave the Rule 5 presentment requirement without any teeth, for as the Government again is forced to admit, if there is no *McNabb-Mallory* there is no apparent remedy for delay in presentment. One might not care if the prompt presentment requirement were just some administrative nicety, but in fact the rule has always mattered in very practical ways and still does. As we said, it stretches back to the common law, when it was "one of the most important" protections "against unlawful arrest." Today presentment is the point at which the judge is required to take several key steps to foreclose Government overreaching: informing the defendant of the charges against him, his right to remain silent, his right to counsel, the availability of bail, and any right to a preliminary hearing; giving the defendant a chance to consult with counsel; and deciding between detention or release.

In a world without *McNabb-Mallory*, federal agents would be free to question suspects for extended periods before bringing them out in the open, and we have always known what custodial secrecy leads to. * * * "[C]ustodial police interrogation, by its very nature, isolates and pressures the individual," and there is mounting empirical evidence that these pressures can induce a frighteningly high percentage of people to confess to crimes they never committed.

556 U.S. at 320–21, 129 S.Ct. at 1570.

3.   **Violation of Fourth Amendment Right to Probable Cause Determination.** Under Gerstein v. Pugh, 420 U.S. 103, 95 S.Ct. 854 (1975), an unindicted defendant arrested without a warrant has a Fourth Amendment right to a "prompt" judicial determination of probable cause. County of Riverside v. McLaughlin, 500 U.S. 44, 111 S.Ct. 1661 (1991), made clear that promptness generally requires such probable cause determinations be made within 48 hours of arrests. These determinations may—but need not—be made when the defendants go before magistrates pursuant to the statutory provisions discussed in note 2, above. If an arrested defendant is not provided with the probable cause determination required under *Gerstein* and *McLaughlin*, is a confession given during that detention—and after the defendant was entitled to a probable cause determination—inadmissible as the fruit of the Fourth Amendment violation?

The issue was noted but not addressed by the Supreme Court in Powell v. Nevada, 511 U.S. 79, 84–85, 114 S.Ct. 1280, 1283–84 (1994). Justice

Thomas, joined by the Chief Justice, argued in *Powell* that the Court should reach the issue. He further offered an analysis that would render suppression inappropriate in some and perhaps all such cases. Petitioner Powell was arrested on November 3, 1989 after he brought a badly injured child to a hospital for treatment. On November 7, he made a statement admitting abusing the child. Later on the 7th, a magistrate determined the arrest was supported by probable cause; the magistrate relied upon facts recited in a "declaration of arrest" prepared by officers within an hour of Powell's arrest. On these facts, Justice Thomas reasoned, the November 7th statement need not be suppressed:

> [S]uppression of petitioner's statement would not be appropriate because the statement was not a product of the *McLaughlin* violation.
>
> Our decisions make clear "that evidence will not be excluded as 'fruit' [of an unlawful act] unless the illegality is at least the 'but for' cause of the discovery of the evidence." * * *
>
> Contrary to petitioner's arguments, the violation of *McLaughlin* (as opposed to his arrest and custody) bore no causal relationship whatsoever to his November 7 statement. The timing of the probable cause determination would have affected petitioner's statement only if a proper hearing at or before the 48-hour mark would have resulted in a finding of no probable cause. Yet, as the Magistrate found, the police had probable cause to suspect petitioner of child abuse, and there is no suggestion that the delay in securing a determination of probable cause permitted the police to gather additional evidence to be presented to the Magistrate. On the contrary, the Magistrate based his determination on the facts included in the declaration of arrest that was completed within an hour of petitioner's arrest. Thus, if the probable cause determination had been made within 48 hours as required by *McLaughlin*, the same information would have been presented, the same result would have been obtained, and none of the circumstances of petitioner's custody would have been altered.
>
> Moreover, it cannot be argued that the *McLaughlin* error somehow made petitioner's custody unlawful and thereby rendered the statement the product of unlawful custody. Because the arresting officers had probable cause to arrest petitioner, he was lawfully arrested at the hospital. The presumptively unconstitutional delay in securing a judicial determination of probable cause during a period of lawful custody did not render that custody illegal. We have never suggested that lawful custody becomes unlawful due to a failure to obtain a prompt judicial finding of probable cause—that is, probable cause does not disappear if not judicially determined within 48 hours.

511 U.S. at 89–91 114 S.Ct. at 1286–87 (Thomas, J., dissenting). Since the confession was not the product of illegal governmental activity, he added, "conventional attenuation principles are inapplicable in this case * * * ."

EDITORS' NOTE: PROPOSALS FOR REFORM OF CONFESSION LAW

Continuing dispute concerning constitutional and non-constitutional legal requirements for law enforcement and interrogation has given rise to a number of proposals for reform in this area. Some have been implemented, at least on a limited basis. The wisdom of these proposals, of course, cannot be fully addressed without considering the substance of existing law as developed in the remainder of this chapter. But that material is best considered in light of these alternative or additional possible ways of dealing with the problems the doctrines explored in this chapter are intended to address.

Recording of Interrogations and Confessions

Recording of custodial interrogation and suspects' resulting statements has long been urged by some. The Model Code of Pre-Arraignment Procedure, for example, proposed a requirement that sound recordings be made of warnings, waivers, questioning, and statements made in response to questioning. Model Code of Pre-Arraignment Procedure § 130.4(3) (Official Draft 1975). An extensive argument for videotaping was made in Leo, The Impact of Miranda Revisited, 86 J.Crim.L. & Crim. 621, 681–92 (1996).

The Alaska Supreme Court read the state's constitutional due process demand as requiring electronic recording of custodial interrogations. Stephan v. State, 711 P.2d 1156, 1162 (Alaska 1985). The Connecticut Supreme Court reviewed the case law in State v. Lockhart, 298 Conn. 537, 4 A.3d 1176 (2010), and noted that no other state court has held recording constitutionally required. *Lockhart* refused to read the Connecticut state constitutional requirement of due process as demanding recording.

Some state courts have adopted recording requirements pursuant to their supervisory authority. In Commonwealth v. DiGiambattista, 442 Mass. 423, 813 N.E.2d 516 (2004), for example, the court held on this basis as follows:

> [W]hen the prosecution introduces evidence of a defendant's confession or statement that is the product of a custodial interrogation or an interrogation conducted at a place of detention (e.g., a police station), and there is not at least an audiotape recording of the complete interrogation, the defendant is entitled (on request) to a jury instruction advising that the State's highest court has expressed a preference that such interrogations be recorded whenever practicable, and cautioning the jury that, because of the absence of any recording of the interrogation in the case before them, they should weigh evidence of the defendant's alleged statement with great caution and care.

442 Mass. at 447–448, 813 N.E.2d 516. In *Lockhart*, the Connecticut court declined to so exercise its supervisory authority largely on the basis that rules of this sort are more appropriate for legislative formulation.

Some states have adopted statutory recording requirements. Illinois has enacted a statute, effective in 2005, providing as follows:

§ 103–2.1. When statements by accused may be used.

* * *

(b) An oral, written, or sign language statement of an accused made as a result of a custodial interrogation at a police station or other place of detention shall be presumed to be inadmissible as evidence against the accused in any criminal proceeding * * * unless:

(1) an electronic recording is made of the custodial interrogation; and

(2) the recording is substantially accurate and not intentionally altered.

* * *

(d) If the court finds, by a preponderance of the evidence, that the defendant was subjected to a custodial interrogation in violation of this Section, then any statements made by the defendant during or following that non-recorded custodial interrogation, even if otherwise in compliance with this Section, are presumed to be inadmissible in any criminal proceeding against the defendant except for the purposes of impeachment.

(e) Nothing in this Section precludes the admission * * * of a statement made during a custodial interrogation by a suspect who requests, prior to making the statement, to respond to the interrogator's questions only if an electronic recording is not made of the statement, provided that an electronic recording is made of the statement of agreeing to respond to the interrogator's question, only if a recording is not made of the statement * * *. Nothing in this Section precludes the admission of a statement, otherwise inadmissible under this Section, that is used only for impeachment and not as substantive evidence.

(f) The presumption of inadmissibility of a statement made by a suspect at a custodial interrogation at a police station or other place of detention may be overcome by a preponderance of the evidence that the statement was voluntarily given and is reliable, based on the totality of the circumstances.

* * *

A May 12, 2014 Memo from the Deputy Attorney General of the United States established a federal policy that custodial statements of persons arrested by federal law enforcement officers are to be recorded if recording equipment is available. Certain exceptions apply. The memo stressed that the policy "does not create any rights or benefits, substantive or procedural, enforceable at law or in equity, in any manner, civil or criminal, by any party against the United States * * * or any * * * person * * * ."

News stories reported that the 2014 memo replaced prior policy set out in a 2006 memo which barred recording of statements. The prior policy was defended in part on grounds that recordings could disclose officers' interrogation methods, interfere with officers' effective use of rapport-building interrogation techniques, and discourage suspects from talking. It might also give jurors an unfavorable impression of federal officers. M. Schmidt, In Policy Change, Justice Dept. to Require Recording of Interrogations, New York Times, May 22, 2014.

Recordings may alter officers' conduct. For example, the Dallas, Texas police department decided to begin videotaping statements by homicide suspects, but only after training sessions for the detectives conducted by prosecutors. "[V]ideotapes, particularly of hours of interrogation leading up to a confession, can backfire on a detective who isn't trained to understand fully how their behavior will appear to jurors." Another person interviewed explained the need for training by commenting, "Some interrogators are more professional than others." Jason Trehan, Police to videotape confessions, *Dallas Morning News*, May 30, 2005, p. 9A.

Use of Expert Testimony on the Effects of Interrogation and Suspects' Decisions to Confess

Whatever restrictions are placed on the admissibility of confessions, it is inevitable that at many trials the triers of fact will have to address the credibility and perhaps also the voluntariness of confessions the defendants are shown to have been made. To what extent should defendants be able to introduce expert testimony in support of contentions that confessions they gave were involuntary, inaccurate, or both? Do defendants have any constitutional right to introduce such evidence?

In some cases, defendants have offered experts to testify only as to the occurrence and perhaps the frequency of false confessions. In others, the experts offer to testify that certain interrogation techniques tend to be associated with resulting false confessions and that particular characteristics of persons being interrogated—such as youth or developmental disability—tend to result in those persons giving false confessions. The experts may even be offered to testify as to the risk of false confessions created by the interrogation at issue in the case or as to an opinion as to whether the confession at issue in the case is accurate and reliable.

In a considerable number of cases defendants have offered testimony by persons who have done extensive research and writing on interrogation and false confessions, particularly Doctors Richard Leo, a psychologist, and Richard Ofshe who holds a Ph.D. in sociology.

Courts are divided on the limits placed by the law on trial judges' considerable discretion to exclude such testimony on a variety of grounds.

An Indiana trial judge was found to have erred in excluding the testimony of Dr. Ofshe, offered by the defense as an expert in the field of the "social psychology of police interrogation and false confessions." Police interrogators had falsely told the mentally retarded suspect his fingerprints had been found at the scene of the charged murder and the victim may have died from natural causes. Dr. Ofshe would have testified these techniques tend to persuade even innocent suspects that convictions are inevitable and ease the difficulty of admitting to involvement by persuading suspects that authorities may believe the actions involved were not criminal. He would also have testified that mentally impaired suspects are less able than other suspects to appreciate the long-range consequences of confessions, easier than other suspects to persuade to see the facts as asserted by interrogators, and generally more suggestible and more likely to give false confessions than other suspects. Dr. Ofshe's testimony, the defense claimed, was necessary to enable jurors to understand why the mentally retarded defendant "would succumb to the lies" although innocent of the crime. The Indiana Supreme Court agreed and explained:

> [T]he general substance of Dr. Ofshe's testimony would have assisted the jury regarding the psychology of relevant aspects of police interrogation and the interrogation of mentally retarded persons, topics outside common knowledge and experience. * * * We hold that excluding the proffered expert testimony in its entirety deprived the defendant of the opportunity to present a defense.

Miller v. State, 770 N.E.2d 763, 773–74 (Ind.2002).

At least one court has held that defendants' federal constitutional right to challenge the credibility of confession evidence, as established in Crane v. Kentucky, 476 U.S. 683, 106 S.Ct. 2142 (1986) (discussed earlier in this chapter), gives defendants a right to introduce some such expert testimony. People v. Lopez, 946 P.2d 478, 482–83 (Colo.App.1997), cert. denied. Others have held it admissible under general evidence law. Hannon v. State, 84 P.3d 320, 353 (Wyo.2004).

A number of courts, however, have held such expert testimony inadmissible or at least that trial judges did not err in rejecting specific offers of this sort of expert testimony. A trial judge might find that the effect of interrogation techniques upon the likelihood that an innocent person would confess is within the competence of jurors unassisted by expert testimony. See Commonwealth v. Tolan, 453 Mass. 634, 648, 904

N.E.2d 397, 410 (Mass.2009). One court held that in light of *Crane* and other authority, "a criminal defendant against whom a confession will be admitted may be permitted to introduce expert psychological or psychiatric testimony bearing on his or her ability to respond reliably to interrogation." It added, however, that "[i]t is essential, however, that the testimony actually tell jurors something they would not otherwise know from their usual human experience * * * ." State v. Oliver, 280 Kan. 681, 702, 124 P.3d 493, 508 (2005).

A trial judge might find that given the extent and nature of the research done in the area, an expert's proposed testimony was itself not established as reliable. People v. Kowalski, 2010 WL 3389741 (Mich.App.2010) (per curiam) (unreported) ("The principles and methodologies used by [the expert offered by the defendant] to arrive at his opinion that certain interrogation techniques correlate with false confessions were not shown to be reliable."); State v. Craven, 18 Neb.App. 633, 648, 790 N.W.2d 225, 236 (2010) (expert's "theory regarding false confessions was still being tested and subjected to peer review and publication, had no known rate of error, and had no specific standards to control its operation").

Whether the results of existing research can be—or will be in a particular case—presented in a manner that will enable jurors or judges to use it may be open to question. One trial judge, choosing to exclude such expert testimony, commented that the witness's "intricate testimony and explanation of coercive motivators, which in his opinion can lead to a false confession, was extremely confusing." People v. Rosario, 20 Misc.3d 401, 409, 862 N.Y.S.2d 719, 725 (N.Y.Sup.2008).

Courts have been particularly reluctant to permit defense experts to give testimony that can be construed as invading the province of the jury to assess credibility. For example, after the Indiana Supreme Court's decision in *Miller*, discussed above, an intermediate Indiana court held:

> We conclude that *Miller* generally [held] that * * * experts * * * may testify on the general subjects of coercive police interrogation and false or coerced confessions. The expert may not, however, comment about the specific interrogation in controversy in a way that may be interpreted by the jury as the expert's opinion that the confession in that particular case was coerced.

Fox v. State, 881 N.E.2d 733 (Ind.App.2008) (unpublished). The import of such testimony, one court explained, is to tell the jury to "disregard the confession and credit the defendant's testimony that his confession was a lie." Such testimony, it continued, usurps a critical function of the jury. United States v. Benally, 541 F.3d 990, 995 (10th Cir.2008). The Kansas Supreme court in *Oliver*, discussed earlier, made clear the testimony it held admissible must "remain hypothetical or theoretical" and "[i]t must stop short of expressing the expert's judgment on the defendant's reliability in the specific instance of the confession submitted for the jury's consideration." *Oliver*, 280 Kan. at 712, 124 P.3d at 508.

Judicial Review of Offered Confessions for Reliability

Some propose that trial judges be required to scrutinize offers of confession evidence for the reliability of the proffered confession. Richard A. Leo, Steven A. Drizin, Peter J. Neufeld, Bradley R. Hall, Amy Vatner, Bringing Reliability Back In: False Confessions and Legal Safeguards In the Twenty-First Century, 2006 Wis. L. Rev. 479, for example, offered a revised version of the approach suggested in Richard J. Ofshe & Richard A. Leo, The Social Psychology of Police Interrogation: The Theory and Classification of True and False Confessions. 16 Stud. L. Pol. & Soc'y 189 (1997).

Existing evidence law authorizes trial judges to exclude evidence upon a determination that the probative value of the evidence is outweighed by the risk of unfair or undue prejudice. Leo and his co-authors propose that trial judges exercise this power to review confession evidence that is offered by the prosecution and survives and challenges on voluntariness or other grounds. Leo et al. suggest specifically:

> Judges evaluating the reliability of confessions * * * should weigh three factors: 1) whether the confession contains nonpublic information that can be independently verified, would only be known by the true perpetrator or an accomplice, and cannot likely be guessed by chance; 2) whether the suspect's confession led the police to new evidence about the crime; and 3) whether the suspect's postadmission narrative "fits" (or fails to fit) with the crime facts and existing objective evidence.

2006 Wis. L. Rev. at 531. Defendants should have the burden of producing some evidence that the confession is unreliable. The prosecution should have the ultimate burden of persuading the judge— by a preponderance of the evidence—that the probative value of the confession is not outweighed by the risk of unfair or undue prejudice.

The proposal assumes that interrogations would be recorded and that trial courts, aiding by such recordings, could resolve challenges under the proposed standard with reasonable efficiency.

B. THE REQUIREMENT OF "VOLUNTARINESS"

EDITORS' INTRODUCTION: CONTENT AND CURRENT SIGNIFICANCE OF THE VOLUNTARINESS REQUIREMENT

Because of the widespread publicity given the *Miranda* decision, contemporary discussions of "confession law" tend to revolve around the *Miranda* requirements. An adequate understanding of the reasons for the "*Miranda* revolution," however, demands acquaintance with pre-*Miranda* voluntariness law.

In addition, the voluntariness requirement is not without current significance. If *Miranda* does not apply to a given situation, the voluntariness requirement is likely to be the major consideration in determining whether a confession can be used in evidence. If a confession is inadmissible to prove a defendant's guilt because of the *Miranda* requirements, its availability to impeach the defendant's credibility—should the defendant testify at trial—apparently depends in part upon the voluntariness of the admission. Even if *Miranda* applies to a situation, there is a high likelihood that the effectiveness of the suspect's waiver of the rights to silence and to counsel will be at issue. Traditional voluntariness law undoubtedly bears upon the appropriate resolution of such matters. Further, if a suspect has given several confessions and *Miranda* was violated only during the elicitation of the first, the admissibility of the later confessions depends largely or entirely upon their voluntariness.

Current Content of the Voluntariness Requirement.

The content of the federal constitutional requirement of voluntariness has evolved as that requirement developed. In Blackburn v. Alabama, 361 U.S. 199, 80 S.Ct. 274 (1960), the Supreme Court observed that "a complex of values underlies the stricture against use by the state of confessions which, by way of convenient shorthand, this Court terms involuntary, and the role played by each in any situation varies according to the particular circumstances of the case." The Court commented further upon these values:

> The abhorrence of society to the use of involuntary confessions does not turn alone on their inherent untrustworthiness. It also turns on the deep-rooted feeling that the police must obey the law while enforcing the law; that in the end life and liberty can be as much endangered from illegal methods used to convict those thought to be criminals as from the actual criminals themselves. Accordingly, the actions of police in obtaining confessions * * * come under scrutiny * * * .

Spano v. New York, 360 U.S. 315, 320–21, 79 S.Ct. 1202, 1205–06 (1959).

Brown and many early cases involved "coerced" confessions—that is, confessions stimulated by improper violence or the threat of such violence. In *Brown,* for example, police beat the suspects and told them such beatings would continue until the suspects provided confessions of the substance desired by the officers. But in subsequent cases the Court extended the prohibition against involuntary confessions far beyond such coerced statements.

Need for Coercive Law Enforcement Conduct.

A major limitation of the due process requirement was applied in Colorado v. Connelly, 479 U.S. 157, 107 S.Ct. 515 (1986). Connelly introduced evidence that he suffered from a mental illness and, as a result, had heard a voice he believed was that of God, telling him he had to admit to a murder or commit suicide. The state courts held the resulting confession involuntary and inadmissible because Connelly's decision to confess did not reflect a meaningfully free choice. Justice Brennan, joined by Justice Marshall agreed, reasoning that due process voluntariness requires that a confession reflect "the exercise of free will" and Connelly's did not. A trial court's use of the confession would constitute state action. Justice Brennan continued:

> Minimum standards of due process should require that the trial court find substantial indicia of reliability, on the basis of evidence extrinsic to the confession itself, before admitting the confession of a mentally ill person into evidence. I would require the trial court to make such a finding on remand.

479 U.S. at 183, 107 S.Ct. at 530.

The *Connelly* majority, however, held the Colorado courts had erred. The due process requirement is implicated, the Court explained, only where a confession fails to reflect a free choice because of coercive governmental conduct. None was shown by the evidence before it. Due process voluntariness does not impose a general requirement of free will or reliability:

> [S]uppressing [Connelly]'s statements would serve absolutely no purpose in enforcing constitutional guarantees. The purpose of excluding evidence seized in violation of the Constitution is to substantially deter future violations of the Constitution. Only if we were to establish a brand new constitutional right—the right of a criminal defendant to confess to his crime only when totally rational and properly motivated—could respondent's present claim be sustained.

> We have previously cautioned against expanding "currently applicable exclusionary rules by erecting additional barriers to placing truthful and probative evidence before state juries. . . ." We abide by that counsel now. "[T]he central purpose of a criminal trial is to decide the factual question of the defendant's guilt or innocence," and while we have previously held that exclusion of evidence may be necessary to protect constitutional guarantees, both the necessity for the collateral inquiry and the exclusion of evidence deflect a criminal trial from its basic purpose. [Connelly] would now have us require sweeping inquiries into the state of mind of a criminal defendant who has confessed, inquiries quite divorced from any coercion brought to bear on the defendant by the State. We think the Constitution rightly leaves this sort of inquiry to be resolved by state laws governing the admission of evidence and erects no standard of its own in this area. A statement rendered by one in the condition of respondent might be proved to be quite unreliable, but this is a matter to be governed by the evidentiary laws of the forum, see, *e.g.,* Fed.Rule Evid. 601, and not by the Due

Process Clause of the Fourteenth Amendment. "The aim of the requirement of due process is not to exclude presumptively false evidence, but to prevent fundamental unfairness in the use of evidence, whether true or false." *Lisenba v. California,* 314 U.S. 219, 236, 62 S.Ct. 280, 290, 86 L.Ed. 166 (1941).

We hold that coercive police activity is a necessary predicate to the finding that a confession is not "voluntary" within the meaning of the Due Process Clause of the Fourteenth Amendment.

479 U.S. at 166–167, 107 S.Ct. at 521–22. "The most outrageous behavior by a private party seeking to secure evidence against a defendant," it noted, "does not make that evidence inadmissible under the Due Process Clause."

The Court did seem to suggest that at least in some circumstances coercive police activity might be found if interrogating officers were aware of the suspect's impairment and exploited that in their questioning.

It indicated further that if evidence shows the coercive police activity necessary to trigger due process analysis, the suspect's impairment would be properly considered in deciding whether the effect of that activity was to render a particular statement involuntary.

Also at issue in *Connelly* were statements made later to which *Miranda* applied. These and issues they raised are considered later in this chapter.

Beyond Physical Coercion—Overbearing of the Will.

"[C]oercion can be mental as well as physical" the Court noted in Blackburn v. Alabama, "and * * * the blood of the accused is not the only hallmark of an unconstitutional inquisition." In Spano v. New York, the Court observed:

> [A]s * * * the methods used to extract confessions [become] more sophisticated, our duty to enforce federal constitutional protections does not cease. It only becomes more difficult because of the more delicate judgments to be made.

360 U.S. at 321, 79 S.Ct. at 1206.

In cases lacking overt brutality, the Court has applied a "totality of the circumstances" analysis. Justice Frankfurter articulated the classic statement of this approach:

> No single litmus-paper test for constitutionally-impermissible interrogation has been evolved: neither extensive cross questioning * * *; nor undue delay in arraignment * * *; nor failure to caution a prisoner * * *; nor refusal to permit communication with friends and legal counsel at stages in the proceeding when the prisoner is still only a suspect * * * .

Each of these factors, in company with all of the surrounding circumstances—the duration and conditions of detention (if the confessor has been detained), the manifest attitude of the police towards him, his physical and mental state, the diverse pressures which sap or sustain his powers of resistance and self-control—is relevant. The ultimate test remains * * * : * * * Is the confession the product of an essentially free and unconstrained choice by its maker? * * * [I]f his will has been overborne and his capacity for self-determination critically impaired, the use of his confession offends due process.

Culombe v. Connecticut, 367 U.S. 568, 601–02, 81 S.Ct. 1860, 1878–79 (1961).

Under this approach, the courts have been reluctant to characterize particular interrogation techniques as necessarily impermissible. In Bobby v. Dixon, ___ U.S. ___, 132 S.Ct. 26 (2011) (per curiam), for example, the federal court below had held that proof that interrogating officers had urged him to "cut a deal" before his accomplice did so clearly established Dixon's confession was involuntary. This, the Supreme Court held, was error: "[N]o holding of this Court suggests, much less clearly establishes, that police may not urge a suspect to confess before another suspect does so * * * ." ___ U.S. at ___, 132 S.Ct. at 30.

Greenwald v. Wisconsin, 390 U.S. 519, 88 S.Ct. 1152 (1968) (per curiam), illustrated application of the "totality of the circumstances" test. Although the case was decided by the Supreme Court after *Miranda*, *Miranda*'s nonretroactivity meant that *Miranda* did not govern the admissibility of the confession. The facts were as follows:

[Greenwald], who has a ninth-grade education, was arrested on suspicion of burglary shortly before 10:45 on the evening of January 20, 1965. He was taken to a police station. He was suffering from high blood pressure, a condition for which he was taking medication twice a day. [He] had last taken food and medication, before his arrest, at 4 p.m. He did not have medication with him at the time of the arrest. At the police station [he] was interrogated from 10:45 until midnight. He was not advised of his constitutional rights. [He] repeatedly denied guilt. No incriminating statements were made at this time.

[He] was booked and fingerprinted and, sometime after 2 a.m., he was taken to a cell in the city jail. A plank fastened to the wall served as his bed. [He] claims he did not sleep. At 6 a.m., [he] was led from the cell to a "bullpen." At 8:30 he was placed in a lineup. At 8:45, his interrogation recommenced. It was conducted by several officers at a time, in a small room. [Greenwald] testified that in the course of the morning he was not offered food and that he continued to be without medication.

For an hour or two he refused to answer any questions. When he did speak, it was to deny, once again, his guilt.

Sometime after 10 a.m., [Greenwald] was asked to write out a confession. He refused, stating that "it was against my constitutional rights" and that he was "entitled to have a lawyer." These statements were ignored. No further reference was made to an attorney, by [Greenwald] or by the police officers.

At about 11 a.m. [Greenwald] began a series of oral admissions culminating in a full oral confession at about 11:30. At noon he was offered food. The confession was reduced to writing about 1 p.m. Just before the confession was reduced to writing, [he] was advised of his constitutional rights. According to his testimony, he confessed because "I knew they weren't going to leave me alone until I did."

Considering the totality of these circumstances, a majority of the Court held the Wisconsin Supreme Court had erred in finding that Greenwald's statements "were the product of his free and rational choice." Justice Stewart, joined by two other members of the Court, read the circumstances as adequately supporting the state court's conclusion:

[Greenwald] was nearly 30 years old and was by no means a stranger to the criminal law. He was questioned for little more than an hour one evening and for less than four hours the next morning. He was neither abused nor threatened and was promised no benefit for confessing. * * * [H]e himself testified that, during his interrogation, "he knew he had a constitutional right to refuse to answer any questions, * * * he knew anything he said could be used against him, and * * * he knew he had a constitutional right to retain counsel." Moreover, * * * [he] himself testified that at no time between his arrest and his confession did he express to anyone a desire for food or for medication.

390 U.S. at 521–22, 88 S.Ct. at 1154 (Stewart, J., dissenting).

As applied in cases such as *Greenwald*, does the voluntariness case law provide a meaningful standard for determining the admissibility of confessions? Judge Posner of the Seventh Circuit suggested not:

[W]hether a confession is voluntary is not really a fact, but a characterization. There is indeed no "faculty of will" inside our heads that has two states, on and off, such that through careful reconstruction of events the observer can determine whether the switch was on when the defendant was confessing. * * *

[C]ourts have not been successful in devising a standard that will determine in a consistent fashion when confessions should be excluded on grounds of involuntariness. Of course if the confession is unreliable, it should go out, along with other unreliable evidence. It is on this basis that confessions extracted by torture are excluded. But in most cases in which a confession is sought to be excluded because involuntary, there is little likelihood that the inducements placed before the defendant were so overpowering as to induce an untrue confession. The courts in such cases retreat to the proposition that a confession, to be admissible, must be the product of a free choice. [B]ut [this] is just the faculty of will approach, and, as the courts are beginning to suspect, it leads nowhere. Taken seriously it would require the exclusion of virtually all fruits of custodial interrogation, since few choices to confess can be thought truly "free" when made by a person who is incarcerated and is being questioned by armed officers without the presence of counsel or anyone else to give him moral support. The formula is not taken seriously. * * * [V]ery few incriminating statements, custodial or otherwise, are held to be involuntary, though few are the product of a choice that the interrogators left completely free.

United States v. Rutledge, 900 F.2d 1127, 1128–29 (7th Cir.1990) (Posner, J.).

Promises.

The traditional requirement of voluntariness mandated exclusion of a confession obtained as a result of a promise or inducement, made by a person in a position of authority, concerning the criminal charges to which the defendant confessed. See generally, Dix, Mistake, Ignorance, Expectation of Benefit, and the Modern Law of Confessions, 1975 Wash.U.L.Q. 275 (1975). In Bram v. United States, 168 U.S. 532, 18 S.Ct. 183 (1897), the Supreme Court appeared to incorporate this traditional requirement into the due process voluntariness standard.

The Supreme Court addressed the modern constitutional significance of promises in Arizona v. Fulminante, 499 U.S. 279, 111 S.Ct. 1246 (1991). Fulminante was a prisoner in a federal correctional facility and had begun to receive "rough treatment" from other inmates because of a rumor he had killed a child. Sarivola was a fellow inmate who was also an informant for the Federal Bureau of Investigation. Federal agents encouraged Sarivola to elicit information about the killing from Fulminante. Sarivola then offered to protect Fulminante from other inmates if Fulminante told him about the matter. Fulminante admitted the killing to Sarivola. At Fulminante's trial for the murder of the child, the prosecution successfully offered his confession to Sarivola. On appeal, the Arizona Supreme Court reversed, holding the confession inadmissible. The Supreme Court granted review to consider the State's contention that the Arizona Supreme Court had incorrectly applied a standard under which the confession was involuntary upon proof that "but for" the "promise" by Sarivola, Fulminante would not have made the confession.

The Court noted the *Bram* language but made clear that this 1897 discussion's statement of voluntariness was no longer accurate federal constitutional law:

> Although the Court noted in *Bram* that a confession cannot be obtained by " 'any direct or implied promises, however slight, nor by the exertion of any improper influence,' " it is clear this passage from *Bram* * * * does not state the standard for determining the voluntariness of a confession * * * .

499 U.S. at 285, 111 S.Ct. at 1251. It further found, however, that the Arizona court had properly applied a totality of the circumstances analysis. Although the question was a "close one," the majority concluded, the Arizona court acceptably found the confession involuntary:

> The Arizona Supreme Court found a credible threat of physical violence unless Fulminante confessed. Our cases have made clear that a finding of coercion need not depend upon actual violence by a government agent; a credible threat is sufficient. * * * [T]he Arizona Supreme Court found that it was fear of physical violence, absent protection from his friend (and Government agent) Sarivola, which motivated Fulminante to confess. Accepting the Arizona court's finding, permissible on this record, that there was a credible threat of physical violence, we agree with its conclusion that Fulminante's will was overborne in such a way as to render his confession the product of coercion.

499 U.S. at 287, 111 S.Ct. at 1252–53.

In applying voluntariness analyses that weigh promises of leniency in favor of a finding of inadmissibility, courts often distinguish promises from mere admonitions to tell the truth and similar communications that do not militate significantly if at all against admissibility. Impermissible coercion is not established, one court summarized, by an officer's assurance that the defendant's cooperation will be considered and/or helpful, a mere suggestion that cooperation may result in more lenient treatment, an offer to help if the defendant confesses, or an admonition that telling the truth will result in a benefit that flows naturally from being truthful. State v. Jones, 2015-Ohio-4116, ¶ 19, 43 N.E.3d 833, 845 (App.2015). On the other hand, an officer's "promise" that if the defendant confessed to involvement in the events under investigation he would be charged with attempted robbery rather than attempted murder was coercive conduct rendering the confession inadmissible. Squire v. State, 193 So.3d 105, 108–09 (Fla.App. 2016).

Some state courts, sometimes implementing statutory provisions to this effect, have indicated that a promise of a benefit or leniency will render a confession involuntary if that promise is one that could, or is likely to, cause a person to falsely confess. E.g., State v. Sharp, 289 Kan. 72, 82, 210 P.3d 590, 598–99 (Kan.2009).

Courts have given particular significance to so-called *false* promises. E.g., Alexander v. DeAngelo, 329 F.3d 912, 918 (7th Cir.2003) (despite rule that officers may "actively mislead" a suspect, a confession induced by a false promise of leniency may be deemed coerced and therefore inadmissible). A confession given in return for the officer's promise to keep it confidential, for example, may be inadmissible as the product of a false promise. See State v. Dodge, 17 A.3d 128, 133–34 (Me.2011). One court explained:

> The reason we treat a false promise differently than other somewhat deceptive police tactics (such as cajoling and duplicity) is that a false promise has the unique potential to make a decision to speak irrational and the resulting confession unreliable. Police conduct that influences a rational person who is innocent to view a false confession as more beneficial than being honest is necessarily coercive, because of the way it realigns a suspect's incentives during interrogation. "An empty prosecutorial promise could prevent a suspect from making a rational choice by distorting the alternatives among which the person under interrogation is being asked to choose." The ultimate result of a coercive interrogation is unreliable.

United States v. Villalpando, 588 F.3d 1124, 1128 (7th Cir.2009).

As the principal case following makes clear, promise aspects of voluntariness continue to present courts with difficulties.

Deception.

Despite the case law's traditionally rigid prohibition against promises, American courts developed no similar voluntariness rule barring police officers from deceiving suspects during interrogation, at least when that deception involves factual matters. "False statements by officers concerning evidence, as contrasted with threats or promises, have been tolerated in confession cases generally, because such statements do not affect the reliability of the confession." State v. Smith, 698 S.E.2d 556 (N.C.App.2010) (unpublished), quoting from *State v. Jackson,* 308 N.C. 549, 574, 304 S.E.2d 134, 148 (1983).

The Supreme Court did not address the relationship between deception and the federal due process standard until Frazier v. Cupp, 394 U.S. 731, 89 S.Ct. 1420 (1969). Although *Frazier* was decided after *Miranda, Miranda*'s requirements did not apply to the confession at issue in *Frazier*. Therefore the confession's admissibility turned upon its Due Process voluntariness.

Police interrogated Frazier; he denied committing the offense and claimed to have been with his cousin, Rawls, on the night of the crime. The officer then falsely told Frazier that Rawls had confessed to the murder. Subsequently, Frazier decided to make a statement. The trial court, over defense objection, admitted the statement at Frazier's trial.

The Supreme Court found no violation of the due process standard. It noted that Frazier had received a "partial warning" of his constitutional rights, the questioning was of short duration, and Frazier was "a mature individual of normal intelligence." Without citation of authority or discussion of the relevant considerations, the Court then commented, "The fact that the police misrepresented the statement that Rawls made is, while relevant, insufficient in our view to make this otherwise voluntary confession inadmissible."

Lower courts tend to follow the approach taken in *Frazier*, although sometimes with discomfort. "While 'we expressly disapprove of the tactics of making deliberate and intentionally false statements to suspects in an effort to obtain a statement,'" one court stated, "the use of such aggressive interrogation techniques is just one factor to be considered in analyzing the totality of the circumstances." Commonwealth v. Neves, 474 Mass. 355, 362, 50 N.E.3d 428, 436 (2016).

Some lower courts have at least suggested that deception will itself render a confession involuntary and inadmissible if, but only, it is deception "of a type reasonably likely to produce an untrue statement." People v. Scott, 52 Cal.4th 452, 481, 129 Cal.Rptr.3d 91, 257 P.3d 703, 727 (2011). Courts have been more receptive to attacks based on deception concerning matters other than the nature and amount of evidence authorities have of the suspect's guilt. Officers may, for example, misrepresent that the suspect's refusal to confess will result in the arrest of vulnerable members of the suspect's family. It has been suggested that such misrepresentations are a greater threat to voluntariness because—unlike the case regarding deception concerning evidence—the suspect lacks personal knowledge that would enable him to recognize the inaccurately of the officers' representations. See Brisbon v. United States, 957 A.2d 931, 944–49 (D.C.2008).

* * *

The principal case in this section reflects a lower court's effort to apply the voluntariness requirement to what might be regarded as bargaining between a suspect and law enforcement officers. When the Supreme Court later addressed the case, the Court did not reach the issue addressed in the opinions reprinted here.

Moore v. Czerniak[1]

Ninth Circuit Court of Appeals, 2009.
574 F.3d 1092.

■ Before: STEPHEN REINHARDT, MARSHA S. BERZON, and JAY S. BYBEE, CIRCUIT JUDGES.

■ REINHARDT, CIRCUIT JUDGE:

[This is an appeal from petitioner Randy Moore's unsuccessful effort to get federal habeas corpus relief from his Oregon conviction for felony murder. The conviction was based upon Moore's plea of no contest, made on the advice of counsel who had not moved to suppress the taped confession Moore gave to Josephine County, Oregon officers at the Josephine County Sheriff's department.

Moore contends his conviction was fatally tainted by defense counsel's ineffective assistance under *Strickland v. Washington,* 466 U.S. 668, 104 S.Ct. 2052 (1984). To prevail on a claim of ineffective assistance of counsel under *Strickland,* Moore must demonstrate both that his counsel's representation was deficient—in other words, that it "fell below an objective standard of reasonableness"—and that the deficiency was prejudicial. To show prejudice, Moore must demonstrate that "there is a reasonable probability that, but for counsel's unprofessional errors, the result of the proceeding would have been different. A reasonable probability is a probability sufficient to undermine confidence in the outcome." In the context of a plea bargain, we specifically ask whether there is a reasonable probability that, but for counsel's deficient performance, the petitioner would have gone to trial rather than accept the plea bargain offered by the state.]

In December 1995, petitioner Randy Moore, his half-brother Lonnie Woolhiser, and his friend Roy Salyer were allegedly involved in the assault, kidnapping, and death of Kenneth Rogers. After arresting Salyer and booking him in the county jail, the investigating police officers asked Moore and Woolhiser to come to the police station for questioning. The two were separated and interviews were conducted by different police detectives. Moore provided a brief statement about stopping by Rogers's motor home, waiting while Woolhiser and Salyer went in to talk to Rogers, and then leaving with Woolhiser and Salyer. After making this statement, Moore was advised of and invoked his *Miranda* rights. Subsequently, as the district court found, both Moore and Woolhiser were released on the condition that they speak with their older brother Raymond Moore ("Raymond"), and return to the station at 1:00 p.m. the following day.

The police officers had good reason for directing Moore and Woolhiser to speak with Raymond. Raymond had a personal and working relationship with the investigating officers. Moreover, these officers had

---

1   [Some portions of the opinions that appeared in footnotes have been editorially inserted into the text of those opinions. Eds.]

been involved in the investigation of a murder charge against Raymond that resulted from a separate killing. The charge was dropped when Raymond cooperated with the officers and explained that the killing was perpetrated in self-defense. Raymond testified later that because Moore and Woolhiser told him that Rogers's death was an accident, he believed that the police officers would do the same for his brother and half-brother as they had for him, if they cooperated in the same manner he had.

The next day, after speaking with Raymond, Moore and Woolhiser spent the morning unsuccessfully trying to obtain legal representation. When they called the police station at 1:10 p.m., the police promptly ordered them to return for further questioning: "they told us that if we were not there by 3:00 they would come get us—[ ] and our family would not like the way they did it and they—we knew what they meant." In accordance with the police officers' commands, Moore and Woolhiser returned to the police station that afternoon, without counsel. They were accompanied by Raymond, and also by Woolhiser's girlfriend, Debbie Ziegler.

When the four arrived at the police station, the investigating officers began another round of questioning. Moore interrupted at the very beginning of that questioning to request counsel: "You see . . . until I, I have to be able to talk to somebody that's on my side, you know, for me, to be able to go tell nobody . . . I don't trust my judgment right now." When the police officers ignored Moore's request, Woolhiser reiterated by stating, "You know, we'd just like to talk to somebody, you know." Moore then stated that he wanted to, "[a]s quick as possible, talk to a lawyer," which was followed by Raymond's confirmation of that request: "If there was some way we could maybe get an attorney in here for a consultation." Eventually, in response, the police officers told Moore and Woolhiser that they were not entitled to counsel at that time unless they could afford it themselves. The police officers then promptly proceeded with the interrogation.

During the interrogation, the police officers told Moore and Woolhiser that they "would go to bat for [them] as long as [they] got the truth," to which Moore responded: "See that's what I want to hear." At this point, Raymond interrupted the questioning to vouch for the officers' assurances, stating that "I know in my, this is for myself, saying, there was once an officer, and I said hey, look, I want out, I did something and been doing something. I want out of this, I want a chance. And this officer said, okay, Ray, I'll go to bat for you. And that officer's your captain." Building on Raymond's account, one of the interrogating officers asked, "But he did go to bat for you[?]," to which Raymond responded, "That's exactly right. . . . I talked to him and he stood behind his word one hundred percent and he's probably one of the best friends I have in the world."

After Raymond's comments, the interrogating officers emphasized that the police could be similarly helpful to Moore and Woolhiser if they confessed. Moore first hesitated, but then indicated that he would be willing to talk. At this point, one of the officers told Moore, "Okay, so that you know you're going to get a fair shake from us alright, I want to verify that with our DA that he is not going and [sic] turn around and jam you. I want him to tell me right now on the phone that you can change your mind and he will accept it. So there's no jammin' down the road, okay?" The officer then left to obtain the verification that the DA would not "jam" Moore so long as he confessed.

When the officer returned, he told Moore that he had spoken with the DA—"our Deputy DA actually"—and then proceeded to elicit Moore's confession. Before doing so, however, he extracted several statements from Moore regarding his custody status and the voluntariness of the confession he was about to give. In response to a series of questions, Moore agreed with the officers that he had voluntarily returned to the police station, that he was not in custody, that the police had offered nothing in exchange for his confession other than that they would make a "recommendation[ ]" to the District Attorney, and that he understood his right to counsel and was waiving it. In short, as one of the interrogating officers explained: "[t]he main thing is we want everybody on this recording to know that you guys are not in custody . . . [a]nd this is not an . . . in custody interrogation type of thing."

In the recorded confession that he then made, Moore described how he, Salyer, and Woolhiser went to Rogers's home after Salyer informed the two that Rogers had stolen property from his cabin. Moore stated that Woolhiser confronted Rogers about the theft, assaulted him, and placed him in the trunk of a car. They then drove Rogers to a remote wooded area and began to walk him blindfolded up a hill. At some point during this walk, Woolhiser handed Moore a loaded gun. Moore explained that they had no intention of killing Rogers; they were simply going to frighten him by leaving him on top of the hill and forcing him to find his way back home. As the four climbed the hill, however, Rogers stumbled and fell back into Moore, causing the gun in his hands to discharge. As a result, Rogers died of an accidental gunshot wound to the head.

Following his confession, Moore was appointed counsel and charged with one count of felony murder with a firearm. He entered a plea of no contest, and was given a mandatory sentence of twenty-five years imprisonment * * * . Moore appealed his sentence to the Oregon Court of Appeals, which affirmed without opinion, and to the Oregon Supreme Court, which denied review.

Shortly thereafter, Moore filed a petition for state post-conviction relief, alleging, *inter alia,* that he had been denied effective assistance of counsel because his lawyer had failed to file a motion to suppress his confession. The state court held an evidentiary hearing at which Moore and his brother Raymond testified. Raymond recalled that the detectives "made it appear" that Moore and Woolhiser were not in custody, but that it was clear from the circumstances that they were not free to leave. He also testified that he advised the pair to confess their involvement in Rogers's death because he understood that the police had promised leniency: "[B]asically what I had deducted [sic] from what they had said was that they would work for [Moore] like they had worked for me to change my life around."

Moore also testified that he understood the officers' statements to be an assurance that his crime would be charged as an accidental killing rather than felony murder. He stated that the officers "left me believing that the D.A. had agreed not to ja[m] us down the road. . . . [W]hen the detective went and talked to the D.A. to make sure he wasn't going to ja[m] me, I thought there was an agreement that they were going to charge me with accidental death and the D.A. had agreed to it because he didn't come back saying that he did not agree, and that's what he went there for." Moreover, Moore explained that during the interrogation, he did not feel free to leave, in part because detectives had made it clear on the evening prior to the interview that Salyer had already been charged and that they were going to be booked that day.

After the evidentiary hearing, the state court filed an unpublished order denying Moore's post-conviction petition. * * * [T]he state court * * * reasoned [in part] that even if a motion to suppress had been filed and granted, it would have been "fruitless" because Moore "had previously confessed his participation in the crime to his brother (Raymond Moore) and another friend [Debbie Ziegler]." From this, the state court concluded that Moore suffered no prejudice because "[b]oth Raymond Moore and [Ziegler] could have been called as witnesses to repeat petitioner's confession." * * *

In December 2001, Moore petitioned the United States District Court for the District of Oregon for a writ of habeas corpus. He raised, *inter alia,* the ineffective assistance of counsel claim that was denied in the state courts. Adopting the magistrate judge's findings and recommendation, the district court found that * * * [Moore] had "confessed to Rogers' murder based on [a] false promise" of leniency, which "rendered [his] confession involuntary." Nevertheless, the court concluded that "counsel's failure to seek suppression did not necessarily fall below an objective standard of reasonableness" because of Moore's prior confessions to Raymond Moore and Debbie Ziegler and the potential adverse testimony of Salyer. On that basis, the district court ultimately held that the post-conviction court's conclusion that there had not been a constitutional violation was "neither contrary to, nor an unreasonable application of, *Strickland v. Washington.*"

This appeal followed. * * *

Moore's trial counsel stated [he did not file a motion to suppress in part[2] because] counsel believed * * * " * * * the statement was voluntary." * * *

Moore urges * * * a motion to suppress his confession would have been meritorious [because] his confession was involuntary, having been extracted as the result of a promise of leniency made by the interrogating officers. The state court * * * did not * * * address the involuntariness question. On federal habeas review, the district court * * * found that a motion to suppress would have been meritorious on the involuntariness ground. Critically, the state does not challenge the district court's determination on appeal. Thus, * * * we simply accept as correct the district court's finding that Moore's confession was involuntary—and, consequently, that a motion to suppress would have been meritorious on that ground.

We note, however, that had the state contested the district court's voluntariness determination, we could not conclude that the district court had erred * * * in finding that Moore's confession was made in response to a false promise that the charges against him would be reduced if he confessed to accidentally killing Rogers. The officers repeatedly told Moore that they would "go to bat for him" if he confessed. More important, the officers reminded Moore of the experience of his brother Raymond, whose murder charges had been dismissed at their instigation when Raymond explained that the killing was accidental, and used Raymond's own personal reaffirmation of the events to convince Moore that his treatment would follow in the same vein. Throughout the interrogation, the officers implied that if he agreed to talk, Moore would receive the same treatment his brother did—that is, that the charges against him would be dropped, or, more likely, reduced from murder to a lesser offense. The officers also purported to clear the arrangement with the District Attorney, reassuring Moore that he would be taken care of as long as he told the truth. Given these facts, we fully agree with the district court's conclusion that the officers created an implied promise that Moore would not be charged with intentional murder or felony murder if he confessed to Rogers's accidental killing, and that this promise was "sufficiently compelling to overbear [Moore's] will."

Having determined that a motion to suppress Moore's confession, had it been filed, would have been meritorious, we must now consider whether counsel's failure to file such a suppression motion was objectively unreasonable. We conclude that it was.

* * *

It has long been clear that *Strickland*'s prejudice prong requires no more than a "show[ing] that there is a reasonable probability that, but

---

[2] [Those portions of the opinions addressing counsel's failure to seek suppression on the ground that Moore was actually in custody and thus had been denied his right to counsel are omitted. Eds.]

for counsel's unprofessional errors, the result of the proceeding would have been different." * * *

The probability that Moore would not have pled to a felony murder charge with a mandatory twenty-five-year sentence had his counsel filed a motion to suppress the taped confession is more than "sufficient to undermine confidence in the outcome" under *Strickland.* Without Moore's formal, taped confession, the state's case would have been far weaker. * * *

* * *

* * * We conclude that Moore was prejudiced by his counsel's failure to file the suppression motion and that, because counsel's performance fell below an objective standard of reasonableness, he received ineffective assistance of counsel under *Strickland.* * * * Accordingly, Moore is entitled to a writ of habeas corpus directing the state to permit him to withdraw his plea or to release him from custody. Accordingly, we reverse the district court and remand for the issuance of the writ.

Reversed and Remanded.

■ BERZON, CIRCUIT JUDGE, concurring:

I concur in Judge Reinhardt's result and almost all of his opinion.

* * * Because the state has, by forfeiture, acknowledged that Moore's confession was involuntary for the purposes of this appeal, I see no reason to reach that issue de novo. I therefore do not concur in [that portion] of the majority opinion, which does so. * * *

■ BYBEE, CIRCUIT JUDGE, dissenting:

* * * I agree with the majority that the question of voluntariness * * * is not properly before us. I note that, were the issue preserved, a persuasive argument could be made that the confession was in fact given voluntarily.

The district court based its finding of involuntariness on an implied promise of leniency that the police allegedly gave to Moore. Yet, to use Moore's own words, the officers promised him "[n]othing other [than] helping the best [they] could." This offer to recommend leniency to the district attorney is inadequate to establish that "all of the attendant circumstances" indicate that " 'the defendant's will was overborne at the time he confessed.' " * * * *see* * * * *United States v. Guerrero,* 847 F.2d 1363, 1366 (9th Cir.1988) ("An interrogating agent's promise to inform the government prosecutor about a suspect's cooperation does not render a subsequent statement involuntary, even when it is accompanied by a promise to recommend leniency or by speculation that cooperation will have a positive effect."). The record demonstrates that the police could not have promised anything other than a recommendation of leniency— and certainly could not promise a reduction of charges—because Moore had not been formally booked or charged when he made his confession.

Since the state—inexplicably—has not pressed this issue on appeal, I proceed on the assumption that Moore has demonstrated that his confession was involuntarily given. * * *

* * * Moore is plainly guilty of felony murder, or worse. He took a fair deal from the prosecutor on the advice of competent counsel. Justice was served. There is no reason for us to up-end the orderly administration of justice in Oregon * * * .

I respectfully dissent.

NOTES

1.   The Supreme Court granted review. Belleque v. Moore, 559 U.S. 1004, 130 S.Ct. 1882 (2010). One brief to the Court addressed an aspect of the voluntariness issue:

> The Court of Appeals majority interprets the police officers statements that they would "go to bat" for Moore if he told the truth, along with references to his brother's case in which charges were dropped, as promises to give Moore immunity or at least charge him with something less than murder. This interpretation is not credible. In the brother's case, he said the killing was self-defense, not a crime at all, and that statement was apparently believed. In other words, the brother made a statement, the statement was deemed to be true, and he was not charged with anything *more* than he confessed to, which was justifiable homicide and not a crime at all. A reasonable person would not infer by analogy that speaking to the police would result in being charged with *less* than the crime confessed to. Similarly, the police statements that they would "go to bat" for Moore and not "jam" him are reasonably interpreted to be promises not to *overcharge* him rather than promises to *undercharge* him.
>
> In this case, we also have the habeas petitioner's testimony as to what he thought the officers had promised him. Far from establishing his case of a false promise of leniency, his own testimony refutes it.
>
> "About where the detectives told me that if it was an accident, they would go before the D.A. on my behalf and see to it that I was charged with an accident. And when he did go to the D.A. to ensure the D.A. didn't jam me for later on down the road, he came back. And then after we told him those statements, they charged us with murder anyhow."
>
> Moore himself unmistakably states that he was not expecting that a truthful statement of what happened would result in his being charged with less than the crime he admitted to. He thought that if he stated that the death of Rogers was accidental, then he would be charged with accidental death. He was not promised leniency, much less immunity. He was promised he would not be overcharged.

So understood, the promise was kept. Moore's statement confessed to all the elements of felony murder, which does not require proof of intent to kill. He was not "jammed," *i.e.*, charged with any greater offense. Clearly, Moore was greatly surprised to learn that his dubious statement of accidental shooting was actually a confession to murder under Oregon's felony murder rule. However, matters internal to the defendant's mind do not convert proper police conduct into coercion. See *Colorado v. Connelly,* 479 U.S. 157, 170 (1986). Moore expected he would be charged with the accidental death of Rogers, and he was. It is the felony murder law, not a breach of promise by the police or prosecutors, that makes this charge "murder anyhow."

Brief Amicus Curiae of the Criminal Justice Legal Foundation in Support of Petitioner, at 27–28.

2.   The Supreme Court ultimately held that the state courts did not act unreasonably in concluding that Moore's attorney acted competently in deciding that a motion to suppress the confession—even if successful—would have been futile because of the other evidence possessed by the prosecution. Thus the Ninth Circuit erred in holding that Moore was entitled to federal habeas corpus relief. The Court expressly noted it was not reaching whether Moore's attorney acted reasonably in concluding that a motion to suppress the confession would have been likely to fail. Premo v. Moore, 562 U.S. 115, 124, 131 S.Ct. 733, 741 (2011).

3.   **Adequacy of Voluntariness Requirement.** Was the voluntariness requirement insufficient to protect suspects' interests during custodial interrogation? Schulhofer, Confessions and the Court, 79 Mich.L.Rev. 865, 869–72 (1981), summarized a number of defects which critics found in the due process voluntariness requirement. It failed to provide specific guidance to law enforcement on which questioning tactics were and were not permissible. The "elusive task of balancing" invited trial judges to give weight to their subjective preferences and discouraged appellate review; judicial review of police activity was therefore impaired. Often, the critical issue was one of fact—what happened in the interrogation room—resulting in "swearing matches" between officers and defendants; defendants generally lost. And despite the requirement, considerable pressure was placed on suspects to confess, those with special weaknesses were especially susceptible to such pressure, and even physical brutality was not effectively enough discouraged.

C. SELF-INCRIMINATION AND *MIRANDA*'S RIGHT TO COUNSEL

The Supreme Court began in Escobedo v. Illinois, 378 U.S. 478, 84 S.Ct. 1758 (1964), to shift away from the voluntariness requirement as the major federal constitutional means of addressing what it perceived to be the continuing problems posed by police questioning of suspects in custody. This shift was completed two years later in Miranda v. Arizona, 384 U.S. 436, 86 S.Ct. 1602 (1966).

The *Miranda* decision itself is presented in the first unit of this subchapter. The second unit addresses the task of determining those situations to which *Miranda* applies. The next presents one aspect of *Miranda* that has undergone considerable evolution—the right to prevent questioning. Unit four considers what has become a major problem area in *Miranda* law—the existence and validity of waivers of the *Miranda* rights. In the fifth unit, attention is turned to a particularly troublesome problem concerning remedy—a defendant's potential right to exclusion of evidence obtained as a factual result of an inadmissible confession. Finally, the last unit considers the impact of the *Miranda* requirements.

1. THE *MIRANDA* DECISION

EDITORS' INTRODUCTION: THE *MIRANDA* RIGHTS

Miranda v. Arizona is, of course, one of the most widely-known and controversial decisions of the Warren Court. To put the decision in doctrinal perspective, it is necessary to understand that before *Miranda* there was substantial support for the proposition that police interrogation did not—directly, at least—implicate the Fifth Amendment privilege against compelled self-incrimination. The privilege, it was widely considered, applied only where the suspect could be the subject of "legal compulsion," that is, compulsion authorized by law, to answer questions. In a courtroom or before a grand jury a witness can be penalized for contempt of court for refusing to respond to questions; thus the court applies "legal" compulsion to the witness and consequently the situation implicated the privilege. Police officers, on the other hand, have no legal right to impose penalties upon suspects who refuse to answer the officers' questions. Consequently, although police interrogation could give rise to an involuntary confession, it could not directly violate the Fifth Amendment privilege.

In addition, even where the privilege against compelled self-incrimination applies, it is, as a general rule, violated only if a person first specifically claims a right under the privilege to refuse to answer a question and then is nevertheless encouraged or required to answer. Unless the person first claims the privilege, he has not been "compelled" to incriminate himself within the meaning of the privilege. It follows from this, of course, that—again, as a general rule—the government has no obligation before or during questioning to inform the person of the privilege. The person has the obligation to assert the privilege. See Minnesota v. Murphy, 465 U.S. 420, 427, 104 S.Ct. 1136, 1142 (1984).

Miranda first determined that police custodial interrogation of a person implicated interests of the person protected by the Fifth Amendment, and thus that provision. The Court then proceeded to define the requirements of the Fifth Amendment in this context.

Subsequent judicial discussion and development of *Miranda* sometimes emphasized the identification of so-called "*per se*" rules. The precise meaning of this characterization of some *Miranda* requirements is not always clear. Perhaps, however, it is best considered as describing the relationship between a legal requirement and the exclusionary remedy. A *per se* requirement, then, is one that, when violated, automatically demands the exclusion of resulting evidence. Police violation of other requirements, on the other hand, may not require exclusion of resulting evidence unless other considerations apply. In the *Miranda* context, for example, violation of some requirements announced in the decision or subsequent case law might require the exclusion of resulting evidence only if it rendered the suspect's waiver of the right to remain silent involuntary or otherwise ineffective.

Whatever the terminology used, it is important in identifying and understanding the *Miranda* rights to separate two matters. One, of course, is the contents of the requirements which case law places upon law enforcement officers. The other, however, is the relationship between violation of these requirements and the admissibility of suspects' self-incriminating statements and other evidence obtained as the result of such statements.

Miranda v. Arizona

Supreme Court of the United States, 1966.
384 U.S. 436, 86 S.Ct. 1602.

■ MR. CHIEF JUSTICE WARREN delivered the opinion of the Court.

The cases before us raise questions which go to the roots of our concepts of American criminal jurisprudence: the restraints society must observe consistent with the Federal Constitution in prosecuting individuals for crime. More specifically, we deal with the admissibility of statements obtained from an individual who is subjected to custodial police interrogation and the necessity for procedures which assure that the individual is accorded his privilege under the Fifth Amendment to the Constitution not to be compelled to incriminate himself.

* * *

Our holding will be spelled out with some specificity in the pages which follow but briefly stated it is this: the prosecution may not use statements, whether exculpatory or inculpatory, stemming from custodial interrogation of the defendant unless it demonstrates the use of procedural safeguards effective to secure the privilege against self-incrimination. By custodial interrogation, we mean questioning initiated by law enforcement officers after a person has been taken into custody or otherwise deprived of his freedom of action in any significant way. As for the procedural safeguards to be employed, unless other fully effective means are devised to inform accused persons of their right of silence and to assure a continuous opportunity to exercise it, the following measures are required. Prior to any questioning, the person must be warned that he has a right to remain silent, that any statement he does make may be used as evidence against him, and that he has a right to the presence of an attorney, either retained or appointed. The defendant may waive effectuation of these rights, provided the waiver is made voluntarily, knowingly and intelligently. If, however, he indicates in any manner and at any stage of the process that he wishes to consult with an attorney before speaking there can be no questioning. Likewise, if the individual is alone and indicates in any manner that he does not wish to be interrogated, the police may not question him. The mere fact that he may have answered some questions or volunteered some statements on his own does not deprive him of the right to refrain from answering any further inquiries until he has consulted with an attorney and thereafter consents to be questioned.

I.

* * *

An understanding of the nature and setting of * * * in-custody interrogation is essential to our decisions today. The difficulty in depicting what transpires at such interrogations stems from the fact that in this country they have largely taken place incommunicado. From extensive factual studies undertaken in the early 1930's, including the famous Wickersham Report to Congress by a Presidential Commission, it is clear that police violence and the "third degree" flourished at that time. In a series of cases decided by this Court long after these studies, the police resorted to physical brutality—beatings, hanging, whipping— and to sustained and protracted questioning incommunicado in order to extort confessions. * * *

[Situations involving brutality] are undoubtedly the exception now, but they are sufficiently widespread to be the object of concern. Unless a proper limitation upon custodial interrogation is achieved—such as these decisions will advance—there can be no assurance that practices of this nature will be eradicated in the foreseeable future.

* * *

[T]he modern practice of in-custody interrogation is psychologically rather than physically oriented. * * * "[T]his Court has recognized that coercion can be mental as well as physical, and that the blood of the accused is not the only hallmark of an unconstitutional inquisition." *Blackburn v. State of Alabama*, 361 U.S. 199, 206, 80 S.Ct. 274, 279, 4 L.Ed.2d 242 (1960). Interrogation still takes place in privacy. Privacy results in secrecy and this in turn results in a gap in our knowledge as to what in fact goes on in the interrogation rooms. A valuable source of information about present police practices, however, may be found in various police manuals and texts which document procedures employed with success in the past, and which recommend various other effective tactics. These texts are used by law enforcement agencies themselves as guides. It should be noted that these texts professedly present the most enlightened and effective means presently used to obtain statements through custodial interrogation. By considering these texts and other data, it is possible to describe procedures observed and noted around the country.

The officers are told by the manuals that the "principal psychological factor contributing to a successful interrogation is privacy—being alone with the person under interrogation." The efficacy of this tactic has been explained as follows:

> "If at all practicable, the interrogation should take place in the investigator's office or at least in a room of his own choice. The subject should be deprived of every psychological advantage. In his own home he may be confident, indignant, or recalcitrant. He is more keenly aware of his rights and more reluctant to tell of his indiscretions or criminal behavior within the walls of his home. Moreover his family and other friends are nearby, their presence lending moral support. In his office, the investigator possesses all the advantages. The atmosphere suggests the invincibility of the forces of the law."

To highlight the isolation and unfamiliar surroundings, the manuals instruct the police to display an air of confidence in the suspect's guilt and from outward appearance to maintain only an interest in confirming certain details. The guilt of the subject is to be posited as a fact. The interrogator should direct his comments toward the reasons why the subject committed the act, rather than court failure by asking the subject whether he did it. Like other men, perhaps the subject has had a bad family life, had an unhappy childhood, had too much to drink, had an unrequited desire for women. The officers are instructed to minimize the moral seriousness of the offense, to cast blame on the victim or on society. These tactics are designed to put the subject in a psychological state where his story is but an elaboration of what the police purport to know already—that he is guilty. Explanations to the contrary are dismissed and discouraged.

The texts thus stress that the major qualities an interrogator should possess are patience and perseverance. One writer describes the efficacy of these characteristics in this manner:

> "In the preceding paragraphs emphasis has been placed on kindness and stratagems. The investigator will, however, encounter many situations where the sheer weight of his personality will be the deciding factor. Where emotional appeals and tricks are employed to no avail, he must rely on an oppressive atmosphere of dogged persistence. He must interrogate steadily and without relent, leaving the subject no prospect of surcease. He must dominate his subject and overwhelm him with his inexorable will to obtain the truth. He should interrogate for a spell of several hours pausing only for

the subject's necessities in acknowledgment of the need to avoid a charge of duress that can be technically substantiated. In a serious case, the interrogation may continue for days, with the required intervals for food and sleep, but with no respite from the atmosphere of domination. It is possible in this way to induce the subject to talk without resorting to duress or coercion. The method should be used only when the guilt of the subject appears highly probable."

The manuals suggest that the suspect be offered legal excuses for his actions in order to obtain an initial admission of guilt. Where there is a suspected revenge-killing, for example, the interrogator may say:

"Joe, you probably didn't go out looking for this fellow with the purpose of shooting him. My guess is, however, that you expected something from him and that's why you carried a gun—for your own protection. You knew him for what he was, no good. Then when you met him he probably started using foul, abusive language and he gave some indication that he was about to pull a gun on you, and that's when you had to act to save your own life. That's about it, isn't it, Joe?"

Having then obtained the admission of shooting, the interrogator is advised to refer to circumstantial evidence which negates the self-defense explanation. This should enable him to secure the entire story. One text notes that "Even if he fails to do so, the inconsistency between the subject's original denial of the shooting and his present admission of at least doing the shooting will serve to deprive him of a self-defense 'out' at the time of trial."

When the techniques described above prove unavailing, the texts recommend they be alternated with a show of some hostility. One ploy often used has been termed the "friendly-unfriendly" or the "Mutt and Jeff" act:

" * * * In this technique, two agents are employed. Mutt, the relentless investigator, who knows the subject is guilty and is not going to waste any time. He's sent a dozen men away for this crime and he's going to send the subject away for the full term. Jeff, on the other hand, is obviously a kindhearted man. He has a family himself. He has a brother who was involved in a little scrape like this. He disapproves of Mutt and his tactics and will arrange to get him off the case if the subject will cooperate. He can't hold Mutt off for very long. The subject would be wise to make a quick decision. The technique is applied by having both investigators present while Mutt acts out his role. Jeff may stand by quietly and demur at some of Mutt's tactics. When Jeff makes his plea for cooperation, Mutt is not present in the room."

The interrogators sometimes are instructed to induce a confession out of trickery. The technique here is quite effective in crimes which require identification or which run in series. In the identification situation, the interrogator may take a break in his questioning to place the subject among a group of men in a lineup. "The witness or complainant (previously coached, if necessary) studies the lineup and confidently points out the subject as the guilty party." Then the questioning resumes "as though there were now no doubt about the guilt of the subject." A variation on this technique is called the "reverse lineup":

> "The accused is placed in a lineup, but this time he is identified by several fictitious witnesses or victims who associated him with different offenses. It is expected that the subject will become desperate and confess to the offense under investigation in order to escape from the false accusations."

The manuals also contain instructions for police on how to handle the individual who refuses to discuss the matter entirely or who asks for an attorney or relatives. The examiner is to concede him the right to remain silent. "This usually has a very undermining effect. First of all, he is disappointed in his expectation of an unfavorable reaction on the part of the interrogator. Secondly, a concession of this right to remain silent impresses the subject with the apparent fairness of his interrogator." After this psychological conditioning, however, the officer is told to point out the incriminating significance of the suspect's refusal to talk:

> "Joe, you have a right to remain silent. That's your privilege and I'm the last person in the world who'll try to take it away from you. If that's the way you want to leave this, O. K. But let me ask you this. Suppose you were in my shoes and I were in yours and you called me in to ask me about this and I told you, 'I don't want to answer any of your questions.' You'd think I had something to hide, and you'd probably be right in thinking that. That's exactly what I'll have to think about you, and so will everybody else. So let's sit here and talk this whole thing over."

Few will persist in their initial refusal to talk, it is said, if this monologue is employed correctly.

In the event that the subject wishes to speak to a relative or an attorney, the following advice is tendered:

> "[T]he interrogator should respond by suggesting that the subject first tell the truth to the interrogator himself rather than get anyone else involved in the matter. If the request is for an attorney, the interrogator may suggest that the subject save himself or his family the expense of any such professional service, particularly if he is innocent of the offense under investigation. The interrogator may also add, 'Joe, I'm only looking for the truth, and if you're telling the truth, that's it. You can handle this by yourself.'"

From these representative samples of interrogation techniques, the setting prescribed by the manuals and observed in practice becomes clear. In essence, it is this: To be alone with the subject is essential to prevent distraction and to deprive him of any outside support. The aura of confidence in his guilt undermines his will to resist. He merely confirms the preconceived story the police seek to have him describe. Patience and persistence, at times relentless questioning, are employed. To obtain a confession, the interrogator must "patiently maneuver himself or his quarry into a position from which the desired objective may be attained." When normal procedures fail to produce the needed result, the police may resort to deceptive stratagems such as giving false legal advice. It is important to keep the subject off balance, for example, by trading on his insecurity about himself or his surroundings. The police then persuade, trick, or cajole him out of exercising his constitutional rights.

Even without employing brutality, the "third degree" or the specific stratagems described above, the very fact of custodial interrogation exacts a heavy toll on individual liberty and trades on the weakness of individuals. * * *

In those cases before us today * * * we might not find the defendants' statements to have been involuntary in traditional terms. * * * The fact remains that in none of these cases did the officers undertake to afford appropriate safeguards at the outset of the interrogation to insure that the statements were truly the product of free choice.

It is obvious that such an interrogation environment is created for no purpose other than to subjugate the individual to the will of his examiner. This atmosphere carries its own badge of intimidation. To be sure, this is not physical intimidation, but it is equally destructive of human dignity. The current practice of incommunicado interrogation is at odds with one of our Nation's most cherished principles—that the individual may not be compelled to incriminate himself. Unless adequate protective devices are employed to dispel the compulsion inherent in custodial surroundings, no statement obtained from the defendant can truly be the product of his free choice.

From the foregoing, we can readily perceive an intimate connection between the privilege against self-incrimination and police custodial questioning. * * *

II.

* * *

The question in these cases is whether the [Fifth Amendment] privilege is fully applicable during a period of custodial interrogation. * * * We are satisfied that all the principles embodied in the privilege apply to informal compulsion exerted by law-enforcement officers during in-custody questioning. An individual swept from familiar surroundings into police custody, surrounded by antagonistic forces, and subjected to the techniques of persuasion described above cannot be otherwise than under compulsion to speak. As a practical matter, the compulsion to speak in the isolated setting of the police station may well be greater than in courts or other official investigations, where there are often impartial observers to guard against intimidation or trickery.

* * *

III.

* * * We have concluded that without proper safeguards the process of in-custody interrogation of persons suspected or accused of crime contains inherently compelling pressures which work to undermine the individual's will to resist and to compel him to speak where he would not otherwise do so freely. In order to combat these pressures and to permit a full opportunity to exercise the privilege against self-incrimination, the accused must be adequately and effectively apprised of his rights and the exercise of those rights must be fully honored.

It is impossible for us to foresee the potential alternatives for protecting the privilege which might be devised by Congress or the States in the exercise of their creative rulemaking capacities. Therefore we cannot say that the Constitution necessarily requires adherence to any particular solution for the inherent compulsions of the interrogation process as it is presently conducted. Our decision in no way creates a constitutional straitjacket which will handicap sound efforts at reform, nor is it intended to have this effect. We encourage Congress and the States to continue their laudable search for increasingly effective ways of protecting the rights of the individual while promoting efficient enforcement of our criminal laws. However, unless we are shown other procedures which are at least as effective in apprising accused persons of their right of silence and in assuring a continuous opportunity to exercise it, the following safeguards must be observed.

At the outset, if a person in custody is to be subjected to interrogation, he must first be informed in clear and unequivocal terms that he has the right to remain silent. For those unaware of the privilege, the warning is needed simply to make them aware of it—the threshold requirement for an intelligent decision as to its exercise. More important, such a warning is an absolute prerequisite in overcoming the inherent pressures of the interrogation atmosphere. It is not just the subnormal or woefully ignorant who succumb to an interrogator's imprecations, whether implied or expressly stated, that the interrogation will continue until a confession is obtained or that silence in the face of accusation is itself damning and will bode ill when presented to a jury. Further, the warning will show the individual that his interrogators are prepared to recognize his privilege should he choose to exercise it.

The Fifth Amendment privilege is so fundamental to our system of constitutional rule and the expedient of giving an adequate warning as to the availability of the privilege so simple, we will not pause to inquire in individual cases whether the defendant was aware of his rights without a warning being given. Assessments of the knowledge the defendant possessed, based on information as to his age, education, intelligence, or prior contact with authorities, can never be more than speculation; a warning is a clearcut fact. More important, whatever the background of the person interrogated, a warning at the time of the interrogation is indispensable to overcome its pressures and to insure that the individual knows he is free to exercise the privilege at that point in time.

The warning of the right to remain silent must be accompanied by the explanation that anything said can and will be used against the individual in court. This warning is needed in order to make him aware not only of the privilege, but also of the consequences of forgoing it. It is only through an awareness of these consequences that there can be any assurance of real understanding and intelligent exercise of the privilege. Moreover, this warning may serve to make the individual more acutely aware that he is faced with a phase of the adversary system—that he is not in the presence of persons acting solely in his interest.

The circumstances surrounding in-custody interrogation can operate very quickly to overbear the will of one merely made aware of his privilege by his interrogators. Therefore, the right to have counsel present at the interrogation is indispensable to the protection of the Fifth Amendment privilege under the system we delineate today. Our aim is to assure that the individual's right to choose between silence and speech remains unfettered throughout the interrogation process. A once-stated warning, delivered by those who will conduct the interrogation, cannot itself suffice to that end among those who most require knowledge of their rights. A mere warning given by the interrogators is not alone sufficient to accomplish that end. * * * Even preliminary advice given to the accused by his own attorney can be swiftly overcome by the secret interrogation process. * * * Thus, the need for counsel to protect the Fifth Amendment privilege comprehends not merely a right to consult with counsel prior to questioning, but also to have counsel present during any questioning if the defendant so desires.

The presence of counsel at the interrogation may serve several significant subsidiary functions as well. If the accused decides to talk to his interrogators, the assistance of counsel can mitigate the dangers of untrustworthiness. With a lawyer present the likelihood that the police will practice coercion is reduced, and if coercion is nevertheless exercised the lawyer can testify to it in court. The presence of a lawyer can also help to guarantee that the accused gives a fully accurate statement to the police and that the statement is rightly reported by the prosecution at trial.

An individual need not make a preinterrogation request for a lawyer. While such request affirmatively secures his right to have one, his failure to ask for a lawyer does not constitute a waiver. No effective waiver of the right to counsel during interrogation can be recognized unless specifically made after the warnings we here delineate have been given. The accused who does not know his rights and therefore does not make a request may be the person who most needs counsel. * * *

Accordingly we hold that an individual held for interrogation must be clearly informed that he has the right to consult with a lawyer and to have the lawyer with him during interrogation under the system for protecting the privilege we delineate today. As with the warnings of the right to remain silent and that anything stated can be used in evidence against him, this warning is an absolute prerequisite to interrogation. No amount of circumstantial evidence that the person may have been aware of this right will suffice to stand in its stead. Only through such a warning is there ascertainable assurance that the accused was aware of this right.

If an individual indicates that he wishes the assistance of counsel before any interrogation occurs, the authorities cannot rationally ignore or deny his request on the basis that the individual does not have or cannot afford a retained attorney. The financial ability of the individual has no relationship to the scope of the rights involved here. The privilege against self-incrimination secured by the Constitution applies to all individuals. The need for counsel in order to protect the privilege exists for the indigent as well as the affluent. In fact, were we to limit these constitutional rights to those who can retain an attorney, our decisions today would be of little significance. The cases before us as well as the vast majority of confession cases with which we have dealt in the past involve those unable to retain counsel. While authorities are not required to relieve the accused of his poverty, they have the obligation not to take advantage of indigence in the administration of justice. * * *

In order fully to apprise a person interrogated of the extent of his rights under this system then, it is necessary to warn him not only that he has the right to consult with an attorney, but also that if he is indigent a lawyer will be appointed to represent him. Without this additional warning, the admonition of the right to consult with counsel would often be understood as meaning only that he can consult with a lawyer if he has one or has the funds to obtain one. The warning of a right to counsel would be hollow if not couched in terms that would convey to the indigent—the person most often subjected to interrogation—the knowledge that he too has a right to have counsel present. As with the warnings of the right to remain silent and of the general right to counsel, only by effective and express explanation to the indigent of this right can there be assurance that he was truly in a position to exercise it.[43]

---

[43] While a warning that the indigent may have counsel appointed need not be given to the person who is known to have an attorney or is known to have ample funds to secure one, the expedient of giving a warning is too simple and the rights involved too important to engage in *ex post facto* inquiries into financial ability when there is any doubt at all on that score.

Once warnings have been given, the subsequent procedure is clear. If the individual indicates in any manner, at any time prior to or during questioning, that he wishes to remain silent, the interrogation must cease.[44] At this point he has shown that he intends to exercise his Fifth Amendment privilege; any statement taken after the person invokes his privilege cannot be other than the product of compulsion, subtle or otherwise. Without the right to cut off questioning, the setting of in-custody interrogation operates on the individual to overcome free choice in producing a statement after the privilege has been once invoked. If the individual states that he wants an attorney, the interrogation must cease until an attorney is present. At that time, the individual must have an opportunity to confer with the attorney and to have him present during any subsequent questioning. If the individual cannot obtain an attorney and he indicates that he wants one before speaking to police, they must respect his decision to remain silent.

* * *

If the interrogation continues without the presence of an attorney and a statement is taken, a heavy burden rests on the government to demonstrate that the defendant knowingly and intelligently waived his privilege against self-incrimination and his right to retained or appointed counsel. * * * This Court has always set high standards of proof for the waiver of constitutional rights, Johnson v. Zerbst, 304 U.S. 458, 58 S.Ct. 1019, 82 L.Ed. 1461 (1938), and we reassert these standards as applied to in-custody interrogation. Since the State is responsible for establishing the isolated circumstances under which the interrogation takes place and has the only means of making available corroborated evidence of warnings given during incommunicado interrogation, the burden is rightly on its shoulders.

An express statement that the individual is willing to make a statement and does not want an attorney followed closely by a statement could constitute a waiver. But a valid waiver will not be presumed simply from the silence of the accused after warnings are given or simply from the fact that a confession was in fact eventually obtained. * * * Moreover, where in-custody interrogation is involved, there is no room for the contention that the privilege is waived if the individual answers some questions or gives some information on his own prior to invoking his right to remain silent when interrogated.

Whatever the testimony of the authorities as to waiver of rights by an accused, the fact of lengthy interrogation or incommunicado incarceration before a statement is made is strong evidence that the accused did not validly waive his rights. In these circumstances the fact

---

[44] If an individual indicates his desire to remain silent, but has an attorney present, there may be some circumstances in which further questioning would be permissible. In the absence of evidence of overbearing, statements then made in the presence of counsel might be free of the compelling influence of the interrogation process and might fairly be construed as a waiver of the privilege for purposes of these statements.

that the individual eventually made a statement is consistent with the conclusion that the compelling influence of the interrogation finally forced him to do so. It is inconsistent with any notion of a voluntary relinquishment of the privilege. Moreover, any evidence that the accused was threatened, tricked, or cajoled into a waiver will, of course, show that the defendant did not voluntarily waive his privilege. The requirement of warnings and waiver of rights is a fundamental with respect to the Fifth Amendment privilege and not simply a preliminary ritual to existing methods of interrogation.

The warnings required and the waiver necessary in accordance with our opinion today are, in the absence of a fully effective equivalent, prerequisites to the admissibility of any statement made by a defendant. * * *

Our decision is not intended to hamper the traditional function of police officers in investigating crime. When an individual is in custody on probable cause, the police may, of course, seek out evidence in the field to be used at trial against him. Such investigation may include inquiry of persons not under restraint. General on-the-scene questioning as to facts surrounding a crime or other general questioning of citizens in the factfinding process is not affected by our holding. It is an act of responsible citizenship for individuals to give whatever information they may have to aid in law enforcement. In such situations the compelling atmosphere inherent in the process of in-custody interrogation is not necessarily present.

In dealing with statements obtained through interrogation, we do not purport to find all confessions inadmissible. Confessions remain a proper element in law enforcement. Any statement given freely and voluntarily without any compelling influences is, of course, admissible in evidence. The fundamental import of the privilege while an individual is in custody is not whether he is allowed to talk to the police without the benefit of warnings and counsel, but whether he can be interrogated. There is no requirement that police stop a person who enters a police station and states that he wishes to confess to a crime, or a person who calls the police to offer a confession or any other statement he desires to make. Volunteered statements of any kind are not barred by the Fifth Amendment and their admissibility is not affected by our holding today.

* * *

V.

Because of the nature of the problem and because of its recurrent significance in numerous cases, we have to this point discussed the relationship of the Fifth Amendment privilege to police interrogation without specific concentration on the facts of the cases before us. We turn now to these facts to consider the application to these cases of the constitutional principles discussed above. In each instance, we have concluded that statements were obtained from the defendant under circumstances that did not meet constitutional standards for protection of the privilege.

No. 759. Miranda v. Arizona

On March 13, 1963, petitioner, Ernesto Miranda, was arrested at his home and taken in custody to a Phoenix police station. He was there identified by the complaining witness. The police then took him to "Interrogation Room No. 2" of the detective bureau. There he was questioned by two police officers. The officers admitted at trial that Miranda was not advised that he had a right to have an attorney present. Two hours later, the officers emerged from the interrogation room with a written confession signed by Miranda. At the top of the statement was a typed paragraph stating that the confession was made voluntarily, without threats or promises of immunity and "with full knowledge of my legal rights, understanding any statement I make may be used against me."

At his trial before a jury, the written confession was admitted into evidence over the objection of defense counsel, and the officers testified to the prior oral confession made by Miranda during the interrogation. Miranda was found guilty of kidnapping and rape. He was sentenced to 20 to 30 years' imprisonment on each count, the sentences to run concurrently. On appeal, the Supreme Court of Arizona held that Miranda's constitutional rights were not violated in obtaining the confession and affirmed the conviction. In reaching its decision, the court emphasized heavily the fact that Miranda did not specifically request counsel.

We reverse. From the testimony of the officers and by the admission of respondent, it is clear that Miranda was not in any way apprised of his right to consult with an attorney and to have one present during the interrogation, nor was his right not to be compelled to incriminate himself effectively protected in any other manner. Without these warnings the statements were inadmissible. The mere fact that he signed a statement which contained a typed-in clause stating that he had "full knowledge" of his "legal rights" does not approach the knowing and intelligent waiver required to relinquish constitutional rights.

* * *

[The Court's discussion of the facts of the other cases is omitted. Editors.]

■ MR. JUSTICE CLARK, dissenting in Nos. 759, 760, and 761, and concurring in the result in No. 584.

* * * Since there is at this time a paucity of information and an almost total lack of empirical knowledge on the practical operation of requirements truly comparable to those announced by the majority, I would be more restrained lest we go too far too fast.

* * *

Custodial interrogation has long been recognized as "undoubtedly an essential tool in effective law enforcement." *Haynes v. State of Washington*, 373 U.S. 503, 515, 83 S.Ct. 1336, 1344, 10 L.Ed.2d 513 (1963). Recognition of this fact should put us on guard against the promulgation of doctrinaire rules. * * *

The rule prior to today * * * depended upon "a totality of circumstances evidencing an involuntary * * * admission of guilt." * * *

I would continue to follow that rule. Under the "totality of circumstances" rule * * *, I would consider in each case whether the police officer prior to custodial interrogation added the warning that the suspect might have counsel present at the interrogation, and further, that a court would appoint one at his request if he was too poor to employ counsel. In the absence of warnings, the burden would be on the State to prove that counsel was knowingly and intelligently waived or that in the totality of the circumstances, including the failure to give the necessary warnings, the confession was clearly voluntary.

* * *

■ [The dissenting opinions of JUSTICE HARLAN, with whom JUSTICES STEWART and WHITE joined, and of JUSTICE WHITE, with whom JUSTICES HARLAN and STEWART joined, are omitted.]

NOTES

1. **Terminology of the Warnings.** How much deviation from the language used by the majority in *Miranda* is permissible in giving suspects *Miranda* warnings? In California v. Prysock, 453 U.S. 355, 101 S.Ct. 2806 (1981) (per curiam), the sixteen year old suspect was warned and questioned in the presence of his mother. The officer first told Prysock "you have the right to remain silent," "if you give up your right to remain silent, anything you say can and will be used as evidence against you in a court of law," and "you have the right to talk to a lawyer before you are questioned, have him present with you while you are being questioned, and all during the questioning." He was also told, "you have the right to have a lawyer appointed to represent you at no cost to yourself." This was all tape recorded. There was then a brief off-the-record discussion between the suspect's mother and the officer. The officer later testified that in this discussion, the mother asked if a lawyer would be available later if the suspect did not request one at this time. According to the officer, he responded by saying:

> That he would have an attorney when he went to Court. And that he could have one at this time if he wished one. He could terminate the statement at any time he so desired.

Following the warnings, Prysock consented to questioning without an attorney and admitted the killing. This confession was later used against him in his murder trial, and he was convicted. On appeal, however, the intermediate California appellate court reversed. Emphasizing its view that the rigidity of the *Miranda* requirements affords police clear guidance, the court held Prysock had not been adequately informed that the services of a free attorney were available to him prior to the impending questioning. The Supreme Court reversed. It read the state court as establishing "a flat rule that the content of *Miranda* warnings be a virtual incantation of the precise language contained in the *Miranda* opinion" and holding the warnings here defective because of the order in which they were given. In fact, the Court stressed, "no talismanic incantation" is required to satisfy *Miranda*. The warnings given Prysock adequately conveyed to him that he had a right to an appointed attorney prior to and during questioning.

In Duckworth v. Eagan, 492 U.S. 195, 109 S.Ct. 2875 (1989), Eagan was given warnings that, in regard to the right to counsel, included:

> You have a right to talk to a lawyer for advice before we ask you any questions, and to have him with you during questioning. You have this right to the advice and presence of a lawyer even if you cannot afford to hire one. We have no way of giving you a lawyer, but one will be appointed for you, if you wish, if and when you go to court. If you wish to answer questions now without a lawyer present, you have the right to stop answering questions at any time. You also have the right to stop answering at any time until you've talked to a lawyer.

By a 5-to-4 vote, the Supreme Court held this complied with *Miranda*. Chief Justice Rehnquist wrote for the Court rejecting Eagan's argument that the "if and when you go to court" phrase rendered the warning confusing and insufficient:

> First, this instruction accurately described the procedure for the appointment of counsel in Indiana. Under Indiana law, counsel is appointed at the defendant's initial appearance in court, and formal charges must be filed at or before that hearing. We think it must be relatively commonplace for a suspect, after receiving *Miranda* warnings, to ask when he will obtain counsel. The "if and when you go to court" advice simply anticipates that question. Second, *Miranda* does not require that attorneys be producible on call, but only that the suspect be informed, as here, that he has the right to an attorney before and during questioning, and that an attorney would be appointed for him if he could not afford one. The Court in *Miranda* emphasized that it was not suggesting that "each police station must have a 'station house lawyer' present at all times to advise prisoners." If the police cannot provide appointed counsel, *Miranda* requires only that the police not question a suspect unless he waives his right to counsel. Here, [Eagan] did just that.

495 U.S. at 204, 109 S.Ct. at 2880–81.

The written warnings at issue in Florida v. Powell, 559 U.S. 50, 130 S.Ct. 1195 (2010), were as follows:

> You have the right to remain silent. If you give up the right to remain silent, anything you say can be used against you in court. You have the right to talk to a lawyer before answering any of our

questions. If you cannot afford to hire a lawyer, one will be appointed for you without cost and before any questioning. You have the right to use any of these rights at any time you want during this interview.

Two members of the Court regard the warning as inadequate because "[t]he more natural reading of the warning * * *, which (1) contained a temporal limit and (2) failed to mention his right to the presence of counsel in the interrogation room, is that Powell only had the right to consult with an attorney before the interrogation began, not that he had the right to have an attorney with him during questioning." 559 U.S. at 73, 130 S.Ct. at 1211 (Stevens, J., dissenting). The Court, however, held the warning sufficient:

> The [warning] informed Powell that he had "the right to talk to a lawyer before answering any of [their] questions" and "the right to use any of [his] rights at any time [he] want[ed] during th[e] interview." The first statement communicated that Powell could consult with a lawyer before answering any particular question, and the second statement confirmed that he could exercise that right while the interrogation was underway. In combination, the two warnings reasonably conveyed Powell's right to have an attorney present, not only at the outset of interrogation, but at all times.

559 U.S. at 62, 130 S.Ct. at 1204–05.

2. **Impeachment Use of Confessions Violating *Miranda*.** The "impeachment exception" to many exclusionary sanctions, discussed in Chapter 1, has been applied to confessions in a manner distinguishing between the requirements of *Miranda* and voluntariness.

The majority in Harris v. New York, 401 U.S. 222, 91 S.Ct. 643 (1971), acknowledged language in *Miranda* could be read as barring the use of a confession obtained in violation of *Miranda* for any purpose. Nevertheless, the Court held in *Harris* that a statement obtained after a warning failing to inform the defendant of his right to appointed counsel could be used to impeach the defendant when he took the stand at trial and testified in a manner inconsistent with the statement. "[T]he trustworthiness of the evidence satisfies legal standards," the majority commented, and the confession would undoubtedly aid the jury in evaluating the defendant's credibility as well as determining whether he perjured himself during testimony. Turning to the need to exclude such confessions as a means of deterring violation of the *Miranda* requirements, the majority concluded "sufficient deterrence flows when the evidence in question is made unavailable to the prosecution in its case in chief."

In Oregon v. Hass, 420 U.S. 714, 95 S.Ct. 1215 (1975), Hass was arrested and given complete *Miranda* warnings. Although Hass said he wanted to telephone a lawyer, an officer continued to interrogate him without the presence of counsel; he made an incriminating statement. This statement was used for impeachment at trial after Hass took the stand and testified to facts contrary to those in the confession. The Supreme Court found no impropriety in use of the statement at Hass's trial. The dissent contended the case was distinguishable from *Harris*:

> [A]fter *Harris*, police had some incentive for following *Miranda* by warning an accused of his right to remain silent and his right to counsel. If the warnings were given, the accused might still make a statement which could be used in the prosecution's case in chief. [But where the warnings are given and the suspect indicates a desire for counsel], police have almost no incentive for following *Miranda*'s requirement that "[i]f the individual states that he wants an attorney, the interrogation must cease until an attorney is present." * * * If the requirement is followed there will almost surely be no statement since the attorney will advise the accused to remain silent. If, however, the requirement is disobeyed, the police may obtain a statement which can be used for impeachment if the accused has the temerity to testify in his own defense.

420 U.S. at 725, 95 S.Ct. at 1222 (Brennan, J., dissenting). Thus the need to exclude the confession to encourage compliance with *Miranda* was greater in the case before the Court than in *Harris*. The majority, in contrast, characterized the possibility of an officer proceeding on the basis suggested by the dissent as "speculative." "If, in a given case," it concluded, "the officer's conduct amounts to an abuse, that case, like those involving coercion or duress, may be taken care of when it arises measured by the traditional standards for evaluating voluntariness and trustworthiness."

Mincey v. Arizona, 437 U.S. 385, 98 S.Ct. 2408 (1978), reaffirmed that involuntary statements could not be used even for impeachment of a testifying defendant. This is apparently because such statements—unlike the statements in *Harris* and *Hass*—do not satisfy legal standards of trustworthiness.

3. **Warning Efforts Frustrated by the Suspect.** Suppose the suspect frustrates efforts by officers to comply with *Miranda*?

In United States v. Patane, 542 U.S. 630, 124 S.Ct. 2620 (2004), a federal officer arrested Patane and began advising him of his *Miranda* rights. When the officer finished admonishing Patane that he had the right to remain silent, Patane interrupted by asserting that he knew his rights. Without further efforts to comply with *Miranda*, the officer began questioning Patane. The Supreme Court analyzed the case on the assumption that *Miranda* had been violated. Justice Thomas's plurality opinion noted that the Government conceded the officer's conduct rendered Patane's statements in response to the questioning inadmissible. 542 U.S. at 635 n. 1, 124 S.Ct. at 2625 n. 1.

4. **Use of Suspects' Silence to Impeach.** A defendant's silence under circumstances in which a reasonable, innocent person would have denied guilt is, generally speaking, admissible to prove the defendant's guilt as a "tacit" confession. See McCormick, Evidence § 161 (7th ed. 2013). *Miranda*, however, imposes some limitations on the admissibility of such silence. In Doyle v. Ohio, 426 U.S. 610, 96 S.Ct. 2240 (1976), Doyle was charged with sale of marijuana based on a transaction arranged by one

Bonnell, a police informant. None of the narcotics agents who had the transaction under surveillance actually saw the alleged transfer of the marijuana from Doyle to Bonnell. At trial, Doyle took the stand and testified that the arrangement had actually been for Bonnell to sell marijuana to him. On cross examination, the prosecution elicited Doyle's admission that after being arrested and given the *Miranda* warnings he had not told this version of the incident to the arresting officers. Reversing Doyle's conviction, the Supreme Court held that silence after being given the *Miranda* warnings could not be used even for impeachment. Silence after *Miranda* warnings cannot, under *Doyle*, even be used to rebut a defendant's claim of insanity. Wainwright v. Greenfield, 474 U.S. 284, 106 S.Ct. 634 (1986).

In Fletcher v. Weir, 455 U.S. 603, 102 S.Ct. 1309 (1982) (per curiam), the Court characterized *Doyle* as resting not upon the ambiguity of suspects' silence but the fundamental unfairness of using silence against defendants after they have received governmental assurances that there is a right to remain silent. The Court found no federal constitutional barrier to the use of a defendant's silence after arrest but before *Miranda* warnings, at least where silence was used to impeach the defendant after he took the witness stand at trial and testified to an exculpatory version of the events. Where the *Miranda* warnings were not given, the Court reasoned, no assurances of a right to remain silent were provided and thus there is no unfairness in using the defendants' silence. Whether in such situations a defendant's silence is a sufficiently reliable indicator he lied during direct examination, the Court commented, is a decision each State is entitled to make as a matter of State evidence law policy.

Doyle imposes no federal constitutional bar to the use of *prearrest* silence to impeach a testifying defendant. Jenkins v. Anderson, 447 U.S. 231, 100 S.Ct. 2124 (1980). Nor does *Miranda* bar questioning of a testifying defendant concerning inconsistent statements made after arrest and receipt of *Miranda* warnings. Such a defendant has chosen to speak rather than remain silent so there is no impermissible use of silence as prohibited by *Doyle*. Anderson v. Charles, 447 U.S. 404, 100 S.Ct. 2180 (1980) (per curiam).

5. **Use of Precustodial Silence as Evidence of Guilt.** The Supreme Court returned to silence in Salinas v. Texas, ___ U.S. ___, 133 S.Ct. 2174 (2013). Salinas was tried for murder. He did not testify. The prosecution was permitted to introduce evidence that after being visited at home by officers he agreed to hand over his shotgun for analysis and to accompany the officers to the station for questioning. The questioning at the station was described as follows:

> [Salinas's] interview with the police lasted approximately one hour. All agree that the interview was noncustodial, and the parties litigated this case on the assumption that he was not read *Miranda* warnings. For most of the interview, [Salinas] answered the officer's questions. But when asked whether his shotgun "would match the shells recovered at the scene of the murder," [Salinas] declined to answer. Instead, [Salinas] "[l]ooked down at the floor, shuffled his feet, bit his bottom lip, cl[e]nched his hands in his lap,

[and] began to tighten up." After a few moments of silence, the officer asked additional questions, which [Salinas] answered.

___ U.S. at ___, 133 S.Ct. at 2178 (plurality opinion). Over objection, prosecutors were permitted to use Salinas's reaction to the officer's question about the shotgun matching the shells as evidence of his guilt.

Justice Breyer, joined by three other justices, reasoned in dissent that this violated a Fifth Amendment bar to prosecutors "commenting on an individual's silence where that silence amounts to an effort to avoid becoming 'a witness against himself.'" He explained:

> I would hold that Salinas need not have expressly invoked the Fifth Amendment. The context was that of a criminal investigation. Police told Salinas that and made clear that he was a suspect. His interrogation took place at the police station. Salinas was not represented by counsel. The relevant question—about whether the shotgun from Salinas' home would incriminate him—amounted to a switch in subject matter. And it was obvious that the new question sought to ferret out whether Salinas was guilty of murder.
>
> These circumstances give rise to a reasonable inference that Salinas' silence derived from an exercise of his Fifth Amendment rights.

___ U.S. at ___, 133 S.Ct. at 2189 (Breyer, J., dissenting). He added: "[M]any, indeed most, Americans are aware that they have a constitutional right not to incriminate themselves by answering questions posed by the police during an interrogation conducted in order to figure out the perpetrator of a crime." Reliance upon silence, the dissenters concluded, should be barred where—as in *Salinas* —the circumstances of the silence give rise to a reasonable or fair inference that the silence reflected an exercise of the Fifth Amendment right to avoid providing authorities with self-incriminating information. ___ U.S. at ___, 133 S.Ct. at 2190.

The dissenters' position was, however, rejected by a split majority of five justices.

In a plurality opinion announcing the judgment of the Court, Justice Alito, joined by the Chief Justice and Justice Kennedy, noted that the prohibition against use of a person's reliance upon the privilege against self-incrimination generally applies only when the person has expressly invoked the privilege. Under *Miranda*, "a suspect who is subjected to the 'inherently compelling pressures' of an unwarned custodial interrogation need not invoke the privilege," Justice Alito explained, "because 'a witness' failure to invoke the privilege must be excused where governmental coercion makes his forfeiture of the privilege involuntary.'" But that is not the case when—as in *Salinas*—the person is not in custody. Salinas's failure to expressly invoke the privilege, the plurality reasoned, meant he was entitled to no relief. ___ U.S. at ___, 133 S.Ct. at 2180 (plurality opinion). Consequently, the case presented no need to address whether the Fifth Amendment bars prosecutors' use of *effective* reliance on the privilege—by express invocation—during a precustodial interview. ___ U.S. at ___, 133 S.Ct. at 2179.

Justice Thomas, joined by Justice Scalia, agreed Salinas was not entitled to relief but on a different ground. A criminal defendant is not "compelled * * * to be a witness against himself" within the meaning of the Fifth Amendment, he reasoned, "simply because a jury has been told that it may draw an adverse inference from his silence." In such situations the defendant has not been compelled to give self-incriminating testimony. Insofar as the Court's case law bars any use of silence in reliance on the privilege, Justice Thomas continued, it rests on an "indefensible foundation," and thus he "would not extend it to a defendant's silence during a precustodial interview." ___ U.S. at ___, 133 S.Ct. at 2184 (Thomas, J., concurring in the judgment). So, even if Salinas had expressly invoked his privilege as the plurality would require, his claim to relief would fail because the prosecutors' actions did not compel Salinas to give self-incriminating testimony.

6.   **Congressional Effort to "Overrule" *Miranda*.** Two years after *Miranda* was decided, Congress purported to reject the case's exclusionary remedy. As part of the Omnibus Crime Control and Safe Streets Act of 1968, Congress enacted 18 U.S.C. § 3500, titled "Admissibility of Confessions," applicable in federal prosecutions. Under this statute, the admissibility of an out-of-court incriminating statement was to be determined solely by whether it was "voluntarily given." In determining voluntariness, the trial judge was to consider the totality of the circumstances including "whether or not [the] defendant was advised or knew that he was not required to make any statement and that any such statement could be used against him, * * ** whether or not such defendant had been advised prior to questioning of his right to the assistance of counsel; and * * * whether or not such defendant was without the assistance of counsel when questioned and when giving such confession." No one factor, however, needed to be conclusive.

The effectiveness of this provision did not reach the Supreme Court until Dickerson v. United States, 530 U.S. 428, 120 S.Ct. 2326 (2000), in which the trial judge found the confession at issue to have been made voluntarily but without the warnings required by *Miranda*. The court of appeals held the statement admissible under the statute. A split Supreme Court reversed, holding that Congress lacked the power to overrule *Miranda* and make admissible a confession such as this that *Miranda* required be suppressed. *Miranda*, the majority confirmed, was a constitutional decision beyond legislative power to modify. Continuing, the Court explained:

> Whether or not we would agree with *Miranda*'s reasoning and its resulting rule, were we addressing the issue in the first instance, the principles of *stare decisis* weigh heavily against overruling it now. While " '*stare decisis* is not an inexorable command,' " particularly when we are interpreting the Constitution, "even in constitutional cases, the doctrine carries such persuasive force that we have always required a departure from precedent to be supported by some 'special justification.' "

> We do not think there is such justification for overruling *Miranda*. *Miranda* has become embedded in routine police practice to the point where the warnings have become part of our national

culture. While we have overruled our precedents when subsequent cases have undermined their doctrinal underpinnings, we do not believe that this has happened to the *Miranda* decision. If anything, our subsequent cases have reduced the impact of the *Miranda* rule on legitimate law enforcement while reaffirming the decision's core ruling that unwarned statements may not be used as evidence in the prosecution's case in chief.

530 U.S. at 443–44, 120 S.Ct. at 2336.

EDITORS' NOTE: IDENTIFYING AND DISTINGUISHING THE *MIRANDA* RIGHTS

Analysis of issues arising in the development and application of *Miranda* may be furthered by identifying and distinguishing among the possible "rights" of a person faced with custodial interrogation.

Miranda removed any doubt that persons undergoing custodial interrogation have a Fifth Amendment right to avoid compelled self-incrimination. This clearly means they have a right to not respond to the interrogation by making self-incriminating admissions.

In addition *Miranda* appeared to hold that such suspects—unlike witnesses in a judicial proceeding—have a right to remain completely silent. This seems to mean they have the right to refuse to answer any questions whether the answers would be incriminating or not.

The decision also made clear that such suspects have a right to counsel even during the interrogation. Further, they have a right to certain admonitions or warnings.

To what extent does *Miranda* give persons faced with possible custodial interrogation a right not to be interrogated at all? To the extent that suspects do have such a right, is it only a limited one incident to other rights? It might, for example, apply only to persons who do not waive the right to counsel and bar interrogation only until counsel is present. Or it might be a general—and in a sense an "ultimate"—one that entitles the suspect to be free of any efforts to persuade that suspect to give up the other rights.

2. APPLICABILITY OF *MIRANDA*

EDITORS' INTRODUCTION: "THRESHOLD" ISSUES AND EXCEPTIONS

Soon after the *Miranda* decision, the Court rejected arguments that its requirements be limited to stationhouse interrogation or at least not applied to custodial questioning conducted in surroundings familiar to the suspect. Orozco v. Texas, 394 U.S. 324, 89 S.Ct. 1095 (1969), held *Miranda* applicable to questioning of Orozco in his own bedroom by four officers who entered the bedroom and awoke, arrested, and questioned him.

Nevertheless, the *Miranda* opinion itself made clear that the requirements established by the case did not apply to all out-of-court confessions or statements by defendants. Rather, those requirements must be respected only in situations involving both "custody" and "interrogation." When these threshold requirements for the application of *Miranda* are met is addressed in the two subsections that follow.

The Court has also considered arguments for exceptions releasing officers from the *Miranda* requirements in situations involving what is at least "technically" custodial interrogation.

Public Safety Exception

A "public safety" exception to the *Miranda* requirements, applicable despite the existence of both custody and interrogation, was adopted and applied in New York v. Quarles, 467 U.S. 649, 104 S.Ct. 2626 (1984).

In *Quarles*, a woman approached two New York police officers and reported that she had just been raped by a man who entered a nearby supermarket carrying a gun. Upon arrival at the supermarket, one officer (Kraft) entered the store and the other radioed for assistance. Officer Kraft quickly observed Quarles, who met the woman's description. Apparently upon seeing Officer Kraft, Quarles ran towards the rear of the store. Kraft drew his weapon and pursued Quarles. Although he lost sight of Quarles for several seconds, Officer Kraft soon saw him again and ordered Quarles to stop and place his hands over his head. Several other officers had since arrived. Kraft approached Quarles and, upon frisking him, discovered he was wearing an empty shoulder holster. Quarles was handcuffed. Kraft then, without providing any *Miranda* warnings, asked Quarles where the gun was. Nodding in the direction of some empty cartons, Quarles responded by saying, "The gun is over there." Kraft searched the area and found a loaded .38 caliber revolver. Quarles was then warned under *Miranda* and agreed to answer questions without an attorney present. In response to questions by Kraft, Quarles admitted ownership of the gun and explained how he had acquired it. Before Quarles' trial for criminal possession of a weapon, the trial court considered the admissibility of the revolver, his pre-warning statement, "The gun is over there," and his post-warning admissions. Both the gun and the pre-warning statement were held inadmissible because of Officer Kraft's failure to comply with *Miranda* before asking about the gun's location; the post-warning admissions were excluded as tainted by the preceding *Miranda* violation.

By a five-to-four vote, the Supreme Court reversed. *Miranda* had not been violated, it held, because Officer Kraft's actions came within a "narrow exception" to *Miranda* for situations in which the officer's question is prompted by concern for the public safety. This exception, Justice Rehnquist explained for the Court, is consistent with *Miranda*'s rationale. In most situations, the cost of respecting *Miranda*'s requirements is the possibility of fewer convictions; this cost is acceptable given the value of the *Miranda* requirements in protecting the underlying right to freedom from compelled self-incrimination. But where in addition compliance with the *Miranda* requirement poses an immediate risk to public safety, the cost becomes unacceptably high:

> We decline to place officers such as Officer Kraft in the untenable position of having to consider, often in a matter of seconds, whether it best serves society for them to ask the necessary questions without the *Miranda* warnings and render whatever probative evidence they uncover inadmissible, or for them to give the warnings in order to preserve the admissibility of evidence they might uncover but possibly damage or destroy their ability to obtain that evidence and neutralize the volatile situation confronting them.

467 U.S. at 657–58, 104 S.Ct. at 2632. On the facts before it, the Court found sufficient risk to public safety. Officer Kraft had reason to believe the gun was somewhere in the store where it might be retrieved by an accomplice of Quarles or discovered by a store employee or customer.

The Supreme Court observed it was presented with no claim that Quarles's pre-warning statement was "actually compelled by police conduct which overcame his will to resist." Quarles was free to argue on remand that his statement was "coerced under traditional due process standards." The Court's holding, Justice Rehnquist emphasized, was not a rejection of this argument; he explained, "we merely reject the * * * argument * * * that the statement must be *presumed* compelled because of Officer Kraft's failure to read [Quarles] his *Miranda* warnings." 467 U.S. at 655 n. 5, 104 S.Ct. at 2631 n. 5 (emphasis in original).

Routine Booking Question Exception

A plurality of the Court recognized another exception in Pennsylvania v. Muniz, 496 U.S. 582, 110 S.Ct. 2638 (1990). After his arrest for drunk-driving, Muniz was taken to the stationhouse. During the ensuing procedure, and without complying with *Miranda*, an officer asked Muniz his name, address, height, weight, eye color, date of birth, and current age. This was videotaped. Justice Brennan, writing for a plurality of four justices, explained why the plurality regarded his answers admissible:

> We agree with amicus United States * * * that Muniz's answers to these * * * questions are * * * admissible because the questions fall within a "routine booking question" exception which exempts from *Miranda*'s coverage questions to secure the "biographical data necessary to complete booking or pretrial services." Brief for the United States as Amicus Curiae 12 * * * . The state court found that the first seven questions were "requested for recordkeeping purposes only," and therefore the questions appear reasonably related to the police's administrative concerns. In this context, therefore, the * * *

questions * * * fall outside the protections of *Miranda* and the answers thereto need not be suppressed.

495 U.S. at 601–02, 110 S.Ct. at 2650. He added:

> As amicus United States explains, "[r]ecognizing a 'booking exception' to *Miranda* does not mean, of course, that any question asked during the booking process falls within that exception. Without obtaining a waiver of the suspect's *Miranda* rights, the police may not ask questions, even during booking, that are designed to elicit incriminatory admissions." Brief for United States as Amicus Curiae 13.

495 U.S. at 602 n. 14, 110 S.Ct. at 2650 n. 14.

* * *

Although these exceptions may render *Miranda* inapplicable to some situations, the major limitations on the scope of the decision arise from the requirements of, first, interrogation and, second, custody. The following two subsections address these prerequisites to the application of *Miranda*.

a.   THE REQUIREMENT OF "INTERROGATION"

Unless a suspect in custody is subjected to "interrogation," *Miranda* has no applicability. Thus when a statement is "volunteered" by a suspect in custody, it is admissible despite the failure to comply with *Miranda* requirements.

Rhode Island v. Innis

Supreme Court of the United States, 1980.
446 U.S. 291, 100 S.Ct. 1682.

■ MR. JUSTICE STEWART delivered the opinion of the Court.

* * * The issue in this case is whether the respondent was "interrogated" in violation of the standards promulgated in the *Miranda* opinion.

I.

On the night of January 12, 1975, John Mulvaney, a Providence, R. I., taxicab driver, disappeared after being dispatched to pick up a customer. His body was discovered four days later buried in a shallow grave in Coventry, R. I. He had died from a shotgun blast aimed at the back of his head.

On January 17, 1975, shortly after midnight, the Providence police received a telephone call from Gerald Aubin, also a taxicab driver, who reported that he had just been robbed by a man wielding a sawed-off shotgun. Aubin further reported that he had dropped off his assailant near Rhode Island College in a section of Providence known as Mount Pleasant. While at the Providence police station waiting to give a statement, Aubin noticed a picture of his assailant on a bulletin board. Aubin so informed one of the police officers present. The officer prepared a photo array, and again Aubin identified a picture of the same person. That person was the respondent. Shortly thereafter, the Providence police began a search of the Mount Pleasant area.

At approximately 4:30 a. m. on the same date, Patrolman Lovell, while cruising the streets of Mount Pleasant in a patrol car, spotted the respondent standing in the street facing him. When Patrolman Lovell stopped his car, the respondent walked towards it. Patrolman Lovell then arrested the respondent, who was unarmed, and advised him of his so-called *Miranda* rights. While the two men waited in the patrol car for other police officers to arrive, Patrolman Lovell did not converse with the respondent other than to respond to the latter's request for a cigarette.

Within minutes, Sergeant Sears arrived at the scene of the arrest, and he also gave the respondent the *Miranda* warnings. Immediately thereafter, Captain Leyden and other police officers arrived. Captain Leyden advised the respondent of his *Miranda* rights. The respondent stated that he understood those rights and wanted to speak with a lawyer. Captain Leyden then directed that the respondent be placed in a "caged wagon," a four-door police car with a wire screen mesh between the front and rear seats, and be driven to the central police station. Three officers, Patrolmen Gleckman, Williams, and McKenna, were assigned to accompany the respondent to the central station. They placed the respondent in the vehicle and shut the doors. Captain Leyden then instructed the officers not to question the respondent or intimidate or coerce him in any way. The three officers then entered the vehicle, and it departed.

While en route to the central station, Patrolman Gleckman initiated a conversation with Patrolman McKenna concerning the missing shotgun. As Patrolman Gleckman later testified:

> "A. At this point, I was talking back and forth with Patrolman McKenna stating that I frequent this area while on patrol and [that because a school for handicapped children is located nearby,] there's a lot of handicapped children running around in this area, and God forbid one of them might find a weapon with shells and they might hurt themselves."

Patrolman McKenna apparently shared his fellow officer's concern:

> "A. I more or less concurred with him [Gleckman] that it was a safety factor and that we should, you know, continue to search for the weapon and try to find it."

* * *

The respondent then interrupted the conversation, stating that the officers should turn the car around so he could show them where the gun was located. At this point, Patrolman McKenna radioed back to Captain Leyden that they were returning to the scene of the arrest, and that the respondent would inform them of the location of the gun. At the time the respondent indicated that the officers should turn back, they had traveled no more than a mile, a trip encompassing only a few minutes.

The police vehicle then returned to the scene of the arrest where a search for the shotgun was in progress. There, Captain Leyden again advised the respondent of his *Miranda* rights. The respondent replied that he understood those rights but that he "wanted to get the gun out of the way because of the kids in the area in the school." The respondent then led the police to a nearby field, where he pointed out the shotgun under some rocks by the side of the road.

On March 20, 1975, a grand jury returned an indictment charging the respondent with the kidnapping, robbery, and murder of John Mulvaney. Before trial, the respondent moved to suppress the shotgun and the statements he had made to the police regarding it. * * * [T]he trial court sustained the admissibility of the shotgun and testimony related to its discovery. That evidence was later introduced at the respondent's trial, and the jury returned a verdict of guilty on all counts.

* * *

II

* * *

In the present case, the parties are in agreement that the respondent was fully informed of his *Miranda* rights and that he invoked his *Miranda* right to counsel when he told Captain Leyden that he wished to consult with a lawyer. It is also uncontested that the respondent was "in custody" while being transported to the police station.

The issue, therefore, is whether the respondent was "interrogated" by the police officers in violation of the respondent's undisputed right under *Miranda* to remain silent until he had consulted with a lawyer. In resolving this issue, we first define the term "interrogation" under *Miranda* before turning to a consideration of the facts of this case.

A

The starting point for defining "interrogation" in this context is, of course, the Court's *Miranda* opinion. There the Court observed that "[b]y custodial interrogation, we mean *questioning* initiated by law enforcement officers after a person has been taken into custody or otherwise deprived of his freedom of action in any significant way." This passage and other references throughout the opinion to "questioning" might suggest that the *Miranda* rules were to apply only to those police interrogation practices that involve express questioning of a defendant while in custody.

We do not, however, construe the *Miranda* opinion so narrowly. The concern of the Court in *Miranda* was that the "interrogation environment" created by the interplay of interrogation and custody would "subjugate the individual to the will of his examiner" and thereby undermine the privilege against compulsory self-incrimination. The police practices that evoked this concern included several that did not involve express questioning. For example, one of the practices discussed in *Miranda* was the use of lineups in which a coached witness would pick the defendant as the perpetrator. This was designed to establish that the defendant was in fact guilty as a predicate for further interrogation. A variation on this theme discussed in *Miranda* was the so-called "reverse line-up" in which a defendant would be identified by coached witnesses as the perpetrator of a fictitious crime, with the object of inducing him to confess to the actual crime of which he was suspected in order to escape the false prosecution. The Court in *Miranda* also included in its survey of interrogation practices the use of psychological ploys, such as to "posi[t]" "the guilt of the subject," to "minimize the moral seriousness of the offense," and "to cast blame on the victim or on society." It is clear that these techniques of persuasion, no less than express questioning, were thought, in a custodial setting, to amount to interrogation.

This is not to say, however, that all statements obtained by the police after a person has been taken into custody are to be considered the product of interrogation. * * * It is clear * * * that the special procedural safeguards outlined in *Miranda* are required not where a suspect is simply taken into custody, but rather where a suspect in custody is subjected to interrogation. "Interrogation," as conceptualized in the *Miranda* opinion, must reflect a measure of compulsion above and beyond that inherent in custody itself.

We conclude that the *Miranda* safeguards come into play whenever a person in custody is subjected to either express questioning or its functional equivalent. That is to say, the term "interrogation" under *Miranda* refers not only to express questioning, but also to any words or actions on the part of the police (other than those normally attendant to arrest and custody) that the police should know are reasonably likely to elicit an incriminating response from the suspect. The latter portion of this definition focuses primarily upon the perceptions of the suspect, rather than the intent of the police. This focus reflects the fact that the *Miranda* safeguards were designed to vest a suspect in custody with an added measure of protection against coercive police practices, without regard to objective proof of the underlying intent of the police. A practice that the police should know is reasonably likely to evoke an incriminating response from a suspect thus amounts to interrogation.[7] But, since the police surely cannot be held accountable for the unforeseeable results of their words or actions, the definition of interrogation can extend only to

---

[7]   This is not to say that the intent of the police is irrelevant, for it may well have a bearing on whether the police should have known that their words or actions were reasonably likely to evoke an incriminating response. In particular, where a police practice is designed to elicit an incriminating response from the accused, it is unlikely that the practice will not also be one which the police should have known was reasonably likely to have that effect.

words or actions on the part of police officers that they *should have known* were reasonably likely to elicit an incriminating response.[8]

B

Turning to the facts of the present case, we conclude that the respondent was not "interrogated" within the meaning of *Miranda*. It is undisputed that the first prong of the definition of "interrogation" was not satisfied, for the conversation between Patrolmen Gleckman and McKenna included no express questioning of the respondent. Rather, that conversation was, at least in form, nothing more than a dialogue between the two officers to which no response from the respondent was invited.

Moreover, it cannot be fairly concluded that the respondent was subjected to the "functional equivalent" of questioning. It cannot be said, in short, that Patrolmen Gleckman and McKenna should have known that their conversation was reasonably likely to elicit an incriminating response from the respondent. There is nothing in the record to suggest that the officers were aware that the respondent was peculiarly susceptible to an appeal to his conscience concerning the safety of handicapped children. Nor is there anything in the record to suggest that the police knew that the respondent was unusually disoriented or upset at the time of his arrest.[9]

The case thus boils down to whether, in the context of a brief conversation, the officers should have known that the respondent would suddenly be moved to make a self-incriminating response. Given the fact that the entire conversation appears to have consisted of no more than a few offhand remarks, we cannot say that the officers should have known that it was reasonably likely that Innis would so respond. This is not a case where the police carried on a lengthy harangue in the presence of the suspect. Nor does the record support the respondent's contention that, under the circumstances, the officers' comments were particularly "evocative." It is our view, therefore, that the respondent was not subjected by the police to words or actions that the police should have known were reasonably likely to elicit an incriminating response from him.

The Rhode Island Supreme Court erred * * * in equating "subtle compulsion" with interrogation. That the officers' comments struck a responsive cord is readily apparent. Thus, it may be said, as the Rhode Island Supreme Court did say, that the respondent was subjected to "subtle compulsion." But that is not the end of the inquiry. It must also

---

[8] Any knowledge the police may have had concerning the unusual susceptibility of a defendant to a particular form of persuasion might be an important factor in determining whether the police should have known that their words or actions were reasonably likely to elicit an incriminating response from the suspect.

[9] The record in no way suggests that the officers' remarks were *designed* to elicit a response. It is significant that the trial judge, after hearing the officers' testimony, concluded that it was "entirely understandable that [the officers] would voice their concern [for the safety of the handicapped children] to each other."

be established that a suspect's incriminating response was the product of words or actions on the part of the police that they should have known were reasonably likely to elicit an incriminating response.[10] This was not established in the present case.

* * *

■ MR. JUSTICE STEVENS, dissenting.

* * *

[I]n order to give full protection to a suspect's right to be free from any interrogation at all [after he has invoked his right to cut off questioning], the definition of "interrogation" must include any police statement or conduct that has the same purpose or effect as a direct question. Statements that appear to call for a response from the suspect, as well as those that are designed to do so, should be considered interrogation. By prohibiting only those relatively few statements or actions that a police officer should know are likely to elicit an incriminating response, the Court today accords a suspect considerably less protection. Indeed, * * * this new definition will almost certainly exclude every statement that is not punctuated with a question mark from the concept of "interrogation."

* * *

In any event, I think the Court is clearly wrong in holding, as a matter of law, that Officer Gleckman should not have realized that his statement was likely to elicit an incriminating response. * * *

The Court's assumption that criminal suspects are not susceptible to appeals to conscience is directly contrary to the teachings of police interrogation manuals, which recommend appealing to a suspect's sense of morality as a standard and often successful interrogation technique. Surely the practical experience embodied in such manuals should not be ignored in a case such as this in which the record is devoid of any evidence—one way or the other—as to the susceptibility of suspects in general or of Innis in particular.

Moreover, there is evidence in the record to support the view that Officer Gleckman's statement was intended to elicit a response from Innis. Officer Gleckman, who was not regularly assigned to the caged wagon, was directed by a police captain to ride with respondent to the police station. Although there is a dispute in the testimony, it appears that Gleckman may well have been riding in the back seat with Innis. The record does not explain why, notwithstanding the fact that respondent was handcuffed, unarmed, and had offered no resistance

---

[10] By way of example, if the police had done no more than to drive past the site of the concealed weapon while taking the most direct route to the police station, and if the respondent, upon noticing for the first time the proximity of the school for handicapped children, had blurted out that he would show the officers where the gun was located, it could not seriously be argued that this "subtle compulsion" would have constituted "interrogation" within the meaning of the *Miranda* opinion.

when arrested by an officer acting alone, the captain ordered Officer Gleckman to ride with respondent. It is not inconceivable that two professionally trained police officers concluded that a few well-chosen remarks might induce respondent to disclose the whereabouts of the shotgun. This conclusion becomes even more plausible in light of the emotionally charged words chosen by Officer Gleckman ("God forbid" that a "little girl" should find the gun and hurt herself).

NOTES

1. *Innis* was applied in Arizona v. Mauro, 481 U.S. 520, 107 S.Ct. 1931 (1987). Mauro was arrested after he approached authorities, volunteered he had killed his young son, and led authorities to the victim's body. At the stationhouse, he was advised of his *Miranda* rights. He told officers he did not want to make any more statements until his lawyer was present. Questioning then ceased. Meanwhile, Mauro's wife, who had been questioned by other officers, asked to speak to him. After discussion, the officer in charge (Sergeant Allen) permitted this. Mrs. Mauro was taken to the office in which Mauro was held. The couple was told they could speak only if an officer remained present and the officer—Detective Manson—then placed a tape recorder in plain sight. A brief conversation ensued in which Mrs. Mauro expressed despair regarding the situation and Mauro urged his wife not to answer questions until a lawyer was present. At trial, Mauro presented a defense of insanity. The state then in rebuttal sought to prove the conversation between Mauro and his wife to show that Mauro was functioning in a sane fashion. The defense objected that the conversation was the result of "interrogation" conducted in violation of *Miranda* because Mauro had invoked his right to counsel which barred further "interrogation" until a lawyer was present. Nevertheless, the evidence was admitted. By a 5–4 vote, the Supreme Court found no *Miranda* defect. The majority noted some uncertainty in the record as to whether Mauro was given advance notice that his wife would be coming to speak with him. Assuming no notice was provided, however, the Court explained:

> The sole issue * * * is whether the officers' * * * actions rose to the level of interrogation—that is, in the language of *Innis,* whether they were the "functional equivalent" of police interrogation. We think it is clear under both *Miranda* and *Innis* that Mauro was not interrogated. * * * Detective Manson asked Mauro no questions about the crime or his conduct. Nor is it suggested—or supported by any evidence—that Sergeant Allen's decision to allow Mauro's wife to see him was the kind of psychological ploy that properly could be treated as the functional equivalent of interrogation.
>
> There is no evidence that the officers sent Mrs. Mauro in to see her husband for the purpose of eliciting incriminating statements. * * * [T]he weakness of Mauro's claim that he was interrogated is underscored by examining the situation from his perspective. We doubt that a suspect, told by officers that his wife will be allowed to speak to him, would feel that he was being coerced to incriminate

himself in any way. * * * Officers do not interrogate a suspect simply by hoping that he will incriminate himself. * * * Mauro was not subjected to compelling influences, psychological ploys, or direct questioning. Thus, his voluntered statements cannot properly be considered the result of police interrogation.

481 U.S. at 527–29, 107 S.Ct. at 1935–37. Justice Stevens, joined by Justices Brennan, Marshall and Blackmun, dissented.

2.   **Request for Submission to Blood Alcohol Test.** In *Innis,* the Court indicated "interrogation" did not include police words or activity "normally attendant to arrest and custody." In South Dakota v. Neville, 459 U.S. 553, 103 S.Ct. 916 (1983), relying on this *Innis* dictum, the Court held that a request a suspect submit to a blood alcohol test is not "interrogation." Justice O'Connor explained for the Court:

> The police inquiry * * * is highly regulated by state law, and is presented in virtually the same words to all suspects. It is similar to a police request to submit to fingerprinting or photography.

459 U.S. at 564 n. 15, 103 S.Ct. at 923 n. 15.

b.   THE REQUIREMENT OF "CUSTODY"

EDITORS' INTRODUCTION: *MIRANDA*'S CUSTODY PREREQUISITE

The requirement of custody has given rise to more Supreme Court consideration than the requirement of interrogation. In Oregon v. Mathiason, 429 U.S. 492, 97 S.Ct. 711 (1977) (per curiam), the Court made clear that the need for custody was firm. *Miranda* would not be applied where custody was lacking, *Mathiason* held, even if the situation presented a "coercive environment" in some sense.

When custody exists has presented a source of continuing controversy. In *Mathiason*, the Court concluded a parolee who appeared at a police station in response to an officer's request for a discussion was not in custody for purposes of *Miranda*. The majority explained, "*Miranda* warnings are required only where there has been such a restriction on a person's freedom as to render him 'in custody.'"

The Court developed and applied the *Mathiason* standard for custody in California v. Beheler, 463 U.S. 1121, 103 S.Ct. 3517 (1983) (per curiam). Beheler himself called police after he and several others attempted to rob a drug dealer and one of the others killed the dealer. He admitted his participation and consented to a search of his backyard; the murder weapon was located there, as he said it would be. That evening, he agreed to accompany officers to the stationhouse. The officers told him he was not under arrest. During a thirty-minute interview, he again acknowledged his participation. He was told his statement would be evaluated by the district attorney and he was then permitted to leave. The stationhouse statement was admitted over defense objection at Beheler's trial for aiding and abetting first degree murder. An intermediate California appellate court, however, held admission of the statement violated *Miranda,* reasoning that the prosecution had failed to meet its burden of establishing lack of custody. *Mathiason* was distinguished on several grounds: (a) the interview with Beheler took place soon after the offense, while that with Mathiason occurred 25 days after the crime under investigation; (b) the officers had more information implicating Beheler than had been available against Mathiason at the time of his interview; (c) Beheler had been drinking and was emotionally upset; and (d) Beheler was not a parolee and therefore lacked a parolee's incentive to cooperate with law enforcement officers by voluntarily consenting to an interview.

The Supreme Court reversed. Under *Mathiason,* it explained, "the ultimate inquiry is simply whether there is a 'formal arrest or restraint on freedom of movement' of the degree associated with a formal arrest." Considerations (a) and (b) summarized above, it continued, are irrelevant to this inquiry. Properly framed, the issue presented "is whether *Miranda* warnings are required if the suspect is not placed under arrest, voluntarily comes to the police station, and is allowed to leave unhindered by the police after a brief interview." Since its past decisions clearly directed a negative answer, the Court reversed the decision of the California appellate tribunal.

Similarly, a probationer who appeared at his probation officer's office in response to her request for a meeting with the officer was not in custody under *Mathiason* and *Beheler*. Minnesota v. Murphy, 465 U.S. 420, 104 S.Ct. 1136 (1984).

In 1994, the Court returned to the custody problem in Stansbury v. California, 511 U.S. 318, 114 S.Ct. 1526 (1994) (per curiam). Officers investigating the rape and murder of a ten-year old girl learned that on the day of her death the victim had been seen talking to Stansbury, an ice cream truck driver. At 11:00 p.m., four officers went to Stansbury's trailer home and asked if he would accompany them to the police station to answer some questions. He agreed. During subsequent questioning conducted without *Miranda* warnings, Stansbury made incriminating admissions. The state court held the statement nevertheless admissible, stressing in part that suspicion had not focused on Stansbury until he made the statement. The Supreme Court responded:

> Our decisions make clear that the initial determination of custody depends on the objective circumstances of the interrogation, not on the subjective views harbored by either the interrogating officers or the person being questioned. * * *
>
> [A] police officer's subjective view that the individual under questioning is a suspect, if undisclosed, does not bear upon the question whether the individual is in custody for purposes of *Miranda*. The same principle obtains if an officer's undisclosed assessment is that the person being questioned is not a suspect. In either instance, one cannot expect the person under interrogation to probe the officer's innermost thoughts. Save as

they are communicated or otherwise manifested to the person being questioned, an officer's evolving but unarticulated suspicions do not affect the objective circumstances of an interrogation or interview, and thus cannot affect the *Miranda* custody inquiry. * * *

An officer's knowledge or beliefs may bear upon the custody issue if they are conveyed, by word or deed, to the individual being questioned. Those beliefs are relevant only to the extent they would affect how a reasonable person in the position of the individual being questioned would gauge the breadth of his or her " 'freedom of action.' " Even a clear statement from an officer that the person under interrogation is a prime suspect is not, in itself, dispositive of the custody issue, for some suspects are free to come and go until the police decide to make an arrest. The weight and pertinence of any communications regarding the officer's degree of suspicion will depend upon the facts and circumstances of the particular case. In sum, an officer's views concerning the nature of an interrogation, or beliefs concerning the potential culpability of the individual being questioned, may be one among many factors that bear upon the assessment whether that individual was in custody, but only if the officer's views or beliefs were somehow manifested to the individual under interrogation and would have affected how a reasonable person in that position would perceive his or her freedom to leave. (Of course, instances may arise in which the officer's undisclosed views are relevant in testing the credibility of his or her account of what happened during an interrogation; but it is the objective surroundings, and not any undisclosed views, that control the *Miranda* custody inquiry.)

511 U.S. at 523–25, 114 S.Ct. at 1529–30. The state court's analysis suggested the court may have regarded the officers' subjective beliefs regarding Stansbury's status "as significant in and of themselves, rather than as relevant only to the extent they influenced the objective conditions surrounding his interrogation." Nevertheless, the parties disagreed on whether the objective facts in the record supported a finding that Stansbury was in custody. Concluding the state court should consider this question in the first instance, the Supreme Court reversed the judgment of the state tribunal and remanded the case "for further proceedings not inconsistent with this opinion."

The nature of the custody determination was again addressed in J.D.B. v. North Carolina, 564 U.S. 261, 131 S.Ct. 2394 (2011). J.D.B. was a 13-year-old seventh grade middle school student. A uniformed school resource police officer interrupted his class, removed him from the classroom, and escorted him to a conference room. In that room were—in addition to the resource officer—an assistant principal, an administrative intern, and a police juvenile investigator. J.D.B. was questioned for 30–45 minutes about a break-in and a larceny, and he made oral admissions and wrote out an incriminating statement. Failure to comply with the *Miranda* requirements did not affect the admissibility of the admissions and statements, the state courts held, because J.D.B. was not in custody. J.D.B.'s age, the North Carolina Supreme Court reasoned, was not relevant to whether he was in custody.

By a 5-to-4 vote, the Supreme Court held the state tribunal erred in its analysis. Generally, Justice Sotomayor explained for the majority, whether a suspect is "in custody" is an objective question:

> The benefit of the objective custody analysis is that it is "designed to give clear guidance to the police." Police must make in-the-moment judgments as to when to administer *Miranda* warnings. By limiting analysis to the objective circumstances of the interrogation, and asking how a reasonable person in the suspect's position would understand his freedom to terminate questioning and leave, the objective test avoids burdening police with the task of anticipating the idiosyncrasies of every individual suspect and divining how those particular traits affect each person's subjective state of mind.

564 U.S. at 271, 131 S.Ct. at 2402.

Nevertheless, the age of a child-suspect must be considered in determining whether the suspect was in custody, "[s]o long as the child's age was known to the officer at the time of the interview, or would have been objectively apparent to any reasonable officer * * * ." The *J.D.B.* majority explained:

> [A] reasonable child subjected to police questioning will sometimes feel pressured to submit when a reasonable adult would feel free to go. We think it clear that courts can account for that reality without doing any damage to the objective nature of the custody analysis.

564 U.S. at 272, 131 S.Ct. at 2403.

This, the majority continued, is not inconsistent with the discussion in Yarborough v. Alvarado, 541 U.S. 652, 124 S.Ct. 2140 (2004):

> [A] child's age differs from other personal characteristics that, even when known to police, have no objectively discernible relationship to a reasonable person's understanding of his freedom of action. *Alvarado*, holds, for instance, that a suspect's prior interrogation history with law enforcement has no role to play in the custody analysis because such experience could just as easily lead a reasonable person to feel free to walk away as to feel compelled to stay in place. Because the effect in any given case would be "contingent [on the] psycholog[y]" of the individual suspect, the Court explained, such experience cannot be considered without compromising the objective nature of the custody analysis. A child's age, however, is different. Precisely

because childhood yields objective conclusions * * * considering age in the custody analysis in no way involves a determination of how youth "subjectively affect[s] the mindset" of any particular child.

564 U.S. at 275, 131 S.Ct. at 2404–05.

Justice Alito, writing for the four *J.D.B* dissenters, found the majority's result "fundamentally inconsistent" with the need for clarity in *Miranda* law:

> Age * * * is in no way the only personal characteristic that may correlate with pliability, and in future cases the Court will be forced to choose between two unpalatable alternatives. It may choose to limit today's decision by arbitrarily distinguishing a suspect's age from other personal characteristics—such as intelligence, education, occupation, or prior experience with law enforcement—that may also correlate with susceptibility to coercive pressures. Or, if the Court is unwilling to draw these arbitrary lines, it will be forced to effect a fundamental transformation of the *Miranda* custody test—from a clear, easily applied prophylactic rule into a highly fact-intensive standard resembling the voluntariness test that the *Miranda* Court found to be unsatisfactory.

564 U.S. at 283, 131 S.Ct. at 2409 (Alito, J., dissenting). Further, the dissenters argued that suspects unusually sensitive to law enforcement pressure because of their age or other characteristics could be adequately protected by those suspects' ability to challenge the voluntariness of their statements:

> The voluntariness inquiry is flexible and accommodating by nature, and the Court's precedents already make clear that "special care" must be exercised in applying the voluntariness test where the confession of a "mere child" is at issue. If *Miranda*'s rigid, one-size-fits-all standards fail to account for the unique needs of juveniles, the response should be to rigorously apply the constitutional rule against coercion to ensure that the rights of minors are protected. There is no need to run *Miranda* off the rails.

564 U.S. at 297–98, 131 S.Ct. at 2418.

Stansbury, *Alverado*, and *J.D.B.* emphasized suspects' perceptions regarding their ability to break off interactions with police. Nevertheless, the following principal case makes clear that custody does not depend entirely upon whether a reasonable person would believe himself unable to do this.

Berkemer v. McCarty

Supreme Court of the United States, 1984.
468 U.S. 420, 104 S.Ct. 3138.

■ JUSTICE MARSHALL delivered the opinion of the Court.

This case presents two related questions: First, does our decision in *Miranda v. Arizona*, 384 U.S. 436, 86 S.Ct. 1602, 16 L.Ed.2d 694 (1966), govern the admissibility of statements made during custodial interrogation by a suspect accused of a misdemeanor traffic offense? Second, does the roadside questioning of a motorist detained pursuant to a traffic stop constitute custodial interrogation for the purposes of the doctrine enunciated in *Miranda?*

I

A

The parties have stipulated to the essential facts. On the evening of March 31, 1980, Trooper Williams of the Ohio State Highway Patrol observed respondent's car weaving in and out of a lane on Interstate Highway 270. After following the car for two miles, Williams forced respondent to stop and asked him to get out of the vehicle. When respondent complied, Williams noticed that he was having difficulty standing. At that point, "Williams concluded that [respondent] would be charged with a traffic offense and, therefore, his freedom to leave the scene was terminated." However, respondent was not told that he would be taken into custody. Williams then asked respondent to perform a field sobriety test, commonly known as a "balancing test." Respondent could not do so without falling.

While still at the scene of the traffic stop, Williams asked respondent whether he had been using intoxicants. Respondent replied that "he had consumed two beers and had smoked several joints of marijuana a short time before." Respondent's speech was slurred, and Williams had difficulty understanding him. Williams thereupon formally placed respondent under arrest and transported him in the patrol car to the Franklin County Jail.

At the jail, respondent was given an intoxilyzer test to determine the concentration of alcohol in his blood. The test did not detect any alcohol whatsoever in respondent's system. Williams then resumed questioning respondent in order to obtain information for inclusion in the State Highway Patrol Alcohol Influence Report. Respondent answered affirmatively a question whether he had been drinking. When then asked if he was under the influence of alcohol, he said, "I guess, barely." Williams next asked respondent to indicate on the form whether the marihuana he had smoked had been treated with any chemicals. In the section of the report headed "Remarks," respondent wrote, "No ang[el] dust or PCP in the pot. Rick McCarty."

At no point in this sequence of events did Williams or anyone else tell respondent that he had a right to remain silent, to consult with an attorney, and to have an attorney appointed for him if he could not afford one.

B

Respondent was charged with operating a motor vehicle while under the influence of alcohol and/or drugs * * * . Under Ohio law, that offense is a first-degree misdemeanor and is punishable by fine or imprisonment for up to 6 months. Incarceration for a minimum of 3 days is mandatory.

Respondent moved to exclude the various incriminating statements he had made to Patrolman Williams on the ground that introduction into evidence of those statements would violate the Fifth Amendment insofar as he had not been informed of his constitutional rights prior to his interrogation. When the trial court denied the motion, respondent pleaded "no contest" and was found guilty. He was sentenced to 90 days in jail, 80 of which were suspended, and was fined $300, $100 of which were suspended.

On appeal [in the state courts, respondent's conviction was affirmed.]

Respondent then filed an action for a writ of habeas corpus in the District Court for the Southern District of Ohio. The District Court dismissed the petition * * * .

A divided panel of the Court of Appeals for the Sixth Circuit reversed, holding that "*Miranda* warnings must be given to *all* individuals prior to custodial interrogation, whether the offense investigated be a felony or a misdemeanor traffic offense." * * *

We granted certiorari * * * .

II

* * *

In the years since the decision in *Miranda,* we have frequently reaffirmed the central principle established by that case: if the police take a suspect into custody and then ask him questions without informing him of the rights enumerated above, his responses cannot be introduced into evidence to establish his guilt.

Petitioner asks us to carve an exception out of the foregoing principle. When the police arrest a person for allegedly committing a misdemeanor traffic offense and then ask him questions without telling him his constitutional rights, petitioner argues, his responses should be admissible against him. We cannot agree.

One of the principal advantages of the doctrine that suspects must be given warnings before being interrogated while in custody is the clarity of that rule. * * * The exception to *Miranda* proposed by petitioner would substantially undermine this crucial advantage of the doctrine.

The police often are unaware when they arrest a person whether he may have committed a misdemeanor or a felony. * * * It would be unreasonable to expect the police to make guesses as to the nature of the criminal conduct at issue before deciding how they may interrogate the suspect.

* * *

We hold * * * that a person subjected to custodial interrogation is entitled to the benefit of the procedural safeguards enunciated in *Miranda,* regardless of the nature or severity of the offense of which he is suspected or for which he was arrested.

The * * * statements made by respondent at the County Jail were inadmissible. There can be no question that respondent was "in custody" at least as of the moment he was formally placed under arrest and instructed to get into the police car. Because he was not informed of his constitutional rights at that juncture, respondent's subsequent admissions should not have been used against him.

III

To assess the admissibility of the self-incriminating statements made by respondent prior to his formal arrest, we are obliged to address a second issue concerning the scope of our decision in *Miranda:* whether the roadside questioning of a motorist detained pursuant to a routine traffic stop should be considered "custodial interrogation." Respondent urges that it should, on the ground that *Miranda* by its terms applies whenever "a person has been taken into custody *or otherwise deprived of his freedom of action in any significant way.*" Petitioner contends that a holding that every detained motorist must be advised of his rights before being questioned would constitute an unwarranted extension of the *Miranda* doctrine.

It must be acknowledged at the outset that a traffic stop significantly curtails the "freedom of action" of the driver and the passengers, if any, of the detained vehicle. Under the law of most States, it is a crime either to ignore a policeman's signal to stop one's car or, once having stopped, to drive away without permission. Certainly few motorists would feel free either to disobey a directive to pull over or to leave the scene of a traffic stop without being told they might do so. * * *

However, we decline to accord talismanic power to the phrase in the *Miranda* opinion emphasized by respondent. Fidelity to the doctrine announced in *Miranda* requires that it be enforced strictly, but only in those types of situations in which the concerns that powered the decision are implicated. Thus, we must decide whether a traffic stop exerts upon a detained person pressures that sufficiently impair his free exercise of his privilege against self-incrimination to require that he be warned of his constitutional rights.

Two features of an ordinary traffic stop mitigate the danger that a person questioned will be induced "to speak where he would not otherwise do so freely." First, detention of a motorist pursuant to a traffic stop is presumptively temporary and brief. The vast majority of roadside detentions last only a few minutes. A motorist's expectations, when he sees a policeman's light flashing behind him, are that he will be obliged to spend a short period of time answering questions and waiting while the officer checks his license and registration, that he may then be given a citation, but that in the end he most likely will be allowed to continue on his way. In this respect, questioning incident to an ordinary traffic stop is quite different from stationhouse interrogation, which frequently is prolonged, and in which the detainee often is aware that questioning will continue until he provides his interrogators the answers they seek.[27]

Second, circumstances associated with the typical traffic stop are not such that the motorist feels completely at the mercy of the police. To be sure, the aura of authority surrounding an armed, uniformed officer and the knowledge that the officer has some discretion in deciding whether to issue a citation, in combination, exert some pressure on the detainee to respond to questions. But other aspects of the situation substantially offset these forces. Perhaps most importantly, the typical traffic stop is public, at least to some degree. Passersby, on foot or in other cars, witness the interaction of officer and motorist. This exposure to public view both reduces the ability of an unscrupulous policeman to use illegitimate means to elicit self-incriminating statements and diminishes the motorist's fear that, if he does not cooperate, he will be subjected to abuse. The fact that the detained motorist typically is confronted by only one or at most two policemen further mutes his sense of vulnerability. In short, the atmosphere surrounding an ordinary traffic stop is substantially less "police dominated" than that surrounding the kinds of interrogation at issue in *Miranda* itself, and in the subsequent cases in which we have applied *Miranda*.

In both of these respects, the usual traffic stop is more analogous to a so-called "*Terry* stop," see *Terry v. Ohio*, 392 U.S. 1, 88 S.Ct. 1868, 20 L.Ed.2d 889 (1968), than to a formal arrest. Under the Fourth Amendment, we have held, a policeman who lacks probable cause but whose "observations lead him reasonably to suspect" that a particular person has committed, is committing, or is about to commit a crime, may detain that person briefly in order to "investigate the circumstances that provoke suspicion." "[T]he stop and inquiry must be 'reasonably related in scope to the justification for their initiation.'" Typically, this means that the officer may ask the detainee a moderate number of questions to determine his identity and to try to obtain information confirming or dispelling the officer's suspicions. But the detainee is not obliged to respond. And, unless the detainee's answers provide the officer with

---

[27] The brevity and spontaneity of an ordinary traffic stop also reduces the danger that the driver through subterfuge will be made to incriminate himself. One of the investigative techniques that *Miranda* was designed to guard against was the use by police of various kinds of trickery—such as "Mutt and Jeff" routines—to elicit confessions from suspects. A police officer who stops a suspect on the highway has little chance to develop or implement a plan of this sort.

probable cause to arrest him, he must then be released. The comparatively nonthreatening character of detentions of this sort explains the absence of any suggestion in our opinions that *Terry* stops are subject to the dictates of *Miranda.* The similarly noncoercive aspect of ordinary traffic stops prompts us to hold that persons temporarily detained pursuant to such stops are not "in custody" for the purposes of *Miranda.*

Respondent contends that to "exempt" traffic stops from the coverage of *Miranda* will open the way to widespread abuse. Policemen will simply delay formally arresting detained motorists, and will subject them to sustained and intimidating interrogation at the scene of their initial detention. * * * The net result, respondent contends, will be a serious threat to the rights that the *Miranda* doctrine is designed to protect.

We are confident that the state of affairs projected by respondent will not come to pass. It is settled that the safeguards prescribed by *Miranda* become applicable as soon as a suspect's freedom of action is curtailed to a "degree associated with formal arrest." If a motorist who has been detained pursuant to a traffic stop thereafter is subjected to treatment that renders him "in custody" for practical purposes, he will be entitled to the full panoply of protections prescribed by *Miranda.*

Admittedly, our adherence to the doctrine just recounted will mean that the police and lower courts will continue occasionally to have difficulty deciding exactly when a suspect has been taken into custody. Either a rule that *Miranda* applies to all traffic stops or a rule that a suspect need not be advised of his rights until he is formally placed under arrest would provide a clearer, more easily administered line. However, each of these two alternatives has drawbacks that make it unacceptable. The first would substantially impede the enforcement of the nation's traffic laws—by compelling the police either to take the time to warn all detained motorists of their constitutional rights or to forgo use of self-incriminating statements made by those motorists—while doing little to protect citizens' Fifth Amendment rights. The second would enable the police to circumvent the constraints on custodial interrogations established by *Miranda.*

Turning to the case before us, we find nothing in the record that indicates that respondent should have been given *Miranda* warnings at any point prior to the time Trooper Williams placed him under arrest. For the reasons indicated above, we reject the contention that the initial stop of respondent's car, by itself, rendered him "in custody." And respondent has failed to demonstrate that, at any time between the initial stop and the arrest, he was subjected to restraints comparable to those associated with a formal arrest. Only a short period of time elapsed between the stop and the arrest. At no point during that interval was respondent informed that his detention would not be temporary. Although Trooper Williams apparently decided as soon as respondent stepped out of his car that respondent would be taken into custody and charged with a traffic offense, Williams never communicated his intention to respondent. A policeman's unarticulated plan has no bearing on the question whether a suspect was "in custody" at a particular time; the only relevant inquiry is how a reasonable man in the suspect's position would have understood his situation. Nor do other aspects of the interaction of Williams and respondent support the contention that respondent was exposed to "custodial interrogation" at the scene of the stop. From aught that appears in the stipulation of facts, a single police officer asked respondent a modest number of questions and requested him to perform a simple balancing test at a location visible to passing motorists. Treatment of this sort cannot fairly be characterized as the functional equivalent of formal arrest.

We conclude, in short, that respondent was not taken into custody for the purposes of *Miranda* until Williams arrested him. Consequently, the statements respondent made prior to that point were admissible against him.

IV

[W]e agree with the Court of Appeals that respondent's postarrest statements should have been suppressed but conclude that respondent's prearrest statements were admissible * * * .

Accordingly, the judgment of the Court of Appeals is

Affirmed.

NOTES

1. **Modified Warnings for Field Stop Situations.** Insofar as a suspect subjected to a nonarrest detention is not "in custody," *Miranda* is entirely inapplicable. But are there—or should there be—any requirements for interrogation in such circumstances, other than the apparent demand that any resulting admissions be voluntary? Should, for example, the Court have considered whether a modified version of *Miranda* rights might be required by risks posed to suspects' Fifth Amendment interests in traffic stop situations? Might this be required when nonarrest detention is rather an investigatory field stop concerning a serious offense?

The American Law Institute's Model Code of Pre-Arraignment Procedure proposed the following alternatives to govern questioning during nonarrest stops for investigation:

(5) *Questioning of Suspects.*

(a) *Warnings.* If a law enforcement officer stops any person who he suspects or has reasonable cause to suspect may have committed a crime, the officer shall warn such person as promptly as is reasonable under the circumstances, and in any case before engaging in any sustained questioning

(i) that such person is not obligated to say anything, and anything he says may be used in evidence against him,

(ii) that within twenty minutes he will be released unless he is arrested.[,]

[(iii) that if he is arrested he will be taken to a police station where he may promptly communicate by telephone with counsel, relatives or friends, and

(iv) that he will not be questioned unless he wishes, and that if he wishes to consult a lawyer or have a lawyer present during questioning, he will not be questioned at this time, and that after being taken to the stationhouse a lawyer will be furnished him prior to questioning if he is unable to obtain one.]

(b) *Limitations on Questioning.* No law enforcement officer shall question a person detained pursuant to the authority of this Section who he suspects or has reasonable cause to suspect may have committed a crime, if such person has indicated in any manner that he does not wish to be questioned, or that he wishes to consult counsel before submitting to any questioning.

A Model Code of Pre-Arraignment Procedure § 110.2 (Official Draft 1975).

2. **Post-Conviction Incarceration as "Custody."** When does questioning of a suspect already incarcerated trigger *Miranda*? The issue was addressed in Howes v. Fields, ___ U.S. ___, 132 S.Ct. 1181 (2012), involving a suspect (Fields) already incarcerated on a criminal conviction. Fields was escorted from his cell by a corrections officer to a conference room where he was questioned for five to seven hours by two sheriff's deputies concerning a crime committed before he was imprisoned. The deputies informed him several times he was free to leave and return to his cell at any time, although it was clear such leaving would require a correctional officer to escort him. The Supreme Court rejected a proposed "categorical rule * * * that a prisoner is always in custody for purposes of *Miranda* whenever a prisoner is isolated from the general prison population and questioned about conduct outside the prison." Rather:

When a prisoner is questioned, the determination of custody should focus on all of the features of the interrogation. These include the language that is used in summoning the prisoner to the interview and the manner in which the interview is conducted.

___ U.S. at ___, 132 S.Ct. at 1192. The ultimate question is—apparently— whether a reasonable person would have felt free to terminate the interview and leave.

Applying this analysis, the majority concluded Fields was not in custody. He was told and reminded he could return to his cell whenever he wanted. The interview occurred in a well-lit, average-sized conference room and the door was sometime left open. The deputies neither physically-restrained nor threatened him. Fields himself acknowledged he was "not uncomfortable."

3. INVOKING *MIRANDA* RIGHTS

EDITORS' INTRODUCTION: INVOKING THE *MIRANDA* RIGHTS AND BARRING INTERROGATION

Post-*Miranda* case law has suffered from some confusion between the prosecution's need to prove waivers of some or all *Miranda* rights and the effect of evidence that a defendant may have affirmatively invoked one or more of his *Miranda* rights. Invoking the rights is considered in this subchapter; waiver matters are addressed in the next.

To the extent that *Miranda* gives a suspect a right to not be interrogated, this may be triggered by—and perhaps only by—a defendant's affirmative invocation of one of the other rights, such as the right to remain silent or the right to counsel.

Effect of Invoking the Right to Silence

The effect of a suspect's invocation of the *Miranda* right to silence was addressed in Michigan v. Mosley, 423 U.S. 96, 96 S.Ct. 321 (1975). After being arrested, Mosley was warned and apparently made whatever waivers were required to permit interrogation about certain robberies. He responded he did not want to answer any questions about the robberies and the interrogation ended. Later, another officer again approached and warned him and solicited his waivers. During this interrogation, Mosley made incriminating admissions. The admissibility of those admissions, the Court reasoned, depended on whether what might be called the second officer's "reapproach" of Mosley violated *Miranda*:

> [This] turns almost entirely on the interpretation of a single passage in the *Miranda* opinion * * *:
>
>> Once warnings have been given, the subsequent procedure is clear. If the individual indicates in any manner, at any time prior to or during questioning, that he wishes to remain silent, the interrogation must cease. At this point he has shown that he intends to exercise his Fifth Amendment privilege; any statement taken after the person invokes his privilege cannot be other than the product of compulsion, subtle or otherwise. Without the right to cut off questioning, the setting of in-custody interrogation operates on the individual to overcome free choice in producing a statement after the privilege has been once invoked.
>
> This passage states that "the interrogation must cease" when the person in custody indicates that "he wishes to remain silent." It does not state under what circumstances, if any, a resumption of questioning is permissible. The passage could be literally read to mean that a person who has invoked his "right

to silence" can never again be subjected to custodial interrogation by any police officer at any time or place on any subject. Another possible construction of the passage would characterize "any statement taken after the person invokes his privilege" as "the product of compulsion" and would therefore mandate its exclusion from evidence, even if it were volunteered by the person in custody without any further interrogation whatever. Or the passage could be interpreted to require only the immediate cessation of questioning, and to permit a resumption of interrogation after a momentary respite.

It is evident that any of these possible literal interpretations would lead to absurd and unintended results. To permit the continuation of custodial interrogation after a momentary cessation would clearly frustrate the purposes of *Miranda* by allowing repeated rounds of questioning to undermine the will of the person being questioned. At the other extreme, a blanket prohibition against the taking of voluntary statements or a permanent immunity from further interrogation, regardless of the circumstances, would transform the *Miranda* safeguards into wholly irrational obstacles to legitimate police investigative activity, and deprive suspects of an opportunity to make informed and intelligent assessments of their interests. Clearly, therefore, neither this passage nor any other passage in the *Miranda* opinion can sensibly be read to create a per se proscription of indefinite duration upon any further questioning by any police officer on any subject, once the person in custody has indicated a desire to remain silent.

423 U.S. at 100–03, 96 S.Ct. at 325–26.

The prosecution may under *Mosley* have greater difficulty showing that a suspect effectively waived his rights if the facts show that the suspect was reapproached after invoking the right to silence; this is considered later in this chapter. But a suspect who invokes only the right to silence is protected by no absolute prohibition against officers reapproaching him.

Effect of Invoking the Right to Counsel—The Edwards Rule

Six years after *Mosley* the Court considered the effect of a suspect's invoking the right to counsel during questioning properly initiated under *Miranda*. Edwards v. Arizona, 451 U.S. 477, 101 S.Ct. 1880 (1981), addressing this issue, gave rise to what is often called the *Edwards* Rule.

On January 19, Edwards was arrested on a complaint charging a variety of crimes. He was properly interrogated by several officers and discussed the possibility of "making a deal." Eventually he said to the interrogating officer, "I want an attorney before making a deal." Questioning ceased and he was taken to a jail cell. The Supreme Court explained what happened next:

At 9:15 the next morning, two detectives, colleagues of the officer who had interrogated Edwards the previous night, came to the jail and asked to see Edwards. When the detention officer informed Edwards that the detectives wished to speak with him, he replied that he did not want to talk to anyone. The guard told him that "he had" to talk and then took him to meet with the detectives. The officers identified themselves, stated they wanted to talk to him, and informed him of his *Miranda* rights. Edwards was willing to talk, but he first wanted to hear the taped statement of the alleged accomplice who had implicated him. After listening to the tape for several minutes, * * * [h]e * * * implicated himself in the crime.

The Court held that his incriminating statement was inadmissible. It explained:

> *Miranda* itself indicated that the assertion of the right to counsel was a significant event and that once exercised by the accused, "the interrogation must cease until an attorney is present." * * * We reconfirm th[is] view[ ] and, to lend [it] substance, emphasize that it is inconsistent with *Miranda* and its progeny for the authorities, at their instance, to reinterrogate an accused in custody if he has clearly asserted his right to counsel.
>
> [T]he officers conducting the interrogation on the evening of January 19 ceased interrogation when Edwards requested counsel as he had been advised he had the right to do. * * * [W]ithout making counsel available to Edwards, the police returned to him the next day. This was not at his suggestion or request. Indeed, Edwards informed the detention officer that he did not want to talk to anyone. At the meeting, the detectives told Edwards that they wanted to talk to him and again advised him of his *Miranda* rights. Edwards stated that he would talk, but what prompted this action does not appear. * * * We think it is clear that Edwards was subjected to custodial interrogation on January 20 * * * , and that this occurred at the instance of the authorities. His statement made without having had access to counsel, did not amount to a valid waiver and hence was inadmissible.

451 U.S. at 485–87, 101 S.Ct. at 1883–84.

Edwards distinguished *Mosley* on the basis that the request made in *Mosley*—"a request to remain silent"—was not the request for counsel that triggers the *Miranda* bar to all further interrogation.

Edwards has been treated as recognizing and implementing a right on the part of those who have invoked their right to counsel not to be interrogated until and unless counsel is present. Neither *Edwards* nor the cases following it distinguished between interrogation in the common sense of that term—questioning aimed at eliciting a self-incriminating admission—and what might usefully be called a "reapproach" to a suspect—an approach to a suspect designed to persuade the suspect to submit to questioning without counsel's presence. Apparently *Edwards* regarded a reapproach in this sense as interrogation barred by the suspect's invocation of the right to counsel.

Essentially, then, *Edwards* holds that if a suspect invokes the right to counsel, until the attorney is present the suspect cannot be subjected to efforts to persuade him to admit guilt (literal interrogation), or even an inquiry as to whether he would—without counsel—submit to such efforts to persuade him to admit guilt (a reapproach not involving literal interrogation).

Duration of the Edwards Bar to Interrogation

The duration of the *Edwards* bar to interrogation was addressed in Maryland v. Shatzer, 599 U.S. 98, 130 S.Ct. 1213 (2010). On August 7, 2003, officers questioned Shatzer about a child sexual abuse offense. Shatzer was at the time of the questioning imprisoned after conviction for an unrelated child molestation offense. When Shatzer invoked his right to counsel, the interrogation stopped and Shatzer was returned to the general prison population. On March 2, 2006 officers approached Shatzer—still imprisoned on the same conviction but in a different institution—and sought to question him about the sexual abuse matter. He was warned, waived his rights, and was questioned. Five days later, on March 7, officers returned, warned him and obtained waivers, and administered a polygraph test Shatzer had agreed on March 2 to take. After the test, he admitted the offense. The state court held that Shatzer's actions in 2003 triggered *Edwards*, and the bar to reapproaching Shatzer was still applicable in March of 2006. Thus his statement was inadmissible.

The Supreme Court reversed. It reasoned that the rationale for the *Edwards* presumption of involuntariness does not apply in situations such as *Shatzer*:

> It is easy to believe that a suspect may be coerced or badgered into abandoning his earlier refusal to be questioned without counsel in the paradigm *Edwards* case. That is a case in which the suspect has been arrested for a particular crime and is held in uninterrupted pretrial custody while that crime is being actively investigated. After the initial interrogation, and up to and including the second one, he remains cut off from his normal life and companions, "thrust into" and isolated in an "unfamiliar," "police-dominated atmosphere," where his captors "appear to control [his] fate." * * *
>
> When * * * a suspect has been released from his pretrial custody and has returned to his normal life for some time before the later attempted interrogation, there is little reason to think

that his change of heart regarding interrogation without counsel has been coerced. He has no longer been isolated. He has likely been able to seek advice from an attorney, family members, and friends. And he knows from his earlier experience that he need only demand counsel to bring the interrogation to a halt; and that investigative custody does not last indefinitely. In these circumstances, it is far fetched to think that a police officer's asking the suspect whether he would like to waive his *Miranda* rights will any more "wear down the accused," than did the first such request at the original attempted interrogation—which is of course not deemed coercive. * * * Uncritical extension of *Edwards* to this situation would not significantly increase the number of genuinely coerced confessions excluded.

599 U.S. at 106–08, 130 S.Ct. at 1220–21. As a result, it continued:

The protections offered by *Miranda*, which we have deemed sufficient to ensure that the police respect the suspect's desire to have an attorney present the first time police interrogate him, adequately ensure that result when a suspect who initially requested counsel is reinterrogated after a break in custody that is of sufficient duration to dissipate its coercive effects. * * * We think it appropriate to specify a period of time to avoid the consequence that continuation of the *Edwards* presumption "will not reach the correct result most of the time." It seems to us that period is 14 days. That provides plenty of time for the suspect to get reacclimated to his normal life, to consult with friends and counsel, and to shake off any residual coercive effects of his prior custody.

599 U.S. at 110, 130 S.Ct. at 1222–23.

Shatzer, of course, was not actually released from incarceration. The Court made clear that—assuming Shatzer was in custody during the questioning—Shatzer's retention in the general prison population was not custody. Thus his return to the general prison population constituted a break in custody. Consequently, "[b]ecause Shatzer experienced a break in *Miranda* custody lasting more than two weeks between the first and second attempts at interrogation, *Edwards* does not mandate suppression of his March 2006 statements." 599 U.S. at 116, 130 S.Ct. at 1227.

Edwards Rule Not "Offense Specific"

Edwards' prohibition against further interrogation applies even if officers reapproach the suspect concerning an offense unrelated to that under discussion when the suspect invoked his right to counsel. In this sense, the *Edwards* Fifth Amendment rule—unlike the Sixth Amendment *Edwards*-like rule discussed in Subchapter D of this chapter—is not "offense specific."

This was established in Arizona v. Roberson, 486 U.S. 675, 108 S.Ct. 2093 (1988). Officers called to the scene of a break-in arrested Roberson for the burglary. This took place on April 16, 1985. After the arresting officer gave him his *Miranda* warnings, Roberson responded that he "wanted a lawyer before answering any questions." The officer noted this in his written report. Three days later, another officer approached Roberson, who was still in custody, regarding a burglary committed on April 15. This officer had not read the arresting officer's report and was unaware Roberson had invoked his right to counsel. After warning Roberson and questioning him, the second officer obtained from Roberson an admission to the April 15 offense.

A majority of the Supreme Court held this statement was inadmissible under *Edwards*. Once a suspect invokes his right to counsel, Justice Stevens reasoned for the Court, *Edwards* bars further interrogation (until a lawyer is provided) even if that subsequent interrogation concerns an offense unrelated to the offense involved in the first interrogation session. Roberson's invocation of his right to counsel during questioning about the April 16 break-in, therefore, barred the second officer from reapproaching him even though that reapproach concerned the separate April 15 offense. The rationale for *Edwards*—that a suspect's invocation of the right to counsel raises a "presumption" that the suspect believes himself incapable of undergoing questioning without the help of an attorney—applies even if the further interrogation concerns a different offense. The rigid *Edwards* rule is justified in order to vigorously discourage police activity creating an especially high risk of an involuntary waiver; the Court found no basis for concluding "that police engaged in separate investigations will be any less eager than police involved in only one inquiry to question a suspect in custody." Suspects like Roberson might have good reason to speak with police about a different offense or at least to learn from police what the new investigation concerns so they can decide whether or not to make a statement, the Court acknowledged. But:

> the suspect, having requested counsel, can determine how to deal with the separate investigations with counsel's advice. Further, even if the police have decided temporarily not to provide counsel, they are free to inform the suspect of the facts of the second investigation as long as such communication does not constitute interrogation.

486 U.S. at 687, 108 S.Ct. at 2101. The second officer's ignorance that Roberson had invoked his right to counsel was of no significance, the Court continued. *Edwards* focuses upon the suspect's state of mind rather than that of the officer. *Miranda* creates a "need to determine whether the suspect has requested counsel." This need exists whether further investigation concerns the same or a different offense or the same or a different interrogator. Failure to honor a request for counsel, the

Court concluded, "cannot be justified by the lack of diligence of a particular officer."

Justice Kennedy, joined by the Chief Justice, dissented. When officers reapproach a suspect concerning a separate crime, he reasoned, "the danger of badgering is minimal and insufficient to justify a rigid *per se* rule." Suspects' interests, in this type of situation, are adequately protected by the officers' need to provide the "known and tested warnings" and the prosecution's obligation to prove any waivers were voluntary. When persons are arrested for one offense, it is frequently learned that they are "wanted for questioning" with regard to other offenses. The majority's approach, Justice Kennedy complained, will often bar officers, even those representing a jurisdiction other than the arresting one, from such questioning. "The majority's rule is not necessary to protect the rights of suspects, and it will in many instances deprive our nationwide law enforcement network of a legitimate investigative technique now routinely used to resolve major crimes." 486 U.S. at 688, 108 S.Ct. at 2102 (Kennedy, J., dissenting).

Suspect Initiated Discussion

Edwards described its holding as inapplicable to situations in which "the accused himself initiates further communications, exchanges or conversations with the police." This qualification to the *Edwards* rule was developed in Oregon v. Bradshaw, 462 U.S. 1039, 103 S.Ct. 2830 (1983) (plurality opinion).

Bradshaw was asked to accompany a police officer to the station for further investigation of a traffic accident in which one Reynolds, a minor, had been killed. After being given full *Miranda* warnings, Bradshaw acknowledged furnishing Reynolds with liquor but denied other involvement. He was then placed under arrest for furnishing liquor to a minor and again advised of his *Miranda* rights. A police officer informed him that the officer believed Bradshaw was driving the vehicle in which Reynolds had been killed. After denying this, Bradshaw said, "I do want an attorney before it goes very much further." The officer immediately stopped the conversation.

"Sometime later" officers transported Bradshaw about ten or fifteen miles to a jail. Before or during this trip, Bradshaw asked one of the officers, "Well, what is going to happen to me?" The officer responded, "You do not have to talk to me. You have requested an attorney and I don't want you talking to me unless you so desire because anything you say—because—since you have requested an attorney, you know, it has to be at your own free will." Bradshaw stated he understood. A conversation then took place between Bradshaw and the officer concerning where Bradshaw would be taken and the offense with which he would be charged. The officer suggested Bradshaw take a lie detector test and Bradshaw agreed. The next day, after an officer again read him the *Miranda* rights, Bradshaw took the test. Afterwards, he admitted driving the vehicle and passing out because of intoxication. At his subsequent trial, his post-polygraph test statement was admitted into evidence. A state appellate tribunal, however, held admission of the confession violated *Edwards* and reversed.

Without an opinion of the Court, the Supreme Court reversed. The Court's judgment was announced in an opinion authored by Justice Rehnquist and joined in by three other justices. In this plurality opinion, Justice Rehnquist explained:

> [In *Edwards,*] we held that after the right to counsel had been asserted by an accused, further interrogation of the accused should not take place "unless the accused himself initiates further communication, exchanges, or conversations with the police." This was in effect a prophylactic rule, designed to protect an accused in police custody from being badgered by police officers * * * .
>
> But even if a conversation taking place after the accused had "expressed his desire to deal with the police only through counsel," is initiated by the accused, where reinterrogation follows, the burden remains upon the prosecution to show that subsequent events indicated a waiver of the Fifth Amendment right to have counsel present during the interrogation.

462 U.S. at 1044, 103 S.Ct. at 2834. A suspect "initiates" a conversation under *Edwards* only by inquiries which can "be fairly said to represent a desire on the part of an accused to open up a more generalized discussion relating directly or indirectly to the investigation." Other inquiries, such as requests for water to drink or access to a telephone, are "routine incidents of the custodial relationship" and generally do not amount to an initiation of a conversation within the meaning of *Edwards*.

No violation of the *Edwards* "rule" took place in *Bradshaw*, Justice Rehnquist then concluded:

> Although ambiguous, [Bradshaw's] question in this case as to what was going to happen to him evinced a willingness and a desire for a generalized discussion about the investigation; it was not merely a necessary inquiry arising out of the incidents of the custodial relationship. It could reasonably have been interpreted by the officer as relating generally to the investigation.

462 U.S. at 1045–46, 103 S.Ct. at 2835. Progressing to whether the waiver was valid, Justice Rehnquist found no reason to dispute the conclusions of the lower courts that the waiver was voluntary and intelligent.

Justice Powell provided the fifth vote to affirm. He did not join Justice Rehnquist's opinion but concurred on the ground the issue should be the voluntariness of Bradshaw's waiver and the record showed the waiver was voluntary.

Justice Marshall, joined by three other members of the Court, dissented. He agreed with Justice Rehnquist that under *Edwards* an accused "initiates" further communication with police—and thus renders the bar to interrogation inapplicable—only by conduct demonstrating a desire to discuss the subject matter of the investigation. But, he added, this "obviously" means "communication or dialogue *about the subject matter of the criminal investigation.*" (emphasis in original). Turning to the facts before the Court, Justice Marshall construed Bradshaw's inquiry as expressing no more than a desire to find out where the officers were taking him. It did not concern the subject matter of the investigation and therefore did not express a desire to discuss that subject matter. As a result, the officer's actions violated *Edwards' per se* rule and the subsequent confession was inadmissible under *Miranda*.

* * *

The significant effect of a suspect's successful invocation of the right to counsel makes clear the importance of the standard for determining when such an invocation occurs. That is addressed in the case that follows.

<h2 style="text-align:center">Davis v. United States</h2>

Supreme Court of the United States, 1994.
512 U.S. 452, 114 S.Ct. 2350.

■ JUSTICE O'CONNOR delivered the opinion of the Court.

In *Edwards v. Arizona*, 451 U.S. 477, 101 S.Ct. 1880, 68 L.Ed.2d 378 (1981), we held that law enforcement officers must immediately cease questioning a suspect who has clearly asserted his right to have counsel present during custodial interrogation. In this case we decide how law enforcement officers should respond when a suspect makes a reference to counsel that is insufficiently clear to invoke the *Edwards* prohibition on further questioning.

I

Pool brought trouble—not to River City, but to the Charleston Naval Base. Petitioner, a member of the United States Navy, spent the evening of October 2, 1988, shooting pool at a club on the base. Another sailor, Keith Shackleton, lost a game and a $30 wager to petitioner, but Shackleton refused to pay. After the club closed, Shackleton was beaten to death with a pool cue on a loading dock behind the commissary. The body was found early the next morning.

The investigation by the Naval Investigative Service (NIS) gradually focused on petitioner. Investigative agents determined that petitioner was at the club that evening, and that he was absent without authorization from his duty station the next morning. The agents also learned that only privately owned pool cues could be removed from the club premises, and that petitioner owned two cues—one of which had a bloodstain on it. The agents were told by various people that petitioner either had admitted committing the crime or had recounted details that clearly indicated his involvement in the killing.

On November 4, 1988, petitioner was interviewed at the NIS office. As required by military law, the agents advised petitioner that he was a suspect in the killing, that he was not required to make a statement, that any statement could be used against him at a trial by court-martial, and that he was entitled to speak with an attorney and have an attorney present during questioning. Petitioner waived his rights to remain silent and to counsel, both orally and in writing.

About an hour and a half into the interview, petitioner said, "Maybe I should talk to a lawyer." According to the uncontradicted testimony of one of the interviewing agents, the interview then proceeded as follows:

> "[We m]ade it very clear that we're not here to violate his rights, that if he wants a lawyer, then we will stop any kind of questioning with him, that we weren't going to pursue the matter unless we have it clarified is he asking for a lawyer or is he just making a comment about a lawyer, and he said, [']No, I'm not asking for a lawyer,' and then he continued on, and said, 'No, I don't want a lawyer.'"

After a short break, the agents reminded petitioner of his rights to remain silent and to counsel. The interview then continued for another hour, until petitioner said, "I think I want a lawyer before I say anything else." At that point, questioning ceased.

At his general court-martial, petitioner moved to suppress statements made during the November 4 interview. The Military Judge denied the motion * * * . Petitioner was convicted on one specification of unpremeditated murder * * * . The Navy-Marine Corps Court of Military Review affirmed.

The United States Court of Military Appeals granted discretionary review and affirmed. The court recognized that the state and federal courts have developed three different approaches to a suspect's ambiguous or equivocal request for counsel:

> "Some jurisdictions have held that any mention of counsel, however ambiguous, is sufficient to require that all questioning cease. Others have attempted to define a threshold standard of clarity for invoking the right to counsel and have held that comments falling short of the threshold do not invoke the right to counsel. Some jurisdictions . . . have held that all interrogation about the offense must immediately cease whenever a suspect mentions counsel, but they allow interrogators to ask narrow questions designed to clarify the earlier statement and the [suspect's] desires respecting counsel."

Applying the third approach, the court held that petitioner's comment was ambiguous, and that the NIS agents properly clarified petitioner's wishes with respect to counsel before continuing questioning him about the offense.

* * *

II

[W]e held in *Miranda v. Arizona*, 384 U.S. 436, 469–473, 86 S.Ct. 1602, 1625–1627, 16 L.Ed.2d 694 (1966), that a suspect subject to custodial interrogation has the right to consult with an attorney and to have counsel present during questioning, and that the police must explain this right to him before questioning begins. * * * If the suspect effectively waives his right to counsel after receiving the *Miranda* warnings, law enforcement officers are free to question him. But if a suspect requests counsel at any time during the interview, he is not subject to further questioning until a lawyer has been made available or the suspect himself reinitiates conversation. This "second layer of prophylaxis for the *Miranda* right to counsel," is "designed to prevent police from badgering a defendant into waiving his previously asserted *Miranda* rights." * * * "It remains clear, however, that this prohibition on further questioning—like other aspects of *Miranda*—is not itself required by the Fifth Amendment's prohibition on coerced confessions, but is instead justified only by reference to its prophylactic purpose." *Connecticut v. Barrett*, [479 U.S. 523, 528, 107 S.Ct. 828, 832, 93 L.Ed.2d 920 (1987)].

The applicability of the " 'rigid' prophylactic rule" of *Edwards* requires courts to "determine whether the accused *actually invoked* his right to counsel." *Smith v. Illinois*, [469 U.S. 91, 95, 105 S.Ct. 490, 492 83 L.Ed.2d 488 (1984) (per curiam)] (emphasis added). To avoid difficulties of proof and to provide guidance to officers conducting interrogations, this is an objective inquiry. Invocation of the *Miranda* right to counsel "requires, at a minimum, some statement that can reasonably be construed to be an expression of a desire for the assistance of an attorney." *McNeil v. Wisconsin*, [501 U.S. 171, 178, 111 S.Ct. 2204, 2209, 115 L.Ed.2d 158 (1991)]. But if a suspect makes a reference to an attorney that is ambiguous or equivocal in that a reasonable officer in light of the circumstances would have understood only that the suspect might be invoking the right to counsel, our precedents do not require the cessation of questioning.

Rather, the suspect must unambiguously request counsel. * * * Although a suspect need not "speak with the discrimination of an Oxford don," he must articulate his desire to have counsel present sufficiently clearly that a reasonable police officer in the circumstances would understand the statement to be a request for an attorney. If the statement fails to meet the requisite level of clarity, *Edwards* does not require that the officers stop questioning the suspect.

We decline petitioner's invitation to extend *Edwards* and require law enforcement officers to cease questioning immediately upon the making of an ambiguous or equivocal reference to an attorney. The rationale underlying *Edwards* is that the police must respect a suspect's wishes regarding his right to have an attorney present during custodial interrogation. But when the officers conducting the questioning reasonably do not know whether or not the suspect wants a lawyer, a rule requiring the immediate cessation of questioning "would transform the *Miranda* safeguards into wholly irrational obstacles to legitimate police investigative activity," because it would needlessly prevent the police from questioning a suspect in the absence of counsel even if the suspect did not wish to have a lawyer present. * * *

We recognize that requiring a clear assertion of the right to counsel might disadvantage some suspects who—because of fear, intimidation, lack of linguistic skills, or a variety of other reasons—will not clearly articulate their right to counsel although they actually want to have a lawyer present. But the primary protection afforded suspects subject to custodial interrogation is the *Miranda* warnings themselves. * * * A suspect who knowingly and voluntarily waives his right to counsel after having that right explained to him has indicated his willingness to deal with the police unassisted. Although *Edwards* provides an additional protection—if a suspect subsequently requests an attorney, questioning must cease—it is one that must be affirmatively invoked by the suspect.

In considering how a suspect must invoke the right to counsel, we must consider the other side of the *Miranda* equation: the need for effective law enforcement. Although the courts ensure compliance with the *Miranda* requirements through the exclusionary rule, it is police officers who must actually decide whether or not they can question a suspect. The *Edwards* rule—questioning must cease if the suspect asks for a lawyer—provides a bright line that can be applied by officers in the real world of investigation and interrogation without unduly hampering the gathering of information. But if we were to require questioning to cease if a suspect makes a statement that might be a request for an attorney, this clarity and ease of application would be lost. Police officers would be forced to make difficult judgment calls about whether the suspect in fact wants a lawyer even though he has not said so, with the threat of suppression if they guess wrong. We therefore hold that, after a knowing and voluntary waiver of the *Miranda* rights, law enforcement officers may continue questioning until and unless the suspect clearly requests an attorney.

Of course, when a suspect makes an ambiguous or equivocal statement it will often be good police practice for the interviewing officers to clarify whether or not he actually wants an attorney. That was the procedure followed by the NIS agents in this case. Clarifying questions help protect the rights of the suspect by ensuring that he gets an attorney if he wants one, and will minimize the chance of a confession being suppressed due to subsequent judicial second-guessing as to the meaning of the suspect's statement regarding counsel. But we decline to adopt a rule requiring officers to ask clarifying questions. If the suspect's statement is not an unambiguous or unequivocal request for counsel, the officers have no obligation to stop questioning him.

* * *

The courts below found that petitioner's remark to the NIS agents "Maybe I should talk to a lawyer" was not a request for counsel, and we see no reason to disturb that conclusion. The NIS agents therefore were not required to stop questioning petitioner, though it was entirely proper for them to clarify whether petitioner in fact wanted a lawyer. Because there is no ground for suppression of petitioner's statements, the judgment of the Court of Military Appeals is

Affirmed.

■ JUSTICE SOUTER, with whom JUSTICE BLACKMUN, JUSTICE STEVENS, and JUSTICE GINSBURG join, concurring in the judgment.

* * *

I agree with the majority that the Constitution does not forbid law enforcement officers to pose questions (like those directed at Davis) aimed solely at clarifying whether a suspect's ambiguous reference to counsel was meant to assert his Fifth Amendment right. Accordingly I concur in the judgment affirming Davis's conviction, resting partly on evidence of statements given after agents ascertained that he did not wish to deal with them through counsel. I cannot, however, join in my colleagues' further conclusion that if the investigators here had been so inclined, they were at liberty to disregard Davis's reference to a lawyer entirely, in accordance with a general rule that interrogators have no legal obligation to discover what a custodial subject meant by an ambiguous statement that could reasonably be understood to express a desire to consult a lawyer. * * * The concerns of fairness and practicality that have long anchored our *Miranda* case law point to a different response: when law enforcement officials "reasonably do not know whether or not the suspect wants a lawyer," they should stop their interrogation and ask him to make his choice clear.

* * *

[A]s the majority expressly acknowledges, criminal suspects who may (in *Miranda*'s words) be "thrust into an unfamiliar atmosphere and run through menacing police interrogation procedures, would seem an odd group to single out for the Court's demand of heightened linguistic care." A substantial percentage of them lack anything like a confident command of the English language; many are "woefully ignorant;" and many more will be sufficiently intimidated by the interrogation process or overwhelmed by the uncertainty of their predicament that the ability to speak assertively will abandon them.⁴ * * *

[I]t is easy, amidst the discussion of layers of protection, to lose sight of a real risk in the majority's approach, going close to the core of what the Court has held that the Fifth Amendment provides. The experience of the timid or verbally inept suspect (whose existence the Court acknowledges) may not always closely follow that of the defendant in *Edwards v. Arizona* (whose purported waiver of his right to counsel, made after having invoked the right, was held ineffective, lest police be tempted to "badge[r]" others like him). * * * When a suspect understands his (expressed) wishes to have been ignored (and by hypothesis, he has said something that an objective listener could "reasonably," although not necessarily, take to be a request), in contravention of the "rights" just read to him by his interrogator, he may well see further objection as futile and confession (true or not) as the only way to end his interrogation.

* * *

The other justification[ ] offered for the "requisite level of clarity" rule [is] that, whatever its costs, it will * * * maintain the "ease of application," that has long been a concern of our *Miranda* jurisprudence. * * *

As for practical application, while every approach, including the majority's, will involve some "difficult judgment calls,"⁷ the rule argued for here would relieve the officer of any responsibility for guessing "whether the suspect in fact wants a lawyer even though he hasn't said so." To the contrary, it would assure that the "judgment call" will be made by the party most competent to resolve the ambiguity, who our case law has always assumed should make it: the individual suspect.

As a practical matter, of course, the primary arbiters of "clarity" will be the interrogators themselves, who tend as well to be courts' preferred source in determining the precise words a suspect used. And when an inculpatory statement has been obtained as a result of an unrecorded,

---

⁴ Social science confirms what common sense would suggest, that individuals who feel intimidated or powerless are more likely to speak in equivocal or nonstandard terms when no ambiguity or equivocation is meant. See W. O'Barr, Linguistic Evidence: Language, Power, and Strategy in the Courtroom 61–71 (1982). Suspects in police interrogation are strong candidates for these effects. Even while resort by the police to the "third degree" has abated since *Miranda*, the basic forms of psychological pressure applied by police appear to have changed less. Compare, e.g., *Miranda*, supra, 384 U.S., at 449, 86 S.Ct., at 1615 (" '[T]he principal psychological factor contributing to a successful interrogation is privacy' ") (quoting F. Inbau & J. Reid, Criminal Interrogations and Confessions 1 (1962)), with F. Inbau, J. Reid, & J. Buckley, Criminal Interrogation and Confessions 24 (3d ed. 1986) ("The principal psychological factor contributing to a successful interrogation is privacy").

⁷ In the abstract, nothing may seem more clear than a "clear statement" rule, but in police stations and trial courts the question, "how clear is clear?" is not so readily answered. When a suspect says, "uh, yeah, I'd like to do that" after being told he has a right to a lawyer, has he "clearly asserted" his right? Compare *Smith v. Illinois*, [469 U.S. 91, 97, 105 S.Ct. 490, 493, 83 L.Ed.2d 488 (1984) (per curiam)] (statement was " 'neither indecisive nor ambiguous' ") (citation omitted), with id., at 101, 105 S.Ct., at 495 496 (REHNQUIST, J., dissenting) (questioning clarity) * * *

incommunicado interrogation, these officers rarely lose "swearing matches" against criminal defendants at suppression hearings.

* * *

Our cases are best respected by a rule that when a suspect under custodial interrogation makes an ambiguous statement that might reasonably be understood as expressing a wish that a lawyer be summoned (and questioning cease), interrogators' questions should be confined to verifying whether the individual meant to ask for a lawyer. While there is reason to expect that trial courts will apply today's ruling sensibly (without requiring criminal suspects to speak with the discrimination of an Oxford don) and that interrogators will continue to follow what the Court rightly calls "good police practice" * * * , I believe that the case law under *Miranda* does not allow them to do otherwise.

NOTES

1. **Presence of Attorney Required Under *Edwards*.** In Minnick v. Mississippi, 498 U.S. 146, 111 S.Ct. 486 (1990), a majority rejected a contention that the *Edwards* bar to reapproaching a suspect who has invoked the right to counsel should cease to apply after the suspect has consulted with the attorney:

> [W]e * * * hold that when counsel is requested, interrogation must cease, and officials may not reinstate interrogation without counsel present, whether or not the accused has consulted with his attorney.

498 U.S. at 153, 111 S.Ct. at 491.

2. **"Anticipatory" Invocation of the Right to Counsel.** The dissenters in McNeil v. Wisconsin, 501 U.S. 171, 111 S.Ct. 2204 (1991), suggested lawyers, on behalf of their clients, will routinely and at the first court appearance announce that their clients are invoking *Miranda* rights and thus prevent officers from approaching those clients and seeking to interrogate them without counsel. Responding, Justice Scalia questioned whether these and other "anticipatory" invocations of *Miranda* rights would be effective:

> We have * * * never held that a person can invoke his *Miranda* rights anticipatorily, in a context other than "custodial interrogation"—which a preliminary hearing will not always, or even usually, involve. If the *Miranda* right to counsel can be invoked at a preliminary hearing, it could be argued, there is no logical reason why it could not be invoked by a letter prior to arrest, or indeed even prior to identification as a suspect. Most rights must be asserted when the government seeks to take the action they protect against. The fact that we have allowed the *Miranda* right to counsel, once asserted, to be effective with respect to future custodial interrogation does not necessarily mean that we will allow it to be asserted initially outside the context of custodial interrogation, with similar future effect.

501 U.S. at 182 n. 3, 111 S.Ct. at 2211 n. 3.

In Montejo v. Louisiana, 556 U.S. 778, 797, 129 S.Ct. 2079, 2091 (2009), the majority appeared to embrace the view that a person cannot invoke the *Miranda* rights anticipatorily. *Montejo* is discussed in Subchapter D.

An aspect of the issue arose in Bobby v. Dixon, ___ U.S. ___, 132 S.Ct. 26 (2011) (per curiam). Archie Dixon was a suspect in a murder investigation. He came to the police station on November 4, 1993 to retrieve his car, which had been impounded on apparently unrelated grounds. A detective approached him, gave him *Miranda* warnings, and asked to talk with him about the missing murder victim. Dixon declined to answer questions without his lawyer present. He then left the station. Five days later, he was arrested for a crime related to the murder. The court below had held that because Dixon had invoked the right to counsel at the first encounter, officers were barred from approaching him as they did after his arrest. A unanimous Supreme Court responded:

> That is plainly wrong. It is undisputed that Dixon was not in custody during his chance encounter with police on November 4. And this Court has "never held that a person can invoke his *Miranda* rights anticipatorily, in a context other than 'custodial interrogation.'" *McNeil v. Wisconsin,* 501 U.S. 171, 182, n. 3, 111 S.Ct. 2204, 115 L.Ed.2d 158 (1991); see also *Montejo v. Louisiana,* 556 U.S. 778, ___, 129 S.Ct. 2079, 2090, 173 L.Ed.2d 955 (2009) ("If the defendant is not in custody then [*Miranda* and its progeny] do not apply").

___ U.S. at ___, 132 S.Ct. at 29.

3. **Invoking the Right to Remain Silent.** In Berghuis v. Thompkins, 560 U.S. 370, 130 S.Ct. 2250 (2010), reprinted in part later in this chapter, the Court addressed whether the *Davis* analysis was appropriate when a defendant claimed to have invoked the right to remain silent rather than the right to counsel. It explained the facts which Thompkins argued showed he invoked the right to remain silent:

> Officers began an interrogation. At no point during the interrogation did Thompkins say that he wanted to remain silent, that he did not want to talk with the police, or that he wanted an attorney. Thompkins was "[l]argely" silent during the interrogation, which lasted about three hours. He did give a few limited verbal responses, however, such as "yeah," "no," or "I don't know." And on occasion he communicated by nodding his head. Thompkins also said that he "didn't want a peppermint" that was offered to him by the police and that the chair he was "sitting in was hard."

Rejecting Thompkins's contention, the majority held he had not invoked his right to silence so as to require interrogation to cease. It explained:

> There is good reason to require an accused who wants to invoke his or her right to remain silent to do so unambiguously. A requirement of an unambiguous invocation of *Miranda* rights results in an objective inquiry that "avoid[s] difficulties of proof and

. . . provide[s] guidance to officers" on how to proceed in the face of ambiguity. If an ambiguous act, omission, or statement could require police to end the interrogation, police would be required to make difficult decisions about an accused's unclear intent and face the consequence of suppression "if they guess wrong." Suppression of a voluntary confession in these circumstances would place a significant burden on society's interest in prosecuting criminal activity. Treating an ambiguous or equivocal act, omission, or statement as an invocation of *Miranda* rights "might add marginally to *Miranda*'s goal of dispelling the compulsion inherent in custodial interrogation." But "as *Miranda* holds, full comprehension of the rights to remain silent and request an attorney are sufficient to dispel whatever coercion is inherent in the interrogation process."

Thompkins did not say that he wanted to remain silent or that he did not want to talk with the police. Had he made either of these simple, unambiguous statements, he would have invoked his " 'right to cut off questioning.' " Here he did neither, so he did not invoke his right to remain silent.

560 U.S. at 381–82, 130 S.C. at 2260.

4. WAIVER OF *MIRANDA* RIGHTS

EDITORS' INTRODUCTION: *MIRANDA* WAIVER ISSUES

As *Miranda* was developed in later decisions, the role of waivers in *Miranda* law increased. This subchapter explores waiver-related issues. Part (a) considers what if any words or conduct that are relied upon as waivers is required. Part (b) addresses the constitutional effectiveness of an adequately proved waiver. First, however, some more general inquiries are appropriate.

Distinguishing Different Waivers. Discussions sometimes assume that only one waiver or set of waivers can be at issue. But this may not be the case. The Editors' Note: Identifying and Distinguishing *Miranda* Rights, earlier in this chapter, suggested that *Miranda* may be viewed as establishing a number of different rights. A defendant may waive some but not others. Or possible waivers of different rights may occur at different times under different circumstances.

Suppose a suspect, after officers gave her the required warnings, agrees to talk with officers in the absence of an attorney. After two hours of discussion, the suspect makes a self-incriminating admission. She has arguably at the beginning of these events waived her right to silence and her right to have counsel present during custodial interrogation. If her right not to incriminate herself is to be distinguished from these rights, that right was probably waived—if at all—only considerably later before or during her decision to make the incriminating admission.

Burden of Proof. The burden of proof regarding *Miranda* waivers was addressed in Colorado v. Connelly, 479 U.S. 157, 107 S.Ct. 515 (1986). The state court had held that the prosecution must establish waivers of the rights to counsel and to remain silent by "clear and convincing evidence." Agreeing that the prosecution bears the burden of proof, the Supreme Court held this burden of proof is by only a preponderance of the evidence. Lego v. Twomey, 404 U.S. 477, 92 S.Ct. 619 (1972), the Court noted, established that the prosecution need prove the voluntariness of a confession only by a preponderance of the evidence. "[A] waiver of the auxiliary protections established in *Miranda*," *Connelly* reasoned "should require no higher a burden of proof."

Scope of Waiver. The scope of an effective waiver, especially one of the right to counsel, may raise difficult questions. One such problem was presented by Wyrick v. Fields, 459 U.S. 42, 103 S.Ct. 394 (1982). Fields had agreed to a polygraph test and had waived his right to counsel during that procedure. After the examination, the agent who administered the examination told Fields there had been some deceit and asked Fields if he could explain why his answers were bothering him. In the resulting discussion, Fields made incriminating admissions. He argued that neither he nor the lawyer who advised him prior to the waiver anticipated questioning after the examination and, therefore, his waiver of counsel had not extended to such post-examination questioning. Rejecting this contention, the Court explained:

> [I]t would have been unreasonable for Fields and his attorneys to assume that Fields would not be informed of the polygraph readings and asked to explain any unfavorable results. Moreover, Fields had been informed that he could stop the questioning at any time, and could request at any time that his lawyer join him. Merely disconnecting the polygraph equipment could not remove this knowledge from Fields' mind.

459 U.S. 47–48, 103 S.Ct. at 396. Does this mean that the scope of a waiver is not defined by what the defendant actually understood it would cover but rather by what, in the exercise of reasonable care, he should have known it would be treated by police as covering?

Limited or Qualified Waiver. Can a suspect limit what police officers can do during an interrogation session by qualifying or limiting the waiver? One Supreme Court decision suggests so.

In Connecticut v. Barrett, 479 U.S. 523, 107 S.Ct. 828 (1987), Barrett signed an acknowledgment that he had been given the *Miranda* warnings. He then stated to the officers several times that he would not give them any written statement, at least until his lawyer was present. He added, however, that he had "no problem" in talking with them about the incident for which he had been arrested. During the following interrogation sessions, he made oral admissions of involvement in a sexual assault. At trial, testimony concerning these admissions was permitted over defense objection. The state appellate court—

emphasizing that requests for counsel are not to be narrowly construed—held that Barrett's response to his *Miranda* warnings invoked his right to counsel and the subsequent conversations resulting in his oral admissions constituted prohibited interrogation without the presence of an attorney. The Supreme Court reversed:

> Barrett's limited requests for counsel * * * were accompanied by affirmative announcements of his willingness to speak with the authorities. The fact that officials took the opportunity provided by Barrett to obtain an oral confession is quite consistent with the Fifth Amendment. *Miranda* gives the defendant a right to choose between speech and silence, and Barrett chose to speak. * * * Here * * * Barrett made clear his intentions, and they were honored by police. To conclude that [Barrett] invoked his right to counsel for all purposes requires not a broad interpretation of an ambiguous statement, but a disregard of the ordinary meaning of [Barrett's] statement.

479 U.S. at 529–30, 107 S.Ct. at 832. Justice Brennan concurred, explaining "a partial waiver of the right to counsel, without more, invariably will be ambiguous." But he continued, Barrett's partial waiver of counsel was accompanied by express waiver of his right to silence, which removed the ambiguity.

a.   THE "WAIVER" REQUIRED

EDITORS' INTRODUCTION: NEED FOR PROOF OF A "WAIVER"

As *Miranda* makes clear, the constitutionally-required foundation for admissibility of a self-incriminating statement made during custodial interrogation is proof that the defendant "knowingly and intelligently waived his privilege against self-incrimination and [unless a lawyer was present during the interrogation] his right to retained or appointed counsel." The *Miranda* majority clearly believed that counsel's presence when a suspect decides to confess would reduce the difficulty of determining whether that waiver of the right to remain silent was effective. In most cases, however, counsel will not have been present during the interrogation. Consequently, waiver issues have become more prominent in *Miranda* law.

Analysis is helped by distinguishing between the need for the prosecution to prove two different matters. First is that the defendant actually made a choice that might constitute waiver. Second is that a choice proved to have been made by the defendant was effective. The two inquiries raise different concerns. What is necessary to prove a choice, for example, is a much different question than what is necessary to prove that a choice was sufficiently voluntary and intelligent and therefore effective.

An "express" statement by a defendant that he does not want an attorney present during interrogation is not a necessary aspect of proof of waiver. What is required is less clear.

In North Carolina v. Butler, 441 U.S. 369, 99 S.Ct. 1755 (1979), defendant Butler was warned and orally acknowledged he understood the rights. When asked to sign a written documents setting out a waiver, he replied, "I will talk to you but I am not signing any forms." The state court held that *Miranda* was violated when the officers began interrogation. Under *Miranda*, it reasoned, "waiver of the right to counsel during interrogation will not be recognized unless such waiver is 'specifically made' after the *Miranda* warnings have been given."

The Supreme Court held the state tribunal erred in applying a *per se* rule requiring an express waiver. "[A] court may find an intelligent and understanding rejection of counsel in situations where the defendant did not expressly state as much," Justice Stewart explained for the Court. He continued:

> The question is not one of form, but rather whether the defendant in fact knowingly and voluntarily waived the rights delineated in *Miranda*. * * * [M]ere silence is not enough. That does not mean that the defendant's silence, coupled with an understanding of his rights and a course of conduct indicating waiver, may never support a conclusion that a defendant has waived his rights. * * * [I]n at least some cases waiver can be clearly inferred from the actions and words of the person interrogated.

441 U.S. at 373, 99 S.Ct. at 1757.

Under *Butler*, waiver can be "implied" or "inferred." What this means is somewhat uncertain.

Berghuis v. Thompkins

Supreme Court of the United States, 2010.
560 U.S. 370, 130 S.Ct. 2250.

■ JUSTICE KENNEDY delivered the opinion of the Court.

* * *

I

A

On January 10, 2000, a shooting occurred outside a mall in Southfield, Michigan. Among the victims was Samuel Morris, who died from multiple gunshot wounds. The other victim, Frederick France, recovered from his injuries and later testified. Thompkins, who was a suspect, fled. About one year later he was found in Ohio and arrested there.

Two Southfield police officers traveled to Ohio to interrogate Thompkins, then awaiting transfer to Michigan. The interrogation began around 1:30 p.m. and lasted about three hours. The interrogation was conducted in a room that was 8 by 10 feet, and Thompkins sat in a chair that resembled a school desk (it had an arm on it that swings around to provide a surface to write on). At the beginning of the interrogation, one of the officers, Detective Helgert, presented Thompkins with a form derived from the *Miranda* rule. It stated:

"NOTIFICATION OF CONSTITUTIONAL RIGHTS AND STATEMENT

"1. You have the right to remain silent.

"2. Anything you say can and will be used against you in a court of law.

"3. You have a right to talk to a lawyer before answering any questions and you have the right to have a lawyer present with you while you are answering any questions.

"4. If you cannot afford to hire a lawyer, one will be appointed to represent you before any questioning, if you wish one.

"5. You have the right to decide at any time before or during questioning to use your right to remain silent and your right to talk with a lawyer while you are being questioned."

Helgert asked Thompkins to read the fifth warning out loud. Thompkins complied. Helgert later said this was to ensure that Thompkins could read, and Helgert concluded that Thompkins understood English. Helgert then read the other four *Miranda* warnings out loud and asked Thompkins to sign the form to demonstrate that he understood his rights. Thompkins declined to sign the form. The record contains conflicting evidence about whether Thompkins then verbally confirmed that he understood the rights listed on the form.

Officers began an interrogation. At no point during the interrogation did Thompkins say that he wanted to remain silent, that he did not want to talk with the police, or that he wanted an attorney. Thompkins was "[l]argely" silent during the interrogation, which lasted about three hours. He did give a few limited verbal responses, however, such as "yeah," "no," or "I don't know." And on occasion he communicated by nodding his head. Thompkins also said that he "didn't want a peppermint" that was offered to him by the police and that the chair he was "sitting in was hard."

About 2 hours and 45 minutes into the interrogation, Helgert asked Thompkins, "Do you believe in God?" Thompkins made eye contact with Helgert and said "Yes," as his eyes "well[ed] up with tears." Helgert asked, "Do you pray to God?" Thompkins said "Yes." Helgert asked, "Do you pray to God to forgive you for shooting that boy down?" Thompkins answered "Yes" and looked away. Thompkins refused to make a written confession, and the interrogation ended about 15 minutes later.

Thompkins was charged with first-degree murder, assault with intent to commit murder, and certain firearms-related offenses. He moved to suppress the statements made during the interrogation. He argued * * * that he had not waived his right to remain silent * * * . The trial court denied the motion.

* * *

The jury found Thompkins guilty on all counts. He was sentenced to life in prison without parole.

B

* * *

Thompkins appealed [on the ground that the trial court ered in refusing] to suppresss his pretrial statements under *Miranda* [*v. Arizona*, 384 U.S. 436, 86 S.Ct.1602, 16 L.Ed.2d 694 (1966)]. The Michigan Court of Appeals rejected the *Miranda* claim, ruling that Thompkins had * * * had waived [his right to remain silent]. * * * The Michigan Supreme Court denied discretionary review.

Thompkins filed a petition for a writ of habeas corpus in the United States District Court for the Eastern District of Michigan. The District Court rejected Thompkins's *Miranda* * * * claim[ ]. It noted that, under the Antiterrorism and Effective Death Penalty Act of 1996 (AEDPA), a federal court cannot grant a petition for a writ of habeas corpus unless the state court's adjudication of the merits was "contrary to, or involved an unreasonable application of, clearly established Federal law." The District Court * * * held * * * that the Michigan Court of Appeals was not unreasonable in determining that Thompkins had waived his right to remain silent.

The United States Court of Appeals for the Sixth Circuit reversed * * * . The Court of Appeals ruled that the state court, in rejecting Thompkins's *Miranda* claim, unreasonably applied clearly established federal law and based its decision on an unreasonable determination of the facts. The Court of Appeals acknowledged that a waiver of the right to remain silent need not be express, as it can be " 'inferred from the actions and words of the person interrogated.' " The panel held, nevertheless, that the state court was unreasonable in finding an implied waiver in the circumstances here. The Court of Appeals found that the state court unreasonably determined the facts because "the evidence demonstrates that Thompkins was silent for two hours and forty-five minutes." According to the Court of Appeals, Thompkins's "persistent silence for nearly three hours in response to questioning and repeated invitations to tell his side of the story offered a clear and unequivocal message to the officers: Thompkins did not wish to waive his rights."

* * *

III

* * *

B

We * * * consider whether Thompkins waived his right to remain silent. * * * [T]he accused's statement during a custodial interrogation is inadmissible at trial unless the prosecution can establish that the accused "in fact knowingly and voluntarily waived [*Miranda*] rights" when making the statement. The waiver inquiry "has two distinct dimensions": waiver must be "voluntary in the sense that it was the product of a free and deliberate choice rather than intimidation, coercion, or deception," and "made with a full awareness of both the nature of the right being abandoned and the consequences of the decision to abandon it."

Some language in *Miranda* could be read to indicate that waivers are difficult to establish absent an explicit written waiver or a formal, express oral statement. * * *

The course of decisions since *Miranda,* informed by the application of *Miranda* warnings in the whole course of law enforcement, demonstrates that waivers can be established even absent formal or express statements of waiver that would be expected in, say, a judicial hearing to determine if a guilty plea has been properly entered. * * *

The prosecution * * * does not need to show that a waiver of *Miranda* rights was express. An implicit waiver of the "right to remain silent" is sufficient to admit a suspect's statement into evidence. [*North Carolina v. Butler*, 441 U.S. 369, 99 S.Ct. 1755, 60 L.Ed.2d 286 (1979),] made clear that a waiver of *Miranda* rights may be implied through "the defendant's silence, coupled with an understanding of his rights and a course of conduct indicating waiver." The Court in *Butler* therefore "retreated" from the "language and tenor of the *Miranda* opinion," which "suggested that the Court would require that a waiver . . . be 'specifically made.' "

If the State establishes that a *Miranda* warning was given and the accused made an uncoerced statement, this showing, standing alone, is insufficient to demonstrate "a valid waiver" of *Miranda* rights. The prosecution must make the additional showing that the accused understood these rights. Where the prosecution shows that a *Miranda* warning was given and that it was understood by the accused, an accused's uncoerced statement establishes an implied waiver of the right to remain silent.

Although *Miranda* imposes on the police a rule that is both formalistic and practical when it prevents them from interrogating suspects without first providing them with a *Miranda* warning, it does not impose a formalistic waiver procedure that a suspect must follow to relinquish those rights. As a general proposition, the law can presume that an individual who, with a full understanding of his or her rights, acts in a manner inconsistent with their exercise has made a deliberate choice to relinquish the protection those rights afford. The Court's cases have recognized that a waiver of *Miranda* rights need only meet the standard of *Johnson v. Zerbst,* 304 U.S. 458, 464, 58 S.Ct. 1019, 82 L.Ed. 1461 (1938). As *Butler* recognized, *Miranda* rights can therefore be waived through means less formal than a typical waiver on the record in a courtroom, given the practical constraints and necessities of interrogation and the fact that *Miranda*'s main protection lies in advising defendants of their rights.

The record in this case shows that Thompkins waived his right to remain silent. There is no basis in this case to conclude that he did not understand his rights; and on these facts it follows that he chose not to invoke or rely on those rights when he did speak. First, there is no contention that Thompkins did not understand his rights; and from this it follows that he knew what he gave up when he spoke. There was more than enough evidence in the record to conclude that Thompkins understood his *Miranda* rights. Thompkins received a written copy of the *Miranda* warnings; Detective Helgert determined that Thompkins could read and understand English; and Thompkins was given time to read the warnings. Thompkins, furthermore, read aloud the fifth warning, which stated that "you have the right to decide at any time before or during questioning to use your right to remain silent and your right to talk with a lawyer while you are being questioned." (capitalization omitted). He was thus aware that his right to remain silent would not dissipate after a certain amount of time and that police would have to honor his right to be silent and his right to counsel during the whole course of interrogation. Those rights, the warning made clear, could be asserted at any time. Helgert, moreover, read the warnings aloud.

Second, Thompkins's answer to Detective Helgert's question about whether Thompkins prayed to God for forgiveness for shooting the victim is a "course of conduct indicating waiver" of the right to remain silent. If Thompkins wanted to remain silent, he could have said nothing in response to Helgert's questions, or he could have unambiguously invoked his *Miranda* rights and ended the interrogation. The fact that Thompkins made a statement about three hours after receiving a *Miranda* warning does not overcome the fact that he engaged in a course of conduct indicating waiver. Police are not required to rewarn suspects from time to time. Thompkins's answer to Helgert's question about praying to God for forgiveness for shooting the victim was sufficient to show a course of conduct indicating waiver. This is confirmed by the fact that before then Thompkins had given sporadic answers to questions throughout the interrogation.

Third, there is no evidence that Thompkins's statement was coerced. Thompkins does not claim that police threatened or injured him during the interrogation or that he was in any way fearful. The interrogation was conducted in a standard-sized room in the middle of the afternoon. It is true that apparently he was in a straight-backed chair for three hours, but there is no authority for the proposition that an interrogation of this length is inherently coercive. Indeed, even where interrogations of greater duration were held to be improper, they were accompanied, as this one was not, by other facts indicating coercion, such as an incapacitated and sedated suspect, sleep and food deprivation, and threats. The fact that Helgert's question referred to Thompkins's religious beliefs also did not render Thompkins's statement involuntary. "[T]he Fifth Amendment privilege is not concerned 'with moral and psychological pressures to confess emanating from sources other than official coercion.'" In these circumstances, Thompkins knowingly and voluntarily made a statement to police, so he waived his right to remain silent.

* * *

The judgment of the Court of Appeals is reversed, and the case is remanded with instructions to deny the petition.

It is so ordered.

■ JUSTICE SOTOMAYOR, with whom JUSTICE STEVENS, JUSTICE GINSBURG, and JUSTICE BREYER join, dissenting.

The Court concludes today that a criminal suspect waives his right to remain silent if, after sitting tacit and uncommunicative through nearly three hours of police interrogation, he utters a few one-word responses. * * * [This, and the other proposition announced today,] mark a substantial retreat from the protection against compelled self-incrimination that *Miranda v. Arizona,* 384 U.S. 436, 86 S.Ct. 1602, 16 L.Ed.2d 694 (1966), has long provided during custodial interrogation. The broad rules the Court announces today are also troubling because they are unnecessary to decide this case, which is governed by the deferential standard of review set forth in the Antiterrorism and Effective Death Penalty Act of 1996 (AEDPA) 28 U.S.C. § 2254(d). * * * I believe Thompkins is entitled to relief under AEDPA on the ground that his statements were admitted at trial without the prosecution having carried its burden to show that he waived his right to remain silent * * * .

I

* * *

Thompkins' federal habeas petition is governed by AEDPA, under which a federal court may not grant the writ unless the state court's adjudication of the merits of the claim at issue "was contrary to, or involved an unreasonable application of, clearly established Federal law, as determined by the Supreme Court of the United States," or "was based on an unreasonable determination of the facts in light of the evidence presented in the State court proceeding." §§ 2254(d)(1), (2).

The relevant clearly established federal law for purposes of § 2254(d)(1) begins with our landmark *Miranda* decision * * * .

Even when warnings have been administered and a suspect has not affirmatively invoked his rights, statements made in custodial interrogation may not be admitted as part of the prosecution's case in chief "unless and until" the prosecution demonstrates that an individual "knowingly and intelligently waive[d] [his] rights." "[A] heavy burden rests on the government to demonstrate that the defendant knowingly and intelligently waived his privilege against self-incrimination and his right to retained or appointed counsel." The government must satisfy the "high standar[d] of proof for the waiver of constitutional rights [set forth in] *Johnson v. Zerbst,* 304 U.S. 458, 58 S.Ct. 1019, 82 L.Ed. 1461 (1938)."

The question whether a suspect has validly waived his right is "entirely distinct" as a matter of law from whether he invoked that right. The questions are related, however, in terms of the practical effect on the exercise of a suspect's rights. A suspect may at any time revoke his prior waiver of rights—or, closer to the facts of this case, guard against the possibility of a future finding that he implicitly waived his rights—by invoking the rights and thereby requiring the police to cease questioning.

II

A

* * *

Rarely do this Court's precedents provide clearly established law so closely on point with the facts of a particular case. Together, *Miranda* and *Butler* establish that a court "must presume that a defendant did not waive his right[s]"; the prosecution bears a "heavy burden" in attempting to demonstrate waiver; the fact of a "lengthy interrogation" prior to obtaining statements is "strong evidence" against a finding of valid waiver; "mere silence" in response to questioning is "not enough"; and waiver may not be presumed "simply from the fact that a confession was in fact eventually obtained."

It is undisputed here that Thompkins never expressly waived his right to remain silent. His refusal to sign even an acknowledgment that he understood his *Miranda* rights evinces, if anything, an intent not to waive those rights. That Thompkins did not make the inculpatory statements at issue until after approximately 2 hours and 45 minutes of interrogation serves as "strong evidence" against waiver. *Miranda* and *Butler* expressly preclude the possibility that the inculpatory statements themselves are sufficient to establish waiver.

In these circumstances, Thompkins' "actions and words" preceding the inculpatory statements simply do not evidence a "course of conduct indicating waiver" sufficient to carry the prosecution's burden. Although the Michigan court stated that Thompkins "sporadically" participated in the interview, that court's opinion and the record before us are silent as to the subject matter or context of even a single question to which Thompkins purportedly responded, other than the exchange about God and the statements respecting the peppermint and the chair. Unlike in

Butler, Thompkins made no initial declaration akin to "I will talk to you." Indeed, Michigan and the United States concede that no waiver occurred in this case until Thompkins responded "yes" to the questions about God. I believe it is objectively unreasonable under our clearly established precedents to conclude the prosecution met its "heavy burden" of proof on a record consisting of three one-word answers, following 2 hours and 45 minutes of silence punctuated by a few largely nonverbal responses to unidentified questions.

B

Perhaps because our prior *Miranda* precedents so clearly favor Thompkins, the Court today goes beyond AEDPA's deferential standard of review and announces a new general principle of law. Any new rule, it must be emphasized, is unnecessary to the disposition of this case. * * *

The Court concludes that when *Miranda* warnings have been given and understood, "an accused's uncoerced statement establishes an implied waiver of the right to remain silent." More broadly still, the Court states that, "[a]s a general proposition, the law can presume that an individual who, with a full understanding of his or her rights, acts in a manner inconsistent with their exercise has made a deliberate choice to relinquish the protection those rights afford."

These principles flatly contradict our longstanding views that "a valid waiver will not be presumed ... simply from the fact that a confession was in fact eventually obtained," and that "[t]he courts must presume that a defendant did not waive his rights." * * * At best, the Court today creates an unworkable and conflicting set of presumptions that will undermine *Miranda*'s goal of providing "concrete constitutional guidelines for law enforcement agencies and courts to follow." At worst, it overrules *sub silentio* an essential aspect of the protections *Miranda* has long provided for the constitutional guarantee against self-incrimination.

* * *

Today's dilution of the prosecution's burden of proof to the bare fact that a suspect made inculpatory statements after *Miranda* warnings were given and understood takes an unprecedented step away from the "high standards of proof for the waiver of constitutional rights" this Court has long demanded. When waiver is to be inferred during a custodial interrogation, there are sound reasons to require evidence beyond inculpatory statements themselves. *Miranda* and our subsequent cases are premised on the idea that custodial interrogation is inherently coercive. Requiring proof of a course of conduct beyond the inculpatory statements themselves is critical to ensuring that those statements are voluntary admissions and not the dubious product of an overborne will.

Today's decision thus ignores the important interests *Miranda* safeguards. The underlying constitutional guarantee against self-incrimination reflects "many of our fundamental values and most noble aspirations," our society's "preference for an accusatorial rather than an inquisitorial system of criminal justice"; a "fear that self-incriminating statements will be elicited by inhumane treatment and abuses" and a resulting "distrust of self-deprecatory statements"; and a realization that while the privilege is "sometimes a shelter to the guilty, [it] is often a protection to the innocent." For these reasons, we have observed, a criminal law system "which comes to depend on the 'confession' will, in the long run, be less reliable and more subject to abuses than a system relying on independent investigation." "By bracing against 'the possibility of unreliable statements in every instance of in-custody interrogation,'" *Miranda*'s prophylactic rules serve to "'protect the fairness of the trial itself.'" Today's decision bodes poorly for the fundamental principles that *Miranda* protects.

Today's decision turns *Miranda* upside down. Criminal suspects must now unambiguously invoke their right to remain silent—which, counterintuitively, requires them to speak. At the same time, suspects will be legally presumed to have waived their rights even if they have given no clear expression of their intent to do so. Those results, in my view, find no basis in *Miranda* or our subsequent cases and are inconsistent with the fair-trial principles on which those precedents are grounded. Today's broad new rules are all the more unfortunate because they are unnecessary to the disposition of the case before us. I respectfully dissent.

NOTE

Thompkins appeared to involve only the *Miranda* right to remain silent and not the right to counsel. But does the decision—particularly part III(C) of the Court's opinion—reflect a determination or assumption by the Court that the prosecution need not prove that the defendant made at least an "implied" waiver of the right to counsel before interrogation begins?

The United States, in an amicus curiae brief, took the position that Davis v. United States, 512 U.S. 452, 114 S.Ct. 2350 (1994), reprinted in the last subchapter, applies to a suspect who is considering in the first instance whether to invoke his rights following warnings as well as one who initially waived his rights and then reconsiders. Using different standards in the two situations, it reasoned, "would create uncertainties in an area in which the Court has stressed the need for clear 'guidance to police officers conducting interrogations.' *Davis*, 412 U.S. at 458–459." Brief for the United States as Amicus Curiae Supporting Petitioner, at 15–16. The brief continued:

> After a suspect receives his *Miranda* warnings, he may invoke them, thereby ending the interview, or he may waive them and make statements to the police. But he may also take no action to invoke or waive his right, instead waiting to see how the interview unfolds. In those circumstances, the police may conduct interrogation—*i.e.*, may make statements reasonably likely to elicit an incriminating response.

Brief for the United States, at 19–20.

Perhaps the *Thompkins* majority accepted the United States' contention that this reflected the state of the law.

b.   EFFECTIVENESS OF A WAIVER

EDITORS' INTRODUCTION: EFFECTIVENESS OF *MIRANDA* WAIVERS

Waiver under *Miranda* requires proof both that the defendant made the necessary choice to give up the right and that this choice was constitutionally effective.

The criteria to be used in determining the effectiveness of *Miranda* waivers were distinguished and to some extent developed in Edwards v. Arizona, 451 U.S. 477, 101 S.Ct. 1880 (1981).

Before making his oral confession, given during a custodial interrogation, Edwards insisted he did not want his confession recorded because it could then be used against him in court. The interrogating detectives explained that an unrecorded oral confession could also be used against him. Edwards then made an incriminating statement. Prior to trial, defense counsel moved to suppress the confession on the ground that, despite the detectives' efforts, Edwards did not understand the admissibility of an oral confession and therefore the waiver of his rights was not knowingly made. The trial judge found the confession to have been "voluntary" and denied the motion to suppress. On appeal, the Arizona Supreme Court regarded the applicable standard as that discussed in Schneckloth v. Bustamonte, 412 U.S. 218, 93 S.Ct. 2041 (1973) (reprinted in Chapter 5), dealing with the voluntariness of a consent to search. It posed the question as whether, based on the totality of the circumstances, the trial court's conclusions that the defendant's action in confessing was knowing and intelligent and that his will had not been overborne were "clear and manifest error." It found no such error.

The Supreme Court held that the Arizona Supreme Court had not adequately considered whether Edwards had effectively relinquished his right to counsel. Under *Miranda*, it explained, the "voluntariness" of a consent or an admission, on the one hand, and the existence of a knowing and intelligent waiver, on the other, "are discrete inquiries." However sound the state court's conclusion regarding the "voluntariness" of Edwards' confession, that tribunal did not adequately address the *Miranda* waiver issue:

> [W]aivers of counsel must not only be voluntary, but must also constitute a knowing and intelligent relinquishment or abandonment of a known right or privilege * * * . [N]either the trial court nor the Arizona Supreme Court undertook to focus on whether Edwards understood his right to counsel and intelligently and knowingly relinquished it. It is thus apparent

that the decision below misunderstood the requirement for finding a valid waiver of the right to counsel * * * .

451 U.S. at 482–84, 101 S.Ct. at 1883–84.

Under *Edwards*, the effectiveness of *Miranda* waivers clearly requires separate consideration of voluntariness and intelligence.

Voluntariness. The prosecution must prove a suspect's *Miranda* waivers were "voluntary." But what does this mean? How does the standard for determining voluntariness in this context compare with the criterion under the due process standard for determining the voluntariness of a confession?

Colorado v. Connelly, 479 U.S. 157, 107 S.Ct. 515 (1986), discussed in Subchapter B of this chapter on general due process voluntariness, also addressed the voluntariness of *Miranda* waivers. After passing on the admissibility of the Connelly's confessions made before he was placed in custody, the Court assumed that once Officer Anderson handcuffed Connelly *Miranda* became applicable. It then turned to the state court's determination that Connelly had not effectively waived his *Miranda* rights regarding statements he made under custodial interrogation:

> The Supreme Court of Colorado in addressing this question relied on the testimony of the court-appointed psychiatrist to the effect that [Connelly] was not capable of making a "free decision with respect to his constitutional right of silence * * * and his constitutional right to confer with a lawyer before talking to the police."
>
> We think that the Supreme Court of Colorado erred in importing into this area of constitutional law notions of "free will" that have no place there. There is obviously no reason to require more in the way of a "voluntariness" inquiry in the *Miranda* waiver context than in the Fourteenth Amendment confession context. The sole concern of the Fifth Amendment, on which *Miranda* was based, is governmental coercion. * * * The voluntariness of a waiver of this privilege has always depended on the absence of police overreaching, not on "free choice" in any broader sense of the word. * * *
>
> [Connelly] urges this Court to adopt his "free will" rationale, and to find an attempted waiver invalid whenever the defendant feels compelled to waive his rights by reason of any compulsion, even if the compulsion does not flow from the police. But such treatment of the waiver issue would "cut this Court's holding in [*Miranda*] completely loose from its own explicitly stated rationale." *Miranda* protects defendants against government coercion leading them to surrender rights protected by the Fifth Amendment; it goes no further than that. [Connelly's] perception of coercion flowing from the "voice of God," however important or significant such a perception might

be in other disciplines, is a matter to which the United States Constitution does not speak.

479 U.S. at 169–71, 107 S.Ct. at 523–24.

Intelligence. Edwards made clear that the requirement of an intelligent or knowing waiver is separate from, and requires different proof than, the need for voluntariness.

Perhaps this should have been clear from Tague v. Louisiana, 444 U.S. 469, 100 S.Ct. 652 (1980). Tague's confession given during custodial interrogation was offered at his trial for robbery. At a pretrial hearing on the admissibility of the statement, the officer who had taken the confession testified that he had read Tague the *Miranda* rights from a card, that he could not presently remember what those rights were, that he could not recall whether he had asked Tague whether he understood the rights, and that he "couldn't say yes or no" whether he rendered any tests to determine whether Tague was literate or otherwise capable of understanding the rights. The confession was admitted and Tague was convicted. On appeal, the Supreme Court of Louisiana affirmed, reasoning that "absent a clear and readily apparent lack thereof, it can be presumed that a person has capacity to understand [the *Miranda* rights], and the burden is on the one claiming a lack of capacity to show that lack." Without oral argument and in a *per curiam* opinion, the Supreme Court reversed. The Louisiana courts had impermissibly relied upon a presumption that one given the *Miranda* warnings understands the rights involved; such a presumption is inconsistent with the burden placed by *Miranda* on the state to show a knowing and intelligent waiver of the rights. Turning to the facts of the case, the Court continued:

> In this case no evidence at all was introduced to prove that [Tague] knowingly and intelligently waived his rights before making the inculpatory statement. The statement was therefore inadmissible.

441 U.S. at 471, 100 S.Ct. at 653. As *Edwards* reaffirmed the next year, *Tague* held that the prosecution must address and prove that a *Miranda* waiver was intelligent.

But what precisely must a suspect know or understand in order to render intelligent his decisions to forego the assistance of counsel, his right to remain silent, or both? The principal case in this subsection addresses this question.

Suppose a defendant's waiver is "unintelligent," but for reasons not attributable to law enforcement officers' misconduct. *Connelly* made clear a *Miranda* waiver cannot be rendered *involuntary* by the defendant's mental impairment, where there is no law enforcement misconduct. Is it possible, however, that even in the absence of police misconduct, such mental impairment might nevertheless prevent a suspect from adequately understanding his right to counsel and therefore render his decision to relinquish it *unintelligent*?

In *Connelly,* the Supreme Court noted the Colorado Supreme Court's opinion could be read as finding Connelly's waiver invalid "on other grounds." This was apparently a reference to the state court's comment that Connelly's mental impairment had rendered him unable to make an "intelligent" decision. The Colorado court's analysis was influenced by "its mistaken view of 'voluntariness' in the constitutional sense," the *Connelly* majority stated. It thus reversed the state court's judgment "in its entirety," although it commented that on remand the state court was free to reconsider other issues in a manner not inconsistent with the opinion of the Court. Justice Brennan, dissenting, construed the majority's comment as permitting the state court to find that despite the absence of any official compulsion, Connelly's mental illness demonstrated that the prosecution had failed to meet *Miranda's* requirement of a knowing and intelligent waiver.

The year before the principal case reprinted in this subchapter, the Supreme Court considered a contention that a *Miranda* waiver is ineffective if the suspect made earlier admissions in violation of *Miranda* and did not know those earlier admissions could not be used as evidence against him. Oregon v. Elstad, 470 U.S. 298, 105 S.Ct. 1285 (1985). Rejecting the argument, it explained in part: "[W]e have not held that the *sine qua non* for a knowing and voluntary waiver of the right to remain silent is a full and complete appreciation of all of the consequences flowing from the nature and the quality of the evidence in the case." 470 U.S. at 317, 105 S.Ct. at 1297. Elstad had argued in these situations *Miranda* required an additional admonition, apparently conveying that any earlier admissions could not be used as evidence. The Court reasoned that a requirement of such a warning would not be practical, given the difficulty officers would have in determining whether they or other officers had committed a breach of *Miranda* procedures.

Moran v. Burbine

Supreme Court of the United States, 1986.
475 U.S. 412, 106 S.Ct. 1135.

■ JUSTICE O'CONNOR delivered the opinion of the Court.

After being informed of his rights pursuant to *Miranda v. Arizona,* 384 U.S. 436, 86 S.Ct. 1602, 16 L.Ed.2d 694 (1966), and after executing a series of written waivers, respondent confessed to the murder of a young woman. * * * The question presented is whether either the conduct of the police or respondent's ignorance of the attorney's efforts to reach him taints the validity of the waivers and therefore requires exclusion of the confessions.

I

On the morning of March 3, 1977, Mary Jo Hickey was found unconscious in a factory parking lot in Providence, Rhode Island. Suffering from injuries to her skull apparently inflicted by a metal pipe found at the scene, she was rushed to a nearby hospital. Three weeks later she died from her wounds.

Several months after her death, the Cranston, Rhode Island police arrested respondent and two others in connection with a local burglary. Shortly before the arrest, Detective Ferranti of the Cranston police force had learned from a confidential informant that the man responsible for Ms. Hickey's death lived at a certain address and went by the name of "Butch." Upon discovering that respondent lived at that address and was known by that name, Detective Ferranti informed respondent of his *Miranda* rights. When respondent refused to execute a written waiver, Detective Ferranti spoke separately with the two other suspects arrested on the breaking and entering charge and obtained statements further implicating respondent in Ms. Hickey's murder. At approximately 6:00 p.m., Detective Ferranti telephoned the police in Providence to convey the information he had uncovered. An hour later, three officers from that department arrived at the Cranston headquarters for the purpose of questioning respondent about the murder.

That same evening, at about 7:45 p.m., respondent's sister telephoned the Public Defender's Office to obtain legal assistance for her brother. Her sole concern was the breaking and entering charge, as she was unaware that respondent was then under suspicion for murder. She asked for Richard Casparian who had been scheduled to meet with respondent earlier that afternoon to discuss another charge unrelated to either the break-in or the murder. As soon as the conversation ended, the attorney who took the call attempted to reach Mr. Casparian. When those efforts were unsuccessful, she telephoned Allegra Munson, another Assistant Public Defender, and told her about respondent's arrest and his sister's subsequent request that the office represent him.

At 8:15 p.m., Ms. Munson telephoned the Cranston police station and asked that her call be transferred to the detective division. In the words of the Supreme Court of Rhode Island * * * the conversation proceeded as follows:

> "A male voice responded with the word 'Detectives.' Ms. Munson identified herself and asked if Brian Burbine was being held; the person responded affirmatively. Ms. Munson explained to the person that Burbine was represented by attorney Casparian who was not available; she further stated that she would act as Burbine's legal counsel in the event that the police intended to place him in a lineup or question him. The unidentified person told Ms. Munson that the police would not be questioning Burbine or putting him in a lineup and that they were through with him for the night. Ms. Munson was not informed that the Providence Police were at the Cranston police station or that Burbine was a suspect in Mary's murder."

At all relevant times, respondent was unaware of his sister's efforts to retain counsel and of the fact and contents of Ms. Munson's telephone conversation.

Less than an hour later, the police brought respondent to an interrogation room and conducted the first of a series of interviews concerning the murder. Prior to each session, respondent was informed of his *Miranda* rights, and on three separate occasions he signed a written form acknowledging that he understood his right to the presence of an attorney and explicitly indicating that he "[did] not want an attorney called or appointed for [him]" before he gave a statement. Uncontradicted evidence at the suppression hearing indicated that at least twice during the course of the evening, respondent was left in a room where he had access to a telephone, which he apparently declined to use. Eventually, respondent signed three written statements fully admitting to the murder.

Prior to trial, respondent moved to suppress the statements. The court denied the motion, finding that respondent had received the *Miranda* warnings and had "knowingly, intelligently, and voluntarily waived his privilege against self-incrimination [and] his right to counsel." Rejecting the contrary testimony of the police, the court found that Ms. Munson did telephone the detective bureau on the evening in question, but concluded that "there was no * * * conspiracy or collusion on the part of the Cranston Police Department to secrete this defendant from his attorney." In any event, the court held, the constitutional right to request the presence of an attorney belongs solely to the defendant and may not be asserted by his lawyer. Because the evidence was clear that respondent never asked for the services of an attorney, the telephone call had no relevance to the validity of the waiver or the admissibility of the statements.

The jury found respondent guilty of murder in the first degree, and he appealed to the Supreme Court of Rhode Island. A divided court rejected his contention that the Fifth and Fourteenth Amendments to the Constitution required the suppression of the inculpatory statements and affirmed the conviction. * * *

After unsuccessfully petitioning the United States District Court for the District of Rhode Island for a writ of habeas corpus, respondent appealed to the Court of Appeals for the First Circuit. That court reversed. * * *

We granted certiorari to decide whether a prearraignment confession preceded by an otherwise valid waiver must be suppressed either because the police misinformed an inquiring attorney about their plans concerning the suspect or because they failed to inform the suspect of the attorney's efforts to reach him. * * *

* * *

II

* * *

Respondent * * * contends * * * that the confessions must be suppressed because the police's failure to inform him of the attorney's telephone call deprived him of information essential to his ability to knowingly waive his Fifth Amendment rights. In the alternative, he suggests that to fully protect the Fifth Amendment values served by *Miranda,* we should extend that decision to condemn the conduct of the Providence police. We address each contention in turn.

A

Echoing the standard first articulated in *Johnson v. Zerbst,* 304 U.S. 458, 464, 58 S.Ct. 1019, 1023, 82 L.Ed. 1461 (1938), *Miranda* holds that "[t]he defendant may waive effectuation" of the rights conveyed in the warnings "provided the waiver is made voluntarily, knowingly and intelligently." The inquiry has two distinct dimensions. First the relinquishment of the right must have been voluntary in the sense that it was the product of a free and deliberate choice rather than intimidation, coercion or deception. Second, the waiver must have been made with a full awareness both of the nature of the right being abandoned and the consequences of the decision to abandon it. Only if the "totality of the circumstances surrounding the interrogation" reveal both an uncoerced choice and the requisite level of comprehension may a court properly conclude that the *Miranda* rights have been waived.

Under this standard, we have no doubt that respondent validly waived his right to remain silent and to the presence of counsel. The voluntariness of the waiver is not at issue. As the Court of Appeals correctly acknowledged, the record is devoid of any suggestion that police resorted to physical or psychological pressure to elicit the statements. Indeed it appears that it was respondent, and not the police, who spontaneously initiated the conversation that led to the first and most damaging confession. Nor is there any question about respondent's comprehension of the full panoply of rights set out in the *Miranda* warnings and of the potential consequences of a decision to relinquish them. Nonetheless, the Court of Appeals believed that the "[d]eliberate or reckless" conduct of the police, in particular their failure to inform respondent of the telephone call, fatally undermined the validity of the otherwise proper waiver. We find this conclusion untenable as a matter of both logic and precedent.

Events occurring outside of the presence of the suspect and entirely unknown to him surely can have no bearing on the capacity to comprehend and knowingly relinquish a constitutional right. Under the analysis of the Court of Appeals, the same defendant, armed with the same information and confronted with precisely the same police conduct, would have knowingly waived his *Miranda* rights had a lawyer not telephoned the police station to inquire about his status. Nothing in any of our waiver decisions or in our understanding of the essential components of a valid waiver requires so incongruous a result. No doubt the additional information would have been useful to respondent; perhaps even it might have affected his decision to confess. But we have never read the Constitution to require that the police supply a suspect with a flow of information to help him calibrate his self interest in deciding whether to speak or stand by his rights. Once it is determined that a suspect's decision not to rely on his rights was uncoerced, that he at all times knew he could stand mute and request a lawyer, and that he was aware of the state's intention to use his statements to secure a conviction, the analysis is complete and the waiver is valid as a matter of law. The Court of Appeals' conclusion to the contrary was in error.

Nor do we believe that the level of the police's culpability in failing to inform respondent of the telephone call has any bearing on the validity of the waiver. In light of the state-court findings that there was no "conspiracy or collusion" on the part of the police, we have serious doubts about whether the Court of Appeals was free to conclude that their conduct constituted "deliberate or reckless irresponsibility." But whether intentional or inadvertent, the state of mind of the police is irrelevant to the question of the intelligence and voluntariness of respondent's election to abandon his rights. Although highly inappropriate, even deliberate deception of an attorney could not possibly affect a suspect's decision to waive his *Miranda* rights unless he were at least aware of the incident. Nor was the failure to inform respondent of the telephone call the kind of "trick[ery]" that can vitiate the validity of a waiver. Granting that the "deliberate or reckless" withholding of information is objectionable as a matter of ethics, such conduct is only relevant to the constitutional validity of a waiver if it deprives a defendant of knowledge essential to his ability to understand the nature of his rights and the consequences of abandoning them. Because respondent's voluntary decision to speak was made with full awareness and comprehension of all the information *Miranda* requires the police to convey, the waivers were valid.

B

At oral argument respondent acknowledged that a constitutional rule requiring the police to inform a suspect of an attorney's efforts to reach him would represent a significant extension of our precedents. He contends, however, that the conduct of the Providence police was so inimical to the Fifth Amendment values *Miranda* seeks to protect that we should read that decision to condemn their behavior. Regardless of any issue of waiver, he urges, the Fifth Amendment requires the reversal of a conviction if the police are less than forthright in their dealings with an attorney or if they fail to tell a suspect of a lawyer's unilateral efforts to contact him. Because the proposed modification ignores the underlying purposes of the *Miranda* rules and because we think that the decision as written strikes the proper balance between society's legitimate law enforcement interests and the protection of the defendant's Fifth

Amendment rights, we decline the invitation to further extend *Miranda's* reach.

At the outset, while we share respondent's distaste for the deliberate misleading of an officer of the court, reading *Miranda* to forbid police deception of an *attorney* "would cut [the decision] completely loose from its own explicitly stated rationale." As is now well established, "[t]he * * * *Miranda* warnings are 'not themselves rights protected by the Constitution but [are] instead measures to insure that the [suspect's] right against compulsory self-incrimination [is] protected.'" Their objective is not to mold police conduct for its own sake. Nothing in the Constitution vests in us the authority to mandate a code of behavior for state officials wholly unconnected to any federal right or privilege. The purpose of the *Miranda* warnings instead is to dissipate the compulsion inherent in custodial interrogation and, in so doing, guard against abridgement of the suspect's Fifth Amendment rights. Clearly, a rule that focuses on how the police treat an attorney—conduct that has no relevance at all to the degree of compulsion experienced by the defendant during interrogation—would ignore both *Miranda's* mission and its only source of legitimacy.

Nor are we prepared to adopt a rule requiring that the police inform a suspect of an attorney's efforts to reach him. While such a rule might add marginally to *Miranda's* goal of dispelling the compulsion inherent in custodial interrogation, overriding practical considerations counsel against its adoption. As we have stressed on numerous occasions, "[o]ne of the principal advantages" of *Miranda* is the ease and clarity of its application. We have little doubt that the approach urged by respondent and endorsed by the Court of Appeals would have the inevitable consequence of muddying *Miranda's* otherwise relatively clear waters. The legal questions it would spawn are legion: To what extent should the police be held accountable for knowing that the accused has counsel? Is it enough that someone in the station house knows, or must the interrogating officer himself know of counsel's efforts to contact the suspect? Do counsel's efforts to talk to the suspect concerning one criminal investigation trigger the obligation to inform the defendant before interrogation may proceed on a wholly separate matter? We are unwilling to modify *Miranda* in manner that would so clearly undermine the decision's central "virtue of informing police and prosecutors with specificity * * * what they may do in conducting [a] custodial interrogation, and of informing courts under what circumstances statements obtained during such interrogation are not admissible."

Moreover, problems of clarity to one side, reading *Miranda* to require the police in each instance to inform a suspect of an attorney's efforts to reach him would work a substantial and, we think, inappropriate shift in the subtle balance struck in that decision. Custodial interrogations implicate two competing concerns. On the one hand, "the need for police questioning as a tool for effective enforcement of criminal laws" cannot be doubted. Admissions of guilt are more than merely "desirable"; they are essential to society's compelling interest in finding, convicting and punishing those who violate the law. On the other hand, the Court has recognized that the interrogation process is "inherently coercive" and that, as a consequence, there exists a substantial risk that the police will inadvertently traverse the fine line between legitimate efforts to elicit admissions and constitutionally impermissible compulsion. *Miranda* attempted to reconcile these opposing concerns by giving the *defendant* the power to exert some control over the course of the interrogation. Declining to adopt the more extreme position that the actual presence of a lawyer was necessary to dispel the coercion inherent in custodial interrogation, the Court found that the suspect's Fifth Amendment rights could be adequately protected by less intrusive means. Police questioning, often an essential part of the investigatory process, could continue in its traditional form, the Court held, but only if the suspect clearly understood that, at any time, he could bring the proceeding to a halt or, short of that, call in an attorney to give advice and monitor the conduct of his interrogators.

The position urged by respondent would upset this carefully drawn approach in a manner that is both unnecessary for the protection of the Fifth Amendment privilege and injurious to legitimate law enforcement. Because, as *Miranda* holds, full comprehension of the rights to remain silent and request an attorney are sufficient to dispel whatever coercion is inherent in the interrogation process, a rule requiring the police to inform the suspect of an attorney's efforts to contact him would contribute to the protection of the Fifth Amendment privilege only incidentally, if at all. This minimal benefit, however, would come at a substantial cost to society's legitimate and substantial interest in securing admissions of guilt. Indeed, the very premise of the Court of Appeals was not that awareness of Ms. Munson's phone call would have dissipated the coercion of the interrogation room, but that it might have convinced respondent not to speak at all. Because neither the letter nor purposes of *Miranda* require this additional handicap on otherwise permissible investigatory efforts, we are unwilling to expand the *Miranda* rules to require the police to keep the suspect abreast of the status of his legal representation.

We acknowledge that a number of state courts have reached a contrary conclusion. * * * Nothing we say today disables the States from adopting different requirements for the conduct of its employees and officials as a matter of state law. We hold only that the Court of Appeals erred in construing the Fifth Amendment to the Federal Constitution to require the exclusion of respondent's three confessions.

IV

Finally, respondent contends that the conduct of the police was so offensive as to deprive him of the fundamental fairness guaranteed by the Due Process Clause of the Fourteenth Amendment. Focusing primarily on the impropriety of conveying false information to an attorney, he invites us to declare that such behavior should be condemned as violative of canons fundamental to the " 'traditions and conscience of our people.' " *Rochin v. California*, 342 U.S. 165, 169, 72 S.Ct. 205, 208, 96 L.Ed. 183 (1952). We do not question that on facts more egregious than those presented here police deception might rise to a level of a due process violation. * * * We hold only that, on these facts, the challenged conduct falls short of the kind of misbehavior that so shocks the sensibilities of civilized society as to warrant a federal intrusion into the criminal processes of the States.

We hold therefore that the Court of Appeals erred in finding that the Federal Constitution required the exclusion of the three inculpatory statements. Accordingly, we reverse and remand for proceedings consistent with this opinion.

So ordered.

■ JUSTICE STEVENS, with whom JUSTICE BRENNAN and JUSTICE MARSHALL join, dissenting.

Well-settled principles of law lead inexorably to the conclusion that the failure to inform Burbine of the call from his attorney makes the subsequent waiver of his constitutional rights invalid. * * * [T]his Court has sometimes relied on a case-by-case totality of the circumstances analysis. We have found, however, that some custodial interrogation situations require strict presumptions against the validity of a waiver. *Miranda* established that a waiver is not valid in the absence of certain warnings. * * * In these circumstances, the waiver is invalid as a matter of law * * * . Like the failure to give warnings * * * , police deception of a suspect through omission of information regarding attorney communications greatly exacerbates the inherent problems of incommunicado interrogation and requires a clear principle to safeguard the presumption against the waiver of constitutional rights. As in those situations [involving a failure to warn], the police deception should render a subsequent waiver invalid.

* * *

The Court makes the * * * argument that requiring police to inform a suspect of his attorney's communications to and about him is not required because it would upset the careful "balance" of *Miranda*. Despite its earlier notion that the attorney's call is an "outside event" that has "no bearing" on a knowing and intelligent waiver, the majority does acknowledge that information of attorney Munson's call "would have been useful to respondent" and "might have affected his decision to confess." Thus, a rule requiring the police to inform a suspect of an attorney's call would have two predictable effects. It would serve "*Miranda*'s goal of dispelling the compulsion inherent in custodial interrogation" and it would disserve the goal of custodial interrogation because it would result in fewer confessions. By a process of balancing these two concerns, the Court finds the benefit to the individual outweighed by the "substantial cost to society's legitimate and substantial interest in securing admissions of guilt."

The Court's balancing approach is profoundly misguided. The cost of suppressing evidence of guilt will always make the value of a procedural safeguard appear "minimal," "marginal," or "incremental." Indeed, the value of any trial at all seems like a "procedural technicality" when balanced against the interest in administering prompt justice to a murderer or a rapist caught redhanded. The individual interest in procedural safeguards that minimize the risk of error is easily discounted when the fact of guilt appears certain beyond doubt.

What is the cost of requiring the police to inform a suspect of his attorney's call? It would decrease the likelihood that custodial interrogation will enable the police to obtain a confession. This is certainly a real cost, but it is the same cost that this Court has repeatedly found necessary to preserve the character of our free society and our rejection of an inquisitorial system. * * *

If the Court's cost benefit analysis were sound, it would justify a repudiation of the right to a warning about counsel itself. * * *

* * *

The possible reach of the Court's opinion is stunning. For the majority seems to suggest that police may deny counsel all access to a client who is being held. * * * [I]t has been widely accepted that police may not simply deny attorneys access to their clients who are in custody. * * * The Court today seems to assume that this view was error—that, from the federal constitutional perspective, the lawyer's access is, as a question from the Court put it in oral argument, merely "a matter of prosecutorial grace." * * *

* * *

In my judgment, police interference in the attorney-client relationship is the type of governmental misconduct on a matter of central importance to the administration of justice that the Due Process Clause prohibits. Just as the police cannot impliedly promise a suspect that his silence will not be used against him and then proceed to break that promise, so too police cannot tell a suspect's attorney that they will not question the suspect and then proceed to question him. Just as the government cannot conceal from a suspect material and exculpatory evidence, so too the government cannot conceal from a suspect the material fact of his attorney's communication.

* *

I respectfully dissent.

NOTES

1. **Knowledge of Subject Matter of Interrogation.** Knowledge of the subjects officers will pursue during an interrogation is not essential to an effective waiver of the *Miranda* rights concerning that interrogation.

In Colorado v. Spring, 479 U.S. 564, 107 S.Ct. 851 (1987), an informant told officers of the federal Bureau of Alcohol, Tobacco, and Firearms (ATF) that John Spring was engaged in the transportation of stolen firearms and admitted to the informant he had once shot a companion during a hunting trip in Colorado. The agents set up a "sting" operation in Kansas City, Missouri, and, during a purchase of firearms from Spring, the agents arrested him. Agents advised of his *Miranda* rights at the scene of the arrest. After being taken to the ATF office in Kansas City, he was again advised of his rights and signed a written form stating he understood and waived his rights and he was willing to answer questions and make a statement. After questioning him about the firearms transaction, the ATF agents asked Spring about homicides. He "ducked his head" and mumbled, "I shot another guy once." The Colorado Supreme Court held that Spring's waiver of *Miranda* rights during the interview with ATF agents was not voluntary and intelligent because the agents failed to inform him that the questioning would involve the homicide.

The Supreme Court reversed, reasoning that no violation of *Miranda* occurred:

> [T]here is no allegation that Spring failed to understand the basic privilege guaranteed by the Fifth Amendment. Nor is there any allegation that he misunderstood the consequences of speaking freely to the law enforcement officials. * * * [T]he trial court was indisputably correct in finding that Spring's waiver was made knowingly and intelligently within the meaning of *Miranda*.
>
> * * *
>
> * * * We have held that a valid waiver does not require that an individual be informed of all information "useful" in making his decision or all information that "might . . . affec[t] his decision to confess." *Moran v. Burbine*, 475 U.S. [412, 422, 106 S.Ct. 1135, 1142, 89 L.Ed.2d 410 (1986)]. * * * [This] additional information could affect only the wisdom of a *Miranda* waiver, not its essentially voluntary and knowing nature. Accordingly, the failure of law enforcement officials to inform Spring of the subject matter of the interrogation could not affect Spring's decision to waive his Fifth Amendment privilege in a constitutionally significant manner.
>
> * * *
>
> [W]e hold that a suspect's awareness of all the possible subjects of questioning in advance of interrogation is not relevant to determining whether the suspect voluntarily, knowingly, and intelligently waived his Fifth Amendment privilege.

479 U.S. at 575–77, 107 S.Ct. at 858–59.

2.   **Waiver by Suspect Reapproached After Invoking Right to Silence.** A suspect who invokes the right to remain silent raises no bar to being reapproached by officers, as is discussed in Subchapter C(3) of this chapter. Under Michigan v. Mosley, 423 U.S. 96, 96 S.Ct. 321 (1975), however, the fact that the suspect was reapproached after so invoking that right may increase the prosecution's burden of proving that his waivers were effective.

After Mosley was arrested, a Detective Cowie sought to question him about a specific robbery of a White Tower Restaurant. When Mosley said he did not want to answer any questions about the robbery, Cowie ceased the questioning and had Mosley taken to a cell. Several hours later, another officer—Detective Hill—had Mosley brought to an interrogation room for questioning concerning the fatal shooting of one Leroy Williams during a robbery of the 101 Ranch Bar. Hill gave Mosley *Miranda* warnings and Mosley signed a notification form. During the following 15 minute interrogation, Mosley admitted being involved in the slaying. Addressing the prosecution's ability to use that admission in evidence, the Supreme Court first determined that a suspect's invocation of his right to remain silent "can[not] sensibly be read to create a *per se* proscription of indefinite duration upon any further questioning by any police officer on any subject, once the person in custody has indicated a desire to remain silent." It then continued:

> We * * * conclude that the admissibility of statements obtained after the person in custody has decided to remain silent depends under *Miranda* on whether his "right to cut off questioning" was "scrupulously honored."

> A review of the circumstances leading to Mosley's confession reveals that his "right to cut off questioning" was fully respected in this case. Before his initial interrogation, Mosley was carefully advised that he was under no obligation to answer any questions and could remain silent if he wished. He orally acknowledged that he understood the *Miranda* warnings and then signed a printed notification-of-rights form. When Mosley stated that he did not want to discuss the robberies, Detective Cowie immediately ceased the interrogation and did not try either to resume the questioning or in any way to persuade Mosley to reconsider his position. After an interval of more than two hours, Mosley was questioned by another police officer at another location about an unrelated holdup murder. He was given full and complete *Miranda* warnings at the outset of the second interrogation. He was thus reminded again that he could remain silent and could consult with a lawyer, and was carefully given a full and fair opportunity to exercise these options. The subsequent questioning did not undercut Mosley's previous decision not to answer Detective Cowie's inquiries. Detective Hill did not resume the interrogation about the White Tower Restaurant robbery * * * , but instead focused exclusively on the Leroy Williams homicide, a crime different in nature and in time and place of occurrence from the robberies for which Mosley had been arrested and interrogated by Detective Cowie. Although

it is not clear from the record how much Detective Hill knew about the earlier interrogation, his questioning of Mosley about an unrelated homicide was quite consistent with a reasonable interpretation of Mosley's earlier refusal to answer any questions about the robberies.

This is not a case, therefore, where the police failed to honor a decision of a person in custody to cut off questioning, either by refusing to discontinue the interrogation upon request or by persisting in repeated efforts to wear down his resistance and make him change his mind. In contrast to such practices, the police here immediately ceased the interrogation, resumed questioning only after the passage of a significant period of time and the provision of a fresh set of warnings, and restricted the second interrogation to a crime that had not been a subject of the earlier interrogation.

423 U.S. at 104–06, 96 S.Ct. 326–27.

3. **Empirical Information on Suspects' Understanding of** *Miranda.* Consideration of whether the Supreme Court has most appropriately formulated *Miranda* waiver law may be facilitated by information concerning what suspects might in actual fact understand as a result of *Miranda* warnings.

Grisso, Juveniles' Capacity to Waive Miranda Rights: An Empirical Analysis, 68 Cal.L.Rev. 1134 (1980), for purposes of comparison with juveniles, studied the results of giving *Miranda* warnings to 203 adult parolees and 57 adults employed in custodial services and university and hospital maintenance crews. He concluded a significant proportion of these adults did not learn the underlying rights from the *Miranda* warnings. 42.3% of the subjects were able accurately to paraphrase all four of the *Miranda* rights after the warning; 57.7% were not. The most commonly misunderstood part of the warning concerned the right to the presence of counsel; 14.6% of the subjects were unable to paraphrase this accurately. In an effort to avoid the effect of facility in verbal expression, Griss administered a true-false test containing 12 questions to the subjects. 76.5% received a score of 10–12 correct responses; another 18.9% scored 7 to 9 correct answers. But 4.6% of the subjects scored only 5 or 6 correct answers. A further test consisted of questioning the subjects concerning a hypothetical interrogation situation. 89–95% of the subjects recognized the adversarial nature of the interrogation, the role of the subject's lawyer in it, and the lawyers' need for full information concerning the events. But many of the subjects failed to understand the effect which the privilege against self-incrimination would have later in the courtroom. 42.9% believed that they would have to later explain their criminal involvement in court if questioned by the judge. This suggests a significant proportion of *Miranda* waivers may be influenced by the suspects' perception that they will later be compelled to answer questions concerning the situation. Such suspects might reason that since they will have to explain the situation to authorities at some point, they might as well do it during police questioning.

4.   **Effect of Deception on Effectiveness of Waivers.** What is the effect of police officers' deception before or during interrogation to which *Miranda* applies? The issue was urged in *Spring*, discussed in note 1 above, but the Court held that it was not raised. The ATF agents' failure to inform Spring that he would be questioned about the homicide did not constitute "trickery." Therefore it was not addressing, the Court noted, the validity of waivers when law enforcement officials made "an affirmative misrepresentation * * * as to the scope of the interrogation * * * ."

Miranda itself contains language suggesting that waivers are rendered ineffective by proof that the defendant "was * * * tricked * * * into [the] waiver." Frazier v. Cupp, discussed in the Editors' Introduction to Subchapter B of this chapter, addressed the effect of deception upon due process voluntariness. Although it was decided after *Miranda*, *Frazier* did not acknowledge potential tension between its holding and the discussion in *Miranda*. Perhaps, then, *Frazier*'s approach is not necessarily applicable when the issue is the validity of a *Miranda* waiver. Often, however, courts assume that the *Frazier* approach applies under *Miranda*. Thus, officers' use of deception is simply one of the factors to consider in deciding whether, on the totality of the circumstances, *Miranda* waivers are voluntary. Commonwealth v. Holley, 79 Mass.App.Ct. 542, 547–548, 947 N.E.2d 606, 612 (Mass.App.), review denied 460 Mass. 1107, 950 N.E.2d 439 (2011).

5.   **Intoxication.** What effect does a suspect's intoxication have upon the effectiveness of a waiver of the *Miranda* rights? In Berkemer v. McCarty, 468 U.S. 420, 104 S.Ct. 3138 (1984), reprinted in Subchapter C(2)(b) of this chapter, the Court noted:

> [W]e are asked to consider what a State must do in order to demonstrate that a suspect who might have been under the influence of drugs or alcohol when subjected to custodial interrogation nevertheless understood and freely waived his constitutional rights. * * * We prefer to defer resolution of [this matter] to a case in which law enforcement authorities have at least attempted to inform the suspect of rights to which he is indisputably entitled.

468 U.S. at 434 n. 21, 104 S.Ct. at 3147 n. 21. In light of *Connelly*, discussed in the Editors' Introduction to this subchapter, is intoxication relevant at all in the absence of law enforcement overreaching of some sort?

5. "FRUITS" OF A CONFESSION INADMISSIBLE UNDER *MIRANDA* AND "QUESTION FIRST" TACTICS

EDITORS' INTRODUCTION

Supreme Court case law firmly establishes that when a defendant shows a violation of his Fourth Amendment rights, this requires—subject to exceptions—exclusion of what is often called all "fruit of the poisonous tree." This requirement, and various limitations and exceptions that might affect it, were developed in Chapter 1.

Miranda's exclusionary sanction need not impose an identical requirement. In fact, it does not. The case law may, however, distinguish situations in which the challenged fruit is an out-of-court incriminating admission made after *Miranda* requirements are met and those in which the fruit is some other type of evidence, such as items located and seized as a result of an interrogation conducted in violation of *Miranda*.

Whether the Fifth Amendment requires suppression of physical evidence obtained by using statements of a suspect themselves inadmissible because they were elicited in violation of *Miranda* was addressed in United States v. Patane, 542 U.S. 630, 124 S.Ct. 2620 (2004).

Officers arrested Patane and without complying with *Miranda* asked him about a .40 Glock pistol the officers had been told Patane possessed. Patane informed the officers the gun was in his bedroom and gave them permission to retrieve it. They did. The lower federal courts held the gun inadmissible.

A split five-to-four majority of the Supreme Court reversed. Justice Thomas, joined by the Chief Justice and Justice Scalia, explained in a plurality opinion that the "fruit of the poisonous tree" rule of Fourth Amendment jurisprudence did not apply because *Miranda*, properly read, made clear there was no poisonous tree in this situation. A *Miranda* violation occurs only if police fail to comply with *Miranda*'s directives *and* a resulting statement is admitted into evidence. Failure to give the *Miranda* warnings itself does not violate a suspect's constitutional rights or the *Miranda* rule. "The *Miranda* rule is not a code of police conduct * * * ." 542 U.S. at 637, 124 S.Ct. at 2626 (plurality opinion of Thomas, J., announcing the judgment of the court).

An analysis considering any possible need to deter police conduct, the plurality asserted, would be improper here, because in these situations there is nothing the Court can properly consider as needing to be deterred. Mere unwarned questionings of suspects, when not accompanied by actual use of resulting self-incriminating statements, are not actions the Court can properly act to discourage or deter.

The five-justice majority was made up of those joining Justice Thomas's opinion and Justice Kennedy, joined by Justice O'Connor. Justice Kennedy explained for himself and Justice O'Connor:

> [I]t is sufficient to note that the Government presents an even stronger case for admitting the evidence obtained as the result of Patane's unwarned statement [than was presented in prior cases permitting use of evidence obtained following an unwarned interrogation]. Admission of nontestimonial physical fruits (the Glock in this case) * * * does not run the risk of admitting into trial an accused's coerced incriminating statements against himself. In light of the important probative value of reliable physical evidence, it is doubtful that exclusion

can be justified by a deterrence rationale sensitive to both law enforcement interests and a suspect's rights during an in-custody interrogation. Unlike the plurality, however, I find it unnecessary to decide whether the detective's failure to give Patane the full *Miranda* warnings should be characterized as a violation of the *Miranda* rule itself, or whether there is "[any]thing to deter" so long as the unwarned statements are not later introduced at trial.

542 U.S. at 645, 124 S.Ct. at 2631 (Kennedy, J., concurring in the judgment).

Three dissenters argued that the majority mischaracterized the issue:

> The issue actually presented today is whether courts should apply the fruit of the poisonous tree doctrine lest we create an incentive for the police to omit *Miranda* warnings, before custodial interrogation. In closing their eyes to the consequences of giving an evidentiary advantage to those who ignore *Miranda,* the majority adds an important inducement for interrogators to ignore the rule in that case.

* * *

> There is no way to read this case except as an unjustifiable invitation to law enforcement officers to flout *Miranda* when there may be physical evidence to be gained. * * * I respectfully dissent.

542 U.S. at 645–47, 124 S.Ct. at 2631–32 (Souter, J., dissenting). Justice Breyer, dissenting separately, would have applied the approach he took in the principal case reprinted following this Introduction. Since the lower courts made no explicit finding that the officers acted in good faith, he would have applied a rule requiring exclusion of physical evidence obtained from unwarned questioning. 542 U.S. at 647–48, 124 S.Ct. at 2632 (Breyer, J., dissenting).

State law, of course, may be require exclusion where *Patane* does not. The Supreme Judicial Court of Massachusetts concluded in Commonwealth v. Martin, 444 Mass. 213, 827 N.E.2d 198 (2005), for example, that the state constitutional privilege against self-incrimination required a common-law rule of evidence excluding physical evidence obtained as a result of unwarned statements where state constitutional law required the *Miranda* warnings for those statements to be admissible. It explained:

> To apply the *Patane* analysis to the broader rights embodied in [the state constitutional provision] would have a corrosive effect on them, undermine the respect we have accorded them, and demean their importance to a system of justice chosen by the citizens of Massachusetts in 1780.

444 Mass. at 219, 827 N.E.2d at 203. A similar result was reached in State v. Peterson, 181 Vt. 436, 923 A.2d 585 (2007).

Where the challenged fruit of a statement inadmissible under *Miranda* is another self-criminating statement presents a somewhat more difficult question. This is explored in the following case.

Missouri v. Seibert

Supreme Court of the United States, 2004.
542 U.S. 600, 124 S.Ct. 2601.

■ JUSTICE SOUTER announced the judgment of the Court and delivered an opinion, in which JUSTICE STEVENS, JUSTICE GINSBURG, and JUSTICE BREYER join.

This case tests a police protocol for custodial interrogation that calls for giving no warnings of the rights to silence and counsel until interrogation has produced a confession. Although such a statement is generally inadmissible, since taken in violation of *Miranda v. Arizona*, 384 U.S. 436, 86 S.Ct. 1602, 16 L.Ed.2d 694 (1966), the interrogating officer follows it with *Miranda* warnings and then leads the suspect to cover the same ground a second time. The question here is the admissibility of the repeated statement. * * *

I

Respondent Patrice Seibert's 12-year-old son Jonathan had cerebral palsy, and when he died in his sleep she feared charges of neglect because of bedsores on his body. In her presence, two of her teenage sons and two of their friends devised a plan to conceal the facts surrounding Jonathan's death by incinerating his body in the course of burning the family's mobile home, in which they planned to leave Donald Rector, a mentally ill teenager living with the family, to avoid any appearance that Jonathan had been unattended. Seibert's son Darian and a friend set the fire, and Donald died.

Five days later, the police awakened Seibert at 3 a.m. at a hospital where Darian was being treated for burns. In arresting her, Officer Kevin Clinton followed instructions from Rolla, Missouri, officer Richard Hanrahan that he refrain from giving *Miranda* warnings. After Seibert had been taken to the police station and left alone in an interview room for 15 to 20 minutes, Hanrahan questioned her without *Miranda* warnings for 30 to 40 minutes, squeezing her arm and repeating "Donald was also to die in his sleep." After Seibert finally admitted she knew Donald was meant to die in the fire, she was given a 20-minute coffee and cigarette break. Officer Hanrahan then turned on a tape recorder, gave Seibert the *Miranda* warnings, and obtained a signed waiver of rights from her. He resumed the questioning with "Ok, 'trice, we've been talking for a little while about what happened on Wednesday the twelfth, haven't we?," and confronted her with her prewarning statements:

Hanrahan: "Now, in discussion you told us, you told us that there was a[n] understanding about Donald."

Seibert: "Yes."

Hanrahan: "Did that take place earlier that morning?"

Seibert: "Yes."

Hanrahan: "And what was the understanding about Donald?"

Seibert: "If they could get him out of the trailer, to take him out of the trailer."

Hanrahan: "And if they couldn't?"

Seibert: "I, I never even thought about it. I just figured they would."

Hanrahan: " 'Trice, didn't you tell me that he was supposed to die in his sleep?"

Seibert: "If that would happen, 'cause he was on that new medicine,' you know. . . ."

Hanrahan: "The Prozac? And it makes him sleepy. So he was supposed to die in his sleep?"

Seibert: "Yes."

After being charged with first-degree murder for her role in Donald's death, Seibert sought to exclude both her prewarning and postwarning statements. At the suppression hearing, Officer Hanrahan testified that he made a "conscious decision" to withhold *Miranda* warnings, thus resorting to an interrogation technique he had been taught: question first, then give the warnings, and then repeat the question "until I get the answer that she's already provided once." He acknowledged that Seibert's ultimate statement was "largely a repeat of information . . . obtained" prior to the warning.

The trial court suppressed the prewarning statement but admitted the responses given after the *Miranda* recitation. A jury convicted Seibert of second-degree murder. On appeal, the Missouri Court of Appeals affirmed, treating this case as indistinguishable from *Oregon v. Elstad,* 470 U.S. 298, 105 S.Ct. 1285, 84 L.Ed.2d 222 (1985).

The Supreme Court of Missouri reversed, holding that "[i]n the circumstances here, where the interrogation was nearly continuous, . . . the second statement, clearly the product of the invalid first statement, should have been suppressed." The court distinguished *Elstad* on the ground that warnings had not intentionally been withheld there * * * .

We granted certiorari * * * .

III

* * *

The technique of interrogating in successive, unwarned and warned phases raises a new challenge to *Miranda*. Although we have no statistics on the frequency of this practice, it is not confined to Rolla, Missouri. An officer of that police department testified that the strategy of withholding *Miranda* warnings until after interrogating and drawing out a confession was promoted not only by his own department, but by a national police training organization and other departments in which he had worked. Consistently with the officer's testimony, the Police Law Institute, for example, instructs that "officers may conduct a two-stage interrogation. . . . At any point during the pre-*Miranda* interrogation, usually after arrestees have confessed, officers may then read the *Miranda* warnings and ask for a waiver. If the arrestees waive their *Miranda* rights, officers will be able to repeat any *subsequent* incriminating statements later in court." Police Law Institute, Illinois Police Law Manual 83 (Jan.2001–Dec.2003), http:// www.illinoispolice law.org/training/lessons/ILPLMIR.pdf (as visited Dec. 31, 2003, and available in the Clerk of Court's case file) (hereinafter Police Law Manual) (emphasis in original).[2] The upshot of all this advice is a question-first practice of some popularity, * * * sometimes in obedience to departmental policy.

IV

When a confession so obtained is offered and challenged, attention must be paid to the conflicting objects of *Miranda* and question-first. *Miranda* addressed "interrogation practices . . . likely . . . to disable [an individual] from making a free and rational choice" about speaking, and held that a suspect must be "adequately and effectively" advised of the choice the Constitution guarantees. The object of question-first is to render *Miranda* warnings ineffective by waiting for a particularly opportune time to give them, after the suspect has already confessed.

Just as "no talismanic incantation [is] required to satisfy [*Miranda*'s] strictures," *California v. Prysock,* 453 U.S. 355, 359, 101 S.Ct. 2806, 69 L.Ed.2d 696 (1981) *(per curiam),* it would be absurd to think that mere recitation of the litany suffices to satisfy *Miranda* in every conceivable circumstance. "The inquiry is simply whether the warnings reasonably 'conve[y] to [a suspect] his rights as required by *Miranda*.'" *Duckworth v. Eagan,* 492 U.S. 195, 203, 109 S.Ct. 2875, 106 L.Ed.2d 166 (1989) (quoting *Prysock, supra,* at 361). The threshold issue when interrogators question first and warn later is thus whether it would be reasonable to find that in these circumstances the warnings could function "effectively" as *Miranda* requires. Could the warnings effectively advise the suspect that he had a real choice about giving an admissible statement at that juncture? Could they reasonably convey that he could choose to stop talking even if he had talked earlier? For unless the warnings could place

---

[2]   Emphasizing the impeachment exception to the *Miranda* rule * * *, some training programs advise officers to omit *Miranda* warnings altogether or to continue questioning after the suspect invokes his rights. * * *

It is not the case, of course, that law enforcement educators en masse are urging that *Miranda* be honored only in the breach. Most police manuals do not advocate the question-first tactic * * * .

a suspect who has just been interrogated in a position to make such an informed choice, there is no practical justification for accepting the formal warnings as compliance with *Miranda,* or for treating the second stage of interrogation as distinct from the first, unwarned and inadmissible segment.[4]

There is no doubt about the answer that proponents of question-first give to this question about the effectiveness of warnings given only after successful interrogation, and we think their answer is correct. By any objective measure, applied to circumstances exemplified here, it is likely that if the interrogators employ the technique of withholding warnings until after interrogation succeeds in eliciting a confession, the warnings will be ineffective in preparing the suspect for successive interrogation, close in time and similar in content. After all, the reason that question-first is catching on is as obvious as its manifest purpose, which is to get a confession the suspect would not make if he understood his rights at the outset; the sensible underlying assumption is that with one confession in hand before the warnings, the interrogator can count on getting its duplicate, with trifling additional trouble. Upon hearing warnings only in the aftermath of interrogation and just after making a confession, a suspect would hardly think he had a genuine right to remain silent, let alone persist in so believing once the police began to lead him over the same ground again.[5] A more likely reaction on a suspect's part would be perplexity about the reason for discussing rights at that point, bewilderment being an unpromising frame of mind for knowledgeable decision. What is worse, telling a suspect that "anything you say can and will be used against you," without expressly excepting the statement just given, could lead to an entirely reasonable inference that what he has just said will be used, with subsequent silence being of no avail. Thus, when *Miranda* warnings are inserted in the midst of coordinated and continuing interrogation, they are likely to mislead and "depriv[e] a defendant of knowledge essential to his ability to understand the nature of his rights and the consequences of abandoning them."

---

[4] Respondent Seibert argues that her second confession should be excluded from evidence under the doctrine known by the metaphor of the "fruit of the poisonous tree," developed in the Fourth Amendment context * * *: evidence otherwise admissible but discovered as a result of an earlier violation is excluded as tainted, lest the law encourage future violations. But the Court in *Elstad* rejected the * * * fruits doctrine for analyzing the admissibility of a subsequent warned confession following "an initial failure . . . to administer the warnings required by *Miranda.*" * * * In a sequential confession case, clarity is served if the later confession is approached by asking whether in the circumstances the *Miranda* warnings given could reasonably be found effective. If yes, a court can take up the standard issues of voluntary waiver and voluntary statement; if no, the subsequent statement is inadmissible for want of adequate *Miranda* warnings, because the earlier and later statements are realistically seen as parts of a single, unwarned sequence of questioning.

[5] It bears emphasizing that the effectiveness *Miranda* assumes the warnings can have must potentially extend through the repeated interrogation, since a suspect has a right to stop at any time. It seems highly unlikely that a suspect could retain any such understanding when the interrogator leads him a second time through a line of questioning the suspect has already answered fully. The point is not that a later unknowing or involuntary confession cancels out an earlier, adequate warning; the point is that the warning is unlikely to be effective in the question-first sequence we have described.

Moran v. Burbine, 475 U.S. 412, 424, 106 S.Ct. 1135, 89 L.Ed.2d 410 (1986). By the same token, it would ordinarily be unrealistic to treat two spates of integrated and proximately conducted questioning as independent interrogations subject to independent evaluation simply because *Miranda* warnings formally punctuate them in the middle.

V

Missouri argues that a confession repeated at the end of an interrogation sequence envisioned in a question-first strategy is admissible on the authority of *Oregon v. Elstad,* 470 U.S. 298, 105 S.Ct. 1285, 84 L.Ed.2d 222 (1985), but the argument disfigures that case. In *Elstad,* the police went to the young suspect's house to take him into custody on a charge of burglary. Before the arrest, one officer spoke with the suspect's mother, while the other one joined the suspect in a "brief stop in the living room," where the officer said he "felt" the young man was involved in a burglary. The suspect acknowledged he had been at the scene. This Court noted that the pause in the living room "was not to interrogate the suspect but to notify his mother of the reason for his arrest," and described the incident as having "none of the earmarks of coercion." The Court, indeed, took care to mention that the officer's initial failure to warn was an "oversight" that "may have been the result of confusion as to whether the brief exchange qualified as 'custodial interrogation' or . . . may simply have reflected . . . reluctance to initiate an alarming police procedure before [an officer] had spoken with respondent's mother." At the outset of a later and systematic station house interrogation going well beyond the scope of the laconic prior admission, the suspect was given *Miranda* warnings and made a full confession. In holding the second statement admissible and voluntary, *Elstad* rejected the "cat out of the bag" theory that any short, earlier admission, obtained in arguably innocent neglect of *Miranda,* determined the character of the later, warned confession; on the facts of that case, the Court thought any causal connection between the first and second responses to the police was "speculative and attenuated." Although the *Elstad* Court expressed no explicit conclusion about either officer's state of mind, it is fair to read *Elstad* as treating the living room conversation as a good-faith *Miranda* mistake, not only open to correction by careful warnings before systematic questioning in that particular case, but posing no threat to warn-first practice generally.

The contrast between *Elstad* and this case reveals a series of relevant facts that bear on whether *Miranda* warnings delivered midstream could be effective enough to accomplish their object: the completeness and detail of the questions and answers in the first round of interrogation, the overlapping content of the two statements, the timing and setting of the first and the second, the continuity of police personnel, and the degree to which the interrogator's questions treated the second round as continuous with the first. In *Elstad,* it was not unreasonable to see the occasion for questioning at the station house as presenting a markedly different experience from the short conversation at home; since a reasonable person in the suspect's shoes could have seen the station house questioning as a new and distinct experience, the *Miranda* warnings could have made sense as presenting a genuine choice whether to follow up on the earlier admission.

At the opposite extreme are the facts here, which by any objective measure reveal a police strategy adapted to undermine the *Miranda* warnings.[3] The unwarned interrogation was conducted in the station house, and the questioning was systematic, exhaustive, and managed with psychological skill. When the police were finished there was little, if anything, of incriminating potential left unsaid. The warned phase of questioning proceeded after a pause of only 15 to 20 minutes, in the same place as the unwarned segment. When the same officer who had conducted the first phase recited the *Miranda* warnings, he said nothing to counter the probable misimpression that the advice that anything Seibert said could be used against her also applied to the details of the inculpatory statement previously elicited. In particular, the police did not advise that her prior statement could not be used.[4] Nothing was said or done to dispel the oddity of warning about legal rights to silence and counsel right after the police had led her through a systematic interrogation, and any uncertainty on her part about a right to stop talking about matters previously discussed would only have been aggravated by the way Officer Hanrahan set the scene by saying "we've been talking for a little while about what happened on Wednesday the twelfth, haven't we?" The impression that the further questioning was a mere continuation of the earlier questions and responses was fostered by references back to the confession already given. It would have been reasonable to regard the two sessions as parts of a continuum, in which it would have been unnatural to refuse to repeat at the second stage what had been said before. These circumstances must be seen as challenging the comprehensibility and efficacy of the *Miranda* warnings to the point that a reasonable person in the suspect's shoes would not have understood them to convey a message that she retained a choice about continuing to talk.[5]

VI

Strategists dedicated to draining the substance out of *Miranda* cannot accomplish [this] by training instructions * * * . Because the question-first tactic effectively threatens to thwart *Miranda*'s purpose of

---

[3] Because the intent of the officer will rarely be as candidly admitted as it was here (even as it is likely to determine the conduct of the interrogation), the focus is on facts apart from intent that show the question-first tactic at work.

[4] We do not hold that a formal addendum warning that a previous statement could not be used would be sufficient to change the character of the question-first procedure to the point of rendering an ensuing statement admissible, but its absence is clearly a factor that blunts the efficacy of the warnings and points to a continuing, not a new, interrogation.

[5] Because we find that the warnings were inadequate, there is no need to assess the actual voluntariness of the statement.

reducing the risk that a coerced confession would be admitted, and because the facts here do not reasonably support a conclusion that the warnings given could have served their purpose, Seibert's postwarning statements are inadmissible. The judgment of the Supreme Court of Missouri is affirmed.

It is so ordered.

■ JUSTICE BREYER, concurring.

In my view, the following simple rule should apply to the two-stage interrogation technique: Courts should exclude the "fruits" of the initial unwarned questioning unless the failure to warn was in good faith. Cf. *Oregon v. Elstad,* 470 U.S. 298, 309, 318, n. 5, 105 S.Ct. 1285, 84 L.Ed.2d 222 (1985); *United States v. Leon,* 468 U.S. 897, 104 S.Ct. 3405, 82 L.Ed.2d 677 (1984). I believe this is a sound and workable approach to the problem this case presents. Prosecutors and judges have long understood how to apply the "fruits" approach, which they use in other areas of law. And in the workaday world of criminal law enforcement the administrative simplicity of the familiar has significant advantages over a more complex exclusionary rule.

I believe the plurality's approach in practice will function as a "fruits" test. The truly "effective" *Miranda* warnings on which the plurality insists, will occur only when certain circumstances—a lapse in time, a change in location or interrogating officer, or a shift in the focus of the questioning—intervene between the unwarned questioning and any postwarning statement.

I consequently join the plurality's opinion in full. I also agree with JUSTICE KENNEDY'S opinion insofar as it is consistent with this approach and makes clear that a good-faith exception applies.

■ JUSTICE KENNEDY, concurring in the judgment.

* * * Although I agree with much in the careful and convincing opinion for the plurality, my approach does differ in some respects, requiring this separate statement.

The *Miranda* rule has become an important and accepted element of the criminal justice system. At the same time, not every violation of the rule requires suppression of the evidence obtained. Evidence is admissible when the central concerns of *Miranda* are not likely to be implicated and when other objectives of the criminal justice system are best served by its introduction. Thus, we have held that statements obtained in violation of the rule can be used for impeachment, so that the truth finding function of the trial is not distorted by the defense, that there is an exception to protect countervailing concerns of public safety, and that physical evidence obtained in reliance on statements taken in violation of the rule is admissible. These cases, in my view, are correct. They recognize that admission of evidence is proper when it would further important objectives without compromising *Miranda*'s central concerns. Under these precedents, the scope of the *Miranda* suppression remedy depends on a consideration of those legitimate interests and on whether admission of the evidence under the circumstances would frustrate *Miranda*'s central concerns and objectives.

Oregon v. Elstad, 470 U.S. 298, 105 S.Ct. 1285, 84 L.Ed.2d 222 (1985), reflects this approach. * * * The Court held that, although a *Miranda* violation made the first statement inadmissible, the postwarning statements could be introduced against the accused because "neither the general goal of deterring improper police conduct nor the Fifth Amendment goal of assuring trustworthy evidence would be served by suppression" given the facts of that case.

In my view, *Elstad* was correct in its reasoning and its result. *Elstad* reflects a balanced and pragmatic approach to enforcement of the *Miranda* warning. An officer may not realize that a suspect is in custody and warnings are required. The officer may not plan to question the suspect or may be waiting for a more appropriate time. Skilled investigators often interview suspects multiple times, and good police work may involve referring to prior statements to test their veracity or to refresh recollection. In light of these realities it would be extravagant to treat the presence of one statement that cannot be admitted under *Miranda* as sufficient reason to prohibit subsequent statements preceded by a proper warning. * * *

This case presents different considerations. The police used a two-step questioning technique based on a deliberate violation of *Miranda*. The *Miranda* warning was withheld to obscure both the practical and legal significance of the admonition when finally given. As JUSTICE SOUTER points out, the two-step technique permits the accused to conclude that the right not to respond did not exist when the earlier incriminating statements were made. The strategy is based on the assumption that *Miranda* warnings will tend to mean less when recited midinterrogation, after inculpatory statements have already been obtained. This tactic relies on an intentional misrepresentation of the protection that *Miranda* offers and does not serve any legitimate objectives that might otherwise justify its use.

Further, the interrogating officer here relied on the defendant's prewarning statement to obtain the postwarning statement used against her at trial. The postwarning interview resembled a cross-examination. The officer confronted the defendant with her inadmissible prewarning statements and pushed her to acknowledge them. (" 'Trice, didn't you tell me that he was supposed to die in his sleep?'"). This shows the temptations for abuse inherent in the two-step technique. Reference to the prewarning statement was an implicit suggestion that the mere repetition of the earlier statement was not independently incriminating. The implicit suggestion was false.

The technique used in this case distorts the meaning of *Miranda* and furthers no legitimate countervailing interest. * * * When an interrogator uses this deliberate, two-step strategy, predicated upon violating *Miranda* during an extended interview, postwarning statements that are related to the substance of prewarning statements must be excluded absent specific, curative steps.

The plurality concludes that whenever a two-stage interview occurs, admissibility of the postwarning statement should depend on "whether the *Miranda* warnings delivered midstream could have been effective enough to accomplish their object" given the specific facts of the case. This test envisions an objective inquiry from the perspective of the suspect, and applies in the case of both intentional and unintentional two-stage interrogations. In my view, this test cuts too broadly. *Miranda*'s clarity is one of its strengths, and a multifactor test that applies to every two-stage interrogation may serve to undermine that clarity. I would apply a narrower test applicable only in the infrequent case, such as we have here, in which the two-step interrogation technique was used in a calculated way to undermine the *Miranda* warning.

The admissibility of postwarning statements should continue to be governed by the principles of *Elstad* unless the deliberate two-step strategy was employed. If the deliberate two-step strategy has been used, postwarning statements that are related to the substance of prewarning statements must be excluded unless curative measures are taken before the postwarning statement is made. Curative measures should be designed to ensure that a reasonable person in the suspect's situation would understand the import and effect of the *Miranda* warning and of the *Miranda* waiver. For example, a substantial break in time and circumstances between the prewarning statement and the *Miranda* warning may suffice in most circumstances, as it allows the accused to distinguish the two contexts and appreciate that the interrogation has taken a new turn. Alternatively, an additional warning that explains the likely inadmissibility of the prewarning custodial statement may be sufficient. No curative steps were taken in this case, however, so the postwarning statements are inadmissible and the conviction cannot stand.

For these reasons, I concur in the judgment of the Court.

■ JUSTICE O'CONNOR, with whom THE CHIEF JUSTICE, JUSTICE SCALIA, and JUSTICE THOMAS join, dissenting.

The plurality devours *Oregon v. Elstad,* 470 U.S. 298, 105 S.Ct. 1285, 84 L.Ed.2d 222 (1985), even as it accuses petitioner's argument of "disfigur[ing]" that decision. I believe that we are bound by *Elstad* to reach a different result, and I would vacate the judgment of the Supreme Court of Missouri.

I

On two preliminary questions I am in full agreement with the plurality. First, the plurality appropriately follows *Elstad* in concluding that Seibert's statement cannot be held inadmissible under a "fruit of the poisonous tree" theory. Second, the plurality correctly declines to focus its analysis on the subjective intent of the interrogating officer.

* * *

* * * I [also] believe that the approach espoused by JUSTICE KENNEDY is ill advised. JUSTICE KENNEDY would extend *Miranda's* exclusionary rule to any case in which the use of the "two-step interrogation technique" was "deliberate" or "calculated." This approach untethers the analysis from facts knowable to, and therefore having any potential directly to affect, the suspect. Far from promoting "clarity," the approach will add a third step to the suppression inquiry. In virtually every two-stage interrogation case, in addition to addressing the standard *Miranda* and voluntariness questions, courts will be forced to conduct the kind of difficult, state-of-mind inquiry that we normally take pains to avoid.

II

The plurality's adherence to *Elstad,* and mine to the plurality, end there. Our decision in *Elstad* rejected * * * the argument that the "lingering compulsion" inherent in a defendant's having let the "cat out of the bag" required suppression. * * * [T]oday's plurality [reasons]: "[T]he coercive impact of the unconstitutionally obtained statement remains, because in a defendant's mind it has sealed his fate. It is this impact that must be dissipated in order to make a subsequent confession admissible."

We rejected this theory outright. We did so not because we refused to recognize the "psychological impact of the suspect's conviction that he has let the cat out of the bag," but because we refused to "endo[w]" those "psychological effects" with "constitutional implications." To do so, we said, would "effectively immuniz[e] a suspect who responds to pre-*Miranda* warning questions from the consequences of his subsequent informed waiver," an immunity that "comes at a high cost to legitimate law enforcement activity, while adding little desirable protection to the individual's interest in not being *compelled* to testify against himself." The plurality might very well think that we struck the balance between Fifth Amendment rights and law enforcement interests incorrectly in *Elstad;* but that is not normally a sufficient reason for ignoring the dictates of *stare decisis.*

I would analyze the two-step interrogation procedure under the voluntariness standards central to the Fifth Amendment and reiterated in *Elstad. Elstad* commands that if Seibert's first statement is shown to have been involuntary, the court must examine whether the taint dissipated through the passing of time or a change in circumstances: "When a prior statement is actually coerced, the time that passes between confessions, the change in place of interrogations, and the change in identity of the interrogators all bear on whether that coercion has carried over into the second confession." In addition, Seibert's second statement should be suppressed if she showed that it was involuntary despite the *Miranda* warnings. Although I would leave this analysis for the Missouri courts to conduct on remand, I note that, unlike the officers in *Elstad,* Officer Hanrahan referred to Seibert's unwarned statement during the second part of the interrogation when she made a statement at odds with her unwarned confession. (" 'Trice, didn't you tell me that he was supposed to die in his sleep?"). Such a tactic may bear on the voluntariness inquiry.

* * *

Because I believe that the plurality gives insufficient deference to *Elstad* and that JUSTICE KENNEDY places improper weight on subjective intent, I respectfully dissent.

NOTE

Seibert was applied in Bobby v. Dixon, 565 U.S. 23, 132 S.Ct. 26 (2011) (per curiam), resulting from an investigation into the murder of Chris Hammer and various offenses committed by taking Hammer's car, selling it, and forging Hammer's signature on the payment check. The morning of November 9, 1993, Dixon was taken into custody. Dixon had once—after being warned—refused to speak with police, so the officers decided not to warn him. From 11:30 a.m. to 3:30 p.m. they questioned him sporadically for a total of about 45 minutes. In the course of this, the officers indicated that another suspect—Tim Hoffner—was providing information. Dixon admitted selling the car and forging the check signature but denied any knowledge of Hammer's location. He was then moved to another facility and booked for forgery.

At 7:30 p.m., after police recovered Hammer's body, Dixon was brought back to the station. Before questioning started, Dixon said he had heard police found a body and asked whether Hoffner was in custody. He was told Hoffner was not in custody. Dixon then said, "I talked to my attorney, and I want to tell you what happened." The officers warned him and obtained a signed written waiver of the *Miranda* rights. After a second *Miranda* warning, Dixon gave, and officers recorded, an admission to participating in the murder of Hammer. The confession to forgery was inadmissible. But did the state court err in admitting against Dixon his recorded statement acknowledging guilt of the murder?

A unanimous Supreme Court held—in a per curiam opinion—that the recorded statement was admissible despite *Seibert.* The Court did not explicitly articulate the standards it was applying in light of the split among the justices in *Seibert.* It explained:

> In this case, no two-step interrogation technique of the type that concerned the Court in *Seibert* undermined the *Miranda* warnings Dixon received. In *Seibert,* the suspect's first, unwarned interrogation left "little, if anything, of incriminating potential left unsaid," making it "unnatural" not to "repeat at the second stage what had been said before." But in this case Dixon steadfastly

maintained during his first, unwarned interrogation that he had "[n]othing whatsoever" to do with Hammer's disappearance. Thus, unlike in *Seibert,* there is no concern here that police gave Dixon *Miranda* warnings and then led him to repeat an earlier murder confession, because there was no earlier confession to repeat. Indeed, Dixon *contradicted* his prior unwarned statements when he confessed to Hammer's murder. Nor is there any evidence that police used Dixon's earlier admission to forgery to induce him to waive his right to silence later: Dixon declared his desire to tell police what happened to Hammer before the second interrogation session even began. * * * [T]here was simply "no nexus" between Dixon's unwarned admission to forgery and his later, warned confession to murder.

Moreover, in *Seibert* the Court was concerned that the *Miranda* warnings did not "effectively advise the suspect that he had a real choice about giving an admissible statement" because the unwarned and warned interrogations blended into one "continuum." Given all the circumstances of this case, that is not so here. Four hours passed between Dixon's unwarned interrogation and his receipt of *Miranda* rights, during which time he traveled from the police station to a separate jail and back again; claimed to have spoken to his lawyer; and learned that police were talking to his accomplice and had found Hammer's body. Things had changed. Under *Seibert*, this significant break in time and dramatic change in circumstances created "a new and distinct experience," ensuring that Dixon's prior, unwarned interrogation did not undermine the effectiveness of the *Miranda* warnings he received before confessing to Hammer's murder. 542 U.S., at 615, 124 S.Ct. 2601; see also *id.,* at 622, 124 S.Ct. 2601 (KENNEDY, J., concurring in judgment) ("For example, a substantial break in time and circumstances between the prewarning statement and the *Miranda* warning may suffice in most circumstances, as it allows the accused to distinguish the two contexts and appreciate that the interrogation has taken a new turn").

The admission of Dixon's murder confession was consistent with this Court's precedents: Dixon received *Miranda* warnings before confessing to Hammer's murder; the effectiveness of those warnings was not impaired by the sort of "two-step interrogation technique" condemned in *Seibert;* and there is no evidence that any of Dixon's statements was the product of actual coercion.

___ U.S. at ___, 132 S.Ct. at 31–32.

6.   IMPACT OF *MIRANDA*

EDITORS' NOTE: THE EFFECT OF *MIRANDA*

Despite the outcry following the *Miranda* decision, some evidence suggests its impact was relatively slight. Early research efforts and the problems of such studies are summarized and discussed in The American Law Institute's, A Model Code of Pre-Arraignment Procedure Part II (Study Draft No. 1, 1968). See also Medalie, Zeitz and Alexander, Custodial Police Interrogation in our Nation's Capitol: The Attempt to Implement Miranda, 66 Mich.L.Rev. 1347 (1968).

Project, Interrogations in New Haven: The Impact of Miranda, 76 Yale L.J. 1519 (1965), compared the success of interrogations involving warnings and others in which the suspects received no warnings. Paradoxically, the questioning was *more* successful in those cases in which the subject was warned. The researchers' analysis of the conduct of 81 warned suspects suggested the warning affected the interrogation result for only eight. Three refused to talk; two of these had received advice of counsel. Three others made oral incriminating statements but refused to sign written statements. One admitted his guilt but refused to sign a statement implicating others, and another confessed after consulting an attorney and being advised to do so. The minor impact of the warnings, the study concluded, was not surprising in light of the process observed:

> In the first place, although most interrogations were not intimidating, they were designed to discourage any initiative on the part of the suspect. * * * [T]he warnings * * * were often intoned in a manner designed to minimize or negate their importance and effectiveness. * * * [U]nless the detectives made it absolutely clear what the warning meant—which they rarely did—most suspects appeared unable to grasp their significance.
>
> Perhaps equally important, almost every person arrested * * * had committed the crime for which he was arrested and knew that the police had evidence of this. When he remained silent, the police would confront him with the evidence. Most suspects apparently felt compelled to give some alibi. Usually they lied and in doing so were caught in their lie. From then on the process was all downhill—from the suspect's point of view. Once a suspect said anything he usually had taken the first step towards incriminating himself.
>
> In addition * * * , the warnings did not have an impact on a number of suspects who, knowing they were guilty, apparently saw no point in denying their guilt. Perhaps previous exposure to the process made them believe silence was futile—several of the defendants we interviewed expressed this belief.
>
> Finally, the warnings had no apparent impact on the behavior of the suspects who seemingly believed they were giving exculpatory statements. * * * Most of those who began by attempting to justify their actions ended by incriminating themselves to some degree.

Id. at 1571–72.

Seeburger and Wettick, *Miranda* in Pittsburgh—A Statistical Study, 29 U.Pitt.L.Rev. 1 (1967), compared cases before and after *Miranda* and produced somewhat different results. The percentage of cases in which suspects made confessions dropped from 54.4% to 37.5% after *Miranda*; in robbery cases, the drop was from 62.4% to 36.7%. The percentage of cases in which confessions were necessary for conviction did not decrease after *Miranda*. Nevertheless, the conviction rate did not drop significantly after *Miranda*. This, the authors suggested, might be explained by grand juries' refusals to indict in the post-*Miranda* cases in which the defendants gave no confessions and in which a confession was essential to conviction, or by the dismissal of these cases at arraignment. Turning to the clearance rate for the crimes studied, the authors concluded the post-*Miranda* clearance rate actually exceeded the pre-*Miranda* rate by a small percentage.

The Seeburger and Wettick study was conducted soon after the *Miranda* decision. It may, then, reflect in part problems of transition as law enforcement adjusted to the new requirements. Certainly the study does not reflect any effects of post-*Miranda* decisions reducing the effect of the seminal case. Nevertheless, some changes seem certain to have occurred after—and perhaps—because of *Miranda*. Gerald Caplan has noted widespread agreement (although no firm evidence) on some matters:

> Before *Miranda*, charges of physical force, questioning in relays, and sustained incommunicado detention were common; after *Miranda*, they became far less frequent.

Caplan, Book Review, 93 Yale L.J. 1375, 1382–83 (1984).

A reexamination of the empirical studies conducted on *Miranda* challenged the widespread perception that these studies indicated only minimal results. Cassell, *Miranda*'s Social Costs: An Empirical Reassessment, 90 Nw.U.L.Rev. 387 (1966). Professor Cassell contended that "the existing empirical data supports the tentative estimate that *Miranda* has led to lost cases against almost four percent of all criminal suspects in this country who are questioned." A "lost case," he explained, is one in which a confession is needed to convict and, because of *Miranda*, the suspect did not confess. While a lost case is not necessarily one that would have resulted in a conviction, Professor Cassell added, most of the lost cases are probably ones that would have resulted in convictions. Finding that the data permits a "very rough" quantitative estimate of the effect of *Miranda* on plea bargaining, he concluded the decision resulted in more favorable plea bargains in about the same percent of cases. Id. At 445–46.

Turning to the significance of the various *Miranda* requirements, he concluded that advising suspects of their right to remain silent does not appear the critical factor. Instead, he argued, the rules barring questioning explain the results, given that about 20% of suspects invoke their rights and thus cannot be questioned. In the absence of the *Miranda* "cutoff" rules, he indicated, officers could be expected to successfully persuade some of these suspects to make incriminating statements. He also suggested *"Miranda's* greatest cost" is its blocking of searches for new approaches to custodial interrogation that might better reconcile society's need to apprehend offenders and suspects' interest in avoiding coercive questioning. Although *Miranda* purported to invite exploration of alternatives, he argued, the Court's failure to indicate the acceptability of specific alternatives rendered the invitation an empty one.

Professor Cassell acknowledged the drop in the confession rate might be a benefit rather than a cost of *Miranda* if it reflected the results of police inability to use coercive techniques. He concluded, however, that although direct evidence is lacking the indirect indications suggest it is "quite unlikely" that a reduction in police coercion explains the confession rate drop he attributed to *Miranda*. Id., at 478.

Professor Cassell and a colleague themselves conducted a study of the effect of *Miranda* in Salt Lake City, Utah by examining a sample of felony cases presented to the District Attorney for screening and possible prosecution and comparing the results with what they concluded were general pre-*Miranda* facts. Cassell and Hayman, Police Interrogation in the 1990s: An Empirical Study of the Effects of *Miranda*, 43 U.C.L.A.L.Rev. 839 (1966). 21% of the Salt Lake City suspects were not questioned, leading the authors to conclude that questioning rates have declined since *Miranda*. Of those questioned, 83.7% waived their *Miranda* rights, 7.0% requested an attorney, 4.7% invoked their right to silence, and another 4.7% refused to execute a waiver or otherwise invoked their rights. Turning to the productivity of questioning, the study concluded that successful questioning—questioning producing a statement useful to the prosecution—occurred in 33.3% of all the cases and in 42.2% of the cases in which the suspects were questioned. After determining that the available evidence indicated a 55% to 60% success rate in interrogations before *Miranda*, the authors concluded that their data suggested *"Miranda* has hampered law enforcement efforts to obtain incriminating statements." The strength of the evidence police had at the time of the questioning was strongly correlated with the productivity of questioning; questioning was productive in 55.6% of cases in which the available evidence was overwhelming and in only 26.3% of the cases in which it was weak.

Cassell would respond to what he believes to be the current state of affairs by eliminating the right of suspects to counsel during prearraignment interrogation, imposing no requirement of a waiver of rights before interrogation, and eliminating the requirement that interrogation halt upon the suspect's request for counsel or assertion of the right to remain silent. He would require a modified warning telling a suspect he has a right to silence and anything he says can be used as evidence. The suspect would also be told he has a right to be represented when brought before a judge and that the judge will appoint an attorney if necessary. He would add the admonition that the officers are required to bring the suspect before the judge without unnecessary delay. Balancing this retreat from *Miranda*, he would require the videotaping of all stationhouse interrogations and audiotaping of field custodial interrogations.

Professor Schulhofer responded at length to Professor Cassell in Schulhofer, *Miranda*'s Practical Effect: Substantial Benefits and Vanishingly Small Social Costs, 90 Nw.U.L.Rev. 500 (1996). He reevaluated the empirical studies and concluded that *Miranda* has been shown to have resulted in lost convictions "in at most 0.78% of serious criminal cases." Does this suggest *Miranda* has so little impact it is not worth defending? Schulhofer claimed not, reasoning that *Miranda* has changed the nature of interrogation and the basis for suspects' confessing. Modern police questioning, he argued, has become "an elaborate 'confidence game,'" in which the officer dupes the suspect into believing he can help himself by revealing information. As a result:

> [T]oday's suspects typically confess not because of fear of mistreatment but primarily because of misplaced confidence in their own ability to talk their way out of trouble. * * * [C]onfessions are now most the result of persuasion and the suspect's overconfidence, not of pressure and fear.

90 Nw.U.L.Rev. at 561–62. Cassell replied in Cassell, All Benefits, No Costs: The Grand Illusion of Miranda's Defenders, 90 Nw.U.L.Rev. 1084 (1996). See also, Thomas, Plain Talk About the *Miranda* Empirical Debate: A "Steady-State" Theory of Confessions, 43 U.C.L.A. L. Rev. 933 (1996).

Professor Cassell and a colleague have also challenged the conventional wisdom that *Miranda* neither caused nor was followed by a sustained fall in the clearance rate for major offenses. Paul G. Cassell and Richard Fowles, Handcuffing the Cops? A Thirty-year Perspective on *Miranda*'s Harmful Effect on law Enforcement, 50 Stan.L.Rev. 1055 (1998). They subjected clearance rate data to regression analysis, and concluded *Miranda* affected clearance rates for robbery, larceny, vehicle theft, and burglary, but not for homicide, rape or assault. Specifically:

> [W]ithout *Miranda*, the number of crimes cleared would have been substantially higher—by as much as 6.6–29.7% for robbery, 6.2–28.9% for burglary, 0.4–11.9% for larceny, and 12.8–45.4% for vehicle theft. * * * As many as 36,000 robberies, 82,000 burglaries, 163,000 larcenies, and 78,000 vehicle thefts remain uncleared each year as a result of *Miranda*.

Id., at 1126.

Lawyer-sociologist Richard Leo conducted research of a quite different kind. His results were reported in Leo, Inside the Interrogation Room, 86 J.Crim. & Crim. 266 (1996). Leo observed 122 interrogations of felony suspects in an unidentified city and reviewed sixty videotaped interrogations from two other localities. Of the 175 suspects to whose interrogations *Miranda* applied, 38 (22%) invoked their rights. Leo noted that this is a higher percentage than is assumed by "conventional wisdom." Of the suspects who waived their rights (and who were therefore interrogated), more than three-fourths (76%) made some sort of incriminating statement and about one-third made full confessions. In only four cases, he concluded, did police tactics constitute coercion, and even in these the coercion was psychological rather than physical.

Suspects with felony criminal records, Leo reported, were four times as likely as those with no record to invoke *Miranda* rights. He found no relationship between success of the interrogation and the class, race, or gender of the suspects, victims, or officers, the age of the suspects, the strength of the evidence against the suspects, or the suspect's criminal record. Success of the interrogation was related to the number of tactics officers used and the length of the interrogation—the longer the interrogation and the more tactics used, the more fruitful the interrogation.

Distinguishing among techniques, Leo noted that in almost all cases officers confronted the suspect with existing evidence of his guilt and appealed to his self-interest. In 30% of the cases, officers confronted the suspect with *false* evidence of guilt. Leo found that success tended to be achieved by (1) identifying contradictions in the suspect's denial of involvement; (2) offering a moral justification or psychological excuse for the criminal behavior; (3) praise or flattery; (4) appealing to the suspect's conscience; and (5) appealing to the importance of cooperating with authorities.

Whether a suspect made an incriminating statement or not had a significant effect on the processing of the case. Suspects who made such statements were 20% more likely to be charged, 24% less likely to have charges dismissed, 25% more likely to have their cases resolved by plea bargaining (which meant a conviction in 98% of the cases), and 26% more likely to be convicted.

Leo commented further on the implications of his research in Leo, The Impact of *Miranda* Revisited, 86 J.Crim.L. & Crim. 621 (1996). He suggested compliance with *Miranda* is often a social process orchestrated to predispose suspects towards voluntarily waiving their rights. Leo described the detectives he observed employing three kinds of "subtle psychological strategies." The first was "conditioning," a process in which the officer makes pleasant small talk with the suspect or strikes up a conversation about some point of common interest (such as sports), sometimes while going through the routine booking questions. These practices, Leo concluded, were "intended to disarm the suspect, to lower his anxiety levels, to improve his opinion of the detective, and to create a social psychological setting conducive to both a *Miranda* waiver as well as to subsequent admissions."

A second strategy—which Leo called "de-emphasizing"—consisted of downplaying the potential importance of the *Miranda* rights. This was accomplished in either or both of two ways. One involved "blending the *Miranda* warning into the ebb and flow of pre-interrogation conversation by not doing or saying anything unusual when reading the warnings so that the suspect paid no special attention to the admonition." The other method of de-emphasizing was to call the suspect's attention to the "anomalous status" of the warnings, as by characterizing them as a mere formality required prior to questioning or by suggesting the suspect himself can probably recite them as a result of television viewing.

The third strategy—persuasion—consisted of explicit although often subtle attempts to persuade the suspect to waive the rights. For example, officers sometimes emphasized that the police already had the victim's side of the story and thus suggested that this would become in some sense an "official" version unless the suspect talked to the officers. Alternatively, officers sometimes indicated the purpose of the session was to inform the suspect of the evidence against him and what was likely to happen. They would then add that this could be done only if the suspect waived the rights.

Leo suggested the effectiveness of these techniques is more important in explaining why so many suspects waive their *Miranda* rights than other possibilities sometimes offered, such as suggestions that suspects do not actually understand the rights or are impermissibly induced to waive them. These negotiating strategies developed by police to minimize *Miranda*'s potential obstacle, he concluded, "usually remain within the letter of *Miranda*, but frequently they straddle the ambiguous margins of legality."

D. SIXTH AMENDMENT RIGHT TO COUNSEL

EDITORS' INTRODUCTION: SIXTH AMENDMENT RIGHT TO COUNSEL DURING POLICE QUESTIONING

In a series of cases beginning with Massiah v. United States, 377 U.S. 201, 84 S.Ct. 1199 (1964), the Supreme Court held the Sixth Amendment right to counsel applied to law enforcement undercover efforts to elicit self-incriminating statements occurring after the investigation had progressed to a certain point. This is considered further in Chapter 8. In Brewer v. Williams, 430 U.S. 387, 97 S.Ct. 1232 (1977), however, the Court held that the Sixth Amendment also applied to overt police interrogations occurring after the case had progressed far enough to trigger that provision. As the principal case in this section makes clear, this holding presented the Court with the difficult task of determining how suspects' rights are affected when their *Miranda* rights are supplemented (or perhaps preempted) by the Sixth Amendment right to counsel.

The Court's application of the Sixth Amendment to overt interrogation raises several other issues. One, of course, is when in this context the Sixth Amendment attaches. Another is the extent to which the Sixth Amendment embodies a prohibition against reapproaching a suspect as is imposed by the Fifth Amendment right to counsel under Edwards v. Arizona, 451 U.S. 477, 101 S.Ct. 1880 (1981).

Attachment of the Sixth Amendment. In *Williams,* the Court noted some uncertainty as to when the progress of an investigation triggered the Sixth Amendment but stated it certainly provides its protection "at or after the time that judicial proceedings have been initiated against [a suspect]—'whether by way of formal charge, preliminary hearing, information or arraignment.' Kirby v. Illinois, [406 U.S. 682, 689, 92 S.Ct. 1877, 1882 (1972)]." The Court's citation to *Kirby,* an eyewitness identification decision, indicated attachment of the Sixth Amendment to interrogations poses the same problem raised by application of the provision to lineups and similar law enforcement techniques; this is considered in Chapter 9.

In *Williams,* a magistrate had issued an arrest warrant for Williams. Police took him into custody on that warrant and presented before a judge. Williams was then "committed" to confinement in jail. Thus, the Court held, judicial proceedings had been initiated. In Edwards v. Arizona, 451 U.S. 477, 480 n. 7, 101 S.Ct. 1880, 1882–83 n. 7 (1981), however, the Court noted but did not reach the prosecution's contention that under Arizona state law adversary judicial proceedings did not begin until the filing of an indictment or information or perhaps at a preliminary hearing if one was held.

Michigan v. Jackson, 475 U.S. 625, 106 S.Ct. 1404 (1986), announced that "arraignment" triggers the Sixth Amendment right. Police questioned Jackson after he was arrested and "arraigned." The State argued that judicial proceedings had not been initiated, but the Court responded, "In view of the clear language in our decisions about the significance of arraignment, the State's argument is untenable." Unfortunately, *Jackson* did not make clear what the Court meant by the term "arraignment."

In Rothgery v. Gillespie County, 554 U.S. 191, 128 S.Ct. 2578 (2008), the Court held that the Sixth Amendment attached when: (1) the defendant had been arrested; (2) a peace officer filed with a magistrate a sworn document that recited that the defendant was charged with a specified felony; (3) the defendant appeared before the magistrate; (4) the magistrate informed the defendant of the charge against him and set bail; and (5) the defendant was jailed until he posted the bail set. In this situation, the appearance before the magistrate reflected the initiation of adversary judicial proceedings. The Court explicitly rejected an argument that the Sixth Amendment attached only if a prosecutor was involved in, or at least aware of, the proceedings.

Does the Sixth Amendment attach if no document referring to a charge offense has been filed? *Rothgery* purported to simply apply what the Court described as its holdings that "the right to counsel guaranteed by the Sixth Amendment applies in the first appearance before a judicial officer at which a defendant is told of the formal accusation against him and restrictions are imposed on his liberty." Later, the Court observed that "an accusation filed with a judicial officer is sufficiently formal," at least "when the accusation prompts arraignment and restrictions on the accused's liberty to facilitate the prosecution."

The Court has refused to move application of the provision to an earlier point. In Moran v. Burbine, 475 U.S. 412, 106 S.Ct. 1135 (1986) (reprinted in part earlier in this chapter), the defendant argued that Sixth Amendment applied to his interrogation. He acknowledged that "adversary judicial proceedings" had not yet begun, but urged that in some situations at least the Sixth Amendment is triggered before that point. Specifically, he argued the importance of custodial interrogation is such that the Sixth Amendment creates a right to noninterference with an attorney's dealings with a client-suspect if the attorney-client relationship has been formed and custodial interrogation begins. The Supreme Court, however, rejected the proposition that an attorney-client relationship independently triggers the Sixth Amendment right to counsel:

> As a practical matter, it makes little sense to say that the Sixth Amendment right to counsel attaches at different times depending on the fortuity of whether the suspect or his family happened to have retained counsel prior to interrogation. More importantly, the suggestion that the existence of an attorney-client relationship itself triggers the protections of the Sixth Amendment misconceives the underlying purpose of the right to counsel. The Sixth Amendment's intended function is not to wrap a protective cloak around the attorney-client relationship for its own sake any more than it is to protect a suspect from the consequences of his own candor. Its purpose, rather, is to assure than in any "criminal prosecutio[n]," U.S. Const., Amdt. 6, the accused shall not be left to his own devices in facing the " 'prosecutorial forces of organized society.' " *Maine v. Moulton,* [474 U.S. 159, 169, 106 S.Ct. 477, 484, 88 L.Ed.2d 481 (1985)]. By its very terms, it becomes applicable only when the government's role shifts from investigation to accusation. * * * [L]ooking to the initiation of adversary judicial proceedings, far from being mere formalism, is fundamental to the proper application of the Sixth Amendment right to counsel. * * * [U]ntil such time as the " 'government has committed itself to prosecute, and . . . the adverse positions of the government and defendant have solidified' " the Sixth amendment right to

counsel does not attach. [*United States v. Gouveia*, 467 U.S. 180, 189, 104 S.Ct. 2292, 2298, 81 L.Ed.2d 146 (1984)].

475 U.S. at 430–32, 106 S.Ct. at 1145–46.

Application of Edwards *Rule.* In *Jackson,* the Court held the *Edwards* rule as developed in the *Miranda* context, see Subchapter C(3) of this chapter, also applied in Sixth Amendment situations. This prohibition against reapproach of a suspect who invokes the right to counsel applies somewhat differently where it arises because the suspect has invoked the Sixth Amendment right to counsel.

Police arrested the two defendants in *Jackson* and presented them before a magistrate for "arraignment." At this arraignment the defendants requested that counsel be appointed for them. The records left unclear whether the magistrate first offered to appoint counsel and, if so, in what terms; those records also left uncertain the terms of the defendants' requests for counsel. Later, while the defendants were still in custody, they were approached by police officers, given *Miranda* warnings, and—apparently after agreeing to submit to questioning without counsels' presence—made incriminating statements. A majority of the Supreme Court agreed with the Michigan Supreme Court that the Sixth Amendment required the suppression of these statements. The arraignment caused the defendants' Sixth Amendment right to counsel to attach, so the issue was whether the officers reapproach violated a Sixth Amendment version of the *Edwards* rule. The Sixth Amendment right to counsel includes an *Edwards*-like prohibition against reapproach, because "the Sixth Amendment right to counsel at a postarraignment interrogation requires at least as much protection as does the Fifth Amendment right to counsel at any custodial interrogation." The State argued that the defendants did not trigger this bar to any approach by officers seeking to interrogate the defendants; the defendants could have intended their request for counsel to refer only to counsel for trial and other formal legal purposes and not for purposes of representation during further questioning. But the Court responded:

> [I]t is the State that has the burden of establishing a valid waiver. Doubts must be resolved in favor of protecting the constitutional claim. This settled approach to questions of waiver requires us to give a broad, rather than a narrow, interpretation to a defendant's request for counsel—we presume that the defendant requests the lawyer's services at every critical stage of the prosecution. We thus reject the State's suggestion * * * .

475 U.S. at 633, 106 S.Ct. at 1409. In a footnote, the Court commented further:

> In construing respondents' request for counsel, we do not, of course, suggest that the right to counsel turns on such a request. Rather, we construe the defendant's request for counsel as an

extremely important fact in considering the validity of a subsequent waiver in response to police-initiated interrogation.

475 U.S. at 633 n. 6, 106 S.Ct. at 1409 n. 6. The Court summarized its holding:

> We * * * hold that, if police initiate interrogation after a defendant's assertion, at an arraignment or similar proceeding, of his right to counsel, any waiver of the defendant's right to counsel for that police-initiated interrogation is invalid.

475 U.S. at 636, 106 S.Ct. at 1411.

But the *Edwards* rule as applied in some Sixth Amendment situations has less impact than it has when applied in *Miranda* contexts. If a suspect invokes the right to counsel during police questioning to which *Miranda* applies, *Edwards* as construed in *Roberson* (discussed in Subchapter C(3) of this chapter) means that officers cannot reapproach the suspect until a lawyer is present even if the subject of their inquiries is a different offense. In McNeil v. Wisconsin, 501 U.S. 171, 111 S.Ct. 2204 (1991), the Supreme Court held that in the Sixth Amendment context *Edwards* was not so broad.

Police arrested McNeil for a West Allis, Wisconsin armed robbery and brought him before a court commissioner on that charge. McNeil was represented by a public defender at this appearance. The commissioner set bail and scheduled a preliminary examination. Subsequently, officers approached McNeil seeking to question him about a robbery-murder committed in Caledonia, Wisconsin. After the officers warned McNeil under *Miranda,* he waived his rights and made several statements admitting participation in the Caledonia crimes. The Supreme Court assumed the Sixth Amendment right to counsel attached by virtue of McNeil's court appearance. It also assumed by appearing with counsel McNeil invoked his Sixth Amendment right with regard to the West Allis robbery. But it rejected McNeil's claim that under *Edwards* and *Roberson* this meant that the officers were barred from reapproaching him concerning the Caledonia crimes.

The Sixth Amendment right to counsel, the *McNeil* majority explained, "is offense-specific." It does not attach until prosecution commences, and its *Edwards* effect is similarly "offense-specific." Thus a suspect's invocation of the Sixth Amendment right to counsel does not bar officers from reapproaching the suspect regarding offenses as to which he does not yet have a Sixth Amendment right to counsel. McNeil "provided the statements at issue here before his Sixth Amendment right to counsel with respect to the Caledonia offenses had been (or could have been) invoked." Therefore, the Sixth Amendment did not bar the use of those statements against him.

Sixth Amendment Edwards *Rule and Intertwined Offenses.* The offense for which officers approached McNeil was apparently unrelated to that on which his Sixth Amendment right to counsel had attached.

Texas v. Cobb, 532 U.S. 162, 121 S.Ct. 1335 (2001), addressed the effect of *McNeil* where the offenses as to which the Sixth Amendment right to counsel has attached and that for which officers reapproach the suspect are related or "intertwined." In *Cobb*, a mother and her young daughter were reported missing after their residence was burglarized. Cobb was indicted for the burglary and accepted appointed counsel. Officers approached him and questioned him about the murders of the mother and her daughter; he admitted the killings. His confession was used in his prosecution for the capital murder of more than one person in a single transaction. Cobb's Sixth Amendment right to counsel had attached on the burglary charge, the state court reasoned. Because the murders were closely related factually to—or "factually interwoven with"—the burglary, the Sixth Amendment attached regarding those offenses as well. Since the police had not obtained counsel's permission to approach Cobb without counsel's presence, the state tribunal concluded, the confession was obtained in violation of the Sixth Amendment, and its use required reversal of the conviction.

The Supreme Court reversed, holding Cobb's confession admissible. *McNeil* "meant what it said"—"that the Sixth Amendment is 'offense specific.' " But the Court added:

> Although it is clear that the Sixth Amendment right to counsel attaches only to charged offenses, we have recognized in other contexts that the definition of an "offense" is not necessarily limited to the four corners of a charging instrument. In *Blockburger v. United States,* 284 U.S. 299, 52 S.Ct. 180, 76 L.Ed. 306 (1932), we explained that "where the same act or transaction constitutes a violation of two distinct statutory provisions, the test to be applied to determine whether there are two offenses or only one, is whether each provision requires proof of a fact which the other does not." We have since applied the *Blockburger* test to delineate the scope of the Fifth Amendment's Double Jeopardy Clause, which prevents multiple or successive prosecutions for the "same offence." We see no constitutional difference between the meaning of the term "offense" in the contexts of double jeopardy and of the right to counsel. Accordingly, we hold that when the Sixth Amendment right to counsel attaches, it does encompass offenses that, even if not formally charged, would be considered the same offense under the *Blockburger* test.

532 U.S. at 172–73, 121 S.Ct. at 1343. Burglary requires proof of entry into or remaining in premises and capital murder does not; capital murder requires proof of killing more than one person and burglary does not. Therefore, the murders were not the same offense as the burglary and the fact that Cobb's Sixth Amendment right to counsel had attached to the burglary charge did not mean it also attached on the murder

charge. Consequently, Cobb had no Sixth Amendment right implicated by the officers' approach concerning the murders.

Modification of the Sixth Amendment Version of the Edwards *Rule.* *Jackson*'s application of the *Edwards* rule in the Sixth Amendment context was dramatically modified by a 5-to-4 vote in Montejo v. Louisiana, 556 U.S. 778, 129 S.Ct. 2079 (2009). At issue in *Montejo* was the effect of the Sixth Amendment on a defendant who had apparently made no request for counsel but nevertheless was appointed an attorney at a preliminary appearance before the trial court.

The *Jackson* rule, Justice Scalia's *Montejo* majority opinion reasoned, must be that after the Sixth Amendment attaches and a defendant is actually represented by counsel, police cannot initiate interrogation without the lawyer being present. This "would prevent police-initiated interrogation entirely once the Sixth Amendment right attaches, at least in those States that appoint counsel promptly without request from the defendant." Addressing the merits of *Jackson* so construed, the Court continued:

> What does the *Jackson* rule actually achieve by way of preventing unconstitutional conduct? * * * [T]he purpose of the rule is to preclude the State from badgering defendants into waiving their previously asserted rights. The effect of this badgering might be to coerce a waiver, which would render the subsequent interrogation a violation of the Sixth Amendment. Even though involuntary waivers are invalid even apart from *Jackson*, mistakes are of course possible when courts conduct case-by-case voluntariness review. A bright-line rule like that adopted in *Jackson* ensures that no fruits of interrogations made possible by badgering-induced involuntary waivers are ever erroneously admitted at trial.

> But without *Jackson*, how many would be? The answer is few if any. The principal reason is that the Court has already taken substantial other, overlapping measures toward the same end. Under *Miranda*'s prophylactic protection of the right against compelled self-incrimination, any suspect subject to custodial interrogation has the right to have a lawyer present if he so requests, and to be advised of that right. Under *Edwards'* prophylactic protection of the *Miranda* right, once such a defendant "has invoked his right to have counsel present," interrogation must stop. And * * * no subsequent interrogation may take place until counsel is present, "whether or not the accused has consulted with his attorney."

> These three layers of prophylaxis are sufficient. Under the *Miranda-Edwards* * * * line of cases (which is not in doubt), a defendant who does not want to speak to the police without counsel present need only say as much when he is first approached and given the *Miranda* warnings.

556 U.S. at 794, 129 S.Ct. at 2089–90. The *Jackson* rule consequently was overruled.

* * *

When the Sixth Amendment is triggered, what effect does it have upon the legal status of a suspect undergoing custodial interrogation, above and beyond what is dictated by *Miranda* and the Fifth Amendment? Justice Marshall has suggested waivers of the Sixth Amendment right to counsel should be subjected to greater scrutiny than waivers of *Miranda* rights. A waiver of the former, he urged, should require a greater comprehension of the consequences than a waiver of the latter. See Fields v. Wyrick, 464 U.S. 1020, 1022–23, 104 S.Ct. 556, 557 (1983) (Marshall, J., dissenting from denial of certiorari). The following case, to some extent, confronts this general question.

Patterson v. Illinois

Supreme Court of the United States, 1988.
487 U.S. 285, 108 S.Ct. 2389.

■ JUSTICE WHITE delivered the opinion of the Court.

In this case, we are called on to determine whether the interrogation of petitioner after his indictment violated his Sixth Amendment right to counsel.

I

Before dawn on August 21, 1983, petitioner and other members of the "Vice Lords" street gang became involved in a fight with members of a rival gang, the "Black Mobsters." Some time after the fight, a former member of the Black Mobsters, James Jackson, went to the home where the Vice Lords had fled. A second fight broke out there, with petitioner and three other Vice Lords beating Jackson severely. The Vice Lords then put Jackson into a car, drove to the end of a nearby street, and left him face down in a puddle of water. Later that morning, police discovered Jackson, dead, where he had been left.

That afternoon, local police officers obtained warrants for the arrest of the Vice Lords, on charges of battery and mob action, in connection with the first fight. One of the gang members who was arrested gave the police a statement concerning the first fight; the statement also implicated several of the Vice Lords (including petitioner) in Jackson's murder. A few hours later, petitioner was apprehended. Petitioner was informed of his rights under *Miranda v. Arizona*, 384 U.S. 436, 86 S.Ct. 1602, 16 L.Ed.2d 694 (1966), and volunteered to answer questions put to him by the police. Petitioner gave a statement concerning the initial fight between the rival gangs, but denied knowing anything about Jackson's death. Petitioner was held in custody the following day, August 22, as law enforcement authorities completed their investigation of the Jackson murder.

On August 23, a Cook County grand jury indicted petitioner and two other gang members for the murder of James Jackson. Police officer Michael Gresham, who had questioned petitioner earlier, removed him from the lockup where he was being held, and told petitioner that because he had been indicted he was being transferred to the Cook County jail. Petitioner asked Gresham which of the gang members had been charged with Jackson's murder, and upon learning that one particular Vice Lord had been omitted from the indictments, asked: "[W]hy wasn't he indicted, he did everything." Petitioner also began to explain that there was a witness who would support his account of the crime.

At this point, Gresham interrupted petitioner, and handed him a *Miranda* waiver form. The form contained five specific warnings, as suggested by this Court's *Miranda* decision, to make petitioner aware of his right to counsel and of the consequences of any statement he might make to police. Gresham read the warnings aloud, as petitioner read along with him. Petitioner initialed each of the five warnings, and signed the waiver form. Petitioner then gave a lengthy statement to police officers concerning the Jackson murder; petitioner's statement described in detail the role of each of the Vice Lords—including himself—in the murder of James Jackson.

Later that day, petitioner confessed involvement in the murder for a second time. This confession came in an interview with Assistant State's Attorney (ASA) George Smith. At the outset of the interview, Smith reviewed with petitioner the *Miranda* waiver he had previously signed, and petitioner confirmed that he had signed the waiver and understood his rights. Smith went through the waiver procedure once again: reading petitioner his rights, having petitioner initial each one, and sign a waiver form. In addition, Smith informed petitioner that he was a lawyer working with the police investigating the Jackson case. Petitioner then gave another inculpatory statement concerning the crime.

Before trial, petitioner moved to suppress his statements, arguing that they were obtained in a manner at odds with various constitutional guarantees. The trial court denied these motions, and the statements were used against petitioner at his trial. The jury found petitioner guilty of murder, and petitioner was sentenced to a 24-year prison term.

On appeal, petitioner argued that he had not "knowingly and intelligently" waived his Sixth Amendment right to counsel before he gave his uncounseled postindictment confessions. Petitioner contended that the warnings he received, while adequate for the purposes of protecting his *Fifth* Amendment rights as guaranteed by *Miranda,* did not adequately inform him of his *Sixth* Amendment right to counsel. The Illinois Supreme Court, however, rejected, this theory * * * .

II

There can be no doubt that petitioner had the right to have the assistance of counsel at his postindictment interviews with law enforcement authorities. Our cases make it plain that the Sixth Amendment guarantees this right to criminal defendants.[3] Petitioner asserts that the questioning that produced his incriminating statements violated his Sixth Amendment right to counsel in two ways.

A

Petitioner's first claim is that because his Sixth Amendment right to counsel arose with his indictment, the police were thereafter barred from initiating a meeting with him. He equates himself with a preindictment suspect who, while being interrogated, asserts his Fifth Amendment right to counsel; under *Edwards v. Arizona*, 451 U.S. 477, 101 S.Ct. 1880, 68 L.Ed.2d 378 (1981), such a suspect may not be questioned again unless he initiates the meeting.

* * *

At bottom, petitioner's theory cannot be squared with our rationale in *Edwards,* the case he relies on for support. * * * Preserving the integrity of an accused's choice to communicate with police only through counsel is the essence of *Edwards* and its progeny—not barring an accused from making an *initial* election as to whether he will face the State's officers during questioning with the aid of counsel, or go it alone. If an accused "knowingly and intelligently" pursues the latter course, we see no reason why the uncounseled statements he then makes must be excluded at his trial.

B

Petitioner's principal and more substantial claim is that questioning him without counsel present violated the Sixth Amendment because he did not validly waive his right to have counsel present during the interviews. Since it is clear that after the *Miranda* warnings were given to petitioner, he not only voluntarily answered questions without claiming his right to silence or his right to have a lawyer present to advise him but also executed a written waiver of his right to counsel during questioning, the specific issue posed here is whether this waiver was a "knowing and intelligent" waiver of his Sixth Amendment right.[4] See *Brewer v. Williams,* [430 U.S. 387, 401, 404, 97 S.Ct. 1232, 1240–41, 1242, 51 L.Ed.2d 424 (1977)]; *Johnson v. Zerbst*, 304 U.S. 458, 464–465, 58 S.Ct. 1019, 1023, 82 L.Ed. 1461 (1938).

In the past, this Court has held that a waiver of the Sixth Amendment right to counsel is valid only when it reflects "an intentional relinquishment or abandonment of a known right or privilege." In other words, the accused must "kno[w] what he is doing" so that "his choice is

---

[3]   We note as a matter of some significance that petitioner had not retained, or accepted by appointment, a lawyer to represent him at the time he was questioned by authorities. Once an accused has a lawyer, a distinct set of constitutional safeguards aimed at preserving the sanctity of the attorney-client relationship takes effect. The State conceded as much at argument.

[4]   * * * [T]he voluntariness of petitioner's confession is not before us.

made with eyes open." In a case arising under the Fifth Amendment, we described this requirement as "a full awareness [of] both the nature of the right being abandoned and the consequences of the decision to abandon it." *Moran v. Burbine*, 475 U.S. 412, 421, 106 S.Ct. 1135, 1141, 89 L.Ed.2d 410 (1986). Whichever of these formulations is used, the key inquiry in a case such as this one must be: Was the accused, who waived his Sixth Amendment rights during postindictment questioning, made sufficiently aware of his right to have counsel present during the questioning, and of the possible consequences of a decision to forgo the aid of counsel? In this case, we are convinced that by admonishing petitioner with the *Miranda* warnings, respondent has met this burden and that petitioner's waiver of his right to counsel at the questioning was valid.

First, the *Miranda* warnings given petitioner made him aware of his right to have counsel present during the questioning. By telling petitioner that he had a right to consult with an attorney, to have a lawyer present while he was questioned, and even to have a lawyer appointed for him if he could not afford to retain one on his own, Officer Gresham and ASA Smith conveyed to petitioner the sum and substance of the rights that the Sixth Amendment provided him. * * * There is little more petitioner could have possibly been told in an effort to satisfy this portion of the waiver inquiry.

Second, the *Miranda* warnings also served to make petitioner aware of the consequences of a decision by him to waive his Sixth Amendment rights during postindictment questioning. Petitioner knew that any statement that he made could be used against him in subsequent criminal proceedings. This is the ultimate adverse consequence petitioner could have suffered by virtue of his choice to make uncounseled admissions to the authorities. This warning also sufficed—contrary to petitioner's claim here—to let him know what a lawyer could "do for him" during the postindictment questioning: namely, advise petitioner to refrain from making any such statements. By knowing what could be done with any statements he might make, and therefore, what benefit could be obtained by having the aid of counsel while making such statements, petitioner was essentially informed of the possible consequences of going without counsel during questioning. If petitioner nonetheless lacked "a full and complete appreciation of all of the consequences flowing" from his waiver, it does not defeat the State's showing that the information it provided to him satisfied the constitutional minimum.

Our conclusion is supported by petitioner's inability, in the proceedings before this Court, to articulate with precision what additional information should have been provided to him before he would have been competent to waive his right to counsel. All that petitioner's brief and reply brief suggest is petitioner should have been made aware of his "right under the Sixth Amendment to the broad protection of counsel"—a rather nebulous suggestion—and the "gravity of [his] situation." But surely this latter "requirement" (if it is one) was met when Officer Gresham informed petitioner that he had been formally charged with the murder of James Jackson. Under close questioning on this same point at argument, petitioner likewise failed to suggest any meaningful additional information that he should have been, but was not, provided in advance of his decision to waive his right to counsel. * * *

As a general matter, then, an accused who is admonished with the warnings prescribed by this Court in *Miranda,* has been sufficiently apprised of the nature of his Sixth Amendment rights, and of the consequences of abandoning those rights, so that his waiver on this basis will be considered a knowing and intelligent one.[9]

C

We consequently reject petitioner's argument, which has some acceptance from courts and commentators, that since "the sixth amendment right [to counsel] is far superior to that of the fifth amendment right" and since "[t]he greater the right the greater the loss from a waiver of that right," waiver of an accused's Sixth Amendment right to counsel should be "more difficult" to effectuate than waiver of a suspect's Fifth Amendment rights. While our cases have recognized a "difference" between the Fifth Amendment and Sixth Amendment rights to counsel, and the "policies" behind these Constitutional guarantees, we have never suggested that one right is "superior" or "greater" than the other, nor is there any support in our cases for the notion that because a Sixth Amendment right may be involved, it is more difficult to waive than the Fifth Amendment counterpart.

Instead, we have taken a more pragmatic approach to the waiver question—asking what purposes a lawyer can serve at the particular stage of the proceedings in question, and what assistance he could provide to an accused at that stage—to determine the scope of the Sixth Amendment right to counsel, and the type of warnings and procedures that should be required before a waiver of that right will be recognized.

At one end of the spectrum, we have concluded there is no Sixth Amendment right to counsel whatsoever at a postindictment photographic display identification, because this procedure is not one at

---

[9] This does not mean, of course, that all Sixth Amendment challenges to the conduct of postindictment questioning will fail whenever the challenged practice would pass constitutional muster under *Miranda.* For example, we have permitted a *Miranda* waiver to stand where a suspect was not told that his lawyer was trying to reach him during questioning; in the Sixth Amendment context, this waiver would not be valid. See *Moran v. Burbine,* 475 U.S., at 424, 428, 106 S.Ct. at 1142–43, 1145. Likewise a surreptitious conversion between an undercover police officer and an indicted suspect would not give rise to any *Miranda* violation as long as the "interrogation" was not in a custodial setting; however, once the accused is indicted, such questioning would be prohibited.

Thus, because the Sixth Amendment's protection of the attorney-client relationship—"the right to rely on counsel as a 'medium' between [the accused] and the State"—extends beyond *Miranda's* protection of the Fifth Amendment right to counsel, there will be cases where a waiver which would be valid under *Miranda* will not suffice for Sixth Amendment purposes.

which the accused "require[s] aid in coping with legal problems or assistance in meeting his adversary." At the other extreme, recognizing the enormous importance and role that an attorney plays at a criminal trial, we have imposed the most rigorous restrictions on the information that must be conveyed to a defendant, and the procedures that must be observed, before permitting him to waive his right to counsel at trial. In these extreme cases, and in others that fall between these two poles, we have defined the scope of the right to counsel by a pragmatic assessment of the usefulness of counsel to the accused at the particular proceeding, and the dangers to the accused of proceeding without counsel. An accused's waiver of his right to counsel is "knowing" when he is made aware of these basic facts.

Applying this approach, it is our view that whatever warnings suffice for *Miranda*'s purposes will also be sufficient in the context of postindictment questioning. The State's decision to take an additional step and commence formal adversarial proceedings against the accused does not substantially increase the value of counsel to the accused at questioning, or expand the limited purpose that an attorney serves when the accused is questioned by authorities. With respect to this inquiry, we do not discern a substantial difference between the usefulness of a lawyer to a suspect during custodial interrogation, and his value to an accused at postindictment questioning.

Thus, we require a more searching or formal inquiry before permitting an accused to waive his right to counsel at trial than we require for a Sixth Amendment waiver during postindictment questioning—*not* because postindictment questioning is "less important" than a trial (the analysis that petitioner's "hierarchical" approach would suggest)—but because the full "dangers and disadvantages of self-representation," during questioning are less substantial and more obvious to an accused than they are at trial. Because the role of counsel at questioning is relatively simple and limited, we see no problem in having a waiver procedure at that stage which is likewise simple and limited. So long as the accused is made aware of the "dangers and disadvantages of self-representation" during postindictment questioning, by use of the *Miranda* warnings, his waiver of his Sixth Amendment right to counsel at such questioning is "knowing and intelligent."

III

Before confessing to the murder of James Jackson, petitioner was meticulously informed by authorities of his right to counsel, and of the consequences of any choice not to exercise that right. On two separate occasions, petitioner elected to forgo the assistance of counsel, and speak directly to officials concerning his role in the murder. Because we believe that petitioner's waiver of his Sixth Amendment rights was "knowing and intelligent," we find no error in the decision of the trial court to permit petitioner's confessions to be used against him. Consequently, the judgment of the Illinois Supreme Court is

Affirmed.

■ JUSTICE BLACKMUN, dissenting.

I agree with most of what Justice Stevens says in his dissenting opinion. I, however, merely would hold that after formal adversary proceedings against a defendant have been commenced, the Sixth Amendment mandates that the defendant not be " 'subject to further interrogation by the authorities until counsel has been made available to him, unless the accused himself initiates further communication, exchanges, or conversations with the police.' "

* * *

■ JUSTICE STEVENS, with whom JUSTICE BRENNAN and JUSTICE MARSHALL join, dissenting.

The Court should not condone unethical forms of trial preparation by prosecutors or their investigators. In civil litigation it is improper for a lawyer to communicate with his or her adversary's client without either notice to opposing counsel or the permission of the court. An attempt to obtain evidence for use at trial by going behind the back of one's adversary would be not only a serious breach of professional ethics but also a manifestly unfair form of trial practice. In the criminal context, the same ethical rules apply and, in my opinion, notions of fairness that are at least as demanding should also be enforced.

* * *

The question that this case raises * * * is at what point in the adversary process does it become impermissible for the prosecutor, or his or her agents, to conduct such private interviews with the opposing party? Several alternatives are conceivable: when the trial commences, when the defendant has actually met and accepted representation by his or her appointed counsel, when counsel is appointed, or when the adversary process commences. In my opinion, the Sixth Amendment right to counsel demands that a firm and unequivocal line be drawn at the point at which adversary proceedings commence.

* * *

Today, however * * * the Court backs away from the significance previously attributed to the initiation of formal proceedings. In the majority's view, the purported waiver of counsel in this case is properly equated with that of an unindicted suspect. * * * Given the significance of the initiation of formal proceedings and the concomitant shift in the relationship between the state and the accused, I think it quite wrong to suggest that *Miranda* warnings—or for that matter, any warnings offered by an adverse party—provide a sufficient basis for permitting the undoubtedly prejudicial—and, in my view, unfair—practice of permitting trained law enforcement personnel and prosecuting attorneys to communicate with as-of-yet unrepresented criminal defendants.

* * *

[W]ithout a careful discussion of the pitfalls of proceeding without counsel, the Sixth Amendment right cannot properly be waived. An adversary party, moreover, cannot adequately provide such advice. As a result, once the right to counsel attaches and the adversary relationship between the state and the accused solidifies, a prosecutor cannot conduct a private interview with an accused party without "dilut[ing] the protection afforded by the right to counsel." * * *

I therefore respectfully dissent.

NOTES

1. **Interference with Counsel's Efforts.** A *Patterson* footnote cited Moran v. Burbine, 475 U.S. 412, 428, 106 S.Ct. 1135, 1144 (1986) (reprinted in Subchapter C(4)(b) of this chapter). In *Burbine*, the Court "readily agreed" that once the Sixth Amendment right to counsel attached, "it follows that the police may not interfere with the efforts of a defendant's attorney to act as a 'medium' between [the suspect] and the State' during the interrogation." *Burbine*'s waiver, apparently, would not have been effective if the events had occurred after his Sixth Amendment right to counsel had attached.

2. **Deliberate Elicitation.** In Fellers v. United States, 540 U.S. 519, 124 S.Ct. 1019 (2004), the facts were as follows:

> On February 24, 2000, after a grand jury indicted petitioner for conspiracy to distribute methamphetamine, Lincoln Police Sergeant Michael Garnett and Lancaster County Deputy Sheriff Jeff Bliemeister went to petitioner's home in Lincoln, Nebraska, to arrest him. The officers knocked on petitioner's door and, when petitioner answered, identified themselves and asked if they could come in. Petitioner invited the officers into his living room.

> The officers advised petitioner they had come to discuss his involvement in methamphetamine distribution. They informed petitioner that they had a federal warrant for his arrest and that a grand jury had indicted him for conspiracy to distribute methamphetamine. The officers told petitioner that the indictment referred to his involvement with certain individuals, four of whom they named. Petitioner then told the officers that he knew the four people and had used methamphetamine during his association with them.

> After spending about 15 minutes in petitioner's home, the officers transported petitioner to the Lancaster County jail. There, the officers advised petitioner for the first time of his rights under *Miranda* * * * . Petitioner and the two officers signed a *Miranda* waiver form, and petitioner then reiterated the inculpatory statements he had made earlier, admitted to having associated with other individuals implicated in the charged conspiracy, and admitted to having loaned money to one of them even though he suspected that she was involved in drug transactions.

The district court suppressed the statements Fellers made at his home but admitted those made at the jail. On appeal, the Court of Appeals affirmed. It held that no Sixth Amendment violation occurred at Fellers' home because "the officers did not interrogate" Fellers there.

Before the Supreme Court, the Government defended the result below on the ground that the officers were simply informing Fellers of the basis for his arrest:

> [T]he government did not deliberately elicit statements from petitioner at the time of his arrest so as to raise any Sixth Amendment issue. The officers did not ask petitioner questions, or encourage him to reveal incriminating information. Rather, the officers simply informed petitioner, in a single continuous statement, that they were there "to discuss" his involvement in methamphetamine distribution, that he had been indicted for conspiring to distribute methamphetamine, that the officers had an arrest warrant, and that the charges concerned petitioner's involvement with certain individuals. Courts have long held that informing a person of the charges that support his arrest is not an interrogation tactic or its equivalent, but is routine police practice that is consistent with the Federal Rules of Criminal Procedure. * * *

> [P]etitioner contends that the officer's use of the word "discuss" to introduce his brief description of the indictment constituted an "invitation * * * to discuss pending charges." Taken in context, the record indicates that Bliemeister merely used colloquial language to inform petitioner that he wished to tell petitioner about the charges that he faced. Although one meaning of the word "discuss" denotes speaking about a topic with another person, another common use of the word denotes speaking about a topic to another person, as a lecture or speech would "discuss" a topic.

Brief for the United States, at 8, 18.

A unanimous Supreme Court rejected this and reversed:

> The Court of Appeals erred in holding that the absence of an "interrogation" foreclosed petitioner's claim that the jailhouse statements should have been suppressed as fruits of the statements taken from petitioner at his home. First, there is no question that the officers in this case "deliberately elicited" information from petitioner. Indeed, the officers, upon arriving at petitioner's house, informed him that their purpose in coming was to discuss his involvement in the distribution of methamphetamine and his association with certain charged co-conspirators. Because the ensuing discussion took place after petitioner had been indicted, outside the presence of counsel, and in the absence of any waiver of petitioner's Sixth Amendment rights, the Court of Appeals erred in holding that the officers' actions did not violate the Sixth Amendment standards established in *Massiah* and its progeny.

540 U.S. at 524–25, 124 S.Ct. at 1023.

The specific issue in *Fellers*, of course, was the admissibility of the statements made at the jail. Regarding that, the Court held:

> The Court of Appeals did not reach the question whether the Sixth Amendment requires suppression of petitioner's jailhouse statements on the ground that they were the fruits of previous questioning conducted in violation of the Sixth Amendment deliberate-elicitation standard. We have not had occasion to decide whether the rationale of [*Oregon v. Elstad*, 470 U.S. 298, 105 S.Ct. 1285, 84 L.Ed.2d 222 (1985), discussed in *Missouri v. Seibert*, 542 U.S. 600, 124 S.Ct. 2601 (2004) as reprinted in Subchapter C(5) of this chapter] applies when a suspect makes incriminating statements after a knowing and voluntary waiver of his right to counsel notwithstanding earlier police questioning in violation of Sixth Amendment standards. We therefore remand to the Court of Appeals to address this issue in the first instance.

540 U.S. at 525, 124 S.Ct. at 1023.

3. **Impeachment Use.** A statement elicited in violation of a defendant's Sixth Amendment right to counsel, the Court held in Kansas v. Ventris, 556 U.S. 586, 129 S.Ct. 1841 (2009), can be used to impeach a defendant who testifies at trial. The Court found the analysis it had used in recognizing impeachment exceptions to other constitutional rules applicable here:

> [P]reventing impeachment use of statements taken in violation of [the Sixth Amendment] would add little appreciable deterrence. Officers have significant incentive to ensure that they and their informants comply with the Constitution's demands, since statements lawfully obtained can be used for all purposes rather than simply for impeachment. And the *ex ante* probability that evidence gained in violation of [the Sixth Amendment] would be of use for impeachment is exceedingly small. An investigator would have to anticipate both that the defendant would choose to testify at trial (an unusual occurrence to begin with) *and* that he would testify inconsistently despite the admissibility of his prior statement for impeachment. Not likely to happen—or at least not likely enough to risk squandering the opportunity of using a properly obtained statement for the prosecution's case in chief.

556 U.S. at 593f, 129 S.Ct. at 1847.

CHAPTER 7

UNDERCOVER INVESTIGATIONS

Analysis

A.   Entrapment
B.   Elicitation of Self-Incriminating Statements
C.   Undercover Activities as "Searches" (and Related Matters)

EDITORS' INTRODUCTION: UNDERCOVER LAW ENFORCEMENT ACTIVITIES AND SPECIAL CONCERNS

Police undercover investigations present a sufficiently unique situation to deserve separate consideration. Such investigations pose unusually difficult problems for legal control of law enforcement conduct. Since undercover activities inherently involve deception, officers' actions may infringe upon subjects' interest in privacy more than do other types of law enforcement investigatory conduct. In addition, however, undercover investigations necessarily involve low visibility decisionmaking. Consequently, decisions whether to conduct such investigations or to use particular investigatory techniques in particular investigations are comparatively less open to scrutiny, evaluation, and control.

Many analyses of undercover investigations—both legal discussions and others—fail to carefully identify the underlying concerns. The risk that undercover investigations will stimulate criminal acts which would not otherwise be committed is, of course, among the considerations. In addition, such investigations may unjustifiably infringe upon subjects' interest in privacy. Deception—or other activities always or sometimes involved in undercover work—may bring a law enforcement agency into public disrepute because some regard these tactics as inherently "wrong" when employed by government agencies. These concerns might be further refined—what the subjects' interest in "privacy" is, for example, obviously could be more carefully developed. Too often, however, discussions fail to make any effort whatsoever to define and evaluate the real underlying concerns.

Perhaps because of this failure to identify and discuss the underlying considerations, the legal situation of undercover investigations and specific techniques used in such investigations is confused. Many doctrines relate to undercover police work but judicial opinions and other discussions often suggest available legal tools are inadequate to deal with problems presented by some undercover police activity. This chapter is divided into sections each focusing upon a doctrine affecting undercover investigations. First, the traditional law of entrapment is presented.

Next explored is the Sixth Amendment right to counsel and its effect upon the elicitation and overhearing by undercover personnel of self-incriminating admissions made by defendants. Finally, the third section addresses the application of the Fourth Amendment's right to be free from unreasonable searches and seizures in this context.

Two categories of undercover law enforcement activities are usefully distinguished. The first involves surveillance by an undercover investigator. Surveillance may be visual observation or involve overhearing communications. It may lead to the officer gaining possession of physical evidence, as where the subject of the surveillance, unaware of the agent's official status, entrusts items to the agent.

Surveillance must be contrasted with the other category of investigation, consisting of the undercover investigator actively stimulating the subject of the investigation to commit an offense at a time and place which make it feasible or easier for law enforcement officers to obtain proof of commission of the offense. L. Tiffany, D. McIntyre and D. Rotenberg, Detection of Crime 273 (1967) and Rotenberg, The Police Detection Practice of Encouragement: Lewis v. United States and Beyond, 4 Hous.L.Rev. 609 (1967), used the phrase "encouragement" to describe this tactic. Dix, Undercover Investigations and Police Rulemaking, 53 Texas L.Rev. 203, 215 (1975), preferred the phrase, "an offer * * * of the opportunity to commit an offense under controlled conditions." Whatever the practice is called, however, it raises considerations different than—or perhaps additional to—those triggered by surveillance. Tactics within both categories involve deception and therefore some possible invasion of the subject's expectation of privacy. The manipulation of the subject involved in encouragement, however, arguably constitutes a significantly greater invasion of that interest. In addition, encouragement creates a greater danger of stimulating the commission of offenses that would not otherwise be committed and of involving police agents in the commission of criminal acts.

A. ENTRAPMENT

EDITORS' INTRODUCTION: ENTRAPMENT AS A LIMIT ON LAW ENFORCEMENT ACTIVITY

Traditional law has responded to some concerns regarding undercover investigations with the doctrine of entrapment. There is, however, some reason to doubt whether entrapment provides an effective incentive for law enforcement to avoid misuse of undercover investigations.

Much dispute regarding entrapment law revolves around whether the controlling standard should be the "subjective" or the "objective" one. The Supreme Court's case law defining the entrapment defense under federal criminal law is a leading model supporting the subjective approach. In the principal case in this subchapter, the Court adheres to its traditional subjective approach.

Traditional entrapment, as a defense on the merits to a criminal charge, may be less appropriate than other legal doctrines as a means of discouraging inappropriate law enforcement conduct.

United States v. Russell

Supreme Court of the United States, 1973.
411 U.S. 423, 93 S.Ct. 1637.

■ MR. JUSTICE REHNQUIST delivered the opinion of the Court.

Respondent Richard Russell was charged in three counts of a five count indictment returned against him and codefendants John and Patrick Connolly. After a jury trial in the District Court, in which his sole defense was entrapment, respondent was convicted on all three counts of having unlawfully manufactured and processed methamphetamine ("speed") and of having unlawfully sold and delivered that drug * * * . He was sentenced to concurrent terms of two years in prison for each offense, the terms to be suspended on the condition that he spend six months in prison and be placed on probation for the following three years. On appeal the United States Court of Appeals for the Ninth Circuit, one judge dissenting, reversed the conviction solely for the reason that an undercover agent supplied an essential chemical for manufacturing the methamphetamine which formed the basis of respondent's conviction. The court concluded that as a matter of law "a defense to a criminal charge may be founded upon an intolerable degree of governmental participation in the criminal enterprise." We granted certiorari, and now reverse that judgment.

There is little dispute concerning the essential facts in this case. On December 7, 1969, Joe Shapiro, an undercover agent for the Federal Bureau of Narcotics and Dangerous Drugs, went to respondent's home on Whidbey Island in the State of Washington where he met with respondent and his two codefendants, John and Patrick Connolly. Shapiro's assignment was to locate a laboratory where it was believed that methamphetamine was being manufactured illicitly. He told the respondent and the Connollys that he represented an organization in the Pacific Northwest that was interested in controlling the manufacture and distribution of methamphetamine. He then made an offer to supply the defendants with the chemical phenyl-2-propanone, an essential ingredient in the manufacture of methamphetamine, in return for one-half of the drug produced. This offer was made on the condition that Agent Shapiro be shown a sample of the drug which they were making and the laboratory where it was being produced.

During the conversation Patrick Connolly revealed that he had been making the drug since May 1969 and since then had produced three pounds of it. John Connolly gave the agent a bag containing a quantity of methamphetamine that he represented as being from "the last batch that we made." Shortly thereafter, Shapiro and Patrick Connolly left respondent's house to view the laboratory which was located in the Connolly house on Whidbey Island. At the house Shapiro observed an empty bottle bearing the chemical label phenyl-2-propanone.

By prearrangement Shapiro returned to the Connolly house on December 9, 1969, to supply 100 grams of propanone and observe the chemical reaction. When he arrived he observed Patrick Connolly and the respondent cutting up pieces of aluminum foil and placing them in a large flask. There was testimony that some of the foil pieces accidentally fell on the floor and were picked up by the respondent and Shapiro and put into the flask.[3] Thereafter Patrick Connolly added all of the necessary chemicals, including the propanone brought by Shapiro, to make two batches of methamphetamine. The manufacturing process having been completed the following morning, Shapiro was given one-half of the drug and respondent kept the remainder. Shapiro offered to buy, and the respondent agreed to sell, part of the remainder for $60.

About a month later Shapiro returned to the Connolly house and met with Patrick Connolly to ask if he was still interested in their "business arrangement." Connolly replied that he was interested but that he had recently obtained two additional bottles of phenyl-2-propanone and would not be finished with them for a couple of days. He provided some additional methamphetamine to Shapiro at that time. Three days later Shapiro returned to the Connolly house with a search warrant and, among other items, seized an empty 500-gram bottle of propanone and a 100-gram bottle, not the one he had provided, that was partially filled with the chemical.

There was testimony at the trial of respondent and Patrick Connolly that phenyl-2-propanone was generally difficult to obtain. At the request of the Bureau of Narcotics and Dangerous Drugs, some chemical supply firms had voluntarily ceased selling the chemical.

At the close of the evidence, and after receiving the District Judge's standard entrapment instruction,[4] the jury found the respondent guilty on all counts charged. On appeal the respondent conceded that the jury could have found him predisposed to commit the offenses, but argued that on the facts presented there was entrapment as a matter of law. The Court of Appeals agreed, although it did not find the District Court had misconstrued or misapplied the traditional standards governing the

---

[3] Agent Shapiro did not otherwise participate in the manufacture of the drug or direct any of the work.

[4] The District Judge stated the governing law on entrapment as follows: "Where a person has the willingness and the readiness to break the law, the mere fact that the government agent provides what appears to be a favorable opportunity is not entrapment." He then instructed the jury to acquit respondent if it had a "reasonable doubt whether the defendant had the previous intent or purpose to commit the offense * * * and did so only because he was induced or persuaded by some officer or agent of the government." No exception was taken by respondent to this instruction.

entrapment defense. Rather, the court in effect expanded the traditional notion of entrapment, which focuses on the predisposition of the defendant, to mandate dismissal of a criminal prosecution whenever the court determines that there has been "an intolerable degree of governmental participation in the criminal enterprise." In this case the court decided that the conduct of the agent in supplying a scarce ingredient essential for the manufacture of a controlled substance established that defense.

This new defense was held to rest on either of two alternative theories. One theory is based on * * * lower court decisions which have found entrapment, regardless of predisposition, whenever the government supplies contraband to the defendants. The second theory, a nonentrapment rationale, is based on a recent Ninth Circuit decision that reversed a conviction because a government investigator was so enmeshed in the criminal activity that the prosecution of the defendants was held to be repugnant to the American criminal justice system. *Greene v. United States*, 454 F.2d 783 (C.A.9 1971). The court below held that these two rationales constitute the same defense and that only the label distinguishes them. In any event, it held that "[b]oth theories are premised on fundamental concepts of due process and evince the reluctance of the judiciary to countenance 'overzealous law enforcement.'"

This Court first recognized and applied the entrapment defense in *Sorrells v. United States*, 287 U.S. 435, 53 S.Ct. 210, 77 L.Ed. 413 (1932). In *Sorrells*, a federal prohibition agent visited the defendant while posing as a tourist and engaged him in conversation about their common war experiences. After gaining the defendant's confidence the agent asked for some liquor, was twice refused, but upon asking a third time the defendant finally capitulated, and was subsequently prosecuted for violating the National Prohibition Act.

Chief Justice Hughes, speaking for the Court, held that as a matter of statutory construction the defense of entrapment should have been available to the defendant. Under the theory propounded by the Chief Justice, the entrapment defense prohibits law enforcement officers from instigating criminal acts by persons "otherwise innocent in order to lure them to its commission and to punish them." Thus, the thrust of the entrapment defense was held to focus on the intent or predisposition of the defendant to commit the crime. "[I]f the defendant seeks acquittal by reason of entrapment he cannot complain of an appropriate and searching inquiry into his own conduct and predisposition as bearing upon that issue."

Justice Roberts concurred in the result but was of the view "that courts must be closed to the trial of a crime instigated by the government's own agents." The difference in the view of the majority and the concurring opinions is that in the former the inquiry focuses on the predisposition of the defendant, whereas in the latter the inquiry focuses on whether the government "instigated the crime."

In 1958 the Court again considered the theory underlying the entrapment defense and expressly reaffirmed the view expressed by the *Sorrells* majority. *Sherman v. United States*, 356 U.S. 369, 78 S.Ct. 819, 2 L.Ed.2d 848 (1958). In *Sherman* the defendant was convicted of selling narcotics to a government informer. As in *Sorrells* it appears that the government agent gained the confidence of the defendant and, despite initial reluctance, the defendant finally acceded to the repeated importunings of the agent to commit the criminal act. On the basis of *Sorrells,* this Court reversed the affirmance of the defendant's conviction.

In affirming the theory underlying *Sorrells,* Chief Justice Warren for the Court, held that "[t]o determine whether entrapment has been established, a line must be drawn between the trap for the unwary innocent and the trap for the unwary criminal." Justice Frankfurter stated in a concurring opinion that he believed Justice Roberts had the better view in *Sorrells* and would have framed the question to be asked in an entrapment defense in terms of "whether the police conduct revealed in the particular case falls below standards * * * for the proper use of governmental power."

In the instant case respondent asks us to reconsider the theory of the entrapment defense as it is set forth in the majority opinions in *Sorrells* and *Sherman*. His principal contention is that the defense should rest on constitutional grounds. He argues that the level of Shapiro's involvement in the manufacture of the methamphetamine was so high that a criminal prosecution for the drug's manufacture violates the fundamental principles of due process. The respondent contends that the same factors that led this Court to apply the exclusionary rule to illegal searches and seizures, and confessions should be considered here. But he would have the Court go further in deterring undesirable official conduct by requiring that any prosecution be barred absolutely because of the police involvement in criminal activity. The analogy is imperfect in any event, for the principal reason behind the adoption of the exclusionary rule was the government's "failure to observe its own laws." * * * [T]he government's conduct here violated no independent constitutional right of the respondent. Nor did Shapiro violate any federal statute or rule or commit any crime in infiltrating the respondent's drug enterprise.

Respondent would overcome this basic weakness in his analogy to the exclusionary rule cases by having the Court adopt a rigid constitutional rule that would preclude any prosecution when it is shown that the criminal conduct would not have been possible had not an undercover agent "supplied an indispensable means to the commission of the crime that could not have been obtained otherwise, through legal or illegal channels." Even if we were to surmount the difficulties attending the notion that due process of law can be embodied in fixed rules, and those attending respondent's particular formulation, the rule he proposes would not appear to be of significant benefit to him. For on the record presented it appears that he cannot fit within the terms of the very rule he proposes.

The record discloses that although the propanone was difficult to obtain it was by no means impossible. The defendants admitted making the drug both before and after those batches made with the propanone supplied by Shapiro. Shapiro testified that he saw an empty bottle labeled phenyl-2-propanone on his first visit to the laboratory on December 7, 1969. And when the laboratory was searched pursuant to a search warrant on January 10, 1970, two additional bottles labeled phenyl-2-propanone were seized. Thus, the facts in the record amply demonstrate that the propanone used in the illicit manufacture of methamphetamine not only *could* have been obtained without the intervention of Shapiro but was in fact obtained by these defendants.

While we may some day be presented with a situation in which the conduct of law enforcement agents is so outrageous that due process principles would absolutely bar the government from invoking judicial processes to obtain a conviction, cf. *Rochin v. California*, 342 U.S. 165, 72 S.Ct. 205, 96 L.Ed. 183 (1952), the instant case is distinctly not of that breed. Shapiro's contribution of propanone to the criminal enterprise already in process was scarcely objectionable. The chemical is by itself a harmless substance and its possession is legal. While the government may have been seeking to make it more difficult for drug rings, such as that of which respondent was a member, to obtain the chemical, the evidence described above shows that it nonetheless was obtainable. The law enforcement conduct here stops far short of violating that "fundamental fairness, shocking to the universal sense of justice," mandated by the Due Process Clause of the Fifth Amendment.

The illicit manufacture of drugs is not a sporadic, isolated criminal incident, but a continuing, though illegal, business enterprise. In order to obtain convictions for illegally manufacturing drugs, the gathering of evidence of past unlawful conduct frequently proves to be an all but impossible task. Thus in drug-related offenses law enforcement personnel have turned to one of the only practicable means of detection: the infiltration of drug rings and a limited participation in their unlawful present practices. Such infiltration is a recognized and permissible means of apprehension; if that be so, then the supply of some item of value that the drug ring requires must, as a general rule, also be permissible. For an agent will not be taken into the confidence of the illegal entrepreneurs unless he has something of value to offer them. Law enforcement tactics such as this can hardly be said to violate "fundamental fairness" or "shocking to the universal sense of justice."

Respondent also urges, as an alternative to his constitutional argument, that we broaden the nonconstitutional defense of entrapment in order to sustain the judgment of the Court of Appeals. This Court's opinions in *Sorrells v. United States*, supra, and *Sherman v. United*

States, supra, held that the principal element in the defense of entrapment was the defendant's predisposition to commit the crime. Respondent conceded in the Court of Appeals, as well he might, "that he may have harbored a predisposition to commit the charged offenses." Yet he argues that the jury's refusal to find entrapment under the charge submitted to it by the trial court should be overturned and the views of Justices Roberts and Frankfurter, concurring in *Sorrells* and *Sherman,* respectively, which make the essential element of the defense turn on the type and degree of governmental conduct, be adopted as the law.

We decline to overrule these cases. *Sorrells* is a precedent of long standing that has already been once reexamined in *Sherman* and implicitly there reaffirmed. Since the defense is not of a constitutional dimension, Congress may address itself to the question and adopt any substantive definition of the defense that it may find desirable.

Critics of the rule laid down in *Sorrells* and *Sherman* have suggested that its basis in the implied intent of Congress is largely fictitious, and have pointed to what they conceive to be the anomalous difference between the treatment of a defendant who is solicited by a private individual and one who is entrapped by a government agent. Questions have been likewise raised as to whether "predisposition" can be factually established with the requisite degree of certainty. Arguments such as these, while not devoid of appeal, have been twice previously made to this Court, and twice rejected by it, first in *Sorrells* and then in *Sherman.*

We believe that at least equally cogent criticism has been made of the concurring views in these cases. Commenting in *Sherman* on Justice Roberts' position in *Sorrells* that "although the defendant could claim that the Government had induced him to commit the crime, the Government could not reply by showing that the defendant's criminal conduct was due to his own readiness and not to the persuasion of government agents," Chief Justice Warren quoted the observation of Judge Learned Hand in an earlier stage of that proceeding:

> " 'Indeed, it would seem probable that, if there were no reply [to the claim of inducement], it would be impossible ever to secure convictions of any offences which consist of transactions that are carried on in secret.' "

Nor does it seem particularly desirable for the law to grant complete immunity from prosecution to one who himself planned to commit a crime, and then committed it, simply because government undercover agents subjected him to inducements which might have seduced a hypothetical individual who was not so predisposed. * * *

Several decisions of the United States district courts and courts of appeals have undoubtedly gone beyond this Court's opinions in *Sorrells* and *Sherman* in order to bar prosecutions because of what they thought to be for want of a better term "overzealous law enforcement." But the defense of entrapment enunciated in those opinions was not intended to give the federal judiciary a "chancellor's foot" veto over law enforcement practices of which it did not approve. The execution of the federal laws under our Constitution is confined primarily to the Executive Branch of the Government, subject to applicable constitutional and statutory limitations and to judicially fashioned rules to enforce those limitations. We think that the decision of the Court of Appeals in this case quite unnecessarily introduces an unmanageably subjective standard which is contrary to the holdings of this Court in *Sorrells* and *Sherman.*

Those cases establish that entrapment is a relatively limited defense. It is rooted not in any authority of the Judicial Branch to dismiss prosecutions for what it feels to have been "overzealous law enforcement," but instead in the notion that Congress could not have intended criminal punishment for a defendant who has committed all the elements of a prescribed offense, but who was induced to commit them by the government.

* * *

Respondent's concession in the Court of Appeals that the jury finding as to predisposition was supported by the evidence is, therefore, fatal to his claim of entrapment. He was an active participant in an illegal drug manufacturing enterprise which began before the government agent appeared on the scene, and continued after the government agent had left the scene. He was, in the words of *Sherman,* supra, not an "unwary innocent" but an "unwary criminal." The Court of Appeals was wrong, we believe, when it sought to broaden the principle laid down in *Sorrells* and *Sherman.* Its judgment is therefore reversed.

Reversed.

■ MR. JUSTICE STEWART, with whom MR. JUSTICE BRENNAN and MR. JUSTICE MARSHALL join, dissenting.

It is common ground that "[t]he conduct with which the defense of entrapment is concerned is the *manufacturing* of crime by law enforcement officials and their agents." *Lopez v. United States*, 373 U.S. 427, 434, 83 S.Ct. 1381, 1385, 10 L.Ed.2d 462 (1963). For the Government cannot be permitted to instigate the commission of a criminal offense in order to prosecute someone for committing it. * * * It is to prevent this situation from occurring in the administration of federal criminal justice that the defense of entrapment exists. But the Court has been sharply divided as to the proper basis, scope, and focus of the entrapment defense, and as to whether, in the absence of a conclusive showing, the issue of entrapment is for the judge or the jury to determine.

I.

In *Sorrells v. United States*, supra, and *Sherman v. United States*, supra, the Court took what might be called a "subjective" approach to the defense of entrapment. In that view, the defense is predicated on an unexpressed intent of Congress to exclude from its criminal statutes the prosecution and conviction of persons, "otherwise innocent," who have been lured to the commission of the prohibited act through the Government's instigation. * * * The Court today adheres to this approach.

The concurring opinion of Mr. Justice Roberts, joined by Justices Brandeis and Stone, in the *Sorrells* case, and that of Mr. Justice Frankfurter, joined by Justices Douglas, Harlan, and Brennan, in the *Sherman* case, took a different view of the entrapment defense. In their concept, the defense is not grounded on some unexpressed intent of Congress to exclude from punishment under its statutes those otherwise innocent persons tempted into crime by the Government, but rather on the belief that "the methods employed on behalf of the Government to bring about conviction cannot be countenanced." Thus, the focus of this approach is not on the propensities and predisposition of a specific defendant, but on "whether the police conduct revealed in the particular case falls below [the] standards, to which common feelings respond, for the proper use of governmental power." Phrased another way, the question is whether—regardless of the predisposition to crime of the particular defendant involved—the governmental agents have acted in such a way as is likely to instigate or create a criminal offense. Under this approach, the determination of the lawfulness of the Government's conduct must be made—as it is on all questions involving the legality of law enforcement methods—by the trial judge, not the jury.

In my view, this objective approach to entrapment advanced by the concurring opinions in *Sorrells* and *Sherman* is the only one truly consistent with the underlying rationale of the defense. Indeed, the very basis of the entrapment defense itself demands adherence to an approach that focuses on the conduct of the governmental agents, rather than on whether the defendant was "predisposed" or "otherwise innocent." I find it impossible to believe that the purpose of the defense is to effectuate some unexpressed congressional intent to exclude from its criminal statutes persons who committed a prohibited act, but would not have done so except for the Government's inducements. * * *

The purpose of the entrapment defense, then, cannot be to protect persons who are "otherwise innocent." Rather, it must be to prohibit unlawful governmental activity in instigating crime. * * * If that is so, then whether the particular defendant was "predisposed" or "otherwise innocent" is irrelevant; and the important question becomes whether the Government's conduct in inducing the crime was beyond judicial toleration.

Moreover, a test that makes the entrapment defense depend on whether the defendant had the requisite predisposition permits the introduction into evidence of all kinds of hearsay, suspicion, and rumor—all of which would be inadmissible in any other context—in order to prove the defendant's predisposition. It allows the prosecution, in offering such proof, to rely on the defendant's bad reputation or past criminal activities, including even rumored activities of which the prosecution may have insufficient evidence to obtain an indictment, and to present the agent's suspicions as to why they chose to tempt this defendant. This sort of evidence is not only unreliable, as the hearsay rule recognizes; but it is also highly prejudicial, especially if the matter is submitted to the jury, for, despite instructions to the contrary, the jury may well consider such evidence as probative not simply of the defendant's predisposition, but of his guilt of the offense with which he stands charged.

More fundamentally, focusing on the defendant's innocence or predisposition has the direct effect of making what is permissible or impermissible police conduct depend upon the past record and propensities of the particular defendant involved. Stated another way, this subjective test means that the Government is permitted to entrap a person with a criminal record or bad reputation, and then to prosecute him for the manufactured crime, confident that his record or reputation itself will be enough to show that he was predisposed to commit the offense anyway.

* * *

[W]hen the agents' involvement in criminal activities goes beyond the mere offering of such an opportunity and when their conduct is of a kind that could induce or instigate the commission of a crime by one not ready and willing to commit it, then—regardless of the character or propensities of the particular person induced—I think entrapment has occurred. For in that situation, the Government has engaged in the impermissible manufacturing of crime, and the federal courts should bar the prosecution in order to preserve the institutional integrity of the system of federal criminal justice.

II.

In the case before us, I think that the District Court erred in submitting the issue of entrapment to the jury, with instructions to acquit only if it had a reasonable doubt as to the respondent's predisposition to committing the crime. Since, under the objective test of entrapment, predisposition is irrelevant and the issue is to be decided by the trial judge, the Court of Appeals, I believe, would have been justified in reversing the conviction on this basis alone. But since the appellate court did not remand for consideration of the issue by the District Judge under an objective standard, but rather found entrapment as a matter of law and directed that the indictment be dismissed, we must reach the merits of the respondent's entrapment defense.

Since, in my view, it does not matter whether the respondent was predisposed to commit the offense of which he was convicted, the focus must be, rather, on the conduct of the undercover government agent. What the agent did here was to meet with a group of suspected producers of methamphetamine, including the respondent; to request the drug; to offer to supply the chemical phenyl-2-propanone in exchange for one-half of the methamphetamine to be manufactured therewith; and, when that offer was accepted, to provide the needed chemical ingredient, and to purchase some of the drug from the respondent.

It is undisputed that phenyl-2-propanone is an essential ingredient in the manufacture of methamphetamine; that it is not used for any other purpose; and that, while its sale is not illegal, it is difficult to obtain, because a manufacturer's license is needed to purchase it, and because many suppliers, at the request of the Federal Bureau of Narcotics and Dangerous Drugs, do not sell it at all. It is also undisputed that the methamphetamine which the respondent was prosecuted for manufacturing and selling was all produced on December 10, 1969, and that all the phenyl-2-propanone used in the manufacture of that batch of the drug was provided by the government agent. In these circumstances, the agent's undertaking to supply this ingredient to the respondent, thus making it possible for the Government to prosecute him for manufacturing an illicit drug with it, was, I think, precisely the type of governmental conduct that the entrapment defense is meant to prevent.

* * *

I would affirm the judgment of the Court of Appeals.

NOTES

1. **Predisposition Independent of the Undercover Investigation.** The Supreme Court's application of federal entrapment law in Jacobson v. United States, 503 U.S. 540, 112 S.Ct. 1535 (1992), may have imposed new demands on some undercover activity. Specifically, federal entrapment law may now require the Government to respond to a claim of entrapment by showing the defendant's predisposition was independent of— and perhaps existed before—the undercover investigation.

In 1984, federal postal inspectors examining the records of a California book store found the name of a customer, Keith Jacobson. Jacobson, a Nebraska farmer, had purchased by mail two magazines Bare Boys I and Bare Boys II before federal legislation made criminal receipt through the mail of sexually explicit depictions of children. In January 1985 a postal inspector sent Jacobson a letter purporting to come from the fictitious American Hedonist Society. The letter included a membership application and represented that the Society believed that its members had the "right to read what we desire, the right to discuss similar interests with those who share our philosophy, and finally that we have the right to seek pleasure without restrictions being placed on us by outdated puritan morality." Jacobson joined the organization and returned a sexual attitude questionnaire asking him to rank on a scale of one to four his enjoyment of various sexual materials, one being "really enjoy," two being "enjoy," three being "somewhat enjoy," and four being "do not enjoy." He ranked the entry "[p]re-teen sex" as a two, but indicated he was opposed to pedophilia.

In May 1986, Jacobson was sent a solicitation from a second fictitious consumer research company, "Midlands Data Research," seeking a response from those who "believe in the joys of sex and the complete awareness of those lusty and youthful lads and lasses of the neophite [sic] age." He responded: "Please feel free to send me more information, I am interested in teenage sexuality. Please keep my name confidential." Postal authorities then sent him material purporting to come from another fictitious unit, "Heartland Institute for a New Tomorrow" or HINT. The material explained HINT was "an organization founded to protect and promote sexual freedom and freedom of choice. We believe that arbitrarily imposed legislative sanctions restricting your sexual freedom should be rescinded through the legislative process." A survey was enclosed and in response Jacobson indicated his interest in "[p]reteen sex-homosexual" material was above average, but not high.

A Government "prohibited mail specialist" began writing to Jacobson, using the pseudonym "Carl Long." The letters employed a tactic known as "mirroring," in which the investigator reflects interests expressed by the person under investigation. Jacobson indicated his primary interest was in "male-male items," and elaborated

> "As far as my likes are concerned, I like good looking young guys (in their late teens and early 20's) doing their thing together."

After writing two letters, Jacobson discontinued the correspondence.

In March 1987, a second Government agency, the Customs Service, using the fictitious name "Produit Outaouais," mailed Jacobson a brochure advertising photographs of young boys engaging in sex. Petitioner placed an order that was never filled.

The Postal Service then wrote to Jacobson as the "Far Eastern Trading Company Ltd." Its letter began:

> "As many of you know, much hysterical nonsense has appeared in the American media concerning 'pornography' and what must be done to stop it from coming across your borders. This brief letter does not allow us to give much comments; however, why is your government spending millions of dollars to exercise international censorship while tons of drugs, which makes yours the world's most crime ridden country are passed through easily."

It continued:

> "[W]e have devised a method of getting these to you without prying eyes of U.S. Customs seizing your mail * * * . After consultations with American solicitors, we have been advised that once we have posted our material through your system, it cannot be opened for any inspection without authorization of a judge."

Jacobson responded with a request for more information, and was sent a catalogue. He ordered Boys Who Love Boys, a pornographic magazine depicting young boys engaged in various sexual activities. Postal authorities arranged a controlled delivery of a photocopy of the magazine, and Jacobson was arrested.

Jacobson was prosecuted for violating the Child Protection Act of 1984 by receiving through the mails a visual depiction involving a minor engaged in sexually explicit conduct. At trial, he asserted a defense of entrapment.

He testified that, when he received the initial Bare Boys magazines, he was shocked because he expected to receive photographs of young men 18 years or older. A search of Jacobson's home revealed no evidence that Jacobson collected or was actively interested in child pornography. When asked why he placed the order for Boys Who Love Boys, he responded:

> "Well, the statement was made of all the trouble and the hysteria over pornography and I wanted to see what the material was. It didn't describe the—I didn't know for sure what kind of sexual action they were referring to in the Canadian letter * * * ."

The jury rejected his defense and convicted him.

The Supreme Court, by a 5 to 4 vote, reversed. Since the Government did not dispute its inducing Jacobson's commission of the offense, the majority explained, it had the burden of proving him predisposed to violate the law before the Government directed its attention to him. It failed to do so:

> [A]lthough he had become predisposed to break the law by May 1987, it is our view that the Government did not prove that this predisposition was independent and not the product of the attention that the Government had directed at [Jacobson] since January 1985.

> The prosecution's evidence of predisposition falls into two categories: evidence developed prior to the Postal Service's mail campaign, and that developed during the course of the investigation. The sole piece of preinvestigation evidence is petitioner's 1984 order and receipt of the Bare Boys magazines. But this is scant if any proof of petitioner's predisposition to commit an illegal act, the criminal character of which a defendant is presumed to know. * * *

> Furthermore, petitioner was acting within the law at the time he received these magazines. * * * Evidence of predisposition to do what once was lawful is not, by itself, sufficient to show predisposition to do what is not illegal, for there is a common understanding that most people obey the law even when they disapprove of it. * * *

> The prosecution's evidence gathered during the investigation also fails to carry the Government's burden. [Jacobson's] responses to the many communications prior to the ultimate criminal act were at most indicative of certain personal inclinations, including a predisposition to view photographs of preteen sex and a willingness to promote a given agenda by supporting lobbying organizations. Even so, [his] responses hardly support an inference that he would commit the crime of receiving child pornography through the mails. * * *

> On the other hand, the strong arguable inference is that, by waving the banner of individual rights and disparaging the legitimacy and constitutionality of efforts to restrict the availability of sexually explicit materials, the Government not only excited

petitioner's interest in sexually explicit materials banned by law but also exerted substantial pressure on petitioner to obtain and read such material as part of a fight against censorship and the infringement of individual rights. * * *

Because * * * the prosecution failed, as a matter of law, to adduce evidence to support the jury verdict that petitioner was predisposed, independent of the Government's acts and beyond a reasonable doubt, to violate the law by receiving child pornography through the mails, we reverse the Court of Appeals' judgment affirming the conviction of Keith Jacobson.

503 U.S. at 550–54, 112 S.Ct. at 1541–43.

The dissenters indicated the majority held "Government conduct may be considered to create a predisposition to commit a crime, even before any Governmental action to induce the commission of the crime." This, they maintained, changed federal entrapment doctrine which has traditionally asked whether the defendant was predisposed before the Government induced the commission of the crime. They predicted the majority's approach would be often relied upon by defendants:

[A]fter this case, every defendant will claim that something the Government agent did before soliciting the crime "created" a predisposition that was not there before. For example, a bribe taker will claim that the description of the amount of money available was so enticing that it implanted a disposition to accept the bribe later offered. A drug buyer will claim that the description of the drug's purity and effects was so tempting that it created the urge to try it for the first time. In short, the Court's opinion could be read to prohibit the Government from advertising the seductions of criminal activity as part of its sting operation, for fear of creating a predisposition in its suspects. * * *

503 U.S. at 557, 112 S.Ct. at 1545 (O'Connor, J., dissenting).

2. **Provision of Contraband for Offense.** The phenyl-2-propanone provided to the defendants by the officer in *Russell* was not contraband, i.e., its possession by persons like the defendants was not itself criminal. Suppose officers provide contraband for use in the commission of an offense?

In Hampton v. United States, 425 U.S. 484, 96 S.Ct. 1646 (1976), Hampton and Hutton, a Drug Enforcement Administration informant, sold heroin to federal undercover officers. At his trial for distribution of heroin, Hampton testified Hutton provided the heroin and suggested selling it; other testimony suggested Hampton provided the drug. The defense requested an instruction that Hampton was entitled to acquittal if the jury found the heroin sold supplied to Hampton by a government informer. The instruction was denied, Hampton was convicted, and appeal followed. The Supreme Court, with Justice Stevens not participating, affirmed but without an opinion of the Court. Justice Rehnquist, joined by the Chief Justice and Justice White, concluded *Russell* "ruled out the possibility that the defense of entrapment could ever be based upon governmental misconduct in a case, such as this one, where the predisposition of the defendant to commit the crime was established." He continued:

> The limitations of the Due Process Clause of the Fifth Amendment come into play only when the Government activity in question violates some protected right of the *defendant*. Here, * * * the police, the Government informant, and the defendant acted in concert with one another. * * * If the police engage in illegal activity in concert with a defendant beyond the scope of their duties the remedy lies, not in freeing the equally culpable defendant, but in prosecuting the police under the applicable provisions of state or federal law. But the police conduct here no more deprived defendant of any right secured to him by the United States Constitution than did the police conduct in *Russell* deprive Russell of any rights.

425 U.S. at 490–91, 96 S.Ct. at 1650. Justice Powell, joined by Justice Blackmun, concurred in the judgment. Given that the phenyl-2-propanone in *Russell* was difficult to obtain and useful only in the manufacture of methamphetamine, he found no difference between providing it and providing heroin. *Russell*, he concluded, controlled. Turning to the Due Process argument, he acknowledged "the doctrinal and practical difficulties of delineating limits to police involvement in crimes that do not focus upon predisposition, as Government participation ordinarily will be fully justified in society's 'war with the criminal classes.' " But given that Hampton's Due Process claim could be rejected as controlled by *Russell*, he was unwilling to join the plurality's broad language rejecting such claims in all cases of government involvement in crime.

3. **Expansive Objective "Due Process" Formulations of Entrapment.** The objective approach to entrapment as generally construed provides for the defense only if the officers' conduct violates objective limits designed to discourage law enforcement conduct tending to generate the commission of crime. The Supreme Court of Alaska, for example, defined entrapment under its objective standard as follows:

> [U]nlawful entrapment occurs when a public law enforcement official * * * induces another person to commit * * * an offense by persuasion which would be effective to persuade an average person, other than one who is ready and willing, to commit such an offense.

Grossman v. State, 457 P.2d 226, 229 (Alaska 1969).

Some courts, however, impose more rigorous limits on undercover investigations, often on due process related grounds but in terms that include entrapment phraseology. The Florida Supreme Court, for example, held that a defendant was entitled, under the Florida constitutional requirement of due process, to rely on "[t]he defense of outrageous government conduct or objective entrapment." Munoz v. State, 629 So.2d 90, 98 (Fla.1993). State v. Vallejos, 123 N.M. 739, 945 P.2d 957 (1997), recognized "objective entrapment," based on due process as guaranteed by the New Mexico Constitution, under which a defendant is entitled to dismissal of the prosecution if the judge determines the law enforcement conduct employed in the investigation so exceeded the standards of proper investigation that the public's confidence in the fair and honorable administration of justice would be shaken by such conduct.

A Florida court summarized that state's application of due process objective entrapment:

> Cases finding a due process violation based on outrageous government conduct have one common thread: affirmative and unacceptable conduct by law enforcement or its agent. In [*State v. Glosson*, 462 So.2d 1082, 1082 (Fla.1985)], a sheriff's department employed an informant to conduct a reverse-sting drug operation. As consideration, the informant was promised ten percent of the proceeds from any civil forfeitures arising out of a successful prosecution. The informant's testimony and cooperation were necessary for a successful prosecution. Because of the "enormous financial incentive not only to make criminal cases, but also to color his testimony or even commit perjury in pursuit of the contingent fee," the supreme court found a due process violation. The supreme court further stated, "[t]he due process rights of all citizens require us to forbid criminal prosecutions based upon the testimony of vital state witnesses who have what amounts to a financial stake in criminal convictions."
>
> In [*State v. Williams*, 623 So.2d 462, 463 (Fla.1993)], the defendant was arrested during a reverse sting operation by the Broward County Sheriff's Office for purchasing crack cocaine within 1,000 feet of a school. The supreme court reversed the defendant's conviction, finding a due process violation where the Sheriff's Office illegally manufactured the crack cocaine. [*S*]*ee also Farley v. State*, 848 So.2d 393, 398 (Fla. 4th DCA 2003) (holding that law enforcement's manufacture of child pornography as part of an email solicitation, coupled with promises of protection from government interference, was a violation of due process). Similarly, in *Madera v. State*, 943 So.2d 960, 962 (Fla. 4th DCA 2006), the defendant's due process rights were violated when the informant pretended to be romantically interested in the defendant and induced him to purchase drugs with promises of sex and pleas that she needed the drugs to cope with cancer.

Bist v. State, 35 So.3d 936, 940 (Fla.App.), review denied 46 So.3d 565 (Fla. 2010).

State v. Grubb, 319 N.J.Super. 407, 725 A.2d 707 (1999), found the drug defendant entitled to acquittal under "common law objective entrapment." It emphasized the investigating officers had insufficient justification for targeting and investigating the defendant as a criminal suspect. The investigation was triggered when another suspect, who became an informant, reported that he had a deal pending to purchase Clenbuterol from Grubb, but the officers failed to conduct sufficient inquiry to determine that Clenbuterol was not a steroid as the officers suspected. The *Grubb* court also stressed the officers exercised insufficient supervision over the informant.

B. ELICITATION OF SELF-INCRIMINATING STATEMENTS

EDITORS' INTRODUCTION: APPLICATION OF THE FIFTH AND SIXTH AMENDMENTS TO UNDERCOVER INVESTIGATIONS

The two major federal constitutional limits on law enforcement officers' ability to elicit self-incriminating admissions from suspects are the Fifth Amendment prohibition against compelled self-incrimination, as developed in Miranda v. Arizona, 384 U.S. 436, 86 S.Ct. 1602 (1966), and the Sixth Amendment right to counsel. Both doctrines, as they apply to general law enforcement questioning of suspects, are developed in Chapter 6. When self-incriminating admissions are obtained or overheard by undercover officers or informants working as agents of officers, the situation—and the law—is considerably different.

Does an undercover officer passively overhearing self-incriminating admissions made by a suspect engage in action that triggers self-incrimination protection? This was addressed in Hoffa v. United States, 385 U.S. 293, 87 S.Ct. 408 (1966), reprinted in part later in this chapter. *Hoffa* considered the argument that testimony by a government informer concerning incriminating admissions made by the defendant in the former's presence violated the defendant's Fifth Amendment privilege against compelled self-incrimination. It was clear that if the informer had disclosed his status he would not have been permitted by the defendant to overhear the conversations. The Court held:

> [A] necessary element of compulsory self-incrimination is some kind of compulsion. * * * [No] claim has been or could be made that [Hoffa's] incriminating statements were the product of any sort of coercion, legal or factual. The * * * conversations * * * were wholly voluntary. For that reason, if for no other, it is clear that no right protected by the Fifth Amendment privilege against compulsory self-incrimination was violated in this case.

384 U.S. at 304, 87 S.Ct. at 414–15.

Does *Miranda* apply when an undercover officer or informant actively persuades a suspect to make incriminating admissions? This was addressed in Illinois v. Perkins, 496 U.S. 292, 110 S.Ct. 2394 (1990). Police learned from a former prison acquaintance of Perkins that Perkins had admitted a homicide. Upon locating Perkins in a local jail, police placed the former acquaintance and an undercover officer in the same cellblock. After the former acquaintance introduced them, the officer engaged Perkins in conversations and encouraged Perkins to admit the offense and relate details of its commission. Failure to comply with *Miranda* in this process, the Court held, did not render Perkins's admissions subject to suppression. It explained:

> Conversations between suspects and undercover agents do not implicate the concerns underlying *Miranda*. The essential ingredients of a "police-dominated atmosphere" and compulsion

are not present when an incarcerated person speaks freely to someone he believes to be a fellow inmate. Coercion is determined from the perspective of the suspect. * * * When a suspect considers himself in the company of cellmates and not officers, the coercive atmosphere is lacking. * * * When the suspect has no reason to think that the listeners have official power over him, it should not be assumed that his words are motivated by the reaction he expects from his listeners. * * *

> *Miranda* forbids coercion, not mere strategic deception by taking advantage of a suspect's misplaced trust in one he supposes to be a fellow prisoner. * * *

496 U.S. at 296–97, 110 S.Ct. at 2397.

As a result of these decisions, federal constitutional regulation of law enforcement conduct in this area is achieved through the Sixth and Fourteenth Amendments right to counsel. The seminal case is Massiah v. United States, 377 U.S. 201, 84 S.Ct. 1199 (1964). Massiah, Colson, and others were arrested and indicted for drug offenses; Massiah and Colson were released on bail. Massiah retained a lawyer. Unknown to Massiah, Colson decided to cooperate with the government agents in their continuing investigation, and permitted the installation of a radio transmitter in his car. One evening, Colson and Massiah had a lengthy conversation while sitting in Colson's parked automobile. A federal agent listened over his radio to the conversation, which included several incriminating admissions by Massiah. At Massiah's trial, the agent was permitted to testify as to these admissions. The Supreme Court held this constitutional error:

> We hold that [Massiah] was denied the basic protection of [the Sixth Amendment right to counsel] when there was used against him at his trial evidence of his own incriminating words, which federal agents had deliberately elicited from him after he had been indicted and in the absence of his counsel.

377 U.S. at 206, 84 S.Ct. at 1203. The principal case in this section explores the ramifications of *Massiah*.

United States v. Henry

Supreme Court of the United States, 1980.
447 U.S. 264, 100 S.Ct. 2183.

■ MR. CHIEF JUSTICE BURGER delivered the opinion of the Court.

We granted certiorari to consider whether respondent's Sixth Amendment right to the assistance of counsel was violated by the admission at trial of incriminating statements made by respondent to his cellmate, an undisclosed government informant, after indictment and while in custody.

I.

The Janaf Branch of the United Virginia Bank/Seaboard National in Norfolk, Va., was robbed in August 1972. Witnesses saw two men wearing masks and carrying guns enter the bank while a third man waited in the car. No witnesses were able to identify respondent Henry as one of the participants. About an hour after the robbery, the getaway car was discovered. Inside was found a rent receipt signed by one "Allen R. Norris" and a lease, also signed by Norris, for a house in Norfolk. Two men, who were subsequently convicted of participating in the robbery, were arrested at the rented house. Discovered with them were the proceeds of the robbery and the guns and masks used by the gunman.

Government agents traced the rent receipt to Henry; on the basis of this information, Henry was arrested in Atlanta, Ga., in November 1972. Two weeks later he was indicted for armed robbery under 18 U.S.C.A. § 2113(a) and (d). He was held pending trial in the Norfolk City Jail. Counsel was appointed on November 27.

On November 21, 1972, shortly after Henry was incarcerated, government agents working on the Janaf robbery contacted one Nichols, an inmate at the Norfolk City Jail, who for some time prior to this meeting had been engaged to provide confidential information to the Federal Bureau of Investigation as a paid informant. Nichols was then serving a sentence on local forgery charges. The record does not disclose whether the agent contacted Nichols specifically to acquire information about Henry or the Janaf robbery.

Nichols informed the agent that he was housed in the same cellblock with several federal prisoners awaiting trial, including Henry. The agent told him to be alert to any statements made by the federal prisoners, but not to initiate any conversation with or question Henry regarding the bank robbery. In early December, after Nichols had been released from jail, the agent again contacted Nichols, who reported that he and Henry had engaged in conversation and that Henry had told him about the robbery of the Janaf bank. Nichols was paid for furnishing the information.

When Henry was tried in March 1973, an agent of the Federal Bureau of Investigation testified concerning the events surrounding the discovery of the rental slip and the evidence uncovered at the rented house. Other witnesses also connected Henry to the rented house, including the rental agent who positively identified Henry as the "Allen R. Norris" who had rented the house and had taken the rental receipt described earlier. A neighbor testified that prior to the robbery she saw Henry at the rented house with John Luck, one of the two men who had by the time of Henry's trial been convicted for the robbery. In addition, palm prints found on the lease agreement matched those of Henry.

Nichols testified at trial that he had "an opportunity to have some conversations with Mr. Henry while he was in the jail," and that Henry told him that on several occasions he had gone to the Janaf Branch to see which employees opened the vault. Nichols also testified that Henry described to him the details of the robbery and stated that the only evidence connecting him to the robbery was the rental receipt. The jury was not informed that Nichols was a paid government informant.

On the basis of this testimony, Henry was convicted of bank robbery and sentenced to a term of imprisonment of 25 years. On appeal he raised no Sixth Amendment claims. His conviction was affirmed, and his petition to this Court for a writ of certiorari was denied.

On August 28, 1975, Henry moved to vacate his sentence * * * . At this stage, he stated that he had just learned that Nichols was a paid government informant and alleged that he had been intentionally placed in the same cell with Nichols so that Nichols could secure information about the robbery. Thus, Henry contended that the introduction of Nichols' testimony violated his Sixth Amendment right to the assistance of counsel. The District Court denied the motion without a hearing. The Court of Appeals, however, reversed and remanded for an evidentiary inquiry into "whether the witness [Nichols] was acting as a government agent during his interviews with Henry."

On remand, the District Court requested affidavits from the government agents. An affidavit was submitted describing the agent's relationship with Nichols and relating the following conversation:

> "I recall telling Nichols at this time to be alert to any statements made by these individuals [the federal prisoners] regarding the charges against them. I specifically recall telling Nichols that he was not to question Henry or these individuals about the charges against them, however, if they engaged him in conversation or talked in front of him, he was requested to pay attention to their statements. I recall telling Nichols not to initiate any conversations with Henry regarding the bank robbery charges against Henry, but that if Henry initiated the conversations with Nichols, I requested Nichols to pay attention to the information furnished by Henry."

The agent's affidavit also stated that he never requested anyone affiliated with the Norfolk City Jail to place Nichols in the same cell with Henry.

The District Court again denied Henry's § 2255 motion, concluding that Nichols' testimony at trial did not violate Henry's Sixth Amendment right to counsel. The Court of Appeals reversed and remanded, holding that the actions of the government impaired the Sixth Amendment rights of the defendant under *Massiah v. United States*, 377 U.S. 201, 84 S.Ct. 1199, 12 L.Ed.2d 246 (1964). The court noted that Nichols had engaged in conversation with Henry and concluded that if by association, by general conversation, or both, Nichols had developed a relationship of trust and confidence with Henry such that Henry revealed incriminating information, this constituted interference with the right to the assistance of counsel under the Sixth Amendment.

II.

* * *

The question here is whether under the facts of this case, a government agent "deliberately elicited" incriminating statements from Henry within the meaning of *Massiah*. Three factors are important. First, Nichols was acting under instructions as a paid informant for the government; second, Nichols was ostensibly no more than a fellow inmate of Henry; and third, Henry was in custody and under indictment at the time he was engaged in conversation by Nichols.

The Court of Appeals viewed the record as showing that Nichols deliberately used his position to secure incriminating information from Henry when counsel was not present and held that conduct attributable to the government. Nichols had been a paid government informant for more than a year; moreover, the FBI agent was aware that Nichols had access to Henry and would be able to engage him in conversations without arousing Henry's suspicion. The arrangement between Nichols and the agent was on a contingent fee basis; Nichols was to be paid only if he produced useful information. This combination of circumstances is sufficient to support the Court of Appeals' determination. Even if the agent's statement is accepted that he did not intend that Nichols would take affirmative steps to secure incriminating information, he must have known that such propinquity likely would lead to that result.

The Government argues that the federal agents instructed Nichols not to question Henry about the robbery. Yet according to his own testimony, Nichols was not a passive listener; rather, he had "some conversations with Mr. Henry" while he was in jail and Henry's incriminatory statements were "the product of this conversation." * * *

* * *

It is undisputed that Henry was unaware of Nichols' role as a government informant. The Government argues that this Court should apply a less rigorous standard under the Sixth Amendment where the accused is prompted by an undisclosed undercover informant than where the accused is speaking in the hearing of persons he knows to be government officers. That line of argument, however, seeks to infuse Fifth Amendment concerns against compelled self-incrimination into the Sixth Amendment protection of the right to the assistance of counsel. An accused speaking to a known government agent is typically aware that his statements may be used against him. The adversary positions at that stage are well established; the parties are then "arms length" adversaries.

When the accused is in the company of a fellow inmate who is acting by prearrangement as a government agent, the same cannot here be said. Conversation stimulated in such circumstances may elicit information that an accused would not intentionally reveal to persons known to be government agents. Indeed, the *Massiah* Court noted that if the Sixth Amendment "is to have any efficacy it must apply to indirect and surreptitious interrogations as well as those conducted in the jailhouse." The Court pointedly observed that Massiah was more seriously imposed upon because he did not know that his codefendant was a government agent.

Moreover, the concept of a knowing and voluntary waiver of Sixth Amendment rights does not apply in the context of communications with an undisclosed undercover informant acting for the government. In that setting Henry, being unaware that Nichols was a government agent expressly commissioned to secure evidence, cannot be held to have waived his right to the assistance of counsel.

Finally Henry's incarceration at the time he was engaged in conversation by Nichols is also a relevant factor. As a ground for imposing the prophylactic requirements in *Miranda v. Arizona*, 384 U.S. 436, 467, 86 S.Ct. 1602, 1624, 16 L.Ed.2d 694 (1966), this Court noted the powerful psychological inducements to reach for aid when a person is in confinement. While the concern in *Miranda* was limited to custodial police interrogation, the mere fact of custody imposes pressures on the accused; confinement may bring into play subtle influences that will make him particularly susceptible to the ploys of undercover government agents. The Court of Appeals determined that on this record the incriminating conversations between Henry and Nichols were facilitated by Nichols' conduct and apparent status as a person sharing a common plight. That Nichols had managed to gain the confidence of Henry, as the Court of Appeals determined, is confirmed by Henry's request that Nichols assist him in his escape plans when Nichols was released from confinement.

Under the strictures of the Court's holdings on the exclusion of evidence, we conclude that the Court of Appeals did not err in holding that Henry's statements to Nichols should not have been admitted at trial. By intentionally creating a situation likely to induce Henry to make incriminating statements without the assistance of counsel, the government violated Henry's Sixth Amendment right to counsel. This is not a case where, in Justice Cardozo's words, "the constable blundered," *People v. Defore*, 242 N.Y. 13, 21, 150 N.E. 585, 587 (1926); rather, it is one where the "constable" planned an impermissible interference with the right to the assistance of counsel.

The judgment of the Court of Appeals for the Fourth Circuit is affirmed.

■ MR. JUSTICE BLACKMUN, with whom MR. JUSTICE WHITE joins, dissenting.

* * *

I.

Massiah mandates exclusion only if a federal agent "deliberately elicited" statements from the accused in the absence of counsel. The word "deliberately" denotes intent. *Massiah* ties this intent to the act of elicitation, that is, to conduct that draws forth a response. Thus *Massiah*, by its own terms, covers only action undertaken with the specific intent to evoke an inculpatory disclosure.

* * *

[W]hile claiming to retain the "deliberately elicited" test, the Court really forges a new test that saps the word "deliberately" of all significance. The Court's extension of *Massiah* would cover even a "negligent" triggering of events resulting in reception of disclosures. This approach, in my view, is unsupported and unwise.

* * *

II.

In my view, the Court not only missteps in forging a new *Massiah* test; it proceeds to misapply the very test it has created. The new test requires a showing that the agent created a situation "likely to induce" the production of incriminatory remarks, and that the informant in fact "prompted" the defendant. Even accepting the most capacious reading of both this language and the facts, I believe that neither prong of the Court's test is satisfied.

A.   *"Likely to Induce."* In holding that Coughlin's actions were likely to induce Henry's statements, the Court relies on three facts: a contingent fee arrangement; Henry's assumption that Nichols was just a cellmate; and Henry's incarceration.

* * *

* * *   I question whether the existence of a contingent fee arrangement is at all significant. The reasonable conclusion of an informant like Nichols would be that, whatever the arrangement, he would *not* be remunerated if he breached his promise; yet the Court asks us to infer that Coughlin's conversation with Nichols "likely would lead" Nichols to engage in the very conduct which Coughlin told him to avoid.

The Court also emphasizes that Henry was "unaware that Nichols was a government agent." One might properly assign this factor some importance, were it not for *Brewer v. Williams*, 430 U.S. 387, 97 S.Ct. 1232, 51 L.Ed.2d 424 (1977). In that case, the Court explicitly held that the fact "[t]hat the incriminating statements were elicited surreptitiously in the *Massiah* case, and otherwise here, is *constitutionally irrelevant*." (Emphasis added.) The Court's teeter-tottering with this factor in *Massiah* analysis can only induce confusion.

Finally, the Court notes that Henry was incarcerated when he made his statements to Nichols. The Court's emphasis of the "subtle influences" exerted by custody, however, is itself too subtle for me. This is not a case

ELICITATION OF SELF-INCRIMINATING STATEMENTS

of a custodial encounter with police, in which the Government's display of power might overcome the free will of the accused. The relationship here was "social" and relaxed. Henry did not suspect that Nichols was connected with the FBI. Moreover, even assuming that "subtle influences" might encourage a detainee to talk about his crime, there are certainly counterbalances of at least equal weight. Since, in jail, "official surveillance has traditionally been the order of the day," and a jailmate has obvious incentives to assist authorities, one may expect a detainee to act with corresponding circumspection. * * *

* * *

B. *"Prompting."* All Members of the Court agree that Henry's statements were properly admitted if Nichols did not "prompt" him. The record, however, gives no indication that Nichols "stimulated" Henry's remarks with "affirmative steps to secure incriminating information." Certainly the known facts reveal nothing more than "a jailhouse informant who had been instructed to overhear conversations and to engage a criminal defendant in some conversations." The scant record demonstrates only that Nichols "had 'an opportunity to have some conversations with Mr. Henry while he was in the jail.'" "Henry had engaged [Nichols] in conversation," "had requested Nichols' assistance," and "had talked to Nichols about the bank robbery charges against him." Thus, we know only that Nichols and Henry had conversations, hardly a startling development, given their location in the same cellblock in a city jail. We know nothing about the nature of these conversations, particularly whether Nichols subtly or otherwise focused attention on the bank robberies. Indeed, to the extent the record says anything at all, it supports the inference that it was Henry, not Nichols, who "engaged" the other "in some conversations," and who was the moving force behind any mention of the crime. I cannot believe that *Massiah* requires exclusion when a cellmate previously unknown to the defendant and asked only to keep his ears open says: "It's a nice day," and the defendant responds: "It would be nicer if I hadn't robbed that bank." * * *

■ MR. JUSTICE REHNQUIST, dissenting.

* * *

The doctrinal underpinnings of *Massiah* have been largely left unexplained, and the result in this case, as in *Massiah*, is difficult to reconcile with the traditional notions of the role of an attorney. Here, as in *Massiah*, the accused was not prevented from consulting with his counsel as often as he wished. No meetings between the accused and his counsel were disturbed or spied upon. And preparation for trial was not obstructed. * * *

Once the accused has been made aware of his rights, it is his responsibility to decide whether or not to exercise them. If he voluntarily relinquishes his rights by talking to authorities, or if he decides to disclose incriminating information to someone whom he mistakenly believes will not report it to the authorities, he is normally accountable for his actions and must bear any adverse consequences that result. Such information has not in any sense been obtained because the accused's will has been overborne, nor does it result from any "unfair advantage" that the State has over the accused: the accused is free to keep quiet and to consult with his attorney if he so chooses. In this sense, the decision today and the result in *Massiah* are fundamentally inconsistent with traditional notions of the role of the attorney that underlie the Sixth Amendment right to counsel.

* * *

* * * This Court has never held that an accused is constitutionally protected from his inability to keep quiet, whether or not he has been encouraged by third party citizens to voluntarily make incriminating remarks. I do not think the result should be different merely because the government has encouraged a third party informant to report remarks obtained in this fashion. When an accused voluntarily chooses to make an incriminatory remark in these circumstances, he knowingly assumes the risk that his confidant may be untrustworthy.

* * *

The fact that police carry on undercover activities should not automatically be transmuted because formal criminal proceedings have begun. * * * [T]he mere bringing of formal proceedings does not necessarily mean that an undercover investigation or the need for it has terminated. A person may be arrested on the basis of probable cause arising in the immediate aftermath of an offense and during early stages of investigation, but before the authorities have had an opportunity to investigate fully his connection with the crime. And for the criminal, there is no rigid dichotomy between the time before commencement of former criminal proceedings and the time after such proceedings have begun. Once out on bail the accused remains free to continue his criminal activity, and very well may decide to do so. * * * I would hold that the Government's activity here is merely a continuation of their lawful authority to use covert operations in investigating a criminal case after formal proceedings have commenced.

NOTES

1. **Passive Informants.** If an informant overhears an incriminating admission by a defendant but did not elicit it, does the Sixth Amendment bar the use of this admission? The principal case suggests not, and this has been reaffirmed.

In Kuhlmann v. Wilson, 477 U.S. 436, 106 S.Ct. 2616 (1986), Wilson was arrested and arraigned on charges relating to a robbery-murder. He was placed in a cell with prisoner Benny Lee; the cell provided them with a view of the garage at which the crimes were committed. Unknown to Wilson, Lee had entered into an arrangement under which he agreed to listen to Wilson's conversations and report them to police. Lee was instructed not to ask Wilson any questions but to "keep his ears open." Wilson soon told Lee that, although he was present at the robbery and murder, he did not know the perpetrators and was not involved in the crime. According to his later testimony, Lee responded that the story "didn't sound too good" and "things didn't look too good for him." At another point, Lee testified he had told Wilson, "[Y]ou better come up with a better story because that one doesn't sound too cool to me * * * ." Several days later, Wilson told Lee another version of the events, admitting guilty participation. At Wilson's state trial, the trial judge found Wilson's admissions to Lee "spontaneous" and "unsolicited" and admitted them. In subsequent federal habeas corpus litigation, the Supreme Court held Wilson entitled to no relief. Acknowledging that it had never expressly addressed whether the Sixth Amendment bars the admission of statements overheard yet not elicited by an informant, the majority resolved the issue:

> [T]he primary concern of the *Massiah* line of decisions is secret interrogation by investigatory techniques that are the equivalent of direct police interrogation. Since "the Sixth Amendment is not violated whenever—by luck or happenstance—the State obtains incriminating statements from the accused after the right to counsel has attached," a defendant does not make out a violation of that right simply by showing that an informant, either through prior arrangement or voluntarily, reported his incriminating statements to the police. Rather, the defendant must demonstrate that the police and their informant took some action, beyond merely listening, that was designed deliberately to elicit incriminating remarks.

477 U.S. at 459, 106 S.Ct. at 2630. The record in the case, the majority concluded, did not permit a federal habeas corpus court to find, under this standard, Wilson's Sixth Amendment rights violated.

2. **Target Suspected of Several Crimes.** Special problems are presented when a suspect is believed involved in multiple crimes. If the suspect's Sixth Amendment right to counsel under *Massiah* and *Henry* attaches, may law enforcement officers nevertheless seek to elicit admissions to other offenses under investigation?

In Maine v. Moulton, 474 U.S. 159, 106 S.Ct. 477 (1985), both Moulton and one Colson were indicted for theft by receiving stolen property. Colson contacted police; he reported that he had received anonymous threatening telephone calls and that Moulton suggested the two kill Gary Elwell, a state witness. Other witnesses in the case reported to authorities that they had also received threats. The police made and Colson accepted a deal under which he would cooperate with authorities in return for no further charges being brought against him. During later telephone conversations with Colson, Moulton suggested the two meet to plan their defense to the charges. For purposes of this meeting, Colson was equipped with a body wire transmitter to record what was said; according to police testimony, the device was provided for Colson's safety in the event Moulton realized he was cooperating with authorities and to record any further threats to witnesses

Moulton might make. During the conversation, Moulton offered that the plan for killing Elwell would not work. There was extended discussion concerning the falsification of alibis and Colson encouraged Moulton to make a number of incriminating admissions concerning the crime for which he had been indicted. At Moulton's later theft trial, the state successfully offered into evidence those portions of the recorded conversations in which Moulton made admissions concerning the crime charged. One portion of the discussion concerning false alibis was admitted, but no part of the conversation concerning the killing of the witness was offered. Moulton was convicted.

The Supreme Court reversed, reasoning that admission of the conversations violated Moulton's Sixth Amendment rights as developed in *Massiah* and *Henry*. The majority rejected the prosecution's argument that the evidence was admissible because the police activity was legitimately intended to investigate matters other than the theft offense for which Moulton was indicted—the threats to Colson and Moulton's plan to kill Elwell:

> To allow the admission of evidence obtained from the accused in violation of his Sixth Amendment right whenever the police assert an alternative, legitimate reason for their surveillance invites abuse by law enforcement personnel in the form of fabricated investigations and risks the evisceration of the Sixth Amendment right recognized in *Massiah*. * * * Consequently, incriminating statements pertaining to pending charges are inadmissible at the trial of those charges, notwithstanding the fact that the police were also investigating other crimes, if, in obtaining this evidence, the State violated the Sixth Amendment by knowingly circumventing the accused's right to the assistance of counsel.

474 U.S. at 180, 106 S.Ct. at 489. Because Moulton's *Massiah* right was violated, the use of the evidence in his theft trial was improper. The Court also offered:

> On the other hand, to exclude evidence pertaining to charges as to which the Sixth Amendment right to counsel had not attached at the time the evidence was obtained, simply because other charges were pending at that time, would unnecessarily frustrate the public's interest in the investigation of criminal activities.

474 U.S. at 180, 106 S.Ct. at 489. It added:

> Incriminating statements pertaining to other crimes, as to which the Sixth Amendment right has not yet attached are, of course, admissible at the trial of those offenses.

474 U.S. at 180 n. 16, 106 S.Ct. at 489 n. 16.

C. UNDERCOVER ACTIVITIES AS "SEARCHES" (AND RELATED MATTERS)

The Fourth Amendment's prominence in federal constitutional regulation of other aspects of law enforcement investigatory behavior suggests the provision would be appropriate as a means of limiting, but not prohibiting, certain aspects of undercover investigations. This, of course, would be possible only if some or all of the activities of undercover officers and agents constituted "searches" or "seizures" within the meaning of the Fourth Amendment. Whether this is or should be the case is explored in this subchapter.

Generally, the courts have rejected arguments that undercover officers require probable cause or even reasonable suspicion to target a suspect and offer the suspect an opportunity to commit an offense under circumstances making proof of the offense easier. United States v. Aibejeris, 28 F.3d 97, 99 (11th Cir.1994); United States v. Harvey, 991 F.2d 981, 989–93 (2d Cir.1993); Commonwealth v. Mance, 539 Pa. 282, 286–89, 652 A.2d 299, 301–02 (1995).

Hoffa v. United States

Supreme Court of the United States, 1966.
385 U.S. 293, 87 S.Ct. 408.

■ MR. JUSTICE STEWART delivered the opinion of the Court.

Over a period of several weeks in the late autumn of 1962 there took place in a federal court in Nashville, Tennessee, a trial by jury in which James Hoffa was charged with violating a provision of the Taft-Hartley Act. That trial, known in the present record as the Test Fleet trial, ended with a hung jury. The petitioners now before us—James Hoffa, Thomas Parks, Larry Campbell, and Ewing King—were tried and convicted in 1964 for endeavoring to bribe members of that jury. The convictions were affirmed by the Court of Appeals. A substantial element in the Government's proof that led to the convictions of these four petitioners was contributed by a witness named Edward Partin, who testified to several incriminating statements which he said petitioners Hoffa and King had made in his presence during the course of the Test Fleet trial. Our grant of certiorari was limited to the single issue of whether the Government's use in this case of evidence supplied by Partin operated to invalidate these convictions.

* * *

The controlling facts can be briefly stated. The Test Fleet trial, in which James Hoffa was the sole individual defendant, was in progress between October 22 and December 23, 1962, in Nashville, Tennessee. James Hoffa was president of the International Brotherhood of Teamsters. During the course of the trial he occupied a three-room suite in the Andrew Jackson Hotel in Nashville. One of his constant companions throughout the trial was the petitioner King, president of the Nashville local of the Teamsters Union. Edward Partin, a resident of Baton Rouge, Louisiana, and a local Teamsters Union official there, made repeated visits to Nashville during the period of the trial. On these visits he frequented the Hoffa hotel suite, and was continually in the company of Hoffa and his associates, including King, in and around the hotel suite, the hotel lobby, the courthouse, and elsewhere in Nashville. During this period Partin made frequent reports to a federal agent named Sheridan concerning conversations he said Hoffa and King had had with him and with each other, disclosing endeavors to bribe members of the Test Fleet jury. Partin's reports and his subsequent testimony at the petitioners' trial unquestionably contributed, directly or indirectly, to the convictions of all four of the petitioners.

The chain of circumstances which led Partin to be in Nashville during the Test Fleet trial extended back at least to September of 1962. At that time Partin was in jail in Baton Rouge on a state criminal charge. He was also under a federal indictment for embezzling union funds, and other indictments for state offenses were pending against him. Between that time and Partin's initial visit to Nashville on October 22 he was released on bail on the state criminal charge, and proceedings under the federal indictment were postponed. On October 8, Partin telephoned Hoffa in Washington, D. C., to discuss local union matters and Partin's difficulties with the authorities. In the course of this conversation Partin asked if he could see Hoffa to confer about these problems, and Hoffa acquiesced. Partin again called Hoffa on October 18 and arranged to meet him in Nashville. During this period Partin also consulted on several occasions with federal law enforcement agents, who told him that Hoffa might attempt to tamper with the Test Fleet jury, and asked him to be on the lookout in Nashville for such attempts and to report to the federal authorities any evidence of wrongdoing that he discovered. Partin agreed to do so.

After the Test Fleet trial was completed, Partin's wife received four monthly installment payments of $300 from government funds, and the state and federal charges against Partin were either dropped or not actively pursued.

[W]e proceed upon the premise that Partin was a government informer from the time he first arrived in Nashville on October 22, and that the Government compensated him for his services as such. It is upon that premise that we consider the constitutional issues presented.

* * *

I.

It is contended that only by violating the petitioner's rights under the Fourth Amendment was Partin able to hear the petitioner's incriminating statements in the hotel suite, and that Partin's testimony was therefore inadmissible * * * . The argument is that Partin's failure to disclose his role as a government informer vitiated the consent that the petitioner gave to Partin's repeated entries into the suite, and that by listening to the petitioner's statements Partin conducted an illegal "search" for verbal evidence.

The preliminary steps of this argument are on solid ground. A hotel room can clearly be the object of Fourth Amendment protection as much as a home or an office. The Fourth Amendment can certainly be violated by guileful as well as by forcible intrusions into a constitutionally protected area. And the protections of the Fourth Amendment are surely not limited to tangibles, but can extend as well to oral statements.

Where the argument falls is in its misapprehension of the fundamental nature and scope of Fourth Amendment protection. What the Fourth Amendment protects is the security a man relies upon when he places himself or his property within a constitutionally protected area, be it his home or his office, his hotel room or his automobile. There he is protected from unwarranted governmental intrusion. And when he puts something in his filing cabinet, in his desk drawer, or in his pocket, he has the right to know it will be secure from an unreasonable search or an unreasonable seizure. * * *

In the present case, however, it is evident that no interest legitimately protected by the Fourth Amendment is involved. It is obvious that the petitioner was not relying on the security of his hotel suite when he made the incriminating statements to Partin or in Partin's presence. Partin did not enter the suite by force or by stealth. He was not a surreptitious eavesdropper. Partin was in the suite by invitation, and every conversation which he heard was either directed to him or knowingly carried on in his presence. The petitioner, in a word, was not relying on the security of the hotel room; he was relying upon his misplaced confidence that Partin would not reveal his wrongdoing. As counsel for the petitioner himself points out, some of the communications with Partin did not take place in the suite at all, but in the "hall of the hotel," in the "Andrew Jackson Hotel lobby," and "at the courthouse."

Neither this Court nor any member of it has ever expressed the view that the Fourth Amendment protects a wrongdoer's misplaced belief that a person to whom he voluntarily confides his wrongdoing will not reveal it. Indeed, the Court unanimously rejected that very contention less than four years ago in *Lopez v. United States*, 373 U.S. 427, 83 S.Ct. 1381, 10 L.Ed.2d 462. * * * In the words of the dissenting opinion in *Lopez*, "The risk of being overheard by an eavesdropper or betrayed by an informer or deceived as to the identity of one with whom one deals is probably inherent in the conditions of human society. It is the kind of risk we necessarily assume whenever we speak."

Adhering to these views, we hold that no right protected by the Fourth Amendment was violated in the present case.

* * *

IV.

Finally, the petitioner claims that even if there was no violation [of any of his specific federal constitutional rights], the judgment of conviction must nonetheless be reversed. The argument is based upon the Due Process Clause of the Fifth Amendment. The "totality" of the Government's conduct during the Test Fleet trial operated, it is said, to

" 'offend those canons of decency and fairness which express the notions of justice of English-speaking peoples even toward those charged with the most heinous offenses' (*Rochin v. [People of] California*, 342 U.S. 165, 169 [72 S.Ct. 205, 208, 96 L.Ed. 183])."

The argument boils down to a general attack upon the use of a government informer as "a shabby thing in any case," and to the claim that in the circumstances of this particular case the risk that Partin's testimony might be perjurious was very high. Insofar as the general attack upon the use of informers is based upon historic "notions" of "English-speaking peoples," it is without historical foundation. In the words of Judge Learned Hand, "Courts have countenanced the use of informers from time immemorial; in cases of conspiracy, or in other cases when the crime consists of preparing for another crime, it is usually necessary to rely upon them or upon accomplices because the criminals will almost certainly proceed covertly. * * * " *United States v. Dennis*, 2 Cir., 183 F.2d 201, at 224.

This is not to say that a secret government informer is to the slightest degree more free from all relevant constitutional restrictions than is any other government agent. It *is* to say that the use of secret informers is not *per se* unconstitutional.

The petitioner is quite correct in the contention that Partin, perhaps even more than most informers, may have had motives to lie. But it does not follow that his testimony was untrue, nor does it follow that his testimony was constitutionally inadmissible. The established safeguards of the Anglo-American legal system leave the veracity of a witness to be tested by cross-examination, and the credibility of his testimony to be determined by a properly instructed jury. At the trial of this case, Partin was subjected to rigorous cross-examination, and the extent and nature of his dealings with federal and state authorities were insistently explored. The trial judge instructed the jury, both specifically and generally, with regard to assessing Partin's credibility. The Constitution does not require us to upset the jury's verdict.

Affirmed.

NOTES

1.   **Use of Transmitters or Recorders.** If an undercover agent uses electronic devices, does the investigation involve a search? Should it make any difference whether the undercover agent merely records a conversation with the suspect, or causes it to be transmitted for hearing (and perhaps recording) by others?

In United States v. White, 401 U.S. 745, 91 S.Ct. 1122 (1971), White was charged with drug transactions with a government informer, Harvey Jackson. Jackson had carried a radio transmitter concealed on his person and nearby government agents listened to the transaction by this means. At trial, Jackson was not available and, over objection, the trial judge permitted the government agents to testify to what they overheard; White was convicted. On appeal, the Court of Appeals read On Lee v. United States, 343 U.S. 747, 72 S.Ct. 967 (1952), as holding that use of such a transmitting device did not make Jackson's conduct a search. But it further read Katz v. United States, 389 U.S. 347, 88 S.Ct. 507 (1967), as overruling *On Lee*. Under *Katz*, it continued, Jackson's activity was a search conducted without a warrant. Therefore the agents' testimony was inadmissible. The Supreme Court reversed. In an opinion announcing the judgment of the Court and joined by three other members of the Court, Justice White relied upon two grounds. First, the Court of Appeals erred in reading *Katz* as overruling *On Lee*:

> If the conduct and revelations of an agent operating without electronic equipment do not invade the defendant's constitutionally justifiable expectations of privacy, neither does a simultaneous recording of the same conversation made by the agent or by others from transmissions received from the agent to whom the defendant is talking and whose trustworthiness the defendant necessarily risks.

401 U.S. at 751, 91 S.Ct. at 1126. Second, under Desist v. United States, 394 U.S. 244, 89 S.Ct. 1030 (1969), *Katz* was not to be applied to surveillance which—like that in *On Lee*—took place before the decision in *Katz*. Judged by pre-*Katz* law, i.e., *On Lee*, the facts presented no search.

Justices Harlan, Marshall, and Douglas dissented separately; each expressed the view that *Desist* was wrongly decided and should not be followed. All also took the position that *On Lee* should no longer be regarded as controlling, and that Jackson's activity implicated the Fourth Amendment. Justice Harlan explained:

> The critical question * * * is whether under our system of government, as reflected in the Constitution, we should impose on our citizens the risk of the electronic listener or observer without at least the protection of a warrant requirement.
>
> This question must, in my view, be answered by assessing the nature of a particular practice and the likely extent of its impact on the individual's sense of security balanced against the utility of the conduct as a technique of law enforcement. * * *
>
> The impact of the practice of third-party bugging must, I think, be considered such as to undermine that confidence and sense of security in dealing with one another that is characteristic of individual relationships between citizens in a free society. It goes beyond the impact on privacy occasioned by the ordinary type of "informer" investigation * * *. The argument of the plurality opinion, to the effect that it is irrelevant whether secrets are revealed by the mere tattletale or the transistor, ignores the differences occasioned by third-party monitoring and recording which insures full and accurate disclosure of all that is said, free of the possibility of error and oversight that inheres in human reporting.

401 U.S. at 786–87, 91 S.Ct. at 1143. Overruling *On Lee*, he stressed, would not end third-party monitoring of informants but rather prevent law enforcement officers from engaging in the practice "unless they first had probable cause to suspect an individual of involvement in illegal activities and had tested their version of the facts before a detached judicial officer." Justice Harlan noted that recording of a transaction by an informer-participant (without transmission of it to others) was not at issue. He observed, however, that such a situation might be distinguished on the ground the informer may renege and not provide the recording to the Government; where transmission of the conversation is involved, however, the intrusion involved in providing the government with a documented record of the conversation "is instantaneous."

Justice Marshall expressed the view that in light of *Katz*, *On Lee* "cannot be considered viable." Justice Douglas' general discussion strongly suggested he would regard either participant recording or transmission as a search.

Justice Brennan concurred in the result on the ground that, under *Desist*, the case was controlled by *On Lee*. But he further offered that in his view "current Fourth Amendment jurisprudence interposes a warrant requirement not only in cases of third-party electronic monitoring * * * but also in cases of electronic recording by a government agent of a face-to-face conversation with a criminal suspect." Justice Black also concurred in the result only. He expressed disagreement with the plurality's reliance upon *Desist* because, in his view, exclusionary rule cases should be applied retroactively. But relying upon his dissent in *Katz*, he took the position that eavesdropping by electronic means cannot constitute a search (i.e., *Katz* was wrongly decided) and therefore Jackson's activities did not constitute a search for Fourth Amendment purposes.

Does *White* settle the issue of transmission of a conversation by an undercover agent? Justices Brennan, Douglas, Marshall and Harlan expressed the view that Jackson's conduct constituted a search under the Fourth Amendment; the four Justices in the plurality were obviously committed to the opposite position. Justice Black's action can be characterized as a refusal to address the effect of *Katz* upon this situation because he regarded *Katz* as wrongly decided.

Despite the Government's apparent victory in *White*, on October 16, 1972, the United States Attorney General issued a memorandum requiring Department of Justice approval for all consensual monitoring of nontelephone conversations by federal departments or agencies. If fewer than 48 hours are available to obtain such approval or if exigent circumstances preclude an effort to secure Department of Justice approval, the head of the department or agency (or someone designated by the head) may authorize the action. In United States v. Caceres, 440 U.S. 741, 99 S.Ct. 1465 (1979), the Supreme Court refused to require the exclusion in a federal criminal trial of evidence obtained in violation of Internal Revenue Service regulations adopted pursuant to the Attorney General's memorandum.

2. **Literal "Searches" Conducted by Undercover Officers.** Is the Fourth Amendment applicable if an undercover officer engages in a more

traditional "search," as contrasted with the efforts to overhear conversations involved in *Hoffa*? The leading case is Gouled v. United States, 255 U.S. 298, 41 S.Ct. 261 (1921). Army intelligence personnel suspected Gouled of involvement in a scheme to defraud the Government. They discovered an enlisted man assigned to intelligence, Cohen, was a business associate of Gouled and directed him to visit Gouled to see what he could learn. The formal certificate before the Supreme Court stated that Cohen came to Gouled's office during his absence on the pretense of making a friendly call, gained admission to the office, and—in a manner not detailed—found and seized a certain document later admitted at trial. The Solicitor General, however, urged this version of the facts was not supported by the only evidence directly bearing upon the matter, Cohen's own testimony. Cohen testified that Gouled was in his office when he arrived and the two chatted; when Gouled stepped out for a moment, Cohen took the document at issue from the top of Gouled's desk. The Court's opinion stated that Cohen "pretending to make a friendly call upon the defendant gained admission to his office and in his absence * * * seized and carried away" the document. It is not clear whether Gouled, if present at the time of Cohen's visit, was aware of Cohen's status as an army intelligence agent.

The Court held that the manner in which the document was obtained constituted an unreasonable search within the meaning of the Fourth Amendment.

> [W]hether entrance to the home or office of a person suspected of crime be obtained * * * by stealth, or through social acquaintance, or in the guise of a business call, and whether the owner be present or not when [the officer] enters, any search and seizure subsequently and secretly made in his absence falls within the scope of the prohibition of the Fourth Amendment * * * .

255 U.S. at 306, 41 S.Ct. at 264.

Gouled can be read as holding only that if an undercover officer obtains consent to enter premises or to inspect items through deception, the offficer cannot exceed the scope of that consent. Thus the decision may rest upon the proposition that Cohen's entry into the office, although pursuant to consent obtained by deception, was permissible. When he approached the desk, rummaged through the papers (if he did so), or seized the document, however, he exceeded the scope of that consent and his conduct was no longer supportable on the basis of the consent. It is also possible, however, to read *Gouled* more broadly as imposing or at least suggesting more stringent limitations upon some undercover activities.

CHAPTER 8

GRAND JURY INVESTIGATIVE FUNCTIONS

Analysis

A. Introduction
B. The Subpoena Power
C. Questioning and the Privilege Against Compelled Self-Incrimination

---

The grand jury serves two distinct functions. One is a screening function; the grand jury evaluates evidence supporting possible charges and returns an indictment only in those cases in which the evidence amounts to at least probable cause to believe the accused committed the offense. The other is an investigatorial function: the grand jury sometimes develops information that is of value in determining whether grounds for a charge exist and—perhaps incidentally—in proving that charge at the defendant's criminal trial. The second function is the subject of this chapter.

A. INTRODUCTION

EDITORS' INTRODUCTION: GRAND JURY INVESTIGATIVE POWERS

The unique advantage the grand jury has as an investigatorial agency is its subpoena power. Unlike police officers or prosecutors, the grand jury can compel persons, under threat of contempt, to appear, be sworn, and—in absence of a legal privilege—to accurately answer questions. Note, The Grand Jury—Its Investigatory Powers and Limitations, 37 Minn.L.Rev. 586, 606 (1953). See also, Note, The Grand Jury as an Investigatory Body, 74 Harv.L.Rev. 590 (1961). In addition, a grand jury subpoena can direct persons to bring with them papers, documents, or physical items for production to the grand jury. A subpoena directing appearance for oral testimony is often called a subpoena *ad testificandum*, while a subpoena directing the production of items is called a subpoena *duces tecum*. See State ex rel. Pollard v. Criminal Court, 263 Ind. 236, 329 N.E.2d 573 (1975).

Investigatory Role

The grand jury's investigatory role developed out of its function in screening charges. Although the government often presented a proposed criminal charge to the grand jury for consideration, grand juries were traditionally free to act on their own knowledge and return charges on this basis. Costello v. United States, 350 U.S. 359, 362, 76 S.Ct. 406, 408

(1956). Moreover, the grand jury could develop its own information even in the absence of a proposed criminal charge submitted by the government. See Hale v. Henkel, 201 U.S. 43, 26 S.Ct. 370 (1906). The authority to subpoena witnesses and documents developed as an aid in performing the duty to develop information to use in deciding whether to return formal criminal charges. The Supreme Court has commented:

> [T]he grand jury * * * plays an important role in fair and effective law enforcement * * * . Because its task is to inquire into the existence of possible criminal conduct and to return only well-founded indictments, its investigative powers are necessarily broad. "It is a grand inquest, a body with powers of investigation and inquisition, the scope of whose inquiries is not to be limited narrowly by questions of propriety or forecasts of the probable results of the investigation, or by doubts whether any particular individual will be found properly subject to an accused action of crime." *Blair v. United States*, 250 U.S. 273, 282, 39 S.Ct. 468, 471, 63 L.Ed. 979 (1919). Hence, the grand jury's authority to subpoena witnesses is not only historic * * * but essential to its task.

Branzburg v. Hayes, 408 U.S. 665, 687–88, 92 S.Ct. 2646, 2660 (1972).

The traditional absence of legal limitations upon the grand jury's inquiries—both their scope and method—is justified on the need for full information, the absence of danger of abuse of the power due in large part to the lay composition of the groups, and the difficulty of imposing such limitations without unduly impeding the work of the bodies. In Costello v. United States, for example, the Court described the grand jury as "a body of laymen, free from technical rules, acting in secret, pledged to indict no one because of prejudice and to free no one because of special favor." Clearly the Court regarded the solemn nature of grand jury service and the absence of a professional or occupational bias in favor of law enforcement as sufficient to prevent abuse of the grand jury's investigatorial powers—at least in light of the disruption and cost entailed in any efforts to regulate those powers by legal means.

Grand Jury Subpoena Power

The grand jury typically has the authority to invoke the subpoena power of the court which called the grand jury into existence. It may subpoena witnesses to testify or—by use of a subpoena *duces tecum*—to produce documents or other physical things. A subpoena may direct the person to submit to a procedure (such as the taking of a saliva sample) or to more actively participate in a procedure (such as by providing a handwriting sample).

In theory, perhaps, the grand jury decides whether to compel appearance of a witness and the court determines whether to issue the subpoena. But in practice the situation may be far different:

[A]lthough like all federal court subpoenas grand jury subpoenas are issued in the name of the district court over the signature of the clerk, they are issued pro forma and in blank to anyone requesting them. The court exercises no prior control whatsoever over their use. * * * [A]lthough grand jury subpoenas are occasionally discussed as if they were instrumentalities of the grand jury, they are in fact almost universally instrumentalities of the United States Attorney's office or of some other investigative or prosecutorial department of the executive branch.

In re Grand Jury Proceedings, 486 F.2d 85, 90 (3d Cir.1973). This description of practice has been repeated. E.g., In re Grand Jury Proceeding Related to M/V DELTUVA, 752 F.Supp.2d 173, 177 (D.Puerto Rico 2010).

A grand jury may not itself punish an actual or potential witness for failing to respond to the subpoena or for declining to answer questions. Only the court which called the grand jury into existence can exercise contempt power. See 28 U.S.C.A. § 1826. In the federal system, the scenario often develops as follows: A witness appears before the grand jury but refuses to answer questions put. The refusal is brought to the attention of the judge, who considers the witness's reasons, if any, for refusing to answer. The judge then orders the witness to testify. The witness is returned to the grand jury room. If the witness persists in refusing to respond, the matter goes back to the judge and contempt proceedings begin. See Note, Coercive Contempt and the Federal Grand Jury, 79 Colum.L.Rev. 735, 746 n. 83 (1979).

In the contempt proceeding, the witness has an opportunity to assert defenses, i.e., any legal reason for declining to answer. 28 U.S.C.A. § 1826(a) provides for contempt sanctions if a witness has refused to comply with a court order "without just cause." If found in contempt, the witness may be confined until s/he is willing to comply. But such confinement cannot, generally, extend beyond the term of the grand jury. Shillitani v. United States, 384 U.S. 364, 86 S.Ct. 1531 (1966). A witness found in contempt can also be given a "criminal contempt" penalty, which generally provides no provision for escape from the penalty by complying with the initial order or directive. The Supreme Court indicated in *Shillitani*, however, that the lower federal courts should regard so-called "civil" contempt as the preferred response to an uncooperative witness.

Prior to compliance with a grand jury subpoena, a person on whom a subpoena has been served can challenge the subpoena by a motion "quash" the subpoena in the court which called the grand jury into existence. The criteria to be applied in such proceedings is considered in the Notes following the case in the first subchapter that follows.

Independence of Grand Jury

Perhaps the major issue in structuring grand jury investigation tools is the extent to which some characteristics of the body render it less susceptible to abuse than other investigatorial agencies. It is traditionally regarded as an independent body, in part because its screening and indictment functions assume such independence; this independence is assumed carry over into its use of the subpoena power for purposes of investigation.

Detractors of the grand jury argue that it is in fact not independent because prosecutors tend to dominate grand juries. Prosecutors are generally given the right to be present during the investigatory stages of the grand jury process, although they may not remain in the chamber for the jury's deliberation and vote on a proposed indictment. E.g., Fed.R.Crim.Pro. 6(d). Although prosecutors have no formal legal power to control the grand jury, they have immense practical authority. Prosecutors generally propose avenues of inquiry, subpoena witnesses, question witnesses when they appear, and advise the grand jurors concerning all matters. One commentator, after noting the "plain fact" of the prosecutor's dominance over the grand jury, concluded:

> The real evil of the grand jury system—its viciousness, if you will—lies not so much in the fact that the grand jury is * * * the prosecutor's alter ego, as it does in our pretensions that it is actually an informed and independent quasi-judicial organ, a pretension which misrepresents the prosecutor's unilateral action as the product of stately proceedings conducted by judicial standards. Therefore, * * * the grand jury * * * ironically * * * encourages abuses by allowing the prosecuting authority to carry on its work with complete anonymity and with effects greatly magnified by the accompanying judicial rites.

Antell, The Modern Grand Jury: Benighted Supergovernment, 51 A.B.A.J. 153, 156 (1965).

"One Man" Grand Juries

A number of jurisdictions have curious procedures for judicial participation in the investigation of suspected criminal offenses that somewhat resembles the traditional grand jury. These procedures are more streamlined because they provide for inquiry by single judges. See Conn.Gen.Stat. §§ 54–47b–54–47(h) (providing for "investigatory grand jury" that may consist of a single judge); Kan. Stat. Ann. § 22–3101 (providing for what is termed an "inquisition" by a single judge); Mich.Con.Law § 767.3. In some jurisdictions, a judge functioning in this capacity is labeled a "special inquiry" judge. See Idaho Code §§ 19–1116– 19–1123; Wash.Rev.Code Ann. § 10.27.170. More traditionally, judges operating under such a procedure are referred to as "one man" grand juries. See In re Slattery, 310 Mich. 458, 461, 17 N.W.2d 251, 252 (1945).

The judge typically has the power to subpoena witnesses, compel testimony with the contempt power, and grant immunity to witnesses. At the conclusion of the inquiry, the judge may issue a report or direct the apprehension of the suspect (if probable cause is found), but does not appear to have authority to return formal charges. Authority to bring formal charges remains in the traditional grand jury, if the jurisdiction affords defendants the right to grand jury indictment, or in the prosecutor. See In re Judicial Inquiry Number 2005–02, 293 Conn. 247, 252, 977 A.2d 166, 169 (Conn.2009) ("investigatory grand jury" cannot indict but conducts an inquiry and makes a report to the court).

The rationale for this procedure was discussed by the Michigan Supreme Court in In re Colacasides, 379 Mich. 69, 150 N.W.2d 1 (1967):

> Experience has demonstrated * * * that regularly constituted law enforcement agencies sometimes are unable effectively and lawfully to enforce the laws, particularly with respect to corrupt conduct by officers of government and conspiratorial criminal activity on an organized and continuing basis. Our experience has also demonstrated that the common-law 23-man grand jury is unwieldy and ineffective for the investigation of such crimes in a modern, industrialized, and mobile society. It has demonstrated also that corruption in government and organized crime are susceptible to discovery and prosecution if the investigative body has the power to compel some participants therein to testify by enforcing attendance of witness by subpoena and granting immunity from prosecution, but police agencies in this country do not possess such extraordinary power. * * * Traditionally in this country, such extraordinary power has been entrusted only to judicial officers. * * *

> This dilemma has been resolved * * * by [the] unique one-man grand jury, comprised of a judicial officer who can properly exercise the subpoena power and the power to grant immunity to compel testimony. * * *

379 Mich. at 89–90, 150 N.W.2d at 11.

If procedural protections for suspects in police investigations are properly relaxed in traditional grand jury inquiries, is such relaxation also appropriate when the inquiry is conducted by such a one man grand jury or special inquiry judge? A Michigan court read that state's statutes as permitting a witness to have counsel present during questioning by a one man grand jury but not during an appearance before a traditional grand jury. Responding to the argument that this difference violated the equal protection rights of persons appearing before traditional grand juries, the court summarily concluded "the significant differences" between the two types of proceedings justified the different rights to counsel. People v. Blachura, 59 Mich.App. 664, 667, 229 N.W.2d 877, 879 (1975).

Prosecutorial Subpoena Power

Some jurisdictions provide prosecutors with some subpoena power. See Oman v. State, 737 N.E.2d 1131, 1136 n. 4 (Ind.2000) (listing state statutes "authorizing prosecutors to issue pre-charge investigative subpoenas"). Some provide for prosecutors to themselves issue subpoenas and others authorize them to obtain subpoenas from courts. Michigan permits trial courts to authorize prosecutors to issue subpoenas. Mich. Com. L. §§ 767A.2–767A.3.

Under the Comprehensive Drug Abuse Prevention and Control Act of 1970, the Attorney General has the power to subpoena witnesses, compel testimony, and require the production of records. 21 U.S.C.A. § 876. This authority has been delegated to special agents in charge of the Drug Enforcement Administration. Such agents' exercise of the subpoena power was upheld in United States v. Hossbach, 518 F.Supp. 759 (E.D.Pa.1980).

* * *

This chapter contains two subchapters covering two aspects of the grand jury's investigatory function. The first addresses the subpoena power and the extent to which it is subject to Fourth Amendment requirements placed upon law enforcement investigation. The second considers the applicability of the Fifth Amendment privilege against compelled self-incrimination in this context and more specifically the need to afford grand jury witnesses the procedural incidents of that privilege applying in traditional law enforcement investigations.

B. THE SUBPOENA POWER

A person required by subpoena to appear before a grand jury to testify or participate in the grand jury's investigation could reasonably be regarded as seized within the meaning of the Fourth Amendment. If this is the nature of compelled appearance and participation, the courts would have to consider the circumstances under which such seizures are "reasonable" for Fourth Amendment purposes. The Fourth Amendment significance of grand juries' exercise of the subpoena power is the major issue addressed by the cases in this section.

United States v. Dionisio

Supreme Court of the United States, 1973.
410 U.S. 1, 93 S.Ct. 764.

■ MR. JUSTICE STEWART delivered the opinion of the Court.

A special grand jury was convened in the Northern District of Illinois in February 1971, to investigate possible violations of federal criminal statutes relating to gambling. In the course of its investigation the grand jury received in evidence certain voice recordings that had been obtained pursuant to court orders.

The grand jury subpoenaed approximately 20 persons, including the respondent Dionisio, seeking to obtain from them voice exemplars for comparison with the recorded conversations that had been received in evidence. Each witness was advised that he was a potential defendant in a criminal prosecution. Each was asked to examine a transcript of an intercepted conversation, and to go to a nearby office of the United States Attorney to read the transcript into a recording device. The witnesses were advised that they would be allowed to have their attorneys present when they read the transcripts. Dionisio and other witnesses refused to furnish the voice exemplars, asserting that these disclosures would violate their rights under the Fourth and Fifth Amendments.

The Government then filed separate petitions in the United States District Court to compel Dionisio and the other witnesses to furnish the voice exemplars to the grand jury. The petitions stated that the exemplars were "essential and necessary" to the grand jury investigation, and that they would "be used solely as a standard of comparison in order to determine whether or not the witness is the person whose voice was intercepted * * * ."

Following a hearing, the district judge rejected the witnesses' constitutional arguments and ordered them to comply with the grand jury's request. He reasoned * * * there would be no Fourth Amendment violation, because the grand jury subpoena did not itself violate the Fourth Amendment, and the order to produce the voice exemplars would involve no unreasonable search and seizure within the proscription of that Amendment * * * . When Dionisio persisted in his refusal to respond to the grand jury's directive, the District Court adjudged him in civil contempt and ordered him committed to custody until he obeyed the court order, or until the expiration of 18 months.

The Court of Appeals for the Seventh Circuit reversed. It * * * concluded that to compel the voice recordings would violate the Fourth Amendment. In the Court's view, the grand jury was "seeking to obtain the voice exemplars of the witnesses by the use of its subpoena powers because probable cause did not exist for their arrest or for some other, less unusual, method of compelling the production of the exemplars." The Court found that the Fourth Amendment applied to grand jury process, and that "under the fourth amendment law enforcement officials may not compel the production of physical evidence absent a showing of the reasonableness of the seizure. * * * "

* * *

The Court of Appeals held that the Fourth Amendment required a preliminary showing of reasonableness before a grand jury witness could be compelled to furnish a voice exemplar, and that in this case the proposed "seizures" of the voice exemplars would be unreasonable because of the large number of witnesses summoned by the grand jury and directed to produce such exemplars. We disagree.

The Fourth Amendment guarantees that all people shall be "secure in their persons, houses, papers, and effects, against unreasonable searches and seizures * * * ." Any Fourth Amendment violation in the present setting must rest on a lawless governmental intrusion upon the privacy of "persons" rather than on interference with "property relationships or private papers." *Schmerber v. California*, 384 U.S. 757, 767, 86 S.Ct. 1826, 1833, 16 L.Ed.2d 908. In *Terry v. Ohio*, 392 U.S. 1, 88 S.Ct. 1868, 20 L.Ed.2d 889, the Court explained the protection afforded to "persons" in terms of the statement in *Katz v. United States*, 389 U.S. 347, 88 S.Ct. 507, 19 L.Ed.2d 576, that "the Fourth Amendment protects people, not places," and concluded that "wherever an individual may harbor a reasonable 'expectation of privacy,' * * * he is entitled to be free from unreasonable governmental intrusion."

[T]he obtaining of physical evidence from a person involves a potential Fourth Amendment violation at two different levels—the "seizure" of the "person" necessary to bring him into contact with government agents, and the subsequent search for and seizure of the evidence. * * * The constitutionality of the compulsory production of exemplars from a grand jury witness necessarily turns on the same dual inquiry—whether either the initial compulsion of the person to appear before the grand jury, or the subsequent directive to make a voice recording is an unreasonable "seizure" within the meaning of the Fourth Amendment.

It is clear that a subpoena to appear before a grand jury is not a "seizure" in the Fourth Amendment sense, even though that summons may be inconvenient or burdensome. Last Term we again acknowledged what has long been recognized, that "[c]itizens generally are not constitutionally immune from grand jury subpoenas * * * ." *Branzburg v. Hayes*, 408 U.S. 665, 682, 92 S.Ct. 2646, 2656, 33 L.Ed.2d 626.

* * *

[This is] recent reaffirmation[ ] of the historically grounded obligation of every person to appear and give his evidence before the grand jury. "The personal sacrifice involved is a part of the necessary contribution of the individual to the welfare of the public." *Blair v. United States*, 250 U.S. 273, 281, 39 S.Ct. 468, 471, 63 L.Ed. 979. And while the duty may be "onerous" at times, it is "necessary to the administration of justice."

The compulsion exerted by a grand jury subpoena differs from the seizure effected by an arrest or even an investigative "stop" in more than civic obligation. For, as Judge Friendly wrote for the Court of Appeals for the Second Circuit:

> "The latter is abrupt, is effected with force or the threat of it and often in demeaning circumstances, and, in the case of arrest, results in a record involving social stigma. A subpoena is served in the same manner as other legal process; it involves no stigma

whatever; if the time for appearance is inconvenient, this can generally be altered; and it remains at all times under the control and supervision of a court." *United States v. Doe (Schwartz)* 457 F.2d 895, 898 (1972).

* * *

This is not to say that a grand jury subpoena is some talisman that dissolves all constitutional protections. The grand jury cannot require a witness to testify against himself. * * * The Fourth Amendment provides protection against a grand jury subpoena *duces tecum* too sweeping in its terms "to be regarded as reasonable." *Hale v. Henkel*, 201 U.S. 43, 76, 26 S.Ct. 370, 379, 50 L.Ed. 652. And last Term, in the context of a First Amendment claim, we indicated that the Constitution could not tolerate the transformation of the grand jury into an instrument of oppression: "Official harassment of the press undertaken not for purposes of law enforcement but to disrupt a reporter's relationship with his news sources would have no justification. Grand juries are subject to judicial control and subpoenas to motions to quash. We do not expect courts will forget that grand juries must operate within the limits of the First Amendment as well as the Fifth." *Branzburg v. Hayes*, 408 U.S. 665, 707–708, 92 S.Ct. 2646, 2669–2670, 33 L.Ed.2d 626.

But we are here faced with no such constitutional infirmities in the subpoena to appear before the grand jury or in the order to make the voice recordings. There is * * * no valid Fifth Amendment claim. There was no order to produce private books and papers, and no sweeping subpoena *duces tecum*. And even if *Branzburg* be extended beyond its First Amendment moorings and tied to a more generalized due process concept, there is still no indication in this case of the kind of harassment that was of concern there.

The Court of Appeals found critical significance in the fact that the grand jury had summoned approximately 20 witnesses to furnish voice exemplars. We think that fact is basically irrelevant to the constitutional issues here. The grand jury may have been attempting to identify a number of voices on the tapes in evidence, or it might have summoned the 20 witnesses in an effort to identify one voice. But whatever the case, "[a] grand jury's investigation is not fully carried out until every available clue has been run down and all witnesses examined in every proper way to find if a crime has been committed * * * ." *United States v. Stone*, 2 Cir., 429 F.2d 138, 140. As the Court recalled last Term, "Because its task is to inquire into the existence of possible criminal conduct and to return only well-founded indictments, its investigative powers are necessarily broad." *Branzburg v. Hayes*, 408 U.S., at 688, 92 S.Ct., at 2659. The grand jury may well find it desirable to call numerous witnesses in the course of an investigation. It does not follow that each witness may resist a subpoena on the ground that too many witnesses have been called. Neither the order to Dionisio to appear, nor the order to make a voice recording was rendered unreasonable by the fact that many others were subjected to the same compulsion.

But the conclusion that Dionisio's compulsory appearance before the grand jury was not an unreasonable "seizure" is the answer to only the first part of the Fourth Amendment inquiry here. Dionisio argues that the grand jury's subsequent directive to make the voice recording was itself an infringement of his rights under the Fourth Amendment. We cannot accept that argument.

In *Katz v. United States*, supra, we said that the Fourth Amendment provides no protection for what "a person knowingly exposes to the public, even in his own home or office * * * ." The physical characteristics of a person's voice, its tone and manner, as opposed to the content of a specific conversation, are constantly exposed to the public. Like a man's facial characteristics, or handwriting, his voice is repeatedly produced for others to hear. No person can have a reasonable expectation that others will not know the sound of his voice, any more than he can reasonably expect that his face will be a mystery to the world. * * *

Since neither the summons to appear before the grand jury, nor its directive to make a voice recording infringed upon any interest protected by the Fourth Amendment, there was no justification for requiring the grand jury to satisfy even the minimal requirement of "reasonableness" imposed by the Court of Appeals. A grand jury has broad investigative powers to determine whether a crime has been committed and who has committed it. The jurors may act on tips, rumors, evidence offered by the prosecutor, or their own personal knowledge. No grand jury witness is "entitled to set limits to the investigation that the grand jury may conduct." And a sufficient basis for an indictment may only emerge at the end of the investigation when all the evidence has been received.

> "It is impossible to conceive that * * * the examination of witnesses must be stopped until a basis is laid by an indictment formally preferred, when the very object of the examination is to ascertain who shall be indicted." *Hale v. Henkel*, 201 U.S. 43, 65, 26 S.Ct. 370, 375, 50 L.Ed. 652.

Since Dionisio raised no valid Fourth Amendment claim, there is no more reason to require a preliminary showing of reasonableness here than there would be in the case of any witness who, despite the lack of any constitutional or statutory privilege, declined to answer a question or comply with a grand jury request. Neither the Constitution nor our prior cases justify any such interference with grand jury proceedings.[14]

---

[14] Mr. Justice Marshall in dissent suggests that a preliminary showing of "reasonableness" is required where the grand jury subpoenas a witness to appear and produce handwriting or voice exemplars, but not when it subpoenas him to appear and testify. Such a distinction finds no support in the Constitution. The dissent argues that there is a potential Fourth Amendment violation in the case of a subpoenaed grand jury witness because of the asserted intrusiveness of the initial subpoena to appear—the possible stigma from a grand jury appearance and the

The Fifth Amendment guarantees that no civilian may be brought to trial for an infamous crime "unless on a presentment or indictment of a Grand Jury." This constitutional guarantee presupposes an investigative body "acting independently of either prosecuting attorney or judge," whose mission is to clear the innocent, no less than to bring to trial those who may be guilty. Any holding that would saddle a grand jury with minitrials and preliminary showings would assuredly impede its investigation and frustrate the public's interest in the fair and expeditious administration of the criminal laws. * * * The grand jury may not always serve its historic role as a protective bulwark standing solidly between the ordinary citizen and an overzealous prosecutor, but if it is even to approach the proper performance of its constitutional mission, it must be free to pursue its investigations unhindered by external influence or supervision so long as it does not trench upon the legitimate rights of any witness called before it.

Since the Court of Appeals found an unreasonable search and seizure where none existed, and imposed a preliminary showing of reasonableness where none was required, its judgment is reversed and this case is remanded to that Court for further proceedings consistent with this opinion.

It is so ordered.

United States v. Mara

Supreme Court of the United States, 1973.
410 U.S. 19, 93 S.Ct. 774.

■ MR. JUSTICE STEWART delivered the opinion of the Court.

The respondent, Richard J. Mara, was subpoenaed to appear before the September 1971 Grand Jury in the Northern District of Illinois that was investigating thefts of interstate shipments. On two separate occasions he was directed to produce handwriting and printing exemplars to the grand jury's designated agent. Each time he was advised that he was a potential defendant in the matter under investigation. On both occasions he refused to produce the exemplars.

The Government then petitioned the United States District Court to compel Mara to furnish the handwriting and printing exemplars to the grand jury. * * * The District Judge rejected the respondent's contention that the compelled production of such exemplars would constitute an unreasonable search and seizure, and he ordered the respondent to provide them. When the witness continued to refuse to do so, he was adjudged to be in civil contempt and was committed to custody until he obeyed the court order or until the expiration of the grand jury term.

The Court of Appeals for the Seventh Circuit reversed. * * *

---

inconvenience of the official restraint. But the initial directive to appear is as intrusive if the witness is called simply to testify as it is if he is summoned to produce physical evidence.

We have held today in *Dionisio*, that a grand jury subpoena is not a "seizure" within the meaning of the Fourth Amendment, and further, that that Amendment is not violated by a grand jury directive compelling production of "physical characteristics" which are "constantly exposed to the public." Handwriting, like speech, is repeatedly shown to the public, and there is no more expectation of privacy in the physical characteristics of a person's script than there is in the tone of his voice. * * * Consequently the Government was under no obligation here, any more than in *Dionisio*, to make a preliminary showing of "reasonableness."

Indeed, this case lacks even the aspects of an expansive investigation that the Court of Appeals found significant in *Dionisio*. In that case 20 witnesses were summoned to give exemplars; here there was only one. The specific and narrowly drawn directive requiring the witness to furnish a specimen of his handwriting violated no legitimate Fourth Amendment interest. The District Court was correct, therefore, in ordering the respondent to comply with the grand jury's request.

Accordingly, the judgment of the Court of Appeals is reversed, and this case is remanded to that court for further proceedings consistent with this opinion.

It is so ordered.

■ MR. JUSTICE MARSHALL, dissenting [in both *Dionisio* and *Mara*.]

* * *

The Court concludes that the exemplars sought from the respondents are not protected by the Fourth Amendment because respondents have surrendered their expectation of privacy with respect to voice and handwriting by knowingly exposing these to the public. But even accepting this conclusion, it does not follow that the investigatory seizures of respondents, accomplished through the use of subpoenas ordering them to appear before the grand jury—and thereby necessarily interfering with their personal liberty—are outside the protection of the Fourth Amendment. To the majority, though, "[i]t is clear that a subpoena to appear before a grand jury is not a 'seizure' in the Fourth Amendment sense, even though that summons may be inconvenient or burdensome." With due respect, I find nothing "clear" about so sweeping an assertion.

There can be no question that investigatory seizures effected by the police are subject to the constraints of the Fourth and Fourteenth Amendments. * * * [T]he present cases involve official investigatory seizures which interfere with personal liberty. The Court considers dispositive, however, the fact that the seizures were effected by the grand jury, rather than the police. I cannot agree.

* * *

In the present cases * * * it was not testimony that the grand juries sought from respondents, but physical evidence. The Court glosses over this important distinction from its prior decisions, however, by artificially bifurcating its analysis of what is taking place in these cases—that is, by effectively treating what is done with individuals once they are before the grand jury as irrelevant in determining what safeguards are to govern the procedures by which they are initially compelled to appear. Nonetheless, the fact remains that the historic exception to which the Court resorts is not necessarily as broad as the context in which it is now employed. Hence, I believe that the question we must consider is whether an extension of that exception is warranted, and if so, under what conditions.

* * *

The Court seems to reason that the exception to the Fourth Amendment for grand jury subpoenas directed at persons is justified by the relative unintrusiveness of the grand jury process on an individual's liberty. The Court * * * suggests that arrests or even investigatory "stops" are inimical to personal liberty because they may involve the use of force; they may be carried out in demeaning circumstances; and at least an arrest may yield the social stigma of a record. By contrast, we are told, a grand jury subpoena is a simple legal process, which is served in an unoffensive manner; it results in no stigma; and a convenient time for appearance may always be arranged. The Court would have us believe, in short, that, unlike an arrest or an investigatory "stop," a grand jury subpoena entails little more inconvenience than a visit to an old friend. Common sense and practical experience indicate otherwise.

It may be that service of a grand jury subpoena does not involve the same potential for momentary embarrassment as does an arrest or investigatory "stop." But this difference seems inconsequential in comparison to the substantial stigma which—contrary to the Court's assertion—may result from a grand jury appearance as well as from an arrest or investigatory seizure. Public knowledge that a man has been summoned by a federal grand jury investigating, for instance, organized criminal activity can mean loss of friends, irreparable injury to business, and tremendous pressures on one's family life. Whatever nice legal distinctions may be drawn between police and prosecutor, on the one hand, and the grand jury, on the other, the public often treats an appearance before a grand jury as tantamount to a visit to the station house. Indeed, the former is frequently more damaging than the latter, for a grand jury appearance has an air of far greater gravity than a brief visit "downtown" for a "talk." The Fourth Amendment was placed in our Bill of Rights to protect the individual citizen from such potentially disruptive governmental intrusion into his private life unless conducted reasonably and with sufficient cause.

Nor do I believe that the constitutional problems inherent in such governmental interference with an individual's person are substantially alleviated because one may seek to appear at a "convenient time." * * * No matter how considerate a grand jury may be in arranging for an individual's appearance, the basic fact remains that his liberty has been officially restrained for some period of time. In terms of its effect on the individual, this restraint does not differ meaningfully from the restraint imposed on a suspect compelled to visit the police station house. Thus, the nature of the intrusion on personal liberty caused by a grand jury subpoena cannot, without more, be considered sufficient basis for denying respondents the protection of the Fourth Amendment.

* * *

Thus, the Court's decisions today can serve only to encourage prosecutorial exploitation of the grand jury process, at the expense of both individual liberty and the traditional neutrality of the grand jury. Indeed, by holding that the grand jury's power to subpoena these respondents for the purpose of obtaining exemplars is completely outside the purview of the Fourth Amendment, the Court fails to appreciate the essential difference between real and testimonial evidence in the context of these cases, and thereby hastens the reduction of the grand jury into simply another investigative device of law enforcement officials. By contrast, the Court of Appeals, in proper recognition of these dangers, imposed narrow limitations on the subpoena power of the grand jury which are necessary to guard against unreasonable official interference with individual liberty but which would not impair significantly the traditional investigatory powers of that body.

The Court of Appeals in *Mara* did not impose a requirement that the Government establish probable cause to support a grand jury's request for exemplars. It correctly recognized that "examination of witnesses by a grand jury need not be preceded by a formal charge against a particular individual," since the very purpose of the grand jury process is to ascertain probable cause. * * * [I]t ruled only that the request for physical evidence such as exemplars should be subject to a showing of reasonableness. This "reasonableness" requirement has previously been explained by this Court, albeit in a somewhat different context, to require a showing by the Government that: (1) "the investigation is authorized by Congress"; (2) the investigation "is for a purpose Congress can order"; (3) the evidence sought is "relevant"; and (4) the request is "adequate, but not excessive, for the purposes of the relevant inquiry." See *Oklahoma Press Publishing Co. v. Walling*, 327 U.S. 186, 209, 66 S.Ct. 494, 506, 90 L.Ed. 614 (1946). This was the interpretation of the "reasonableness" requirement properly adopted by the Court of Appeals. And, in elaborating on the requirement that the request not be "excessive," it added that the Government would bear the burden of showing that it was not conducting "a general fishing expedition under grand jury sponsorship."

These are not burdensome limitations to impose on the grand jury when it seeks to secure physical evidence, such as exemplars, that has traditionally been gathered directly by law enforcement officials. The essence of the requirement would be nothing more than a showing that the evidence sought is relevant to the purpose of the investigation and that the particular grand jury is not the subject of prosecutorial abuse— a showing that the Government should have little difficulty making, unless it is in fact acting improperly. Nor would the requirement interfere with the power of the grand jury to call witnesses before it, to take their testimony, and to ascertain their knowledge concerning criminal activity. It would only discourage prosecutorial abuse of the grand jury process. The "reasonableness" requirement would do no more in the context of these cases than the Constitution compels—protect the citizen from unreasonable and arbitrary governmental interference, and ensure that the broad subpoena powers of the grand jury which the Court now recognizes are not turned into a tool of prosecutorial oppression.

I would therefore affirm the Court of Appeals' decisions reversing the judgments of contempt against respondents and order the cases remanded to the District Court to allow the Government an opportunity to make the requisite showing of "reasonableness" in each case. To do less is to invite the very sort of unreasonable governmental intrusion on individual liberty that the Fourth Amendment was intended to prevent.[11]

NOTES

1. **Limits on Grand Jury Subpoena Power.** Trial courts that have convened grand juries can often entertain motions to quash subpoenas issued in connection with the grand jury's investigations. This provides some opportunity for judicial review of subpoenas, especially those seeking the production of documents or items.

Under Federal Rule of Criminal Procedure 17(c), a person served with a subpoena commanding the production of papers or other objects (a subpoena *duces tecum*) may move the court to quash or modify the subpoena on the grounds that "compliance would be unreasonable or oppressive." Application of the provision to grand jury subpoenas was addressed in United States v. R. Enterprises, Inc., 498 U.S. 292, 111 S.Ct. 722 (1991). A federal grand jury investigating allegations of interstate transportation of obscene materials issued subpoenas to R. Enterprises and two other companies owned by Martin Rothstein; the subpoenas called for production of records. All three companies moved to quash the subpoenas, primarily on the ground they called for material irrelevant to the grand jury's investigation; the district court denied the motions. The Court of Appeals, however, reversed. In United States v. Nixon, 418 U.S. 683, 94 S.Ct. 3090 (1974), the Supreme Court held that a subpoena calling for production of documents before trial is to be enforced only if the party seeking it shows relevancy, admissibility and specificity. The Court of Appeals in *R. Enterprises* held that these standards were also applicable to grand jury

---

[11] * * * [A] requirement that the Government establish the "reasonableness" of the request for an exemplar would hardly be so burdensome as the Court suggests. As matters stand, if the suspect resists the request, the Government must seek a judicial order directing that he comply with the request. Thus, a formal judicial proceeding is already necessary. The question whether the request is "reasonable" would simply be one further matter to consider in such a proceeding.

subpoenas *duces tecum* and those issued in the case did not meet the standards.

The Supreme Court reversed. Given the function of the grand jury, Justice O'Connor explained, the *Nixon* standards do not apply to grand jury subpoenas. Rule 17(c) imposes a requirement of "reasonableness" on grand jury subpoenas, she continued, and the Court's task was to fashion a standard for reasonableness in the context of grand jury proceedings:

> [T]he law presumes, absent a strong showing to the contrary, that a grand jury acts within the legitimate scope of its authority. Consequently, a grand jury subpoena issued through normal channels is presumed to be reasonable, and the burden of showing unreasonableness must be on the recipient who seeks to avoid compliance. * * * [W]here, as here, a subpoena is challenged on relevancy grounds, the motion to quash must be denied unless the district court determines that there is no reasonable possibility that the category of materials the Government seeks will produce information relevant to the general subject of the grand jury's investigation.

498 U.S. at 300–01, 111 S.Ct. at 728. The subpoenas at issue were not challenged as too indefinite or calling for overly burdensome production, and consequently the Court did not consider such claims.

A person served with a subpoena may not know the general subject matter of the grand jury's investigation, the Court noted. Therefore, even if such a person has a valid claim to have the subpoena quashed he may not be able to make the showing necessary under the standard set out by the Court. *R. Enterprises, Inc.* did not resolve this difficulty. The Court suggested, however, that in a case where unreasonableness is alleged, the District Court might be justified in requiring the Government to reveal the general subject matter of the investigation before requiring the challenging party to carry its burden of persuasion. To discourage subpoena challenges as a means of achieving discovery, Justice O'Connor added, such disclosure might be required *in camera*.

Turning to the facts of the case, the Court noted all three companies were owned by one person and did business in the same area. One of the three, further, shipped sexually explicit material into the district of concern to the grand jury. From these undisputed facts the District Court could have properly concluded there was a reasonable possibility the records would produce information relevant to the grand jury's investigation into the interstate transportation of obscene material. Thus the District Court correctly denied the motions to quash the subpoenas.

2. **Use of Subpoena for Intrusive Evidence Gathering.** A few courts have held that at least the ordinary grand jury subpoena process is unavailable to secure certain evidence that could otherwise be obtained only by a search reasonable under Fourth Amendment standards. In In re Grand Jury Proceeding, 455 F.Supp.2d 1281 (D.N.M.2006), for example, the petitioner—already incarcerated—moved to quash a federal grand jury subpoena ordering him to appear before a grand jury and provide a saliva

sample. The grand jury was investigating a possible violation of a federal statute prohibiting retaliation against witnesses, victims, and informants.

The District Judge noted that neither *Dionisio* nor *Mara* involved compelled submission to a bodily intrusion constituting a search under Fourth Amendment law. He continued:

> Given the lack of controlling authority and district courts' divergence on this issue, one tenet is clear: the reasonableness of a particular subpoena seeking a bodily intrusion warrants a "case-by-case approach." [*Winston v. Lee,* 470 U.S. 753, 760, 105 S.Ct. 1611 (1985)]. In essence, * * * *Winston* recognized a fact-based continuum of "reasonableness" with "probable cause" being the threshold requirement.

> Applying the *Winston* Court's fact-based analysis here, the grand jury subpoena seeks physical evidence from Petitioner that constitutes a "search." While Petitioner has a recognized privacy interest in his saliva, it is a less significant intrusion than a compelled blood sample. His Fourth Amendment dignitary concern must be weighed against the grand jury's important role in criminal investigations.

> Having received the exhibits attached to the Government's Response, it appears that the Government will not need to gather additional information to make a probable cause showing. Accordingly, this Court is hard pressed to see how requiring a warrant here would impede the grand jury's investigation in any regard.

> As noted above, Petitioner is incarcerated and the grand jury seeks Petitioner's DNA for ordinary law enforcement purposes. Therefore, no recognized exception to the warrant rule applies that, coupled with demonstrated probable cause, would justify bypassing the requirement's procedural protections.

> Under these particular circumstances, requiring the Government to obtain a valid warrant would not hinder or delay the grand jury proceedings. As such, the subpoena duces tecum is not the proper procedural vehicle to obtain a saliva sample from Petitioner. The Court underscores, however, that its holding is limited to the underlying facts.

455 F.Supp.2d at 1285–86.

Some state courts have also developed limits on the grand jury subpoena process, sometimes as a matter of state constitutional law. An Oklahoma court, for example, held that a subpoena for a blood sample should issue only if the grand jury foreman submits to the trial judge an affidavit permitting the judge to find that probable cause exists to believe the sample would result in developing evidence of criminal activity. Woolverton v. Multi-County Grand Jury, 859 P.2d 1112 (Okla.Crim.App.1993). See also, In the Matter of a Grand Jury Investigation, 427 Mass. 221, 692 N.E.2d 56 (1998) (when grand jury subpoena seeks blood sample, Fourth Amendment and state constitution are satisfied if the grand jury is shown to have a reasonable basis for believing resulting tests will significantly aid it in investigating circumstances it has good reason to believe involve crime).

3. **Subpoena Directives to Cooperate with Police or Prosecutors.** To what extent can a grand jury subpoena direct a witness not to appear or produce items before the grand jury but rather to cooperate with police or prosecutors?

In Perez v. United States, 968 A.2d 39 (D.C.2009), Perez contended the prosecutor improperly manipulated the grand jury process by serving subpoenas to force witnesses to come into the U.S. Attorney's Office for repeated questioning without presenting them before the grand jury. He also complained the witnesses were paid witness fees even though they had not testified before the grand jury. By using these tactics, Perez argued, the prosecutor intimidated and wore down the witnesses into giving false testimony to the grand jury that was favorable to the government.

The appellate court responded:

> We adopt the views of the D.C. Circuit and other federal appellate courts that the use of subpoenas intended for grand jury witnesses for the purpose of prosecutorial investigation is improper. We note that it is also improper for the government to pay fees to witnesses called to the U.S. Attorney's Office solely for prosecutorial interrogation. Under 28 U.S.C. § 1821, witnesses in federal court are to be paid a fee only for attending court or a deposition. * * *
>
> We do not mean to imply that prosecutors may not interview witnesses prior to their appearance before a grand jury in order to prepare the witness for giving testimony, provided there is no intimidation or abuse of the grand jury subpoena process for the purpose of conducting discovery. While the prosecutor may organize the testimony of potential witnesses in order to present the government's case to the grand jury in an orderly and comprehensible manner and need not present all potential witnesses to the grand jury, "[t]he prosecutor may *not* conduct [preliminary] interviews for an improper purpose such as to harass witnesses or as a means to conduct criminal or civil discovery."

968 A.2d 61–62. The record in *Perez* showed abuse of the grand jury process, as it showed the prosecutor caused several subpoenas to be served on one witness and conducted at least five interviews before presenting him to the grand jury. Perez was entitled to no relief, however, because the abuse did not lead to subornation of perjured testimony that was presented at trial by the prosecutor.

One court has condemned the use of "forthwith" subpoenas *duces tecum*, in which the person served is directed to comply forthwith by providing the items listed to the serving officer as agent of the grand jury. In re John Doe Grand Jury Proceedings, 717 A.2d 1129 (R.I.1998). But is it improper for officers serving such a subpoena to offer to save the witness the trouble of appearing by accepting the specified documents? United States v. Mower, 2010 WL 1813789 (D. Utah 2010) (no).

4. **Use of Grand Jury for Trial Preparation.** A few limitations upon the grand jury's investigatory power are widely acknowledged. It is improper, for example, for a grand jury to take testimony for purposes of pursuing civil remedies available to the government. United States v. Procter & Gamble Co., 356 U.S. 677, 78 S.Ct. 983 (1958).

Similarly, once a defendant has been indicted the prosecution cannot use the grand jury for the sole or dominant purpose of preparing for trial on that indictment. The prosecution may, however, use the grand jury to investigate yet-uncharged persons or to determine whether to bring new or superseding charges against an indicted defendant. A defendant challenging use of a grand jury on this ground must prove the prosecution was improperly motivated. See United States v. Dupree, 781 F. Supp.2d 115 (E.D.N.Y. 2011) (in light of *in camera* review of letter from prosecutors, indicted defendant failed to show that continued grand jury investigation was inappropriate).

One court refused to apply the "sole or dominant purpose" test to pre-indictment use of the grand jury. State v. Francis, 191 N.J. 571, 926 A.2d 305 (N.J.2007). Instead, "the standard applicable to claims of pre-indictment grand jury abuse must be whether the evidence sought by the State via the grand jury was relevant to the crimes under investigation, that is, did the evidence sought have 'a tendency in reason to prove or disprove any fact of consequence to the determination of the action.'" Under this approach, the prosecution may have abused the grand jury when, before indictment, it called the capital murder defendant's mother as a witness and asked her about discussions she had with a social worker employed by a mitigation firm hired by defendant's counsel to assist in the defendant's defense. 191 N.J. at 594, 926 A.2d at 319 (remanding for trial court to determine whether information sought was relevant to crimes under investigation).

5. **Self-Incrimination Privilege to Resist Production of Documents.** Grand jury subpoenas *duces tecum* direct the subpoenaed witness to produce documents or other items. Does the Fifth Amendment privilege against compelled self-incrimination justify such a witness in refusing to produce the described documents or items for the grand jury?

Despite language to the contrary in Boyd v. United States, 116 U.S. 616, 634–35, 6 S.Ct. 524, 534 (1886), Fisher v. United States, 425 U.S. 391, 96 S.Ct. 1569 (1976), held the Fifth Amendment did not protect *the contents* of a document. Any self-incriminating admissions made by putting them in the document occur before the subpoena. Thus, those admissions are not compelled by the subpoena. But, Justice White continued for the Court in *Fisher*, compliance with a summons or subpoena for documents may have incriminating and communicative aspects. Compliance with the subpoena may constitute tacit acknowledgments: (1) that the documents described in the subpoena exist and are in the person's possession; and (2) that the produced documents are the ones described and thus constitute an "implicit authentication" of the documents produced. The acknowledged facts may be incriminating. Further, he observed, the act of complying—or the act of production of the documents—is clearly "compelled." But whether particular tacit acknowledgments are both "testimonial" and "incriminating" are questions without categorical answers. Both matters depend upon the facts and circumstances of particular cases or classes of cases.

The Court then turned to tax cases like the ones before the Court in which subpoenas seek from taxpayers' lawyers work papers of the taxpayers' accountants that might incriminate the taxpayers. Justice White first noted the attorney-client privilege permitted the attorneys to resist production if—but only if—the clients could do so. In these cases, however, the client-taxpayers had no right to resist. The Government will already know of the papers' existence and the subjects' access to them; the act of production's confirmation that the documents exist and that the taxpayers have access to them will not significantly add to what the Government knew. Seeking preparation and delivery of the papers by the accountant is not illegal; any testimonial admission to these facts by the act of production, therefore, posed no realistic threat of incriminating the taxpayer. Tacit acknowledgment of the described documents' existence and their possession will not justify noncompliance.

Turning to the danger of implicit authentication by the act of production, *Fisher* noted the taxpayers lacked firsthand knowledge as to the preparation of the documents, could not vouch for their accuracy, and therefore would not be competent to authenticate them. If the documents were eventually offered as evidence of the taxpayers' guilt in a criminal trial, they would not be admissible without authenticating testimony other than evidence the taxpayer produced them in response to the subpoena. "Without more," Justice White reasoned, "responding to the subpoena in the circumstance before us would not appear to represent a substantial threat of self-incrimination." 425 U.S. at 413, 96 S.Ct. at 1582.

A witness was held entitled to resist production of subpoenaed documents in United States v. Doe, 465 U.S. 605, 104 S.Ct. 1237 (1984). Grand jury subpoenas issued directing Doe to produce certain records of his businesses. The government conceded these records were or might be incriminating. The district court quashed the subpoenas and the Supreme Court upheld this action. The facts made a sufficient showing that under *Fisher* the act of producing the documents would involve testimonial self-incrimination. By the act of producing any described documents he had in his possession, Doe would acknowledge—in a testimonial fashion—such documents did exist and they were in his possession. Further, his acknowledgments might relieve the government of the need for other evidence to authenticate those documents should they be offered against Doe in a criminal prosecution. The Court noted the Government was not foreclosed from rebutting this possibility by producing evidence the existence, possession and authentication of the documents were "foregone conclusion[s]," and therefore Doe's act of production would not significantly add to what the Government already knew and had. But no such evidence was produced. Unlike the situation in *Fisher*, the record in *Doe* failed to establish the act of production would have only minimal testimonial value and would not operate to incriminate. As a result, Doe's acts necessary for production of the subpoenaed documents were privileged by the Fifth Amendment. He could not be compelled to produce them.

The *Doe* majority further commented that production of the documents could be compelled if Doe was granted immunity from the use of evidence which might be created by his acts in producing the documents. Immunity as a means of eliminating the risk of "incrimination" is discussed later in this chapter.

C. QUESTIONING AND THE PRIVILEGE AGAINST COMPELLED SELF-INCRIMINATION

As the Supreme Court's opinion in *Dionisio* recognized, there is universal agreement that the Fifth Amendment privilege against compelled self-incrimination is available to a witness appearing before a grand jury. There is also agreement a witness can, in reliance upon this privilege, decline to answer specific questions put by the jurors or the prosecutor. The major questions concern the extent to which the privilege or sound policy requires that various procedures be followed to implement the right to avoid compelled self-incrimination. The Fifth and Fourteenth Amendments, as developed in Chapter 6, mean a suspect undergoing custodial interrogation by police must be afforded the right to the presence of counsel and warnings designed to assure he is aware of the rights to silence and to counsel. Should Fifth Amendment law impose identical or similar requirements when a suspect is interrogated before a grand jury?

There are also additional questions raised by the grand jury process. One who has been taken into custody and questioned by police generally has notice that he or she is a suspect in the investigation, since police do not do this to persons not a target of their investigation. But the grand jury may subpoena witnesses not suspected of criminal involvement, so a person subpoenaed cannot infer from the subpoena that he is a suspect. In light of this lack of notice, does or should one suspected of involvement—a "target"—have the right to be warned of that fact when called to testify before the grand jury?

United States v. Washington
Supreme Court of the United States, 1977.
431 U.S. 181, 97 S.Ct. 1814.

■ MR. CHIEF JUSTICE BURGER delivered the opinion of the Court.

The question presented in this case is whether testimony given by a grand jury witness suspected of wrongdoing may be used against him in a later prosecution for a substantive criminal offense when the witness was not informed in advance of his testimony that he was a potential defendant in danger of indictment.

(1)

The facts are not in dispute. Zimmerman and Woodard were driving respondent's van truck when a Washington, D. C., policeman stopped them for a traffic offense. Seeing a motorcycle in the rear of the van which he identified as stolen, the officer arrested both men and impounded respondent's vehicle. When respondent came to reclaim the van, he told police that Zimmerman and Woodard were friends who were driving the van with his permission.

He explained the presence of the stolen motorcycle by saying that while driving the van himself he had stopped to assist an unknown motorcyclist whose machine had broken down. Respondent then allowed the motorcycle to be placed in his van to take it for repairs. Soon after this the van stalled and he walked to a nearby gasoline station to call Zimmerman and Woodard for help, leaving the van with the unknown motorcyclist. After reaching Zimmerman by phone, respondent waited at the gasoline station for his friends, then returned to the spot he had left the van when they failed to appear; by that time the van had disappeared. Respondent said he was not alarmed, assuming his friends had repaired the van and driven it away. Shortly thereafter, Zimmerman and Woodard were arrested with the stolen motorcycle in the van.

Not surprisingly, the officer to whom respondent related this tale was more than a little skeptical; he told respondent he did not believe his story, and advised him not to repeat it in court, "because you're liable to be in trouble if you [do so]." The officer also declined to release the van. Respondent then repeated this story to an Assistant United States Attorney working on the case. The prosecutor, too, was dubious of the account; nevertheless, he released the van to respondent. At the same time, he served respondent with a subpoena to appear before the grand jury investigating the motorcycle theft.

When respondent appeared before the grand jury, the Assistant United States Attorney in charge had not yet decided whether to seek an indictment against him. The prosecutor was aware of respondent's explanation, and was also aware of the possibility that respondent could be indicted by the grand jury for the theft if his story was not believed.

The prosecutor did not advise respondent before his appearance that he might be indicted on a criminal charge in connection with the stolen motorcycle. But respondent, after reciting the usual oath to tell the truth, was given a series of other warnings, as follows:

"Q. * * *

"You have a right to remain silent. You are not required to say anything to us in this Grand Jury at any time or to answer any question."[2]

---

[2] This was an obvious overstatement of respondent's constitutional rights; the very purpose of the grand jury is to elicit testimony, and it can compel answers, by use of contempt powers, to all except self-incriminating questions.

After the oral warnings, respondent was also handed a card containing all the warnings prescribed by *Miranda v. Arizona*, 384 U.S. 436, 86 S.Ct. 1602, 16 L.Ed.2d 694 (1966), and a waiver form acknowledging that the witness waived the privilege against compelled self-incrimination. Respondent signed the waiver.

"Anything you say can be used against you in Court.

"You have the right to talk to a lawyer for advice before we question you and have him outside the Grand Jury during any questioning.

"If you cannot afford a lawyer and want one a lawyer will be provided for you.

"If you want to answer questions now without a lawyer present you will still have the right to stop answering at any time.

"You also have the right to stop answering at any time until you talk to a lawyer.

"Now, do you understand those rights, sir?

"A. Yes, I do.

"Q. And do you want to answer questions of the Grand Jury in reference to a stolen motorcycle that was found in your truck?

"A. Yes, sir.

"Q. And do you want a lawyer here or outside the Grand Jury room while you answer those questions?

"A. No, I don't think so."

In response to questions, respondent again related his version of how the stolen motorcycle came to be in the rear of his van. Subsequently, the grand jury indicted respondent, Zimmerman, and Woodard for grand larceny and receiving stolen property.

Respondent moved to suppress his testimony and quash the indictment, arguing that it was based on evidence obtained in violation of his Fifth Amendment privilege against compelled self-incrimination. The Superior Court for the District of Columbia suppressed the testimony * * * holding that before the Government could use respondent's grand jury testimony at trial, it had first to demonstrate that respondent had knowingly waived his privilege against compelled self-incrimination. Notwithstanding the comprehensive warnings described earlier, the court found no effective waiver had been made, holding that respondent was not properly advised of his Fifth Amendment rights. The court thought the Constitution required, at a minimum, that

"inquiry be made of the suspect to determine what his educational background is, and what his formal education is and whether or not he understands that this is a constitutional privilege and whether he fully understands the consequences of what might result in the event that he does waive his constitutional right and in the event that he does make incriminatory statements * * * ."

The court also held that respondent should have been told that his testimony could lead to his indictment by the grand jury before which he was testifying, and could then be used to convict him in a criminal prosecution.

The District of Columbia Court of Appeals affirmed the suppression order. That court also took the position that "the most significant failing of the prosecutor was in not advising [respondent] that he was a potential defendant. Another shortcoming was in the prosecutor's waiting until after administering the oath in the cloister of the grand jury before undertaking to furnish what advice was given."[1]

(2)

The implicit premise of the District of Columbia Court of Appeals' holding is that a grand jury inquiry, like police custodial interrogation, is an "interrogation of persons suspected or accused of crime [that] contains inherently compelling pressures which work to undermine the individual's will to resist and to compel him to speak where he would not otherwise do so freely." *Miranda v. Arizona*, 384 U.S. 436, 467, 86 S.Ct. 1602, 1624, 16 L.Ed.2d 694 (1966). But this Court has not decided that the grand jury setting presents coercive elements which compel witnesses to incriminate themselves. Nor have we decided whether any Fifth Amendment warnings whatever are constitutionally required for grand jury witnesses; moreover, we have no occasion to decide these matters today, for even assuming that the grand jury setting exerts some pressures on witnesses generally or on those who may later be indicted, the comprehensive warnings respondent received in this case plainly satisfied any possible claim to warnings. Accordingly, respondent's grand jury testimony may properly be used against him in a subsequent trial for theft of the motorcycle.

Although it is well settled that the Fifth Amendment privilege extends to grand jury proceedings, it is also axiomatic that the Amendment does not automatically preclude self-incrimination, whether spontaneous or in response to questions put by government officials. * * * Absent some officially coerced self-accusation, the Fifth Amendment privilege is not violated by even the most damning admissions. Accordingly, unless the record reveals some compulsion, respondent's incriminating testimony cannot conflict with any constitutional guarantees of the privilege.[2]

---

[1] Though both courts below found no effective waiver of Fifth Amendment rights, neither court found, and no one suggests here, that respondent's signing of the waiver-of-rights form was involuntary or was made without full appreciation of all the rights of which he was advised. The Government does not challenge, and we do not disturb, the finding that at the time of his grand jury appearance respondent was a potential defendant whose indictment was considered likely by the prosecution.

[2] In *Miranda*, the Court saw as inherently coercive any police custodial interrogation conducted by isolating the suspect with police officers; therefore, the Court established a *per se* rule that all incriminating statements made during such interrogation are barred as "compelled." All *Miranda's* safeguards, which are designed to avoid the coercive atmosphere,

The Constitution does not prohibit every element which influences a criminal suspect to make incriminating admissions. * * * Of course, for many witnesses the grand jury room engenders an atmosphere conducive to truth telling, for it is likely that upon being brought before such a body of neighbors and fellow citizens, and having been placed under a solemn oath to tell the truth, many witnesses will feel obliged to do just that. But it does not offend the guarantees of the Fifth Amendment if in that setting a witness is more likely to tell the truth than in less solemn surroundings. The constitutional guarantee is only that the witness be not *compelled* to give self-incriminating testimony. The test is whether, considering the totality of the circumstances, the free will of the witness was overborne.

(3)

After being sworn, respondent was explicitly advised that he had a right to remain silent and that any statements he did make could be used to convict him of crime. It is inconceivable that such a warning would fail to alert him to his right to refuse to answer any question which might incriminate him. This advice also eliminated any possible compulsion to self-incrimination which might otherwise exist. To suggest otherwise is to ignore the record and reality. Indeed, it seems self-evident that one who is told he is free to refuse to answer questions is in a curious posture to later complain that his answers were compelled. Moreover, any possible coercion or unfairness resulting from a witness' misimpression that he must answer truthfully even questions with incriminatory aspects is completely removed by the warnings given here. Even in the presumed psychologically coercive atmosphere of police custodial interrogation, *Miranda* does not require that any additional warnings be given simply because the suspect is a potential defendant; indeed, such suspects are potential defendants more often than not.

Respondent points out that unlike one subject to custodial interrogation, whose arrest should inform him only too clearly that he is a potential criminal defendant, a grand jury witness may well be unaware that he is targeted for possible prosecution. While this may be so in some situations, it is an overdrawn generalization. In any case, events here clearly put respondent on notice that he was a suspect in the motorcycle theft. He knew that the grand jury was investigating that theft and that his involvement was known to the authorities. Respondent was made abundantly aware that his exculpatory version of events had been disbelieved by the police officer, and that his friends, whose innocence his own story supported, were to be prosecuted for the theft. The interview with the prosecutor put him on additional notice that his implausible story was not accepted as true. The warnings he received in the grand jury room served further to alert him to his own potential

---

rest on the overbearing compulsion which the Court thought was caused by isolation of a suspect in police custody. * * *

criminal liability. In sum, by the time he testified respondent knew better than anyone else of his potential defendant status.

However, all of this is largely irrelevant, since we do not understand what constitutional disadvantage a failure to give potential defendant warnings could possibly inflict on a grand jury witness, whether or not he has received other warnings. It is firmly settled that the prospect of being indicted does not entitle a witness to commit perjury, and witnesses who are not grand jury targets are protected from compulsory self-incrimination to the same extent as those who are. Because target witness status neither enlarges nor diminishes the constitutional protection against compelled self-incrimination, potential-defendant warnings add nothing of value to protection of Fifth Amendment rights.

* * *

(4)

Since warnings were given, we are not called upon to decide whether such warnings were constitutionally required. However, the District of Columbia Court of Appeals held that whatever warnings are required are insufficient if given "in the cloister of the grand jury." That court gave no reason for its view that warnings must be given outside the presence of the jury, but respondent now advances two justifications. First, it could be thought that warnings given to respondent before the grand jury came too late, because of the short time to assimilate their significance, and because of the presence of the grand jurors. But respondent does not contend that he did not understand the warnings given here. In any event, it is purely speculative to attribute any such effects to warnings given in the presence of the jury immediately before taking the stand. If anything, the proximity of the warnings to respondent's testimony and the solemnity of the grand jury setting seem likely to increase their effectiveness.

Second, respondent argues that giving the oath in the presence of the grand jury undermines assertion of the Fifth Amendment privilege by placing the witness in fear that the grand jury will infer guilt from invocation of the privilege. But this argument entirely overlooks that the grand jury's historic role is an investigative body; it is not the final arbiter of guilt or innocence. Moreover, it is well settled that invocation of the Fifth Amendment privilege in a grand jury proceeding is not admissible in a criminal trial, where guilt or innocence is actually at stake.

The judgment of the Court of Appeals is reversed, and the cause is remanded for further proceedings not inconsistent with this opinion.

Reversed and remanded.

■ MR. JUSTICE BRENNAN, with whom MR. JUSTICE MARSHALL joins, dissenting.

* * *

I would hold that a failure to warn the witness that he is a potential defendant is fatal to an indictment of him when it is made unmistakably to appear, as here, that the grand jury inquiry became an investigation directed against the witness and was pursued with the purpose of compelling him to give self-incriminating testimony upon which to indict him. I would further hold that without such prior warning and the witness' subsequent voluntary waiver of his privilege, there is such gross encroachment upon the witness' privilege as to render worthless the values protected by it unless the self-incriminating testimony is unavailable to the Government for use at any trial brought pursuant to even a valid indictment.

NOTES

1. **Perjury Prosecutions.** Insofar as the Fifth Amendment privilege against compelled self-incrimination applies in grand jury proceedings, it provides no license to commit perjury.

In United States v. Wong, 431 U.S. 174, 97 S.Ct. 1823 (1977), the defendant was called before a grand jury investigating police corruption. She was warned of her privilege against self-incrimination and then denied giving money to police officers or discussing gambling activities with them. Subsequently, she was indicted for perjury on the basis of these statements, which were false. At a hearing on her motion to dismiss the indictment, she convinced the District Judge that because of her limited command of English she had not understood the warning concerning the Fifth Amendment privilege and, further, had believed she was required to answer all questions. The district judge suppressed her testimony before the grand jury and the Court of Appeals affirmed. A unanimous Supreme Court reversed:

> [T]he Fifth Amendment privilege does not condone perjury. It grants a privilege to remain silent without risking contempt but it "does not endow the person who testifies with a license to commit perjury." * * * The failure to provide a warning of the privilege, in addition to the oath to tell the truth, does not call for a different result.

431 U.S. at 178, 97 S.Ct. at 1825. The Court also rejected the argument that the failure to provide an effective warning violated due process requirements of fundamental fairness: "perjury is not a permissible way of objecting to the Government's [unfair or oppressive] questions."

2. **Statutory Rights of Grand Jury Targets or "Subjects".** There is wide variation concerning the rights, if any, a target of a grand jury investigation has under state case law and legislation concerning testimony before the grand jury. Utah, for example, distinguishes between witnesses who are "subjects" ("a person whose conduct is within the scope of the grand jury's investigation, and that conduct exposes the person to possible criminal

prosecution") and one who is a "target" ("a person who appears before the grand jury either voluntarily or pursuant to subpoena for the purpose of providing testimony or evidence for the grand jury's use in discharging its responsibilities"). Utah §§ 77–10a–1, 77–10a–13. A target is afforded more protection than a subject.

Often those witnesses who are targets must be warned of that fact, at least if they are subpoenaed. Indiana, for example, requires that a subpoena issued to a target "shall * * * contain a statement informing the target that * * * he is a subject of the grand jury investigation * * * ." Ind. St. § 35–34–2–5, Sec. 5(a)(1). Utah requires that at the time of appearance a subject be told he is a subject and "the general scope of the grand jury's investigation." A target, in contrast, must be told he is a target, authorities are "in possession of substantial evidence linking him to the commission of a crime for which he could be charged" and "the general nature of that charge and of the evidence that would support the charge."

New Mexico statutes require a person who is a target of a grand jury inquiry be advised of that fact and be given an opportunity to testify. N.M.Stat.Ann. § 31–6–11(B). Further, the target is not to be subpoenaed "except where it is found by the prosecuting attorney to be essential to the investigation." N.M.Stat.Ann. § 31–6–12(B).

3. **Constitutional Right to Counsel.** Under *Miranda*, a suspect has the right to the presence of counsel during custodial police interrogation. As the Supreme Court suggested in *Washington*, the Court has not extended this right to questioning before the grand jury. In United States v. Mandujano, 425 U.S. 564, 96 S.Ct. 1768 (1976), the grand jury witness (and subsequent perjury defendant) was informed that if he desired he could have the assistance of counsel, but his lawyer could not be inside the grand jury room. "[T]hat statement," the Supreme Court commented, "was plainly a correct recital of the law." The Court has subsequently, citing *Mandujano*, explained, "A grand jury witness has no constitutional right to have counsel present during the grand jury proceeding, and no decision of this Court has held that a grand jury witness has a right to have her attorney present outside the jury room." Conn and Najera v. Gabbert, 526 U.S. 286, 292, 119 S.Ct. 1292, 1296 (1999). It added that it "need not decide today whether * * * a right [to have an attorney present outside the grand jury room] exists."

4. **Statutory Rights to Counsel.** A number of jurisdictions presently provide for at least some grand jury witnesses to have counsel present during questioning. The Colorado statute providing for representation attempts to address a number of potential problems counsel might create:

> Any witness subpoenaed to appear and testify before a grand jury or to produce books, papers, documents, or other objects before such grand jury shall be entitled to assistance of counsel during any such time that such witness is being questioned in the presence of such grand jury, and counsel may be present in the grand jury room with his client during such questioning. However, counsel for the witness shall be permitted only to counsel the witness and shall not

make objections, arguments, or address the grand jury. Such counsel may be retained by the witness or may, for any person financially unable to obtain adequate assistance, be appointed * * * . An attorney present in the grand jury room shall take an oath of secrecy. If the court, at an in camera hearing, determines that counsel was disruptive, then the court may order counsel to remain outside the courtroom when advising his client. * * *

Colo.Rev.Stat. § 16–5–204(4)(d). Kansas provides by statute that any grand jury witness is entitled to have counsel present and adds:

(2)   Counsel for any witness may be present while the witness is testifying and may interpose objections on behalf of the witness. He shall not be permitted to examine or cross-examine his client or any other witness before the grand jury.

Kan.Stat.Ann. § 22–3009.

The Massachusetts statute, Mass.Rev.Stat. ch. 277, § 14A, specifies further, "no witness may refuse to appear for reason of unavailability of counsel for that witness."

5.   **Immunity.** A witness's Fifth Amendment right to decline to respond to questions in the grand jury context as well as in other situations depends upon the answers' "incriminatory" nature. If no danger of incrimination exists, there is no self-incrimination privilege to refuse an answer. The danger of incrimination can be removed by the expiration of the period of limitations for the offenses at issue, an executive pardon for them or—as is more frequently the case—an effective grant of immunity from prosecution. Brown v. Walker, 161 U.S. 591, 16 S.Ct. 644 (1896). In Ullmann v. United States, 350 U.S. 422, 76 S.Ct. 497 (1956), for example, a grand jury witness asserted testifying would result in loss of his job, expulsion from a labor union, ineligibility for a passport and general public opprobrium. Despite a grant of immunity from prosecution, he urged, he had a right to refuse to provide information to a grand jury. Rejecting the argument, the Court stressed that the Fifth Amendment protects only against criminal liability. For a grant of immunity to be effective, it added, "the immunity granted need only remove those sanctions which generate the fear justifying invocation of the privilege * * * ."

The major question presented by grants of immunity is the type of immunity required to render the privilege inapplicable. Specifically, must the immunity be from prosecution for the offenses which the answers concern (so-called "transactional immunity," because the immunity is from criminal prosecution for the transaction concerning which the person is required to testify)? Or, is immunity from the use of the answers (so-called "use immunity") is sufficient? The matter was addressed in Kastigar v. United States, 406 U.S. 441, 92 S.Ct. 1653 (1972). Kastigar had been called before a federal grand jury and was granted immunity under 18 U.S.C.A. §§ 6002, 6003. Section 6003 authorizes a federal district judge to issue an order requiring a person to give testimony or provide information if: (a) the person has refused to give testimony or provide information in a proceeding before a court or grand jury of the United States; and (b) the United States attorney requests the order. A person who testifies or provides information under such an order is entitled to certain immunity under Section 6002, which provides as follows:

> Whenever a witness refuses, on the basis of his privilege against self-incrimination, to testify or provide other information in a proceeding before or ancillary to—
>
>> (1)   a court or grand jury of the United States, * * * and the person presiding over the proceeding communicates to the witness an order issued under [Section 6003], the witness may not refuse to comply with the order on the basis of his privilege against self-incrimination; but no testimony or other information compelled under the order (or any information directly or indirectly derived from such testimony or other information) may be used against the witness in any criminal case, except a prosecution for perjury, giving a false statement, or otherwise failing to comply with the order.

Kastigar nevertheless declined to answer the questions and consequently was found in contempt of court. The Supreme Court upheld the contempt citation, concluding the grant of immunity was sufficient and, therefore, Kastigar had no Fifth Amendment basis for refusing to answer:

> The statute's explicit proscription of the use in any criminal case of "testimony or other information compelled under the order (or any information directly or indirectly derived from such testimony or other information)" is consonant with Fifth Amendment standards. We hold that such immunity from use and derivative use is coextensive with the scope of the privilege against self-incrimination, and therefore is sufficient to compel testimony over a claim of the privilege. While a grant of immunity must afford protection commensurate with that afforded by the privilege, it need not be broader. Transactional immunity, which accords full immunity from prosecution for the offense to which the compelled testimony relates, affords the witness considerably broader protection than does the Fifth Amendment privilege. The privilege has never been construed to mean that one who invokes it cannot subsequently be prosecuted. Its sole concern is to afford protection against being "forced to give testimony leading to the infliction of 'penalties affixed to * * * criminal acts.' " Immunity from the use of compelled testimony, as well as evidence derived directly and indirectly therefrom, affords this protection. It prohibits the prosecutorial authorities from using the compelled testimony in any respect, and it therefore insures that the testimony cannot lead to the infliction of criminal penalties on the witness.

406 U.S. at 453, 92 S.Ct. at 1661.

Kastigar argued that persons compelled to testify who were later prosecuted would experience difficulty in determining whether evidence offered against them was derived from their compelled testimony. In response, the Court held after a grant of use immunity, a prosecuted witness can require the Government to prove its evidence was not derived from compelled testimony. A defendant creates the Government's obligation by demonstrating the prosecution concerns a matter as to which he was compelled to testify under a grant of use immunity. The prosecution then has the burden of showing that its evidence has a legitimate source independent of the compelled testimony and is therefore not tainted by that testimony. Justice Marshall, dissenting, argued the majority's holding fails to sufficiently protect an immunized witness. As a practical matter, a criminal defendant cannot effectively challenge a prosecution claim that evidence offered at trial has a source independent of prior compelled testimony. Only transactional immunity, he concluded, can effectively protect such persons from the use of their testimony and its "fruits."

6. **Immunity and Perjury.** Immunity does not protect against prosecution for or proof of perjury committed during immunized testimony. Applying this position, the Supreme Court has permitted extensive use of compelled testimony in perjury proceedings.

In United States v. Apfelbaum, 445 U.S. 115, 100 S.Ct. 948 (1980), Apfelbaum was called before a federal grand jury to testify concerning a suspected robbery and extortion. He invoked his privilege against self-incrimination, was granted immunity under 18 U.S.C.A. § 6002, and testified concerning a number of matters. Subsequently, he was charged with perjury on the basis that during his grand jury testimony he had falsely denied attempting to locate one Harry Brown during December, 1975 and loaning Brown money. At trial, the government introduced over objection portions of Apfelbaum's grand jury testimony other than that charged in the indictment as perjured testimony. This testimony concerned his relationship and discussions with Brown, a trip on another occasion to Florida to visit Brown, and similar matters; the government argued this evidence put the allegedly perjured statements "in context" and proved that Apfelbaum knew they were false. Apfelbaum was convicted. On appeal, he successfully argued the federal statute and the Fifth Amendment prohibited, even in a perjury trial, the use of immunized testimony not specifically the basis for the perjury charge. The Supreme Court reversed the Court of Appeals.

After considering the legislative history of the immunity statute, the Court concluded Congress intended to permit use of both truthful and false statements made during immunized testimony, if use of such statements was permitted by the Fifth Amendment. It then turned to the defendant's argument that the Fifth Amendment prohibited the use of immunized testimony except for the "corpus delicti" or "core" of a perjury charge. The Court of Appeals held that use of defendant's immunized testimony must be limited to that charged as perjury on the following rationale: A grant of immunity must be coextensive with Fifth Amendment protection; this means a defendant must be placed in as near a position as possible to that which he would have occupied had he retained the privilege. The need to prevent perjury requires a narrow exception to this rule permitting the use of perjured testimony in a prosecution for that perjury. But because an immunized witness would not have given the other testimony had he retained the privilege, this other, i.e., nonperjured, testimony must not be used even in a perjury prosecution where it is relevant to guilt. The Supreme Court rejected the Court of Appeals' rationale. It reasoned that for a grant of immunity to provide protection coextensive with that of the privilege, it need not treat the witness as if he had remained silent. As long as the use of immunized testimony is limited to perjury prosecution, the exception is sufficiently narrow. "[W]e hold," the Court concluded, "that neither the statute nor the Fifth Amendment requires that the admissibility of immunized testimony be governed by any different rules than other testimony at a trial for making false statements."

Justices Brennan, Blackmun, and Marshall concurred, preferring to withhold comment on situations not before the Court. Specifically, they expressed reservation concerning the admissibility of immunized testimony in a prosecution for perjury allegedly committed after immunized testimony rather than, as in *Apfelbaum*, during immunized testimony.

CHAPTER 9

EYEWITNESS IDENTIFICATION

Analysis

A. The Scientific Background
B. Federal Constitutional Issues
C. Other Evidentiary and Procedural Safeguards Against Unreliable Eyewitness Testimony

---

The prosecution in criminal trials often relies upon eyewitness identification evidence—evidence that persons who saw the charged crimes committed believe the defendants on trial were the perpetrators. This evidence may be of several sorts. The eyewitness may testify that the witness recalls the appearance of the perpetrator, and then—in the courtroom—the witness compares that memory with the defendant's appearance. Finally, the witness specifies that based on that in-court process the witness believes the defendant was the perpetrator. This is an "in-court" identification—the identification and the process of developing it purport to occur in court while the witness is on the witness stand. Alternatively, or in addition, the prosecution may offer evidence that before trial began the witness observed the defendant—perhaps in a lineup or a showing of photographs—and at that time identified the defendant as the perpetrator. This is a pretrial and out-of-court identification.

The general rule is that eyewitness identification testimony is not only admissible but often sufficient to support a conviction. E.g., People v. Rodriguez, 408 Ill.App.3d 782, 794, 945 N.E.2d 666, 676 (2011) ("A single witness's identification of the accused is sufficient to sustain a conviction if, as here, the witness viewed the accused under circumstances permitting a positive identification.").

A major concern has been that an eyewitness's conclusion that the defendant on trial was the perpetrator will be based not upon the witness's reliable comparison of the witness's memory with the defendant's appearance but rather upon other influences conveying to the witness that the witness should identify the defendant on trial. Suggestiveness of this sort may come from many sources, including—but certainly not limited to—signals from law enforcement personnel as to whom the officers believe committed the offense and thus should be identified by the witness.

Concern regarding the accuracy and impact of eyewitness testimony has been supported by exoneration of convicted persons on the basis of DNA analysis. In many of these cases inaccurate eyewitness identification testimony was used by the prosecution and apparently not identified by judges or juries as inaccurate. A study of the first 200 exonerations, for example, reported that "[t]he overwhelming number of convictions of the innocent involved eyewitness identification—158 of 200 cases (79%). * * * In fifty-six cases (28%), the victim's identification testimony was the central evidence supporting the conviction." Brandon L. Garrett, Judging Innocence, 108 Colum. L. Rev. 55, 78–79 (2008).

An eyewitness's in-court identification testimony is, of course, generally admissible. Courts have divided on the admissibility of evidence of a pretrial out-of-court identification, although in 1967 the Supreme Court noted a trend towards admitting prior identifications at least if the eyewitness is available for cross-examination at trial. Gilbert v. California, 388 U.S. 263, 274 n. 3, 87 S.Ct. 1951, 1957 n. 3 (1967). This trend is obviously influenced at least in part by judicial (and legislative) perceptions that the trial context is itself quite suggestive and by comparison out-of-court identifications may be made under conditions rendering them more reliable than in-court identifications. See United States v. Elemy, 656 F.2d 507, 508 (9th Cir.1981). Courts, however, have generally refused to condition the prosecution's ability to use in-court identification testimony upon the prosecution's having—at least where feasible—tested the witness's ability to identify the perpetrator at a nonsuggestive pretrial identification procedure. E.g., State v. Brooks, 294 So.2d 503, 504 (La.1974) ("We know of no law * * * granting [criminal defendants] the right to a lineup prior to an in-court identification.").

The major Supreme Court decisions, considered in Subchapter B of this chapter, direct the focus of constitutional analysis upon whether pretrial procedures have been deficient in such a way and to such an extent as to render inadmissible either or both identifications made at those procedures or later during in-court testimony by the witness.

Several courts have recently addressed more critically what is sometimes called "first time in-court identification testimony," testimony in which the witness is asked for the first time in court during trial to identify the defendant as the perpetrator. In State v. Dickson, 141 A.3d 810, 322 Conn 410 (2016), for example, the Connecticut Supreme Court held that such situations involve as much official suggestiveness as some defective law enforcement lineups and similar procedures and thus they trigger the due process prohibition against use of testimony tainted by such suggestiveness. (The due process case law is discussed in Subchapter B(2) of this chapter.) Another court explained:

> The presence of the defendant in the court room is likely to be understood by the eyewitness as confirmation that the prosecutor, as a result of the criminal investigation, believes that the defendant is the person whom the eyewitness saw commit the crime. Under such circumstances, eyewitnesses may identify the defendant out of reliance on the prosecutor and in conformity with what is expected of them rather than because their memory is reliable.

Commonwealth v. Crayton, 470 Mass. 228, 237, 21 N.E.3d 157, 166–67 (2014).

Specifically, *Dickson* held as follows:

> In cases in which there has been no pretrial identification * * * and the state intends to present a first time in-court identification, the state must first request permission to do so from the trial court. The trial court may grant such permission only if it determines that there is no factual dispute as to the identity of the perpetrator, or the ability of the particular eyewitness to identify the defendant is not at issue. * * *
>
> If the trial court determines that the state will not be allowed to conduct a first time identification in court, the state may request permission to conduct a nonsuggestive identification procedure, namely, at the state's option, an out-of-court lineup or photographic array, and the trial court ordinarily should grant the state's request. If the witness previously has been unable to identify the defendant in a nonsuggestive identification procedure, however, the court should not allow a second nonsuggestive identification procedure unless the state can provide a good reason why a second bite at the apple is warranted. If the eyewitness is able to identify the defendant in a nonsuggestive out-of-court procedure, the state may then ask the eyewitness to identify the defendant in court.

141 A.2d at 835–36, 322 Conn. at 445–46. *Crayton* reached a similar result under "[c]ommon law principles of fairness" rather than constitutional due process.

Both *Dickson* and *Crayton* rejected the traditional in-court process as an appropriate model regarding the manner of developing and presenting eyewitness identification testimony and instead established a fair pretrial identification procedure as a principle foundation for such testimony. They also shifted the emphasis of challenges from an inquiry into whether authorities had done something deficient enough to warrant exclusion to whether authorities can establish affirmatively that they used a procedure designed to reasonably assure the reliability of in-court identification testimony.

This chapter begins by exploring the scientific information available relating to eyewitness testimony issues. It next considers the Supreme Court's federal constitutional case law and then other responses of the law to the issues and problems presented.

A. THE SCIENTIFIC BACKGROUND

The United States Supreme Court's basic case law on the constitutional issues raised by eyewitness identification, considered later in this chapter, was decided in 1967. But, "[a] great upsurge in eyewitness memory research began in the early 1970s, and much of this research has revealed a disturbingly high error rate and ever more ways in which eyewitness identifications and recollections are susceptible to error." Michael R. Leippe, The Case for Expert Testimony About Eyewitness Memory, 1 Psychol. Pub. Pol'y & L. 909 (1995).

In 2008, the New Jersey Supreme Court granted review in a case challenging then-existing state law standards for determining the admissibility of eyewitness testimony. State v. Henderson, 195 N.J. 521, 950 A.2d 907 (2008). In February of 2009, the court determined that the factual record was inadequate to resolve the issues presented. Consequently, it remanded for a plenary hearing on whether the assumptions and other factors reflected in current eyewitness identification law "remain valid and appropriate in light of recent scientific and other evidence * * * ." State v. Henderson, 39 A.3d 147, 209 N.J. 507 (N.J.2009). On remand, a special master conducted proceedings that resulted in a report issued June 18, 2010. The report and an extensive record were transmitted to the New Jersey Supreme Court. On August 24, 2011, that court decided two cases addressing the matter. State v. Henderson, 208 N.J. 208, 27 A.3d 872 (2011); State v. Chen, 208 N.J. 307, 27 A.3d 930 (2011).

In the portions of *Henderson* that follow, the court summarized its conclusions regarding the current state of scientific evidence on the considerations that should affect eyewitness identification law. The specific resolution of the legal questions presented in *Henderson* and *Chen* are addressed later in this chapter.

State v. Henderson

Supreme Court of New Jersey, 2011.
208 N.J. 208, 27 A.3d 872.

■ CHIEF JUSTICE RABNER delivered the opinion of the Court.

* * * How Memory Works

Research * * * has refuted the notion that memory is like a video recording, and that a witness need only replay the tape to remember what happened. Human memory is far more complex. * * * [M]emory is a constructive, dynamic, and selective process.

The process of remembering consists of three stages: acquisition—"the perception of the original event"; retention—"the period of time that passes between the event and the eventual recollection of a particular piece of information"; and retrieval—the "stage during which a person recalls stored information." Elizabeth F. Loftus, *Eyewitness Testimony* 21 (2d ed.1996). As the Special Master observed,

> [a]t each of those stages, the information ultimately offered as "memory" can be distorted, contaminated and even falsely imagined. The witness does not perceive all that a videotape

would disclose, but rather "get[s] the gist of things and constructs a "memory" on "bits of information . . . and what seems plausible." The witness does not encode all the information that a videotape does; memory rapidly and continuously decays; retained memory can be unknowingly contaminated by post-event information; [and] the witness's retrieval of stored "memory" can be impaired and distorted by a variety of factors, including suggestive interviewing and identification procedures conducted by law enforcement personnel.

* * *

Science has proven that memory is malleable. The body of eyewitness identification research further reveals that an array of variables can affect and dilute memory and lead to misidentifications.

Scientific literature divides those variables into two categories: system and estimator variables. System variables are factors like lineup procedures which are within the control of the criminal justice system. Estimator variables are factors related to the witness, the perpetrator, or the event itself—like distance, lighting, or stress—over which the legal system has no control.

* * *

Along with those variables, a concept called relative judgment * * * helps explain how people make identifications and raises concerns about reliability. Under typical lineup conditions, eyewitnesses are asked to identify a suspect from a group of similar-looking people. "[R]elative judgment refers to the fact that the witness seems to be choosing the lineup member who most resembles the witnesses' memory *relative* to other lineup members." Gary L. Wells, *The Psychology of Lineup Identifications,* 14 *J. Applied Soc. Psychol.* 89, 92 (1984) (emphasis in original). As a result, if the actual perpetrator is not in a lineup, people may be inclined to choose the best look-alike. Psychologists have noted that "[t]his is not a surprising proposition." Also not surprising is that it enhances the risk of misidentification.

A. System Variables

We begin with variables within the State's control.

1. Blind Administration

An identification may be unreliable if the lineup procedure is not administered in double-blind or blind fashion. Double-blind administrators do not know who the actual suspect is. Blind administrators are aware of that information but shield themselves from knowing where the suspect is located in the lineup or photo array.

Dr. [Gary] Wells[, who holds a Ph.D. in Experimental Social Psychology and serves as a Professor of Psychology at Iowa State University,] testified that double-blind lineup administration is "the single most important characteristic that should apply to eyewitness identification" procedures. Its purpose is to prevent an administrator from intentionally or unintentionally influencing a witness' identification decision.

Research has shown that lineup administrators familiar with the suspect may leak that information "by consciously or unconsciously communicating to witnesses which lineup member is the suspect." * * * Psychologists refer to that phenomenon as the "expectancy effect": "the tendency for experimenters to obtain results they expect . . . because they have helped to shape that response." * * *

Even seemingly innocuous words and subtle cues—pauses, gestures, hesitations, or smiles—can influence a witness' behavior. Yet the witness is often unaware that any cues have been given.

* * *

2. Pre-Identification Instructions

[I]nstructions to the witness [may state] that the suspect may or may not be in the lineup or array and that the witness should not feel compelled to make an identification. * * *

Pre-lineup instructions help reduce the relative judgment phenomenon * * *. Without an appropriate warning, witnesses may misidentify innocent suspects who look more like the perpetrator than other lineup members.

* * *

3. Lineup Construction

The way that a live or photo lineup is constructed can also affect the reliability of an identification. Properly constructed lineups test a witness' memory and decrease the chance that a witness is simply guessing.

A number of features affect the construction of a fair lineup. First, the Special Master found that "mistaken identifications are more likely to occur when the suspect stands out from other members of a live or photo lineup." As a result, a suspect should be included in a lineup comprised of look-alikes. The reason is simple: an array of look-alikes forces witnesses to examine their memory. In addition, a biased lineup may inflate a witness' confidence in the identification because the selection process seemed easy.

Second, lineups should include a minimum number of fillers. The greater the number of choices, the more likely the procedure will serve as a reliable test of the witness' ability to distinguish the culprit from an innocent person. * * * [N]o magic number exists, but there appears to be general agreement that a minimum of five fillers should be used.

Third, based on the same reasoning, lineups should not feature more than one suspect. As the Special Master found, "if multiple suspects are in the lineup, the reliability of a positive identification is difficult to assess, for the possibility of 'lucky' guesses is magnified."

The record is unclear as to whether the use of fillers that match a witness' pre-lineup description is more reliable than fillers that resemble an actual suspect (to the extent there is a difference between the two). * * * Further research may help clarify this issue.

* * *

4.   * * * Feedback * * *

Information received by witnesses both before and after an identification can affect their memory. * * * [M]emories can be altered by pre-identification remarks.

Confirmatory or post-identification feedback presents the same risks. It occurs when police signal to eyewitnesses that they correctly identified the suspect. That confirmation can reduce doubt and engender a false sense of confidence in a witness. Feedback can also falsely enhance a witness' recollection of the quality of his or her view of an event.

There is substantial research about confirmatory feedback. A meta-analysis of twenty studies encompassing 2,400 identifications found that witnesses who received feedback "expressed significantly more . . . confidence in their decision compared with participants who received no feedback." The analysis also revealed that "those who receive a simple post-identification confirmation regarding the accuracy of their identification significantly inflate their reports to suggest better witnessing conditions at the time of the crime, stronger memory at the time of the lineup, and sharper memory abilities in general."

[E]yewitness confidence is generally an unreliable indicator of accuracy, but * * * research show[s] that *highly* confident witnesses can make accurate identifications 90% of the time. * * * .

[T]o the extent confidence may be relevant in certain circumstances, it must be recorded in the witness' own words before any possible feedback. * * *

5.   Multiple Viewings

Viewing a suspect more than once during an investigation can affect the reliability of the later identification. The problem * * * is that successive views of the same person can make it difficult to know whether the later identification stems from a memory of the original event or a memory of the earlier identification procedure.

* * *

Multiple identification procedures that involve more than one viewing of the same suspect * * * can create a risk of "mugshot exposure" and "mugshot commitment." Mugshot exposure is when a witness initially views a set of photos and makes no identification, but then selects someone—who had been depicted in the earlier photos—at a later identification procedure. A meta-analysis of multiple studies revealed that although 15% of witnesses mistakenly identified an innocent person viewed in a lineup for the first time, that percentage increased to 37% if the witness had seen the innocent person in a prior mugshot. Kenneth A. Deffenbacher et al., *Mugshot Exposure Effects: Retroactive Interference, Mugshot Commitment, Source Confusion, and Unconscious Transference,* 30 *Law & Hum. Behav.* 287, 299 (2006).

Mugshot commitment occurs when a witness identifies a photo that is then included in a later lineup procedure. Studies have shown that once witnesses identify an innocent person from a mugshot, "a significant number" then "reaffirm[ ] their false identification" in a later lineup— even if the actual target is present.

* * *

6. Simultaneous v. Sequential Lineups

Lineups are presented either simultaneously or sequentially. Traditional, simultaneous lineups present all suspects at the same time, allowing for side-by-side comparisons. In sequential lineups, eyewitnesses view suspects one at a time.

[T]he science supporting one procedure over the other remains inconclusive * * * .

Some experts believe that the theory of relative judgment helps explain the results; with sequential lineups, witnesses cannot compare photos and choose the lineup member that best matches their memory. * * *

Other experts, including Dr. [Roy] Malpass, [who holds a Ph.D., and is a Professor of Psychology and Criminal Justice at the University of Texas, El Paso, where he runs the university's Eyewitness Identification Research Lab,] are unconvinced. They believe that researchers have not yet clearly shown that sequential presentation is the "active ingredient" in reducing misidentifications.

7. Composites

When a suspect is unknown, eyewitnesses sometimes work with artists who draw composite sketches. Composites can also be prepared with the aid of computer software or non-computerized "tool kits" that contain picture libraries of facial features.

* * *

It is not clear * * * what effect the process of making a composite has on a witness' memory—that is, whether it contaminates or confuses a witness' memory of what he or she actually saw. * * *

8. Showups

Showups are essentially single-person lineups: a single suspect is presented to a witness to make an identification. Showups often occur at the scene of a crime soon after its commission. * * *

[A]s the Special Master found, "the risk of misidentification is not heightened if a showup is conducted immediately after the witnessed event, ideally within two hours" because "the benefits of a fresh memory seem to balance the risks of undue suggestion."

* * *

B.   Estimator Variables

Unlike system variables, estimator variables are factors beyond the control of the criminal justice system. They can include factors related to the incident, the witness, or the perpetrator. * * *

1.   Stress

Even under the best viewing conditions, high levels of stress can diminish an eyewitness' ability to recall and make an accurate identification. The Special Master found that "while moderate levels of stress improve cognitive processing and might improve accuracy, an eyewitness under high stress is less likely to make a reliable identification of the perpetrator." * * *

Scientific research affirms that conclusion. * * *

[Charles A. Morgan III et al., *Accuracy of Eyewitness Memory for Persons Encountered During Exposure to Highly Intense Stress,* 27 Int'l J.L. & Psychiatry 265 (2004),] concluded that

> [c]ontrary to the popular conception that most people would never forget the face of a clearly seen individual who had physically confronted them and threatened them for more than 30 min[utes], . . . [t]hese data provide robust evidence that eyewitness memory for persons encountered during events that are personally relevant, highly stressful, and realistic in nature may be subject to substantial error.

* * *

2.   Weapon Focus

When a visible weapon is used during a crime, it can distract a witness and draw his or her attention away from the culprit. "Weapon focus" can thus impair a witness' ability to make a reliable identification and describe what the culprit looks like if the crime is of short duration.

* * *

3.   Duration

Not surprisingly, the amount of time an eyewitness has to observe an event may affect the reliability of an identification. * * *

There is no measure to determine exactly how long a view is needed to be able to make a reliable identification. * * *

4.   Distance and Lighting

It is obvious that a person is easier to recognize when close by, and that clarity decreases with distance. We also know that poor lighting makes it harder to see well. Thus, greater distance between a witness and a perpetrator and poor lighting conditions can diminish the reliability of an identification.

* * *

5. Witness Characteristics

Characteristics like a witness' age and level of intoxication can affect the reliability of an identification.

[C]hildren between the ages of nine and thirteen who view target-absent lineups are more likely to make incorrect identifications than adults. Showups in particular "are significantly more suggestive or leading with children."

Some research also shows that witness accuracy declines with age. * * *

6. Characteristics of Perpetrator

Disguises and changes in facial features can affect a witness' ability to remember and identify a perpetrator. * * *

Disguises as simple as hats have been shown to reduce identification accuracy.

* * *

7. Memory Decay

Memories fade with time. * * * [M]emory decay "is irreversible"; memories never improve. As a result, delays between the commission of a crime and the time an identification is made can affect reliability. * * *

[T]he more time that passes, the greater the possibility that a witness' memory of a perpetrator will weaken. However, researchers cannot pinpoint precisely when a person's recall becomes unreliable.

8. Race-Bias

[A] witness may have more difficulty making a cross-racial identification.

9. Private Actors

[P]rivate—that is, non-State—actors can affect the reliability of eyewitness identifications, just as the police can. * * * Studies show that witness memories can be altered when co-eyewitnesses share information about what they observed. Those studies bolster the broader finding "that post-identification feedback does not have to be presented by the experimenter or an authoritative figure (e.g. police officer) in order to affect a witness' subsequent crime-related judgments." Feedback and suggestiveness can come from co-witnesses and others not connected to the State.

* * *

Private actors can also affect witness confidence. In one study, after witnesses made identifications—all of which were incorrect—some witnesses were either told that their co-witness made the same or a different identification. Confidence rose when witnesses were told that their co-witness agreed with them, and fell when co-witnesses disagreed.

* * *

10. Speed of Identification

The Special Master also noted that the speed with which a witness makes an identification can be a reliable indicator of accuracy. The State agrees. * * *

Laboratory studies offer mixed results. * * *

EDITORS' NOTE: JUROR AWARENESS OF THE SCIENCE

To what extent do jurors share the scientific knowledge available regarding eyewitness testimony? *Henderson* addressed the evidence on the perceptions of average persons who are likely to reflect juror understanding:

> Using survey questionnaires and mock-jury studies, experts have attempted to discern what lay people understand, and what information about perception and memory are beyond the ken of the average juror. Based on those studies, the Special Master found "that laypersons are largely unfamiliar" with scientific findings and "often hold beliefs to the contrary." Defendant and amici agree. The State does not. The State argues that the sources the Special Master cited are unreliable, and that jurors generally understand how memory functions and how it can be distorted.
>
> * * *
>
> Survey questionnaires provide the most direct evidence of what jurors know about memory and eyewitness identifications. Researchers conducting the surveys ask jurors questions about memory and system and estimator variables. The results can then be compared to expert responses in separate surveys.
>
> Survey studies have generated varied results. The Special Master relied on data from a 2006 survey (the "Benton Survey") that asked 111 jurors in Tennessee questions about eyewitness identification and memory. *See* Tanja Rapus Benton et al., *Eyewitness Memory Is Still Not Common Sense: Comparing Jurors, Judges and Law Enforcement to Eyewitness Experts,* 20 *Applied Cognitive Psychol.* 115, 118 (2006). Juror responses differed from expert responses on 87% of the issues. Among other issues, only 41% of jurors agreed with the importance of pre-lineup instructions, and only 38% to 47% agreed with the effects of the accuracy-confidence relationship, weapon focus, and cross-race bias. By comparison, about nine of ten experts agreed on the effects of all of those issues.

The State disputes the Benton study for various reasons and instead highlights results from Canadian surveys conducted in 2009, which showed a substantially higher level of juror understanding. *See* J. Don Read & Sarah L. Desmarais, *Expert Psychology Testimony on Eyewitness Identification: A Matter of Common Sense?, in Expert Testimony on the Psychology of Eyewitness Identification,* at 115, 120–27. The majority of jury-eligible participants in those surveys agreed with experts on the importance of lineup instructions, the accuracy-confidence relationship, cross-race bias, and weapon focus. *See id.* at 121–22. Still, as the survey authors acknowledged, "substantial differences in knowledge and familiarity between experts and laypersons were readily apparent for 50% of the eyewitness topics." Id. at 127.

Mock-jury studies provide another method to try to discern what jurors know. * * * In one mock-jury experiment, researchers showed jurors different versions of a videotaped mock trial about an armed robbery of a liquor store. Brian L. Cutler et al., *Juror Sensitivity to Eyewitness Identification Evidence,* 14 *Law & Hum. Behav.* 185, 186–87 (1990). To test how sensitive jurors were to the effect of weapon focus, some heard an eyewitness testify that the defendant pointed a gun at her during the robbery, while others heard that the gun was hidden in the robber's jacket. Similarly, some jurors heard the eyewitness declare that she was 80% confident that she had correctly identified the robber, while others heard that she was 100% confident. Researchers used similar methods to test reactions to eight other system and estimator variables.

The study revealed that mock-jurors "were insensitive to the effects of disguise, weapon presence, retention interval, suggestive lineup instructions, and procedures used for constructing and carrying out the lineup" but "gave disproportionate weight to the confidence of the witness." Stated otherwise, eyewitness confidence "was the most powerful predictor of verdicts" regardless of other variables. The authors thus concluded that jurors do "not evaluate eyewitness memory in a manner consistent with psychological theory and findings."

Neither juror surveys nor mock-jury studies can offer definitive proof of what jurors know or believe about memory. But they reveal generally that people do not intuitively understand all of the relevant scientific findings. * * *

208 N.J. at 272–74, 27 A.3d at 909–11.

B. FEDERAL CONSTITUTIONAL ISSUES

EDITORS' INTRODUCTION: THE SUPREME COURT'S EYEWITNESS TRILOGY

In 1967, the United States Supreme Court decided a trilogy of eyewitness identification cases designed to deal constitutionally with some risks of eyewitness identification. These decisions, and the constitutional requirements they established, are considered in the present subchapter. The first two cases, United States v. Wade, 388 U.S. 218, 87 S.Ct. 1926 (1967), and Gilbert v. California, 388 U.S. 263, 87 S.Ct. 1951 (1967), dealt with the right to counsel, the subject of the first unit following. The third, Stovall v. Denno, 388 U.S. 293, 87 S.Ct. 1967 (1967), indicated a pretrial identification procedure could be so suggestive that using testimony of the witness who participated in the procedure violated due process of law. This is the subject of the second unit.

1. ASSISTANCE OF COUNSEL

Much as the Supreme Court regarded the right to counsel as the appropriate vehicle for dealing with problems raised by law enforcement interrogation techniques, the Court also called that right into play to combat some difficulties with pretrial identification procedures. Consider what the Court anticipated would be the role of counsel in lineups and similar identification procedures. Does the right to counsel mean the right to have counsel at least heard regarding objections to the manner in which an identification procedure is conducted?

In addition, consider the effect of a violation of the right to counsel at a lineup upon the admissibility of later testimony. Specifically, consider the difference between the effect of a violation on in-court identification testimony by the witness and upon testimony as to an identification made by the witness at the lineup.

United States v. Wade
Supreme Court of the United States, 1967.
388 U.S. 218, 87 S.Ct. 1926.

■ MR. JUSTICE BRENNAN delivered the opinion of the Court.

The question here is whether courtroom identifications of an accused at trial are to be excluded from evidence because the accused was exhibited to the witnesses before trial at a postindictment lineup conducted for identification purposes without notice to and in the absence of the accused's appointed counsel.

The federally insured bank in Eustace, Texas, was robbed on September 21, 1964. A man with a small strip of tape on each side of his face entered the bank, pointed a pistol at the female cashier and the vice president, the only persons in the bank at the time, and forced them to fill a pillowcase with the bank's money. The man then drove away with an accomplice who had been waiting in a stolen car outside the bank. On March 23, 1965, an indictment was returned against respondent, Wade, and two others for conspiring to rob the bank, and against Wade and the accomplice for the robbery itself. Wade was arrested on April 2, and counsel was appointed to represent him on April 26. Fifteen days later an FBI agent, without notice to Wade's lawyer, arranged to have the two bank employees observe a lineup made up of Wade and five or six other prisoners and conducted in a courtroom of the local county courthouse. Each person in the line wore strips of tape such as allegedly worn by the robber and upon direction each said something like "put the money in the bag," the words allegedly uttered by the robber. Both bank employees identified Wade in the lineup as the bank robber.

At trial the two employees, when asked on direct examination if the robber was in the courtroom, pointed to Wade. The prior lineup identification was then elicited from both employees on cross-examination. At the close of testimony, Wade's counsel moved for a judgment of acquittal or, alternatively, to strike the bank officials' courtroom identifications on the ground that conduct of the lineup, without notice to and in the absence of his appointed counsel, violated his Fifth Amendment privilege against self-incrimination and his Sixth Amendment right to the assistance of counsel. The motion was denied, and Wade was convicted. The Court of Appeals for the Fifth Circuit reversed the conviction and ordered a new trial at which the in-court identification evidence was to be excluded, holding that, though the lineup * * * held as it was, in the absence of counsel, already chosen to represent appellant, was a violation of his Sixth Amendment rights * * * .

I.

Neither the lineup itself nor anything shown by this record that Wade was required to do in the lineup violated his privilege against self-incrimination. * * * *Schmerber v. State of California*, 384 U.S. 757, 761, 86 S.Ct. 1826, 1830, 16 L.Ed.2d 908. [This part of the Court's holding is discussed in Chapter 2. Editors.]

* * *

II.

[I]t is urged that the assistance of counsel at the lineup was indispensable to protect Wade's most basic right as a criminal defendant—his right to a fair trial at which the witnesses against him might be meaningfully cross-examined.

The Framers of the Bill of Rights envisaged a broader role for counsel than under the practice then prevailing in England of merely advising his client in "matters of law," and eschewing any responsibility for "matters of fact." * * * This * * * is reflected in the scope given by our decisions to the Sixth Amendment's guarantee to an accused of the assistance of counsel for his defense. When the Bill of Rights was adopted, there were no organized police forces as we know them today. The accused confronted the prosecutor and the witnesses against him, and the evidence was marshaled, largely at the trial itself. In contrast, today's law enforcement machinery involves critical confrontations of the accused by the prosecution at pretrial proceedings where the results might well settle the accused's fate and reduce the trial itself to a mere formality. In recognition of these realities of modern criminal prosecution, our cases have construed the Sixth Amendment guarantee to apply to "critical" stages of the proceedings. The guarantee reads: "In all criminal prosecutions, the accused shall enjoy the right * * * to have the Assistance of Counsel *for his defence.*" (Emphasis supplied.) The plain wording of this guarantee thus encompasses counsel's assistance whenever necessary to assure a meaningful "defence."

[W]e [have] * * * recognized that the period from arraignment to trial was "perhaps the most critical period of the proceedings * * * ," during which the accused "requires the guiding hand of counsel * * * ," if the guarantee is not to prove an empty right. * * *

* * *

[Our decisions reflect the] principle that in addition to counsel's presence at trial, the accused is guaranteed that he need not stand alone against the State at any stage of the prosecution, formal or informal, in court or out, where counsel's absence might derogate from the accused's right to a fair trial. The security of that right is as much the aim of the right to counsel as it is of the other guarantees of the Sixth Amendment— the right of the accused to a speedy and public trial by an impartial jury, his right to be informed of the nature and cause of the accusation, and his right to be confronted with the witnesses against him and to have compulsory process for obtaining witnesses in his favor. The presence of counsel at such critical confrontations, as at the trial itself, operates to assure that the accused's interests will be protected consistently with our adversary theory of criminal prosecution.

In sum, the principle of [the Sixth Amendment right to counsel] requires that we scrutinize *any* pretrial confrontation of the accused to determine whether the presence of his counsel is necessary to preserve the defendant's basic right to a fair trial as affected by his right meaningfully to cross-examine the witnesses against him and to have effective assistance of counsel at the trial itself. It calls upon us to analyze whether potential substantial prejudice to defendant's rights inheres in the particular confrontation and the ability of counsel to help avoid that prejudice.

III.

The Government characterizes the lineup as a mere preparatory step in the gathering of the prosecution's evidence, not different—for Sixth Amendment purposes—from various other preparatory steps, such as systematized or scientific analyzing of the accused's fingerprints, blood sample, clothing, hair, and the like. We think there are differences which preclude such stages being characterized as critical stages at which the accused has the right to the presence of his counsel. Knowledge of the techniques of science and technology is sufficiently available, and the variables in techniques few enough, that the accused has the opportunity for a meaningful confrontation of the Government's case at trial through the ordinary processes of cross-examination of the Government's expert witnesses and the presentation of the evidence of his own experts. The denial of a right to have his counsel present at such analyses does not therefore violate the Sixth Amendment; they are not critical stages since there is minimal risk that his counsel's absence at such stages might derogate from his right to a fair trial.

IV.

But the confrontation compelled by the State between the accused and the victim or witnesses to a crime to elicit identification evidence is peculiarly riddled with innumerable dangers and variable factors which might seriously, even crucially, derogate from a fair trial. The vagaries of eyewitness identification are well-known; the annals of criminal law are rife with instances of mistaken identification. * * * A major factor contributing to the high incidence of miscarriage of justice from mistaken identification has been the degree of suggestion inherent in the manner in which the prosecution presents the suspect to witnesses for pretrial identification. * * * Suggestion can be created intentionally or unintentionally in many subtle ways. And the dangers for the suspect are particularly grave when the witness' opportunity for observation was insubstantial, and thus his susceptibility to suggestion the greatest.

Moreover, "[i]t is a matter of common experience that, once a witness has picked out the accused at the lineup, he is not likely to go back on his word later on, so that in practice the issue of identity may (in the absence of other relevant evidence) for all practical purposes be determined there and then, before the trial."

The pretrial confrontation for purpose of identification may take the form of a lineup, also known as an "identification parade" or "showup," as in the present case, or presentation of the suspect alone to the witness * * *. It is obvious that risks of suggestion attend either form of confrontation and increase the dangers inhering in eyewitness identification. But as is the case with secret interrogations, there is serious difficulty in depicting what transpires at lineups and other forms of identification confrontations. * * * [T]he defense can seldom reconstruct the manner and mode of lineup identification for judge or jury at trial. Those participating in a lineup with the accused may often be police officers; in any event, the participants' names are rarely recorded or divulged at trial. The impediments to an objective observation are increased when the victim is the witness. Lineups are prevalent in rape and robbery prosecutions and present a particular hazard that a victim's understandable outrage may excite vengeful or spiteful motives. In any event, neither witnesses nor lineup participants are apt to be alert for conditions prejudicial to the suspect. And if they were, it would likely be of scant benefit to the suspect since neither witnesses nor lineup participants are likely to be schooled in the detection of suggestive influences.[13] Improper influences may go undetected by a suspect, guilty or not, who experiences the emotional tension which we might expect in one being confronted with potential accusers. Even when he does observe abuse, if he has a criminal record he may be reluctant to take the stand and open up the admission of prior convictions. Moreover any protestations by the suspect of the fairness of the lineup made at trial are likely to be in vain; the jury's choice is between the accused's unsupported version and that of the police officers present. In short, the accused's inability effectively to reconstruct at trial any unfairness that occurred at the lineup may deprive him of his only opportunity meaningfully to attack the credibility of the witness' courtroom identification.

What facts have been disclosed in specific cases about the conduct of pretrial confrontations for identification illustrate both the potential for substantial prejudice to the accused at that stage and the need for its revelation at trial. * * * [S]tate reports, in the course of describing prior identifications admitted as evidence of guilt, reveal numerous instances of suggestive procedures, for example, that all in the lineup but the suspect were known to the identifying witness, that the other participants in a lineup were grossly dissimilar in appearance to the suspect, that only the suspect was required to wear distinctive clothing which the culprit allegedly wore, that the witness is told by the police that they have caught the culprit after which the defendant is brought before the witness alone or is viewed in jail, that the suspect is pointed out before or during a lineup, and that the participants in the lineup are asked to try on an article of clothing which fits only the suspect.

The potential for improper influence is illustrated by the circumstances, insofar as they appear, surrounding the prior identifications in the three cases we decide today. In the present case, [for example,] the testimony of the identifying witnesses elicited on cross-examination revealed that those witnesses were taken to the courthouse and seated in the courtroom to await assembly of the lineup. The courtroom faced on a hallway observable to the witnesses through an open door. The cashier testified that she saw Wade "standing in the hall" within sight of an FBI agent. Five or six other prisoners later appeared in the hall. The vice president testified that he saw a person in the hall in the custody of the agent who "resembled the person that we identified as the one that had entered the bank."

---

[13] An additional impediment to the detection of such influences by participants, including the suspect, is the physical conditions often surrounding the conduct of the lineup. In many, lights shine on the stage in such a way that the suspect cannot see the witness. In some a one-way mirror is used and what is said on the witness' side cannot be heard.

The few cases that have surfaced therefore reveal the existence of a process attended with hazards of serious unfairness to the criminal accused and strongly suggest the plight of the more numerous defendants who are unable to ferret out suggestive influences in the secrecy of the confrontation. We do not assume that these risks are the result of police procedures intentionally designed to prejudice an accused. Rather we assume they derive from the dangers inherent in eyewitness identification and the suggestibility inherent in the context of the pretrial identification. * * *

Insofar as the accused's conviction may rest on a courtroom identification in fact the fruit of a suspect pretrial identification which the accused is helpless to subject to effective scrutiny at trial, the accused is deprived of that right of cross-examination which is an essential safeguard to his right to confront the witnesses against him. And even though cross-examination is a precious safeguard to a fair trial, it cannot be viewed as an absolute assurance of accuracy and reliability. Thus in the present context, where so many variables and pitfalls exist, the first line of defense must be the prevention of unfairness and the lessening of the hazards of eyewitness identification at the lineup itself. The trial which might determine the accused's fate may well not be that in the courtroom but that at the pretrial confrontation, with the State aligned against the accused, the witness the sole jury, and the accused unprotected against the overreaching, intentional or unintentional, and with little or no effective appeal from the judgment there rendered by the witness—"that's the man."

Since it appears that there is grave potential for prejudice, intentional or not, in the pretrial lineup, which may not be capable of reconstruction at trial, and since presence of counsel itself can often avert prejudice and assure a meaningful confrontation at trial, there can be little doubt that for Wade the postindictment lineup was a critical stage of the prosecution at which he was "as much entitled to such aid [of counsel] * * * as at the trial itself." Thus both Wade and his counsel should have been notified of the impending lineup, and counsel's presence should have been a requisite to conduct of the lineup, absent an "intelligent waiver." No substantial countervailing policy considerations have been advanced against the requirement of the presence of counsel. Concern is expressed that the requirement will forestall prompt identifications and result in obstruction of the confrontations. As for the first, we note that in [this] case[ ] * * *, counsel had already been appointed and no argument is made * * * that notice to counsel would have prejudicially delayed the confrontation[ ]. Moreover, we leave open the question whether the presence of substitute counsel might not suffice where notification and presence of the suspect's own counsel would result in prejudicial delay.[27] And to refuse to recognize the right to counsel for

---

[27] Although the right to counsel usually means a right to the suspect's own counsel, provision for substitute counsel may be justified on the ground that the substitute counsel's

fear that counsel will obstruct the course of justice is contrary to the basic assumptions upon which this Court has operated in Sixth Amendment cases. * * * In our view counsel can hardly impede legitimate law enforcement; on the contrary, for the reasons expressed, law enforcement may be assisted by preventing the infiltration of taint in the prosecution's identification evidence.[28] That result cannot help the guilty avoid conviction but can only help assure that the right man has been brought to justice.

Legislative or other regulations, such as those of local police departments, which eliminate the risks of abuse and unintentional suggestion at lineup proceedings and the impediments to meaningful confrontation at trial may also remove the basis for regarding the stage as "critical." But neither Congress nor the federal authorities have seen fit to provide a solution. * * *

V.

We come now to the question whether the denial of Wade's motion to strike the courtroom identification by the bank witnesses at trial because of the absence of his counsel at the lineup required, as the Court of Appeals held, the grant of a new trial at which such evidence is to be excluded. We do not think this disposition can be justified without first giving the Government the opportunity to establish by clear and convincing evidence that the in-court identifications were based upon observations of the suspect other than the lineup identification. Where, as here, the admissibility of evidence of the lineup identification itself is not involved, a *per se* rule of exclusion of courtroom identification would be unjustified.[32] A rule limited solely to the exclusion of testimony concerning identification at the lineup itself, without regard to admissibility of the courtroom identification, would render the right to counsel an empty one. The lineup is most often used, as in the present case, to crystallize the witnesses' identification of the defendant for future reference. We have already noted that the lineup identification will have that effect. The State may then rest upon the witnesses' unequivocal courtroom identification, and not mention the pretrial identification as part of the State's case at trial. Counsel is then in the predicament in which Wade's counsel found himself—realizing that possible unfairness at the lineup may be the sole means of attack upon the unequivocal courtroom identification, and having to probe in the dark in an attempt to discover and reveal unfairness, while bolstering the

---

presence may eliminate the hazards which render the lineup a critical stage for the presence of the suspect's *own* counsel.

[28] Concern is also expressed that the presence of counsel will force divulgence of the identity of government witnesses whose identity the Government may want to conceal. To the extent that this is a valid or significant state interest there are police practices commonly used to effect concealment, for example, masking the face.

[32] We reach a contrary conclusion in *Gilbert v. California*, [discussed in the notes following this case], as to the admissibility of the witness' testimony that he also identified the accused at the lineup.

government witness' courtroom identification by bringing out and dwelling upon his prior identification. Since counsel's presence at the lineup would equip him to attack not only the lineup identification but the courtroom identification as well, limiting the impact of violation of the right to counsel to exclusion of evidence only of identification at the lineup itself disregards a critical element of that right.

We think it follows that the proper test to be applied in these situations is that quoted in *Wong Sun v. United States*, 371 U.S. 471, 488, 83 S.Ct. 407, 417, 9 L.Ed.2d 441, " '[W]hether, granting establishment of the primary illegality, the evidence to which instant objection is made has been come at by exploitation of that illegality or instead by means sufficiently distinguishable to be purged of the primary taint.' Maguire, Evidence of Guilt, 221 (1959)." Application of this test in the present context requires consideration of various factors; for example, the prior opportunity to observe the alleged criminal act, the existence of any discrepancy between any prelineup description and the defendant's actual description, any identification prior to lineup of another person, the identification by picture of the defendant prior to the lineup, failure to identify the defendant on a prior occasion, and the lapse of time between the alleged act and the lineup identification. It is also relevant to consider those facts which, despite the absence of counsel, are disclosed concerning the conduct of the lineup.

* * *

On the record now before us we cannot make the determination whether the in-court identifications had an independent origin. This was not an issue at trial, although there is some evidence relevant to a determination. That inquiry is most properly made in the District Court. We therefore think the appropriate procedure to be followed is to vacate the conviction pending a hearing to determine whether the in-court identifications had an independent source, or whether, in any event, the introduction of the evidence was harmless error, and for the District Court to reinstate the conviction or order a new trial, as may be proper.

The judgment of the Court of Appeals is vacated and the case is remanded to that court with direction to enter a new judgment vacating the conviction and remanding the case to the District Court for further proceedings consistent with this opinion. It is so ordered.

Judgment of Court of Appeals vacated and case remanded with direction.

NOTES

1.   In actual fact, no further proceedings took place in the trial court. The case was remanded to the district court which scheduled a hearing. Wade, however, absconded and never appeared. Interview With Weldon Holcomb, Counsel for Wade, May, 1991.

2. **Per Se Rule of Inadmissibility for Testimony Concerning Identification Made at Pretrial Procedure.** In Gilbert v. California, 388 U.S. 263, 87 S.Ct. 1951 (1967), a companion case to *Wade*, the Court also concluded that a pretrial lineup had been conducted in violation of Gilbert's Sixth Amendment right to counsel. Unlike in *Wade*, however, at trial in *Gilbert* the prosecution solicited from one of the eyewitnesses on direct examination that he had picked Gilbert out of the pretrial lineup. The Supreme Court characterized that testimony as "the direct result of the illegal lineup 'come at by exploitation of [the primary] illegality.' * * * . The State is therefore not entitled to an opportunity to show that testimony had an independent source. Only a *per se* exclusionary rule as to such testimony can be an effective sanction to assure law enforcement authorities will respect the accused's constitutional right to the presence of counsel at the critical lineup."

3. **Attachment of Right to Counsel.** The right to counsel recognized in *Wade* applies only if the identification procedure is conducted after the Sixth Amendment right to counsel attaches. When does this occur? The case law on this is presented in Subchapter D of Chapter 6. The interrogation case law also applies to attachment of the Sixth Amendment for *Wade-Gilbert* purposes.

4. **Photo Showings.** To what extent does the right to counsel apply at investigatory procedures not involving a physical confrontation between the defendant and a potential prosecution witness?

In United States v. Ash, 413 U.S. 300, 93 S.Ct. 2568 (1973), the Court held counsel is not required at a photo array showing. Witnesses to a bank robbery were shown five color photographs shortly before trial and long after Ash had been indicted. Finding no violation of the right to counsel, the Court distinguished *Wade* and *Gilbert*. The opportunities for suggestion and the difficulty of reconstructing a suggestive lineup were used in *Wade* only to address whether—assuming a right to counsel at the lineup existed—providing counsel only at trial would be sufficient, the Court explained. Whether the right to counsel attached at the lineup in the first place was determined in *Wade* by the Court's conclusion the lineup constituted a "trial-like confrontation" requiring assistance of counsel to counterbalance any prosecution "overreaching." The critical question, therefore, is whether a photo showing is a "trial-like confrontation" in this sense.

Addressing that question, the Court noted a defendant has no right to be present at the showing of a photo display and most likely will not be present. Thus the showing is not a "trial-like adversary confrontation." There is no possibility that the defendant might be "misled" by his lack of familiarity with the law or overpowered by his professional adversary. Both sides have equal access to witnesses for purposes of showing them photographs. The traditional counterbalance in the American adversary system for the prosecution's ability to interview witnesses and to show them photographs is the equal ability of defense counsel to seek and interview witnesses himself. While counsel's ability to do this does not remove all potential for abuse, "it does remove any inequality in the adversary process itself and thereby fully satisfies the historical spirit of the Sixth

Amendment's right to counsel guarantee." The primary safeguard against abuses of pretrial identification, the Court noted, is the ethical responsibility of the prosecutor. "If that safeguard fails, review remains available under the due process standards." The majority then concluded, "We are not persuaded that the risks inherent in the use of photographs are so pernicious that an extraordinary system of safeguards is required."

2.   PROHIBITION AGAINST IMPERMISSIBLY SUGGESTIVE PROCEDURES

EDITORS' INTRODUCTION: THE DUE PROCESS PROHIBITION AGAINST EXCESSIVE SUGGESTIVENESS

The third case of the 1967 identification trilogy, Stovall v. Denno, 388 U.S. 293, 87 S.Ct. 1967 (1967), recognized a due process right to have excluded eyewitness testimony tainted by certain excessively suggestive pretrial procedures.

Stovall arose out of an attack upon a husband and wife in the kitchen of their home at about midnight, August 23, 1961. The intruder stabbed both; the husband died but the wife, stabbed 11 times, survived. On the basis of evidence found at the scene, Stovall was arrested and arraigned on August 24. The wife underwent surgery on that date for her wounds and there was still substantial question as to whether she would survive. About noon on August 25, Stovall was brought to the wife's hospital room. He was handcuffed to one of five police officers who accompanied him; two prosecutors were also there. Stovall, the only Black in the room, was required to repeat a few words for voice identification; no one could later recall what words he said. After a police officer asked if Stovall "was the man," the wife identified him. At Stovall's later trial, the wife testified that he was the person who assaulted the couple. Stovall was convicted. The Supreme Court held the right to counsel announced in *Wade* and *Gilbert* did not apply retroactively, so the failure to accord Stovall the right to assistance of a lawyer at the confrontation did not entitle him to relief.

Nevertheless, the Court found potential merit in Stovall's alternative claim that "the confrontation conducted in this case was so unnecessarily suggestive and conducive to irreparable mistaken identification that he was denied due process of law." This, the Court commented, "is a recognized ground of attack upon a conviction independent of any right to counsel claim." Whether a violation of due process of law occurred, however, depends upon "the totality of the circumstances" surrounding the confrontation. Stressing the victim's condition made the confrontation "imperative," however, the Court found no due process defect in *Stovall*.

In a number of subsequent cases the Court considered claims that pretrial procedure's suggestiveness rendered witnesses' testimony unavailable to the prosecution as a matter of due process. It has generally found such claims without merit. See Neil v. Biggers, 409 U.S. 188, 93 S.Ct. 375 (1972); Coleman v. Alabama, 399 U.S. 1, 90 S.Ct. 1999 (1970); Simmons v. United States, 390 U.S. 377, 88 S.Ct. 967 (1968).

Only in Foster v. California, 394 U.S. 440, 89 S.Ct. 1127 (1969), did the Court find a violation of the due process standard. Foster was arrested for the late-night robbery of a Western Union office; the only employee present when the two robbers entered was Joseph David, the late-night manager. The following then occurred:

> David was called to the police station to view a lineup. There were three men in the lineup. One was [Foster]. He is a tall man—close to six feet in height. The other men were short—five feet, five or six inches. [Foster] wore a leather jacket which David said was similar to the one he had seen underneath the coveralls worn by the robber. After seeing this lineup, David could not positively identify [Foster] as the robber. He "thought" he was the man, but he was not sure. David then asked to speak to [Foster], and [Foster] was brought into an office and sat across from David at a table. Except for prosecuting officials there was no one else in the room. Even after this one-to-one confrontation David still was uncertain whether [Foster] was one of the robbers: "truthfully—I was not sure," he testified at trial. A week or 10 days later, the police arranged for David to view a second lineup. There were five men in that lineup. [Foster] was the only person in the second lineup who had appeared in the first lineup. This time David was "convinced" [Foster] was the man.

At trial, David identified Foster as one of the robbers and testified to his identification of Foster at the second lineup; Foster was convicted. Finding the suggestive elements in the identification procedure "made it all but inevitable that David would identify [Foster] whether or not he was in fact 'the man,'" the Court concluded the procedure "so undermined the reliability of the eyewitness identification as to violate due process."

Manson v. Brathwaite

Supreme Court of the United States, 1977.
432 U.S. 98, 97 S.Ct. 2243.

■ MR. JUSTICE BLACKMUN delivered the opinion of the Court.

This case presents the issue as to whether the Due Process Clause of the Fourteenth Amendment compels the exclusion, in a state criminal trial, apart from any consideration of reliability, of pretrial identification evidence obtained by a police procedure that was both suggestive and unnecessary. This Court's decisions in *Stovall v. Denno*, 388 U.S. 293, 87 S.Ct. 1967, 18 L.Ed.2d 1199 (1967), and *Neil v. Biggers*, 409 U.S. 188, 93 S.Ct. 375, 34 L.Ed.2d 401 (1972), are particularly implicated.

I.

Jimmy D. Glover, a fulltime trooper of the Connecticut State Police, in 1970 was assigned to the Narcotics Division in an undercover capacity. On May 5 of that year, about 7:45 p. m., e.d.t., and while there was still daylight, Glover and Henry Alton Brown, an informant, went to an apartment building at 201 Westland, in Hartford, for the purpose of purchasing narcotics from "Dickie Boy" Cicero, a known narcotics dealer. Cicero, it was thought, lived on the third floor of that apartment building. Glover and Brown entered the building, observed by backup Officers D'Onofrio and Gaffey, and proceeded by stairs to the third floor. Glover knocked at the door of one of the two apartments served by the stairway.[2] The area was illuminated by natural light from a window in the third floor hallway. The door was opened 12 to 18 inches in response to the knock. Glover observed a man standing at the door and, behind him, a woman. Brown identified himself. Glover then asked for "two things" of narcotics. The man at the door held out his hand, and Glover gave him two $10 bills. The door closed. Soon the man returned and handed Glover two glassine bags.[3] While the door was open, Glover stood within two feet of the person from whom he made the purchase and observed his face. Five to seven minutes elapsed from the time the door first opened until it closed the second time.

Glover and Brown then left the building. This was about eight minutes after their arrival. Glover drove to headquarters where he described the seller to D'Onofrio and Gaffey. Glover at that time did not know the identity of the seller. He described him as being "a colored man, approximately five feet eleven inches tall, dark complexion, black hair, short Afro style, and having high cheekbones, and of heavy build. He was wearing at the time blue pants and a plaid shirt." D'Onofrio, suspecting from this description that respondent might be the seller, obtained a photograph of respondent from the Records Division of the Hartford Police Department. He left it at Glover's office. D'Onofrio was not acquainted with respondent personally but did know him by sight and had seen him "[s]everal times" prior to May 5. Glover, when alone, viewed the photograph for the first time upon his return to headquarters on May 7; he identified the person shown as the one from whom he had purchased the narcotics.

---

[2]   It appears that the door on which Glover knocked may not have been that of the Cicero apartment. Petitioner concedes, in any event, that the transaction effected "was with some other person than had been intended."

[3]   This was Glover's testimony. Brown later was called as a witness for the prosecution. He testified on direct examination that, due to his then use of heroin, he had no clear recollection of the details of the incident. On cross-examination, as in an interview with defense counsel the preceding day, he said that it was a woman who opened the door, received the money, and thereafter produced the narcotics. On redirect, he acknowledged that he was using heroin daily at the time, that he had had some that day, and that there was "an inability to recall and remember events."

The toxicological report on the contents of the glassine bags revealed the presence of heroin. The report was dated July 16, 1970.

Respondent was arrested on July 27 while visiting at the apartment of a Mrs. Ramsey on the third floor of 201 Westland. This was the apartment at which the narcotics sale had taken place on May 5.[4]

Respondent was charged, in a two-count information, with possession and sale of heroin * * * . At his trial in January 1971, the photograph from which Glover had identified respondent was received in evidence without objection on the part of the defense. Glover also testified that, although he had not seen respondent in the eight months that had elapsed since the sale, "there [was] no doubt whatsoever" in his mind that the person shown on the photograph was respondent. Glover also made a positive in-court identification without objection.

No explanation was offered by the prosecution for the failure to utilize a photographic array or to conduct a lineup.

Respondent, who took the stand in his own defense, testified that on May 5, the day in question, he had been ill at his Albany Avenue apartment ("a lot of back pains, muscle spasms * * * a bad heart * * * high blood pressure * * * neuralgia in my face, and sinus,") and that at no time on that particular day had he been at 201 Westland. His wife testified that she recalled, after her husband had refreshed her memory, that he was home all day on May 5. Doctor Wesley M. Vietzke, an internist and assistant professor of medicine at the University of Connecticut, testified that respondent had consulted him on April 15, 1970, and that he took a medical history from him, heard his complaints about his back and facial pain, and discovered that he had high blood pressure. The physician found respondent, subjectively, "in great discomfort." Respondent in fact underwent surgery for a herniated disc at L5 and S1 on August 17.

The jury found respondent guilty on both counts of the information. He received a sentence of not less than six nor more than nine years. His conviction was affirmed *per curiam* by the Supreme Court of Connecticut.

Fourteen months later, respondent filed a petition for habeas corpus in the United States District Court for the District of Connecticut. He alleged that the admission of the identification testimony at his state trial deprived him of due process of law to which he was entitled under the Fourteenth Amendment. The District Court * * * dismissed respondent's petition. On appeal, the United States Court of Appeals for the Second Circuit reversed [and ordered relief granted].

In brief summary, the court felt that evidence as to the photograph should have been excluded, regardless of reliability, because the

---

[4]   Respondent testified: "Lots of times I have been there before in that building." He also testified that Mrs. Ramsey was a friend of his wife, that her apartment was the only one in the building he ever visited, and that he and his family, consisting of his wife and five children, did not live there but at 453 Albany Avenue, Hartford.

examination of the single photograph was unnecessary and suggestive. And, in the court's view, the evidence was unreliable in any event. We granted certiorari.

* * *

IV.

Petitioner at the outset acknowledges that "the procedure in the instant case was suggestive [because only one photograph was used] and unnecessary" [because there was no emergency or exigent circumstance]. The respondent, in agreement with the Court of Appeals, proposes a *per se* rule of exclusion that he claims is dictated by the demands of the Fourteenth Amendment's guarantee of due process. He rightly observes that this is the first case in which this Court has had occasion to rule upon strictly post-*Stovall* out-of-court identification evidence of the challenged kind.

[In *Biggers*, the victim had identified the defendant at a one-on-one showup conducted before the Supreme Court's decision in *Stovall*. The "central question," *Biggers* indicated, "was whether under the 'totality of the circumstances' the identification was reliable even though the confrontation procedure was suggestive." Since the testimony presented "no substantial likelihood of misidentification," that testimony was properly admitted into evidence. The question now before the Court is whether a stricter standard should be applied where the identification procedure was conducted after the Court's decision in *Stovall*.]

[T]he Courts of Appeals appear to have developed at least two approaches to such evidence. The first, or *per se* approach, employed by the Second Circuit in the present case, focuses on the procedures employed and requires exclusion of the out-of-court identification evidence, without regard to reliability, whenever it has been obtained through unnecessarily suggest[ive] confrontation procedures.[10] The justifications advanced are the elimination of evidence of uncertain reliability, deterrence of the police and prosecutors, and the stated "fair assurance against the awful risks of misidentification."

The second, or more lenient, approach is one that continues to rely on the totality of the circumstances. It permits the admission of the confrontation evidence if, despite the suggestive aspect, the out-of-court identification possesses certain features of reliability. Its adherents feel that the *per se* approach is not mandated by the Due Process Clause of the Fourteenth Amendment. This second approach, in contrast to the other, is ad hoc and serves to limit the societal costs imposed by a

---

[10] Although the *per se* approach demands the exclusion of testimony concerning unnecessarily suggestive identifications, it does permit the admission of testimony concerning a subsequent identification, including an in-court identification, if the subsequent identification is determined to be reliable. The totality approach, in contrast, is simpler: if the challenged identification is reliable, then testimony as to it and any identification in its wake is admissible.

sanction that excludes relevant evidence from consideration and evaluation by the trier of fact.

* * *

The respondent here stresses * * * the need for deterrence of improper identification practice, a factor he regards as preeminent. Photographic identification, it is said, continues to be needlessly employed. He notes that the legislative regulation "the Court had hoped [*United States v. Wade*, 388 U.S. 218, 239, 87 S.Ct. 1926, 1938–1939, 18 L.Ed.2d 1149 (1967),] would engender," has not been forthcoming. He argues that a totality rule cannot be expected to have a significant deterrent impact; only a strict rule of exclusion will have direct and immediate impact on law enforcement agents. Identification evidence is so convincing to the jury that sweeping exclusionary rules are required. Fairness of the trial is threatened by suggestive confrontation evidence, and thus, it is said, an exclusionary rule has an established constitutional predicate.

There are, of course, several interests to be considered and taken into account. The driving force behind *United States v. Wade*, 388 U.S. 218, 87 S.Ct. 1926, 18 L.Ed.2d 1149 (1967), *Gilbert v. California*, 388 U.S. 263, 87 S.Ct. 1951, 18 L.Ed.2d 1178 (1967) (right to counsel at a postindictment lineup), and *Stovall*, all decided on the same day, was the Court's concern with the problems of eyewitness identification. Usually the witness must testify about an encounter with a total stranger under circumstances of emergency or emotional stress. The witness' recollection of the stranger can be distorted easily by the circumstances or by later actions of the police. Thus, *Wade* and its companion cases reflect the concern that the jury not hear eyewitness testimony unless that evidence has aspects of reliability. It must be observed that both approaches before us are responsive to this concern. The *per se* rule, however, goes too far since its application automatically and peremptorily, and without consideration of alleviating factors, keeps evidence from the jury that is reliable and relevant.

The second factor is deterrence. Although the *per se* approach has the more significant deterrent effect, the totality approach also has an influence on police behavior. The police will guard against unnecessarily suggestive procedures under the totality rule, as well as the *per se* one, for fear that their actions will lead to the exclusion of identifications·as unreliable.

The third factor is the effect on the administration of justice. Here the *per se* approach suffers serious drawbacks. Since it denies the trier reliable evidence, it may result, on occasion, in the guilty going free. Also, because of its rigidity, the *per se* approach may make error by the trial judge more likely than the totality approach. And in those cases in which the admission of identification evidence is error under the *per se* approach but not under the totality approach—cases in which the identification is reliable despite an unnecessarily suggestive identification procedure—reversal is a Draconian sanction.[13] Certainly, inflexible rules of exclusion that may frustrate rather than promote justice have not been viewed recently by this Court with unlimited enthusiasm.

We therefore conclude that reliability is the linchpin in determining the admissibility of identification testimony * * *. The factors to be considered * * * include the opportunity of the witness to view the criminal at the time of the crime, the witness' degree of attention, the accuracy of his prior description of the criminal, the level of certainty demonstrated at the confrontation, and the time between the crime and the confrontation. Against these factors is to be weighed the corrupting effect of the suggestive identification itself.

V.

We turn, then, to the facts of this case and apply the analysis:

1.   The opportunity to view. Glover testified that for two to three minutes he stood at the apartment door, within two feet of the respondent. The door opened twice, and each time the man stood at the door. The moments passed, the conversation took place, and payment was made. Glover looked directly at his vendor. It was near sunset, to be sure, but the sun had not yet set, so it was not dark or even dusk or twilight. Natural light from outside entered the hallway through a window. There was natural light, as well, from inside the apartment.

2.   The degree of attention. Glover was not a casual or passing observer, as is so often the case with eyewitness identification. Trooper Glover was a trained police officer on duty—and specialized and dangerous duty—when he called at the third floor of 201 Westland in Hartford on May 5, 1970. Glover himself was a Negro and unlikely to perceive only general features of "hundreds of Hartford black males," as the Court of Appeals stated. It is true that Glover's duty was that of ferreting out narcotics offenders and that he would be expected in his work to produce results. But it is also true that, as a specially trained, assigned, and experienced officer, he could be expected to pay scrupulous attention to detail, for he knew that subsequently he would have to find and arrest his vendor. In addition, he knew that his claimed observations would be subject later to close scrutiny and examination at any trial.

3.   The accuracy of the description. Glover's description was given to D'Onofrio within minutes after the transaction. It included the vendor's race, his height, his build, the color and style of his hair, and the high cheekbone facial feature. It also included clothing the vendor wore. No claim has been made that respondent did not possess the physical characteristics so described. D'Onofrio reacted positively at once. Two

---

[13] Unlike a warrantless search, a suggestive preindictment identification procedure does not in itself intrude upon a constitutionally protected interest. Thus, considerations urging the exclusion of evidence deriving from a constitutional violation do not bear on the instant problem.

days later, when Glover was alone, he viewed the photograph D'Onofrio produced and identified its subject as the narcotics seller.

4.   The witness' level of certainty. There is no dispute that the photograph in question was that of respondent. Glover, in response to a question whether the photograph was that of the person from whom he made the purchase, testified: "There is no question whatsoever." This positive assurance was repeated.

5.   The time between the crime and the confrontation. Glover's description of his vendor was given to D'Onofrio within minutes of the crime. The photographic identification took place only two days later. We do not have here the passage of weeks or months between the crime and the viewing of the photograph.

These indicators of Glover's ability to make an accurate identification are hardly outweighed by the corrupting effect of the challenged identification itself. Although identifications arising from single-photograph displays may be viewed in general with suspicion, we find in the instant case little pressure on the witness to acquiesce in the suggestion that such a display entails. D'Onofrio had left the photograph at Glover's office and was not present when Glover first viewed it two days after the event. There thus was little urgency and Glover could view the photograph at his leisure. And since Glover examined the photograph alone, there was no coercive pressure to make an identification arising from the presence of another. The identification was made in circumstances allowing care and reflection.

Although it plays no part in our analysis, all this assurance as to the reliability of the identification is hardly undermined by the facts that respondent was arrested in the very apartment where the sale had taken place, and that he acknowledged his frequent visits to that apartment.

Surely, we cannot say that under all the circumstances of this case there is "a very substantial likelihood of irreparable misidentification." Short of that point, such evidence is for the jury to weigh. We are content to rely upon the good sense and judgment of American juries, for evidence with some element of untrustworthiness is customary grist for the jury mill. Juries are not so susceptible that they cannot measure intelligently the weight of identification testimony that has some questionable feature.

Of course, it would have been better had D'Onofrio presented Glover with a photographic array including "so far as practicable * * * a reasonable number of persons similar to any person then suspected whose likeness is included in the array." The use of that procedure would have enhanced the force of the identification at trial and would have avoided the risk that the evidence would be excluded as unreliable. But we are not disposed to view D'Onofrio's failure as one of constitutional dimension to be enforced by a rigorous and unbending exclusionary rule. The defect, if there be one, goes to weight and not to substance. * * *

The judgment of the Court of Appeals is reversed.

It is so ordered.

■ MR. JUSTICE MARSHALL, with whom MR. JUSTICE BRENNAN joins, dissenting.

Today's decision can come as no surprise to those who have been watching the Court dismantle the protections against mistaken eyewitness testimony erected a decade ago * * * .

* * *

[I]n determining the admissibility of the * * * identification in this case, the Court considers two alternatives, a *per se* exclusionary rule and a totality-of-the circumstances approach. The Court weighs three factors in deciding that the totality approach * * * should be applied. In my view, the Court wrongly evaluates the impact of these factors.

First, the Court acknowledges that one of the factors, deterrence of police use of unnecessarily suggestive identification procedures, favors the *per se* rule. Indeed, it does so heavily, for such a rule would make it unquestionably clear to the police they must never use a suggestive procedure when a fairer alternative is available. I have no doubt that conduct would quickly conform to the rule.

Second, the Court gives passing consideration to the dangers of eyewitness identification recognized in the *Wade* trilogy. It concludes, however, that the grave risk of error does not justify adoption of the *per se* approach because that would too often result in exclusion of relevant evidence. In my view, this conclusion totally ignores the lessons of *Wade*. The dangers of mistaken identification are, as *Stovall* held, simply too great to permit unnecessarily suggestive identifications. * * * [T]he Court's opinion today points to [no] contrary empirical evidence. Studies since *Wade* have only reinforced the validity of its assessment of the dangers of identification testimony. While the Court is "content to rely on the good sense and judgment of American juries," the impetus for *Stovall* and *Wade* was repeated miscarriages of justice resulting from juries' willingness to credit inaccurate eyewitness testimony.

Finally, the Court errs in its assessment of the relative impact of the two approaches on the administration of justice. The Court relies most heavily on this factor, finding that "reversal is a Draconian sanction" in cases where the identification is reliable despite an unnecessarily suggestive procedure used to obtain it. Relying on little more than a strong distaste for "inflexible rules of exclusion," the Court rejects the *per se* test. * * *

[I]mpermissibly suggestive identifications are not merely worthless law enforcement tools. They pose a grave threat to society at large in a more direct way than most governmental disobedience of the law. For if the police and the public erroneously conclude, on the basis of an unnecessarily suggestive confrontation, that the right man has been caught and convicted, the real outlaw must still remain at large. Law enforcement has failed in its primary function and has left society unprotected from the depredations of an active criminal.

For these reasons, I conclude that adoption of the *per se* rule would enhance, rather than detract from, the effective administration of justice. In my view, the Court's totality test will allow seriously unreliable and misleading evidence to be put before juries. Equally important, it will allow dangerous criminals to remain on the streets while citizens assume that police action has given them protection. According to my calculus, all three of the factors upon which the Court relies point to acceptance of the *per se* approach.

* * *

Since I [believe that a *per se* approach] should govern this case, but that even if it does not, the facts here reveal a substantial likelihood of misidentification in violation of respondent's right to due process of law, I would affirm the grant of habeas corpus relief. Accordingly, I dissent from the Court's reinstatement of respondent's conviction.

NOTES

1. **Independent Source.** If a witness identifies a defendant at a pretrial procedure found unconstitutionally suggestive, does the independent source analysis used in the right to counsel cases apply? May the prosecution nevertheless introduce in-court identification testimony if it persuades the judge by clear and convincing evidence that this testimony would have an "independent source"—that is, that the testimony would be untainted by the defective procedure? In Foster v. California, 394 U.S. 440, 89 S.Ct. 1127 (1969), discussed in the Editors' Introduction to this subchapter, Justice Black, dissenting, found the Court's case law ambiguous on that point.

Arguably the Court's post-*Foster* cases resolve Justice Black's concern indirectly. *Braithwaite* approved *Biggers'* analysis in which testimony concerning an out-of-court identification made at an impermissibly suggestive procedure is admissible if it presents "no substantial likelihood of misidentification." In contrast, where a case involves an in-court identification by a witness who made an identification of the defendant at an impermissibly suggestive pretrial procedure, the testimony is admissible if it presents "no substantial likelihood of *irreparable* misidentification." Simmons v. United States, 390 U.S. 377, 384, 88 S.Ct. 967, 971 (1968) (emphasis supplied). This focus upon irreparable misidentification arguably leaves open the possibility that events between an inadmissible out-of-court identification and a later in-court identification might so reduce the risk of unreliability as to make the in-court identification testimony admissible although testimony regarding the out-of-court identification remains inadmissible.

Where the prosecution presents in-court identification testimony by a witness who identified the defendant at a unconstitutionally suggestive pretrial procedure, in other words, the issue may not be independent source. Rather, it may be whether the unnecessarily suggestive pretrial identification procedure gave rise to a substantial likelihood of *irreparable* misidentification.

2. **Unreliability Arising from Non-Police Sources.** The Supreme Court was asked to require as a federal constitutional matter pretrial screening for reliability of eyewitness testimony possibly influenced by suggestive circumstances not arranged by law enforcement officers. Perry v. New Hampshire, 565 U.S. 228, 132 S.Ct. 716 (2012). Perry emphasized the Court's statement in *Brathwaite* that "reliability is the linchpin in determining the admissibility of identification testimony." He argued that "[i]f reliability is the linchpin of admissibility under the Due Process Clause, * * * it should make no difference whether law enforcement was responsible for creating the suggestive circumstances that marred the identification."

In *Perry*, an eyewitness—shortly after witnessing the crime—glanced out a window and observed an officer talking with Perry under circumstances suggesting the officer believed Perry to be the perpetrator of the crime. Nothing suggested that law enforcement officers intended this observation to occur. Later, the witness identified Perry as the person she saw committing the crime. Perry argued that the trial court had a duty under the *Stovall* line of cases to consider whether the witness's testimony was reliable and to permit the jury to hear the testimony only if it was reliable.

The Court declined to expand the *Stovall* line of decisions as urged by Perry. A primary purpose of the due process rule, it reasoned, is to discourage unnecessarily suggestive law enforcement procedures. Reliability comes into play only when in particular situations the need for such deterrence may be outweighed by the value of permitting juries to consider identification testimony despite such improper law enforcement procedures. If there is no unnecessarily suggestive law enforcement activity, this primary purpose is not invoked and the situation presents no need for considering whether nevertheless the evidence at issue is sufficiently reliable to permit the trier of fact to consider it on guilt or innocence.

Further, the Court reasoned, Perry's proposed approach would require expanding due process reliability review to any situation in which any factor raised questions about the reliability of eyewitness testimony. No logical line could be drawn between accidental law enforcement suggestiveness and considerations such as the passage of time between witnessing a crime and identifying a suspect or the witness's distance from the perpetrator. Thus the position urged upon the Court "would * * * entail a vast enlargement of the reach of due process as a constraint on law enforcement conduct." This the *Perry* majority found unacceptable. It explained:

> We have concluded in other contexts * * * that the potential unreliability of a type of evidence does not alone render its introduction at the defendant's trial fundamentally unfair. We reach a similar conclusion here: The fallibility of eyewitness evidence does not, without the taint of improper state conduct, warrant a due process rule requiring a trial court to screen such

evidence for reliability before allowing the jury to assess its creditworthiness.

Our unwillingness to enlarge the domain of due process * * * rests, in large part, on our recognition that the jury, not the judge, traditionally determines the reliability of evidence. We also take account of other safeguards built into our adversary system that caution juries against placing undue weight on eyewitness testimony of questionable reliability. These protections include the defendant's Sixth Amendment right to confront the eyewitness. Another is the defendant's right to the effective assistance of an attorney, who can expose the flaws in the eyewitness' testimony during cross-examination and focus the jury's attention on the fallibility of such testimony during opening and closing arguments. Eyewitness-specific jury instructions, which many federal and state courts have adopted, likewise warn the jury to take care in appraising identification evidence. The constitutional requirement that the government prove the defendant's guilt beyond a reasonable doubt also impedes convictions based on dubious identification evidence.

State and federal rules of evidence, moreover, permit trial judges to exclude relevant evidence if its probative value is substantially outweighed by its prejudicial impact or potential for misleading the jury. In appropriate cases, some States also permit defendants to present expert testimony on the hazards of eyewitness identification evidence.

565 U.S. at 245–46 132 S.Ct. at 728–29.

C. OTHER EVIDENTIARY AND PROCEDURAL SAFEGUARDS AGAINST UNRELIABLE EYEWITNESS TESTIMONY

EDITORS' INTRODUCTION: OTHER LEGAL RESPONSES TO UNRELIABILITY

The empirical evidence summarized in those portions of *Henderson* reprinted at the first subchapter of this chapter have stimulated increasing concern whether existing legal doctrines and procedure provide adequate protection against convictions based on unreliable eyewitness identification testimony. Specifically, current law may rely too heavily upon the existence and approach of the federal constitutional law presented in the second subchapter of this chapter. This subchapter explores other possible legal responses to the issues posed by eyewitness identification testimony.

Trial courts are widely regarded as having discretionary authority to exclude evidence based on a determination that juries are unlikely to be able to accurately assess its credibility. This authority is explicitly provided for in Rule 403 of the Federal Rules of Evidence and the many state rules based on it. Rule 403 permits trial judge to exclude relevant evidence "if its probative value is substantially outweighed by the danger of unfair prejudice, confusion of the issues, or misleading the jury, or by considerations of undue delay, waste of time, or needless presentation of cumulative evidence." Among the relevant considerations in a Rule 403 analysis are whether jurors can assess the credibility of evidence offered and the cost and risks of confusion of what may be necessary to equip jurors to make such assessments. See United States v. Graziano, 558 F.Supp.2d 304, 325–26 (E.D.N.Y.2008) (holding inadmissible evidence that the defendant offered to take a polygraph in part because "any attempt to inform the jury as to [the] factors [relevant to the significance of such an offer] would undoubtedly lead to juror confusion that would substantially outweigh the probative value [of the evidence]").

Might some eyewitness testimony be subject to challenge on this basis? A trial judge has been held to have a duty to scrutinize testimony of a child witness under the Rule 403 approach. This scrutiny is sufficient to protect a defendant from "the frailty of a child's memories, the tendency of a child to form false memories that he or she believes to be true, and a child's susceptibility to suggestion that may taint the child's memory." Ex parte Brown, 74 So.3d 1039 (Ala.2011).

Of course, trial courts are—perhaps understandably—reluctant to find that jurors will be unable to assess the credibility of commonly-used testimony.

This subchapter reprints those portions of the New Jersey Supreme Court's *Henderson* opinion in which the court addressed the appropriate state law response to the increased empirical information developed since the major federal constitutional decisions of the Supreme Court in this area.

State v. Henderson

Supreme Court of New Jersey, 2011.
208 N.J. 208, 27 A.3d 872.

■ CHIEF JUSTICE RABNER delivered the opinion of the Court.

I.   Introduction

In the thirty-four years since the United States Supreme Court announced a test for the admission of eyewitness identification evidence, which New Jersey adopted soon after, a vast body of scientific research about human memory has emerged. That body of work casts doubt on some commonly held views relating to memory. It also calls into question the vitality of the current legal framework for analyzing the reliability of eyewitness identifications. *See Manson v. Brathwaite*, 432 U.S. 98, 97 S.Ct. 2243, 53 L. Ed.2d 140 (1977); *State v. Madison*, 109 N.J. 223, 536 A.2d 254 (1988).

In this case, * * * we remanded the case and appointed a Special Master to evaluate scientific and other evidence about eyewitness identifications. * * *

II. Facts and Procedural History

A. Facts

In the early morning hours of January 1, 2003, Rodney Harper was shot to death in an apartment in Camden. James Womble witnessed the murder but did not speak with the police until they approached him ten days later.

Womble and Harper were acquaintances who occasionally socialized at the apartment of Womble's girlfriend, Vivian Williams. On the night of the murder, Womble and Williams brought in the New Year in Williams' apartment by drinking wine and champagne and smoking crack cocaine. Harper had started the evening with them but left at around 10:15 p.m. Williams also left roughly three hours later, leaving Womble alone in the apartment until Harper rejoined him at 2:00 to 2:30 a.m.

Soon after Harper returned, two men forcefully entered the apartment. Womble knew one of them, co-defendant George Clark, who had come to collect $160 from Harper. The other man was a stranger to Womble.

While Harper and Clark went to a different room, the stranger pointed a gun at Womble and told him, "Don't move, stay right here, you're not involved in this." He remained with the stranger in a small, narrow, dark hallway. Womble testified that he got a look at the stranger, but not a real good look. Womble also described the gun pointed at his torso as a dark semiautomatic.

Meanwhile, Womble overheard Clark and Harper argue over money in the other room. At one point, Harper said, "do what you got to do," after which Womble heard a gunshot. Womble then walked into the room, saw Clark holding a handgun, offered to get Clark the $160, and urged him not to shoot Harper again. As Clark left, he warned Womble, "Don't rat me out, I know where you live."

Harper died from the gunshot wound to his chest on January 10, 2003. Camden County Detective Luis Ruiz and Investigator Randall MacNair were assigned to investigate the homicide, and they interviewed Womble the next day. Initially, Womble told the police that he was in the apartment when he heard two gunshots outside, that he left to look for Harper, and that he found Harper slumped over in his car in a nearby parking lot, where Harper said he had been shot by two men he did not know.

The next day, the officers confronted Womble about inconsistencies in his story. Womble claimed that they also threatened to charge him in connection with the murder. Womble then decided to come clean. He admitted that he lied at first because he did not want to rat out anyone and didn't want to get involved out of fear of retaliation against his elderly father. Womble led the investigators to Clark, who eventually gave a statement about his involvement and identified the person who accompanied him as defendant Larry Henderson.

The officers had Womble view a photographic array on January 14, 2003. That event lies at the heart of this decision * * *. Ultimately, Womble identified defendant from the array, and Investigator MacNair prepared a warrant for his arrest. Upon arrest, defendant admitted to the police that he had accompanied Clark to the apartment where Harper was killed, and heard a gunshot while waiting in the hallway. But defendant denied witnessing or participating in the shooting.

A grand jury in Camden County returned an indictment charging Henderson and Clark with the following offenses: first-degree murder, second-degree possession of a firearm for an unlawful purpose, fourth-degree aggravated assault, third-degree unlawful possession of a weapon, and possession of a weapon having been convicted of a prior offense.

B.   Photo Identification and * * * Hearing

As noted above, Womble reviewed a photo array at the Prosecutors Office on January 14, 2003, and identified defendant as his assailant. The trial court conducted a pretrial * * * hearing to determine the admissibility of that identification. Investigator MacNair, Detective Ruiz, and Womble all testified at the hearing. Cherry Hill Detective Thomas Weber also testified.

Detective Weber conducted the identification procedure because, consistent with guidelines issued by the Attorney General, he was not a primary investigator in the case. *See* Office of the Attorney Gen., N.J. Dep't of Law and Pub. Safety, *Attorney General Guidelines for Preparing and Conducting Photo and Live Lineup Identification Procedures* 1 (2001) (Attorney General Guidelines or Guidelines). * * *

Ruiz and MacNair gave Weber an array consisting of seven "filler" photos and one photo of defendant Henderson. The eight photos all depicted headshots of African-American men between the ages of twenty-eight and thirty-five, with short hair, goatees, and, according to Weber, similar facial features. At the hearing, Weber was not asked whether he knew which photograph depicted the suspect. (Later at trial, he said he did not know.)

The identification procedure took place in an interview room in the Prosecutor's Office. At first, Weber and Womble were alone in the room. Weber began by reading the following instructions off a standard form:

> In a moment, I will show you a number of photographs one at a time. You may take as much time as you need to look at each one of them. You should not conclude that the person who committed the crime is in the group merely because a group of

photographs is being shown to you. The person who committed the crime may or may not be in the group, and the mere display of the photographs is not meant to suggest that our office believes the person who committed the crime is in one of the photographs. You are absolutely not required to choose any of the photographs, and you should feel not obligated to choose any one. The photographs will be shown to you in random order. I am not in any way trying to influence your decision by the order of the pictures presented. Tell me immediately if you recognize the person that committed the crime in one of the photographs. All of the photographs will be shown to you even if you select a photograph.

Please keep in mind that hairstyles, beards, and mustaches are easily changed. People gain and lose weight. Also, photographs do not always show the true complexion of a person. It may be lighter or darker than shown in the photograph. If you select a photograph, please do not ask me whether I agree with or support your selection. It is your choice alone that counts. Please do not discuss whether you selected a photograph with any other witness who may be asked to look at these photographs.

To acknowledge that he understood the instructions, Womble signed the form.

Detective Weber pre-numbered the eight photos, shuffled them, and showed them to Womble one at a time. Womble quickly eliminated five of the photos. He then reviewed the remaining three, discounted one more, and said he wasn't 100 percent sure of the final two pictures. * * *

Weber left the room with the photos and informed MacNair and Ruiz that the witness had narrowed the pictures to two but could not make a final identification. MacNair and Ruiz testified at the hearing that they did not know whether defendant's picture was among the remaining two photos.

MacNair and Ruiz entered the interview room to speak with Womble. According to MacNairs testimony at the * * * hearing, he and Ruiz believed that Womble was holding back—as he had earlier in the investigation—based on fear. Ruiz said Womble was nervous, upset about his father.

In an effort to calm Womble, MacNair testified that he just told him to focus, to calm down, to relax and that any type of protection that [he] would need, any threats against [him] would be put to rest by the Police Department. Ruiz added, "just do what you have to do, and we'll be out of here." In response, according to MacNair, Womble said he "could make [an] identification."

MacNair and Ruiz then left the interview room. * * * When Weber returned to the room, he reshuffled the eight photos and again displayed them to Womble sequentially. This time, when Womble saw defendant's photo, he slammed his hand on the table and exclaimed, "[t]hat's the mother [ ] there." From start to finish, the entire process took fifteen minutes.

Womble did not recant his identification, but during the * * * hearing he testified that he felt as though Detective Weber was "nudging" him to choose defendant's photo, and "that there was pressure" to make a choice.

After hearing the testimony, the trial court applied the two-part *Manson/Madison* test to evaluate the admissibility of the eyewitness identification. The test requires courts to determine first if police identification procedures were impermissibly suggestive; if so, courts then weigh five reliability factors to decide if the identification evidence is nonetheless admissible.

The trial court first found that the photo display itself was "a fair makeup." Under the totality of the circumstances, the judge concluded that the photo identification was reliable. The court found that there was "nothing in this case that was improper, and certainly nothing that was so suggestive as to result in a substantial likelihood of misidentification at all." The court also noted that Womble displayed no doubts about identifying defendant Henderson, that he had the opportunity to view defendant at the crime scene, and that Womble fixed his attention on defendant "because he had a gun on him."

C. Trial

The following facts—relevant to Wombles identification of defendant—were adduced at trial after the court determined that the identification was admissible: Womble smoked two bags of crack cocaine with his girlfriend in the hours before the shooting; the two also consumed one bottle of champagne and one bottle of wine; the lighting was pretty dark in the hallway where Womble and defendant interacted; defendant shoved Womble during the incident; and Womble remembered looking at the gun pointed at his chest. Womble also admitted smoking about two bags of crack cocaine each day from the time of the shooting until speaking with police ten days later.

At trial, Womble * * * testified that when he first looked at the photo array, he did not see anyone he recognized. As he explained, "[m]y mind was drawing a blank . . . so I just started eliminating photos." To make a final identification, Womble said that he "really had to search deep." He was nonetheless "sure" of the identification.

Womble had no difficulty identifying defendant at trial eighteen months later. From the witness stand, Womble agreed that he had no doubt that defendant—the man in the courtroom wearing "the white dress shirt"—is the man who held [him] at bay with a gun to [his] chest.

* * *

Neither Clark nor defendant testified at trial. The primary evidence against defendant, thus, was Womble's identification and Detective MacNair's testimony about defendants-post-arrest statement.

At the close of trial on July 20, 2004, the court relied on the existing model jury charge on eyewitness identification and instructed the jury as follows:

> [Y]ou should consider the observations and perceptions on which the identification is based, and Womble's ability to make those observations and perceptions. If you determine that his out-of-court identification is not reliable, you may still consider Womble's in-court identification of Gregory Clark and Larry Henderson if you find that to be reliable. However, unless the identification here in court resulted from Womble's observations or perceptions of a perpetrator during the commission of an offense rather than being the product of an impression gained at an out-of-court identification procedure such as a photo lineup, it should be afforded no weight. The ultimate issues of the trustworthiness of both in-court and out-of-court identifications are for you, the jury to decide.
>
> To decide whether the identification testimony is sufficiently reliable evidence . . . you may consider the following factors:
>
> First of all, Womble's opportunity to view the person or persons who allegedly committed the offense at the time of the offense; second, Womble's degree of attention on the alleged perpetrator when he allegedly observed the crime being committed; third, the accuracy of any prior description of the perpetrator given [b]y Womble; fourth, you should consider the fact that in Womble's sworn taped statement of January 11th, 2003 to the police . . ., Womble did not identify anyone as the person or persons involved in the shooting of Rodney Harper. . . .
>
> Next, you should consider the degree of certainty, if any, expressed by Womble in making the identification. . . .[3]
>
> You should also consider the length of time between Womble's observation of the alleged offense and his identification. . . . You should consider any discrepancies or inconsistencies between identifications. . . .
>
> Next, the circumstances under which any out-of-court identification was made including in this case the evidence that during the showing to him of eight photos by Detective Weber

---

[3] After defendant's conviction, this Court decided *State v. Romero,* 922 A.2d 693, 191 N.J. 59, 76 (2007), which held that jurors are to be warned that "a witness's level of confidence, standing alone, may not be an indication of the reliability of the identification."

he did not identify Larry Henderson when he first looked at them and later identified Larry Henderson from one of those photos.

. . . You may also consider any other factor based on the evidence or lack of evidence in the case which you consider relevant to your determination whether the identification made by Womble is reliable or not.

* * *

[T]he jury acquitted defendant of murder and aggravated manslaughter, and convicted him of reckless manslaughter, aggravated assault, and two weapons charges. In a bifurcated trial the next day, the jury convicted defendant of the remaining firearms offense: possession by a previously convicted person. The court sentenced him to an aggregate eleven-year term of imprisonment * * *. Defendant appealed his conviction and sentence.

D. Appellate Division

The Appellate Division presumed that the identification procedure in this case was impermissibly suggestive under the first prong of the *Manson/Madison* test. The court reversed and remanded for a new * * * hearing to determine whether the identification was nonetheless reliable under the test's second prong.

* * *

E.   Certification and Remand Order

We granted the State's petition for certification, and also granted leave to appear as amicus curiae to the Association of Criminal Defense Lawyers of New Jersey (ACDL) and the Innocence Project (collectively "amici"). * * * [W]e "concluded that an inadequate factual record exist[ed] on which [to] test the current validity of our state law standards on the admissibility of eyewitness identification." We therefore remanded the matter * * *.

[T]he following parties participated in the remand hearing: the Attorney General, the Public Defender (representing defendant), and amici.

* * *

VIII.   Parties' Arguments
* * *

[D]efendant and the ACDL initially proposed two alternative frameworks to replace *Manson/Madison*. Among other arguments, they analogized to *Miranda v. Arizona,* 384 U.S. 436, 86 S.Ct. 1602, 16 L. Ed.2d 694 (1966), and argued that eyewitness evidence should be excluded per se if an identification procedure violated the Attorney General Guidelines or if a judge found other evidence of suggestiveness.

[T]hey now urge this Court to require a reliability hearing in every case in which the State intends to present identification evidence. At the hearing, they submit that a wide range of system and estimator variables would be relevant, and the State should bear the burden of establishing reliability. * * *

The Innocence Project proposes a different scheme along the following lines: defendants would first have to allege that an identification was unreliable; the burden would then shift to the State to prove, in essence, that neither estimator nor system variables rendered the identification unreliable—to be accomplished through testimony of the eyewitness about the circumstances under which she saw the perpetrator, and proof from law enforcement about the identification procedure used; the burden would next shift back to the defendant to prove by a preponderance of evidence "that there exists a substantial probability of a mistaken identification"; and if the court does not suppress the evidence, defendant could file motions to seek to limit or redact identification testimony and present expert testimony at trial.

* * *

Finally, the Innocence Project encourages this Court to adopt comprehensive jury instructions that are easy to understand, so that jurors can evaluate eyewitness evidence appropriately. The Innocence Project maintains that those instructions should be read to the jury both *before* an eyewitness' testimony and at the conclusion of the case. If at the end of trial the court doubts the accuracy of an identification, the Innocence Project argues that the judge should give a cautionary instruction to treat that evidence with great caution and distrust.

The State argues that the Innocent Project's proposal would invite an unnecessary pretrial fishing expedition in every criminal case involving eyewitness evidence. Instead, the State contends that the initial burden should remain on defendants to show some evidence of suggestiveness, which the State claims is not an onerous threshold.

IX. Legal Conclusions

* * *

B. The *Manson/Madison* Test Needs to Be Revised

[T]he *Manson* Court's two-part test rested on three assumptions: (1) that it would adequately measure the reliability of eyewitness testimony; (2) that the test's focus on suggestive police procedure would deter improper practices; and (3) that jurors would recognize and discount untrustworthy eyewitness testimony.

* * *

The hearing [below] revealed that *Manson/Madison* does not adequately meet its stated goals: it does not provide a sufficient measure for reliability, it does not deter, and it overstates the jury's innate ability to evaluate eyewitness testimony.

First, under *Manson/Madison,* defendants must show that police procedures were "impermissibly suggestive" before courts can consider estimator variables that also bear on reliability. As a result, although evidence of relevant estimator variables * * * is routinely introduced at pretrial hearings, their effect is ignored unless there is a finding of impermissibly suggestive police conduct. In this case, for example, the testimony at the * * * hearing related principally to the lineup procedure. Because the court found that the procedure was not "impermissibly suggestive," details about the witness' use of drugs and alcohol, the dark lighting conditions, the presence of a weapon pointed at the witness' chest, and other estimator variables that affect reliability were not considered at the hearing. (They were explored later at trial.)

Second, under *Manson/Madison,* if a court finds that the police used impermissibly suggestive identification procedures, the trial judge then weighs the corrupting effect of the process against five "reliability" factors. But three of those factors—the opportunity to view the crime, the witness' degree of attention, and the level of certainty at the time of the identification—rely on self-reporting by eyewitnesses; and research has shown that those reports can be skewed by the suggestive procedures themselves and thus may not be reliable. Self-reporting by eyewitnesses is an essential part of any investigation, but when reports are tainted by a suggestive process, they become poor measures in a balancing test designed to bar unreliable evidence.

Third, rather than act as a deterrent, the *Manson/Madison* test may unintentionally reward suggestive police practices. The irony of the current test is that the more suggestive the procedure, the greater the chance eyewitnesses will seem confident and report better viewing conditions. Courts in turn are encouraged to admit identifications based on criteria that have been tainted by the very suggestive practices the test aims to deter.

Fourth, the *Manson/Madison* test addresses only one option for questionable eyewitness identification evidence: suppression. Yet few judges choose that ultimate sanction. An all-or-nothing approach does not account for the complexities of eyewitness identification evidence.

Finally, *Manson/Madison* instructs courts that "the reliability determination is to be made from the totality of the circumstances in the particular case." In practice, trial judges routinely use the test's five reliability factors as a checklist. The State maintains that courts may consider additional estimator variables. Even if that is correct, there is little guidance about which factors to consider, and courts and juries are often left to their own intuition to decide which estimator variables may be important and how they matter.

As a result of those concerns, we now revise the State's framework for evaluating eyewitness identification evidence.[10]

C. Revised Framework

Remedying the problems with the current *Manson/Madison* test requires an approach that addresses its shortcomings: one that allows judges to consider all relevant factors that affect reliability in deciding whether an identification is admissible; that is not heavily weighted by factors that can be corrupted by suggestiveness; that promotes deterrence in a meaningful way; and that focuses on helping jurors both understand and evaluate the effects that various factors have on memory—because we recognize that most identifications will be admitted in evidence.

Two principal changes to the current system are needed to accomplish that: first, the revised framework should allow all relevant system *and* estimator variables to be explored and weighed at pretrial hearings when there is some actual evidence of suggestiveness; and second, courts should develop and use enhanced jury charges to help jurors evaluate eyewitness identification evidence.

The new framework also needs to be flexible enough to serve twin aims: to guarantee fair trials to defendants, who must have the tools necessary to defend themselves, and to protect the State's interest in presenting critical evidence at trial. With that in mind, we first outline the revised approach for evaluating identification evidence and then explain its details and the reasoning behind it.

First, to obtain a pretrial hearing, a defendant has the initial burden of showing some evidence of suggestiveness that could lead to a mistaken identification. That evidence, in general, must be tied to a system—and not an estimator—variable.

Second, the State must then offer proof to show that the proffered eyewitness identification is reliable—accounting for system and estimator variables—subject to the following: the court can end the hearing at any time if it finds from the testimony that defendant's threshold allegation of suggestiveness is groundless. * * *

Third, the ultimate burden remains on the defendant to prove a very substantial likelihood of irreparable misidentification. To do so, a defendant can cross-examine eyewitnesses and police officials and present witnesses and other relevant evidence linked to system and estimator variables.

Fourth, if after weighing the evidence presented a court finds from the totality of the circumstances that defendant has demonstrated a very substantial likelihood of irreparable misidentification, the court should suppress the identification evidence. If the evidence is admitted, the

---

[10]   We have no authority, of course, to modify *Manson*. The expanded protections stem from the due process rights guaranteed under the State Constitution. * * *

court should provide appropriate, tailored jury instructions, as discussed further below.

To evaluate whether there is evidence of suggestiveness to trigger a hearing, courts should consider the following non-exhaustive list of system variables:

1.   *Blind Administration.* Was the lineup procedure performed double-blind? If double-blind testing was impractical, did the police use a technique * * * to ensure that the administrator had no knowledge of where the suspect appeared in the photo array or lineup?

2.   *Pre-Identification Instructions.* Did the administrator provide neutral, pre-identification instructions warning that the suspect may not be present in the lineup and that the witness should not feel compelled to make an identification?

3.   *Lineup Construction.* Did the array or lineup contain only one suspect embedded among at least five innocent fillers? Did the suspect stand out from other members of the lineup?

4.   *Feedback.* Did the witness receive any information or feedback, about the suspect or the crime, before, during, or after the identification procedure?

5.   *Recording Confidence.* Did the administrator record the witness' statement of confidence immediately after the identification, before the possibility of any confirmatory feedback?

6.   *Multiple Viewings.* Did the witness view the suspect more than once as part of multiple identification procedures? Did police use the same fillers more than once?

7.   *Showups.* Did the police perform a showup more than two hours after an event? Did the police warn the witness that the suspect may not be the perpetrator and that the witness should not feel compelled to make an identification?

8.   *Private Actors.* Did law enforcement elicit from the eyewitness whether he or she had spoken with anyone about the identification and, if so, what was discussed?

9.   *Other Identifications Made.* Did the eyewitness initially make no choice or choose a different suspect or filler?

The court should conduct a * * * hearing only if defendant offers some evidence of suggestiveness. If, however, at any time during the hearing the trial court concludes from the testimony that defendant's initial claim of suggestiveness is baseless, and if no other evidence of suggestiveness has been demonstrated by the evidence, the court may exercise its discretion to end the hearing. Under those circumstances, the court need not permit the defendant or require the State to elicit more evidence about estimator variables; that evidence would be reserved for the jury.

By way of example, assume that a defendant claims an administrator confirmed an eyewitness' identification by telling the witness she did a "good job." That proffer would warrant a * * * hearing. Assume further that the administrator credibly denied any feedback, and the eyewitness did the same. If the trial court finds that the initial allegation is completely hollow, the judge can end the hearing absent any other evidence of suggestiveness. In other words, if no evidence of suggestiveness is left in the case, there is no need to explore estimator variables at the pretrial hearing. Also, trial courts always have the authority to direct the mode and order of proofs, and they may exercise that discretion to focus pretrial hearings as needed.

If some actual proof of suggestiveness remains, courts should consider the above system variables as well as the following non-exhaustive list of estimator variables to evaluate the overall reliability of an identification and determine its admissibility:

1. *Stress.* Did the event involve a high level of stress?

2. *Weapon Focus.* Was a visible weapon used during a crime of short duration?

3. *Duration.* How much time did the witness have to observe the event?

4. *Distance and Lighting.* How close were the witness and perpetrator? What were the lighting conditions at the time?

5. *Witness Characteristics.* Was the witness under the influence of alcohol or drugs? Was age a relevant factor under the circumstances of the case?

6. *Characteristics of Perpetrator.* Was the culprit wearing a disguise? Did the suspect have different facial features at the time of the identification?

7. *Memory Decay.* How much time elapsed between the crime and the identification?

8. *Race-Bias.* Does the case involve a cross-racial identification?

Some of the above estimator variables overlap with the five reliability factors outlined in *Neil v. Biggers,* [409 U.S. 188, 93 S.Ct. 375, 34 L.Ed.2d 401 (1972),] which we nonetheless repeat:

9. *Opportunity to View the Criminal at the Time of the Crime.*

10. *Degree of Attention.*

11. *Accuracy of Prior Description of the Criminal.*

12. *Level of Certainty Demonstrated at the confrontation.* Did the witness express high confidence at the time of the identification before receiving any feedback or other information?

13. *The Time Between the Crime and the Confrontation.* (Encompassed fully by "memory decay" above.)

The above factors are not exclusive. Nor are they intended to be frozen in time. We recognize that scientific research relating to the reliability of eyewitness evidence is dynamic * * * . * * *

We adopt this approach over the initial recommendation of defendant and the ACDL that any violation of the Attorney General Guidelines should require per se exclusion of the resulting eyewitness identification. Although that approach might yield greater deterrence, it could also lead to the loss of a substantial amount of reliable evidence. We believe that the more flexible framework outlined above protects defendants' right to a fair trial at the same time it enables the State to meet its responsibility to ensure public safety.

D. Pretrial Hearing

[T]o obtain a pretrial hearing, a defendant must present some evidence of suggestiveness. Pretrial discovery, which this opinion has enhanced in certain areas, would reveal, for example, if a line-up did not include enough fillers, if those fillers did not resemble the suspect, or if a private actor spoke with the witness about the identification. Armed with that and similar information, defendants could request and receive a hearing.

The hearing would encompass system and estimator variables upon a showing of some suggestiveness that defendant can support. * * *

But concerns about estimator variables alone cannot trigger a pretrial hearing; only system variables would. This approach differs from the procedure * * * proposed by defendant and amici, which would essentially require pretrial hearings in every case involving eyewitness identification evidence. Several reasons favor [his] approach * * * .

First, we anticipate that eyewitness identification evidence will likely not be ruled inadmissible at pretrial hearings solely on account of estimator variables. For example, it is difficult to imagine that a trial judge would preclude a witness from testifying because the lighting was "too dark," the witness was "too distracted" by the presence of a weapon, or he or she was under "too much" stress while making an observation. How dark is too dark as a matter of law? How much is too much? What guideposts would a trial judge use in making those judgment calls? In all likelihood, the witness would be allowed to testify before a jury and face cross-examination designed to probe the weaknesses of her identification. Jurors would also have the benefit of enhanced instructions to evaluate that testimony—even when there is no evidence of suggestiveness in the case. As a result, a pretrial hearing triggered by, and focused on, estimator variables would likely not screen out identification evidence and would largely be duplicated at trial.

Second, courts cannot affect estimator variables; by definition, they relate to matters outside the control of law enforcement. More probing pretrial hearings about suggestive police procedures, though, can deter inappropriate police practices.

Third, * * * suggestive behavior can distort various other factors that are weighed in assessing reliability. That warrants a greater pretrial focus on system variables.

Fourth, we are mindful of the practical impact of today's ruling. Because defendants will now be free to explore a broader range of estimator variables at pretrial hearings to assess the reliability of an identification, those hearings will become more intricate. They will routinely involve testimony from both the police and eyewitnesses, and that testimony will likely expand as more substantive areas are explored. Also, trial courts will retain discretion to allow expert testimony at pretrial hearings.

* * *

[T]rial courts should make factual findings at pretrial hearings about relevant system and estimator variables to lay the groundwork for proper jury charges and to facilitate meaningful appellate review.

* * *

E. Trial

[J]uries will continue to hear about all relevant system and estimator variables at trial, through direct and cross-examination and arguments by counsel. In addition, when identification is at issue in a case, trial courts will continue to "provide[ ] appropriate guidelines to focus the jury's attention on how to analyze and consider the trustworthiness of eyewitness identification." * * * [W]e direct that enhanced instructions be given to guide juries about the various factors that may affect the reliability of an identification in a particular case.

Those instructions are to be included in the court's comprehensive jury charge at the close of evidence. In addition, instructions may be given during trial if warranted. For example, if evidence of heightened stress emerges during important testimony, a party may ask the court to instruct the jury midtrial about that variable and its effect on memory. Trial courts retain discretion to decide when to offer instructions.

* * *

Expert testimony may also be introduced at trial, but only if otherwise appropriate. The *Rules of Evidence* permit expert testimony to "assist the trier of fact to understand the evidence or to determine a fact in issue." N.J.R.E. 702. Expert testimony is admissible if it meets three criteria:

> (1) the intended testimony must concern a subject matter that is beyond the ken of the average juror; (2) the field testified to must be at a state of the art such that an expert's testimony could be sufficiently reliable; and (3) the witness must have sufficient expertise to offer the intended testimony.

Those criteria can be met in some cases by qualified experts seeking to testify about the import and effect of certain variables * * * . That said, experts may not opine on the credibility of a particular eyewitness.

* * *

We anticipate * * * , that with enhanced jury instructions, there will be less need for expert testimony. Jury charges offer a number of advantages: they are focused and concise, authoritative (in that juries hear them from the trial judge, not a witness called by one side), and cost-free; they avoid possible confusion to jurors created by dueling experts; and they eliminate the risk of an expert invading the jury's role or opining on an eyewitness' credibility. That said, there will be times when expert testimony will benefit the trier of fact. We leave to the trial court the decision whether to allow expert testimony in an individual case.

Finally, in rare cases, judges may use their discretion to redact parts of identification testimony * * * . For example, if an eyewitness' confidence was not properly recorded soon after an identification procedure, and evidence revealed that the witness received confirmatory feedback from the police or a co-witness, the court can bar potentially distorted and unduly prejudicial statements about the witness' level of confidence from being introduced at trial.

X. Revised Jury Instructions

[W]e ask the Criminal Practice Committee and the Committee on Model Criminal Jury Charges to draft proposed revisions to the current charge on eyewitness identification and submit them to this Court for review before they are implemented. Specifically, we ask them to consider all of the system and estimator variables * * * for which we have found scientific support that is generally accepted by experts, and to modify the current model charge accordingly.

* * *

XI. Application

We return to the facts of this case. After Womble, the eyewitness, informed the lineup administrator that he could not make an identification from the final two photos, the investigating officers intervened. They told Womble to focus and calm down, and assured him that the police would protect him from retaliation. "Just do what you have to do," they instructed. From that exchange, Womble could reasonably infer that there was an identification to be made, and that he would be protected if he made it. The officers conveyed that basic message to him as they encouraged him to make an identification.

The suggestive nature of the officers' comments entitled defendant to a pretrial hearing, and he received one. Applying the *Manson/Madison* test, the trial judge admitted the evidence. We now remand to the trial court for an expanded hearing consistent with the principles outlined in this decision. Defendant may probe all relevant system and estimator variables at the hearing. In addition to suggestiveness, the trial court should consider Womble's drug and alcohol use immediately before the confrontation, weapon focus, and lighting, among other relevant factors.

We express no view on the outcome of the hearing. * * *

XIV. Judgment

[W]e * * * remand to the trial court for further proceedings consistent with this opinion.

■ JUSTICES LONG, LAVECCHIA, ALBIN, RIVERA-SOTO and HOENS join in CHIEF JUSTICE RABNER's opinion.

NOTES

1.   On remand, the trial court found the defendant failed to demonstrate a very substantial likelihood of misidentification and this was upheld on appeal. State v. Henderson, 433 N.J. Super. 94, 109–10, 77 A.3d 536, 545–46 (2013), cert. denied 217 N.J. 590, 91 A.3d 25 (2014).

2.   **Private Party Suggestiveness.** The *Henderson* court, in another decision the same day, addressed the effect of private party suggestiveness. State v. Chen, 208 N.J. 307, 27 A.3d 930 (2011). In *Chen*, the assault victim's husband suggested to the victim that Chen might be her assailant and showed her several photographs of Chen. The court held that "[c]ertain basic evidence rules form the bedrock of [the] principle" that "[c]ourts have a gatekeeping role to ensure that unreliable, misleading evidence is not admitted." This role applies where the source of potential unreliability or potential for misleading is nongovernmental. Private actors, however, cannot be expected to respond to the possibility that their actions may affect the admissibility of evidence. Thus the law applicable when private action is the basis for a defendant's challenge to evidence must be somewhat adjusted. The need to deter misconduct by police is not a consideration the principal concern of the courts must be reliability.

Chen held that the *Henderson* approach is to be applied in these private actor situations with one modification: A defendant is entitled to a hearing only upon production of "some evidence of *highly* suggestive circumstances." It explained specifically:

> [B]ehavior that would trigger a * * * hearing if engaged in by a law enforcement officer would not automatically require a * * * hearing unless the conduct was highly suggestive in its context. Thus, for example, if a police officer conducting a photo array asked, "Are you sure the attacker wasn't wearing glasses?" that procedure would compel a * * * hearing. The same words uttered in conversation by a friend with no apparent knowledge or authority, though, would not warrant a hearing. By contrast, if an eyewitness provided a detailed identification to a fellow eyewitness, those highly suggestive comments would require exploration at a hearing.

208 N.J. at 328, 27 A.3d at 943. On the facts of *Chen*, the actions of the victim's husband were sufficient to trigger a hearing.

3.   **Expert Testimony.** Many courts are more favorably inclined than the *Henderson* court regarding expert testimony, sometimes as a result of a shift in the law, in judicial attitude, or both. See State v. Guilbert, 306 Conn 218, 226, 49 A.3d 705, 715 (2012) (overruling prior case law and holding that "expert testimony on eyewitness identification is admissible upon a determination by the trial court that the expert is qualified and the proffered testimony is relevant and will aid the jury"); Commonwealth v. Walker, 625 Pa 450, 455, 92 A.3d 766, 769 (2014) ("we hold that, in Pennsylvania, the admission of expert testimony regarding eyewitness identification is no longer *per se* impermissible, and join the vast majority of jurisdictions which leave the admissibility of such expert testimony to the discretion of the trial court"). In People v. Enis, 139 Ill.2d 264, 564 N.E.2d 1155 (1990), the Illinois Supreme Court expressed skepticism and caution against the overuse of such testimony, with the result the court commented in People v. Lerma, 2016 IL 118496, ¶ 24, 47 N.E.3d 985, 993 (2016), "that the exclusion of such testimony remains the common practice in Illinois to this day." *Lerma*, however, noted that since *Enis* the underlying research has become well settled and well supported. Reflecting a much different attitude, *Lerma* announced that the research on eyewitness identification is "in appropriate cases a perfectly proper subject for expert testimony." It went on to hold that in the case before the court, the trial judge's exclusion of expert testimony offered by the defendant was an abuse of discretion and reversible error.

INDEX

References are to Pages